D1072211

CHILDHOOD Psychopathology

CHILDHOOD Psychopathology

AN ANTHOLOGY OF

BASIC READINGS

EDITED BY

SAUL I. HARRISON

AND JOHN F. McDERMOTT

INTERNATIONAL UNIVERSITIES PRESS, INC.

NEW YORK NEW YORK

Second Printing, 1973

Third Printing, 1974

Fourth Printing, 1975

Fifth Printing 1976

Library of Congress Catalog Card Number: 76–141808
ISBN: 0–8236–5660–8

Manufactured in the United States of America

CONTENTS

PART I
DEVELOPMENT

Preface ix
Introduction–Albert C. Cain xi
1 The Innate and the Experiential in Child Development–John D. Benjamin 2
2 Critical Periods in the Development of Social Behavior in Puppies –John P. Scott 20
3 Some Aspects of Neurophysiology of the Newborn and Their Implications for Child Development–Julius B. Richmond and Earle L. Lipton 39
4 Behavior Problems Revisited: Findings of Anterospective Study –Stella Chess, Alexander Thomas, and Herbert G. Birch 56
5 Excerpt from *The First Five Years of Life*–Arnold Gesell 66
6 The Etiological Significance of Sexual Life–Sigmund Freud . . . 79
7 Comments on the Formation of Psychic Structure–Heinz Hartmann, Ernst Kris, and Rudolph Loewenstein 83
8 Eight Ages of Man–Erik H. Erikson 109
9 The Concept of Developmental Lines–Anna Freud 133
10 The Stages of the Intellectual Development of the Child–Jean Piaget 157
11 The Relation of Affectivity to Intelligence in the Mental Development of the Child–Jean Piaget 167
12 Trends in Infant Care–Martha Wolfenstein. 176
13 Social Class and Parent-Child Relationships: An Interpretation –Melvin L. Kohn 189
14 Continuities and Discontinuities in Cultural Conditioning–Ruth Benedict 203
15 The Mystique of Adolescence–Joseph B. Adelson 214
16 Puberty and Adolescence–Peter Blos 221

PART II
DEVELOPMENTAL DISORDERS

17 Hospitalism—René A. Spitz 237
18 Hospitalism: A Follow-up Report—René A. Spitz 258
19 Childhood Mourning and Its Implications for Psychiatry—John Bowlby 263
20 Maternal Overprotection—David M. Levy 290
21 The Psychoanalytic Study of Infantile Feeding Disturbances—Anna Freud 296
22 On the Sleep Disturbances of Early Childhood—Selma Fraiberg 310
23 Oppositional Syndromes and Oppositional Behavior—David M. Levy 340
24 Anlage of Productiveness in Boys: Womb Envy—John B. Nelson 360

PART III
NEUROTIC DISORDERS

25 Irrational Fears and Phobias—O. Spurgeon English and Gerald H. Pearson 375
26 Conditioned Emotional Reactions—John B. Watson and Rosalie Rayner 382
27 The Etiology and Treatment of Children's Phobias: A Review —Stanley Rachman and Charles G. Costello 394
28 School Phobia—Adelaide M. Johnson, Eugene I. Falstein, Stanislaus A. Szurek, and Margaret Svendsen 410
29 Enuresis: A Study in Etiology—Margaret W. Gerard 418
30 Hysteria in Childhood—James T. Proctor 431

PART IV
LEARNING DISORDERS

31 Difficulties in Learning—O. Spurgeon English, and Gerald H. Pearson 445
32 A Research Approach to Reading Retardation—Ralph D. Rabinovitch, Arthur L. Drew, Russell N. DeJong, Winifred Ingram, and Lois Withey 457
33 Psychoanalytic Contributions to the Problems of Reading Disabilities—Phyllis Blanchard 487

PART V
ANTISOCIAL DISORDERS

34 Underlying Causes of Delinquency—August Aichhorn 507
35 Sanctions for Superego Lacunae of Adolescents—Adelaide M. Johnson 522

36 Ego Disturbances—Fritz Redl 532

37 Some Current Theories of Delinquent Subcultures—Richard A. Cloward and Lloyd E. Ohlin 540

PART VI

PSYCHOPHYSIOLOGIC DISORDERS

38 Anorexia Nervosa—William W. Gull 567

39 The Role of Bodily Illness in the Mental Life of Children—Anna Freud 572

40 Disturbed Communication in Eating Disorders—Hilde Bruch . . . 585

41 The Asthmatic Child and the Psychosomatic Problem of Asthma: Toward a General Theory—Peter H. Knapp 591

42 An Experimental Approach to the Psychopathology of Childhood: Encopresis—E. James Anthony 610

PART VII

CHILDHOOD PSYCHOSIS

43 Childhood Schizophrenia—Lauretta Bender 628

44 Early Infantile Autism—Leo Kanner, and Leonard I. Lesser . . . 647

45 On Child Psychosis and Schizophrenia: Autistic and Symbiotic Infantile Psychoses—Margaret S. Mahler 670

46 An Investigation of Childhood Schizophrenia: A Retrospective View—William Goldfarb 688

47 The Space Child—Rudolf Ekstein and Dorothy G. Wright 710

PART VIII

MENTAL RETARDATION

48 First Developments of the Young Savage of Aveyron—Jean M. Itard 726

49 Mental Retardation in Historical Perspective—Howard W. Potter 733

50 The Hidden I.Q.—Frank Reissman 744

51 Effects of Adoption on Children from Institutions—Harold M. Skeels 756

52 Parents' Feelings about Retarded Children—Leo Kanner 761

PART IX

BRAIN DYSFUNCTION

53 Psychiatric Implications of Brain Damage in Children—Leon Eisenberg 774

54 Effects of Intensive Psychotherapy on Epileptic Children—Louis A. Gottschalk 788

55 Epidemiologic Studies on the Complication of Pregnancy and the Birth Process—Benjamin Pasamanick and Hilda Knobloch 825

PREFACE

THIS ANTHOLOGY stems from our teaching experience with courses in child psychopathology given at undergraduate, graduate, and professional levels. Our students came from such diverse fields as child psychiatry, developmental and clinical psychology, special education, psychiatric social work, and pediatrics. Together with the rewards and pleasures of teaching these courses, we found that even though backed by relatively rich university library resources we experienced repeated frustration in trying to master the sheer logistics of making available to our students the array of readings assigned. There are, inevitably, gaps in any library's holdings, limits to the number of copies of journals libraries can stack, as well as difficulties in obtaining reprints in large numbers. We also discovered that the students felt a need for copies of their own, on which they could underline, annotate, jot down puzzlements and acid remarks, and draw implications or frowning faces.

Wrestling with these and related problems stimulated us to survey a large number of other training centers regarding their form, content, and didactic approaches with similar courses. The responses made it clear that our problems were shared by colleagues in similar educational settings. Our solution was to develop a sourcebook of readings. This, after extensive screening of the literature and trial runs made with the assistance of our students, we have done.

Once we recognized the need for such a collection of readings, the issue of criteria for the selection of papers became paramount. Although we admit to having had our initial, personal favorites, many of these did not survive the repeated screening and culling of the literature which led to the final selection reprinted here. We employed several criteria in addition to that of intrinsic excellence. We gave strong preference to original articles rather than reviews, "interpretations," or restatements; to papers of classic or nascent classic status, and to representation of major contributors to each of the fields. Although all-inclusiveness was impossible, we sought broad coverage of key syndromes, and similar breadth in range of viewpoints and theories on major issues in child psychopathology. We regret that inevitable limitations of space and, in some instances, unavailability of reprint rights, meant certain valuable papers could not be included. The same limitations of space have, in a few instances, demanded that we use only part of an article. Wherever we have abridged, however, we have preserved the author's original wording.

Beliefs and commitments of another nature also substantially influenced the selection of writings and the content of the editorial commentaries. The book reflects our firm belief that developmental concepts and data are essential to understanding the nature of childhood psychopathology: thus the prevalence of articles written from this point of view. Similarly reflected is the importance we attribute, in a field vulnerable to the shifting winds of doctrine, to affording the students an opportunity to attain historical perspective. We have sought to achieve this by including papers stating classic positions along with their subsequent revisions, critiques, or reformulations. We have also attempted to suggest our own sense of the many elements and spheres of study that must be integrated for a scientifically adequate and professionally applicable understanding of childhood psychopathology.

One last word regarding our introductory commentaries. Our efforts therein are threefold. First, the commentaries should help the student gain perspective by placing the paper in proper context. Second, in a field in which so much remains unknown, the commentaries' appropriate function is as much to raise as to answer questions, as much to focus or clarify issues as to resolve them. Finally, the commentary references are intended to guide the student who wishes to pursue a subject beyond the confines of this volume.

We are much indebted and will long remain grateful to all those who helped make this book possible. Our special thanks to our colleague, Dr. Albert C. Cain; to colleagues in other training centers who so liberally shared with us their teaching approaches and experiences; to the students who bore with our trial runs of various sets of readings and were so open and direct in their evaluations and comments; to the authors of papers who were so generous in their unconditional willingness to permit reprinting of their writings; and to the secretaries, Miss Alexis Archibald, Mrs. Rosalie Gee, Mrs. Elizabeth Houston, Mrs. Katherine Shugg, Mrs. Carol Adams and Miss Pam Cramer, so understanding of our whims, illegible handwriting, and impatience amid their steady, invaluable assistance in the preparation of this manuscript.

Saul I. Harrison
John F. McDermott

INTRODUCTION

It is a personal pleasure to introduce readers to the writing of colleagues. It is a special delight to introduce a book whose pragmatic purposes and conceptual intent one can enthusiastically endorse, a book whose usefulness to professionals and students alike is so manifest.

It would be praiseworthy enough an undertaking simply to have sieved exhaustively through our widely scattered literature with the care and good judgement the editors have obviously exercised. To have juggled so successfully the multiple selection criteria of comprehensiveness, classic status, current relevance, and general excellence within the compact boundaries of a single volume is all the more to be appreciated. Further dividends are to be found in the editors' introductory and interstitial remarks, which lead the reader into an ever-widening circle of concepts and issues.

Each of these efforts—and successes—in and of themselves would have sufficed to create a worthy sourcebook. But perhaps most of all the editors are to be congratulated for their insistence, in their selection of readings and their own comments, upon the multiple points of view, investigatory approaches, scholarly disciplines, and sources of data necessary to the modern study of child psychopathology. Thus, I welcome the reader to a sourcebook which is not merely eminently needed and useful, but enriching.

Albert C. Cain

PART 1
DEVELOPMENT

The choice of papers reprinted in this section proceeds from our conviction that a knowledge of the concepts and data of normal development is vital to an understanding of the emotionally disturbed child. Those concepts and data now stem not only from the clinician's office, but from such varied perspectives as neurophysiology, ethology, psychology, anthropology, and sociology. Papers which follow articulate the view that the child is a complex biosocial organism, constantly affected by both patterned and accidental forces in his milieu. The critical nature of the interaction of constitutional factors and environment, from the psychobiological primary unit of mother and infant forward, is described within a developmental frame of reference.

The developmental point of view sees the child as an incomplete, ever-evolving organism passing through the developmental sequences, each of which has relevance to those preceding and succeeding it. Inherent in this point of view is a focus on the fluid quality of many features of the child's personality organization. Clearly, normative data and a sense of the wide range of normal variation are vital as a foundation for the developmental point of view. Perhaps even more important is a heavy emphasis on interrelated developmental sequences: the relevance of current states for later developmental phases and, conversely, the implications of subsequent developmental tasks for current development. Character traits, symptoms, and ego capacities are thus evaluated, not by means of static assessments, but in terms of balances between progressive and regressive forces, differentiation between transitory and permanent deviations and the extent to which any given state contains a threat to normal development. This developmental frame of reference encompasses psychosexual stages as well as the evolution of object relations, affects, defensive structures, and ego functions. Further, it includes neurophysiologic mechanisms, psychological impulses, fantasy, thought processes and observable behavior.

The readings in this section reflect the recent, heightened awareness of sociocultural factors influencing the child's development, shaping such varied phenomena as motoric styles, values, language usage, motivations, modes of gratification, and patterns of relationship.

THE INNATE AND THE EXPERIENTIAL IN CHILD DEVELOPMENT

JOHN D. BENJAMIN

The late John Benjamin is equally well known for his scholarly contributions to psychoanalytic research methodology (1950, 1959) and for his major role in reviving interest in the concept of constitution in psychoanalysis (1965). Prior to Benjamin's efforts, the concept of constitution in the psychoanalytic literature, if not utterly neglected or subjected to abuse, was, for the most part, relegated to a brief passing reference. Its principal employment was in ad hoc *explanations of clinical phenomena and focused particularly on libido theory and erogenous zones. Until the last decade, it played an almost equally subordinate role in developmental psychology and theories of child development.*

In this paper, Benjamin presents a history of the concept of constitution in relation to psychoanalytic thinking, and he further refines the concept, stressing the relationship between constitution and environment.

Like Montagu's (1950), his was a dynamic concept of constitution, one emphasizing the developmental vicissitudes of constitutional elements. The renaissance *of this concept has led to numerous fruitful contributions in the study of such constitutional variables in personality and psychopathology as autonomic reactivity, congenital activity level, styles of dealing with internal and external stimuli, response to novel situations, sensory thresholds, etc. (Korner, 1964; Thomas et al., 1963; Bridger and Reiser, 1959; Lipton and Steinschneider, 1964; Fries and Woolf, 1953).*

In a relatively small series of publications over a number of years, I have repeatedly found myself referring to the topic of this presentation, the interactions of the innate and the experiential in development, as a

Reprinted from *Lectures on Experimental Psychiatry,* ed, H. W. Brosin. Pittsburgh: University of Pittsburgh Press, 1961, pp. 19–42.

problem central to the whole of developmental theory (1950, 1952, 1958a, 1959, 1958b; Benjamin and Tennes, 1958).

The obstacles to adequate conceptualizations about genetic factors in personality development are, even more than elsewhere, only in small part intellectual ones. The emotional investments in what I have called second order convictions (1958a) on one or the other side of this notorious pseudo-dichotomy are extraordinarily great, with many psychological, social, and cultural roots (1952, 1958a). As a result, we find a paucity of research designs capable of giving us the sort of data we need for better theory, and with it, better empiric research. If this is not exactly a vicious circle, it is at least a vitiating one; and one that, as in so many areas of applied psychobiological investigation (1958a), stands in marked and unhappy contrast to the exciting progress of recent years in fundamental biology, including basic genetics.

It would be well to delimit our topic in several respects. The whole emphasis of this discussion will be on *interactions between* the innate and the experiential, and not on the one *or* the other. We assume that most complex adaptive or non-adaptive behaviors are importantly co-determined by innate and experiential variables as well as by innate and experiential universals and near universals; and set ourselves the task of first raising, in the hope of eventually answering, questions about the differential modes and degrees of participation and the different mechanisms of interactions involved (1959). From this point of view the only appropriate answer to the question: 'nature *or* nurture?' is—nuts!

I should probably also comment at this point on an essentially unimportant matter, my use of the term interaction rather than the currently popular term transaction. My reason for this choice is simple. Perhaps the Deweyian concept "transaction", as defined and used by Bentley (Dewey and Bentley, 1949; Benjamin, 1958b, does express more accurately the complexities of what actually goes on in human organisms between biological, psychological, and social levels of organization (1952); and thus, by not quite accurate analogy, between the innate and the experiential. I say perhaps, because not only have I no idea whether or not this is true, but also know no way to find out. For as far as I can see, we have no methods for investigating transactions as defined. Whenever we try to do so, it turns out that we are investigating interactions after all. So I prefer to use the simpler and more operational term.

It is obvious, I believe, that there are a number of different investigative approaches to the field of inquiry under discussion, ranging, for example, from genetic behavioral investigations, without immediate consideration of the biochemical mechanisms involved, through the further study of biopsychological relationships, without immediate consideration of genetics as such, through basic chemical genetics, without immediate reference to behavior, to developmental behavioral studies, with primary concentration on the interactions of the apparently innate with the experiential. It is clear that more knowledge and better methods in all of these fields, and others as well, is needed before even approximate answers to some of our questions will be available, in terms of both normal and psychopathological varieties of behavior. Although my interest in all these fields is great, and I have a tangential investigative involvement in some of them, my discussion here will be primarily restricted to my own field of competence, that of investigating normal and psychopathological development within the overall framework of modern developmental psychoanalytic theory.

No attempt can be made at an historical summary of philosophic or general scientific thought on our topic. I think, however, that a brief review of psychoanalytic thinking on the subject is indicated.

Freud's earliest concerns with this problem occupied a substantial part of his writings in the 1890's (1894, 1895, 1896a, 1896b, 1896c, 1897, 1898), most of this dealing with the role of hereditary and experiential factors in the causation of the psychoneuroses, and particularly of hysteria. In partial consonance with the opinions prevalent in French and German medicine at the time, he ascribed an important predisposing factor to heredity; but laid increasingly great weight, initially, upon actual life experiences, one of his earliest major contributions. Here it is necessary, however, to emphasize the highly restricted meaning which Freud gave to the concept of pathogenic experience at that time. Having gone far beyond Breuer in his repeated finding that infantile sexuality was regularly involved in the development of hysterial symptoms, he restricted his use of the concept of pathogenic experience almost exclusively to traumata in the sexual sphere, to seductions by parents or others during early childhood. Much has been written, by Freud himself (1905a, 1905b, 1914b, 1922, 1924a, 1925a) as well as by others (e.g. Abraham, 1907; Jones, 1924, 1953; Kris, 1950b, 1954), particularly recently, about the significance for the development of psychoanalysis of Freud's discovery (1897) that this formulation, on which he had laid such great weight, was not a tenable one; that many of the seductions had not occurred in reality, but were the products of fantasies of his patients. Freud himself repeatedly, and throughout his lifetime, referred to this "momentous error," as he termed it (1905a), as a turning point in his thinking. There can be no doubt that this was true, leading, as it did, to the discovery of unconscious fantasies and of the Oedipus, and to the first formulations of drive theory and infantile sexuality. What concerns us here, however, is not the history of psychoanalysis as a whole, but of Freud's thinking on the subject of heredity and experience. From this point of view, the recognition of "the momentous error" had a remarkable impact for Freud. Having discovered that actual experiences of seduction in early childhood, while certainly of importance (1924a), were not as common in the psychoneuroses as he had once thought they were, they could, therefore, no longer be considered as a "specific aetiology." For the time being Freud ignored all other sorts of experiences except as precipitating factors, and admitted, somewhat ruefully, that "the factors of constitution and heredity necessarily gained the upper hand once more" (1905a p. 275), and that "the factor of hereditary predisposition regains a sphere of influence from which I had made it my business to oust it" (1897, p. 216).

To be sure, he repeatedly, in subsequent writings, stressed the importance of childhood experience in general, as compared to later experiences; but this was much more often in terms of the *universal* experiences inherent in being a member of the human species than it was in terms of *variable* experiences as major factors in ego development. Thus, at various times, the experience of birth, the protracted helplessness of the human infant, the loss of the breast, toilet training experiences, and, more generally, the demands of reality for drive restraint were given major emphases in shaping personality (1923, 1926); less often was there that emphasis on variability in these and other experiential processes, and their impact on development, that one finds in the majority of Freud's successors, both within analysis, and, in this country particularly, in child psychiatry, in dynamic psychiatry in general, in much learning theory, and in social and educational psychology. That much of this environmentalism had roots in American culture which were independent of Freud, is, I think, demonstrable (Benjamin, 1952); but it is ironical that not only the highly productive but also the one-sided and extreme versions of environmentalism can also be traced in part to the influence of Freud's great mistrust of the relatively much greater acceptance of psychoanalysis in this country as compared to Europe, was to a significant extent determined, or at least reinforced, by the environmentalist interpretations given to his work here. I say it is ironical because of the frequency nowadays with which psychoanalysis is reproached with environmentalism. Granted that there is some inconsistency in this as in other aspects of Freud's writings, I think there would be at least as much justification, and probably a good deal more, if one were to reproach him with an *underestimation* of the role of experience.

In provisionally relegating variations in real life experiences to a relatively subordinate position, Freud was led to what seems to me to be the most remarkable paradox in the whole of his thinking–his Lamarckian views on heredity, which persisted throughout the remainder of his life. I am tempted to describe what happened in this respect in the following unquestionably over-simplified formulation: Freud, with his outstanding clinical-observational as well as theoretical gifts, was so impressed with the role of experience in the production of psychopathological states, that when he found that he could not verify a specific simple traumatic experiential hypothesis, rather than looking for more complex combinations of chronic repetitive experiences as pathogenic, he displaced the role of *highly specific experience* from the ontogenetic to the phylogenetic (1913b). With this maneuver, the distinction between the innate and the experiential, which had occupied him to such a great extent in his earliest writings, became, in one sense at least, a meaningless one. The innate *was* the experiential! The usefulness of this much more "momentous error" for Freud's own development lay, of course, in the emphasis it gave to the universality, or near universality, of some conscious and unconscious fantasies; and even more importantly, to the tendencies of fantasies, and the drives they represent, to organize and shape individual experience to a significant degree (cf. Abraham, 1907). In this sense, then, biologically naive as it was, it had some positive impact on the development of psychoanalysis as a whole, in the manner previously discussed. But it obviously failed completely to account for individual variability in development; variability *both* in the innate and in the experiential.

Freud's most explicit formulation of how he perceived the relationships of hereditary to experiential determinants of pathological behaviors was advanced in his famous concept of the *complemental series.* Although first given under this name in the Three Essays (1905b), and restated in the Introductory Lectures (1916–17), he had said essentially the same thing in an earlier paper on Heredity and the Aetiology of the Neuroses (1896b). The principle laid down was a simple one: the stronger the hereditary disposition toward a form of psychopathology, the less need was there for actual life experiences to bring it out; and, conversely, at the other extreme, sufficiently pathogenic experiences could lead to the same nosological results in the absence of any appreciable predisposition on an hereditary basis.

In between these two extremes varying proportions of the two sets of determinants could be found. It will be noted that although the derivation of this principle was an empiric one, the empiricism was purely on the side of experiences: i.e., hereditary factors were never directly studied by Freud, and could not be. What was thought by him to be constitutional was neither derived from prevailing opinion in German and French medicine at that time, based on what I have elsewhere called prescientific concepts of heredity (Benjamin, 1952, 1958a); or was defined as hereditary by virtue of the fact that the experiences hypothesized as being necessary for its occurrence could not be demonstrated to have occurred.

It is also of some interest for our purposes to note that the translation of Ergänzungsreihe as complemental series makes the conceptualization sound more interactive than it actually was. The term supplemental series would better portray the basic thesis advanced, that undefined hereditary predispositions and specific experiences can supplement, or take the place of each other, in the production of psychopathological phenomena. It is clear that Freud's initial conception, following his formulations of drive theory (1900, 1905b, 1915a), and one that with some modifications persisted throughout his work (1940), was that the hereditary variability in predispositions was a function of variability in the instinctual drives and their sources in different erogenous zones. More of this shortly, in the context of later ego-psychological developments in psychoanalysis.

Whatever the limitations of the complemental series formulation, it had the great virtue of militating against over-simplified single factor etiological thinking in such a complex area as personality functioning, while at the same time not succumbing to a scientifically nihilistic pseudo-philosophic denial of etiology as a scientific problem (Benjamin, 1952). To quote myself from a recent paper (1959): "Although his (Freud's) conceptualizations of the nature of the relationships between the constitutional and the experiential, and between the biological and the psychological were necessarily different from those which seem most strategic to pursue today, the basic thesis advanced in this concept appears at present to be as well supported by clinical experience, and as much neglected in most etiological investigations, as it was when he first formulated it" (p. 70). Although, as implied, I believe it to be a highly limited conceptualization, it may well turn out, for example, to be directly applicable to the problem of genetic factors in the so-called schizophrenias (1952, 1958a). Perhaps the process-reactive dichotomy (1944) may prove to be a continuum of this sort, and perhaps not.

A major turning point in the history of psychoanalytic thinking on the subject of the innate in personality development was initiated through the development of psychoanalytic ego-psychology, first through Freud himself (1923); then through Nunberg (1930), Waelder (1930), Anna Freud (1936), and others; and still later, and most incisively, through the conceptual contributions of Hartmann, alone and with his collaborators (1939, 1950, 1953; Hartmann, Kris and Loewenstein, 1947; Kris, 1952), of Erikson (1950, 1953, 1956), of Rapaport (1951b, 1958, 1959a), of Spitz (1957), and others. Again, we must somewhat arbitrarily restrict ourselves to the specific topic under consideration. I bring the topic of modern psychoanalytic ego-psychology into this discussion solely because one of its outstanding characteristics, distinguishing it sharply from earlier psychoanalytic conceptualizations of ego development, is the recognition, or assumption, that there are important innate as well as experiential *ego roots* (Rapaport, 1959a).

There was, of course, a great deal of empiric evidence for this assumption from outside the field of psychoanalysis long before the first serious attempt to integrate it with psychoanalytic findings and into psychoanalytic theory as a whole. With this latter step, in which Hartmann through his major contribution (1939) played the leading role, and to which he, Erikson, Rapaport and others have subsequently contributed significantly, psychoanalysis is in a more favorable position than formerly to systematically integrate and utilize the many highly pertinent data from the behavioral and biological sciences in approaching a unified developmental and psychopathological theory. I personally think that Hartmann and Rapaport, in contradistinction to Erikson, have somewhat overshot the mark in their emphasis on the innate, the autonomous, the conflict free in ego development in general, and in the nature of drive restraining forces in particular. In any case, this strategically and scientifically necessary corrective to the extreme environmentalism of much learning theory, educational psychology, and dynamic psychiatry has opened the way for, but does not in itself constitute, empiric investigation of just how the innate and the experiential do interact in the varieties of normal and psychopathological developments.

I mentioned briefly above how Freud conceptualized variability in the innate in terms of the instinctual drives and their somatic sources. Although his predominant emphasis for many years as regards ego development was in terms of universal experiences, of the demands of reality for drive restraint, there are repeated indications in his later writings (e.g. 1923, 1926) that he recognized the importance of innate factors in ego development also. Nevertheless, it was possible for him in his last major publication, the Outline (1940), to restate his older position with the words: "The id–contains everything that is inherited, that is present at birth, that is fixed in the constitution–above all, therefore, the instincts–."

I quote this passage not so much to illustrate how Freud, like everyone else, could occasionally contradict himself (cf. Schur, 1953), but to point up another consideration, one equally pertinent to our topic. I refer to psychoanalytic drive theory. For if the innate was formerly underrated as a factor in ego development, it seems equally clear to me that it has been somewhat overrated in so-called instinct theory. If one accepts, as I do, Freud's own position as regards the psychological nature of instinctual drives, their non-identity with their somatic sources; if the unconscious *wish* aspect of the drive is emphasized (1898, 1915a), as it repeatedly was by Freud, in contrast to needs (tissue states) on the biological level; then it follows, I think, that the immutability and permanence of instinctual drives, also repeatedly emphasized by Freud (e.g. 1900, 1926, 1940), cannot be taken too literally; that one must think of changes in drive organization not only in terms of maturation and differentiation but also in terms of learning as co-determined by experience; that no instinctual drive is completely determined by innate variables or constants alone. If, then, one finds it useful and profitable, as I do, to conduct empiric investigation within the framework of basic psychoanalytic theory (1959), difficult as this may be (Escalona, 1952a), one comes to the conclusion that drive theory as well as the theory of ego development demand consideration of both the innate and the experiential, and their interactions.

I should now like to bring a number of fragments of investigative problems which have arisen in the course of our long term studies of development. I have selected these solely for their pertinence to our specific and delimited topic. Some of them have been discussed in other publications (1959, 1958b); a few are barely under way as empiric studies, and are mentioned here for the first time.

(1) We have been increasingly impressed in our infant observations with what we have termed a maturational crisis occurring at around three to four weeks of age in full term infants (1958b). As compared with neonates, babies at this age show a marked increase in overall sensitivity to external stimulation. (This occurs irrespective of individual variability in the predominance and use of sensory modalities, which will constitute a separate topic for our discussion.) Without intervention of a mother figure for help in tension reduction, the infant tends to become overwhelmed by stimuli, with increased crying and other motor manifestations of undifferentiated negative affect. With adequate mothering, in this sense, the phenomenon may be masked in terms of pure observation, and elicitable only through experimentation. On purely behavioral grounds, with no direct genetic evidence, and with as yet only suggestively supporting

neurophysiological data (E.E.G.), we conceptualize this crisis as a function of a rapid rate of maturation of sensory apparatuses at this time, with a resultant increase in tension accumulation through external stimulation. Independent observations by David and Appell (1958) on the behavior of infants temporarily separated from their families since birth, and without adequate mothering in this caretaking sense, point up the frequent occurrence of negative behavioral changes at this same age period.

We have reason to hypothesize from our own small sample within the range of so-called normal mother-child relationships that the absence of adequate tension reduction during this "critical period" has important results in helping to create an increased predisposition to anxiety (Benjamin, 1958b; Freud, 1926; Greenacre, 1941). The number of children followed long enough in our studies is as yet too small to permit statistical confirmation of this precursor relationship to later anxiety manifestations. Since these are of course also importantly dependent upon later experiences, and possibly on other innate variables also, a larger population of subjects will be necessary for a rigorous correlational demonstration of the validity of this proposition. Although this is one of the problems that plague us in our overall studies of personality development, I have discussed it in some detail elsewhere (1959), and it need not concern us further here. For the behaviors as described, if correctly conceptualized, serve to illustrate one sort of interaction between the innate and the experiential, whether or not they are correlationally predictive of later behaviors. In this case, the interaction can formally be described as one between an assumed innate universal (i.e. the rapid rate of maturation of sensory apparatuses at this age) and a demonstrated experiential variable (i.e., the help in tension reduction given by the mother or mother surrogate at the time). It also illustrates the obvious necessity for including under the concept of the innate many phenomena which are not observable at birth, but require physiological maturation of organs and systems in order to be manifested. I mention the obvious only to emphasize the extreme importance of considerations of *timing* for those much more complex interactions of maturation and experience which must, and in part have, replaced the earlier more naive and simplicist propositions about the impact of such experiences as weaning, toilet training, sexual education and the like on personality development, without reference to the *when* of the experiences in terms of individual maturational rates.

For purposes of semantic clarity, we restrict our use of the term maturation to those growth processes for which it can either be reasonably assumed or actually demonstrated that somatic maturation underlies the behavioral changes, a usage in consonance with traditional psychological terminology and with some psychoanalytic writings, but to be distinguished from the more general use of the word to denote those processes through which a so-called mature personality is achieved. Now it is a truism, of no great interest for our specific purposes, that maturational processes in our restricted sense, like everything else that is innate, also need an environment in which to develop. There is interest in the question, however, as to how the *rate* of maturation is affected, if at all, by variations in the environment, physical or psychological. My second example of an investigative problem, in this case barely under way, represents a sort of paradigmatic and oversimplified approach to this problem on a physiological level.

(2) As is well known to all who observe infants, it is often difficult during the first few weeks of life to tell at first glance whether a neonate is awake or asleep. Nothing, in fact, could be further from the truth than the concept, advanced largely by those who have never really looked at babies, that the life of the young infant consists simply of suckling, satiation, deep sleep, awakening with hunger, and then the same cycle over again. As many students of infancy have noted (cf. Peiper, 1956), and as P. Wolff (1959) in particular has recently emphasized in his careful studies of neonatal behavior, there are at least three differentiatable levels of sleep in these earliest days of life. They are best characterized by variations in the depth, rate, and rhythm of respiration, and, in deep sleep, by lowered responsivity to most external stimuli, and by a *heightened* tendency to elicited and spontaneous startles.

If one now turns to electroencephalographic recordings for help in distinguishing between the sleeping and the awake neonate, one finds that none is forthcoming. For the first three to five weeks of life, no electroencephalographic sleep patterns are seen (Garsche, 1953), although diffuse slowing and the absence of muscle artifacts can sometimes permit a differentiation. But these have nothing to do with a sleep pattern as such. At about four weeks, on the average, the first signs of such a pattern appear, and develop rapidly.

We have here, then, a clear-cut instance of a maturational process; and one with a fairly constant rate. Our question is: to what extent is this rate independent of experience; in this case the experience of extra-uterine life? There is some evidence, I should add, that something very much like neonatal sleep occurs in the last weeks of intra-uterine existence (Peiper, 1956).

We are attempting to answer this question through current investigation comparing the gestational ages of premature with full term infants with respect to the first appearance of the sleep pattern. Although the design is a maximally simple one, the interpretation of the results may be somewhat less so, for a variety of technical reasons, including the possibility of other complications of prematurity affecting maturational rates. Assuming that we find any regularity in the results, they could range from the finding that the initiation and rate of maturation was largely independent of extra-uterine influences, as would be indicated, for example, if thirty week prematures should not show a sleep pattern until thirteen to fifteen weeks post partum; to the other extreme of total dependence upon such extra-uterine influences, as would be indicated by a three to five weeks post partum appearance in all or most of the subjects. In between these two extremes, we should be able to estimate an approximate degree of interdependence of the two factors, if such exists. Our first provisional results point in the direction of a heavy weighting toward the extra-uterine factor; i.e., the appearance of bursts of sleep spindles at a much earlier gestational age in the prematures.

From a formal point of view, we are here examining the interaction of an innate universal with an experiential universal. That such a formal categorization, useful and even necessary as I think it is in the complex field under discussion, nevertheless cannot begin fully to describe the rich variety of interactions to be found, is well illustrated by our next example. This will take us into more familiar territory, to a stage of development where we can already see the beginnings, rather than merely the precursors, of the ego as we understand it psychoanalytically; one where we can empathize more easily with the infant. I refer to the phenomenon of the social smiling response. Here, as in the first of our examples, we would again formally characterize the interaction as one between an innate delayed maturational universal and an experiential variable. Yet the maturational factor is of a different nature.

(3) As is well known, social smiling, occurring classically at the age of two to two-and-a-half months, but often seen somewhat earlier also in our and others' experience, has been demonstrated in careful studies by Kaila (1932) and by Spitz and Wolf (1946) to be elicitable not only by the human face, but by schematic representations of it in the form of a configuration of two eyes, a nose, and a forehead. Apart from the question of whether this so-called eye-schema is the *only* stimulus to smiling at this age, a statement which we have every reason to challenge, there is no doubt whatsoever that the human face is by far the most frequent stimulus for this sort of smiling—hence the name *social* smiling.

Since the smile can also be elicited by the eye-schema in inanimate form, we agree fully with Spitz that this smiling response to the face is a *delayed maturational innate releaser mechanism* in ethological terms, with the schema as the *key stimulus.*

In a publication in preparation I am presenting systematic evidence to support the hypothesis, however, that both the timing and the nature of this smiling are not *only* maturationally determined, but are significantly co-determined also by previous experiences with the mother or mother surrogates as sources first of tension reduction, and later of undifferentiated positive affect.

The data supporting this hypothesis include correlations between independent ratings of tension reduction by the mother and the timing and frequency of the smiling response, as well as observations of much earlier smiling to varying stimuli, achieving a high degree of negative predictability (1959) as to when smiling will not occur; that is, when there are other and independent evidences of undifferentiated negative affect.

Some of Lorenz's observations (1958) lend independent support to this thesis of an experientially modifiable I.R.M., in that he gives examples from his studies of late appearing maturational I.R.M's requiring conditioning over longer periods of time, as contrasted with the rapidity of imprinting. (I shall resist the temptation to enter here into a discussion of the central importance of the natural history of smiling for many basic aspects of personality theory; a subject about which much has been written from different theoretical points of view; e.g. by Spitz (1946b, 1957, 1959), Spitz and Wolf, Meili (1957, 1959), Goldstein (1957), Buytendijk (1947), and Piaget (1952). I shall permit myself the undocumented comment, however, that as far as a theory of affects is concerned, the development of the smiling response affords, as I see it, a refutation of the Schopenhauerian thesis, at one time apparently subscribed to by Freud also, that pleasure is nothing more than the absence of pain.)

(4) In a recent publication (1959) I have discussed a group of observations, and propositions derived from them, concerning the predictive implications of individual differences between infants with respect to sensory modalities and their uses. It would not be appropriate, I think, merely to repeat this material here; and to expand upon it would take far more time than is available. Since it has considerable pertinence to our topic, however, I do not wish to skip over it entirely, and shall therefore include some of it in a maximally condensed form.

The general topic of sensorimotor behavior in infants and young children has received much attention, from various points of view and from a large number of investigators, including Piaget (1952, 1954), Bergman and Escalona (1949), Escalona (1952b, 1959), Katherine Wolf (1953), Werner (1957), Meili (1957), and P. Wolff (1959). The special interest which I and my close associate and collaborator in all our studies, Katherine Tennes, have brought to this field lies in two areas: (1) hypothesized relationships between sensorimotor behaviours and later choices of defense mechanisms; and (2) their predictive value for the strength and dynamic impact of *infantile separation anxiety*—a behavior which we have found necessary and useful to distinguish from the related but not identical *stranger anxiety* (1959, 1958b).

I shall omit details of both sets of hypotheses. While a satisfactory demonstration of validity for the first is still lacking, and will in any event require longer follow up of our cases, we have considerable though not yet conclusive evidence for the validity of the second, in the form of a series of predictions and outcomes.

Since experiences are also demonstrably of the greatest importance in determining these phenomena, which, in turn, are of such significance in normal and pathological development, both these sets of hypotheses, if validated, would represent significant examples of a different formal relationship than we have as yet exemplified: the interaction of innate *variables* with experiential variables.

A word of reservation about the use of the term *innate* in this example is perhaps indicated. Although it is entirely plausible that we are here dealing with individual differences due to genetic variability, it is possible that intra-uterine, natal, and very early post-natal experiences may contribute importantly to them. Only actual genetic investigation of these sensory phenomena, preferably for this sort of problem with twin methods, could give us a definitive answer to this question; and this has not yet, to my knowledge, been undertaken.

(5) With my fifth and last example, we enter an area of greater theoretical complexity than any we have discussed so far: the field of cognitive functioning in general, and of conceptual thinking in particular, *as they relate to the rest of developmental and personality theory.* Of major significance in terms of descriptive psychopathology (1944) as well as of normal developmental theory, cognition has long been somewhat of a stepchild in dynamic psychiatry and clinical psychoanalyses, perhaps because of having attained the reputation of being "undynamic," the harshest epithet at our disposal! Now it is true that some of the most important and creative work in the field of cognitive development has been done by investigators, such as Piaget (1952, 1954) and Werner (1957),

whose theoretical systems are essentially *nonmotivational* in nature; and that this fact sets certain limits to the explanatory and predictive power of these systems as such. At the same time, however, their data and conceptualizations strongly challenge the motivational developmental theorist and investigator to examine more thoroughly the developmental relationships between motivations (drives), affects, object relations, defenses, and conflict in general, and the autonomous (Hartmann, 1939; Rapaport, 1951b, 1958) and "epigenetic" aspects of development. The psychoanalytic theory of thinking, as first formulated by Freud, and subsequently developed by Hartmann and others, but most particularly by Rapaport (1950, 1951a), offers us, in my opinion, a highly useful though far from validated framework for such studies.

For the past several years, we have been working on the further development of *methods* suitable for investigating various aspects of cognitive development, and on the testing of these instruments on various populations of subjects (Ricciuti and Benjamin 1957). I shall not report on these here nor on the first provisional results of their application to normal and psychopathological populations at different ages. Here I wish merely to outline, in the form of questions, a few areas of great interest to us, and of pertinence to our overall topic, with no discussion of underlying theory, or research methods and design, or, for that matter, of the probabilities, with available methods, of getting any definitive answers at all to the sort of questions we are asking. All of this must be reserved for future communication; and, more important, for future work.

1. To what extent are the difficulties in conceptual thinking found in some psychopathological states in children and adults, a function of disturbances in early and later object relationships—particularly the mother-infant relationship; and to what extent does the inverse hold true, that the disturbances in object relationships are in part due to innate deficiencies in areas of functioning including the cognitive and its precursors? The derivation of this question from older work on formal thinking disorders in schizophrenia as well as more recent studies of childhood psychosis is clear.

2. More generally, in terms of normal developmental variability, can we relate any defined and assessed variables in early parent-child relationships to longitudinally assessed aspects of cognitive functioning and its precursors; and what sort of interactions can we postulate? What are the motivational and timing parameters in the development of such functions as discrimination, perception, and sorting ability? What, if any, differences can systematically be found between the infant's cognitive performances

on tasks with highly cathected as compared to relatively neutral objects? As I have commented elsewhere (1959), this last question suggests the repetition of some of Piaget's experiments with systematic variation of object cathexes.

3. A survey of the existing literature on the development of concept formation in children, as well as our own work to date, strongly suggests that there is a sharp acceleration in the curve of ability to perform certain abstract tasks, particularly sorting, at about six years of age, plus or minus half a year. Disregarding for the moment the highly complicating factor of learning and of practice effects in general through kindergarten and school experience; assuming that the choice of six years as the starting age for school may well be, on the contrary, a function of a primarily maturational development of these capacities; and planning to control this complicating factor through a rather simple experimental design, involving preschool versus non-preschool subjects; we ask the following question: to what extent does the resolution of the Oedipus conflict determine this spurt in abstract abilities; and, again inversely, to what extent does a relatively autonomous maturational increase in these capacities co-determine the resolution of the Oedipus conflict? If both these possibilities seem like highly implausible speculations to some of you, I would ask you to think about what the categorization of mother and father as members of a class of adults, rather than as "the" adults, might mean.

These examples, and particularly the last one, are brought to illustrate more complex and therefore more typical, paradigms of interaction than the relatively simple ones presented earlier. Here we are dealing with true dynamic interactions, back and forth, between innate and experiential variables and universals, in various combinations, and with the forces involved acting on an organism constantly changing over time as a function of these and other forces.

While it is possible to make approximate mathematical models of such complex systems, the limitations of our measures and therefore of our empiric knowledge are not thereby overcome. What I would most emphasize here is that in such interactive conceptualizations, the role of the innate is just as dynamic, no more and no less, than is that of the experiential. It is a common error to think otherwise, to conceive of what is inherited as something inert and static, upon which forces derived from experience alone exert a non-reciprocal influence. The same error is often made with respect to the biological in the study of bio-psychological relationships.

One more related consideration, and I shall have gone as far as I can in this presentation, short of a systematic and detailed analysis of the problem. We have every reason, empirically, to state the following: not only can innate differences in drive organization, in ego functions, and in maturational rates determine different responses to objectively identical experiences; *but they can also help determine what experiences will be experienced, and how they will be perceived* (1959). [1]

Conclusion

I should like to conclude these remarks on a more personal and informal note. For what seems like a long time I have advocated, first in teaching and training, and then in publications, giving greater attention to constitutional and genetic factors in normal and pathological development than these have generally been accorded in our psychiatric and psychological culture.

Although there is still a good deal of disinterest or even aversion among many dynamic psychiatrists toward problems of innate factors in mental illness, partly as a continuing reaction against the pre-scientific concepts of the direct hereditary causation of the psychoses in late 19th century continental psychiatry (1952, 1958a), the gap is slowly lessening, as it is also between dynamic and descriptive and dynamic and biological psychiatry (1950, 1952, 1958a).

In psychoanalysis proper, the influence of such men as Hartmann, Kris, Rapaport, and Erikson, among others, has made an interest in the innate respectable again, if still far from popular. Yet, promising as these developments are, I find some causes for discomfort in the present scene, too; and in the opposite direction. It seems to me that there are an increasing number of colleagues in psychiatry and in the biological sciences who are in effect reverting to an over-estimation of the role of heredity in mental illness; or, rather, to old fashioned undifferentiated concepts of how genetic factors may be related to personality in general and to various mental disorders in particular; reverting, accordingly, to a serious *under-estimation* of the role of experience in producing normal and deviant behaviors.

I have recently discussed (1958a) the present status of genetic research in schizophrenia, and the large number of questions it has left unanswered, in spite of reasonably convincing evidence that for some schizophrenias at least such factors are of major importance. Without wishing to

[1] The work of Mirsky on pepsinogen levels, and some of his conceptualizations about their interactions with early experience (1953), is a nice example of one sort of possible codetermination of this sort.

deny the possibility that some forms of psychosis may turn out to be primarily genetically determined in the specific and restricted sense that some forms of neurological disease and of feeble-mindedness are, there is as yet no evidence whatsoever that warrants the genetic comparison of any psychosis with, say, a Huntington's chorea or a phenylketonuric idiocy. Be that as it may, what I have been talking about in this presentation in terms of the interactions of the experiential with the innate in no way justifies a lessening of interest in the role of experiences, nor a lessening of convictions about their importance, in shaping personality. On the contrary it should logically lead to intensified study of *what* experiences in interaction with *what* innate variables and universals at *what* time lead to *what* behaviors.

There is ample experimental evidence by this time that experience alone can produce marked variations in behavior in genetically homogeneous animals (cf. Beach, 1954; Scott, 1957; and references cited there). I have had the personal satisfaction of instigating (1950) and participating in (Bernstein, 1957; Ruegamer et al., 1954) some of this experimental work.

Even without such evidence, however, those of you who, like me, have their primary identifications with the clinic, whether in clinical research or therapy or both, know on the basis of evidence, and not just of convictions (1958a), that behaviors often do change as a result of experiences leading to unlearning and new learning, whether in therapy or in the world outside the clinic; and that they can change significantly and permanently, not just in a transitory fashion. Recognition of the importance of innate factors, then, no more justifies psychotherapeutic nihilism than the demonstrable importance of experience warrants a wishful overestimation of what we *can* accomplish therapeutically. Moreover, the fact that we can completely fail in the therapy of many cases is in itself no proof, or disproof, that innate factors are responsible for the failure. The undoing of the effects of very early experiences can be a formidable enough task in itself.

It is appropriate at this point to return to Freud. As in several areas, he was somewhat inconsistent also in his appraisal of what psychoanalytic therapy could accomplish, and what its limitations were. At times he unquestionably overrated it; at others, as in his late paper, Analysis Terminable and Interminable (1937), he brought a dispassionate and profound realism to bear on the subject, while maintaining a basic and, I think, justified therapeutic optimism. In other late passages (1926, 1933), though, he predicted that the time would come when the chief function of the analyst would be to give the biochemists and endocrinologists exact indications as to what drugs should be used, which he surely meant as an id directed form of therapy. Now it is entirely conceivable, I think, and have so written (1952), that with continued progress in chemical genetics a time will come when it will be possible to prevent and ameliorate primarily or partially genetically determined diseases through the administration of the appropriate constitutive or adaptive enzymes or other functional macromolecules, or substances designed to influence systems dependent on these. But that this could in itself undo the effects of pathogenic experiences without simultaneous unlearning and new learning, whether through psychotherapy or through other means, implies a degree and type of reductionism to which few of us could subscribe, and which contradicts much of what Freud himself wrote on psychopathology and on therapy.

In the same period of Freud's life (1933), he formulated the goal of therapeutic analysis, as of normal development, in those moving words: "Where id was, there shall ego be". Since id, for Freud, meant, as we have seen, the innate, and since ego development, in his conceptualization, was largely a function of experience, he was here formulating a major triumph of life experiences, including therapeutic experience, over the innate.

So did another genius, more explicitly if less professionally; and with an optimism which far exceeded Freud's, and mine, but which, like the passage I have just quoted, serves as an inspiring if not quite realistic goal for all of us who are concerned with the positive and negative impacts of experience on personality. Lucretius, poet, philosopher and intuitive scientist, wrote (1951): "Though education may apply a similar polish to various individuals, it still leaves fundamental traces of their several temperaments. It must not be supposed that innate vices can be completely eradicated: one man will still incline more readily to outbursts of rage; another will give way a little sooner to fear; a third will accept some contingencies too impassively. And in a host of other ways men must differ one from another in temperament and so also in the resultant behavior. To unfold here the secret causes of these differences is beyond my power. I cannot even find names for the multiplicity of atomic shapes that give rise to this variety of types. But I am clear that there is one relevant fact I can affirm: the lingering traces of inborn temperament that cannot be eliminated by philosophy are so slight that there is nothing to prevent men from leading a life worthy of the gods" (pp. 105–106).

Of course, we must remember that there have been some few mutations since the time of Lucretius.

CRITICAL PERIODS IN THE DEVELOPMENT OF SOCIAL BEHAVIOR IN PUPPIES

JOHN P. SCOTT

Scott's writings (1958, 1958; 1962), along with the parallel work of investigators such as Harlow (1958, 1962), Lorenz (1952, 1965), and Tinbergen (1951), have restored studies of animal behavior to a prominent place in psychology and psychiatry. The concept of a critical period represents a special illustration of the effect of early experience upon later behavior. In essence, it refers to a limited period in the organism's early life, during which specific patterns of environmental stimuli ("input," "stimulus nutriment") are a prerequisite for its continued normal development. Deficiencies or gross disturbances in such early experiences within the critical period lead to various developmental distortions or stunted capacities. If the required experiences occur subsequent to the critical period, the deficit is not "made up"; the pathological course is not reversed.

Having obvious analogies in embryology, this concept's major applications to psychological development were initially limited almost exclusively to the realm of object relations. The hypothesis was that relative absence or gross deficiencies of mothering in vulnerable periods of infancy produced irreversible arrests and distortions in the infant's later development (Bowlby, 1961; Spitz, 1945, 1947). Recently, the critical period concept has received further documentation from animal experiments and ethology (Denenberg, 1964; Hess, 1962; Moltz, 1960; Sluckin, 1965). Still the subject of lively debate, it has been explored or applied across a broad range of developmental phenomena, such as perception and cognition. It is suggested that the critical period concept may well prove crucial to the understanding of a wide spectrum of normal and aberrant development.

As part of a program for the study of heredity and social behavior in dogs, the author and his colleagues have made a thorough study of the

Reprinted from *Psychosomatic Medicine,* 20, 1958, pp. 42–54.

development of social behavior in puppies, with the idea of finding out the times at which heredity was most likely to exert its effects. As we did so, we also observed that there were certain periods in which environmental factors were particularly likely to affect behavior. As a result we have, from time to time, reported evidence on what we have called the critical hypothesis (Scott, Fredericson and Fuller, 1951; Scott and Marston, 1950b). This idea is one which is basically related to certain clinical ideas concerning the effect of early experience on later mental health and behavioral adjustment. It is therefore important that it be clearly understood.

Critical Period Hypothesis

What is the critical period hypothesis? In the first place it is in certain respects no longer a hypothesis, but a well-established generalization which can be stated as follows: All highly social animals which have been so far studied show early in life a limited period in which the group of animals with which the individual will form positive social relationships is determined. To take a few of many examples, the slave-making ants raid the nests of other species for eggs and larvae. As the captive ants grow up, they become attached to their captors and take care of their young and no longer recognize their own species. The experiments of Lorenz (1935) with the newly hatched greylag geese which quickly form social bond with the first moving object they see, whether goose or human, have dramatized the findings of Heinroth and others that contact with the young birds in the proper state of development establishes a strong social relationship, regardless of the species concerned. Lambs that are taken at birth and raised on the bottle form social relations with people rather than other sheep and become as a result quite unsheeplike in many respects. The dog is particularly interesting because the process of socialization with human beings is a normal part of its life as a domestic animal. Dogs are more closely attached to people than are many animals, and develop a relationship which is in many ways similar to the human parent-child relationship. Furthermore, the critical period for socialization in the dog does not begin at birth, but approximately three weeks later (1953).

The existence of critical periods for the process of primary socialization can therefore be taken as established. Other parts of the critical period hypothesis, namely, that there exist certain periods of sensitivity to psychological damage, still remain as hypotheses and need a great deal more experimental evidence before they are accepted.

The existence of critical periods of any sort implies certain subsidiary hypotheses. The first of these is that the critical period has a physical basis and results from the state of anatomical, psychological, and physiological development of the animal. The second is that hereditary variability between species will affect the course of development. We have found, in a limited survey of different forms, that such differences are great, and they do not consist simply of the condensation or elongation of a standard type of development. The order of developmental events may even be reversed in different species. It does look, and this is the third hypothesis, as if the social development of any particular species is strongly correlated with the social organization of the adult (1951). For example, in dogs there is a close association between mother and puppies during the first three weeks in life, but since the permanent social relations of the puppy are formed after this period and at a time when the mother leaves the litter for long periods, the result is that the strongest relationships are formed with the litter mates. This relationship is in turn the basis of pack organization of adult dogs and wolves. A final hypothesis is that there should be genetic variability in the course of development *within a species,* which means that the time of onset of critical periods and their relative sensitivity should vary from individual to individual. This paper will be chiefly concerned with the evidence which we have been able to gather regarding the physical basis of the critical period for primary socialization in the puppy.

Normal Development

I shall first describe the normal course of social development in the puppy. The newborn pup is a very immature animal, being both blind and deaf, and unable to move except in a slow crawl. Its movements are slow and shaky, and its reflexes sometimes occur seconds after stimulation. In spite of being deaf, it whines loudly if cold or without food. Its chief needs appear to be warmth, milk, and elimination, and these are taken care of by reflex behavior. If moved away from the mother, the puppy will crawl, usually in a circle, throwing the head from side to side. If it comes into contact with the mother, it attempts to nurse. When it succeeds, it pushes with its head and forepaws and also with the hind feet. In doing this it touches and so stimulates the other puppies in the litter. Any touch will initiate exploratory movements. The mother also frequently stimulates the puppies by nosing them and licking the genital and anal areas. This produces reflex elimination as well as stimulating the pups to exploratory movement and nursing.

This is the typical behavior of puppies in the *neonatal period.* No immediate change is observed in their behavior. They gradually grow somewhat stronger and quicker, until the opening of the eyes, which typically occurs just before two weeks of age. This marks the beginning of the *transition period,* one of very rapid change and development. At its beginning the eyes open, and at its end the puppy gives a startled reaction to sound. It can walk instead of crawl, and can move backward as well as forward. Its first teeth appear, it takes solid food, and it begins to urinate and defecate without assistance by the end of the period, which typically occurs just before three weeks of age.

At approximately three weeks of age, the puppy first begins to notice other individuals at a distance and shows evidence of conditioning and habit formation. This is the beginning of the period of *socialization,* in which its primary social relationships are formed. At almost the same time, the mother begins to leave the puppies unattended so that there is a tendency for the strongest relationships to be developed with the litter mates rather than the mother. During the next few weeks it is easy for the human observer to form a positive social relationship with the puppy. This period of primary socialization comes to an end somewhere around seven to 10 weeks of age, which is the normal period of weaning. This does not mean that the puppies are self-sufficient with regard to food. Studies of wolves show that the pups are not able to hunt at all until four months of age, and are not really independent until six months of age (Murie, 1944). In the domestic dog, food is normally supplied by man, but in the wild state it is provided by the hunting parents. This period, which ends with the sexual maturity of the puppy, is called the *juvenile* period. In some of our domestic breeds estrus of the females occurs as early as five months, but in the ancestral wolves this does not happen until the end of the second year.

We can see that there might be several critical periods affecting the development of new social relations: that of primary socialization at three weeks, that when sexual relations are established at the end of the juvenile period, and that when the parental relationships are established as a new generation of pups is born. We are here concerned primarily with the first of these periods, the period of primary socialization, because we can make the assumption that the end of the primary social relationships will strongly affect the degree of adaptation and adjustment in later relationships.

Anatomical Basis for Social Behavior

Function is of course related to form, and form in turn to the process of growth. Let us examine the anatomical changes which accompany changes in social behavior. In the young pups there are three sorts of external changes which are easy to follow, the eruption of the teeth, the opening of the eyes, and the opening of the external ear canal. The last is somewhat harder to follow and is probably less reliable than the other two.

All the following data are based on observations of purebred puppies reared under the standard conditions of our long-term experiment on genetics and social behavior (Scott and Fuller, 1950a). The total numbers differ slightly from table to table because complete information was not gathered on all animals in the early part of the experiment.

The first teeth to appear are the canines, followed shortly by the incisors, which all come in together, except that the corresponding upper teeth come in before the lower. No animals show teeth at two weeks, nearly half have some teeth by three weeks, and nearly all have at least the upper canines through the gums by four weeks of age. An eruption of the teeth therefore coincides with the beginning of the period of socialization.

The teeth erupt the earliest in basenjis and beagles (Table 1), and wirehaired terriers are definitely slower than all the rest. The shelties are unusual in that the lower teeth develop relatively fast, and, in certain animals, the lower canines actually appear before the upper.

The eyes typically open at about two weeks of age or slightly before. Very few are partly open at one week, the majority are open at two weeks, and all animals have the eyes completely open by three weeks of age (Table 2). The opening of the eye is the first external sign of the transition period. Eighty-five per cent of the purebred puppies have the eyes partly open at two weeks, and we can estimate the average time at 13 days. There is, however, individual variability and differences between breeds. The eyes open earliest in cocker spaniels and beagles, a little later in basenjis, and much slower in shelties and wirehaired terriers.

The opening of the ears is a more prolonged process and comes a little later than that of the eyes. Over half the animals show the ears at least partly open at two weeks, and all are completely open at four weeks. The differences between strains are not great. The shelties appear to be the most rapid, and the wirehaired terriers the slowest, with the other breeds being intermediate and showing only slight differences.

The variability of any of these events which can be precisely timed, such as the eruption of the teeth or opening of the eyes, has a range of approximately one week in normal animals. The wirehaired fox terriers appear to be definitely slower in all respects, but in the other breeds the speed of development is not correlated in the different traits. It looks as if there can be separate variability in any one of these characters. One might expect that the development of all the teeth would be correlated, but even here the shelties show a relatively more rapid development of teeth in the lower jaw than do the other strains.

TABLE 1

ERUPTION OF UPPER CANINE TEETH

Breed	No.	%Erupted at 2 weeks	3 weeks	4 weeks
Basenji	51	0	79	100
Beagle	54	0	74	100
Cocker spaniel	67	0	22	100
Sheltie	30	0	30	100
Wirehaired fox terrier	31	0	14	89
TOTAL	233	0	47	99

TABLE 2

OPENING OF THE EYE

Breed	No.	% Completely open at 1 week	2 weeks	3 weeks
Basenji	43	0	65	100
Beagle	49	0	94	100
Cocker spaniel	51	2	94	100
Sheltie	25	0	31	100
Wirehaired fox terrier	27	0	11	100
TOTAL	195	0.5	67*	100

* Average with equal weight for breeds = 59.

Function of the Sense Organs

Histological studies of the development of the puppy eye (Blume, in preparation) indicate that the retina is not fully developed at the time of the opening of the eyes, nor even by three weeks of age. However, it can be shown that the eye responds to light at a much earlier age. Some puppies will give a winking reflex to light at birth, long before the eyes open. This appears to happen most frequently in those breeds which have red hair color and light skin pigment.

As soon as the eyes open and the pupil can be clearly seen, we can demonstrate a pupillary reflex when a strong light is shown into the eye. At the same time the nystagmus reflex can also be observed. If the puppy's head is moved slowly sideways, the eyes roll or flick back and forth. This, however, is probably a reflex controlled by the nonauditory portion of the acoustic nerve rather than by sight. Incidentally, puppies do not show nystagmus in reaction to a moving object or rotating cylinder held in front of them.

The above reflexes concerned with eye function appear early in development, but it is probable that these are responses to light and darkness, and that the capacity to perceive images is not developed until four or five weeks of age.

The onset of function in the ears is much more definite. Only one per cent of the puppies give a startle reaction to sound by two weeks of age, and 74 per cent give a reaction at three weeks of age. We may therefore estimate that the average time is about 19.5 days. There is considerable genetic variability between the breeds, and the wirehaired terriers have the highest percentage of animals which give a definite startle reaction.

As with the eyes, there is no evidence that the puppies use their ears in finer ways at first. The tendency to startle to all sorts of loud sounds persists for a week or two.

All the puppies gave some reaction to odors at birth. They give reliable avoidance reflexes to two substances, oil of anise and a proprietary drug used as a dog repellant, which is a compound related to citronella. Eighty-three per cent of all puppies gave the avoidance response to the repellant, and a smaller number to oil of anise. Harman (private communication) found that the parts of the brain connected with olfaction were unmyelinated at birth, and it is probably that these reactions to odor are largely connected with the sense of taste rather than true olfaction. In the human subject, both substances can be detected in both the nose and throat. There is some observational evidence that hungry puppies react to the smell of milk in the neonatal stage, but we have no definite evidence on this point.

With regard to other senses, puppies definitely react to pain and touch at birth. The majority of all newborn animals give a "winking reflex" to touch and nearly all of them show this by one week of age.

In general the function of the sense organs at birth is quite limited, but all senses are at least partially functional at approximately three weeks. Prior to the beginning of the period of socialization, it is impossible for the animal to be stimulated by many environmental changes. Those stimuli which are effective are ones which set off the reflexes connected with eating and other vital processes. In effect, the very young puppy is insulated from many sorts of environmental stimulation.

Development of the Central Nervous System

Observation of puppies in the neonatal and transition stages gives no indication that the animals learn in the way that adults do. For example, a puppy placed on the scales may crawl to the edge and fall off. When he is put in the situation repeatedly, he does the same thing time and again, with no improvement in adjustment.

The only change in behavior for some time after birth is that the puppies become somewhat faster and stronger in their simple behavioral reactions. Fuller et al, (1950) found that the avoidance behavior of puppies could be easily conditioned to sounds shortly before three weeks of age. This could not be done previously, and the change in an individual animal's behavior occurred from one day to the next. This change is, of course, related to the development of the function of hearing, but no conditioning to other sensory stimuli could be obtained at earlier ages. Responses were given to taste and touch but did not produce conditioning. James and Cannon (1952) confirmed Fuller's results and found that the avoidance reaction to a mild electric shock is restricted to the part stimulated by 28 days of age, indicating that psychological development is still going on.

Harman (private communication) has made histological examination of the brains of young puppies and finds that the newborn brain is myelinated in very few places, those corresponding to the parts associated with the observed reflex patterns of behavior. This lack of myelination may account for the slow movements of the young puppies, as contrasted with their more rapid responses at later ages.

A measure of actual function of the developing nervous system was obtained by Charles and Fuller (1956) by taking the EEG of puppy brains at different ages. At birth the puppy brain has almost no waves at all, and there is no differentiation between sleeping and waking states. At three weeks, corresponding to the other differences in behavior noted above, the sleeping and waking states are differentiated, and the amplitude of waves is increased. The adult form of the EEG is achieved at approximately eight weeks of age, which is shortly after the earliest time at which mothers normally wean their pups.

Another measure of nervous development is the heart rate (Fig. 1). At first glance this might be considered a purely physiological response. However, the heart is actually a very sensitive indicator of both body activity and various kinds of emotions. As will be seen on the graph, the heart rate of the newborn puppies is very high and stays this way through the second week. Then it takes a very decided dip at from three to six weeks, coming back up to the early level around seven weeks of age. Thereafter the heart rate slowly declines toward the adult level. These general changes seem to be independent of breed. The first change occurs at the beginning of socialization, and its end occurs at seven weeks, coinciding approximately with the time of the adult EEG. We can suppose that this is the period when complete cortical connections are established with the hypothalamus. We can conclude that the period from three to seven weeks is an especially sensitive one for emotional reactions, which corresponds to observation of overt behavior. We might also speculate that, since the cortex is not completely developed, emotional reactions during this time might be less permanently learned. On the other hand, they might be more disturbing because complete cortical control has not been established. We have here a fascinating field for further precise experiments on the effects of early experience.

The development of the nervous system and its associated psychological abilities goes through several stages. The puppy definitely does not come into the world with all its psychological abilities developed. He is in fact, quite immature at birth and for the next three weeks. We would expect, and have found (Scott et al. 1951), that it would be extremely difficult to produce psychological trauma upon very young puppies and that any future effects on their behavior produced at this time would have to be made by physiological or anatomical injury.

These results raise the question of what the situation is in the human infant. Human development is obviously different from that of the puppy, but we have every indication that the neonatal human infant has a nervous system which is decidedly undeveloped. We need to know more about the origin of learning abilities in human infants before we can talk authoritatively about the effects of early experience. It is not too much to suggest that it would be contrary to the general law of biological adaptation to find that the nervous system was highly sensitive to psychological damage at such a period as birth. This, however, does not invalidate the possibility of anatomical birth injuries.

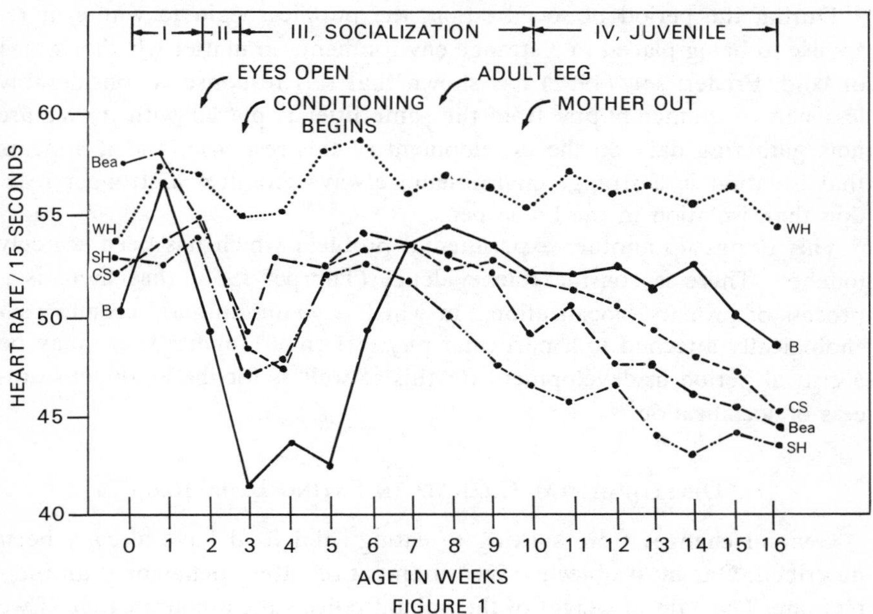

FIGURE 1

Average heart rates at different periods in development. Note that the breeds show a lower rate during the early part of the period of socialization than they do either earlier or later. The heart rate change probably measures the puppy's emotional reaction to being picked up, and indicates unusual emotional sensitivity at this age.

Social Behavior

The most obvious social behavior of young puppies is vocalization. This response is obviously related to various sorts of social contacts. The type of behavior involved is et-epimeletic, or calling for care and attention. In any situation in which the puppy is unable to adapt, the puppy substitutes this reaction for any attempt at adjustment on its own part. Newborn puppies whine repeatedly until they begin to nurse. Fredericson (1952) has shown that, besides hunger, the sensation of cold is the stimulus most likely to produce whining. In addition, puppies will whine loudly if accidentally hurt. All these things can be alleviated by social contact.

During the early stages of development, the number of whines made by the puppies while being weighed for a period of one minute was counted. In general the response decreases, so that by four weeks of age most of the puppies make no noise at all. The response is chiefly due to contact with the cold scales, and there is evidence of breed differences, the beagle reacting with relatively small numbers of noises.

During the period of socialization, the puppies begin to whine in response to being placed in a strange environment, no matter whether warm or cold. Fredericson (1952) has shown that this response is considerably lessened if another puppy from the same litter is placed with it. We are now gathering data on the development of this response, and it appears that isolation in a strange environment always produces a stronger reaction than isolation in the home pen.

This brings up another experimental problem which has been scarcely touched. There is considerable evidence (Thorpe, 1956) that there is a process of primary "localization," in which a young animal becomes psychologically attached to a particular physical environment. There may be a critical period in development for this as well as for the analogous process of socialization.

Developmental Changes in Eating Behavior

General changes from sucking to eating solid food have already been described. Our most objective measurement of eating behavior is an indirect one. The gain in weight of the animal reflects the amount eaten. If we chart the weekly gains of puppies we find, as we might expect, that the rate of gain declines week by week. However, there is a definite change in the nature of this curve at three weeks of age. The curve before this time is entirely dependent upon the milk supply of the mother. Afterwards the puppy has the possibility of eating solid food, and we would expect that the decline in the growth would be less rapid as soon as solid food was available. However, there is probably a psychological factor involved also. Puppies pay no attention to solid food if they get plenty of milk from the mother, even beyond the age of three weeks. This was definitely the case in our F_2 hybrids which were fed by F_1 mothers having an abundance of milk, even in excess of what the pups could use. In their case also, the rate of decline of growth was halted after three weeks, indicating that the animals were taking in more food (Fig. 2). We may conclude that because of their ability to be conditioned the animals now learn to eat, increasing their food motivation.

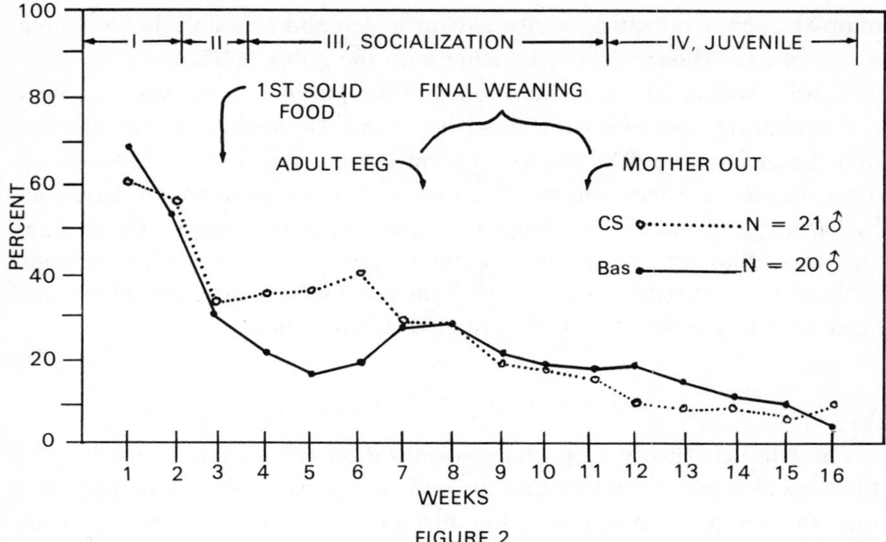

FIGURE 2

Weekly percentage gain of weight in male cocker spaniel and basenji pups. Note the change in the slope of the curve at 3 weeks. This reflects both the taking of solid food and increased food motivation resulting from learning and habit formation. The difference between the two breeds reflects a genetic difference in palatability of the food supplied.

This idea is supported by observations on hand-fed puppies. During the neonatal stage they are quite difficult to feed by ordinary means. It is hard to get them to take a nursing bottle, and they have a tendency to stop before the stomach is filled. They can be laboriously fed by a dropper, but the easiest and most practical way to insure adequate feeding is to inject milk into the stomach through a tube. The explanation is that natural feeding is stimulated by specific primary stimuli or releasers which activate certain reflexes and simple patterns of behavior. Puppies become more active and more responsive to external stimuli if hungry, but hunger has little relation to the amount of food taken.

During the transition period, between two and three weeks, the pups are much more easy to feed. They will readily take a bottle, and, if placed near a dish, they can clumsily lap the food. However, they will not take adequate amounts if the dish of warm milk is simply left with them. They still have to be stimulated by fresh food and handling several times a day in order to be properly nourished.

By contrast, puppies older than three weeks of age are relatively easy to feed, particularly because a supply of food can be left with them and they will continue to eat adequate amounts.

We can draw several conclusions from these observations. One is that puppies cannot be satisfactorily fed on a demand schedule before three weeks of age. Maternal care, together with the reflex behavior of the puppies, will provide adequate nutrition, but the puppy has not yet become a self-regulating organism with regard to eating. He needs external stimulation. Later on, when the ability to form associations and habits is developed, the hunger mechanisms, together with motivation to eat produced by learning, are sufficient to regulate the eating of the puppy in a satisfactory way. This, of course, poses certain questions regarding the reasons back of the necessity for handling human infants, a problem which has been raised by Spitz (1951), Ribble (1944), and others.

Feeding and Socialization

The simplest theory of primary socialization is that this relationship is built up through the association of food with a particular individual, and that the relationship can develop further based on this original bond. Brodbeck (1954) tested this by rearing cocker spaniel puppies which were mechanically fed, and comparing their behavior with that of puppies fed by hand. In both cases the experimenter spent an equal amount of time playing with the pups. The result was that the pups which had never been fed by people still showed strong attraction to the experimenter. This indicates that feeding is not the only element in the formation of a social bond.

On various occasions we have observed puppies which, through some accident to the mother or deficiency in her milk supply, were underfed. Young pups that are well-fed are fat and lethargic. In contrast, the underfed animals are active, show more interest in people, and seem to show an earlier expression of many behavior traits than do the normal ones. An opportunity to check this finding occurred recently in connection with an experiment of John A. King, in which he fed two groups of basenji puppies by hand twice a day during the period of socialization. One group was given as much as it could eat, and food was left in the dish so that it could eat later. The other group was given considerably less and its weight was much lower. Both groups were given a handling test which measures responses of the puppy to a human handler.

With puppies raised in a different situation in which most of the food comes from the mother but in which there is considerable handling from five weeks on, there is a big decline of the timidity score between five and seven weeks, which may be taken as a measure of the process of socialization. In the experimental pups, whose contacts with people were started at four weeks and confined to feeding, the timidity score at five weeks averaged very nearly as low as the other animals at seven weeks. The average score stayed slightly higher than the controls in subsequent weeks, but not significantly so. At an early age, and using a genetic type of animal susceptible to the development of timidity, animals which are totally dependent for food show a greater degree of socialization than those only partially dependent.

Another obvious result was that there was a differentiation between the reaction to the person who did the feeding and another person who did not. This difference appeared more strongly as the pups grew older. All this indicates that the process of feeding does contribute importantly to social relationships but does not constitute the whole process.

The difference between the hungry and nonhungry animals was not as great as had been anticipated. There was a great deal of individual variability in behavior. However, hungry animals did show a consistently greater proportion of investigation and food begging in their responses than did the controls.

Sucking Frustration

D. M. Levy's experiment on puppies (1934) indicated that the canine equivalent of thumb sucking could be produced by sucking frustration. Levy's experiment extended over a relatively long period in the development of the puppy, including the transition period and the early part of the period of socialization. Because of the importance of sucking in early development and its disappearance later, there should be a limited period in which this effect could be produced.

Ross, Fisher, and King (in preparation) experimented with this possibility, using the technique of sudden weaning, after which the pups could obtain food only by lapping or eating solid food. The experiment was done on a group of 34 experimental and 24 control animals. None of the experimental puppies developed spontaneous body sucking, but they did show an increased tendency to suck a finger of the experimenter. When this was analyzed in relation to age of the puppy, it was found that all the puppies weaned between the ages of 10 and 18 days showed more finger sucking than the controls. After this date, many experimental animals were as low as the controls, although there were some indications of smaller effects. There were no effects at all by the time the animals were five weeks of age.

We can draw two conclusions. One is that there is an obvious change in the puppies' behavior with regard to sucking at the beginning of the period of socialization. Up to this time, a puppy deprived of its mother will mouth. After this point, it shows very little tendency to suck. The simplest explanation is that the power to discriminate between objects which give nourishment and those which do not has been developed.

The other conclusion is that the simple and sudden deprivation of the opportunity to nurse does not by itself produce the neurotic form of body sucking. Whether there is a critical period for this latter phenomenon has yet to be determined.

Heredity Variability

As can be seen in Table 3, there is considerable evidence that hereditary variability in development exists, both between individuals and between breeds. For example, cocker spaniels are the first to open their eyes, are slow to develop the startle response to sound, and are intermediate between the other breeds with regard to the development of teeth. The wirehaired terriers were the slowest to develop in every trait observed except the startle reaction to sound, in which they are fastest. There is every indication that the different sense organs and anatomical characteristics vary in the speed of development independently of each other. There is no one highly correlated pattern of development which is slowed down or speeded up as a unit.

Assuming that the age of onset of each developmental event falls into a normal curve, we can estimate the average time and variability of each event. As seen by Table 1, there is approximately three days' difference between the fastest and slowest breeds. Eighty-six per cent of all animals should fall within a range of one week. If anything, these estimates of variability are probably too great, since they are based on the one per cent or so of animals which are as much as a week away from the normal.

The species as a whole shows a developmental pattern which is not departed from except in cases of gross abnormality. Events occur in the general order described in the early part of this paper, so that we can speak of definite periods of development. We can set the beginning of the transition period at 13 days with a normal range of three or four days on either side. Similarly, we can place the beginning of the period of socialization at approximately 19.5 days with a similar range of variability. This means that when experimental procedures are employed in which time is the experimental variable, close attention must be paid to the breed and the state of individual development. Two litters of puppies of exactly the same chronological age could give completely different results.

TABLE 3
ESTIMATED DEVELOPMENTAL AGES IN DAYS FOR SIGNIFICANT EVENTS

Breed	Mean and Standard Deviation		
	Eyes completely open	Ears startle to sound	Teeth Eruption, upper canines
Basenji	13.1	19.6	18.6
Beagle	11.0	18.7	19.1
Cocker spaniel	11.0 ± 1.9	20.2 ± 2.9	23.3
Sheltie	15.2	20.3	22.6
Wirehaired fox terrier	16.9	17.8 ± 2.2	24.3 ± 3.0
TOTAL	13.0 ± 2.3	19.5 ± 2.3	20.8 ± 2.9

Conclusions

At the beginning of this paper I stated that there is a definite critical period for the process of socialization, and that it must rest on a physical basis. The data which I have just presented show that there is a definite physical basis in the dog, and that there are two important points where sudden changes occur. One of these is the point just before three weeks, where there are changes in the ability to be conditioned, in the EEG, in the emotional responses indicated by the heart rate, in the ability to hear, and in the growth rate and method of nutrition. The other point, at seven to eight weeks, is so far defined only by the adult EEG and the change in emotional reaction measured by the heart rate. Final weaning sometimes occurs as early as this date.

To summarize, the puppy before three weeks of age is highly insulated from its environment by the immature state of development of the sense organs, by the lack of ability for conditioning, and by maternal care. From three to seven weeks, the puppy is in an extremely interesting stage in which its sense organs and cerebral cortex are not yet completely developed but in which it has extremely sensitive emotional reactions and is capable of making associations. This is the time when primary socialization normally takes place and during which it is easiest for a dog owner to establish a strong social bond. These facts provide us with an experimental opportunity to analyze some of the theories of the effects of early experience on later social adjustment and mental health.

Comparing these with results on human babies, we see that we need more fundamental facts about human development. We know a great deal about babies from birth until 10 days of age. After this time mothers and babies leave the hospital and disappear into the home where there is little opportunity for scientific study. Facts and information are very scarce until about the age of two years, when the babies begin to emerge from the home and appear in nursery school. It is precisely this period in which we are most likely to find the period corresponding to the primary period of socialization in the dog, if it exists. As I mentioned above, one of the most important basic facts yet to be adequately described is the development of simple learning ability in young infants.

One of the biggest problems in predicting human development is the element of individual variability in behavior. The study of development in the different dog breeds, where we should get the maximum possible variability in development, gives us some hint as to what we might expect in human beings. There is considerable individual variability and variability between dog strains. However, the timing does not vary a great deal in terms of the length of the period of development. The changes at three weeks of age in puppies appear to take place within a week for all animals. If we assume that the life span of a dog is one sixth that of a human, we might expect a human range of variability of six weeks. Actually, the possible range in early development is probably considerably less than this.

The existence of a critical period for primary socialization is so widespread in the animal kingdom that there is every reason for suspecting that a similar period exists in human development. If so, we are faced with a number of questions:

1. When? In other animals, the critical period may occur immediately after birth or hatching, or fairly late in development, as it does in the puppy. The human infant is somewhat more mature than a puppy at birth, but far less so than a lamb. We would expect that the critical period would not begin immediately after birth, and the evidence that we have indicates that it may begin as early as a month or six weeks, or as late as five or six months. However, any social relationship depends on the behavior of two individuals, and the period immediately after birth may be a critical one for the mother, although the evidence from adoptions indi-

cates that mothers can form a strong social relationship at other times.

2. How long? The period of primary socialization certainly lasts as long as the period of complete dependency on the mother, up to one and a half or two years, and possibly even longer.

3. By what means? The positive behavioral mechanisms which establish primary social relationships, such as feeding, contact, handling, and the like, are difficult to understand without experimental data. Likewise, we would expect to find negative mechanisms which prevent the socialization of infants to strangers, such as the anxiety or fear reaction to strangers as described by Spitz (1950). Their understanding would be immensely important as a means for bringing about a better identification with other human beings and a broader range of tolerance.

4. Why? This brings us down to the primary data in this paper, and raises the question of the physical basis of critical periods in the human infant. As I have indicated above, animal experiments indicate the type of thing we should look for: the development of sensory and motor organs, the development of the central nervous system and the power of simple learning, the development of social behavior patterns, and the development of individual hereditary differences. We have much information on the first two, and far less on the rest. It is this kind of evidence which is the easiest to get on human subjects, and without this firm foundation we shall never be on safe ground.

Seen in this light, our study on the dog provides the opportunity for the experimental analysis of environmental and hereditary influence on an undeveloped nervous system. The dog is an animal which is capable of forming a type of social relationship with people very similar to the human parent-child relationship. We should be able to find out whether early emotional experiences produce lasting effects. Without evidence, it is just as logical to suppose that an immature nervous system would be less severely affected. It will take a long time and will be a laborious and expensive job to obtain the needed facts, but we should eventually be able to bring the phenomena of early social experience out of the realm of conjecture into that of established scientific fact.

Summary

1. The existence of a critical period for the establishment of primary social relationships is a well-established phenomenon in social animals. This paper has dealt with the physical and hereditary basis of the critical period in the dog.

2. Normal social development in the puppy can be divided into several periods based on changes in social relationships. Several of these may be critical, but the most important is that of primary socialization, beginning about three weeks of age.

3. The beginning of this period is accompanied by certain anatomical changes: the eruption of the teeth and the opening of the ears. Eyes open at an earlier date.

4. Its beginning is also closely associated with the appearance of the function of the ears. The senses of touch and taste (including tasting gases) are present at birth. The eye is sensitive to light before it opens, but not completely functional until some time after.

5. Changes in the heart rate appear which correspond to changes in the EEG and ability to be conditioned.

6. At three weeks, there is a change in the rate of growth which may be attributed to both additional food and to a psychological change in food motivation.

7. Experimental evidence indicates that feeding is an important factor in socialization, but not the only factor.

8. There is a marked change in the fingersucking response of weaned puppies at an age corresponding to the beginning of the critical period.

9. Hereditary variability of the exact time of onset of the critical period exists both between individuals and between breeds. However, the functional variability appears to be smaller than that in the accompanying anatomical changes.

10. In the period immediately following birth, the puppy is strongly protected from psychological influences. During the critical period it becomes highly sensitive, at a time when the sense organs and nervous system are still not completely developed. The exact effects of experience during this time are still to be determined.

11. These data suggest facts which must be ascertained in order to establish the existence and duration of a similar critical period in human infants. They also suggest ways in which important clinical theories can be experimentally tested.

SOME ASPECTS OF NEUROPHYSIOLOGY OF THE NEWBORN AND THEIR IMPLICATIONS FOR CHILD DEVELOPMENT

JULIUS B. RICHMOND AND EARLE L. LIPTON

Richmond and Lipton's article is more than a valuable, compact, personal review of infant neurophysiology. It presents their own work on neonate autonomic reactivity (Lipton and Steinschneider, 1964) and contains, at the same time, a plea for more direct empirical data (less reconstructive-retrospective, adultomorphic "speculation") on infant development, as well as for recognition of developmental neurophysiology as one of the building blocks of child development and child psychiatry. The call for more infant research is being met increasingly from many different quarters (Wolff, 1959, 1966; Stevenson, 1967; Pavenstedt, 1962; Siegel, 1967, 1968; Foss, 1961, 1963, 1965), and such data are gradually coming into child psychiatry's field of vision. Many psychoanalytic developmental workers, while quick to attack the reconstructive, speculative qualities of some of Melanie Klein's extravagances regarding infant development, are ready to welcome—indeed gather—empirical data on infants from other than clinical sources. They see these as integrative with, rather than superior to or obviating the need for, reconstruction-based theories of early development.

Developmental neurology and neurophysiology remain in a rudimentary stage (Peiper, 1963; Paine, 1965; Scheifel and Scheifel, 1964) and are still relatively neglected throughout much of child-psychiatric education, practice, and research. As they gradually do become integrated, Richmond and Lipton will have served us well by their repeated emphasis that central variables be considered within a consistently interactional approach, with our efforts best directed to exploration of the interaction between intrinsic and environmental variables, rather than to question of which has priority.

Reprinted from *Dynamic Psychopathology in Childhood,* ed. L. Jessner and E. Pavenstedt. New York: Grune & Stratton, 1959, pp. 78–105.

The clinician who works with children is necessarily concerned with the development of object relations, the ego, personality, and social and cultural patterns of adaptation. For a deeper understanding of these developmental phenomena it becomes necessary to learn more of the building blocks out of which they are formed. The study of the development of relationships in the human infant should logically carry us back to embryonic and fetal subjects, but since this is not feasible, we have concerned ourselves mainly with newborn infants.

Because of the infant's incapacity to communicate at a verbal level, psychologically oriented studies of the newborn infant are relatively few. Indeed, studies of newborn infants can only be *oriented* psychologically, since data collection must necessarily be physiologic (including motor behavior) or biochemical. The problem of conceptualizing what is transpiring within the infant psychologically can lead to adultomorphic speculations on which theoretical formulations are then based. Because of the limitations of our knowledge concerning infant development, efforts should be expended toward the accumulation of data on which more effective theoretical formulations may be based. It is hoped, however, that as new formulations develop they will be modest and in keeping with the data rather than premature elaborations from the data. It is anticipated that direct observations of infants will obviate the need to rely on speculations derived from retrospective data from older children and adults.

In considering early infant development, it is helpful to visualize a model which incorporates various levels of communication between parents and infant. If we view a hierarchy of communications which influence parent-infant interaction, we may see the social and cultural backgrounds of the parents as having determined the feelings of the parents (their individual psychology) in relationship to the infant. The communication to the infant, in terms of how he is fed, clothed, fondled, and diapered, is physiologic. This relationship may be represented diagrammatically as follows:

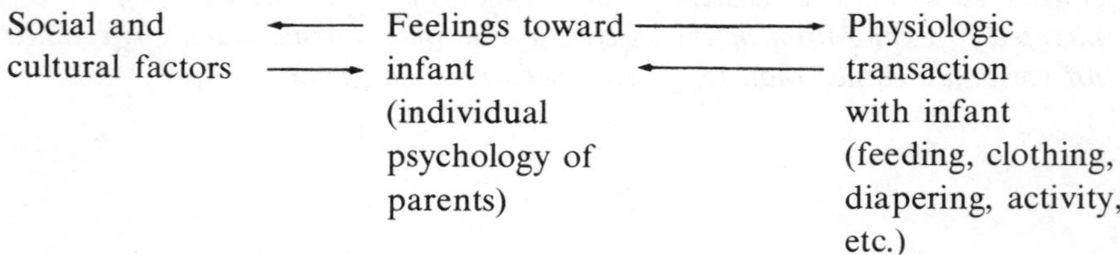

The complexity of nonverbal forms of communication leaves us without a functional language for describing parent-infant interaction (Spitz,

1957). This complexity has been indicated by Benedek (1956) in her statement that, "Growth, neurophysiologic maturation, and psychosexual development are intrinsically interwoven processes" (p. 390). Thus, at various ages, depending upon the state of neurophysiologic maturation, the process of communication will vary. The development of object relationships, for example, is facilitated by visual maturation.

Knowledge of newborn neurophysiology can be helpful in several ways: (1) it may provide us with more understanding of constitutional differences at birth; (2) it may provide us with data concerning inter-individual differences at birth which may be related to developmental patterns in the growing organism; and (3) it may provide us with basic data concerning the physiology of emotional development. In this connection, Engel (1954) has indicated: "Indeed, the inescapable fact is that there is as yet no physiology of the mother-infant symbiotic unit, or of object relationship. Nothing is known of the physiology of separation, grief, and depression; other than embryology, there is no real comparative physiology of growth and development; the physiology of moods and affects is incomplete; there is no physiology of love, and only meager knowledge of sexual processes, erotic phenomena, and sexuality. Yet, much evidence suggests that such processes are concerned in intimate but obscure ways with the development of a wide variety of somatic changes, including pathologic changes" (p. 370).

In order to facilitate a better understanding of the physiology of emotions, it is essential that we have adequate data concerning the newborn in order that these data may serve as a baseline for further studies and for the development of theory. Our presentation will concern itself, therefore, with significant data available concerning the central and autonomic nervous systems of the newborn infant. If these data help in the formulation of theory, they will have served their purpose.

CNS Immaturity at Birth

The brain of the human newborn infant is comparatively large, but it is histologically and biochemically quite immature. Its weight of 300 to 350 grams is nearly that of adult primates (chimpanzee, 350 grams; gorilla, 450 grams; orangutan, 240 grams). Within two years the brain weight nearly trebles, and by six years of age 95 per cent of the mature weight (1200-1300 grams) has been attained. Since water content decreases after birth, future comparative studies should include data on solid tissue weight.

Conel's (1939) studies of the cerebral cortex of the young infant have provided us with more information on the development of the cortex than we have concerning other parts of the brain. The inner cellular layers of the cortex are the more advanced at birth; this is particularly true of the anterior and posterior central gyrus areas. In the motor cortex the most advanced areas are those which control neck and shoulder movements. Progressive complex arborization of dendritic processes during the first few months of life was found with no evidence of a quantitative cellular increase. Thus, cellular endowment is fixed at birth, but complex morphologic changes continue for a long period. Since it is now generally accepted that neurons are connected in a network and not merely in a linear series, and that nerve impulses pass about the connections in a circular, more or less continuing fashion, the potential significance of this growing arborization for the development of the infant may be appreciated (Gerard, 1955). Certainly, the pediatrician is well aware of the disorganizing effects of central nervous system infections and other insults on the orderly pattern of development.

The relative slowness of the maturation of the central nervous system may well be a leading factor in man's ultimate developmental attainments. The extreme flexibility of his thought processes appears to evolve through prolonged scanning of the environment with simultaneous and subsequent integration through complex processes of association. Hebb (1949) has stated that

> the process of perceptual learning must be thought of as establishing a control of association-area activity by sensory events. The larger the association areas, both absolutely and relative to the size of the sensory projection areas, the slower the establishment of such a control must be and the less rigid and complex its final form [p. 123].

This would tend to explain the rapid early learning in lower species and the slower primary learning in man.

Myelin first appears in the fetus at four months gestation, and there is subsequently a progressive appearance of the material in certain tracts of the cord. The motor root fibers precede the dorsal roots in this regard. The principal fiber tracts of the brain stem and spinal cord are myelinated at birth but little or no myelin is found in the cortex. In fact there is little in the cerebral hemispheres until six to nine months of age, and pyramidal tract myelinization is not completed until five to six years of age (Arey, 1944; Kennedy, 1957).

In the past, attempts have been made to correlate the initial functional activity of the nervous system with the appearance of myelin, synaptic thresholds, development of neurofibrillae, and other phenomena. It has been established that neurons can convey impulses prior to myelinization. Conel (1939) has avoided making any such correlations, for it would appear that the relationships among many of these, in addition to biochemical factors, interacting in complex fashion are responsible for the development of neural function.

After early embryonic life, mammals show essentially no regenerative capacity in the central nervous system (Hooker, 1950). Experimental insults to the developing neural crest of lower species result in irreversible damage to central and peripheral neural structures. In this manner, Yntema and Hammond (1955) have demonstrated the derivation and migration of gastrointestinal ganglion cells from neural crest tissue. Once the enzyme systems presumed to be responsible for the capacity for regeneration in some inframammalian species have been definitely established, we may hope for comparable data concerning the time at which embryonic nerve tissue loses this capacity.

Advances in the field of enzyme chemistry have resulted in many studies of the developing nervous system in animals. Cholinesterase, acetylcholine and porphyrin concentration in various sites has been tentatively correlated by some authors with function and with neural differentiation (Kluver, 1955; Shen, 1957). Few studies have been performed on human tissue in varying stages of development. Richter's excellent review (1955) indicates the directions which such work might take as a result of provocative animal studies. Studies of the rat and guinea pig show critical periods of histologic, enzyme and electrical activity change. These occur in the prenatal period of the guinea pig and postnatally in the rat, which is considerably less mature at birth.

During the first four years of life it is estimated that more than one half the total body oxygen consumption is by the brain (Richter, 1955). This may be correlated with the rapidity of growth during these early years. It appears that enzyme systems concerned with glucose oxidation first appear in lower centers during fetal life. These energy supplying mechanisms continue to increase after birth. Anaerobic glycolysis, still present in the newborn, may account for the greater ability to withstand hypoxic insults as compared to the adult (Kennedy, 1957).

The enzyme systems change as the "metabolism of growth" is replaced by the "metabolism of function" (Richter, 1955). The adult brain has a much reduced capacity to synthesize or utilize proteins and lipids and is almost wholly dependent upon carbohydrate. This factor plus the rapidly developing blood-brain barrier allows for relatively greater homeostasis in the brain than any other organ.

Environmental Influence on Structure and Function

From available evidence it would appear that the neonate brain has certain advantages in its relatively immature and less differentiated state. There has been considerable clinical speculation that the relative infrequency of cerebral palsy and other neurologic disorders as a consequent of hypoxia and other insults is due to the immature brain's capacity to recuperate with a minimum of residual damage and to the facility with which other brain areas compensate for any loss of function which may occur (Kennard, 1948; Kennedy, 1957).

Experimentally, environmental stimulation appears to have some effect upon ultimate structure and function under normal circumstances of development. Langworthy's studies (1933) in kittens revealed that myelinization may be significantly influenced by neuronal function. The optic nerve of the eye blindfolded from birth histologically manifested less myelinization than that of the contralateral, stimulated eye. In similar fashion, LeGros Clark (1947) demonstrated a failure of development of certain retinal cells in animals restricted to an environment of blue light from birth.

Rao (1955) found that vascularity of the visual cortex was decreased by the removal of eyes in neonate rats. Apparently, human premature infants whose eyes have been exposed to light since birth show more mature optic nerve development than full-term infants of an equivalent age at the time of death (Kennard, 1948). These types of studies seem to give support to the contention that even after the fetal stage, environmental stimulation (or lack thereof) can modify developing structure in the central nervous system.

Evidence of the importance of afferent impulses in influencing function comes from the stimulating work of Weiss (1950). Motor neurons, separated from their associated muscles by section of their axons, given rise to less selective impulses. If regeneration occurs into a different muscle, the neuronal discharges become less general and diffuse and subsequently take on characteristics determined by the new muscle. Thus, a muscle exercises an effect upon its associated motor neurons that determines their central selectivity.

Central afferent connections may play a vital role in the early generalized behavior of the organism. Specificity of response and inhibition of mass activity may well relate to increasing afferent impulses. Barron (1950) indicates that: ". . . in ontogeny, the arrival of afferents within the neuronal field of the limb efferents is associated–in the sheep, for example–with the dissociation of the limb from activity patterns of the trunk initiated through stimulation of the maxillary division of the trigeminal".

Hebb's experiments (1955) suggest that early sensory stimulation (or at least relationships with others) is needed for the development of the ability to learn later from experience. Puppies raised in solitary confinement had little capacity to avoid painful stimuli after repeated exposure, unlike control animals raised in the usual environment. Their responses were inappropriate, unorganized and panicky. Spitz (1957) compares this with the later learning difficulty observed in children who had experienced affect-deprivation in infancy.

Studies of the postoperative recovery of sight in cases of congenital blindness (cataract) indicate that despite the presence of considerable development in other aspects of behavior, the first visual learning is extremely inefficient and often amazingly difficult and delayed (Hebb, 1949). This is confirmed by Riesen's studies (1947) of chimpanzees reared in darkness who could not for a long period discriminate even the moving, white-clad attendant from any other part of their environment. Less integration is apparently required in insects or rats reared in darkness since they discriminate visually with little if any delay under such experimental circumstances. This further illustrates the relatively more rapid primary learning in lower species referred to by Hebb (1949), who observed that "the human baby takes six months, the chimpanzee four months, before making a clear distinction visually between friend and enemy. Evidently, this is a period of learning as well as of maturation, not just a matter of waiting until certain neural structures are fully grown, with learning then at a typical adult rate."

Neonate Capacity for Sensation and Response

The onset of motor behavior is at eight weeks gestation in the human fetus. Patterned responses to tactile stimulation occur first, followed at nine and a half weeks by unprovoked spontaneous movements (Hooker, 1939). By fourteen weeks most of the neonate reflexes are at least represented. After this, movements are less stereotyped and responses become more specifically related to the areas stimulated. Proprioception, taste, olfaction, audition and vision are potentially functional senses prior to birth according to studies in premature infants (Carmichael, 1954).

The problem of whether findings in the fetus so tested really represent the true fetal state has been expressed by Barcroft. He stated that hypoxia in the extrauterine state may account for some of the responses and activities observed. Data from these observations have served as the basis for discussions which debate whether behavior develops through individuation of partial patterns from an initial total pattern, as proposed by Coghill (1929), or through the progressive integration of initial simple reflexes as suggested by Windle (1962). Barron (1950), in an incisive discussion, has integrated these views on the basis of current neurophysiologic principles; the reader is referred to his paper for elucidation.

The newborn reacts to light but little is known about the ability to differentiate stimuli in terms of wave length, complexity of form, etc. As with audition, responses depend upon intensity and duration. There is evidence of visual fixation on objects and pursuit movements (Graham, et al., 1956). Such observations demonstrate a "certain amount of ability to orient in the environment and to localize the sources of excitation" (Pratt, 1954).

Pitch discrimination has not been definitely established on the basis of behavioral response. Short intense stimuli produce lid reflexes, autonomic changes and gross muscular responses. Decreasing response occurs with repetition. Tones of greater intensity and duration tend to decrease motor activity. Response to sound varies according to the physiologic state of the infant, with little reactivity during nursing. These observations have been utilized as a gross test for hearing in the newborn infant (Richmond, et al., 1953).

Infants react vigorously to various odors and seem to indicate "pleasure" by sucking and licking and "displeasure" by grimacing, head turning, etc. The neonate differentiates certain taste qualities; sucking with a sugar stimulus, stopping when salt or bitter stimuli are presented.

Reactions to pressure, pain, and thermal stimuli have been studied, but little is known of differential sensitivity of various cutaneous areas. Thermal stimuli often produce local responses, though extreme cold often leads to withdrawal movements, while warmth may lead to movement towards the stimulus. The authors' studies of heart rate and skin temperature responses to the stimulation of various skin areas are described later. Many additional observations of neonate sensitivity and neuromuscular behavior are to be found in Pratt's review (1954), the observations of Gesell (1947), McGraw (1946), and many other workers.

Despite this evidence of considerable sensitivity to external stimuli, Carmichael (1954) believes "it is the internal stimuli which account for most of the mobility of the infant." It is our general impression, however, that under usual home and nursery conditions the neonate probably is responding to external stimuli a much larger proportion of the time than has been stated in the past. Some of our experimental data which follow tend to support our view.

Autonomic Function

Our interest in children with disorders commonly designated as psychosomatic (ulcerative colitis, peptic ulcer, asthma, eczema) has led us to an inquiry into the genesis of the psychophysiologic disturbance in these children (Mohr, et al., 1955). Our present state of knowledge does not permit us to define the precise contributions of constitutional predisposition which may influence organ involvement, or environmental factors which may be implicated in specific organ response. This is, of course, the "nature vs. nurture" controversy; no attempt is made to provide a solution of this problem, for we feel that we are concerned with the interaction of these forces rather than the priority of one over the other.

For a better understanding, data are necessary which will contribute toward some clarification of these problems. An editorial in *Psychosomatic Medicine* (1953) summarized the current developments in this field as follows:

> Earlier studies devoted to a kind of descriptive typology seem now over-simplified. They have given way to more carefully contrived and controlled experimental ones and to the accumulation of more soundly tested data. This is a healthy development that should lead, in time, to much needed theoretical formulations in this complicated field where interacting forces of many kinds are at work [p. 373].

In an effort to define constitutional factors more clearly, we have felt the need to investigate the "functional constitution," of the individual in terms of autonomic reactivity in the early life of the infant. We have, therefore, directed our attention to such studies in newborn infants. The problems concerned with autonomic studies generally and this age group specifically are formidable. The studies to be presented, therefore, while lacking in direct application to clinical work, are essential for the elaboration of theory and as building blocks on which long-term observations of children may be based.

It is significant to emphasize that these studies are important not alone for a better understanding of "psychosomatic disorders", but are also basic to learning more of the development of cortico-autonomic relationships. These relationships have implications for an understanding of the physiology of emotions, particularly if the physiologic data can be correlated with psychological interaction of parents and child. Studies of patterns of response in early life should ultimately offer a better understanding of the genesis of the physiology of anxiety, anger, and other emotional states. This has implications for the child's development of concepts concerning his relationship to his body as an object, emerging ego patterns, and personality development.

Because of the relative lack of information concerning autonomic function in the neonate, we have found it necessary to study its general characteristics. This has led to many methodologic problems, both in the laboratory and in the analysis of data, which can be dealt with only briefly in this presentation. For more extended discussion, the reader is referred to a recent paper (Lipton, Richmond, et al., 1958). Our data are derived from a population of newborn infants in order to discern general patterns of autonomic reactivity as well as the variations within the individual.

General Characteristics of Neonate Autonomic Activity

In one of our experiments, 32 infants were studied in a constant temperature environment (Lipton, Richmond and Lustman, 1955). Each was stimulated with thirteen different stimuli applied in the same order. These consisted of one minute of (1) tactile stimulation (to and fro) of the lips, abdomen, genitalia and anus; (2) air jet of constant velocity on the same areas; (3) cold (25° C) and warm (45° C) immersion of the foot and ankle; (4) sudden lowering of the body to elicit a startle reflex; and (5) restraint of both arms, and all extremities. Heart rate, recorded on an EKG, was measured for one minute periods before and during stimulation. Skin temperature studies were performed simultaneously.

Relationship between Prestimulus Level and Response. The heart rate change with stimulation showed an inverse relationship to the prestimulus rate in this population data. Greatest increments in rate occurred at the lower prestimulus levels. This is a confirmation of the observations of Lacey and Wilder which have been labeled: "the law of initial values" (1956). Presumably this represents a homeostatic control of the autonomic nervous system by means of feedback or self-regulatory mechanisms.

These data emphasize that in studies of the autonomic nervous system it is essential to know the state of the organism prior to stimulation in order to interpret the response appropriately.

Differential Responses to Varying Stimuli. The correlations between heart rate, prestimulus level, and algebraic change in rate all are statistically significant. Cold immersion produced greater responses than air on the abdomen, and air on the anal region gave less reaction. Thus, one observes that the reactions are not "all or none" and that seemingly identical stimuli applied to different body sites produce different orders of response. Stroking of the abdomen similarly was more productive of increase in rate than stroking the anus. In fact, the latter stimulus often resulted in a slowing of the heart rate. We are not yet in a position to explain these differences neurophysiologically.

Influence of Internal State upon Reactivity. In a subsequent study, repeated stimuli were presented to each of ten neonates before and after feedings during their first five days of life (Lipton, Richmond, et al. 1958). Here we found, not only that tactile stimulation of the oral mucosa produced greater heart rate response than similar stimulation of the abdominal skin, but that both heart rate level and algebraic change in rate were greater when the infant was presumably hungry. These findings emphasize that mild stimuli which simulate daily life experience of the newborn infant are productive of responses.

The neonate is responsive to his external environment when apparently asleep and may be especially reactive when irritable and apparently hungry. However, there are occasional periods during sleep, during intense rage-like behavior, during the "resting states" described subsequently, and during feeding when responsivity is minimal or lacking. We have few data during these refractory-like states. We are in the process of studying other autonomic functions to determine whether the organism is generally or differentially refractory to stimuli during these periods.

Relationships between Somatic and Visceral Responses. We have found a high correlation between change in motor activity (when quantified by Brownfield's technique 1956) and change in heart rate. Sometimes, however, as when sucking, the infants' heart rate may increase although overt muscular activity other than sucking ceases.

In these studies, we have observed a rise in heart rate, and a change in depth and rate of respiration, often occurring within less than one second after a motor response.

We do not present these findings in terms of cause and effect but only note the remarkable association of somatic and autonomic responses. This may be of importance in those studies in which we seek to determine the autonomic concomitants of emotion. Engel, Reichsmann, and Segal (1956a) noted, for instance, that highest gastric acid secretion occurred when the infant Monica actively participated with her external environment (as in contentment, joy, irritation or rage) and often showed greatest muscular activity. They cautiously stated: "Whether the increased gastric secretion may be merely part of a general increase in the physiologic activity of the body and not have the specific meaning we have proposed cannot be settled from a consideration of the data of this study" (p. 396). They subsequently stated that these physiologic observations are "the biologic anlage of processes that may later have psychological expression" (p. 397).

From these studies of a neonate population we may conclude the following: (1) that responses vary according to the stimulus, (2) that responses vary according to the state of the infant prior to stimulation, (3) there would appear to be a considerable degree of sensitivity to mild stimuli such as minimal touch of mucous membrane and skin areas, and (4) there appears to be a close relationship between autonomic and neuromuscular responses.

Differences Between Neonates

Much of past work has delineated responses of newborn populations with little in the way of comparing individual infants. The more recent studies of Fries (1953), Brownfield (1956), and Graham et al. (1956), seem to indicate differences between infants in spontaneous activity and in response to stimulation.

Brownfield (1956), observing and sampling motor activity during the first week in the hospital nursery, derived spontaneous activity scores from 100 infants. These showed a symmetric distribution. Quiet babies slept more, showed almost the same activity when awake, but less vocalizing than the active babies. The latter were especially vocal, active, and awake before feedings. There was a correlation between spontaneous activity and activity in response to an auditory stimulus.

Her conclusion that this may mean the quiet baby has less sensitivity to hunger and other stimuli must be tempered by the knowledge that babies vary considerably in caloric needs and in ability to nurse; and similarly, mothers vary in their ability to provide proper stimulation and breast milk. Quiet babies may be more satiated during these early days. Other physiologic factors will be discerned and taken into account as studies of this nature are continued in the future.

Differences in Range of Heart Rate

A striking example of differences between neonates was the findings in our recent study of nonidentical female twins who were quite mature at birth though both were just under five pounds. One twin was usually very quiet and inactive while the other was generally vocal and active, particularly prior to feedings. Their ranges of heart rate before and during stimulation were quite different, with little overlap. They were repeatedly tested before and after feedings during the experiment described previously.

The mother, who had had three previous children, spontaneously commented upon the distinct differences between these twins. She repeated these observations three months later when the more active baby was still the most vocal at feeding time when the other remained relatively quiet and "complacent." Comparative longitudinal studies of behavior seem to have documented the clinician's long awareness that infants are considerably different at birth (Wolf, 1953) and mothers' observations that subsequent fetuses often show differences in motility in utero.

The different heart rate ranges of the 32 infants described previously are seen in Figure 1 (Lipton, Richmond, and Lustman, 1955). Our subsequent studies have demonstrated that repeated observations of individual neonates show considerable variations in rate from period to period, but that over-all, distinct, interindividual differences in mean heart rate are striking, as in the twins referred to above.

Differences in Response Patterns

When the regression lines for ten individual neonates are plotted showing the relationship between prestimulus and stimulus heart rate, one observes different slopes. This indicates that some infants show greater responses at their lower ranges of prestimulus heart rate than others. We found, as did Bridger and Reiser (1959), that the points (prestimulus levels) at which no response to stimulation usually resulted also differed. We also found less predictable responses and thus greater scatter and lower correlations in some individuals. These observations may prove of value in testing for interindividual differences in autonomic reactivity. We are currently studying individual infants in terms of their total response patterns at various levels of prestimulus activity to ascertain more interrelationships. The relationship between stimulus-induced response and prestimulus level is not always described best as a linear correlation. Unfortunately, we are not yet prepared to amplify these statements since data for the solutions to these problems are not yet available.

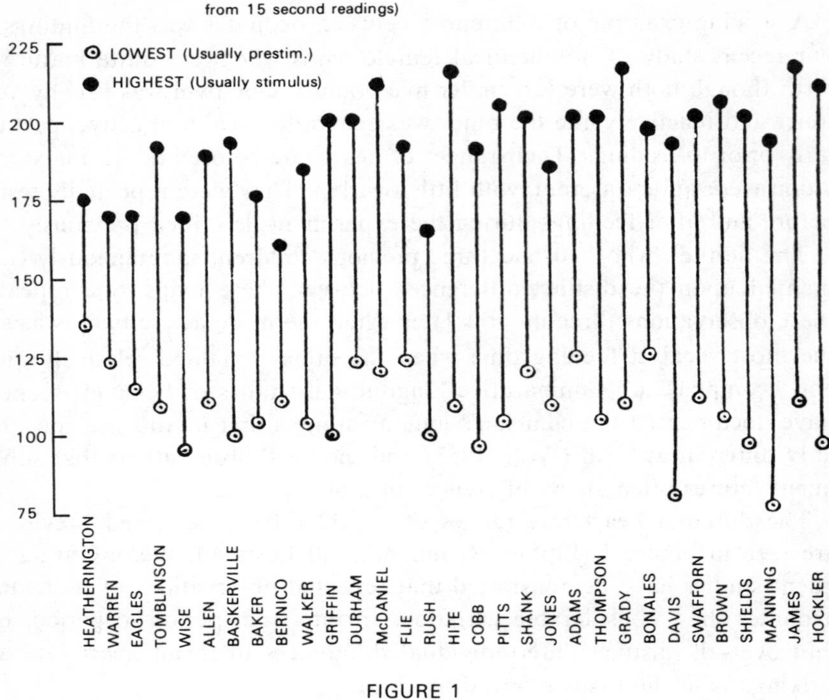

FIGURE 1

Ranges of heart rate noted in newborns tested under comparable conditions. Extreme rates, below 80 or above 200 beats per minute, had rarely before been noted in normal newborns. Highest rates usually accompanied the cold immersion test.

We have been impressed by the changes in motor and autonomic activity that may immediately follow cessation of stimulation. These may correlate with the "OFF" electroencephalographic changes described by Ellingson (1958) at the end of photic stimulation, since we have sometimes observed only a poststimulus cardiac change with this particular stimulus. Some infants appear to continue to react to a stimulus for a long period after it has stopped; others return rather quickly to the prestimulus level. For a complete understanding of homeostatic response patterns, observations should go beyond the period of stimulation–a commonly neglected source of data.

Studies have purported to demonstrate that individuals manifest different patterns of autonomic end organ reactivity. In order to deal with this problem adequately, it would be necessary to have considered prestimulus values, which few investigators have done. We believe that the autonomic endowment in this regard can be described in the newborn period if one preserves an approach which accounts for the prestimulus state of the organism. Such observations will provide further measures of inter-individual differences and, in longitudinal studies of child development, permit more appropriate interpretation of data.

Other Experimental Approaches

The extension of our knowledge concerning neurophysiologic development and behavior of the human newborn will depend upon the accumulation of data from a variety of sources. Because, ethically, human subjects are not subjected to hazardous experimentation, studies of spontaneous behavior, congenital anomalies, central and autonomic nervous system injuries, and animal behavior and physiology will be necessary.

Infants born with anomalies can provide excellent investigation opportunities. Thus, by modern methods, including electroencephalography, the observation that neonatal behavior simulates that of a brain stem preparation such as is observed in the anencephalic monster would be open to serious challenge (Kennedy, 1957). In addition to the study of the central nervous system anomalies, detailed studies of newborn infants having experienced possible central nervous system trauma, such as have been carried out by Graham and colleagues (1956), are in order. The occurrence of anomalies such as tracheoesophageal fistula provide natural experimental models, as has been demonstrated by the work of Engel et al. (1956a). The study of the significance of sucking for later development might be critically studied in infants with gastrostomies or who are tube-fed for some physical reason starting in the newborn period.

Studies of children with specific sensory defects have been very informative. Studies of sightless children might delineate factors other than visual which may be associated with the development of the social smiling response. The impact of a hearing defect on the development of object relationships and personality could be studied in infants and children with congenital deafness, if recognized early.

Observation of conditioned responses in the newborn is important in understanding patterns of learning. Although the details are not available, Russian investigators have stated that the earliest conditioned reflex is "that expressed in sucking movements when the child is in the lactation position at the breast. This appears at three to four weeks of age. The conditioned reflex is a reflex to a complex stimulus with many components: visual (sight of breast and mother's face), aural (the mother's voice), kinesthetic (position of the body), etc." (Elkonin, 1957, p. 51).

Within several weeks, conditioning was reported to occur with isolated visceral, tactile, or aural stimuli. Kasatkin noted a conditioned aural reflex in prematures during the first half of the second month of life, irrespective of the degree of prematurity. He states (Elkonin, *ibid.),* "It is evident, therefore, that the functional maturity of the cerebral cortex depends upon its actual functioning: this alone can explain its earlier maturity in premature infants." For more detailed consideration of conditioning the reader is referred to the view by Carmichael (1954).

Animal studies relating to variations in maternal care of the newborn are helpful in establishing a better understanding of mother-newborn relationships and their implications for later development. Thus, Seitz (1954) has studied the effect of litter size on later behavior in the rat. Scott (1950b) has observed the significance of early human contact for puppies as being critical for the development of their capacity to form relationships with human beings in later life. Dr. Helen Blauvelt (1955) of our group, in her observations of goats at the Cornell Behavior Farm Laboratory, has demonstrated considerable biological deterioration following separation in the newborn period.

Also from our group and the Cornell Behavior Farm Laboratory, Hersher et al. (1958) have observed the effects on later behavior of separation of newborn kids from their goat mothers for one-half to two hours immediately following birth. Observations were made on the relationship when the kids attained two and three months of age.

In these studies none of the separated mothers accepted their own kids in the normal manner. Half of this group nursed no young, neither their own nor others, during the observational periods (the "rejecting" pattern), and the other half nursed kids indiscriminately, suckling other kids as long or longer than their own (the "discriminate" pattern). The majority of the nonseparated group exhibited normal nursing behavior, nursing their own kids but not others. None of the nonseparated mothers nursed indiscriminately, although one third were "rejecting."

The effect of early separation on maternal care thus varies among individuals, some mothers reacting to separation by rejecting all kids and other mothers reacting by exhibiting highly maternal, though nonindividual-specific behavior. Thus, the immediate postpartum period is critical to the development of maternal behavior in goats, but the behavior which normally develops during that time consists of at least two factors, maternalism and individual care, and the former may develop in the absence of the latter.

Discussion

The data presented indicate the fragmentary nature of our knowledge concerning the neurophysiology of the newborn. Certainly, the knowledge available has relatively little clinical application. Further studies of this period will be basic to our understanding of the development of behavior; without such studies we remain limited largely to retrospective speculations concerning this period of life.

From studies of the biochemistry and physiology of the central and autonomic nervous systems of the newborn, we can hope to learn more of the development of neural units and their emergence into more complex neural patterns which ultimately will have significance for the development of consciousness, memory, learning, and feelings. Although no series of dramatic experiments will tell us the precise moment when the infant develops an awareness that experiences from his environment mean "other than I" or "mother", we can direct efforts toward a better understanding of how this awareness emerges. As he begins to have a greater sense of separation of self from his environment, he also develops a relationship to his body as an object. Disorders in the development of this relationship may be observed in children with psychotic or psychosomatic disorders.

Though strikingly immature, the central nervous system of the human infant has within it infinite and unique potentialities for development. Whether these potentialities are fulfilled will be determined by its interaction with stimuli, in the form of life experiences. The direction and pattern of behavior will be determined not alone by the quality and quantity of these experiences but by their *timing* as well. For clinicians, called upon to influence the direction of the development of behavior more effectively, a deeper understanding of this brief, but developmentally significant, period is needed. In part, this understanding will depend upon research in neonatal neurophysiology and its implications for later child development.

BEHAVIOR PROBLEMS REVISITED: FINDINGS OF AN ANTEROSPECTIVE STUDY

STELLA CHESS, ALEXANDER THOMAS, AND HERBERT G. BIRCH

The New York longitudinal studies of individuality in behavioral development reported by the husband and wife team of Chess and Thomas along with various co-workers (1960, 1963a, 1963b, 1968a, 1968b) represents to many a vital continuing endeavor to understand and refine the concept, constitution ("primary reactivity"), and to apply it in a developmental and clinical framework (see Richmond and Lipton, 1959; Benjamin, 1961). Advancing from the earlier work of Fries and Woolf (1953) who studied congenital activity types and hypothesized a relationship to future personality development, these investigators have focused on "temperament," a popular term with ancient scientific roots in Hippocrates' humoral theory. The authors' revival of scientific interest in temperament entailed the delineation of nine subcategories of primary reactivity which can be accurately identified at three months of age and remain consistent thereafter. Like Bender (1947) they conceive of the emotional component as a superimposed reaction, secondary to the primary dissonance between the parent and child's individual temperament. This should be compared to the perspective articulated in the report emanating from the Yale University Child Study Center's longitudinal study of child development (Coleman, Kris and Provence, 1953) in which the same parents' attitudes were observed to vary in correlation with their children's developmental progress.

The authors' attempts to define and delineate certain aspects of constitution have contributed to more specific use of the term by clinicians. It has led to their serious consideration of primary innate factors as an important positive variable in diagnostic assessment and treatment planning. While the emphasis in applying the findings of the New York longitudinal study has been on identifying temperamental patterns in order to facilitate parental understanding and effective dealing with individual differences of children, Chess (1968a) has attempted also to apply these concepts to specific clinical problems such as interferences in the processes of learning. This is reminis-

Reprinted from *Journal of the American Academy of Child Psychiatry,* 6, 1967, pp. 321–331.

cent of Bergman and Escalona's (1949) correlation of unusual sensitivities in children with subsequent psychotic development.

Viewing maladaptive temperamental-environmental interaction as decisive in the development of behavior disorders has stimulated the authors to think increasingly in terms of guidance *rather than* treatment *of parents. In an earlier publication (Chess, Thomas, Rutter and Birch, 1963b) the authors speculated that some of the complex intrapsychic explanations of the origin of behavioral disturbances might serve to fill gaps in anterospective developmental data collected prior to the onset of difficulties and, therefore, uncontaminated by therapeutic need and retrospective distortion.*

A number of theoretical formulations have been advanced to explain the origin and nature of behavior problems in childhood. These have included the constitutionalist view in which the symptoms of disturbance are considered to be the direct expression of a predetermined constitutional pattern in the child, the psychoanalytic view in which disturbance is seen as the outcome of conflicts between instinctual drive seeking expression and satisfaction and repressing forces seeking to inhibit or contain them, the learning theory approach in which symptoms are viewed as conditioned maladaptive learned patterns based on conditioned reflex formations, and the culturist view in which symptoms are considered to be the more or less direct expression of sociocultural influences.

A unique opportunity to investigate the genesis and evolution of behavior problems and to test the validity of these theories has presented itself during the course of our New York longitudinal study of individuality in behavioral development. In this study, in progress since 1956, 39 of the 136 children who have been followed from the earliest months of life onward by a variety of data-gathering techniques have developed behavior disturbances of various types and varying degrees of severity.

Until now, none of the numerous studies in the field has provided a body of evidence sufficient to validate one or another of the extant theoretical formulations. Aside from any other questions as to the adequacy of the data offered as evidence, the approaches have relied primarily on data gathered retrospectively. A number of recent studies, including several from our own center, have revealed significant distortions in retrospective parental reports on the early developmental histories of their children

(Robbins, 1963; Wenar, 1963; Chess et al., 1966). It has become clear that retrospective data are insufficient for the study of the genesis of behavior disorders and that anterospective data gathered by longitudinal developmental studies are essential.

Previous longitudinal studies—at Berkeley (MacFarlane et al., 1954), the Fels Institute (Kagan and Moss, 1962), Yale (Kris, 1957), and Topeka (Murphy et al., 1962)—have made certain contributions to the understanding of the evolution of behavior disorders. The possible significance of temperamental characteristics of the child in interaction with parental functioning has been indicated. A lack of correlation between the child's patterns of psychodynamic defenses and the occurrence of behavioral dysfunction has been found. Symptoms typical of various age-periods have been tabulated, their vicissitudes over time traced, and correlations among different symptoms determined. However, each of these studies has been limited either by small sample size, which has not permitted generalization of the findings, or by the absence of systematic psychiatric evaluation of the children, which has severely restricted the possibility of categorizing the behavior disturbance and of making meaningful correlations with the longitudinal behavioral data.

Our New York longitudinal study has had available, by contrast, both a total sample of substantial size and the data resulting from independent clinical psychiatric evaluation in all of the children with behavior problems. The data on the total sample include information gathered longitudinally and anterospectively at sequential age levels from early infancy onward on the nature of the child's own individual characteristics of functioning at home, in school, and in standard test situations; on parental attitudes and child care practices; on special environmental events and the child's reactions to such events; and on intellectual functioning. In addition, psychiatric evaluation has been done on each child presenting symptoms by the staff child psychiatrist. Wherever necessary, neurological examination or special testing, such as perceptual tests, have been done. Clinical follow-up of each child with a problem has also been carried out systematically.

Details of the data-gathering procedures and of the techniques of data analysis have been reported elsewhere (Chess et al., 1962; Thomas et al., 1963). Since the developmental data were gathered before the child was viewed as a problem by either the parent or the psychiatrist, they were uncontaminated by the distortions which inevitably attend retrospective histories obtained after the appearance of the behavioral disturbance. Data as to environmental influences, such as parental practices and attitudes, changes in family structure, illnesses and hospitalization, and the character of the school situation, were also obtained in advance of the behavioral disturbance and so were also not distorted by the fact of pathology.

The size of the sample and the nature of the data have made possible various quantitative analyses comparing children with and without behavior problems as well as individual longitudinal case studies. In all our analyses we have been concerned with tracing the ontogenesis and development of each behavioral disturbance in terms of the interaction of temperament and environment, as well as the influence of additional factors in specific cases, such as brain damage, physical abnormalities, and characteristics of intellectual functioning. *Temperament,* in our usage, refers to the behavioral style of the individual child and contains no inferences as to genetic, endocrine, somatologic, or environmental etiologies. It is a phenomenological term used to describe the characteristic tempo, energy expenditure, focus, mood, and rhythmicity typifying the behaviors of the individual child, independently of their contents. We have used nine categories of reactivity within which to subsume temperamental attributes. They are activity level, rhythmicity, adaptability, approach-withdrawal, intensity of reaction, quality of mood, sensory threshold, distractibility, and persistence and attention span. [1] A child's temperamental organization, therefore, represents his characteristic mode of functioning with respect to these features of behavioral organization. It refers to the *how* rather than to the *what* or the *why* of behavior. No implications of permanence or immutability attach to such a conception.

The prevalence rate of behavior problems in our study population approximates that found in other studies (Lapouse and Monk, 1958; Glidewell et al., 1963). The types of symptoms were typical of those usually coming to notice in preschool and early school age children of middle-class highly educated parents.

In each of the thirty-nine children with behavior problems the psychiatric assessment has been followed by a detailed culling of all the anterospective data from early infancy onward for pertinent information on temperament, environmental influences, and the sequences of symptom appearance and development. It has been possible in each case to trace the ontogenesis of the behavioral disturbances in terms of the interaction of temperament and environment. Temperament alone did not produce behavioral disturbance. Instances of children of closely similar tempera-

[1] See Thomas et al. (1963) for criteria of each of the nine categories and for details of the scoring method.

mental structure to the children with behavior problems were found in the normally functioning group. Rather, it appeared that both behavioral disturbance as well as behavioral normality were the result of the interaction between the child with a given patterning of temperament and significant features of his developmental environment. Among these environmental features intrafamilial as well as extrafamilial circumstances such as school and peer group were influential. In several cases, additional special factors such as brain damage or physical abnormality were also operative in interaction with temperament and environment to produce symptoms of disturbed development.

A number of case summaries illustrating typical interactive patterns of development in children with and without behavior problems have been presented in several previous publications (Chess et al., 1963; Birch et al., 1964). At this time we would like to present some of the characteristic temperamental patterns found among the children, the environmental demands which are typically stressful for children with each of these temperamental constellations, and the parental and other environmental approaches which intensify such stressful demands to the point of symptom formation. Symptoms manifested by the children included tantrums, aggressive behavior, habit disorders, fears, learning difficulties, nonparticipation in play activities with other children, and lack of normal assertiveness.

A temperamental pattern which produced the greatest risk of behavior problem development comprises the combination of irregularity in biological functions, predominantly negative (withdrawal) responses to new stimuli, nonadaptability or slow adaptability to change, frequent negative mood, and predominantly intense reactions. As infants, children with this pattern show irregular sleep and feeding patterns, slow acceptance of new foods, prolonged adjustment periods to new routines, and frequent periods of loud crying. Their laughter, too, is characteristically loud. Mothers find them difficult to care for, and pediatricians frequently refer to them as the "difficult infants." They are not easy to feed, to put to sleep, to bathe, or to dress. New places, new activities, strange faces—all may produce initial responses of loud protest or crying. Frustration characteristically produces a violent tantrum. These children approximate 10 per cent of the total study population but comprise a significantly higher proportion of the behavior problem group (Rutter et al., 1964). The stressful demands for these children are typically those of socialization, namely, the demands for alteration of spontaneous responses and patterns to conform to the rules of living of the family, the school, the peer group, etc. It is also characteristic of these children that once they do learn the rules, they function easily, consistently, and energetically.

We have found no evidence that the parents of the difficult infants are essentially different from the other parents. Nor do our studies suggest that the temperamental characteristics of the children are caused by the parents. The issue is rather that the care of these infants makes special requirements upon their parents for unusually firm, patient, consistent, and tolerant handling. Such handling is necessary if the difficult infant is to learn to adapt to new demands with a minimum of stress. If the new demand is presented inconsistently, impatiently, or punitively, effective change in behavior becomes stressful and even impossible. Negativism is a not infrequent outcome of such suboptimal parental functioning.

The problems of managing a difficult child not infrequently highlight a parent's individual reaction to stress. The same parents who are relaxed and consistent with an easy child may become resentful, guilty, or helpless with a difficult child, depending on their own personality structures. Other parents, by contrast, who do not feel guilty or put upon by the child's behavior may learn to enjoy the vigor, lustiness, and "stubbornness" of a difficult infant.

At the opposite end of the temperamental spectrum from the difficult infant is the child who is regular, responds positively to new stimuli (approaches), adapts quickly and easily to change, and shows a predominantly positive mood of mild or moderate intensity. These are the infants who develop regular sleep and feeding schedules easily, take to most new foods at once, smile at strangers, adapt quickly to a new school, accept most frustrations with a minimum of fuss, and learn the rules of new games quickly. They are aptly called "easy babies" and are usually a joy to their parents, pediatricians, and teachers. By contrast to the difficult infant, the easy child adapts to the demands for socialization with little or no stress and confronts his parents with few if any problems in handling. However, although these children do as a group develop significantly fewer behavior problems proportionately than do the difficult infants, their very ease of adaptability may under certain circumstances be the basis for problem behavior development. Most typically we have seen this occur when there is a severe dissonance between the expectations and demands of the intra- and extrafamilial environments. The child first adapts easily to the standards and behavioral expectations of the parent in the first few years of life. When he moves actively into functional situations outside the home, such as in peer play groups and school, stress and malfunctioning will develop if the extrafamilial standard and demands conflict sharply with the patterns learned in the home. As a typical example, the parents of one such child had a high regard for individuality of expression and disapproval of any behavior or attitude in their child which they identified as stereotypical or lacking in imagination. Self-expression was encouraged and conformity and attentiveness to rules imposed by others discouraged even when this resulted in ill manners and a disregard of the desires of others. As the child grew older she became increasingly isolated from her peer group because of continuous insistence on her own preferences. In school her progress was grossly unsatisfactory because of difficulty in listening to directions. The parents were advised to restructure their approach, to place less emphasis on individuality and instead to teach her to be responsive to the needs of others and to conform constructively in behavior in class and in activities with her peers. The parents, acutely aware of the child's growing social isolation and the potential seriousness of her educational problem, carried out this plan consistently. At follow-up, six months later, the child had adapted to the new rules easily, the conflict between standards within and without the home had become minimal, and she had become an active member of a peer group and had caught up to grade level in academic work.

It is certainly true that a severe dissonance between intra- and extrafamilial environment demands and expectations may produce stress and disturbance in psychological development for many types of youngsters, including the difficult child. In our case series, however, it has been most readily apparent as a dominant pathogenic factor in these easy children.

Another important temperamental constellation comprises the combination of negative responses of mild intensity to new stimuli with slow adaptability after repeated contact. Children with this pattern differ from the difficult infants in that their withdrawal from the new is quiet rather than loud. They also usually do not have the irregularity of function, frequent negative mood expression, and intense reactions of the difficult infants. The mildly expressed withdrawal from the new is typically seen with the first encounter with the bath, a new person, a stranger, or a new place. With the first bath the child lies still and fusses mildly, with a new food he turns his head away quietly and lets it dribble out of his mouth, with a stranger who greets him loudly he clings to his mother. If given the opportunity to re-experience new situations without pressure, such a child gradually comes to show quiet and positive interest and involvement. This characteristic sequence of response has suggested the appellation "Slow to Warm Up" as an apt if inelegant designation for these children. A key issue in their development is whether parents and teachers allow them to make an adaptation to the new at their own tempo or insist on the immediate positive involvement which is difficult or impossible for the slow-to-warm-up children. If the adult recognizes that the slow adaptation to a new school, new peer group or new academic subject reflects the child's normal temperamental style, patient encouragement is likely. If, on the contrary, the child's slow warm-up is interpreted as timidity or lack of interest, adult impatience and pressure on the child for quick adaptation may occur. The child's reaction to this stressful pressure is typically an intensification of his withdrawal tendency. If this increased holding back in turn stimulates increased impatience and pressure on the part of the parent or teacher, a destructive child-environment interactive process will be set in motion.

In several other instances in our study population, nursery school teachers have interpreted the child's slow initial adaptation as evidence of underlying anxiety. In still another case, an elementary school teacher estimated that a child's slow initial mastery of a new accelerated academic program indicated inadequate intellectual capacity. In these cases, the longitudinal behavioral records documented a slow warm-up temperamental style and made possible the recommendation that judgment be suspended until the child could have a longer period of contact with the new situation. The subsequent successful mastery of the demands of the new situation clarified the issue as one of temperamental style and not psychopathology or lack of intellectual capacity.

A contrast to the slow-to-warm-up child is the very persistent child who is most likely to experience stress not with his initial contact with a situation but during the course of his ongoing activity after the first positive adaptation has been made. His quality of persistence leads him to resist interference or attempts to divert him from an activity in which he is absorbed. If the adult interference is arbitrary and forcible, tension and frustration tend to mount quickly in these children and may reach explosive proportions.

Type-specific stress and maladaptive child-environment patterns can be identified for other temperamental patterns, such as the very distractible or highly active child, but the scope of this presentation does not permit their description.

Currently influential psychoanalytic theories of the ontogenesis of behavior problems place primary emphasis on the role of anxiety, intrapsychic conflict, and psychodynamic defenses. Our findings do not support these concepts. Our data suggest that anxiety, intrapsychic conflict, and psychodynamic defenses, when they do appear in the course of behavior problem development, are secondary phenomena which result from the stressful, maladaptive character of an unhealthy temperament-environment interaction. Once any or all of these secondary factors appear they can add a new dimension to the dynamics of the child-environment interaction and substantially influence the subsequent course of the behavior problem. It is not surprising that in retrospective studies which begin when the child already presents an extensively elaborated psychological disturbance the prominent phenomena of anxiety and conflict should be labeled as primary rather than secondary influences. Also, if the fact of temperamental individuality is not given serious attention, certain temperamental patterns, such as those of the difficult child or the child with a slow warm-up are easily misinterpreted as the result of anxiety or as defenses against anxiety.

Our findings also challenge the validity of the currently prevalent assumption that a child's problem is a direct reaction of a one-to-one kind to unhealthy maternal influences. The slogan "To meet Johnny's mother is to understand his problem" expresses an all too frequent approach in which a study of the mother is substituted for a study of the complex factors which may have produced a child's disturbed development, of which parental influences are only one. Elsewhere we have described this unidirectional preoccupation of psychologists and psychiatrists with the pathogenic role of the mother as the "Mal de Mère" syndrome (Chess, 1964). The harm done by this preoccupation has been enormous. Innumerable mothers have been unjustly burdened with deep feelings of guilt and inadequacy as a result of being incorrectly held exclusively or even primarily responsible for their children's problems. Diagnostic procedures have tended to be restricted to a study of the mother's assumed noxious attitudes and practices, with investigations in other directions conducted in a most cursory fashion, or not at all. Treatment plans have focused on methods of changing maternal attitudes and ameliorating the effects of presumed pathogenic maternal attitudes on the child and have ignored other significant etiological factors.

Our data on the origin and development of behavior problems in children emphasize the necessity to study the child—his temperamental characteristics, neurological status, intellectual capacities, and physical handicaps. The parents should also be studied rather than given global labels such as rejecting, overprotective, anxious, etc. Parental attitudes and practices are usually selective and not global, with differentiated characteristics in different areas of the child's life and with marked variability from child to child. Parent-child interaction should be analyzed not only for parental influences on the child but just as much for the influence of the child's individual characteristics on the parent. The influence of other intra- and extrafamilial environmental factors should be estimated in relation to the interactive pattern with each specific child with his individual characteristics rather than in terms of sweeping generalizations.

Our finding that an excessively stressful maladaptive temperament-environment interaction constitutes a decisive element in the development of behavior problems suggests that treatment should emphasize the modification of the interactive process so that it is less stressful and more adaptive. This requires first of all an identification of the pertinent temperamental and environmental issues. Parents can then be armed with this knowledge in the service of modifying their interactive pattern with the child in a healthy direction. Parent guidance rather than parent treatment should be the first aim. If the parent cannot learn to understand his child and utilize this understanding effectively, it then becomes pertinent to inquire into the factors which may be responsible for such a failure of parent guidance. In our experience such failures are in a minority. Most parents do appear able to cooperate in a parent guidance program. When this is accomplished, the parent and psychiatrist can truly become allies in the treatment of the child's problem.

EXCERPT FROM
THE FIRST FIVE YEARS OF LIFE

ARNOLD GESELL

While the work of Gesell and his colleagues receives less and less attention from clinicians, his contributions—clinical, experimental, and theoretical—have played a unique role in our intellectual heritage (Kanner, 1960). His contributions to child development range far beyond his numerous useful studies of handicapped children, visual and postural development, handedness, and twins. He created a widely used developmental test, or "scale," as he would prefer to call it, and introduced new methods of child study. He is best known for his historically important observations of the normal development of infants and young children (Gesell and Gesell, 1912; Gesell and Thompson, 1934; Gesell, 1940a; Gesell and Amatruda, 1941; Gesell and Ilg, 1946; Gesell et al., 1956). Although he organized his research in terms of a four-fold division of behavior—motor, language, adaptive, personal-social—he insisted that we not lose sight of the integrated organism. At a time when Watsonian environmentalism ruled the field, Gesell, while not insensitive to the role of the environment, emphasized benign innate forces as providing the impetus for growth and development. He addressed himself repeatedly to the child's realization of its growth potential by way of maturationally regulated, "preordained," orderly paths.

From time to time, Gesell mentioned individual differences in maturational pace. Yet, as in the selection which follows—a brief "bird's-eye survey" of a portion of preschool development from one of his major books—he too often tied specific behavioral developments and changes to chronological age. Consequently, the broad range of normal variation fades into the background. To be sure, his samples were limited, his methodology flawed—by today's standards—and his generalizations overstated (Stolz, 1958). Nevertheless, the careful ordering of his observations and his vivid descriptions of behavior and development continue to prove useful and to fill an otherwise crippling gap in our knowledge of child development.

Reprinted from *The First Five Years of Life.* New York: Harper Bros., 1940, pp. 46–57.

Four Years Old

THREE was transitional. Four is well on his way. THREE, being transitional, is somewhat more quaint and naive. Four is more sophisticated and even a bit dogmatic because of his amateur command of words and ideas. His verbal assertiveness may deceive us into crediting him with more knowledge than he actually possesses. His propensity to speak out, to produce, to create, makes him highly responsive to psychological examination. These interesting traits also make him more transparent to observation.

Motor Characteristics

Four is a more facile runner than THREE. He is also more able to break up the regular rhythms of his stride. He can make a fair running broad jump and a standing broad jump. THREE'S jump is usually limited to a downward and upward leap—another instance in which the motor command of the vertical dimension apparently precedes command of the horizontal. Four can also skip, at least after a lame duck fashion. But he cannot hop—much less hop-skip-jump in sequence. He can, however, maintain a one-legged equilibrium much longer than can THREE. He can balance himself on one foot for several seconds, and usually in another half-year he can hop. His improved body equilibrium is shown in his excellent performance on the 6 cm. walking board. He rarely has to step off with both feet to regain his balance.

Four likes to try motor stunts which are not too difficult. He enjoys accomplishment. This well-defined interest in feats and tasks is a somewhat new developmental symptom, which offers a clue to the psychology of the four-year-old.

His new athletic feats are based on a greater independence of his leg musculature. Here, as elsewhere, the principle of individuation is at work. There is less totality in his bodily responses; legs, trunk, shoulders, arms react somewhat less in unison. This makes his joints seem more mobile. Whereas at two and at three he would merely toss or hurl a ball in a propulsive manner (with much torso participation), he can now swing back a more independent arm and execute a strong overhand throw.

He finds pleasure in feats of fine coordination as well. He can take a knitting-needle spear and thrust it with well-directed aim into a small hole, smiling with success. He can button his clothes and lace his shoes with ease. He gestures with more refinement and precision. In his drawing he may give concentrated attention to the representation of an isolated detail. His copy of a circle is more circumscribed than at three years, and characteristically is executed in a clockwise direction, appropriate to a more strongly entrenched right-handedness. In the manipulation of fine objects like the pellet, however, unilateral preference is not so dominant.

Motor command of the oblique dimension is still imperfect. Four cannot copy a diamond from a model, although he can combine a vertical and horizontal stroke into a cross. Between parallel lines a centimeter apart he can trace a paper a diamond-shape pathway. Imitating a demonstration, he can thrice fold a piece of paper, making an oblique crease on the last fold. This is a definite advance beyond THREE, in whom a neuromotor blind spot still obscures the oblique axis.

Adaptive

A lamb was nursing. "What is the lamb getting from its mother?" The metropolitan four-year-old who answered, "Gasoline," was more intellectual than appears at first blush. In a vague yet concrete way he knew that gasoline is a source of energy. Gasoline makes things, including lambs, go. Four has powers of generalization and of abstraction which he exercises much more frequently and deliberately than does THREE. THREE, to be sure, generalizes such relationships as *in, on, under,* etc.; he distinguishes between *one* and *many;* he seeks and finds resemblances among physical objects; but he does not ask the numerous and varied questions with which Four plies his elders.

These questions of the four-year-old reflect not a hunger for information but rather an inveterate impulse to conceptualize the multiplicities of nature and of the social world. THREE is an enumerator, a designator. So is Four, but with a dim intent to generalize and to order his experience. He is even beginning to sense himself as only one among many. He is less circumscribed than THREE. He has a definite consciousness of kind, of his own kind. Once during a psychological examination he asked, "Do you spank children who don't finish?" A revealing question, which discloses that the four-year-old realizes his equivalence with other children who come to the Clinic under similar circumstances. This realization denotes a fundamental noetic attitude which pervades his intellectual life and raises the level of his social life.

His intellectual processes, however, are narrow in scope. He has very meager comprehension of the past and the future, and even in stories he manifests very little interest in plot. He can count to four or more by rote, but his number concept barely goes beyond *one, two,* and *many.* He may have an imaginary playmate, but his communings with this companion are sketchy rather than organized. Even in his dramatic play he does not long sustain a role. He may, as *dramatis persona,* kiss his wife good-by as he leaves for his downtown office, but the next moment finds him fishing beside a brook. His questions often are equally kaleidoscopic; nevertheless they serve to clear up confusion for him.

We underestimate the vastness of his *terra incognita.* An intelligent four-year-old, while building a playhouse, was heard to say, "Houses do not have tails." This lucid judgment was the sober product of an inquiring mind. Four has a busy rather than a profound mind. His thinking is consecutive and combinative rather than synthetic. Confronted by the two parallel Binet lines he says, "This is the big one; this is the little one"; he does not make one summary comparative judgment; he makes two consecutive judgments. Likewise in making an esthetic choice between pretty and ugly, he refers in turn to each member of the comparative pair.

He is so literal in this thinking that analogies when used by a storyteller tend to befuddle him, and yet out of his own motor experience he can create metaphors which are so fresh and startling that they suggest poetic imagery (to the adult!). When he listens to stories he is literally moved in a muscular sense, for he tends to re-enact in his body postures and gestures what is told.

There is a primitive mixture of symbolization and of naive literalness in his drawings. A typical drawing of a man consists of a head and two appendages and possibly two eyes. The torso usually does not appear until FIVE. There is overweening interest in the individual parts as they are drawn. Unity may be achieved by making a circle to surround the parts.

When presented with an incomplete drawing of a man, he can supply three missing parts. If he supplies an eye, he comments, "Now he can see!" With similar literalness he represents the movements of a steam shovel through dramatic imitation.

He matches eight of the ten test forms. He imitates the construction of a five-block gate, inserting a keystone block diagonally. In his spontaneous play with blocks he builds in both vertical and horizontal dimensions, names his constructions, and sometimes exploits them dramatically. He likes to create and to produce by first intention. He likes to go from one thing to another, rather than to repeat. His mind is lively and covers much ground.

Language

Questioning is at a peak at Four. A bright four-year-old can elaborate and improvise questions almost endlessly. Perhaps this is a developmental form of practice in the mechanics of speech, inasmuch as the four-year-old still tends to articulate in a somewhat infantile manner. His volubility serves to make him more fluent and facile.

Sometimes apparently he chatters along in order to maintain social rapport, and to attract attention. He also likes to play on words in a clownish way, particularly if he has an audience. He enjoys crude malapropisms and can perpetrate them for humor's sake. For example, "Cedar rabbits!" instead of "Cedar Rapids."

Why and *How* frequently appear in the questions, but Four is by no means always interested in explanations. He is more interested to note how the answers fit his own thoughts. He is, however, less apt than THREE to ask questions to which he already knows the answers. Much of his questioning is virtually a soliloquy by means of which he projects one verbal construction after another, concurrently rearranging his images and reformulating relationships. He is not building coherent logical structures, but combining facts, fancies, and phrases to strengthen his command of words and clauses. He makes declarations and running comments as profusely as he frames questions, using with aptness (and sometimes with marked ineptitude) such expressions as, "I don't *even* know that. You *almost* hit him. *Now* I will make *something* else; I can make something different. They are *like* the other one, *but* the other one is bigger. That one *too.*" Such grammar, and such parts of speech, imply a considerable degree of relational and even abstract thinking. They are much more recondite than were nouns, verbs, or prepositions. The wonder is that Four acquires mastery over them so rapidly. How long did it take the race to achieve even the "simple" notion of *too?*

Four is verbal rather than verbose. He is also after a manner prolix. He tends to elaborate replies. "What scratches?" "A cat," says FIVE who knows that a responsive answer alone is desired. But Four names the cat and tells about his dog as well. Such associative thinking is a developmental kind of prolixity, pardonable in the preschool child.

The speech of Four is forthright. He does not like to repeat things. He says flatly, "I did that before." He has a certain crispness as well as garrulity. He can carry on long and involved conversations. He can tell a lengthy story, mixing truth and fiction. He can flounder as helplessly as adults do in discussions of war and crime. For example:

> *Arthur (age four years):* "Soldiers are bad people. They kill others."
> *Betty (age four years):* "Soldiers aren't bad. But if someone does something

wrong, they shoot them. If some naughty person catches a bird, then the soldiers shoot them."

Arthur (unconvinced): "Well, if England catches a bird, then the soldiers shoot England."

No wonder that Bernard Shaw wanted to get us back to Methuselah. Part Five of Shaw's *Metabiological Pentateuch* is dated 31,920 A.D. Under this distance dispensation newborn children will be as mature as our youth now are at seventeen years, and these children will become adults (by present-day standards) at the age of four years. Our norms of preschool development will then need revision!

Personal-Social Behavior

Four presents an interesting combination of independence and sociability. His self-reliance in his personal habits, his assertiveness, a certain "bossiness," his emphatic dogmatisms conspire to make him seem more stalwart and independent than THREE. During the examination he also displays a kind of maturity wanting in THREE. Four is much less apt to leave the table than is THREE, although Four may shuffle his feet and wriggle a good deal during the examination. Ordinarily he is quite willing to go into the examination room without his mother and during the examination there is much less smiling reference to the examiner. THREE shows much more tendency toward communicative smiling, due to a normal kind of social dependence which Four is now transcending. In reaction to the individual tests, Four goes about each appointed task more carefully; he has more drive; makes more uninvited comments; and may even pursue his comments and questions to such an extent that the examiner will find himself examined. This imparts to Four a pleasant if not always convincing plausibility.

In his home life he needs much less care. He is able to dress and undress himself with very little assistance, laces his shoes (but is unable to tie them), combs his own hair with some supervision, and brushes his own teeth. In eating he likes to choose his own menu; he can be very conversational without interfering with his eating. He needs little direction; indeed, he can even set the table well.

In many instances Four no longer naps during the day. If he continues to nap it is a long nap of one to one-and-a-half hours. He tries to put off going to bed at night but falls sleep in a short time and no longer needs to take things to bed with him. He sleeps through the night without having to get up.

Four goes to the toilet by himself and needs very little help. He manages his clothes without much difficulty. He likes to go to the bathroom when others are there to satisfy new curiosities which are awakening.

His play similarly reflects a balanced mixture of self-dependency and sociability. He takes less enjoyment than THREE in solitary and purely parallel types of play. He makes a greater number of social approaches and spends more time in social contacts with the play group. Associative group play rather than parallel play is characteristic of Four. He prefers a group of two or three children. He shares possessions brought from home. He suggests turns in play but he is by no means consistently orderly. Indeed, he often makes sudden "silly" sallies and purposefully perpetrates wrong behavior. But this is not so much because of antisocial impulses as it is to evoke social reactions in others. He enjoys evoking such reactions and can be very "bossy" in directing others. His dramatic play is less desultory and wayward than that of THREE, but it is often harum-scarum in its reckless changes of scene and of impersonations.

Four is talkative. His sentences are replete with the first personal pronoun. But many of these egoistic statements prove to have a definite social reference and social context. He is very good at supplying alibis: "I cannot make it because my mother won't let me." "I cannot make it because I don't want to." The significant fact is that he should be interested in alibis at all. Such interest is social. It denotes an awareness of the attitudes and opinions of others. His self-criticisms and self-appraisals also have social implications: "I am mad." "I said I don't know." "I said it too many times." "I have good ideas, don't I?" "I was very fast, wasn't I?" "I put that nice, didn't I?" "Certainly I can make it." "Do you want to see how quickly I find the things?" "I know everything!" "I am smart. Am I smarter than you?" Four also criticizes others: "Mother, doesn't he talk funny?" "You mustn't say 'ain't,' " etc.

Despite his growing reasoning powers and his critical capacities, he is prone to so-called unreasonable fears such as fear of the dark, fear of old men, fear of a rooster, fear of feathers and pieces of cotton. Fears of this kind serve to remind us that Four is not so mature as his speech sometimes suggests.

Four is also reputed to be a fabricator. His fabrications, like his bossiness, his dogmatic assertiveness, his alibis, his rationalizations, and his clowning, all spring from a consciousness of social milieu and from maturing social insight. For the time being they may be regarded as developmental symptoms which usually have a favorable connotation. Because of his immaturity Four is unable to make realistic distinctions between truth and fable. His brave excursions into the unknown will in time supply him with adequate social orientations, if his deviations from the "truth" are not too clumsily handled by his superiors, who passed through a comparable stage of confusion when they were Four.

Five Years Old

The period of early childhood is coming to a relative close at 5 years. The five-year-old may not be ready for the technicalities or abstractions of reading, writing, and sums for another two years. But he is no longer tied to apron strings. He endures and even enjoys the separation from home demanded by a kindergarten. He is more self-contained and self-dependent than FOUR who is still deeply immersed in elementary explorations of the physical and social world. Five has a better understanding of this world and of his own identity in it. Society likewise recognizes a budding social maturity, and provides increasing opportunities for group behavior. Fascist governments have not found the five-year-old too young to regiment in uniforms, to marshal in battalions preparatory to group behavior which will be required in later years. Five is more of "a little man" than FOUR.

Motor Characteristics

Five is more agile than Four and more controlled in general bodily activity. Five has a more mature sense of balance, which makes him seem more sure and less given to caution on the playground.

Four can skip in a lame duck manner. Five skips smoothly and jumps as well. He conducts himself with more self-reliant abandon. He can negotiate a 4 cm. walking board usually with a two-feet step down, or a one-foot slip. He can stand on one foot and even balance himself on his toes for several seconds or more.

These tokens of motor maturity, including a well-developed sense of equilibrium and an increased social adaptability, make Five a more ready pupil than FOUR in the teaching of dancing and of physical exercises and evolutions.

His spontaneous postural demeanor gives an impression of relative finish and completeness. Under wholesome conditions his postural attitudes show natural grace. Ease and economy of movement are present in his finer coordinations as well. He can pluck a dozen pellets one by one and drop them deftly into a bottle in about twenty seconds, typically with a preferred hand.

Five, in comparison with FOUR, shows greater precision and command of tools. Five can wield a brush for his teeth and a comb for his hair; he can wash his face. FOUR needs much more supervision than Five in these domestic duties. Five also dawdles less, partly because of his greater motor maturity.

Five likewise wields a crayon with greater assurance and definitiveness. He draws a recognizable man. His straight strokes show an increased neuro-motor command over the following axes: downward vertical, left to right horizontal, downward oblique. The vertical is most facile; the oblique, least. He has difficulty with the obliques required in the copying of a diamond, but he is quite equal to copying a square and a triangle. He shows interest and some competence in washing dishes. He keeps better time to music when he dances. Such motor abilities suggest that the neuromotor system is now well advanced in its development. Musical prodigies may approach an adult level of motor virtuosity as early as the fifth year.

Adaptive Behavior

The relative motor maturity of Five is reflected in the free, adaptive manner in which he solves simple problems involving geometric and spatial relations. He is not unduly confused by the problem of a diagonally cut visiting card, and reorients the two halves to make a rectangle out of the triangles. He solves the Goddard formboard with directness and dispatch, adjusting movement to perception, and rarely using the method of kinesthetic trial and error still frequently seen at Three and Four. He can insert in sequence a series of nested boxes, making immediate practical judgments as to succession and orientation.

Other characteristic abilities rest on a comparable perceptiveness of order, form, and detail. He is able to put his toys away in an orderly manner. His drawing of a man shows differentiation of parts with a certain completeness from head to feet. He adds eyes and even ears to an incomplete man. If he draws a flag, he delineates pole, stars, and stripes. He is realistic.

It is significant that in his play, he likes to finish what he has started. FOUR is much less sensitive to incompleteness and to inconclusiveness. FOUR may be rambling and prolix. Both in mentation and conversation. Five shows conclusiveness and autocriticism.

In apprehension of number, also, Five displays increased discriminativeness. Whereas FOUR had concepts of *one, two,* and *many,* Five can intelligently count ten objects, and can do a few simple concrete sums within the magnitude of his age (5). And he can tell his age.

Sense of time and duration are more developed in Five. He can carry a plot in a story and repeat a long sequence accurately. He can carry over a play project from one day to another, which is correlated with a more vivid appreciation of yesterdays and tomorrows. He has a clearer remembrance of and interest in places remote. Furthermore, he can carry a melody. And when he paints or draws, an idea in the mind precedes the production on paper.

This relationship between idea and execution is much more ambiguous in FOUR who often draws first and names afterwards. Indeed, FOUR may supply two or three different names to the same drawing. The psychomotor arc in FOUR is fluid and permeable in both directions. Five is more executive, more sensible, more accurate, more relevant, more practical. He is in these respects more adultish.

There is a vein of seriousness in Five which makes him less hospitable to fanciful fables and grotesque fairy tales than children of riper maturity who have a stable footing in realities. He is ready and eager to know realities, but is not equal to the double task of discrimination which excessive romancing entails. His method of drawing reflects the same realism. He aims at something definite with the first stroke of the pencil, whereas FOUR (like Polonius and the clouds) reinterprets his drawing as he goes along, changing designations to conform with the strokes *after* they are made. This difference epitomizes a significant gain in intellect. Add to this access of realism an increase of attention span, and many of the distinctive features of the psychology of Five are accounted for. Intellectually he seems well oriented, but close examination of his verbalized judgments and notions discloses amazing forms of immaturity in his thinking.

Language

In speech, too, Five is much more grown up than FOUR. Five talks without infantile articulation. His answers to questions are more succinct and to the point. His own questions are fewer and more relevant. He asks questions for information and not merely for social intercourse or for practice in the art of speaking. He is no longer an experimental apprentice in this art, but makes serious inquiries, "What is this for?" "How does this work?" "What does it mean?" "Who made those (referring to test objects)?"

Parents are less annoyed by the questions of Five than those of FOUR because the questions are more meaningful. Five really wants to know. His questions and answers betray an interest in the practical mechanisms of the universe. He is a pragmatist. His definitions are in terms of use: *A horse is to ride; a fork to eat.* Fairy tales with excessive unrealities vex and confuse him. He is serious and empirical. His imagination is not so footloose as it was a year ago, nor as it will be a few years hence. Five has an ear as well as an eye for details. This shows itself in language. He can single out one word and ask its meaning, whereas FOUR would react to the sentence as a whole, without analysis of component words.

Language is now essentially complete in structure and form. Five has assimilated the syntactical conventions and expresses himself in correct, finished sentences. He uses all types of sentences, including complex sentences with hypothetical and conditional clauses. He uses conjunctions somewhat more freely than FOUR, but in general the relative frequency of parts of speech is similar to that of FOUR. Vocabulary is greater by several hundred words (1,500 at Four, versus 2,200 at Five, on an average); usage more accurate and much more elaborate. Five follows linguistic custom rather than the naive movement of thought which determines word order in Two.

FOUR is rather more literal and concrete than Five. FOUR, having heard it said of a pair of gloves that "one" was as good as "the other," wanted to know which is the one, and which the other. Five might be capable of the required abstraction. The following dialogue also shows that Five has a bit of edge on FOUR when it comes to abstract cerebration:

> *Four:* "I know that Pontius Pilate is a tree."
> *Five:* "No, Pontius Pilate is not a tree at all."
> *Four:* "Yes, it was a tree, because it says: 'He suffered under Pontius Pilate,' so it must have been a tree."
> *Five:* "No, I am sure Pontius Pilate was a person and not a tree."
> *Four:* "I know he was a tree, because he suffered under a tree—a big tree."
> *Five:* "No, he was a person but he was a very pontious person."

The dramatic play of Five is full of practical dialogue and commentary which has to do with the everyday functions of business, kitchen, grocery store, transportation, garage. Bright five-year-old children may even dramatize natural phenomena in which sun, moon, stars, wind, clouds, etc., figure as characters. There is a good deal of talk in these impersonations,—an effort to clear ideas and to capture relationships through words rather than to indulge make-believe. Even the renderings of death, killing, sickness, surgery, and accidents are factual instead of emotional in spirit.

The preoccupation with community situations in group play reflects an intellectual effort to understand social organization. But much of the talk is in essence a form of "collective monologue," and does not bear upon causal or logical relationships. Not until the age of Seven or later do such relationships figure in conversation. Genuine interchange of ideas remains limited. Although Five is clarifying the world in which he lives through a discriminating and even analytic use of words, his thinking is still so self-confined that he cannot suppress his own point of view even temporarily, in order to realize by reciprocity the point of view of others. He distinguishes his left and right hand in his own person, but not in other persons. He also lacks synthetic capacity. He will be Seven or older before he understands the simple mechanism of a bicycle and before he comprehends that pedals, chain, and gear are necessary to make the wheels go. He lacks the power of explicit reasoning. He makes no distinction between the physical and psychical; he confuses physical causality with psychological motivation. He is so egocentric (in Piaget's sense) that he is unconscious of himself, unaware of his own thinking as a subjective process separate from the objective world. Hence his animism. Hence an intellectual innocence which is profoundly primitive in spite of deceptively mature facility in grammar and speech.

Personal-Social Behavior

Within his capacities, Five is relatively independent and self-sufficient. One can easily imagine a self-operating Lilliputian village of five-year-olds, which would require only a moderate degree of external control. Five is already mature enough to fit into a simple type of culture. (Perhaps it is for this reason that the adjective "adultish" characterizes him aptly.)

He is dependable and obedient in the household. Normally he gives little trouble in sleep, toilet habits, in dressing, and in the duties of everyday life. He shows interest in sweeping and in washing and wiping dishes. He is protective toward younger playmates and siblings. In underprivileged homes the five-year-old frequently shows remarkable competence and responsibility in sharing the care of an infant.

If Five gets lost in a big city he can tell his name and address. He plays checkers with the policemen while he waits to be claimed. Adults may marvel at his "calmness." If he exhibits indifference in distressful and tragic situations it is because his emotional organization is limited by the self-engrossment which has already been noted in his intellectual reactions. He is innocent of certain complex emotions because he is still simply organized. But in less complicated situations he clearly displays attractive emotional traits and attitudes: seriousness, purposefulness, patience, persistence, carefulness, generosity, outgoing sociability, friendliness, poise, pride in accomplishment, pride in going to school, satisfaction in artistic production, pride in possession. He has a certain capacity for friendships. He plays in groups of two to five with new sociability. He also plays with imaginary companions. He is very social and talkative during meals. He quarrels rather less than FOUR. He can be spurred into increased activity under the stress of rivalry. But he shows a positive amenability and docility. A vein of politeness and tactfulness even emerges in his speech.

Tricycle and sled are favorite outdoor toys. Crayon and scissors have an increased appeal. His horizon is widening. He likes to go on excursions. Sometimes he even makes collections of objects.

Five, even more than FOUR, prefers associative play to solitary and parallel types of play. He definitely desires companions and enjoys group projects, requiring construction of houses, garages, switch yards, and city planning. Although he does not have a sophisticated appreciation of cooperation, he is sensitive to social situations. He likes clothes. He likes to dress up in masquerade. He likes to make an impression on his companions. He is also beginning to realize that these companions sometimes cheat in play. So he himself may develop mild deceptions and fabrications. He has an elementary sense of shame and disgrace, and of status. He is more conscious than hitherto of cultural and other differences in the two sexes. He is capable of anxiety and of "unreasonable" fears, but typically he is stable and well adjusted in his emotional life, as he is in his intellectual outlook. Self-assurance, confidence in others, and social conformability are cardinal personal-social traits at five.

THE ETIOLOGICAL SIGNIFICANCE OF SEXUAL LIFE

SIGMUND FREUD

These paragraphs, which Freud wrote for an encyclopedia in 1922, contain a condensed statement of early versions of psychoanalytic theory—the existence of childhood sexuality (in a special, broadened sense of the term sexuality); the importance of the early years of development; the continuity of normal and abnormal childhood and adulthood; the marked influence of unconscious mental functioning and of fantasy; the Oedipus complex; and, more generally phrased, a psychology of conflicts, of instinctual drives and their vicissitudes (Sterba, 1942; Fenichel, 1945b).

Much has already occurred, and is to come, by way of revisions in psychoanalytic theory with regard to ego and superego structures, the conflict-free sphere of ego functioning, autonomous ego development, instinctual drives, object relations, social reality and adaptation to it, etiologic agents and paths of maladaptation, a broadening and rephrasing of psychosexual theory, discarding or revamping of certain aspects of energic drive discharge and libidinal concepts. Nevertheless, many of Freud's original concepts continue to constitute the core of our understanding of human development and its disturbances (A. Freud, 1936; Hartmann, 1958b, 1964a; Erikson, 1950; Gill, 1967; Holt, 1967; Schur, 1966; Arlow and Brenner, 1964; Marmor, 1968).

Infantile Sexuality.—As a result of its aetiological researches, psycho-analysis found itself in the position of dealing with a subject the very existence of which had scarcely been suspected previously. Science had become accustomed to consider sexual life as beginning with puberty and regarded manifestations of sexuality in children as rare signs of abnormal

From two encyclopedia articles. *Standard Edition,* 18:243-246, London: Hogarth Press. Reprinted with permission of Sigmund Freud Copyrights Ltd., the Estate of Mr. James Strachey, and the Hogarth Press Ltd.

precocity and degeneracy. But now psychoanalysis revealed a wealth of phenomena, remarkable, yet of regular occurrence, which made it necessary to date back the beginning of the sexual function in children almost to the commencement of extra-uterine existence; and it was asked with astonishment how all this could have come to be overlooked. The first glimpses of sexuality in children had indeed been obtained through the analytic examination of adults and were consequently saddled with all the doubts and sources of error that could be attributed to such a belated retrospect; but subsequently (from 1908 onwards) a beginning was made with the analysis of children themselves and with the unembarrassed observation of their behaviour, and in this way direct confirmation was reached for the whole factual basis of the new view.

Sexuality in children showed a different picture in many respects from that in adults, and, surprisingly enough, it exhibited numerous traces of what, in adults, were condemned as *'perversions'*. It became necessary to enlarge the concept of what was sexual, till it covered more than the impulsion towards the union of the two sexes in the sexual act or towards provoking particular pleasurable sensations in the genitals. But this enlargement was rewarded by the new possibility of grasping infantile, normal and perverse sexual life as a single whole.

The analytic researches carried out by the writer fell, to begin with, into the error of greatly overestimating the importance of *seduction* as a source of sexual manifestations in children and as a root for the formation of neurotic symptoms. This misapprehension was corrected when it became possible to appreciate the extraordinarily large part played in the mental life of neurotics by the activities of *fantasy,* which clearly carried more weight in neurosis than did external reality. Behind these fantasies there came to light the material which allows us to draw the picture which follows of the development of the sexual function.

The Development of the Libido.—The sexual instinct, the dynamic manifestation of which in mental life we shall call *'libido',* is made up of component instincts into which it may once more break up and which are only gradually united into well-defined organizations. The sources of these component instincts are the organs of the body and in particular certain specially marked *erotogenic zones;* but contributions are made to libido from every important functional process in the body. At first the individual component instincts strive for satisfaction independently of one another, but in the course of development they become more and more convergent and concentrated. The first (pre-genital) stage of organization to be discerned is the *oral* one, in which—in conformity with the suckling's predominant interest—the oral zone plays the leading part. This is followed by the *sadistic-anal* organization, in which the *anal* zone and the component instinct of *sadism* are particularly prominent; at this stage the difference between the sexes is represented by the contrast between active and passive. The third and final stage of organization is that in which the majority of the component instincts converge under the *primacy of the genital zones.* As a rule this development is passed through swiftly and unobtrusively; but some individual portions of the instincts remain behind at the prodromal stages of the process and thus give rise to *fixations* of libido, which are important as constituting predispositions for subsequent irruptions of repressed impulses and which stand in a definite relation to the later development of neuroses and perversions.

The Process of Finding an Object and the Oedipus Complex.—In the first instance the oral component instinct finds satisfaction by attaching itself to the sating of the desire for nourishment; and its object is the mother's breast. It then detaches itself, becomes independent and at the same time *autoerotic,* that is, it finds an object in the child's own body. Others of the component instincts also start by being autoerotic and are not until later diverted on to an external object. It is a particularly important fact that the component instincts belonging to the genital zone habitually pass through a period of intense autoerotic satisfaction. The component instincts are not all equally serviceable in the final genital organization of libido; some of them (for instance, the anal components) are consequently left aside and suppressed, or undergo complicated transformations.

In the very earliest years of childhood (approximately between the ages of two and five) a convergence of the sexual impulses occurs of which, in the case of boys, the object is the mother. This choice of an object, in conjunction with a corresponding attitude of rivalry and hostility towards the father, provides the content of what is known as the *Oedipus complex,* which in every human being is of the greatest importance in determining the final shape of his erotic life. It has been found to be characteristic of a normal individual that he learns to master his Oedipus complex, whereas the neurotic subject remains involved in it.

The Diphasic Onset of Sexual Development.—Towards the end of the fifth year this early period of sexual life normally comes to an end. It is succeeded by a period of more or less complete *latency,* during which ethical restraints are built up, to act as defences against the desires of the Oedipus complex. In the subsequent period of *puberty,* the Oedipus complex is revivified in the unconscious and embarks upon further modifications. It is only at puberty that the sexual instincts develop to their full intensity; but the direction of that development, as well as all the predispositions for it, have already been determined by the early efflorescence of sexuality during childhood which preceded it. This diphasic development of the sexual function–in two stages, interrupted by the latency period–appears to be a biological peculiarity of the human species and to contain the determining factor for the origin of neuroses.

COMMENTS ON THE FORMATION OF PSYCHIC STRUCTURE

HEINZ HARTMANN, ERNST KRIS,
AND RUDOLPH M. LOEWENSTEIN

The contributions of Hartmann, Kris, and Loewenstein—both individually and collectively—to psychoanalytic theory are legion (Hartmann, 1964a; Kris, 1952; Loewenstein, 1957; Hartmann, Kris, and Loewenstein, 1964b), and have been well recognized (Rapaport, 1959b; Loewenstein, 1966; Rangell, 1965; A. Freud, 1958). Although this paper begins with a statement of intention to clarify terminology, a much-needed task in psychoanalytic theory (Sandler, 1962; Harrison, 1970), it proceeds far beyond that intention. It summarizes decades of substantial modification of psychoanalytic theory, declares an unequivocal commitment (too readily neglected in many psychoanalytic quarters) to verification, and seeks to enlarge the data base and range of methodologies relevant for psychoanalysis. Most of all, in accordance with the genetic point of view in psychoanalysis (Hartmann and Kris, 1945), the authors give an account of the formation of ego and superego structures—their origins, energy sources, constituents, interrelationships, and the maturational and environmental influences shaping them.

Concern with clarification of terms is unpopular amongst psychoanalysts and rare in psychoanalytic writing. This is partly due to Freud's example. Semantics could hardly be the concern of the great explorer and some inconsistency in the usage of words may well be considered the prerogative of genius. [1] It is a different matter when a generation or two of scientists assume a similar prerogative; then scientific communication may tend to suffer and controversy to dissolve into soliloquies of individuals or groups. The latter conditions seem to prevail in recent psychoanalytic

Reprinted from *The Psychoanalytic Study of the Child,* 2. New York: International Universities Press, 1947, pp. 11–38.

[1] See also E. Kris (1947a), a contribution written at the same time as this paper.

writing and clarification of terminology may well be one of the means to counteract it.

Psychoanalysis has developed under social conditions rare in science. Small teams of private practitioners everywhere formed the nuclei of larger professional groups. During the early stages of team work, written communication was supplemented to such an extent by personal contact on an international scale—mainly by training analyses with the few instructors—that mutual understanding was not endangered by uncertainties of terminology. With the increase of the number of psychoanalysts, that condition was bound to change. The situation of the 1940's is hardly reminiscent of the period of early team work; large groups of psychoanalysts work in ever looser contact with each other and the diffusion of psychoanalytic concepts in psychiatry, their extension into psychosomatic medicine, social work and various educational and psychological techniques opens up new vistas of development. Every step in this development, every new context in which psychoanalytic propositions are being tested or used raises anew the problem of adequate communication. Since scientific communication is impaired by ambiguity of meaning, the need for clarification has become urgent.

Psychoanalytic hypotheses have undergone far-reaching modifications in Freud's own work and in that of his earlier collaborators. The importance of some of these reformulations was in many instances underrated at the time of their publication; and we believe that the importance of the most radical and farsighted ones, suggested in Freud's *Inhibitions, Symptoms and Anxiety,* has not yet been fully appreciated. Briefly, since a structural viewpoint was introduced into psychoanalytic thinking, hypotheses established previously must be reintegrated. The task of synchronization is larger than it might seem at first. For the newcomer the study of psychoanalysis will remain cumbersome until this is accomplished: he can hardly turn to any one book or any one presentation. While psychoanalysis has reached the "handbook stage," no handbook exists. [2] In order to grasp the systematic cohesion of psychoanalysis as a theory, the student has to study its development. This detour alone seems to guarantee full understanding; it is a detour which only a few devoted workers choose. Yet without it, there is some danger that part of what has been presented in many years of psychoanalytic writings is lost to the student, that rediscoveries of what once was discarded for valid reasons may occur ever more frequently, but also that the degree of relevance of various hypotheses

[2] This point was made by Hartmann at the Symposium on Present Trends in Psychoanalytic Theory and Practice, at the Psychoanalytic Congress in Detroit, 1943.

may not always clearly be established and a systematic understanding of hypotheses seems to indicate that shifts in emphasis are unavoidable. Without these shifts, progress in insight tends to be retarded at a moment which otherwise lends itself uniquely to concentrated efforts to research. In restating some of the most general propositions of psychoanalysis, we have such concentrated efforts of research in mind.

In the writings of Freud and of other psychoanalysts, a large number of assumptions are tacitly implied, partly because the atmosphere of team work made full explicitness seem unnecessary; partly because the novelty of the clinical phenomena suggested global rather than detailed explanation. Thus, in turning to any one statement in the literature on a given subject, the student is likely to find incompletely stated hypotheses, and those who rely on random quotations from Freud's work have an easy time obscuring his meaning. When verification of hypotheses is at stake, incomplete statements are bound to encumber the way. Yet verification is essential in many areas; in none so much as in genetic questions (Hartmann and Kris, 1945). In the present paper we attempt to formulate just those propositions that are concerned with the formation of psychic structure; and within this group we select some that may be considered as models; i.e., many parallel hypotheses are being used in other areas of psychoanalytic theory. Our selection of propositions is also guided by consideration of actual or potential misunderstandings. We are therefore less concerned with problems of libidinal development, its stages and its manifestations, and more with some problems of ego development and superego formation, and with the part played by maturation in these developments.

The Structural Concepts

Precursors of structural concepts appeared in Freud's work when, at the end of the nineteenth century, he implemented his first startling discoveries by explanatory concepts which his subject matter had forced upon him. That subject matter was the study of psychic conflict.

The concept of psychic conflict is integral to many religious systems and many philosophical doctrines. Ever more frequently since the days of enlightenment had the great masters of intuitive psychology, had writers, poets, and philosophers described the life of man as torn between conflicting forces. Freud's contribution conquered this area for the rule of science. The study of psychic conflict in general, and more specifically that of the pathognomic nature of certain conflicts, suggested that the forces opposing each other in typical conflict situations were not grouped at random; rather that the groups of opposing forces possessed an inner cohesion or organization. These impressions were undoubtedly stimulated by a topic that in the 1880's and 1890's played a considerable part in French psychiatry: that of multiple personality.[3] The intermittent eruptions observed in these cases supported the idea that other less dramatic manifestations of mental illness could be understood in terms of "man divided against himself".

Freud's first approach to this division and his first understanding of its implications was guided by the physicalist school in the German physiology of his time (Bernfeld, 1944), and by the evolutionist thinking of Darwinism. Under these influences he tentatively suggested his first formulations on the nature of "the psychic apparatus" whose complex functions would account for the kind of bewildering phenomena that had emerged; disturbances of memory, indirect expression of impulses in symptoms or symbols, the nature of dreams, fantasy and delusion; all these appeared in a new context, once the limitation of psychology to consciousness had been abandoned; all had to be explained in the light of the clinical study of conflict situations.

We shall not describe in detail here how, in a set of reformulations, the first hypotheses concerning the psychic apparatus were gradually modified; how step by step the concepts emerged which in the early 1920's Freud introduced under the names of "id", "ego", and "superego". These three psychic substructures or systems are not conceived of as independent parts of personality that invariably oppose each other, but as three centers of psychic functioning that can be characterized according to their developmental level, to the amount of energy vested in them, and to their demarcation and interdependence at a given time. Under specific conditions one of the centers may expand its area, and another or the two others may recede; more correctly, we should say that functions exercised by one of the systems may temporarily be more or less influenced by one of the others.

Thus, three of the foremost functions of the ego, *thinking, perception* and *action,* are frequently put into the service of either the id or the superego.

Thinking may be used for the gratification of instinctual as well as self-critical tendencies. In pathological cases, e.g., in compulsive thinking, it can become a substitute for masturbation. In psychoses, e.g., in paranoic delusions, it is overwhelmed by id and superego functions.

[3] See in this connection Azam (1876), Binet (1892), Bourru and Burot (1888), Camuset (1882), Dufay (1876), Janet (1876).

Perception may be used for the gratification of instinctual wishes in scoptophilic activity. In pathological cases, it might lead to hysterical disturbances of vision. In dreams and in psychoses perception is modified in a different sense; hallucinatory phenomena are perceptions without objects in the outside world. The perceptual function in these cases can be used by both the id and the superego.

Normal actions may serve instinctual gratification or superego demands, completely disregarding the interests of the ego. In pathological cases, interference of these systems may lead to hysterical symptoms, e.g., paralyses. In extreme cases, in catatonic states, for instance, motor activity loses even residues of ego functions–its coordination into deliberate acts.

In using more precise formulations, we have indicated the criteria used in defining the three substructures: the psychic systems are defined by the functions attributed to them.

A word need be said here as to how these definitions were arrived at. Definitions are matters of "convenience", and convenience in science consists of an adequate relation to the observed facts. Freud established his definitions of the psychic systems after careful and repeated scrutiny of his clinical material. That material suggested that in a typical psychic conflict one set of functions is more frequently on "the one side" than on "the other side" of the conflict. Functions that we find "together on one side" have common characteristics or properties. The relatedness is one of frequency.

Functions of the id center around the basic needs of man and their striving for gratification. These needs are rooted in instinctual drives and their vicissitudes (we do not here deal wih these drives themselves and the theory of instincts as developed by Freud). Functions of the id are characterized by the great mobility of cathexes of the instinctual tendencies and their mental representatives, i.e., by the operation of the primary process. Its manifestations are condensation, displacement, and the use of special symbols.

Functions of the ego center around the relation to reality. In this sense, we speak of the ego as of a specific organ of adjustment. It controls the apparatus of motility and perception; it tests the properties of the present situation at hand, i.e., of "present reality", and anticipates properties of future situations. The ego mediates between these properties and requirements, and the demands of the other psychic organizations.

Functions of the superego center around moral demands. Self-criticism, sometimes heightened to incentives to self-punishment, and the formation of ideas, are essential manifestations of the superego.

In adopting the *functions* exercised in mental processes as the decisive criterium for defining the psychic systems, Freud used physiology as his model in concept formation. However, this does not imply any correlation of any one of the systems to any specific physiological organization or group of organs, though Freud considered such a correlation as the ultimate goal of psychological research. Psychological terminology, he assumed, has to be maintained as long as it cannot be adequately substituted by physiological terminology.[4] It seems that the time for such substitution has not yet come. We therefore do not dwell, in the following, on parallels between the psychic systems in Freud's definition and certain organizations of the central nervous system.

The structural concepts of psychoanalysis have met with much criticism. It has been said that through their use clinical description has been obscured, since the terms were dramatic in an anthropomorphic sense (Glover, 1930; Masserman, 1946). Clearly, whenever dramatization is encountered, metaphorical language has crept into scientific discourse and that there is danger in the use of metaphor in science hardly needs to be demonstrated; danger, it should be added, to which Freud (1933) himself drew our attention. However, it remains a problem worth some further discussion, under what conditions the danger outweighs the advantage. The danger obviously begins if and when metaphor infringes upon meaning: in the case in point, when the structural concepts are anthropomorphized. Then the functional connotation may be lost and one of the psychic systems may be substituted for the total personality. There are cases in psychoanalytic literature where dramatizations have led to anthropomorphisms of this kind. To quote one conspicuous example: in Alexander's *Psychology of the Total Personality* (1930a), the id, ego and superego have indeed become exalted actors on the psychic stage.

In order to illustrate the vicissitudes of meaning in this area, we select as an example the Freudian sentence: "The Ego presents itself to the Superego as love object." The metaphor expresses the relations of two psychic organizations by comparing it to a love relation between individuals, in which the one is the lover and the other the beloved. However, the sentence expresses an important clinical finding: self-love can easily and does, under certain conditions, substitute for love of another person. Self-love in this formulation indicates that approval of the self by the superego concerns the self in lieu of another person.

[4] *Jenseits des Lustprinzips,* Gesammelte Werke, XIII, p. 65. The English translation *(Beyond the Pleasure Principle)* by omitting one word, fails to render Freud's meaning.

We replace the word "ego" in Freud's text by the word "self." We do so since the ego is defined as part of the personality, and since Freud's use of the word is ambiguous. He uses "ego" in reference to a psychic organization and to the whole person. Before we can attempt to reformulate Freud's proposition, it is essential to go one step further. In a more rigorous sense, we find it advisable not to speak of "approval" or "disapproval" by the superego, but simply to speak of different kinds and degrees of tension between the two psychic organizations, according to the presence or absence of conflict between their functions. Approval would be characterized by a diminution of tension; disapproval by its increase.

There can be little doubt that a reformulation of this kind that tries to restrict the use of metaphors, considerably impoverishes the plasticity of language, as compared to Freud's mode of expression. Man frequently experiences self-satisfaction as if an inner voice expressed approval, and self-reproaches as if the inner voice expressed reprobation (Loewenstein, 1938). Thus the metaphorical expression comes closer to our immediate understanding, since the anthropomorphism it introduces corresponds to human experience. Our reformulation shows that not the concepts which Freud introduced are anthropomorphic, but that the clinical facts he studied and described led us to understand what part anthropomorphism plays in introspective thinking.

When the French psychiatrists of the nineteenth century turned to the clinical study of human conflict, they used a metaphorical language of their own. Their descriptive skill lives in the papers of Pierre Janet and others; it has rarely been emulated in the descriptive psychiatry of other schools. But the metaphorical language of descriptive psychiatry did not permit in the nineteenth century, and no reformulation in terms of existential psychology will permit in the twentieth century, the step from empathy to causal explanation. This step became possible only after conceptual tools had been adopted which permitted a more generalized penetration of the phenomena; a penetration that becomes possible only at some distance from immediate experience. This was the function of Freud's structural concepts. If we use these concepts in a strict sense, the distance from experience grows. Freud's metaphorical usage of his own terms was clearly intended to bridge this gap. It might thus be said that Freud's usage bears the imprint of the clinical source from which the concepts were originally derived, the imprint of the communication with the patients. Requirements of communication may ever again suggest richness of metaphor, but metaphors should not obscure the nature of the concepts and their function in psychoanalysis as a science. That function is to facilitate explanatory constructs. Briefly, the structural concepts are amongst our most valuable tools, since they stand in a genetic context.

The Formation of Psychic Structure

Whenever in psychoanalysis we use biological concepts, we are faced with one of three cases. First, the case of immediate borrowing: we refer to a biological or physiological phenomenon and use the terms current in these sciences; for instance, when we refer to the physiological changes within the personality at the age of puberty as distinguished from the concomitant psychological processes of adolescence. Second, a term may be borrowed, but its meaning may be changed by the context in which it is used and new properties may accrue. A case in point is the term "regression". Through its use in psychoanalysis, it has acquired meanings far transcending those in its original neurological setting. Third, biological terms may be used in a different context. Their definition is taken over from the old context, since the requirements of the new are similar to those in which they have originated.

In describing developmental functions, child psychology and psychoanalysis use the concept of differentiation and integration. [5] Differentiation indicates the specialization of a function; integration, the emergence of a new function out of previously not coherent sets of functions or reactions. The terms maturation and development are not always so clearly distinguished. We use both terms here in the sense that maturation indicates the processes of growth that occur relatively independent of environmental influences; development indicates the processes of growth in which environment and maturation interact more closely.

The relation between stimulus and response becomes, during growth, ever more specific. One might say that a specific structure of stimulus response correlations is characteristic of a specific phase through which the child goes. Thus a stimulus that was of little relevance in one phase of its development may be of decisive relevance in another. The best known examples of this correlation can be found in the way children react to sexual experiences. Their reactions depend upon both the nature of the experience and the stage of the child's development. The "Wolfman's" observation of the primal scene at the age of one-and-a-half became of pathogenic importance only at the age of three when specific conflicts reactivated this memory (Freud, 1918).

[5] For closer definitions see Allport (1937).

Differentiation and integration in the child's early phases of development are partly regulated by maturational sequence, but even where they are influenced by environmental conditions, we are compelled to assume a principle regulating their interaction (Hartmann, 1939). Thus acceleration of certain integrative processes may become pathological. Premature ego development, for example, may in this sense be considered as one of the factors predisposing to obsessional neurosis. The regulation of this interaction can be attributed to a principle of balance, one that does not work in the cross-section only, but that regulates balance of development.

The Undifferentiated Phase [6]

We assume that the essential elements in the structure of personality exist in children of our civilization at the age of five or six. Developmental processes occurring after that age can be described as modifications, as enrichment, or, in pathological cases, as restriction of the then existing structure. Developmental processes before that age can be described in terms of formation of this structure. In introducing his concepts of psychic structure, Freud speaks of a gradual differentiation of the ego from the id; as an end result of this process of differentiation the ego, as a highly structured organization, is opposed to the id. Freud's formulation has obvious disadvantages. It implies that the infant's equipment existing at birth is part of the id. It seems however that the innate apparatus and reflexes cannot all be part of the id, in the sense generally accepted in psychoanalysis. We suggest a different assumption, namely that of an undifferentiated phase during which both the id and the ego gradually are formed. The difference is not merely one of words. The new formulation permits a better explanation of some of the basic properties of both id and ego. During the undifferentiated phase there is maturation of apparatuses that later will come under the control of the ego, and that serve motility, perception, and certain thought processes. [7] Maturation in these areas proceeds without the total organization we call ego; only after ego formation will these functions be fully integrated. To the degree to which differentiation takes place man is equipped with a specialized organ of adaptation, i.e, with the ego. This does not mean that there do not remain in the id certain elements that further the "maintenance" or preservation of the individual (Loewenstein, 1940). However, the differentiation accounts for the nature of the instinctual drives of man, sharply distinguished as they are

[6] This section follows Hartmann (1939).

[7] For a somewhat divergent discussion of these problems see Hendrik (1942).

from animal instincts. One gains the impression that many manifestations of the id are further removed from reality than any comparable behavior of animals. The instincts of the animal (Lashley, 1938) mediate its adjustment to the reality in which it lives and their properties determine the extent of the possible adaptation. With man, adjustment is mainly entrusted to an independent organization. One may raise the question whether, early in the infant's life, a residual equipment of "instincts" exists, that later loses its function of adjusting to the environment.

The Self and the Environment

We have refrained from indicating at what time during early infancy the successive steps leading to structural differentiation take place, and from what time the psychic systems of id and ego oppose and supplement each other. While we do not wish to draw rigid chronological lines, we shall summarize some of the steps in the child's growth, which lead to the formation of the ego and partly represent its earliest functions. The first and most fundamental of these steps concerns the ability of the infant to distinguish between his self and the world around him. At birth, environmental circumstances have suddenly changed; the organism grows no longer under conditions of total shelter from all disturbances from outside, and no longer, comparatively speaking, under conditions of total gratification of all basic needs. The most essential part of the new environment is the infant's mother; she controls the physical properties of the environment, providing shelter, care and food.

The nature of the biological equipment of the infant, and the nature of its environment account for the fact that the infant's first reactions are related to indulgence and deprivation experienced at the hands of its mother. Freud assumes that as long as all needs are gratified, i.e., under "total" indulgence, the infant tends to experience the source of satisfaction as part of the self; partial deprivation thus is probably an essential condition for the infant's ability to distinguish between the self and the object. The classical example concerns the child's relation to the feeding breast or its substitutes. To the extent to which indulgence prevails, comprehension of the breast as part of the self is dominant; to the extent to which deprivation is experienced, or indulgence delayed, the distinction becomes possible. That distinction, however, seems to become impossible unless a certain amount of gratification is allowed for. There is some reason to believe that the neutral term "distinction" may be preceded by or cover a number of highly significant experiences: they may range from expectation of or longing for gratification, to feelings of disappointment, and even rage against the source of frustration.

Deprivation, we have said, is a necessary, but clearly not a sufficient condition for the establishment of the distinction between the self and the object. The process of distinguishing has a cognitive or perceptual side; it is thus dependent on the maturation of the child's perceptual equipment. Moreover, psychoanalysis works with the hypothesis of another necessary condition, which concerns the distribution of psychic energy. Freud assumed that with the newborn, psychic energy is concentrated upon the self (primary narcissism). When we state that an object in the external world is experienced as part of the self, we imply that the object partakes in its narcissistic cathexis. When we speak of a distinction between the self and the external object, we assume that the object which is experienced as independent from the self has retained cathexis in spite of the separation; we infer that primary narcissistic cathexis has been transformed into object cathexis.

These processes we here describe are not accomplished in one step; they proceed in ever repeated trial experiences. Some of these trials follow a pattern established by the physiological organization of man; predominant modes of this pattern are incorporation and ejection; its psychological counterparts are introjection and projection.

These processes seem to accompany the earliest sequences of indulgence and deprivation in the child's life.

> . . . the course of gratification of instinctual needs during the period immediately following birth can be presented as follows: the instinctual need—crying—gratification. The next possible step in the course of the process would be: instinctual need—hallucinated gratification which does not suffice—crying which brings on the real gratification; the child can then sleep again [Benedek, 1938, p. 201].

We have no means to assess what might happen if even under such early conditions indulgence were maximized; no conditions of infancy have been observed in which nursing procedures occur that could be described in these terms; they do not exist in human society, and would have to be created for the purpose of an experiment. We are better informed on consequences of intensive deprivation, and have learned recently that the prolonged absence of maternal care, or the lack of adequate stimulation (from the first quarter of the first year of life) tends to produce irreversible retardations that even affect maturation (Durfee and Wolf, 1933; Spitz, 1945). It seems reasonable to assume that the infant's apparatus of control and adjustment are given their best training chances at a distance considerably closer to the maximum of indulgence than to that of deprivation. As the maturation of the apparatus proceeds, the child shows signs of expectation and recognition; he turns his head towards the mother's breast, searches for the breast when put in a feeding position, and between the third and fifth month of his life, he learns to anticipate the feeding situation without crying. He recognizes his mother while she prepares his food. (For a good summary, see Benedek, p. 207.)

As the child learns to distinguish between himself and the mother, he develops understanding for her communications. Little is known about the detailed processes by which this understanding is established; reactions to the actual handling of the child by the mother, to touch and bodily pressure, certainly play a part; gradually, the understanding of the child for the mother's facial expression grows. It seems probably that experiences concerning emotive processes and expressive movements in the infant itself form the basis or are a necessary condition for the infant's understanding of the mother's expression (Freud, 1905c; Schilder, 1935). But the cognitive side of the process, the understanding of signs of communication, is part of the libidinal tie existing between the two. The identification of the child with the mother that we assume to exist at an early stage, gradually develops into an object relation. [8] The mother, as the first love object, is the object most highly cathected in the child's world, and the child's earliest learning proceeds partly by identifying with this object. In this connection we mention Freud's latest suggestion on the subject, communicated in 1940 in a paper by Ruth M. Brunswick: Freud indicates the possibility that the development of the child's activity is decisively influenced by the identification with the nursing mother. Maturational changes proceeding during the second half of the first year give the child further control of his own body and enable him partly to master the inanimate objects in his life space. [9] Some kind of anticipation of future events plays its part in each of these operations. They represent a central function of the ego; that which makes the transfer from the pleasure principle to the reality principle possible. The two regulatory principles of mental functioning express two tendencies of man. The one strives toward the immediate and unconditional gratification of demands; the other ac-

[8] Balint (1937) and others assume, in addition, the existence of an early object relation in the newly born infant. We do not decide how far this assumption is warranted. Freud's theory of "primary narcissism" seems still best to account for facts observable immediately after birth.

[9] We do not however follow Hendrick (1942) in assuming the existence of an "instinct to master."

cepts the limitations of reality, postponing gratification in order to make it more secure (Freud, 1911).

Various theories have attempted to explain the relation of the two principles (Ferenczi, 1926b; French, 1936). No explanation is satisfactory unless we assume that the transition from one principle to the other is rendered possible by the formation of the ego, which enters the process as an independent variable (Hartmann, 1939; see also Mahler, 1945).

Some Influences on Ego Formation

The development of the ego proceeds along with that of the child's object relations. Amongst the factors that threaten object relations and thereby endanger the stability of the child's ego functions, we here discuss ambivalence. Theories on the origin of ambivalence are in part identical with those concerning the origin of aggression. Thus Freud (1930) considers the possibility that ambivalence arises as a necessary protection of the individual against destructive impulses bound within the self; their externalization would then be a prerequisite of survival. Some of the characteristics of ambivalence, the rapid oscillation from manifestations of positive to manifestations negative attitudes in infant and child suggests another possibility: one might assume that the intermittent changes between projection and introjection, which were necessary concomitants of the infant's trials to establish a distinction between the self and the environment survive as a tendency towards and away from the human object. Better founded in observable fact, and not necessarily in contradiction with these assumptions, is another explanation: without discussing the problem whether or not instinctual drives tending towards destructive aims are part of the original equipment of man, one may be satisfied to assume that in the earliest phases of the infant's life any transition from indulgence to deprivation tends to elicit aggressive responses. The child's ambivalence towards his first love objects, one might say, corresponds to their position within the continuum leading from indulgence to deprivation (Ferenczi, 1926b). All human relations would, according to this suggestion, be permanently colored by the fact that the earliest love relations in the child's life were formed at a time when those whom the child loves are those to whom it owes both indulgence and deprivation.

However tempting it might be to assume a correlation between the frequency and intensity of the infant's deprivational experiences, and the frequency and intensity of the child's aggressive impulses as manifested in his ambivalence, evidence does not support such simple conclusions. Too many variables exist that tend to obscure the issue, except possibly in extreme cases such as described by Bender, Schilder, and Kaiser (1936), who were exposed to neglect and hostility, in an environment hardly interested in their survival. In less extreme cases, the complexity of the emotional processes can hardly be overestimated. Deprivations in earliest infancy are unavoidable in that the rising intensity of demand of the crying child waiting for the mother is experienced as deprivation; deprivations on this level are, as we have said, essential incentives for the distinction of the world from the self. At a later stage, when the child learns to exchange immediate for future indulgence, he is again exposed to a deprivational experience, one that, as we shall see, is a prerequisite for the formation of the world of thought and the further development of his ego. The child delays his demands in order to comply with the mother's request. There can be little doubt that the better assured the child is that indulgence will follow the postponement of demands, the more easily will the deprivation be tolerated. (Benedek, in this connection, stresses the importance of the element of confidence.) And yet one cannot overlook the fact that each of the basic demands of the child, the fulfillment of which is postponed, contain both libidinal and aggressive impulses. They are linked to every one of the dominant biological functions, to the nutritive as well as the eliminative, and both libidinal and aggressive tendencies find their expression on the oral and anal level of libidinal development. Any attempt to study the child's reaction to deprivation should therefore take at least three aspects into account: the nature of deprivation, its timing, and the modes of its administration.

The situation seems clearest where the third point is concerned. The mother's role is a double one. She sets the premium on learning: in order to retain her love, the child has to comply. Secondly, once the ego organization is established, by the consistency of her requests the mother supports the child's ego in his struggle against his impulses. Both roles are best fulfilled if education is conducted in an atmosphere of loving attention, i.e., if no conscious or unconscious manifestiations of aggression on the part of the adult elicit counter-aggression of the child. We do not discuss here the problem of how the child senses the adult's hostility—even when it is carefully controlled—but we assume that the child's capacity to perceive it is greater than has been assumed until recently, and that this capacity develops at an extremely early age. [10]

The effect of the adult's attitude upon the child when administering deprivation has been studied in the set-up of restraint situations. The

[10] For problems later in the child's life, see Burlingham (1935).

child does not only experience deprivation when one of his demands is denied—the demand for food, care or attention—but also when the adult interferes with one of his spontaneous activities, whether they serve the gratification of a drive or the solution of a problem. In the child's life, various types of activities tend to be not as sharply delimited from each other as they normally are with the adult. All action is closer to instinctual drives; problem-solving and fantasy play tend to interact; even the older child eats while it plays, and may at any moment shift from one type of gratification to the other. Many attempts to "stop the child from doing something" restrict, therefore, processes that are highly cathected. In order to characterize these manifold occurrences, we speak of restraint situations.

By and large, the child tends to react to restraint by some manifestation of aggression. However, that response is not regular. Infants swaddled during long periods of the first year of life are said not to show any more pronounced proclivity to aggression than infants who could move their bodies freely (Greenacre, 1944). This finding seems to suggest that early swaddling, especially if it is a part of a cultural tradition, and not the expression of an individual preference of the mother, does not stimulate aggressive response, since it does not interrupt an activity but prevents one (Buxbaum, 1947a).

The assumption that early in childhood the interruption of activity rather than the prevention, may be a crucial experience—though the point should be generalized only with care—leads us to the hypothesis that many kinds of "practising" activities are highly cathected, and thus indirectly to the proposition that interruption of practice, prevention of what one calls "completion of the act" is likely to upset the balance in psychic energy. This proposition is generally true of man's life; a host of experiments on act completion with normal adults and one set of experiments with obsessional patients has given ample evidence in this area (Zeigarnik, 1927; Hartmann, 1933; Gerö, 1933). The similarity in the behavior of child and adult extends even to those cases where the completion is prevented by failure: a child who fails in handling a toy properly, or who fails to solve a problem he has set himself, may turn from activity to rage-like reactions. Frustrations imposed upon adults by unsolvable problems elicit a similar response—except that their frustration tolerance is greater.

However, the relevant point in our context is that the child's tendency to aggressive outbursts when he experiences restraint can easily be modified by the behavior of the restraining adult: friendly restraint tends to reduce aggressive response. One distracts a child best by loving attention. Cathexis directed towards action is thus transformed into object cathexis. The importance of this area of problems is considerable, since the sequence of restraint of the child's spontaneous activities and decrease of aggressive impulses in the child affects many learning situations.

We do not here attempt to enter into the question of what contributions psychoanalysis might make to a general theory of learning, or how the presentation of certain psychoanalytic hypotheses could profit in general, if formulated in terms of learning. We briefly note that learning processes may lead to the gratification of instinctual impulses, since they make the mastery of reality possible, but that, at the same time, they represent an essential requisite for the development of the child's defenses against danger. As far as the child's early experiences in learning are concerned, psychoanalytic hypotheses tend to take mainly four factors into account: first, the stage of maturation of the apparatuses; second, the reaction of the environment; third, the tolerance for deprivation; and fourth, the various types of gratification afforded by the processes of learning and the satisfactions that can be obtained as consequences of mastery. Among the specific learning situations that tend to become crucial for the child's life, as a sort of model in which ego control is developed, we wish to discuss habit training.

There are plausible reasons of a physiological and psychological order to which we may refer in an attempt to account for the extreme importance of this specific situation in the child's life. The demand for control of habits has two phases; it involves the demand for retention and for elimination. Compliance therefore involves two opposite innervations of both the voluntary urethral and anal sphincters. On the other hand, the same innervation may at various times express opposite things—compliance at one time; defiance at the other. [11]

Compliance is facilitated when the child understands the adult's request, and when the muscular apparatus itself is fully developed. The recent tendency to postpone habit training to the second year of life takes these factors into account. But not only the intellectual capacity and the muscular apparatus have matured: another maturational process, that of the libidinal cathexis of the anal zone, takes place approximately at the same time. Learning takes place at a time when the stimulation of the anal passage is likely to create intense sexual experiences. [12] The situation

[11] A somewhat similar viewpoint has been suggested by Erikson (1940).

[12] It is possible that "premature" toilet training could accelerate the libidinal cathexis of the zone.

of the child during the period of toilet training represents in a nutshell the nature of its conflict situation at that age. That conflict situation is threefold: first, there is the conflict between two instinctual tendencies, that of elimination and retention (instinctual conflict); second, there is the conflict between either one of these tendencies, and the child's attempts to control them and to time his function: it is a conflict between the id and the ego (structural conflict); and third, there is the conflict with the external world that has made the structural conflict necessary: the mother's request for timing of elimination.

The power of this request rests in the premium which the mother offers: approval or disapproval in all their manifold intensities. Approval may range from the mother's smile to caresses or gifts, disapproval from the disappearance of the smile to spanking. But again, it is not the intensity, or not only the intensity of approval or disapproval that is relevant; not the tangible manifestations of indulgences and deprivation, since whatever the intensity of manifestation, the threat of disapproval embodies the greatest danger in the child's life.

At the end of the first year, in the early phases of ego development, the child has formed lasting object relations; his attachment can outlast deprivation, and libidinal energy directed toward the love object has been partly transformed into aim-inhibited libidinal energy, transient into permanent cathexis.

As long as the demand for immediate indulgence prevails, any absence of those on whose care the child depends is experienced as a threat; gradually, as ego development proceeds, abstraction from the concrete situation becomes possible. The threat becomes, to some extent, independent of the presence or absence of the mother. These two stages coexist in the child's life for a long time and are embodied in a variety of highly complex situations. Freud (1926) comprehended these situations in the formulation that the fear of losing the love object is supplemented by the fear of losing love. Thus, one might say that the child in acquiring this new security acquires also a new kind of vulnerability; anxiety may now invade its life under new conditions.

The meaning of fear itself undergoes parallel transformations: it has been integrated into the child's structural equipment. Originally, fear is a reflex-like response to danger, i.e., to changes that tend to evoke feelings of helplessness; later, it acts as a signal that warns of changes to come. It is only when the ego cannot act upon the warning of the signal, that the intensity of anxiety grows and the state of anxiety may develop. That change in the function of anxiety is another instance of what we shall call later the extension of the inner world: anxiety as a signal can operate only when the child has learned to anticipate the future.

Only since in 1926 Freud introduced the concept of the danger situation, has the full impact of the problem of the child's defense against danger been studied in some detail. In the present context, two aspects of the problem of defense deserve our particular attention: we have said that in order to retain the love of his environment, the child learns to control his instinctual drives: this means that the differentiation between id and ego becomes ever more complete as the child grows, and that those of the child's defenses that are directed against the power of his drives serve to maintain that differentiation. The vicissitudes of these conflicting forces can be studied in the instances of regressive behavior, and of sudden eruptions of instinctual impulses in the child's early life: we do not here enter into this area of problems, since they require a discussion of the functions and the strength of the ego.

The term "defense" should not suggest the misapprehension that the process here referred to is either pathological or only of a negative importance. Rather is it correct to say that the human personality is formed by psychic mechanisms which serve, also, the purpose of defense. Some of these mechanisms first operate in other areas; thus projection and introjection are used in order to establish the distinction between the self and the non-self; regression, as a regular and temporary transformation of psychic functioning, accompanies the daily cycle from awakeness to sleep; and denial of the unpleasant represents probably an initial phase in the elimination of all disturbing stimuli. These and other mechanisms, which in the infant's life serve the function of adjustment and may be rooted in the reflex equipment of the newborn, may later function as mechanism of defense and thus produce changes in the child's personality (Hartmann, 1939). Some of these changes are only temporary, others may become permanent. The ego may develop a preference for one or the other kind of defense, use it in coping with both the id and the outer world, and later the superego; thus in all, or many, of its functions, the ego may bear the imprint of the reaction to early danger situations (Anna Freud, 1936). Certain mechanisms of defense regularly leave their traces in a permanent modification of the structure of personality: repression and identification are cases in point.

There is no reason here to state anew Freud's hypotheses concerning repression (1915b) and its consequences for the dynamics, the economy and the structuralization of the personality. Suffice it to say that with the existence of repression the demarcation between id and ego is drawn more sharply and maintained by counter-cathexes.

It is different with identification. Whereas repression is a specific mechanism, not previously operating—unless we assume the tendency to denial to be its precursor, as we well may—identification has been one of the major, if not the major mechanism contributing to the child's early formation of personality; secondly, and under the pressure of danger, it can also be used for purposes of defense. But the two functions, the primary function of identification, its part in growing, and its secondary function, as a defense against danger, can hardly ever be sharply distinguished. The roots of identification can be traced to those impulses of the id, which strive towards incorporation; the psychological mechanism of identification is a correlate of and is built upon the model of this striving. In the earliest phases of the child's ego development, the child relies upon the adult in his dealing with the external world; he participates in their reactions and thus acquires their methods of solving problems and coping with emergencies. The impact of identification on the child's ego development is not known in detail. Our impressions are clearest in regard to moral behavior.

In taking over the parent's attitudes, the child strengthens his resistance against the onslaught of instinctual demands that he has learned to consider as undesirable. He pays for this greater security with the sense of guilt in case of failure, and acquires the precarious faculty of using the archaic mechanism of turning the drive against the self for auto-punitive purposes. The siding with the parents' requests, the acceptance of their demands as part of what the child wishes himself strengthens his ego against id impulses. This security also plays its part in the organization of the child's intellectual world.

The maturational sequence of the child's growing intellectual capacities is known in great detail. There is an interrelation of this maturation with the formation of psychic structure; the maturational factors in this connection concern the apparatuses that the ego controls. The relationship of the child to the world around him changes in character when the reality principle, at least in part, replaces the pleasure principle. That "replacement" may be described as a process of learning. The child gradually becomes aware of probable changes in his environment; the anticipation of the future centers on considerations such as these: "When I behave in a certain way, my environment will react in a certain way"—and thus behavior can be regulated in order to meet expectations.

This step becomes possible only if and when the urgency of demands can be reduced, when, as we said, future gratification can be substituted for immediate gratification. As a consequence, experience with those whom the child loves is no longer exclusively in terms of indulgence or deprivation. The child's attachment to them can outlast deprivation and they gain characteristics of their own that the child tries to understand. In studying this process with respect to the distribution of psychic energy, we have said that libidinal energy has been transformed into aim-inhibited libidinal energy; with respect to the child's ego functions, we may say that the child has learned to establish objective criteria and use them in action and thought.

The child's thoughts are not only concerned with the problem of finding new ways in order to gain formerly valued gratifications. This clearly plays a part; the child "learns" in order to obtain the candy and in order to elicit the parents' caresses. But there are new pleasures corresponding to each level of development. Moreover, the mastery of difficulties, the solving of problems, becomes a novel source of delight. And thinking itself yields gratification. Thought processes can operate on various levels; thought and fantasy interact. The child can imagine and pretend; he can, in his fantasies, re-enact his relationship with his environment; he can play at being an adult—briefly, the child has created a world of his own.

His independence from the outer world, his resistance to immediate reactions to stimuli, has led to an enlargement of his inner, his intellectual world.

Superego Formation

The processes of differentiation and integration in early childhood show the constant interaction between maturational and developmental factors. The processes leading to the formation of the third psychic organization, the superego, are to a higher degree independent of maturation. There is no specific apparatus whose maturation is essential for the growth of conscience; only a certain stage of development of intellectual life forms an essential precondition. But though the formation of the superego is the result of social influences and of processes of identification, these processes take place under the pressure of a specific situation in the child's life that is brought about by maturation.

The child reaches the phallic phase of its sexual development usually in the third or fourth year. (We here discuss these problems only as they concern the male child.) The manifestations in behavior of the cathexis of and the interest in the genital zone are manifold; the higher frequency of genital masturbation, the greater desire for physical contact with others, particularly with members of the opposite sex, and the predominance of tendencies towards phallic exhibitionism are outstanding examples. Other manifestations frequently interacting with those of behavior pertain to fantasy life. That interaction has best been studied where masturbatory activity is concerned. The link between fantasies of sexual activities with incestuous objects, and of fantasies of being prevented from or punished for such activities (by castration or its equivalent) account for the fact that masturbation during the phallic phase frequently acquires a crucial significance for symptom- and character-formation.

The reaction of the environment to the manifestation of the boy's demand during the phallic phase is no less decisive than the reaction to his earlier strivings. As far as incestuous demands are concerned, deprivation at this stage is regular. The boy's reaction to the new deprivational experience, however, can as a rule not be sharply isolated from his previous experiences in indulgence and deprivation. The intensity of his reaction to deprivation is at this stage partly under the shadows of the past. This relation is in many cases, if not regularly, sharpened by the phenomena of regression: under the pressure of the oedipal conflict, the boy tends temporarily to return to earlier phases of his libidinal development.

The Oedipus constellation itself, best studied under conditions of western civilization, is replete with a series of unavoidable conflicts: the phallic demands of the boy directed against the mother are not only doomed to meet with partial rejection or restraint on her part, but they involve the boy in inescapable conflict with his father. That conflict represents a complete structure: there is the boy's hostility against the rival and his fear of the father's retaliation; the climax of this fear is the fear of castration. There also is the fear that the boy's hostility may actually endanger the father, who outside the area of conflict is a love object of paramount importance.

Freud originally stressed the idea of a phylogenetic factor, predisposing the individual to castration fear. Hartmann and Kris (1945) have formulated alternative views, as follows:

> . . . Freud argues that the intensity of the fear of castration experienced by the male child in our civilization is unaccountable if we consider it as a reaction to the actual threats to which the boy is being exposed in the phallic phase; only the memory of the race will explain it. To this, we are inclined to reply with Freud's own arguments. While in many cases the child in our civilization is no longer being threatened with castration, the intensity of the veiled aggression of the adult against the child may still produce the same effect. One might say that there always is "castration" in the air. Adults who restrict the little boy act according to patterns rooted in their own upbringing. However symbolic or distant from actual castration their threats might be, they are likely to be interpreted by the little boy in terms of his own experi-

> ences. The tumescent penis with which he responds in erotic excitement, that strange phenomenon of a change in a part of his body that proves to be largely independent of his control, leads him to react not to the manifest content but rather to the latent meaning of the restriction with which his strivings for mother, sister, or girl-playmate meet. And then, what he may have seen frequently before, the genitals of the little girl, acquire a new meaning as evidence and corroboration of that fear. However, the intensity of fear is not only linked to his present experience, but also to similar experiences in his past. The dreaded retaliation of the environment revives memories of similar anxieties when desires for other gratifications were predominant and when the supreme fear was not that of being castrated but that of not being loved [pp. 21–22].

The importance of castration fear in the economy of man's anxiety is best illustrated by the fact that it even affects man's attitude to death. Like all higher organisms, man fears death, but this fear is colored by all previous conditions that have evoked anxiety; particularly by the fear of castration and by the "fear of the superego". The formation of the superego and its specific relation to the situation of the child during the phallic phase has been frequently discussed. We approach the problem from one point of view: we ask ourselves to what degree earlier experience in the same area, i.e., that of moral conduct, can be related to the formation of the superego. The identification with the parents and the compliance with their demands exists, as we have said, at an earlier stage of the boy's development. So does the feeling of guilt in case of failure to comply with the parents' requests; and even actions as a result of hostility turned towards the self occur in the younger child. In order to differentiate the functions of the superego from their precursors, we sharply distinguish two aspects of the process of superego formation.

First, the child identifies with the parents in a new way in order to escape the conflict between love, hate and guilt and the torments of anxiety. He does not identify with the parents as they are, but with the idealized parent, i.e., the child purifies their conduct in his mind and the identification proceeds as if they were consistently true to the principles they explicitly profess or aspire to observe. Hence Freud's formulation, the child identifies with the superego of the parents.

It would be erroneous to assume that idealization of the parents starts at this age; it rather reflects the concomitant stage of the child's mentation and is possibly linked to its original ambivalence. All primitive mental operations tend to sharpen contrasts and to "agglutinate values" (Hartmann, 1947). The child's proclivity in this area has been repeatedly studied. However, it seems that at the pre-phallic stage, idealization is predominantly concerned with the area of puissance: the child aggrandizes the parents in order magically to partake in their protection and power. At the end of the phallic phase, under the pressure of the fear of castration, idealization concerns moral behavior.

Second: the process of identification that takes place is different from previous processes of identification, through the concomitant change in the economy of psychic energy. The newly acquired identifications of the child retain permanently part of the cathexis previously attached to the objects. The relative independence from the objects on the one hand and from the ego on the other constitutes the superego as an organization, distinct from either the id or the ego.

In the course of this process, libidinal energy is desexualized: the dangerous, or sexual part of the boy's attachment to the mother is sublimated and partly used in idealization. The aggressive attitudes towards the father are internalized; they become the force with which the demands of the superego are equipped.

The clearest manifestation of the existence of the newly formed organization is that as a consequence a new anxiety situation is introduced in the child's life. The fear of loss of the love object or of loss of love, in the pre-phallic phase, the fear of castration in the phallic phase, are supplemented, but naturally not supplanted by a new fear; the new factor, that of superego anxiety, creates the possibility for the child's moral independence of his environment. Man has acquired an inner voice.

The development of personality is not concluded at this point, and we feel that the potentialities of its transformation throughout latency and adolescence have for some time been underrated in psychoanalytic writings. But it seems that the basic structure of the personality and the basic functional interrelation of the systems have been fixed to some extent. The child does not stop growing and developing, but after that age both growth and development modify an existing structure. The newly formed superego organization is exposed to many conflicting demands. At first, it tends to be over-rigid. It does not compromise—it rather yields. The over-rigidity expresses itself in its "moral absolutism" (Piaget, 1932b). Psychoanalytic observation adds that at this stage, early in latency, obsessional symptoms are highly frequent amongst children.

Throughout latency, one can watch a gradual adjustment of superego functions. That adjustment is partly due to the growth of intellectual comprehension, and educational or religious indoctrination, but partly also to the fact that the function of the superego is less endangered; therefore it needs less protection. The pubertal change creates new dangers;

they reactivate the situation that once led to superego formations. The ensuing polarization of behavior between asceticism and indulgence has repeatedly been described (Anna Freud, 1936). Less clearly has it been realized that at this stage a new set of ideals is frequently chosen. They become part of the adolescent's conscious moral equipment (ego ideal). Again, that choice is not sudden. Throughout latency, the child has identified with many models—teachers; friends; policemen; leaders in battle, state or community; and the whole set of images that his culture makes available. But during adolescence, identifications gain a new impact; they become more compelling, and the need for support from outside is greater.

Hence the obvious importance of cultural conditions for the function of the superego. We do not enter into the area of problems that exist here; we do not discuss under what conditions idealism and cynicism tend to develop as transitory phases of development, and how gradually balance is re-established. We only point to one alternative: if social values rapidly change, if new values do not fully substitute for old ones, if no new conduct ideals supplement the older structure of the superego, then we may be faced with behavior in the adult that maximizes compliance with what "the neighbors" do. The intensity with which ideas are invested in a society assured of its social values may manifest itself then in a compulsory drive to be exactly like "the others are". Conformity then has become the supreme good.

The Data of Observation

The genetic hypotheses here discussed represent a selection from those formulated by psychoanalysts in order to explain the formation of psychic structure. Without saying so explicitly, we have also frequently implied dynamic propositions; in the context of the system of psychoanalytic psychology, as in any other scientific system, hypotheses support each other, and where support is at default, there is room for doubt. Whether in science one retains any one hypothesis, a set of hypotheses, or even the assumptions and concepts that hold the system together, depends on their usefulness as tools in the causal explanation of the phenomena studied.

Freud, and those with him, who based upon the assumptions and concepts of psychoanalysis definite genetic propositions, were, on the whole, faced with four sets of specific data that they attempted to integrate. We enumerate these data according to their probable importance at the time:

1. The reconstruction of life histories in psychoanalytic observation.

2. The study of regressive phenomena in normal, but mainly in pathological behavior, largely in the study of neuroses and psychoses.

3. Observations on child development.

4. Data from history and anthropology mainly interpreted in the light of evolutionism and used for the formulation of "prehistoric" constructs. These constructs were then linked to ontogenetic observations.

In partially reformulating some of these hypotheses, we have not only tried to eliminate terminological impasses and certain contradictions within the systematic cohesion of hypotheses. We have also attempted implicitly to re-evaluate, to some extent, the contributions of the data. The difference can be stated as follows:

We have avoided all connection between ontogenetic hypotheses and prehistoric constructs; we did so not because we doubt the importance of such constructs as sources of valuable clues, but because we doubt their value within the more rigorous set of hypotheses that aim at verification by empirical procedures. On the other hand, we tried to allow for a better integration between the three other types of data, those gained from the study of regressive phenomena in general, from psychoanalytic reconstructions and from direct observation of the growing child. All three are essential and their interrelation in the formulation of psychoanalytic hypotheses deserves some more detailed discussion.

In order to explain the earliest processes of differentiation and integration, we turn to the study of phenomena that we attribute to regression to these stages. Thus, the loss of the distinction between the self and the non-self is familiar from many psychotic processes. The schizophrenic experience of the emptiness of the external world, and many other hallucinatory and delusionary processes, as well as the psychological aspect of sleep, are explained according to Freud's hypothesis as a withdrawal of cathexis from the world to the self. These phenomena and their opposites supply the models for the hypothesis of transformations of object cathexis into narcissistic cathexis, and vice versa.

On the other hand, the fact that the distinction between the self and the outer world gradually develops, and the ways and time intervals in which it develops, belong to a series of data which can be ascertained by the study of infant and child behavior. The importance of these latter data is, we believe, indicated by some of our reformulations, for instance, by those that stress the importance of maturational processes.

Only in exceptional cases have we directly referred to the data themselves; their systematic integration with psychoanalytic observations and hypotheses represents a task for monographic studies in many areas. The data now available will not suffice. Only studies in child development, guided by these psychoanalytic hypotheses, can supply a better empirical foundation. As far as studies in this area proceed, they prove to be of great value. That value will increase when they fully deal with the communication between the child and the mother in the pre-verbal stage, or in the earliest verbal stages. What we need is an observational check on our hypotheses concerning object formation. Similarly, hypotheses concerning the reactions of mother and child to toilet training, and many other hypotheses concerning early childhood, could be formulated more concretely and probably more correctly if observational data were more ample.

Observations of this kind will still not replace the findings of psychoanalytic reconstruction. In the observation of the behavior detail, the potential importance of one experience cannot always be seen. Retrospective investigation alone can elucidate that importance.

Thus we repeat what has been said elsewhere, that the systematic study of large numbers of life histories from birth on, based on an integration of many skills of observation, permits the greatest chance for verification or falsification of hypotheses. There are areas in which objective observations cannot, as yet, contribute to the formulation of hypotheses; but they are often eminently useful in excluding hypotheses that are in contradiction to observation.

EIGHT AGES OF MAN

Erik H. Erikson

This paper contains many of the essentials of Erikson's manifold contributions to the study of human development (1950, 1951, 1954, 1958, 1959). He broadens and extends psychoanalytic psychosexual theory by adding systematic consideration of the modes related to erogenous zones, and seeks to trace their transformation into enduring behavioral modalities. In so doing, he focuses on the mutual regulation of development through the interaction between the child-rearing agents (the latter, conceptualized as representatives of their society), and thereby inevitably heightens psychoanalytic consideration of the actual characteristics of the social institutions shaping and forming that interaction.

As Erikson extends psychoanalytic developmental theory through the full life cycle, he underlines and interrelates the individual's vital need for a sense of inner sameness and continuity, and his need for a wider social "belongingness"—major features of an individual's sense of identity, a central issue for Erikson. Thus Erikson articulates the full life cycle actively intermeshed with the social context, while broadening psychoanalytic psychosexual theory to a psychosocial theory of sequential developmental stages, each based on the integration of earlier stages, each with its own typical instinctual vicissitudes, stresses, nuclear conflicts, developmental tasks, social modes, growth potentials, and possible psychopathological resolutions.

Basic Trust vs. Basic Mistrust

The first demonstration of social trust in the baby is the ease of his feeding, the depth of his sleep, the relaxation of his bowels. The experi-

Reprinted from *Childhood and Society* (2nd Ed.). New York: Norton, 1963, pp. 247–274 by permission of Erik H. Erikson, Norton & Company, Inc., and Chatto & Windus, Ltd.

ence of a mutual regulation of his increasingly receptive capacities with the maternal techniques of provision gradually helps him to balance the discomfort caused by the immaturity of homeostasis with which he was born. In his gradually increasing waking hours he finds that more and more adventures of the senses arouse a feeling of familiarity, of having coincided with a feeling of inner goodness. Forms of comfort, and people associated with them, become as familiar as the gnawing discomfort of the bowels. The infant's first social achievement, then, is his willingness to let the mother out of sight without undue anxiety or rage, because she has become an inner certainty as well as an outer predictability. Such consistency, continuity, and sameness of experience provide a rudimentary sense of ego identity which depends, I think, on the recognition that there is an inner population of remembered and anticipated sensations and images which are firmly correlated with the outer population of familiar and predictable things and people.

What we here call trust coincides with what Therese Benedek has called confidence. If I prefer the word "trust," it is because there is more naiveté and more mutuality in it: an infant can be said to be trusting where it would go too far to say that he has confidence. The general state of trust, furthermore, implies not only that one has learned to rely on the sameness and continuity of the outer providers, but also that one may trust oneself and the capacity of one's own organs to cope with urges; and that one is able to consider oneself trustworthy enough so that the providers will not need to be on guard lest they be nipped.

The constant tasting and testing of the relationship between inside and outside meets its crucial test during the rages of the biting stage, when the teeth cause pain from within and when outer friends either prove of no avail or withdraw from the only action which promises relief: biting. Not that teething itself seems to cause all the dire consequences sometimes ascribed to it. As outlined earlier, the infant now is driven to "grasp" more, but he is apt to find desired presences elusive: nipple and breast, and the mother's focused attention and care. Teething seems to have a prototypal significance and may well be the model for the masochistic tendency to assure cruel comfort by enjoying one's hurt whenever one is unable to prevent a significant loss.

In psychopathology the absence of basic trust can best be studied in infantile schizophrenia, while lifelong underlying weakness of such trust is apparent in adult personalities in whom withdrawal into schizoid and depressive states is habitual. The reestablishment of a state of trust has been found to be the basic requirement for therapy in these cases. For no matter what conditions may have caused a psychotic break, the bizarreness and withdrawal in the behavior of many very sick individuals hides an attempt to recover social mutuality by a testing of the borderlines between senses and physical reality, between words and social meanings.

Psychoanalysis assumes the early process of differentiation between inside and outside to be the origin of projection and introjection which remain some of our deepest and most dangerous defense mechanisms. In introjection we feel and act as if an outer goodness had become an inner certainty. In projection, we experience an inner harm as an outer one: we endow significant people with the evil which actually is in us. These two mechanisms, then, projection and introjection, are assumed to be modeled after whatever goes on in infants when they would like to externalize pain and internalize pleasure, an intent which must yield to the testimony of the maturing senses and ultimately of reason. These mechanisms are, more or less normally, reinstated in acute crises of love, trust, and faith in adulthood and can characterize irrational attitudes toward adversaries and enemies in masses of "mature" individuals.

The firm establishment of enduring patterns for the solution of the nuclear conflict of basic trust versus basic mistrust in mere existence is the first task of the ego, and thus first of all a task for maternal care. But let it be said here that the amount of trust derived from earliest infantile experience does not seem to depend on absolute quantities of food or demonstrations of love, but rather on the quality of the maternal relationship. Mothers create a sense of trust in their children by that kind of administration which in its quality combines sensitive care of the baby's individual needs and a firm sense of personal trustworthiness within the trusted framework of their culture's life style. This forms the basis in the child for a sense of identity which will later combine a sense of being "all right," of being oneself, and of becoming what other people trust one will become. There are, therefore (within certain limits previously defined as the "musts" of child care), few frustrations in either this or the following stages which the growing child cannot endure if the frustration leads to the ever-renewed experience of greater sameness and stronger continuity of development, toward a final integration of the individual life cycle with some meaningful wider belongingness. Parents must not only have certain ways of guiding by prohibition and permission; they must also be able to represent to the child a deep, an almost somatic conviction that there is a meaning to what they are doing. Ultimately, children become neurotic not from frustrations, but from the lack or loss of societal meaning in these frustrations.

But even under the most favorable circumstances, this stage seems to introduce into psychic life (and become prototypical for) a sense of inner division and universal nostalgia for a paradise forfeited. It is against this powerful combination of a sense of having been deprived, of having been divided, and of having been abandoned—that basic trust must maintain itself throughout life.

Each successive stage and crisis has a special relation to one of the basic elements of society, and this for the simple reason that the human life cycle and man's institutions have evolved together. In this chapter we can do little more than mention, after the description of each stage, what basic element of social organization is related to it. This relation is two-fold: man brings to these institutions the remnants of his infantile mentality and his youthful fervor, and he receives from them—as long as they manage to maintain their actuality—a reinforcement of his infantile gains.

The parental faith which supports the trust emerging in the newborn, has throughout history sought its institutional safeguard (and, on occasion, found its greatest enemy) in organized religion. Trust born of care is, in fact, the touchstone of the *actuality* of a given religion. All religions have in common the periodical childlike fortune as well as spiritual health; some demonstration of man's smallness by way of reduced posture and humble gesture; the admission in prayer and song of misdeeds, of misthoughts, and of evil intentions; fervent appeal for inner unification by divine guidance; and finally, the insight that individual trust must become a common faith, individual mistrust a commonly formulated evil, while the individual's restoration must become part of the ritual practice of many, and must become a sign of trustworthiness in the community.[1] We have illustrated how tribes dealing with one segment of nature develop a collective magic which seems to treat the Supernatural Providers of food and fortune as if they were angry and must be appeased by prayer and self-torture. Primitive religions, the most primitive layer in all religions, and the religious layer in each individual, abound with efforts at atonement which try to make up for vague deeds against a maternal matrix and try to restore faith in the goodness of one's strivings and in the kindness of the powers of the universe.

Each society and each age must find the institutionalized form of reverence which derives vitality from its world-image—from predestination to indeterminacy. The clinician can only observe that many are proud to be

[1] This is the communal and psychosocial side of religion. Its often paradoxical relation to the spirituality of the individual is a matter not to be treated briefly and in passing (See Erikson, 1958).

without religion whose children cannot afford their being without it. On the other hand, there are many who seem to derive a vital faith from social action or scientific pursuit. And again, there are many who profess faith, yet in practice breathe mistrust both of life and man.

AUTONOMY VS. SHAME AND DOUBT

In describing the growth and the crises of the human person as a series of alternative basic attitudes such as trust vs. mistrust, we take recourse to the term a "sense of," although, like a "sense of health," or a "sense of being unwell," such "senses" pervade surface and depth, consciousness and the unconscious. They are, then, at the same time, ways of *experiencing* accessible to introspection; ways of *behaving,* observable by others; and unconscious *inner states* determinable by test and analysis. It is important to keep these three dimensions in mind, as we proceed.

Muscular maturation sets the stage for experimentation with two simultaneous sets of social modalities: holding on and letting go. As is the case with all of these modalities, their basic conflicts can lead in the end to either hostile or benign expectations and attitudes. Thus, to hold can become a destructive and cruel retaining or restraining, and it can become a pattern of care: to have and to hold. To let go, too, can turn into an inimical letting loose of destructive forces, or it can become a relaxed "to let pass" and "to let be".

Outer control at this stage, therefore, must be firmly reassuring. The infant must come to feel that the basic faith in existence, which is the lasting treasure saved from the rages of the oral stage, will not be jeopardized by this about-face of his, this sudden violent wish to have a choice, to appropriate demandingly, and to eliminate stubbornly. Firmness must protect him against the potential anarchy of his as yet untrained sense of discrimination, his inability to hold on and to let go with discretion. As his environment encourages him to "stand on his own feet," it must protect him against meaningless and arbitrary experiences of shame and of early doubt.

The latter danger is the one best known to us. For if denied the gradual and well-guided experience of the autonomy of free choice (or if, indeed, weakened by an initial loss of trust) the child will turn against himself all his urge to discriminate and to manipulate. He will overmanipulate himself, he will develop a precocious conscience. Instead of taking possession of things in order to test them by purposeful repetition, he will become obsessed by his own repetitiveness. By such obsessiveness, of course, he then learns to repossess the environment and to gain power by stubborn and minute control, where he could not find large-scale mutual regulation. Such hollow victory is the infantile model for a compulsion neurosis. It is also the infantile source of later attempts in adult life to govern by the letter, rather than by the spirit.

Shame is an emotion insufficiently studied, because in our civilization it is so early and easily absorbed by guilt. Shame supposes that one is completely exposed and conscious of being looked at: in one word, self-conscious. One is visible and not ready to be visible; which is why we dream of shame as a situation in which we are stared at in a condition of incomplete dress, in night attire, "with one's pants down." Shame is early expressed in an impulse to bury one's face, or to sink, right then and there, into the ground. But this, I think, is essentially rage turned against the self. He who is ashamed would like to force the world not to look at him, not to notice his exposure. He would like to destroy the eyes of the world. Instead he must wish for his own invisibility. This potentiality is abundantly used in the educational method of "shaming" used so exclusively by some primitive peoples. Visual shame precedes auditory guilt, which is a sense of badness to be had all by oneself when nobody watches and when everything is quiet—except the voice of the superego. Such shaming exploits an increasing sense of being small, which can develop only as the child stands up and as his awareness permits him to note the relative measures of size and power.

Too much shaming does not lead to genuine propriety but to a secret determination to try to get away with things, unseen—if, indeed, it does not result in defiant shamelessness. There is an impressive American ballad in which a murderer to be hanged on the gallows before the eyes of the community, instead of feeling duly chastened, begins to berate the onlookers, ending every salvo of defiance with the words, "God damn your eyes." Many a small child, shamed beyond endurance, may be in a chronic mood (although not in possession of either the courage or the words) to express defiance in similar terms. What I mean by this sinister reference is that there is a limit to a child's and an adult's endurance in the face of demands to consider himself, his body, and his wishes as evil and dirty, and to his belief in the infallibility of those who pass such judgment. He may be apt to turn things around, and to consider as evil only the fact that they exist: his chance will come when they are gone, or when he will go from them.

Doubt is the brother of shame. Where shame is dependent on the consciousness of being upright and exposed, doubt, so clinical observation leads me to believe, has much to do with a consciousness of having a front and a back—and especially a "behind." For this reverse area of the body, with its aggressive and libidinal focus in the sphincters and in the buttocks, cannot be seen by the child, and yet it can be dominated by the will of others. The "behind" is the small being's dark continent, as area of the body which can be magically dominated and effectively invaded by those who would attack one's power of autonomy and who would designate as evil those products of the bowels which were felt to be all right when they were being passed. This basic sense of doubt in whatever one has left behind forms a substratum for later and more verbal forms of compulsive doubting; this finds its adult expression in paranoiac fears concerning hidden persecutors and secret persecutions threatening from behind (and from within the behind).

This stage, therefore, becomes decisive for the ratio of love and hate, cooperation and willfulness, freedom of self-expression and its suppression. From a sense of self-control without loss of self-esteem comes a lasting sense of good will and pride; from a sense of loss of self-control and of foreign overcontrol comes a lasting propensity for doubt and shame.

If, to some reader, the "negative" potentialities of our stages seem overstated throughout, we must remind him that this is not only the result of a preoccupation with clinical data. Adults, and seemingly mature and unneurotic ones, display a sensitivity concerning a possible shameful "loss of face" and fear of being attacked "from behind" which is not only highly irrational and in contrast to the knowledge available to them, but can be of fateful import if related sentiments influence, for example, interracial and international policies.

We have related basic trust to the institution of religion. The lasting need of the individual to have his will reaffirmed and delineated within an adult order of things which at the same time reaffirms and delineates the will of others has an institutional safeguard in the *principle of law and order*. In daily life as well as in the high courts of law—domestic and international—this principle apportions to each his privileges and his limitations, his independence on the part of adults around him gives to the child of good will the confident expectation that the kind of autonomy fostered in childhood will not lead to undue doubt or shame in later life. Thus the sense of autonomy fostered in the child and modified as life progresses, serves (and is served by) the preservation in economic and political life of a sense of justice.

Initiative vs. Guilt

There is in every child at every stage a new miracle of vigorous unfolding, which constitutes a new hope and a new responsibility for all. Such is the sense and the pervading quality of initiative. The criteria for all these senses and qualities are the same: a crisis, more or less beset with fumbling and fear, is resolved, in that the child suddenly seems to "grow together" both in his person and in his body. He appears "more himself," more loving, relaxed and brighter in his judgment, more activated and activating. He is in free possession of a surplus of energy which permits him to forget failures quickly and to approach what seems desirable (even if it also seems uncertain and even dangerous) with undiminished and more accurate direction. Initiative adds to autonomy the quality of undertaking, planning and "attacking" a task for the sake of being active and on the move, where before self-will, more often than not, inspired acts of defiance or, at any rate, protested independence.

I know that the very word "initiative" to many, has an American, and industrial connotation. Yet, initiative is a necessary part of every act, and man needs a sense of initiative for whatever he learns and does, from fruit-gathering to a system of enterprise.

The ambulatory stage and that of infantile genitality add to the inventory of basic social modalities that of "making," first in the sense of "being on the make." There is no simpler, stronger word for it; it suggests pleasure in attack and conquest. In the boy, the emphasis remains on phallic-intrusive modes; in the girl it turns to modes of "catching" in more aggressive forms of snatching or in the milder form of making oneself attractive and endearing.

The danger of this stage is a sense of guilt over the goals contemplated and the acts initiated in one's exuberant enjoyment of new locomotor and mental power: acts of aggressive manipulation and coercion which soon go far beyond the executive capacity of organism and mind and therefore call for an energetic halt on one's contemplated initiative. While autonomy concentrates on keeping potential rivals out, and therefore can lead to jealous rage most often directed against encroachments by younger siblings, initiative brings with it anticipatory rivalry with those who have been there first and may, therefore, occupy with their superior equipment the field toward which one's initiative is directed. Infantile jealousy and rivalry, those often embittered and yet essentially futile attempts at demarcating a sphere of unquestioned privilege, now come to a climax in a final contest for a favored position with the mother; the usual failure leads to resignation, guilt, and anxiety. The child indulges in fantasies of being a giant and a tiger, but in his dreams he runs in terror for dear life. This, then, is the stage of the "castration complex," the intensified fear of finding the (now energetically erotized) genitals harmed as a punishment for the fantasies attached to their excitement.

Infantile sexuality and incest taboo, castration complex and superego all unite here to bring about that specifically human crisis during which the child must turn from an exclusive, pregenital attachment to his parents to the slow process of becoming a parent, a carrier of tradition. Here the most fateful split and transformation in the emotional powerhouse occurs, a split between potential human glory and potential total destruction. For here the child becomes forever divided in himself. The instinct fragments which before had enhanced the growth of his infantile body and mind now become divided into an infantile set which perpetuates the exuberance of growth potentials, and a parental set which supports and increases self-observation, self-guidance, and self-punishment.

The problem, again, is one of mutual regulation. Where the child, now so ready to overmanipulate himself, can gradually develop a sense of moral responsibility, where he can gain some insight into the institutions, functions, and roles which will permit his responsible participation, he will find pleasurable accomplishment in wielding tools and weapons, in manipulating meaningful toys—and in caring for younger children.

Naturally, the parental set is at first infantile in nature: the fact that human conscience remains partially infantile throughout life is the core of human tragedy. For the superego of the child can be primitive, cruel, and uncompromising, as may be observed in instances where children overcontrol and overconstrict themselves to the point of self-obliteration; where they develop an over-obedience more literal than the one the parent has wished to exact; or where they develop deep regressions and lasting resentments because the parents themselves do not seem to live up to the new conscience. One of the deepest conflicts in life is the hate for a parent who served as the model and the executor of the superego, but who (in some form) was found trying to get away with the very transgressions which the child can no longer tolerate in himself. The suspiciousness and evasiveness which is thus mixed in with the all-or-nothing quality of the superego, this organ of moral tradition, makes moral (in the sense of moralistic) man a great potential danger to his own ego—and to that of his fellow men.

In adult pathology, the residual conflict over initiative is expressed either in hysterical denial, which causes the repression of the wish or the abrogation of its executive organ by paralysis, inhibition, or impotence; or in overcompensatory showing off, in which the scared individual, so eager to "duck," instead "sticks his neck out." Then also a plunge into psychosomatic disease is now common. It is as if the culture had made a man over-advertise himself and so identify with his own advertisement that only disease can offer him escape.

But here, again, we must not think only of individual psychopathology, but of the inner powerhouse of rage which must be submerged at this stage, as some of the fondest hopes and the wildest phantasies are repressed and inhibited. The resulting self-righteousness—often the principal reward for goodness—can later be most intolerantly turned against others in the form of persistent moralistic surveillance, so that the prohibition rather than the guidance of initiative becomes the dominant endeavor. On the other hand, even moral man's initiative is apt to burst the boundaries of self-restriction, permitting him to do to others, in his or in other lands, what he would neither do nor tolerate being done in his own home.

In view of the dangerous potentials of man's long childhood, it is well to look back at the blueprint of the life-stages and to the possibilities of guiding the young of the race while they are young. And here we note that according to the wisdom of the ground plan the child is at no time more ready to learn quickly and avidly, to become bigger in the sense of sharing obligation and performance than during this period of his development. He is eager and able to make things cooperatively, to combine with other children for the purpose of constructing and planning, and he is willing to profit from teachers and to emulate ideal prototypes. He remains, of course, identified with the parent of the same sex, but for the present he looks for opportunities where work-identification seems to promise a field of initiative without too much infantile conflict or oedipal guilt and a more realistic identification based on a spirit of equality experienced in doing things together. At any rate, the "oedipal" stage results not only in the oppressive establishment of a moral sense restricting the horizon of the permissible; it also sets the direction toward the possible and the tangible which permits the dreams of early childhood to be attached to the goals of an active adult life. Social institutions, therefore, offer children of this age an economic ethos, in the form of ideal adults recognizable by their uniforms and their functions, and fascinating enough to replace, the heroes of picture book and fairy tale.

Industry vs. Inferiority

Thus the inner stage seems all set for "entrance into life," except that life must first be school life, whether school is field or jungle or classroom. The child must forget past hopes and wishes, while his exuberant imagination is tamed and harnessed to the laws of impersonal things—even the three R's. For before the child, psychologically already a rudimentary parent, can become a biological parent, he must begin to be a worker and potential provider. With the oncoming latency period, the normally advanced child forgets, or rather sublimates, the necessity to "make" people by direct attack or to become papa and mama in a hurry: he now learns to win recognition by producing things. He has mastered the ambulatory field and the organ modes. He has experienced a sense of finality regarding the fact that there is no workable future within the womb of his family, and thus becomes ready to apply himself to given skills and tasks, which go far beyond the mere playful expression of his organ modes or the pleasure in the function of his limbs. He develops a sense of industry—i.e., he adjusts himself to the inorganic laws of the tool world. He can become an eager and absorbed unit of a productive situation. To bring a productive situation to completion is an aim which gradually supersedes the whims and wishes of play. His ego boundaries include his tools and skills: the work principle (Hendrick, 1942) teaches him the pleasure of work completion by steady attention and persevering diligence. In all cultures, at this stage, children receive some *systematic instruction,* although it is by no means always in the kind of school which literate people must organize around special teachers who have learned how to teach literacy. In preliterate people and in non-literate pursuits much is learned from adults who become teachers by dint of gift and inclination rather than by appointment, and perhaps the greatest amount is learned from older children. Thus the *fundamentals of technology* are developed, as the child becomes ready to handle the utensils, the tools, and the weapons used by the big people. Literate people, with more specialized careers, must prepare the child by teaching him things which first of all make him literate, the widest possible basic education for the greatest number of possible careers. The more confusing specialization becomes, however, the more indistinct are the eventual goals of initiative; and the more complicated social reality, the vaguer are the father's and mother's role in it. School seems to be a culture all by itself, with its own goals and limits, its achievements and disappointment.

The child's danger, at this stage, lies in a sense of inadequacy and inferiority. If he despairs of his tools and skills or of his status among his tool partners, he may be discouraged from identification with them and with a section of the tool world. To lose the hope of such "industrial" association may pull him back to the more isolated, less tool-conscious familial rivalry of the oedipal time. The child despairs of his equipment in the tool world and in anatomy, and considers himself doomed to mediocrity or inadequacy. It is at this point that wider society becomes significant in its ways of admitting the child to an understanding of meaningful roles in its technology and economy. Many a child's development is disrupted when family life has failed to prepare him for school life, or when school life fails to sustain the promises of earlier stages.

Regarding the period of a developing sense of industry, I have referred to *outer and inner hindrances* in the use of new capacities but not to aggravations of new human drives, nor to submerged rages resulting from their frustration. This stage differs from the earlier ones in that it is not a swing from an inner upheaval to a new mastery. Freud calls it the latency stage because violent drives are normally dormant. But it is only a lull before the storm of puberty, when all the earlier drives re-emerge in a new combination, to be brought under the dominance of genitality.

On the other hand, this is socially a most decisive stage: since industry involves doing things beside and with others, a first sense of division of labor and of differential opportunity, that is, a sense of the *technological ethos* of a culture, develops at this time. We have pointed in the last section to the danger threatening individual and society where the schoolchild begins to feel that the color of his skin, the background of his parents, or the fashion of his clothes rather than his wish and his will to learn will decide his worth as an apprentice, and thus his sense of *identity*—to which we must now turn. But there is another, more fundamental danger, namely man's restriction of himself and constriction of his horizons to include only his work to which, so the Book says, he has been sentenced after his expulsion from paradise. If he accepts work as his only obligation, and "what works" as his only criterion of worthwhileness, he may become the conformist and thoughtless slave of his technology and of those who are in a position to exploit it.

Identity vs. Role Confusion

With the establishment of a good initial relationship to the world of skills and tools, and with the advent of puberty, childhood proper comes to an end. Youth begins. But in puberty and adolescence all samenesses and continuities relied on earlier are more or less questioned again, because of a rapidity of body growth which equals that of early childhood and because of the new addition of genital maturity. The growing and developing youths, faced with this physiological revolution within them, and with tangible adult tasks ahead of them are now primarily concerned with what they appear to be in the eyes of others as compared with what they feel they are, and with the question of how to connect the roles and skills cultivated earlier with the occupational prototypes of the day. In their search for a new sense of continuity and sameness, adolescents have to refight many of the battles of earlier years, even though to do so they must artificially appoint perfectly well-meaning people to play the roles of adversaries; and they are ever ready to install lasting idols and ideals as guardians of a final identity.

The integration now taking place in the form of ego identity is, as pointed out, more than the sum of the childhood identifications. It is the accrued experience of the ego's ability to integrate all identifications with the vicissitudes of the libido, with the aptitudes developed out of endowment, and with the opportunities offered in social roles. The sense of ego identity, then, is the accrued confidence that the inner sameness and continuity prepared in the past are matched by the sameness and continuity of one's meaning for others, as evidenced in the tangible promise of a "career."

The danger of this stage is role confusion.[2] Where this is based on a strong previous doubt as to one's sexual identity, delinquent and outright psychotic episodes are not uncommon. If diagnosed and treated correctly, these incidents do not have the same fatal significance which they have at other ages. In most instances, however, it is the inability to settle on an occupational identity which disturbs individual young people. To keep themselves together they temporarily overidentify, to the point of apparent complete loss of identity, with the heroes of cliques and crowds. This initiates the stage of "falling in love," which is by no means entirely, or even primarily, a sexual matter—except where the mores demand it. To a considerable extent adolescent love is an attempt to arrive at a definition of one's identity by projecting one's diffused ego image on another and by seeing it thus reflected and gradually clarified. This is why so much of young love is conversation.

Young people can also be remarkably clannish, and cruel in their exclusion of all those who are "different," in skin color or cultural background, in tastes and gifts, and often in such petty aspects of dress and gesture as have been temporarily selected as *the* signs of an in-grouper or

[2] See Erikson (1956).

out-grouper. It is important to understand (which does not mean condone or participate in) such intolerance as a defense against a sense of identity confusion. For adolescents not only help one another temporarily through much discomfort by forming cliques and by stereotyping themselves, their ideals, and their enemies; they also perversely test each other's capacity to pledge fidelity. The readiness for such testing also explains the appeal which simple and cruel totalitarian doctrines have on the minds of the youth of such countries and classes as have lost or are losing their group identities (feudal, agrarian, tribal, national) and face world-wide industrialization, emancipation, and wider communication.

The adolescent mind is essentially a mind of the *moratorium,* a psychosocial stage between childhood and adulthood, and between the morality learned by the child, and the ethics to be developed by the adult. It is an ideological mind—and, indeed, it is the ideological outlook of a society that speaks more clearly to the adolescent who is eager to be affirmed by his peers, and is ready to be confirmed by rituals, creeds, and programs which at the same time define what is evil, uncanny, and inimical. In searching for the social values which guide identity, one therefore confronts the problems of *ideology* and *aristocracy,* both in their widest possible sense which connotes that within a defined world image and a predestined course of history, the best people will come to rule and rule develops the best in people. In order not to become cynically or apathetically lost, young people must somehow be able to convince themselves that those who succeed in their anticipated adult world thereby shoulder the obligation of being the best. We will discuss later the dangers which emanate from human ideals harnessed to the management of super-machines, be they guided by nationalistic or international, communist or capitalist ideologies.

Intimacy vs. Isolation

The strength acquired at any stage is tested by the necessity to transcend it in such a way that the individual can take chances in the next stage with what was most vulnerably precious in the previous one. Thus, the young adult, emerging from the search for and the insistence or identity, is eager and willing to fuse his identity with that of others. He is ready for intimacy, that is, the capacity to commit himself to concrete affiliations and partnerships and to develop the ethical strength to abide by such commitments, even though they may call for significant sacrifices and compromises. Body and ego must now be masters of the organ modes and of the nuclear conflicts, in order to be able to face the fear of ego loss in situations which call for self-abandon: in the solidarity of close affiliations, in orgasms and sexual unions, in close friendships and in physical combat, in experiences of inspiration by teachers and of intuition from the recesses of the self. The avoidance of such experiences because of a fear of ego loss may lead to a deep sense of isolation and consequent self-absorption.

The counterpart of intimacy is distantiation: the readiness to isolate and, if necessary, to destroy those forces and people whose essence seems dangerous to one's own, and whose "territory" seems to encroach on the extent of one's intimate relations. Prejudices thus developed (and utilized and exploited in politics and in war) are a more mature outgrowth of the blinder repudiations which during the struggle for identity differentiate sharply and cruelly between the familiar and the foreign. The danger of this stage is that intimate, competitive, and combative relations are experienced with and against the selfsame people. But as the areas of adult duty are delineated, and as the competitive encounter, and the sexual embrace, are differentiated, they eventually become subject to the *ethical sense* which is the mark of the adult.

Strictly speaking, it is only now that *true genitality* can fully develop; for much of the sex life preceding these commitments is of the identity-searching kind, or is dominated by phallic or vaginal strivings which make of sex-life a kind of genital combat. On the other hand, genitality is all too often described as a permanent state of reciprocal sexual bliss. This then, may be the place to complete our discussion of genitality.

For a basic orientation in the matter I shall quote what has come to me as Freud's shortest saying. It has often been claimed, and bad habits of conversation seem to sustain the claim, that psychoanalysis as a treatment attempts to convince the patient that before God and man he has only one obligation: to have good orgasms, with a fitting "object," and that regularly. This, of course, is not true. Freud was once asked what he thought a normal person should be able to do well. The questioner probably expected a complicated answer. But Freud, in the curt way of his old days, is reported to have said: "Lieben und arbeiten" (to love and to work). It pays to ponder on this simple formula; it gets deeper as you think about it. For when Freud said "love" he meant *genital* love, and genital *love;* when he said love *and* work, he meant a general work-productiveness which would not preoccupy the individual to the extent that he loses his right or capacity to be a genital and a loving being. Thus we may ponder, but we cannot improve on "the professor's" formula.

Genitality, then, consists in the unobstructed capacity to develop an orgastic potency so free of pregenital interferences that genital libido (not just the sex products discharged in Kinsey's "outlets") is expressed in heterosexual mutuality, with full sensitivity of both penis and vagina, and with a convulsion-like discharge of tension from the whole body. This is a rather concrete way of saying something about a process which we really do not understand. To put it more situationally: the total fact of finding, via the climactic turmoil of the orgasm, a supreme experience of the mutual regulation of two beings in some way takes the edge off the hostilities and potential rages caused by the oppositeness of male and female, of fact and fancy, of love and hate. Satisfactory sex relations thus make sex less obsessive, overcompensation less necessary, sadistic controls superfluous.

Preoccupied as it was with curative aspects, psychoanalysis often failed to formulate the matter of genitality in a way significant for the processes of society in all classes, nations, and levels of culture. The kind of mutuality in orgasm which psychoanalysis has in mind is apparently easily obtained in classes and cultures which happen to make a leisurely institution of it. In more complex societies this mutuality is interfered with by so many factors of health, of tradition, of opportunity, and of temperament, that the proper formulation of sexual health would be rather this: A human being should be potentially able to accomplish mutuality of genital orgasm, but he should also be so constituted as to bear a certain amount of frustration in the matter without undue regression whenever emotional preference or considerations of duty and loyalty call for it.

While psychoanalysis has on occasion gone too far in its emphasis on genitality as a universal cure for society and has thus provided a new addiction and a new commodity for many who wished to so interpret its teachings, it has not always indicated all the goals that genitality actually should and must imply. In order to be of lasting social significance, the utopia of genitality should include:

1. mutuality of orgasm
2. with a loved partner
3. of the other sex
4. with whom one is able and willing to share a mutual trust
5. and with whom one is able and willing to regulate the cycles of
    a. work
    b. procreation
    c. recreation
6. so as to secure to the offspring, too, all the stages of a satisfactory development.

It is apparent that such utopian accomplishment on a large scale cannot be an individual or, indeed, a therapeutic task. Nor is it a purely sexual matter by any means. It is integral to a culture's style of sexual selection, cooperation, and competition.

The danger of this stage is isolation, that is the avoidance of contacts which commit to intimacy. In psychopathology, this disturbance can lead to severe "character-problems". On the other hand, there are partnerships which amount to an isolation à deux, protecting both partners from the necessity to face the next critical development–that of generativity.

Generativity vs. Stagnation

In this book the emphasis is on the childhood stages, otherwise the section on generativity would of necessity be the central one, for this term encompasses the evolutionary development which has made man the teaching and instituting as well as the learning animal. The fashionable insistence on dramatizing the dependence of children on adults often blinds us to the dependence of the older generation on the younger one. Mature man needs to be needed, and maturity needs guidance as well as encouragement from what has been produced and must be taken care of.

Generativity, then, is primarily the concern in establishing and guiding the next generation, although there are individuals who, through misfortune or because of special and genuine gifts in other directions, do not apply this drive to their own offspring. And indeed, the concept generativity is meant to include such more popular synonyms as *productivity* and *creativity,* which, however, cannot replace it.

It has taken psychoanalysis some time to realize that the ability to lose oneself in the meeting of bodies and minds leads to a gradual expansion of ego-interests and to a libidinal investment in that which is being generated. Generativity thus is an essential stage on the psychosexual as well as on the psychosocial schedule. Where such enrichment fails altogether, regression to an obsessive need for pseudo-intimacy takes place, often with a pervading sense of stagnation and personal impoverishment. Individuals, then, often begin to indulge themselves as if they were their own–or one another's–one and only child; and where conditions favor it, early invalidism, physical or psychological, becomes the vehicle of self-concern. The mere fact of having or even wanting children, however, does not "achieve" generativity. In fact, some young parents suffer, it seems, from the retardation of the ability to develop this stage. The reasons are often to be found in early childhood impressions; in excessive self-love based on a too strenuously self-made personality; and finally (and here we return to the beginnings) in the lack of some faith, some "belief in the species," which would make a child appear to be a welcome trust of the community.

As to the institutions which safeguard and reinforce generativity, one can only say that all institutions codify the ethics of generative succession. Even where philosophical and spiritual tradition suggests the renunciation of the right to procreate or to produce, such early turn to "ultimate concerns," wherever instituted in monastic movements, strives to settle at the same time the matter of its relationship to the Care for the creatures of this world and to the Charity which is felt to transcend it.

If this were a book on adulthood, it would be indispensable and profitable at this point to compare economic and psychological theories (beginning with the strange convergencies and divergencies of Marx and Freud) and to proceed to a discussion of man's relationship to his production as well as to his progeny.

Ego Integrity vs. Despair

Only in him who in some way has taken care of things and people and has adapted himself to the triumphs and disappointments adherent to being, the originator of others or the generator of products and ideas—only in him may gradually ripen the fruit of these seven stages. I know no better word for it than ego integrity. Lacking a clear definition, I shall point to a few constituents of this state of mind. It is the ego's accrued assurance of its proclivity for order and meaning. It is a post-narcissistic love of the human ego—not of the self—as an experience which conveys some world order and spiritual sense, no matter how dearly paid for. It is the acceptance of one's one and only life cycle as something that had to be and that, by necessity, permitted of no substitutions: it thus means a new, a different love of one's parents. It is a comradeship with the ordering ways of distant times and different pursuits, as expressed in the simple products and sayings of such times and pursuits. Although aware of the relativity of all the various life styles which have given meaning to human striving, the possessor of integrity is ready to defend the dignity of his own life style against all physical and economic threats. For he knows that an individual life is the accidental coincidence of but one life cycle with but one segment of history; and that for him all human integrity stands or falls with the one style of integrity of which he partakes. The style of integrity developed by his culture or civilization thus becomes the "patrimony of his soul," the seal of his moral paternity of himself (". . . pero el honor/Es patrimonio del alma": Calderón). In such final consolidation, death loses its sting.

The lack or loss of this accrued ego integration is signified by fear of death: the one and only life cycle is not accepted as the ultimate of life. Despair expresses the feeling that the time is now short, too short for the attempt to start another life and to try out alternate roads to integrity. Disgust hides despair, if often only in the form of "a thousand little disgusts" which do not add up to one big remorse: *"mille petits dégoûts de soi, dont le total ne fait pas un remords, mais un gêne obscure."* (Rostand)

Each individual, to become a mature adult, must to a sufficient degree develop all the ego qualities mentioned, so that a wise Indian, a true gentleman, and a mature peasant share and recognize in one another the final stage of integrity. But each culture entity, to develop the particular style of integrity suggested by its historical place, utilizes a particular combination of these conflicts, along with specific provocations and prohibitions of infantile sexuality. Infantile conflicts become creative only if sustained by the firm support of cultural institutions and of the special leader classes representing them. In order to approach or experience integrity, the individual must know how to be a follower of image bearers in religion and in politics, in the economic order and in technology, in aristocratic living and in the arts and sciences. Ego integrity, therefore, implies an emotional integration which permits participation by followership as well as acceptance of the responsibility of leadership.

Webster's Dictionary is kind enough to help us complete this outline in a circular fashion. Trust (the first of our ego values) is here defined as "the assured reliance on another's integrity," the last of our values. I suspect that Webster had business in mind rather than babies, credit rather than faith. But the formulation stands. And it seems possible to further paraphrase the relation of adult integrity and infantile trust by saying that healthy children will not fear life if their elders have integrity enough not to fear death.

An Epigenetic Chart

In this book the emphasis is on the childhood stages. The foregoing conception of the life cycle, however, awaits systematic treatment. To prepare this, I shall conclude with a diagram. In this, as in the diagram of pregenital zones and modes, the diagonal represents the normative sequence of psychosocial gains made as at each stage one more nuclear conflict adds a new ego quality, a new criterion of accruing human strength. Below the diagonal there is space for the precursors of each of these solutions, all of which begin with the beginning; above the diagonal there is space for the designation of the derivatives of these gains and their transformations in the maturing and the mature personality.

The underlying assumptions for such charting are (1) that the human personality in principle develops according to steps predetermined in the growing person's readiness to be driven toward, to be aware of, and to interact with, a widening social radius, and (2) that society, in principle, tends to be so constituted as to meet and invite this succession of potentialities for interaction and attempts to safeguard and to encourage the proper rate and the proper sequence of their enfolding. This is the "maintenance of the human world."

But a chart is only a tool to think with, and cannot aspire to be a prescription to abide by, whether in the practice of child-training, in psychotherapy, or in the methodology of child study. In the presentation of the psychosocial stages in the form of an *epigenetic chart* analogous to the one employed for an analysis of Freud's psychosexual stages, we have definite and delimited methodological steps in mind. It is one purpose of this work to facilitate the comparison of the stages first discerned by Freud as sexual to other schedules of development (physical, cognitive). But any one chart delimits one schedule only, and it must not be imputed that our outline of the psychosocial schedule is intended to imply obscure generalities concerning other aspects of development—or, indeed, of existence. If the chart, for example, lists a series of conflicts or crises, we do not consider all development a series of crises: we claim only that psychosocial development proceeds by critical steps—"critical" being a characteristic of turning points, of moments of decision between progress and regression, integration and retardation.

It may be useful at this point to spell out the methodological implications of an epigenetic matrix. The more heavily-lined squares of the diagonal signify both a sequence of stages and a gradual development of component parts: in other words, the chart formalizes a progression through time of a differentiation of parts. This indicates (1) that each critical item of psychosocial strength discussed here is systematically related to all others, and that they all depend on the proper development in the proper sequence of each item; and (2) that each item exists in some form before its critical time normally arrives.

If I say, for example, that a favorable ratio of basic trust over basic mistrust is the first step in psychosocial adaptation, a favorable ratio of autonomous will over shame and doubt, the second, the corresponding diagrammatic statement expresses a number of fundamental relations that exist between the two steps, as well as some facts fundamental to each. Each comes to its ascendance, meets its crisis, and finds its lasting solution during the stage indicated. But they all must exist from the beginning in some form, for every act calls for an integration of all. Also, an infant may show something like "autonomy" from the beginning in the particular way in which he angrily tries to wriggle himself free when tightly held. However, under normal conditions, it is not until the second year that he begins to experience the whole *critical opposition of being an autonomous creature and being a dependent one;* and it is not until then that he is ready for a decisive encounter with his environment, an environment which, in turn, feels called upon to convey to him its particular ideas and concepts of autonomy and coercion in ways decisively contributing to the character and the health of his personality in his culture. It is this encounter, together with the resulting crisis, that we have tentatively described for each stage. As to the progression from one stage to the next, the diagonal indicates the sequence to be followed. However, it also makes room for variations in tempo and intensity. An individual, or culture, may linger excessively over trust and proceed from I 1 over I 2 to II 2, or an accelerated progression may move from I 1 over II 1 to II 2. Each such acceleration or relative retardation, however, is assumed to have a modifying influence on all later stages.

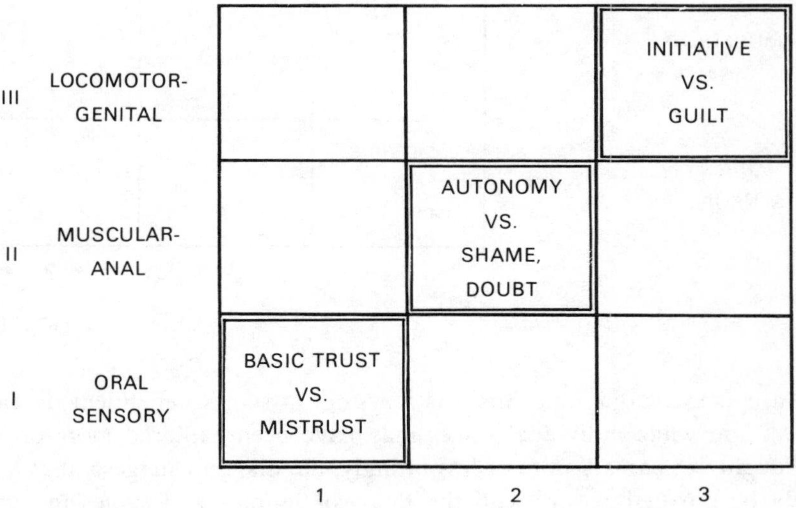

III	LOCOMOTOR-GENITAL			INITIATIVE VS. GUILT
II	MUSCULAR-ANAL		AUTONOMY VS. SHAME, DOUBT	
I	ORAL SENSORY	BASIC TRUST VS. MISTRUST		
		1	2	3

FIGURE 1

		1	2	3
VIII	MATURITY			
VII	ADULTHOOD			
VI	YOUNG ADULTHOOD			
V	PUBERTY AND ADOLESCENCE			
IV	LATENCY			
III	LOCOMOTOR-GENITAL			INITIATIVE VS. GUILT
II	MUSCULAR-ANAL		AUTONOMY VS. SHAME, DOUBT	
I	ORAL SENSORY	BASIC TRUST VS. MISTRUST		

FIGURE 2

An epigenetic diagram thus lists a system of stages dependent on each other; and while individual stages may have been explored more or less thoroughly or named more or less fittingly, the diagram suggests that their study be pursued always with the total configuration of stages in mind. The diagram invites, then, a thinking through of all its empty boxes: if we have entered Basic Trust in I 1 and Integrity in VIII 8, we leave the ques-

				EGO INTEGRITY VS. DESPAIR
			GENERATIVITY VS. STAGNATION	
		INTIMACY VS. ISOLATION		
	IDENTITY VS. ROLE CONFUSION			
INDUSTRY VS. INFERIORITY				
4	5	6	7	8

tion open, as to what trust might have become in a stage dominated by the need for integrity even as we have left open what it may look like and, indeed, be called in the stage dominated by a striving for autonomy (II 1). All we mean to emphasize is that trust must have developed in its own right, before it becomes something more in the critical encounter in which autonomy develops—and so on, up the vertical. If, in the last stage

(VIII 1), we would expect trust to have developed into the most mature *faith* that an aging person can muster in his cultural setting and historical period, the chart permits the consideration not only of what old age can be, but also what its preparatory stages must have been. All of this should make it clear that a chart of epigenesis suggests a global form of thinking and rethinking which leaves details of methodology and terminology to further study. [3]

[3] To leave this matter truly open, certain misuses of the whole conception would have to be avoided. Among them is the assumption that the sense of trust (and all the other "positive" senses postulated) is an *achievement*, secured once and for all at a given state. In fact, some writers are so intent on making an *achievement scale* out of these stages that they blithely omit all the "negative" senses (basic mistrust, etc.) which are and remain the dynamic counterpart of the "positive" ones through life. The assumption that on each stage a goodness is achieved which is impervious to new inner conflicts and to changing conditions is, I believe, a projection on child development of that success ideology which can so dangerously pervade our private and public daydreams and can make us inept in a heightened struggle for a meaningful existence in a new, industrial era of history. The personality is engaged with the hazards of existence continuously, even as the body's metabolism copes with decay. As we come to diagnose a state of relative strength and the symptoms of an impaired one, we face only more clearly the paradoxes and tragic potentials of human life.

The stripping of the stages of everything but their "achievements" has its counterpart in attempts to describe or test them as "traits" or "aspirations" without first building a systematic bridge between the conception advanced throughout this book and the favorite concepts of other investigators. If the foregoing sounds somewhat plaintive, it is not intended to gloss over the fact that in giving to these strengths the very designations by which in the past they have acquired countless connotations of superficial goodness, affected niceness, and all too strenuous virtue, I invited misunderstandings and misuses. However, I believe, that there is an intrinsic relationship between ego and language and that despite passing vicissitudes certain basic words retain essential meanings.

I have since attempted to formulate for Julian Huxley's *Humanist Frame* (1961) blueprint of essential strengths which evolution has built both into the ground plan of the life stages and into that of man's institutions. While I cannot discuss here the methodological problems involved (and aggravated by my use of the term "basic virtues"), I should append the list of these strengths because they are really the lasting outcome of the "favorable ratios" mentioned at every step of the chapter on psychosocial stages. Here they are:

Basic Trust vs. Basic Mistrust: Drive and *Hope*
Autonomy vs. Shame and Doubt: Self-Control and *Willpower*
Initiative vs. Guilt: Direction and *Purpose*
Industry vs. Inferiority: Method and *Competence*
Identity vs. Role Confusion: Devotion and *Fidelity*
Intimacy vs. Isolation: Affiliation and *Love*
Generativity vs. Stagnation: Production and *Care*
Ego Integrity vs. Despair: Renunciation and *Wisdom*

The italicized words are called *basic* virtues because without them, and their re-emergence from generation to generation, all other and more changeable systems of human values lose their spirit and their relevance. Of this list, I have been able so far to give a more detailed account only for Fidelity (1963). But here again, the list represents a total conception within which there is much room for a discussion of terminology and methodology.

THE CONCEPT OF DEVELOPMENTAL LINES

Anna Freud

Anna Freud, in the course of exploring some potential preventive applications of psychoanalytic theory, reviews the problems in the assessment of child development which have long concerned her and others (A. Freud, 1945, 1962; Nagera, 1966a; G.A.P., 1966; Ackerman, 1953). In contrast to Gesell (1940a) she urges great caution in basing expectations on a child's chronological age, in focusing on external behavior, or relying on our often misleading adult definitions of a child's reality. She recommends, as would Piaget (1929, 1954; Flavell, 1963), that we attempt rather to attune ourselves to the child's own interpretation of his world, one which depends upon the development of his mental organization. Through the integrative concept of lines of development, Anna Freud emphasizes the fundamental importance of the interaction *of the gradually evolving individual constituents of personality development—their commingling, their progression and regression. Her approach demonstrates balance, including as it does, consideration of libidinal and aggressive drives, object relations, ego and superego structures, and the particularly marked influence of environmental as well as maturational forces.*

The Translation of External Events into Internal Experience

Analysts, so far as they are regarded as child experts, are confronted by the public with a multitude of questions as they arise normally during the upbringing of any child and concern all the decisions about the child's life which can become problematic to the parents. That they refer to everyday situations is no reason why the answers to them should be left to the analytically untaught, who deal habitually with normal mental life (such as the parents themselves, pediatricians, nurses, nursery school teachers,

Reprinted from: *Normality and Pathology in Childhood: Assessments of Development.* New York: International Universities Press, 1965, pp. 56–92.

teachers, welfare workers, school officers, etc.). In fact, the questions which are raised circumscribe the very areas within which the psychoanalytic theories can be applied profitably to preventive work. The following are some examples:

Should the mother of a young infant have his sole care, and does the introduction of any kind of mother substitute imply a threat to his development? Where she has sole care, when can she be permitted for the first time to leave the infant for a short spell for the benefit of a holiday, for her husband, older children, her own parents, etc.? What are the advantages of breast feeding versus bottle feeding, or of feeding by demand versus feeding by the clock? What is the best age for beginning toilet training? At what age do children actually benefit from the inclusion of other adults or of playmates? What is the right age for entry into nursery school? If surgery has to be performed (for necessary repairs, for circumcision, tonsillectomy, etc.), and if there is a choice of date, is it better to let this happen earlier or later? What type of schooling (formal or informal) is suited best to which type of child? When should sexual enlightenment be introduced? Are there any ages when the arrival of a sibling will be more easily tolerated than at other times? What about the autoerotic activities? Should sucking, masturbation, etc., be permitted without checking, and should the same apply to sex play among the children? What about the freedom of aggression? When and in what way should an adopted child be told about adoption, and does information about the natural parents have to be included? What are the pros and cons concerning day or boarding school? And finally: is there a specific moment during the adolescent process when it is helpful for the young person to "remove" (Katan, 1937) himself bodily from home, in addition to his emotional estrangement from his parents?

When faced with any, even the apparently simplest of these questions, the analyst's reaction has to be a double one. It is obviously not enough for him to point out that there are no general answers which fit all children, only particular ones to fit a given child; to warn against basing solutions on chronological age, since children differ as much in the rate of their emotional and social growth as they differ in their physical milestones and their mental ages; or even to assess the developmental level of the child on whose behalf he is consulted. Considerations of this kind constitute only one part of his assignment, and perhaps the easier one. The other and no less essential half consists of assessing the psychological meaning of the experience or demand to which the parents intend to subject the child. While the parents may view their plans in the light of reason, logic, and practical necessity, the child experiences them in terms of his psychic reality, i.e., according to the phase-adequate complexes, affects, anxieties, and fantasies which are aroused by them. It therefore becomes the analyst's task to point out to the parents the discrepancies which exist between the adult's and the child's interpretation of events and to explain the latter on the basis of the specific modes and levels of functioning which are characteristic of the infantile mind.

Four Areas of Difference Between Child and Adult

There are several areas in the child's mind from which such "misunderstandings" of adult actions are known to arise.

There is, for one, the *egocentricity* which governs the infant's relations with the object world. Before the phase of object constancy has been reached, the object, i.e., the mothering person, is not perceived by the child as having an existence of her own; she is perceived only in terms of a role assigned to her within the framework of the child's needs and wishes. Accordingly, whatever happens in or to the object is understood from the aspect of satisfaction or frustration of these wishes. Every preoccupation of the mother, her concerns with other members of the family, with work or outside interests, her depressions, illnesses, absences, even her death, are transformed thereby into experiences of rejection and desertion. On the same basis, the birth of a sibling is understood as unfaithfulness of the parents, as dissatisfaction with and criticism of the child's own person—in short, as a hostile act to which the child in his turn answers with hostility and disappointment, expressed either in excessive demandingness or in emotional withdrawal with its adverse consequences.

There is, secondly, the very *immaturity* of the infantile *sexual apparatus* which leaves the child no choice but to translate adult genital happenings into pregenital events. This accounts for parental intercourse being misunderstood as a scene of brutal violence, and opens the door for all the difficulties of identifying with either the alleged victim or alleged aggressor which reveal themselves later in the growing child's uncertainty about his own sexual identity. It also accounts, as has been well known for a considerable period, for the comparative failure and parental disappointments in sexual enlightenment. Instead of accepting the sexual facts as reasonably as they are given, the child cannot help but translate them into the terms which are commensurate with his experience, i.e., turn them into the so-called "infantile sexual theories" of impregnation through the mouth (as in fairy tales), birth through the anus, castration of the female partner through intercourse, etc.

Thirdly, there are those occasions where the child's misapprehension of events is based; not on an absolute lack of reasoning on his part, but on economic factors, i.e., on the *relative weakness of secondary process* thinking compared with the strength of impulses and fantasies. A young child after the toddler stage, for example, may be well able to grasp the significance of medical events, to recognize the role of doctor or surgeon as a beneficent one, the necessity for medicines whatever their taste, the need for dietary or motor restrictions, etc. Only this understanding cannot be expected to maintain itself. As the visit to the doctor or an impending operation come nearer, reason goes by the board, and the child's mind is swamped by fantasies of mutilation, castration, violent assault, etc. Being kept in bed becomes imprisonment; the diet is felt as intolerable oral deprivation; the parents who permit these things to happen to the child (in their presence or absence) cease to be protective figures and are turned into hostile ones against whom the child's own anger, rage, hostility can be released. [1]

Finally, there are some basic differences between the functioning of the child's mind and that of the adult, and these are significant in this respect. I mention as their most important representative the different *evaluation of time* at the various age levels. The sense of the length or shortness of a given time period seems to depend on the measuring being carried out by way of either id or ego functioning. Id impulses are by definition intolerant of delay and waiting; the later attitudes are introduced by the ego of which postponement of action (by interpolation of the thought processes) is as characteristic as urgency of fulfillment is of the id. How a child will experience a given time period will depend therefore not on the actual duration, measured objectively by the adult, by the calendar and by the clock, but on the subjective inner relations of either id or ego dominance over his functioning. It is these latter factors which will decide whether the intervals set for feeding, the absence of the mother, the duration of nursery attendance, of hospitalization, etc., will seem to the child short or long, tolerable or intolerable, and as a result will prove harmless or harmful in their consequence.

The child's egocentricity, the immaturity of his sex life, the preponderance of id derivatives over ego responses, his different evaluation of time are characteristics of the infantile mind which may account for many of

[1] See in this respect also Anna Freud (1952), Joyce Robertson (1956).

the parents' apparent insensibilities, i.e., for their difficulty in translating external occurrences into internal experience. Information about a child's history at the diagnostic stage is therefore given by them in a cursory and misleading manner. Reports may contain an account of "a battle about breast feeding which was soon terminated"; a toddler's "initial refusal to accept a mother substitute during the mother's illness"; a boy's "turning his back on the mother momentarily when she returned from the maternity hospital with the new baby"; a child's "passing unhappiness in the hospital," etc.[2]

It requires all the ingenuity of the diagnostician, and sometimes a period of analytic treatment, to reconstruct from descriptions of this kind the dynamic struggles which lie behind the surface picture and which, more often than not, have been responsible for changing the whole course of the child's emotional life from attachment to the parents to withdrawal from them, from love and good-will to resentment and hostility, from the feeling of being cherished to a feeling of rejection and worthlessness, etc.

The Concept of Developmental Lines

For useful answers to the parents' questions concerning developmental issues, the external decisions under consideration need thus to be translated into their internal implications. As mentioned above, this cannot be done if drive and ego development are viewed in isolation from each other, necessary as this is for purposes of clinical analysis and theoretical dissection.

So far, in our psychoanalytic theory, the development sequences are laid down only with regard to particular, circumscribed parts of the child's personality. Concerning the development of the sexual drive, for example, we possess the sequence of libidinal phases (oral, anal, phallic, latency period, preadolescence, adolescent genitality) which, in spite of considerable overlapping, correspond roughly with specific ages. With regard to the aggressive drive, we are already less precise and are usually content to correlate specific aggressive expressions with specific libidinal phases (such as biting, spitting, devouring with orality; sadistic torturing, hitting, kicking, destroying with anality; overbearing, domineering, forceful behavior with the phallic phase; inconsiderateness, mental cruelty, dissocial outbursts with adolescence, etc.). On the side of the ego, the analytically known stages and levels of the sense of reality, in the chronology of defense activity and in the growth of a moral sense, lay down a norm.

[2] Examples quoted from the Diagnostic Service of the Hampstead Child-Therapy Clinic.

The intellectual functions themselves are measured and graded by the psychologist by means of the age-related scales of the various intelligence tests.

Without doubt we need more for our assessments than these selected developmental scales which are valid for isolated parts of the child's personality only, not for its totality. What we are looking for are the basic interactions between id and ego and their various developmental levels, and also age-related sequences of them which, in importance, frequency, and regularity, are comparable to the maturational sequence of libidinal stages or the gradual unfolding of the ego functions. Naturally, such sequences of interaction between the two sides of the personality can be best established where both are well studied, as they are, for example, with regard to the libidinal phases and aggressive expressions on the id side and the corresponding object-related attitudes on the ego side. Here we can trace the combinations which lead from the infant's complete emotional dependence to the adult's comparative self-reliance and mature sex and object relationships, a gradated developmental line which provides the indispensable basis for any assessment of emotional maturity or immaturity, normality or abnormality.

Even if perhaps less easily established, there are similar lines of development which can be shown to be valid for almost every other area of the individual's personality. In every instance they trace the child's gradual outgrowing of dependent, irrational, id- and object-determined attitudes to an increasing ego mastery of his internal and external world. Such lines—always contributed to from the side of both id and ego development—lead, for example, from the infant's suckling and weaning experiences to the adult's rational rather than emotional attitude to food intake; from cleanliness training enforced on the child by environmental pressure to the adult's more or less ingrained and unshakable bladder and bowel control; from the child's sharing possession of his body with his mother to the adolescent's claim for independence and self-determination in body management; from the young child's egocentric view of the world and his fellow beings to empathy, mutuality, and companionship with his contemporaries; from the first erotic play on his own and his mother's body by way of the transitional objects (Winnicott, 1953) to the toys, games, hobbies, and finally to work, etc.

Whatever level has been reached by any given child in any of these respects represents the results of interaction between drive and ego-superego development and their reaction to environmental influences, i.e., between maturation, adaptation, and structuralization. Far from being theoretical abstractions, developmental lines, in the sense here used, are historical realities which, when assembled, convey a convincing picture of an individual child's personal achievements or, on the other hand, of his failures in personality development.

Prototype of a Developmental Line: From Dependency to Emotional Self-Reliance and Adult Object Relationships

To serve as the prototype for all others, there is one basic developmental line which has received attention from analysts from the beginning. This is the sequence which leads from the newborn's utter dependence on maternal care to the young adult's emotional and material self-reliance—a sequence for which the successive stages of libido development (oral, anal, phallic) merely form the inborn, maturational base. The steps on this way are well documented from the analyses of adults and children, as well as from direct analytic infant observations. They can be listed, roughly, as follows:

(1) The biological unity between the mother-infant couple, with the mother's narcissism extending to the child, and the child including the mother in his internal "narcissistic milieu" (Hoffer, 1952), the whole period being further subdivided (according to Mahler, 1952) into the autistic, symbiotic, and separation-individuation phases with significant danger points for developmental disturbances lodged in each individual phase;

(2) the part object (Melanie Klein), or need-fulfilling, anaclitic relationship, which is based on the urgency of the child's body needs and drive derivatives and is intermittent and fluctuating, since object cathexis is sent out under the impact of imperative desires, and withdrawn again when satisfaction has been reached;

(3) the stage of object constancy, which enables a positive inner image of the object to be maintained, irrespective of either satisfactions or dissatisfactions;

(4) the ambivalent relationship of the preoedipal, anal-sadistic stage, characterized by the ego atitudes of clinging, torturing, dominating, and controlling the love objects;

(5) the completely object-centered phallic-oedipal phase, characterized by possessiveness of the parent of the opposite sex (or vice versa), jealousy of, and rivalry with, the parent of the same sex, protectiveness, curiosity, bids for admiration, and exhibitionistic attitudes; in girls a

phallic-oedipal (masculine) relationship to the mother preceding the oedipal relationship to the father;

(6) the latency period, i.e., the postoedipal lessening of drive urgency and the transfer of libido from the parental figures to contemporaries, community groups, teachers, leaders, impersonal ideals, and aim-inhibited, sublimated interests, with fantasy manifestations giving evidence of disillusionment with, and denigration of, the parents ("family romance," twin fantasies, etc.);

(7) the preadolescent prelude to the "adolescent revolt," i.e., a return to early attitudes and behavior, especially of the part-object, need-fulfilling, and ambivalent type;

(8) the adolescent struggle around denying, reversing, loosening, and shedding the tie to the infantile objects, defending against pregenitality, and finally establishing genital supremacy with libidinal cathexis transferred to objects of the opposite sex, outside the family.

While the details of these positions have long been common knowledge in analytic circles, their relevance for practical problems is being explored increasingly in recent years. As regards, for example, the much-discussed consequences of a child's separation from the mother, the parents, or the home, a mere glance at the unfolding of the developmental line will be sufficient to show convincingly why the common reactions to, respectively, the pathological consequences of such happenings are as varied as they are, following the varying psychic reality of the child on the different levels. Infringements of the biological mother-infant tie (phase 1), for whatever reason they are undertaken, will thus give rise to separation anxiety (Bowlby, 1960b) proper; failure of the mother to play her part as a reliable need-fulfilling and comfort-giving agency (phase 2) will cause breakdowns in individuation (Mahler, 1952) or anaclitic depression (Spitz, 1946), or other manifestations of deprivation (Alpert, 1959), or precocious ego development (James, 1960), or what has been called a "false self" (Winnicott, 1955). Unsatisfactory libidinal relations to unstable or otherwise unsuitable love objects during anal sadism (phase 4) will disturb the balanced fusion between libido and aggression and give rise to uncontrollable aggressivity, destructiveness, etc. (A. Freud, 1949). It is only after object constancy (phase 3) has been reached that the external absence of the object is substituted for, at least in part, by the presence of an internal image which remains stable; on the strength of this achievement temporary separations can be lengthened, commensurate with the advances in object constancy. Thus, even if it remains impossible to name the chronological age when separations can be tolerated, according to the developmental line it can be stated when they become phase-adequate and non-traumatic, a point of practical importance for the purposes of holidays for the parents, hospitalization of the child, convalescence, entry into nursery school, etc. [3]

There are other practical lessons which have been learned from the same developmental sequence, such as the following:

that the clinging attitudes of the toddler stage (phase 4) are the result of preoedipal ambivalence, not of maternal spoiling;

that it is unrealistic on the part of parents to expect of the preoedipal period (up to the end of phase 4) the mutuality in object relations which belongs to the next level (phase 5) only;

that no child can be fully integrated in group life before libido has been transferred from the parents to the community (phase 6). Where the passing of the Oedipus complex is delayed and phase 5 is protracted as the result of an infantile neurosis, disturbances in adaptation to the group, lack of interest, school phobias (in day school), extreme homesickness (in boarding school) will be the order of the day;

that reactions to adoption are most severe in the later part of the latency period (phase 6) when, according to the normal disillusionment with the parents, all children feel as if adopted and the feelings about the reality of adoption merge with the occurrence of the "family romance";

that sublimations, foreshadowed on the oedipal level (phase 5) and developed during latency (phase 6), may be lost during preadolescence (phase 7), not through any developmental or educational failure, but owing to the phase-adequate regression to early levels (phases 2, 3, and 4);

that it is as unrealistic on the part of the parents to oppose the loosening of the tie to the family or the young person's battle against pregenital impulses in adolescence (phase 8) as it is to break the biological tie in phase 1, or oppose pregenital autoerotism in the phases 1, 2, 3, 4, and 7.

Some Developmental Lines Toward Body Independence

That the ego of an individual begins first and foremost as a body ego does not imply that bodily independence of the parents is reached earlier than emotional or moral self-reliance. On the contrary: the mother's narcissistic possessiveness of her infant's body is matched from the child's

[3] If, by "mourning" we understand, not the various manifestations of anxiety, distress, and malfunction which accompany object loss in the earliest phases, but the painful, gradual process of detaching libido from an internal image, this, of course, cannot be expected to occur before object constancy (phase 3) has been established.

side by his archaic wishes to merge with the mother and by the confusion concerning body limits which arises from the fact that, in early life, the distinctions between the internal and external world are based not on objective reality but on the subjective experiences of pleasure and unpleasure. Thus, while the mother's breast, or face, hands, or hair, may be treated (or maltreated) by the infant as parts of his own organization, his hunger, his tiredness, his discomforts are her concern as much as they are his own. Although for the whole of early childhood the child's life will be dominated by body needs, body impulses, and their derivatives, the quantities and the qualities of satisfactions and dissatisfactions are determined not by himself but by environmental influence. The only exceptions to this rule are the autoerotic gratifications which from the beginning are under the child's own management and, therefore, provide for him a certain circumscribed measure of independence of the object world. In contrast to these, as will be shown below, the processes of feeding, sleeping, evacuation, body hygiene, and prevention of injury and illness have to undergo complex and lengthy developments before they become the growing individual's own concern.

From Suckling to Rational Eating.—A long line has to be passed through before a child arrives at the point where, for example, he can regulate his own food intake actively and rationally, quantitatively and qualitatively, on the basis of his own needs and appetites and irrespective of his relations to the provider of food, and of conscious and unconscious fantasies. The steps on the way are approximately as follows:

(1) Being nursed at the breast or bottle, by the clock or on demand, with the common difficulties about intake caused partly by the infant's normal fluctuations of appetite and intestinal upsets, partly by the mother's attitudes and anxieties regarding feeding; interference with need satisfaction caused by hunger periods, undue waiting for meals, rationing or forced feeding set up the first—and often lasting—disturbances in the positive relationship to food. Pleasure sucking appears as a forerunner, by-product of, substitute for, or interference with, feeding;

(2) weaning from breast or bottle, initiated either by the infant himself or according to the mother's wishes. In the latter instance, and especially if carried out abruptly, the infant's protest against oral deprivation has adverse results for the normal pleasure in food. Difficulties may occur over the introduction of solids, new tastes and consistencies being either welcomed or rejected;

(3) the transition from being fed to self-feeding, with or without implements, "food" and "mother" still being identified with each other;

(4) self-feeding with the use of spoon, fork, etc., the disagreements with the mother about the quantity of intake being shifted often to the form of intake, i.e., table manners; meals as a general battleground on which the difficulties of the mother-child relationship can be fought out; craving for sweets as a phase-adequate substitute for oral sucking pleasures; food fads as a result of anal training, i.e., of the newly acquired reaction formation of disgust;

(5) gradual fading out of the equation food-mother in the oedipal period. Irrational attitudes toward eating are now determined by infantile sexual theories, i.e., fantasies of impregnation through the mouth (fear of poison), pregnancy (fear of getting fat), anal birth (fear of intake and output), as well as by reaction formations against cannibalism and sadism;

(6) gradual fading out of the sexualization of eating in the latency period, with pleasure in eating retained or even increased. Increase in the rational attitudes to food and self-determination in eating, the earlier experiences on this line being decisive in shaping the individual's food habits in adult life, his taste, preferences, as well as eventual addictions or aversions with regard to food and drink.

The infant's reactions to the changes in phase 2 (i.e., to weaning and to the introduction of new tastes and consistencies) reflect for the first time his leaning toward either progression and adventurousness (when new experiences are welcomed) or a tenacious clinging to existing pleasures (when every change is experienced as threat and deprivation). It is to be expected that, whichever attitude dominates the feeding process will also become important in other developmental areas.

The equation, food-mother, which persists through phases 1-4, provides the rational background for the mother's subjective conviction that every food refusal of the child is aimed at her personally, i.e., expresses the child's rejection of her maternal care and attention, a conviction which causes much oversensitiveness in handling the feeding process and underlies the battle about food on the mother's side. It explains also why in these phases food refusal and extreme food fads can be circumvented by temporarily substituting a stranger, i.e., a noncathected or differently cathected person, for the maternal figure in the feeding situation. Children will then eat, in hospital, in nursery school, or as visitors, but this will not cure their eating difficulties at home, in the presence of the mother. It explains also why traumatic separations from the mother are often followed by refusal of food (rejection of the mother substitute), or by greed and overeating (treating food as a substitute for mother love).

The eating disturbances of phase 5, which are not related to an external object, but are caused by internal, structural conflicts, are not affected by either the material presence or the material absence of the mother, a fact which can be utilized for differential diagnosis.

After phase 6, when the arrangements for food intake have become the mature individual's personal concern, the former food battle with the mother may be replaced by internal disagreements between the manifest wish to eat and an unconsciously determined inability to tolerate certain foods, i.e., the various neurotic food fads and digestive upsets.

From Wetting and Soiling to Bladder and Bowel Control.—Since the desired aim on this line is not the comparatively intact survival of drive derivatives, but the control, modification, and transformation of the urethral and anal trends, the conflicts between id, ego, superego, and environmental forces become particularly obvious.

(1) The duration of the first phase, during which the infant has complete freedom to wet and soil, is determined not maturationally but environmentally, i.e., by the mother's timing of her interference, in which she in her turn is under the influence of personal needs, familial, social, or medical conventions. Under present conditions, this phase may last from a few days (training from birth based on reflex action) to two or three years (training based on object relatedness and ego control).

(2) In contrast to phase one, the second phase is initiated by a step in maturation. The dominant role in drive activity passes from the oral to the anal zone, and due to this transition the child stiffens his opposition to any interference with concerns which have become emotionally vital to him. Since in this phase the body products are highly cathected with libido, they are precious to the child and are treated as "gifts" which are surrendered to the mother as a sign of love; since they are cathected also with aggression, they are weapons by means of which rage, anger, disappointment can be discharged within the object relationship. In correspondence to this double cathexis of the body products, the toddler's entire attitude toward the object world is dominated by ambivalence, i.e., by violent swings between love and hate (libido and aggression not fused with each other). This again is matched on the ego side by curiosity directed toward the inside of the body, pleasure in messing, molding, play with retaining, emptying, hoarding, as well as dominating, possessing, destroy-

ing, etc. While the trends shown by the children in this phase are fairly uniform, the actual events vary with the differences in the mother's attitude. If she succeeds in remaining sensitive to the child's needs and as identified with them as she is usually with regard to feeding, she will mediate sympathetically between the environmental demand for cleanliness and the child's opposite anal and urethral tendencies; in that case toilet training will proceed gradually, uneventfully, and without upheavals. On the other hand, such empathy with the child in the anal stage may be impossible for the mother due to her own training, her own reaction formations of disgust, orderliness, and punctiliousness, or other obsessional elements in her personality. If she is dominated by these, she will represent the demand for urethral and anal control in a harsh and uncompromising manner, and a major battle will ensue, with the child as intent to defend his right over unrestricted evacuation as the mother is on achieving cleanliness and regularity, and with them the rudiments and *sine qua non* of socialization.

(3) In a third phase the child accepts and takes over the mother's and the environment's attitudes to cleanliness and, through identification, makes them an integral part of his ego and superego demands; from then onward, the striving for cleanliness is an internal, not an external, precept, and inner barriers against urethral and anal wishes are set up through the defense activity of the ego, in the well-known form of repression and reaction formation. Disgust, orderliness, tidiness, dislike of dirty hands guard against the return of the repressed; punctuality, conscientiousness, and reliability appear as by-products of anal regularity; inclinations to save, to collect, give evidence of high anal evaluation displaced to other matters. In short, what takes place in this period is the far-reaching modification and transformation of the pregenital anal drive derivatives which—if kept within normal limits—supply the individual personality with a backbone of highly valuable qualities.

It is important to remember in respect to these achievements that they are based on identifications and internalizations and, as such, are not fully secure before the passing of the oedipus complex. Preoedipal anal control remains vulnerable and, especially in the beginning of the third phase, remains dependent on the objects and the stability of positive relations to them. For example, a child who is trained to use the chamberpot or toilet in his home does not exchange them automatically for unfamiliar ones, away from the mother. A child who is severely disappointed in his mother, or separated from her, or suffering from object loss in any form, may not only lose the internalized urge to be clean but also reactivate the aggressive use of elimination. Both together will result in incidents of wetting and soiling which appear as "accidents."

(4) It is only in a fourth phase that bladder and bowel control become wholly secure. This is brought about when the concern for cleanliness is disconnected from object ties and attains the status of a fully neutralized, autonomous ego and superego concern. [4]

From Irresponsibility to Responsibility in Body Management.—That the satisfaction of such essential physical needs as feeding and evacuation [5] remains for years under external control and emerges from it in such slow steps corresponds well with the equally slow and gradual manner in which children assume responsibility for the care of their own body and its protection against harm. As described at length elsewhere (A. Freud, 1952), the well-mothered child leaves these concerns largely to the mother, while he allows himself attitudes of indifference and unconcern, or, as a weapon in a battle with her, downright recklessness. It is only the badly mothered or the motherless who adopt the mother's role in health matters and play "mother and child" with their own bodies as the hypochondriacs do.

On the positive progressive line, here too, there are several consecutive phases to be distinguished from each other, though our present knowledge of them is more sketchy than in other areas.

(1) What comes first, as a maturational step in the first few months of life, is an alteration in the direction of aggression from being lived out on the body to being turned toward the external world. This vital step sets limits to self-injury from biting, scratching, etc., although indications of such tendencies can also be seen in many children as genuine remnants at later ages. [6] The normal forward move happens partly due to the setting up of the pain barrier, partly due to the child's answering to the mother's libidinal cathexis of his body with a narcissistic cathexis of his own (according to Hoffer, 1950a).

(2) What makes itself felt next are the advances in ego functioning such as orientation in the external world, understanding of cause and effect, control of dangerous wishes in the service of the reality principle. Together with the pain barrier and the narcissistic cathexis of the body, these

[4] See Hartmann (1950) on "secondary autonomy of the ego."

[5] Also sleep.

[6] Such remnants should not be confused with the later "turning of aggression against the self," which is not a defect in maturation but a defense mechanism used by the ego under the impact of conflict.

newly acquired functions protect the child against such external dangers as water, fire, heights, etc. But there are many instances of children where—owing to a deficiency in any one of these ego functions—this advance is retarded so that they remain unusually vulnerable and exposed, if not protected by the adult world.

(3) What comes last, normally, is the child's voluntary endorsement of the rules of hygiene and of medical necessities. So far as the avoidance of unwholesome food, overeating, and keeping the body clean are concerned, this is inconclusive here since the relevant attitudes belong to the vicissitudes of the oral and anal component instinct rather than to the present line. It is different with the avoidance of ill-health or the compliance with doctor's orders concerning the intake of medicines, and motor or dietary restrictions. Fear, guilt, castration anxiety, of course, may motivate any child to be careful (i.e., fearful) for the safety of his body. But when not under the influence of these, normal children will be remarkably uncompromising and obstructive in health matters. According to their mothers' frequent complaints, they behave as if they claimed it as their right to endanger their health, while they left it to their mothers to protect and restore it, an attitude which lasts often until the end of adolescence and may represent the last residue of the original symbiosis between child and mother.

Further Examples of Developmental Lines

There are many other examples of developmental lines, such as the two given below, where every step is known to the analyst, and which can be traced without difficulty, either through working backward by reconstruction from the adult picture, or through working forward by means of longitudinal analytic exploration and observation of the child.

From Egocentricity to Companionship.—When describing a child's growth in this particular respect, a sequence can be traced which runs as follows:

(1) a selfish narcissistically orientated outlook on the object world, in which other children either do not figure at all or are perceived only in their role as disturbers of the mother-child relationship and rivals for the parents' love;

(2) other children related to as lifeless objects, i.e., toys which can be handled, pushed around, sought out, and discarded as the mood demands, with no positive or negative response expected from them;

(3) other children related to as helpmates in carrying out a desired task such as playing, building, destroying, causing mischief of some kind,

etc., the duration of the partnership being determined by the task, and secondary to it;

(4) other children as partners and objects in their own right, whom the child can admire, fear, or compete with, whom he loves or hates with whose feelings he identifies, whose wishes he acknowledges and often respects, and with whom he can share possessions on a basis of equality.

In the first two phases, even if cherished and tolerated as the baby by older siblings, the toddler is by necessity asocial, whatever efforts to the contrary the mother may make; community life at this stage may be endured but will not be profitable. The third stage represents the minimum requirement for socialization in the form of acceptance into a home community of older siblings or entry into a nursery group of contemporaries. But it is only the fourth stage which equips the child for companionship, enmities and friendships of any type and duration.

From the Body to the Toy and from Play to Work.—(1) Play begins with the infant as an activity yielding erotic pleasure, involving the mouth, the fingers, vision, the whole surface of the skin. It is carried out on the child's own body (autoerotic play) or on the mother's body (usually in connection with feeding), with no clear distinction between the two, and with no obvious order or precedence in this respect.

(2) The properties of the mother's and the child's body are transferred to some soft substance, such as a nappy, a pillow, a rug, a teddy, which serves as the infant's first plaything, the transitional object (according to Winnicott, 1953) which is cathected both with narcissistic and with object libido.

(3) Clinging to one specific transitional object develops further into a more indiscriminate liking for soft toys of various kinds which, as symbolic objects, are cuddled and maltreated alternately (cathected with libido and aggression). That they are inanimate objects, and therefore do not retaliate, enables the toddler to express the full range of his ambivalence toward them.

(4) Cuddly toys fade out gradually, except at bedtime, when—in their capacity as transitional objects—they continue to facilitate the child's passing from active participation in the external world to the narcissistic withdrawal necessary for sleep.

In daytime, their place is taken increasingly by play material which does not itself possess object status, but which serves ego activities and the fantasies underlying them. Such activities either directly gratify a component instinct or are invested with displaced and sublimated drive energies, their chronological sequence being approximately the following:

(a) toys offering opportunities for ego activities such as filling-emptying, opening-shutting, fitting in, messing, etc., interest in them being displaced from the body openings and their functions:
(b) movable toys providing pleasure in motility;
(c) building material offering equal opportunities for construction and destruction (in correspondence with the ambivalent trends of the anal-sadistic phase);
(d) toys serving the expression of masculine and feminine trends and attitudes, to be used
    (i) in solitary role play,
    (ii) for display to the oedipal object (serving phallic exhibitionism),
    (iii) for staging the various situations of the oedipus complex in group play (provided that stage 3 on the developmental line toward companionship has been reached).

Expression of masculinity can be taken over also by the ego activities of gymnastics and acrobatics, in which the child's entire body and its skillful manipulation represent, display, and provide symbolic enjoyment from phallic activities and phallic mastery.

(5) Direct or displaced satisfaction from the play activity itself gives way increasingly to the pleasure in the finished product of the activity, a pleasure which has been described in academic psychology as pleasure in task completion, in problem solving, etc. By some authors it is taken as the indispensable prerequisite for the child's successful performance in school (Buhler, 1935).

The exact manner in which this pleasure in achievement is linked with the child's instinctual life is still an open question in our theoretical thinking, although various operative factors seem unmistakable, such as imitation and identification in the early mother-child relationship, the influence of the ego ideal, the turning of passive into active as a mechanism of defense and adaptation, and the inner urge toward maturation, i.e., toward progressive development.

That pleasure in achievement, linked only secondarily with object relations, is present in very young children as a latent capacity is demonstrated in a practical manner by the successes of the Montessori method. In this nursery school method the play material is selected so as to afford the child the maximum increase in self-esteem and gratification by means of task completion and independent problem solving, and children can be observed to respond positively to such opportunities almost from the toddler stage onward.

Where this source of gratification is not tapped to the same degree with the help of external arrangements, the pleasure derived from achievement in play remains more directly connected with praise and approval given by the object world, and satisfaction from the finished product takes first place at a later date only, probably as the result of internalization of external sources of self-esteem.

(6) Ability to play changes into ability to work[7] when a number of additional faculties are acquired, such as the following:

(a) to control, inhibit, or modify the impulses to use given materials aggressively and destructively (not to throw, to take apart, to mess, to hoard), and to use them positively and constructively instead (to build, to plan, to learn, and–in communal life–to share);

(b) to carry out preconceived plans with a minimum regard for the lack of immediate pleasure yield, intervening frustrations, etc., and the maximum regard for the pleasure in the ultimate outcome;

(c) to achieve thereby not only the transition from primitive instinctual to sublimated pleasure, together with a high grade of neutralization of the energy employed, but equally, the transition from the pleasure principle to the reality principle, a development which is essential for success in work during latency, adolescence, and in maturity.

Derived from the line from the body to the toy and from play to work and based predominantly on its later stages are a number of allied activities which are significant for personality development, such as daydreaming, games, and hobbies.

Daydreaming: When toys and the activities connected with them fade into the background, the wishes formerly put into action with the help of material objects, i.e., fulfilled in play, can be spun out imaginatively in the form of conscious daydreams, a fantasy activity which may persist until adolescence, and far beyond it.

[7] What is attempted here is not a definition of work with all its social as well as psychological implications, but merely a description of the advances in ego development and drive control which seem to be the necessary forerunners of any individual's acquisition of the capacity to work.

Games: Games derive their origin from the imaginative group activities of the oedipal period (see stage 4, d, iii) from which they develop into the symbolic and highly formalized expression of trends toward aggressive attack, defense, competition, etc. Since they are governed by inflexible rules to which the individual participant has to submit, they cannot be entered successfully by any child before some adaptation to reality and some frustration tolerance have been acquired and, naturally, not before stage 3 on the developmental line toward companionship has been reached.

Games may require equipment (as distinct from toys). Since this is in many instances of symbolic phallic, i.e., masculine-aggressive, significance, it is highly valued by the child.

In many competitive games the child's own body and the body skills themselves play the role of indispensable tools.

Proficiency and pleasure in games are thus a complex achievement, dependent on contributions from many areas of the child's personality, such as the endowment and intactness of the motor apparatus; a positive cathexis of the body and its skills; acceptance of companionship and group life; positive employment of controlled aggression in the service of ambition, etc. Correspondingly, functioning in this area is open to an equally large number of disturbances which may result from developmental difficulties and inadequacies in any of these areas, as well as from the phase-determined inhibitions of anal aggression and phallic-oedipal masculinity.

Hobbies: Halfway between play and work is the place of the hobbies, which have certain aspects in common with both activities. With play they share a number of characteristics:

(a) of being undertaken for purposes of pleasure with comparative disregard for external pressures and necessities;

(b) of pursuing displaced, i.e., sublimated, aims, but aims which are not too far removed from the gratification of either erotic or aggressive drives;

(c) of pursuing these aims with a combination of unmodified drive energies plus energies in various states and degrees of neutralization.

With working attitudes as described above, the hobbies share the important feature of a preconceived plan being undertaken in a reality-adapted way and carried on over a considerable period of time, if necessary in the face of external difficulties and frustrations.

Hobbies appear for the first time at the beginning of the latency period (collecting, spotting, specializing of interests), undergo any number of changes of content, but may persist as this specific form of activity throughout life.

Correspondence Between Developmental Lines

If we examine our notions of average normality in detail, we find that we expect a fairly close correspondence between growth on the individual developmental lines. In clinical terms this means that, to be a harmonious personality, a child who has reached a specific stage in the sequence toward emotional maturity (for example, object constancy), should have attained also corresponding levels in his growth toward bodily independence (such as bladder and bowel control, loosening of the tie between food and mother), in the lines toward companionship, constructive play, etc. We maintain this expectation of a norm even though reality presents us with many examples to the contrary. There are numerous children, undoubtedly, who show a very irregular pattern in their growth. They may stand high on some levels (such as maturity of emotional relations, bodily independence, etc.) while lagging behind in others (such as play where they continue to cling to transitional objects, cuddly toys, or development of companionship where they persist in treating contemporaries as disturbances or inanimate objects). Some children are well developed toward secondary thought, speech, play, work, community life while remaining in a state of dependency with regard to the management of their own bodily processes, etc.

Such imbalance between developmental lines causes sufficient friction in childhood to justify a closer inquiry into the circumstances which give rise to it, especially into the question how far it is determined by innate and how far by environmental reasons.

As in all similar instances, our task is not to isolate the two factors and to ascribe to each a separate field of influence, but to trace their interactions, which may be described as follows:

We assume that with all normally endowed, organically undamaged children the lines of development indicated above are included in their constitution as inherent possibilities. What endowment lays down for them on the side of the id are, obviously, the maturational sequences in the development of libido and aggression; on the side of the ego, less obviously and less well studied, certain innate tendencies toward organization, defense, and structuralization; perhaps also, though we know less still about this, some given quantitative differences of emphasis on progress in one direction or another. For the rest, that is, for what singles out individual lines for special promotion in development, we have to look to accidental environmental influences. In the analysis of older children and the reconstructions from adult analysis we have found these forces embodied in the parents' personalities, their actions and ideals, the family atmosphere, the impact of the cultural setting as a whole. In the analytic observation of young infants it has been demonstrated that it is the individual mother's interest and predilection which act as stimulants. In the beginning of life, at least, the infant seems to concentrate on the development along those lines which call forth most ostensibly the mother's love and approval, i.e., her spontaneous pleasure in the child's achievement and, in comparison, to neglect others where such approval is not given. This implies that activities which are acclaimed by the mother are repeated more frequently, become libidinized, and thereby stimulated into further growth.

For example, it seems to make a difference to the timing of speech development and the quality of early verbalization if a mother, for reasons of her own personality structure, makes contact with her infant not through bodily channels but through talking. Some mothers find no pleasure in the growing infant's adventurousness and bodily unruliness and have their happiest and most intimate moments when the infant smiles. We have seen at least one such mother whose infant made constant and inordinate use of smiling in his approaches to the whole environment. It is not unknown that early contact with the mother through her singing has consequences for the later attitudes to music and may promote special musical aptitudes. On the other hand, marked disinterest of the mother in the infant's body and his developing motility may result in clumsiness, lack of grace in movement, etc.

It was known in psychoanalysis, long before such infant observations, that depressive moods of the mother during the first two years after birth create in the child a tendency to depression (although this may not manifest itself until many years later). What happens is that such infants achieve their sense of unity and harmony with the depressed mother not by means of their developmental achievements but by producing the mother's mood in themselves.

All this means no more than that tendencies, inclinations, predilections (including the tendency to depression, to masochistic attitudes, etc.) which are present in all human beings can be eroticized and stimulated toward growth through forming emotional links between the child and his first object.

The disequilibrium between developmental lines which is created in this manner is not pathological as such. Moderate disharmony does no more than prepare the ground for the innumerable differences as they exist among individuals from an early date, i.e., it produces the many *variations of normality* with which we have to count.

Applications: Entry into Nursery School as an Illustration—To return to the problems and queries raised by parents which are mentioned above:

With the foregoing points in mind, the child analyst can cease to answer them on the basis of the child's chronological age, a factor which is inconclusive psychologically; or on the basis of the child's intellectual grasp of the situation, which is a one-sided view diagnostically. Instead, he can think in terms of basic psychological differences between the mature and immature and in terms of lines of development. The child's readiness to meet events such as the birth of a sibling, hospitalization, school entry, etc., is seen then as the direct outcome of his developmental progress on all the lines which have a bearing on this specific experience. If the appropriate stations have been reached, the happening will be constructive and beneficial to the child; if this is not the case, either on all or on some of the lines concerned, the child will feel bewildered and overtaxed and no effort on the part of the parents, teachers, nurses will prevent his distress, unhappiness, and sense of failure which often assume traumatic proportions.

Such a "diagnosis of the normal child" can be illustrated by a practical example, taking—as one for many—the question under which developmental circumstances a child is ready to leave his home surroundings temporarily for the first time, to give up his close proximity to the mother and enter group life in a nursery school without undue distress and with benefit to himself.

Required Status on the Line "From Dependency to Emotional Self-Reliance".—In the not-too-distant past it was assumed that a child who had reached the age of three years six months should be able to separate from his mother on the first day of entry at the outer door of the nursery school building and should adapt to the new physical surroundings, the new teacher, and the new playmates all in one morning. A blind eye was turned toward the distress of the new entrants; their crying for their mothers, their initial lack of participation and cooperation were considered of little significance. What happened under those conditions was that most children went through an initial stage of extreme unhappiness, after which they settled down to nursery school routine. Some others reversed this sequence of events. They began with a period of acquiescence and apparent enjoyment which then, to the surprise of parents and teacher, was followed a week later by intense unhappiness and a breakdown in participation. In their case, the delayed reaction was due to a slower intellectual grasp of the external circumstances. What seems important with regard to both types of reaction is the fact that, formerly, no thought was given to the way the individual children were affected internally by their respective periods of distress and desolation, and—more important still—that the latter were accepted as inevitable.

As seen from our present point of view, they are inevitable only if developmental considerations are neglected. If, at nursery school entry, a child of whatever chronological age still finds himself at stage one or two of this developmental line, separation from home and mother, even for short periods, is not age adequate and offends against his most vital need; protest and suffering under these conditions are legitimate. If he has reached *object constancy* at least (stage 3), separation from the mother is less upsetting, he is ready to reach out to new people and to accept new ventures and adventures. Even then, the change has to be introduced gradually, in small doses, the period of independence must not be too long, and, in the beginning, return to the mother should be open to his choice.

Required Status on the Line Toward Bodily Independence.—Some children are extremely uncomfortable in nursery school because they find themselves unable to enjoy any food or drink which they are given, or to use the lavatory for urination or defecation. This does not depend on the type of food offered or on the lavatory arrangements themselves, although the child himself usually uses their strangeness as a rationalization. The real difference between the child's function or disfunction in these respects is the developmental one. On the eating line at least stage 4 of self-feeding should have been reached; on the line to bowel and bladder control, the attitude toward cleanliness belonging to stage 3.

Required Status on the Line Toward Companionship.—Any child will be a disturbing element in the nursery school group, and unhappy in himself, before he has attained the stage where other children can be related to at least as helpmates in play (stage 3). He will be a constructive, leading member in the group as soon as he learns to accept other children as partners in their own right, a step which enables him also to form real friendships (stage 4). In fact, if development in this respect is at a lower level, he either should not be accepted in nursery school or, if he has entered, he should be permitted to interrupt attendance.

Required Status on the Line from Play to Work.—The child usually enters nursery school at the beginning of the stage when "play material serves ego activities and the fantasies underlying them" (stage 4), and he climbs up the ladder of development gradually, through the sequence of toys and materials, until at the end of nursery school life he reaches the beginning of "work", which is a necessary prerequisite for entry into elementary school. In this respect it is the task of the teacher throughout to match the child's needs for occupation and expression with the material offered and not to create a sense either of boredom or of failure by lagging too far behind or by anticipating needs before they arise.

So far as the child's ability to *behave* adequately in nursery school is concerned, this depends not on any of the developmental lines described, but in general on the interrelations between his id and ego.

Somewhere in her mind, even the most tolerant nursery school teacher carries the image of the "ideal" nursery child who exhibits no outward signs of impatience or restlessness; who asks for what he wants instead of grabbing it; who can wait for his turn; who is satisfied with his fair share; who does not throw temper tantrums but can stand disappointments. Even if no single child will ever display all these forms of behavior, they will be found in the group, in one or the other pupil, with regard to one or the other aspect of daily life. In analytic terms this means that, at this period, the children are on the point of learning how to master their affects and impulses instead of being at the mercy of them. The developmental tools at their disposal in this respect belong above all to ego growth: advance from primary process to secondary process functioning, i.e., to be able to interpolate thought, reasoning, and anticipation of the future between wish and action directed toward fulfillment (Hartmann, 1947); advance from the pleasure principle to the reality principle. What comes to the help of the child from the side of the id is the age-adequate—probably organically determined—lessening in the urgency of the drives.

No young child should be expected to maintain his best level of performance or behavior for any length of time. But such temporary declines in the level of functioning, even if they occur easily and frequently, do not affect a child's eligibility for nursery school entrance.

THE STAGES OF THE INTELLECTUAL DEVELOPMENT OF THE CHILD

JEAN PIAGET

The voluminous writings of Piaget (1928, 1929, 1930, 1932a, 1932b, 1952, 1954) have only recently had their deserved welcome and impact on American psychology, child psychiatry, and education. The remarkable range of his investigations and contributions—including developmental aspects of language, perception, moral standards, motor behavior, intelligence, and cognition—suggests that the frequent designations of Piaget as a "cognitive theorist" are perhaps too narrow. His ultimate goal has been to create and elaborate an empirical genetic epistemology—concepts and data detailing how man comes to know his world, how his thought processes and interactions with the world gradually evolve, how he achieves approximate "correspondences" between his inner picture and the actual structure of reality. Much that is central to Piaget's work is visible in this selection—the strong adaptational orientation, the motor-action derived origins of cognition, the concept of the organism passing through an invariant series of cognitive stages (only loosely tied to ages), and the mechanisms of transition between those stages.

Piaget's typical methodological approaches, while attractive to clinicians, have raised disquiet among, and have come under attack by, less naturalistic American investigators, those accustomed to more experimental, statistical approaches. Yet his work has stimulated a remarkable outpouring of research, much of which has been confirmatory. Piaget is not a theorist of personality development; he leaves to others concern regarding the implications of his work for psychopathology. Recent years have seen exciting achievements in interrelating his concepts with psychoanalytic developmental theory (Wolff, 1960; Gouin-Décarie, 1965) and applying them to child psychopathology (Anthony, 1956, 1957).

A consideration of the stages of the development of intelligence should be preceded by asking the question, What is intelligence? Unfortunately,

Reprinted with permission from *Bulletin of the Menninger Clinic,* 26, 1962, pp. 120–128, we find ourselves confronted by a great number of definitions. For Claparède (1917b), intelligence is an adaptation to new situations. When a situation is new, when there are no reflexes, when there are no habits to rely on, then the subject is obliged to search for something new. That is to say, Claparède defines intelligence as groping, as feeling one's way, trial-and-error behavior. We find this trial-and-error behavior in all levels of intelligence, even at the superior level, in the form of hypothesis testing. As far as I am concerned, this definition is too vague, because trial and error occurs in the formation of habits and also in the earliest established reflexes: when a newborn baby learns to suck.

Karl Buhler (1942) defines intelligence as an act of immediate comprehension; that is to say, an insight. Buhler's definition is also very precise, but it seems to me too narrow. I know that when a mathematician solves a problem, he ends by having an insight, but up to that moment he feels, or gropes for, his way; and to say that the trial-and-error behavior is not intelligent and that intelligence starts only when he finds the solution to the problem, seems a very narrow definition. I would, therefore, propose to define intelligence, not by a static criterion as in previous definitions, but by the direction that intelligence follows in its evolution, and then I would define intelligence as a form of equilibration, or forms of equilibration, toward which all cognitive functions lead.

But I must first define equilibration. Equilibration in my vocabulary is not an exact and automatic balance, as it would be in Gestalt theory; I define equilibration principally as a compensation for an external disturbance.

When there is an external disturbance, the subject succeeds in compensating for this by an activity. The maximum equilibration is thus the maximum of the activity, and not a state of rest. It is a mobile equilibration, and not an immobile one. So equilibration is defined as compensation; compensation is the annulling of a transformation by an inverse transformation. The compensation which intervenes in equilibration implies the fundamental idea of reversibility, and this reversibility is precisely what characterizes the operations of the intelligence. An operation is an internalized action, but it is also a reversible action. But an operation is never isolated; it is always subordinated to other operations; it is part of a more inclusive structure. Consequently, we define intelligence in terms of operations, coordination of operations.

Take, for example, an operation like addition: Addition is a material action, the action of reuniting. On the other hand, it is a reversible action, because addition may be compensated by subtraction. Yet addition leads to a structure of the whole. In the case of numbers, it will be the structure that the mathematicians call a "group." In the case of addition of classes which intervene in the logical structure it will be a more simple structure that we will call a grouping, and so on.

Consequently, the study of the stages of intelligence is first a study of the formation of operational structures. I shall define every stage by a structure of a whole, with the possibility of its integration into succeeding stages, just as it was prepared by preceding stages. Thus, I shall distinguish four great stages, or four great periods, in the development of intelligence: first, the sensori-motor period before the appearance of language; second, the period from about two to seven years of age, the preoperational period which precedes real operations; third, the period from seven to 12 years of age, a period of concrete operations (which refers to concrete objects); and finally after 12 years of age, the period of formal operations, or positional operations.

Sensorimotor Stage

Before language develops, there is behavior that we can call intelligent. For example, when a baby of 12 months or more wants an object which is too far from him, but which rests on a carpet or blanket, and he pulls it to get to the object, this behavior is an act of intelligence. The child uses an intermediary, a means to get to his goal. Also, getting to an object by means of pulling a string when the object is tied to the string, or when the child uses a stick to get the object, are acts of intelligence. They demonstrate in the sensorimotor period a certain number of stages which go from simple reflexes, from the formation of the first habits, up to the coordination of means and goals.

Remarkable in this sensori-motor stage of intelligence is that there are already structures. Sensorimotor intelligence rests mainly on actions, on movements and perceptions without language, but these actions are coordinated in a relatively stable way. They are coordinated under what we may call schemata of action. These schemata can be generalized in actions and are applicable to new situations. For example, pulling a carpet to bring an object within reach constitutes a schema which can be generalized to other situations when another object rests on a support. In other words, a schema supposes an incorporation of new situations into the previous schemata, a sort of continuous assimilation of new objects or new situations to the actions already schematized. For example, I presented to one of my children an object completely new to him—a box of cigarettes, which is not a usual toy for a baby. The child took the object, looked at it, put it in his mouth, shook it, then took it with one hand and hit it with the other hand, then rubbed it on the edge of the crib, then shook it again, and gave the impression of trying to see if there were noise. This behavior is a way of exploring the object, of trying to understand it by assimilating it to schemata already known. The child behaves in this situation as he will later in Binet's famous vocabulary test, when he defines by usage, saying, for instance, that a spoon is for eating, and so on.

But in the presence of a new object, even without knowing how to talk, the child knows how to assimilate, to incorporate this new object into each of his already developed schemata which function as practical concepts. Here is a structuring of intelligence. Most important in this structuring is the base, the point of departure of all subsequent operational constructions. At the sensorimotor level, the child constructs the schema of the permanent object.

The knowledge of the permanent object starts at this point. The child is not convinced at the beginning that when an object disappears from view, he can find it again. One can verify by tests that object permanence is not yet developed at this stage. But there is there the beginning of a subsequent fundamental idea which starts being constructed at the senso-ri-motor level. This is also true of the construction of the ideas of space, of time, of causality. What is being done at the sensorimotor level concerning all the foregoing ideas will constitute the substructure of the subsequent, fully achieved ideas of permanent objects, of space, of time, of causality.

In the formation of these substructures at the sensorimotor level, it is very interesting to note the beginning of a *reversibility,* not in thought, since there is not yet representation in thought, but in action itself. For example, the formation of the conception of space at the sensori-motor stage leads to an amazing decentration if one compares the conception of space at the first weeks of the development with that at one and one-half to two years of age. In the beginning there is not one space which contains all the objects, including the child's body itself; there is a multitude of spaces which are not coordinated: there are the buccal space, the tactilo-kinesthetic space, the visual and auditory spaces; each is separate, and each is centered essentially on the body of the subject and on actions. After a few months, however, after a kind of Copernican evolution, there is a total reversal, a decentration such that space becomes homogeneous, a one-and-only space that envelops the others. Then space becomes a container that envelops all objects, including the body itself; and after that, space is mainly coordinated in a structure, a coordination of positions and displacements, and these constitute what the geometricians call a "group"; that is to say, precisely a reversible system. One may move from A to B, and may come back from B to A; there is the possibility of returning, of reversibility. There is also the possibility of making detours and combinations which give a clue to what the subsequent operations will be when thought will supersede the action itself.

Pre-Operational Stage

From one and one-half to two years of age, a fundamental transformation in the evolution of intelligence takes place in the appearance of symbolic functions. Every action of intelligence consists in manipulating significations (or meanings) and whenever (or wherever) there are significations, there are on the one hand the "significants" and on the other the "significates." This is true in the sensorimotor level, but the only significants that intervene there are perceptual signs or signals (as in conditioning) which are undifferentiated in regard to the significate; for example, a perceptual cue, like distance, which will be a cue for the size of the distant object, or the apparent size of an object, which will be the cue for the distance of the object. There, perhaps, both indices are different aspects of the same reality, but they are not yet differentiated significants. At the age of one and one-half to two years a new class of significants arises, and these significants are differentiated in regard to their significates. These differentiations can be called symbolic function. The appearance of symbols in a children's game is an example of the appearance of new significants. At the sensorimotor level the games are nothing but exercises; now they become symbolic play, a play of fiction; these games consist in representing something by means of something else. Another example is the beginning of delaying imitation, an imitation that takes place not in the presence of the original object but in its absence, and which consequently constitutes a kind of symbolization or mental image.

At the same time that symbols appear, the child acquires language; that is to say, there is the acquisition of another phase of differentiated significants, verbal signals, or collective signals. This symbolic function then brings great flexibility into the field of intelligence. Intelligence up to this point refers to the immediate space which surrounds the child and to the present perceptual situation; thanks to language, and to the symbolic functions, it becomes possible to invoke objects which are not present perceptually, to reconstruct the past, or to make projects, plans for the future, to think of objects not present but very distant in space—in short, to span spatio-temporal distances much greater than before.

But this new stage, the stage of representation of thought which is superimposed on the sensorimotor stage, is not a simple extension of what was referred to at the previous level. Before being able to prolong, one must in fact reconstruct, because behavior in words is a different thing from representing something in thought. When a child knows how to move around in his house or garden by following the different successive cues around him, it does not mean that he is capable of representing or reproducing the total configuration of his house or his garden. To be able to represent, to reproduce something, one must be capable of reconstructing this group of displacements, but at a new level, that of the representation of the thought.

I recently made an amusing test with Nel Szeminska. We took children of four to five years of age who went to school by themselves and came back home by themselves, and asked them if they could trace the way to school and back for us, not in design, which would be too difficult, but like a construction game, with concrete objects. We found that they were not capable of representation; there was a kind of motor-memory, but it was not yet a representation of a whole—the group of displacements had not yet been reconstructed on the plan of the representation of thought. In other words, the operations were not yet formed. There are representations which are internalized actions, but actions still centered on the body itself, on the activity itself. These representations do not allow the objective combinations, the decentrated combinations that the operations would. The actions are centered on the body. I used to call this egocentrism; but it is better thought of as lack of reversibility of action.

At this level, the most certain sign of the absence of operations which appear at the next stage is the absence of the knowledge of conservation. In fact, an operation refers to the transformation of reality. The transformation is not of the whole, however; something constant is always untransformed. If you pour a liquid from one glass to another there is transformation; the liquid changes form, but its liquid property stays constant. So at the pre-operational level, it is significant from the point of view of the operations of intelligence that the child has not yet a knowledge of conservation. For example, in the case of liquid, when the child pours it from one bottle to the other, he thinks that the quantity of the liquid has changed. When the level of the liquid changes, the child thinks the quantity has changed—there is more or less in the second glass than in the first.

And if you ask the child where the larger quantity came from, he does not answer this question. What is important for the child is that perceptually it is not the same thing any more. We find this absence of conservation in all object properties, in the length, surface, quantity, and weight of things.

This absence of conservation indicates essentially that at this stage the child reasons from the configuration. Confronted with a transformation, he does not reason from the transformation itself; he starts from the initial configuration, then sees the final configuration, compares the two but forgets the transformation, because he does not know how to reason about it. At this stage the child is still reasoning on the basis of what he sees because there is no conservation. He is able to master this problem only when the operations are formed, and these operations, which we have already sensed at the sensorimotor level, are not formed until around seven to eight years of age. At that age the elementary problems of conservation are solved, because the child reasons on the basis of the transformation per se, and this requires a manipulation of the operation. The ability to pass from one stage to the other and be able to come back to the point of departure, to manipulate the reversible operations, which appears around seven to eight years of age, is limited when compared with the operations of the superior level only in the sense that they are concrete. That is to say, the child can manipulate the operations only when he manipulates the object concretely.

Stage of Concrete Operations

The first operations of the manipulation of objects, the concrete operations, deal with logical classes and with logical relations, or the number. But these operations do not deal yet with propositions, or hypotheses, which do not appear until the last stage.

Let me exemplify these concrete operations: the simplest operation is concerned with classifying objects according to their similarity and their difference. This is accomplished by including the subclasses within larger and more general classes, a process that implies inclusion. This classification, which seems very simple at first, is not acquired until around seven to eight years of age. Before that, at the pre-operational level, we do not find logical inclusion. For example, if you show a child at the pre-operational level a bouquet of flowers of which one half is daisies and the other half other flowers and you ask him if in this bouquet there are more flowers or more daisies, you are confronted with this answer, which seems extraordinary until it is analyzed: The child cannot tell you whether there are more flowers than daisies; either he reasons on the basis of the whole or of the part. He cannot understand that the part is complementary to the rest, and he says there are more daisies than flowers, or as many daisies as flowers, without understanding this inclusion of the subclass, the daisies, in the class of flowers. It is only around seven to eight years of age that a child is capable of solving a problem of inclusion.

Another system of operation that appears around seven to eight years of age is the operation of serializing; that is, to arrange objects according to their size, or their progressive weight. It is also a structure of the whole, like the classification which rests on concrete operations, since it consists of manipulating concrete objects. At this level there is also the construction of numbers, which is, too, a synthesis of classification and seriation. In numbers, as in classes, we have inclusion, and also a serial order, as in serializing. These elementary operations constitute structures of wholes. There is no class without classification; there is no symmetric relation without serialization; there is not a number independent of the series of numbers. But the structures of these wholes are simple structures, groupings in the case of classes and relations, which are already groups in the case of numbers, but very elementary structures compared to subsequent structures.

Stage of Formal Operations

The last stage of development of intelligence is the stage of formal operations or propositional operations. At about eleven to twelve years of age we see great progress; the child becomes capable of reasoning not only on the basis of objects, but also on the basis of hypotheses, or of propositions.

An example which neatly shows the difference between reasoning on the basis of propositions and reasoning on the basis of concrete objects comes from Burt's tests. Burt asked children of different ages to compare the colors of the hair of three girls: Edith is fairer than Susan, Edith is darker than Lilly; who is the darkest of the three? In this question there is seriation, not of concrete objections, but of verbal statements which supposes a more complicated mental manipulation. This problem is rarely solved before the age of 12.

Here a new class of operations appear which is superimposed on the operations of logical class and number, and these operations are the propositional operations. Here, compared to the previous stage, are fundamental changes. It is not simply that these operations refer to language, and then to operations with concrete objects, but that these operations have much richer structures.

The first novelty is a combinative structure; like mathematical structures, it is a structure of a system which is superimposed on the structure of simple classifications or seriations which are not themselves systems, because they do not involve a combinative system. A combinative system permits the grouping in flexible combinations of each element of the system with any other element of that system. The logic of propositions supposes such a combinative system. If children of different ages are shown a number of colored disks and asked to combine each color with each other two by two, or three by three, we find these combinative operations are not accessible to the child at the stage of concrete operations. The child is capable of some combination, but not of all the possible combinations. After the age of 12, the child can find a method to make all the possible combinations. At the same time he acquires both the logic of mathematics and the logic of propositions, which also supposes a method of combining.

A second novelty in the operations of propositions is the appearance of a structure which constitutes a group of four transformations. Hitherto there were two reversibilities: reversibility by inversion, which consists of annulling, or canceling; and reversibility which we call reciprocity, leading not to cancellation, but to another combination. Reciprocity is what we find in the field of a relation. If A equals B, by reciprocity B equals A. If A is smaller than B, by reciprocity B is larger than A. At the level of propositional operations a new system envelops these two forms of reversibility. Here the structure combines inversion and reversibility in one single but larger and more complicated structure. It allows the acquisition of a series of fundamental operational schemata for the development of intelligence, which schemata are not possible before the constitution of this structure.

It is around the age of 12 that the child, for example, starts to understand in mathematics the knowledge of proportions, and becomes capable of reasoning by using two systems of reference at the same time. For example, if you advance the position of a board and a car moving in opposite directions, in order to understand the movement of the board in relation to the movement of the car and to other movement, you need a system of four transformations. The same is true in regard to proportions, to problems in mathematics or physics, or to other logical problems.

The four principal stages of the development of intelligence of the child progress from one stage to the other by the construction of new operational structures, and these structures constitute the fundamental instrument of the intelligence of the adult.

THE RELATION OF AFFECTIVITY TO INTELLIGENCE IN THE MENTAL DEVELOPMENT OF THE CHILD

JEAN PIAGET

It is incontestable that affect plays an essential role in the functioning of intelligence. Without affect there would be no interest, no need, no motivation; and consequently, questions or problems would never be posed, and there would be no intelligence. Affectivity is a necessary condition in the constitution of intelligence but, in my opinion, not a sufficient one.

We can consider in two very different ways the relations between affectivity and intelligence. The very essence of intelligence is the progressive formation of operational or preoperational structures. As for the relation between intelligence and affect, we can postulate that affect does, or may cause the formation of cognitive structures. Many authors have presented such a thesis, for example, Odier (1956) in his study of the relations between psychoanalysis and my studies in child psychology. Odier maintained that the schema of the permanent object, the discoveries that the baby makes concerning the permanence of the object when it disappears from his visual field, is caused by feelings, by object relations. That is to say, it is due to the affective relations of the child with the object or the person involved. In other words, the affective relations of the child with the mother-object, or other persons, are responsible for the formation of a cognitive structure.

The French psychologist Wallon thinks that emotion is a source of knowledge. A student of Wallon, Malrieux, went as far as to say that the estimation of distance, or the perception of distance, is due to the desire to reach distant objects, and not to the distance of the objects.

A second interpretation is that affect explains the acceleration or retardation of the formation of structures—acceleration in the case of interest, and need; retardation when affective states are obstacles to intellectual development, as in the excellent studies by Spitz on hospitalism. In this interpretation, affectivity explains the acceleration or the retardation, but

Reprinted with permission of Jean Piaget from *Bulletin of the Menninger Clinic,* 26, 1962, pp. 129–137, copyright by the Menninger Foundation.

not the cause of structure formation. Although a necessary condition, affectivity is not a sufficient condition in structure formation which, in cognition, is autonomous. For example, in an arithmetical structure like 7 plus 5 equal 12, the understanding of the equality may be retarded by certain affective situations, or it may be accelerated where interest is involved. In either case, the subject will end by accepting that 7 plus 5 equal 12. This shows a structure independent of affect, even though its construction may be motivated, and by consequence accelerated or retarded, by feelings, interest, and affect.

Affect can lead to errors, and because of certain affective troubles, a child may accept for a moment that 7 plus 5 equal 11, or 13 and not 12. But this is not an equilibrated structure. Even if affect leads to momentary deviations, purely cognitive factors will eventually correct such a structure, independently of affect.

Of the two interpretations, I choose the second and I will try to demonstrate genetically that affectivity may lead to acceleration or retardation, but it is not the cause of the formation of cognitive structures. Considering first whether affectivity precedes the functions of the cognitive structures, I shall show that the stages of affectivity correspond exactly to the stages of the development of the structures; that is to say, there is correspondence, and not succession.

First we must agree that at no level, at no stage, even in the adult, can we find a behavior or a state which is purely cognitive without affect nor a purely affective state without a cognitive element involved. There is no such thing as a purely cognitive state.

For example, take the most refined form of thought: a mathematician who demonstrates a new theorem. As much as such behavior is intellectual from one aspect, it is necessarily affective from another. If the mathematician spends his time with it, it is because it interests him; he gets pleasure out of it, he feels enthusiasm for it, even passion, and this is affective. In working, he has to direct his effort; he can accelerate his demonstration by greater effort, or, on the contrary, feel fatigued, or slow down. This regulation of his work is affective and when he finishes, he will feel joy in case of success, sorrow or depression in case of failure.

There are no acts of intelligence, even of practical intelligence, without interest at the point of departure and affective regulation during the entire course of an action, without joy at success, or sorrow at failure. Likewise, at the perceptual level we have affective motivations. What we perceive is a function of attention regulation, which is pretty much motivated by needs and interests.

Just as there is no purely cognitive state, there is no purely affective state, no matter how elementary it may be. A state of emotion, for example—and emotion is one of the most elementary forms of affect—supposes a discrimination and, therefore, a cognitive element. In sympathy, friendship or love, there are elements of discrimination and mutual comprehension. The instincts necessarily include cognitive elements. Tinbergen and Lorenz have found evidence, through studies of instinctive behavior, of perceptual signals, or innate releasing mechanisms, which are cognitive.

Thus, affectivity does not precede knowledge, and knowledge never precedes affectivity. They are parallel to each other. What is, then, the relation between the two? Claparède (1933) said that in behavior, it is affect that fixes the goals, while intelligence supplies the means. This is certainly true in general, but there is also a comprehension of the goal; and in the means there is also the value of the means, which is not only cognitive, but affective.

Janet (1937) proposed another theory. In every behavior we must distinguish the primary action and the secondary action. The primary action is the regulation, which Janet calls secondary action; that is to say, the regulation of the primary action, which is actually the regulation of forces present at the moment, reinforces them or puts a brake to them according to success or failure. Janet calls this regulation the economy of the action. On the one hand there is the subject-object relation, the structure of the action; on the other hand there is affectivity, which would be the economy, or the regulating of the forces.

Lewin (1935, 1936, 1948) makes an analogous interpretation, but in different words. His theory of the total field, which includes affectivity as well as cognitive functions, is analogous to that of Gestalt theory: The perceptual field includes on the one hand a structure, the perceptual or cognitive elements, and on the other hand a force, which is the affective element.

All the authors agree that in all behavior the structure is cognitive, and the force, or the economy, is affective. Therefore, affect cannot be the cause of a cognitive structure, any more than intelligence can be the cause of affect, because a structure is not the cause of this energy, this force, and vice versa. Between the two is a relation of correspondence, and not of causality. This relationship I will examine in four stages starting with the sensori-motor stage.

From the cognitive point of view, the sensori-motor stage is characterized by a clear evolution in the sense of decentration, a complete inversion of what goes on at the beginning with what goes on toward the end of that period.

The *initial state* is characterized by the absence of permanent objects. The universe consists of a series of momentary and moving pictures. There is not one space, but a series of spaces centered on the body of the child, and there is no causality between objects, but a causality by action that is neither objectified nor localized in space. The *final state* is a universe of permanent objects, of one space, one causality between objects.

A parallel decentration takes place from the affective point of view. Affectively, if we take what the psychoanalysts say, is at the beginning centered on the body itself. During the oral stage and anal stage, there is a focusing of affectivity on certain regions of the body, then on activity in general; psychoanalysts call this focusing primary narcissism. Then there is decentration only in the sense of object relations, in the choice of the object, in the fixation of affectivity on the mother. Therefore, also, from the affective point of view, a decentration, an inversion of direction occurs; this is an astonishing parallelism to cognitive development.

This crucial stage, which cognitively is the construction of the permanent object, and which affectively is the constitution of object relations, has been studied experimentally by Gouin-Décarie (1965). Her study deals not with three children, as my own observations have, but with 90 babies from the first month to about two years of age. She has constructed a scale of 10 items concerning object relations, and also a scale concerning the construction of the permanent object based on the developmental stages as I have described them.

At the beginning of the first of the initial stages, from the cognitive point of view, there is no object for the child. A child of four and a half to five months starts grasping what he sees. You give him an object, and the child grasps it; then if you cover the object with a handkerchief at the moment when the child's hand is already moving in the direction of the object, he pulls his hand back as if the object did not exist anymore, as if by disappearing from view it had vanished.

It is there that we have our point of departure. From there we find an intermediate level which allows us to confirm this interpretation about the absence of the object. We find that if you put a baby between two screens and hide the object under the left screen at the moment he is trying to get the object, the child looks there for it; then if you hide the object under the right screen, the child, instead of looking under the right screen, will look again under the left. That is because it is not yet a localized object;

there is a beginning of searching, a beginning of permanence, which is only the continuation of the action, without localization.

Finally, there is a third level where the object is looked for in connection with its displacements and its localization.

These three levels, which I described, Madame Décarie found again in an astonishing way, and always in succession. That is, behavior of the second level is never reached without all the previous behavior from the first to the second level having been reached. There is, then, a constant succession, without fluctuation. It is, however, essential to note that this construction of the object is joined at the same time with that of space, of time, of causality. There is a solidarity of development in the construction of these four concepts as each one is constructed jointly with the others. The construction of the object is joined with that of space because the object is not really constituted except when it is localized, and to be localized it must be situated in relation to a group of displacements; joined with time because these displacements are made successively, which require an objective order of successions in order to find the object; and joined with causality because there is then a causality objectified and localized in space.

Gouin-Décarie also studied the stages of object relations according to Freudian theory. She found successive stages beginning with a confusion of the ego and the external world, in a dualistic universe, as Baldwin would say. Then she found more precise beginnings of object relations, beginning with interest in a smiling face, or different smiling faces, as Spitz has shown, and finally object relations, as such. Here, again, Madame Décarie distinguishes a certain number of stages, but the striking thing is that she finds no consistent successions; there is a statistical regularity, but with fluctuations; this is understandable because the stages, as I have conceived them, are primarily defined in terms of a successive integration. In Freudian theory, a stage is characterized by a dominant feature. In the oral stage there is no reason why there should not be anal behavior, and vice versa. In cognitive behavior, a progressive integration occurs with a consequent succession and not simply a dominance.

So, what is the relation between the construction of the cognitive object on the one hand and the object relation on the other? There is a parallelism, but intelligence cannot explain affect and vice versa. My hypothesis is that it is impossible to explain affect by intelligence, that is, we cannot say intelligence is the cause of affectivity; and on the other hand, it seems impossible to explain the construction of the permanent object by the feelings as such. Feelings explain the interest for the object, but the structure of the object is related to space, time, and causality. Can we maintain that these four ideas—object, time, space, causality—are engendered by the interest or the feeling for the external object? This would be much too simple to maintain. The facts show two parallel structures, the affective aspect and the cognitive aspect which are complementary, but without the one being the cause of the other.

In both structures there is decentration, but a decentration which is at the same time cognitive and affective, and we cannot consider one of these two aspects the cause of the other. There are also retardations and accelerations in both. The research of Spitz on hospitalized infants (1945, 1946c) has shown the necessity of a normal affective relation between mother and child. When such a relationship does not exist, intellectual development does not take place. This does not mean that one is the cause of the other. If there is no interest for the object, there will be a retardation of the intellectual structures, because there is no motivation. So, affectivity is a necessary condition for, but not a cause of, intellectual development. Development of cognitive and affective structures are complementary and parallel in this stage, but there is no evidence of causality between them.

From the point of view of intelligence, the second stage has three essential characteristics: First, the appearance of symbolic function and of representation. Second, thought is tied partially to language and rests on the interindividual communications; it is not strictly individual any more. Third, there are still no operations, and consequently, no conservation.

From the affective point of view, we find corresponding characteristics: First, the appearance of representative affects; that is to say, affects that are tied both to interindividual values, and values that subsist outside of the perceptual field, and by consequence are attached to representations. For example, sympathy and antipathy are feelings based on mutual value judgments between individuals, that subsist beyond the immediate perceptual contact; they subsist even in the absence of the individuals. It is the same with feelings based upon self-evaluation, for example, the feelings of superiority or inferiority, which are, of course, individual, but are always related to comparisons with other individuals, and are consequently interindividual. The feelings of the parental complexes, the oedipus complex, the superego, influence the affective life during its entirety, as psychoanalysis has shown. The question is how these infantile feelings can influence the rest of the affective development of the individual. Classical psychoanalysis explained this by saying it was essentially feelings attached to unconscious representations conserved in the unconscious which made possible subsequent identifications. Would it not be simpler to suppose that the element that insures the subsequent permanence of these feelings is simply an element of reaction, that we have to do here with schemata of reaction, like the sensori-motor schemata, but more complex, since the child has already reached the level of representation, schemata about objects or persons?

In this stage, schemata of objects and of persons exist constantly in the cognitive reactions of the child: for example, the schemata of reactions we have acquired in connection with our parents–schemata of submission, obedience, or revolt, with all the intermediate feelings. These schemata are always both affective and cognitive at the same time. The schemata related to objects are connected to the ego with action and have both an affective and cognitive aspect; but the schemata related to persons also have both a cognitive and affective aspect, since persons are centers of causality and are sources of all kinds of cognitive ideas as well as of feelings. In that case, the permanence of infantile feelings would be due simply to the permanence of the schemata, and would not necessarily be unconscious representations of feelings that are being conserved as such. The permanence would be insured by the schemata, and every time a situation similar to the one that had been experienced appeared, there would be a reformation of similar feelings as a function of the schemata; for example, submission to or revolt against a teacher who resembled one's father–the permanence in this case being essentially a permanence of reaction more than a representative of content or feelings preserved in the unconscious as such.

The great problem is knowing if there exists in the field of feelings something that corresponds to conservation in the cognitive field, and mainly, if there is something that corresponds to reversible operations. An operation is a reversible action that transforms reality while conserving one of the aspects of this reality. In the affective field, we find the equivalent of operational structures and consequently conservation, but we find it in a particular section of affective life: moral sentiments. Moral feelings seem to pertain essentially to a conservation of values by a process analogous to what the logical structure is to the cognitive field. But transposed in terms of affectivity, this process is the obligation, the moral obligation, equivalent to the logical structure, which imposes values instead of imposing relations of verification, as if true in the cognitive field. The moral values in this hypothesis would consist of a conservation of values. So in the second stage, which is preoperational from the cognitive point of view—and where consequently there is still neither conservation nor operations—what is there from the point of moral feelings?

Moral feelings are well described by psychoanalysts as a function of the superego. Pierre Bodel spoke of them in different words, as the respect of the child for the adult, a unilateral respect which makes the child abide by the discipline imposed by the adult. These feelings exist in the second stage, but we find pure conservation of them only in the subsequent stage. For example, when you examine the moral feeling of a six- to seven-year-old child, you find that he is perfectly sensible to certain orders and rules imposed by the parents, and shows the beginning of moral feelings; but when the parents are gone, these rules or orders are not obeyed. There is no conservation of these orders when there is no material control. What we find mostly is that orders imposed and accepted at this level are not yet generalized.

Long ago I studied the moral judgment of the child, the ideas a child has about lying. The child very early accepts the order not to lie, that he must tell the truth, but he accepts it without any kind of generalization. When I asked children younger than seven to eight years if it were permissible to lie to playmates, and especially if it were worse to lie to peers than to adults, I found a great difference between a child of the pre-operational level and a child older than eight. Children about seven or eight will tell you that it is not permitted to lie to anybody, including their peers; and when you ask them if it is worse to lie to a peer or to an adult, they will say that it is worse to lie to a playmate because to them one is never forced to lie, while one may find himself in a difficult situation with an adult and there is nothing one can do but lie. Children of the preoperational level will tell you that to tell the truth is an obligation toward adults, but that you can lie to a peer or fool him since this was never prohibited. The instruction not to lie is accepted at the precise moment, for the precise situation in which it was given, without any kind of generalization. Thus, even in the field of moral feeling we cannot speak of conservation at the preoperational level.

At the third stage, from the cognitive point of view, a great novelty appears: the constitution of the operations of intelligence, and with these operations, the constitution of conservation imposed by the functioning of the operational structures.

Added to the preceding affective forms are new feelings in the field of moral feelings, which are equivalent to conservation in the field of intelligence. In fact, around seven to eight years of age, a morality of reciprocity appears. It is no longer the morality of obedience, an obedience that was guided by imitation, but a morality of reciprocity. Reciprocal morality is also an autonomous morality, in that it is related to transactions between partners, without subordination to superior orders. At this level the best example of a moral feeling based on reciprocity is the feeling of justice between children of the same age, between playmates; this feeling of justice is independent of the instructions and orders of adults.

Do we find, at this level of concrete operations, the equivalent of an operation in the affective field also? This might be answered by saying the equivalent is will. We can draw a narrow parallel between will and the problem of operations: The will constitutes the equivalent of the cognitive operation; but it is an operation dealing with the energetic aspect of behavior, therefore, an affective operation.

The fourth stage is the stage of the formal or propositional operations; that is to say, the stage during which the child becomes capable of reasoning on different hypotheses, on the possible, on the probable, and not just on the real, the concrete.

From the affective point of view, new feelings are added to preceding feelings and correspond to these new operational structures. They are feelings I will call ideological. These feelings are not attached to particular persons or only to material realities but attached to social realities and to essentially ideal realities, such as feelings about one's country, about humanitarianism or social ideals, and religious feelings.

It is at this last stage that we can place what we call the formation of personality. This term, personality, is often abused, and we must not confuse it with the ego. Personality is the superior synthesis of the affective life; it is the synthesis achieved at the moment when the individual becomes capable of becoming a member of the society of adults, in a society already formed, and where he plays a role that he, himself, has chosen and which allows the individual to group and regulate the whole of his values.

TRENDS IN INFANT CARE

MARTHA WOLFENSTEIN

Our field is woefully deficient in a sense of its own history. Wolfenstein is one of the few (see also Stendler, 1950; Miller and Swanson, 1958; Olden, 1952) to place current rearing practices in historical perspective. Along with Aries (1965), Mead (1954b, 1955), and Erikson (1950), she has also sought to place them in cultural perspective.

However we interpret the modifications and reversals Wolfenstein records, whether in terms of newly evolving concepts of childhood, changes in the social structure or in the history of ideas, or the return of the repressed (and/or suppressed), their implications are clear. Small wonder that we encounter parental and political confusion, uncertainty, and anxiety about appropriate child-rearing practices when our professional lore on the subject abounds with conflicting, ill-synthesized conglomerations of facts, affect-laden attitudes, values, beliefs, and goals—only some of which are conscious and capable of easy articulation. Worse yet, many professionals make little effort to clarify for themselves—much less for their "audience" of parents—the actual scientific bases for the changing winds of child-rearing doctrine. And they pay equally little attention to the probable consequences of pressing new recommendations upon parents who have been nurtured on diametrically opposite tenets.

In our culture, where we tend to believe persistently that the latest is the best, we often fail to reckon sufficiently with the residues of the past. We behave as if convictions of a year or two ago had been banished without a trace once they have been contradicted by the most recent discovery. This is particularly so with our ideas about child training. We rarely pause to look back (no one likes to recall past errors) to realize the tre-

Reprinted from *American Journal of Orthopsychiatry,* 23, 1953, pp. 120–130.

mendous changes which have taken place in these ideas in the last few decades. But overlooking does not abolish the things that are thus passed over. In all of us—parents, teachers, pediatricians, child psychologists, therapists—there are the accumulated ideas of a number of periods which have passed in rapid succession. And these ideas, insofar as they are not sorted out, cause considerable uncertainty and conflict.

In the fall of 1951, the United States Children's Bureau issued a new edition of the bulletin *Infant Care,* which first appeared in 1914 and which subsequently underwent several drastic revisions. This would seem to be a good occasion for surveying the changes which have appeared during these years in this most widely circulated child care publication.

I shall deal here mainly with the trends in severity and mildness in handling the impulses of the child, as manifested in the areas of thumb-sucking, weaning, masturbation, and bowel and bladder training. I shall not undertake to judge the correctness of the procedures recommended at one time or another. Nor shall I attempt to trace the various influences (of behaviorism, Gesell, psychoanalysis, etc.) which may be observed. What I wish to bring out are facts of social history. I should like to show the sharp contrasts between what mothers of the twenties and those of the forties were told about the best way to bring up their babies (for instance, in the twenties bowel training was to be completed by eight months; in the forties it was to be begun at eight months or later). Marked shifts have also occurred in much shorter periods of time (in 1938, the bulletin still showed a stiff cuff that could be bound on the baby's arm so that he could not bend his elbow to get his thumb in his mouth; in 1942, mothers were told that thumb-sucking is a harmless pleasure that should not be interfered with). It would require further research to determine to what extent mothers were influenced by these ideas (from mother to daughter, or the same mother with an older and a younger child). However, we may suppose that a considerable number of mothers have participated in these changing attitudes. I shall try to show that the fluctuations of opinion in this field are related not only to advances in knowledge, but also in part to unresolved conflicts in our feelings about the child's impulses.

Let me indicate first the main trends through time which we may observe in various editions of *Infant Care.* (This account is based on the editions of 1914, 1921, 1929, 1938, 1942, 1945 and 1951. I omit those of 1926 and 1940, which I was unable to obtain.) In the first period, 1914–21, the danger of the child's autoerotic impulses was acutely felt. Thumb-sucking and masturbation, if not promptly and rigorously interfered with, would grow beyond control and permanently damage the child. While he was in bed, he was to be bound down hand and foot so that he could not suck his thumb, touch his genitals, or rub his thighs together.

In the next period, 1929–38, the focus of severity shifts. Autoerotism seems less dangerous. Now it is bowel training which must be carried out with great determination as early as possible. Severity in this area increases as compared with the previous period. This is accompanied by a pervasive emphasis on regularity, doing everything by the clock. Weaning and the introduction of solid foods are also to be accomplished with great firmness, never yielding for a moment to the baby's resistance. The main danger which the baby presented at this time was that of dominating the parents. Successful child training meant winning out against the child in the struggle for domination.

In 1942–45, all this was changed. The child became remarkably harmless, in effect devoid of sexual or dominating impulses. His main active aim was to explore his world; autoerotism was an incidental by-product of such exploration. When not engaged in his exploratory undertakings, the baby needs attention and care; and giving these when he demands them, far from making him a tyrant, will make him less demanding later on. At this time mildness is advocated in all areas; thumb-sucking and masturbation are not to be interfered with; weaning and toilet training are to be accomplished later and more gently.

In 1951 there is an attempt to continue this mildness, but not without some conflicts and misgivings. Autoerotic activities become even more harmless and negligible. Sucking is a permissible though low-grade pleasure (a poor substitute for being held or fed or talked to) and the pacifier (explicitly taboo, 1914–38; not mentioned, 1942–45) is now restored. Rocking and head-banging (not masturbation) are the puzzling things which babies may do in bed and from which they seem to get some satisfaction; perhaps they do it out of boredom. Masturbation is mentioned only in connection with toilet training. While on the toilet, the baby may touch his genitals. This does not amount to anything (not even pleasure), but if it bothers the mother she may give the child a toy. Here the tolerance for autoerotism seems to require increasing denial of its nature. Requirements in toilet training become even more easygoing than in the preceding period. But the anxiety of 1929 that the child may dominate the parents reappears. If one picks up the child whenever he cries, he may become a tyrant. And in the area of toilet training, gentleness is urged out of the consideration that if the mother tries to be tough she cannot win. If she seems to be fighting the child, he can really hold out against her. Thus we get, if we compare 1929 with 1951, the same anxiety about the child's possible domination combined with extremely polarized approaches toward toilet training, on the one hand very strict, on the other, very mild. Neither the problems of the child's autoerotism nor of his possible domination seem to have been quite solved.

To document the foregoing points: In the 1914 edition of *Infant Care* (p. 62), masturbation is called an "injurious practice"; it "easily grows beyond control . . . children are sometimes wrecked for life." "It must be eradicated . . . treatment consists in mechanical restraints." In the 1921 revision (pp. 45-46), this is already toned down a bit: "a common habit . . . it grows worse if left uncontrolled." The mechanical restraints are slightly moderated; the nightgown sleeves must still be pinned down, but it is no longer specified (as it was in 1914) that the child's legs should be tied to opposite sides of the crib. In 1929, the atmosphere is much more relaxed: this "early period of what may be called sex awareness will pass away unless it is emphasized by unwise treatment on the part of adults." Physical restraints are now considered of little value. "Occupation and diversion" are the best treatment. The baby may be given a toy to hold until he goes to sleep (1929 ed., pp. 60–61). The 1938 revision (p. 49) anticipates the exploratory theme which subsequently becomes central: children "discover accidentally" that they can get pleasure from touching their genitals. The point about spontaneous recovery is repeated. In 1942, we are told: "Babies want to handle and investigate everything that they can see and reach. When a baby discovers his genital organs he will play with them . . . A wise mother will not be concerned about this." Also, "see that he has a toy to play with and he will not need to use his body as a plaything" (1942 ed., p. 60). There is no change in 1945. In the 1951 edition (p. 87), we read: "Sometimes a baby handles his genitals when he is sitting on the toilet, or at other times when he is undressed. This is a common thing, and usually will not amount to anything if let alone. But sometimes it is disturbing to mothers, so if you feel uncomfortable about it you can try giving him a toy to hold while he's on the toilet seat. Don't confuse him by saying, 'No, No.' " The increased moderation in handling masturbation in the course of these years is accompanied by an increasingly diluted version of the activity. From expressing an urgent and dangerous impulse of the child, masturbation becomes an act about which the child has no feelings and which is only inexplicably embarrassing to the mother.

The alarm about thumb-sucking is somewhat less extreme than that about masturbation in the beginning, but it persists longer. Thus, while mechanical restraints in connection with masturbation are abandoned in

1929, such restraints are still recommended to combat thumb-sucking as late as 1938. In 1914–21, mothers are cautioned that thumb-sucking deforms the mouth and causes constant drooling. "Thumb or finger must be persistently and constantly removed from the mouth and the baby's attention diverted to something else." Thus diversion, a relatively mild technique which is not yet envisaged in the case of masturbation, is considered at least partially effective against thumb-sucking. However, it is not enough; sleeves should also be "pinned or sewed down over the offending hand for several days and nights or the hand put in a cotton mitten." The zeal of the mother to keep the child's hand inaccessible is considered so great that the following caution is added: "The baby's hands should be set free now and then, especially if he is old enough to use his hands for his toys, and at meal times to save as much unnecessary strain on his nerves as possible, but with the approach of sleeping time the hand must be covered" (1914 ed., p. 61; no change in 1921). At this time also the use of a pacifier is called a "disgusting habit" which the adults are to blame for introducing. The pacifier "must be destroyed." "Thumb and finger sucking babies will rebel fiercely at being deprived of this comfort when they are going to sleep, but this must be done if the habit is to be broken up" (1914 ed., pp. 58 and 61; 1921 is about the same). Thus in the period of open struggle against the baby's oral pleasures the ferocity of this drive is fully acknowledged.

In 1929-38, thumb-sucking retains the same hazards and is to be treated by the same methods. However, it is described in a more reassuring way. "When the baby first discovers his finger or thumb he naturally starts sucking it." "It is a natural habit . . . it should not excite parents unduly." While mechanical restraints are still recommended, there is a greater emphasis on diversion: "The best way to break up the habit is to keep the hands occupied with some toy" (1929 ed., pp. 59–60). In 1942–45, the exploratory motive becomes central; thumb-sucking like masturbation becomes an incident in the baby's exploration of his world. "A baby explores everything within his reach. He looks at a new object, feels it, squeezes it, and almost always puts it in his mouth." The baby "knows how to suck because he has learned to get food that way, and naturally he sucks on anything he puts in his mouth." No interference with thumb-sucking is required: "Usually children will outgrow the habit unless too much fuss is made . . . as he grows older other interests and pleasures take the place of sucking" (1942 ed., pp. 59–60; 1945 ed. is the same). Oral drives have now lost their fierce tenacity; they are easily outcompeted by other interests. The baby is now much more attracted by things around him than by his own body.

In 1951, thumb-sucking has become even more permissible and even more devalued as a satisfaction. When the baby is "tired or hungry or doesn't have anything interesting to watch or do, he may try to get a little pleasure out of his thumb or fingers. Sucking is a poor substitute for being held, or talked to, or fed; but it is better than nothing." Where the motivation for pleasure sucking had been first a fierce specific urge, later a more bland diffuse exploratory impulse, it is not more apt to arise from "loneliness or boredom." Thus as the attitude toward the child's impulses becomes increasingly permissive these impulses are depicted as increasingly weak and weary. It is now a matter for wonder that thumb-sucking was ever objected to. "Why do so many of us have this strong feeling against what is so perfectly natural for babies to do?" Why such a strong feeling against such a trivial impulse? Even the pacifier is now permitted. The damaging effect of early sucking on jaw formation is denied (1951 ed., pp. 56–57).

From 1914 through 1945 breast feeding was emphatically recommended. However, from 1921 on there was an increasing implicit apprehension that mothers did not want to breast-feed their children. This was expressed in warnings against too early weaning, review and refutation of an increasing number of arguments which mothers might give for early weaning, and the assertion that only a very few extreme circumstances could justify it. Concurrently with these doubts about the mother's willingness to nurse, there developed, however, an increasingly severe attitude toward the child who was to be weaned. Weaning, once the time had come to initiate it, was to be carried out according to a strict schedule and no backsliding was to be permitted. The mother was to refuse the breast and later the bottle with great firmness; the baby would yield and take the proffered substitutes. This trend was reversed in 1942–45, when the temporal pace of weaning was to be adapted to the baby's needs in such a way that the experience would be one of glad growing up and not of deprivation. The anxiety about the mother's unwillingness to nurse continued, however, at this time. It is only in 1951 that mothers are granted an honorable exemption from breast feeding if they prefer it that way. "If a mother isn't happy nursing her baby, and does it only because she thinks it is her duty, it may be better all around for her baby to be bottle fed. Mothers who find bottle feeding easier should feel comfortable about doing it that way" (1951 ed., p. 17). The adaptation of weaning procedure to the baby's needs continues to be recommended. Thus in the latest period both mother and baby are treated indulgently in this area.

In 1914 there seemed to be little anxiety that mothers would wean their babies too soon. However, there was great stress on gradualness in weaning. No precise time schedule was given. A first bottle might be introduced at five months to give the baby plenty of time to get used to it; weaning might be completed by one year (1914 ed., pp. 55–56). In 1921 the anxiety about too early weaning set in. Where previously mothers were told that the baby might be weaned by one year, they are now warned that he should not be weaned before six months. Attention is focused on the minimal nursing period. After six months a normal baby can be weaned if necessary, though preferably weaning should be postponed till about nine months. Once initiated, it "need not take more than two weeks." The mother is advised to persist in getting the baby to take the artificial food even if he refuses it at first: "the child will finally yield" (1921 ed., pp. 58–59). This anticipates the struggle for dominance of the next period. Some fairly serious disturbance about the breast seems indicated in 1921. This is suggested by the only two illustrations in this edition: one a close-up of a breast from which milk is being expressed by hand, the other a diagram of the baby's teeth. If one may speculate on these two images, they would seem to say that the breast had better be preserved from the infant's destructive jaws. We may recall in passing that in the twenties the preferred female body image was one in which the breasts were unnoticeable. There would seem to have been a marked conflict at this time about both the erotic and the maternal uses of the breast. In *Infant Care,* this is reflected in the apprehension that women will not want to breast-feed their children. It is stressed that there are few legitimate excuses for not nursing the child (although the illustrations unwittingly tell a different story). However, once it is time to wean the baby, the mother can be very firm about withholding the breast.

In the 1929 edition (pp. 74–76), we find a further elaboration of inadequate reasons which are often given for too early weaning. "Many babies are weaned unnecessarily because the breast milk looks blue or is thought to be 'too thin.'" That is, the mother is dissatisfied with what her breasts can produce. Mothers are urged to continue breast-feeding their babies until they are seven or eight months old "even if only one or two feedings a day are given and the other feedings are artificial." Weaning, once begun, should follow a strict schedule, and is to be completed by the end of the ninth or beginning of the tenth month. The dominance orientation of this period is evident in the way that weaning is to be carried out. "If the baby refuses the bottle or cup the mother must not give in and allow him to nurse." She must offer the cup or bottle regularly according to the weaning schedule. "Soon the baby will give in and take the cup or bottle. The mother must not get excited or upset if the baby refuses, because he will finally yield." The 1938 revision continues and even slightly intensifies this rigor.

In 1942–45 for the first time the emotional impact of weaning on the baby is acknowledged. Giving up the breast "is a big step for the baby in growing up. Later steps will be easier if the baby finds this one pleasant." If the transition to the bottle is sufficiently gradual, "he will take the step forward gladly. If the change is made suddenly he may resist it." Thus instead of firmly overriding the baby's resistance, the mother should now avoid rousing it. The tempo of weaning is to be adapted to individual needs rather than follow a preconceived schedule. The transition from the bottle to the cup is "also a big problem for the baby. . . . Let him take his time. . . . It makes little difference at exactly what age bottle feeding is given up for good. It makes a great deal of difference to the baby's mental and emotional health that he does not feel cheated out of something important to him, but that he does feel that he is giving up a baby way for a grown-up way" (1945 ed., pp. 47–50). A new consideration is introduced in connection with weaning: the mother may want to wean the baby sooner than she would otherwise, in order to return to work. However, she is advised to discuss this with the father; perhaps they can arrange for her to stay home and "nurse their baby, especially when they realize what a good start in life breast feeding will give the baby" (pp. 70–71). This invocation of the father as the arbiter over the breast, the one who is to grant and ensure the baby's right to it, suggests that both the erotic and maternal associations of the breast have been re-established.

In 1951 the long-term intransigence about breast feeding is relaxed: the mother should not feel guilty if she prefers to bottle-feed her baby from the first. However, sometimes a mother who really wants to breast-feed her baby is prevented by the doctor. "Sometimes doctors and hospitals take very lightly a mother's earnest insistence that she intends to nurse her baby" (1951 ed., p. 17). It is now the doctor rather than the father who becomes a more impersonal and also more grudging arbiter over the breast. It is again stressed, as in the preceding period, that weaning should be gradual and adapted to the readiness of the individual child to give up the pleasure of sucking. The child should be compensated by "a little extra attention" for the loss of this satisfaction. Where there is "no set time at which the baby should be drinking his milk from a cup," there is now some anxiety that the transition to the cup may be too long postponed. The situation may arise where mothers "are at a loss what to do when their baby gets so used to the bottle that at 18 or 20 months, or even later, when he's fast getting beyond seeming like a baby, he still insists on having the bottle" (pp. 43–44). This expresses a conflict which pervades the 1951 edition. The view had been advanced in 1942–45 that early full gratification facilitates later acceptance of limitations. In 1951 doubts about this have rearisen. May not continued gratification lead to addiction and increasingly intensified demands? Thus while on some points (notably thumb-sucking and acceptance of baby's preferences in solid foods) it is held that indulgence will not spoil the baby but just the reverse, on other points (continued bottle feeding, picking up the baby when he cries) there is the apprehension that gratification will intensify the baby's demands. Also a new issue is now raised about weaning to the cup: Should not the breast-fed baby be weaned directly to the cup rather than through a transitional stage of bottle feeding? It would seem that there has been a displacement of conflicting feelings here. Up to this time there was the troubled issue whether to breast-feed or bottle-feed in the first place, with heavy arguments for breast feeding. Now the uncertainty attaches to the question whether to wean to the cup or to the bottle. In other words, the issue breast versus bottle has been replaced by bottle versus cup. (Such displacements as an indication of unresolved problems are frequent in this literature. In 1929, for instance when a more easy-going line was being advanced on masturbation, the danger of obsessive preoccupation was displaced to the toy which was to be given the child to keep his hands occupied in bed. It was feared he might become excessively attached to one toy, and parents were advised to vary these bedtime distractions [1927 ed., pp. 60–66].)

Recommended procedures in bowel training have shown sharp fluctuations. In the twenties there was increasing severity. Subsequently there was a trend in the opposite direction; from 1938 through 1951 increasing mildness has been recommended. Thus where in 1921 the mother was to take up the task of bowel training as soon as she recovered from her confinement, in 1951 the mother is told: "Many babies are not ready to start learning bowel control by the end of the first year" (p. 86). In this latter phase flexibility has replaced rigidity in the training schedule. In the earlier period the value of regular bowel habits for health and character was emphasized. Now what is stressed is the negativism which the mother risks provoking in her child if she tries to force him to be trained against his will.

In 1914 bowel training was to be begun "by the third month or even earlier." The mother was to use "the utmost gentleness. . . . Scolding and punishment will serve only to frighten the child and to destroy the natural impulses, while laughter will tend to relax the muscles and to promote an easy movement." The chamber was to be presented "persistently each day" at the same hour. It is emphasized that establishing bowel regularity will be a great saving of trouble to the mother and "of untold value to the child, not only in babyhood, but throughout the whole life" (1914 ed., p. 51). Increased severity is evidenced in the 1921 revision (pp. 42–44) in demanding an earlier beginning of bowel training: "as early as the end of the first month . . . as soon as the mother takes charge of the baby after her confinement she should begin upon this task." The time for the completion of bowel training is now specified: almost any baby can be trained so that there are no more soiled diapers after the end of the first year. The time that the baby is to be placed on the chamber each day is specified more rigidly: "no varying the time by five minutes." Gentleness and laughter are no longer mentioned; the warning against scolding and punishment drops out. The nuisance for the mother in training the child is expressed more strongly. Where in 1914 this training required "much time and patience" from the mother, it now takes "unlimited patience." The value of establishing and maintaining bowel regularity is that it prevents "endless misery from constipation in the adult."

In 1929 the demand for bowel control is most rigorous. "Almost any baby can be trained so that there are no more soiled diapers to wash after he is six to eight months old." The requirement of absolute regularity, not varying the time for the movement by five minutes from one day to the next, continues (1929 ed., pp. 57–58). The demand for regularity, doing everything "by the clock" now pervades the daily routine. In 1938, there is a reversal in the trend. We hear no more about beginning bowel training at one month. Now it may be begun "as early as six months" (the time when the mother of 1929 might already expect the baby to be completely trained). The time for completion of training is now put at one year. The specification about not varying the time by five minutes drops out, and instead we find that the baby should be put on the chamber "each day for a short period" (1938 ed., pp. 47–48). Correspondingly the general clockboundness of 1929 is moderated. The lifelong value of good bowel habits is not explicitly asserted in 1929 or 1938. Instead there is a general statement that training in regularity of eating and elimination is also character building.

In 1942–45 bowel training is to commence still later, "usually at eight or ten months," and the time for completing it is left indefinite. The baby cannot really cooperate in the training until his muscles have matured. If one waits until this time training becomes easy. Efforts of the mother to catch the baby at the right moment, before he can actively participate, are disparaged; it is the mother, not the baby, who is trained in this case. Bowel training should not be begun at the same time as weaning since one or the other may be hard for the baby to accept (1945 ed., pp. 53–54). Neither the lifelong value of bowel regularity nor its indirect relation to character building is mentioned any more. All that remains is a very general statement (carried over since 1929) that early habits form the basis for later health, happiness and efficiency.

As we have noted, in 1942–45 the handling of the infant in all areas has become very gentle. This tendency is continued and even carried further in 1951. The advocacy is increased leniency is most marked in respect to bowel training. This is also the aspect of the mother-child relation which is seen as most fraught with emotional hazards. "Why do we stress this [bowel training] so much? Because you can so easily make trouble for yourself and the baby if you start training too early. A child can get to feeling that his mother is his enemy if she urges on him things he is not ready for. . . . Let him sit on his toilet chair only a few moments the first few times. . . . As he gets used to his new seat, you can keep him on a little longer, but never more than five minutes." (Note how the theme of "five minutes" recurs, but in a very different way from the twenties' "not varying the time by five minutes.") "You don't want him to get to hate this new routine. Much of the trouble mothers have . . . comes because the babies get the idea this is a battle. . . . This is once when a baby has the upper hand. No mother can *make* her child move his bowels. . . . A lot depends on her not letting him get to feel this is a hateful bore. . . . What you're after is not having fewer diapers to wash, but having a baby who feels like working with you instead of against you." In view of all this the commencement of bowel training is postponed to a considerably later time. "Most babies are not ready to start learning bowel control by the end of the first year. One and a half or two years is a much more common time for them to learn willingly" (1951 ed., pp. 86–87).

The handling of bladder training is not correlated exactly with that of bowel training. In 1929 when severity in bowel training was at its height, severity in bladder training decreased as compared with the preceding period (1921 ed., pp. 42–45; 1929 ed., pp. 58–59). Urination here seems to have more a genital than an anal association (we may recall that severity toward masturbation also decreased at this time. Masturbation was explicitly associated with bed-wetting in the 1929 revision pp. 60–61 as an early habit which would be easily outgrown. Incidentally, masturbation was associated with thumb-sucking in 1942–45, and with defecation in 1951). Intolerance toward wetting was most intense in 1921; from 1929 on the attitude became steadily gentler.

The increase or decrease in severity in the various areas which we have considered may be roughly indicated in Table 1.

In respect to masturbation and thumb-sucking, the curve of severity shows a consistently declining direction. In weaning and bowel training, we find a U-curve, rising in the twenties and subsequently declining. However, this table refers only to the overt procedures which are recommended (when to begin toilet training or weaning, whether to use mechanical restraints against thumb-sucking or masturbation, etc.). It does not indicate the range of conflicting emotional attitudes which are expressed in more subtle ways (as in the altered conception of autoerotic drives, etc.).

TABLE 1

Severity in the handling of:	From 1914 to 1921	From 1921 to 1929	From 1929 to 1938	From 1938 to 1942-45	From 1942-45 to 1951
Masturbation	Decreases	Decreases	Constant	Decreases	Constant
Thumb-sucking	Constant	Decreases	Constant	Decreases	Decreases
Weaning	Increases	Increases	Constant	Decreases	Constant
Bowel training	Increases	Increases	Decreases	Decreases	Decreases
Bladder training	Increases	Decreases	Decreases	Decreases	Decreases

The problem of making scientific insight widely accessible is nowhere more pertinent than in child training. The efforts of the authors of the *Infant Care* bulletins illustrate the difficulty of the undertaking. In the last decade, they have been telling mothers to behave with great tolerance toward the child's autoerotic impulses, his urge to suck, his soiling and wetting. But what has become of the feelings which not so long ago were being expressed with a clear conscience in strenuous struggle against these same impulses in the child? These feelings have certainly not been worked through or transformed, but seem much more to be suppressed or repressed. The mother of 1914 or 1921 was supposed to know that children masturbate in bed, and was told to eradicate his wickedness. The mother of 1951, who is told that masturbation does not amount to anything, is not supposed to know that children masturbate in bed, but may only notice that they sometimes touch their genitals while on the toilet. She is permitted to feel uncomfortable when she observes this and may give the child a toy to relieve her own feelings. But the mother who feels uncomfortable and so must distract her baby may convey, albeit covertly and indecisively, considerable disapproval. And so with other things; changes in behavior too quickly superposed on less quickly alterable feelings may fail to obtain the hoped-for results. The problem remains of how to help people to face the realities of human nature and yet to treat it gently.

SOCIAL CLASS AND PARENT-CHILD RELATIONSHIPS: AN INTERPRETATION

MELVIN L. KOHN

In the process of articulating one major interpretation of the relationship of social-class variables to parent-child interaction, Kohn acquaints us with a substantial portion of relevant social-class literature. We have progressed well beyond the early, simplistic view of social-class differences as a dichotomy based on permissiveness versus prohibition. Although we still tend to focus on the young child, we now study a far broader range of contrasting phenomena (thus Kohn's holistic emphasis on "different conditions of life"), and bend our efforts toward explaining the variables intervening between, or underlying, social-class membership and child-rearing practices. Kohn, in addition to asking "what," asks "why." He suggests a fresh avenue of approach to the effect of social class on parent-child relationships.

The social sciences and psychiatry have contributed multidimensional studies, both qualitative and quantitative, of the total atmosphere of lower-class children's lives (Reissman et al., 1964; Greenblatt et al., 1967; Riese, 1962; Reissmann, 1962). Studies with a language- and cognitive focus have appeared (Deutsch, 1965; Cazden, 1966); the previously almost unacknowledged lowest stratum of society has finally entered our field of vision (Harrington, 1962; Pavenstedt, 1965; Minuchin, 1968); and there have been attempts to reconceptualize the very nature of the sociopsychologically relevant economic divisions in our society (Miller and Swanson, 1958). At the same time, others have begun to study the role of social-class variables in the incidence, etiology, diagnosis, and treatment of childhood psychopathology (Harrison et al., 1965; McDermott et al., 1965).

This essay is an attempt to interpret, from a sociological perspective, the effects of social class upon parent-child relationships. Many past discussions of the problem seem somehow to lack this perspective, even though the problem is one of profound importance for sociology. Because

Reprinted from *American Journal of Sociology,* 68, 1963, pp. 471–480, by permission of the University of Chicago Press.

most investigators have approached the problem from an interest in psychodynamics, rather than social structure, they have largely limited their attention to a few specific techniques used by mothers in the rearing of infants and very young children. They have discovered, *inter alia,* that social class has a decided bearing on which techniques parents use. But, since they have come at the problem from this perspective, their interest in social class has not gone beyond its effects for this very limited aspect of parent-child relationships.

The present analysis conceives the problem of social class and parent-child relationships as an instance of the more general problem of the effects of social structure upon behavior. It starts with the assumption that social class has proved to be so useful a concept because it refers to more than simply educational level, or occupation, or any of the large number of correlated variables. It is so useful because it captures the reality that the intricate interplay of all these variables creates different levels of the social order. Members of different social classes, by virtue of enjoying (or suffering) different conditions of life, come to see the world differently—to develop different conceptions of social reality, different aspirations and hopes and fears, different conceptions of the desirable.

The last is particularly important for present purposes, for from people's conceptions of the desirable—and particularly from their conceptions of what characteristics are desirable in children—one can discern their objectives in child-rearing. Thus, conceptions of the desirable—that is, values [1]—become the key concept for this analysis, the bridge between position in the larger social structure and the behavior of the individual. The intent of the analysis is to trace the effects of social class position on parental values and the effects of values on behavior.

Since this approach differs from analyses focused on social class differences in the use of particular child-rearing techniques, it will be necessary to re-examine earlier formulations from the present perspective. Then three questions will be discussed, bringing into consideration the limited available data that are relevant: What differences are there in the values held by parents of different social classes? What is there about the conditions of life distinctive of these classes that might explain the differences in their values? What consequences do these differences in values have for parents' relationships with their children?

[1] "A value is a conception, explicit or implicit, distinctive of an individual or characteristic of a group, of the desirable which influences the selection from available modes, means, and ends of action" (Kluckhohn, 1951). Also see R. M. Williams' (1951) discussion of values, chapter xi, and his discussion of social class and culture (p. 101).

Social Class

Social classes will be defined as aggregates of individuals who occupy broadly similar positions in the scale of prestige (Williams, 1951). In dealing with the research literature, we shall treat occupational position (or occupational position as weighted somewhat by education) as a serviceable index of social class for urban American society. And we shall adopt the model of social stratification implicit in most research, that of four relatively discrete classes: a "lower class" of unskilled manual workers, a "working class" of manual workers in semiskilled and skilled occupations, a "middle class" of white-collar workers and professionals, and an "elite," differentiated from the middle class not so much in terms of occupation as of wealth and lineage.

Almost all the empirical evidence, including that from our own research, stems from broad comparisons of the middle and working class. Thus we shall have little to say about the extremes of the class distribution. Furthermore, we shall have to act as if the middle and working classes were each homogeneous. They are not, even in terms of status considerations alone. There is evidence, for example, that within each broad social class, variations in parents' values quite regularly parallel gradations of social status. Moreover, the classes are heterogeneous with respect to other factors that affect parents' values, such as religion and ethnicity. But even when all such considerations are taken into account, the empirical evidence clearly shows that being on one side or the other of the line that divides manual from non-manual worker, has profound consequences for how one rears one's children. [2]

Stability and Change

Any analysis of the effects of social class upon parent-child relationships should start with Urie Bronfenbrenner's analytic review of the studies that had been conducted in this country during the twenty-five years up to 1958 (1958). From the seemingly contradictory findings of a number of studies, Bronfenbrenner discerned not chaos but orderly change: there have been changes in the child-training techniques employed by middle-class parents in the past quarter-century; similar changes have been

[2] These, and other assertions of fact not referred to published sources, are based on research my colleagues and I have conducted. For the design of this research and the principal substantive findings see Kohn (1959a, 1959b) and Kohn and Carroll (1960). I should like to express my appreciation to my principal collaborators in this research, John A. Clausen and Eleanor E. Carroll.

taking place in the working class, but working-class parents have consistently lagged behind by a few years; thus, while middle-class parents of twenty-five years ago were more "restrictive" than were working-class parents, today the middle-class parents are more "permissive"; and the gap between the classes seems to be narrowing.

It must be noted that these conclusions are limited by the questions Bronfenbrenner's predecessors asked in their research. The studies deal largely with a few particular techniques of child-rearing, especially those involved in caring for infants and very young children, and say very little about parents' over-all relationships with their children, particularly as the children grow older. There is clear evidence that the past quarter-century has seen change, even faddism, with respect to the use of breast feeding or bottle feeding, scheduling or not scheduling, spanking or isolating. But when we generalize from these specifics to talk of a change from "restrictive" to "permissive" practices—or, worse yet, of a change from "restrictive" to "permissive" parent-child relationships—we impute to them a far greater importance than they probably have, either to parents or to children. [3]

There is no evidence that recent faddism in child-training techniques is symptomatic of profound changes in the relations of parents to children in either social class. In fact, as Bronfenbrenner notes, what little evidence we do have points in the opposite direction: the over-all quality of parent-child relationships does not seem to have changed substantially in either class (1958). In all probability, parents have changed techniques in service of much the same values, and the changes have been quite specific. These changes must be explained, but the enduring characteristics are probably even more important.

Why the changes? Bronfenbrenner's interpretation is ingenuously simple. He notes that the changes in techniques employed by middle-class parents have closely paralleled those advocated by presumed experts, and he concludes that middle-class parents have changed their practices *because* they are responsive to changes in what the experts tell them is right and proper. Working-class parents, being less educated and thus less directly responsive to the media of communication, followed behind only later. [4]

Bronfenbrenner is almost undoubtedly right in asserting that mid-

[3] Furthermore, these concepts employ a priori judgments about which the various investigators have disagreed radically. See Sears, Maccoby and Levin (1957) and Littman, Moore and Pierce-Jones (1957).

[4] Bronfenbrenner gives clearest expression to this interpretation, but it has been adopted by others, too. See, e.g., White (1957).

dle-class parents have followed the drift of presumably expert opinion. But why have they done so? It is not sufficient to assume that the explanation lies in their greater degree of education. This might explain why middle-class parents are substantially more likely than are working-class parents to *read* books and articles on child-rearing, as we know they do. [5] But they need not *follow* the experts' advice. We know from various studies of the mass media that people generally search for confirmation of their existing beliefs and practices and tend to ignore what contradicts them.

From all the evidence at our disposal, it looks as if middle-class parents not only read what the experts have to say but also search out a wide variety of other sources of information and advice: they are far more likely than are working-class parents to discuss child-rearing with friends and neighbors, to consult physicians on these matters, to attend Parent-Teacher Association meetings, to discuss the child's behavior with his teacher. Middle-class parents seem to regard child-rearing as more problematic than do working-class parents. This can hardly be a matter of education alone. It must be rooted more deeply in the conditions of life of the two social classes.

Everything about working-class parents' lives—their comparative lack of education, the nature of their jobs, their greater attachment to the extended family—conduces to their retaining familiar methods. [6] Furthermore, even should they be receptive to change, they are less likely than are middle-class parents to find the experts' writings appropriate to their wants, for the experts predicate their advice on middle-class values. Everything about middle-class parents' lives, on the other hand, conduces to their looking for new methods to achieve their goals. They look to the experts, to other sources of relevant information, and to each other not for new values but for more serviceable techniques.[7] And within the lim-

[5] This was noted by John E. Anderson in the first major study of social class and family relationships ever conducted, and has repeatedly been confirmed (1936).

[6] The differences between middle- and working-class conditions of life will be discussed more fully later in this paper.

[7] Certainly middle-class parents do not get their values from the experts. In our research, we compared the values of parents who say they read Spock, Gesell, or other books on child-rearing, to those who read only magazine and newspaper articles, and those who say they read nothing at all on the subject. In the middle class, these three groups have substantially the same values. In the working class, the story is different. Few working-class parents claim to read books or even articles on child-rearing. Those few who do have values much more akin to those of the middle class. But these are atypical working-class parents who are very anxious to attain middle-class status. One suspects that for them the experts provide a sort of handbook to the middle class; even for them, it is unlikely that the values come out of Spock and Gesell.

its of our present scanty knowledge about means-ends relationships in child-rearing, the experts have provided practical and useful advice. It is not that educated parents slavishly follow the experts but that the experts have provided what the parents have sought.

To look at the question this way is to put it in a quite different perspective: the focus becomes not specific techniques nor changes in the use of specific techniques but parental values.

Values of Middle- and Working-Class Parents

Of the entire range of values one might examine, it seems particularly strategic to focus on parents' conceptions of what characteristics would be most desirable for boys or girls the age of their own children. From this one can hope to discern the parents' goals in rearing their children. It must be assumed, however, that a parent will choose one characteristic as more desirable than another only if he considers it to be both important, in the sense that failure to develop this characteristic would affect the child adversely, and problematic, in the sense that it is neither to be taken for granted that the child will develop that characteristic nor impossible for him to do so. In interpreting parents' value choices, we must keep in mind that their choices reflect not simply their goals but the goals whose achievement they regard as problematic.

Few studies, even in recent years, have directly investigated the relationship of social class to parental values. Fortunately, however, the results of these few are in essential agreement. The earliest study was Evelyn Millis Duvall's pioneering inquiry of 1946. Duvall characterized working-class (and lower middle-class) parental values as "traditional"—they want their children to be neat and clean, to obey and respect adults, to please adults. In contrast to this emphasis on how the child comports himself, middle-class parental values are more "developmental"—they want their children to be eager to learn, to love and confide in the parents, to be happy, to share and cooperate, to be healthy and well.

Duvall's traditional-developmental dichotomy does not describe the difference between middle- and working-class parental values quite exactly, but it does point to the essence of the difference: working-class parents want the child to conform to externally imposed standards, while middle-class parents are far more attentive to his internal dynamics.

The few relevant findings of subsequent studies are entirely consistent with this basic point, especially in the repeated indications that working-class parents put far greater stress on obedience to parental commands than do middle-class parents.[8] Our own research, conducted in 1956–57, provides the evidence most directly comparable to Duvall's (1946). We, too, found that working-class parents value obedience, neatness, and cleanliness more highly than do middle-class parents, and that middle-class parents in turn value curiosity, happiness, consideration, and—most importantly—self-control more highly than do working-class parents. We further found that there are characteristic clusters of value choice in the two social classes: working-class parental values center on conformity to external proscriptions, middle-class parental values on *self*-direction. To working-class parents, it is the overt act that matters: the child should not transgress externally imposed rules; to middle-class parents, it is the child's motives and feelings that matter: the child should govern himself.

In fairness, it should be noted that middle- and working-class parents share many core values. Both, for example, value honesty very highly—although, characteristically, "honesty" has rather different connotations in the two social classes, implying "truthfulness" for the middle-class. The common theme, of course, is that parents of both social classes value a decent respect for the rights of others; middle- and working-class values are but variations on this common theme. The reason for emphasizing the variations rather than the common theme is that they seem to have far-ranging consequences for parents' relationships with their children and thus ought to be taken seriously.

It would be good if there were more evidence about parental values—data from other studies, in other locales, and especially, data derived from more than one mode of inquiry. But, what evidence we do have is consistent, so that there is at least some basis for believing it is reliable. Furthermore, there is evidence that the value choices made by parents in these inquiries are not simply a reflection of their assessments of their own children's deficiencies or excellences. Thus, we may take the findings of these studies as providing a limited, but probably valid, picture of the parents' generalized conceptions of what behavior would be desirable in their preadolescent children.

Explaining Class Differences in Parental Values

That middle-class parents are more likely to espouse some values, and

[8] Alex Inkeles has shown that this is true not only for the United States but for a number of other industrialized societies as well (1960).

working-class parents other values, must be a function of differences in their conditions of life. In the present state of our knowledge, it is difficult to disentangle the interacting variables with a sufficient degree of exactness to ascertain which conditions of life are crucial to the differences in values. Nevertheless, it is necessary to examine the principal components of class differences in life conditions to see what each may contribute.

The logical place to begin is with occupational differences, for these are certainly pre-eminently important, not only in defining social classes in urban, industrialized society, but also in determining much else about people's life conditions.[9] There are at least three respects in which middle-class occupations typically differ from working-class occupations, above and beyond their obvious status-linked differences in security, stability of income, and general social prestige. One is that middle-class occupations deal more with the manipulation of interpersonal relations, ideas, and symbols, while working-class occupations deal more with the manipulation of things. The second is that middle-class occupations are more subject to self-direction, while working-class occupations are more subject to standardization and direct supervision. The third is that getting ahead in middle-class occupations is more dependent upon one's own actions, while in working-class occupations it is more dependent upon collective action, particularly in unionized industries. From these differences, one can sketch differences in the characteristics that make for getting along, and getting ahead, in middle- and working-class occupations. Middle-class occupations require a greater degree of self-direction; working-class occupations, in larger measure, require that one follow explicit rules set down by someone in authority.

Obviously, these differences parallel the differences we have found between the two social classes in the characteristics valued by parents for children. At minimum, one can conclude that there is a congruence between occupational requirements and parental values. It is, moreover, a reasonable supposition, although not a necessary conclusion, that middle- and working-class parents value different characteristics in children *because* of these differences in their occupational circumstances. This supposition does not necessarily assume that parents consciously train their children to meet future occupational requirements; it may simply be that their own occupational experiences have significantly affected parents'

[9] For a thoughtful discussion of the influence of occupational role on parental values see Aberle and Naegele (1952).

conceptions of what is desirable behavior, on or off the job, for adults or for children. [10]

These differences in occupational circumstances are probably basic to the differences we have found between middle- and working-class parental values, but taken alone they do not sufficiently explain them. Parents need not accord pre-eminent importance to occupational requirements in their judgments of what is most desirable. For a sufficient explanation of class differences in values, it is necessary to recognize that other differences in middle- and working-class conditions of life reinforce the differences in occupational circumstances at every turn.

Educational differences, for example, above and beyond their importance as determinants of occupation, probably contribute independently to the differences in middle- and working-class parental values. At minimum, middle-class parents' greater attention to the child's internal dynamics is facilitated by their learned ability to deal with the subjective and the ideational. Furthermore, differences in levels and stability of income undoubtedly contribute to class differences in parental values. That middle-class parents still have somewhat higher levels of income, and much greater stability of income, makes them able to take for granted the respectability that is still problematic for working-class parents. They can afford to concentrate, instead, on motives and feelings—which, in the circumstances of their lives, are more important.

These considerations suggest that the differences between middle- and working-class parental values are probably a function of the entire complex of differences in life conditions characteristic of the two social classes. Consider, for example, the working-class situation. With the end of mass immigration, there has emerged a stable working class, largely derived from the manpower of rural areas, uninterested in mobility into the middle class, but very much interested in security, respectability, and the en-

[10] Two objections might be raised here. (1) Occupational experiences may not be important for a mother's values, however crucial they are for her husband's, if she has had little or no work experience. But even those mothers who have had little or no occupational experience know something of occupational life from their husbands and others, and live in a culture in which occupation and career permeate all of life. (2) Parental values may be built not so much out of their own experiences as out of their expectations of the child's future experiences. This might seem particularly plausible in explaining working-class values, for their high valuation of such stereotypically *middle-class* characteristics as obedience, neatness, and cleanliness might imply that they are training their children for a middle-class life they expect the children to achieve. Few working-class parents, however, do expect (or even want) their children to go on to college and the middle-class jobs for which a college education is required. (This is shown in Hyman [1953], and confirmed in unpublished data from our own research.)

joyment of a decent standard of living.[11] This working class has come to enjoy a standard of living formerly reserved for the middle class, but has not chosen a middle-class style of life. In effect, the working class has striven for, and partially achieved, an American dream distinctly different from the dream of success and achievement. In an affluent society, it is possible for the worker to be the traditionalist—politically, economically, and, most relevant here, in his values for his children.[12] Working-class parents want their children to conform to external authority because the parents themselves are willing to accord respect to authority, in return for security and respectability. Their conservatism in child-rearing is part of a more general conservatism and traditionalism.

Middle-class parental values are a product of a quite different set of conditions. Much of what the working class values, they can take for granted. Instead, they can—and must—instil in their children a degree of self-direction that would be less appropriate to the conditions of life of the working class.[13] Certainly, there is substantial truth in the characterization of the middle-class way of life as one of great conformity. What must be noted here, however, is that *relative to* the working class, middle-class conditions of life require a more substantial degree of independence of action. Furthermore, the higher levels of education enjoyed by the middle class make possible a degree of internal scrutiny difficult to achieve without the skills in dealing with the abstract that college training sometimes provides. Finally, the economic security of most middle-class occupations, the level of income they provide, the status they confer, allow one to focus his attention on the subjective and the ideational. Middle-class conditions of life both allow and demand a greater degree of self-direction than do those of the working class.

[11] See, e.g., Miller and Riessman (1961).

[12] Relevant here is Seymour Martin Lipset's somewhat disillusioned "Democracy and Working-Class Authoritarianism" (1959).

[13] It has been argued that as larger and larger proportions of the middle class have become imbedded in a bureaucratic way of life—in distinction to the entrepreneurial way of life of a bygone day—it has become more appropriate to raise children to be accommodative than to be self-reliant. But this point of view is a misreading of the conditions of life faced by the middle-class inhabitants of the bureaucratic world. Their jobs require at least as great a degree of self-reliance as do entrepreneurial enterprises. We tend to forget, nowadays, just how little the small- or medium-sized entrepreneur controlled the conditions of his own existence and just how much he was subjected to the petty authority of those on whose pleasure depended the survival of his enterprise. And we fail to recognize the degree to which monolithic-seeming bureaucracies allow free play for—in fact, require—individual enterprise of new sorts: in the creation of ideas, the building of empires, the competition for advancement.

At any rate, our data show no substantial differences between the values of parents from bureaucratic and entrepreneurial occupational worlds, in either social class. But see Miller and Swanson (1958).

Consequences of Class Differences in Parents' Values

What consequences do the differences between middle- and working-class parents' values have for the ways they raise their children?

Much of the research on techniques of infant- and child-training is of little relevance here. For example, with regard to parents' preferred techniques for disciplining children, a question of major interest to many investigators, Bronfenbrenner summarizes past studies as follows: "In matters of discipline, working-class parents are consistently more likely to employ physical punishment, while middle-class families rely more on reasoning, isolation, appeals to guilt, and other methods involving the threat of loss of love (Bronfenbrenner, 1958). This, if still true, [14] is consistent with middle-class parents' greater attentiveness to the child's internal dynamics, working-class parents' greater concern about the overt act. For present purposes, however, the crucial question is not *which* disciplinary method parents prefer, but when and why they use one or another method of discipline.

The most directly relevant available data are on the conditions under which middle- and working-class parents use physical punishment. Working-class parents are apt to resort to physical punishment when the direct and immediate consequences of their children's disobedient acts are most extreme, and to refrain from punishing when this might provoke an even greater disturbance (1959b). Thus, they will punish a child for wild play when the furniture is damaged or the noise level becomes intolerable, but ignore the same actions when the direct and immediate consequences are not so extreme. Middle-class parents, on the other hand, seem to punish or refrain from punishing on the basis of their interpretation of the child's intent in acting as he does. Thus, they will punish a furious outburst when the context is such that they interpret it to be a loss of self-control, but will ignore an equally extreme outburst when the context is such that they interpret it to be merely an emotional release.

It is understandable that working-class parents react to the consequences rather than to the intent of their children's actions: the important thing is that the child not transgress externally imposed rules. Correspondingly, if middle-class parents are instead concerned about the child's motives and feelings, they can and must look beyond the overt act to why the child acts as he does. It would seem that middle- and working-class values direct parents to see their children's misbehavior in quite different

[14] Later studies, including our own, do not show this difference.

ways, so that misbehavior which prompts middle-class parents to action does not seem as important to working-class parents, and vice versa.[15] Obviously, parents' values are not the only things that enter into their use of physical punishment. But unless one assumes a complete lack of goal-directedness in parental behavior, he would have to grant that parents' values direct their attention to some facets of their own and their children's behavior, and divert it from other facets.

The consequences of class differences in parental values extend far beyond differences in disciplinary practices. From a knowledge of their values for their children, one would expect middle-class parents to feel a greater obligation to be *supportive* of the children, if only because of their sensitivity to the children's internal dynamics. Working-class values, with their emphasis upon conformity to external rules, should lead to greater emphasis upon the parents' obligation to impose constraints.[16] And this, according to Bronfenbrenner, is precisely what has been shown in those few studies that have concerned themselves with the overall relationship of parents to child: "Over the entire twenty-five-year period studied, parent-child relationships in the middle-class are consistently reported as more acceptance and equalitarian, while those in the working-class are oriented toward maintaining order and obedience" (Bronfenbrenner, 1958).

This conclusion is based primarily on studies of *mother*-child relationships in middle- and working-class families. Class differences in parental values have further ramifications for the father's role.[17] Mothers in each class would have their husbands play a role facilitative of the child's development of the characteristics valued in that class: Middle-class mothers want their husbands to be supportive of the children (especially of sons), with their responsibility for imposing constraints being of decidedly secondary importance; working-class mothers look to their husbands to be considerably more directive—support is accorded far less importance and constraint far more. Most middle-class fathers agree with their wives and

[15] This is not to say that the methods used by parents of either social class are necessarily the most efficacious for achievement of their goals.

[16] The justification for treating support and constraint as the two major dimensions of parent-child relationships lies in the theoretical argument of Parsons and Bales (1955), and the empirical argument of Schaefer (1959).

[17] From the very limited evidence available at the time of his review, Bronfenbrenner tentatively concluded: "though the middle-class father typically has a warmer relationship with the child, he is also likely to have more authority and status in family affairs" (1958). The discussion here is based largely on subsequent research, especially "Social Class and the Allocation of Parental Responsibilities" (1958).

play a role close to what their wives would have them play. Many working-class fathers, on the other hand, do not. It is not that they see the constraining role as less important than do their wives, but that many of them see no reason why they should have to shoulder the responsibility. From their point of view, the important thing is that the child be taught what limits he must not transgress. It does not much matter who does the teaching, and since mother has primary responsibility for child care, the job should be hers.

The net consequence is a quite different division of parental responsibilities in the two social classes. In middle-class families, mother's and father's roles usually are not sharply differentiated. What differentiation exists is largely a matter of each parent taking special responsibility for being supportive of children of the parent's own sex. In working-class families, mother's and father's roles are more sharply differentiated, with mother almost always being the more supportive parent. In some working-class families, mother specializes in support, father in constraint; in others, perhaps in most, mother raises the children, father provides the wherewithal. [18]

Thus, the differences in middle- and working-class parents' values have wide ramifications for their relationships with their children and with each other. Of course, many class differences in parent-child relationships are not directly attributable to differences in values; undoubtedly the very differences in their conditions of life that make for differences in parental values reinforce, at every juncture, parents' characteristic ways of relating to their children. But one could not account for these consistent differences in parent-child relationships in the two social classes without reference to the differences in parents' avowed values.

Conclusion

This paper serves to show how complex and demanding are the problems of interpreting the effects of social structure on behavior. Our inquiries habitually stop at the point of demonstrating that social position correlates with something, when we should want to pursue the question, "Why?" What are the processes by which position in social structure

[18] Fragmentary data suggest sharp class differences in the husband-wife relationship that complement the differences in the division of parental responsibilities discussed above. For example, virtually no working-class wife reports that she and her husband ever go out on an evening or weekend without the children. And few working class fathers do much to relieve their wives of the burden of caring for the children all the time. By and large, working-class fathers seem to lead a largely separate social life from that of their wives; the wife has full-time responsibility for the children, while the husband is free to go his own way.

molds behavior? The present analysis has dealt with this question in one specific form: Why does social class matter for parents' relationships with their children? There is every reason to believe that the problems encountered in trying to deal with that question would recur in any analysis of the effects of social structure on behavior.

In this analysis, the concept of "values" has been used as the principal bridge from social position to behavior. The analysis has endeavored to show that middle-class parental values differ from those of working-class parents; that these differences are rooted in basic differences between middle- and working-class conditions of life; and that the differences between middle- and working-class parental values have important consequences for their relationships with their children. The interpretive model, in essence, is: social class–conditions of life–values–behavior.

The specific of the present characterization of parental values may prove to be inexact; the discussion of the ways in which social-class position affects values is undoubtedly partial; and the tracing of the consequences of differences in values for differences in parent-child relationships is certainly tentative and incomplete. I trust, however, that the perspective will prove to be valid and that this formulation will stimulate other investigators to deal more directly with the processes whereby social structure affects behavior.

CONTINUITIES AND DISCONTINUITIES IN CULTURAL CONDITIONING

Ruth Benedict

This paper, one of Benedict's classical contributions (see also 1934, 1946), brings to bear on the study of human development a highly useful cross-cultural frame of reference. This perspective makes possible a more meaningful, objective study of child development in our society (Mead and Wolfenstein, 1955). It makes us aware of how much of what we take for granted in our child-rearing orientation is essentially arbitrary rather than natural and necessary. Similarly, it demonstrates that much of what we assume to be truly universal in development (whether because presumably it is based in physiology, or "somehow" intrinsic to human nature) is, instead, cultural artifact, merely one of many equally available alternatives open to a given individual or society.

Cultural continuities and discontinuities have also been discussed by Mead (1954a). The subject, in turn, focuses attention on the special role of transitional periods (Van Gennep, 1960), not just the already well-recognized one of adolescence (note the contrasts here between Benedict and Blos [1962]), but the numerous other developmentally crucial transitions faced in our society—entering school and the world of work, marriage, parenthood, middle age, the moment in time when children go out on their own, retirement, and old age. Such transitions require far greater study of their growth-inducing as well as regressive, pathological potentials, and of the manner in which societies do or do not recognize, facilitate, or further burden the adaptations demanded.

All cultures must deal in one way or another with the cycle of growth from infancy to adulthood. Nature has posed the situation dramatically: on the one hand, the newborn baby, physiologically vulnerable, unable to

Reprinted from *A Study of Interpersonal Relations,* ed. P. Mullahy. New York: Hermitage Press, 1949, pp. 297–308.

fend for itself, or to participate of its own initiative in the life of the group, and on the other, the adult man or woman. Every man who rounds out his human potentialities must have been a son first and a father later, and the two roles are physiologically in great contrast; he must first have been dependent upon others for his very existence, and later he must provide such security for others. This discontinuity in the life cycle is a fact of nature and is inescapable. Facts of nature, however, in any discussion of human problems, are ordinarily read off not at their bare minimal but surrounded by all the local accretions of behavior to which the student of human affairs has become accustomed in his own culture. For that reason it is illuminating to examine comparative material from other societies in order to get a wider perspective on our own special accretions. The anthropologist's role is not to question the facts of nature, but to insist upon the interposition of a middle term between "nature" and "human behavior"; his role is to analyse that term, to document local man-made doctorings of nature and to insist that these doctorings should not be read off in any one culture as nature itself. Although it is a fact of nature that the child becomes a man, the way in which this transition is effected varies from one society to another, and no one of these particular cultural bridges should be regarded as the "natural" path to maturity.

From a comparative point of view our culture goes to great extremes in emphasizing contrasts between the child and the adult. The child is sexless, the adult estimates his virility by his sexual activities; the child must be protected from the ugly facts of life, the adult must meet them without psychic catastrophe; the child must obey, the adult must command this obedience. These are all dogmas of our culture, dogmas which, in spite of the facts of nature, other cultures commonly do not share. In spite of the physiological contrasts between child and adult, these are cultural accretions.

It will make the point clearer if we consider one habit in our own culture in regard to which there is not this discontinuity of conditioning. With the greatest clarity of purpose and economy of training, we achieve our goal of conditioning everyone to eat three meals a day. The baby's training in regular food periods begin at birth, and no crying of the child and no inconvenience to the mother is allowed to interfere. We gauge the child's psychological make-up and at first allow it food oftener than adults, but, because our goal is firmly set and our training consistent, before the child is two years old it has achieved the adult schedule. From the point of view of other cultures, this is as startling as the fact of three-year-old babies perfectly at home in deep water is to us. Modesty is another sphere in which our child training is consistent and economical; we waste no time in clothing the baby and, in contrast to many societies where the child runs naked till it is ceremonially given its skirt or its pubic sheath at adolescence, the child's training fits it precisely for adult conventions.

In neither of these aspects of behavior is there need for an individual in our culture to embark before puberty, at puberty or at some later date upon a course of action which all his previous training has tabued. He is spared the unsureness inevitable in such a transition.

The illustration I have chosen may appear trivial, but in larger and more important aspects of behavior our methods are obviously different. Because of the great variety of child training in different families in our society, I might illustrate continuity of conditioning from individual life histories in our culture, but even these, from a comparative point of view, stop far short of consistency and I shall therefore confine myself to describing arrangements in other cultures in which training, which with us is idiosyncratic, is accepted and traditional and does not therefore involve the same possibility of conflict. I shall choose childhood rather than infant and nursing situations not because the latter do not vary strikingly in different cultures but because they are nevertheless more circumscribed by the baby's physiological needs than is its later training. Childhood situations provide an excellent field in which to illustrate the range of cultural adjustments which are possible within a universally given, but not so drastic, set of physiological facts.

The major discontinuity in the life cycle is of course that the child who is at one point a son must later be a father. These roles in our society are strongly differentiated; a good son is tractable, and does not assume adult responsibilities; a good father provides for his children and should not allow his authority to be flouted. In addition the child must be sexless so far as his family is concerned, whereas the father's sexual role is primary in the family. The individual in one role must revise his behavior from almost all points of view when he assumes the second role.

I shall select for discussion three such contrasts that occur in our culture between the individual's role as child and as father: 1. responsible–non-responsible status role. 2. dominance–submission. 3. contrasted sexual role. It is largely upon our cultural commitments to these three contrasts that the discontinuity in the life cycle of an individual in our culture depends.

Responsible–Non-Responsible Status Role

The techniques adopted by societies which achieve continuity during the life cycle in this sphere in no way differ from those we employ in our uniform conditioning to three meals a day. They are merely applied to other areas of life. We think of the child as wanting to play and the adult as having to work, but in many societies the mother takes the baby daily in her shawl or carrying net to the garden or to gather roots, and adult labor is seen, even in infancy, from the pleasant security of its position in close contact with its mother. When the child can run about, it accompanies its parents still, doing tasks which are essential and yet suited to its powers, and its dichotomy between work and play is not different from that its parents recognize, namely the distinction between the busy day and the free evening. The tasks it is asked to perform are graded to its powers and its elders wait quietly by, not offering to do the task in the child's place. Everyone who is familiar with such societies has been struck by the contrast with our child training. Dr. Ruth Underhill tells me of sitting with a group of Papago elders in Arizona when the man of the house turned to his little three-year-old granddaughter and asked her to close the door. The door was heavy and hard to shut. The child tried, but it did not move. Several times the grandfather repeated, "Yes, close the door." No one jumped to the child's assistance. No one took the responsibility away from her. On the other hand there was no impatience, for, after all, the child was small. They sat gravely waiting till the child succeeded and her grandfather gravely thanked her. It was assumed that the task would not be asked of her unless she could perform it, and having been asked, the responsibility was hers alone just as if she were a grown woman.

The essential point of such child training is that the child is from infancy continuously conditioned to responsible social participation, while at the same time the tasks that are expected of it are adapted to its capacity. The contrast with our society is very great. A child does not make any labor contribution to our industrial society except as it competes with an adult; its work is not measured against its own strength and skill but against high-geared industrial requirements. Even when we praise a child's achievement in the home we are outraged if such praise is interpreted as being of the same order as praise of adults. The child is praised because the parent feels well disposed, regardless of whether the task is well done by adult standards, and the child acquires no sensible standard by which to measure its achievement. The gravity of a Cheyenne Indian family ceremoniously making a feast out of the little boy's first snowbird is at the furthest remove from our behavior. At birth the little boy was presented with a toy bow, and from the time he could run about serviceable bows suited to his stature were specially made for him by the man of the family. Animals and birds were taught him in a graded series beginning with those most easily taken, and as he brought in his first of each species his family duly made a feast of it, accepting his contribution as gravely as the buffalo his father brought. When he finally killed a buffalo, it was only the final step of his childhood conditioning, not a new adult role with which his childhood experience had been at variance.

The Canadian Ojibwa show clearly what results can be achieved. This tribe gains its livelihood by winter trapping and the small family of father, mother, and children live during the long winter alone on their great frozen hunting grounds. The boy accompanies his father and brings in his catch to his sister as his father does to his mother; the girl prepares the meat and skins for him just as his mother does for her husband. By the time the boy is 12, he may have set his own line of traps on a hunting territory of his own and return to his parent's house only once in several months—still bringing the meat and skins to his sister. The young child is taught consistently that it has only itself to rely upon in life, and this is as true in the dealings it will have with the supernatural as in the business of getting a livelihood. This attitude he will accept as a successful adult just as he accepted it as a child (Landes, 1938).

Dominance–Submission

Dominance–submission is the most striking of those categories of behavior where like does not respond to like but where one type of behavior stimulates the opposite response. It is one of the most prominent ways in which behavior is patterned in our culture. When it obtains between classes, it may be nourished by continuous experience; the difficulty in its use between children and adults lies in the fact that an individual conditioned to one set of behavior in childhood must adopt the opposite as an adult. Its opposite is a pattern of approximately identical reciprocal behavior, and societies which rely upon continuous conditioning characteristically invoke this pattern. In some primitive cultures the very terminology of address between father and son, and more commonly, between grandchild and grandson or uncle and nephew, reflects this attitude. In such kinship terminologies one reciprocal expresses each of these relationships so that son and father, for instance, exchange the same term with one another, just as we exchange the same term with a cousin. The child later will exchange it with his son. "Father–son," therefore, is a continuous relationship he enjoys throughout life. The same continuity, backed up by verbal reciprocity, occurs far oftener in the grandchild-grandson relationship or that of mother's brother–sister's son. When these are "joking" relationships, as they often are, travellers report wonderingly upon the liberties and pretensions of tiny toddlers in their dealings with these family elders. In place of our dogma of respect to elders, such societies employ in these cases a reciprocity as nearly identical as may be. The teasing and practical joking the grandfather visits upon his grandchild, the grandchild returns in like coin; he would be led to believe that he failed in propriety if he did not give like for like. If the sister's son has right of access without leave to his mother's brother's possessions, the mother's brother has such rights also to the child's possessions. They share reciprocal privileges and obligations which in our society can develop only between age mates.

From the point of view of our present discussion, such kinship conventions allow the child to put in practice from infancy the same forms of behavior which it will rely upon as an adult; behavior is not polarized into a general requirement of submission for the child and dominance for the adult.

It is clear from the techniques described above, by which the child is conditioned to a responsible status role, that these depend chiefly upon arousing in the child the desire to share responsibility in adult life. To achieve this, little stress is laid upon obedience but much stress upon approval and praise. Punishment is very commonly regarded as quite outside the realm of possibility, and natives in many parts of the world have drawn the conclusion from our usual disciplinary methods that white parents do not love their children. If the child is not required to be submissive however, many occasions for punishment melt away; a variety of situations which call for it do not occur. Many American Indian tribes are especially explicit in rejecting the ideal of a child's submissive or obedient behavior. Prince Maximilian von Wied who visited the Crow Indians over a hundred years ago describes a father's boasting about his young son's intractability even when it was the father himself who was flouted; "He will be a man," his father said. He would have been baffled at the idea that his child should show behavior which would obviously make him appear a poor creature in the eyes of his fellows if he used it as an adult. Dr. George Devereux tells me of a special case of such an attitude among the Mohave at the present time. The child's mother was white and protested to its father that he must take action when the child disobeyed and struck him. "But why?" the father said, "he is little. He cannot possibly injure me." He did not know of any dichotomy according to which an adult expects obedience and a child must accord it. If his child had been docile he would simply have judged that it would become a docile adult—an eventuality of which he would not have approved.

Child training which brings about the same result is common also in other areas of life than that of reciprocal kinship obligations between child and adult. There is a tendency in our culture to regard every situation as having in it the seeds of a dominance-submission relationship. Even where dominance-submission is patently irrelevant, we read in the dichotomy, assuming that in every situation there must be one person dominating another. On the other hand some cultures, even when the situation calls for leadership, do not see it in terms of dominance-submission. To do justice to this attitude it would be necessary to describe their political and especially their economic arrangements, for such an attitude to persist must certainly be supported by economic mechanisms that are congruent with it. But it must also be supported by—or what comes to the same thing, express itself in—child training and familial situations.

Contrasted Sexual Role

Continuity of conditioning in training the child to assume responsibility and to behave no more submissively than adults is quite possible in terms of the child's physiological endowment if his participation is suited to his strength. Because of the late development of the child's reproductive organs, continuity of conditioning in sex experience presents a difficult problem. So far as their belief that the child is anything but a sexless being is concerned, they are probably more nearly right than we are with an opposite dogma. But the great break is presented by the universally sterile unions before puberty and the presumably fertile ones after maturations. This physiological fact no amount of cultural manipulation can minimize or alter, and societies therefore which stress continuous conditioning most strongly sometimes do not expect children to be interested in sex experience until they have matured physically. This is striking among American Indian tribes like the Dakota; adults observe great privacy in sex acts and in no way stimulate children's sexual activity. There need be no discontinuity, in the sense in which I have used the term, in such a program if the child is taught nothing it does not have to unlearn later. In such cultures adults view children's experimentation as in no way wicked or dangerous but merely as innocuous play which can have no serious consequences. In some societies such play is minimal and the children manifest little interest in it. But the same attitude may be taken by adults in societies where such play is encouraged and forms a major activity among small children. This is true among most of the Melanesian cultures of Southeast New Guinea; adults go as far as to laugh off sexual affairs within the prohibited class if the children are not mature, saying that since they cannot marry there can be no harm done.

It is this physiological fact of the difference between children's sterile unions and adults' presumably fertile sex relations which must be kept in mind in order to understand the different mores which almost always govern sex expression in children and in adults in the same culture. A great many cultures with preadolescent sexual license require marital fidelity, and a great many which value pre-marital virginity in either male or female arrange their marital life with great license. Continuity in sex experience is complicated by factors which it was unnecessary to consider in the problems previously discussed. The essential problem is not whether or not the child's sexuality is consistently exploited—for even where such exploitation is favored in the majority of cases the child must seriously modify his behavior at puberty or at marriage. Continuity in sex expression means rather that the child is taught nothing it must unlearn later. If the cultural emphasis is upon sexual pleasure the child who is continuously conditioned will be encouraged to experiment freely and pleasurably, as among the Marquesans (Linton, unpublished); if emphasis is upon reproduction, as among the Zuni of New Mexico, childish sex proclivities will not be exploited, for the only important use which sex is thought to serve in his culture is not yet possible to him. The important contrast with our child training is that although a Zuni child is impressed with the wickedness of premature sex experimentation he does not run the risk as in our culture of associating this wickedness with sex itself rather than with sex at his age. The adult in our culture has often failed to unlearn the wickedness or the dangerousness of sex, a lesson which was impressed upon him strongly in his most formative years.

Discontinuity in Conditioning

Even from this very summary statement of continuous conditioning, the economy of such mores is evident. In spite of the obvious advantages, however, there are difficulties in its way. Many primitive societies expect as different behavior from an individual as child and as adult as we do, and such discontinuity involves a presumption of strain.

Many societies of this type however minimize strain by the techniques they employ, and some techniques are more successful than others in ensuring the individual's functioning without conflict. It is from this point of view that age-grade societies reveal their fundamental significance. Age-graded cultures characteristically demand different behavior of the individual at different times of his life, and persons of a like age-grade are grouped into a society whose activities are all oriented toward the behavior desired at that age. Individuals "graduate" publicly and with honor from one of these groups to another. Where age society members are enjoined to loyalty and mutual support, and are drawn not only from the local group, but from the whole tribe as among the Arapaho, or even from other tribes as among the Wagawaga of Southeast New Guinea, such an institution has many advantages in eliminating conflicts among local groups and fostering intratribal peace. This seems to be also a factor in the tribal military solidarity of the similarly organized Masai of East Africa. The point that is of chief interest for our present discussion, however, is that by this means an individual who at any time takes on a new set of duties and virtues is supported not only by a solid phalanx of age mates but by the traditional prestige of the organized "secret" society into which he has now graduated. Fortified in this way, individuals in such cultures often swing between remarkable extremes of opposite behavior without apparent psychic threat. For example, the great majority exhibit prideful and non-conflicted behavior at each stage in the life cycle even when a prime of life devoted to passionate and aggressive head hunting must be followed by a later life dedicated to ritual and to mild and peaceable civic virtues (Elkin, unpublished).

Our chief interest here, however, is in discontinuity which primarily affects the child. In many primitive societies such discontinuity has been fostered, not because of economic or political necessity or because such discontinuity provides for a socially valuable division of labor, but because of some conceptual dogma. The most striking of these are the Australian and Papuan cultures where the ceremony of the "Making of Man" flourishes. In such societies it is believed that men and women have opposite and conflicting powers, and male children, who are of undefined status, must be initiated into the male role. In Central Australia the boy child is of the woman's side, and women are tabu in the final adult stages of tribal ritual. The elaborate and protracted initiation ceremonies of the Arunta therefore snatch the boy from the mother, dramatize his gradual repudiation of her. In a final ceremony he is reborn as a man out of the men's ceremonial "baby pouch." The men's ceremonies are ritual statements of a masculine solidarity, carried out by fondling one another's *churingas,* the material symbol of each man's life, and by letting out over one another blood drawn from their veins. After this warm bond among men has been established through the ceremonies, the boy joins the men in the men's house and participates in tribal rites (Spencer and Gillen, 1927; Róheim 1932). The enjoined discontinuity has been tribally bridged.

West of the Fly River in southern New Guinea there is a striking development of this Making of Men cult which involves a childhood period of passive homosexuality. Among the Keraki (Williams, 1936) it is thought that no boy can grow to full stature without playing the role for some years. Men slightly older take the active role, and the older man is a jealous partner. The life cycle of the Keraki Indians includes, therefore, in succession, passive homosexuality, active homosexuality and heterosexuality. The Keraki believe that pregnancy will result from post-pubertal passive homosexuality and see evidences of such practices in any fat man whom, even as an old man, they may kill or drive out of the tribe because of their fear. The ceremony that is of interest in connection with the present discussion takes place at the end of the period of passive homosexuality. This ceremony consists in burning out the possibility of pregnancy from the boy by pouring lye down his throat, after which he has no further protection if he gives way to the practice. There is no technique for ending active homosexuality, but this is not explicitly tabu for older men; heterosexuality and children however are highly valued. Unlike the neighboring Marindanim who share their homosexual practices, Keraki husband and wife share the same house and work together in the gardens.

I have chosen illustrations of discontinuous conditioning where it is not too much to say that the cultural institutions furnish adequate support to the individual as he progresses from role to role or interdicts the previous behavior in a summary fashion. The contrast with arrangements in our culture is very striking, and against this background of social arrangements in other cultures the adolescent period of *Sturm und Drang* with which we are so familiar becomes intelligible in terms of our discontinuous cultural institutions and dogmas rather than in terms of physiological necessity. It is even more pertinent to consider these comparative facts in relation to maladjusted persons in our culture who are said to be fixated at one or another pre-adult level. It is clear that if we were to look at our social arrangements as an outsider, we should infer directly from our family institutions and habits of child training that many individuals would not "put off childish things"; we should have to say that our adult activity demands traits that are interdicted in children, and that, far from redoubling efforts to help children bridge this gap, adults in our culture put all the blame on the child when he fails to manifest spontaneously the new behavior or, over-stepping the mark, manifests it with untoward belligerence. It is not surprising that in such a society many individuals fear to use behavior which has up to that time been under a ban, and trust instead, though at great psychic cost, to attitudes that have been exercised with approval during their formative years. Insofar as we invoke a physiological scheme to account for these neurotic adjustments, we are led to overlook the possibility of developing social institutions which would lessen the social cost we now pay; instead we elaborate a set of dogmas which prove inapplicable under other social conditions.

THE MYSTIQUE OF ADOLESCENCE

JOSEPH B. ADELSON

Our special fascination with the adolescent, no doubt heightened by recent waves of campus turmoil and the emergence of "hippies" and "street people," is well reflected in proliferating theories of adolescent development (Muus, 1962; Miller, 1969; Weiner, 1970). Earlier attacks (Mead, 1939) on the classical Sturm und Drang *concepts of adolescence have been joined by theory and data from varied clinical and research sources (Friedenberg, 1959; Silber et al., 1961; Adelson, 1966; Masterson, 1967; Offer, 1967). In the emerging revised picture of adolescence, some would emphasize the prolongation of adolescence, the disappearance of adolescence, the coping adaptive equipment of adolescents, the impact of ecological factors upon adolescence, the greater incidence of "normal" or "competent" adolescents. Adelson, in this penetrating appraisal, focuses on the psychosocial continuity and constriction of the modal adolescent rather than on disruption, disorder, and resynthesis. In contrast with traditional views (Blos, 1962), he details the typical adolescent's avoidance of fully joining the generation conflict, and his settling for cheap autonomies in lieu of genuine detachment, individuation, and change.*

In recent years the adolescent has come to weigh oppressively on the American consciousness. Just a few years ago he was of little substance in our collective imaginings, in fiction, and in the mass media. He was represented as a figure of fun: callow, flighty, silly; given to infatuations, wild enthusiasms, and transient moodiness. His prototype was Andy Hardy, Henry Aldrich. Or he was sometimes seen as a latter-day and rather harmless Werther: sensitive, emotionally afflicted, overly sentimental. In either case, the figure was seen as lovable, though sometimes exasperat-

Reprinted from *Psychiatry,* 27, 1964, pp. 1–5 by special permission of the William Alanson White Psychiatric Foundation, Inc.

ing, and not to be taken too seriously. He would get over it—whatever *it* might be—in time. I shall call this type the adolescent as Fool.[1] The Fool exists outside the world of adult happenings; he is blessedly innocent of complication, guilt, or responsibility. He is a fool not in being duped, but because he is unrelated to the intrigues and corruptions, or the moral seriousness, of adulthood. He inhabits an Eden of preresponsibility.

These days two new images, weightier and more ominous, have superseded the Fool figure, and between them they divide the contemporary sense of the adolescent. One of these I shall call the adolescent as Visionary. He is distinguished by a purity of moral vision which allows him to perceive or state the moral simplicity hidden by adult complication. In the way of prophets, he is also a Victim. He is betrayed, exploited, or neglected by the adult world. His needs go unrecognized by adults too busy in their own affairs; or, as an innocent bystander, he may be victimized by adult corruption. The prototypes here are J. D. Salinger's adolescents, Holden Caulfield, or Franny Glass. Whereas the Fool is essentially unrelated to the adult world, the Visionary-Victim is connected to it in being passive and powerless. Perceptive, articulate, morally precocious, his only resources are insight and knowledge, and the strength which may eventually accrue from them.

The antitype to the Visionary is the newest and most disturbing representation of the adolescent as Victimizer. Leather-jacketed, cruel, sinister, and amoral, he is the nemesis-hero of a new genre of fiction and film. A man accidentally incurs the hatred of some hoodlum youths who threaten to kill him. He appeals to the police for protection, but they are impotent to help him. The story ends as the night closes in, and the man, alone and helpless, awaits his death at the hands of the youths. The story's mood is paranoid; the adolescent is the persecutor, the killer. This adolescent stands in utter contrast to the Visionary; one is innocent, the other evil; one is powerless, the other omnipotent.

The emergence of these images makes it clear that the adolescent occupies a peculiarly intense place in American thought and feeling.[2] As

[1] Compare Klapp (1962).

[2] Yet this is not to say that these motifs have been restricted either to American thought, or to the representation of adolescence. The themes of saintliness and violence have been endemic in recent European writing as well, and have also figured in the depiction of post-adolescent prototypes—for example, the Beats as "holy barbarians". An interesting variation is seen in the effort to fuse saintliness and violence, as in the writings of Jean Genet, Norman Mailer, and William Burroughs.

prophet and victim, he joins and replaces the child-innocent who once played these roles exclusively. As victimizer, he is the carrier of the society's projections; sadistic and sexual motives are imputed to him, and he joins or replaces the gangster, the Negro, and other projective enemies. Nor is it only in our dark imaginings that these adolescent types hold so central a place. A good deal of recent social thought sees in the adolescent's character and situation the key to our moral and social pathology. Curiously, it is in its response to the adolescent that the social criticism of the Left is joined by the social criticism of the Right. Both see our youth as reflecting what is most ignoble and most portentous in our time.

I have stressed this mystique of adolescence because it has influenced both work and thought in the social sciences. The attention of social scientists has been captured by two conspicuous but atypical enclaves of adolescence, drawn from extreme and opposing ends of the social-class continuum, and representing exceptional solutions to the adolescent crisis. The victimizer corresponds, of course, to the delinquent. The visionary-victim corresponds—though this may not be apparent at first—to the sensitive, articulate, intense, intelligent type of upper-middle-class adolescent on whom the psychoanalytic theory of adolescence is almost exclusively based.

Now in most ways these two adolescent types could not be more dissimilar. The estranged lower-class youngster relies largely on alloplastic solutions to the adolescent crisis, living out mutely, in urgent yet aimless acts of violence or bravado, a sullen resentment against the middle-class world and its values. The estranged upper-middle-class youngster is largely autoplastic in response, subject to acute intrapsychic upheavals which are expressed in neurotic symptoms, affect storms, character eccentricities, and a general value ferment. Paradoxically, these two extremes are alike, and their alikeness is in being different from the normative adolescent—that is, the socially modal adolescent. The extremes are alike in showing an unusual degree of independence from the family; they are alike in disaffection, in acting out or thinking out a discontent with the social order; they are alike, above all, in their adoption of radical solutions to that key problem of adolescence, the task of ego-synthesis. I want to suggest that one cannot generalize these processes to the adolescent population at large. The adolescent at the extremes responds to the instinctual and psychosocial upheaval of puberty by disorder, by failures of ego synthesis, by a tendency to abandon earlier values and object-attachments. In the normative response to adolescence, however, there is more commonly an avoidance of inner and outer conflict, a premature identity consolidation, ego and ideological constriction, and a general unwillingness to take psychic risks. [3]

Now having stated my thesis, let me pause here to say something about its origins. These conclusions derive from a national survey of adolescent boys and girls. [4] A colleague and I studied, by means of a rather extensive semistructured interview, 3,000 youngsters, including about 1,000 boys between 14 and 16, and about 2,000 girls between 12 and 18. Let me say at once that we were very much aware of the limitations of this sort of interview; one must write questions suitable for the lowest common denominator, and the interview setting is one which maximizes cautious, shallow, and platitudinous responses. But we were, if anything, hypersensitive to these problems, and mined the questionnaire with a great number and variety of projective items. Thanks to IBM technology, we were buried in data; but I want to bypass a discussion of specific findings and approach these interviews as personal documents, to consider them impressionistically, discursively, clinically. The great advantage of this kind of project is that it permits study of those adolescents who make up the middle majority, who evoke neither grief nor wonder, and who all too often escape notice. When one looks at the normative forms of the adolescent experience, one is led to think twice about the received version of adolescence.

Let me begin with the question of autonomy and conflict. Many writers take the position that at puberty the child is under great pressure to detach himself from the family emotionally, to find a pattern of disengagement. The instinctual revival brings with it a return of oedipal dangers and temptations. The home is a hothouse, and the youngster must discover a way out, a means of escaping his dependent status in the family and, even more urgently, the dimly recognized drives and feelings toward his parents. The psychosexual irritation pushes the child from home, leading him to negotiate or battle with the parents for greater freedom. The conflict of generations is joined. Theorists add to this the psychosocial pull of the child's need to be his own man, to forge an individual identity—those needs which draw him toward the future. These forces give the adolescent peer group its critical importance. Peer group and culture supplant the family as the locus of authority and the giver of norms. Through his immersion in the peer group, through the incorporation of

[3] It should be clear that I am speaking here of institutionalized patterns, rather than voluntaristic "choices."

[4] A full report on this research, in co-authorship with Elizabeth Douvan, will be published shortly by John Wiley. A report on one aspect can be found in Douvan and Adelson (1958).

peer ideals and values, the youngster gains the support he needs to win autonomy from the family. And the peer group provides a haven in which the delicate task of self-exploration and self-definition can be accomplished. [5]

This view of adolescence has a good deal to recommend it, but my reading of the interviews suggests that it needs revision in some important particulars. It exaggerates the degree of conflict between parent and child; it wrongly estimates the autonomy issue; and it misinterprets the role of the peer group. The normative adolescent tends to avoid overt conflict with his family. This is not to say that conflict is not present, but it is largely unconscious conflict—undersurface resentments which do not necessarily liberate or enlarge the personality, but which, paradoxically, increase the child's docility toward his parents. Even when one does find overt conflict, one senses that it has an *as if* quality to it, that it is a kind of war game, with all the sights and sounds of battle but without any bloodshed. More often than not, the conflicts center on trivia, on issues of taste—clothing, grooming, and the like. It can be argued that these issues are trivial only to the adult, that they are of great symbolic importance in the adolescent's quest for autonomy. True; but one can reply that parent and child play out an empty ritual of disaffection, that they agree to disagree only on token issues, on teen issues, and in doing so are able to side-step any genuine encounter of differences.

Much the same is true of autonomy. There are autonomies and autonomies. The American adolescent asks for, and is freely given, an unusual degree of behavioral freedom—the right to come and go, to share in setting rules, and so on. But it is far more problematic whether he asks for or achieves a high degree of emotional autonomy, and it is even more doubtful whether he manages much in the way of value autonomy. Indeed, the ease with which the adolescent acquires behavioral freedom may tend to interfere with the achievement of emotional and ideological freedom, for reasons I will mention in a moment. As to the peer group, its supposed functions—as an arena for the confrontation of the self, for the testing and trying out of identities—are present for many adolescents, but for many more the peer group is used for the learning and display of sociability and social skills. The peer culture is all too often a kind of playpen, designed to keep children out of harm's way and out of parents' hair. It may not work out this way; the children may begin throwing toys at each other, or—what is worse—may begin throwing

[5] A full yet succinct review of this general position can be found in Spiegel (1951).

them at the grownups in the living room. But generally it does work out just this way. The peer group, with its artificial amusements and excitements, more often than not acts to hinder differentiation and growth.

This is especially evident in the area of values and ideology. The traditional idea of the adolescent experience holds that the youngster becomes involved in an intense concern with ethics, political ideology, religious belief, and so on. The moral parochialism of early childhood was thought to be smashed by the moral fervor and incipient cosmopolitanism of adolescence. The youngster's need to detach himself from the family and its view of the moral and social order, his need to redo the ego-superego constellation, his need to find new and more appropriate ego ideals, his need to use ideology as a solution for instinctual problems—all these needs came together, so it was thought, to produce a value crisis somewhere in the course of the adolescent career. This pattern can be found in adolescence, but it is found in a bold, sometimes stubborn, often unhappy minority. Our interviews confirm a mounting impression from other studies that American adolescents are on the whole not deeply involved in ideology, nor are they prepared to do much individual thinking on value issues of any generality. Why is this so? I would guess because to think anew and differently endangers the adolescent's connection to the community—his object attachments—and complicates the task of ego synthesis.

Let me sum up in the language of personality theory. The inherent tensions of adolescence are displaced to and discharged within the matrix of peer-group sociability. Intrapsychically the defenses and character positions adopted are those which curtail experience and limit the growth and differentiation of the self—repression, reaction-formation, and certain forms of ego restriction. These modes of dealing with inner and outer experience join to produce a pseudoadapative solution of the adolescent crisis, marked by cognitive stereotypy, value stasis, and interpersonal conformity. It is a solution which is accomplished by resisting conflict, resisting change, resisting the transformation of the self. It settles for a modest, sluggish resynthesis of the ego that closely follows the lines of the older organization of drives, defenses, values, and object-attachments. It is characterized by an avoidance of identity-diffusion through identity-coarctation.

One is left to wonder whether this form of adolescence is a new thing in this country, or whether Americans have always been falsely bemused by one or another mystique of adolescence. Of course we cannot know; if, as this paper has suggested, today's adults have egregiously misunderstood the adolescents they see before their very eyes, then it would be prudent, to say the least, to avoid generalizations about historically earlier patterns of adolescence. In all likelihood, the degree of tension and disorder has always been more apparent than real. It is always more likely that passion, defiance, and suffering will capture the fancy, and that the amiable, colorless forms of adaptation will be ignored.

And yet—and yet—one feels nevertheless that the contemporary modes of adolescence do involve something new, that Friedenberg (1959), among others, is correct in saying that adolescence is disappearing as the period during which the individual can achieve a decisive articulation of the self. If this is so—and granting how large an *if* this is—then perhaps one important reason that can be singled out is the extraordinary attenuation of today's adolescence. Given the long preparation required for advanced technical training, given the uselessness of the adolescent in the labor market, parent and child settle down for a long, long period of time during which the child will, in one way or another, remain a dependent being. Traditionally, adolescence has been the age in which the child readied himself to leave home; accounts of adolescence in the earlier part of this century often describe a decisive encounter between father and son, a decisive testing of wills, in which the son makes a determined bid for autonomy, either by leaving home, or threatening to do so, and meaning it. The adolescent then had little of the freedom he has today; he was kept under the parental thumb, but he used his captivity well, to strengthen himself for a real departure and a real autonomy. Nowadays, the adolescent and his parents are both made captive by their mutual knowledge of the adolescent's dependency. They are locked in a room with no exit, and they make the best of it by an unconscious *quid pro quo,* in which the adolescent forfeits his adolescence, and instead becomes a teen-ager. He keeps the peace by muting his natural rebelliousness, through transforming it into structured and defined techniques for getting on people's nerves. The passions, the restlessness, the vivacity of adolescence are partly strangled and partly drained off in the mixed childishness and false adulthood of the adolescent teen culture.

PUBERTY AND ADOLESCENCE

Peter Blos

Blos' article—the introductory chapter of his book (1962)—in contrast to Adelson's preceding paper, falls well within the traditional boundaries of psychoanalytic concepts of adolescence, to which Blos has been a major contributor (1941, 1954, 1958). Although he uses data from child development research and is keenly aware of the influences of social factors in shaping adolescents, Blos places ultimate reliance on data gathered from the application of psychoanalytic technique to patients in Western societies. His emphasis focuses on intrapsychic aspects of psychosexual maturation, and he defines adolescence as, "the psychological process of adaptation to pubescence." He presents a condensed introductory account of adolescence, couched essentially in classic psychoanalytic terms of strong id—weak ego, of "emotional turmoil" and "profound upheaval," of loss, isolation, and apprehensive steps forward.

At no time have observers of human development failed to recognize the momentous significance of the physical and psychological dimensions of puberty. Sexual maturation has always given this stage of growth a signal importance to which the personality transformations of this period were directly and causally related. However, not until the psychology of early childhood had been explored and systematized through psychoanalysis was it possible to understand puberty in its psychological aspects: it is to these aspects that we refer when we speak of *adolescence.* The elucidations of early childhood linked adolescence genetically to earlier periods of life; thus puberty was instated into a continuum of psychological development. We came to recognize adolescence as the terminal stage of

Reprinted with permission of the Macmillan Company from *On Adolescence: A Psychoanalytic Interpretation* by P. Blos. New York: Free Press, 1962, pp. 1–14, © the Free Press of Glencoe, Inc., 1962.

the fourth phase of psychosexual development, the genital phase, which had been interrupted by the latency period.

The psychoanalytic knowledge of childhood was first derived by reconstruction from the analysis of adults and later confirmed and elaborated by child analysis and direct observation. What we have learned about adolescence is almost wholly the result of clinical studies of adolescents themselves. This source of information will undoubtedly be enriched and elaborated through memory and reconstruction of adolescence in the analysis of adults. It appears that certain psychic spheres and processes inaccessible to analysis during adolescence can more easily and succinctly be investigated in retrospect through the derivatives of the adolescent period analyzed at a later age. The reconstruction of adolescence in adult analysis has recently received explicit attention, and indeed is increasingly considered a requisite component of a total genetic reconstruction.

The biological event of puberty gives rise to a new drive and ego organization. In this process we recognize the developmental model of early childhood, wherein mental organizations were formed in association with physiological functions, thus establishing the erogenous zones of the body. The term puberty is used here to denote the physical manifestations of sexual maturation: e.g., prepuberty refers to the period just preceding the development of primary and secondary sex characters. The term adolescence is used to denote the psychological processes of adaptation to the condition of pubescence. Consequently, the phase of preadolescence, which makes its appearance at a given state of physical maturation, remains independent in its course: e.g., the phase of preadolescence can continue overly long, unaffected by the progression of physical maturation.

The fact remains that pubescent change or the state of sexual maturation influences the rise and decline of certain interests and attitudes; this has been borne out by statistical studies (Stone and Baker, 1939). They have shown that a greater proportion of postmenarchial as compared with premenarchial girls gave responses indicating heterosexual interests and interests in adornment and display of person; on the other hand, they revealed a disinterest in participation in games and activities requiring vigorous or strenuous activity; they engaged in or were interested in imaginative and day-dreaming activities. Such findings, of course, do not reveal intrinsic characteristics of the pubertal condition; however, they do demonstrate how sexual maturation initiates shifts and changes in the mental life of the pubescent child. The quality and content of these changes is immensely flexible; it is left to the sociologist to record and study their manifestations. It is the concern of this study to abstract from the manifest mental content those psychological processes which can be considered specific to the various phases of adolescence.

In the days of prepsychoanalytic psychology, puberty was considered the time of onset, physically and emotionally, of sexual development. The analytic insight into early childhood has corrected this view, and the onset of sexuality in early childhood has become an accepted fact. Freud (1905b) described in broad outlines the phases of psychosexual development in the *Three Essays on the Theory of Sexuality,* and offered the first psychoanalytic concept of puberty: he applied the genetic principle to the period of puberty. As early as 1898, Freud has already stated that it is erroneous to suppose that the child's sexual life begins with the onset of puberty.

Psychoanalysis has always spoken of two prominent periods in the development of sexuality, namely, early childhood and puberty. Both phases emerge under the tutelage of physiological functions, such as nursing in infancy and genital masturbation in puberty. Instinctual drives at the dawn of life enlist the perceptomotor apparatus for the reduction of tension. Consequently the child soon becomes inextricably interwoven with his environment, on which need gratification depends. The long duration of the child's dependency is what makes man human. In this process the development of memory, causality, conscience, and fantasy make thinking and conflict possible. Thus abundant alternative solutions to the pressures of instinctual drives make their appearance. The variability of the object of instinctual drives has always been described by psychoanalysis as almost infinite, while the aim has a far greater constancy. It is no surprise to see that the psychological representation of the environment, including attendant conflictual anxiety, soon stands in the way of any simple solution to drive-satisfaction; in other words, the total personality becomes gradually involved in the maintenance of a psychosomatic homeostasis.

During the period of growth—comprising roughly the first two decades of life—there is progressive personality differentiation and integration. Differentiating processes are effected by maturational stimulants simultaneously acting from within and from without in supplementary and complementary fashion, and are integrated in conformity with the maturational schedule of the body and of the psychic apparatuses. The capacity to assess, reconcile, and accommodate internal and external stimuli, benign and dangerous, enables the ego to live in relative harmony with drive, superego, and environment.

We must keep in mind that the complex phenomena of adolescence are built on specific antecedents which reside in early childhood. If we can recognize the survival of these basic organizations in their derivative forms, we shall be able to discern psychic origins and to study the formation of psychic structures.

Infancy is governed by the pleasure-pain principle, which loses its supremacy as the infant's trust in the mother as the comforter of its physical or emotional distress grows stronger. This basic life situation is of lasting influence and is apt to be revived in critical situations during later years.

The function of regulating anxiety is performed by the parents—particularly the mother—in the early years and is partly taken over by the child as fantasy life develops and soothing activities—sucking, stroking, masturbation, play, and body movement—progressively become subject to the child's volition. Thus the child unrelentlessly pursues new ways to master anxiety, ways in which play activities with fantasy content and psychological meaning move into the foreground of importance. The distinction of inside and outside reality, of me and not-me, signals the child's growing separation from the mother and a lessening of dependency. The differentiation takes a decisive turn at about two years of age, initiating the process of individuation; it ordinarily has achieved a degree of stability at about the age of three. Mobility, language, and social experiences widen the child's life space and bring to his awareness the desirability of being like others, most important, like the parent or sibling. This forward push into life fills the four- or five-year-old with the desire to take father's or mother's place or either one's alternately, indeed simultaneously. A logical consequence of the child's dependency on the adult makes him believe that taking the role of the parent of the same sex will afford him the desired attributes of the displaced parent, attributes which are so highly admired and envied by the young child. Reality renders the attainment of these wishes futile, however, and the child must settle reluctantly for the promise that the future will bring him the fulfillments he must forego at this stage. The child permanently preserves his aspirations and his defeats by making the parent a part of himself; therefore the superego has been defined as "the heir of the oedipus complex" (Freud, 1923).

The period intervening between the early bloom of infantile sexuality and pubescent genital sexuality is referred to as the latency period. "Complete dependence on the parents ceases and identification begins to take the place of object-love" (A. Freud, 1936). Consequently, formal learning and group life attract more of the child's attention; social consciousness carries the child beyond the family confines, while family-centeredness continues to exert its influence. No new sexual aim arises during the years of about five to ten, namely from the end of early childhood to the beginning of puberty. These years constitute the latency period for which the lack of a new sexual aim is characteristic rather than the complete lack of sexual activity. There exists abundant evidence that all through middle childhood sexual activity or fantasy continue to exist in one form or another. The latency child acquires strength and competence in mastering both reality and instinct (sublimation) with the support of educational influences. These achievements are the fruit of the latency period; without their availability—or, to put it differently, without having passed through the latency period—the child will be defeated by puberty. The precondition for the adolescent process to evolve is a successful passage through the latency period.

The biphasic development of sexuality prolongs childhood and represents a uniquely human condition, which in great measure is responsible for man's cultural attainments. At the present time there is a tendency to prolong adolescence, due to the complexities of modern life. This of course cannot be without effect on the young individual and often overtaxes his adaptive potential.

Adolescence is most prominently characterized by physical changes, changes which are reflected in all facets of behavior. Not only is it true that adolescents of both sexes are deeply affected by the physical changes taking place in their own bodies—but on a more subtle and unconscious plane, the process of pubescence affects the development of their interests, their social behavior and the quality of their affective life. These patterns should not of course be regarded as the direct results of physiological factors, for no direct parallel can be established between adolescent changes occurring simultaneously in the anatomical, physiological, mental, and emotional development. Dispositions already existent before puberty will always affect the outcome.

There are, however, certain intrinsic features of the pubescent growth process which are relevant for an understanding of adolescent behavior and which therefore deserve our attention. Observers of adolescents have always been struck by the wide range in onset, duration, and termination of pubescence. A different tempo of physiological changes exists in different adolescents which is part of the individual's total growth pattern. Chronological age does not provide a valid criterion for physical maturation. Among the hundred boys studied by Stolz (1951) there are ten who were two or more years retarded and an equal number who were two or more years accelerated in appropriate male structural and functional characteristics, described in terms of chronological age norms. Among girls a span of five years, from eleven to sixteen—with the mean menarchial age of 13.5 in the United States—constitutes the age range in which menarche occurs (Gallagher, 1960). Statistical studies have shown that the age of menarche has been slightly lowered during the last generation (Shuttleworth, 1938), and that the average height of the present generation of adolescent boys who have attained final stature is greater than that of their fathers. Not only is the individual variability of growth striking, but also the changes between generations have to be taken into account, since in adolescents there are always two generations significantly and crucially intertwined.

Of course a certain stage of development prevails in each age group; and this majority, supported by outside influences, tends to set the standard for physical appropriateness for the group. In relation to precocity and retardation, Stolz (1951) has noted that only in one or two cases of the hundred boys he studied was there evidence that precocity contributed to maladjustment, but eight of the ten retarded boys gave evidence of emotional insecurity. Generally, it can be said that those adolescents who enter pubescence early go through it rapidly, while the later maturing child progresses at a slower rate.

It is well known that girls begin their pubertal development and attain full growth at an earlier age than boys. "Girls gain in height at an accelerating rate from nine to twelve years, whereas boys do so from eleven to fourteen years. This results in the fact that girls are taller than boys between eleven and thirteen years" (Stuart, 1945, p. 668). This difference in physical development between the sexes has an obvious significance for grouping children. Usually children are grouped in accordance with their chronological age level; consequently, children of the same age who are at different stages of physical development are put together in situations which demand social and mental co-operation as well as competition. The individual adolescent always lives within a group of age-mates who vary widely in physical development and in interests. This condition is responsible for the many forms of imitative and "as-if" behavior to which the adolescent resorts in order to keep within the expected pattern of conduct and to protect the social compatibility with the peer group to which he belongs.

In addition to the discrepancies in onset and duration of pubescence among a group of adolescents, the individual's own pattern of growth is not uniform throughout his body. Each organ system is affected by growth in a characteristic way; in terms of the total life span of the individual, each system consistently performs it function optimally. But during pubescence, extreme accelerations and retardations in the growth of particular organ systems produce an uneven distribution of growth within the total organism. Increase in body bulk may not be paralleled by a proportionate increase in breadth or in height; nor do primary and secondary sex characteristics develop at equal rates. This lack of uniformity in physical development, called *asymmetrical growth,* often puts extreme demands upon the physical and mental adaptivity of the individual. In this connection it has to be realized that growth often occurs as a sequence of sudden changes rather than as a gradual smooth progression. "The adolescent spurt [of growth in height] occurs during the tenth year in girls and during the thirteenth year in boys" (Stuart, 1946, p. 670). Growth spurts in relation to height, weight, musculature, and the development of primary and secondary sex characteristics may be accompanied by relevant emotional states. A change of one's body image, and a re-evaluation of the self in the light of new physical powers and sensations are two of the psychological consequences of the change in physical status. (These consequences are described below, in relation to the phases of adolescence.) And because the physical changes occurring during puberty are so marked and visible, the adolescent inevitably tends to compare his own bodily development with that of his contemporaries.

The majority of adolescents are concerned at one time or another with the normality of their physical status; the absence of clearcut age norms as far as adolescent physiology is concerned merely adds to their uncertainty. Physical differences among individuals of a comparable maturity level—and these differences are even greater in a group of the same age level—manifest themselves among girls in variations of the menstrual cycle and in breast development, among boys in variations of genital development, voice change, and facial hair. Such striking indications of sexual maturation imbue physical growth with highly personal meanings.

Physical development, furthermore, does not always progress appropriately—it sometimes assumes features characteristic of the opposite sex. This seems to be less disturbing to girls than boys, perhaps because of the tendency among some groups of girls to prefer a boyish body build, a build also appreciated by boys. Boys are much more concerned (and so are their parents) when they manifest characteristics inappropriate to their sex. The development of the breast in boys (Grenlich et al., 1942; Gallagher, 1960) tends to stimulate and accentuate bisexual fantasies and drives. The breast development is described by Stuart (1946) as "an elevation of the nipples in a slightly full areola. Occasionally, a mass of firm, sharply demarcated tissue several centimeters in diameter underlies this areola and gives the appearance of true breast development. This occurs about the time when dense, dark pubic hair is present at the base of the penis and when axillary hair is beginning to appear. This tissue disappears after a variable number of months, depending on its degree and development." In this connection it should also be mentioned that the preadolescent boy tends to adiposity of the lower torso which emphasizes feminine body contours. This condition normally disappears with accelerated growth in height.

Menarche is usually considered the sign that the girl has achieved sexual maturity. In fact this event really signals that the maturation of the reproductive organs is underway but is by no means complete. "It is now accepted that menstruation begins in most girls before their ovaries are capable of producing mature ova, and ovulation may take place before the uterus is mature enough to support normal gestation. This brings about a period of adolescent sterility" (Benedek, 1959a, pg. 730–731). This period of post-menarchial sterility can last for a year or longer (Josselyn, 1954).

Pubescence is often marked by physical symptoms which make the afflicted adolescent acutely self-conscious of his changing body. Acne, a disfiguring skin condition, and various forms of dysmenorrhea are likely to interfere with the adolescent's desire to grow up. Obesity of different degrees and types, especially prevalent among girls, leads to experimentation with diets.

Often, the adolescent reacts to medical examination with self-conscious reluctance, which is prompted by the fear that the physician may discover inappropriate or abnormal developmental characteristics. Also, the prospect of being examined is apt to intensify his masturbation conflicts, sexual fantasies, and the accompanying feelings of guilt.

One difficulty which arises in any discussion of adolescence stems from the fact that there are many ways of completing the adolescent process successfully and thus achieving a stable ego and drive organization. Furthermore, the time span of this development is as relative as the adaptive processes involved in the attainment of maturity are complex. When ritualization and formalization relieve an individual from achieving his own resolution of the exigencies of growing up, no idiosyncratic and personal adjustment has to be sought; little choice is open, and conflict is minimal. However, in cultures where tradition and custom exert no unchallenged influence over the individual, the adolescent has to achieve by personal resourcefulness the adaptation that institutionalization does not offer him. On the other hand, this lack of institutionalized patterning opens up the opportunity for individual development, for the creation of a unique, highly original and personal variant on tradition. The increase in psychological differentiation during adolescence is necessarily attended by an increase in psychic lability; this condition is reflected by adolescent emotional disturbances of varying seriousness and crippling effects, transient or permanent.

It has been possible—with due allowance for some variability—to establish age norms of child development in early childhood. (In fact, the younger the child, the narrower the variability.) A normative assessment of adolescents must, however, be vague and incongruous. The high degree of plasticity so characteristic for adolescence works against this approach. It is true that there are sequential patterns of maturation in adolescence, but their relatedness to age is loose. Behavior at this age is a complex phenomenon which is highly dependent on the individual life history and on the milieu in which the adolescent grows up. However, if we regard adolescence as a maturational period in which each individual has to work through the exigencies of his total life experiences in order to arrive at a stable ego and drive organization, then any study of adolescence must attempt to clarify those processes which lead to new psychic formations or to psychic restructuring.

In many societies these new formations are conventionalized by traditional sanctions and taboos. The initiation rites which anthropologists have so abundantly recorded are eloquent witnesses to the fact that at puberty a profound reorganization of ego and libido positions occurs; and some societies do provide models on which the adolescent can pattern his personal resolution. By doing this, the society absorbs the maturational push of puberty into its organization and puts it to use for its own purposes. The designation of a new role and status offers the adolescent a self-image which is definite, reciprocal, and groupbound; at the same time, the societal assimilation of the maturing child is promoted. Without this kind of environmental complementation or reinforcement, the adolescent's self-image loses clarity and cohesiveness; consequently he requires constant restitutive and defensive operations to maintain it.

Forms of institutionalized status have changed through the ages and in different societies; they will not concern us in this study. We shall, in fact, restrict our investigations to Western culture, because only in this society have adolescents been studied with psychoanalytic methods. In contrast to many other cultures, modern Western society has progressively eliminated the ritualized or institutionalized assimilation of the adolescent. Religious remnants of such practices still exist; but they now have shrunk to historical, isolated relics out of step with the schedules of status change in all other areas of modern life.

There is still no societal agreement in Western culture as to the age at which an individual ceases to be a child, or ceases to be an adolescent and becomes an adult. The age definition of maturity has varied at different times, and it varies today in different localities. State laws differ considerably in defining the age of economic competence, as well as the age appropriate for obtaining a driver's licence, getting married, and sustaining criminal liability. It is no wonder that under these contradictory and flexible societal conditions youth itself has created its own social forms and experiential patterns. The current "youth" or "peer cultures" are idiomatic expressions of adolescent needs. The adolescent has been forced, so to say, into a self-chosen and self-made way of life. All these efforts of youth are attempts to transform a biological event into a psychosocial experience.

Too little attention has been paid to the fact that adolescence, not only in spite of, but rather because of, its emotional turmoil, often affords spontaneous recovery from debilitating childhood influences, and offers the individual an opportunity to modify or rectify childhood exigencies which threatened to impede his progressive development. The regressive processes of adolescence permit the remodeling of defective or incomplete earlier developments; new identifications and counter-identifications play an important part in this. The profound upheaval associated with the emotional reorganization of adolescence thus harbors a beneficial potential: "The potentialities for formation of personality during latency and adolescence have been underrated in psychoanalytic writing" (Hartmann et al., 1946). Fenichel (1945a) hinted at a similar concept: "Experience in puberty may solve conflicts or shift conflicts into a final direction; moreover, they may give older and oscillating constellations a final and definitive form." Erikson (1956) has suggested that we look at adolescence not as an affliction, but as a "*normative crisis,* i.e., a normal phase of increased conflict characterized by a seeming fluctuation in ego strength, and yet also by a high growth potential. . . . What under prejudiced scrutiny may appear to be the onset of a neurosis, often is but an aggravated crisis which might prove to be self-liquidating and, in fact, contributive to the process of identity formation" (p. 72). One might add that the definitive settling of conflicts at the end of adolescence means either that they lose their disturbing quality because they have been characterologically stabilized, or they solidify into permanently debilitating symptoms or character disorders. We shall return to this complex process in the discussion of the terminal stage of adolescence.

Adolescence is here viewed as the sum total of all attempts at adjustment to the stage of puberty, to the new set of inner and outer—endogenous and exogenous—conditions which confront the individual. The urgent necessity to cope with the novel condition of puberty evokes all the modes of excitation, tension, gratification, and defense that ever played a role in previous years—that is, during the psychosexual development of infancy and early childhood. This infantile admixture is responsible for the bizarreness and the regressive character of adolescent behavior; it is the typical expression of the adolescent struggle to regain or to retain a psychic equilibrium which has been jolted by the crisis of puberty. The significant emotional needs and conflicts of early childhood must be recapitulated before new solutions with qualitatively different instinctual aims and ego interests can be found. This is why adolescence has been called a second edition of childhood; both periods have in common the fact that "a relatively strong id confronts a relatively weak ego" (A. Freud, 1936). It must be kept in mind that the pregenital phases of sexual organization are still at work trying to assert themselves; they interfere intermittently with the progress toward maturity. The gradual advancement during adolescence toward the genital position and heterosexual orientation is only the continuation of a development which temporarily came to a standstill at the decline of the oedipal phase, a standstill which accentuates the biphasic sexual development in man.

We witness at adolescence a second step in individuation, the first one having occurred toward the end of the second year when the child experiences the fateful distinction between "self" and "non-self." A similar yet far more complex individuation experience occurs during adolescence, which leads in its final step to a sense of identity. Before the adolescent can consolidate this formation, he must pass through stages of self-consciousness and fragmented existence. The oppositional, rebellious, and resistive strivings, the stages of experimentation, the testing of the self by going to excess—all these have a positive usefulness in the process of self-definition. "This is not me" represents an important step in the achievement of individuation and in the establishment of autonomy; at an earlier age, it is condensed into a single word—"No!"

Adolescent individuation is accompanied by feelings of isolation, loneliness, and confusion. Individuation brings some of the dearest megalomaniacal dreams of childhood to an irrevocable end. They must now be relegated entirely to fantasy: their fulfillments can never again be considered seriously. The realization of the finality of the definite limitation to individual existence itself—this realization creates a sense of urgency, fear, and panic. Consequently, many an adolescent tries to remain indefinitely in a transitional phase of development; this condition is called *prolonged adolescence.*

The adolescent's slow severence of the emotional ties to his family, his fearful or exhilarated entrance into the new life which beckons him, these experiences are among the profoundest in human existence. Only poets have been able to express adequately the quality of these feelings, their depth and scope. Sherwood Anderson has given a moving impression of the stage of mind of an adolescent about to leave his home town, Winesburg, Ohio. His mother has just died; he is on his way to the big city where he must make a life for himself. The night before his departure he walks through the familiar streets of his town. Strange thoughts and feelings well up in him, arousing a desire for clarity, for awareness, for a link to past and future—briefly, he experiences that self-consciousness of existence which marks the entrance into adulthood.

> George Willard, the Ohio village boy, was fast growing into manhood and new thoughts had been coming into his mind. All that day, amid the jam of people at the Fair, he had gone about feeling lonely. He was about to leave Winesburg to go away to some city where he hoped to get work on a city newspaper and he felt grown up. The mood that had taken possession of him was a thing known to men and unknown to boys. He felt old and a little tired. Memories awoke in him. To his mind his new sense of maturity set him apart, made him a half-tragic figure. He wanted someone to understand the feeling that had taken possession of him after his mother's death.
>
> There is a time in the life of every boy when he for the first time takes the backward view of life. Perhaps that is the moment where he crosses the line into manhood. The boy is walking through the street of his town. He is thinking of the future and of the figure he will cut in the world. Ambitions and regrets awake within him. Suddenly something happens; he stops under a tree and waits as for a voice calling his name. Ghosts of old things creep into his consciousness; the voices outside of himself whisper a message concerning the limitations of life. From being quite sure of himself and his future he becomes not at all sure. If he be an imaginative boy a door is torn open and for the first time he looks out upon the world, seeing, as though they marched in procession before him, the countless figures of men who before his time have come out of nothingness into the world, lived their lives and again disappeared into nothingness. The sadness of sophistication has come to the boy. With a little gasp he sees himself as merely a leaf blown by the wind through the streets of his village. He knows that in spite of all the stout talk of his fellows he must live and die in uncertainty, a thing blown by the winds, a thing destined like corn to wilt in the sun. He shivers and looks eagerly about. The

> eighteen years he has lived seem but a moment, a breathing space in the long march of humanity. Already he hears death calling. With all his heart he wants to come close to some other human, touch someone with his hands, be touched by the hand of another. If he prefers that the other be a woman, that is because he believes that a woman will be gentle, that she will understand. He wants most of all, understanding. [1]

Anderson is describing the end of the adolescent process: childhood has receded into history, into memory; a new time perspective with a circumscribed past and a limited future sets life between birth and death. For the first time it becomes conceivable that one will age, as one's parents did and one's grandparents before them. The consciousness of one's age becomes suddenly different from that of childhood. George's mourning is like a symbol for the deep losses which adolescence entails. Alone and surrounded by man's eternal fear of abandonment and panic, the familiar and life-old need for human closeness awakens; love and understanding are expected to rekindle the trust in life, to blow away the fears of isolation and death. The limitless future of childhood shrinks to realistic proportions, to one of limited chances and goals; but, by the same token, the mastery of time and space and the conquest of helplessness afford a hitherto unknown promise of self-realization. This is the human condition of adolescence which the poet has laid bare.

[1] Reprinted from Sherwood Anderson, *Winesburg, Ohio,* by permission of The Viking Press, Inc.

PART II

DEVELOPMENTAL DISORDERS

During the 1950's, a goodly number of people regarded with a certain condescension those who preoccupied themselves with the classification of psychopathological disorders, assuming that such an interest in descriptive psychiatry necessarily reflected a sacrifice of psychodynamic and psychogenetic considerations. Lately, however, with an increasing recognition that the quality of genetic and dynamic considerations may suffer if descriptive and nosological clarity are lacking, there has been a renewal of interest in the assessment, diagnosis, and classification of psychopathology.

Throughout the course of these pendulum swings, the classification of childhood psychopathology has invariably lagged behind adult psychiatric nosology. In part, we can attribute this lag to the longer history of adult psychiatry. More important, perhaps, are the inherent differences between children and adults, differences which render classification of childhood psychopathology far more difficult. The constant development and change in children results in a fluidity which militates against static classification. Nor does the prolonged dependency of childhood, which requires consideration of parents and other environmental factors, make classification easier. In addition, children tend to be motor-minded, so that their pathological adaptations entail efforts to change the environment (alloplastic adaptation) rather than themselves (autoplastic adaptation). Then too, the child's limited capacity for formalized insight hinders his ability to cooperate with the clinician's attempts to classify him. The difficulty is further compounded by the potentially greater impact of organic disorders on children, as compared with adults. We could cite other differences, all of which would have as a common denominator the same overriding influence of the developmental dimension (see A. Freud, 1965; Kessler, 1966; MacFarlane et al., 1962; Nagera, 1966a).

Until relatively recently, clinicians derived most of their concepts of normal and deviant development in children from clinical work with adult psychiatric patients, so that the newly formulated classification proposed in the G.A.P. Report (1966) was innovative in suggesting "healthy responses" and "developmental deviations" as major diagnostic categories. Coupling these two categories with the Committee's renamed category of "reactive disorder" describes the readings we have grouped in this section under the heading of Developmental Disorders. These disorders stem from either environmental interferences with maturational timetables, or conflicts with the environment engendered by developmental progress. Although the developmental disorders may produce clinical manifestations superficially indistinguishable from those produced by neurotic disorders, the conflicts underlying them are different. Conflicts producing neurotic disorders are between internal psychological forces or systems within the personality, whereas the conflicts producing developmental disorders are primarily between the environment and maturational forces.

The selection of articles in this section by no means encompasses all developmental disorders. To have included them all would have been beyond the scope of this presentation. Some neglected here, such as those connected with toilet training, speech, and language, for example, receive attention elsewhere in this volume. That what we term developmental disorders make an appearance in other sections of this volume testifies to the inadequacy of our attempts, to date, at classification, and to the tentativeness of the etiology of so many childhood disturbances. Our ignorance is frankly acknowledged in a statement which preceded the classification proposed by the G.A.P. Committee: "As yet, no all-encompassing, unequivocally accepted conceptual framework exists within which the intricate interrelationships among somatic, intellectual, emotional, and social processes and phenomena in the developing child can be comprehended and organized in a thoroughly logical, all-inclusive fashion" (p. 173).

HOSPITALISM

RENÉ A. SPITZ

In these two widely quoted articles on hospitalism, Spitz, known for his interest in the relationships between normal and pathological infant development (Spitz, 1964a, 1957, 1959, 1965; Spitz and Wolf, 1946), describes an "experiment in nature" which he recorded on film and quantified by formally testing babies at the time they suffered maternal deprivation. These papers, which should be supplemented by viewing Spitz's vivid film, "Grief: A Peril in Infancy," report the developmental quotients of four groups of babies. The experimental group was raised in a hygienic but emotionally sterile foundling home. The key control group was raised in a nursery maintained in a prison for delinquent women, where the babies' mothers had little else to occupy them other than mothering their children. There were two additional control groups, comprised of babies raised in family homes in communities near the foundling home and the prison.

Spitz's studies demonstrated that the babies in the emotionally sterile foundling home did poorly in all respects. Their development was retarded, their death rate shockingly high. Those in the prison nursery started with developmental quotients lower than those of the other groups. In terms of developmental progress, however, they joined the family-reared babies in the community as they outdistanced by far the maternally deprived foundling-home group.

Spitz subsequently (1946a) described nursery babies after they were deprived of maternal attention. They frequently developed a syndrome which he labeled, "anaclitic depression," his description of which resembled in many respects Bowlby's (1961) later descriptions of babies' responses to object loss.

Like other studies of the effects of maternal deprivation—ranging from Skeel's (1938a, 1938b, 1938c; 1965) reports, Goldfarb's (1955) and A. Freud and Burlingham's (1944) observations, to the investigations reported by Provence and Lipton (1962)—Spitz's papers have stimulated a variety of serious

Reprinted from *The Psychoanalytic Study of the Child,* 1, 1945, pp. 53–74; 2, 1946, pp. 113–117. New York: International Universities Press.

methodological questions. The validity of many of these methodological concerns, as well as findings from studies of children raised in environments that appear inadequate (Caldwell, 1967) and from animal studies (Harlow, 1959, 1962b), do not detract from the impressiveness of the evidence that maternal deprivation is a serious pathogenic agent. Establishing a one-to-one relationship between cause and effect is difficult (Casler, 1961; World Health Organization, 1962; Yarrow, 1961); some children are more vulnerable than others, and the dramatic results described are by no means inevitable.

"En la Casa de Niños Expositos el niño
se va poniendo triste y muchos de ellos
mueren de tristeza."
(1760, *from the diary of a Spanish bishop.*)

The Problem

The term *hospitalism* designates a vitiated condition of the body due to long confinement in a hospital, or the morbid condition of the atmosphere of a hospital. The term has been increasingly pre-empted to specify the evil effect of institutional care of infants placed in institutions from an early age, particularly from the psychiatric point of view. [1] This study is especially concerned with the effect of continuous institutional care of infants under one year of age, for reasons other than sickness. The model of such institutions is the foundling home.

Medical men and administrators have long been aware of the shortcomings of such charitable institutions. At the beginning of our century one of the great foundling homes in Germany had a mortality rate of 71.5 per cent in infants in the first year of life (Schlossman, 1920). In 1915 Chapin (1915a) enumerated ten asylums in the larger cities of the United States, mainly on the Eastern seaboard, in which the death rates of infants admitted during their first year of life varied from 31.7 per cent to 75 per cent by their second year. In a discussion in the same year before the American Pediatric Association (Chapin, 1915b), Dr. Knox of Baltimore stated that in the institutions of that city 90 per cent of the infants died by the end of their first year. He believed that the remaining 10 per cent probably were saved because they had been taken out of the institution in time. Dr. Shaw of Albany remarked in the same discussion that the mortality rate of Randalls Island Hospital was probably 100 per cent.

[1] *Hospitalism* tends to be confused with *hospitalization,* the temporary confinement of a seriously ill person to a hospital.

Conditions have since greatly changed. At present, the best American institutions, such as Bellevue Hospital, New York City, register a mortality rate of less than 10 per cent (Bakwin, 1942), which compares favorably with the mortality rate of the rest of the country. While these and similar results were being achieved both here and in Europe, physicians and administrators were soon faced with a new problem: they discovered that institutionalized children practically without exception developed subsequent psychiatric disturbances and became asocial, delinquent, feebleminded, psychotic, or problem children. Probably the high mortality rate in the preceding period had obscured this consequence. Now that the children survived, the other drawbacks of institutionalization became apparent. They led in this country to the widespread stubstitution of institutional care by foster home care.

The first investigation of the factors involved in the psychiatric consequences of institutional care of infants in their first year was made in 1933 in Austria by H. Durfee and K. Wolf (1933). Further contributions to the problem were made by L. G. Lowrey (1940), L. Bender and H. Yarnell (1941b), H. Bakwin (1942), and W. Goldfarb (1943, 1944a, 1944b; Goldfarb and Klopfer, 1944). The results of all these investigations are roughly similar:

Bakwin found greatly increased susceptibility to infection, in spite of high hygienic and nutritional standards. Durfee and Wolf found that children under three months show no demonstrable impairment in consequence of institutionalization; but that children who had been institutionalized for more than eight months during their first year show such severe psychiatric disturbances that they cannot be tested. Bender, Goldfarb, and Lowrey found that after three years of institutionalization, the changes effected are irreversible. Lowrey found that whereas the impairment of children hospitalized during their first year seems irremediable, that of children hospitalized in the second or third year can be corrected.

Two factors, both already stressed by Durfee and Wolf, are made responsible by most of the authors for the psychological injury suffered by these children.

First: Lack of stimulation. The worst offenders were the best equipped and most hygienic institutions, which succeeded in sterilizing the surroundings of the child from germs, but which at the same time sterilized the child's psyche. Even the most destitute of homes offers more mental stimulation than the usual hospital ward.

Second: The presence or absence of the child's mother. Stimulation by the mother will always be more intensive than even that of the best trained nursery personnel (Ripin, 1930). Those institutions in which the mothers were present had better results than those where only trained child nurses were employed. The presence of the mothers could compensate even for numerous other shortcomings.

We believe that further study is needed to isolate clearly the various factors operative in the deterioration subsequent to prolonged care in institutions. The number of infants studied by Bakwin, Durfee and Wolf, and Lowrey in single institutions is very small; Bender and Yarnell, and Goldfarb did not observe infants in the first twelve months of life. We are not questioning here whether institutions should be preferred to foster homes, a subject now hardly ever discussed—the decision can by implication be deduced from the results of the studies of the Iowa group in their extensive research on the "Nature Versus Nurture" controversy (Skeels, 1938) Skeels et al., 1940, 1938; Skodak, 1939; Stoddard, 1940; Updegraff, 1932). It may seem surprising that, in the course of this controversy, no investigation has covered the field of the first year of life in institutions. [2] All Iowa investigators studied either children in foster homes or children over one year of age, using their findings for retrospective interpretations. [3] They did not have at their disposal a method of investigation that would permit the evaluation and quantification of development, mental or otherwise, during the first year of life. Their only instrument is the I.Q., which is unreliable (Simpson, 1939), and not applicable during the first year. However, the baby tests worked out by Hetzer and Wolf (1928) fill the gap, providing not only a quotient for intelligence but also quantifiable data for development as a whole, such as indication of Developmental Age and of a Developmental Quotient. They provide, furthermore, quantifiable data on six distinct sectors of personality, namely: development of perception, body mastery, social relations, memory, relations to inanimate objects, and intelligence (which in the first year is limited to understanding of relations between and insight into the functions of objects).

[2] Woodworth (1941), in discussing the results of the Child Welfare Research Station of the State University of Iowa, makes the following critical remarks: "The causes of the inferior showing of orphanage children are obviously open to debate. . . . It would seem that a survey and comparative study of institutional homes for children would be instructive . . ." (p. 71)

[3] Jones (1940) takes exception to this method as follows: "It seems probable that we shall turn from retrospective surveys of conditions assumed to have had a prior influence, and shall prefer to deal with the current and cumulative effects of specific environmental factors. It may also be expected that our interest will shift to some extent from mass statistical studies . . . to investigations of the dynamics of the growth process in individuals" (p. 455).

With the help of these data ("dimensions"), a profile (personality curve) is constructed from which relevant conclusions can be drawn and, with the help of which, children can be compared with one another. Averages of development in any one sector or in all of them can be established for given environments. Finally, the relevant progresses of one and the same child in the several sectors of its personality can be followed up. The profiles present a cross-section of infantile development at any given moment; but they also can be combined into longitudinal curves of the developmental progress of the child's total personality as well as of the various sectors of the personality.

The aim of my research is to isolate and investigate the pathogenic factors responsible for the favorable or unfavorable outcome of infantile development. A psychiatric approach might seem desirable; however, infant psychiatry is a discipline not yet existent: its advancement is one of the aims of the present study.

MATERIAL [4]

With this purpose in mind, a long-term study of 164 children was undertaken.[5] In view of the findings of previous investigations, this study was largely limited to the first year of life and confined to two institutions, in order to embrace the total population of both (130 infants). Since the two institutions were situated in different countries of the Western hemisphere, a basis of comparison was established by investigating non-institutionalized children of the same age group in their parents' homes

[4] It is interesting to note that independently of our approach to this problem (mapped out and begun in 1936) Woodworth (1941) recommends a research program on extremely similar lines as being desirable for the better understanding of the problem of heredity and environment:

> Orphanages. Present belief, based on a certain amount of evidence, regards the orphanages as an unfavorable environment for the child, but the causes are not well understood. Two general projects may be suggested.
>
> (a) A survey of institutional homes for children with a view to discovering the variations in their equipment and personnel and in their treatment of the children, with some estimate of the results achieved.
>
> (b) Experimental studies in selected orphanages which retain their children for a considerable time, with a view to testing out the effects of specific environmental factors. For example, the amount of contact of the child with adults could be increased for certain children for the purpose of seeing whether this factor is important in mental development. It is conceivable that an orphanage could be run so as to become a decidedly favorable environment for the growing child, but at present we do not know how this result could be accomplished [pp. 90–91].

[5] I wish to thank K. Wolf, Ph.D., for her help in the experiments carried out in "Nursery" and in private homes, and for her collaboration in the statistical evaluation of the results.

in both countries. A total of 34 of these were observed. We thus have four environments (See Table 1).

PROCEDURE

In each case an anamnesis was made which whenever possible included data on the child's mother; and in each case the Hetzer-Wolf baby tests were administered. Problems cropping up in the course of our investigations for which the test situations did not provide answers were subjected to special experiments elaborated for the purpose. Such problems referred, for instance, to attitude and behavior in response to stimuli offered by inanimate objects, by social situations, etc. All observations of unusual or unexpected behavior of a child were carefully protocoled and studied.

TABLE 1

Environment	Institution No. 1 *	Corresponding private background†	Institution No. 2	Corresponding private background
Number of Children	69	11	61	23

* Institution No. 1 will from here on be called "Nursery"; institution No. 2, "Foundling Home".

† The small number of children observed in this particular environment was justified by the fact that it has been previously studied extensively by other workers; our only aim was to correlate our results with theirs. However, during the course of one year each child was tested at least at regular monthly intervals.

A large number of tests, all the experiments, and some of the special situations were filmed on 16mm. film. A total of 31,500 feet of film preserve the results of our investigation to-date. In the analysis of the movies, the following method was applied: Behavior was filmed at sound speed, i.e., 24 frames per second. This makes it possible to slow action down during projection to nearly one third of the original speed so that it can be studied in slow motion. A projector with additional handdrive also permits study of the films frame by frame, if necessary, to reverse action and to repeat projection of every detail as often as required. Simultaneously the written protocols of the experiments are studied and the two observations compared.

Results

For the purpose of orientation we established the average of the Developmental Quotients for the first third of the first year of life for each of the environments investigated. We contrasted these averages with those for the last third of the first year. This comparison gives us a first hint of the significance of environmental influences for development (See Table 2).

TABLE 2

Type of Environment	Cultural and Social Background	Developmental Quotients	
		Average of first four months	Average of last four months
Parental Home	Professional	133	131
	Village Population	107	108
Institution	"Nursery"	101.5	105
	"Foundling home"	124	72

Children of the first category come from professional homes in a large city; their Developmental Quotient, high from the start, remains high in the course of development.

Children in the second category come from an isolated fishing village of 499 inhabitants where conditions of nutrition, housing, hygienic and medical care are very poor indeed; their Developmental Quotient in the first four months is much lower and remains at a lower level than that of the previous category.

In the third category, "Nursery," the children were handicapped from birth by the circumstances of their origin, which will be discussed below. At the outset their Developmental Quotient is even somewhat lower than that of the village babies; in the course of their development they gain slightly.

In the fourth category, "Foundling Home," the children are of an unselected urban (Latin) background. Their Developmental Quotient on admission is below that of our best category but much higher than that of the other two. The picture changes completely by the end of the first year, when their Developmental Quotient sinks to the astonishingly low level of 72.

Thus the children in the first three environments were at the end of their first year on the whole well-developed and normal, whether they were raised in their progressive middle-class family homes (where obviously optimal circumstances prevailed, and the children were well in advance of average development), or in an institution, or a village home, where the development was not brilliant but still reached a perfectly normal and satisfactory average. The children in the fourth environment, though starting at almost as high a level as the best of the others, had spectacularly deteriorated.

The children in Foundling Home showed all the manifestations of hospitalism, both physical and mental. In spite of the fact that hygiene and precautions against contagion were impeccable, the childred showed, from the third month on, extreme susceptibility to infection and illness of any kind. There was hardly a child in whose case history we did not find reference to otitis media, or morbilli, or varicella, or eczema, or intestinal disease of one kind or another. No figures could be elicited on general mortality; but during my stay an epidemc of measles swept the institution, with staggeringly high mortality figures, notwithstanding liberal administration of convalescent serum and globulins, as well as excellent hygienic conditions. Of a total of 88 children up to the age of two-and-a-half, 23 died. It is striking to compare the mortality among the 45 children up to 1½ years, to that of the 43 children ranging from one-and-a-half to two-and-a-half years: usually, the *incidence* of measles is low in the younger age group, but among those infected the mortality is higher than that in the older age group; since in the case of Foundling Home every child was infected, the question of incidence does not enter; however, contrary to expectation, the mortality was much higher in the older age group. In the younger group, six died, i.e., approximately 13 per cent. In the older group, 17 died, i.e., close to 40 per cent. The significance of these figures become apparent when we realize that the mortality from measles during the first year of life on the community in question, outside the institution, was less than one-half per cent.

In view of the damage sustained in all personality sectors of the children during their stay in this institution, we believe it licit to assume that their vitality (whatever that may be), their resistance to disease, was also progressively sapped. In the ward of the children ranging from 18 months to two-and-a-half years, only two of the twenty-six surviving children speak a couple of words. The same two are able to walk. A third child is beginning to walk. Hardly any of them can eat alone. Cleanliness habits have not been acquired, and all are incontinent.

In sharp contrast to this is the picture offered by the oldest inmates in Nursery, ranging from eight to 12 months. The problem here is not whether the children walk or talk by the end of the first year; the problem with these 10-month-olds is how to tame the healthy toddlers' curiosity and enterprise. They climb up the bars of the cots after the manner of South Sea Islanders climbing palms. Special measures to guard them from harm have had to be taken after one 10-month-old actually succeeded in diving right over the more than two-foot railing of the cot. They vocalize freely and some of them actually speak a word or two. And all of them understand the significance of simple social gestures. When released from their cots, all walk with support and a number walk without it.

What are the differences between the two institutions that result in the one turning out normally acceptable children and the other showing such appalling effects?

A. SIMILARITIES: [6]

1. Background of the children.—Nursery is a penal institution in which delinquent girls are sequestered. When, as is often the case, they are pregnant on admission, they are delivered in a neighboring maternity hospital, and, after the lying-in period, their children are cared for in Nursery from birth to the end of their first year. The background of these children provides for a markedly negative selection since the mothers are mostly delinquent minors as a result of social maladjustment or feeble-mindedness, or because they are psychically defective, psychopathic, or criminal. Psychic normalcy and adequate social adjustment is almost excluded.

The other institution is a foundling home pure and simple. A certain number of the children housed have a background not much better than that of the Nursery children; but a sufficiently relevant number come from socially well-adjusted, normal mothers whose only handicap is inability to support themselves and their children (which is no sign of maladjustment in women of Latin background). This is expressed in the average of the Developmental Quotients of the two institutions during the first four months, as shown in Table 2.

The background of the children in the two institutions does not therefore favor Nursery; on the contrary, it shows a very marked advantage for Foundling Home.

2. Housing Conditions.—Both institutions are situated outside the city, in large spacious gardens. In both, hygienic conditions are carefully main-

[6] Under this heading we enumerate not only actual similarities but also differences that are of no etiological significance for the deterioration in Foundling Home. These differences comprise two groups: differences of no importance whatever, and differences that actually favor the development of children in Foundling Home.

tained. In both, infants at birth and during the first 6 weeks are segregated from the older babies in a special newborns' ward to which admittance is only permitted in a freshly sterilized smock after hands are washed. In both institutions, infants are transferred from the newborns' ward after two or three months to the older babies' wards where they are placed in individual cubicles, which in Nursery are completely glass enclosed, in Foundling Home glass enclosed on three sides and open at the end. In Foundling Home the children remain in their cubicles up to 15 to 18 months; in Nursery they are transferred after the 6th month to rooms containing four to five cots each.

One-half of the children in Foundling Home are located in a dimly lighted part of the ward; the other half, in the full light of large windows facing southeast with plenty of sun coming in. In Nursery all the children have well-lighted cubicles. In both institutions the walls are painted in a light neutral color, giving a white impression in Nursery, a gray-green impression in Foundling Home. In both, the children are placed in white painted cots. Nursery is financially the far better provided one: we usually find here a small metal table with the paraphernalia of child care, as well as a chair in each cubicle; whereas in Foundling Home it is the exception if a low stool is to be found in the cubicles which usually contain nothing but the child's cot.

3. Food.—In both institutions adequate food is excellently prepared and varied according to the needs of the individual child at each age; bottles from which children are fed are sterilized. In both institutions a large percentage of the younger children are breast-fed. In Nursery this percentage is smaller, so that in most cases a formula is soon added, and in many cases weaning takes place early. In Foundling Home all children are breast-fed as a matter of principle as long as they are under three months unless disease makes a deviation from this rule necessary.

4. Clothing.—Clothing is practically the same in both institutions. The children have adequate pastel-colored dresses and blankets. The temperature in the rooms is appropriate. We have not seen any shivering child in either set-up.

5. Medical Care.—Foundling Home is visited by the head physician and the medical staff at least once a day, often twice, and during these rounds the chart of each child is inspected as well as the child itself. For special ailments a laryngologist and other specialists are available; they also make daily rounds. In Nursery no daily rounds are made, as they are not necessary. The physician sees the children when called.

Up to this point it appears that there is very little significant difference between the children of the two institutions. Foundling Home shows, if anything, a slight advantage over Nursery in the matter of selection of admitted children, of breast-feeding, and of medical care. It is in the items that now follow that fundamental differences become visible.

B. DIFFERENCES:

1. Toys.—In Nursery it is the exception when a child is without one or several toys. In Foundling Home my first impression was that not a single child had a toy. This impression was later corrected. In the course of time, possibly in reaction to our presence, more and more toys appeared, some of them quite intelligently fastened by a string above the baby's head so that he could reach it. By the time we left, a large percentage of the children in Foundling Home had a toy.

2. Visual Radius.—In Nursery the corridor running between the cubicles, though rigorously white and without particular adornment, gives a friendly impression of warmth. This is probably because trees, landscape, and sky are visible from both sides and because a bustling activity of mothers carrying their children, tending them, feeding them, playing with them, chatting with each other with babies in their arms, is usually present. The cubicles of the children are enclosed, but the glass panes of the partitions reach low enough for every child to be able at any time to observe everything going on all around. He can see into the corridor as soon as he lifts himself on his elbows. He can look out of the windows and can see babies in the other cubicles by just turning his head; witness the fact that whenever the experimenter plays with a baby in one of the cubicles the babies in the two adjoining cubicles look on fascinated, try to participate in the game, knock at the panes of the partition, and often begin to cry if no attention is paid to them. Most of the cots are provided with widely-spaced bars that are no obstacle to vision. After the age of six months, when the child is transferred to the wards of the older babies, the visual field is enriched as a number of babies are then together in the same room and accordingly play with each other.

In Foundling Home the corridor into which the cubicles open, though full of light on one side at least, is bleak and deserted, except at feeding time when five to eight nurses file in and look after the children's needs.

Most of the time nothing goes on to attract the babies' attention. A special routine of Foundling Home consists in hanging bed sheets over the foot and the side railing of each cot. The cot itself is approximately 18 inches high. The side railings are about 20 inches high; the foot and head railings are approximately 28 inches high. Thus, when bed sheets are hung over the railings, the child lying in the cot is effectively screened from the world. He is completely separated from the other cubicles, since the glass panes of the wooden partitions begin six to eight inches higher than even the head railing of the cot. The result of this system is that each baby lies in solitary confinement up to the time when he is able to stand up in his bed, and that the only object he can see is the ceiling.

3. *Radius of Locomotion.*—In Nursery the radius of locomotion is circumscribed by the space available in the cot, which up to about 10 months provides a fairly satisfactory range.

Theoretically the same would apply to Foundling Home. But in practice this is not the case for, probably owing to the lack of stimulation, the babies lie supine in their cots for many months and a hollow is worn into their mattresses. By the time they reach the age when they might turn from back to side (approximately the seventh month), this hollow confines their activity to such a degree that they are effectively prevented from turning in any direction. As a result we find most babies, even at 10 and 12 months, lying on their backs and playing with the only object at their disposal, their own hands and feet.

4. *Personnel.*—In Foundling Home there is a head nurse and five assistant nurses for a total of forty-five babies. These nurses have the *entire* care of the children on their hands, except for the babies so young that they are breast-fed. The latter are cared for to a certain extent by their own mothers or by wetnurses; but after a few months they are removed to the single cubicles of the general ward where they share with at least seven other children the ministrations of *one* nurse. It is obvious that the amount of care one nurse can give to an individual child when she has eight children to manage is small indeed. These nurses are unusually motherly, baby-loving women; but of course the babies of Foundling Home nevertheless lack all human contact for most of the day.

Nursery is run by a head nurse and her three assistants whose duties do not include the care of the children, but consist mainly in teaching the children's mothers in child care and in supervising them. The children are fed, nursed, and cared for by their own mothers or, in those cases where the mother is separated from her child for any reason, by the mother of another child, or by a pregnant girl who in this way acquires the necessary experience for the care of her own future baby. Thus in Nursery each child has the full-time care of his own mother, or at least that of the substitute which the very able head nurse tries to change about until she finds someone who really likes the child.

Discussion

To say that every child in Nursery has a full-time mother is an understatement, from a psychological point of view. However modern a penal institution may be, and however constructive and permissive its re-educative policies, the deprivation it imposes upon delinquent girls is extensive. Their opportunities for an outlet for their interests, ambitions, activity, are very much impoverished. The former sexual satisfactions as well as the satisfactions of competitive activity in the sexual field, are suddenly stopped: regulations prohibit flashy dresses, vivid nail polish, or extravagant hair-do's. The kind of social life in which the girls could show off has vanished. This is especially traumatic as these girls become delinquent because they have not been able to sublimate their sexual drives, to find substitute gratifications, and therefore do not possess a pattern for relinquishing pleasure when frustrated. In addition, they do not have compensation in relations with family and friends, as formerly they had. These factors, combined with the loss of personal liberty, the deprivation of private property, and the regimentation of the penal institution, all add up to a severe narcissistic trauma from the time of admission; and they continue to affect the narcissistic and libidinal sectors during the whole period of confinement.

Luckily there remain a few safety valves for their emotions: (1) the relationship with wardens, matrons and nurses; (2) with fellow prisoners; (3) with the child. In the relationship with the wardens, matrons, and nurses, who obviously represent parent figures, much of the prisoner's aggression and resentment is bound. Much of it finds an outlet in the love and hate relationship to fellow prisoners where all the phenomena of sibling rivalry are revived.

The child, however, becomes for them the representative of their sexuality, a product created by them, an object they own, which they can dress up and adorn, on which they can lavish their tenderness and pride, and of whose accomplishments, performance, and appearance they can boast. This is manifested in the constant competition among them as to who has the better dressed, more advanced, more intelligent, better looking, the heavier, bigger, more active–in a word, the better baby.[7] For their own persons they have more or less given up the competition for love, but they are intensely jealous of the attention given to their children by the matrons, wardens, and fellow prisoners.

It would take an exacting experimenter to invent an experiment with conditions as diametrically opposed in regard to the mother-child relationship as they are in these two institutions. Nursery provides each child with a mother to the nth degree, a mother who gives the child everything a good mother does and, beyond that, everything else she has.[8] Foundling Home does not give the child a mother, even a substitute-mother, but only an eighth of a nurse.

We are now in a position to approach more closely and with better understanding the results obtained by each of the two institutions. We have already cited a few: we mentioned that the Developmental Quotient of Nursery achieves a normal average of about 105 at the end of the first year, whereas that of the Foundling Home sinks to 72; and we mentioned the striking difference of the children in the two institutions at first sight. Let us first consider the point at which the developments in the two institutions deviate (Figure 1).

On admission the children of Foundling Home have a much better average than the children of Nursery; their hereditary equipment is better than that of the children of delinquent minors. But while Foundling Home shows a rapid fall of the developmental index, Nursery shows a steady rise. They cross between the 4th and 5th months, and from that point on the curve of the average Developmental Quotient of the Foundling Home drops downward with increasing rapidity, never again to rise (Curve I).

The point where the two curves cross is significant. The time when the children in Foundling Home are weaned is the beginning of the 4th month. The time lag of one month in the sinking of the index below nor-

[7] The psychoanalytically oriented reader of course realizes that for these girls in prison the child has become a hardly disguised phallic substitute. However, for the purposes of this article I have carefully avoided any extensive psychoanalytic interpretation, be it ever so tempting, and limited myself as closely as possible to results of direct observations of behavior. At numerous other points it would be not only possible but natural to apply analytic concepts; that is reserved for future publication.

[8] For the nonpsychoanalytically oriented reader we note that this intense mother-child relationship is not equivalent to a relationship based on love of the child. The mere fact that the child is used as phallic substitute implies what a large part unconscious hostility plays in the picture.

mal is explained by the fact that the Quotient represents a cross-section including all sectors of development, and that attempts at compensation are made in some of the other sectors.

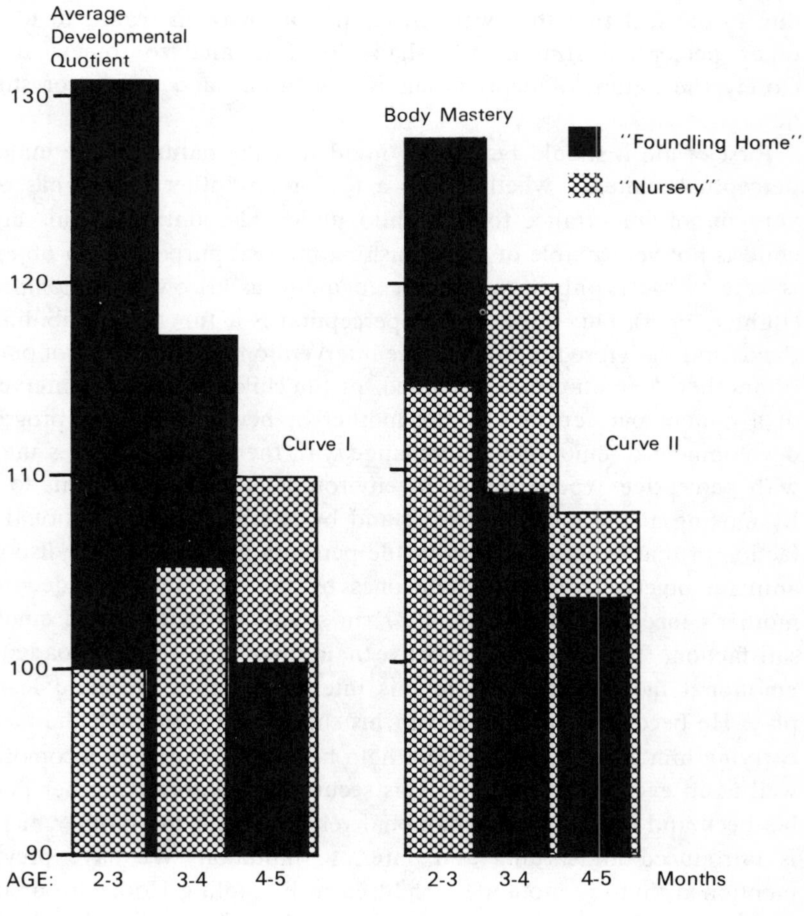

FIGURE 1

However, when we consider the sector of Body Mastery (Curve II), which according to Wolf is most indicative for the mother-child relationship, we find that the curves of the children in Nursery cross the Body

Mastery curve of the Foundling Home children between the 3rd and 4th month. The inference is obvious. As soon as the babies in Foundling Home are weaned, the modest human contacts which they have had during nursing at the breast stop, and their development falls below normal.

One might be inclined to speculate as to whether the further deterioration of the children in Foundling Home is not due to other factors also, such as the perceptual and motor deprivations from which they suffer. It might be argued that the better achievement of the Nursery children is due to the fact that they were better provided for in regard to toys and other perceptual stimuli. We shall therefore analyze somewhat more closely the nature of deprivations in perceptual and locomotor stimulation.

First of all, it should be kept in mind that the nature of the inanimate perceptual stimulus, whether it is a toy or any other object, has only a very minor importance for the child under 12 months. At this age the child is not yet capable of distinguishing the real purpose of an object. He is able to use it only in a manner adequate to his own functional needs (Buhler, 1928). Our thesis is that perception is a function of libidinal cathexis and therefore the result of the intervention of an emotion of one kind or another. [9] Emotions are provided for the child through the intervention of a human partner, i.e., by the mother or her substitute. A progressive development of emotional interchange with the mother provides the child with perceptive experiences of its environment. The child learns to grasp by nursing at the mother's breast and by combining the emotional satisfaction of that experience with tactile perceptions. He learns to distinguish animate objects from inanimate ones by the spectacle provided by his mother's face (Gesell and Ilg, 1937) in situations fraught with emotional satisfaction. The interchange between mother and child is loaded with emotional factors, and it is in this interchange that the child learns to play. He becomes acquainted with his surroundings through the mother's carrying him around; through her help he learns security in locomotion as well as in every other respect. This security is reinforced by her being at his beck and call. In these emotional relations with the mother, the child is introduced to learning and, later, to imitation. We have previously mentioned that the motherless children in Foundling Home are unable to speak, to feed themselves, or to acquire habits of cleanliness: it is the security provided by the mother in the field of locomotion, the emotional

[9] This is stating in psychoanalytic terms the conviction of most modern psychologists, beginning with Compayré (1893) and shared by such familiar authorities in child psychology as Stern (1930) and Buhler (1942) and, in animal psychology, Tolman (1932).

bait offered by the mother calling her child, that "teaches" him to walk. When this is lacking, even children two to three years old cannot walk.

The children in Foundling Home have, theoretically, as much radius of

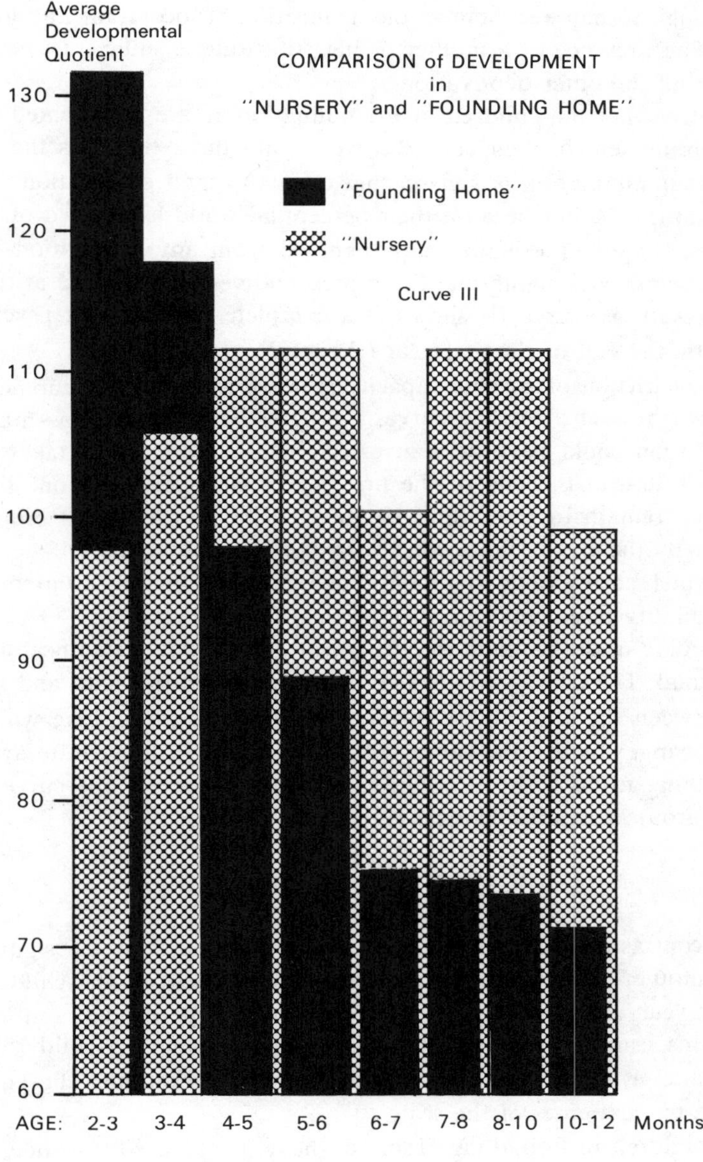

FIGURE 2

locomotion as the children in Nursery. They did not at first have toys, but they could have exerted their grasping and tactile activity on the blankets, on their clothes, even on the bars of the cots. We have seen children in Nursery without toys; they are the exception—but the lack of material is not enough to hamper them in the acquisition of locomotor and grasping skills. The presence of a mother or her substitute is sufficient to compensate for all the other deprivations.

It is true that the children in Foundling Home are condemned to solitary confinement in their cots. But we do not think that it is the lack of perceptual stimulation *in general* that counts in their deprivation. We believe that they suffer because their perceptual world is emptied of human partners, that their isolation cuts them off from any stimulation by any persons who could signify mother-representatives for the child at this age. The result, as Curve III shows, is a complete restriction of psychic capacity by the end of the first year (Figure 2).

This restriction of psychic capacity is not a temporary phenomenon. It is, as can be seen from the curve, a progressive process. How much this deterioration could have been arrested if the children were taken out of the institution at the end of the first year is an open question. The fact that they remain in Foundling Home probably furthers this progressive process. By the end of the second year, the Developmental Quotient sinks to 45, which corresponds to a mental age of approximately 10 months and would qualify these children as imbeciles.

The curve of the children in Nursery does not deviate significantly from the normal. The curve sinks at two points, between the sixth and seventh and between the 10th and 12th months. These deviations are within the normal range; their significance will be discussed in a separate article. It has nothing to do with the influence of institutions, for the curve of the village group is nearly identical (Figure 3).

Provisional Conclusions

The contrasting pictures of these two institutions show the significance of the mother-child relationship for the development of the child during the first year. Deprivations in other fields, such as perceptual and locomotor radius, can all be compensated by adequate mother-child relations. "Adequate" is not here a vague general term. The examples chosen represent the two extremes of the scale.

The children in Foundling Home do have a mother—for a time, in the beginning—but they must share her immediately with at least one other child, and from three months on, with seven other children. The quantitative factor here is evident. There is a point under which the mother-child relations cannot be restricted during the child's first year without inflicting irreparable damage. On the other hand, the exaggerated mother-child relationship in Nursery introduces a different quantitative factor. To anyone familiar with the field, is surprising that Nursery should achieve such excellent results, for we know that institutional care is destructive for children during their first year; but in Nursery the destructive factors have been compensated by the increased intensity of the mother-child relationship.

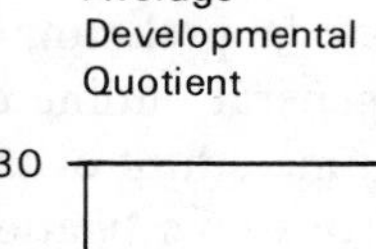

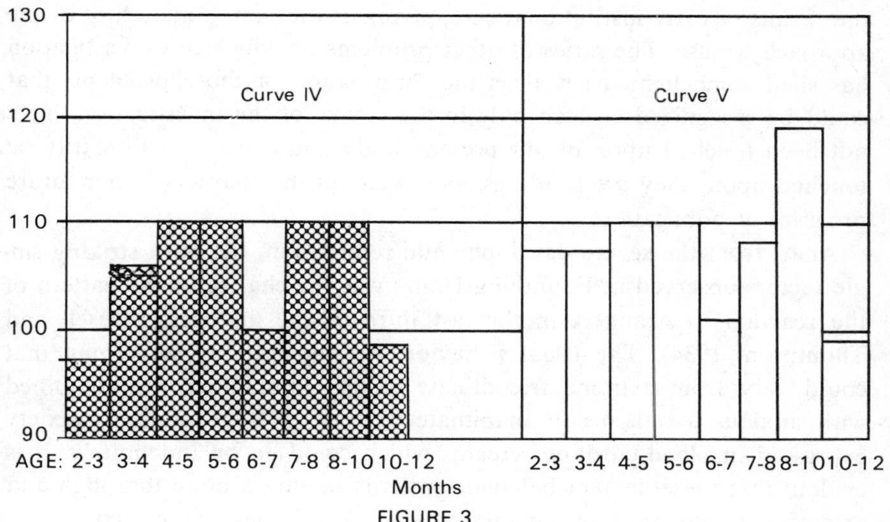

FIGURE 3

These findings should not be construed as a recommendation for overprotection of children. In principle, the libidinal situation of Nursery is almost as undesirable as the other extreme in Foundling Home. Neither in the nursery of a penal institution nor a foundling home for parentless children can the normal libidinal situation that obtains in a family home be expected. The two institutions have here been chosen as experimental set-ups for the purpose of examining variations in libidinal factors ranging from extreme frustration to extreme gratification. That the extreme frustration practised in Foundling Home has deplorable consequences has been shown; the extreme gratification in Nursery can be tolerated by the children housed there for two reasons: (1) The mothers have the benefit of the intelligent guidance of the head nurse and her assistants, and the worst exaggerations are thus corrected. (2) Children during their first year of life can stand the ill effects of such a situation much better than at a later age. In this respect Nursery has wisely limited the duration of the children's stay to the first twelve months. For children older than this, we should consider a libidinal set-up such as that in Nursery very dangerous indeed.

Further Problems

This is the first of a series of publications on the results of a research project on infancy that we are conducting. As such, it is a preliminary report. It is not intended to show more than the most general outline of the results of early institutional care, giving at the same time a hint of the approach we use. The series of other problems on which this investigation has shed some light, as well as the formulation of those problems that could be recognized as such only in the course of the investigation, have not been touched upon in our present study and can only summarily be touched upon; they are headings, as it were, of the chapters of our future program of publication.

Apart from the severe developmental retardation, the most striking single factors observed in Foundling Home was the change in the pattern of the reaction to strangers in the last third of the first year (Gesell and Thompson, 1934). The usual behavior was replaced by something that could vary from extreme friendliness to any human partner combined with anxious avoidance of inanimate objects, to a generalized anxiety expressed in blood-curdling screams which could go on indefinitely. It is evident that these deviant behavior patterns require a more thorough and extensive discussion than our present study would have permitted.

We also observed extraordinary deviations from the normal in the time of appearance and disappearance of familiar developmental patterns, and certain phenomena unknown in the normal child, such as bizarre stereotyped motor patterns distinctly reminiscent of the stereotypy in catatonic motility. These and other phenomena observed in Foundling Home require an extensive discussion in order to determine which are to be classified as maturation phenomena which appear even under the most unfavorable circumstances, and which appear with commensurate retardation when retardation is general; or which can be considered as the first symptoms of the development of serious psychiatric disturbances. In connection with this problem, a more thorough discussion of the rapidity with which the Developmental Quotients recede in Foundling Home is intended.

Another study is to deal with the problems created by the enormous overprotection practised in Nursery.

And finally, the rationale of the one institutional routine as against that of the other will have to be discussed in greater detail. This study will offer the possibility of deciding how to compensate for unavoidable changes in the environment of children orphaned at an early age. It will also shed some light on the social consequences of the progressive disruption of home life caused by the increase of female labor and by the demands of war; we might state that we foresee in the course of events a corresponding increase in asociality, in the number of problem and delinquent children, of mental defectives, and of psychotics.

It will be necessary to take into consideration in our institutions, in our charitable activities, in our social legislation, the overwhelming importance of adequate and satisfactory mother-child relationship during the first year, if we want to decrease the unavoidable and irreparable psychiatric consequences deriving from neglect during this period.

HOSPITALISM: A FOLLOW-UP REPORT

René A. Spitz

The striking picture of the infants studied in Foundling Home encouraged us to make every effort to get whatever information we could on the further development of the individual children. Distance made it impossible for the author to attend to this personally. The investigator who assisted in the original study was therefore directed to ascertain, at regular intervals, certain objectively observable facts on all those infants who were still available. He visited Foundling Home, during the two years following our own study, at four-monthly intervals. On these occasions, equipped with a questionnaire prepared by the author, he asked the nursing personnel a series of questions. He observed each child's general behavior and tried to make contact with each. He took some motion pictures of them and a set of stills at the end of the two years. Finally, some bodily measurements, namely, weight, height, and occipital circumference, were taken.

The questions referred to three principal sectors of personality:

1) Bodily performance: the gross indicator used was whether the child could sit, stand, or walk.

2) Intellectual capacity to handle materials: the gross indicator used was whether the child was capable of eating food alone with the help of a spoon and whether he could dress alone.

3) Social relations: these were explored by ascertaining the number of words spoken by each child and by finding out whether he was toilet trained.

We are only too well aware that the resulting information is inadequate for a thorough study. As will be seen, however, even this inadequate follow-up yields a number of instructive data.

As is usually the case in follow-up investigations, only a relatively small number of the children originally seen could be checked on. Two years ago, when we first visited the ward reserved for the children from birth to one-and-a-half years and the ward for children from one-and-a-half to three years, a total of 91 children were present. In the course of the first year, 27 of these died of various causes, among which were an epidemic of measles, intercurrent sickness, and cachexia; by the end of the second year, another seven of those originally seen had died; this represents a total mortality of over 37 per cent in a period of two years.

Thirty-six children could not be learned about because 23 had been taken back to their families, seven had been adopted (mostly by their own illegitimate parents), two had been placed in children's institutions, and four could not be accounted for.

At the time of this writing,[1] 21 children of those originally seen are still at the institution. Of these the youngest is two years of age, the oldest four years and one month. The data on their development are as follows:

1) Bodily development:	
Incapable of any locomotion:	5
Sit up unassisted (without walking):	3
Walk assisted:	8
Walk unassisted:	5
Total	21
2) Handling materials:	
Cannot eat alone with spoon:	12
Eat alone with spoon:	9
Total	21
Cannot dress alone:	20
Dresses alone:	1
Total	21
3) Adaptation to demands of environment:	
Not toilet trained in any way:	6
Toilet trained, partially:[2]	15
Total	21
4) Speech development:	
Cannot talk at all:	6
Vocabulary: 2 words:	5
Vocabulary: 3 to 5 words:	8
Vocabulary: a dozen words:	1
Uses sentences:	1
Total	21

[1] June 12, 1946.

[2] These children are trained "to a certain extent." According to my observer many of the so-called "toilet-trained" children were found to soil in their beds: their training appears to be limited to their making use of the toilet when put on it.

As seen from these data, the mental development of these 21 children is extraordinarily retarded, compared to that of normal children between the ages of two and four, who move, climb, and babble all day long, and who conform to, or struggle against, the educational demands of the environment. This retardation, which amounts to a deterioration, is borne out by the weights and heights of these children, as well as by their pictures.

Normal children, by the end of the second year weigh, on the average, 26½ pounds, and the length is 33½ inches. At the time of this writing, 12 of the children in Foundling Home range in age between 2.4 and 2.8; 4, between 2.8 and 3.2; and 5, between 3.2 and 4.1. But of all of these children, only three fall into the weight range of a normal *two-year-old* child, and only two have attained the length of a normal child of that age. All others fall below the normal two-year-level–in one case, as much as 45 per cent in weight and five inches in length. In other words, the physical picture of these children impresses the casual observer as that of children half their age.

In our previous article on the subject, we expressed the suspicion that the damage inflicted on the infants in Foundling Home by their being deprived of maternal care, maternal stimulation, and maternal love, as well as by their being completely isolated, is irreparable. One follow-up confirms this assumption. After their fifteenth month, these children were put into more favorable environmental conditions than before, i.e., in the ward for the other children. This is a large room, sunny, without the partitions which in the ward for the younger children isolated the infants from each other and from every environmental stimulus. Three to five nurses are constantly in the room, and they chat with each other and with the children. The children are also taken out of their cots and placed on the floor. Thus they have infinitely more active stimulation than they previously experienced in the ward for younger children. Notwithstanding this improvement in environmental conditions, the process of deterioration has proved to be progressive. It would seem that the developmental imbalance caused by the unfavorable environmental conditions during the children's first year produces a psychosomatic damage that cannot be repaired by normal measures. Whether it can be repaired by therapeutic measures remains to be investigated.

We have advisedly spoken of psychosomatic damage. From the figures given above, it can be seen, quite apart from the inadequate psychic and physical development, all these children showed a seriously decreased resistance to disease and an appalling mortality. Those who survived were all far below the age-adequate weight reached by normal children of comparable age.

In view of these findings we once again examined the data on Nursery, the institution compared to Foundling Home in our previous article. The organization of Nursery did not permit a follow-up extended to the fifth year, as did that of Foundling Home. As a rule children leave Nursery when they are a full year old. However, a certain number of exceptions are made in this rule, and in the course of our study of Nursery, which now covers a period of three-and-a-half years, 29 children were found who stayed longer than a year. The age at which these left varied from the thirteenth to the eighteenth month (1.1 to 1.6) This means that the oldest of them was *half-a-year younger* than the youngest child in our follow-up in Foundling Home, *and two-and-a-half years younger than the oldest.* In spite of this enormous difference in age, the Nursery children all ran lustily around on the floor; some of them dressed and undressed themselves; they fed themselves with a spoon; nearly all spoke a few words; they understood commands and obeyed them; and the older ones showed a certain consciousness of toilet requirements. All of them played lively social games with each other and with the observers. The more advanced ones imitated the activities of the nurses, sweeping the floor, carrying and distributing diapers, etc. In all these children, tests showed that the developmental quotients which in the eleventh and twelfth months had receded somewhat, [3] not only came up to the normal age level, but in most cases surpassed it by far.

But the gross physical picture alone, as expressed by the figures on morbidity and mortality of the children in Nursery, is sufficiently striking. During the three-and-a-half years of our study of Nursery we had occasion to follow 122 infants, each for approximately a full year. [4] During this time *not a single child died.* The institution was visited by no epidemic. Intercurrent sickness was limited, on the whole, to seasonal colds, which in a moderate number developed into mild respiratory involvement; there was comparatively little intestinal disturbance; the most disturbing illnes was eczema. The unusually high level of health maintained

[3] See p. 253. The average retardation in the developmental quotient was approximately 12 points during the eleventh and twelfth month; to be discussed in a later publication.

[4] Exceptions to this are six children who because of circumstances in their families left before their tenth month. This is more than counterbalanced by the group of 29 children who stayed longer than one year.

in Nursery impelled us to look into its past record. We investigated the files of Nursery for ten years prior to the beginning of our work there. We found that during the whole of the last fourteen years a total of three children have died: one of pneumonia at the age of three months; and two of pyloric stenosis, the first at the age of one month, the second after several operations at the age of nine months.

It is in the light of these findings, which show what can be achieved in an institution under favorable circumstances and adequate organization, that the consequences of the methods used in Foundling Home should be evaluated.

CHILDHOOD MOURNING AND ITS IMPLICATIONS FOR PSYCHIATRY

John Bowlby

It is appropriate that Adolf Meyer, the founder of psychobiology, which stressed for psychiatry the importance of the patient's life history, should be memorialized by this discussion of the effects on adults of object loss during childhood. Such a discussion is a natural outcome of Bowlby's earlier work (1946, 1951), which included his well-known demonstration that maternal deprivation was common in the backgrounds of juvenile thieves, and the forceful monograph he wrote at the request of the World Health Organization summarizing the interrelationships between maternal care and mental health. This monograph stimulated controversy that persists as Bowlby has gone on to investigate in greater depth the processes by which psychopathology follows maternal deprivation (Bowlby, 1969).

In the paper that follows, Bowlby reviews his conception of the child's response to object loss: successive stages of protest, despair, and detachment. He considers the dynamics analogous to those in adult mourning (Bowlby, 1960a), a hypothesis that generated a lively and productive exchange with Anna Freud (1960a), Spitz (1960), and Schur (1960).

Bowlby's investigation of the processes leading to psychopathology has intensified his interest in the early development of human relationships. In another study on the attachments between mother and child (1958), he has drawn on the work of ethologists such as Lorenz (1950) and experimental observations such as Harlow's (1959) laboratory work with monkeys.

The mental hygiene movement in the second quarter of this century was founded on the proposition that childhood experiences directly shaped the adult. As the years have gone by and more knowledge has accumulated, efforts to correlate the type of feeding, weaning, toilet training, etc. during childhood with eventual adult personality features has not been as fruitful as the correlation between the experiences of early separation from a parent and subsequent psychopathology (Nagera, 1969). Recognizing that correla-

Reprinted with permission from *American Journal of Psychiatry,* 118, 1961, pp. 481–498.

tion is not proof of causality; Bowlby summarizes, in this paper, the psychiatric implications of childhood bereavement.

Without minimizing the apparent pathogenic influence of object loss during childhood, we would like to note that studies of the effects of parent-child separation generally fail to refer to possible psychic advantages that might accrue as a consequence of coping successfully with brief separations. Is it not valid to question whether the overprotected youngsters whom Levy (1943, this volume) studied would have fared better if they had had more opportunities for learning how to adapt to life's inevitable separations?

For half a century or more there has existed a school of thought that has believed that experiences of infancy and childhood play a large part in determining whether or not an individual grows up prone to develop psychiatric illness. To the growth of this school Adolf Meyer made a great contribution. Insisting that the psychiatric patient is a human being and that his disturbed thought, feeling and behaviour must be seen in the context of the environment in which he is living and has lived, Adolf Meyer bade us pay attention to all the complex details of the patient's life history as possible clues to his illness. "The most valuable determining feature is, as a rule, the *form of evolution* of the [symptom] complex, the time and duration and circumstances of its development." Though I find no evidence that Adolf Meyer was greatly interested in experiences of earliest childhood, they lie plainly within his field of vision and are indeed a logical extension of his work.

Over the years, the belief that experiences of early childhood are of much consequence for the development of psychiatric illness has grown in strength. Nevertheless, the basic hypothesis has always been a subject of sharp controversy. Some have contended that the hypothesis is mistaken—that psychiatric illness has its roots elsewhere than in early childhood; whilst those who believe the hypothesis to be fruitful are still at sixes and sevens regarding precisely what experiences are relevant. Much of the controversy arises from the difficulty of conducting satisfactory research in this area—a difficulty turning largely on the long gap in time between the events thought to be of consequence and the onset of the declared illness. For the science of psychopathology, therefore, the problem posed is how best to explore the area in order to reach firmer ground. My plan is to give an account of recent developments in one line of investigation, that which has set out to understand the effect on personality development of loss of maternal care in early childhood.

In the past 20 years much evidence has accumulated that points to a causal relationship between loss of maternal care in the early years and disturbed personality development (Bowlby, 1951). Many common deviations seem to follow an experience of this kind–from delinquent character formation to a personality prone to anxiety states and depressive illness. Although there are some psychiatrists who still challenge this general conclusion, a more usual attitude is to accept that there is probably something in it and to ask for more information. A particular request has been for an hypothesis which can provide a plausible explanation of how it is that the ill effects attributed to separation and deprivation come to follow such experiences. Since it is to an attempt to fill this gap that I have been devoting myself in recent years, my plan is to present a sketch of where the evidence seems to be leading.

In judging my thesis I must ask you to bear in mind that the inquiry does not follow the usual practice of psychiatric research which starts with a more or less defined clinical syndrome and attempts then to delineate the underlying pathology. Instead, it starts with a class of experience, loss of mother figure in infancy and early childhood, and attempts thence to trace the psychological and psychopathological processes that commonly result. In physiological medicine, a shift of this kind in research orientation has occurred long since. In studies, for example, of the pathology of chronic infection of the lungs, the investigator is no longer likely to start with a group of cases all showing chronic infection and attempt to discover the infective agent or agents that are at work. It is more likely he will start with a specified agent, perhaps tubercle or actinomycosis or some newly identified virus, in order to study the physiological and physiopathological processes to which it gives rise. In so doing he may discover many things which are not immediately relevant to chronic infective pulmonary conditions. Not only may he throw light on certain acute infections and sub-clinical conditions, but he is almost sure to discover that infections of other organs besides lungs are the work of the pathogenic organism he has selected for study. No longer is his center of interest a particular clinical syndrome: it has become instead the manifold sequelae of a particular pathogenic agent.

The pathogenic agent the effects of which I shall be discussing is loss of mother figure during the period between about six months and six years of age. During the early months of life, the infant is learning to discriminate a particular figure, usually his mother, and is developing a strong liking to be in her company. After about six months he shows his preferences in unmistakable fashion (Schaffer, 1958). Throughout the latter half of his first year and during the whole of his second and third he is closely attached to his mother figure, which means that he is content in her company and distressed in her absence. Even momentary separations often lead him to protest, and longer ones always do. After the third birthday the strength of the attachment commonly diminishes, though for some further years it remains strong. From about his first birthday onwards other figures also, for example father or grandmother, may become important to him so that his attachment is not confined to a single figure. Nevertheless, there is usually a well-marked preference for some one person. In the light of phylogeny it is likely that the instinctual bonds that tie human young to a mother figure are built on the same general pattern as in other mammalian species (Bowlby, 1958; Harlow, 1959; Rollman-Branch, 1960).

The majority of children suffer little disruption of this primary attachment in their early years. They live with their mother figure and, during the relatively brief periods when she is absent, are cared for by a familiar subordinate figure. On the other hand, a minority does experience disruptions. Their mother may desert or die; they may be left in hospital or institution; they may be handed from one mother figure to another. Disruptions may be long or short, single or repeated. The experiences that belong under the general heading of maternal deprivation are thus multifarious, and no one investigation can study them all. If, therefore, effective research is to be done, for each project the experience to be studied must be fairly narrowly defined.

As regards research strategies, the investigator has a choice (Ainsworth and Bowlby, 1954). An obvious possibility is to examine a sample of older children and adults who had the experience in their early years with a comparable sample who did not have the experience. Although brilliantly adopted by Goldfarb (1955), this strategy has many practical difficulties. The principle ones are locating a suitable sample, selecting and examining appropriate controls, and finding reliable instruments to measure the features of personality that are expected to show differences. An alternative approach is to study the child's responses at the time of, and in the period immediately subsequent to, the experience. After spending several not very productive years following the first strategy, it is the second on which my research group has concentrated during most of the past decade. It has been much more rewarding.

SEPARATION FROM MOTHER AND CHILDHOOD MOURNING

The basic data with which we have been concerned are observations of the behaviour of healthy children of a defined age, namely in their second and third years, undergoing a defined experience, namely stays of limited duration in residential nurseries or hospital wards and there cared for in traditional ways. This means that the child is removed from the care of his mother figure and all subordinate figures and also from his familiar environment, and is cared for, instead, in a strange place by a succession of unfamiliar people. Further data are derived from observations of his behaviour in his home during the months after his return and from reports of it from his parents. Thanks to the work of James Robertson and Christoph Heinicke we have now a considerable body of observations, some of which have been published (Bowlby, 1953; Heinicke, 1956; Robertson, 1953a, 1953b; Robertson and Bowlby, 1952). Because observations by a number of other workers (Aubry, 1955; Burlingham and Freud, 1942, 1944; Illingworth and Holt, 1955; Prugh, D., et al., 1953; Roudinesco et al., 1952; Schaffer and Callender, 1959), record substantially similar sequences of response, we feel fairly confident of the common patterns.

In the setting described a child of 15 to 30 months who has had a reasonably secure relationship to his mother and has not previously been parted from her will commonly show a predictable sequence of behaviour. This can be broken into three phases according to what attitude to his mother is dominant. We have described them as phases of Protest, Despair and Detachment. [1] At first, with tears and anger he demands his mother back and seems hopeful he will succceed in getting her. This phase of Protest may last several days. Later he becomes quieter, but to the discerning eye it is clear that as much as ever he remains preoccupied with his absent mother and still yearns for her return; but his hopes have faded and he is in the phase of Despair. Often these two phases alternate: hope turns to despair and despair to renewed hope. Eventually, however, a greater change occurs. He seems to forget his mother so that when she comes for him he remains curiously uninterested in her and may seem even not to recognize her. This is the phase of Detachment. In each of these phases the child is prone to tantrums and episodes of destructive behaviour, often of a disquietingly violent kind.

The child's behaviour on return home depends on the phase reached

[1] In certain earlier papers the term "Denial" was used to denote the third phase. It has many disadvantages, however, and has been abandoned.

during the period of separation. Usually for a while he is unresponsive and undemanding; to what degree and for how long turns on the length of the separation and the frequency of visits. For example, when he has been away unvisited for a few weeks or months and so has reached the early stages of detachment, it is likely that unresponsiveness will persist from an hour to a day or more. When at length it breaks the intense ambivalence of his feelings for his mother is made manifest. There is a storm of feeling, intense clinging and, whenever his mother leaves him, even for a moment, acute anxiety and rage. Thenceforward, for weeks or months his mother may be subjected to impatient demands for her presence and angry reproaches when she has been absent. When, however, he has been away for a period of more than six months or when separations have been repeated, so that he has reached an advanced stage of detachment, there is danger that he may remain detached and so never recover his affection for his parents. [2]

Now, in interpreting these data and in relating them to psychopathology a key concept is that of mourning. There is, indeed, good reason to believe that the sequence of responses described–Protest, Despair and Detachment–is a sequence that, in one variant or another, is characteristic of all forms of mourning. Following unexpected loss there seems always to be a phase of protest during which the bereaved person is striving, either in actuality or in thought and feeling, to recover the lost object and is reproaching it for desertion. During this and the succeeding phase of despair, feelings are ambivalent while mood and action vary from an immediate expectancy expressed in an angry demand for the object's return to a despair expressed in subdued pining–or even not expressed at all. Though alternating hope and despair may continue for a long time, at length there develops some measure of emotional detachment from the object lost. After having undergone disorganization in the phase of Despair, behaviour in this phase becomes reorganized on the basis of the object's permanent absence. Though this picture of healthy mourning is not altogether familiar to psychiatrists, evidence that it is a true one seems compelling (Bowlby, 1961b).

If this view is correct, the responses of young children on removal to hospital or institution must be regarded simply as variants of basic

[2] Many variables influence the child's behaviour during and after separation and this makes a brief schematic exposition difficult. The description given applies especially to the behaviour of children who are unvisited and are cared for by nurses or others who have little insight or sympathy for his fretting. It seems likely that free visiting and more insightful care can mitigate the processes described, but there is as yet little reliable information about this.

mourning processes. Irrespective of age, it seems, the same kind of responses occur and in the same sequence. Like adults, infants and young children who have lost a loved object experience grief and go through periods of mourning (Bowlby, 1960a). There appear to be only two interrelated differences. One is that in the young the time scale is abbreviated, though much less so than has sometimes been thought. The other, in which lies the significance for psychiatry, is that in childhood the processes leading to detachment are very apt to develop prematurely, inasmuch as they coincide with and mask strong residual yearning for and anger with the lost object, both of which persist, ready for expression, at an unconscious level. Because of this premature onset of detachment, the mourning processes of childhood habitually take a course that in older children and adults is regarded as pathological.

Once we recognize that the separation of a young child from his loved mother figure commonly precipitates processes of mourning of a pathological sort, we are able to relate our findings to those of many other inquiries. On the one hand are the findings of workers who have taken the grief of adults as a starting point for a study of psychopathology (Engel, 1961; Jacobson, 1957; Lindemann, 1944). On the other are those of the more numerous investigators who have followed the traditional pattern of psychiatric research that starts with a sick patient and tries to discern what have been the preceding events of causal significance, and who have advanced the hypothesis that loss of loved object is in some way pathogenic.

Inquiries that have pointed to loss of loved object as probably pathogenic are of several kinds. First, there are the very numerous studies, of which Freud's *Mourning and Melancholia* is the prototype, that relate a psychiatric syndrome of relatively acute onset, such as anxiety state, depressive illness, or hysteria, to a more or less recent bereavement, and postulate that the clinical picture is to be understood as the result of mourning having taken a pathological course. Next are the studies, almost equally numerous, that relate a psychiatric syndrome of more chronic degree, such as a tendency to episodic depression or a difficulty in experiencing feelings, to a loss that occurred in the patient's adolescence or earlier childhood. Thirdly, there is the extensive psychoanalytic literature that seeks to relate a proneness towards psychiatric illness in later life with some failure of psychic development in early childhood. Fourthly, there is a steadily accumulating series of papers that show a raised incidence of childhood bereavement in the lives of those who subsequently develop psychiatric illness; and, finally, the striking observation that individuals are apt to become mentally ill at an age which appears to be determined by an episode in their childhood when they suffered the loss of a parent—the so-called anniversary reactions.

Urges to Recover and to Reproach Lost Object: Their Role in Psychopathology

Now I wish to draw your attention to anger as an immediate, common and perhaps invariable response to loss. Instead of anger indicating that mourning is running a pathological course—a view suggested by Freud and rather commonly held—evidence makes it clear that anger, including anger with the lost object, is an integral part of the grief reaction. The function of this anger appears to be to add punch to the strenuous efforts, both to recover the lost object and to dissuade it from deserting again, that are the hallmarks of the first phase of mourning. Since this phase has not only been given little attention hitherto but appears crucial for an understanding of psychopathology, it is necessary to explore it more fully.

Because in cases of death an angry effort to recover the lost object is so obviously futile, there has been a tendency to regard it as itself pathological. I believe this to be profoundly mistaken. So far from being pathological, the evidence suggests that the overt expression of this powerful urge, unrealistic and hopeless though it may be, is a necessary condition for mourning to run a healthy course. Only after every effort has been made to recover the lost object, it seems, is the individual in a mood to admit defeat and to orient himself afresh to a world from which the loved object is accepted as irretrievably missing. Protest, including an angry demand for the object's return and reproach against it for deserting, is as much a part of the *adult's* response to loss, especially a sudden loss, as of the young child's.

This may seem puzzling. How comes it that such demands and reproaches should be made even when the object is so plainly beyond recall? Why such gross realism? There is, I believe, a good answer: it stems from evolution theory.

In the first place, a review of the behavioural responses to loss that are shown by infra-human species—birds, lower mammals and primates—suggests that these responses have ancient biological roots. Though not well recorded, such information as is available shows that many if not all the features described for humans—anxiety and protest, despair and disorganization, detachment and reorganization—are the rule also in many lower species.[3]

In the second place, it is not difficult to see why these responses should have been evolved. In the wild, to lose contact with the immediate family group is extremely dangerous, especially for the young. It is, therefore, in the interests of both individual safety and species reproduction that there should be strong bonds tying together the members of a family or of an extended family; and this requires that every separation, however brief, should be responded to by an immediate, automatic and strong effort both to recover the family, especially the member to whom attachment is closest, and to discourage that member from going away again. For this reason, it is suggested, the inherited determinants of behaviour (often termed instinctual) have evolved in such a way that the standard reponses to loss of a loved object are always urges first to recover it and then to scold it. If, however, the urges to recover and scold are automatic responses built into the organism, it follows that they will come into action in response to *any* and *every* loss and without discriminating between those that are really retrievable and those, statistically rare, that are not. It is an hypothesis of this kind, I believe, that explains why a bereaved person commonly experiences a compelling urge to recover the object, even when he knows the attempt to be hopeless, and to reproach it, even when he knows reproach to be irrational.

If, then, neither the futile effort to recover the lost object nor angry reproaches against it for deserting are signs of pathology, in what ways, we may ask, is pathological mourning distinguished from healthy? Examination of the evidence suggests that one of the main characteristics of pathological mourning is nothing less than an inability to express overtly these urges to recover and scold the lost object, with all the yearning for and anger with the deserting object that they entail. Instead of its overt expression, which, though stormy and fruitless, leads on to a healthy outcome, the urges to recover and reproach, with all their ambivalence of feeling, have become split off and repressed. Thenceforward, they have continued as active systems within the personality but, unable to find

[3] Evidence is reviewed by Bowlby (1961b) and Pollock (1961). To give an example quoted by Pollock: A male chimpanzee who had lost his mate is recorded to have made repeated efforts to arouse her. He yelled with rage and at times expressed his anger by snatching at the short hairs of his head. Later there was crying and mourning. As time wore on he became more closely attached to his keeper and more angry than he had been hitherto when the keeper left him.

overt and direct expression, have come to influence feeling and behaviour in strange and distorted ways; hence many forms of character disturbance and neurotic illness.

Let me give a brief illustration of one such form, drawn from a case reported by Helene Deutsch (1937). When he came for analysis in his early thirties, this man was without apparent neurotic difficulties. The clinical picture, however, was one of a wooden and affectionless character. Helene Deutsch describes how

> he showed complete blocking of affect without the slightest insight . . . He had no love relationships, no friendships, no real interests of any sort. To all kinds of experience he showed the same dull and apathetic reaction. There was no endeavour and no disappointment . . . There were no reactions of grief at the loss of individuals near to him, no unfriendly feelings and no aggressive impulses [p. 18].

How did this barren and crippled personality develop? In the light of an hypothesis regarding childhood mourning, the history together with material stemming from analysis enable us to construct a plausible account.

First, history: when he was five years old his mother had died, and it was related that he had reacted to her loss without any feeling. Thenceforward, moreover, he had retained no recollection of any events prior to her death. Secondly, material from analysis: he described how through several years of later childhood he used to leave his bedroom door open "in the hope that a large dog would come to him, be very kind to him, and fulfill all his wishes." Associated with this fantasy was a vivid childhood memory of a bitch which had left her puppies alone and helpless when she had died shortly after their birth. Although in this fantasy the hidden longing for his lost mother seems plainly evident, it was not expressed in a simple direct way. Instead, all memories of his mother had disappeared from consciousness and, insofar as any conscious affects towards her could be discerned, they were hostile.

To explain the course of development in this case, the hypothesis I am advancing (and one that is not very different from Helene Deutsch's) is that, following his mother's death, instead of there being a full expression of his desire for his mother's return and anger at her desertion, his mourning had moved on precipitately to a condition of detachment. In so doing the yearning and the anger had become locked inside him, potentially active but shut off from the world, and only the remainder of his personality had been left free for further development. As a result he grew up gravely impoverished. If this hypothesis is valid, the task of treatment is to help the patient to recover his latent longing for his lost mother and his latent anger with her for deserting him, in other words to return to the first phase of mourning with all its ambivalence of feeling which at the time of the loss had either been omitted or scamped. The experience of many analysts, well illustrated in a paper by Root (1957), suggests that it is in fact only in this way that such a person can be restored to a life of feeling and attachment.

Strong support for this hypothesis comes from our observations of young children separated from their mothers and unvisited, especially from what we know of the early stages of detachment that follow protest and despair. Once the separated child has entered the phase of detachment he seems no longer preoccupied with his missing mother and instead to have adapted satisfactorily in his new surroundings. When his mother comes to fetch him, so far from greeting her, he seems hardly to know her and, so far from clinging to her, remains remote and unresponsive; it is a condition that most mothers find distressing and incomprehensible. Provided the separation has not lasted too long, however, it is reversible, and it is in what happens after reversal that special interest lies.

After the child has been back with his mother a few hours or a few days, the detached behaviour is replaced, not only by all the old attachment, but by attachment of greatly heightened intensity. From this it is clear that during detachment the ties binding him to his mother have not quietly faded, as is suggested by Anna Freud (1960a), [4] nor has there been a simple forgetting. On the contrary, the data strongly suggest that during the phase of detachment the responses that bind the child to his mother and lead him to strive to recover her are subject to a defensive process. In some way they are removed from consciousness, but remain latent and ready to become active again, at high intensity, when circumstances change. [5] This means that in infants and young children the experience of separation habitually initiates defensive processes which lead to yearning for the lost object and reproach for its desertion both to become unconscious. Another way of stating it is that, in early childhood, loss is responded to by processes of mourning that habitually take a course that in adults is deemed pathological.

[4] In an earlier publication (Burlingham and Freud, 1942), however, Anna Freud adopted a viewpoint similar to that taken here.

[5] The change of circumstance required varies with the stage to which detachment has progressed. When the child is still in the early phases, renewed attachment usually follows reunion with his mother: when he is in an advanced stage analytic treatment is likely to be required.

The question that now arises is whether the defensive processes that are so striking following loss in childhood are different in kind from what is seen in healthy mourning or whether they occur in healthy mourning also but with some difference of form or timing. Evidence suggests that they do occur (Bowlby, 1961b), but that in the healthy process their onset is delayed. As a result the urges to recover the lost object and to reproach it have time enough for expression so that, through repeated failure, they are gradually relinquished or, in terms of learning theory, extinguished. What appears to happen in childhood (and in the pathological mourning of later years), on the other hand, is that the development of defensive processes is accelerated. As a result, the urges to recover and to reproach the lost object have no chance to be extinguished and instead persist, with consequences that are serious.

Let us return briefly to apply these ideas to Helene Deutsch's patient. Following his mother's death when he was five, it seems, both longing and anger had disappeared from his conscious self. The fantasy of the visit from the dog shows, however, that they persisted nonetheless at an unconscious level. This and evidence from other cases suggest that, although immobilized, both his love and his anger had remained directed towards the recovery of his dead mother. Thus, locked in the service of a hopeless cause, they had been lost to the developing personality. With loss of mother had gone loss also of his feeling life.

Two common technical terms are in use to denote the processes at work: fixation and repression. Unconsciously the child remains fixated on the lost mother: his urges to recover and to reproach her, and the ambivalent emotions connected with them, have undergone repression.

Another defensive process, closely ralated to and alternative to repression, also occurs following loss. This is "splitting of the ego." In such cases one part of the personality, secret but conscious, denies that the object is really lost and maintains, instead, either that there is still communication with it or that it will soon be recovered; whilst simultaneously another part of the personality shares with friends and relatives the knowledge that the object is irretrievably lost. Incompatible though they be, the two parts may co-exist over many years. As in the case of repression, ego splits lead also to psychiatric illness.

Why in some cases the part still yearning to recover the lost object should be conscious and in others it should be unconscious is unclear. So too are the conditions which lead some bereaved children to develop satisfactorily whilst others do not. [6] What seems certain, however, is that the

[6] This is a problem that Josephine Hilgard is studying (1960).

precipitate onset of the defensive processes, repression or splitting, with the resulting fixation, is initiated much more readily in childhood than in more mature years. In this fact lies a main explanation, I suggest, of why and how it is that experiences of loss in early childhood lead to faulty personality development and proneness to psychiatric illness.

The hypothesis I am advancing, therefore, is that in the young child the experience of separation from mother figure is especially apt to evoke psychological processes of a kind that are as crucial for psychopathology as are inflammation and its resulting scar tissue to physiopathology. This does not mean that a crippling of personality is the inevitable result; but it does mean that, as in the case, say, of rheumatic fever, scar tissue is all too often formed which in later life leads to more or less severe dysfunction. The processes in question, it seems, are pathological variants of those that characterize healthy mourning.

Although this is a theoretical position that is closely akin to many others already in the field, it appears nonetheless to be different from them. Its strength lies in relating the pathological responses with which we are confronted in older patients to responses to loss that are actually to be observed in early childhood, thereby providing a more solid link between psychiatric conditions of later life and childhood experience. Let us turn now to compare this formulation with some of its predecessors.

Two Traditions in Psychoanalytic Theorizing

During this century a number of psychoanalysts and psychiatrists have sought to relate psychiatric illness, loss of a loved object, pathological mourning and childhood experience. Almost all have taken as their starting point the sick patient.

It is more than 60 years since Freud first adumbrated the idea that both hysteria and melancholia are manifestations of pathological mourning following more or less recent bereavement (1897), and more than 40 years since in *Mourning and Melancholia* he advanced the hypothesis in a systematic way (1917). Since then there have been a host of other studies, all of which in different ways support it; recently this literature has been ably reviewed by Parkes (1959). Clinical experience and a reading of the evidence leaves little doubt of the truth of the main proposition—that much psychiatric illness is an expression of pathological mourning—or that such illness includes many cases of anxiety state, depressive illness, and hysteria, and also more than one kind of character disorder. Plainly there has been discovered here a large and important field; for it to be explored fully much further work is required.

Controversy begins when we come to consider why some individuals and not others respond to loss in these pathological ways: and it is amongst hypotheses that seek to account for the origin of such differential responsiveness that the one I am advancing belongs.

A hypothesis that has influenced all later workers with a psychological orientation was outlined by Abraham (1924a). As a result of analyzing several melancholic patients, he came to the conclusion that "in the last resort melancholic depression is derived from disagreeable experiences in the childhood of the patient." He therefore postulated that, during their childhood, melancholics have suffered from what he termed a "primal parathymia." In these passages, however, Abraham never uses the words grief and mourning; nor is it clear that he recognized that for the young child the experience of losing mother (or of losing her love) is in very truth a bereavement.

Since then, a number of other psychoanalysts, in trying to trace the childhood roots of depressive illness and of personalities prone to develop it, have drawn attention to unhappy experiences in the early years of their parents' lives. Except in the tradition of theorizing initiated by Melanie Klein, however, few have conceptualized the experiences in terms of bereavement and pathological mourning. Nevertheless, when we come to study the experiences to which they refer, it seems evident that this is the frame of reference that best fits them. I will give as examples three patients described in the literature.

In 1936 Gerö reported two patients suffering from depression. One of them, he concluded, had been "starved of love" as a child; the other had been sent to a residential nursery and had only returned home when he was three. Each showed intense ambivalence toward any object that was loved, a condition which, Gerö believed, could be traced to the early experience. In the second case, he speaks of both a fixation on the mother and an inability to forgive her for the separation. Edith Jacobson, in her extensive writing on the psychopathology of depression, draws regularly on a female patient, Peggy, whose analysis she describes in two papers (1943, 1946). On referral, Peggy, aged 24, was in a state of severe depression with suicidal impulses and depersonalization; these symptoms had been precipitated by a loss, actually the loss of her lover. The childhood experience on which Edith Jacobson places major emphasis occurred when Peggy was three-and-a-half years old. At this time her mother went to hospital to have a new baby, whilst she and her father stayed with the maternal grandmother. Quarrels developed, and father departed. "The child was left alone, disappointed by her father and eagerly awaiting her mother's return. However, when the mother did return it was with the baby." Peggy recalled feeling at this time "This was not my mother, it was a different person" (an experience that we know is not uncommon in young children who have separated from their mothers for a few weeks). It was soon after this, Edith Jacobson believed, that "the little girl broke down in her first deep depression."

Now it may be questioned both whether the experiences in these patients' early childhoods were accurately recalled and also whether the analysts were right in attributing to them so much significance for their patients' emotional development. But, if we accept, as I am inclined to do, both the validity of the experiences and their significance, I believe the concept of pathological mourning to be the one best fitted both describe how the patient responded at the time and to relate the experience of childhood to the psychiatric illness of adult life. Neither author utilizes this concept, however. Instead, both use concepts such as "disappointment" and "disillusionment" which appear to have a different significance.

Several other analysts, whilst in greater or lesser degree alive to the pathogenic role of such experiences in childhood, also do not identify the child's response to loss with mourning. One is Fairbairn (1952). A second is Stengel who, in his studies of compulsive wandering (1939, 1941, 1943), draws special attention to the urge to recover the lost object. A third is the present writer in his earlier work (1946, 1951). Others are Anna Freud (1960a) and René Spitz (1946), both of whom, by disputing the notion that infants and young children mourn, have ruled out as a possibility the hypothesis that neurotic and psychotic character developments are sometimes the result of mourning in childhood having taken a pathological course.

A main reason why the child's response to loss is so often not identified with mourning appears to be a tradition that confines the concept "mourning" to processes that have a healthy outcome. Although this usage, like any other, is legitimate, it has one grave disadvantage: logically it becomes impossible to discuss, as such, any variants of mourning that may seem pathological. The consequent difficulties are illustrated by Helene Deutsch, already quoted (1937). In her discussion there is firm recognition both of the central place of childhood loss in the production of symptoms and character deviations and also of a defense mechanism which, following loss, may lead to an absence of affect. Nevertheless, although she relates this mechanism to mourning, it is represented more as an alternative to, than as a pathological variant of, mourning. Whilst at first sight this distinction may appear one merely of terminology, it is of more significance. For to regard the defensive process following childhood loss as an alternative to mourning is to miss, both that defensive processes of similar kinds but of lesser degree and later onset enter also into healthy mourning, and also that what is pathological is not so much the defensive processes themselves as their intensity and the prematurity of their onset.

Similarly, although Freud was on the one hand deeply interested in the pathogenic role of mourning and on the other, especially in his later years, was also aware of the pathogenic role of childhood loss, he seems, nonetheless, never to have put his finger on childhood mourning and its disposition to take a pathological course as concepts which link these two sets of ideas together. This is well illustrated in his discussion of the splitting of the ego in the defensive process, to which he was giving special attention at the end of his life (1938).

In one of his papers, Freud describes two patients in whom an ego split had followed loss of father.

> In the analysis of two young men, I learnt that each—one when he was two years old and the other when he was ten—had failed to take cognizance of the death of his beloved father . . . and yet neither of them had developed a psychosis. Thus a piece of reality which was undoubtedly important had been disavowed by the ego . . . [But] it was only one current in their mental life that had not recognized their father's death; there was another current which took full account of the fact that the attitude which fitted in with the wish and the attitude which fitted in with reality [namely that the father was dead], existed side by side [1927, pp. 156–157].

In this and related papers, however, Freud does not relate his discovery of such splits in the ego to the pathology of mourning in general nor to childhood mourning in particular. He did recognize them, nevertheless, as the not uncommon sequelae of bereavements in early life. "I suspect," he remarks when discussing his findings, "that similar occurrences are by no means rare in childhood." Recent statistical studies, we shall see, show that his suspicion was well-founded.

Thus a reading of the literature shows that, despite attributing much pathogenic significance to loss of a parent and to loss of love, in the main tradition of psychoanalytic theorizing, the origin of pathological mourning and of the consequent psychiatric illness in the adult is not connected with the disposition for processes of mourning to take a pathological course when they occur following a loss in infancy and early childhood.

I believe it to have been a major contribution of Melanie Klein (1935,

1940) to have made this connection. Infants and young children mourn and go through phases of depression, she maintains, and their modes of responding at such times are determinants of the way that in later life they will respond to further loss. Certain methods of defense, she believes, are to be understood as "directed against the 'pining' for the lost object." In these respects my approach is identical with hers. Differences arise, however, over the particular experiences that are thought to be of importance, the age at which they are thought to occur, and the nature and origin of anxiety and aggression.

The experiences of loss which Melanie Klein has suggested are pathogenic, all belong to the first year of life and are mostly connected with feeding and weaning. Aggression is regarded as an expression of the death instinct, and anxiety the result of its projection. None of this I find convincing. In the first place the evidence she advances regarding the overwhelming importance of the first year and of weaning is, on scrutiny, far from impressive (Bowlby, 1960a). In the second, her hypotheses regarding aggression and anxiety are not easy to fit into a framework of biological theory (1960b). It is, I believe, because so many find the elaborations, with which Melanie Klein has surrounded the hypothesis regarding the role of childhood mourning, unplausible that the hypothesis itself remains neglected. This is a pity.

My position therefore is that, although I do not regard the details of Melanie Klein's theory of the depressive position as a satisfactory way of explaining why individuals develop in such diverse ways that some respond to later loss with healthy mourning whilst others do so with one or another form of pathological mourning, I nonetheless hold her theory to contain the seeds of a very productive way of ordering the data. The alternative elaborations which I believe the evidence favours are that the most significant object that can be lost is, not the breast, but the mother herself (and sometimes the father), that the vulnerable period is not confined to the first year but extends over a number of years of childhood (as Freud, 1940, held), and that loss of a parent gives rise, not only to primary separation anxiety and grief, but to processes of mourning in which aggression, the function of which is to achieve reunion, plays a major part. Whilst sticking closely to the data, this formulation has the additional merit of fitting readily into biological theory.

Substantial though the differences are between Melanie Klein's standpoint and mine, the area of agreement is also substantial. Both hold as a main hypothesis that processes of mourning occurring in these early years are more apt, than when they occur later in life, to take a pathological course and so to leave the individual thenceforward more prone than others to respond to further loss in a similar way. The version of this theory that I am now advancing appears to be consistent with much of the clinical material published in the literature and already referred to. This includes Freud's cases of splits in the ego, Stengel's cases of compulsive wandering, the depressive patients described by Abraham, Gerö, and Edith Jacobson, and the patients with character defects described by Helene Deutsch, Melanie Klein, Fairbairn, and the present writer. It is also consistent with the numerous studies which have appeared in the past two decades, which show that the incidence of childhood loss in the lives of patients suffering from psychiatric illness and character defeat is significantly higher than in a random sample of the population.

Incidence of Childhood Loss in Psychiatric Patients and Delinquents

In a valuable critique of a dozen statistical papers on this topic available to him at the time of writing in 1958, Gregory remarks that "various selective factors, small samples, and lack of standardization in the recording of data render relatively few comparisons justifiable either with each other" or with data from controls (p. 437). He points out the many pitfalls in making such studies, some of which may exaggerate differences between psychiatric patients and controls, but some of which mask them. Some of the reported data he re-works. After this careful and disinterested examination his conclusions carry weight. The incidence of loss of one or other parent in childhood, he holds, is almost certainly higher in the case of psychiatric patients than it is in the general population.

In considering and comparing the results of the various studies it must be borne in mind that each is concerned, not only with a different kind of patient, but often with a different kind of loss and with losses occurring at different times in the patient's life. This makes for confusion. A special problem arises in connection with age at loss, both because it is so central to our thesis and also because so many different age criteria have been employed. Some authors take a specified age in the late teens or even early twenties and count the losses that occurred at any time before it: others count losses occurring before a specified age somewhere in the early teens. There are a few, however, who divide the years of childhood into a number of age periods and give the incidence of loss for each separately; for example, for the first five years of life, for the second five years, and so on.

Scrutiny of these data makes it clear that only the last type of study is satisfactory, because differences of incidence between patients and controls which are clearcut and significant during one five-year period can be largely or completely hidden when losses occurring during two or more such periods are summated. It is this undifferentiated way of presenting data that almost certainly accounts for some of the negative findings reported (e.g., Ingham, 1949).

Another cause of real difference being masked is the elimination of cases on the score of the inadequacy of data regarding childhood history, since, as Gregory points out, the incidence of early loss in such cases is likely to be raised.

I have selected four studies which appear to have been carefully executed and to give reasonably trustworthy results (see Tables 1, 2, and 3). One of them is concerned with psychiatric inpatients, two with psychiatric outpatients, and one with persistent delinquents. In the first three studies of the indices of loss are the loss of mother and father separately and by death only; in the fourth, the delinquents, the index used is loss of either or both parents and for any of a number of reasons, e.g., death, desertion, separation, divorce.

Barry was one of the first to be interested in this field and has published a number of studies. That of 1949 compares a sample of nearly 1,700 patients who were aged 40 years and under when admitted to a U.S. mental hospital with a control series of subjects derived from life insurance tables; 60% of the patient group were diagnosed as dementia praecox. Figure 1 shows the incidence for the 2 groups of loss of mother through death by the age of the patient at the time of loss. It will be seen that the incidence among patients both in the first five years of life and in the second five years is about double that of the controls; in both cases the difference is statistically significant ($P < .01$). In the age period 10-14, incidence for the patients remains raised but is no longer significant.

Figure 2 shows the incidence for the two groups of loss of father by death. Here again the incidence for the patient group is higher than for the controls, but this time it is less evident. Only in the five-nine year age-period does the difference reach statistical significance ($P < .05$).

In 1960 Barry published another rather similar study. This time he investigated a group of nearly 1000 outpatients with diagnosis either psychoneurosis or psychosomatic illness. For this group the differences in parental death rates are much less marked than for the inpatients. Nevertheless Figure 3 shows that loss of mother in the first five years remains significantly raised ($P < .01$). Incidence of loss of mother at older ages,

TABLE 1

INCIDENCE OF DEATH OF MOTHER BY AGE OF PATIENT AT TIME OF LOSS*

Age at Loss Years	Study by	Incidence of Loss Patients	Controls	Difference	P
		%	%	%	
0-4	Barry	3.80	1.94	1.86 ± 0.45	.01
	Barry and Lindemann	4.12	1.18	2.94 ± 0.63	.01
	Brown	7.30	2.16	5.14 + 1.82	.01
5-9	Barry	4.57	2.08	2.49 ± 0.51	.01
	Barry and Lindemann	2.43	1.97	0.46 ± 1.84	NS
	Brown	6.83	1.55	5.28 ± 1.76	.01
10-14	Barry	3.26	2.5	0.76 ± 0.43	NS
	Barry and Lindemann	2.11	2.35	−0.24	NS
	Brown	6.34	2.04	4.30 ± 1.70	.02

TABLE 2

INCIDENCE OF DEATH OF FATHER BY AGE OF PATIENT AT TIME OF LOSS*

Age at Loss Years	Study by	Incidence of Loss Patients	Controls	Difference	P
		%	%	%	
0-4	Barry	3.32	2.52	0.80 ± 0.43	NS
	Barry and Lindemann	2.32	1.58	0.74 ± 0.49	NS
	Brown	6.95	6.00	0.95 ± 1.79	NS
5-9	Barry	4.04	3.09	0.95 ± 0.48	.05
	Barry and Lindemann	2.55	2.90	−0.38	NS
	Brown	8.45	3.40	5.05 ± 1.96	.01
10-14	Barry	4.99	4.05	0.94 ± 0.53	NS
	Barry and Lindemann	3.80	3.67	0.13	NS
	Brown	12.40	2.52	9.88 ± 2.32	.001

*From Barry (1949), Barry and Lindemann (1960), and Brown (1961).

TABLE 3
INCIDENCE OF FIRST LOSS OF ONE OR BOTH PARENTS
(All Causes) BY AGE OF SUBJECT AT TIME OF LOSS*

Age at Loss Years	Incidence of Loss Delinquent	Non-Delinquent	Difference	P
	%	%	%	
0.4	34	16	18.0 ± 2.67	.001
5-9	17	10.5	6.5 ± 2.16	.01
10-14	9	7	2.0 ± 1.64	NS

*From Glueck and Glueck (1950).

however, and loss of father during each of the age periods (Figure 4) are not very different in the patient group than in the controls.

In 1961 an English psychiatrist, Felix Brown, whose theoretical position regarding the significance of childhood loss is similar to my own, presented figures in which incidence of parental loss in a group of over 200 depressive patients was compared with that of the general population as derived from the census of 1921 (1961). Figure 5 gives his findings for loss of mother by death. The high incidence of loss during all three age periods is striking and significant ($P < .01$ for the younger age groups and $< .02$ for the 10-14 age group). Incidence of loss of father by death (Figure 6) is also high during each age period, though, because of the war of 1914-18, during the youngest age period it is high also for the controls each delinquent was paired with. Incidence of loss for the depressives is above that for the controls to a significant degree ($P < .01$).

The fourth study which I have selected concerns not psychiatric patients but 500 persistently delinquent boys in their early teens. This is perhaps the best of the many studies carried out by the Gluecks (1950). For controls, each delinquent was paired with a non-delinquent boy matched for age, intelligence, national origin and residence (mostly in poor neighborhoods). In this study the criteria of parental loss are extensive and include loss not only by death but by divorce, separation, desertion, and prolonged absence due to illness or imprisonment. Since no breakdown is given as to which parent was lost, Figure 7 shows the incidence of loss of either or both. Here, we are again struck by the raised incidence of loss during the first five years of the delinquents' lives. In fact, in each of the two younger age periods the incidence of loss for the delinquents is significantly higher than for the controls ($P < .01$).

Apart from one British study of psychiatric outpatients published by Norton (1952), where virtually no significant differences in incidence of loss is found, the other studies available (e.g., Oltman, et al., 1952; Wahl, 1954, 1956; Lewis, 1954) all tell the same story. What is so striking is the consistency with which a raised incidence of loss is reported for the first five years of life. It is a finding that strongly supports the view that it is these early years that are the most critical.

Which, if any, of these years show a specially high incidence of parent loss, however, is more difficult to discern because most investigators do no

INCIDENCE OF LOSS BY DEATH*

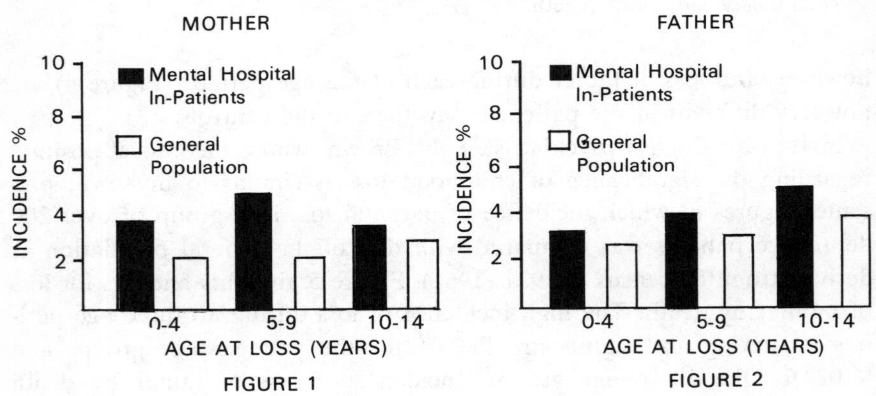

FIGURE 1

FIGURE 2

*From Barry (1949).

INCIDENCE OF LOSS BY DEATH*

MOTHER

FATHER

Psychoneurotics

General Population

INCIDENCE %

10 8 6 4 2

0-4 5-9 10-14

AGE AT LOSS (YEARS)

FIGURE 3

FIGURE 4

*From Barry and Lindemann (1960).

more than group their cases into losses occurring within the whole of a five year period. Only two reports, both by Barry, give figures for each year separately. In one, that on inpatients, the incidence of loss of mother by death remains above the actuarial expectations for each year until about the eighth, after which it drops to the expected level. In the other, on outpatients, the incidence tends to be raised during each of the first three years only. These findings, it will be seen, do nothing to support the view held by some analysts that the first year of life is more critical than those that follow.

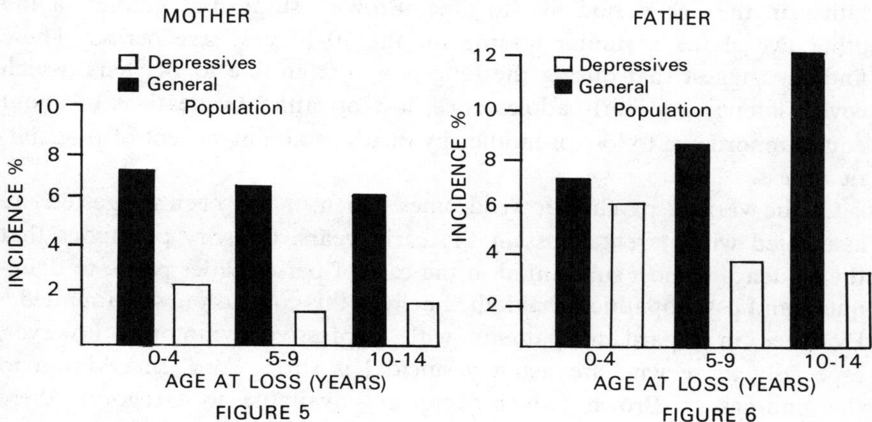

FIGURE 5 FIGURE 6

*From Brown (1961).

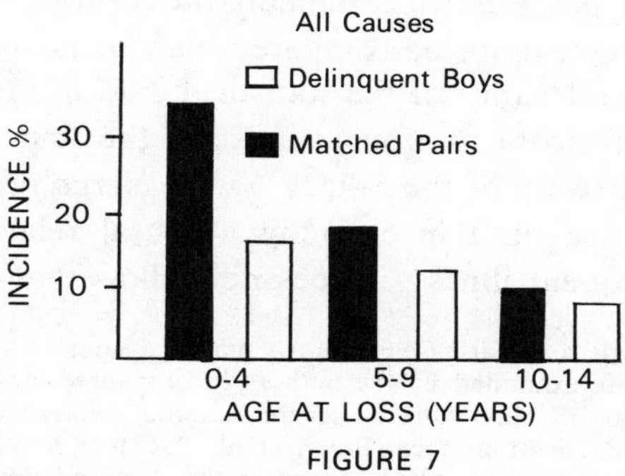

FIGURE 7

*From Glueck and Glueck (1950).

When we come to evaluate the figures for loss of mother and father respectively we find that incidence of loss of mother in the patient groups is more consistently above the expected rate than is incidence of loss of father (Tables 1 and 2). This is shown dramatically when we consider the age period zero to four years. In each of the three studies I have presented, the incidence of loss of mother by death in the first five years is raised in significant degree (in each case $P < .01$). In none of them is the incidence of loss of father by death raised significantly. This strongly supports the view that in regard to the early years it is loss of mother that tells.

As regards later years, two studies (the first of Barry's and the one by Brown) show a raised incidence of loss by death both of mother and of father in the age period five to nine. Brown's study, but neither of the other two shows a similar finding for the 10-14 year age period. These findings suggest that during the long period from five to 14 years, which covers latency and early adolescence, loss of father by death is of about equal importance to loss of mother by death as an antecedent of psychiatric illness.

Of the various psychiatric syndromes which, it has been suggested are associated with parental loss in the early years, Gregory concludes that the evidence is most substantial in the case of personalities prone to delinquent and psychopathic behaviour. I believe this conclusion well-founded.[7] Evidence in regard to patients with depressive symptoms, however, especially those who are actively suicidal is strong also. In addition to the findings of Brown (which were not available to Gregory), there have been a number of reports linking early loss of a parent, both by death and other causes, with suicide or attempted suicide. Among the first to make this connection was Zilboorg (1937); and there is a recent statistical study by Walton (1958). Although Walton's figures go some way to support Zilboorg's hypothesis, unfortunately the form in which he presents them is such that they cannot be compared with those already given.

In considering the relevance of the statistical data to my argument, certain doubts are likely to be in your minds. In the first place, it will be remarked, we must beware of the fallacy *post hoc ergo propter hoc.* In the second, even if we are right in claiming a causal relationship between early loss and subsequent illness, it does not follow that it is always me-

A recent study by Earle and Earle (1961) shows that in a sample of 1423 psychiatric patients under the age of 60, examined by the authors in outpatient clinics, mental hospitals and general hospitals, 100 (7%) had suffered severe maternal deprivation before the age of six years, due either to death of mother (Prugh et al., 1953) or to separations lasting six months or longer (Rollman-Branch, 1960). Amongst the deprived the incidence of sociopathic personality was 27%; amongst the remainder 2.9% ($P. < 01$).

diated by means of the pathological processes that have been described earlier. There are, indeed, two other sorts of process which almost certainly give rise to pathology in some cases. One is the process of identification with parents, which is an integral part of healthy development but which often leads to difficulties after one of them has died.[8] The other sort are evoked by the surviving parent, widow or widower, whose attitude towards the child may change and become pathogenic.

There is another difficulty that the hypothesis must meet. Even if it is true that there is a raised incidence of death of parents in the childhood histories of individuals prone later to develop certain types of personality and certain forms of illness, its absolute incidence is nevertheless low. How, it will be asked, are the other cases to be accounted for? There is more than one possible explanation.

In the first place, in order to base my argument on firm evidence, I have deliberately restricted most of the discussion of statistical data to the incidence of parental *death.* When other causes of parental loss in the early years are included, as they are in the Glueck's study, for many of the cases in which there has been no episode of actual separation in space of child from parent, there is often evidence that there has nonetheless been separation of another and more or less serious kind. Rejection, loss of love (perhaps on advent of a new baby or on account of mother's depression), alienation from one parent by the other, and similar situations, all have as a common factor loss by the child of a parent to love and to attach himself to. If the concept of loss of object is extended to cover loss of love these cases no longer constitute exceptions.

It seems unlikely, however, that such an extension would cover all cases falling within the psychiatric syndromes concerned. If this proves to be so, some other explanation for those not accounted for by the present hypothesis needs to be sought. Perhaps on closer examination the clinical picture of such cases will prove to be different in material degree from those that are accounted for. Alternatively, the clinical conditions may prove to be essentially similar, but the pathological processes in cases not accounted for to have been initiated by events of a different kind. Until these and other possibilities have been explored, problems will remain. Since, however, there is rarely a simple relationship between syndrome, pathological process, and pathogenic experience, the problems are no

[8] Psychiatric disturbance in which identification with a lost parent plays a significant part has for long been a subject of study by analysts. It is particularly clear in anniversary reactions (Hilgard et al., 1959).

different from those which occur constantly in other fields of medical research.

Conclusion

It is probably true that by far the most research in the field of psychiatry today still starts with an end-product, a sick patient, and seeks to unravel the sequence of events, psychological and physiological, that appear to have led to his becoming sick. This results in many suggestive hypotheses but, like any single method of inquiry, has its limitations. One of the hallmarks of an advancing science is exploitation of as many methods as can be devised. When in physiological medicine research was expanded to include the systematic investigation of one or another probable pathogen and its effects, a great harvest of knowledge was garnered. Adolf Meyer, we know, looked forward to the day when the same would be possible in psychiatry. "When we know better what to look out for," he wrote in 1903, "we may undertake studies of *developing* abnormalities which are not insanity yet, and follow them out so as to accumulate material of *actual observation* on which to build a solid theory . . ." (p. 95).

Because of its practical and scientific implications, the study of responses to loss of mother figure in the early years might have appealed to Adolf Meyer. On the practical side he might have been attracted by the vision of our becoming able to develop measures to prevent at least some forms of mental ill-health. On the scientific side he would, no doubt, have valued the opportunities that stem from the identification of an experience of childhood that is probably pathogenic, can be clearly defined, and the effects of which on the developing personality can be systematically studied by direct observation.

There are, of course, many other experiences of childhood besides loss that there is good reason to believe also contribute to the development of disturbed personality and psychiatric illness. Examples are the child's experience of one or another of the various sorts of parental attitude that have long been the subject of concern and therapeutic endeavour in child psychiatric clinics. For each, the research task is, first, to define the experience, secondly, to locate a sample of cases in which it is occurring so that its effects on psychological development may be studied, and finally, to relate the processes that are found to be set in train by it to processes present in patients with declared illness. The consequences of such an expansion of research are far reaching. It is my hope that the illustration of its adoption that has been given will encourage others to try the same route.

The author is much indebted to James Robertson for the observations on which he has drawn, and to him, Robert Hinde, and Anthony Ambrose for discussions in which ideas were clarified. The inquiry was undertaken as part of the work of the Tavistock Child Development Research Unit, which is supported by the National Health Service and by grants from the Foundations Fund for Research in Psychiatry and the Ford Foundation, to which our thanks are due.

MATERNAL OVERPROTECTION

DAVID M. LEVY

Levy, one of the pioneers in American child psychiatry, has made a variety of contributions which range from training child psychiatrists at the Institute of Child Guidance in New York, investigating finger sucking in infancy (1928), to studying the social behavior and sucking reflex of dogs (1934), describing primary affect hunger (1937), exploring different types of psychotherapy for children (1930, 1939, 1940), and investigating a variety of psychopathological states such as oppositional behavior (1955, this volume).

Levy's book, Maternal Overprotection, *from which the following excerpt is taken, is significant in that it was one of the earliest clinical, systematic efforts to observe and record the effects of maternal attitudes on the child's development. Levy sees maternal overprotection, which is often but not always related dynamically to unconscious rejection of the child, as of two sorts, each having its different effect. The* dominating, *overprotective mother can usually be correlated with the dependent, submissive child, whereas the* indulgent, *overprotective mother tends to be linked with demanding, disobedient children.*

A discussion of the concepts of maternal rejection and overprotection raises the question of the vagueness that often accompanies use of these phrases, a vagueness that has been deplored by a number of writers. Kanner, another pioneer American child psychiatrist, wrote a book (1941) defending mothers against what he called "overzealous psychologists." Anna Freud (1955) has urged caution in labeling mothers as "rejecting." Coleman, Kris, and Provence (1952) have convincingly demonstrated at the Yale Child Study Center that maternal attitudes fluctuate in relation to the child's developmental phase, so that blanket statements about a mother's behavior or attitudes are doomed to be imprecise. Benedek (1959b) has wisely written of parenthood as a developmental phase.

Maternal overprotection plays its part in most aspects of child rearing (Buxbaum, 1964). It assumes great importance where physical handicap, mental retardation, psychophysiological disorders, academic inhibition, or

Reprinted from *Maternal Overprotection* by David M. Levy. New York: Columbia University Press, 1943, pp. 37–39, 196–199.

death of a parent exist. In this volume its contribution is implicit, if not explicit, in many of the feeding problems Anna Freud (1947) discusses, in obesity which Bruch (1963) explores, in school phobias (Johnson et al., 1941), and in Mahler's discussion of symbiotic psychosis (1952).

Maternal overprotection is synonymous with excessive maternal care of children. Its manifestations in the mother-child relationship have been grouped, according to the manner in which they occur, under four headings. Three of these concern maternal activity primarily and paraphrase the common observations: 1) "the mother is always there"; 2) "she still treats him like a baby"; and 3) "she won't let him grow up" or "she won't take any risks." These expressions are rendered into the groupings: 1) excessive contact; 2) infantilization; and 3) prevention of independent behavior. All the manifestations of overprotection as revealed by maternal activity are classifiable under the three headings, excepting those which denote anxious behavior.

Maternal anxiety or oversolicitude is indicated in our groupings only when revealed by objective behavior in the mother-child relationship. Since oversolicitude is always manifested in one or more of the three categories already enumerated, the problem of its inclusion is partly solved. Thus, oversolicitude will be manifested by refusal to take risks for the child, by excessive nursing care during illness, and the like. The data furthermore indicate the amount of oversolicitude as measured generally by the type of activity prevented by the mother, the extent of infantilization, the amount of contact.

The child who is ill with a mild case of measles may be exposed to a mother whose harassed look, exaggerated response, tense embracing, and tearful exclamations, "Oh, my baby, my poor sick baby," give evidence of more intensive overprotection than that of a mother in a similar plight, also overprotective, yet emotionally more controlled. The difference in the two mothers is brought out in our study only in so far as the intensity of response is proportional to the factual data. Assuming that the facts recorded under excessive contact, infantilization, and prevention of independent behavior are equal in two given cases, there remains a difference in the quality or intensity of behavior that is not recorded. There is no way of telling with the data at hand how the child's personality is affected by this qualitative difference. At this stage of development in our human relationship studies we must be content with gross differentiation.

The fourth criterion of overprotection is lack of excess of maternal control. The former indicates a breakdown in the mother's ability to modify her child's behavior. In extreme form, the mother is quite subservient to the demands of her nursery despot who has retained full possession of the mother's attention and services as in the first year of life. The latter indicates excessive maternal domination of the child.

When overprotection is revealed by all four criteria, the picture presented is well portrayed by a mother who holds her child tightly with one hand and makes the gesture of pushing away the rest of the world with the other. Her energies are directed to preserving her infant as infant for all time, preserving it from all harm and from contact with the rest of humanity. For her child she will fight hard, make every sacrifice, and aggressively prevent interference with her social monopoly. Her aggression, directed so strongly against the intruder, yields, however, before the child. Towards him she is submissive; her discipline falters when he becomes assertive in the latter half of infancy, and is gradually destroyed.

The picture presents a composite of eleven out of the twenty "pure" cases. It summarizes instances of maternal overprotection in which the negative aspect of the fourth sign, "lack of maternal control," is present. In the remaining nine cases, eight children show an excessively submissive relation to the mother, are obedient to her, and very dependent.

In the group the general picture is that of inadequately modified behavior in respect to infantile power over the mother. The infantile aggression is manifested in having one's way, dominating every situation, manipulating the scene in order to be the central figure, displaying temper when crossed. The overprotection may be described as a process in which infantile power, unmodified, expands into a monstrous growth that tends to subjugate the parents.

In the second group, the dependency phase of the infant's relation to the mother is fostered through lack of development or overmodification of the dominating phase. In regard to infantile aggression, the overprotection in the second group is a process of constriction rather than expansion—a constriction in the growth of aggressive tendencies.

In their clinical manifestations of overprotection, mothers show a distinct difference in the two groups. Mothers of the dominating children are indulgent; mothers of the submissive children are dominating. The statement as it stands is merely a description implied by the meaning of the terms employed. For if a child is submissive to his mother, it is implied that he readily yields to her demands, that he keeps away from the company she forbids, that he goes to bed on time, and the like. She appears to be dominating the child, and the child is submissive to her. On the other hand, if a child goes to bed when he pleases, eats only what happens to suit his fancy, the fact that his behavior toward his mother has been consistently undisciplined implies that she has been consistently indulgent. The fact that the mother has indulged or dominated is implied in the description of the child's behavior as undisciplined or submissive.

The behavior of the indulged overprotected children was featured by disobedience, impudence, tantrums, excessive demands, and varying degrees of tyrannical behavior. The characteristics described were thought to represent accelerated growth of the aggressive components of the personality, and related directly to maternal indulgence. Limitations in the production of extreme tyrannical and possessive behavior at home was explained by varying degrees of parental modification, and external factors.

Most of the indulged overprotected children presented no special problems in school adjustment. This discrepancy between behavior at home and at school was explained by an exceptional and disciplinary attitude towards schoolwork on the part of the mothers; by satisfactions in the classroom related to high intelligence, verbal skill, and help through coaching on the part of the children; also, possibly, to their fear of the school group and a gratification in playing an obedient role. In any event, the adjustment of highly indulged children to classroom discipline indicates a high degree of flexibility in their personalities. When difficulties in classroom behavior occurred, they were consistent with the type of difficulty manifested at home.

Three boys who were disciplinary problems in the classroom were less intelligent than the others and their mothers less concerned about schoolwork.

In contrast with the indulged group, the dominated group responded well to the requirements of classroom behavior in every instance, regardless of I.Q. or of school success.

In all instances but one, difficulties in making friendships with other children occurred. The aggressive children showed, with one exception, "domination" or egocentric difficulties, that is, bossy, selfish, show-off, or cocky behavior. The submissive children showed in all cases but one timidity and withdrawal. There was a remarkable similarity of all the children's difficulty in relationship with their mothers and other children.

Successful adjustment of the indulged overprotected child to camp, as to school, would indicate that his difficulty with playmates could be improved, despite maternal overprotection, if opportunity were afforded for early social experience with children. Difficulties in making friendships were attributed to paucity of contact with children in the preschool age and lack of skill in play and sports, besides the problems inherent in the mother-child relationship. Follow-up studies indicated improvement in this regard during adolescence.

Some form of overt sexual behavior in childhood was noted in six instances, all in the indulged group. No problem in sex abnormality was present. The entire group showed nothing unusual in the frequency or form of masturbation.

Despite the very close attachment, including six cases in which children slept with their mothers long past infancy, follow-up studies into late adolescence or adult life failed to reveal an instance of sex abnormality. This suggests that in maternal indulgent overprotection, the development of heterosexual behavior was hastened rather than delayed, because of lessened inhibitions.

The main outside interest of the overprotected group consisted in reading. There was a notable lack of interest in sports.

Feeding problems occurred in 12 of the 20 cases. The usual variety was manifested; in the form of bad table manners, refusal to eat on schedule, insistence on being fed or coaxed, finickiness and refusal to eat certain foods. There was no instance of inappetence. Practically all the indulged overprotected were maternal indulgence in regard to the feeding.

Nothing unusual was found in regard to sleeping difficulties. Problems related to sleep were in the form of refusal to go to bed, on time or without mother's company. Seven of the eight children who manifested such behavior were in the indulged overprotected group.

No problems in soiling occurred. There were but two cases of enuresis. The number was much less frequent than in other Institute cases. This difference was explained by the greater care exerted by overprotecting mothers. The assumption that the vast majority of problems in enuresis are originally due to neglect in training was supported by special data.

Information regarding cleanliness and care of possessions was available for 11 cases. The four who were very careless in this regard were all in the indulged group. Those noted as neat and careful were all in the dominated group.

Physical examinations revealed that the group of 20 overprotected children was taller and heavier than other Institute of Child Guidance groups in keeping with the high degree of maternal care. Of the group two only may be regarded as quite obese.

Errors of refraction were found in 11 cases. The inference that this relatively large number may have been due to excessive reading could not be determined, through lack of comparable data.

Treatment of organic difficulties seemed clearly related to improvement of social adjustment in two cases. In two others organic factors were apparently reinforcing to the maternal overprotection. In three cases, findings during the physical examination served to overcome maternal apprehension. It was followed in one case by withdrawal of interest in the entire study.

In the cases presented, maternal overprotection appeared to be related directly to increased breast feeding, early bladder control, frequency of tonsillectomy, good nutrition, and probably obesity. It appeared to be related, indirectly, to correction of errors of visual refraction.

Manifestations of personality difficulties were revealed during the physical examination in 14 of the 20 cases. They were seen chiefly in the form of dependency on the mother, sensitivity, shyness, and bids for the examiner's attention.

THE PSYCHOANALYTIC STUDY OF INFANTILE FEEDING DISTURBANCES

Anna Freud

Among the most frequent complaints child clinicians hear from mothers are those having to do with the child's eating habits. It is no surprise, then, that so many theories of psychological development assign a central role to the child's eating and the mother-child interaction surrounding the feeding process. As demonstrated by Brody (1956), feeding behavior is a reliable indicator of many facets of the mother-child relationship. The relevance of feeding behavior for developmental disturbances and food preferences, fads, finickiness, and aversions is obvious. Not as evident, however, is its influence on eventual character structure (Abraham, 1924b; Blum, et al., 1952; Goldman, 1948, 1950) and future neurotic, psychophysiological, and psychotic syndromes.

Although Anna Freud's discussion of infantile feeding disturbances is articulated within a psychoanalytic frame of reference, this does not indicate that the phenomena she is exploring differ from those dealt with in pediatric discussions of feeding disturbances or in behaviorally oriented presentations (Davis, 1928; Gesell and Ilg, 1937; Spock, 1963). The psychoanalytic perspective she employs represents one means of organizing the rich clinical observations she made while working with Viennese and British children. The psychoanalytic orientation also reflects her effort to penetrate psychologically below the surface of the child's behavior.

This report was written when a transition was under way from feeding according to a fixed schedule to feeding based on the baby's demand. Similarly, as the article makes clear, the rigid attitude toward toilet training was yielding to a more flexible approach (Wolfenstein, 1953).

There is an additional point of transition in this article—the development of psychoanalytic theory. Although the article is organized to a considerable extent from the perspective of the traditional psychoanalytic thinking prevalent in the 1940's, it contains many hints of the directions Anna Freud's psy-

Reprinted from *The Psychoanalytic Study of the Child*, 2. New York: International Universities Press, 1946, pp. 119–132.

choanalytic thinking would take. In this study of infantile feeding disturbances published in the 1940's, one can find precursors of her concept of developmental lines which she did not set forth until the 1960's (A. Freud, 1965).

The more severe eating disturbances—anorexia nervosa and obesity—are explored in the section on Psychophysiologic Disorders.

In the psychoanalytic study of children, interest frequently has been concentrated on one or the other of the feeding problems of infancy and childhood. The first disorders of this kind to attract the attention of analytic authors were the upsets of feeding after weaning (Abraham, 1916; Bernfeld, 1929). These were investigated in the beginning indirectly, through the aftereffects for the individual's emotional life as they showed up under analytic treatment of young children. Other feeding problems gradually came into the field of analytic vision. Peto (1937) devoted a paper to the emotional attitude of the mother, as an important factor for the success of breast feeding. Middlemore (1941) made a systematic study of the "suckling situation" between mother and newborn infant and interpreted some of her findings in the light of M. Klein's theories of the conflicts of the oral phase. Jackson (1945) and Mohr (1928) stressed the importance of emotional factors in nutrition work with infants and children. E. Sterba (1941) drew attention to the interrelations between habit training and feeding disorders; Fenichel (1945b), Strachey (1930), Schmideberg (1934) and others, to the connection between feeding inhibitions and inhibitions of intellectual activities. Sylvester (1945), in a case of psychogenic anorexia, traced the influence of the mother-child relationship on the origin and course of the disturbance. Refusal of food owing to the repression of oral sadism and oral introjection has played a large part in the psychoanalytic theory of depressive states and melancholia (see Freud, 1917; Abraham, 1924a; M. Klein, 1932).

Psychoanalytic studies of this kind have been instrumental in shedding light on the origin and meaning of specific feeding disorders, especially of the graver types and those which occur as single symptoms within the framework of a neurotic illness. Less notice was taken of the common feeding difficulties which occur in the everyday life of otherwise normal children. Nor have the findings of the various authors been correlated and systematically applied to the wide field of feeding problems which ranges from manifestations like simple fluctuations of appetite, and transitory food fads, to severe disorders which endanger the child's health, and sometimes its life.

The function of eating serves, primarily, the biological bodily need for nourishment and operates in agreement with the id forces and ego forces which are jointly directed towards the self-preservation of the individual. The function of eating, as such, lies therefore outside the sphere of psychological conflict (see Hartmann's [1939] "konfliktfreie Sphäre"). Eating may, on the other hand, become invested with sexual and aggressive meaning and thereby, secondarily, become the symbolic representative of id forces which are opposed by the ego.

The need for nourishment announces itself to the child's awareness by the sensations of hunger. The painful tension which is created by the sensations of hunger urges the child to take appropriate action (announcing its hunger to the environment by crying, later on asking for food, or helping itself to food). The appeasement of hunger through the intake of nourishment is felt as satisfactory and is accompanied by pleasure. Since the infant's behavior is dominated by the urge to avoid pain and discomfort and to gain pleasure, the urge for self-preservation through feeding is reinforced by the urge to gain pleasure through feeding.

There are, according to these conditions, three main ways in which the function of eating is open to disturbance:

1) through changes in the organism which directly or indirectly affect the organism's drive to survive, or the need for nourishment. (*Organic feeding disturbances.*)
2) through changes in the pleasurable character of the function. (*Nonorganic disturbance of the instinctive process itself.*)
3) through sexualization or aggressive use of the function, which involves the activity of feeding in conflicts with the ego forces and leads to states of neurotic anxiety, inhibition, and symptom formation. (*Neurotic feeding disturbances.*)

Organic Feeding Disturbances

The organic feeding disorders lie outside the field of analytic interest, except in those cases where they become the basis of, or otherwise combine with, nonorganic disorders. In states of severe physical illness, weakness, exhaustion, strain, and in certain states of convalescence, the organism is forced to a lower level of adjustment (Gesell and Ilg, 1937, p. 112), and the need for food, with the accompanying sensations of hunger, is decreased. Some children show a steady sustained appetite even during illness or malaise (Gesell and Ilg, 1937); but with the majority, the appetite falls to a low level with a consequent reduction of intake. Such children are at these times "bad eaters" for physiological reasons.

Where it is necessary, on medical grounds, to urge the child to eat beyond the limits of its appetite, or where mothers, for their own reassurance, force the child to eat against its will, emotional factors may enter into an otherwise simple feeding situation. Eating then becomes symbolic of a struggle between mother and child, in which the child can find an outlet for its passive or active, sadistic or masochistic tendencies towards the mother. To win a victory in this battle may, for the child, become more important than to satisfy its returning appetite. In such cases the phase of "bad eating" outlasts by far the phases of illness and convalescence or may become the starting point for permanent nonorganic feeding troubles. Where the child can be permited in illness to adjust its feeding to the level of its appetite, it will return to its former normal feeding standards as soon as the need for food returns to normal level.

Disturbances of the Instinctive Process

The satisfaction of hunger constitutes the first experience of instinctual gratification in the child's life. An infant who feeds successfully is a contented and "happy" infant. So far as the mother, by providing nourishment, guarantees this satisfaction and thereby provides for a pleasurable experience, the child, its instinctive need, and the environment, are all in perfect harmony.

On the other hand no mother gives food to the child without imposing on it at the same time a feeding regime which constitutes on the part of the environment the first serious interference with an instinctive desire of the child.

The current feeding schedules for the first year of life are based on detailed physiological knowledge of the infant's bodily functioning. The number of mothers who do not follow the advice either of their own pediatricians or of the Medical Officers and nurses of the Welfare Clinics diminishes in England and America from year to year. The mixed diet of the toddlers is, in the middle classes, chosen according to similar advice; in the poorer parts of the population it is left almost entirely in the hands of the mothers and determined by the food habits and circumstances of the other members of the family. With older children, scientific planning of a balanced diet may be introduced again where the child shares in nursery or school meals.

Some feeding regimens are, thus, based on medical-hygienic knowledge;

others are the result of preconceived ideas, sometimes sensible, sometimes outdated, and often superstitious, handed down to mothers by the former generation. In each case they are the embodiment of what a specific environment believes to be wholesome, advantageous and suitable for the various ages. It is a common feature of all the current feeding regimes in our civilization that they take maximum account of the bodily requirements for physiological health, growth, and development, and little or no account of the pleasure which should be an invariable accompaniment and inducement to the feeding process.

The amount of pleasure which an individual child gains from eating depends only partly on the adequate fulfilment of bodily requirements; for an equally large part, it is dependent on the manner in which the food is given. The child finds feeding most pleasurable when it can eat what it likes, how much or how little it likes, and in whatever way it likes. The average feeding regime which regulates the child's meals according to quality, quantity, frequency, and procedure, therefore inevitably interferes with the element of pleasure in all these respects.

In the last decades the feeding schedules for infants have inclined towards strict and fixed hygienic regulation and have left little room for individual fluctuations. Recently many authors show a growing tendency to stress the importance of individualization in the supervision of infant feeding (see Gesell and Ilg, 1937) and to allow for a certain amount of adjustment of the schedule to the individual child. But even with a more flexible feeding regime of this nature, the interference with the natural process will remain considerable. It is inevitable, under conventional feeding conditions, that infants and toddlers are made to cease feeding while they still feel unsatisfied; or that they are urged to continue when they feel that they have had enough; or that they are given foods which are considered necessary for the diet but which they dislike; or that they are offered sweets at moments when they prefer savouries, or savouries when they prefer sweets; that the temperature of liquids or the consistency of solids is not according to preference; that they are passively fed at an age when they desire to handle the food actively; or forced to use implements when they prefer using their fingers, etc. On all these occasions the child will feel displeased, frustrated, uncomfortable, and will connect these painful sensations with the feeding process.

Further discrepancies between an imposed schedule and the child's wishes arise about the incidence of feedings. The former provides for meals at set times, while the wishes turn to food, or the satisfaction connected with it, for ulterior motives too, to allay anxiety, loneliness, longing, boredom, tiredness, or any other emotional upset. This means that for the child food acts as an important general comforter, a function which is disregarded in most feeding schemes. Where the child's wish for food remains unfulfilled at such moments, it feels deeply dissatisfied.

A similar discrepancy exists between child and environment about the question of timing meals. The adult's conception of the length of waiting times after sensations of hunger have appeared is different from the infant's. In infantile life instinctive needs are of overwhelming urgency. There is no organized ego, able to postpone wish-fulfilment with the help of the thought processes or other inhibitory functions. Nothing, therefore, will diminish the painful and distressing tension of the need except immediate satisfaction. Where hungry infants and toddlers are made to wait for their meals, even for minutes, they suffer acute distress to a degree which may prevent them from enjoying the meal when it finally arrives.

On all the occasions enumerated, the child experiences sensations of a disagreeable and painful nature instead of pleasure. Where the disappointments, dissatisfactions and frustrations connected with the feeding experiences become too frequent, they may, in time, outweigh the pleasures and ultimately spoil the child's attitude to the whole feeding process.

Urged by the physiological need of the body and by pressure from the environment, children will continue to eat even when the process of feeding has become dissociated from the powerful urge for pleasure which originally characterizes every instinctive drive. But meal times will then have lost their former attraction and instead be tiresome tasks; forced labor rather than an occasion for wish-fulfillments. The children will then eat slowly instead of greedily; be easily distracted from their meals, or demand to be entertained while eating; object to more types of food and be more distrustful of new foods than they otherwise would; need considerable urging to take in sufficient nourishment; and cannot, as their mothers express it, "be bothered to eat", or will be "too deep in play" to come for their meals. They have become "bad eaters" owing to loss of pleasure in the function. [1]

If doctors, mothers, and nurses are right in taking the child's desire for food as a blind instinctive force, without the discrimination and self-regulation which are essential factors in the parallel feeding situations

[1] In a discussion of these problems in 1933, Dr. Grete Bibring suggested the very widespread reduction in the pleasure of eating in the European children of the twentieth century might well be a consequence of the growing rigidity of the then current schedules of infant feeding.

of young animals, then the imposing of feeding schedules from without, with the loss of pleasure and the eating disturbances consequent on it, are inevitable. On the other hand recent studies on these lines, made under completely changed feeding conditions, do not confirm this distrust in the self-regulating powers of the child's appetite. Davis (1928, 1935a, 1935b) has shown in her experiements with nursing infants, infants of weaning age, and older children in a hospital setting that infants and children can, under carefully regulated conditions, be trusted to make their own choice according to quantity and quality among selected foods rich in the nutritional elements essential to growth, and that under these conditions they will have better appetites, eat more, and have happier mealtimes than children fed in the usual manner. The pleasure which they obtain from the gratification of their appetite will be fully maintained and form an essential element in the smooth functioning of the feeding process.[2]

Neurotic Feeding Disturbances

Eating, more than any other bodily function, is drawn into the circle of the child's emotional life and used as an outlet for libidinal and aggressive tendencies.

a. *The relationship between eating and the stages of object love*:—The newborn infant is self-centered and self-sufficient as a being when it is not in a state of tension. When it is under the pressure of urgent bodily needs, as for instance, hunger, it periodically establishes connections with the environment which are withdrawn again after the needs have been satisfied and the tension is relieved. These occasions are the child's first introduction to experiences of wish-fulfilment and pleasure. They establish centres of interest to which libidinal energy becomes attached. An infant who feeds successfully "loves" the experience of feeding (narcissistic love).

When the child's awareness develops sufficiently to discern other qualities besides those of pain and pleasure, the libido cathexis progresses from the pleasurable experience of feeding to the food which is the source of pleasure. The infant in this second stage "loves" the milk, breast or bottle. (Since, on this level of development, no certain distinctions are made between the child's self and the environment, this libido attachment forms a transitional stage between narcissism and object love.) When its powers of perception permit the child to form a conception of the person through

[2] The author can confirm these findings from experience with toddlers in the Jackson Nursery in Vienna 1937–38 and the Hampstead Nurseries in London 1940–45.

whose agency it is fed, its "love" is transferred to the provider of food, that is, to the mother or mother-substitute (object love).

It is not difficult to pursue the line of development which leads from these crude beginnings of object attachment to the later forms of love. The infant's first love for the mother is directed towards material satisfaction. (Stomach love, cupboard love, egoistic love; "to be fed".) In a next stage object love is still egoistic but directed toward nonmaterial satisfactions, i.e., to receive love, affection, approval from the mother; "to be loved". As the child progresses from the oral and anal to the phallic level, object attachment loses its egoistic character; the qualities of the object increase in libidinal importance while the immediate benefit from the relationship becomes less important. The next and highest stage of development is the ability to love the object regardless of benefit (altruistic love).

Where infants are breast-fed, and the milk and breast are in fact part of the mother and not merely, as with bottle-fed babies, symbolic of her, the transition from narcissism to object love is easier and smoother. The image of food and the mother-image remain merged into one until the child is weaned from the breast.

Psychoanalytic authors have been repeatedly accused of exaggerating the upsets to the feeding situation caused by weaning (see for instance Gesell and Ilg, 1937). Pediatricians and psychologists stress the fact that where weaning takes place in slow stages with the gradual introduction of other foods and other means of feeding (spoon, cup), no shock is felt by the child. In the author's opinion, this is only reliably so where weaning takes place in the first period of narcissistic enjoyment of feeding, when the child's unfavorable reactions are to alterations of the feeding condition which has proved satisfactory and where upsets can be avoided by the avoidance of sudden changes. At the latter stages of developing object relationship, weaning signifies, besides the changes in food and the means of feeding, an entry into a new phase of the mother relationship to which certain children are unable to adjust themselves smoothly. The difficulties on the emotional side may find their outlet as difficulties of adjusting to the new food.

Though food and the mother become separated for the conscious mind of all children from the second year onwards, the identity between the two images remains so far as the child's unconscious is concerned. Much of the child's conflicting behavior towards food does not originate from loss of appetite or a lessened need to eat, etc., but from conflicting emotions towards the mother which are transferred on to the food which is a symbol for her. Ambivalence towards the mother may express itself as fluctuations between over-eating and refusal of food; guilty feelings towards the mother and a consequent inability to enjoy her affection as an inability to enjoy food; obstinacy and hostility towards the mother as a struggle against being fed. Jealousy of the mother's love for the other children of the family may find its outlet in greediness and insatiableness. At the stage of repression of the oedipus complex, refusal of food may accompany, or be substituted for, the inner rejection of the phallic sexual strivings towards the mother.

Eating disturbances of this type normally disappear in adolescence, when repressions of the infantile relation to the parents are revised and solutions for them have to be found on a different level. Where the feeding disorders arising from the child-mother relationship have been especially severe, they may return in adult life in the form of psychosomatic disorders of the stomach or digestive tract.

Mothers, though they do not produce these feeding difficulties in their children, nevertheless may behave in a manner which aggravates the pathogenic elements in the situation. Under the influence of their own unconscious phantasies, they often continue much longer than necessary to act as the connecting link between the child and the food, and, on their side, to treat the food which they offer as if it were a part of themselves; they are pleased and affectionate when the child accepts the food, and as offended when food is rejected as if their love for the child had suffered a rebuff; they beg a badly eating child to eat "for their sake", etc. This attitude of the mother coincides with the unconscious attitude of the child and thereby strengthens the unconscious emotional tendencies which are a threat to feeding. Mothers cannot alter the unconscious phantasies of their children. But they can, by their actions, strengthen the healthy, conscious moves towards the next stage of development. That is, they can give the child direct access to food as early as possible, trust the self-regulating powers of its appetite within sensible limits, and thereby increasingly withdraw from the feeding situation, in the measure in which the child learns to handle food independently.

With children in the preoedipal phase, the feeding disorders of this origin normally disappear when mother and child are separated (away from home, in nursery school, in hospital). In all later phases, the conflicts arising from the mother-relationship persist as inner conflicts, regardless of the mother's presence or behavior. The feeding disorders which are dependent on them then transfer themselves automatically to every available mother substitute.

b. *The relationship between feeding and the oral pleasures:*—The connection between feeding and the oral component of infantile sexuality is so close, and its pathogenic influence so obvious, that analysts often make the mistake of diagnosing all infantile feeding disturbances automatically as "oral disturbances".

From the beginning of suckling the infant derives from the milk flow two different kinds of satisfaction: one from the appeasement of hunger, the other from the stimulation of the mucous membranes of the mouth, The latter, oral, satisfaction remains from then onwards through life a constant accompaniment of every feeding situation. When a mixed diet begins, oral satisfaction is gained from the taste and consistency of the various food substances and plays an important part in the formation of the various individual likes and dislikes for food. (Preference for sweets or salty foods, for hot or cold liquids, etc.) This winning of libidinal pleasure from an otherwise nonlibidinal body function is an added stimulus for the child's feeding, the significance of which cannot be too strongly emphasized. An infant's or toddler's diet in which this element is disregarded (i.e., a drab, dull diet, or one in which too many items are "distasteful" to the child) defeats its own ends by lowering the total gain in satisfaction from the intake of food with a consequent decrease of the child's appetite.

In the oral phase of libido development, oral pleasure, though originally discovered in conjunction with feeding, is sought and reproduced independently of the feeding situation in the numerous forms of thumb-sucking, as an auto erotic oral activity. As such it may be pursued by the infant as a substitute for feeding (while waiting for food or when feeding has to be interrupted before the child is fully satisfied). It may enter into competition with feeding (when infants are unwilling to remove the thumb from the mouth to take the teat of the bottle or the spoon filled with food). It further plays an important part, completely independent of feeding, as a general comforter (like food) before sleep, when the child is lonely, dull, etc.

Through the intimate connection between feeding pleasure, oral pleasure, and the roots of object relationship, oral tendencies become the first carriers of the libidinal attachment to the mother. Oral attitudes are consequently as decisive for shaping the child-mother relationship as the latter is decisive in determining the child's attitude to food.

The oral pleasures are an asset to feeding while the child can enjoy them without interference from the environment or from its own ego forces. When they are repressed, or otherwise rejected by the ego, serious upsets for feeding result. It is impossible for the child to give up or ward off the element of oral enjoyment without losing simultaneously its enjoyment of food and its wish to eat.

c. *The relationship between eating and the aggressive instinct:*—Since Abraham's study (1924b) of the oral-sadistic phase of libido development, the aggressive significance of eating has received constant attention in psychoanalytic literature. According to Abraham oral sadism is at its height after teething, when eating symbolizes an aggressive action against the food which is in this way attacked and consumed, or against the love object that is represented by the food. Melanie Klein and her followers emphasize the significance of oral aggressive phantasies for early childhood and their aftereffects for later normal and abnormal development. (According to Klein, aggressive meaning is attached even to the child's first feeding experiences, independent of the possession of teeth.)

Oral-sadistic (cannibalistic) phantasies are under no circumstances tolerated in consciousness, not even when the ego is immature. They are rejected with the help of all the defense mechanisms available to the child in this early period of life.

The consequences for feeding are inhibitions of eating, refusal to bite, to chew, or to swallow the food. These feeding disorders may reach their height at the toddler stage, though at that time the child still freely uses its teeth for aggressive biting, as a weapon in fights with other children, or to express anger and resentment against the mother.

When the repression or other defense mechanisms used against cannibalistic wishes are not completely successful, the child remains anxious about its oral sadism, not only in the oral phase, but all through childhood, with serious consequences for the pleasure felt in eating. Children of this type feel guilty when they enjoy food and eat only under pressure of need, or under compulsion from the environment, and with no freedom or abandon. They eat slowly and sometimes keep unchewed food in their mouths for long times. They show certain well known dislikes and minor or greater food fads which originate in the fear of hurting or destroying a living creature. They anxiously watch their eggs for possible signs of a partly hatched chicken; they are simultaneously attracted and revolted by the idea of eating sweets, biscuits, cakes, etc., which in their shape imitate a human body, or an animal, or any recognizable part of it; they are not able to eat chickens, rabbits, pigs, etc., which they have known alive. Sometimes a compulsive vegetarianism becomes the last safeguard before a far-reaching eating inhibition is established.

In extreme instances, the defense against oral sadism leads to neurotic self-starvation. In this case the mechanism used is that of turning the aggression away from objects to the individual's own body which is thereby seriously threatened or even destroyed.

d. *The relationship between eating and the anal pleasures:*—While infants are still passively fed they accompany the process with certain movements of their hands or fingers which indicate an impulse towards action. When they are encouraged to help themselves to food or to handle the spoon, it becomes evident that their intention is not directed towards feeding themselves but towards handling the food, playing with it, smearing it over the table or over themselves, etc. It is an error to ascribe this messing of the young child to lack of skill. The child's actions in this respect are deliberate and intentional. They are motivated by the pleasure of smearing, an anal-erotic activity transferred from the excrements to the foodstuffs which are similar to the former in consistency, color, temperature, etc. Behavior of this kind begins approximately at the age of 11 months and reaches its peak at the height of the anal phase of libido development. Where it is tolerated by the environment, the anal pleasure gained from the actions contributes appreciably to the pleasure of feeding. The handling of food which is in the beginning stages merely messy and possessive merges gradually into purposeful actions of self-feeding. Food, which is at first only held tightly or squeezed in the fist, finds its way into the child's mouth, etc. Children who are permitted to develop their self-feeding methods on the basis of this pleasurable anal attitude towards food become skillful in feeding themselves with their hands and fingers earlier than others, and shortly afterwards make an easy transition to the use of the spoon.

Where messing with food is interfered with too strictly by the environment and the child is prevented from adding anal pleasure to the other feeding pleasures, appetite suffers. To keep a child in the anal phase from smearing food necessitates its being kept passively fed for a longer time which has, secondarily, an adverse influence on eventual self-selection of food, on the child's relationship to the mother, etc.

At the period when anal tendencies become repressed and relegated to the unconscious, a whole series of feeding difficulties make their appearance, especially in those cases where habit training has been too sudden or too severe. The reaction formation of disgust, which is set up in consciousness to prevent the return from the unconscious of former wishes to play with excrement, take it into the mouth, etc., is transferred to all those foodstuffs which by their look, touch, or smell remind the child of the now forbidden dirty matter. As a result, many children form violent dislikes of squashy and smeary foods, of green or brown substances, of sausages, occasionally of all sauces and creams, regardless of taste. Where children are forced to eat the foods which disgust them, they react according to the strength of the anal repressions, with being sick, with loss of appetite, with a widening refusal of foods, etc. Where their disgust is understood as an inevitable outcome of the defense against anal urges, and where the resultant food fads are tolerated, the disturbances remain limited to certain substances, and transitory in character. When the anal repressions are firmly established, anxiety with regard to the underlying unconscious tendencies diminishes, and the majority of temporarily "disgusting" foods are readmitted by the child into its diet.

In the interest of the child's appetite, anal pleasure should be permitted to enter into the combination of feeding pleasures, and, for the same and other similar reasons, habit training should be carried out gradually and leniently. This is in contrast to the conventional but psychologically unsound attitude that children should as early as possible be in control of their excretory functions and acquire good table manners.

The intimate connection between the child's behaviour in these two respects can be proved experimentally. Where children in the latency period are urged to make a sudden advance in their table manners, they almost invariably react by regression to smearing and messiness in the lavatory, or vice versa.

Other anal admixtures to the feeding situation arise from a connection, made during the transition from orality to anality, between the ideas of intake of food and output of excrement, and between the body openings which serve the two functions. The feeding disorders which originate from them are of the type described in Editha Sterba's paper (1941). (Retention of food in the mouth as equivalent of retention of stool in the rectum.)

e. The relationship between eating and certain typical fantasies of the phallic phase:—Certain fantasies of the preoedipal and oedipal phase have a specific bearing on the neurotic eating disturbances.

During the conflicts and struggles of the oedipus complex, many children escape anxiety by regressing from the phallic level to the earlier pregenital levels of libido development. This leads to the conception of parental intercourse by mouth, a fantasy which is frequently reinforced by actual observation of fellatio acts. The consequent sexualization of the mouth (by means of genital as well as oral libido), with the repressions following on it, endangers the function of eating by producing hysterical symptoms, as for instance, globus hystericus and hysterical vomiting.

In one of the typical infantile theories of sex, it is asserted that babies are conceived through the mouth (oral conception) and born through the rectum (anal birth), the intestines being substituted for the womb. Anxiety and guilt which become attached to these birth fantasies lead to refusal of food (warding off the wish to be impregnated), to a horror of getting fat (in defense against the fantasy of being with child).

Where fixations to the oral level and the regression to them are especially powerful, the wish to be impregnated takes the form of a fear of being poisoned, which leads to severe eating inhibitions.

Guilt feelings arising from sexual competition with the parents and from death wishes against them lead to the masochistic desire not to grow up which may express itself by means of refusal of food.

The penis envy of the little girl, which may lead to the fantasy of biting off the male genital, combines oral-sadistic with phallic elements. It frequently causes symptoms of hysterical vomiting without reference to specific foods.

Conclusions

The various types of eating disturbances, which have been separated off from each other in this paper for the purpose of theoretical evaluation, are invariably intermixed and interrelated when observed clinically. Organic feeding disorders become the basis for the nonorganic types. Neurotic disturbances arise more easily where loss of pleasure in the function of eating has prepared the ground for them. Considerate handling of the child's feeding, with a reasonable amount of self-determination, to safeguard the child's appetite, makes the function of eating less vulnerable and less favorable ground for neurotic superstructures.

ON THE SLEEP DISTURBANCES OF EARLY CHILDHOOD

SELMA FRAIBERG

Sleep, which every day removes uncounted billions of man hours from consciousness, has recently become an object of intensive psychophysiological investigation. Kleitman (1963), one of the pioneers in this work, reminds us that, whereas we are accustomed to thinking of wakefulness as our natural state, the reverse is probably more accurate: our original, natural state of sleep is interrupted by periods of wakefulness. In fact, the most seasoned observers report difficulty in determining when certain infants are asleep or awake.

Interest in sleep disturbances of children (Harms, 1964) long antedates the recent psychophysiological investigations of sleep. Luce and Segal (1966) point out that almost everyone requires some ritual embodying unspoken, and perhaps unrecognized, feelings in order to sleep. Disturbances in the sleeping pattern during the second year of life are commonplace. Nagera (1966b), in considering sleep disturbances at different developmental levels, notes that prior to age three, and often up to age five, sleep disturbances can be most usefully viewed as a developmental problem which will remit spontaneously or improve with better handling. He adds that sleep disturbances are almost universal in the three- to five-year-olds seen at the Hampstead Clinic—whether tardiness in falling asleep, night waking, anxiety dreams, projective fear of ghosts and wild animals, inability to sleep alone, desire to share the parental bed, sleep phobia, or ritual behavior at bedtime. All observers agree that not only are sleep problems frequent in the second year of life, but that they appear to be on the increase. Whether this seeming increase is real remains a matter of controversy, however. It has been alleged that the frequency of early childhood sleep disturbances has remained constant, but that, in the past, it received less attention from physicians until the advent of chemotherapy in the 1940's eliminated the threat to life that used to accompany infectious diseases. Prior to the availability of antibiotics, it was difficult for pediatricians and family physicians to give much thought to

---

Reprinted from *The Psychoanalytic Study of the Child*, 5. New York: International Universities Press, 1950, pp. 285–309.

well-child care, because their efforts were concentrated on preventing death.

Fraiberg (1952, 1968) has made significant observations on infant behavior and has written a very readable book (1959) about the "magic years" from birth to school age. In the following article, she describes the psychic content inherent in toddlers' sleep disturbances, with emphasis on trauma and anal conflicts as typical influencing factors for this age group. Her observations make clear that there is also evidence of the toddlers' fear of losing control of early ego achievements, a factor that has since been highlighted by others (Maenchen, 1955). In the latter part of the first year of life, infants accomplish much individuated ego development, which is threatened by loss of voluntary control every time they go to sleep. Like Bornstein (1935), Fraiberg perceived her young patients to be particularly threatened by loss of control over their bowel functioning.

To emphasize these factors is not to say that sleep disturbances do not result from a variety of causes, for instance, physical illness disturbs sleep. In describing the parental anxieties that accompany childhood sleep disturbances, Hirschberg (1957) finds it difficult to determine which is primary: the disturbed sleep or the parental anxiety. Nevertheless, it is widely recognized that each factor reinforces the other.

Children in their second year often show a variety of sleep disturbances which range in intensity from a brief waking at night to profound disturbances in certain cases, with wakefulness which may persist for hours or for the entire night. Because night waking occurs so frequently at this age, pediatricians and those who do research in child development have come to regard this problem as typical for the developmental stage. Thus Gesell (1943), in his behavior profiles based on large-scale studies of infants and small children at the Yale Clinic, includes night waking and the reluctance to go to sleep as one of the developmental features of the period from fifteen to thirty months.

In clinical practice we have occasion to study children of this age who suffer severe and exaggerated forms of night waking which almost totally affect the capacity for sleep. Typically, the child wakes screaming after a brief sleep interval, requires long periods of holding, and may return to sleep only after hours of tense wakefulness. Many of these disturbances are progressive and within a few months achieve the proportions of a major illness which dominates the young child's entire mental life. The anxiety spreads to embrace other functions of the developing organism. In the daytime behavior we may observe distortions and transformations of affect. In addition there is usually an arrested developmental picture with failure to acquire new vocabulary or motor skills for the period of the acute phase of the illness.

To the psychologically trained observer, night waking in either its moderate or severe forms would be regarded as a symptom. The fact that a particular symptom should be considered typical for an age is of special interest to us, since we would then expect that its relationship to developmental problems of that period could be investigated and secure for us some additional knowledge of the early mental processes.

In the study that follows I have brought together material from the observation and treatment of a group of small children under two years of age who suffered sleep disturbances of several types and in varying degrees of involvement. In the cases brought for treatment, the sleep disturbance usually had persisted for a long enough time to cause serious concern to the parents. In all these cases, night waking had become an established pattern, beginning with the typical anxiety cry and requiring long periods of holding and comforting by the mother.

For purposes of this discussion it seems desirable to treat separately two conditions which we find to have an important bearing upon the onset of this symptom; i.e., the factor of trauma and the anal conflicts of this age. Illustrative case material will be utilized in both sections. A more detailed case presentation will be made in the third section to illustrate the progression of a sleep disturbance from the level of an early anxiety state to a neurosis.

The Onset of Sleep Disturbance and the Traumatic Situation

Among the children studied, the circumstances of the onset of the sleep disturbance showed a striking feature in each case. To cite a few examples: At 12 months Jimmy begins to waken several times a night with terrifying screams. He clings to his mother as if he cannot bear to let her go. For hours he lies in her arms, tense and fearful. The beginning of his night waking coincides with the period in which his older sister begins vicious and savage attacks upon him. In two other cases, separation from the mother is the exciting cause of the sleep disturbance. At 13 months, Ellen develops a serious type of night waking, during the absence of her mother for a three day period. Following the mother's return, the sleep disturbance continues, in spite of the reassuring presence of her mother.

Peter, at 16 months, wakes several times a night with cries of terror. He is often sleepless for hours. The night waking came on soon after the mother returned from the hospital with a new baby.

We learn of sleep disturbances which follow a tonsillectomy or an injection. And in the case of 15-month-old Danny, the night waking follows an ordinary visit to the doctor's office where he had protested violently against a throat examination and had been restrained. He screams in his sleep before waking, "Let me down! Let me down!" as he had cried out on the examining table.

At 24 months, Sally wakens with terrible cries. She clings to her mother and refuses to go back to sleep, " 'cause then I hear the noises!" The sleep disturbance came on soon after she returned from a two-week visit to her grandparents. Certain observations of the child cause the therapist to suspect that she had observed a sexual act. Through tactful questioning, it is learned that the child slept in the bedroom of her grandparents during her visit. Subsequently the child's observations are brought out in treatment.

These brief examples exclude specific findings in each of these cases. Our only purpose in taking such liberties with our data is that of establishing the primary relationship of the sleep disturbance and a traumatic situation. Yet, as we review the exciting causes of these sleep disturbances, we are struck by the fact that, for the most part, these situations are not exceptional in the life of the child's second year. Attack by a sibling, separation from the mother, a visit to the doctor's office are not unusual events. The same situations may produce anxiety in any child, but not every child develops a sleep disturbance.

It seems necessary, then, to explore this problem from two points of view: first, what factors operate to give such events a traumatic character, and second, in what way does anxiety succeed in breaking through the "protective barriers" of sleep at this early age.

For our purpose, it is necessary to follow the example of Freud and differentiate two types of situations which bring about anxiety. Freud distinguishes a *traumatic* situation and a *danger* situation (1926). The traumatic situation is that of helplessness, the experience of being overwhelmed and indefensible. All anxiety is reducible finally to the original situation of helplessness. Through the memory and recognition of the traumatic situation, the ego may anticipate this situation of helplessness whenever the occasion arises which reproduces the original or prototype of the experience. The second type, which Freud describes as the danger situation, is distinguished by the ego's faculty of anticipation. Its capacity of anticipating danger gives it the advantage of utilizing those methods which it has available for preparation and defense against anxiety.

Normally, the second-year child has already made some progress from the situation of trauma and helplessness to that of anticipation of danger. Where pain is the inevitable result of certain acts, he learns to anticipate the consequences and will either avoid the painful situation or gain control of it through the means available to him. But the child of this age is confronted with a vast array of overwhelming forces. Many of these are unpredictable and beyond his comprehension. He stands up, and a nameless force throws him down. He climbs on the chair, and the temperamental piece of furniture spills him to the floor. He wants the lamp, and the lamp wrestles with him, only to send him crashing to the floor a moment later. His brother kisses him tenderly; his brother delivers a healthy blow to the side of his head. Mama is pleased when he eats his carrots and displeased when he eats the contents of his potty. Some of these factors, while retaining their unpredictability, will yield to scientific investigation. The second-year child begins to learn, for example, that departure is usually followed by return. Others have no rationale and remain for him perversities beyond his comprehension. For these reasons, no child, no matter how tenderly cared for, can escape anxieties. Danger is omnipresent. Animate and inanimate are not differentiated. The furniture is perceived as hostile if it overturns him.

At this age all danger is perceived as an objective threat. But we must now add a subjective factor. Impulses from within the self may bring about an objectively dangerous situation. Certain acts, the child discovers, will bring about his mother's displeasure, and he now fears disapproval in the same way that he fears loss of the mother. Now or earlier, he has submitted to toilet training for no better reason than that it pleases the mother. He willingly becomes partner to a fraud in which mother exclaims over each stool, growing ecstatic as mothers will, only to see this gift of love flushed indifferently down the toilet. To fear of loss of feces is added the danger that through soiling, through refusal to defecate in the pot, he will lose his mother's love. We observe that, even in those cases where toilet training has proceeded without threats or coercion, the child may still perceive a threat through his observation of the fate of his own feces.

At this age then, the child fears loss of the mother and the mother's love, and he fears injury to himself. Yet, if he is reduced to helplessness whenever he loses sight of his mother's face, or if he avoids all motor activities or situations in which he risks injury to himself, we should certainly conclude that we had an abnormal child. That this actually happens in certain cases of very young children is known to us. But what of the normal child? How does he master these traumata and bring them under control?

We are interested then, in the means by which the second-year child commonly defends himself against anxiety. His mother must certainly rank first as guardian of his psychic equilibrium, but now, with his developing independence, his locomotion, and new motor skills, he finds himself more and more in predicaments where his mother can only come to his aid after a minor disaster. He has learned further that certain acts will bring forth the pain of his mother's disapproval and discovers that love and gratification will not always be forthcoming from this very important person. All in all, this developing ego finds the necessity of dealing with certain quantities of anxiety without the aid of his mother, or with minimal support from her.

Freud tells us that the ego gains mastery of the traumatic situation through turning the passive situation of being overwhelmed into the active one of anticipation and preparedness. He has stressed the importance of this binding process in the child's early development. In a memorable example, Freud reports his observations of a game played by an 18-month-old boy (1920b). The child engaged in tireless repetition of a game in which he caused his toy to disappear, or flung it away, then recovered it with exclamations of joy and welcome. In this way, he dramatized departure and return, specifically in relation to his mother, and so mastered one of the universal anxieties of early childhood. In another context, Freud remarks on the familiar "peek-a-boo" games which we play with the small child in which, through hiding the face and uncovering it, we play disappearance and appearance (1926). The spontaneous games of small children and the nursery techniques of the sensitive mother all serve this very important function.

So it is that we play Ring-around-the-Rosy with the child who is learning to stand up or to walk. In the last line we sing "All fall down!", and the child delightedly collapses on the floor. Through such devices he learns to master his fear of falling. "I am not made to fall; I choose to fall." In the same way the child who is repeatedly attacked by an older sibling may avenge himself on some object which offers no risk of retaliation—a stuffed toy, or a piece of furniture. An injury caused by bumping the forehead on a table was always handled expertly by the old-fashioned mother. She would encourage the child to spank the bad table and would kiss the hurt place on the forehead "so it will go away."

The modern mother will say, "But the table did not want to hurt you, darling!" and the child does not believe her.

We could go on to report the toilet games through which the child investigates the mystery of the disappearance of his stool. The mother of a healthy child may expect to find her own precious belongings lodged in the toilet bowl. At this age too, wastebaskets, garbage cans, drawers, as well as the toilet will further the researches of the child, and he behaves comically like the housewife whose careless maid has thrown the silverware out with the garbage. He may retrieve from these excavations some greasy memento which temporarily satisfies him and replaces the original loss. His mother is certain to have difficulty in persuading him to part with it.

In all of these ways, then, the child achieves control of the stimulus through a repetition of the experience in which the passive situation is turned into an active one; he *does* it where before it was *done to* him. The repetitive activity further serves the very important function of bringing about the necessary conditions of anticipation and preparation in the re-created event so that the strength of the stimulus is reduced as the control is increased.

When we now reconsider the events which brought on the sleep disturbances in the cases mentioned, it is apparent that certain of these unexceptional situations assumed the character of traumata because of the failure of the ego to meet the event with the necessary physiological and psychic preparations. Further, we deduce from the appearance of a symptom that this failure was not made good through the restorative measures of the ego in the subsequent period. This brings us to additional considerations in our investigation of the problem. What factors may operate to fix the trauma and promote its effects for a period beyond the critical event itself?

In the case of 15-month-old Danny the sleep disturbance came on following a visit to the doctor's office. He had been restrained on the examining table, his arms and legs held down by the parents, because he refused to permit the doctor to examine his throat. He screams in terror, "Let me down! Let me down!" This marks the beginning of his night waking. He screams in his sleep, "Let me down!", reiterating the terrified cry he used on the examining table. He then awakens and cannot be comforted for hours.

We learn that the reaction of this child to any kind of restraint has always been violent. His developmental history is revealing. He was bottle-fed from birth. Solids were introduced at six weeks, and he refused them. At three months, when he still refused solids, the mother claims that the pediatrician recommended that he be forced to eat. Whether or not such advice was actually given cannot be shown, but, between the ages of three and seven months, mother and baby had been fighting a grim battle. The child was forced to eat while his protesting hands were held down. He immediately vomited, of course. Soon he began to refuse even his bottle. The struggle continued for weeks. At one point when the pediatrician allegedly recommended "starving" the child, Danny demonstrated that he could go for days without food. At seven months, the mother, in alarm at these developments, returned to bottle feeding exclusively, and the child was slowly restored to normal functioning.

Clearly, then, when the physician examined his throat with a tongue depresser at 15 months, the earlier traumatic situation of forced feeding was revived. The child reacted in identical fashion and was then restrained on the examining table while the examination proceeded. Following this incident, the sleep disturbance came which was to continue for months. Thus it appears that even at this early age an experience may assume for the individual a traumatic character if it reproduces the effects of an earlier trauma which overwhelmed the ego and left it helpless.

We are further interested in establishing the relationship between the traumatic event and the sleep disturbance itself. We have already seen that, in those cases in which we could obtain some sort of "report" from the small child, the waking followed what was undoubtedly a dream in which the child was taken back to the scene of the trauma. Before waking, Danny cries out "Let me down!" just as he had during the fateful examination in the doctor's office. In the case of two-year-old Sally, we learn that she wakes up because of "the noises." It is established that she had observed coitus between her grandparents during the visit in which she slept in their room. The noises, then, are the noises of the grandparents. After waking, she refuses to go back to sleep " 'cause then I hear the noises."

In other words, the mechanism and the dream form may be said to closely resemble that of the traumatic neuroses. It would be incorrect and far-fetched to attempt a closer parallel, or to speak of these early disturbances as traumatic neuroses, but in order to investigate this mechanism, we must use our knowledge of the function of the dream in relation to traumatic events. Thus, Freud points out (1920b) that the dreams of the traumatic neuroses do not belong in the category of wish-fulfillment but follow the repetition compulsion. In such dreams in which the patient is brought back to the traumatic situation, the dream work produces a state of apprehension and psychic preparation for the oncoming danger which could not be summoned forth at the time of the critical event. Because these mechanisms failed to prepare the system, the protective barriers collapse under the impact of these excitations, producing a state of helplessness and psychic impotence.

In studying this mechanism on the level of the small child, it appears that the dream function may serve the same purpose as that of the dreams of the traumatic neurosis. In speaking of the latter Freud says, "These dreams are attempts at restoring control of the stimuli, by developing apprehension the omission of which caused the traumatic neurosis" (1920b, p. 32). We have already had occasion to refer to the abreactive devices of this very young child in mastering traumatic situations. We have seen how his play is directed ceaselessly toward repetition of the unpleasurable in order that he may gain control through activity over the situation which earlier had overpowered him. The relationship between this activity to secure mastery through repetition and the dreams of the traumatic neuroses, was established by Freud and provided one basis for his exposition of the theory of repetition compulsion in *Beyond the Pleasure Principle.* Following his discussion of the function of the dream in the traumatic neurosis, Freud puts forth the theory, "Thus . . . the function of dreams which consists in setting aside any motives that might interrupt sleep by fulfilling the wishes of the disturbing impulses, is not their original function. It would not be possible for them to perform that function until the whole of mental life had accepted the dominance of the pleasure principle" (1920b, pp. 32–33). Can we say, then, that this earlier tendency of the child to effect a binding of excitations independent of the pleasure principle will also appear as a dominant principle in his dream mechanism?

Thus far, then, we have established a relationship between the traumatic event and the sleep disturbance. The mechanism appears to be identical with that of the traumatic neuroses in which the dreamer is brought back to the traumatic event and the dream function is that of bringing about a state of apprehension and preparedness, the psychic requirements for control of the stimulus which could not be produced under the conditions of the original event.

On this level, the sleep disturbance is still represented as an attempt in the dream to establish control of a danger which threatens from without. However, when an instinctual wish has been renounced, we have the additional factor that an impulse from within may bring about the objecttively dangerous situation. For this reason, it is necessary further to investigate the nature of these early sleep disturbances when the factor of toilet training has been introduced into the child's life.

The Conflicts of the Anal Period in Relation to the Sleep Disturbance

The conflict between the wish to soil and fear of loss of love appears frequently as the basis of symptom formation in the second year. As a factor in the eating disturbances of early childhood, Editha Sterba has shown how the refusal to eat may be a displacement from the anal sphere, in which the element of refusal is transferred from defecation to eating (1941). As early as the second year, we may also observe a reactive alteration of the instinct in which fear and disgust of dirt replaces the original pleasure. Certain common phobias, for the most part transitory, will appear at this age in the form of a fear of vacuum cleaners, the drain pipe of the bathtub, and other such apparatus, which arouses in the child the fear that he may be swallowed up and caused to disappear like his feces in the toilet.

In the case of a phobia in a two-and-a-half-year-old girl, Bornstein describes an illness which resulted from the conflict between pleasure in soiling and fear of loss of love (1935). The case is of special interest in connection with this study because the neurosis took the form of a *refusal* to go to sleep. The child could sleep only with the aid of sedation and then would fall asleep in a sitting posture with clenched fists and a tense facial expression. Analysis revealed that the child avoided lying down because she was afraid that in this position she could not control the impulse to defecate in bed. A traumatic separation from the mother during the period of toilet training at one year gave rise to the fear that she could lose her mother for soiling. In the interval between one year and 27 months there had been no outbreak of symptoms, although the child's history during this period showed an exceptional preoccupation with tidiness and disgust in connection with dirt. The neurosis broke out at 27 months, when premature sexual excitation brought on an intensification of the soiling conflict. Bornstein brings out similarities between her case and that of Wulff whose report (1928) on an illness in an 18-month-old child revealed identical factors.

In this respect, we find that certain of our cases of night waking can only give further confirmation to the findings of these two authors. However, since our intent in this study is that of exploring the mechanisms which disturb sleep in early childhood and the specific relationship of the early conflicts to night waking, we might examine two such cases in which these factors are clearly discernible.

Ellen was 13 months old when a severe form of night waking came on which resulted in prolonged sleeplessness. Until then the child had had a normal development and had been an unusally cheerful and active infant. She was bottle-fed from birth with some initial difficulties with formula and began her toilet training at eight months. The mother had early exhibited concern about constipation and frequently employed enemas. This same preoccupation with anal functions resulted in an ambitious toilet training. Although no pressures or punitive devices were utilized, something of the mother's insistence must have been communicated to the child because she early achieved a degree of control unusual for her age.

At 13 months Ellen's parents took a week-end holiday and left her in the care of her grandparents. During these three nights, the child, who had never suffered any form of sleep disturbance, was wakeful and screaming almost all night long. She called for her mother constantly. Upon the return of the parents and restoration to her own home, the child's disturbance continued. She wakened in terror several times a night and begged to be held. The sight of her crib filled her with dread and she wept bitterly at bedtime. After the child was home for a week and the night waking grew worse, the mother consulted me.

When I inquired routinely about toilet habits I learned that although Ellen had soiled herself during her stay with her grandparents, she had quickly re-established her "training" when the mother returned, and there was "no difficulty" in that regard. Since I could not visit the child for two days, I offered suggestions to the mother pending a visit. I suggested that the mother play "peek-a-boo" and "bye-bye" games with Ellen during the day, in which mother disappears and comes back, very glad to see the baby, with a hug and a kiss. It was suggested, too, that Ellen be encouraged to take her Teddy bear or lamb to bed with her with a comment that the toy would take care of her. Then I broached the subject of toilet training and suggested that this might be an additional tension at a time when the child was extraordinarily anxious and asked if we could temporarily eliminate this "training." The mother firmly rejected this last idea but did carry out the other two suggestions with results which were better than they deserved to be.

After the first day in which the mother utilized these devices, Ellen slept through the entire night. She had been delighted with the "bye-bye" games and almost exhausted her mother with her frequent requests to play them again and again. At bedtime she chose her lamb to sleep with her. She cuddled up with the lamb in her arms, then, just as she was dozing off, she sat up, placed the lamb on her pillow, then reversed her position in bed by going to sleep with her head at the foot of the bed.

For the next week I received daily reports from the mother. Ellen slept through every night and the mother continued the games and the use of the lamb. Ellen was again cheerful and happy, and all went well. Her mother said that she had continued "very good" so far as toileting was concerned and took this as proof that I must have erred. We were puzzled by this rapid recovery. A month later the mother called to tell me that the sleep disturbance had returned. Ellen was now waking at night in a state of great tension. She would lie rigid in her bed, fists clenched, every muscle taut, whimpering pathetically. She would draw her legs up, squirming and writhing. During the day she had violent outbursts of temper, cried on the slightest provocation, and seemed a changed personality. She was physically well, gave no evidence of illness. Once again I inquired about the toilet training. The mother assured me that that could have nothing to do with it because Ellen had recently begun to have her bowel movements during her afternoon nap! I asked then if the training efforts were continuing, was Ellen being put on the toilet at regular intervals. The mother said that she was continuing this program and that she was certain that the child did not feel any disapproval for her "accidents."

I offered the only advice I could, which was to drop all forms of toilet training, even the subtlest encouragement, and to reassure the child when she awakened from her nap with soiled diapers. Although dubious, the mother followed through on this advice. Almost immediately the child returned to normal sleeping habits. The daytime temper tantrums diminished accordingly. Now convinced of the meaning of the child's symptoms, the mother made no effort to re-establish toilet habits until a later stage. In a three year interval, the sleep disturbance has not recurred.

We are interested, then, in the origins and progress of this sleep disturbance from the time of a traumatic separation from the mother to its later manifestations. We are struck by two factors in the first sleep disturbance which seem unusual. Although it is understandable that a child should react with such anxiety to separation from the mother, we observe that the sleep disturbance continued after the mother's return and that the toilet habits which had typically broken down during the mother's absence, were immediately reestablished. This last factor appears suspicious because it is much more common after such a temporary regression to see mother and child engaged in a tedious retraining process made all the more difficult by the lapse. This child, then, felt it necessary to make an unusual effort to please her mother after her absence. The child commonly experiences the absence of his mother as withdrawal of love. Here the child feels that to maintain the mother's love, to prevent a recurrence of this tragedy, she must keep up her "insurance premiums" and docilely resumes her toilet habits. Also, since the soiling and the mother's absence occurred simultaneously, it is quite possible with the infantile theory of causality, that the child interpreted her mother's absence as withdrawal of love for soiling.

The second period of the sleep disturbance provides further clarification. Now the child was having regular bowel movements during her afternoon nap and produced nothing on the toilet. At night we find anxiety waking with the child tensed and rigid as in the attitude of withholding feces. Here, then, the fear of soiling is evident in the night waking. Although she could permit the soiling during the daytime nap, the anxiety broke out at night because, I believe, the loss of the mother, and the fear of losing her, were associated with the dark. The waking with the cry of fear, and the child's characteristic posture suggests that she had dreamed that she was about to soil, that she *wished* to soil, but the wish was not capable of fulfillment because a previous traumatic loss of the mother exerted a powerful restraint at the crucial moment. In this instance, we might say that the child who has renounced anal pleasures for fear of loss of the mother's love may experience the return of these wishes in the dream, but the dangers which attend the fulfillment of such wishes interrupt the attempts of the dream work and hence interrupt the sleep.

As a further point in our study it is of interest to examine in detail the progression of a single case of sleep disturbance from the level of an anxiety state to a neurosis. In the case which follows, the sleep disturbance came on at thirteen months following certain traumatic events and pursued its course on successive levels of libidinal development.

A Profound Sleep Disturbance in an Eighteen-Month-Old Girl

When Kathie was 13 months old, a critical sleeping disturbance appeared. She wakened several times a night with an anxiety cry and then, for periods ranging from 20 minutes to five or six hours, would lie in her mother's arms, tense and fearful, unable to return to her own bed. Many factors prevented the mother from actively seeking and utilizing help for her daughter at this time. She sought advice from many quarters, tried various unsuccessful methods of handling, and only with the onset of an acute phase of the illness was she finally able to follow through on a therapeutic program for the child.

Kathie was 18 months old at the time her mother consulted me. Five months had elapsed since the onset of the child's illness. The child was now sleepless for the greater part of the night. She was unable to compensate for the loss of sleep through daytime naps so that the physical toll was heavy. At the time I first saw her, her appearance was striking. She had a demure little face, round eyes and tight ringlets over her head. She might have been a pretty child but her skin was yellow, the eyes vacant and staring and there was a flabby fatness about her which one would not find in an active child of her age. Her face was completely dull and expressionless. Although she walked capably at this age, she showed a passivity and a lethargy even in motor activity. During the early visits to her home she sat in a large armchair while her mother talked with me. She would sit quietly, uttering few sounds, completely self-absorbed and listless.

The mother herself was a quiet, restrained young woman, with a carefully articulated speech, controlled affect, and marked fastidiousness of dress and manner. Her distress over the child was real. She herself was physically exhausted following these five months in which her own sleep had averaged only a few hours a night.

Tracing the history of the illness and the child's developmental history, the following factors seemed significant. The nocturnal anxiety attacks began in the 13th month, coinciding with the beginning of vicious physical assaults upon the child by a four-year-old cousin. Joel, who was also a neighbor, was a constant visitor in the house. At this time, the four-year-old boy, initiated severe attacks upon the little girl, striking her, pinching, biting, snatching things from her, and teasing her to the point of hysteria. The relationship between the two children had always been close. There was much confusion in handling these episodes. Kathie's terror and the beginning of the night waking warned the mother that firm measures must be taken to avoid these attacks, but her own relationship to her sister was such that she could not afford to be insistent on methods of handling. Within a month the situation became extremely serious. The attacks grew worse and the night waking more frequent. Now, on the advice of a consultant, the mother restrained Joel and firmly prohibited the attacks. Kathie was given increased mothering and soothing. With these measures, Joel relinquished his hostile assaults. But Kathie's sleep disturbance continued to grow worse, and no amount of comforting from the mother lessened her anxiety. She asked repeatedly to be held by her mother during the day. She showed no interest in toys or games. Her attachment to Joel continued, however, and while he was at school, she would ask for him constantly. When he came to visit, as he did each day, she would greet him with delight.

A further examination of the developmental history revealed the following facts: Kathie had been breast-fed for nine months. There were no feeding problems. During the first five months, she was more wakeful than most infants and required less napping, but the pediatrician felt he could not regard this as unusual. After the fifth month, her sleep requirements were normal. At 13 months the night waking began. At 14 months toilet training was slowly introduced. The mother felt no discernible resistances and the training was easy. Kathie began to take steps at 13 months. At 18 months her speech and articulation were within the normal range of about a dozen words. Kathie had never been separated from her mother for more than an hour or two.

In the first visit to the child's home, I carefully reviewed all these factors with the mother, with no new results. Kathie sat in a big armchair sucking her thumb and staring blankly ahead. At the close of this nonproductive interview, I was preparing to leave when the front door flew open and a four-year-old boy burst into the room. At once the lethargic little girl came to life. "DoDo!" she screamed and waved her arms. Joel swooped down upon her. He rubbed his face against her little belly. She giggled. He kissed her neck. She squealed ecstatically. He tickled her and squeezed her. Kathie's laughter became more and more hysterical. Then he started on her arm. He mouthed her arm from wrist to neck. With each gesture she giggled expectantly. Then he began to take little nips at her arm. More giggles, now a little uncertain. Then he began to bite hard. Suddenly there was a loud outcry from Kathie. He persisted, trying to reassure her. Kathie continued to scream. At this point, the mother asked Joel to leave Kathie alone. There was no alarm in her voice, and I gathered that this was a common occurrence. The mother made no move to interfere although she continued to call to Joel. The noise of Kathie's screaming, Joel's protests, and the mother's calls filled the house. Thinking that for some reason the mother felt she should not act because of my presence, I myself interfered at this point. I was standing near the two children so I reached over and drew Joel to my side. With this, both children stopped momentarily, and then, to my astonishment, Kathie fixed me with an accusing eye and burst into tears again, now calling for "DoDo" to come back to her. "DoDo" screamed his wrath at me while

Kathie's mother picked her up to comfort her. It was plain that no one had welcomed my chivalrous intrusion.

Later, in discussing this incident with the mother, I learned that not only were these incidents common, but the mother had not regarded them as harmful. She usually did interfere when Kathie screamed, but she never had been concerned about the erotic foreplay that preceded the "playful biting" because Joel did this out of love for Kathie and Kathie herself loved it so. Also, the mother explained, such tickling and nuzzling and biting as I had observed was the sort of play Joel himself was accustomed to with his parents.

Our first task, then, was to help the mother understand why such stimulation is harmful to a child. With interpretation to the mother, we worked out a plan in which all such forms of erotic play were to be prohibited by the mother and further, in which play between the two children would be limited to short periods during the day. A few other suggestions were made to the mother pending my return from a brief vacation. I encouraged the mother to help Kathie engage in banging games with pots and pans. Also, in preparation for further work with Kathie, it was suggested that Kathie be allowed to choose a doll or Teddy bear to take to bed with her with the hope of bringing about an identification with a toy which I could use in play.

When I returned two weeks later, there were several new developments. The sleep disturbance had in no way diminished but Kathie had developed a new assertiveness. She had responded to the banging games with relish. Two dolls now began to assume an important role in her play. She had chosen the Teddy bear to sleep with her and had developed a strong attachment for "Bee" (bear) on the basis of their new intimacy. She cuddled him and uttered endearments. On the other hand, an abandoned doll was recovered by Kathie and the doll was battered unmercifully, flung about and scolded. At the same time, our well-trained Kathie, who had always faithfully asked to go to the toilet, began to have several lapses. Her mother handled these casually. Of further interest is the fact that Kathie's table manners suffered a setback. She had begun to throw food and to display outbursts of temper at mealtimes. Yet, with all of these breakdowns in training, the mother exhibited excellent understanding and confidence. It was at this point that suggestions were made to the mother regarding the toilet. It was agreed that no further efforts would be made to "anticipate" bowel movements or encourage the use of the toilet. If Kathie should ask to be taken, she would comply; otherwise training efforts would be abandoned.

During the early visits with Kathie, it was possible to engage her in a relationship to me. My social blunder of the first visit created a well-founded suspicion of me which took a little time to undo. I brought little surprises for her in my purse, candies, trinkets, and the like. Gradually she began to join me in games of hiding. Then the doll and Teddy bear were brought into these games. Her mother was always present of necessity and took an active part then and later in all such activities. Within about four visits we had progressed to a new game with the doll and Teddy bear. We would put the Teddy bear "to bed" in my coat, tucking him in, saying goodnight, and turning off an imaginary light. Then I would make crying noises for the bear whimpering loudly for "Mama." Kathie would then come over to him, pick him up solicitously and hug him. Then she, too, learned to make imitative crying noises and considered this quite a trick.

In the sixth visit, I arrived to find Kathie looking ill and lethargic. Her mother reported a very bad night in which the child had awakened seven or eight times with cries of terror. All morning Kathie had been nursing an injured knee which she received yesterday when she slipped and fell and slightly skinned her knee. Following the slight injury yesterday, she had cried for hours.

We played for a while with the doll and Teddy bear, putting them to sleep and having each wake up crying. Each time Kathie soothed the crying "Bee" (also stands for "baby"). Then she turned to my purse, emptied its contents on the floor, and played with it for awhile. Suddenly in the middle of absorbing play, she burst into a loud wail. Over and over she whimpered "Knee! Knee!" Yet her cry had a manufactured quality about it. Her mother and I expressed quiet sympathy for the knee but she was not comforted. She cried "Hoe! Hoe!" (hold) to her mother, meaning that she wanted to be picked up. We decided not to pick her up but to offer comfort in words. Kathie howled louder and finally produced a bellow of rage.

At this moment, I picked up the bear and began to sob loudly, much louder than Kathie could. Kathie stopped crying and looked up in surprise. I howled lustily, changing roles momentarily to imitate a worried mother trying to comfort the child. Taking advantage of Kathie's surprised silence, I began to interview the bear. "What's the matter, little bear, what's the matter?" I said over and over. Kathie now moved over to my chair. I repeated, "What's the matter, bear?" Kathie spoke up. "DoDo?" she said. "What about DoDo?" I said. "Eye!" Kathie said enigmatically. Her mother and I looked puzzled. Her mother said that she has been saying this for days but they don't know whether she means "eye" or "I". I asked her to show me. "Eye!" Kathie said and covered her eye with her hand. I looked interested. "Head," she continued, and put her hand up instinctively as one does after a blow. Then she lapsed into silence and her hand moved to the genital area where she rubbed herself for a moment. I wasn't sure of what I had seen, so I asked her to repeat it by saying, "Where did DoDo hurt you?" She went through the motions once again, eye, head, genitals. Her mother gave us this much confirmation: Joel had been striking Kathie in the head during the past few days.

Shortly afterward Kathie lost interest in both her knee and the game. As I was getting ready to leave a few minutes later, I noticed Kathie fussing because her hands were sticky from candy I had given her. I took the opportunity to suggest that we spend a few minutes in the sand pile outdoors. Her mother assured me that Kathie would not play with dirt. In the yard I sat beside Kathie and sifted dirt through my fingers, laughing when my hands got sticky. Kathie, now interested, let me pour dirt into her hand. Then she stared thoughtfully at her dirty hands. "Mummy, too!" she commanded. Her mother involuntarily withdrew at this request. I said, "Sure, Mummy too!" and the mother extended her hand while Kathie poured dirt into it. We then had a little party each handing lumps of dirt to the other. It was the first time Kathie had ever touched dirt.

Following this interview, Kathie slept through an entire night for the first time in months.

In the seventh visit, I learned of a particularly bad night preceding this visit in which Kathie had awakened about six times requiring prolonged holding. The last time she woke up in this sequence she whispered in her mother's ear, "Mama, pee-pee!" as if she were telling a secret. Her mother, thinking that she wanted to go to the toilet, took her to the bathroom.

Kathie began the interview on her own initiative. She brought Dolly and Bee to me and told me to cry for them. I picked up the doll and made crying noises. Then Kathie took over.

She picked up the doll and imitated the baby's cry. I asked "What's the matter with Dolly?" "Hoe!" Kathie explained. She pointed to the doll's foot. Both her mother and I were puzzled. Kathie was annoyed that I could not understand and kept repeating, "Hoe!" Next, Kathie sat the doll straight up on the sofa without support. Then Kathie lunged forward and knocked the doll down. She grinned up at me. I suspected this was identification with Joel, and her mother confirmed this. Kathie played this game over and over with more and more vehemence. Each time Kathie made loud crying noises for the doll. Then abruptly she sat the doll up and began to kiss her. The kisses were loud and vehement. Kathie snuggled her face in the doll's neck, and the doll fell over. Kathie laughed triumphantly.

Now she abandoned the doll and began to stride up and down the room. She fell into the role completely and began to take the strides and leaps that so characterized the energetic Joel. Suddenly she stopped. She walked over to the full length mirror on the door and stared at herself for a long time. She lifted up her dress watching her reflection. Now she turned and ran. She approached a table, reached up to get some Kleenex from the box on it and fastidiously wiped herself between the legs. "Pee-pee!" she announced. Then she tossed the tissue into the fireplace. I said, "Yes, Kathie has a pee-pee. Kathie has a nice pee-pee." With this, Kathie ran over to get more Kleenex and picked up the doll. She lifted the doll's dress and wiped her. Then she brought the doll to me and said earnestly and worriedly, "Hoe!" She again pointed to the doll's foot. The doll had cloth feet. I was puzzled. With real annoyance Kathie picked up her own foot and pointed to her shoe. "Hoe!" she said. The shoe was "hoe." Now I understood. The doll had no shoe.

Now I said, "Show me Dolly's pee-pee." Kathie picked up the doll's dress. I said it was a nice pee-pee. Kathie picked up her own dress. "Kathie has a nice pee-pee," I said. With this Kathie took another piece of Kleenex and went over to her mother. She brought the tissue to the mother's lap, making a wiping motion around the genital area. I said, "Yes, Mama has a pee-pee just like Kathie's." She was completely absorbed in this play. Once more she went through the entire sequence, Dolly, Kathie, Mama, and this time added me. I assured her that Kathie was just like Mama, just like "Muh" (her name for me).

Kathie's mother enlightened us further. Yesterday, following the fall that resulted in the skinned knee, Kathie had come into the bathroom earnestly requesting to watch Mama pee-pee. She had stayed long, thoughtfully watching her mother. To a question from me, the mother answered that Joel and Kathie frequently go to the bathroom together, and Kathie during past months had commented frequently on Joel's penis.

Kathie, meantime, was trying to attract our attention. She had picked up the doll and was loudly imitating crying noises. Kathie kissed the doll tenderly, then she solemnly laid the doll "in bed" and put the Teddy bear beside her. Then Kathie climbed up on the couch beside them, put her face next to the doll's and pretended to sleep. Kathie's mother said that this was what had happened last night. When Kathie had awakened the last time, whispering "pee-pee," her mother had taken her to the toilet, put her back in bed with the Teddy bear, and then the exhausted mother put her head down on the pillow beside Kathie and fell asleep.

With the mother's interpolations, we can see how Kathie's pantomime holds together in sequence. She had hurt her knee yesterday. The slight bleeding and pain aroused anxiety. She later went into the bathroom to watch her mother urinate, seeking the answer to a question. All day she was tearful and upset, asking comfort for the injured knee. The night was a very bad one; she was reported to have awakened about six times. The last time she whispered "pee-pee" to her mother, as if in secret, but the mother had interpreted this as a wish to go to the toilet. The pantomime in which the doll cried because she had no shoe probably tells us that she had awakened in terror following a castration dream. That Kathie had faithfully reported the significant events of the preceding day and night is evidenced in the last sequence in which the mother falls asleep beside the child. We could not have asked for better co-operation from an adult patient.

The sequence in which the doll cries because she has no "hoe" is followed by a pantomime in which Kathie imitates and identifies with Joel. This is interrupted by a sudden trip to the mirror where Kathie inspects herself. The comparison between herself and Joel is the basis for her castration anxiety. But further, recalling the sequence in the preceding interview, she blames Joel for an injury to herself. We recall that "DoDo" had allegedly hit her in the eye, the head, and the genital region.

Following this visit, we had a significant improvement in sleeping. In the four-day interval between interviews, Kathie slept through three nights and had awakened only briefly the fourth night. In the meantime, she had refused to have her bowel movements on the pot and had triumphantly given her signal for "potty" after her pants were soiled. Her mother, as planned, reacted casually to this. The mother had also recorded in her notes that Kathie had tried all day yesterday to get her little rag doll to stand up on the table. When she flopped down limply Kathie would yank her by the hair and fling her on the floor.

In this, the eighth interview, Kathie began by playing with the rag doll, vainly trying to get her to stand up. When unsuccessful, she tossed the doll on the floor, as her mother had described. Later she picked up the doll, pointed to her foot, and said "Hurt!" I inspected the doll's foot and said, "Not hurt. Dolly is all right. Nice dolly. Dolly has a nice foot. Dolly has a nice pee-pee."

Thinking I could get behind the "standing up" problem and interpret it more easily in the bathroom, I suggested that Dolly "has to go toidy." Kathie was enthusiastic, asking me to take Bear and Mummy too, and we all went to the bathroom. She put Dolly on the potty and then put Teddy bear on with her. Now Kathie ordered Mummy and me "down" on the floor. Her mother and I crouched down and Kathie crouched down with us. Her mother said to me in astonishment that this was what she used to do when she first began to train Kathie. She would squat on the floor to be on a level with Kathie on her nursery chair. She had not done this for months, yet Kathie remembered!

There was no question about it. Kathie was making encouraging noises for Doll and Bear. Finally she removed them from the potty, peeked inside, congratulated them both like a good mother, and carried them back to the living room.

Although I had started this game in order to interpret the wish to "stand up", Kathie had her own ideas now. The toilet game became very exciting when she introduced her own variation. Now Kathie, without benefit of props like the dolls, began to make grunts as if she wanted to go to the toilet. She smiled up at her mother and me, informing us that this was a game, and ran ahead to the bathroom. There she sat down on the floor *beside* the nursery chair and began to make the noises which served for bowel movement, b-r-u-u-r-p-p. She pretended now that she was moving her bowels on the floor. I laughed as if this were a big joke, and her mother laughed too. Kathie laughed uproariously. Now she arose, took us both by the hand, and led us back to the living room. The moment we sat down, she said, "More!" and began to play the game again. We repeated the game with 12 to 15 trips to the bathroom. Her interest was unflagging to the end.

Following this first display of defiance, we now began to observe a profound struggle in Kathie. In the days that followed, her mother reported that before each bowel movement Kathie tensed and cried. She did not ask to be taken to the potty and was not encouraged to do so. The urge to defecate and the resistance to defecation in a pot brought about a conflict in relation to soiling herself. When this resulted in her soiling her panties, she became even more tearful and whiny. Her mother's casual acceptance of the soiling did not reassure her.

In the following interview, I had an opportunity to observe this behavior closely. Kathie initiated the toilet game which we had played in the previous interview. Once again, we made our several trips to the bathroom while Kathie sat on the floor beside the nursery chair and grunted as if she were defecating. Around the fourth or fifth trip, Kathie suddenly stiffened and began to cry. She called out to her mother that she wanted to "go toidy", and it was obvious that she was no longer playing her game. Her mother walked with her to the bathroom. At the threshold of the bathroom, Kathie began to scream. She sat down on the floor, her body rigid and her fists tightly clenched. Her mother and I stood by offering quiet reassurance. At last the tantrum subsided, and in its place came a bitter weeping. Finally Kathie, still crying, asked her mother to pick her up. In her mother's arms, she now began to point toward the hall. We walked out into the hall. Kathie then pointed to the linen closet. Her mother did not understand, and Kathie's screaming was renewed. I suggested that she wanted something inside. The closet doors were opened, and Kathie began a frenzied pointing. There was an old baby bonnet inside. This was what she wanted. Her mother gave her the bonnet. It was much too small for her, but she perched it absurdly on top of her head and now seemed comforted. "DoDo," she announced with satisfaction. With this, Kathie's mother understood and said that during the last two days Kathie had been snatching Joel's hat from him. The mother had been interested in this "turn about" play, since Joel had always snatched things from Kathie, but had neglected to tell me about it.

Back in the living room, Kathie went directly to the large mirror and inspected herself in the bonnet. She stared at her reflection for several minutes and then burst into heartbreaking sobs. She was inconsolable. Her mother held her in her arms tenderly, but the terrible sobs continued. When she finally began to speak, she repeated over and over, "DoDo. Hat. DoDo. Hat." Now I told her that DoDo had a hat. And DoDo had a pee-pee. He had a pee-pee just like Daddy's. DoDo was a boy. Daddy was a boy. Kathie was a girl. She had a pee-pee just like Mummy. Just like Muh. Kathie was a girl. Mummy was a girl. Muh was a girl. DoDo was a boy. Daddy was a boy. Kathie listened with earnest attention. "Ted?" she inquired. (Her uncle.) I said that Ted was a boy like Daddy, like DoDo. "Nina?" she asked. (Her aunt.) I said that Nina was a girl. Like Mummy. "DoDo?" she asked again. DoDo was a boy like Daddy. "Kattie?" Kathie was a girl. Again and again we went over the long list of relatives and friends until their classification was completed. Her crying had ceased, and she was playing this as a game with me. Now she took the little hat off her head and ordered me to put it on. I did, laughing.

"Muh?" she said. "Muh is a girl just like Kathie." "Mummy!" she said, removing the bonnet from my head and giving it to her mother. Her mother put it on. "Mummy?" said Kathie. "Just like Kathie. Mummy is a girl." She loved the game. We passed the little hat around each trying it on at Kathie's request. From time to time, her mother and I gave her reassurance that she was made just exactly as a little girl should be made and how much we loved her.

As I was leaving that day, in the manner of many an older patient, Kathie brought out the additional necessary piece of information. She brought her doll to me, pointed to the anus and said that this was her "pee-pee."

We are now able to see in the toilet play of the last two interviews how the witholding of feces first expressed revenge and defiance of the mother and, secondly, fear of loss of the feces equated with penis. This was brought out clearly in the last interview when she played her "defiance" game in good spirits, then made a serious request to go to the toilet. At the threshold of the bathroom, the tantrum came on which finally tapered off to inconsolable sobbing and the request for the little hat. The hat sequence also gives us the additional clue that her snatching of DoDo's hat was in revenge for his snatching things from her and that, somewhere in the months in which DoDo had ruthlessly taken things from her, she came to the conclusion that he had taken away her penis.

And now Kathie's nights again became disturbed. For almost a two-week interval between the seventh and tenth interviews, Kathie had either slept through the night or wakened only briefly. But following the last reported interview, Kathie had three bad nights during each of which she wakened with an anguished cry and had to be comforted.

Just prior to the eleventh session which succeeded the hat interview, our work was made easier by the visit of a 22-month-old girl to Kathie's house. Kathie entertained the little girl with all the doll games which we had played together. She also introduced her guest to the toilet game and showed her how she, too, could enjoy the luxury of disobedience combined with a fraudulent obedience. They spent a happy afternoon sitting beside the nursery chair on the floor making grunting noises. When the two little girls decided that they really had to make "pee-pee" their mothers accompanied them to the bathroom where they "took turns" on the nursery chair. Kathie's mother reported that when Kathie and her friend viewed each other with pants down a profound silence ensued. They stared at each other long and searchingly. Sometime afterward, the girls were playing in Kathie's room when the mothers heard loud giggling and noises. When they peeked in to see what was going on, they found the two tiny girls with a drawer-full of hats and bonnets on the floor. They were trying on hats, preening before the mirror and admiring each other noisily.

Kathie's interest in sex differences was now expressed in a variety of games. Thus, she would proudly identify and discriminate between boys and girls, men and women, in picture books and magazines. She began to take pleasure in certain articles of clothing which were "just like Mummy's." Nevertheless, Kathie's conflict about soiling became severe. In spite of her mother's reassurance, each bowel movement brought on a tensing and cries of fear. She would stand stiffly as she had her movement in her pants, crying out pathetically to her mother. When her mother then asked if she wanted the potty, she would scream in protest. On the morning of the eleventh interview, Kathie went through the same procedure, then hit upon a brilliant compromise. She set off for the bathroom alone, ordered her mother to keep out, and closed the door behind her. Sometime later, she called her mother. Her mother found her seated on the nursery chair seemingly quite pleased with herself. The lid of the nursery chair was down and Kathie was sitting on top. She had made her bowel movement in her panties while seated on the closed chair. When I came to visit her in the day, Kathie repeated the performance for my benefit. However, when her mother later said casually that she would give her clean pants, Kathie refused vehemently. We decided to let it go for awhile. Meanwhile, I assured Kathie that she would get a new B.M. every day, but even with this interpretation, she refused to have her panties changed for the rest of that hour.

Within the week that followed Kathie's anxiety about defecation diminished markedly throughout the day, but she continued to wake briefly at night crying out of fear. In the twelfth interview when I tried to create play situations in which to work through some of this material, she ignored me completely. She even refused to play her favorite toilet games. She spent a little time playing in the sand pile with me and was thoroughly spontaneous. There was no longer the fastidious withdrawal from dirt, and she even permitted herself a solemn ritual in which she squatted above a little mound of sand and urinated on it. In the following visit, I introduced plastalene, and she delighted in games in which the dollys made B.M.'s. Yet, as soon as I placed the dolls in bed, she withdrew her attention. When I asked why the dolly was crying, she answered with a phrase which she had recently acquired, "I dunno!"

The brief night waking indicated that there was obviously some residual anxiety which had not been worked through. All evidence pointed to the fact that this elusive fragment belonged to the anal material. The fact that she still disliked having her panties changed after a bowel movement provided one clue. Also, I observed that although she now defecated in her panties with cheerful unconcern, she would not permit me to let the doll do likewise. And, finally, she would not play games in which the dolls woke up at night. From this, I tentatively concluded that the fear of soiling was still the basis of the night waking.

In the thirteenth visit, when she again persistently evaded the doll who woke up crying, I suggested casually that maybe the dolly was afraid that she would make a B.M. in bed. Kathie ignored me. I pursued the play myself, put a piece of plastalene in the doll bed, placed the doll on top and caused her to cry. Then I picked up the doll and remarked casually on the B.M. in bed and reassured the doll that it was all right. Kathie stood by tensely. Suddenly she picked up the doll and ran over to her mother. "Mama, hold!" she cried anxiously. Her mother held the doll as Kathie directed and uttered comforting words to it. I then told Kathie that the dolly was afraid to make a B.M. in bed because she thought her mother would be angry. Her mama would not be angry. And the dolly did not like to see her B.M. go away. But she would get another one every day. Kathie listened intently, then backed away from the scene.

A few moments later, she became absorbed in play with her toy dishes and finally called her mother and me over to sit at the little table. She had picked up all the little pieces of plastalene which we had used in the defecation games, and these were tastefully arranged on the little dishes with a fork and knife alongside. At first she encouraged us to eat with the words of a mother. "Good!" she assured us. "Yum, Yum!" We pretended to eat with deep concentration. "More yumyum!" she would say, pouring a little "milk" from a pitcher onto the plastalene marbles. But soon the tea party fell into great disorder. She became noticeably irritable, ordered her mother and me around, told us to sit here, no sit there, no, not there! Then came tears. She wanted something on top of her chest of drawers. No, she did not want that. She wanted this. No, she didn't want that. And finally she screamed her frustration and wrath at everything and everyone in the room and ended by sitting on the floor sobbing miserably. When it was time for me to leave, she was still in a bad mood and would not be comforted.

That night, Kathie slept through without waking. In fact, it should be said here that this episode marked the end of the anxiety waking.

It then appears that when the nocturnal anxiety returned on the anal level, two components could be discerned. One was the fear of loss of the mother's love for soiling. The other was fear of loss of feces as equated with penis. At the same time, there was the desire to please the mother through being "a big girl" and defecating in the pot. The resulting conflict is dramatically brought forth in the interview reported. Thus, with my two-fold interpretation of the fear of mother's disapproval for soiling and the fear of losing the feces, she reacted at first with a play in which she gave plastalene feces to her mother and me in the tea party. The form of this play, in which she gives the feces as food, probably reveals her own wish to retain the feces through oral incorporation. But then we note the sudden swing in mood, the cacophony of affects, the wanting and not wanting which reveal the strength of the ambivalent tendencies.

In subsequent interviews, we worked over certain details such as the bedtime rituals, the reluctance to have panties changed, and other such matters. Beyond this, there was no further need for help from me. The night waking ceased, and there has been no return of the sleep disturbance in the two and a half years which have elapsed. There has been a close follow-up during this period.

Treatment brought about marked character changes in Kathie. It should be noted that even after the first month, as soon as the anxiety in relation to soiling diminished, we began to see rapid changes. Her vocabulary increased, she became spontaneous and friendly, and played for long hours without needing her mother. At the close of treatment, she had actually advanced beyond her age level in vocabulary, in play, and in social relations. She proved herself competent in dealing with Joel and learned to retaliate actively when he teased or snatched things from her. She became gay and animated and spontaneously friendly and affectionate.

In the case of Kathie, then, we see the evolution of a sleep disturbance from the early stages of anxiety to a complex symptom formation at 18 months. Several features of this care are of special interest here. The conditions which brought about the night waking at 13 months, the later conflict in relation to soiling and the appearance of castration anxiety, represent a sequence in which anxiety accrued on each successive level, sweeping each new libidinal phase into its wake with devastating results.

The effects of the early traumatic situation need little elaboration here. We can see how the attacks of Joel, beginning at 13 months, produced each time a state of helplessness and terror. The mother's uncertain handling of these situations at the beginning must certainly have contributed to the anxiety, since a child of this age must rely in a large measure upon his mother to defend him against danger. It should be noted that these attacks differed from the type we observed at 18 months in which erotic play ended in the biting which was so painful to the child. At this stage, 13 months, the attacks are reported to be frankly hostile and malicious. The erotic factor with its sadistic intent is said to be a later development. In terms of our earlier discussion, it seems probable that the traumatic character of these repeated attacks produced a sleep disturbance which, in its earliest form, was a night waking following a dream in which the trauma was reproduced.

At 14 months, toilet training was introduced. The child's communications to us in treatment establish the fact that bowel control was achieved under the pressure of great anxiety. In her toilet games, we see the refusal to defecate in the pot and, at the same time, fear of soiling. Yet, from the mother's history, we learn that this training was accomplished without any visible resistance from the child. In many cases of emotional disturbance during the second year, we receive such puzzling reports of an uneventful training period. Our first reaction is one of suspicion. Yet, after studying many such cases, I am inclined to believe that this is actually so. The fact can only be explained on the basis that the child produces this absolute obedience to the demands for cleanliness under the influence of anxiety and what is perceived as a real danger of losing the mother's love.

We observe, then, that the sleep disturbance became more severe in the period of toilet training in spite of the fact that the mother's handling of the attacks of Joel resulted in curbing these aggressions and diminishing the objective danger. This suggests, then, that the earlier trauma continued to exert its influence in the child's anticipation of pain, helplessness, and danger, produced by the failure to comply with the mother's demands. It is as if the ego, threatened from without and vulnerable at all points, engages in a treaty with a strong ally whose good favor must be curried at the expense of impoverishment of internal resources.

On this level, the meaning of the sleep disturbance is revealed in our material. The last-analyzed fragment of this layer, which had bound the child to her symptom, was the fear of soiling the bed in her sleep. From this, we deduce that this must have been the original fear which followed upon the introduction of toilet training. As an additional factor, we have fear of loss of feces which plays such a prominent role during this period.

In the third phase of the sleep disturbance we see the effects of Joel's erotic play and the way in which this premature sexual excitation brought on a further development in the course of the anxiety. The little girl was convinced that her penis had been taken away. There are two factors in Joel's erotic play which require investigation. The first is into the nature of the stimulation which brought about a steadily mounting excitement. This excitement remained undischarged at its highest point of pleasure, when the act ended in biting Kathie and the infantile love-making ended in the small child's screams. We know that failure of discharge of sexual excitation may, in itself, bring about anxiety. When we add to this the fact that these novel and highly pleasurable sensations in the genital region necessarily brought about a high valuation of the sexual organ in the little girl, we can see how the groundwork was laid for a new fear. Since Kathie had had many opportunities to observe Joel's penis, we assume that her own genital differences became the source of anxiety, when pleasurable tensions brought about the importance of this zone and when the consequence of such pleasure was pain and injury. From this she reached the conclusion which she reported to us, that "DoDo" had injured her genitals.

From our material, we were able to see how the sleep disturbance in the later stages followed anxiety dreams in which fear of genital injury appeared. From the mother's reports and the play sequence of the seventh visit, we are able to understand that such a dream had caused her to waken in alarm. "Mama, pee-pee!" We recall that this particularly bad night had followed the injury to the knee and the later observation of the mother in the toilet. In her play which recapitulated the whole sequence and included the night and the night waking, we received a report of the dolly who had no shoe, and when this was interpreted, Kathie completed her report of the events of the night to the last detail, which included the mother going to sleep beside the baby.

In this early neurosis, we can follow the development from the first manifestations of anxiety and the night waking through a complicated course in which the symptom was strengthened and elaborated on successive levels of libidinal development. The original trauma, in which injury brought with it the fear of losing the mother (a fear made more urgent by the presence of danger), exerted its influence in the later phase of the illness. The anal material revealed fear of loss of the object both in regard to the mother and feces. This fear produced the conflict about soiling which played a prominent role in the sleep disturbances. Subsequently, the fear of injury and fear of a genital loss combined their forces in typical fashion so that the child concluded that Joel had injured her genitals and had taken away her penis. In this way, external forces reinforced the basic fears throughout, and the night waking, derived from the traumatic situation, continued, including each of the later phases in its course.

SUMMARY

To summarize our findings regarding the sleep disturbance of the second year:

The night waking which is regarded as typical for this age by researchers in child development appears in both its moderate and severe forms. In any case, its characteristic appearance during the second year may be attributed to those developmental tasks and problems of this age which produce anxiety in the child and hence make heavy demands upon the immature ego which strives toward control of the painful stimuli. Night waking, in the cases studied, followed an anxiety dream.

It was seen that in each of the cases reviewed, the night waking first appeared in relation to a traumatic event. The dream mechanism in the early stages of such sleep disturbances is likened to that of the traumatic neuroses, in which the dreamer is brought back to the scene of the trauma and the dream work supplies the conditions of apprehension and anticipation which had failed in their protective functions at the time of the original event. The character of the dream conforms to the child's tendency at this age to gain mastery through repetition.

The conflicts of the anal period play an important role in symptoms of sleep disturbance as well as the other symptoms so common at this age. When pleasure in soiling must be relinquished for fear of loss of the mother's love, the conflicting tendencies may produce another type of anxiety dream which results in interruption of sleep. Here the fear of soiling in sleep breaks through. In two such cases it was seen that the wish to soil was manifest in the dream (from our deductions), but fear of loss of the mother exerted a more potent influence at the critical moment, so that the wish-fulfilling function of the dream failed and anxiety broke through, resulting in the interruption of sleep.

Further, it is noted, that failure to master anxiety on one developmental level will result in a progressive course of the symptom, so that each successive phase of libidinal development comes under the influence of the original trauma and adds its own characteristics to the illness. In one case it was possible to follow the development of the symptom from its origins in a traumatic situation, through the anal period, and finally the beginnings of a prematurely induced castration anxiety.

The study suggests that an understanding of the sleep disturbances of early childhood may provide us with further prophylactic measures. The early detection of serious sleep disturbances will still permit simple environmental measures which can secure good results in most cases. The more evolved symptoms required direct therapy. And for the common varieties of night waking during the second year, there is every reason to believe that if we understand the child's activity more fully, as well as his devices for mastering the typical traumata, we can improve our nursery techniques and, through educational measures, reduce the incidence of sleep disturbance. There is great danger that our present techniques of handling the very young child encourage passivity at a time when he needs all of our help in taking the active position in relation to the dangers which threaten him. By this I do not mean, of course, that we foster a spartan independence, but rather that we understand his behavior and its aims in this critical year and support these tendencies, helping him to abreact through the ancient devices of the nursery.

OPPOSITIONAL SYNDROMES AND OPPOSITIONAL BEHAVIOR

DAVID LEVY

Levy's comprehensive survey of negativism and oppositional behavior specifies that such behavior does not necessarily indicate hostility. Nevertheless, it is difficult to separate exploration of such behavior from the broader concept of aggression, although aggression, of course, need not be hostile. Whether viewed psychoanalytically as an innate drive or, from the perspective of learning theory, as acquired in response to frustration, aggression does appear to be an integral part of the infant's mode of establishing contact with the the world. It may be difficult to prove that the baby in the latter part of the first year of life has an aggressive intent *every time he grabs, squeezes, bites, scratches, pulls, kicks, or hits. There is no question, however, but that those who are targets of his attention often react as if he did. In consequence, one of the first things most babies are taught is that such activity differs from kissing and hugging.*

The ethologist, Lorenz (1966), suggests that there may be a phylogenetic relationship between aggression and love. He points out that enduring bonds between animals of the same species develop only in those species which also manifest aggression within the species, that there are many other species without either intraspecies aggression or bonds, and that some species demonstrate intraspecies aggression without simultaneously developing lasting attachments. But absolutely no species has been observed to develop enduring relationships without simultaneously demonstrating aggression within the species.

Levy asserts that negativism is an integral human maturational process, particularly in the second year of life. Similarly, Goodenough (1931) has observed that angry outbursts reach a peak at that age. Children at that stage are commonly referred to as the "terrible twos." Gesell and Ilg (1943) give a vivid description of the two-and-a-half-year-old contradicting himself. Although this increase in negativism and tantrums is often perceived as being reactive to specific events, and in fact does coincide with increasing

Reprinted from *Psychopathology of Childhood,* ed. P. H. Hoch and J. Zubin. New York: Grune & Stratton, 1955, pp. 204–226.

demands from the environment for conformity, it is difficult to determine which deserves precedence, the child's will or the environment's. In the second year of life, the child does appear to be more vulnerable to frustration, and his aggressive behavior assumes characteristics that impress observers as being more intentional and purposeful. Although not emphasized in Levy's article, toilet training is often given special attention in this context in western culture. Indeed, psychoanalysts, from the perspective of id psychology, have labelled this period the anal phase of development. In terms of ego psychology and object relations development, Mahler (1955, 1963, 1968) has called the same period the separation-individuation phase. In other contexts, it has been called the muscular phase, the verbal phase, the stage of elementary domestic socialization, and the habit-forming stage.

The subject of oppositional syndromes will no doubt be linked in the minds of psychiatrists with the phenomenon of negativism, a form of behavior demonstrated so thoroughly and profusely in catatonia, and described so frequently in the major treatises of psychiatry. No doubt also the subject of oppositional syndromes will be linked in the minds of developmental psychologists and child psychiatrists with the period of resistance, or the stubborn period, as some investigators have phrased it—that trying period for parents beginning in the second year of the life of the child, so replete with the expressions "no! no!" and "I do it myself."

The negativism of the infant and the negativism of the schizophrenic, however normal the former and abnormal the latter, have indeed something in common. Manifestations of negativism in catatonia—of speech, of feeding, of elimination and also of defiance—are to be found in the negativism of infancy and early childhood. Is there a relationship of the two, of the supposedly normal and abnormal, of negativism as seen in the mental hospital and as seen in the home, that bears more than a superficial resemblance?

An answer to this question requires a study of the manifestation of negativism in the early years of life and an attempt to find its meaning in terms of adaptive behavior. Since oppositional syndromes represent selective forms of negativism, clusters of symptoms related to special functions or activities, the same necessity applies to the consideration of that topic and also to generalized forms of oppositional behavior.

In general, it may be said that the term negativistic, or oppositional, or stubborn, or any one of its large number of synonyms is applied most commonly to behavior readily explained as refusal to conform to the ordinary requirements of authority and conventional behavior. The refusal to conform involves also the notion of willful contrariness. The individual who acts in this way is thought to derive some kind of satisfaction in pitting his will against others, in opposing the laws of society, in flaunting his disrespect of the amenities. Oppositional behavior, it can well be imagined, is particularly disturbing to parents and educators. Of its various disturbing effects, it is probably the attack on one's sense of prestige, on one's feeling of position of validity and importance, that arouses the strongest reaction. Since it arouses such strong reaction it is understandable therefore that oppositional behavior is so often regarded as personally motivated, as purposefully defiant, even when no evidence of motivation can be discerned.

A dramatic manifestation can be observed during breast or bottle feeding in the first few days after birth, in the case of the sleeping infant who appears to rebel against awakening and against the insertion of the nipple in his mouth. In this situation the two-day-old infant may be observed pursing his lips, clamping his jaws, and shaking his head vigorously, thereby frustrating all efforts to feed him. Mothers typically regard such behavior as highly motivated. In my records of observations on forty-six breast-feeding mothers, made in a number of hospitals, such expressions as "You bad girl," "You're making me mad," "Don't be stubborn," "Come on, for God's sake," are quite common. The same mothers, however, responded quite differently when they suffered pain due to the infant's sucking. The painful sensations did not evoke critical rejoinders and scolding. Then, mothers hardly ever blamed the baby at all. Presumably that was something the baby couldn't help. Besides, it occurred during vigorous sucking, an achievement which pleased the mother. The baby's failure to suck after the efforts made to get him to do so was a different story. Mothers felt frustrated, sometimes also humiliated, as the expression, "He won't take my milk," reveals. In this situation it was difficult for mothers not to ascribe a motivation to the infant. Indeed, our common way of describing such persistent behavior on the part of the infant, by saying "The baby has a mind of his own," makes this kind of projection extremely tempting.

Ascribing the term oppositional to the baby who resists awakening merely by remaining asleep seems quite subjective, since the resistance may mean nothing more than depth of sleep. Ascribing the term oppositional to such active resistance as clamping the jaws, pursing lips, etc., seem more logical, since the behavior is clearly designed to prevent sucking and appears to be initiated by the infant. As a descriptive term for such behavior the word oppositional or resistant appears more valid, though, as used, it carries the false inference that the infant is acting on the basis of capacities that require the kind of cognition and motivation for which there is no evidence at all in the early months of life.

The newborn infant's capacity to resist a feeding in an active way appears amazing to us, more so than its mouthing and searching movements, with which we are more familiar and regard as natural components of a sucking instinct. In the absence of hunger the lack of response to the stimulus of the nipple would not be at all surprising, nor of the appellation "passive resistance" to this state. The active resistance, however, would imply an inherited neuromuscular pattern of defense, a defense against activation of a function before an appropriate readiness to respond. Along this line of reasoning, the broader question arises of protective devices for all goal-directed behavior in its various phases, at the point of initiation and on through completion of the act.

My next example of behavior, to which the term stubborn is applied, occurs frequently at five to seven months of age. Mothers of young babies at Child Health Stations were asked, Is the baby shy? Can anyone pick him up? Will he go to strangers? When the mother said "yes," the reply was tested by the two physicians and a nurse who were present. When the mother said "no," her reply was tested in the same way. In most cases it was found that babies could be picked up and held in the arms of others until five to seven months of age, at which time they would give evidence of withdrawing, look at the mother, cry, or even push away and struggle to get back into her arms.

These examples may be included in our subject since such behavior, although regarded generally as "shyness," is at times regarded as stubbornness; as stubborn and rather sudden refusal to respond to the receiving gesture of grown-ups to whom the baby was previously so friendly. This period of "shyness" gradually diminishes, and friendliness is often restored within several months. One explanation for its onset is a change in the infant's perception of the mother; from perception of parts to the perception of the whole. Previous to the change, a series of conditioned responses, all strongly reinforced, to various aspects of the mother were developing: responses to the sight of her face, the sound of her cooing, the feel of her during the feeding and embracing, etc. Out of these experiences of the infant the whole mother finally emerges and becomes clearly differentiated from the generalized world of others. Whatever the explanation, the fact remains that there is frequently a pushing away of others and a stronger claim on the mother's presence during this period.

In a number of instances the recoil from strangers and the closeness to the mother attains a persistency that makes it allied to the general problem of negativism. The infant stubbornly withdraws from contact with others and clings tenaciously to the mother. The example is appropriate of the study of negativism that is bound up with dependency. As dependency of the mother increases, from whatever cause, there is in some cases an increasing struggle against separation from her, and also a strengthening through repetition, of persistency in withdrawal from other social contacts.

So far I have considered three kinds of resistances; a passive resistance to being awakened, an active resistance to being fed, and a mixture of passive and active resistance to being separated from social contact. The first two, if resistance to being awakened can be included, have more of the quality of physiologic negativism, to use the term employed by DeJong in his experimental catatonia. The third is more strictly a social form, and also presumably a derivative of dependency problems. In all three emamples there is a common characteristic; namely, a defense against disturbance of a state of being, or, viewed in a social context, a defense against the person who attempts to alter this state.

My next example, the "battle of the spoon," occurs a few months later than the first period of shyness. Commonly at ten or eleven months of age the baby grabs the spoon from the mother's hand and tries to feed itself. However responsive to this display of independence, the spattering of food all over the room poses a problem. Mothers usually solve it by various compromises; letting the baby hold a spoon while they use another, allowing the baby to spoon-feed itself once for several spoon-feedings of their own, etc. Some mothers, as you might expect, remain adamant. They will stand for no nonsense. A feeding is a feeding and not a game, especially one so disastrous to good housekeeping. Then it may happen that unknowingly and unwillingly they are making an experimental contributtion to our subject.

One mother described the difficulty as a hunger strike. At ten months of age her baby suddenly refused to be spoon-fed. The mother's insistence on preventing the baby from doing it himself resulted in his refusal to take the spoon from her hand or his own. The strike was settled amicably after ten days through the intervention of a pediatrician. He advised the mother to put bits of food in front of the baby and let him pick them up with his fingers, which the baby did.

Some babies, in their struggle against interference with their own manipulation of the spoon, even spit out or remove with their fingers food the mother managed to slip into their mouths.

This example of resistance differs from the three previously cited. It represents a struggle for something new rather than a struggle for something old. The initiative of the infant is now involved rather than his inertia. It is an early manifestation of the development of independent behavior which builds up to climax in the second year of life. Before that state is reached there are other noteworthy examples of pushing away the helping hand and going one's own way. That is literally true in the case of a number of infants who will allow no one to help them while learning to walk. They must do it themselves, no matter how many times they fall.

Other forms of resistance that may be seen in the first year of life are concerned with repetitious movements (perseveration). Their importance in the development of muscular control particularly has been studied pre- and postnatally. Self-learning by repetition applies also to psychologic processes. Many of these activities appear to the adult as annoying repetition-compulsions, as the behavior of children who don't know when to stop. Some head-on collisions of infant and grown-up may result. A mother at a health station, in response to a question about her baby's stubbornness, told us about the first clash of wills that occurred when her baby was 12 months old. The baby was then able to walk and get out of her crib and also understand the mother's forbidding gestures. Because of a fever, the doctor advised the mother to keep her baby in bed. She tried to do so but the baby persisted in climbing out. At first the mother said she took it all playfully, each time putting the baby back. As the baby's activity persisted the mother became more serious. She began to scold and applied more pressure in holding the baby down. The mother was getting tired, but the baby seemed to have boundless energy. The mother became as persistent as the baby. "Then, before I knew it," she said, "my hand was red from slapping her behind." She paused and added, "That will never happen again. I'll never fall into that trap again." [1]

The "clash of wills" example serves our purpose for a number of reasons. It illustrates any number of others in which the adult manages to get himself trapped in an untenable position in which he feels compelled to

[1] For a history of the attitudes of social philosophers and educators towards the child's obstinacy see the introductory chapter of Winkler (1929).

break the child's spirit. It illustrates the remarkable strength and also—a point to be considered later—the peculiar automaticity of oppositional mechanisms, which under certain conditions are self-locking, beyond control. The example illustrates how early in life such mechanisms can occur.

We are now ready to consider the period of resistance, or the stubborn period that seems to be fairly concentrated over a six-month span, at ages one and a half to two years. Whatever the measure of noncompliance—the intelligence test, the physical examination, observations of spontaneous behavior, experiments, the clinical case record of ordinary inquiry—all studies confirm the existence of a period in the early childhood of most children in which negativism is more frequent than in the period preceding or following.

At one of our health stations, resistance during the physical examination, consisting of crying and struggling to a degree that made it difficult if not impossible to go on, was classified as type III resistance. About 12 per cent of those examined manifested this type of resistance. Among 800 infants and children ranging in age from a month to 59 months, there were about a hundred whose resistance was of type III. The group age 18 to 23 months had the highest frequency of such resistance. In fact, most of the 100 cases were contained within it. There was a clear rise in frequency as the age of 18 months was reached, and a decided fall in frequency when the age of two years was passed. The findings were also consistent with the mother's accounts of the child's behavior at home (Levy and Tulchin, 1923, 1925a; Levy, 1925, 1951b, 1953).

Of older writings on this subject, reference may be made to James Sully's book, *Studies of Childhood,* published in 1898. He devoted one of his chapters to "Extracts from a Father's Diary," of which one paragraph reads as follows:

> Third year. The moral side of the child's nature appears during this year to have undergone noticeable changes. The most striking fact which comes out in the picture of the boy as painted in the present chapter is the sudden emergence of self-will. He began now to show himself a veritable rebel against parental authority. Thus we read [at age 25 months] that when corrected for slapping Jingo, or other fault, he would remain silent and half laugh in a cold contemptuous way, which must have been shocking to his worthy parents. A month later we hear of an alarming increase in self-will. He would now strike each of these august persons, and follow up sacrilege with a profane laugh.

The "sudden emergence of self-will," so well described in Sully's literary style, can be found in a number of our cases selected from those referred for treatment as well as those seen routinely at child health stations. The following is derived from presumably normal samples at a child health station in response to a question about a three-year-old girl, "When did she start saying 'no!no!, I won't,' or things like that?" The mother replied, "She didn't say I won't. She showed it by first looking at you, so *blank,* as if she doesn't hear you, and she wouldn't do what you asked her to . . . She used to go out with anybody, even strangers . . . She has changed to people. Other people now call her shy. My friends are surprised about it. She changed to them, like she doesn't know them. After awhile she'll talk to them. She has to be thawed out. If it's a stranger she just won't talk to them at all. She was never shy before two months ago." The mother went on to describe the change from compliance to disobedience toward both parents and the mute-like negativism, which she thought had its onset about a year before the more recent shyness toward strangers.

Careful determination of onset, at least within an approximate period of time, is especially important because of the general tendency on the part of informants to relate the onset to an event, such as the birth of the new baby, the nursery school experience, a period of separation from the mother, an illness or fright. The same tendency is very likely true of most of us. We are always in search of connections between events, and feel more comfortable when we can relate the beginnings of negativism to a tangible disturbing experience to which the negativism is a reaction, rather than to a maturational process. In our studies though, it appears very reasonable to assume that negativistic behavior was ushered in by a specific event; more often the events followed such behavior and were thought to be re-enforcing factors. As re-enforcing factors, however, the "events" are quite significant and help to explain the intensity and duration of a negativism which might otherwise have diminished considerably.

Among two-year-olds referred for treatment because of oppositional behavior, a large variety of manifestations are seen. My cases included mutism, food refusal, bowel and bladder refusals (one patient, age 27 months, said to me, "I should move my bowels, but I won't."), oppositeness and inner negativism (asked to sit down, a 26-month-old boy stood up; asked to stand up, he sat down), also instances of opposing one's own wishes, as in the case of a two-year-old who said, "I want to but I won't"; instances of pretending not to understand; and most frequently, as expressed by parents, "persistency in having his own way," "There's no way to make him obey," "You can't talk him out of anything."

Cases were seen in which the child was negativistic to others but not to the mother; in which negativism was the predominant problem and temper tantrums quite secondary, and vice versa. They included one case (unusual) of bowel refusal in an otherwise compliant child. They included cases in which negativism had already been evident in the first year of life, and a few cases in which the onset was sudden and recent. They included cases in which negativism was preceded by shyness, and cases also (and that is a fairly common problem at two years and later) in which there was increased dependency on the mother—an overt representation of conflicting dependent and independent maneuvers.

Negativistic behavior that appears to have its onset with an illness or an operation deserves special mention. In one published case, negativistic behavior became prominent after a minor operation which, through bad handling on the part of the physician, was turned into a frightening episode. The child was then 22 months old. A period of "no," to everything lasted 18 days. During that time her exploring behavior and her interest in people stopped. The improvement in regard to all negativistic manifestations was quite marked within a month of the disturbing experience. Hostility to the mother, however, and increased dependency on her were still present six months later (Levy, 1950). [2]

Oppositional behavior in response to illness, pain, fright and excessive stimuli is commonly observed. In the form of passive resistance, it appears to be a protective device, like physiologic inappetence and general abatement of interest and activity during febrile states. The two-year-old who withdrew from all contact with people and with things after a painful and frightening experience is such an example. Excessive stimuli in the case of children refer particularly to excessive demands by adults for their affection, response and display of brightness; also, requirements of cleanliness, neatness, emotional control and intellectual standards beyond their ability. The problem is thus analogous to the excessive load placed on the back of pack animals. This occasions—in essence the same type of resistance—stubbornness, if not active defiance.

We are now ready to bring all our examples together and consider their common features. A number of them appear to have the common function of resistance to external influence. This influence would determine when an act is to begin, as in the example of sucking stimulation, and

[2] A protective recoil in any situation fraught with anxiety may give rise to behavior regarded as negativistic, which has been observed also in animals. The chimpanzee brought up by the Kelloggs refused to take new playthings they gave her in the early days of the experiment. She would take them herself, however, if the playthings were left on the floor and "she, so to speak, found them herself." The behavior as described may be simply the result of withdrawal from social contact because of anxiety (Kellogg and Kellogg, 1933).

when it is to end, as in the example of awakening the baby and of stopping repeated movements. Without this resistant character the organism's response would be determined entirely by external stimuli. The organism would then have no way of responding to inner stimuli, or, in other words, to inner needs. The capacity to resist external influence thus enables the organism to use and develop inner controls. [3]

The examples of oppositional behavior in response to acute emotional and painful situations are more clearly seen as protective in function, since the individual is thereby enabled to recoil, to barricade himself against noxious influence and win time for recovery.

A number of the examples are readily seen as primarily biologic activities, and what has been said about them might apply equally well if the external influence were of a purely mechanical nature. When the activities are primarily social and concerned with a wide range of behavior, then the principle of autonomy of the act applies equally well, though on a larger scale.

Now we can see the oppositional behavior in the second year of life as a general movement towards the autonomy of the whole person, as the first flowering of self-determination, of which the budding had long been in evidence. The persistency or stubbornness, the assertiveness or refusals that characterize all our examples, have something in common. They are all self-propelling, and resist all obstacles that bar the way.

Animal studies of the separation of mother and young are quite pertinent to our own. To make survival possible, the separation has to be well timed so that the dependency of the young is not terminated too soon. Before this phase arrives there is evidence of behavior that resembles closely the period of resistance. Brückner, a German psychologist, has written extensively on this subject particularly as it pertains to domestic hens. In an article entitled, "Investigations of Animal Psychology," with special reference to "The Dissolution of Family Life," (1933) he noted two principal modes of behavior at the time of the break-up of the relationship between the hen and her chicks, the principle of emancipation and the principle of expulsion. In the first two or three days there is no evidence of either. The hen is constantly on guard and sets up an alarm cry if the chicks walk a few inches away from her perimeter. The relation-

[3] In the pursuit of a goal, which in children often involves a struggle against interruption of play, the "obstacle" is often an inner stimulus. Thus, children interested in play may wait till the last moment before going to the toilet. An extreme example is that of a seven-year-old boy who can never be so deterred if he is in the midst of things: he defecates or urinates on the spot and continues with his activity.

ship is tightly woven and anxious. After three days it begins to loosen. There is more freedom of activity, but for a week or so the hen keeps the chicks in sight and raises the alarm cry if they stray too far away. The maternal bond of chains is transformed, to use Brückner's expression, to a "bond of rubber bands." There is more flexibility but the bond tightens at a certain point and the chicks are pulled back. Thereafter the range of movement grows wider. The chicks stray beyond the hen's vision. They still form a group, however, at times still follow the hen, respond to her clucking when she holds up a special delicacy and also to her alarm cry. During this third stage, which lasts about four to six weeks, the chicks display the kind of independent behavior that reflects Brückner's principle of emancipation, behavior that in humans would be referred to as disobedient, willful, out-of-hand and oppositional. Indeed the principle of emancipation which operates in emancipating the hen from her maternity, as it does the chicks from their dependency, is not necessarily a smooth affair. The hen may cluck desperately without any result. She may spend time searching for her chicks. They in turn may wander all over the place and make no appearance until sundown. At least during their period of growing independence they are bound to come home to roost. This stage is terminated by the hen's own efforts at expelling the brood. She pecks them away consistently for two or three days, even longer. In spite of the fact that the young have been foraging for themselves they keep returning to the hen, though the hen is adamant in expelling them. During this ordeal they appear quite disturbed; according to Brückner, they are in a state of panic. Finally, they take leave of the hen but for some time thereafter the young remain together.

According to Brückner the hen procrastinates before she starts pecking away the brood. Her first pecks may be hesitant and unsure. She may also be discriminating before the pecking goes on in earnest, attacking the larger chicks more strongly than the smaller ones.

Whether the pattern as just described holds true in all its details, and there are numerous variations, the essential principles of emancipation and exclusion are revealed in numerous accounts of the separation of mother and young among birds and mammals. In almost all of them the final exclusion is timed to meet two exigencies: the capacity of the young to manage for themselves and the imminent arrival of the next brood or litter. The first filial generation must be cleared away before the second arrives.

In the human species the analogous problem is seen in a series of partial emancipations and expulsions until the final loosening, if not complete freedom, occurs. The question of the relative frequency of the resistant period and of the time of its occurrence was given special cogency through studies of animal behavior. Why does resistant behavior attain its first peak between the age of eighteen months and two years? Is there also in humans a time relationship of emancipation from dependency and the birth of the next offspring? Busemann (1928, 1929) in an article published in 1930 on the causes of the first stubborn age and other periods of tension, supported the affirmative answer to this question.[4] In a series of cases of uninterrupted pregnancies he found that the most frequent interval between a first and second childbirth was two years. He noted that the sucking stage has been passed by then, the child can eat and drink alone, there is readiness for speech and social activity with other children. The infant type of dependency is over.

In this connection the spontaneous remarks of mothers during their second or later pregnancy is of interest. When a mother knows that her next baby will be no more than a year older than the preceding one she wonders, she says, how she will manage; "It's like having two at the same time," "It doesn't seem fair," etc. When asked how she would feel if the difference were two years instead of one, she replies, "Oh, that's different, it's much easier." She takes it for granted that the difference is quite obvious.

The period of resistance might better be called the first period of independence or even, as some writers have named it, the first puberty,[5] and there are notable resemblances between it and the puberty of adolescence. Evidently the "no-no's" have been more impressive than the words "I do it myself." That there may be an essential relationship between the two, i.e., between negativism and independence, could be determined by comparing children who have never had a period of resistance, with the others. Children of the same family who, according to the mother, differ markedly in respect to the "no-no" period, would present a favorable group for this kind of comparison. Our own data are still scanty on this point. One study comparing two groups of seven-year-old children divided according to the presence or absence of "the stubborn period" has been published by Hetzer (1929). A significant difference in regard to independent behavior was found. Compared with the others, the children

[4] See E. Benjamin (1930). Benjamin regards negativism as due to the change of relationship from mother-infant to family and community. See also Benjamin, (1942). The term "first stubborn age" was employed by Charlotte Bühler (1927).

[5] The term "puberty" was first applied to the infantile period of resistance by Häberlin (1931).

who had not gone through "the stubborn period," according to observations made in the classroom, were much more dependent on the teacher's help than the others.

The finding of a resistant period as a developmental stage in animals, as in men, is based on a study of resemblance of behavior and of function. The differences are revealed in the manifold varieties and subtleties of resistant behavior in the human—differences related to family structure, to intelligence, and to the larger varieties of personality constellations.

As soon as the early resistant forms become modified, numerous patterns appear in relation to any particular form of activity. Thus, the refusal to talk at all may be modified to scanty speech, jumbled speech, slowness or procrastination, and a host of other negativistic speech mechanisms. Refusal to eat may be modified to eating very little, to restricting the choice of food, to dawdling, fussiness, etc. All such patterns may have their origins in sources other than negativism, but eventually may be utilized for that purpose.

Since the mother is the infant's most frequent frustrating agent—a necessary party of her function in protecting and rearing—she is usually the earliest and easiest target for the infant's display of rebellion. Since her relationship, unlike that of the animals, continues for so many years, the rebellious attitude towards her, aided by a variety of conditions familiar to us, can be expressed in an amazing series of vituperative forms. In the study of mother-daughter antagonisms, it is not difficult to trace, in the selection of every particular negativistic performance, something designed particularly to outrage the mother, and with notable success. In humans the problem of negativism is complicated by the problems of adapting to a large variety of relationships over long periods of time. A difference which affects animals as well as men has to do with the individual's available aggression. If we regard the infant's temper tantrum as an outburst of aggression we can say that such displays of aggression are generally increased during the period of resistance. There are, however, marked differences in the relative frequency of tantrums and negativism. Some children reveal little evidence of tantrums, and express their noncompliance almost exclusively in the form of negativism.

In this connection the fact should be noted also that in some children, tantrums in most instances take the form of "silent rage." The rebellious feelings of people under the control of a strong authority, as of submissive people generally, are much more likely to take the safer form of some variety of negativism than that of open aggression. The aggression is concealed in the negativism. It may be used for the same purpose, but is less likely to become the method of choice of the aggressive child or adult. Incapacity of any kind in childhood—clumsiness, for example—also favors the negativistic type of defense, if the child is subject to much criticism on that account.

Animals supposedly show breed differences as well as individual difference in regard to stubbornness. I am not aware of any special investigation of the genetic aspects of this problem among humans. I am impressed by the number of families of our most negativistic children who are noted for the number of obstinate characters they contain, which our informants are happy to talk about, and point to with pride.

The early manifestations of negativism have been represented as protective and self-propelling functions that enable the child to overcome infantile dependency. When first observed they do not appear to be hostile reactions. They appear to be simply a struggle that is part of the process of growth towards self-realization. In time, hostile feelings toward the obstacle appear, whether the obstacle is an object or a human being, and in the case of a human being particularly, negativism may appear largely as hostile behavior.

Inner negativism, a term used in reference to catatonia to denote the reversal of one's own thoughts or wishes, occurs not only in children, as I have described, but also in nonpsychotic adults. In questioning mothers concerning their own stubbornness I have heard some interesting examples. One mother said that when shopping for a dress which she really wants and can afford, the only way she can get herself to buy it is to discuss it with her husband who invariably says no. That enables her to make the purchase.

A number of people utilize opposition as a spur to their own efforts, as an energizer, without which their initiative is inadequate.

Inner negativism, though not in the sense of oppositeness, is used also as a protective device against compliance when a corrective is needed against a strong tendency to yield to the wishes of others or to play a submissive role. The fear of giving up negativistic behavior is sometimes expressed in a similar way by children. In response to the question, "What would happen if you'd give in to your mother just once?" the reply was to the effect that if you give in she will take advantage, make you do everything, and never let you do anything for yourself. Actually, in the case of a child who replied in this way, the modification of his negativism during therapy was followed by a close and quite subservient relationship to his mother. The use of negativism as a protective barrier against submissive tendencies should be given consideration.

Negativistic phenomena of varying degrees are relatively common. They may represent useful outlets of defiance in otherwise well-behaved people who preserve such minor negativistic residues from their childhood as refusal ever to wear an overcoat, or always arriving late at a party. Floyd Allport (1934) has investigated the frequency of specific kinds of nonconformity among samples of the population in various phases of life and finds a similar curve of distribution in most of them. All his groups contain a small percentage who are prone to pass a red light, to violate a factory regulation, to omit a church ritual that is adhered to by the majority, etc.

In our clinical work with adults we are more likely to see the more severe forms of negativism. Among children, the areas of behavior in which negativism is manifested may be more circumscribed. To this area the term "oppositional syndrome" may be applied. Among those whose oppositional behavior is well generalized, the oppositional tactics may be particularly prominent with reference to a special form of activity. The term oppositional syndrome is a convenient label to cover such special forms also. The use of the term "syndrome" may help also to guard us against the tendency to make a diagnosis prematurely.

Some years ago a 12-year-old boy was referred because he was making just passing marks in school in spite of a superior intelligence. In that regard he was unusually consistent, from the first grade to the seventh. In time, he told me that it took lots of planning to manage never to fail and yet never make more than a passing mark. On occasion his parents hired a tutor to help him with his work. The patient soon learned how to dissipate the tutor's efforts by getting him to talk about certain subjects that claimed his interest.

His difficulty in accepting his studies began presumably as a revolt against his mother for sending him to a nursery school. At that time he put up a feeble protest, though he felt it deeply as an act of abandonment. His revenge took the special form of negativism I have described–a revenge of withholding from his mother, whose own scholastic achievement had been high, the gift of good marks in school. The boy was otherwise a dutiful son. His negativism for schoolwork was never quite overcome. It became a system from which he could never extricate himself. He was graduated from college and a professional school, though only with passing marks. Today he is married and holds an important executive position.

At the time of referral there was evidence of rather compulsive neatness, ritualistic behavior and generally an overly organized personality.

He had gone through a long period of resistance in infancy. His mother had the highest standards of ethical behavior and housekeeping. Her relationship to the boy was affectionate. The findings in this case are rather characteristic of many, and reveal also the common relationship of early negativism and compulsive behavior. His Rorschach test also revealed certain characteristic findings—a tendency to turn several plates upside down as soon as they were placed in his hands, generally a high frequency of reversals, one or two plates to which he could not respond at all, and a longer than usual form per cent.

The modification of the original and powerful "no, no" in his case could be traced along various routes, including certain perseverative tendencies, procrastination, negativistic forgetting and dawdling. One of the routes ended in a special syndrome in which the negativism was channelled into a specialized opposition to schoolwork.

I have by now collected a series of such cases and have followed the course of several who have been treated by others. In these cases it would appear that mechanism becomes more powerful than motivation. That may be why such cases are so recalcitrant to psychoanalysis. The patient's full insight into the meaning of his oppositional method is only the beginning of the modifying process, after which we rely primarily on the method of re-education.

In a number of oppositional school syndromes the children were shifted from one nursery school to another, after making an adjustment to the former. In this kind of situation, where the child's protests are in vain and its own problem of meeting new situations fraught with danger, his retaliation is understandable. When out-and-out refusals are not in the cards, negativistic half-refusals become the compromise. In one case a child developed a partial paralysis of the legs which was diagnosed as hysteria. Her selection of the legs was probably due to the fact that much attention had been given her feet since early infancy because of flatness. Numerous neurologic examinations were negative. I mention this case because of the possibility that a negativistic process may be selective enough to be confused with a conversion symptom. The child said during therapy, "I made my legs not to walk, and I thought that when I wanted to I could make them walk again." One of the values of delimiting special forms of negativism into syndromes lies in the finding of characteristic patterns in each of them. Seen only as a general expression of negativistic behavior, we may lose the significance of certain combinations of symptoms and of the special therapeutic problems involved.

Oppositional syndromes are seen in a number of cases of anorexia nervosa. The large preponderance of females, the frequent finding of mother-daughter antagonisms, and the negativistic behavior are well known. The final outcome of some of these cases into full-fledged catatonia may be explained partly as a quantitative variation, an extreme manifestation of the syndrome, with the complications that arise from the consequent withdrawal of all social contact. Otherwise we would have to say that whatever becomes schizophrenia always was schizophrenia, a position that would rule out the notion of quantitative variations in the intensity and duration of negativistic behavior.

Oppositional syndromes are seen also in certain cases of obesity, speech problems, intellectual inhibitions other than the oppositional school syndromes; in fact, in a large number of functional difficulties which need exploring.

What has been called negativism, resistance, and oppositional behavior we see as behavior that has its origin in a basic protective function for biologic as well as social processes. In the clinical pictures which represent an abuse or excess of this function we have lost sight of their original positive values because our attention has been diverted by the disturbing and urgent manifestations of rebellious and hostile behavior. Our attention has also been diverted from the study of the adaptive features of the mechanism, and of the mechanism as such, by our absorbing interest in its motivational and diagnostic aspects.

If we consider as a functional unit of behavior any on-going process that appears to have an initial point and an end point, we have a large variety of units to consider, from the simplest to the most complex. In all of them we may delineate that part of the process which is concerned primarily with the problems of initiating and maintaining goal direction and of removing hindrances to its purpose. In the case of the simplest functional unit—the reflex—this would involve neurophysiologic studies beyond our scope; the persistence of a reflex after interruption by various stimuli would be one example of many related to our problem. The unit of behavior represented by a biologic process involving the satisfaction of a "basic drive" would represent an act of greater complexity. The social act of which the obstacle to goal achievement in another human being, or influences derived from social relationships, represents a still higher degree of complexity. Whether the unitary act considered is short-range or long, an immediate satisfaction or the fulfillment of a life-long ambition, the same aspects of the on-going behavior in terms of goal persistency and reaction to interference can be discerned.

As resistance against modification of an on-going process by external or internal stimuli, we may see the problem as that of the autonomy of the act, as it pertains to neural, biologic or social behavior. Without such autonomy, the act could be so easily inhibited, deflected or terminated that it could hardly function. This principle of autonomy of the act in social behavior has been revealed in the mother-infant relationship as a process of emancipation from the earliest stage of dependency on the parent, a process which the parent has aided. Within the process of emancipation, which is complicated by the numerous factors that bear on any variety of human behavior, a maturational factor has been delineated as its most important feature.

Resistant behavior or negativism serves to favor the individual's separateness and independence. It serves also as a protective function in situations of emotional stress. The recoil in such situation may involve inner as well as outer negativism, cessation of exploratory behavior, social withdrawal and hostility.

As a reaction *vs* interference with self-determined behavior, negativism runs counter to malleability or plasticity. In the same sense it runs counter to suggestibility. Since excessive malleability or suggestibility may be felt by the individual as threatening to his autonomy, as a fear of complete domination by others, he may cultivate negativism as his main protective device. That may be one of the reasons for the clinical finding of negativism and marked suggestibility in the same individual.

In general, it may be said that when negativism is used as a characteristic mode of defense for whatever reason, it favors the development of contrariness, rigidity of personality and social isolation.

In the examination of apparently normal though negativistic children, it may even appear in the form of muscular rigidity of the limb as a reaction against flexion of the knee during examination of the knee reflex. Inasmuch as it involves persistency in attaining a goal regardless of all obstacles, it favors purposive or goal-directed thinking as opposed to undirected, spontaneous thinking. Both kinds characterize normal individuals, even when there is a preponderance of the one kind of thinking as compared with the other. The point at which the preponderance may be regarded as abnormal is determined by clinical criteria.

In the rearing of children, the mother, of necessity, must modify or frustrate many of the child's struggles for self-assertion and self-determination. Under certain conditions (especially when the mother is strict and unloving) hostility may take the form of persistent oppositional behavior and give rise to spiteful reprisals and the development of personality traits that run counter to those of the mother's. A number of oppositional syndromes are determined by the special kinds of reprisals that are selected.

The limitation of negativistic behavior in regard to duration, intensity, areas of function and the number of people concerned, requires, for its explanation, study of the individual case. Numerous syndromes of oppositional behavior may represent an adaptational stage that need never advance any further. The assumption that all of them, and particularly those with obsessional symptoms, represent wild or abortive or developing forms of catatonia, is unproved. The danger of the spread of the oppositional mechanism, viewed psychopathologically, can be understood most readily when it involves all social contacts. Every person is then regarded as hostile and dangerous—at least thwarting—and social isolation follows. In childhood, when the withdrawal tendency is still modifiable, we have the most favorable opportunity to overcome it. The study of the spread of negativism might include also the study of its special lines of direction when one is more pronounced than the others: for example, the special line of persistency, of reliance on one's self alone, of the no-saying phase, etc.

Negativism has been contrasted with aggression and referred to as a more primitive and also safer expression of antagonism. In the form of open defiance it is difficult and probably unnecessary to differentiate it from aggression. As in the case of aggression, numerous modifications of the extreme act are seen. The assault is modified to teasing; the refusal is modified to procrastinating. Any form of negativism can be used as an instrument of, and a substitute for, aggression. It may be said that this is the method of choice of the submissive individual, or of the individual in any situation in which aggressive behavior is regarded as too dangerous. The mixtures of patterns of both forms of behavior depend on the situation and on the available aggression in the personality.

Finally, we must consider briefly the relation of anxiety and negativism. When the infant struggles against the physician during the physical examination he may be expressing in that manner his anxiety about an inoculation rather than oppositional behavior. That differentiation must often be made by parents, physicians and teachers. The question is sometimes put in the form, "Is he anxious or just stubborn?" When we are in doubt, we assume for safety's sake that the answer is anxiety.

In the case of anxiety, the individual may use oppositional tactics as a protection against any situation that may incite it. That is one of the reasons for the conviction on the part of some investigators that the source of negativism is anxiety.

Anxiety, as we see it in relation to negativism, arises most frequently from the feeling of fear and guilt of hostility against the frustrating agent. Since negativism, when expressed in a social relationship, is so often charged with hostility, it is a fertile source of anxiety derived from the fear of loss of the love and support of the social object, the fear of retribution, and the fears emanating from the feelings of the guilt of hostile and shameful behavior.

In closing, I realize that I have yielded to the temptation, in spite of my resolve, of covering too much ground. If, in spite of that fact, I have succeeded in stimulating your interest in the original adaptive function of oppositional behavior, and in its study as a mechanism in its own right, my own on-going and purposive behavior will be completed.

ANLAGE OF PRODUCTIVENESS IN BOYS: WOMB ENVY

JOHN B. NELSON

Nelson discusses a relatively neglected area, that of feminine attributes in young males (Green and Money, 1961). Joining forces with Murphy (1962), he challenges the universal applicability of the equation of passivity with femininity and activity with masculinity (see Bettelheim, 1962; Brody, 1964; Brunswick, 1940; Mead, 1949) and makes a firm distinction between productivity and creativity. Many of the efforts to influence boys to behave in a fashion arbitrarily designated as masculine are viewed as a culturally imposed burden in a home and school environment dominated by women. Kagan (1964) and Maccoby (1966) detail the multifaceted considerations in the development of sex differences.

In keeping with our conviction that a developmental orientation includes consideration of the individual's future as well as his past and present, we believe it appropriate to keep in mind, while reading Nelson's article, the crucial and integral relationship for men, in most cultures, between masculinity and work and the importance of adult sexuality as a goal. Sociological surveys agree with recent psychoanalytic observations that there is a growing number of men who appear to envy females. The sociologists also remind us that today man's sexual responsibilities are increasing as a consequence of the growing equality between the sexes, which is accelerating during the current sexual revolution. Contemporary man has the double burden of satisfying his female sexual partner, who is no longer ignorant about sexuality, as well as himself. In addition, society continues to have greater tolerance for female than for male homosexuality. Thus, the old double standard of sexual behavior was probably easier for men. Over the course of history, men appear to have entertained two sexual views of women. The Victorian one, that woman is repressed, inhibited, and does not enjoy sexuality, is well known. Brenton (1966) asserts that this view was invented by males as a means of coping with an even more ancient and threatening view of female sexuality, one that considered women to be sexually insatiable and thereby potentially capable of turning man to putty. This view, as the Victorian one,

Reprinted from *Journal of the American Academy of Child Psychiatry,* 6, 1956, pp. 213–225.

relieved man of the sexual responsibility now being thrust upon him by the newer equalitarian approach.

It is frequently asserted that the patriarchy of the past was established and maintained primarily through the efforts of females. While this is consistent with the psychological observation that boys derive much of their masculinity from their mothers, the patriarchal heritage continues to saddle growing boys with concepts of rigid sexual differentiation which do not necessarily fit the reality to which they must adapt as adults.

This sociocultural commentary on what is often considered to be a basically biological function is motivated by the complexities of the relationship between the innate and the experiential (Benjamin, 1961, this volume) in the area of sexuality. It has been observed (Money et al., 1955; Stoller, 1968; Harrison, 1970) that in hermaphrodites the sex of assignment and rearing seems to be a more potent determinant of sexual identity than the individual's biology.

For the preschool child, the size, power, and productiveness of the mother loom wonderfully large in reality and fantasy. At times the child stands in awe of this superbeing: such experiences of awe in childhood, coupled with many other factors, may be linked to adult creativity (Greenacre, 1956). Rare are the combinations of constitution and experience resulting in the development of truly creative individuals. Much less rare is the likely association between the drive-engendered activity in children and the activity of the busy and powerful figure of the pregenital mother. By way of the early forms of identification, the activity can become productiveness as the child struggles to emulate the mother. Very likely there is an interrelatedness between creativity and productivity, the former being a very specialized capacity tapping productivity as well as many other aspects of psychic life. The chief ego activity focused upon in this paper will be productiveness: the process of shaping, forming, making, bearing, or yielding something. Creativity, which has been the object of study by many clinicians, will receive little attention. If the literature is any measure, the more common, and therefore less spectacular, topic of productivity has been accorded far less study.

Much of the early experience of the girl with her mother may be transferred to her own future mothering. This influence is often discernible, even though the preoedipal era is well blotted out by infantile amnesia. The sexual identity of the girl is subjected to considerable buffeting during the oedipal, latency, and prepubertal stages. The girl knows, sometimes vaguely and sometimes clearly, that eventually womanhood and motherhood will occur. Despite the developmental stresses and defensive maneuverings, the girl retains a sexual kinship with the mother, a notion of common destiny. This is clearly not so for the boy. Although his oedipal struggle vis-à-vis his mother offers less threat of loss because he continues to keep her as a love object, he perceives the necessity to alter his wishes growing out of the earlier identification. This would be part of the differentiation of sexual role carried out by the boy. The sexual kinship of mother and daughter is realistically possible. The boy, on the other hand, as he becomes the man, will be limited to partial participation in child rearing. He can, of course, produce ideas, works of art, and, most commonly, physical objects.

Girls and women undoubtedly experience penis envy. The penis, capable of direct biological action, becomes symbolic both to girls and boys of active, independent, masculine activities. Why is there no symmetrical term, such as womb envy, for the boy and man? The female focuses on the penis, an organ which actually creates nothing and serves merely as a depositor. Girls and many women seem less aware of the scrotum and its contents, thereby ignoring this organ and its important function of generation and storage of germ plasm. This state of relative ignorance has many roots. One could be the blocking out of awareness of a dependent organ with paired contents because there is a greater resemblance to the external organs of females (breasts and labia) than to the unitary penis. Bell (1961) has written of the importance of the scrotum and its contents in the development of castration anxiety and sexual identity in boys. She suggests that girls may link ideas about their own or mothers' sexuality with notions about the scrotum having a feminine function. Perhaps, in the general reaction to the boy's apparent physical superiority, girls mute their curiosity and awareness of the boy's more "feminine" area. This oversight reminds one of the boy's seeming ignorance of the germinal areas of the female, except that there is a better anatomical reason for this oversight, since the principal parts of the woman's reproductive anatomy is hidden. Both sexes focus on the most obvious externals of the opposite: plain enough for the female's view of the male, but what of the male's view of the female? Professional persons who listen closely to children have heard several answers: the boy expects that females have either lost the penis, will grow one, have it hidden away, or have something better.

The evolving childish theories are more complicated and varied than one theory that exists in many children; both boys and girls imagine the woman's sexuality related to an elusive phallus. The boy must contend with a number of confusing realities as he contemplates his mother. She is large; every part of her body available for casual inspection dwarfs the boy. More specific than her general bulk are her breasts, organs the boy clearly possesses only in minute form. Single organs and paired organs also must pose problems. The boy knows that he has one little penis, but his mother has two big breasts. Furthermore, mother, or a neighbor woman, may have a baby during the boy's early years. The chances are excellent for some kind of exposure to such an event.

The observation of a pregnant woman can be interpreted as the result of mother's phallic qualities, therefore also leaving father and the boy open to childbearing. But there is a strong possibility that another childhood theory evolves: mother is different, she is to be admired, and she becomes further endowed with the magic and power in keeping with the ego and libidinal states characteristic of the age. Grotjahn (1949) attributes the following quote to Zilboorg: "It is not penis envy on the part of the woman, but womb envy on the part of the man, that is psychogenetically older, and therefore, more fundamental." The evidence presented to the boy includes: breasts, babies, big belly, and power. These become connected with the mysteriousness of productivity. The mother's power—the power demonstrated in running the household and supervising the boy's life—may be magically connected with her childbearing capacity. This supposition leaves the boy's childish theory in a far more abstract condition that that of the girl who has seen a penis. The hidden, internal, abstract qualities of the female are embodied in many figures found in poetry, drama, sculpture, and painting.

Children during the pregenital years are not capable of abstraction; for this reason the boy may attempt to form a concrete theory. Little boys have been heard to say: "The baby comes from mother's breasts." Other immature theories proffered have included birth from either end of the alimentary canal, from the head, from the naval, or from external physical objects such as boxes, suitcases, and ovens (folklore). The frequent statement that boys universally consider women castrates and so inferior may well be inaccurate. The boy may often consider that women have "something better," perhaps related to the qualities and organs mentioned above. This attitude could contribute to the widespread reverence for the mother and is no doubt connected to the universal fantasies involved in the phrases: "mother earth," "mother church," and "mother nature."

This paper will attempt to delineate the young boy's reaction to his mother's attributes and feminine functions and to present the thesis that some pressure for productivity in the boy and man has roots in their envy of the woman's feminine functions. Furthermore, I believe that this factor is operative from the pregenital years on. Comments will be made on possible reasons for the general clinical silence in this area and some impressions of why a potentially useful, partial identification with mother is often thwarted, thereby inhibiting productivity in certain men.

Ruth Mack Brunswick (1940) presented a careful study of the preoedipal libidinal development of boys and girls. She describes the dyadic nature of the pregenital relationships, the capacity for triadic relationships not appearing until the occurrence of the instinctual and ego developmental changes of the early phallic phase. The dyadic relationship, by definition, involves a nearly total reliance of the child upon the mother for sustenance, companionship, entertainment, and education. The preoedipal attachment of the boy to his mother is of shorter duration than that of girls because it phases into the oedipal attachment to the same person. Brunswick comments that the boy needs to change neither love object nor sex organ (the girl must deal with mother and father, clitoris and vagina), but he *must* change his attitude toward his mother. This imperative entails a shift from the passive to the active mode, giving rise to the seemingly paradoxical situation that efforts at active mastery by the pregenital boy arise partly out of an identification with the mother. This is an early fundamental identification antedating the later sexual differentiation determined with the onset of the phallic phase. The mother becomes less powerful as the child assumes more independence from the oral-dependent state via his increased muscular strength and control. These changes are all relative since the mother continues to be involved with the preschool child, but the balance often seems reversed as the lively toddler leads, rather than follows, the mother. This liveliness, or aggressiveness, is partially the result of identification with the active and all-powerful adult, although it certainly has strong constitutional components as well.

Out of the searching attention focused on the mother arises the "harmless" (asexual) wish for a baby. This process might be greatly enhanced if mother becomes pregnant while the boy is still in the preoedipal stage of development. Very early, then, the child perceives mother's childbearing capacity as central to her nature and talent. Libidinal changes and changes in aggression characteristic of the anal period appear to strengthen the wish to be like mother and have a baby. Through the boy's phallic strivings which then follow, activity predominating over passivity, the wish changes from receiving from the mother to presenting mother with a baby.

Lampl-de Groot (1947), in her important paper on "The Preoedipal Phase in the Development of the Male Child," traces the bisexual or asexual anal relationship with the mother. It appears that the mother satisfies the passive and active longings of the boy–the latter, of course, should become the dominant expression once the phallic oedipal strivings begin to be solidified. She postulates that the interplay between the passive and active longings strongly influence character formation. The adult man with an imbalance of active and passive wishes is more likely to suffer from a potency disturbance, neurosis, or character deformity. In such men the transition from love for the mother to love for a nontabooed woman is faulty.

Jacobson (1950) wrote of the boy's wish for a baby. She comments that by the second year, some kind of doll or stuffed animal play is common. In it, the child seems to be expressing his wish for autonomy and assertion. The child may well wish for mother to become his baby. Again, as Brunswick earlier stated, Jacobson says that the step in the anal phase is the wish for a baby as an anal production. Here, there must be an equation between breasts, womb (intestines and feces), and baby. This ideation, then, gives way, even before the phallic phase is well under way, as the sexual differences are somewhat more clearly perceived. In both boys and girls, there may be a stage in which they wish to replace father and impregnate mother; thus the emphasis shifts from breast to penis. With the more vivid and forceful enunciation of sexual differences seen in the phallic phase, the girl may accept the baby as a substitute for the penis, thereby identifying with the mother. The boy, seeing the female's apparent plight, turns to an identification with father. This change is of course, related to the important libidinal shift of that developmental period. In normal development, this shift spells the downfall of the earlier passive receptive strivings in a boy. But in this process, the boy must sacrifice the more or less overt wish to have a baby.

Van der Leeuw (1958), writing of the preoedipal phase in males, describes the identification with and jealousy of the child-rearing mother. He underlines the importance of the activity-passivity continuum, believing that the early experiences and partial resolution are central to character formation.

Van der Leeuw's views are in agreement with those of Brunswick, Lampl-de Groot, and Jacobson. These authors are cautious in making direct links between the early experience of the child and his later productivity. Clear connections are difficult, if not impossible, to make because of the lack of verbal expressiveness in the young child and the infantile amnesia of the older child and adult.

These authors all agree that whatever envy the boy develops of the child-rearing capacity of his mother must have its roots in the pregenital era. These early preoedipal years can be roughly compared with the early state of the human fetus—for the first seven weeks of its existence, sexuality is not apparent as the original buds and tubes are undifferentiated. Sexual anatomy appears capable of going either way from this primordial undifferentiated state. Translated to toddler years, the anatomical difference is by then clear, but the meaning to the child is still minimal. The attitude of his parents is already shaped because of their response to the external sexuality of the child and their attitudes will influence the child's unfolding development. The important environmental factor of the parental attitudes will shape, along with his constitution, the unfolding personality of the child according to the epigenetic principle.

It is only during the phallic and oedipal stages that the sex of the parent becomes a really crucial issue. In the early months, the mother is really the child's world and this state continues to a lesser extent for a number of years. The only time throughout childhood, including adolescence, in which a child is in fairly continuously close proximity with one person is this pregenital era. During this time, the child witnesses the mother's usually continuous activity in various phases of mothering, housewifing, and entertaining. Whether this child be a boy or a girl, this is his most concentrated experience with activity, productivity, and perhaps creativity. The boy in subsequent years, as he yearns to identify with his father, often finds this difficult partly because of the periodicity of father's time spent at home and partly because of the vagueness of the father's position in the world as well as in the family. There is usually nothing vague or periodic about the mother's position in the world during the child's early years. The instincts, supported by the ego's cognitive awareness of physical attributes, promote sexual differentiation in later developmental phases and mitigate against the massive accumulation of experience with (and identification with) the mother. The ego of the oedipal and later phases is, of course, far sturdier than that of the pregenital years.

Womb envy derivatives may be observed in oedipal and latency age boys with their sublimated interest in growing plants, breeding and training animals, collecting nests, and so on. These can be manifested as an expression of a temporary or more lasting negative oedipal solution, but they necessarily reach back to the above-described early identification with the mother. Both the internal management and the environmental molding experiences deeply affect the outcome of the child's bisexual heritage.

We can postulate that productiveness, choice of life's work, style of future fathering, and attitudes toward child rearing are all influenced by the early identification with the mother. Motherhood has received far more attention than fatherhood in our literature, and creativity has received more attention than productiveness. In short, there has not been sufficient study of the developmental reverberations of the early mother-boy relationship. Such a statement applies to the general topic of the pregenital relationship of the boy with his mother as well as to the more specific topic of womb envy. Why has there been insufficient study? Perhaps the basic cause is a lack of acceptance of the feminine traits in men, especially the American male, although this reluctance is by no means restricted to citizens of this country. Male analysts and psychiatric supervisors may shy away from this topic and thereby help perpetuate such oversights in training. The literature certainly contains relatively few references to the issues of early productiveness in boys.

In a sampling of training experiences in child psychiatry, we learn that these dynamic issues receive relatively little comment. We are undoubtedly influenced by common cultural values, for instance, the idealized American man is supermasculine and ostensibly free of feminine leanings. However, by virtue of the process of natural selection which leads to one's lifework, the child psychiatrist obviously makes his commitment partially from unconscious needs and fantasies, one of which must be some interest in raising children. Child psychiatrists as a professional group are not noteworthy for their aggressiveness. The disparity between the image of the idealized male and that of the relatively passive tender of children, here oversimplified, may well be dealt with by repression and other defensive maneuvers and result in an inhibition of accurate observation of the patient and of his therapist.

Women in child psychiatry also struggle in varying degrees with important personal issues. Penis envy in girls and castration anxiety in boys have been the two dynamic issues receiving the greater focus in the child psychiatric teaching. However, Jones (1935) states succinctly: "There is a healthy suspicion growing that men analysts have been led to adopt an unduly phallo-centric view of the problems in question, the importance of the female organs being correspondingly underestimated. Women have on their side contributed to the general mystification by their secretive attitude towards their own genitals and by displaying a hardly disguised preference for interest in the male organ" (p. 556). It may be that there has been an unconscious conspiracy of silence in the area of the early child-rearing practices and sexual identification which has influenced child psychiatry practitioners and teachers as well as other adults. The topic cannot be avoided in following female development into adolescence and beyond, but in boys it can be underplayed; and I suggest that this indeed is the case. This whole process is supported by the repression in boys of aspects of infantile sexuality, especially repression of their passive feminine wishes. This development must be partly due to the aversion at a sociocultural level to such leanings, and is therefore enforced at home and in school.

Erikson (1950) describes differences in block play configuration in late latency children. Such elaborate productions are far beyond the early nursery school child. In a series of observations conducted in a day care center for preschool children, I noted much freer bisexual expressive play in boys at the three-year level than in those several years older. It should be noted that many of the children were living in homes dominated by women. Three-and-a-half-year-old boys were quite content to spend fractions of each day working diligently in the kitchen corner of the playroom, mixing and serving pretend foods on the real equipment provided for such play. They also gleefully dressed in women's clothes made available for free play, and it was not uncommon to see a boy tenderly tucking a doll into bed or being concerned with the doll's clothing. There seemed to be little difference between the activity expressed in this play by the boys and by the girls. By the age of five the boys were far busier with vigorous activities, such as truck and train play, and less involved in the female play area. Some evidence of sublimation such as painting could be observed. Among the five-year-olds, there seemed to be one or two boys with marked feminine interests, and information about the home indicated some degree of imbalance in their family constellations.

The behavior of the majority of the five-year-olds certainly suggested a moving away from expressions of identification with the all-powerful mother, at least in the grosser aspects of her childbearing and child-rearing role. Their reality testing is more mature, their perceptions are more discriminating, and their defenses more effective. It can be postulated that much of the activity of these more masculine little boys, which is expressed in more differentiated ways in latency and afterward, may have its roots in this early identification with the active, powerful mother. A boy of seven, whom I observed, had been preoccupied for over a year in growing seeds, in onions sprouting, and in growing animals. His block and car play was replete with towers, movement along roadways and blockades. Yet, he also spent hours making garages and other close enclosures. When he spoke of his long-range ideals, they were masculine. He appeared to present a workable, very comfortable amalgamation of the feminine and masculine, the latter clearly predominating, but the former neither completely lost nor troublesome.

Psychiatrists employ stereotyped concepts about sexual roles, sexual activities, and psychosexual derivatives to adults as well as children. We can observe in many diagnostic conferences a hasty assumption that what is passive is feminine and what is active is masculine. The children with various admixtures of identification may indeed be severely troubled, but there is apt to be little discussion of the specific contributions of each discerned identification area to the child's personality, with a weighing of positive solutions or traits alongside a consideration of the anxiety-provoking and disturbing aspects of the child's mixed identifications. The many children with sexual identification problems in child psychiatry practice commonly present difficulties in being productive. A more modulated, less stereotyped approach to the evaluation and management of these children might often be very helpful.

Lois Murphy, in her book *The Widening World of Childhood* (1962), presents data which she suggests point to the need for much more careful scrutiny of the various trends in the personality development of children. She reports upon the considerable overlap in the areas of activity and passivity in her sampling of preschool children. Some girls were as active as the most active boys, and some boys were as passive as certain of the most passive girls. She writes of the need to define clearly what is passive-passive and what is active-passive; what is really a state of preparation or absorption in the child as contrasted with passivity. She sees activity and receptivity as entirely separate variables which do not belong on a continuum. She believes that some of the boys in her sample were really rather masculine without being extremely active, aggressive youngsters. It is her opinion that creativity can grow out of activity or passivity, but that in most instances both modes are prominent in the creative personality.

But the stereotypes remain, and they are important to our field. Undoubtedly, there are direct dynamic psychological issues involved in the infantile repression that generally buries much of the early identification with the active mother. Part of this process is associated with the libidinal ascendancy of the phallic oedipal urges. The boy demonstrates at this period a libidinal concentration in the area of his body that is considered neither anatomically nor functionally receptive. His phallic intrusiveness leads to aggressive efforts being directed toward the world with a great vigor and energy, and some of this energy may be used in a productive fashion. However, the increasing range and sophistication of his productivity may represent partially a sublimation of his earlier feminine wish to have a baby.

The boy's behaviors are under close scrutiny by his parents, his teachers, and his peers. This fact may account in part for the relative lack of freedom of expression of feminine tendencies in the latency boys, the external social pressure reinforcing the wish to identify with the group and not to be ostracized. In the American culture at all levels, the word "sissy" is a very important and emotional term. In its own symbolic way, it stands for all that wishes to make femininity in a man or boy alien. It is doubtful that one three-and-a-half-year-old boy calls another a "sissy" if he sees him cooking at a stove in a day care center or pushing a baby in a baby carriage. But an eight- or nine-year-old boy, haughty in his manliness, could easily criticize the youngster and his criticism would carry considerable weight. Somehow the "sissy" state seems to become associated with the notion of a taboo even before the concept of homosexuality as such is known to a child.

Prior to the presentation to the boy of the "sissy" problem, the mother and the mother surrogates usually steer the boy more quietly into acceptable activities and they are joined during the preschool year eventually by the father, all tending to sharpen, but also narrow, the sexual role of the child. These external factors of parental and peer attitudes added to the internal psychological pressures upon the boy may lead to a dampening, an inhibition, an interference with the free use of the man's or boy's full potential. This potential has its roots in human bisexuality. It is hard to believe that fatherhood, for instance, with the complex demands it represents from conception onward, is not made more tolerable for a man by some remnant of an identification with an active mother. It is also likely that a husband's empathy for his pregnant or mothering wife is enhanced by such residues.

In psychiatric clinics, men are often seen who are anxiously fighting off their passivity, wearing themselves down in the process with counterphobic or other defensive behavior. They seem to be anxiously negating anything within themselves that might be soft and tender. Their underachievement and diminishing productivity are commonly features of their life style discomfitting to themselves or to their families. Sublimation of their genuine wishes seems unacceptable or impossible; instead they sacrifice the wishes and institute strong countermeasures which persistently break down. This fairly common syndrome is unfortunate for the individual, his wife, and children, and unfortunate for the interference with the man's potential productivity. The child psychiatrist frequently deals with the child and the parent displaying disturbed sexual identification and sexual conflicts. It is, however, sometimes difficult for the psychiatrist to perceive such conflict as admitting of satisfactory solution and attempts at solutions as potentially a healthy process. We probably too often see a boy's activities in growing or caring for things as his wish to be cared for or to be "feminine" and do not consider if they are indicative of a helpful effort at solution of conflicting goals, energies, and images.

Based on the idea expressed in this paper it is possible to raise the following question: Would long-range benefit be derived from a child-rearing philosophy that permits some leeway in the developing boy's identification? Generalization is impossible, but indeed there are many parents, educators, and physicians who appear to favor the development of "pure" sexual identity, free of conflict or "blends." Of interest would be a study of families where there was greater freedom of expression and flexible encouragement of roles than exists in the "average." Perhaps it would be found that in such families there would be confusion of roles or mounting anxiety amounting to interference with productive, adaptive, and relatively comfortable development. However, it would seem well within the realm of possibility that boys raised in a manner permitting some carry-over and some enhancement of useful modification of the early (and subsequent) maternal identification might be found productive, relatively asymptomatic, and in possession of a range of sensitivities and responses not found ordinarily. There is agreement that all guidelines must lead to the male's development of aggressiveness and intrusiveness, guaranteeing continuation of the race—just as the female must accept one of her roles to be bearer of pain and receptor. It would seem possible that these ends could be met without the total dampening of useful partial identification with the opposite sex. Mabel Blake Cohen (1966) has recently written of her wish to encourage a more critical scrutiny of our assumptions about sex-typical behavior.

Our understanding of the effect of opposite sex hormones in each individual is still in the earliest stages. The male level of estrogen is low; studies suggest that it varies during the life cycle. Physiology must exert at least subtle effects on psychological states and vice versa. It would be interesting to measure estrogen levels in the husband of the pregnant wife or in the boy who is preoccupied with a real or fantasy fetus.

The male aversion to feminine traits has been well documented by therapists and sociologists. The various defensive maneuvers utilized to retain a monolithic sexual stance have been equally well documented. This struggle against femininity can, in some men, lead to a paradoxical inhibition of productiveness. The broad topic of sexual identification lies beyond the narrow scope of this paper; however, an Anlage of mature productivity in men is the identification described in this paper. This is an early envy of the mother's power and magic of productivity, linked in part to her femininity, and therefore to her womb, an organ which may not be recognized in name until years later. Because this early envy and emulation pertain to the almost embryonic development of productivity, they deserve fuller understanding.

PART III
NEUROTIC DISORDERS

The word "neurotic" is commonly employed by the general public to describe behavior encompassing the unexpected, disagreeable, annoying, maladaptive, deviant, and even frankly psychotic. In clinical parlance, however, the noun "neurosis," or "psychoneurosis," is reserved to designate specific syndromes, and the adjective "neurotic" is applied to a specific type of conflict which may underlie a variety of syndromes in addition to clinical neuroses. Thus, throughout this volume, the term "neurotic" appears with great frequency, but it is never used with a lack of specificity.

Many of the psychopathological entities discussed in the section of developmental, learning, and antisocial disorders are accompanied by neurotic conflict. In short, neurotic conflicts are far more prevalent than actual psychoneuroses. This is especially true in childhood, when crystallized symptom neuroses are relatively rare (Anthony, 1967). While noting Kraepelin's (1904) failure to mention children in his classic treatise, Cramer (1959) observed that the term neurosis was not applied descriptively and conceptually to children until Freud's report that infantile neurosis was an integral determinant of adult psychoneuroses.

Developmental disorders may stem from conflicts between the child's maturational level and the demands of the external *environment. Psychoneurotic conflicts, although they may evolve out of developmental conflict with the environment, are* internal, *intrapsychic struggles between different aspects of the developing personality (A. Freud, 1965; Nagera, 1966a). Many unconscious neurotic conflicts derive from earlier overt conflicts between the child and significant environmental figures, such as his parents. With personality development and the internalization of environmental standards into superego functioning, and with the repression of the internal drives, these conflicts evolve into intrapsychic ones.*

To outline the matter briefly and schematically: the incompleteness of repression results in upsurges of impulses, which, prior to reaching the level of consciousness, stimulate the signal of anxiety. The vicissitudes eventuating from the emergence of this neurotically induced anxiety constitute the psychoneurosis. Ordinarily, the individual reacts with a variety of ego defense mechanisms, the nature of which dictates the form of the psychoneurosis. It is possible, however, that the anxiety may remain undefended, in which case the neurosis is an anxiety state. In children, the motor elements of anxiety are typically primary, so that, with them, hyperactivity resulting in behavior problems and/or sleep disturbances is the most frequent consequence of such unbound anxiety. Among the possible defense mechanisms is the displacement of anxiety onto an environmental object, such as an animal, which may then assume the aura of danger, and is phobically avoided. In hysteria, the mechanism of conversion is employed, resulting in various somatic symptoms. If the preferred defense mechanism is reaction formation, isolation of affect and ideas, or undoing, one then observes the disagreeable thoughts and rituals typical of the obsessive-compulsive neurosis. Relatively uncommon in childhood is the guilty turning of the impulse against the self in reaction to object loss, and therefore the self-depreciation characteristic of the adult neurotic depressive reaction is rare among children. In recent years, there has been a growing tendency to view depression as a basic ego state analogous to anxiety. In consequence, certain psychoneurotic syndromes are conceptualized as a means of handling the depressive reactions elicited by life's inevitable frustrations and separations.

Although typical neurotic conflicts underlie many learning inhibitions and antisocial behavior disorders, these have other possible causes, as the sections on Learning and Antisocial Behavior Disorders demonstrate. Similarly, it should be noted that enuresis may be caused by a variety of other determinants in addition to neurotic conflicts (Gerard, 1939).

The foregoing formulation rests firmly on a psychoanalytic foundation. It should be noted that psychoneuroses have also been conceptualized within neurophysiological, psychobiological, embryonic (Bender, 1947) and social learning-behavioral frameworks. (Watson and Raynor, 1920; Rachman and Costello, 1961).

IRRATIONAL FEARS AND PHOBIAS

O. SPURGEON ENGLISH AND GERALD H. J. PEARSON

In this excerpt from their popular book, English and Pearson distinguish between ordinary fears and irrational phobias in childhood, and articulate the prevailing psychoanalytic ideas (see Colm, 1959) concerning the development of phobias. Of central importance in this view is the role of anxiety. Indeed, many clinicians have observed that persistent phobias are often preceded by a period of diffuse, unfocused anxiety.

English and Pearson illustrate their point of view with a case report of a little girl who is terrified of dogs. The psychodynamics outlined in their presentation are strikingly similar to those described in Freud's (1909a) famous report, Analysis of a Phobia in a Five-Year-Old Boy. *Freud's patient, Little Hans, also developed an animal phobia, in his case for horses. Little Hans, troubled by a repressed oedipal wish to harm his father, projected his own hostile wishes onto his father and became fearful that the latter wished to attack him. He then displaced this hostility onto horses. These mechanisms relieved Little Hans of anxiety. He was able to avoid horses, whereas avoiding his father and his own feelings would have been impossible.*

The case of Little Hans is well known not only because of the detailed unraveling of the mechanisms of his animal phobia, but also because this was the first reported instance of the psychoanalysis of a child. In fact, it is generally thought to mark the beginning of the modern era of child psychotherapy. In this context, it is worth noting that Freud was not Little Hans's therapist, as Freud at that time thought that only someone close to the child, in this case his father, would be capable of treating the child.

Both Little Hans and the young patient referred to by English and Pearson had been exposed to frightening experiences connected with the animals that subsequently became their phobic objects. The psychoanalytic view deemphasizes such experiences, reasoning that they are likely to produce phobias only if a child is vulnerable by virtue of being in the throes of an emotional conflict. Most clinicians doubt that experience alone is sufficient to cause irrational fears that are permanent enough to merit the clinical des-

ignation of phobia. Very different points of view are expressed in the two selections which follow. However, when we take into account that phobias often continue beyond the time of their psychic need, the concepts and approaches explored in these two readings take on relevance for psychoanalytic propositions that assume children do not have to learn how *to be anxious, but may learn* when *to be anxious.*

Not only does the frequency of fears and phobias vary with age, but their content and mode of expression vary with development. Jersild (1933, 1935a), in his extensive surveys of the external manifestations of childhood fears, reports that, until school age, children's fears tend to be of concrete objects, whereas with further development, fears become focused on anticipated and imaginary dangers. Newborn babies appear to be easily frightened by intense, abrupt sensory stimuli and loss of physical support. Toward the second half of the first year of life, the fear of strangers and other unfamiliar objects assumes precedence. Toddlers are afraid of specific, concrete objects such as animals, while older preschool-age children frequently appear to be concerned about the dark. With increasing development, fears are focused more on anticipated imaginary dangers such as kidnappers, burglars, pain, or physical harm. The mode of expression of the anxiety changes with development from the infant's global body response of organismic distress to the specific fear and panic reactions with which all adults are familiar.

Irrational fears appear in a wide variety of different character structures and in personality contexts ranging from the well integrated to the profoundly psychotic. Just as there are various sources and types of irrational fears, the parents' reactions and involvements with their child's fears may significantly shape the course and nature of these fears.

Childhood is a time of life when the human being is haunted by numerous fears. He is little, weak, and helpless, and the world in which he lives is filled with many objects and situations that can really do him harm. In fact, parents have to spend considerable time warning the child of objects and situations which, however attractive they are to him, are really full of deadly peril. The busy street, fire, sharp knives, sparkling broken glass, electric-light sockets, electric fans, and other appliances—all are fraught with real danger of bodily harm to the child, against which he must be protected until he learns how to protect himself. In addition to these real dangers (which interestingly enough the child often seems to disparage), the world of every child is haunted with unreasonable fears.

He is overafraid of falling, of physical punishment, of accidents and injuries, of dying; he is afraid of rough games, bad people, magic, giants, corpses; of the dark; of being alone; of strange places and persons, deformities, lights and shadows; of strange noises, scary stories and movies; of ghosts, goblins, bogeymen; of birds, insects (harmless or otherwise); of multitudinous objects and situations which in reality either could cause him no injury or are not at all likely to do so.

Jersild et al. (1933, 1935a, 1935b) in their exhaustive study of the subject fround that only 19 of 400 children (comprising 25 boys and 25 girls at each age level between the ages of five and 12) admitted having no fears. The remainder of the 400 admitted one fear and often several. Three-year-olds admitted an average of 5.5 fears; four-year-olds, 6.3; five-year-olds, 4.3; and six-year-olds, 3.2 fears each. Boys of all ages were more commonly afraid of bodily injury, and girls were afraid of the dark, solitude, and strange sights and noises.

The unreality of these fears (for what sensible child could really be afraid of a butterfly, or of the motes floating in a sunbeam, either of which send certain sensible and intelligent children we have seen into a state of severe panic) indicates that they are not really fears but phobias. What is the mechanism of the phobia?

In the *phobia* the child is conscious of a certain feeling tone which we call fear, and he ascribes the feeling tone to the presence of the phobic object or to the dread lest the phobic object become present. No amount of sensible reassurance, even by an adult whom he loves and trusts, can reduce the feeling of panic or can change his assertion that the phobic object is the cause. In order to discuss the reasons for this compulsive type of reaction and the mechanism by which such phobias occur we will refer to a four-year-old girl who had a pronounced phobia of dogs. If one appeared three blocks away she became panic-stricken and rushed into the house or clung to her mother screaming. It made no difference whether the dog was large or small, friendly or hostile, good-natured or vicious; its appearance produced an anxiety attack. This fear of dogs did not follow any attack or injury by one, but began suddenly. When she was convalescing from an attack of pneumonia, she suffered a night terror. In the early hours of the morning she began to scream and did not seem to recognize any person in the room. When her father came toward her she shouted for him to go away. When her mother asked what the matter was, she said there was a dog under her mother's bed. When the father again approached her, she screamed, "Go away. You're a dog." After some little time her terror subsided and she fell asleep quietly. On waking the next morning she was perfectly calm, but from that day on her fear of dogs was present.

What happened to this little girl? She was sexually attracted to her father and as a result was jealous and antagonistic toward the mother who she loved also. She had the wish to destroy the mother and rid herself of her by biting her to pieces. During her severe illness she had received a great deal of very pleasant care, affection, and attention from the mother, to which she responded with love. But she had also received increased care and kindness from the father and some actual physical handling which had increased her sexual attraction to him. The increased desire for the father in turn increased her hostility to the mother. She thinks, "If I were alone with father he would give me all the attention he now does plus all the attention mother gives. So why not plan to get rid of mother altogether?" But the little girl relishes the attention and kindness she gets from her mother. If she got rid of her these would cease. How can she get rid of the mother and keep her at the same time? The problem is too complicated for her immature ego to solve.

Why is this problem impossible to solve, when it is a problem that every human being has to find a solution for, and for which the majority of children do find a satisfactory one? Most children are not exposed to the increase in feeling that was brought about in this little girl by her need for nursing care during her illness. Also, before she took sick she learned that her mother and father were not a united couple. They were superficially on good terms, but the mother was being induced by a former lover (whom she still loved) to leave her husband. On Sundays the mother refused to go with the father to visit his relatives. The father went and took the children; the child realized that this separation on Sundays and holidays was not a matter-of-fact occurrence but resulted from a difference of opinion. It was as if the mother were saying, "I can't get along with your father, let him go his way and I will go mine." At her grandparents' she heard much malicious gossip against the mother, with the constant theme that the father should not have married her and that the mother was not really interested in the father.

The mother stayed with the father for the children's sake and occasionally was troubled by conscious ideas of getting rid of the children. These ideas appeared more frequently in her dreams, indicating that she had a great but unconscious desire to get rid of them. There is no question that the child could sense this underlying feeling since, being largely conscious, it expressed itself in the mother's daily handling of the child. The child then felt somewhat as follows: "She is my mother but it is all right for me to want to get rid of her because she doesn't like me anyway and she really wants to leave father. He would be happier if she did leave. My grandmother and aunts all think so. Surely I would make a better wife for him than mother does and with me he would be much happier."

The child was thus all prepared for the possibility that her desire would come true; that is, she was certain that her wishes were magical and that in a short time they would act, the mother would disappear, and she would be completely happy. She took sick, and she noticed that her mother was greatly concerned, that she did everything possible for her, and that she seemed worried about the illness. (It is to be assumed that the mother would be more anxious than usual because she would feel guilty about the possible fulfillment of her own unconscious wishes to get rid of the child.) This whole situation confused the little girl. She now thought, "I thought my mother hated me as I hated her, but now I find she loves me and tries to make me happy. I must have been mistaken. How could I ever have had such bad thoughts about my dear mother? Perhaps this illness itself and all the discomfort I am suffering are a punishment sent on me for my wickedness. But I still have these bad thoughts of wanting to get rid of mother every time father is nice to me. I have wanted to bite my kind mother at these times. I must be a dog. Perhaps mother is a dog too. Perhaps if she knew what I thought about her she would bite me. I wish I were a dog. Dogs can do all kinds of bad things, things that little girls are forbidden to do. If I were a dog and father were a dog we could do as we liked and then it wouldn't matter about mother. Mother likes dogs. Perhaps father is really a dog part of the day. (It is easy to see here how closely such ideas approach the superstition of the werewolf.) Perhaps mother is a dog part of the day. If they were both dogs I could stay away from them and then would not be so uncomfortable. My father really is a dog." And so, the dog phobia begins.

We do not mean that this little girl thought this all out consciously. We mean that, if her feelings were translated into concepts, the concepts would follow the line stated above. Anyone who knows children knows how frequently they play they are animals. If the adult joins in the game and pretends he is a dog or bear, and if the game becomes too exciting, one can observe the pleasure changing to a thrill and the thrill to a panic, as if the adult were rapidly transformed into the animal he is portraying. The pretense from the child's point of view ceases to be a pretense, and the child suddenly loses all perspective of reality. The child enjoys pretending to be an animal because he admires the animal's courage, skill, power, and freedom from cultural restrictions.

In our opinion, the closer the dread of the phobic object (in this case the dog) approaches a reality dread (in this instance, dogs really may bite or hurt a child), the less serious is the phobia. We have observed instances where the phobic object was something that did not exist in reality–such as a strange dinosaurlike animal–and in those instances the child was very sick emotionally. In all instances the choice of phobic object depends on an accidental concatenation of circumstances (in the case cited above, on the fact that the mother liked dogs) but the formation of the phobia is a result of the projection of the child's insoluble emotional conflict and has nothing to do with the phobic object itself.

This choice of phobic object is important, for both physicians and parents are often misled in regarding the phobic object as of great importance. We are thinking now of the number of instances where parents are certain that the cause of the child's anxiety is a movie he saw, a frightening story he read or heard, perhaps over the radio or on the television. We remember one little girl who developed an acute panic during the movie of *Jack and the Beanstalk.* The parents blamed the movie. Actually the movie would have had no effect on the child whatsoever if she had not been in the throes of an insoluble emotional conflict about her mingled love and hatred of her mother. Often in therapy with a child who has such an idea, it is difficult to get him to realize that his difficulties lie in his feelings about his parents and are not the result of seeing a frightening picture.

All little children have phobias. They disappear when the child has solved his particular emotional conflict. We remember one child who solved his most dramatically. He got out of bed in the middle of the night, shot the bear that troubled him, and was no longer troubled by a phobia of bears. In reality he had apparently acquired enough courage to admit and play out his hatred of his father. These phobias are not prognostically serious but are what Freud calls "the normal neurosis of childhood." They become serious only if circumstances make the child's Oedipus problem insoluble for him. In the case cited above, the insolubility of the problem lay in the fact that the parents had a real marital difficulty and so could not furnish the security of a stable home in which the child is compelled to work through his conflicting feelings to a satisfactory solution. The Oedipus situation was made insoluble by a traumatic experience. It is interesting–although Freud does not make any reference to its importance–that in the first case report in which a child's phobia was analyzed, (1909) the parents of the little boy later separated. Obviously if the separation took place, they had a marital problem at the time of the boy's phobia. Also, in Freud's case of the man who had the recurrent dream of the seven wolves (1918) and who suffered during his childhood from numerous phobias, being particularly panic-stricken by the picture of a wolf in a storybook, there had been definite traumatic experiences: the sight of parental intercourse (the most traumatic of all), the absence of the parents, the seduction by the older sister, and the quarreling between the servants.

The prognosis of the usual phobias of childhood is good. The child grows out of them. Reich (1925) points out that the development of a phobia is a sign that the ego is too weak to control the libidinal strivings. It really implies a splitting of the personality. Sometimes, perhaps always, this splitting is overcome by the accentuation of certain personality traits, which accentuation acts by unifying the personality, and this strengthens the ego. However, the unification may take place at the expense of further repression. This probably takes place with the resolution of all the phobias of childhood and if not too marked does not have a serious later effect; this combination results if the child has not had too many or too severe traumatic experiences. If there have been too many traumatic experiences or if they have been too severe, the phobia may disappear but the healing personality formation will show very serious scars of inhibitions, accentuated repressions, and regressions. Such a personality is predisposed to a breakdown later in life, as occurred in Freud's Wolf Man.

All the phobias of childhood merit consideration, if not necessarily treatment, since they indicate that the child is having difficulty in coming to terms with his inner strivings. It is not sufficient to pass them by with the light statement that he will grow out of them.

CONDITIONED EMOTIONAL REACTIONS

JOHN B. WATSON AND ROSALIE RAYNOR

Following in the tradition of Thorndike's (1911) and Pavlov's (1928a) classical efforts to apply experimental techniques to the study of behavior, Watson is frequently credited with ushering in the modern era of child psychology. Watson discarded introspection, a favorite method of psychological investigation at the time, and considered infants and young children valid subjects for psychological experimentaion. He employed the technique of conditioning and championed a behavioristic approach to psychology and child rearing (Watson, 1919, 1928). As a consequence, many of today's adults were raised under the influence of Watson's ideas about behaviorism.

Reprinted here in its entirety is Watson and Raynor's famous experiment with Albert. Peripheral aspects of their report highlight the contrast in orientation in 1920 with ideas that are rarely questioned today. For instance, compare Spitz's (1945, 1947) and Bowlby's (1961) statements in this volume with Watson and Raynor's remarks about "sheltered environment of the hospital," contrasted with "rough and tumble of the home." Also, from the perspective of modern thinking about experimental design, their statement that they had to remove the baby's thumb from his mouth before a conditioned response could be obtained, neglects the important variable introduced by removing the baby's thumb from his mouth.

Responses like Albert's were not universally observed in all infant subjects; some babies responded to the loud noise by turning toward the direction of the noise and scowling as they continued to play with the animal.

Four years after Watson and Raynor's report was published, M. C. Jones (1924) demonstrated that another infant who, like Albert, had been conditioned to fear furry objects, could be relieved of the fear by means of social imitation and direct reconditioning. These two experiments provide a background for the recent recrudescence of interest in conceptualizing psychopathology and psychotherapy in learning-behavioral theory terms and in applying treatment approaches employing these ideas across wide range of symptomatic behaviors (Wolpe, 1958; Eysenck, 1968; Rachman and Costello, 1961).

Reprinted from *Journal of Experimental Psychology,* 3 (1), 1920, pp. 1–14.

In recent literature, various speculations have been entered into concerning the possibility of conditioning various types of emotional response, but direct experimental evidence in support of such a view has been lacking. If the theory advanced by Watson and Morgan (1917) to the effect that in infancy the original emotional reaction patterns are few, consisting, so far as observed, of fear, rage, and love, then there must be some simple method by means of which the range of stimuli which can call out these emotions and their compounds is greatly increased. Otherwise, complexity in adult response could not be accounted for. These authors, without adequate experimental evidence, advanced the view that this range was increased by means of conditioned reflex factors. It was suggested there that the early home life of the child furnishes a laboratory situation for establishing conditioned emotional responses. The present authors have recently put the whole matter to an experimental test.

Experimental work has been done so far on only one child, Albert B. This infant was reared almost from birth in a hospital environment; his mother was a wet nurse in the Harriet Lane Home for Invalid Children. Albert's life was normal: he was healthy from birth and one of the best developed youngsters ever brought to the hospital, weighing twenty-one pounds at nine months of age. He was on the whole stolid and unemotional. His stability was one of the principal reasons for using him as a subject in this test. We felt that we could do him relatively little harm by carrying out such experiments as those outlined below.

At approximately nine months of age we ran him through the emotional tests that have become a part of our regular routine in determining whether fear reactions can be called out by other stimuli than sharp noises and the sudden removal of support. Tests of this type have been described by the senior author in another place (1919). In brief, the infant was confronted suddenly, and for the first time, successively with a white rat, a rabbit, a dog, a monkey, with masks with and without hair, cotton wool, burning newspapers, etc. A permanent record of Albert's reactions to these objects and situations has been preserved in a motion picture study. Manipulation was the most usual reaction called out. *At no time did this infant ever show fear in any situation.* These experimental records were confirmed by the casual observations of the mother and hospital attendants. No one had ever seen him in a state of fear and rage. The infant practically never cried.

Up to approximately nine months of age we had not tested him with loud sounds. The test to determine whether a fear reaction could be called out by a loud sound was made when he was eight months, twenty-six days of age. The sound was that made by striking a hammer upon a suspended steel bar four feet in length and three-fourths of an inch in diameter. The laboratory notes are as follows:

One of the two experimenters caused the child to turn its head and fixate her moving hand; the other, stationed back of the child, struck the steel bar a sharp blow. The child started violently, his breathing was checked and the arms were raised in a characteristic manner. On the second stimulation the same thing occurred, and in addition the lips began to pucker and tremble. On the third stimulation the child broke into a sudden crying fit. This is the first time an emotional situation in the laboratory has produced any fear or even crying in Albert.

We had expected just these results on account of our work with other infants brought up under similar conditions. It is worth while to call attention to the fact that removal of support (dropping and jerking the blanket upon which the infant was lying) was tried exhaustively upon this infant on the same occasion. It was not effective in younger children. At what age such stimuli lose their potency in producing fear is not known. Nor is it known whether less placid children ever lose their fear of them. This probably depends upon the training the child gets. It is well known that children eagerly run to be tossed into the air and caught. On the other hand, it is equally well known that, in the adult, fear responses are called out quite clearly by the sudden removal of support, if the individual is walking across a bridge, walking out upon a beam, etc. There is a wide field of study here which is aside from our present point.

The sound stimulus, thus, at nine months of age, gives us the means of testing several important factors. I. Can we condition fear of an animal, e.g., a white rat, by visually presenting it and simultaneously striking a steel bar? II. If such a conditioned emotional response can be established, will there be a transfer to other animals or other objects? III. What is the effect of time upon such conditioned emotional responses? IV. If, after a reasonable period, such emotional responses have not died out, what laboratory methods can be devised for their removal?

I. *The establishment of conditioned emotional responses.*—At first there was considerable hesitation upon our part in making the attempt to set up fear reactions experimentally. A certain responsibility attaches to such a procedure. We decided finally to make the attempt, comforting ourselves by the reflection that such attachments would arise anyway as soon as the child left the sheltered environment of the nursery for the rough and tumble of the home. We did not begin this work until Albert was eleven months, three days of age. Before attempting to set up a conditioned response we, as before, put him through all of the regular emotional tests. *Not the slightest sign of a fear response was obtained in any situation.*

The steps taken to condition emotional responses are shown in our laboratory notes.

11 Months 3 Days

1. White rat suddenly taken from the basket and presented to Albert. He began to reach for rat with left hand. Just as his hand touched the animal the bar was struck immediately behind his head. The infant jumped violently and fell forward, burying his face in the mattress. He did not cry, however.

2. Just as the right hand touched the rat the bar was again struck. Again the infant jumped violently, fell forward and began to whimper.

In order not to disturb the child too seriously no further tests were given for one week.

11 Months 10 Days

1. Rat presented suddenly without sound. There was steady fixation but no tendency at first to reach for it. The rat was then placed nearer, whereupon tentative reaching movements began with the right hand. When the rat nosed the infant's left hand, the hand was immediately withdrawn. He started to reach for the head of the animal with the forefinger of the left hand, but withdrew it suddenly before contact. It is thus seen that the two joint stimulations given the previous week were not without effect. He was tested with his blocks immediately afterwards to see if they shared in the process of conditioning. He began immediately to pick them up, dropping them, pounding them, etc. In the remainder of the tests the blocks were given frequently to quiet him and to test his general emotional state. They were always removed from sight when the process of conditioning was under way.

2. Joint stimulation with rat and sound. Started, then fell over immediately to right side. No crying.

3. Joint stimulation. Fell to right side and rested upon hands, with head turned away from rat. No crying.

4. Joint stimulation. Same reaction.

5. Rat suddenly presented alone. Puckered face, whimpered and withdrew body sharply to the left.

6. Joint stimulation. Fell over immediately to right side and began to whimper.

7. Joint stimulation. Started violently and cried, but did not fall over.

8. Rat alone. *The instant the rat was shown the baby began to cry. Almost instantly he turned sharply to the left, fell over on left side, raised himself on all fours and began to crawl away so rapidly that he was caught with difficulty before reaching the edge of the table.*

This was as convincing a case of a completely conditioned fear response as could have been theoretically pictured. In all, seven joint stimulations were given to bring about the complete reaction. It is not unlikely had the sound been of greater intensity or of a more complex clang character that the number of joint stimulations might have been materially reduced. Experiments designed to define the nature of the sounds that will serve best as emotional stimuli are under way.

II. *When a conditioned emotional response has been established for one object, is there a transfer?*—Five days later Albert was again back into the laboratory and tested as follows:

11 Months 15 Days

1. Tested first with blocks. He reached readily for them, playing with them as usual. This shows that there has been no general transfer to the room, table, blocks, etc.

2. Rat alone. Whimpered immediately, withdrew right hand and turned head and trunk away.

3. Blocks again offered. Played readily with them, smiling and gurgling.

4. Rat alone. Leaned over to the left side as far away from the rat as possible, then fell over, getting up on all fours and scurrying away as rapidly as possible.

5. Blocks again offered. Reached immediately for them, smiling and laughing as before.

The above preliminary test shows that the conditoned response to the rat had carried over completely for the five days in which no tests were given. The question as to whether or not there is a transfer was next taken up.

6. Rabbit alone. The rabbit was suddenly placed on the mattress in front of him. The reaction was pronounced. Negative responses began at once. He leaned as far away from the animal as possible, whimpered, then burst into tears. When the rabbit was placed in contact with him he

buried his face in the mattress, then got up on all fours and crawled away, crying as he went. This was a most convincing test.

7. The blocks were next given him, after an interval. He played with them as before. It was observed by four people that he played far more energetically with them than ever before. The blocks were raised high over his head and slammed down with a great deal of force.

8. Dog alone. The dog did not produce as violent a reaction as the rabbit. The moment fixation occurred the child shrank back and as the animal came nearer he attempted to get on all fours but did not cry at first. As soon as the dog passed out of his range of vision he became quiet. The dog was then made to approach the infant's head (he was lying down at the moment). Albert straightened up immediately, fell over to the opposite side and turned his head away. He then began to cry.

9. The blocks were again presented. He began immediately to play with them.

10. Fur coat (seal). Withdrew immediately to the left side and began to fret. Coat put close to him on the left side, he turned immediately, began to cry and tried to crawl away on all fours.

11. Cotton wool. The wool was presented in a paper package. At the end the cotton was not covered by the paper. It was placed first at his feet. He kicked it away but did not touch it with his hands. When his hand was laid on the wool he immediately withdrew it but did not show the shock that the animals or fur coat produced in him. He then began to play with the paper, avoiding contact with the wool itself. He finally, under the impulse of the manipulative instinct, lost some of his negativism to the wool.

12. Just in play W. put his head down to see if Albert would play with his hair. Albert was completely negative. Two other observers did the same thing. He began immediately to play with their hair. W. then brought the Santa Claus mask and presented it to Albert. He was again pronouncedly negative.

11 Months 20 Days

1. Blocks alone. Played with them as usual.

2. Rat alone. Withdrawal of the whole body, bending over to left side, no crying. Fixation and following with eyes. The response was much less marked than on first presentation the previous week. It was thought best to freshen up the reaction by another joint stimulation.

3. Just as the rat was placed on his hand the rod was struck. Reaction violent.

4. Rat alone. Fell over at once to left side. Reaction practically as strong as on former occasion but no crying.

5. Rat alone. Fell over to left side, got up on all fours and started to crawl away. On this occasion there was no crying, but strange to say, as he started away he began to gurgle and coo, even while leaning far over to the left side to avoid the rat.

6. Rabbit alone. Leaned over to left side as far as possible. Did not fall over. Began to whimper but reaction not so violent as on former occasions.

7. Blocks again offered. He reached for them immediately and began to play.

All of the tests so far discussed were carried out upon a table supplied with a mattress, located in a small, well-lighted dark-room. We wished to test next whether conditioned fear responses so set up would appear if the situation were markedly altered. We thought it best before making this test to freshen the reaction both to the rabbit and to the dog by showing them at the moment the steel bar was struck. It will be recalled that this was the first time any effort had been made to directly condition response to the dog and rabbit. The experimental notes are as follows:

8. The rabbit at first was given alone. The reaction was exactly as given in test (6) above. When the rabbit was left on Albert's knees for a long time he began tentatively to reach out and manipulate its fur with forefingers. While doing this the steel rod was struck. A violent fear reaction resulted.

9. Rabbit alone. Reaction wholly similar to that on trial (6) above.

10. Rabbit alone. Started immediately to whimper, holding hands far up, but did not cry. Conflicting tendency to manipulate very evident.

11. Dog alone. Began to whimper, shaking head from side to side, holding hands as far away from the animal as possible.

12. Dog and sound. The rod was struck just as the animal touched him. A violent negative reaction appeared. He began to whimper, turned to one side, fell over and started to get up on all fours.

13. Blocks. Played with them immediately and readily.

On this same day and immediately after the above experiment Albert was taken into the large well-lighted lecture room belonging to the laboratory. He was placed on a table in the center of the room immediately under the skylight. Four people were present. The situation was thus very different from that which obtained in the small dark room.

1. Rat alone. No sudden fear reaction appeared at first. The hands,

however, were held up and away from the animal. No positive manipulatory reactions appeared.

2. Rabbit alone. Fear reaction slight. Turned to left and kept face away from the animal but the reaction was never pronounced.

3. Dog alone. Turned away but did not fall over. Cried. Hands moved as far away from the animal as possible. Whimpered as long as the dog was present.

4. Rat alone. Slight negative reaction.

5. Rat and sound. It was thought best to freshen the reaction to the rat. The sound was given just as the rat was presented. Albert jumped violently but did not cry.

6. Rat alone. At first he did not show any negative reaction. When rat was placed nearer he began to show negative reaction by drawing back his body, raising his hands, whimpering, etc.

7. Blocks. Played with them immediately.

8. Rat alone. Pronounced withdrawal of body and whimpering.

9. Blocks. Played with them as before.

10. Rabbit alone. Pronounced reaction. Whimpered with arms held high, fell over backward and had to be caught.

11. Dog alone. At first the dog did not produce the pronounced reaction. The hands were held high over the head, breathing was checked, but there was no crying. Just at this moment the dog, which had not barked before, barked three time loudly when only about six inches from the baby's face. Albert immediately fell over and broke into a wail that continued until the dog was removed. The sudden barking of the hitherto quiet dog produced a marked fear response in the adult observers!

From the above results it would seem that emotional transfers do take place. Furthermore it would seem that the number of transfers resulting from an experimentally produced conditioned emotional reaction may be very large. In our observations we had no means of testing the complete number of transfers which may have resulted.

III. *The effect of time upon conditioned emotional responses.*—We have already shown that the conditioned emotional response will continue for a period of one week. It was desired to make the time test longer. In view of the imminence of Albert's departure from the hospital we could not make the interval longer than one month. Accordingly no further emotional experimentation was entered into for thirty-one days after the above test. During the month, however, Albert was brought weekly to the laboratory for tests upon right and left-handedness, imitation, general development, etc. No emotional tests whatever were given and during the whole month his regular nursery routine was maintained in the Harriet Lane Home. The notes on the test given at the end of this period are as follows:

1 Year 21 Days

1. Santa Claus mask. Withdrawal, gurgling, then slapped at it without touching. When his hand was forced to touch it, he whimpered and cried. His hand was forced to touch it two more times. He whimpered and cried on both tests. He finally cried at the mere visual stimulus of the mask.

2. Fur coat. Wrinkled his nose and withdrew both hands, drew back his whole body and began to whimper as the coat was put nearer. Again there was the strife between withdrawal and the tendency to manipulate. Reached tentatively with left hand but drew back before contact had been made. In moving his body to one side his hand accidentally touched the coat. He began to cry at once, nodding his head in a very peculiar manner (this reaction was an entirely new one). Both hands were withdrawn as far as possible from the coat. The coat was then laid on his lap and he continued nodding his head and whimpering, withdrawing his body as far as possible, pushing the while at the coat with his feet but never touching it with his hands.

3. Fur coat. The coat was taken out of his sight and presented again at the end of a minute. He began immediately to fret, withdrawing his body and nodding his head as before.

4. Blocks. He began to play with them as usual.

5. The rat. He allowed the rat to crawl towards him without withdrawing. He sat very still and fixated it intently. Rat then touched his hand. Albert withdrew it immediately, then leaned back as far as possible but did not cry. When the rat was placed on his arm he withdrew his body and began to fret, nodding his head. The rat was then allowed to crawl against his chest. He first began to fret and then covered his eyes with both hands.

6. Blocks. Reaction normal.

7. The rabbit. The animal was placed directly in front of him. It was very quiet. Albert showed no avoiding reactions at first. After a few seconds he puckered up his face, began to nod his head and to look intently at the experimenter. He next began to push the rabbit away with his feet, withdrawing his body at the same time. Then as the rabbit came nearer he began pulling his feet away, nodding his head, and wailing "da da".

After about a minute he reached out tentatively and slowly and touched the rabbit's ear with his right hand, finally manipulating it. The rabbit was again placed in his lap. Again he began to fret and withdrew his hands. He reached out tentatively with his left hand and touched the animal, shuddered and withdrew the whole body. The experimenter then took hold of his left hand and laid it on the rabbit's back. Albert immediately withdrew his hand and began to suck his thumb. Again the rabbit was laid in his lap. He began to cry, covering his face with both hands.

8. Dog. The dog was very active. Albert fixated it intensely for a few seconds, sitting very still. He began to cry but did not fall over backwards as on his last contact with the dog. When the dog was pushed closer to him he at first sat motionless, then began to cry, putting both hands over his face.

These experiments would seem to show conclusively that directly conditioned emotional responses as well as those conditioned by transfer persist, although with a certain loss in intensity of the reaction, for a longer period than one month. Our view is that they persist and modify personality throughout life. It should be recalled again that Albert was of an extremely phlegmatic type. Had he been emotionally unstable, probably both the directly conditioned response and those transferred would have persisted through the month unchanged in form.

IV. "Detachment" or removal of conditioned emotional responses.— Unfortunately Albert was taken from the hospital the day the above tests were made. Hence the opportunity of building up an experimental technique by means of which we could remove the conditioned emotional responses was denied us. Our own view, expressed above, which is possibly not very well grounded, is that these responses in the home environment are likely to persist indefinitely, unless an accidental method for removing them is hit upon. The importance of establishing some method must be apparent to all. Had the opportunity been at hand, we should have tried out several methods, some of which we may mention. (1) Constantly confronting the child with those stimuli which called out the responses, in the hopes that habituation would come in corresponding to "fatigue" of reflex when differential reactions are to be set up. (2) By trying to "recondition" by showing objects calling out fear responses (visual) and simultaneously stimulating the erogenous zones (tactual). We should try first the lips, then the nipples and as a final resort the sex organs. (3) By trying to "recondition" by feeding the subject candy or other food just as the animal is shown. This method calls for the food control of the subject. (4) By building up "constructive" activities around the object by imitation and by putting the hand through the motions of manipulation. At this age imitation of overt motor activity is strong, as our present but unpublished experimentation has shown.

Incidental Observations

(a) Thumb sucking as a compensatory device for blocking fear and noxious stimuli.—During the course of these experiments, especially in the final test, it was noticed that whenever Albert was on the verge of tears or emotionally upset generally he would continually thrust his thumb into his mouth. The moment the hand reached the mouth he became impervious to the stimuli producing fear. Again and again, while the motion pictures were being made at the end of the thirty-day rest period, we had to remove the thumb from his mouth before the conditioned response could be obtained. This method of blocking noxious and emotional stimuli (fear and rage) through erogenous stimulation seems to persist from birth onward. Very often in our experiments upon the work adders with infants under ten days of age, the same reaction appeared. When at work upon the adders, both of the infants arms are under slight restraint. Often rage appears. They begin to cry, thrashing their arms and legs about. If the finger gets into the mouth, crying ceases at once. The organism thus apparently from birth, when under the influence of love stimuli, is blocked to all others. [1] This resort to sex stimulation when under the influence of noxious and emotional situations, or when the individual is restless and idle, persists through adolescent and adult life. Albert, at any rate, did not resort to thumb sucking except in the presence of such stimuli. Thumb sucking could immediately be checked by offering him his blocks. These invariably called out active manipulating instincts. It is worth while here to call attention to the fact that Freud's conception of the stimulation of erogenous zones as being the expression of an original "pleasure" seeking principle may be turned about and possibly better described as a compensatory (and often conditioned) device for the blockage of noxious and fear and rage producing stimuli.

[1] The stimulus to love in infants according to our view is stroking of the skin, lips, nipples and sex organs, patting and rocking, picking up, etc. Patting and rocking (when not conditioned) are probably equivalent to actual stimulation of sex organs. In adults of course, as every lover knows, vision, audition and olfaction soon become conditioned by joint stimulation with contact and kinaesthetic stimuli.

(b) Equal primacy of fear, love and possibly rage.—While in general the results of our experiment offer no particular points of conflict with Freudian concepts, one fact out of harmony with them should be emphasized. According to proper Freudians, sex (or in our terminology, love) is the principal emotion in which conditioned responses arise which later limit and distort personality. We wish to take sharp issue with this view on the basis of the experimental evidence we have gathered. Fear is as primal a factor as love in influencing personality. Fear does not gather its potency in any derived manner from love. It belongs to the original and inherited nature of man. Probably the same may be true of rage, although at present we are not so sure of this.

The Freudians, twenty years from now, unless their hypotheses change, when they come to analyze Albert's fear of a sealskin coat—assuming that he comes to analysis at that age—will probably tease from him the recital of a dream which, upon their analysis, will show that Albert at three years of age attempted to play with the pubic hair of the mother and was scolded violently for it. (We are by no means denying that this might in some other case condition it.) If the analyst has sufficiently prepared Albert to accept such a dream when found as an explanation of his avoiding tendencies, and if the analyst has the authority and personality to put it over, Albert may be fully convinced that the dream was a true revealer of the factors which brought about the fear.

It is probable that many of the phobias in psychopathology are true conditioned emotional reactions either of the direct or the transferred type. One may possibly have to believe that such persistence of early conditioned responses will be found only in persons who are constitutionally inferior. Our argument is meant to be constructive. Emotional disturbances in adults cannot be traced back to sex alone. They must be retraced along at least three collateral lines—to conditioned and transferred responses set up in infancy and early youth in all three of the fundamental human emotions.

THE ETIOLOGY AND TREATMENT OF CHILDREN'S PHOBIAS: A REVIEW

STANLEY RACHMAN AND CHARLES G. COSTELLO

Beginning with Watson and Raynor's report (1920) and M. C. Jones's (1924) classical demonstrations that fears can be conditioned and extinguished, learning theory has made a variety of contributions to the treatment of emotional disturbances. These range from Dollard and Miller's (1950) attempt to reconceptualize dynamic psychotherapy in learning theory terms, Mowrer's (1953) moral approach to treatment, and, most recently, to the symptom-oriented mechanistic attempts to alter behavior ostensibly rooted in the nervous system. Eysenck (1960a) asserts that such use of behavior should be designated as behavioral therapy to distinguish it from psychotherapy, which employs psychological methods. Eysenck makes it abundantly clear that systematic symptom-oriented efforts to induce unlearning, inhibition, and extinction of maladaptive behavior by means of desensitization, operant conditioning, aversive conditioning, avoidance learning, reciprocal inhibition, negative practice, and similar approaches are not based on the premise that difficulties such as anxiety-tension states, phobias, enuresis, tics, and sexual disorders may have unconscious determinants. He asserts that symptoms are learned habits without underlying neurotic conflicts, so that if the sympton is extinguished, the neurosis is eliminated.

Rachman and Costello introduce their article on the evidence and theories derived from behavioral therapy of phobias, with a polemic on the psychoanalytic view of childhood phobias. In contrast to English and Pearson's (1963) favorable articulation of a psychoanalytically oriented perspective on childhood phobias, Rachman and Costello present the psychoanalytic view in the worst possible light. Supplementing this is their quotation of Ellis's devastating appraisal of the scientific status of psychoanalysis with no mention of any of the more sober and balanced assessments of the scientific status of psychoanalysis such as those of Benjamin (1959), Escalona (1952a), Guttman (1965), Harrison (1970), Hartmann (1958a), Kris (1947b), Kubie (1960), Lustman (1963), Rapaport (1960), Richfield (1954), Waelder (1962), and Wallerstein (1964), among others.

Reprinted with permission from *American Journal of Psychiatry,* 118, 1961, pp. 97–105.

The authors complain that psychoanalysis is not logical. We think that the charge made against psychoanalysis more properly belongs to human nature. It is not our contention that Rachman and Costello's criticisms of psychoanalysis are invariably invalid. Rather, we feel impelled to note that their wide-swinging attack goes so far as to run the risk of missing the mark. They appear to present a choice between either psychoanalytic theory or behavioral-learning theory. At our current level, of knowledge such a choice is untenable. Deriving benefit from one theory of human behavior does not require excluding everything related to other theories of human behavior.

To fully understand human nature requires information from other frameworks as well—developmental, biological, sociocultural. Rachman and Costello seem to reject such an open-ended approach in that they take to task those psychoanalysts who include behavioral and learning theory elements in their thinking without specifically stating so. Surprisingly, they exclude Freud, whose concept of the secondary or epinosic gain of illness is such an example, while they point to Eisenberg (1957, this volume) who is one of the most articulate critics of psychoanalysis.

The burgeoning interest in the application of modern learning theories to the control of maladaptive behavior is evidenced by a rapidly increasing number of publications. See, for example, Werry and Wollersheim (1967).

The past few years have seen the establishment of two conflicting views regarding phobias in children. Most workers in this field, psychiatrists and psychologists, are influenced to a greater or lesser extent by either the psychoanalytic theory or the behavior theory in their approach to the subject of phobias. For this reason we have restricted our review primarily to these two theories.

Psychoanalytic Theory

The psychoanalytic theory of phobias derives very largely from Freud's case history of Little Hans (1909a) which was published in 1909. The essentials of the phobic theory were presented in this paper and appear to have undergone little change in the past 50 years.

The theory states that the basis for phobic disturbances is the Oedipus Complex. The child desires to possess the mother sexually and is jealous and hostile towards the father. The child fears his father because of these hostile wishes and, in particular, dreads castration. The fear of the avenging father is then projected onto some external and formerly innocuous object. The outbreak of the phobia is generally preceded by a period of privation and/or intensified sexual excitement.

This development of phobias may be analysed into the following components.

1. The child "is fixated at the oedipal or preoedipal level" (E. Klein, 1945, p. 279).

Freud (1925a) states that psychoanalysis has "often showed that animal (phobic object) was a substitute for the father, a substitute on to which the fear of the father derived from the Oedipus complex has been displaced" (p. 123).

(1a) The child has a sexual desire for the mother.

This aspect of the theory is stressed in the case of Little Hans (1909a). In a discussion on the psychogenesis of agoraphobia in childhood, Abraham (1955) illustrates Frued's theory by referring to case material: the phobic child had "an incestuous wish for sexual possession of her (the mother)" (p. 43).

(1b) The child is jealous of, and hostile to, the father.

In the discussions by Abraham mentioned above, he also makes explicit the child's hostility to the father–he had "a death wish against his father" (p. 43).

2. The child fears the father.

Freud (1940) states that "the animals which play a part in the animal-phobias of children are generally father-substitutes" (p. 82).

He also says that "the instinctual impulse subjected to repression here (in animal phobias) is a libidinal attitude to the father, coupled with a dread of him. After repression this impulse vanishes out of consciousness" (1953, p. 107).

(2a) The child has castration fears.

The anxiety experienced by the child when he is confronted by the object of his phobia is a danger signal set off by his ego and the danger which is being signalled in this way is invariably the danger of castration (1926).

And again, "the fear in zoophobia is castration anxiety on the part of the ego" (1926, p. 109).

3. The fears of the father and of castration are projected onto a neutral external object.

Castration anxiety, states Sarason et al. (1960) results in

> the displacement or projection of the dangerous connotations upon an external (previously innocuous) object or situation. After this occurs the original

castration anxiety is elicited by a different object and therefore is expressed only in a distorted form [p. 50].

In Freud's words (1926)" . . . castration anxiety is given another object and a distorted expression–namely that of being bitten by a horse . . . instead of being castrated by the father" (p. 108).

4. The onset of the phobia is often preceded by a period of privation and/or sexual excitement.

"An increase in sexual longing, fear or guilt, reactivates the oedipal or preoedipal fear of sexual injury to the mother . . ." (E. Klein, 1945 p. 279).

Freud (1909a) attaches importance to this precipitant in the Little Hans case as does Bornstein (1935) in the case of Lisa.

5. The onset of the phobia is generally preceded by an anxiety attack which is associated with the phobic object.

Freud (1926) states that "a phobia generally sets in after a first anxiety attack has been experienced in specific circumstances such as in the street or in a train or in solitude." (p. 128) Similarly, Abraham is quoted as stating that "in general, the phobic reaction to a specific object or situation becomes established only after the child has experienced an anxiety attack while interacting in some way with the particular object or situation" (Sarason et al., 1960, p. 49). The initial anxiety attack itself however is produced by castration fears. "The phobic process begins when the ego recognizes the danger of castration and consequently gives a signal of anxiety" (Sarason et al., 1960, pp. 49–50).

6. Phobias only develop in people with disturbed sexual adjustments.

Freud (1895) states that, "The main thing about the problems of the phobias seems to me to be that *when the vita sexualis is normal*–when the specific condition, a disturbance of sexual life in the sense of a deflection of the somatic from the psychical, is not fulfilled–phobias do not appear at all" (p. 134, original italics).

He says further, ". . . my theory can only be refuted when I have been shown phobias where sexual life is normal or even where there is a disturbance of it of a non-specific sort" (p. 134).

Watson and Rayner's (1920) laboratory demonstration of the development of a phobia in little Albert (see below) must bring into question five of the six elements of the psychoanalytic theory, as does the evidence discussed in the works of Wolpe (1958), Eysenck (1960a, 1960b) and H. G. Jones (1960). Point 5, however, approaches close to the learning theory account of phobias described below. The learning theory position is that the onset of the phobia is not merely preceded by an anxiety attack which is associated with the phobic object, but that the anxiety attack is generally the major cause of the phobia.

More generally, Ellis (1950) argues that

> the vague, suppositional and multi-interpretive terms in which the theoretical framework of orthodox analysis is usually stated make it almost impossible to test its concepts by normal psychological methods of investigation [p. 156].

And we may add, it also makes it almost impossible to appraise the internal consistency and logic of psychoanalytic theory—as a theory.

Ellis (1950) has criticized the unscientific nature of psychoanalysis and emphasizes the inadequacies and confusion of the theory, the unreliability of the supportive evidence, the failure to submit any part of the theory or practice of psychoanalysis to acceptable scientific test. One of Ellis's most insistent complaints is against the rampant speculation so common in psychoanalysis. As we hope to demonstrate below, one of Ellis's comments on a passage of Freud's writings seems in fact to be applicable to a large body of psychoanalytic literature. He remarks that, "the ratio of speculative statements to empirically adduced facts . . . is slightly overpowering." (p. 189)

Psychoanalytic Evidence

Clinical evidence serves a double purpose in psychoanalysis. It is used in order to construct the theory and also to support the theory. Some serious deficiencies present in psychoanalytic case material have been discussed in a critical examination of Freud's treatment of the famous Little Hans case (Wolpe and Rachman, 1960). Although the criticisms which we offer here may all be applied equally well to the Little Hans case, we have restricted our comments to other well-known case histories in order to emphasize that these flaws are the rule rather than the exception.

Elaboration

Bornstein (1935) presents an account of a girl of two years four months who developed a phobia of lying down. At one point, Bornstein writes, "She was asked directly what she really had to fear in bed. She replied with a recital of misdeeds having the character of severe self-reproach." The following is an example of what the child said, "See cup ow." Bornstein states that this means ("translated into the language of the adult") "See the cup is broken, has pain (ow) and it is my fault" (p. 97). We suggest that this is an elaboration, particularly the claim that the child felt at fault.

Later we read that the child used to masturbate by rubbing her legs together. Then, the mother reported, she stuck diapers or table napkins between her legs. Bornstein comments, "As if wishing to demonstrate that her genitalia were not 'Ow,' not damaged, that in other words she possessed a male genital" (p. 98).

A more extensive elaboration is given in an account of one of the child's dreams. The child reported the dream thus; "Opa dudu." Bornstein gives as a direct literal translation "Grandpa naughty naughty," but writes also that it "meant that her grandfather had appeared to her in a dream and had either threatened or spanked her" (p. 100). Later the dream was apparently better understood and Bornstein writes, "The little girl's favorite game before she was sick had been the 'Kuckuck game.' This consisted in hiding and then calling "Kuckuck" which the child who still spoke very imperfectly often used to pronounce "Duduck" or really almost "Dudu." The dream therefore said 'Grandfather is hiding, has gone away' " (pp. 100-101).

Further elaborations are given in connection with two incidents. (a) The grandfather on one occasion when out with the child had gone behind a tree and urinated. (b) The grandfather had taken the child's mother away for a short period in order to look after the sick grandmother. "Opa Dudu" finally means "If I am not good, mother will be taken away by grandfather." But over and above this, it expressed the wish that her grandfather would play 'Dudu' again—that is, disappear and expose his penis" (p. 101). We suggest that this also reveals a tendency toward over-elaboration.

Suggestion

Schnurmann (1949) gives an account of a girl, Sandy, who developed a dog phobia at the age of two years five months. At that time (1944) she was in the Hampstead Nursery. One night she had a nightmare: "She told the nurse a dog was in her bed." Schnurmann comments later that,

> As Sandy had up to then not shown any special interest in dogs it seems strange that in the dream the dog was invested with great significance. An explanation may be found in the following facts: "When the nursery children were taken out in a group an encounter with a dog was usually met by some kind of emotion on the part of the other children [p. 266]. The fear of dogs at night continued for the next three nights. Statements like "Out, out, out,

> doggie coming" [p. 257] were made. On the fourth night, Sandy undertook a thorough inspection of her genitais. She was deeply absorbed in this activity and did not take any notice of our presence (two therapists). The worker told her that everything was all right there and that all girls looked like that.

The next day, "On the way to the nursery some of our children started to play with a strange dog. I explained to them that he might bite if they frightened him" (p. 258). It is noteworthy that it was only from this time that the child showed signs of fear of dogs in the street. The main point, however, is that it was only after the worker had drawn the child's special attention to her genitals and after the worker had suggested that the dog might bite, that Sandy herself began to talk about biting. Two nights later Sandy said to the worker, "Bite Annie Bite" (p. 259).

There was a considerable amount of talk about biting for the remainder of the therapy which enabled the therapist to conclude that, "In the nightmare—as it became clear in Sandy's subsequent behavior and remarks—a dog was assaulting Sandy in her bed, injuring her genitals, i.e., biting off her penis" (p. 265).

It is also noteworthy that after Sandy's attention had been drawn to the "rightness" of her genitals she became quite concerned about the rest of her body and clothes—fingers, legs, coat, hat. They all became penis symbols by displacement apparently.

It is felt that, after having given the child the idea that genitals are all right (or all wrong) and also warning her that dogs bite, to regard her subsequent concern with these ideas as confirming the analysis is unsatisfactory and not convincing.

Inversions and Non-Acceptance

A common feature of psychoanalytic case reports is the refusal to accept the patient's accounts and to attach instead a reversed meaning to his testimony. The tendency is clearly illustrated in the case of Frankie, age four and a half, reported by Bornstein (1949). For example, the boy reported a dream in which he, the room and two other persons were falling down. Borstein comments, "Actually, the emphasis on 'going down' was a representation of its opposite being lifted up" (p. 206).

We feel then the psychoanalytic theory of phobias is inadequate for the following reasons: (1) The theory is complex and loosely formulated. (2) The evidence is not related clearly to the theory by means of predictions from the theory. (3) The evidence is manipulated through overelaboration and inversion to fit into the theory and sometimes the patient himself is manipulated by suggestion so that his behavior may fit into the theory.

We will now proceed to an account of an alternative theory–Behavior Theory–which has been presented to account for the development and treatment of phobias.

A Behavior Theory of Phobia

The past decade has seen the growth of a new theory of neurotic behavior which has been developed from learning theory. Expositions of the general theory are provided by Wolpe (1958), Eysenck (1960a, 1960b), H. G. Jones (1960).

The position adopted by this theory is that neurotic behavior is acquired. The process of acquisition implied in the theory is derived from Hull's system.

Wolpe (1958) defines neurotic behavior as "any persistent habit of unadaptive behavior acquired by learning in a physiologically normal organism." Anxiety is "usually the central constituent of this behavior, being invariably present in the causal situations" (p. 32).

In similar vein, Eysenck (1960a) postulates that, "neurotic symptoms are *learned patterns of behavior* which for some reason or another are *unadaptive,*" (p. 5) (original italics). Neurotic behavior patterns persist paradoxically, because they are unpleasant. Having acquired an unpleasant association and reaction to a particular stimulus or situation, the person will tend to avoid exposure to these noxious circumstances. As learned patterns of behavior can only be extinguished by repeated unreinforced evocations, the tendency to avoid the noxious situation often precludes the possibility of a spontaneous disappearance of the neurotic behavior. Furthermore, if the person does come into contact with the noxious stimulus he generally responds by withdrawing. This withdrawal is followed by a reduction in anxiety and will reinforce the avoidance behavior mentioned above. This then is what Eysenck (1960a) refers to as "the vicious circle which protects the conditioned fear response from extinction" (p. 9).

As is the case in all learned responses, neurotic reactions are subject to stimulus generalization. That is, a range of stimuli similar to the original noxious stimulus may also evoke the neurotic reaction.

It should be noted also that neurotic symptoms may under certain circumstances result "not from the learning of an unadaptive response, but from the failure to learn an adaptive response" (Jones, 1960, p. 489). An instance of this type is enuresis nocturna.

The experimental evidence which supports the behavior theory of neurosis is discussed in Wolpe (1958), Eysenck (1960a, 1960b), Jones (1960).

In terms of the behavior theory, *phobias* may be regarded as conditioned anxiety (fear) reactions.

> Any neutral stimulus, simple or complex, that happens to make an impact on an individual at about the time that a fear reaction is evoked acquires the ability to evoke fear subsequently. If the fear at the original conditioning situation is of high intensity, or if the conditioning is repeated a good many times, the conditioned fear will show the persistence that is characteristic of *neurotic* fear; and there will be generalization of fear reactions to stimuli resembling the conditioned stimulus (Wolpe and Rachman, 1960).

The experimental evidence supporting this view of phobias is discussed in Wolpe (1958) and Wolpe and Rachman (1960) and is derived from studies of the behavior of children and of animals. The classical demonstration of the development of a phobia in a child was provided by Watson and Rayner (1920). Having first ascertained that it was a neutral object, the authors presented an 11-month-old boy, Albert, with a white rat to play with. Whenever he reached for the animal the experimenters made a loud noise behind him. After only five trials, Albert began showing signs of fear in the presence of the white rat. This fear then generalized to similar stimuli such as furry objects, cotton wool, white rabbits. The phobic reactions were still present when Albert was tested four months later.

The process involved in this demonstration provides a striking illustration of the manner in which phobias develop and may be represented in this way:

1. Neutral stimulus (rat) → Approach R
2. Painful noise stimulus (UCS) → Fear (UCR)
3. Rat (CS) + noise (UCS) → Fear
4. Rat (CS) → Fear (CR)
5. Rabbit (GS^1) → Fear (GCR)
6. Cotton wool (GS^2) → Fear (GCR)

The essentials of the theory may be summarized in six statements.

1. Phobias are learned responses.
2. Phobic stimuli, simple or complex, develop when they are associated temporarily and spatially with a fear producing state of affairs.

3. Neutral stimuli which are of relevance in the fear-producing situation and/or make an impact on the person in the situation, are more likely to develop phobic qualities than weak or irrelevant stimuli.
4. Repetition of the association between the fear situation and the new phobic stimuli will strengthen the phobia.
5. Associations between high intensity fear situations and neutral stimuli are more likely to produce phobic reactions.
6. Generalization from the original phobic stimulus to stimuli of a similar nature will occur.

Each of these six statements is based on experimental evidence and would also appear to be consistent with clinical experience (Wolpe, 1958; Eysenck, 1960b). All are supported by Wolpe's experiments (1958), and evidence for specific statements is provided by Liddell (1944), Jones (1960), Watson and Rayner (1920), Eysenck (1960b) and Gantt (1944), among others. It can be legitimately argued in fact that these propositions are supported by the full weight of almost all the evidence accumulated in research on the learning process.

Behavior Therapy

The essence of Behavior Therapy is clearly deducible from the theory. If neurotic behavior is acquired (learned) it should be amenable to 'un-learning' in a manner similar to that whereby non-neurotic acquired behavior is extinguished. The two major decremental processes in learning are inhibition and extinction. Numerous therapeutic procedures based on these processes have already been developed (Wolpe, 1958; Eysenck, 1960b), and additional techniques are now under investigation. The indications are that these methods are successful in a variety of neurotic disturbances (Eysenck, 1960a, 1960b; Wolpe, 1958), but a definitive conclusion must be postponed until a properly designed and controlled experimental test has been conducted. Such an investigation admittedly poses serious and difficult practical problems, but on theoretical grounds, behavior therapy is eminently suited for such an investigation. The hypotheses and procedures are clearly defined and manipulable, and a satisfactory study can be expected to provide a relatively unambiguous answer.

Most of the case-reports available to date which deal with the treatment of children's phobias involve the use of Wolpe's "inhibitory therapy." He defines the principle of reciprocal inhibition psychotherapy:

> If a response antagonistic to anxiety can be made to occur in the presence of anxiety-evoking stimuli so that it is accompanied by a complete or partial

> suppression of the anxiety responses, the bond between these stimuli and the anxiety responses will be weakened [Wolpe, 1958, p. 71].

The method may be illustrated by referring to some actual case reports which we summarize briefly here.

> A three-year-old boy, Peter, evinced fear of white rats, rabbits, fur, cotton wool and other stimuli along this continuum. He was treated by Jones (1942b) using deconditioning methods. It was decided to work on the rabbit phobia, as this seemed to be a focus of Peter's fears. Peter was gradually introduced to contacts with a rabbit during his daily play period. He was placed in a play group with three fearless children, and the rabbit was brought into the room for short periods each day. Peter's toleration of the rabbit was gradually improved. The progressive steps observed in the process included: "rabbit in case 12 feet away tolerated . . . in case four feet away tolerated . . . close by in cage tolerated . . . free in room tolerated . . . eventually, fondling rabbit affectionately" [pp. 310–311]. Another measure employed by Jones involved the use of feeding responses. "Through the presence of the pleasant stimulus (food) whenever the rabbit was shown, the fear was eliminated gradually in favor of a positive response" [p. 313].

Using these techniques, Jones overcame not only Peter's fear of rabbits but all the associated fears. The follow-up of this case showed no resurgence of the phobia.

Lazarus and Rachman (1957) describe the treatment of a 14-year-old boy who had suffered from a fear of hospitals and ambulances for four years. The phobia had developed after the prolonged illness and suffering experienced by his mother. She had been taken from the house several times by ambulance and spent over a year in hospitals.

The boy was first trained to relax. Hierarchies of disturbing situations concerning ambulances and hospitals were then constructed, ranging from mildly upsetting to extremely upsetting items. The lowest item in the ambulance hierarchy for example, was a mental image of a derelict ambulance in a scrap-yard, and the highest item an image of sitting beside the driver in a moving ambulance. The therapist then slowly worked up the hierarchies, desensitizing each item by relaxation responses. After 10 interviews, the boy was much improved and was able to visit a hospital. Four months later he was still quite well.

The third case, reported by Lazarus (1960), deals with an eight-year-old boy who developed a fear of moving vehicles two years after having been involved in a motor accident. Initially the therapist rewarded the boy whenever he made a positive comment concerning vehicles, by giving him a piece of his favorite chocolate. By the third interview the boy was able to talk freely about all types of moving vehicles. Next a series of "accidents" with toy motor cars was demonstrated. The boy, John, was given chocolate after each accident. Later John was seated in a stationary vehicle and slow progress (with chocolate feeding reinforcements used at each point) was made until John was able to enjoy motor travel without anxiety.

Lazarus also describes the successful treatment of a case of separation anxiety and a case of dog-phobia. Case reports describing the treatment of phobias in adults are provided in Eysenck (1960b).

Reinterpretation of Psychoanalytic Cases

A further advantage of behavior theory is that is can account for and incorporate a good deal of evidence presented by psychoanalysts. We will illustrate this with several examples from the literature.

A number of psychoanalysts when discussing school phobia have stressed the importance of getting the child back to school early. Eisenberg (1958) writes, "In general, the longer the period of absence from school before therapeutic intervention is attempted the more difficult treatment becomes" (p. 713). In explanation he writes, "Left at home the patient . . . is reinforced to persist in infantile maneuvering by the 'success' of his efforts" (p. 713). This point has also been stressed by the workers at the Judge Baker Guidance Center (Coolidge, et al., 1957; Johnson, et al., 1941; Waldfogel, et al., 1957; Waldfogel, et al., 1959). No attempt is made, however, to incorporate this important aspect of therapy in the psychoanalytic theory. This therapeutic procedure is in a sense even contradictory to the theory insofar as it is symptom-oriented. This failure to account for important data by means of the theory can be added to the list of deficiencies above.

The importance of the early return to school can be accounted for by the behavior theory of phobias in the following manner:

As learned responses (including fear) can be abolished only by extinction or inhibition, no reduction of the school phobia can be expected to occur if the person is entirely isolated from the noxious situation. Furthermore, continued absence from school will certainly reinforce the phobic pattern. It will have this effect because of the reduction in school-anxiety which is produced when the person refrains from attending school. Like all learned behavior, phobic responses are strengthened by drive reduction, in this case, reduction of the anxiety drive.

Another aspect of therapy for school phobias has been stressed by some psychoanalytic writers. Klein (1945) writes:

> The child is told he must go to school every day, but does not have to stay there and does not have to attend the classroom. The child can stay in an office, assist the office staff, read or draw and can leave at any time [p. 267].

This graded approach is another aspect of therapy not in keeping with the general psychoanalytic approach and not accounted for by the theory. It is on the other hand a procedure which directly follows from the behavior theory of phobias.

Though the psychoanalytic case histories referred to in this paper are long and complex, most of the data presented are taken from the analytic sessions, and the phobic situation itself is seldom described adequately. For this reason it is not possible to give precise accounts in terms of behavior theory of the development and treatment of the phobias reported. But one or two general observations can be made.

We referred earlier in this paper to Bornstein's case of the girl who developed a phobia of lying down (1935). From the point of view of behavior theory the following points are of importance. "Training in cleanliness was begun in the sixth month. The child was held over a pot at regular hours" (p. 94). Towards the end of the first year, the child's grandmother took over the toilet training and apparently imposed severe measures. After the age of one year the child wet herself on very few occasions. One of these occasions was the day before her mother's return from an illness, when she wet herself several times. "The members of the household also thought it probable that when this happened they had said to her 'Wait until your mother hears you have wet yourself again! She won't love you any more. She will go right away again and won't want to come back' " (p. 115).

Bornstein comments,

> We believe that she could not allow herself to lie down because she was afraid that when lying down or sleeping she would be unable to control the wish to defecate in bed . . . Moreover we know of a historical factor which had connected the motif 'incontinence' with the motif 'not sitting': *After her illness with diarrhoea the child could no longer sit up* (p. 112, original italics].

Bornstein is referring here to the fact that when the child was seven-months-old she had an attack of diarrhoea which left her so weak that she could no longer sit alone.

From the point of view of behavior theory, the development of the phobia can be accounted for in the following way: Because of her severe toilet training the stimulus to urinate or defecate had become associated with anxiety. The association of defecation with lying down (at the time of her illness) resulted in the act of lying down also producing the anxiety response. The child then attempted to avoid anxiety by sitting up all the time.

Concerning the child's recovery from the phobia, the following observation is noteworthy:

> The child on one occasion refused to resume even a sitting position in bed. As was usual she was left. She soiled herself, the bed was changed and the girl asked her mother to give her a hug which she was given. Then to the mother's astonishment the girl happily lay down in bed for the first time in five weeks [pp. 109–110].

It would seem unlikely that this one association of soiling with an accepting and affectionate response was sufficient to produce a recovery. Although we are not informed whether, after this "astonishing" result, the mother altered her attitude and behavior to her child, we will assume that she used this experience in her future handling of the girl. If she continued to use affection and reassurance to dampen the child's anxiety, such a procedure would almost certainly have brought about a reduction of the phobia.

In the case of Sandy's dog phobia (Schnurmann, 1949) and Frankie's elevator phobia (Bornstein, 1949) we do not have sufficient information to give a convincing account of the development of the phobia. But we have already seen that in both cases the phobic objects were associated with fear producing stimuli. In the case of Sandy, we have the nightmare involving a dog and the therapist's warning that dogs bite. But one may be justified in asking why the child had a nightmare involving a dog in the first place. In the case of Frankie we have the nurse's threats that she would call the elevator man to teach him not to disturb people.

Regarding Sandy's and Frankie's recovery from their phobias we again do not have sufficient information. But it is of interest that Sandy frequently encountered dogs when out walking with the therapist, which would at least present an opportunity for the extinction of the fear response. Secondly Schnurmann writes that on one occasion Sandy played quite happily with a doll's pram, "I asked her whom she had covered with the blankets. She produced a dog. I said, 'A doggie.' Sandy replied, 'No pussy cat'" (p. 260). It is possible that further play with the toy dog would have produced some desensitization. Finally Sandy had played dogs with other children and the therapist, and it is of interest that the phobia ended in the following way: "When on the way to nursery school we met a dog who was on a lead. Sandy at first made a withdrawing movement, then she approached the dog hesitatingly. When another dog came into sight, Sandy walked directly towards him and barked" (pp. 260–261). Sandy responded, in other words, in a manner learned while playing at being dogs.

Conclusions

Mention has been made of May Carver Jones's (1924a, 1924b) classic studies in which she describes her attempt to develop techniques for eliminating children's fears. The significance of this early work is only now becoming recognized. She gives an account of several methods of treatment. Four of these appear to be promising, practical and in accord with present-day learning theory. They are the methods of:

1. Direct conditioning.
2. Social imitation.
3. Systematic distraction and
4. Feeding responses.

The fruitfulness of the behavior theory approach to phobias is well demonstrated if we add to Jones' list the additional new methods which have been, or could be used in overcoming children's phobias. [1]

5. Systematic desensitization (Wolpe)
6. Assertive responses (Wolpe)
7. Relaxation responses (Wolpe)
8. "Pleasant" responses in the life situation–with drug enhancement (Wolpe)

In a suggestive article by Jersild and Holmes (1935b), further possible methods for treatment of children's fears are discussed. From their survey of parent's experiences in dealing with children's fears, Jersild and Holmes suggest these techniques (among others): Prompting the child to acquire skills which will enable him to cope with the feared situation; progressive contact with, and participation in, the feared situation; verbal explanation and reassurance; practical demonstration of fearlessness.

Some of these techniques are already employed by prevailing therapies without receiving explicit acknowledgment.

[1] Naturally, many of these methods are equally applicable to the treatment of adults' phobias.

All these methods certainly provide therapists with a formidable armamentarium to begin with. What is now required is careful, thorough investigation of these methods and above all a major project to establish the degree and permanence of improvements which may be obtained by these techniques.

In the meantime, active therapists may consider conducting their own investigations of these methods when faced with children suffering from phobic conditions. Obviously the choice of the method will depend to a considerable extent on the nature of the phobia. It is worth remembering also that these methods are not mutually exclusive and it is probable that in many cases a combination of these techniques may offer the most promising approach.

SCHOOL PHOBIA

Adelaide M. Johnson, Eugene I. Falstein,
Stanislaus A. Szurek, and Margaret Svendsen

A phobia unique to childhood is the subject of this historically significant paper, noteworthy because it focuses attention on school refusal, a broad clinical category of which school phobia is but one manifestation. [1] *It also marks the initial publication reflecting Johnson's long and productive interest in parental influences on children's psychopathology (Johnson and Szurek, 1952; Giffin, Johnson, and Litin, 1954; Litin, Giffin and Johnson, 1956).*

Subsequent investigators of school refusal have agreed with the authors' emphasis on the significant role of the parents in this syndrome. Indeed, many clinicians suspect that school refusal in a mild form is a relatively frequent occurrence but does not attract professional attention because of judicious parental handling. The anxious tummy-aches experienced by many youngsters each fall on the first day of school are one example.

Johnson and her coauthors highlight three cardinal factors: (1) acute anxiety in the child, (2) an increase in the mother's anxiety, and (3) inadequate resolution of the child's early dependency on the mother. A fourth factor, not specified as such within their report but obviously prominent in their data and in the experience of most clinicians, is the mother's unresolved dependency on her own mother. In short, the mothers and the children share an anxiety about separating from one another. The presence of these factors has since been confirmed by Eisenberg (1958) and in the series of studies at the Judge Baker Guidance Center (Coolidge et al., 1957, 1962; Waldfogel et al., 1957, 1959). The Judge Baker studies have called attention also to maternal conflicts about aggression which appear to be stimulated by the child's striving for independence.

All clinical investigators emphasize the importance of early detection and intervention in school refusal. Therapeutic success is greatly enhanced by

Reprinted from *American Journal of Orthopsychiatry,* 11, 1941, pp. 702–708.

[1] This should be distinguished from truancy, which Johnson (1949) discusses in her paper on "Sanctions for Superego Lacunae in Adolescence."

diminishing the secondary gains to the child as a consequence of staying away from school.

An unresolved paradox deserving further study is the relative infrequency with which serious learning inhibitions (see section on Learning Disorders, this volume) occur in youngsters with a school refusal syndrome.

For years psychiatrists have recognized that there is a type of emotional disturbance in children, associated with great anxiety, that leads to serious absence from school. This is a deep-seated psychoneurotic disorder fairly sharply differentiated from the more frequent and common delinquent variety of school truancy. The syndrome, often referred to as "school phobia," is recognizable by the intense terror associated with being at school. The child may be absent for periods of weeks or months or years, unless treatment is instituted. The children, on fleeing from school, usually go straight home to join the mother. Eventually they refuse to leave the house. When the child is superficially questioned, he cannot verbalize what he fears, and the whole matter appears incomprehensible to parents and teachers. It seems to us that this syndrome is not a clean-cut entity, for one finds overlapping of the phobic tendencies with other neurotic patterns, such as those of an hysterical or obsessive nature.

Although this type of problem is seen fairly frequently in any child guidance clinic and can become very serious, there has been very little written about it. In 1932 Dr. Isra T. Broadwin described this syndrome in his paper entitled, *A Contribution to the Study of Truancy.* The title might suggest that it is only another article on delinquent truancy but it does attempt to describe the psychoneurotic elements in this disorder.

There are all degrees of school phobia ranging from those that are abortive and clear quickly, to those requiring intensive treatment. The severe school phobia that is left untreated may develop into a seriously crippling condition. This is well exemplified by a case of a woman of 31 who was analyzed by one of the writers (E.I.F.). Her first acute anxiety began in the school room at 13 and soon developed into a severe school phobia which was untreated. This rapidly spread to include phobias of many varieties from which the secondary gains were so great that after 18 years they constituted an insurmountable barrier to any very successful analytic therapy.

Fairly intensive clinical experience with eight children treated at the Institute for Juvenile Research has resulted in a somewhat clearer insight into the dynamics of school phobia as well as its therapy. The group studied includes an equal number of male and female children. The age range at time of appearance of the phobia was from six to 14 years of age. The symptoms had existed from 10 days to two years, one eight year old boy never having gone to school. There was no consistent determinant so far as ordinal position was concerned. Intelligence ranged from low average to extremely superior—the majority of the children being in the superior group. In the eight cases studied the four boys were submissive and obedient to their mothers, whereas the girls were aggressively defiant. All of these children had a definite history pointing to the presence of considerable anxiety in their early years, such as night terrors that were striking, promotion anxieties, earlier short periods of phobia regarding school, severe temper tantrums, asthma and eczema. The children came from homes of varied economic levels.

The outstanding common factors in initiation of the school phobia which seem to be operating in all eight cases are, first, *an acute anxiety in the child,* which condition may be caused by organic disease, or by some emotional conflict manifested in hysterical, hypochondriacal, or compulsive symptoms precipitated by arrival of a new sibiling, promotion in school, etc. Second, and equally important, an *increase of anxiety in the mother* due to some simultaneously operating threat to her satisfactions, such as sudden economic deprivation, marital unhappiness, illness, etc. Third, there seems always to be a strikingly poorly resolved early dependency relationship of these children to their mothers. How these three cardinal factors become interrelated in the production of the school phobia will be seen most easily perhaps from study of a case summary and excerpts from others.

Summary of Case

Jack, age nine, the middle child in a family of three, developed school phobia eight months before coming to the Institute. After a mild organic illness associated with unnecessary trips to various medical clinics accompanied by his oversolicitous mother, with two or three months of absence from school the boy refused to return to school and developed hypochondrical complaints, temper tantrums, fears of storms, etc. Soon a full-blown school phobia was very evident. Early in her clinic visits the boy's mother said, "It made me sick to see Jack so pale and anxious, angry and upset. Jack and I had such arguments about his going to school and I became so sick and upset that last spring his father decided it would be better for Jack not to go to school. Jack had always been so lovable—always worried about my illnesses—more than the other two children." The mother stated that people in her community said the boy was "working her" and she felt their view might be justified. Patient was described as "very cuddly, always needing more love than the others." The mother felt "he would have been better off had she devoted all of her time to him."

The child's maternal grandmother had been in bed for years with a hysterical disorder, and was growing increasingly demanding at this time of her younger daughter, the child's mother. The latter suffered from many somatic neurotically conditioned disorders that sent her to bed for days. She was a very dependent, hostile woman and while in a resentful mood, used her illness as a way to punish herself and her mother, to enslave her husband and this boy. Unconsciously she exploited the boy's guilt regarding his resentments toward her in order to bind him to herself. When treatment began at the Institute regularly once a week, she developed more severe disorders which at first were used as an excuse for not making the long trip. The family lived 250 miles from the clinic. She wrote, "I know I'm impeding Jack's progress by not coming in, for my husband can tell you nothing." Though the boy enjoyed his treatment hours from the start, his mother early used every excuse to keep him home. Finally criticism from the school and community operated to increase the mother's anxiety to the point where she came to the clinic regularly. Very quickly she developed a dependent transference to her psychiatrist (male) and subsequently seldom missed treatment hours. The boy was treated in a playroom by a woman psychiatrist. In this situation he lived through in play activity and verbally his conflicts with the family as brought out in relation to the therapist. Relationship interpretations were given to the child as seemed necessary to the resolution of his conflicts.

In the five months of regular weekly treatment hours the patient worked through a great deal of his ambivalence and rivalries toward both parents and siblings. Especially was he concerned early with rage and guilt against the mother because of her demands upon him for obedience and attention, and because of her resentment of any independent strivings. After he had been in treatment for some time he sent her a rather expensive present to cover both Mother's Day and her birthday. The mother complained bitterly to her therapist that Jack was "No longer her dear little Jack who had always given her two separate presents before."

There were periods of fearfulness, especially when his mother would be very sick and, as these were worked through, patient brought out clearly at times his intense hateful wishes against her. As he asserted himself with the mother and turned more to outside interests, the mother interpreted this behavior as a real rejection. Often during treatment it was obvious that the boy felt very unhappy regarding his absence from school, recognized the crippling to himself and felt keenly the blow to his self-esteem when children became critical of him.

The mother discussed with her therapist her own unresolved dependence on her mother, her sister, and the therapist. She discussed also her bulimia when left alone, her longing for love, her feeling of inability to give it to her children, and her competition with Jack for attention, e.g., she often complained that her headaches were worse than his. Her "pride was cut to the quick by Jack's not going to school" and she saw his refusal to go as defiance of her. This led to discussion of her wish to dominate the boy as she was being dominated by her neurotic bedridden mother. Early in the treatment she vacillated in her wish to have Jack home, developed guilt as a result and tried to put the responsibility for forcing him to go to school on Jack's therapist. She also tried to prove that Jack's therapist was inadequate and exploited every opportunity to keep the boy near her. As she worked through her own frustrated, dependent needs with her therapist and felt indulged without criticism, she became much more giving with the children and husband and demanded less appreciation and nursing care. She became able to assert herself with her own mother, to sidestep the mother's attempts to make her guilty and to feel far better physically. After five or six months of treatment the boy returned to school and a year later a detailed letter stated that there was no more trouble with the boy and that the mother was feeling better than she had for years.

Dynamics

Consideration of the dynamics of this case with a few illustrative excerpts from the others seemed to point to the following impressions.

Jack suffered some acute anxiety associated with organic illness which created a tendency to regress to a greater dependency on the mother for the moment. This is the first crucial step in the cycle to follow. The mother herself had been recently more hostile and frustrated because of the increasing demands made by her neurotic mother. This is an equally important factor in the genesis of the disorder.

Study of the early life situations of these mothers always shows an inadequately resolved dependency relationship to their mothers with intense repressed resentments. One recalls that Jack's mother felt she could never give him enough love—that she should have been free to devote all her time to him as a little boy. This with many other similar comments suggests strongly the dependency relationship of Jack to his mother was never well resolved. What happens when Jack's mother, herself recently deprived and needing new satisfactions, begins to renew overindulgence to her child for the gratification it affords him and her? Though gratified to some extent because of the child's revived dependence on her, she feels aroused within her at the same time great resentment regarding granting to anyone that which she was not given. Thus Jack's mother reacted to his bid for renewed dependence with indulgence first and then with hostile envy. She clearly indicated her envy and resentment by competing with him in the sphere of illnesses, her headaches became worse, she felt that he should serve her refreshment in bed, etc. She felt guilty regarding her resentment, however, and sensing his rage at her none too subtle frustrations and begrudging, she began to vacillate in firmness in all situations. Furthermore, his rage aroused in her a recognition of a mirror image of her own reaction to her mother's dependent, infantile demands and begrudgings, and this in turn led to even further guilt and vacillation in firmness on her part. "When he looks so wild and angry and pale," said the mother, "I cannot stand it—it scares me and I give in. I can't make him go to school."

Occurring concomitantly is the ever-present conflict over the child's efforts at independence. The mother of one boy said, "I can't stand to see Bob such a sissy. I want him to stand his own ground like other boys," and a few minutes later commented, "I told him to go to bed at nine o'clock and at nine-thirty he walked into my bedroom fully dressed, hands in pockets and whistling—just defying me—a mother should be considered an authority."

In treatment Jack felt less dependent on his mother and gave her one gift to cover Mother's Day and a birthday which were one day apart. She was angry and complained bitterly. On the one hand, tired and resentful of the child's dependence she urges him to stand on his own feet, but on the other, when he tries this, she resents it as rejection and affront to her authority. In countless subtle ways these mothers create intense guilt in the children for their independent strivings.

What does the child do in these various situations? Sensing his mother's wish to have him dependent again, he at once exploits it. One girl utilized her asthma attacks with the anxiety they aroused in her mother to exploit indulgence to a great degree. One child early inveigled his mother into taking him to Florida to rest, "He looked so sick and pale." When the mother becomes angry regarding the degree to which she is asked to give, the child is furious and more demanding. The same rage appears when the child's attempts at independence are thwarted. All these reactions lead the child to wish to punish the mother in various ways, particularly through not going to school. Sooner or later all these mothers were humiliated and miserable with the criticism leveled at them regarding the child from the community and relatives. As one mother put it, "It is like a knife through my heart." Also the child punishes himself for his hostile rages in a typically self-destructive way by falling behind in school and crippling himself for life, if not treated. All of the children show fears and sensitiveness regarding this. Frequently they will stay indoors all day and be seen on the streets only after children are home from school. Furthermore, being home permits the child to reassure himself and check up to be sure his hostile destructive wishes against the parents, particularly the mother do not ensue. One boy frequently said to his mother with real venom, "You're so old and haggard looking I doubt if you will live long and I want to be with you."

A fundamental step in this vicious circle is finally that of mutual restitution which involves loving, giving, oversolicitousness regarding one another's comforts with the need to be near each other. This constitutes the end and beginning of the circle, and they begin again with mutual indulgence of dependence and of all that we now know follows this first step.

Very early in this chain of events there enters as a factor the school itself. When the teacher, as a more consistent disciplinarian, frustrates the child, she arouses his rage. Being less dependent on the teacher, who is a diluted form of the mother, the child's rage inhibited toward the mother can now find expression through displacement, and the teacher in her milieu becomes the phobic object. To avoid the teacher and school is now the defense against being placed in the situation in which the overwhelming anxiety is aroused. Often a child early complains that the teacher dislikes him.

It must be emphasized that in any clinic dealing with children we encounter countless histories of abortive school phobias and all gradations of transient anxieties with reference to going to school. These constitute the so-called "self-cures" which were possibly brought about by sufficient shift in the balance of life situations to offset anything more serious. A word should be said about the relation of this acute and deep anxiety which produces absence from school and the common form of truance where the child often absents himself from school and dallies here and there about the neighborhood. He does not rush home as the phobic children do. In the cases of phobia where the child hurries home, the reaction seems to be part of a crystallized circle of mutually partially inhibited rages and need to make restitution where dependence and guilt of child is far greater with respect to the mother. In school phobias the mother is, in her vacilating moments, more affectionate, and therefore guilt is greater in the child, whereas in common truancy the child senses far less genuine love from the parent.

Discussion and Conclusion

Just how does this neurosis differentiate itself from other childhood neuroses? The syndrome of school phobia does not seem to us to be a qualitatively new and specific entity. It is a symptom developing under very definite circumstances. First, it appears to us that there is present a history of a poorly resolved dependency relationship between the child and its mother. With this background, two specific factors now enter in to initiate the phobia. There always occurs at the outset in the child some acute anxiety, produced either by organic disease or some external situation which arouses conflict, and manifested in hysterical or compulsive symptoms. Simultaneously the mother must be suffering from some new threat to her security—marital unhappiness, economic deprivation, or demands that she resents. Newly frustrated in her satisfactions, she has need now to exploit the child's acute anxiety and his wish for dependence. On the basis of an early poorly resolved dependency relationship, both readily regress to that earlier period of mutual satisfaction. Now the cycle begins which soon results in the school phobia if the child is of school age, with the teacher, in her milieu, made the phobic object.

ENURESIS: A STUDY IN ETIOLOGY

MARGARET W. GERARD

Control over involuntary urination during sleep is typically achieved prior to school attendance. Only when children continue to wet the bed after that time should they be called enuretic.

The nonscientific literature, as exemplified by letters sent to Abigail Van Buren's advice column (1960) tends to neglect etiology other than laziness and recommends home remedies such as feeding the child raisins or a concoction of magnolia blossoms, swamproot, and chestnuts, sewing a wooden block on the back of the youngster's pajamas so that he cannot sleep on his back, raising the foot of the bed, and concentrating on swimming as an exercise.

By contrast, the scientific literature is more confident in discussing etiology than in recommending effective treatment. The Mowrers (1938) and Lovibond (1964) conceptualized enuresis in learning theory terms and recommended a conditioned response treatment method (see Watson and Raynor, 1920; Rachman and Costello, 1961). Katan (1946) observed that enuretics frequently have the fantasy that their genitals are injured. Michaels' (1955) extensive studies focused on the enuretic's immature, defective capacity to control all varieties of impulses, suggesting to him a relationship with delinquent behavior. Tapia et al. (1960) labeled enuresis a "ubiquitous happenstance" which they considered to be of no consequence if the child appeared otherwise well adjusted.

Altogether too often, enuresis is considered to have one cause and one treatment. Gerard's classic study, which is still valid after more than 30 years, presents the view that enuresis is a symptom which may have a variety of determinants. While two thirds of her sample were considered to be neurotic with specific conflicts regarding sexual identity, she also cites organic diseases of the nervous system or genito-urinary tract, the factor of faulty training, regressive reactions, revengeful motives, and hysterical identification. Most observers agree with Gerard that there are multiple determinants, that the symptom occurs more frequently in boys than in girls, that it tends to disappear around the time of puberty (although the underlying cause may per-

Reprinted from *American Journal of Orthopsychiatry,* 9, 1939, pp. 48–58.

sist), and that there is often a family history of enuresis. Debate continues, however, over whether familial occurrence is actually more frequent than with other psychiatric symptoms, or whether it is simply a matter of being easier to elicit an unequivocal history of bed wetting. Gerard reports many other features that evoke controversy, e.g., depth of sleep, inherent weakness in bladder musculature, the relationship to fluid intake, etc.

For all of those persons treating children's difficulties, whether in a Child Guidance Clinic or in private practice, enuresis is an ever recurring problem. Many theories of etiology have been advanced, and various methods of treatment have been used with occasional success, sometimes permanent, but more frequently temporary. We know also, that without treatment and without apparent cause, enuresis may cease for long periods of time or permanently. This is particularly true as the child enters adolescence and has led to the common attitude expressed as, "Don't worry about his bed wetting. He will stop in puberty."

In literature on the subject, which is voluminous, there are innumerable causes suggested and an equal number of treatment methods recommended. Data offered in support of the theories are frugal and confusing, and one is led to believe that our real knowledge concerning the cause of the symptom is in reverse proportion to the frequency of its occurrence. Although the majority of authors agree that enuresis is psychological in origin, a few claim an organic etiology. The latter divides into neurological and somatic causes. Homburger (1926) claims that it is due to a spina bifida occulta and that enuretics show mental deficiency and other degenerate symptoms. Karlin (1935) contradicts this contention, stating that 54 per cent of normal children evidence spina bifida upon x-ray examination and, that in a study of enuretic children, he found it as a cause only in the cases of extensive involvement of the lumbo-sacral vertebra which evidenced other symptoms of myelodysplasia, such as disturbances in rectal function and in cutaneous sensory perception of the legs and feet. Neurological causes also include Bleyer's (1928) suggestion of a defective cerebral control of the bladder reflex or its disturbance by faulty deep sensation, and Ederer (1933) and Sicard's (1925) contention that enuresis is the result of a local spasm due to hypervagatonia. One should also mention here Schachter's (1933) and others' theory that enuresis results from inadequate conditioned reflex development. Among somatic causes, thickened bladder musculature is suggested by Eserky (1931) and Sturniman (1933), who substantiate their conclusions with the fact that enuresis is more frequent in males than females, and with the statement that anatomically the male bladder musculature is thicker than that of the female. Campbell (1934) found physical causes in two-thirds of 300 cases; the most common finding being that of occlusion of the urethra. Fatigue, offered by Mohr (1929) as one of a variety of causes, is denied by Christoffel (1934), who found, in an extensive study of treatment methods, that tiring the child by active physical exercise in the afternoon markedly decreased the incidence of wetting. Bakwin (1928) claims that enuresis is the result of an irritable bladder and associates it with frequency and urgency. Christoffel (1934), on the other hand, found no such correlation but believes that frequency and urgency are more often associated with diarrhea and represent symptoms of an anxiety neurosis. And finally, Macciotta (1931) maintains that there is a correlation between enuresis and spasmophilia, having noted an increased galvanac response in such cases.

An equal variety of psychological causes is offered. Mohr (1929) mentions suggestion among emotional factors. Poor training in certain cases is claimed by K. Levy (1934), Mohr (1929) and Bakwin (1928), while the last author also includes a wish of a neglected child to gain attention, among possible causes. K. Levy (1934) found some cases developing enuresis as a regressive reaction to love loss. This latter is substantiated by Christoffel (1934) who found that often a cure of the symptom was achieved when a cleanliness routine was given up and affectionate handling of the child was substituted for it; and by Lippman (1932), who found an exessive number of cases in foster homes. The symptoms in these cases, he believes, resulted from the wish of the patient to revenge the new parents for the loss of his real parents. The revenge motive is also upheld by McGuinness (1935), who claims that wetting is an expression of antagonism against parental domination, of children otherwise submissive in their behavior. Both Hamill (1929) and Beverly (1933) state that it is a conduct disorder due to the child's lack of responsibility. In the psychoanalytic literature, we find Freud's early statement (1910) that nocturnal enuresis, when not an accompaniment of epilepsy, is a pollution. K. Levy (1934) agrees with the above, offering as evidence the fact that an infant has an erection just before urination, and that enuresis stops at adolescence when urethral eroticism passes into genital eroticism. She also quotes Sadger (1910, 1918) as claiming an urethral character in enuretics. This is also maintained by Winnicott (1930). Christoffel (1934) likewise believes in the erotic significance of the act, stating that a beginning orgasm can be lost by a sudden urinary need. Enuresis, as a consequence of conflict between active and passive wishes, occurred in a case described by Bornstein (1934), represented an identification of the male with the female in a case of Deutsch (1932), and developed as a result of a sexual trauma in Angel's (1934) case, while Baudouin (1929) found it as a regressive phenomena, a desire to return to the suckling stage in which wetting is uncontrolled.

It seems obvious, from this review of the literature, that enuresis is not a clinical entity to which one can ascribe a single cause, and also that there is no consensus of opinion as to what can be considered enuresis. The word is used, in many instances, to apply to any urination which occurs in places other than that designated for it, that is, the toilet, thus discarding the dictionary definition of "involuntary urination." For clarity in this study, I shall differentiate between incontinence as a result of physical disease–deliberate wetting–and enuresis, or involuntary wetting of psychic origin. The data which I shall discuss in this paper consist of the histories and treatment records of the cases referred to the psychiatric service for wetting over a period of seven years, a total of 72 cases.

In this group are included seven children in which the wetting was definitely found to be due to physical causes. In one case there were grand mal epileptic attacks, and the wetting started two years previously, at the time of onset of the epilepsy. In this case, it was found that nocturnal wetting coincided with a convulsion; that day wetting occurred during the attacks, as would be expected, but also in intervals between attacks. Careful observation during the day, however, disclosed that this interval wetting was accompanied by momentary loss of consciousness without convulsions; evidence of the epileptic causation of all the instances of wetting in this case, and also disclosure of the presence of petit mal attacks as part of the total picture, which had not previously been described. In two other cases of petit mal, it was found that the wetting was associated with the attacks, and, in all three cases, control of the epilepsy by luminal also eliminated wetting. Return of the attacks brought a return of involuntary wetting. I classify these epileptic cases in the group of physical etiology, because, even by those who consider the convulsion as possibly psychic in origin, the involuntary soiling is conceded to be a reflex phenomenon. Bladder infections were found to be present in three cases. Two patients started wetting after their return home following a period of hospitalization for acute pyelocystitis. Frequency, urgency and pain upon urination were associated symptoms, and in each case the patient started for the toilet but wet before arrival. In the one case which was followed in the clinic, wetting ceased when the cystitis was cured. A third case of infective etiology was found to be due to tuberculosis of the bladder. The wetting of this child was in the form of dribbling which occurred night and day. He was aware of the flow but unable to control it, a rather typical finding in tuberculous bladder infections. There was only one case in which spina bifida occulta with its accompanying nerve agenesis could be considered as the cause of the wetting. In this case there was diurnal and nocturnal wetting of which the child insisted he was unaware until he found himself wet. He also had occasional incontinence of feces. Physical examination revealed spina bifida occulta as well as a dilated bladder and rectum, suggesting probable imperfect development of the nerves. In none of our cases was there any evidence of a thickened bladder musculature, noninfective bladder irritability, occlusion of the urethra, hypervagatonia, spasmophilia, or fatigue.

Of the remaining 65 cases, only four could be ascribed to faulty training; the other 61 showed definite diagnosable psychogenic causation. Of the four untrained cases, two were under four years of age. In both, wetting occurred only once during the night in the second or third hours of sleep. Training in the two instances had been started before one year of age by picking the child up at intervals during the night. The time of arousal had never been consistent, and dry nights had only occasionally occurred. In both cases, as in all four, large quantities of fluids were taken at the night meal and the children were put to bed immediately afterwards. The two older cases, brothers, seven and nine years old, had been previously trained, but started wetting after a period of hospitalization for scarlet fever. Wetting occurred at about 10 p.m., two hours after retiring. Treatment had consisted of picking up the children a little before 10 which usually resulted in dry beds, but if left until later they were found to be wet. In these cases it was disclosed that, in the hospital, they had been wakened at 10 for temperature recording and for urination. None of these four children evidenced any neurotic or behavior problems, and treatment by reduction of fluids at the evening meal cleared the symptom within a week for the older children, and within two weeks for the younger ones. The faulty training in these instances might be ascribed to poorly conditioned reflex development, if one wished to so designate it. Wetting occurred at a time when the children had been accustomed to urinate, also, when the bladder was full because of the high fluid intake at the evening meal, and during the period of deepest sleep. In deep sleep, the cortex is depressed relative to the lower parts of the nervous system. Therefore, the increasing stimuli from the filling bladder, which would ordinarily awake the patient before producing reflex evacuation, may then cause reflex emptying before producing wakefulness.

All the remaining cases, 61 in number, presented definite neurotic patterns of which wetting represented one symptom in the syndrome. For five of these, the onset of wetting, both day and night, coincided with the arrival of a sibling in the home. One started wetting five months before the birth of the sibling, at a time when the mother was ill, admitted she had been irritable and had left the patient to the care of a 10-year-old sister. Three others started wetting within the first month after the birth of the sibling, and the last, a four-year-old adopted child, began to wet after a two-year-old boy was taken into the home. All children developed, at the same time, other regressive symptoms, such as food refusal if not fed by the mother, whining, clinging to the mother, and following her around, and, in three cases, hostile attacks upon the sibling. Treatment consisted in simple advice to the mother, aiding her to plan her day in such a way as to give more time and attention to the patient and less care to the sibling in the presence of the patient. Two cases did not return to the clinic. The mothers of the other three reported cessation of wetting and feeding problems as well as a redevelopment of the previous more mature attitudes. Eight other cases, all over five years of age, were children who had never responded to training, wet nightly, occasionally in the day, and in a few instances also defecated in their clothes or bed. One boy of seven defecated in a paper and put it into his mother's soiled clothes bag. All of these children evidence various degrees of stubborn and aggressive behavior. They refused to obey, were critical of, and negativistic toward, food, were antagonistic to their siblings, although four of them got on well in school and were devoted and obedient to their teachers. All, during interviews, were verbally antagonistic toward one or both of their parents, and four admitted deliberate soiling, two stating that they did it to make the parent angry, admitting also that they wakened at night but urinated in their beds instead of going to the toilet. Of interest, in the determination of factors responsible for the development of this stubborn form of wetting, are the frankly admitted attitudes of the parents toward the children. Five mothers openly rejected the children. Three stated that the children had been unwanted in the first place, and the others, that caring for them had been an irritation and a nuisance. These mothers were all dominating characters, nagging, perfectionistic, and unusually punitive and hostile in their disciplinary measures. In the three other cases of this category, the mothers' attitudes were moderately good, but the fathers were cruelly punitive and undertook the major part of the discipline, occasionally with the mothers' interference but usually with her acquiescence. In all of the cases, the children had been restless and irritable from infancy, indicating tension developing early as a response to the rejecting attitude of the parents. Treatment in such instances, as one may easily understand, is difficult, since the symptoms are obviously conscious defense mechanisms of the child against the ever present painful experiences. As long as the experiences continue, the child's immature ego finds no other solution to the problem. Such parents are deeply neurotic, and recognition of the cause of the children's behavior has little effect in changing their real attitude toward them. In only one case was a change of attitude on the part of the parent accomplished, but in this case, the gradual cessation of symptoms and the development of a more adequate personality of the child corroborated our etiological diagnosis. Foster home placement of two of the children with tolerant, easy-going, affectionate foster parents effected a salutary change in behavior and a cessation of wetting. These results confirm the statement already made that the conflict in this type of wetting is not deep and the problems are the result of a conscious reaction to the traumatic environmental situation.

One case is of interest because of the unusual precipitating event and because of the obvious hysterical nature of the symptom. An eight-year-old boy developed occasional nocturnal wetting, diurnal wetting with urgency and frequency, as well as abdominal pains and generalized anxiety, following the death of his father from carcinoma of the bladder. The symptoms of the father during his illness were similar to those developed by the patient. Upon physical examination, the boy evidenced no physical disease. He had been devoted to his father, had been with him much during the latter part of his illness, had witnessed his death, and had reacted with tremendous distress. After the father's death, the mother kept her son constantly with her, slept with him, confided her grief to him, and placed much responsibility upon him. During treatment interviews, the patient disclosed his close identification with the father and an ensuing anxiety about himself. Following a two-month stay in a good summer camp, where he was able to identify with a male counselor as a father substitute, his symptoms disappeared but, unfortunately, reappeared after his return to his mother whose attitude had remained unchanged.

The last group of 46, which makes up, by far, the largest per cent of our nocturnal enuretic cases, and, if one can generalize from our experience, probably represents the most common form of enuresis, presented neuroses, in each of which was found a distinct and similar clinical syndrome, and in which the enuresis was only one of the symptoms. Wetting, in these cases, occurred during sleep or unconsciousness and therefore, according to definition, was true enuresis. In a previous paper (1937), I have presented in more detail than I shall here, the findings in such cases obtained by psychoanalysis. In this study, the six analyzed cases are included as well as 40 more cases studied less intensively but sufficiently long to discern the neurotic pattern. Of interest is the fact that the manifest attitudes of these children were consistent for the boys and for the girls. But of significance is the finding that these attitudes differed strikingly in the two sexes. The boys' attitudes were passive, retiring, and self-depreciatory. Physical activity such as rough play or gymnastics was avoided from fear of physical injury. They were slow and dawdling in their daily activities, as dressing, eating, working in school, and so forth. They demanded more than the normal amount of help and assurance in performing tasks and indulged in evasive petty lying. In school their achievement was below that expected from their intelligence quotient rating, and their behavior indicated inattentiveness and easy distractibility. In many of the cases teachers reported exhibitionistic activities of a non-aggressive type, such as giggling, grimacing, and so forth.

The girls, on the contrary, appeared much more normal in their manifest behavior. All were active children, the majority, leaders among other girls, and they were independent and proficient in performing tasks. In school, their achievement correlated with their intelligence quotient rating, and they were attentive, ambitious, and well behaved. In play, they evidenced a strongly competitive attitude toward boys, associated with a verbal depreciation of males in general. And finally, they were honest and frank in their relations with other individuals. Although the girls, in contrast to the boys, were fearless in daytime activities, both sexes shared a common anxiety, that of nocturnal fears. In some cases this was evidenced by an undifferentiated fear of the dark without fantasy association. In others, the fear was of attack from some fantasied person, either living or ghostly. Twenty-two of the children had definite nightmares which awakened them and led them to seek solace from one or both parents. In 11 of the cases the dream was recurrent and remembered. The others were aware of having dreamt, but had no memory of the dream content.

In summary, the boys behaved as if they were inferior to their fellows, whereas the girls behaved as if they were equal or superior to theirs, but in both sexes a real anxiety expressed itself in nocturnal fear. Besides these manifest attitudes revealed in the case histories of these children, the investigation of the individual cases, both of those completely analyzed and of those studied less completely, disclosed neurotic personality patterns which were similar for the boys and for the girls but differed in the two sexes. In the analyzed cases, as one might suspect, the material was more detailed and more obvious than in the cases less completely studied, but in all of them the patterns were evident. The boys disclosed a preponderance of material indicating a fear of women as dangerous persons who could injure or destroy them if they themselves were active. The mechanism for overcoming this fear was an identification with the woman in the form of a passive attitude and an avoidance of the active role of the male. In the analyzed cases it was found that urination was conceived by them as a passive act. One boy described it as a feeling similar to drifting lazily down a stream in a boat without paddling. Enuresis thus became part of a passive pattern, urine being allowed to flow uncontrolled and without responsibility for the act. Each girl, on the other hand, presented an excessive amount of material which expressed clearly a fear of man as a destructive aggressor who could injure her in his activities. She, in turn, avoided the difficulty by denying men their abilities, eliminating them from her existence, in fantasy, and yet identifying with the active male rather than the passive female. Enuresis in the girl represented an active destructive process rather than a passive flow. As one girl expressed it, "Urine can burn and hurt people. I could use it in a war by flying in a plane and killing the enemy by urinating on them." Of significance also, was the fact that the majority of both girls and boys admitted pleasant bodily sensations during the act of urination, and also the fact that in none of the cases was masturbation indulged in, nor did they or their parents remember the occurrence of actual masturbation after infancy. This leads me to hypothecate that enuresis in this neurotic type acts as a substitute for masturbation, associated in the male with fantasies of passivity, and in the girl, with fantasies of activity. This agrees with Freud's original postulate that nocturnal enuresis, when not occurring during an epileptic attack, represents a pollution. It may also explain the reason for the frequent cessation of enuresis during puberty, since, due to the increased sexual development and its resultant stimulation at this time, actual masturbation is usually indulged in in spite of anxiety or guilt associated with the act, and a symptom substitute is no longer necessary. The material presented by these children disclosed the reason for the substitution of actual masturbation by another act. The fantasies which they associated with sexual stimulation were so destructive that masturbation was too dangerous an indulgence. The choice of the substitute act of urination by the girls can be explained by their identification with men, and their concept of the male sexual act as urination. In the boys, it is less easily explained, but a hint is given to us by three boys who had witnessed menstruation and conceived of it as an involuntary bloody urination. Thus, involuntary urination became a part of the expression of their feminine identification.

Finding these consistent neurotic patterns in such a large number of our group of cases studied, the question naturally presented itself as to what were the experiences of the children which developed these anxieties and which led to such deep emotional conflicts with the attendant pathological solution of the disturbing emotion. With this question in mind, I undertook a detailed study of the developmental experiences of the children and of the attitudes of the persons in the home environment toward the children themselves. Several important factors were disclosed which should aid in explaining the development of the neurosis. For the sake of simplicity in the following discussion of attitudes, I use the word *mother* for the woman caring for the child. In most instances she was the real mother, in other instances she was a grandmother, in some, a stepmother, a foster mother, or a housekeeper. Similarly I use *father* for the real father or paternal figure in the home. In the cases of the girls, no consistent maternal attitude was disclosed. In some cases the mothers were affectionate, kindly persons, fond of the daughter and tolerant toward her. In other cases they were irritable, semi-rejecting mothers, but none were as excessively rejecting and punitive as were those found in the cases of the stubborn negativistic type of wetting. A few of the mothers disclosed jealousy toward their daughters because of the obvious affection of the father for the girl. The fathers in these cases, however, presented an exceptionally similar picture. They were fond of their daughters, affectionate toward them and, in most cases, obviously favored them above the siblings. In 11 of the cases, they were punitive as well, alternating between affectionate advances and criticism with occasional whippings during temper explosions. Four of the fathers had been physically seductive, handling the child's genitals in play while two of this group also exhibited themselves to the patients.

In the case of the boys, the attitudes of the fathers varied as that of the mothers varied toward the girls. Some were easy going, kindly men, some strict disciplinarians, but the majority were ambitious for their sons, constantly set standards of masculine achievement for them, and were irritated and critical of the boy's passive behavior. The majority of the mothers of these boys, on the other hand, were rejecting persons. However, except for a few who openly rejected their sons, the rejection was less blatant than that exhibited by the parents of those cases described early in this paper, in which wetting was a conscious attack upon the rejecting parent. The largest number of mothers of the neurotic enuretic boys were on the whole unconscious of their rejection, but the attitudes were disclosed by their mechanism of overcompensation evidenced in their behavior toward their sons. These women were excessively oversolicitous and fearful of injury of the patient, as well as constantly supervising and directing him in all his activities. In several instances the boy was identified with a consciously rejected husband, and these mothers admitted that they could not love the particular child as much as the others because of the resemblance to the unloved husbands. In two cases, no actual rejection was evidenced by the mother who seemed devoted to their children. These children, however, during interview, expressed the feeling that they were unloved. One gave as a reason for his belief the fact that the mother did not protect him from the father who was rough and often cruel, but usually watched as if she enjoyed the painful play or punishment.

Besides the findings of the seductive attitudes of the fathers in the cases of the girls, and the rejecting attitudes of the mothers in the boys' cases, one other experience of traumatic import appeared with regularity in the case histories: that of a sexual trauma. In the histories of these children, information disclosed the incidence of early actual sexual experiences of a frightening nature in a surprisingly larger percentage of cases than was found in the total number of histories in the clinic. In the majority of instances it had occurred during sex play with other children. Two girls had, at the ages of two and three, been seduced by men to masturbate them, and in four cases already mentioned, the children had been frightened by actual seduction from the fathers. Besides traumatic sexual experiences, a large number of the cases, 28, had slept in their parent's bedroom and were exposed to marital relations, while 11 slept in an adjoining room or an alcove. In such situations, it is common knowledge that children see and hear more than their parents suspect and, as a result, very frequently develop sadistic fantasies and nocturnal fears.

No other experiences could be found in the histories of these cases, or from information from the children during interviews, which occurred with any regularity. However, if one correlates the above data and our knowledge of psychic development with the form of the fantasied fear exhibited in the interviews with the children, it is possible to theorize as to the causative factors which could be responsible for the development of the specific anxiety and its resultant symptoms. Psychoanalytic studies of adults and children have often given us repeated proof that in the early years the child develops a close attachment to the parent of the opposite sex and a resultant wish to possess the exclusive love of that parent. This wish for exclusiveness creates hostile attitudes toward the rival parent which are expressed in destructive fantasies of injury or death of the rival, the well-known Oedipus complex. In our neurotic enuretic cases, we find the concept that sexual intercourse is injurious to the parent of the same sex as the patient. Thus, by a mechanism of projection, the rival is injured or destroyed, not by himself, but by his loved parent. In our case histories we find justifiable reasons for the choice of this particular projection, since these children have been exposed, in most instances, to traumatic sexual experiences and have witnessed coitus between the parents. Such a projection, however, leads to a conflict concerning his own relation to his parent. If such a parent is destructive in love expression, the patient may also be destroyed, if his wish for exclusive love is consummated. The affectionate attitudes of the fathers toward the girls, then, develop expectant fears of sadistic consequences of such affection, making them withdraw from men and attempt to acquire a semblance of safety by identification with men, as if they argued, "If I am a man, then I can make the attacks and not be attacked." The boys, in turn, conceiving the female role as dangerous to the man, may accept the mother's rejecting attitudes as corroboration of evil intent, and they attempt to avoid the danger also by identification, but with the woman, not with the man, and by denying their masculinity. In this way they evade any behavior which might stimulate the woman's attacks. Also, because of the child's sadistic sexual concepts, masturbation fantasies become sadistic, and the wish to avoid harm is probably responsible for the repression of genital masturbation and its substitution by a safer, unconscious act, i.e., urination.

In summarizing the results of the present study, it seems clear that wetting is not a symptom with one etiology similar in all the cases, and which will respond to one form of treatment, but divides itself into several categories. Thus, wetting, both diurnal and nocturnal, occasionally occurred as a result of a physical disorder of the nervous system or of the bladder. Treatment of such cases, naturally, should be directed toward the disease itself, not toward the relief of the symptom. In only a small number of the cases were faulty training methods found to be responsible for wetting. Etiological factors of an emotional nature were present in the majority of cases. A small number of these could be classified as regressive cases in which the wetting developed as part of an episode of total personality regression to a more infantile level of behavior. This regression, in turn, was precipitated by jealousy of a new sibling. A few other cases fell into a category which I may, perhaps, designate as revenge response cases. In these, the child retaliated by wetting or soiling as well as by general stubbornness to a nagging punitive attitude of the mother or person training him. In both of these two types of cases, treatment directed toward relieving or eliminating the traumatic daily occurrences was found to result in the cessation of the wetting symptom and in a favorable personality change, thus corroborating the finding that the symptom, here, was not the result of a deeply unconscious conflict, but of a conscious attitude. Its occurrence during consciousness also excludes it from the category of true enuresis, if one adheres to the classical definition. Only one case in the series could be designated as a hysterical type of case in which the wetting was one expression of a symptom complex resulting from a hysterical form of identification with the father. Treatment of such a case, naturally, should be directed toward the resolution of the total pathological pattern. And finally, in the present study, it was found that the largest number of cases of wetting fell into a group which should be classified as true enuresis because wetting occurred during unconsciousness, that is, during sleep. In these cases the enuresis was one symptom of a syndrome which presented a clear-cut neurotic pattern of behavior and neurotic mechanism development. These disclosed a common etiology, fear of harm from persons of the opposite sex. This fear, in turn, probably developed as a result of three factors working together: destructive wishes toward the rival parent, traumatic sexual experiences, or information and experiences of parental seduction or rejection, depending upon the sex of the patient. Of importance in terms of treatment of the case, this latter group proved resistant to therapy of a superficial nature because the emotion conflict was deeply repressed and partially solved by unhealthy defense mechanisms.

This analysis of the types of wetting and the resulting classification, based upon etiology rather than upon symptom expression, should be of value in aiding one to determine the specific treatment necessary for an individual case. Thus it should be possible to make treatment causal and logical rather than empirical.

HYSTERIA IN CHILDHOOD

JAMES T. PROCTOR

Ever since Hippocrates coined the word to describe the presumed wandering of the uterus to the affected parts of the body, much attention has been focused on hysteria. Interest reached a peak in the latter part of the last and early years of this century, when Charcot (1892), Janet (1907), Bernheim (1897), and others employed hypnosis to demonstrate that hysteria was of psychological origin. These studies influenced Freud, whose initial psychoanalytic explorations, in collaboration with Breuer (1895), involved hysterical patients. Then, the number of articles on hysteria in children waned until 1953, when an entire issue of The Nervous Child *was devoted to childhood hysteria. Recently, as the incidence of hysteria, especially in urban settings, has decreased, there has been less written on the subject as a whole.*

Proctor's scholarly exploration of the relatively high incidence of hysteria in North Carolina focuses on pertinent sociocultural factors. He assumes that the reader is familiar with both the clinical manifestations and intrapsychic determinants. The current tendency to eliminate the use of the label "hysteria" in favor of emphasizing conversion and dissociative features may leave some readers uncertain that hysteria can encompass extreme emotionality, suggestibility, disturbances of sensation and motility, altered states of consciousness, and loss of contact with reality. The psychoanalytic view assumes that the hysterical symptoms–whether they be emotional outbursts, anesthesia, paralysis, blindness, fainting, amnesia, convulsions, or certain hallucinatory phenomena–are the result of the return of repressed oral and/or oedipal conflicts which are converted into symptoms representing a symbolic compromise between both sides of the conflict.

Proctor's conviction of the rival significance of the underlying causes leads him to assert that most of his cases were not carried to "therapeutic termination," even though most of the patients were free of symptoms after brief hospitalization or outpatient care. He is not satisfied with symptomatic relief alone as a justification for "therapeutic termination" because he has little confidence in the permanence of symptom relief which is not based on resolution of the underlying psychodynamic conflicts.

Reprinted from *American Journal of Orthopsychiatry,* 28, 1958, pp. 394–403.

Many casual observers have been impressed by the apparent high incidence of hysteria among psychiatric patients of North Carolina, both children and adults. To explore this clinical observation, 191 unselected, consecutively diagnosed cases in the child psychiatric unit of the Department of Psychiatry, the University of North Carolina School of Medicine, were reviewed and 25 cases of frank conversion and/or dissociative reactions were discovered, an incidence of 13 per cent. This fact stimulated our interest in childhood hysteria and led to 1) review of the literature, 2) comparison of our cases and incidence rate with those from other areas, 3) preliminary analysis of our data and observations concerning treatment, 4) speculation concerning factors involved in our high incidence rate as well as in the choice of and dynamics of the neurosis.

The first review of the American literature was by Sheffield (1898), in which he reported 98 cases of hysteria in children, culled from the literature. This article also describes early mass hysteria in children and refers to epidemics. There have been several subsequent partial reviews (Jensen and Wert, 1945; Kanner, 1948; Robbins and O'Neal, 1953) and the reader is referred to those sources for consideration of the earlier literature; however, there is no good bibliography available pertinent to childhood hysteria, so an extensive one of the various important contributions is included with this article, along with relevant background references.

Caulfield's article (1943) on the Salem Witchcraft Tragedy is illuminating, particularly from a historical vantage. Caulfield quotes excellent contemporary descriptions of the children's hysterical states and offers psychiatric-anthropologic explanation of the genesis. The article by Schuler and Parenton (1943), in which a hysterical epidemic in a Louisiana high school is described, certainly indicates that such epidemics are still possible, although rare in modern times; this article also reviews the literature on hysteric epidemics. Winnicott's book, *Clinical Notes on Disorder of Childhood* (1931), deserves special mention as it has received too little attention in America, although it offers excellent discussions of many psychogenic illnesses of childhood, primarily those with somatic manifestations.

Creak (1938) has categorized the types of childhood hysteria: true conversion, hysterical prolongation of a symptom, "nervous accompaniments" as in asthma, etc. Starr (1953) sets forth some of the psychoanalytic concepts pertinent to hysteria. The careful report by Dawes (1953) on "The Psychoanalysis of a Case of 'Grand Hysteria of Charcot' in a Girl of Fifteen" is noteworthy, as is the unique report by Powers (1955) of amnesia in an 11-year-old boy. Warson and others (1954) report a case of encopresis; from this material they conclude that the syndrome falls between a conversion reaction and a psychosomatic disorder, or that it is a pregenital conversion. For the most part, however, the articles dealing with childhood hysteria are case reports and of only casual interest.

Hysterical disturbances of the eye receive much attention in the literature. Fodor's article (1946), although it deals with an adult patient, is interesting since it demonstrates that color blindness can be hysterical in origin, a conversion not commonly recognized. Other articles deal with hysterical involvement of visual acuity (Beitel, 1939; Francois, 1953; Yasuma, 1951), accommodation (Binois and Salsac, 1951), as well as hysterical blindness (Wolff and Lachman, 1938; Wolpe, 1953) and divergent squint (Beitel, 1939). Diminished visual fields are a characteristic finding and are mentioned in several articles (Francois, 1953; Wolff and Lachman, 1938; Yasuma, 1951). These articles dealing with hysterical disturbances of the eye indicate that often the suggestion implicit in ophthalmologic examination and/or refraction is sufficient to dissipate the symptom (Beitel, 1939; Francois, 1953) and at times (Beitel, 1939) can result in marked behavioral improvement. Wolpe's article (1953) dealing with functional blindness in a four-year-old is unusual in that treatment was carried on very successfully through the father. The circumstances were such that neither the child nor the mother could be brought into active treatment.

Since 1950 there have been a number of articles about hysteria. Purtell and others (1951) published an article dealing with statistical and follow-up studies on hysteria, which has some pertinence to the childhood illness. Yasuma's 1951 article on amblyopia has been noted above. One issue of the *Nervous Child* in 1953, with eight contributors, was devoted to childhood hysteria (Adler, 1953). Wulff's 1951 article deals with problems of preoedipal neurotic manifestations and is a noteworthy contribution. There have also been three articles in French (Binois, 1951; Francois, 1953; Benon, 1953), two dealing with visual disturbances and previously noted, the third dealing with general topics; two articles in Spanish (De Sandoval, 1953; Luisa Palacios et al., 1953), both in 1953, dealing with hysterical paralyses; three articles in Dutch (Van Krevelen, 1953a, 1953b, 1955) dealing with fugues and secondly with a clinical demonstration of two cases of simulated pregnancy (a four-year-old girl and a 12-year-old boy) and another case of pain of conversion origin; two articles in German (Klemm, 1951; Biermann, 1955), one dealing with a hysterical neck contracture in a nine-year-old girl and the other concerning adolescent girls with umbilical pain and the concomitant impregnation, pregnancy and birth fantasies and their projection in the Rorschach. However, these papers in other languages are too general to be of great value to us. Biermann's article in German (1955) is probably an exception, but it came to attention too late for translation and is known only through the abstract.

In view of our 13 per cent incidence, we feel the observations of others that hysteria in childhood is relatively uncommon (Adler, 1953; Creak, 1938; English and Pearson, 1937) must be modified in terms of the area in which the observations are made. Also, in considering various reports, we must allow for different ideas conveyed by a given diagnostic label (Creak, 1938; Robbins and O'Neal, 1953). This is one reason that only the frank conversion and/or dissociative reactions have been chosen in this study, inasmuch as these terms seem to bear a fairly constant meaning, in a descriptive sense at least, from Charcot through Babinski (1908), Janet (1907), the modern descriptionists (Kretschmer, 1926), to the various dynamic schools (Carter, 1937; Fenichel, 1945b). Throughout, I use the terms in the Freudian dynamic sense (Breuer and Freud, 1895; Fenichel, 1945b; Freud, 1908, 1920a, 1925b; Starr, 1953), with the symptom of conversion as a compromise substitute for an instinctual satisfaction, an affect-laden somatic expression that has specific thought representation which can be retranslated from its somatic language to the word language; with dissociation as a return of repressed derivatives of daydreams which take possession of the personality and result in a disturbance of consciousness and reality orientation, although alteration in consciousness may also have unconscious significance of its own. These factors are, of course, oedipal in origin, but the Freudian dynamics are so well known that I am sure there is no need to review them here.

It is somewhat difficult to compare our statistics and incidence rate with those from other areas, owing to a paucity of information in the literature and to difficulty in obtaining current statistics from various child centers. English and Pearson (1937) report only two cases of frank conversion in several thousand cases examined, although they suggest that certain minor conversion symptoms, e.g., diminished hearing, may occur more frequently than suspected (Cobb and Butler, 1949). A study of Robbins and O'Neal (1953), on material from the St. Louis area revealed an incidence of hysteria of 8.3 per cent; but for purposes of their study they incorporated within the diagnosis of hysteria cases of hypochondriasis and mixed psychoneuroses, so that their category is obviously more inclusive than ours. Current statistics from the University of Colorado Children's Diagnostic Center (Stubblefield*), a screening center with a selective intake pol-

*personal communication

icy centering around affect-deprived children, reveal an incidence of hysteria of "less than 5%," but again it is not known if that includes hysteria in an asymptomatic phase, hysterical character disorders, etc. A review of the diagnoses made at the New Orleans Guidance Center revealed no diagnosis of hysteria (Chappuis*), conversion or dissociation, although there were many cases diagnosed as psychoneurotic reactions; this cannot be evaluated without further study. However, frank conversions are certainly seen elsewhere, and statistics from the Massachusetts General Hospital for 1955 reveal three cases of childhood conversion reactions in psychotherapy. Also, Jensen and Wert (1945) reported 16 cases of conversion hysteria at the University of Minnesota Hospital, but did not indicate the relative frequency with which such cases occurred. All of this seems to indicate, however, that the incidence of childhood hysteria is high in North Carolina.

Our cases are often of a dramatic nature, and from perusal of the literature it seems they are often more florid than commonly seen in other areas of this country; for example: ticlike pelvic thrusts associated with a request for circumcision in a 10-year-old Negro boy; paraplegia in an 11-year-old Negro female; dental pain leading to extractions of normal teeth in a nine-year-old white girl; oculogyric phenomenon in a 13-year-old white female (facetiously referred to as clonus of the eye balls by the pediatricians); grotesque giant steps in a 10-year-old Negro boy; recurrent and long-standing dissociative reactions in a 12-year-old white male, one of which was observed directly in the hospital, in which the lad held his testicles, ran up and down the ward apparently out of contact, screaming in terror; a dissociative reaction in an 11-year-old Negro male, in which he fell from a chair and hid under the bed in terror while hallucinating a man without a head. But it is not my purpose here to present a museum of psychopathology, and besides, Janet has a better collection (1907). The latter two cases, dissociative reactions, might suggest schizophrenia; but although they posed diagnostic problems, a careful history in each case, psychiatric evaluation, and psychological tests established them as severe cases of hysteria beyond reasonable doubt.

A comparison of the hysteric group with the total child unit population with respect to age, sex and race is presented in Table 1. Dissociative reactions accounted for 20 per cent of the cases in the hysteric group, with conversion reactions accounting for the other 80 per cent, frank conversion and dissociative features being combined in only one case.

Only one of the cases continues in treatment at this time, and we have

---

*personal communication

been struck by the fact that most of the cases are not carried to therapeutic termination. Of the 24 closed cases in our sample, only two (8%) were actually terminated by agreement: one because of improvement; the other, a 15-year-old girl, because she married and desired to withdraw from treatment, so we acquiesced. Excessive distance from the hospital accounted for dropout in two cases (8%), dissatisfaction with service accounted for one case (4%), and there are four cases (17%) with which we have had no further contact following diagnostic evaluation; i.e., the family has not even been available for an interpretative session. However, in the other 15 closed cases (63% of our sample) the patient was symptom-free following hospitalization or brief contact in the outpatient clinic.

TABLE 1
COMPARISON OF HYSTERIC GROUP
AND TOTAL PATIENT POPULATION OF THE CHILD UNIT

	Age			Sex		
	Under 12 Yrs.	12 Yrs.	13-16 Yrs.	Male	Female	Negro*
Hysteric group (N = 25)	40%†	16%	44%	56%	44%	33%
Child unit total population	55%	9%	36%	63%	37%	10%

* Twenty-seven per cent Negroes in the state's total population.
† The youngest was 7 years 3 months.

It is apparent that symptom alleviation is an important factor in these cases, since with alleviation of the symptom there is a decline in motivation to carry through with more prolonged treatment and its more nebulous goals. The symptoms are at times alleviated very easily. For example, I had been discussing with the pediatric residents the value of strong positive suggestion in dealing with selected minor hysterical symptoms or hysterical superimpositions on organic disease. When the 11-year-old Negro boy with ticlike pelvic thrusts appeared in the pediatric clinic, he was seen briefly in psychiatric consultation and further evaluated physically there before referral to the child psychiatric outpatient clinic. However, the pediatric resident on the case suggested firmly to the lad that his symptoms would disappear, and when the boy was seen for formal evaluation in child psychiatry two or three weeks later, the symptoms had all but disappeared. The boy was picked up in treatment and seen for three interviews, but, inasmuch as he was symptom-free, the mother could see no point in continuing and terminated treatment against advice. This, of course, highlights the importance of the method of dealing with these cases.

There are reports in the literature (Fraga-Arroyo and Herrera, 1947; Walker, 1947) indicating that suggestion, hypnosis, or Amytal, followed by abreaction, support, and reassurance is the treatment of choice; and an occasional follow-up report shows good results from such an approach (Walker, 1947). Even English and Pearson (1937) suggest that this approach should not be disdained, especially where intelligence is low or socioeconomic factors prohibit other types of treatment. Albert Linch (1956) has suggested that because of cultural factors, further and more nebulous modification than symptom alleviation is inconceivable to many patients, and that should such modification occur it might actually result in poor social adaptation in certain local cultural groups. However, follow-up studies (Purtell et al., 1951; Robbins and O'Neal, 1953) on children diagnosed as hysterical reveal a subsequent history of unnecessary hospitalizations, operations, and other illnesses, so we feel that whenever possible the child should be engaged in psychotherapy aimed at alteration of the underlying pathology.

Our contact with hysteria poses many questions for which I have no answers. One question concerns the high incidence of childhood hysteria in our geographic area. We get hints from observations of our culture with its largely rural population distribution, low educational level, and generally low economic status. Weston La Barre (1956) states that ethnographic and psychiatric records indicate that "Tobacco Road" is no artistic caricature, but a faithful portrait of some regions of the South. He speaks further of the intricate interplay of a rigidly compulsive cultural background and the individual's adaptation to it, of the picayune fanaticism of certain rural folk which must be observed to be believed, all of this in context with a description of the faith of the Southern Missionary Baptist as a dour, pleasure-inhibiting, fundamentalist, rural religion which frowns on smoking, drinking, and sex. Our geographic area has been spoken of as the Bible Belt, and even over the radio in the early morning one can hear sermons about hell-fire and damnation, with the firm belief expressed that Christ's return to North Carolina is imminent, with various magical ideas about why he is to return specifically to North Carolina. There is also considerable residual belief in hex doctors, faith healing, and other magic. It is true that these concepts touch only certain segments of the population directly, yet they are ever present, and some universal contamination is inevitable.

Such primitive and repressive attitudes are of course important, but there are the further factors of early stimulation of the child by discussion of original sin, as well as through disapproval of all pleasure, which hint at and perhaps emphasize the desirable nature of these things while at the same time denying them (Caulfield, 1943). Such inconsistencies are often acted out; e.g., it is not uncommon for sex to be taboo, yet to find repeated exposures to the primal scene, the son sleeping with the mother to an advanced age, or the daughter with the father. This results in great stimulation with denial of even verbal discharge, and we are reminded at this point of Freud's ideas about accumulated tension and its relation to hysteria (1920a). It is certainly possible that in a predisposed personality where there is great accumulation of tension because the conflicts cannot be dealt with consciously, particularly that tension which arises over oedipal conflicts, topological regression to primitive modes of discharge, somatization or materialization may occur (Ferenczi, 1926a).

The question of the choice of neurosis or the methods by which conflicts are to be managed also arises, since we seem to see a great deal of hysteria in this area whereas in other areas the disease is seen less often. (I do not have data concerning the relative frequency of various psychiatric disorders in children in our geographic area, but hope to make this the subject of a future report.) We again get some hints from studies such as Abse's concerning hysteria in Indian and English soldiers (1950), where the hysterical picture presented in the Indian soldier was more florid in nature, and where there was the typical *belle indifférence;* yet in the English soldier with conversion hysteria, the symptom picture was less dramatic, and there was nearly always some associated anxiety. Thus, it seems that hysteria is a less satisfactory manner of dealing with anxiety for the more sophisticated Englishman, so that he might well be expected to find other patterns.

In this context the comments of Jules Henry (1947) seem pertinent. He indicates that in the case of any symptom the specific cause will be found in the environment, i.e., the anxiety-producing factor, but further that all behavior is culturally determined; and thus I conclude he also means the manner in which psychic conflicts are managed. Henry's statement supports the observation made by Fenichel (1945b) and others that historically there is no shift in the type of neurosis seen without a concurrent change in the milieu. For example, we no longer see the devil neurosis or St. Vitus dance of a few hundred years ago, presumably because of changes in the morals, manners and mores. In this regard it has been suggested by Waelder (1943) that the shift seen in the types of cases in the population as a whole (from the more florid neurotic-type cases to those presenting a picture more in keeping with the character disorder) results from a real change that has taken place in the parents' management of children. He goes on to suggest that parents' management of children was quite strict in earlier times, with rigid routines and instinctual repression that resulted in neuroses with dramatic symptoms; but that at about the time of World War I, the pendulum swung in the opposite direction, and extreme indulgence without training at all was the order of the day, which produced poor equipment to bear anxiety and frustrations so that the personality was molded in such a way as to avoid any situation that would arouse anxiety. This suggests that such a shift in child-rearing practices has not occurred in our area, and is in keeping with the cultural factors previously noted. All this seems to indicate that we have considerable repressive forces at the oedipal level, generally in excess of that in other areas, plus many cultural segments that are somewhat primitive and unsophisticated in which the relatively transparent hysteric symptoms are culturally acceptable and effective.

These socioanthropologic factors seem to operate in the males' utilization of hysteria. Various observers (Kanner, 1948; Purtell, 1951; Robbins and O'Neal, 1953) have wondered why so few adult male hysterics are seen when the illness is not infrequently diagnosed in boys—you will recall that 56 per cent of our sample were male. Robbins and O'Neal (1953), attempting to determine the longitudinal history of boys diagnosed as hysteric, followed eight such boys into adulthood to find four anxiety neuroses, one psychopathy, one case of alcoholism, one case undiagnosed and one completely well. Thus in their study none of the boys diagnosed as hysteric presented this condition in adulthood. This is probably in large part a cultural phenomenon inasmuch as the dependency, passivity, and oral incorporative phenomena seen in hysteria are considered feminine traits in our society (Marmor, 1953) but are traits which are at least partially acceptable throughout childhood. Hence within the framework of social acceptance and approval, hysteric mechanisms could be readily used by the male in childhood, but not in later life. Such traits are more socially and culturally acceptable for women than men, and thus it would seem that hysteria would be more acceptable to women. In fact, frank hysteria in adults seems preponderant in females at present, and some statistical studies indicate it is largely limited to females (Purtell et al., 1951).

Of course this does not solve the question of the choice of the hysterical neurosis, and some (Federn, 1940; A. Freud, 1936) feel that there is a basic disposition to hysteria; but implicit in this are questions of early ego formation and the relation of such to orality and/or incorporative processes in general. It is probably true that the essential disposition to hysteria has to do with constitutional factors, or at least very early ego development and mother-child relationship (English, 1945; Federn, 1940; A. Freud, 1936; Freud, 1909b; Marmor, 1953); but the further conditions of environmental factors and repressions occurring at the oedipal level seem to be a *sine qua non* for the development of hysteria as we ordinarily conceive it. However, the two factors may well be related since it is also probably true that the parent who creates an excessively difficult oral period, either in the sense of frustration or excessive gratification, is also the parent whose behavior favors the development of a strong Oedipus complex. There are certainly indications that much of the oedipal material presented in hysteria is really an oral-receptive and/or incorporative wish and that the sexuality of the hysteric is a sham in that it expresses the pregenital oral-receptive wish rather than a genital one. These incorporative and/or oral phenomena were somewhat neglected in earlier concepts of hysteria, but more recently the pregenital origins have come into prominence (Federn, 1940; Marmor, 1953).

Basic to the interrelation of oral and oedipal material in hysteria is the fascinating question concerning early childhood affect-laden somatic expression as exemplified by a case report of functional paralysis of an arm in an 18-month-old child (Gillette, 1882) and by a similar case report by Anna Freud on a 27-month-old child (1926). There are also Winnicott's cogent observations concerning convulsive phenomena in the first year of life (1931) and their relation to emotional factors with particular reference to frustrated orality. He demonstrates clearly with case material that infantile convulsions can at times be precipitated and perpetuated by an adverse mother-child relationship, particularly around weaning and other oral frustrations. His suggestions concerning joking interpretations to the mother as a prophylactic measure, his report of the successful treatment of a case of infantile convulsions by allowing the infant to express its anger orally to him, his demonstration of the marked factor of orality in this somatic discharge mechanism are indeed striking and provocative.

Here we can only say that there seems to be in the earliest infant period (under a year) a primitive discharge mechanism in the somatic sphere which appears descriptively identical with hysteria, yet is not hysteria in the topological, dynamic sense as we usually think of it, since in the earliest infant periods there is little distinction between id and ego and hardly any distinction between ego and body or soma (A. Freud, 1936). Here I am reminded of Spitz's term, somato-psyche, which emphasizes the greater somatic component in the "psychogenic diseases in infancy" (1951). In this early psychic structure there is no specific word representation associated with the somatic expression.

From a strictly clinical viewpoint, many cases of affect-laden somatic discharge in infants resemble the corresponding adult hysteria to such an extent that it would seem justified to classify them as such, but the differences are notable. There is a different psychological structure in that the inner conflict between instinctual drives and superego does not exist in the infant, and the symptom picture is not stable and has no rigidly developed structure. The symptoms seem to be essentially constitutional psychic and psychobiological mechanisms used by the primitive, immature psychic apparatus, in which the ego and id are still undifferentiated. Similar transitory symptoms can be discovered in the development of almost every normal child (Spitz, 1951, Wulff, 1951).

Further, it seems that with ego development and a shift from primitive affect-laden somatic expression to the more sublimated way of dealing with the conflict intrapsychically, the basic predisposition to the use of this mechanism and its adult counterpart, hysteria, is usually not marked. However, when predisposition, relative fixation in the early incorporative stages, or the inability to withstand frustration without discharge occurs, it is probably the result of faulty ego development or failure to separate the self from mother, with an ever-readiness to identify with or incorporate mother again and thus to enlarge ego boundaries and strength. When this rescue mechanism persists it results in a heightened suggestibility and autosuggestibility, with a readiness to identify with, and to incorporate, a passing person, idea or even personal fantasy (Federn, 1940; Marmor, 1953). The affect-laden somatic discharge mechanism in the slightly older child—e.g., a paralyzed limb at 18 months (Gillette, 1882), Anna Freud's case at 27 months (1926), blindness at three years (Abt, 1915), and aphonia at four years (Gillette, 1882)—raises questions about when early specific word representation or symbolism begins, as well as early superego formation (or the activity of its precursors), along with considerations of when the Oedipus complex itself really begins. However, it seems that a true neurosis does not begin before latency and consolidation of the superego with its precursors under the impact of the oedipal conflict (M. Klein, 1932; Wulff, 1951). In the person predisposed in the oral phase, the superimposed oedipal conflict may well result in anxieties sufficient to produce topological regression and the "leap from psychic to bodily" materialization, reversion to the primitive mode of somatic discharge.

However, we must also keep in mind that these shifts in the management of anxiety are fluid and capable of changes back and forth at any time, depending on the factors of stress and ego strength (Schur, 1955).

I think that these oral factors have been alluded to many times in the literature, often in the terms of overdependence, ego weakness, or character weakness applied to the hysteric (Abse, 1950). You have probably observed that these terms might well be used in relation to schizophrenia, and I should like to emphasize the similarity between hysteria and schizophrenia in the factors of orality and dissociation, the splitting of the personality which is common to both (Federn, 1940; Marmor, 1953). There is considerable similarity in the two diseases, but it has been suggested by Federn (1940) that the difference lies essentially in the fact that the hysteric represses the split-off or dissociated portion of the ego, while that portion remains conscious in the schizophrenic. Also, to stress the similarity further, there is evidence that cases formerly diagnosed as severe hysteria now tend to be called schizophrenia (Farnham, 1953; Greenacre, 1952b; Harms, 1945). You will recall the two cases I mentioned earlier, diagnosed as hysteric dissociative reactions, which I am sure evoked the question of schizophrenia in your mind. This perhaps indicates more concern with the deep-seated processes underlying symptoms which in an earlier period would with less hesitation have been called hysteric. There is also the factor of current diagnostic "fashion", and schizophrenia is the fashion of the day. Hysteric dissociative reactions always distort the patient's reality orientation to the degree that he reacts to the returning oedipal fantasies rather than to current reality, and occasionally, defense mechanisms we associate with the psychoses appear transitorily. Perhaps we pay too much attention to the transitory psychotic elaborations, rather than to ego strength and the patient's ability to repress the fantasy in the long run and thus to maintain his psychic integrity without resort to the more ominous defense mechanisms. Of course, recurrent episodes in which psychotic mechanisms are active indicate less ego strength and foster the impression of at least an incipient psychosis.

PART IV
LEARNING DISORDERS

Devoting a separate section to learning disorders constitutes a departure from our prevailing nosological framework. Conceptually, focusing on developmental, neurotic, psychophysiologic, and psychotic disorders, which are groups of syndromes, differs from focusing on learning inhibition which is a symptom that may be part of any one of a number of syndromes. We feel, however, that the overwhelming importance of learning in the child's life warrants devoting a special section to this topic.

Child development is inevitably intertwined with the process of learning. When he reaches school age, learning becomes the child's legally prescribed responsibility—in essence, his life's work. It is not surprising, therefore, that learning problems constitute the most common single referral complaint in child guidance clinics. This was true even before the launching of the Soviet Sputnik in the late 1950's stimulated interest in the quality of our country's educational systems. The present older generation, in fact, has seen the median educational accomplishment in the country rise from the completion of elementary school to the completion of high school.

Educators have accumulated a mass of statistical data concerning the learning process and its vicissitudes. Unfortunately, too much of this information is misleading in that it is founded on the assumptions that the I.Q. represents native intellectual capacity, while achievement tests measure academic accomplishments. These assumptions neglect the fact that the I.Q. is affected by many factors (see Riessman, 1962) in addition to native capacity, and among these vital factors is academic achievement. But statistical studies have also produced some findings which accord with observations made by clinicians: that all academic problems, ranging from minor underachievement to illiteracy in high school, are far more common in males (Monroe, 1932; Schaw, 1961); that school problems increase in frequency as the family's socioeconomic status decreases, although why this is so remains a matter of some controversy (Sexton, 1961; Coleman, 1966). As with individual learning problems, the chances of being misled increase considerably if one looks for a single isolated cause.

Learning, which encompasses a variety of processes, has generated a multitude of explanatory theories. All views agree that it is a function of the central nervous system entailing integration of perception, attention, memory, thinking, and recall. Learning theorists have advanced beyond the earlier stimulus-response conditioning view to include motivation, reinforcement, need reduction, etc. Clinicians have observed that formal education can succeed only if the mind is sufficiently organized and if the individual is mature enough to be capable of interest in the world outside himself, at which point curiosity is a strong stimulus. It is essential also that the child recognize the reality of his own limitations, e.g., he has to admit his inability before he can be taught. Pretending to possess a skill interferes with acquisition of that skill. Although learning can be achieved through passive, imitative identification, activity considerably enhances educational processes. A host of other factors has been observed to contribute to, and interfere with, the process of learning, e.g., problems in focusing attention, interfering parental value systems, anxiety, racism, the quality of teaching (Harris, 1961; Holt, 1964; Glasser, 1969; Kozol, 1967).

At the core of formal academic achievement is reading. It follows that reading problems constitute the central learning inhibition. More than 20,000 publications have been devoted to reading inhibitions (see Robinson, 1946; Westman, Arthur, and Scheidler, 1965). The strategic position of reading difficulties in the clinic is made obvious in the following selections.

DIFFICULTIES IN LEARNING

O. Spurgeon English and Gerald H. J. Pearson

Beginning with the conviction that, in an important sense, people learn because they love, English and Pearson emphasize the multiplicity of factors that can interfere with learning. They approach this complex and widespread problem from a differential diagnostic perspective, discussing several of the many possible causes underlying the symptom of learning inhibition. Only such a framework permits the formulation of a differentiated remedial approach that will be specific for the individual child.

In consequence, they offer no single answer to "why Johnny can't read." Instead, they articulate many possible answers to that question, ranging from the factor of difficient intellectual endowment (which is but one aspect of the broader category of mental retardation [see Part VII, this volume]) to learning inhibitions that are a consequence of the intellectually endowed child's effort to adapt. English and Pearson discuss briefly and with authority such controversial factors interfering with learning as inappropriate class placement, efforts to teach a child before he is ready, variable maturational patterns, and mirror reading. They focus also on the effects of physical problems, painful conditioning experiences, disturbances in interpersonal relationships, overindulging the immature child, deflection of attention due to internal and external conflicts and neurosis. Their approach reflects a deep interest in the interrelationships of education and psychoanalysis (Pearson, 1952, 1954).

A child may have difficulty in learning *because his intellectual endowment is lower than that of the average child.* Either as the result of lack of development or of disease or injury to the central nervous system, the cortical centers and the association pathways are not as capable of functioning as they are in the healthy child.

Reprinted from *Emotional Problems of Living,* 3rd ed. New York: Norton, 1963, pp. 334–347.

The causes of intellectual deficiency are discussed in Section H, so that they do not need to be reviewed here. It is not so well understood that an intellectually defective child labors under a difficulty in addition and in contrast to the organic one. He is slow in developing and is not able to identify himself with his parents as rapidly and as efficiently as the average child. Therefore his infantile anxieties are prolonged because he has less than the normal capacity to deal with them. The constant pressure of anxiety further weakens the development of his ego. His parents, moreover, cannot have as much real affection for him as they would for an average child because his defectiveness is a severe blow to their narcissism. In order to avoid the hurt to their narcissism, most parents refuse to recognize that the child is defective intellectually, and they try, usually inadvertently, to distort the history of the child's development and may even go so far as to try to convince the psychiatrist that the child is psychotic instead of feeble-minded. This lack of parental affection further interferes with the development of the child's ego and with his acquisition of the skills for which he really may have capacity. He contacts the real world, therefore, with an ego weakened organically and weakened also by a defect in the ability to identify himself and a defect in the amount of love he receives.

We need not do more than mention that a frequent cause of school difficulty is the fact that *the child is not graded according to his intellectual capacity.* If his level of intelligence is different from that of the class—whether it be higher or lower is immaterial—he does not have the pleasure of success resulting from his efforts, or the pleasure of having to put effort into attaining success. As a result, he works less and less hard; he becomes annoyed because, as he sees it, other children receive preferential treatment—that is, they get higher grades—and this annoyance causes a feeling of hostility toward them and the teachers, which in some instances reaches the height of feeling that he is being persecuted. He expresses his hostile feeling in his behavior, which then gets him into trouble and often results in a real feeling of dislike on the part of other children and the teachers. Their attitude makes him more hostile, and the vicious circle of hostility and counterhostility develops.

Instead of becoming openly hostile the child may try to get away from the irritating situation by truancy. If he goes by himself, he gets into trouble with the school authorities and with his parents, to whom the school complains. If he goes with other children, the same results occur, but in addition he may become associated with a gang of delinquents and himself become one. If he does not withdraw himself physically, he may do so psychically, that is, sit in the classroom and daydream instead of attending to his work. From the psychiatric standpoint this last-mentioned reaction is more likely to result in serious maladjustment than the other two, in which the maladjustment is an open conflict between the individual and society.

The treatment for these cases is a proper regrading. But in the ordinary school setup this would mean that the child would be placed with much younger or much older children, where he would feel a difference in physical size and be treated differently by the other children than if he were with his peers. What he needs is to be placed in a special class or in a school where there are no actual grades—for example, a good progressive school.

Children whose total intellectual endowment is very superior may find difficulty in learning in the average educational setup, as Terman (1916) pointed out long ago. Their failure is the result of boredom. The other children in the class, whose intelligence quotients may be average or slightly above, may take about an hour to understand and master a particular problem which the child with very superior intelligence may be able to conquer in fifteen minutes. For the remaining three-quarters of an hour such a child has nothing to do, and in order not to be restless and disturbing will spend his time in daydreaming. The daydreams soon become more interesting than was the problem solved in the first fifteen minutes, and instead of occupying only the unemployed time they begin to occupy the whole hour. Consequently such children learn little or nothing, and at the end of several months their achievements are far less than those of the other members of the class. On the basis of their poor schoolwork the teacher may believe they are intellectually retarded. They also have omitted learning certain basic fundamentals so that now when confronted by more complex problems, which the others in the class have the basic skills to solve, they fail utterly. This secondary failure drives them into more intensive daydreaming. The diagnosis and management of children whose difficulty in learning is the result of their intellectual endowment is the task of the teacher and the educational psychologist.

In our opinion entrance to school should be preceded not only by a thorough physical examination but also by an estimation of the intellectual capacity, and, ideally, of the emotional status, of the child. If his intellectual level is considerably less than the average he should be placed in a special class for backward children. The children in this class should have made a careful estimation of all their intellectual capabilities and assets, and their educational life should be planned on the results of this estimation. Children whose intellectual capacity is much above the average should be placed either in a special class for intellectually advanced children or in a good progressive school.

In either situation more attention should be given to helping the child in his social and emotional adjustments and in his physical and manual development than to the process of scholastic achievement. Ordinarily a child with a very high intelligence level tends to progress through school too fast. He may even graduate from school at the age of fourteen or fifteen, which is too young to enter college, where he will be unwelcome in the social and recreational activities. With the school program adjusted to his total needs—physical, social, recreational, and emotional, as well as intellectual—these unnecessary and painful difficulties of adjustment could be avoided. (It was to avoid the tendency to have bright children put all their efforts into intellectual accomplishments that Cecil Rhodes wisely laid down the requirements he did for selecting Rhodes scholars.)

If the child is gifted, and also exceptionally gifted along one particular line such as music, an added difficulty arises, for the parents and other interested adults often desire that the exceptional skill be highly developed and forget the other needs of the child. Here perhaps is the reason why so many great musicians and other artists are so often emotionally maladjusted individuals. It should be the care of those who are entrusted with the education of a genius to see that all his needs are met, and not just those of his talent.

Learning readiness is a determinant of learning ability. The abilities to learn to write and to do arithmetic develop as part of a maturational process. At certain ages all children are unable to learn any of these skills. As they grow older one or another ability becomes manifest.

Research educators have come to the conclusion that children are not able to learn to read until they have reached a certain stage of development, and that the age at which this stage is reached is specific for each child. It is therefore useless to try to teach a child to read before this stage is reached. It seems probable that it is reached when the intracortical connections between the various brain centers have reached a stage of maturity. The attainment of this stage is known to educators as *reading readiness* and may take place anywhere between four and ten years of age. If the parent or teacher tries to teach a child to read before the stage of reading readiness, the child does not understand what the whole procedure is about. He tries in order to please the adult, but without result. If the adult gets annoyed by his "stubbornness" or "laziness," the child tries harder, but again without success. Reading therefore becomes associated in his mind with a painful feeling of failure, and when his reading readiness appears, the past association with pain may make him try to avoid any contact with the subject. It may even be years before the pleasure he finds in reading becomes great enough to overcome the memory of the pain of the past. Or he may always be disinclined to read or always be a poor reader. The prevention of such a result will depend on not trying to teach the child to read before he is ready. If a reading disability has resulted from the failure to observe this rule, the child should be given a rest from all reading for awhile and then be retaught to read under pleasant circumstances and in ways that will bring a quick sense of success, which will gradually outweigh the painful memories of past failures.

Similarly there must be a time when the child is incapable of learning to write or of learning to do arithmetic, and also there must be a time when through certain anatomical and physiological maturational processes he becomes capable. In some children this maturational process is completed later than in others, without any pathology being present. The knowledge of this fact, however, is very necessary to educators who then will be able to spare the child the secondary emotional conflicts which would arise because he is forced to *try* to read or to master other skills before he is physiologically able to do so. Such conflicts may intefere with the child ever learning a particular school skill.

Physical impairment (as fatigue, illness, or sensorimotor defect) hinders learning. It is well-known that children who constantly are fatigued because of lack of sleep, overstimulation, and overexertion do not learn as quickly and as effectively as unfatigued children do.

Chronic illnesses, particularly those in which toxic substances are circulating in the blood, or, as in anemia, the oxygen-carrying power of the blood is decreased, result in an impairment of the functions of the cortex, and therefore the child with an average or better than average intelligence has an impaired ability to learn. Intellectual and neurological changes result from vitamin deficiency. In certain cases the child's difficulty in learning is the result of chronic avitaminosis.

Vision and hearing are the sensory organs most used in the learning of academic subjects; therefore, any defect in them—lens defects, partial or total deafness, for example—will interfere with the child's capacity to learn. Often in little children, gross defects of this kind pass unnoticed for a number of years. Such oversight is less common today than it was several years ago because there has been a steady and desirable indoctrination of the public on this subject. However, the effect of slow eye movements on the capacity to learn to read is not yet so well known. Educators are aware that a good reader usually reads rapidly—that is, his eye movements are rapid—while poor readers often read very slowly as a result of slowness in their eye movements and they need exercise to speed up the rapidity of the• eye movements.

The ability to learn to write, draw, model, and make things—that is, the ability to learn to use the hands in creative ways—may also be disturbed from physical causes. Some of these, like chronic illnesses, fatigue, and avitaminosis, we have mentioned already. The effects of gross motor disturbances due to major cortical injuries are so obvious that they need only be mentioned. However, certain cortical or subcortical lesions (involving particularly the cerebellum and the cerebellar association pathways) may occur as the result of birth anoxia, birth hemorrhage, physical trauma, or some type of encephalitis. These may not be evident on clinical examination but may make it impossible for the child to do accurate work.

Orton (1928b) has discussed an important and special type of reading disability—*strephosymbolia.* This condition shows itself in both the child's reading and writing. The child has great difficulty in learning to read because at one time he sees the letter E as E and the word SAW as SAW and at another see E as Ǝ and SAW as WAƧ. At one time he will write NOT as not, at another as ton. Such children actually often read in a mirror better than when looking at the page itself. The reason is that the dominance of one cerebral hemisphere over the other has not been established. Therefore at one time the child tries to elide the sense impression from one half of his cortex, and at another time tries to elide the sense impression from the other half. This uncertainty in dominance is sometimes associated with the fact that the child was innately left-handed and right-brained and was then trained to be right-handed and left-brained, which made it impossible for one cerebral hemisphere to attain definite dominance over the other. Such cases are readily ascertained when tested by the methods developed by Orton, who has also formulated precise methods of treatment for them. All cases of strephosymbolia should be placed in the hands of some person trained in the use of Orton's methods.

A small number of children with reading disabilities who show some of the characteristics of strephosymbolia nevertheless do not respond to the specific tests. The disability is the result of complicated emotional problems concerning the use of language—written, spoken, and read—as a weapon of offense and defense, and results from the child's reactions of guilt and fear about the uses of language. Such cases can be diagnosed and treated only by a psychiatrist, and the ideal treatment is psychoanalysis.

Improper or unpleasant conditioning experiences diminish the capacity to learn. The child may be encouraged to learn by using his desire for pleasure. He may be bribed with rewards he desires, the gratification of which gives him pleasure; or the subject to be learned may be presented in such an interesting fashion that its learning in itself is accomplished by a feeling of pleasure. He may be encouraged by using his desire to avoid pain. This method has been used for many centuries in the form of punishment, the infliction of pain, for not learning. If the child does not learn as quickly and as completely as the teacher feels he should, he suffers real pain so that he quickly comes to associate not learning with pain. This method often miscarries. The child may associate the teacher with the pain and rapidly come to hate him; then he will not learn. Or he may associate the pain with the subject matter to be learned and so may hate the subject and refuse to learn it.

Children whose ability to learn is disturbed by painful conditioning experiences need to be tutored in the subject by a skillful tutor under very pleasant circumstances. If this tutoring is not successful they should be studied by a psychoanalyst. Then tutoring should be supplemented by psychoanalytically oriented psychotherapy either by the school counselor —if he is trained to do this—or by a psychoanalyst, depending on the degree of repression of the conditioning experiences.

Object relations affect the capacity to learn. The need to learn, that is, to acquire ego skill and particularly the ego skills of an academic nature, arises from a number of sources. One important one is the need to identify with the adult. The child envies the power, self-sufficiency, and apparent freedom from fear of the adult and desires to be like him so as not to be tormented with his ever-present feelings of fear, inadequacy, and incapability. This psychic mechanism is one of the most important in the process of education.

The child of school age wishes to be able to do everything his peers do. If he observes that they are learning to read, their motives being as obscure to him as they are to them, he also wishes to learn to read. Competitive envy is a real intrapsychic motive in learning academic and other ego skills. A second more important motive lies in *the child's relationship with his teacher.* If the child loves the teacher, he wants to please him. The best way he knows to please the teacher is to do what the teacher asks, that is, to be like him. Because he loves the teacher and wants the teacher to love him, he identifies with the teacher just as he did as a younger child with his parents. In making this identification he learns the academic skills which he observes the teacher knows. As identification with the teacher takes place because the child loves the teacher, any emotional reaction to the teacher of a different nature—such as hate, anger, or fear—will interfere with the identification, and therefore with the learning process. A certain number of learning difficulties arise because the child hates or fears the teacher either because of the teacher's attitude toward him or because he displaces these feelings from another adult to the teacher.

If the child starts his reading when he has attained the stage of reading readiness, he usually will be interested in learning. However, if he has interpersonal difficulties with his teacher—if the teacher dislikes him, is unnecessarily harsh and brutal, or is too impatient—than he falls into the same emotional reaction. His dislike for the painful experiences at his teacher's hands is carried over to the subject matter, and he begins to dislike that and not want to learn it. He develops a reading disability. For reading disabilities due to this cause, the ideal treatment is tutoring by a person who understands the importance of the interpersonal relationship for learning. Much of the tutoring consists in an introduction to the tutor—an introduction that has as its main purpose the development of a friendly relationship between tutor and child. When this has been accomplished, the retraining in reading proceeds quite rapidly.

In certain cases of reading disability that we have seen, the beginning of the difficulty lay in an unpleasant *relationship between the child and the parent,* who, the child knew, had placed a high value on the ability to read. The child was angry and annoyed at the way he was treated and in revenge struck where he knew it would hurt most, that is, through the reading. Treatment for such cases must follow two routes: the unpleasant interpersonal relation with the parent must be corrected, and, later, the child must be given special tutoring to bring him up to his grade level.

When a child has such an educational difficulty—usually a reading disability, whatever the cause is—we find that he is not as successful in his school progress as other children. As a result he begins to feel inferior. He tries to evade the inadequacy in various ways. He may, for instance, strain his memory prodigiously so that simply by sitting in class, listening to other children read, and paying careful attention to marks that will distinguish the page on which he is reading, he is able by memory to read the whole page with only a few mistakes. If he is confronted by exactly similar words arranged in a slightly different order on a page that has no distinguishing marks, he is totally unable to read it. (We have seen children who had attained the eighth grade who were able actually to read only a very few words.) He may become totally disinterested in all schoolwork and proceed to develop compensations along other lines. He may develop feelings that the teacher is picking on him and that she is responsible for his deficiencies at school. All of these reactions are the result, not the cause, of the reading disability. They may have to be dealt with during any tutoring process, a point of which many parents and teachers seem unaware. The basic essentials of good tutoring are the ability to develop a good interpersonal relationship between the child and tutor and the capacity of the tutor to understand the child's behavior and reactions. It is the presence of this particular ability that makes one tutor successful in his work and another not, rather than whether the tutor knows his subject or uses the most advanced teaching methods.

Intrapsychic conflicts, whether perceived consciously as worries, as feelings of guilt, shame, and embarrassment, or as daydreams, or whether occurring in the unconscious portions of the ego, attract the attention to themselves and deflect it to a greater or less extent from all other external or intrapsychic constellations. Centering of the attention on the academic subjects to be learned and inhibition of the deflection of the attention to other internal or external situations is a necessary mechanism for a successful learning process. This centering may be interfered with by the attention being drawn to other external situations which the child finds important because they would serve as a means of gratification for some pressing instinctual desire or because certain instinctual desires forcibly are attracting the attention to themselves.

The intrapsychic conflicts may be classified into several groups. A boy who could not remain in school because he was worried lest his mother desert him is an example of this type of learning difficulty. Excessive parental quarreling, broken homes, and the like all cause the child to worry; and this worry interferes with his ability to learn. Similarly, if the child's attention is engrossed with conscious feelings of guilt, shame, and embarrassment as the sign of fear of real detection and punishment or of superego disapproval because of some real or fancied "bad" act or failure, he is not able to attend to his schoolwork and the result is a quite serious, although perhaps short-lived, decrease in academic achievement. It is unfortunate that these deflections of attention, from whatever cause, result in the child not learning the particular sections of the subjects being taught at the time the attention is deflected. The results of this lack of learning, however short-lived it may be, show consistently in difficulties in mastering later aspects of the same subjects; the individual may labor under inadequate skills in these subjects for the rest of his life, unless he receives special tutoring in the parts he did not learn. It is the duty of the educator to see that this special tutoring is provided in all these cases after the conflict has been solved.

These conflicts or worries may be the result of conscious feelings of horror and fear. A girl of 12 began to fail in her schoolwork. Shortly before the failure began, she had been told by her friend about the phenomena of childbirth, the friend depicting vividly, and with much exaggeration, the painfulness and bloodiness of labor. The patient formerly had been quite satisfied with her feminine role and was looking forward with eager anticipation to the time when she could be married and have many children. Now these desires and anticipation became terrifying. She had to focus her whole attention on this conscious conflict so that she had no capacity to attend to her academic work, and in consequence it became impossible for her to learn anything.

The child may be engrossed with a conscious conflict about his instinctual desires. A girl of 14 rather suddenly began to fail in her schoolwork. At this time she had become aware of a strong desire to masturbate, to which she succumbed at intervals. After each time, however, she experienced great remorse and fear—so great that she preferred to walk the floor all night lest by getting into bed and trying to go to sleep she might succumb again. Of course the fatigue on the next day interfered with her ability to learn. Her attention was focused night and day on the problem of whether she would masturbate or not and so was deflected from her task of learning. In this case the conflict was due to the strength of her instinctual desires and their demands for gratification. These desires were opposed by her fears of the results of the act and by her feelings that masturbation was morally wrong which were derived from superego prohibitions against the unconscious fantasies during masturbation.

The focusing of attention on daydreams may interfere with the ability to learn. During the first few days or few weeks at boarding school, the learning ability of a child often decreases. If he is questioned, it will be found that he is centering his attention on daydreams about his home and his family and has deflected it from the task of learning. He may not feel the unhappiness or anxiety which other children often feel in the same situation, and which are usually the feelings that accompany homesickness in the first day or so at camp, because he is focusing his attention on pleasant memories; but his ability to learn suffers during this time. This type of focusing of attention on fantasy, and all other conditions in which escape from unpleasant intrapsychic conflicts to fantasy produces a similar focusing of the attention on the fantasy, produce learning difficulties in children.

Another type of focusing attention is a pathological process but results in an increased ability to learn instead of a failure in learning. A boy of 19 explained that when he was younger he had found that if he felt deeply and expressed his feelings he was exposed to constant rebuffs by his parents, who favored his younger brother and who seemed to dislike him. About the age of nine the boy had decided that he would not allow himself to feel anything again but would allow himself to think only. In this he was caricaturing the old adage, "Look before you leap." Instead of responding to a situation with feeling, he thought the whole situation through very carefully before he acted. He focused all his attention on the process of thinking and of learning academic skills to increase his thinking ability. Since he devoted all his time to studying, his school grades were excellent. However, in his adolescence he began to notice that he had no friends, that his colleagues seemed to avoid him and ridiculed his scientific interest. It was this loneliness and unhappiness that brought him to treatment. In this case, in order to avoid many deep-seated and painful intrapsychic conflicts and to avoid the feelings that are inherently a part of daydreaming, the boy focused his attention entirely on learning academic skills.

The child who is *too* interested in his schoolwork and strains too hard at it is often a more pathological case than the one who fails because his attention is deflected away from learning. The diagnosis and treatment of the child who has difficulty in learning, because he is worried or because he is daydreaming, is the task of the trained teacher and the trained school counselor, in those cases—which are in the majority—where the worries and the reasons for the daydreaming are conscious. Carefully planned interviews, through which the child develops confidence in the therapist and discusses his worries, frequently lead to a marked improvement in his ability to learn. The therapist, however, must be sufficiently skilled to distinguish these cases from those in which the learning difficulty is the outstanding symptom of a severe neurosis. These disturbances appear more prominently in adolescence.

Too permissive upbringing contributes to another important type of learning and personality difficulty that is occurring with increasing frequency. In this type is included the new intermediate group of children discussed previously. Educators, and particularly progressive educators, in the last few years, have become aware of a peculiar phenomenon in certain children. These children on entering school seem to lack any interest in learning. Instead of being interested in acquiring knowledge, they seem interested only in the immediate gratification of their desires. Learning to read is boring because it requires effort and interferes with their immediate pleasure. No matter how hard the teacher tries to arouse their interest and hold them to this task by making it pleasurable, the results are slight or nil. In fact, these children will state openly that they do not intend to learn and that the teacher cannot make them. These statements do not sound defiant or stubborn but simply matter-of-fact.

More peculiar still is the fact that such children come from homes which appear to be the best. The parents are interested in the acquisition of knowledge but do not force their children to follow in their footsteps. They interfere as little as possible with the manifestations of the various stages of psychosexual development. Toilet training is done easily and slowly, there is no interference with finger sucking, masturbation, curiosity, or exhibitionism; in short, it seems as if they gave their children every opportunity for successful development. But when the upbringing of these children is studied carefully, two misconceptions are found. The child has been permitted to operate always on the pleasure principle. He has been protected as much as is humanly possible from any pain or any interference with the immediate gratification of his desires. The parents are not only extremely permissive toward his gratification but actually almost turn themselves inside out to see that he is gratified. They do not wish him to experience any pain or anxiety. These children therefore have not learned to tolerate any anxiety, particularly that which arises when the immediate gratification of an instinctual desire is prevented by reality.

This kind of upbringing is one of the typical and most frequent misapplications of Freud's findings. It reverses the whole parent-child relationship, for here the adult identifies with the aggressor, who in this case is the child, instead of vice versa. As a consequence, the development of the defenses of repression, reaction formation, change of aim, and sublimation–in sum the development of the organization of the ego–is greatly retarded. Sexual curiosity is not changed into curiosity about the nonsexual aspect of the world, but remains sexual curiosity, which is gratified constantly. Such children have no energy to learn at their disposal, and their desire to learn cannot be stimulated even by making the subject to be learned as interesting as possible. They will begin to learn only when they are subjected to the slow educational process of being compelled both to postpone immediate gratification of instinctual drives and to tolerate the anxiety which necessarily must arise during this educational procedure. It is therefore the task of the skilled teacher to help them develop their personalities before they can learn.

A RESEARCH APPROACH TO READING RETARDATION

Ralph D. Rabinovitch, Arthur L. Drew,
Russell N. DeJong,
Winifred Ingram, and Lois Withey

The disciplines of psychiatry, neurology, psychology, and remedial reading combined to produce the following report on reading retardation. The investigators started out by attempting to assess the relative therapeutic value of the processes of growth, specific reading instruction, and direct psychotherapy. However, they soon became aware that the concept of a single *clinical entity, "reading retardation," was fallacious (see English and Pearson, 1963). Citing Whitehorn's (1947) assertion that a valuable and accurate psychodynamic description may not have any causal significance, they carefully distinguished reactive emotional problems from basic etiology.*

Based on their study of 250 cases, the authors were able to delineate three major categories: (a) reading retardation due to frank brain damage, manifested by gross neurological deficits, (b) primary reading retardation, in which they suspect a biologically based developmental discrepancy, and (c) secondary reading retardation, which they consider to be reactive to "exogenous" factors such as anxiety, negativism, emotional blocking, and limited school opportunities.

Their lucid report concentrates on instances where all four disciplines agreed on the categorization of the reading problem. It focuses on primary reading retardation, bringing in secondary reading retardation for contrast. The primary group were often totally illiterate and demonstrated a defect in integrative capacity, reflected in their inability to deal with written symbols and to construct and recall gestalts from letter groups. This defect, which was not found in the secondary group, is considered to be the essential differentiation between the two types of reading inhibition. Another significant differentiating point between the primary and secondary groups

Reprinted from *Neurology and Psychiatry in Childhood. Proceedings of the Association on Research in Neurological and Mental diseases,* 34. Baltimore: Williams & Williams, 1956, pp. 363–387.

was the better response of the latter to remedial reading therapy. In contrast to the findings in Blanchard's (1946) reports, these investigators assert that they rarely saw reading retardation as an overdetermined neurotic symptom.

Professional interest in children who have difficulty reading because of a maturational lag in their language development remains very active, as evidenced by the continuing growth of literature on this subject (de Hirsch, Jansky and Langford, 1966; Money, 1966; Thompson, 1966).

Although the reported statistics of incidence vary a good deal, it is likely that at least 10 per cent of children of average intelligence at school in the United States are reading so inadequately for their grade placement as to impair their total adjustment.

Faced with the fact that more than 50 per cent of boys in residential treatment present reading problems, six years ago we began a research study of these difficulties in disturbed children. The initial focus of our project was to assess the relative therapeutic values of the growth process itself, specific reading instruction, and direct psychotherapy in cases of reading inadequacy. It soon become apparent that the concept of a single clinical entity was fallacious and untenable in a research design. The generic term "reading disability" was seen to include a wide variety of clinical entities of apparently different etiology and treatment need. Recognizing this, we embarked on an exploratory program of attempting to define these different entities, and this paper will be concerned with this aspect of our study.

The literature on reading problems in children is extensive, with contributions from many disciplines—notably neurology, psychiatry, education and pediatrics. The total literature is complex and sometimes confusing. One of the difficulties standing in the way of clarity may relate as much to communication as to the concepts meant to be expressed. As early as 1843, Lordat vividly described his own inability to read as a result of a cerebral vascular accident (Riese, 1954). Adding further case material, in 1877 Kussmaul introduced the term "word-blindness." Since this time, innumerable terms have been used, many to describe the same concept. Among these are congenital word blindness (Morgan, 1896), congenital symbolamblyopia (Claiborne, 1906), congenital typholexia (Variot and Lecomte, 1906), congenital alexia (Stephenson, 1907, amnesia visualis verbalis (Witmer, 1907), congenital dyslexia (Rutherford, 1909), developmental alexia (Chance, 1913; J. Jackson, 1944; Orton, 1937), analfabetia partialis (Wolff, 1916), bradylexia (Claparède, 1917), strephosymbolia (Orton,

1928b), constitutional dyslexia (Skydsgaard, 1942), specific dyslexia (Hallgren, 1950), and specific reading disability (Bender and Schilder, 1951). Much simpler, and as such of particular merit, is the term found in the title of Monroe's book, *Children Who Cannot Read* (1932).

In addition to a confusing terminology in relation to reading problems, a wide range of diagnostic criteria has also been used, and this has led to wide variations in estimates of incidence (0.02 to 20 per cent). Some workers, notably Launay (1952a), have urged a broad pedagogic definition. More specific and complex diagnostic formulae are described by Monroe (1932), Ronne (1936), and Skydsgaard (1942), among others. Extensive bibliographies summarizing these varying definitions of the problems are to be found in papers by Bachmann (1927), Solms (1948) and Hallgren (1950).

Through the years the tendency has been to define the clinical entity in terms of its causation and there has been a wide diversity of opinion as to etiology, with three major factors stressed: 1) A neurologic deficit akin to aphasia. 2) A developmental lag depending upon uneven growth in the child and compensated for in time. 3) An emotional disturbance to which the reading problem is secondary.

The earlier workers, including Kussmaul (1877), Broadbent (1872), Kerr (1897), and Morgan (1896), stress the concept of alexia or dyslexia resulting from a specific focal cerebral lesion–usually considered of angular and supramarginal gyrus location. Later workers, notably Bender and Schilder (1951b), Skydsgaard (1942), and Hallgren (1950), in line with the general trend in neurologic thinking, de-emphasize specific localization. They conceive of reading disability as a specific neurologic dysfunction and are more concerned with problems of process description and analysis than with localization.

Although the presence of a primary defect in non-readers is fairly widely recognized, acceptance of this view has been by no means universal. In earlier years some writers considered the problem simply as a symptom of defective intelligence. Others have tended to view severe disturbances in reading at the lower end of the curve representing the reading skill of the normal population and, along similar lines, the concept of a developmental lag, with ultimate spontaneous maturation of function, is stressed by Olson (1949). A more general multifactorial approach has been offered by Monroe (1932) and De Ajuriaguerra (1951a).

Broader explanations have been attempted by some, including frequent physical nonneurologic illness, inadequate or improper teaching (sight or look-say vs. phonic methods), and frequent school changes. Single associated findings derived from case studies, often of small groups, have been suggested as the crucial factor by a number of workers. Reversals in reading and writing, left-handedness, mixed handedness, mixed hand-eye-foot patterns and peripheral visual, and auditory disturbances have all received primary emphasis. Each claim of such single determining factors has been met by later statistical studies refuting the hypothesis (Drews, 1954; Irvine, 1941; Johnston, 1942; M. Jones, 1944; Monroe, 1932; Witty and Kopel, 1939).

Emotional factors as basic in the etiology of reading disorders have been described by many (Blanchard, 1946; Ellis, 1949; Gann, 1945; Laubenthal, 1941; Pearson, 1952; Stewart, 1950). Blau (1946), representing an extreme view, writes: "The language disturbance is secondary and only one of the many symptoms of the personality disorder (p. 153). While many writers recognize such cases in which neurosis is the basic etiologic factor, there is a tendency to limit the group. Thus Blanchard (1946) believes that in about 20 per cent of the total cases, neurosis is the basis of the reading disturbance; in a similar way Gates (1941) suggests the incidence to be 25 per cent. Recently Pearson (1952), disturbed by a trend in psychiatric reporting, has felt it necessary "to re-emphasize it [the organic] because at the present time when there is so much emphasis on the importance of intrapsychic processes in all phases of medicine and education, psychiatrists tend to become overenthusiastic about dynamic intrapsychic processes to the complete neglect of physiological and organic processes, for which they seem to have a psychic blind spot" (p. 328).

While these differences in point of view exist regarding basic etiology, there is general agreement that the presence of a serious impairment in reading leads to reactive emotional disturbance in children. At this point in psychiatric research it is likely that some workers have confused reactive patterns with basic etiology.

Faced with this abundant literature, with its very diffuse and often confusing use of terminology and definition, at the outset of our project we recognized a need for simplification. As our work developed, we felt that the most convenient and valid term was probably the simplest. We should like now to suggest the term *reading retardation* to describe all cases in which the level of reading achievement is two years or more below the mental age obtained in performance tests. We use performance rather than verbal tests as the index of mental age because functioning on the verbal portions of such psychometric tests as the Wechsler or the Binet is significantly affected by the reading inadequacy itself, whereas the performance sub-tests are much less so influenced. The two-year discrepancy between mental and reading age is arbitrary but has the value of limiting the definitive diagnosis to cases showing significant functional reading inadequacy that inevitably affects school adjustment.

In our total caseload, which now numbers some 250 children and adolescents, we have been impressed with the emergence of three major groups:

1. Those in whom the reading retardation is due to frank brain damage manifested by gross neurologic deficits. In these cases there are clearly demonstrable major aphasic difficulties, and they are similar to adult dyslexic syndromes. An example is that of a nine-year-old boy who sustained a severe head injury with prolonged coma, followed by a right hemiparesis and expressive aphasia.

2. Those with no history or gross clinical findings to suggest neurologic disease but in whom the reading retardation is viewed as primary. The defect appears to be in basic capacity to integrate written material and to associate concepts with symbols. On the basis of findings to be presented later in this paper, a neurologic deficit is suspected and, because the defect is basic or biologic in its origin, we have called these cases *primary reading retardation.*

3. Those cases demonstrating reading retardation on standard tests but in whom there appears to be no defect in basic reading learning capacity. These children have a normal potential for learning to read, but this has not been utilized because of *exogenous* factors, common among which are anxiety, negativism, emotional blocking, and limited schooling opportunities. We diagnose these cases as *secondary reading retardation.*

This study will concern itself with groups 2 and 3. Failure to differentiate these two groups, with all cases labelled indiscriminately as reading disabilities, has probably led to the many divergencies in diagnostic and treatment reports in the literature.

We realize that this differentiation may appear oversimplified, and in practice, at this point, it is not always easy or possible to be certain of the specific situation in each case. In some of our children, both primary and secondary factors appear to be operating, and there is at all times a mutual or psychophysiologic unity. On the other hand we have been troubled by a tendency in psychiatric thinking in recent years to so stress the psychosomatic concept that basic causative factors have been forgotten. Too often a dynamic study has been presented indicating relationship distortions in the life of a disturbed child with the *a priori* assumption that these distortions have *caused* the illness. The caution expressed by Whitehorn (1947), in his paper on the concept of "meaning" and "cause" in psychodynamics, is pertinent to this problem of emphasis. Whitehorn points out that in any specific disturbance, a dynamic description of relationships may be accurate and yet have no reference to the basic cause.

The accurate delineation of the etiology of reading retardation in individual cases is of more than academic significance in that treatment requirements are dictated by diagnostic realities (Rabinovitch, 1954)—a fact which, Levy (1951a) points out, has been lost sight of too often in recent years. Lowrey (1950), sharing Levy's concern about "a prevalent anti-diagnostic attitude," comments: "In recent years I have been puzzled by what seems to be a tendency to treat first, and then inquire afterward what was the matter" (p. 676).

In our project we have attempted to isolate differential diagnostic criteria in primary and secondary reading retardations, looking for significant differences in the findings of five examination approaches: 1) psychometric evaluation; 2) achievement testing; 3) psychiatric evaluation; 4) neurological appraisal; 5) response to specific remedial reading therapy.

The hope has been to replace the present subjective evaluation by more objective criteria. Forty cases have been selected for detailed analysis, 20 primary and 20 secondary reading retardations. In all 40 cases the psychiatrist, the clinical psychologist, the neurologist and the remedial reading therapist, each working from his own material, agreed upon the diagnosis. In other cases agreement was not complete; these are not included in this study, since we wished to be as conclusive as possible in our attempt at differentiation. Following is a summary of the findings.

Psychometric Evaluation

In all cases the Wechsler Intelligence Scale was used, in 36 the Children's and in the 4 oldest, the Adult. Wechsler has defined the areas of functioning tapped by the various sub-tests of his Adult Scale. We have applied similar concepts to our interpretation of the meaningfulness of the sub-tests of the Children's Scale. Wechsler suggests that this practice is permissible and clinical necessity has dictated this procedure in the absence of experimental data specifically relating to the Children's Scale.[1] Our results over a period of five years using these interpretations for diagnostic, prognostic and planning purposes have provided reassurance that the two scales are very similar in the psychological factors tapped by the sub-tests. The rationale for the sub-tests is developed by Wechsler (1944, 1949) and amplified by Rapaport (1944).

[1] The following summarizes our initial attempt to investigate the intercorrelations of the sub-tests at various age levels in both the Adult and the Children's Scales. Inspection of the correlation tables given by Wechsler in his manuals reveals that intercorrelations between

Figure 1 lists the sub-tests of the Verbal and Performance Scales and the distribution of functioning of a typical primary and a secondary retardation case.

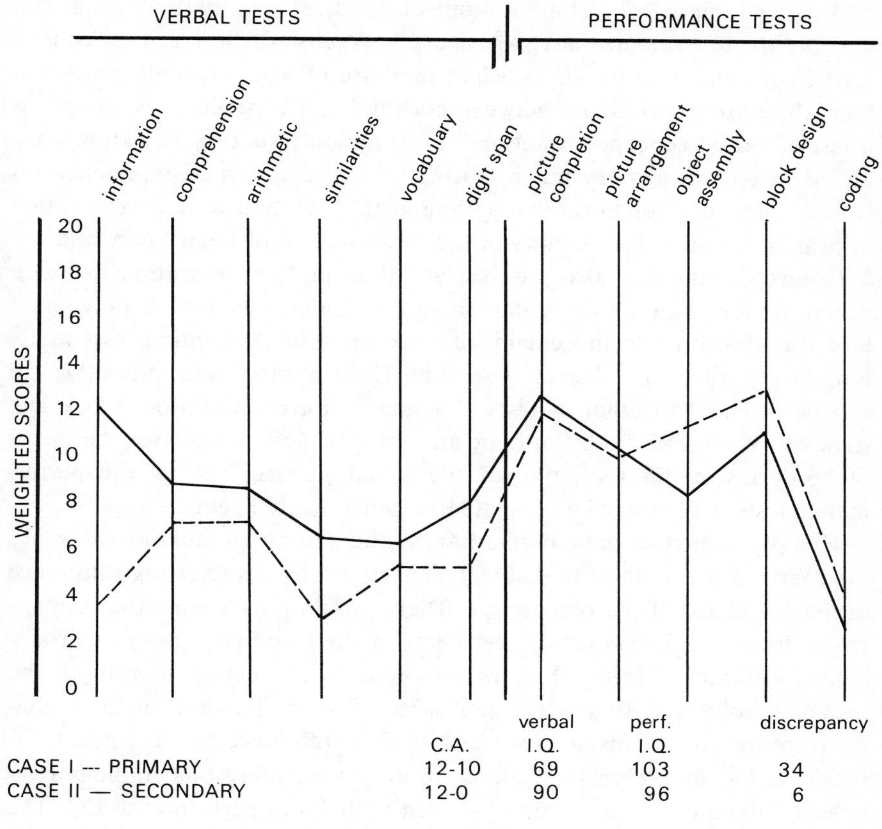

FIGURE 1

Examples of sub-test scatter: Wechsler Intelligence Scale for Children

---

tests are on the average much lower at age 7½ than at ages 10½ and 20–34. The highest intercorrelation at age 7½ is .53, at age 10½, .75 and at age 20–34, .72. Some interesting shifts in the degree of association between tests occur; e.g., at age 7½ the correlation between Similarities and Comprehension ranks tenth, but at age 10½ it ranks eighth and at age 20–34 it ranks first. A similar shift in rank is apparent for intercorrelations between Comprehension and Information, Similarities and Arithmetic, Block Design and Picture Completion and Similarities and Digit Symbol in relation to several other tests. On the other hand the relative importance of the correlation between Arithmetic and Information decreases from rank 1 at age 7½ to rank 5 at age 20–34. These shifts can be explained largely in terms of increasing integration which comes with maturation and practice. They reveal a reorganization in the hierarchy of interrelated functions. Instead of saying that the tasks test different kinds of function at different ages, it should be said that the functions vary in quality and quantity according to the degree of integration, which is in part related to age, and that the tasks test the quality and quantity of integration. (W.I.)

The tests depending most heavily upon the subject's capacity to comprehend and utilize language are Vocabulary, Comprehension, Similarities and Information. Comprehension "suffers least from practice effect" and depends upon a "certain amount of practical information and a general ability to evaluate past experience" (Wechsler). Similarities, considered by Wechsler to be an excellent measure of general intelligence, test "the ability to discriminate between essential and superficial likeness; it is a test of verbal concept formation." Information tests range of knowledge and is in part a memory test revealing "the integration of experiences of words, facts and relationships" (Rapaport). Attention and concentration appear to be the major factors in the Arithmetic and Digit Span tests.

Picture Completion also requires attention and concentration but with visual rather than auditory factors predominant. Picture Arrangement taps the ability to "comprehend and size up a total situation, essentially human or practical." Object Assembly, Digit Symbol and Block Design can be grouped together as tests of visual motor coordination. Block Design, which requires both synthetic and analytic ability, involves the factor of "progressive differentiation of the visual pattern"; of all the performance tests it is most highly related to general intelligence.

The psychometric data derived from the testing of our 40 cases are summarized in Table 1. In Table 1 first we note an interesting difference in the sex factor of the two groups. There are no girls among the primary cases; there are 5 girls (or 25 per cent) in the secondary group. Chronological age ranges from 10 years 3 months to 16 years 3 months in the primary group and 10 years 2 months to 15 years 1 month in the secondary group. The means are 13–1 and 12–3, a difference not significant statistically. On the Wechsler scale there are some interesting findings relative to differences in patterning between verbal and performance I.Q. The mean full scale I.Q.'s are 91.8 for the primary group and 94.6 for the secondary, a difference not significant. The difference between the performance I.Q.'s of 104.1 and 99.8 is also not significant. When we consider the verbal scale, however, we find a highly significant difference with a mean I.Q. in the primary group of 82.0 and 90.9 in the secondary. The level of probability is .01. *Even more significant as a criterion of differentiation is the discrepancy between performance and verbal I.Q., 22.1 as compared with 8.8. The probability is .001. We note then a gross general verbal incapacity relative to intellectual potential in those children with a suspected primary neurologic deficit and a much smaller discrepancy in those whose poor reading is due to emotional or environmental problems.*

TABLE 1
READING RETARDATION

	Primary ♂ 20	Secondary ♂ 15 ♀ 5	Significance
Chronologic age			
Range	10-3 to 16-3	10-2 to 15-1	
Mean	13-1	12.3	$.05 < P < .10$
I.Q.-Wechsler scale			
Full scale			
Range	78 to 111	83 to 107	
Mean	91.8	94.6	.30 $P < .40$
Verbal			
Range	66 to 101	77 to 109	
Mean	82.0	90.9	$P < .01$
Performance			
Range	86 to 121	76 to 111	
Mean	104.1	99.8	$.10 < P < .20$
Discrepancy: performance verbal I.Q. . . .	22.1	8.8	P .001

TABLE 2
PRIMARY READING RETARDATION

Verbal I.Q.	Performance I.Q.	Verbal I.Q.	Performance I.Q.
90	121	90	122
95	121	79	86
95	127	74	94
85	99	72	89
84	103	66	96
95	118	69	93
72	100	79	107
69	101	74	96
84	89	101	113
74	99	93	106

TABLE 3

SECONDARY READING RETARDATION

Verbal I.Q.	Performance I.Q.	Verbal I.Q.	Performance I.Q.
109	103	95	104
91	99	85	100
91	93	80	97
89	99	96	96
92	76	94	100
100	110	77	111
94	96	77	99
96	104	103	105
86	103	81	103
90	96	91	101

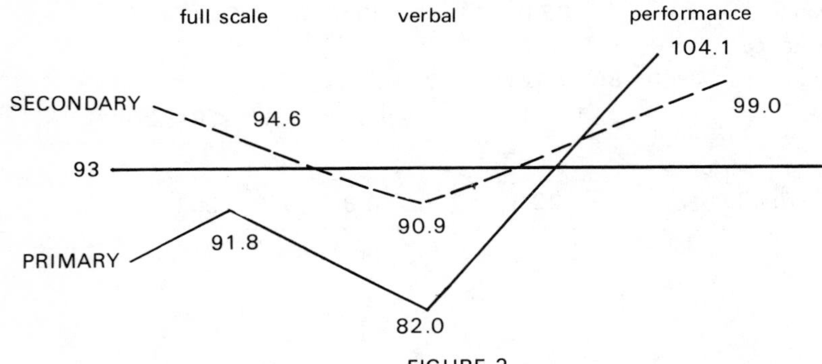

FIGURE 2

Mean full scale, verbal, performance I.Q. levels

Table 2 indicates discrepancies between verbal and performance I.Q. in the individual primary cases. We note for example a verbal of 72 and a performance of 100, 69 and 103, 90 and 122. The range is from 5 to 32 points; the mean is 22.1. It is interesting to observe that in none of the 20 primary cases is the verbal I.Q. higher than the performance. These data suggest how inadequate verbal tests alone are in assessing the intellectual potential of primary non-readers. The fact that in the past such evaluations have been used has seriously clouded our understanding of the problem and has led to distortions in some reported studies.

Table 3 presents a similar chart for the secondary cases. The discrepancies are smaller. The range is from 0 to 34 points; the mean is 8.8. The patient attaining a verbal I.Q. of 77 and a performance I.Q. of 111 (discrepancy 34) was a 13-year-old girl—extremely depressed, inert and with little interest in communicating through speech. In 6 cases the verbal I.Q. is no more than 2 points less than the performance; in 3 cases it is higher. These findings are in sharp contrast to those for the primary group.

Figure 2 summarizes the mean full scale, verbal and performance I.Q. levels of both primary and secondary cases. Again the relatively lower verbal functioning of the primary cases is illustrated.

We were much interested in submitting for statistical analysis the 11 sub-test scores for each case to determine whether any interest pattern of differentiation between the two groups emerged. Statistical analysis suggests some basic differences in the two groups. T-tests reveal that scores on comprehension are maintained in the primary group and decreased in the secondary. Less definitive but suggestive differences are found in results of Picture Arrangement, which is relatively higher in the primary group, and Block Design and Information, both lower in the primary.

Pearsonian coefficients of correlation between the degree of retardation and relative test scores show moderate but significant correlation on two tests for each group. In both groups severity of retardation tends to be reflected in loss of function on Vocabulary tests and in the secondary group in reduced Coding score. Despite drop in reading level, the primary group maintains functioning on Picture Arrangement and the secondary group on Object Assembly.

It is difficult to summarize these findings at this point, and the relationships must be considered tentative because of the smallness of our groups. It appears however that, in those tests involving for the most part social judgment, the secondary group, or those children with general personality problems, show greater relative incapacity than the children with a *primary* reading problem. This latter group, on the other hand, shows a greater tendency to difficulty with abstract or conceptual thinking, verbal and nonverbal. The results to date suggest that further work along these lines will be productive, and this is planned.

Achievement Testing

All cases were given as a minimum the Gates Primary Reading Tests, the Gray Oral Reading Paragraphs, and the Metropolitan Achievement Test, which covered both reading and arithmetic. These tests assess the level of both oral and silent reading, such factors as reading comprehension, method of reading attack, directional orientation, sight or phonic approach, and use of visual or auditory cues.

Quantitative analysis of the test results are summarized in Table 4. The reading age in the primary group is seven years three months, or lowest second grade equivalent.[2] It is higher in the secondary group, the level being eight years 10 months, more than a grade and a half above the primary cases, despite a lower mental age. There is a significantly larger number of children classified as non-readers among the primary cases.

Comparing reading and arithmetic functioning, we find that in both groups the arithmetic level is somewhat higher but only slightly so.

Table 5 summarizes the mean discrepancy between reading age and mental age and between arithmetic age and mental age. In both areas of functioning, the discrepancies are significantly higher in the primary group. These children, it is seen, are functioning at an average reading level more than five years below that expected for their mental age.

TABLE 4
MENTAL AGE, READING AGE, ARITHMETIC AGE

Primary			Secondary		
M.A.	R.A.	A.A.	M.A.	R.A.	A.A.
12-9	7-3	8-7	12-3	8-10	9-11

TABLE 5
MEAN DISCREPANCIES

	Primary	Secondary
	mo.	mo.
Performance mental age: reading age	65.9	41.2
Performance mental age: arithmetic age	50.2	28.3

The primary group, it is seen, functions at a definitely lower level than the secondary in both reading and arithmetic and there are differences as well in the quality of their approach in testing. Many of the primary group fail to recognize even letters. They may be able to repeat the alphabet by rote but are uncertain of individual letters. In their attempts to

[2] It is to be noted that the reported scores are those attained on silent reading tests; the level of oral reading is lower.

read they tend to show no word attack, often recognizing some words but being unable to figure out those they have not memorized. Sometimes they isolate phonics but are unable to incorporate these into a meaningful whole. Many have difficulty maintaining a left-right direction, and reversals are common. In their relationship with the examiner they tend to deny their difficulties and frequently confabulate. Contrary to a view often held, they are little more proficient in arithmetic fundamentals than in reading. They are able to do simple rote problems but appear confused when any abstract number concepts are introduced and often fail to differentiate between larger and smaller. In some cases there is gross impairment in conceptual thinking of the simplest level.

In summary, on the achievement tests, the primary retardations reveal impairment in the most elementary techniques required for reading and the difficulty appears to be in their basic capacity for integrating symbols. Both quantitatively and qualitatively the secondary retardations are different. They are rarely totally illiterate, are capable of a word attack and can usually sound out new words during the testing. Left-right orientation is intact, and reversals are few. Conceptual thinking is not impaired. In general they exhibit a normal process in their reading attempts although their skills are poor.

Psychiatric Evaluation

The psychiatrists and neurologists engaged in the project worked very closely together, and there has been an integration of both examinations with many of the cases being seen first separately and then jointly. There is a good deal of overlapping in the examination techniques, but for purposes of discussion we can separate the essential observations.

It is unfortunately not possible to document psychiatric findings neatly and statistically as in the case of the psychometric and achievement data, and at this point we are obliged to rely as much on our overall clinical view of each case as on any specific criteria. On the other hand our data, we feel, allow for at least a tentative differentiation of primary and secondary cases, and we shall attempt to summarize briefly the pertinent material, beginning with the secondary group.

In general we note a wide range of problems in our secondary group. Usually these children have been referred not because of inability to read but with such complaints as poor general adjustment, delinquency, unwillingness or inability to attend school, psychosomatic disturbance, or schizophrenia. On examination we find a capacity to read with the basic technique apparently intact but *utilized* less effectively than the child's potential should allow. The learning process is impaired by anxiety, depression, neglect, lack of motivation, negativism, or personality disorganization. In the depressed child, for example, psychomotor inertia impairs learning. In the very anxious child, concentration and interest may be reduced. The schizophrenic child reads words, but the context may be lost, and the sound of the word is of more interest than its meaning. Some of these secondary cases have been much neglected and have lacked school opportunities. While the school adjustment is usually poor, the major anxiety is not centered around this area. In summary, learning has been impeded by a core problem unrelated to reading itself and to which the reading retardation is secondary. We have rarely found the reading problem to represent a specific overdetermined neurotic symptom, but view it as part of a larger symptom complex.

There is a qualitative difference in the primary group, not easy to define, but, we feel, clinically evident. These children show marked anxiety about their reading incapacity itself, tend to hold themselves responsible for the problem, feel much guilt, inferiority, and frustration. They tend to be protective and defensive and often confabulate, looking for clues from pictures when asked to read. We have noted a general rigidity in thought process, with difficulty in shifting. Conceptual language is often poor, especially as it relates to orientation involving relative size, number, time and similar abstractions. For example, a 13-year-old boy of superior intellectual potential tells us: "Christmas is in July." When asked to name the months, he does so correctly by rote, but asked which is the hottest month, he replies: "February." He tells us the average American woman is "around seven feet tall." This type of conceptual difficulty is common and was noted as well by the psychologist, the neurologist, and the reading therapist. Some of these children have more specific language difficulty in addition, an aphasia which may be primarily receptive, expressive, or nominal and usually is mixed.

Typical is George, age 15, referred because of delinquency involving running away from home, markedly disruptive behavior in school, school truancy and some stealing. He had had intensive psychiatric treatment in a community clinic over a period of several years without improvement. The family was intact, with some disturbing tensions, and the boy's relationship with his father was uncomfortable. On psychometric testing he attained a performance I.Q. of 96, a verbal I.Q. of 66. He was reading at a 2.1 grade level, more than 7 years retarded for his performance mental age. Neurologic examination revealed some right-left confusion, impaired visual-motor functioning, difficulty in shifting with some tendency to perseveration. Although there was no gross impairment in speech, in the course of the psychiatric interview it became evident that he had difficulty comprehending language. Questions had to be repeated and some he could not understand at all. This disturbance was shown more specifically in formal vocabulary testing. For example, he defined the word "fur" as "hair" and was unable to elaborate. He defined "tint" as "something like a house", confusing tint and tent. The word "brim" he stated had "something to do with a wheel." "Cushion" was called a motor scooter, the patient confusing the word "cushion" with "Cushman." Auditory memory, discrimination, and association are all severely impaired in this boy and his difficulty involves total language function. When the trouble was pointed out to George, he explained that he frequently failed to understand the teacher at school and was now running away because he could no longer tolerate the frustration.

The differentiation of primary and secondary cases is complicated by the fact that neuroses stemming from distorted relationships may be present in both groups. Primary reading problems are probably a good deal more common than we in our Clinic once thought, and we are obliged to be constantly alert to their presence. Impressed with severe neurotic problems in some children, we have not infrequently at first contact failed to diagnose a concomitant and unrelated primary reading or analogous retardation.

Ed, for example, age 16, was referred because of marked asocial withdrawal. He was unable to attend school, secluded himself at home and appeared to have lost all motivation. Initial study indicated problems at two levels. First there was a physical handicap, the result of polio at age 4 years, that had left the patient with fairly marked atrophy and weakness of one shoulder and arm. It was felt that this influenced his social adjustment at school and contributed to his present difficulties. Secondly there was a disturbed family situation, the source of much concern to Ed. Our study led to an accurate defining of the psychodynamics which we assumed had led to the ultimate withdrawal. The patient was of very superior intelligence, with an I.Q. of over 140. He was creative and inquiring and anxious for help. Psychotherapy was undertaken with high expectation for success. After two months no progress was noted, the patient seemed little interested in continuing and began to miss appointments. At this time, more by accident than by plan, we discovered that while he could read at a high level and was superior in mathematics, he had a gross spelling deficiency, almost 12 grades below his functioning in mathematics. He was unable to distinguish vowel sounds and would spell "than," "then," "thin" indiscriminately. He exhibited many reversals in his spelling attempts, would write "Nergo" for "Negro" and then when told it was incorrect would change it to "Nrego." There was marked directional confusion and very poor auditory discrimination and memory. Through the years at school, Ed had covered up his deficiencies as well as he could, but by the time he reached the 11th grade he could no longer manage. He was ashamed to turn in assignments; what written work he did was accomplished extremely slowly, laboriously, and inaccurately. He was strongly motivated for continued schooling but after years of tension could no longer tolerate the frustration his difficulty imposed and finally withdrew completely. When his problem was faced with Ed and an intensive remedial program instituted, he returned to school and graduated with his class. Any treatment for this boy which failed to take into account his specific retardation would not have succeeded, as was clearly demonstrated to us in our early psychotherapy with him.

In this brief report we have attempted to present some of the psychiatric criteria that differentiate primary and secondary retardations. It is, however, important to stress that the psychiatrist cannot work in isolation in this field and must integrate with his findings those of the psychologist, the neurologist and the reading clinic. There is no room for autonomy in either clinical or research work relating to reading and language disorders, and increased definitive understanding will come only from well-integrated collaborative studies.

Neurological Appraisal

On the basis of neurological study, the three groups of reading retardation cases, earlier defined, could be delineated. A number of children, some previously diagnosed and treated as primary emotional disturbances, were found on neurological examination to show unequivocal evidence of central nervous system abnormalities. Frank reflex and motor-system changes, sensory defects, and gross aphasic syndromes were found in various combinations. In these cases the difficulty in reading is considered to represent a dyslexia comparable to the acquired adult dyslexic syndrome. In the preschool group, it is important to note the differences stressed by Strauss (1954) in his insistence on the distinction between loss of language and "lack of language development."

Some of the referring workers had held the view that the reading disability in this group of obviously brain-injured children was not organically determined but had its origin in exogenous emotional factors. Such a view seems to us to ignore the facts and is not supported by present-day knowledge of the nervous system. These erroneously diagnosed cases simply served to re-emphasize the danger of failing to recognize aphasias as important determinants in the educational, social, and personality adjustment of children.

It is the second type of retarded reader, designated primary reading retardation, upon which major interest has focused in the present investigation. These children are characterized by: 1) reading achievement level at least two years below the performance test mental age; 2) absence of historical evidence of either brain damage or disease; 3) no evidence of abnormality in the routine neurological examination; 4) the presence of certain abnormalities in the expanded neurological examination. There is considerable variation from case to case, but we feel that the findings suggest a definite pattern.

On examination, this group of patients shows no detectable abnormalities in cranial nerve function. It should be stressed, however, that the present investigation did not include the elaborate examination of visual function which has been reported by Bender and his associates (1952), nor was it possible within the limits of the present study to extend Bender's methods of investigation to auditory function. It is suggested that such an approach might be profitable for the future.

There were no reflex abnormalities, no evidence of paresis, atrophy, or other deviations of motor function or muscular development. Routine tests of cerebellar function were equally negative for evidences of recognizable disability. However, observation of gait and the performance of motor acts such as dressing, opening and closing doors, and the handling of psychological test materials led to the definite impression of a nonspecific awkwardness and clumsiness in motor function. This observation is difficult to characterize, but has been noted by other workers (Eustis, 1947) and is perhaps best evaluated in relation to other findings to be noted below.

In the sensory examination, no disturbance in touch, pain, temperature, motion and position, deep pain, or vibratory modalities was detected. However, simultaneous stimulation of the face and hand revealed a delay in appreciation of the double nature of this stimulation. Positive or abnormal face-hand responses most frequently occurred to touch stimulation alone. Less frequent were positive responses elicited by both touch and rubbing stimuli. Exsomesthesia was not found, and allesthesia occurred only rarely and inconstantly. Simple forms of displacement and grossly inaccurate localization of the stimulus were more frequent but were extremely variable from examination to examination. These findings were frequently accompanied by other extinction or inattention phenomena, such as the habitual failure to appreciate the simultaneous stimulation of both hands. Graphesthesia and two-point discrimination were impaired in some cases.

In only one instance was anything approaching a true finger or limb agnosia detected, and this could not be confirmed on subsequent examination. However, directional (right-left) confusion was an extremely frequent finding. In a number of instances, confusion between right and left was so gross that the patient was totally unable to differentiate the right from the left side of the body. At other times this confusion of laterality could be demonstrated only by the use of Head's hand-eye-ear test (1926).

In no instance was it possible on the basis of the neurological examination to establish any laterality of abnormal findings which would enable the examiner to implicate one or another hemisphere. Our experiences tend to confirm the conclusions of Goodglass and Quadfasel (1954) that "cerebral laterality for language and handedness are not directly linked and one does not determine the other . . ." (p. 546).

In this group of primary reading retardations mixed hand-eye-foot preference patterns were frequent but were by no means uniformly present. No set pattern of mixed preference could be detected; left eye-right hand or right eye-left hand patterns were seen indiscriminately.

An important part of the neurological examination was the aphasia testing. Chesher's modification of Head's tests was used (1937). When abnormal responses were elicited, additional test items were added to expand the test situation. In no instance was there any disturbance in the ability to name the object pointed to by the examiner or to point to the object upon oral command. In some cases, where previous contact with the patient had suggested some speech disturbance, it was found that if the tests were elaborated there was some hesitation in repeating words. The patient showed a tendency to confuse similar sounding words and to exhibit speech reversals similar to those noted in his reading and writing.

In all cases the ability to read a printed word aloud and to understand a printed word was impaired, as could be expected in a group of poor readers. Here again it was not infrequently necessary to expand the testing beyond the original six objects (cards) routinely used in Chesher's test.

The ability to write spontaneously and to dictation was grossly impaired, as illustrated in Figures 3 and 4. Figure 3 shows a 14-year-old boy's attempt to write to dictation "The boy came home"; he is able to reproduce the initial consonant of each word, but little more—except the word "the," which he knows by rote. The second sentence is his response to "The man went to the store"; again only those words previously memorized are reproduced. He forms letters adequately but his phonic attack is grossly deficient. Figure 4 illustrates the response of a 15-year-old illiterate boy of average intelligence. He has attempted to write to dictation "The boy came home." There is no use of phonics and no capacity at all for written symbolic expression. This patient confabulated and tended to deny his difficulty at first contact.

Despite this gross defect in ability to write spontaneously, the capacity to copy from printed material to script, or vice versa, was either intact or only slightly interfered with. This dissociated form of dysgraphia is similar to that seen in Gerstmann's syndrome (1940; Hermann and Voldby, 1946), and was an almost constant finding in patients with primary reading retardation.

The last part of the aphasia test, the ability to spell aloud, was, as expected, very frequently disturbed; here again, when the test situation was elaborated, reversals and confusion would frequently appear.

When this material is examined, a characteristic pattern emerges. It must be strongly emphasized, however, that rarely, if ever, does a single patient exhibit all these deviations from the normal. Thus right-left confusion, various extinction or inattention phenomena, cortical sensory disturbances, mixed hand-eye preferences, nonspecific motor awkwardness, dissociated dysgraphia, and speech and spelling abnormalities are all variously combined with the reading disturbance.

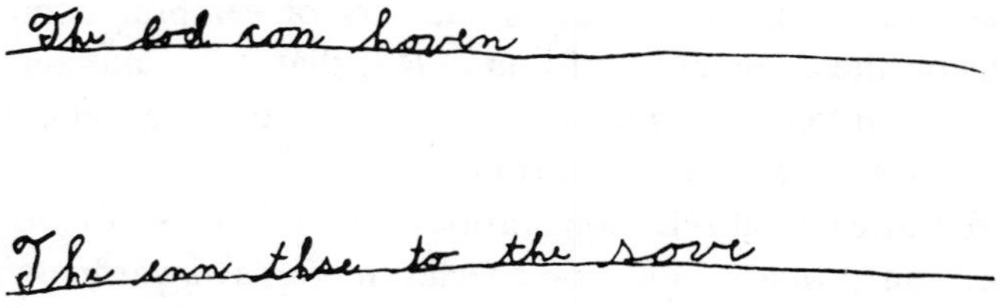

FIGURE 3

Result of an Attempt to Write to Dictation

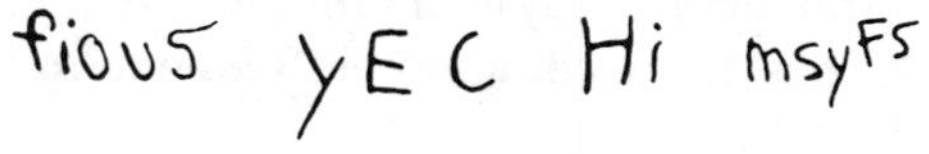

FIGURE 4

Result of an Attempt to Write to Dictation

These, then, are the neurological findings in the cases of primary reading retardation. It is the presence of these findings which distinguishes the primary from the secondary group. In the secondary cases they are not found, except in occasional isolated form.

At this point we should like to discuss the possible significance of the neurological data.

Abnormal face-hand responses have not, to our knowledge, been previously reported in reading retardation cases. The face-hand test has been interpreted in a number of ways and, while not diagnostic of structural brain damage or of specific cerebral localizing significance, it is generally accepted that an abnormal response is indicative of either structural brain damage or a failure of maturation of cortical functioning (Bender, 1952; Cohn, 1951).

Disordered directional selection (right-left confusion) after the age of seven or eight years, another frequent finding in this series, is considered as a disorder of spatial orientation and indicative of parietal lobe pathology (Critchley, 1953). Disordered directional selection has been previously reported in reading retardation cases (Bender and Schilder, 1951; Ellis, 1949).

Orton (1937) was probably the first to stress the theory that failure of dominance or mixed dominance is an important factor in the etiology of reading disability. Mixed hand-foot-eye preferences have been both affirmed (Dearborn, 1931; Eames, 1935; Monroe, 1932; Orton, 1937), and denied (Bennett, 1938; Hildreth, 1945; Johnston, 1942; L. Smith, 1950) as significant in reading disorders. Testing methods have been severely criticized, and considerable skepticism has been expressed of the view that handedness and eyedness are true indicators of cerebral dominance. In this connection the comment by Brain (1945) that ". . . anomaly of handedness is a symptom and not a cause of the disorder underlying the congenital aphasias" (p. 841) is pertinent.

Disordered directional selection, various abnormalities of extinction and inattention, and probably the non-specific motor awkwardness may best be considered as expressions of a disturbed spatial orientation—that is, disorientation in both personal and/or extra-personal space. In the young child, these findings are expected and probably represent functional immaturity of the central nervous system. In the older individual, spatial disorientation of various forms is a not infrequent result of pathology involving the parietal lobe.

The dissociated dysgraphia which is so frequent in the group of primary reading retardations is also found in a recognized clinical syndrome, the Gerstmann syndrome, which is accepted as implying definite parietal lobe pathology. According to Gerstmann (1940) the "pure" syndrome of finger agnosia, right-left disorientation, acalculia and agraphia may be associated with ". . . various other clinical symptoms, such as constructive apraxia, amnestic reduction of word finding, a certain, insignificant disturbance in the capacity to read, impairment of color perception, absence of optokinetic nystagmus and disturbance of equilibrium." These manifestations ". . . can undoubtedly be regarded as arising from involvement of border or neighborhood tissue" (p. 402).

From the viewpoint of the neurologist, it is impossible to avoid comparison of the findings in this group of primary reading retardations and those of acquired dyslexic syndromes seen in parietal lobe lesions. It must be re-emphasized that pure alexia is probably never seen, and, as Critchley (1953) states: "Incomplete clinical examination will naturally endow the alexia with an appearance of isolation or specificity which may well be spurious. Most dyslexia patients prove to be afflicted by other parietal symptoms" (p. 307).

In the present series of cases, neither historical nor clinical neurological evidence permits the assumption of any acquired cerebral lesion. Hallgren (1950), on the basis of a thorough review of the literature and his own genetic studies, was led to the conclusion that there is a definite hereditary factor in many cases of reading retardation. This is a view previously expressed by many earlier workers in the field.

In view of the fact that neither detailed family histories nor entirely satisfactory birth histories were always available in the present case material, it is necessary to admit the possibility that at least some of our cases may have sustained minimal unrecognized birth injury which, according to Gesell and Amatruda (1947), may express "itself in speech difficulty, poorly defined unilateral dominance, and in delayed integration, [and] may later result in a serious difficulty in the acquisition of reading" (p. 239).

Our findings, to date, however, give more credence to the formulation that we are dealing with a developmental discrepancy rather than an acquired brain injury. Our observations further suggest that the dysfunction primarily involves the parietal and parietal-occipital regions. Continued investigation with these cases will, we hope, clarify further many of the issues raised in this discussion, and such work is projected.

Response to Remedial Reading Therapy

The fifth level of differentiation investigated in this study is the child's response to remedial reading therapy, and there is a marked difference in both quality and degree of progress in the two groups. In general, the cases of primary retardation are more difficult to retrain. The learning process is slow and laborious, and the ultimate results are not as great. In the primary cases there is wide variability in performance and behavior during treatment. The process is so difficult because of the nature of the major discrepancies in the child's performance that come to light in treatment. The general approach is rigid. Attention span tends to be short. Directional orientation and such abstract concepts as time and space relationships tend to be poor. Visual and auditory discrimination and memory are often impaired, and because of this there is little carry-over from day to day. Learning needs constant reinforcement; numerous approaches–visual, auditory, kinesthetic and others–have to be introduced. The patients are often discouraged by their slow, uneven progress, and the reading therapist is obliged to devise a constantly-changing succession of new projects and devices to maintain interest. Concomitant psychotherapy does not appear to increase basic reading capacity, although it has helped the child to be maintained in the program and to adapt to his difficulty as he receives specific help.

The general response of the secondary group is more rapid and even, and ultimate progress is usually greater. Because the technique of reading is intact, the reading therapist's role is to motivate the child to utilize an unimpaired capacity; this is a great deal easier than imparting basic techniques. Most of these children have had concomitant psychotherapy in an attempt to handle the basic adjustment problem to which the reading retardation is secondary. Psychotherapy is usually indicated to release the patient's learning potential. We have found that specific reading help is usually also needed to help the child increase the skills in which he is deficient because of earlier blocking, lack of exposure, or practice.

The difference in response to specific therapy in the primary and secondary groups, as well as many of the other factors referred to in this study, can be illustrated in two case reports.

Case 1: Primary Reading Retardation.

Bob was 12 years old when referred to us by a community guidance clinic. He had been in treatment at the clinic for five months because of frequent fighting at school, destructive acting-out, bullying of younger children, lying and stealing. His behavior had led to exclusion from school, he had been in frequent trouble with the police and finally had been made a ward of the Court. The guidance clinic felt that he could not respond to out-patient treatment and referred him for intensive residential therapy.

Bob's family background and experience indicate gross disturbance and trauma. He was never wanted, frequently abused and ultimately totally rejected by his natural parents. He was placed for adoption at age six years, but unfortunately the pattern of rejection continued in this second family, culminating with Bob's being made a ward of the Court at age 12.

Developmental history is not clear in that the natural parents were not available for interview and the adoptive mother had little knowledge of Bob's earlier life. She reported that she was told that birth had been normal and there had been no unusual illnesses during childhood, but there is no possible confirmation of this.

Shortly after his adoption at the age of six, Bob began school. School records indicate an average adjustment in the first grade, with difficulties beginning in second grade and increasing progressively until his exclusion at age 12. He failed completely to learn to read in first grade, was forced to repeat both second and third grades and at age 12 was doing virtually no academic work in the fourth grade. By second grade Bob was aware of his inability to learn to read; from this time on school meant total frustration and unhappiness for him.

In our Clinic, initial diagnostic interview revealed a 12-year-old boy, very large for his age, confused about his relationships, guilty about his delinquencies and in general pathetically lost. On the Children's Wechsler Scale he was found to function at a verbal I.Q. level of 75 and a performance I.Q. of 97. Initial testing in the reading clinic when Bob was age 12 indicated no score on the Gray Oral Paragraphs and a reading age of six years nine months, virtually a nonreading level, on the Metropolitan Achievement Tests. His arithmetic functioning was at an eight-year-four-month level. During the testing he was most anxious and needed much reassurance that no one but his examiner and his doctor would see the test results. There were marked confused in left-right orientation, no phonic attack at all, failure to recognize some letters. In many ways Bob functioned as a preschool child in his attempts at reading. Neurological examination indicated no abnormality on routine testing but almost constant left-right confusion, poor body image concept, poor concept formation and gross inability to read or write.

The total picture indicated that we were dealing with a primary reading retardation of severe proportions, along with a superimposed neurotic problem reactive to relationship distortions, as well as the frustration and failure imposed by his learning defect. Despite all his difficulties he wanted desperately to learn to read, and a program of total therapy including remedial reading was planned for him. Because of his severe delinquency he was treated as an in-patient, received psychotherapy, attended a special school and occupational therapy on the ward and was handled through a planned total 24-hour treatment program. His work in the reading clinic was integrated with the other aspects of the program throughout his stay with us. This report will concern itself with his response to attempts at specific reading therapy:

In reading clinic Bob was at first silent and suspicious. The first phase of re-training was to establish a meaningful relationship with him. This proved relatively easy in that Bob liked his tutor from the beginning, came to trust her and saw in the relationship an opportunity to find help for his illiteracy of which he was deeply ashamed. At first the tutor took him on walks, showed him interesting sights in the town, had cokes and candy with him; office sessions were possible within less than two weeks and, although informal contacts continued, from this point on a definitive structured work program was possible.

Early in his work Bob was able to describe his lack of visual memory and poor visual discrimination. He told how he had tried desperately to remember words he had been taught in the first grade but just could not recognize them when he saw them again. Using this as a cue we decided to attempt an almost straight phonic approach. Because he could not retain the image of whole words, we attempted to teach him the various sounds of the 26 letters of the alphabet and show him how words were formed with various combinations of these letters. However, we did not begin with this letter-by-letter method, knowing from experience that older children are able to grasp phonic principles more easily and to enter into actual reading faster if they first master a few basic sight words. The therapist and Bob chose 50 words with which to work. Criteria were: 1) that they be as different in shape as possible; 2) that they be used frequently in the simple books that Bob would be exposed to; 3) that their meanings be familiar to Bob; 4) that they be suitable ones on which to build basic phonic principles. These words were then studied and reviewed in a variety of ways. A regular game of Parcheesi was played, substituting word cards for the dice. If Bob knew the word he could move his men the designated number of spaces. If he did not know the word, the therapist moved her man. Bingo was also played with words instead of numbers. Flash cards were used, with Bob winning the cards for those words he recognized. We attempted to give him some indication of the shape of various words, drawing frames around each of his 50 words, showing him how words looked when they began with tall consonants, consonants that were below the line, etc.

It soon became apparent that Bob could not retain these words for any length of time without more than visual cues. Therefore a systematic attempt was made to teach him both the name and sound of all the consonants. This was done by drill, by cutting out pictures of articles, the names of which began with certain consonants, by playing the game of "I see something in this room that begins with a 'B' which says 'buh'." Bob had little difficulty differentiating the sounds; his auditory memory and discrimination were much more intact than their visual counterparts. His major difficulty was in letters such as 'b', 'd', 'p', and 'g', involving directional confusion. Special exercises were devised; he would wrote long rows of the four letters and pick out all of one kind; he would print them on the typewriter and explain their differences.

Throughout our work with Bob it was necessary to attempt to create an atmosphere of fun and relaxation during the sessions. He tended to be passive, to withdraw and to acquiesce while he integrated nothing. Much work was done to help him learn to read from left to right. His directional disorientation was extreme, and left-to-right movements were stressed in all phases of our work; the typewriter was particularly helpful here, as only a left-to-right movement was possible.

Gradually, over the first six weeks, Bob mastered some of his sight words; with this accomplishment the first signs of meaningful motivation appeared. As soon as he could read a word for three days in a row, he typed it on a three by four card and filed it in his own file box. It was an important day for Bob when he was able to show all 50 words to his doctor. After initial gains were made, in the subsequent weeks many were lost and Bob tended to return to patterns of reversals and to confuse words of similar length. Constant reinforcement was necessary. Gradually word families were introduced and from "can" Bob went on to "ban," "fan," "man," etc. Beginning consonants were then changed with Bob's 49 other words and his vocabulary began to grow.

Bob had been working with us for about two months when he expressed a desire to "really read something." Short stories with the words in his reading vocabulary were then written for Bob on the primer typewriter. One of the most challenging problems in working with older children is to compose material for them appropriate to their interest and age level and at the same time within the scope of their limited reading competence. Our tutors compose individual books directed around specific interests of children and this was done with Bob. About this time it was felt that Bob was ready for more concentrated teaching of many skills. Rhyming words were introduced and endings were added to known words through play utilizing auditory and visual games. Compound words were introduced through pictures; to form the word "dishpan" we would help Bob find a picture of a dish and one of a pan and he would place them together to illustrate the word. In the fourth month, daily tutoring having continued on the basis of one hour per day, vowel drill was introduced. The therapist would underline all the words in a new passage containing one vowel and numerous exercises were done, such as writing under the picture of a pen the words "pen," "pan," "pin," and having Bob choose the correct one.

After about five months Bob began reading in primers and first grade books, but he had great trouble with abstract words like "where," "there," "what." It is difficult to concretize these and Bob could not read them phonically. At this point a kinesthetic approach was added, with Bob drawing each word in a tray of damp chemical sand and pronouncing it as he wrote it. This process was extremely slow but proved very helpful.

After six months of reading therapy, during which Bob had had concomitant psychotherapy and total treatment in the residential unit, he was placed in a foster home close to the Hospital. Arrangements were made for him to attend a regular junior high school for half-days where he had classes in music, art, physical education, woodshop and science. The school was most cooperative and the plan worked well.

From the eighth to the eleventh month Bob was in an extensive learning plateau. He made no advance and we were obliged to return to earlier work. During this period we concentrated on arithmetic. He had a paper route and was experiencing great difficulty keeping his accounts. We obtained a copy of his records and worked for many hours on keeping weekly records of a very simple type. This was very difficult for Bob, in that he had much confusion about such concepts as "higher" and "lower", "most" and "least," "larger" and "smaller," "shorter" and "longer." We practiced writing numbers up to 100, used pages from arithmetic readiness books for drill, and introduced dominoes to teach groups of numbers. His memory span was so short that frequent drill was necessary and many devices had to be found to keep his interest. His poor visual memory was a major problem and learning was reinforced by using auditory along with visual associations, Bob saying the combination aloud before he was able to arrive at the correct answer by sight.

Bob's reading therapy continued for two and a half years with new techniques gradually introduced. It was very difficult for him to read more than one word at a time and larger units were introduced through the use of a tachistoscopic device. Later came an introduction to punctuation, with the therapist first reading to Bob as he, following the material, noted inflection. Still later he was encouraged to make notebooks, choosing one on the Lewis and Clark expedition and another on the human body. He felt that he was really reading and he was able to collect material on these subjects, dictating his story to the therapist for her to type and for him to add illustrations; he drew very well.

Throughout the two and a half years there were many ups and downs, plateaus and blow-ups, and also many episodes of triumph for Bob. It is difficult to overestimate the importance of the therapeutic relationship established with the reading therapist; it was only through this relationship and its skillful management that he could be motivated to continue the very laborious task he faced. After two and a half years Bob's reading, on standard testing, was at a 4–3 grade level, reflecting slow but significant progress. He was no longer illiterate and able to read sufficiently for simple practical purposes.

The reading therapist's experience with Bob has been described at some length to illustrate the problems and techniques in working with cases of primary retardation. Bob represents one of our most severe and difficult cases; others, while usually less severe, require a similar approach and illustrate the same principles.

Case 2: Secondary Reading Retardation

Alice was admitted to our in-patient service when she was 10 years 10 months of age, referred by a community guidance clinic. She was unable to attend school because of numerous somatic complaints including shortness of breath, dizziness, nausea, severe headaches and pains in the legs. At the time of her admission she had been immobilized at home in a state of virtual invalidism for more than a year. She had never attended school regularly, complaining of feeling sick in kindergarten, and spent long periods at home. Several schools had been tried but on each occasion she would complain that her head hurt or her legs were too weak or that she could not breathe, and her mother was forced to keep her at home. Psychotherapy in the local guidance clinic was attempted but Alice did not respond, and total in-patient treatment was felt indicated.

Alice's family situation was disturbed. She was born out of wedlock and never knew her father. She fantasied him as a brutal, sadistic man and had many night terrors centered around this fantasy. The mother was markedly disturbed, alternately overprotective and neglecting, very unstable in her own emotional expression, and inconsistent in her handling of Alice.

Diagnostic studies at the time of admission revealed a thin, good-looking, 10-year-old girl, markedly anxious and revealing numerous somatic fears. Detailed physical examination indicated no evidence of anomaly or physical disease. Neurological study revealed no abnormalities in the routine or special detailed examinations. In psychometric testing at the time of admission, on the Children's Wechsler Scale, Alice attained a verbal I.Q. of 92 and a performance I.Q. of 76; she was then very slow in her motor functioning, which accounted in large measure for the low performance score. Five months later the test was repeated and now, much improved generally, Alice attained a verbal I.Q. of 100 and a performance I.Q. of 93; this was viewed as a valid assessment of her potential. The subtest patterning was even, with only one score below average, and this involved a test of concentration. In achievement testing at age 10 years 10 months Alice was found to function at a reading level of 8 years 4 months. She read very slowly, recognized few words, but there was no directional confusion, no difficulty in basic appreciation of phonics and both visual and auditory discrimination were intact. Her level of functioning in arithmetic was somewhat lower than that in reading and she appeared to have no familiarity with any thing beyond the simplest arithmetic principles. The patterning of her functioning in testing suggested a normal reading potential, undeveloped because of marked anxiety interfering with the learning process and minimal exposure to learning because of prolonged absence from school. The psychiatric diagnosis was psychoneurosis, severe anxiety state with much internalization and somatization of anxiety. The reading retardation was viewed as secondary to the neurotic problem. A program of intensive psychotherapy along with individual remedial reading tutoring was instituted as part of the total inpatient treatment.

From the first the reading therapist found that Alice could be taught through the usual school methods and there were no complications in our work with her. The problem was to motivate her for learning and then to offer her training in the fundamental reading, spelling and arithmetic skills. Her visual memory and discrimination were excellent, and there was no impairment in auditory memory or discrimination. From the beginning directional orientation was intact and there was no tendency to reversals. It was not necessary to begin at the beginning as with Bob, Alice being able to read second-grade books moderately well. She made many errors, but these were largely due to carelessness–mostly omissions or substitutions. She was able to learn by the whole-word method and many types of word-card games were used to increase her reading vocabulary. She tended to read in a very monotonous voice with poor comprehension. She had no idea of punctuation or units such as sentences and paragraphs; when these were explained she learned readily and was soon reading with much more comprehension.

Once material had been learned there was excellent carry-over from day to day and Alice was able to learn through a visual route with minimal reinforcement from other modalities. Auditory methods were employed to help her sound out long words through phonics, and this was grasped readily.

Alice's reading work was carried on in close association with her direct psychotherapy. The major problem was one of motivation and anxiety that impaired her learning capacity. Separated from her mother and offered an opportunity to express her fantasies and reintegrate experiences in psychotherapy, her anxiety rapidly diminished and she made good progress in her total adjustment within a few months. Her response to reading therapy was equally rapid and steady. In six months Alice gained two years one month in her reading. From this point she needed little further specific help and her gains continued. At the time of last testing Alice's performance mental age was 12–0, her reading age 12–2. She had returned to school in the community and was functioning at an average level in a grade placement appropriate for her age.

This report of techniques of remedial reading and the child's response is typical of the secondary group. The report is much briefer than that for Bob because the techniques are much simpler. The problem in our work with Alice was to release a normal learning potential, a much easier task than that with which we were faced with Bob. Any analysis of the results of specific remedial reading therapy must take into account the differentiation between primary and secondary cases. Both the techniques and ultimate goals are very different, as these two cases demonstrate.

Summary

1. As we attempt to understand and plan for children who cannot read adequately, it seems valid and useful to recognize three major groups: (a) Those in whom the reading retardation is due to frank brain damage manifested by gross neurologic deficits, among which are aphasias of various types; b) Those, with no history of gross clinical findings to suggest

neurologic disease, who present a basic defect in capacity to integrate written material and to associate concepts with symbols. A neurologic deficit is suspected in these cases, and to describe them we have used the term *primary reading retardation;* (c) Those cases demonstrating reading retardation but with normal potential for learning to read; because the reading difficulty is the result of personality or educational neglect factors, we have described these cases as *secondary reading retardation.*

2. Criteria of differentiation of primary and secondary reading retardation are suggested in the data from five examination approaches: psychometric testing, achievement testing, psychiatric evaluation, neurological assessment, and response to remedial reading therapy.

3. In the primary group, the defect appears to be part of a larger disturbance in integration. Our findings suggest that we are dealing with a developmental discrepancy rather than an acquired brain injury. The specific areas of difficulty manifested in the clinical examinations are those commonly associated with parietal and parietaloccipital dysfunction.

4. The goal of research must be to define more clearly the specific defects in primary reading retardation in order to devise optimal techniques for retraining.

5. A clear understanding of the differentiating diagnostic criteria may aid in early case finding in order to implement preventive programs at the kindergarten or first-grade level. This must be viewed as the ultimate goal of our present research.

6. This report presents the findings to date of a continuing study. Further detailed investigation is projected in the five diagnostic areas outlined.

PSYCHOANALYTIC CONTRIBUTIONS TO THE PROBLEMS OF READING DISABILITIES

PHYLLIS BLANCHARD

Blanchard divides children with reading disabilities into those who are neurotic and those who are not. She notes, however, that the youngsters in the second category, regardless of the primary cause of their reading disability, generally suffer from emotional problems resulting from their inability to read. The following article focuses on the children whose reading problems are based on neurotic difficulties. It offers, in addition, a survey of the literature pertaining to the subject.

From her psychoanalytic perspective, Blanchard views reading disability as a neurotic compromise formation. Her position might be contrasted with that expressed by Rabinovitch et al. (1956), who report that they rarely encounter reading retardation as an overdetermined neurotic symptom. Blanchard cites examples wherein words and letters assumed symbolic meanings that interfered with the learning process. Thus, reading can become the equivalent of an anxiously avoided phobic object (see English and Pearson, 1963).

In Blanchard's opinion, reading disability can be traced to conflicts in the child's attitude toward the teacher (as parent surrogate) and to interferences with the sublimation of sexual curiosity and aggression. Additional attention to the role of aggression in learning inhibitions has been rare, even though several observers have noted that aggressive nonlearners are generally brighter than submissive nonlearners (Harris, 1961; Sperry, Ulrich and Staver, 1958; Sontag, Baker and Nelson, 1955). The influence of parental expectations on children's performance, as demonstrated in the Fels study, are well-known (Kagan and Moss, 1959). In the laboratory, Rosenthal (1966) has demonstrated that even the speed with which rats run a maze is correlated with the experimenters' opinions about the rats' intelligence.

Although Blanchard finds that more boys than girls have reading problems, and also stresses the importance of the relationship between student

---

Reprinted from *The Psychoanalytic Study of the Child,* 2. New York: International Universities Press, 1946, pp. 163–187.

and teacher, she does not mention that primary-grade boys learning to read are at the age when resolution of the Oedipus complex is enhanced by identification with a man, but, given a female teacher, they may perceive instruction in reading as an insistence that they identify with a woman.

The child with a reading disability typically is of average or superior intelligence, able to achieve an I.Q. of 90 to 150 (or more) on oral intelligence tests such as the Stanford-Binet, although rating considerably lower on group tests of intelligence which require reading the questions or instructions. Such a child's failures in school are due not to lack of intelligence but to inability to read well; for example, competency in arithmetic computation is rarely affected, since learning to add, subtract, multiply, divide, etc., is not dependent upon ability to read to the same extent that learning many other subjects is dependent on it. Difficulties in writing and spelling words often are associated with reading disabilities, but disabilities for reading and spelling may appear independently of one another.

Reading disabilities are far more common among boys than girls: statistical studies indicate that eighty per cent or more of children with disabilities in reading are boys. We do not yet have an adequate explanation for this. [1]

For the purposes of the present discussion, it will be convenient to divide reading disabilities into two categories–those of neurotic origin, and those arising from non-neurotic sources. Emotional disturbances may of course be present in both neurotic and non-neurotic cases. The distinction between the two types depends upon the fact that in the non-neurotic group, emotional conflicts have developed largely out of the situation of failure in learning to read, which is in itself a cause of chagrin to the child, and as reactions to the attitudes of parents and teachers to the failure. In the neurotic kind of disability, on the other hand, emotional conflicts and

[1] Monroe has suggested that possibly reading defects, like certain biological variations, may occur more frequently in boys because constitutional factors that impede learning to read are largely characteristic of the male sex (1932, p. 98). In the light of psychoanalytic contributions, Blanchard has advanced another hypothesis. She notes that Nunberg (1932) stated, in regard to the earlier psychosexual development of girls, that their active, aggressive strivings tend to be held in check by passive, feminine tendencies, seldom reaching the same strength as in boys. This may mean that boys, more frequently than girls, encounter difficulties in the normal repressive and sublimative processes in connection with the aggressive drives for which reading, according to psychoanalytic theories, is one means of sublimation (Blanchard, 1936a). For the statistics on sex and reading disabilities, see Berman and Bird (1933), Monroe (1932), and other psychological studies of reading disabilities.

difficulties in personality development have preceded the reading disability, which is a neurotic symptom growing from these earlier maladjustments. Gates (1941), who has probably done research over a longer period of time and on larger numbers of cases than anyone else, estimates that in about seventy-five per cent of children with severe reading disabilities, emotional disturbances and personality problems will be present. He states that in about one-fourth of these cases, the emotional and personality difficulties are the cause of the reading disability, while in the other three-fourths they result from the disability for reading.

It is well to emphasize the above statistical data, for while a psychoanalytic orientation enables us to understand the etiology of neurotic reading disabilities and to offer proper therapy for those cases, it is not the approach to be preferred for all. If the figures quoted from Gates are fairly accurate, we may expect that about 20 per cent of reading disabilities will be of the neurotic type, amenable to psychotherapy followed by remedial teaching, but about 80 per cent will be non-neurotic and able to respond to remedial teaching immediately, without its being preceded by psychotherapy. Occasionally, however, even the non-neurotic child suffers from such severe emotional disturbances as a reaction to the failure in reading and the family attitudes toward it, that psychotherapy may be required prior to instituting a program of special methods of instruction.

In the present discussion, we shall be concerned chiefly with the smaller group of reading disabilities (the probable 20 per cent mentioned above) in which the trouble in learning to read is an outgrowth of personality maladjustments and is one of the child's neurotic symptoms. Careful differential diagnosis is necessary in order to determine whether we are dealing with this type of case or whether the reading disability is of a non-neurotic etiology.[2] Diagnostic reading tests alone do not differentiate the neurotic from the non-neurotic child with a reading disability, for the

[2] The etiology may be quite as complicated in the non-neurotic cases as in the neurotic ones, since the disability for reading may arise from a variety of sources. For example, certain neurological conditions may be a primary factor. Nielson (1941) mentions that injury to the angular gyrus of the parietal lobe impairs its function of recognition of symbols, including letters and words; or lesion of Wernicke's area, causing loss of the function of recognition and recall of sounds of words, may result in reading disability, since ordinarily in learning to read the sounds of words must be associated with the visual symbol of the written word. Nielson states, however, that individuals who have suffered destruction of the cortex of the angular gyrus can be taught to read by the Fernald-Keller method which utilizes kinaesthetic factors in learning (1921). Orton's neurological theory of reading disabilities (1937), stressing faulty unilateral cerebral dominance which causes images formed in one side of the brain to conflict with those formed in the other side, is too widely known to need more than passing reference. This hypothesis has been questioned by other investigators because the errors in reading ascribed to a defect in cerebral dominance often are susceptible to alternative explanations not considered by Orton. See, for instance, Schilder (1944). Defects of vision or hear-

same types of errors ordinarily are made by both. Emotional reactions to reading tests may be significant, however, in distinguishing between neurotic responses and attitudes toward the failure in reading resulting from them. Careful medical examinations (including tests of vision and hearing), a developmental history, and a study of the child's personality are important. Only on the basis of data so obtained, as well as the findings from psychological tests, can we formulate an adequate diagnostic opinion as to whether a reading disability in any given case is a neurotic symptom or stems from other sources. If we fail to detect the presence of emotional factors in this kind of diagnostic approach, we shall be made aware of them by the child's inability to respond to remedial teaching, for one characteristic of the neurotic reading disability is the child's failure to

---

ing are probably more frequent etiological factors in reading disabilities than neurological conditions. Gates (1936) has summarized a number of controlled statistical studies which show that vision defects have been found in 44 per cent of reading disability cases as compared to 38 per cent of good readers, while a hearing loss of 15 per cent or more occurred in 30 per cent of reading disability cases but in only 11 per cent of good readers. Left-handedness, left eye and hand dominance or mixed eye and hand dominance, once thought prominent in association with failures in learning to read, appear only 10 per cent more frequently among children having trouble with reading than among those who learn to read satisfactorily (Monroe, 1932).

When children have difficulty in learning to read, attitudes of parents and teachers often are such as to exaggerate the problem until it grows into a real disability. Preston (1939) described the reactions of parents to their children in 100 reading disability cases. Some of the parents were deeply worried and anxious; others thought the children lazy or stubborn; still others were bewildered by the child's not learning to read. Some of the parents were irritable or reproachful, while others scolded or beat the children. Preston (1940) also reported on the attitudes of 32 school principals toward reading disabilities of 40 pupils. Only four of the principals had any insight into the poor reading as cause of poor schoolwork; the other 28 principals ascribed the trouble to low mentality, poor physical condition, or psychopathic or delinquent tendencies; none of these opinions proved correct when the children were examined by physicians and psychologists.

In learning to read or spell words, psychologically speaking, we know that visual, auditory and kinaesthetic sensations, perceptions, and memories are associated in a complex mental activity, involving both analytical and synthetic processes (Bronner, 1921). To put it more simply, in learning to read words, there must be visual perception and recognition of letters and combinations of letters in association with the sounds of these combinations, while the meaning of the word also must be associated with the letter combinations that form it. Perhaps children who learn to read easily employ this complex mental process early in reading. Certainly, in many reading disability cases, the chief cause of trouble has been failure to acquire this approach. One such case is described in detail in the literature, showing how a seven-year-old boy, who chanced to be highly gifted in visual perception and memory, was depending upon these gifts for learning words, never associating the spoken word with the written one. Thus, he could reproduce words that he had seen in writing but was unable to pronounce them and did not know how to say them when he encountered them in reading lessons. (This case appears as Case I, Tommy Nolan, by Blanchard, in *Psychiatric Interviews with Children,* Witmer [1946]).

Besides such possible factors as those indicated above, poor educational training may result in inability to read. Once, in a school survey, tests were given to a whole third grade in which none of the pupils could read due to incompetent teaching in the first and second grades.

learn to read by any method of instruction, given either individually or in a group, until there has been a recovery from his neurosis.

Historical Background (Review of the Literature)

Most of our current knowledge about reading disabilities has been acquired since 1920. Previous to that time, there were some reports in medical literature on cases of "word-blindness" or "word-deafness", but appreciation of the full extent of trouble with reading among school children did not come until the application of psychological tests revealed that many children who would formerly have been considered mentally deficient were in reality failing schoolwork because of lack of reading skill and were of normal or superior intelligence. Contemporaneously with the development of psychological testing methods, techniques for psychoanalytic work with children were being devised under the leadership of Anna Freud. New light on special educational disabilities, including those for reading, came from both clinical psychology and child analysis. Although psychologists had to devote considerable time from 1920 to 1930 to perfecting diagnostic reading tests and conducting statistical studies comparing groups of children with reading disabilities to control groups of good readers (Bronner, 1921; Burt, 1921; Gates, 1922, 1927; Gray, 1922; Hollingworth, 1923; Monroe, 1928), they became aware fairly soon of an association between emotional or personality disturbances and reading disabilities. Simultaneously, psychoanalysis was revealing that there sometimes seemed to be a causal relationship between unconscious emotional conflicts and attitudes and scholastic failures in special subjects.

Psychology and psychoanalysis have been in considerable agreement in including emotional factors in the etiology of some reading disability cases. Thus, Jones (1923) stated that disabilities for a particular school subject were often due to an inhibition of interest because that subject was unconsciously associated with some personally disagreeable idea or topic, and that after the unconscious associations were brought into consciousness through psychoanalysis, the individual was able to master the subject which had been failed previously. At about the same time, Meek (1925) observed that young children showed wide individual differences in their emotional attitudes toward reading even in their first lessons, and Hincks (1926) published a series of case studies in which she emphasized the relationship between reading disabilities and personality maladjustments, stating her belief that in a few of her cases the child's emotional conflicts were significant in the etiology of the disability for reading. Although advancing a neurological explanation for reading disabilities, Orton (1925, 1928a) noted emotional disturbances often coincident with them, but for the most part he considered that the emotional maladjustments grew out of the experience of failure in reading rather than they they preceded it. Gates (1941, 1927, 1936), in his earlier writings, mentioned the possibility that emotional problems and personality maladjustments might be contributing factors in some cases of reading disability and has since given increasing attention to these factors. Blanchard (1928, 1929) reported several cases of reading disability or arithmetical disability where emotional disturbances also were evident, indicating that these disabilities might develop from a child's emotional attitudes toward the subject.

After these beginnings in the nineteen-twenties, the early thirties saw still more study devoted to the role of emotional factors in the production of reading failures. Strachey's article on unconscious factors influencing the reading process appeared in 1930. In 1935 and 1936, papers by Tulchin and by Blanchard reported clinical case summaries showing that some children's difficulty in learning to read was a symptom of emotional conflict or neurotic illness (Blanchard, 1936a, 1935, 1936b; Tulchin, 1935).

In his general theoretical paper, Strachey reviewed the evidence that reading represents a sublimation of oral tendencies, especially those of sadistic and destructive nature. Hence skill in reading breaks down when these oral drives are unstably or incompletely repressed and sublimated: reading threatens to bring about release of too many unsublimated sadistic and destructive oral impulses instead of providing a sublimated outlet for them. Tulchin, in his series of cases, described such emotional factors as emotional instability, resistance to authority, feelings of inadequacy, infantile personality, anxieties, and conflicts arising from family relationships, such as sibling rivalry or marital disharmony between parents, as contributing to reading disability. From her case material, Blanchard arrived at the conclusion that a common etiological factor was difficulty in handling aggression, with excessive guilt and anxiety over hostile, destructive, or sadistic impulses and fantasies, which frequently were oral in form, as suggested by Strachey. Blanchard also described certain similarities between reading disabilities and neurotic symptoms, as the latter are seen in psychoanalysis. The neurotic symptom, from this viewpoint, in one sense originates from an effort to solve ambivalent guilt conflicts; it affords a disguised expression for repressed instinctive drives but at the same time relieves anxiety and guilt about those drives through the self-punishment of illness or securing punishment from others. In like manner, a reading disability often disguises hidden motives; also it satisfies the guilty need for punishment by exposing the child to a situation of failure at school and criticism both there and at home.

In their book *Common Neuroses of Children and Adults* (1937), Pearson and English enumerated four emotional situations that might be a basis for reading disability: (1) Some unpleasant and painful experience may have occurred during the early efforts to learn to read so that the child becomes conditioned against reading or has a negative attitude toward it. (2) If there is great antagonism of a child to a parent, and the parent constantly stresses success in reading, the child may express rebellion through refusing to learn to read, when he dare not openly resist the parent. (3) If a child has been severely inhibited in peeping, his superego may place a ban upon acquiring knowledge by visual means. Reading implies learning things by use of vision, and the inhibition may readily become attached to that subject. (4) Letters and words may come to represent curious anal-sadistic fantasies, and, in attempting to keep these repressed, the child may avoid reading or introduce into it word distortions that afford disguised expressions of the fantasies.

Sylvester and Kunst, after studying thirteen reading disability cases, concluded (1943) that trouble in learning to read is one aspect of disturbances of the exploratory function in the instinctual tendencies, the manifestation of curiosity as an aggressive, self-assertive activity becoming a source of anxiety to the child, with reading disability serving as a defense against this anxiety.

Psychoanalytic Theories as Applied to Reading Disabilities

From the preliminary orientation of the preceding introductory comments and sketchy history of the literature, we come to our chief purpose—a brief review of certain psychoanalytic theories that help to explain how difficulties in reading may sometimes develop out of emotional conflicts and neurotic tendencies. Anna Freud (1935) has described how a young child's training (education) is facilitated by his love of adults and his wish to retain their affection and approval. The child accepts instruction from his parents, in his preschool years, motivated by his love of them and his desire to please them. If the parent-child relationship is a less affectionate one and engenders considerably more than an ordinary amount of friction, the child may express hostility to the parents in negativistic behavior toward their training. We often see this in young children who refuse to be toilet trained or who will not talk although quite capable of doing so.

When the child enters school, the attitudes he has previously had toward parents may be transferred into his relationship with his teachers. If he has liked his parents and been willing to learn what they taught, he will often adopt the same positive attitude toward learning from teachers. On the other hand, when a child has had more than the usual amount of hostility toward parents and reacted negativistically toward their instruction, he may carry over these patterns to his teachers, regardless of whether they are pleasant or unpleasant people in their own right. Sometimes this situation results in the child becoming a disciplinary problem in school, but sometimes he yields to the classroom discipline and centers his negative responses upon learning, either in general or in particular upon learning to read.

A well-known psychoanalytic contribution to education is the concept that learning offers an opportunity for the sublimation of instinctive drives. In the first years of life, the child tends towards fairly free and open expression of sexual curiosity and interests, and of aggression, with the latter often directed against animals or people. During the latter part of his preschool life, if development has been normal, the child begins to control and modify such instinctive behavior. Anna Freud (1943) has spoken particularly of the importance of aggressive drives being sublimated by turning their energy into constructive rather than destructive activities and into the accomplishment of all sorts of tasks. By the time a child enters school, he should at least be started on this road of sublimation of sexual interest and aggression, and his schoolwork offers a chance for further sublimation. If the child has acquired very little capacity for sublimation, he may not be able to take advantage of the opportunity for it afforded by school tasks. He is apt then to develop into a poor student and a behavior problem as well but will be more likely to fail in all subjects than to have a disability for some one, such as reading.

In the reading disability cases, more frequently the child will be suffering from severe unconscious conflicts, with repression of impulses and imperfect capacity to sublimate them, so that much of his energy is used up in maintaining repression and not enough is left over for such a complex mental process as learning to read. Moreover, this type of child often tends to resort to restriction of ego activities in order to escape painful situations and now may utilize this defense mechanism to avoid the painful experience of seeing classmates excel his achievement, giving up all effort to learn to read as a way of evading competition where he knows he will appear inferior to others (A. Freud, 1936). This soon results in the child being so far behind in the subject that he has a real disability for it.

Either traumatic experiences or chronic subjection to excessive emotional strain in the relationship with parents may result in unconscious conflicts that interfere with a child's learning. A good example of a traumatic emotional experience is that of a child who has been separated from one or both parents. In working with the English children during war time, Anna Freud found that loss of parents or separation from them was a severe trauma for the child (1943, 1944); we have known this for some time, too, from our clinical work with children placed in foster homes or institutions and temporarily or permanently separated from their own parents. Such a traumatic experience may be an immediate cause of trouble with learning if the child is emotionally disturbed by it at the time of school entrance or during early school years. Again, the emotions surrounding an earlier traumatic occurrence may be reactivated by some later event of similar nature that revives the memories and feelings associated with the original traumatic situation.

A child suffers from chronic emotional stress when exposed constantly to unfavorable family relationships over a long period of time. One illustration would be the kind of family life in which parents are antagonistic to each other, are constantly quarrelling, and use the child's behavior or disciplinary questions as a means of provoking each other into arguments or criticizing each other. Under these circumstances, a child often feels that he is to blame for the disharmony between the parents and is caught in conflict between guilt over the trouble that he occasions and resentment and hostility toward the parents for the way they are using him. Another familiar illustration is continuous unfavorable comparison of a child with a brother or sister, which results in jealousy and hostility toward the parent and the favored sibling coming into conflict with love for those members of the family.

In these chronically unfavorable family relationships, reading sometimes becomes a focus of the parents' dissatisfactions with the child, especially if the child should chance to have some trouble with it. When the parents' complaints center upon reading, there is all the more likelihood of any mild difficulty growing into a severe disability and becoming one of the neurotic reactions to parental pressures. In these parent-child relationships where there are chronic situations affecting the child's emotional development, psychotherapy for the child is unlikely to be of much benefit unless there is also work with the parent.

It is logical to inquire why children with hostile attitudes towards parents and teachers, or children suffering from emotional conflicts and neurotic repressions, should have trouble in learning to read more frequently than in learning other subjects. Sometimes, of course, a child's emotional problems do interfere with learning some other subject or prevent mastery of any schoolwork at all. But as Gates stated, the majority of failures in the first years of school life are due to reading, and this subject does seem to be a source of far more trouble to children than any other single one. [3] Thus we need to seek for an explanation of these facts.

In the primary grades, learning the fundamentals of reading is a more complicated mental process, probably requiring greater expenditure of energy and better sustained attention than learning the first steps of arithmetic. Hence a child may have enough energy left over from maintaining repressions and may be able to sustain attention sufficiently well to learn his number work but not his first reading lessons. Furthermore, reading is symbolically, for the unconscious, a sublimated aggressive, sadistic activity, according to the psychoanalytic viewpoint (M. Klein, 1931; Strachey, 1930). Therefore, while reading offers an excellent opportunity for the sublimation of aggressive tendencies for a child whose development has been normal so that he is free to sublimate them, for a child whose neurotic conflicts are largely concerned with trying to keep aggressive drives repressed even a sublimated expression and satisfaction through reading may not be permissible to the ego and superego. We shall come to some clinical case material illustrative of this statement a little later.

In his *Psychopathology of Everyday Life,* Freud (1901) explained certain likenesses between errors in speaking or writing and the mechanisms of neurotic symptom formation. The psychoanalytic concept of the neurotic symptom regards it as a compromise between wishes to gratify an impulse and the need to refuse gratification or even to deny that such an impulse exists. In a symbolic manner, the symptom gratifies a repressed instinctive impulse but at the same time disguises both the gratification and the existence of the impulse itself. Freud described many errors of speech or writing that served the same purpose; when we come to case reports, we shall see that errors in reading sometimes afford symbolic gratification or expression of a repressed impulse while concealing it and not admitting its existence. [4]

[3] For statistics, see Gates (1936).

[4] This statement is not intended to imply however, that errors in reading must always resemble a neurotic symptom, for defective vision or some other condition may cause errors in reading that superficially are very similar to the errors resulting from emotional conflicts.

Undoubtedly still another reason why neurotic or emotionally disturbed children are likely to develop disabilities for reading rather than for another subject is the fact that reading content can so easily become associated with emotional conflicts. In the psychoanalytic literature there are many illustrations of the ways in which single words or certain combinations of words become surrounded with a whole constellation of emotionally colored associations, so that a person may seek to evade using those words or forget them. The content of reading, either as it consists of separate words, or contains certain letters, or tells about certain things, may become associated with emotional conflicts already present in the child's life. If this happens, the child may dislike reading because he has found it emotionally disturbing, or refuse to read in order to avoid the danger of recurrence of the emotional disturbance, or when he does read, may be so upset and apprehensive that he will make many mistakes.

For example, if a child pictures the letter C and certain other letters as animals with mouths open ready to bite him, he may want to have nothing to do with reading matter because many words have these letters and recall his fears of being bitten. This actually happened in two cases seen at the clinic. Both children who spoke of letters biting them were struggling to repress hostile wishes toward baby sisters whom they wished to bite or eat up; in one sense, their reactions to the letters were expressions of their feelings of guilt and need to be punished; in another sense, we might say that as usual there was a wish disguised by the fear. [5]

An experimental investigation conducted by two psychologists supports the psychoanalytically derived theory that reading content which is emotionally disturbing leads to difficulties in reading. A study was made of the responses of four students without fear of high places and of six students who did have this fear, when given reading matter that might activate it. Their comprehension and memory for reading material was first tested by a paragraph selected because it seemed to contain nothing that could be associated with high places or falling from them. They were then given a paragraph of similar length and difficulty but describing a person hanging from the top of a tall building by an overall strap caught on a projecting plank, in imminent danger of falling to his death. The four students who were not fearful of high places comprehended and recalled about the same amount from reading both paragraphs. The six students who suffered from a phobia for high places, on the other hand, made mis-

[5] More detailed account of these two cases appears in the paper previously referred to (Blanchard, 1936a).

takes in reading, read more slowly and could recall much less of what they read in the second paragraph describing the man in danger of falling from the top of the tall building (Warren and Jones, 1943).

Many children's books have been carefully edited with the idea of excluding material that might be emotionally disturbing. Obviously, however, since unconscious attitudes of the child are involved, it is impossible to choose reading content free of all emotional coloring, even if it were considered advisable. We cannot protect a child from encountering letters or words that for some reason he has endowed with symbolic significance. Furthermore, story content that activates painful emotions for some individuals will not do so for others (as indicated by the experimental study just mentioned). Thus the same reading content may have an emotional value of one sort for some children but may arouse no emotional response or a quite different emotion for other children. More extensive censorship and editing of children's reading actually could abate neither reading disabilities nor emotional conflicts, for the former are the outgrowth from many possible sources and the latter exist before the child reads disturbing content, indeed, they determine whether he will be disturbed by it. Moreover, if we could succeed in robbing books of emotional stimulus, we should lose one of the greatest incentives to reading, for both children and adults alike read as a means of obtaining emotional excitation and not merely to secure information. This incentive to learning to read has already been partially lost, in our modern times, because radio and movies compete with reading as sources of emotional excitement and satisfaction.

Cases Illustrating Neurotic Reading Disabilities

For purposes of brevity, the following illustrations will not be complete case summaries but will consist of material selected chiefly to clarify points made in the preceding general discussion. Since the selection has been made for research purposes and to illustrate theoretical concepts, no implications as to therapeutic methods and techniques are intended.[6] In some instances, longer case reports have been published previously (in papers referred to in reviewing the literature on reading disabilities).

The first case illustrates a chronically unfavorable parent-child relationship in which the child was under constant emotional strain. For some three years prior to his referral to clinic, the boy had been the object of

[6] Viewpoints on psychotherapy may be found in the author's contributions to the symposium on *Psychiatric Interviews with Children* (H. Witmer, 1946).

his father's anxiety and criticism, focused upon the subject of reading. Why the boy developed difficulty in reading and other neurotic symptoms should be self-evident from the case material presented below.

Case 1. Matthew was a twelve-year-old boy who was repeating fifth grade and still failing the work. He was considered mentally deficient by parents, teachers and classmates but psychological examination showed that he actually was of superior intelligence, with an I.Q. of 133.

The boy's father had had considerable difficulty in his vocational adjustments and had often been unemployed. He displaced anxiety from himself onto worry about the boy's future, stressing success in school as a preparation for later vocational success. When the boy was in third grade, the father began to supervise his schoolwork. Although Matthew's teachers gave him good marks in reading, his father decided that he was poor in this subject. The father came to this conclusion after asking Matthew to read matter that was far too advanced for a third grade pupil. From that time, however, the father centered his anxiety upon the boy's reading and began to tutor him in it. Invariably, he scolded and criticized the boy during these home lessons, so that they always ended with Matthew in tears and his father in a temper. It is not strange, therefore, that the boy made no further progress in reading between the third and fifth grades or that by the time he was in fifth grade, he had a serious reading disability. By then, also, he was so sensitive to criticism that he would burst into tears at the slightest reprimand from a teacher and would fight with any child who said a teasing word to him.

Neither remedial teaching nor psychotherapy helped in this case so long as the boy remained at home, for the father was unable to change in his relationship to the boy, continued to displace anxiety onto him, and could not be induced to forego tutoring him. When the boy went to a boarding school and was thus freed from his father's anxiety and criticisms, he was able to learn to read with the help of individual remedial teaching.

In the following case, we see how a later event may reactivate the unconscious feelings that surrounded an earlier traumatic one.

Case 2. Thomas was an eleven-year-old boy, failing fifth grade for the second time. He had made low ratings on group tests given at school. Individual tests showed that he had an I.Q. of 108 but was handicapped in doing both group tests and schoolwork by a reading disability. He dated the start of his trouble with reading from the first part of third grade, when a teacher whom he liked very much had to go to the hospital for an operation. Since she did not return to the school, Thomas assumed she had died. He explained that he was so worried over the teacher's absence and her supposed death that he could not keep his mind on his work and so fell behind in reading.

This preoccupation with the question of the teacher's possible death becomes more intelligible if we know that when the boy was five years old, his mother had been away in a hospital, for an operation. He did not recall these circumstances about his mother's hospitalization, even when they were mentioned to him; he only remembered about the teacher.

In some of his therapeutic interviews, Thomas wanted to read aloud. It then became obvious that the content of reading often brought up his unconscious emotional conflicts. He would be reading fairly well when suddenly he would begin to make many errors until he stopped and talked of personal matters suggested to him by something he had read. After speaking out what had come into his mind, he could resume reading without excessive mistakes. For example, in reading a story about a dog, Thomas began making errors and continued to do so until he had paused to talk about a dog he once had owned. He had loved his dog very much indeed, he said, but he had not been permitted to keep it. After his dog was given away, he was very lonely; he cried and cried because he wanted his dog back and because he did not know what might be happening to it. "I was afraid my dog might die without my knowing about it," he explained. "It is awful to be wondering whether someone you love is alive or dead."

By the time his therapy ended, he could read without breaking down as described above. According to follow-up reports, during the next two years, his school progress was satisfactory.

The circumstances of the teacher's going to a hospital for an operation evidently revived the boy's feelings about his mother's hospitalization even though he had repressed the memory of his mother's operation and his anxiety about it. Reactivation of the emotional trauma was not the only reason for his trouble with reading, however, for from his interviews it was evident that reading content too frequently tended to stir up his unconscious conflicts. It does not take a very vivid imagination to realize that his feelings about his dog, for instance, were like those he had experienced when his mother was in the hospital. These feelings quite obviously were brought closer to consciousness when he read the story about the dog, even though it was a very cheerful one, just because the content contained the word dog many times repeated.

Case 2 illustrates the statements in the preceding general theoretical formulation concerning the ease with which reading content becomes associated with a child's unconscious emotional conflicts, leading to a breakdown in reading skill, or to an aversion to reading. Our last case is that of a boy whose expressions of sexual curiosity and also of aggression had been stringently restricted. This case shows a reading disability developing from too severe limitations of instinctive drives.

Case 3. Jonathan, eight years old when referred to the clinic, had been living in the same foster home since infancy. He had for some time been a tense, hyperactive child, hardly ever still. After two years in school, he had not learned to read. At first it was difficult to maintain contact with him or carry on any connected conversation for more than a few minutes. It was soon observed that he often hunted among the therapist's books, as if searching for something in particular, but he never would tell what he was looking for, saying that he did not know, which was probably quite true. One day as he rummaged through the books, he came upon *Growing Up.* He seized it with the exclamation, "That's what I wanted," but immediately replaced it upon the shelf, saying he could not read it. When asked if he would like it read to him, he hastily disclaimed any such wish.

For some time after this episode, the interviews were taken up with some of his conflicts about living in a foster home and having no parents of his own. At first he tried to protect himself from the anxiety aroused by the knowledge that his own parents had died when he was a small child, by fantasies that the foster parents were his own. After a while he gave up this defense and admitted the insecurity he felt at having no "real" parents like other children at school. Instead of running aimlessly around the room, he now began to do carpentry, liking to fashion swords, knives and guns out of wood. From his talk about these weapons, it was clear that they were symbols of both masculinity and aggressive tendencies, but he often had to leave them with the therapist because he was sure that his foster mother would object to his having them. Actually, when he did get courage to take home a sword he had made, his foster mother took it away from him. As he complained, she wanted him to act like a girl. His complaint had foundation in fact, for the foster mother told us that she had wanted the placement agency to give her a girl (although she had never mentioned this to the agency) and when receiving a boy instead, she had dressed him like a girl as long as he would tolerate it and still expected him to be feminine in his behavior.

After he had found some relief from the repression of aggression and masculinity imposed by the foster mother, he again sought out the book *Growing Up* and looked at the pictures, asking the therapist to read some of the pages. He was guilty about this until he had talked over how his foster father once read him this book—but behind locked doors and with a stern warning that Jonathan must never talk about these sex education matters with the foster mother or anyone else except the foster father himself. This was only one aspect of the foster father's need to assure himself the sole intimate relationship with the boy; he did not permit Jonathan to play after school with other children, visit them or invite them to his home. Once Jonathan had thrown aside the restriction his foster father had placed upon his speaking of sex matters to other people, his next interviews with the therapist were full of questions and talk about sex and babies, including repetition of all the slang words and phrases he had heard. He concluded this series of interviews by saying, "I wish I could have asked my mother these things and talked about them with her, but I didn't dare because it would have made my father so angry that maybe he wouldn't have kept me. I was afraid he would give me back to the agency." He also told how he had been eager to learn to read when he first went to school, so that he could read *Growing Up* by himself, only he was fearful that the foster father would not have liked his reading it, for he always kept the book locked in his desk.

After the therapy was completed Jonathan was able to learn to read at school without remedial teaching. By then, too, he was ready for a move to another foster home where masculine and aggressive strivings were acceptable. Follow-up reports from the agency indicated that he was developing along normal masculine lines thereafter and when a young adolescent, he was seen for educational guidance tests and interview. At this later date, he could never have been recognized as the same repressed, effeminate boy who had come to the clinic years earlier.

It is interesting to raise a question as to whether this boy would have developed his reading disability as the result of limitation of sexual curiosity alone. To be sure, he was so guilty over wanting to read *Growing Up* and talk about it with his foster mother that he had to resist all reading, but it would seem that repression of aggression was also involved in his avoidance of reading. At least, it was plain in the therapeutic interviews that he could only admit his interest in sex questions, in defiance of his foster father's prohibitions, after relaxation of the repression of masculine, aggressive strivings. Apparently reading was not simply a way of acquiring knowledge but also was an activity that represented aggressive rebellion against the foster father's restrictions, and against his desire to keep the boy to himself.[7] The boy realized that aggression of any kind

[7] In this connection, it is interesting to recall that Freud mentioned the sadistic nature of desire for knowledge in the obsessional neuroses (1913a).

would meet with disapproval from the foster mother, on whom he had been very dependent as a young child. He was afraid also that the foster father might punish rebellious resistance to his domination by refusing to give him a home any longer. Hence it is little wonder that the boy had to repress aggression so completely.

Conclusion

In the clinical cases just presented to illustrate reading disabilities of a psychogenic nature, it seems possible to interpret the material in the light of psychoanalytic theories of reading and learning. But it also appears that there is no single situation or personality maladjustment which can be isolated to explain the development of a reading disability as one of the child's neurotic symptoms. The background may be either traumatic or may reveal chronically unfavorable experiences; the personality difficulties may be severe, (as in the case of Jonathan who was inhibited, passive and effeminate); or maladjustments other than the trouble with reading may be mild enough to be masked from ordinary observation and may become fully apparent only to the professional eye in therapeutic work with the child. These statements might not seem warranted as generalizations on the basis of the comparatively small number of cases included in this paper or reported in previous ones, except for the fact that other investigators have arrived independently at the same conclusions by accumulating statistical data on large numbers of cases. [8]

Both our individual case studies and the statistical findings of other psychologists suggest that a complexity of factors come together in a focal point around reading, particularly where the disability is of emotional origin. In this respect, the neurotic reading disability conforms to the psychoanalytic concept of neurotic symptoms generally as being overdetermined. It also conforms otherwise to psychoanalytic theories of symptom-formation: for the repression of instinctive drives and existence of emotional conflicts forms the setting for the reading disability as well as for other neurotic symptoms; errors in reading may serve as disguised ways of gratifying repressed impulses, just as illness-symptoms serve this

[8] Bell (1945) speaks of research in this field as indicating that reading is related to many different factors and is a highly complex function of the personality; Jackson (1944) reaches a similar conclusion on the basis of his own statistical findings. Gates (1941) states that there is no single personality pattern among pupils of adequate intelligence coexistent with reading disability, but that difficulty in reading may occur in all sorts of personalities, emotional patterns and parental relationships. Moreover, Gates points out, citing examples, that a factor which seems to be a chief cause of a reading disability in one individual may even be a strong motivation for learning to read well in another.

purpose; failure in reading may represent a hidden antagonism to adults expressed in passive resistance rather than in openly rebellious behavior, and thus may also conceal repressed attitudes. To be sure, at other times the failure may result from a wish to avoid reading because it has previously stirred up feelings of guilt or anxiety, but here too, it closely resembles a well-known neurotic tendency toward avoidance of imaginary dangers.

In considering that reading disabilities tend to appear as a center of convergence for several emotional factors, we probably need to take into account the timing of this occurrence. It is reasonable to believe that reading is most apt to become involved in a child's emotional conflicts when these concur with the period of learning the fundamentals of the reading process in the early school grades. Once a firm foundation has been acquired, further proficiency in reading depends more upon enlarging the reading vocabulary than learning new processes, so that disability for this subject is less likely to begin in higher grades, although it may have remained undetected until then. [9] It is possible, therefore, that the time element may have a bearing on whether a special educational disability will be for reading or for some other subject. Since in many cases personality maladjustments of children begin by the time they enter school or soon afterward, this may be one reason why reading disabilities are more frequent than others. But an equally valid reason, already mentioned, is the ease with which reading content, either directly or symbolically, can become associated with unconscious emotional conflicts.

[9] Unlike arithmetic, where fundamental processes (addition, subtraction, multiplication, fractions, decimals, etc.) are being learned, one after another through most of the elementary grades, and lack of mastery of any one process can affect much subsequent work, so that a disability in this subject may develop as readily in later grades as in earlier ones.

PART V

ANTISOCIAL DISORDERS

Man has always been concerned with the antisocial behavior of his progeny. Every older generation, from earliest antiquity, believed delinquency to be on the increase. Now that we keep records, we can make the same statement with more authority. But is the increase real or merely the result of improved techniques in gathering statistics? Can it perhaps be attributed to society's changing concept of what constitutes antisocial behavior, or society's growing intolerance for it? Eissler (1949a) deemphasizes legal and statistical considerations by urging that delinquency be defined psychologically as well as legally. He asserts that the essential criterion as to whether or not a particular behavior is delinquent should be based entirely on the motivation underlying the behavior in question rather than on an arbitrary legal code—"No external feature of behavior can ever be used as a reliable index of delinquency" (p. 5). Unquestionably, assessing the individual motivational factors can be far more important: benign-appearing behavior which is not legally "delinquent" may be indicative of more malignant psychopathological processes than certain legal offenses.

Devoting an entire section to antisocial disorders, as with learning disorders, is again a departure from the prevailing conceptual framework of this volume. Justification is to be found in the great frequency of antisocial maladaptation during childhood and in the special social significance of this symptomatology. Also worthy of note is the important historical role antisocial disorders have played in the development of child psychiatry. Pioneering child-psychiatric work during the first decade of this century was carried out by William Healy (see Healy and Bronner, 1936) under the auspices of the juvenile court in Chicago. The child guidance movement, which started to blossom during the third decade of this century, had its impetus in an effort to cope with juvenile delinquency.

It is estimated that, in the U.S., two per cent of all children become legally delinquent and that one out of every five boys between the ages of 10 and 17 appears in court. Despite the probable statistical artifacts in incidence rates, it seems clear that the frequency rises in proportion to the pros-

perity and complexity of the society; delinquency appears to be more prevalent in cultures on the move. Concomitantly, there is a decrease during economic depression and an increase during times of war. In this country, both the highest and lowest rates occur in minority groups—Blacks and Orientals, respectively.

Theories concerning the causes of antisocial behavior continue to proliferate. Although Lombroso's anatomical theory of a "criminal type" has received little support, the Gluecks (1956) and Sheldon (1949) have demonstrated that delinquents tend to be mesomorphic. Uncertainty remains, however, about the extent to which this muscularity contributes to, or is a consequence of, the delinquency. Very recently, electroencephalographic, neurophysiological, and neurosurgical techniques have been employed to explore physiological bases for certain violent outbursts. The most widely accepted causes of antisocial behavior, however, are to be found in the realm of psychology and sociology (Finch, 1962) and some of the important ones are described and discussed in the readings that follow.

UNDERLYING CAUSES OF DELINQUENCY

AUGUST AICHHORN

Aichhorn was a Viennese schoolteacher who often found himself interested in the psychological make-up of both his students and his fellow teachers. After successfully preventing an infusion of militarism into the Viennese educational system, he became the director of an institution for delinquent boys. In this capacity, he explored therapeutic approaches to delinquency. Eissler (1949a), in a volume dedicated to Aichhorn on the occasion of his 70th birthday, observed that "crime and delinquency had taken their course without hindrance. Punishment, segregation, flogging, and execution were recommended by some; love, humaneness, understanding, mercy, and charity by others. Neither approach satisfied Aichhorn" (p. x).

Aichhorn studied neuropathology and experimental psychology before he came upon psychoanalysis, which he felt supplied the data and method that fulfilled the needs of a teacher working with delinquents. Aichhorn's use of psychoanalysis was thoroughly innovative, so that while his orientation was unquestionably psychoanalytic, his technique differed markedly from typical psychoanalytic treatment. The illustrative case report which follows demonstrates, in Aichhorn's words, "what we can learn about the causes of dissocial behavior without going deeply into the matter as in psychoanalysis." What Aichhorn reports here represents an early form of family therapy, in which he deftly manipulates a supportive relationship to effect a transference cure. Interspersed in the case report are examples of Aichhorn's bold intuitiveness which even employed duplicity in a fashion modern therapists generally avoid, e.g., keeping the boy waiting for two hours in order to test the strength of his emotional attachment.

Although many prominent students praised Aichhorn enthusiastically as a teacher, few seem to have learned to employ his easy, free-swinging therapeutic approach. He nevertheless stimulated many to extend his pioneering psychoanalytic investigations of delinquency. The productive work of Eissler (1949a) and Friedlander (1947) follows in the paths first trod by Aichhorn.

Unlike the delinquents having ego disturbances which Redl (1951) described, Aichhorn's patient should be classified as neurotic delinquent. He is

---

Reprinted from *Wayward Youth* by August Aichhorn. New York: Viking Press, 1935, pp. 92–116.

reminiscent of the character type Freud (1916a) delineated as "criminals from a sense of guilt," subsequently elaborated on by Alexander's (1930b) description of self-punishment as a motive for antisocial behavior.

A factory foreman brought his seventeen-year-old son into the child-guidance clinic because he wanted to put him in an institution. The boy was at this time apprenticed to a shoemaker. From the father we learned certain important facts. Until the previous summer the son had been a good boy who made no trouble at home or in the shop. One day he asked his father for some money, saying that he could get the leather to make himself a pair of shoes cheap. He obtained the money but failed to come home that night, and the family learned the next day that he had not been at the shop. Since such a thing had never happened before, the family was very much concerned, feared that he had met with an accident or had been attacked. They reported his disappearance to the police and inquired about him daily at headquarters. Six days later his mother received word that he had been picked up penniless by the police in another city and was already on his way home. The family was overjoyed at his return, but this pleasure was soon forgotten in the distress over his subsequent behaviour. The boy would not talk. He refused to tell his father why he had left his work or where he had spent the week. He became more obdurate and defiant, and would say nothing more than that he had been to Graz, the city in which he had been picked up. His father became excited, a great scene occurred, and finally he gave his son a severe beating. After this things went from bad to worse. The boy would not work, stayed away from home, hung about the streets or in cafés all day, and stayed out later and later at night. As if this were not enough, he continued to get money out of his father and his employer. His father punished him with increasing severity in the hope of changing his behaviour. Since this only made him worse and drove him further from his family, his mother began to take his part and persuaded her husband to be more gentle with him. This method brought only temporary improvement, and finally his mother's patience was exhausted and his father reverted once more to force. Severity and kindness were tried alternately several times, but the boy only acted worse. The father concluded his remarks to me with the following words: "You can't imagine how awful it is. We've tried to be good to him and we've tried being strict and beating him, but nothing helps. We don't know what to do next. Perhaps if he goes into an institution, they can make something out of him."

Up to this point the father had confined his talk to a description of his son's behaviour and of his efforts to improve him. He had told us nothing of himself nor of the family relationships. Since such knowledge was indispensable to our insight into the problem, I turned the conversation in this direction. The family consisted of the father, the stepmother, a brother two years older who was about to enter the university, and a stepsister of five. The father had been married to the stepmother for twelve years and the five-year-old girl was a child of this marriage. The relationship between the parents, as well as the economic situation, was good. That the boy could have any feeling of inferiority in relation to the older brother seemed to the father out of the question, as the two had always been treated alike and had got along well together until this one began to behave so badly. Now they quarrelled all the time. The father thought that the stepsister was so much younger that there could be no question of jealousy of her. He did not pay much attention to her, was neither very affectionate with her nor unpleasant to her. The father was bitter, and complained that the change in the boy had completely disturbed what had formerly been a peaceful, happy family life. They used to sit around in the evening reading aloud, singing, or playing. Now when he got home at night he heard nothing except his son's misdemeanours, and he often had to go out on the street to look for him. The son had begun to learn the trade of shoemaker against his father's wishes. He had failed in the seventh grade and had refused to repeat the year. All arguments with him were in vain. He insisted on becoming a shoemaker like the stepmother's father. I inquired about the boy's relationship to girls, wondering if that could offer any explanation for his first running away. The father stated definitely that he knew his son's attitude toward girls and that this was impossible. When I asked how he explained this sudden change, he said, "Either the devil's got into him or he's gone crazy."

"Then he would not belong in our institution," I remarked.

The father answered, "Oh, you must not take that remark literally, but this has all happened so suddenly."

I talked to the boy alone. He was a very thin young man who looked somewhat older than his seventeen years. He was well dressed. The following is a part of the conversation, given verbatim.

"Do you know where you are?"

"No."

"In the child-guidance clinic of the Juvenile Court."

"Oh yes. My father wants to put me in a reform school."

"Your father has told me what has happened and I'd like to help you."

"It's no use." He shrugged his shoulders and turned away.

"Certainly it's no use, if you don't want help."

"You can't help me."

"I know you don't have much confidence in me; we don't know each other yet."

"Not that, but anyway it's no use." He showed the same hopeless, uncooperative air.

"Are you willing to talk to me?"

"Why not?"

"I must ask you various questions and I'll make you a proposition."

"What?" The tone betrayed expectation.

"That you don't answer any question you don't like."

"How do you mean?" He was astonished and incredulous.

"The questions you don't like you need not answer or you may tell me it's none of my business."

"Why do you say that?"

"Because I'm not a detective nor a policeman and I don't need to know everything. Anyway you wouldn't tell me the truth if I asked questions you didn't like."

"How do you know that?"

"Because that is what everybody does and you are no exception. I wouldn't tell everything either to someone whom I'd met for the first time."

"But if I talk and tell you lies, will you know that too?"

"No, but that would be too bad. And anyway it isn't necessary because I don't want to force you to answer me."

"At home they always said if I'd talk, nothing bad would happen to me, but when I did it was always much worse. So I quit talking."

"But here it's a little different. I'll be satisfied with what you are willing to tell. But I'd like to be sure you are telling me the truth."

"Good."

"You agree?" I offered him my hand which he took eagerly.

"Agreed."

"What grade were you in when you left school?"

"Seventh."

"Why didn't you go further in school?"

"I failed in three subjects and didn't want to go any more."

"Did your father agree to that?"

"He would have liked it better if I had repeated the grade."

"How did you happen to take up shoemaking?"

"My grandfather is a shoemaker and I wanted to be one too."

"I'm not interested in knowing all about your troubles but how did they begin? Why did you go to Graz?"

"I don't know."

"There must be some reason, though, why you went there. You might just as well have chosen another city."

"I really don't know."

"But it's not so long ago, not even a year. Think a little; maybe it will occur to you.

"Perhaps because my brother went there a year ago with a holiday group." Here he hesitated and became silent.

"Don't you want to tell me something more?" I asked this question after a pause during which I had noticed that the boy was having a battle with himself and was unable to come to a conclusion. He looked me straight in the eyes, then bowed his head, and shaken with sobs, said:

"If you promise you won't tell my father, I'll tell you something."

"Here's my hand on it." He took my hand and shook it vigorously.

"I wanted to kill myself."

"When?"

"Last summer."

"Before you got the money from your father or afterwards?"

"Before."

"Why?"

"My brother went away with mother to visit an aunt, and since I was an apprentice I had to stay at home. I went to work for a week. Then I laid off for three days and suddenly got afraid my father would find it out. Then I wanted to kill myself."

"Did you try to kill yourself?"

"No. I thought I'd go away and never come back. I got the money from my father and started off. When the money was all gone, I didn't know what to do and came back home. At home there was an awful row and since then everything's been all wrong."

"How do you get along with your brother?"

"All right; we used to get along better, but now he is on father's side."

"Do you think the other children are treated better at home than you?"

"No!"

"Doesn't it matter to you that your brother is getting educated and that you are a shoemaker's apprentice?" To this question he made no reply.

He went on to report the following facts. He was four when his mother died. His father remarried a year later. His stepmother was much attached to her father, the shoemaker, who according to the boy must have been a very understanding man. The tender attachment he had had to his own mother he transferred very quickly to the stepmother. The relationship to his father also had been good until the previous year. Despite his present antagonism to his father, he described him as a good man who stayed at home in the evenings, went seldom to beer taverns, and spent a great deal of time with his children. There was no great financial strain.

It is interesting to note how the boy justified the money episode. His father gave the brother money for the trip with his mother; therefore he had a right to the same amount. Had he told his father his true reason for wanting the money, of course it would have been refused. Consequently, he lied. It was not yet clear why he held his father responsible for his becoming a shoemaker. He said: "Father should have known better than I. I was dumb. A fourteen-year-old boy doesn't know what he wants to be. My father should have made me repeat the seventh grade. If he'd only insisted, then I would have obeyed and today I'd still be in school."

After a while I asked him if he thought it was possible for him and his father to come to some understanding. I offered to help. He was sceptical, but not so reluctant as at first. He said, "Oh, I've talked to my father time and again. It's no use." I tried to make him see that his father could not understand him as long as he did not know what he was really thinking. He might let me try to explain to the father. He released me from my promise to say nothing.

The boy went into the next room and sent his father to me. I had to talk with his father a long time before I could make him see that, without knowing it and without meaning to, he had lived with his son and had not been able to understand him. I told him also what the boy had suffered as a result of this situation. At first he listened in astonishment and shook his head incredulously; then he became indignant. Finally, as he began to understand, he was unable to restrain his tears. He apologized and said that he had not wept so since he was a child. I reassured him by saying that it was a natural reaction to such a realization and that I took it as proof of his affection for the boy. He calmed himself and was in such a conciliatory mood that I thought it was an opportune moment to begin to effect an understanding between father and son.

So I called the boy back. I started the conversation and then left them alone, feeling that a third person would only prove a hindrance. After about twenty minutes, I came back to find them both red-eyed and silent. The father said in answer to my look of astonishment, "It's no use, he won't talk." I know that the mentor dare not let himself get angry and I know that I should have been able to understand the father's emotional situation, but I was angry and disappointed in him. I had worked with him for over two hours to show him how the situation had arisen and had tried to show him what he must do to bring the poor boy back into a sympathetic relation to him, and now he was behaving like this! Without looking at the father, I went over to the boy, put my hand on his head, and said, "Never mind, one doesn't always have to talk. Two people can understand each other without saying a word." At that the boy began to cry violently. I do not know just how it happened or who took the initiative, but the next minute they were in each other's arms. I must admit that I too was not untouched by the scene. After things were a little calmer, I wanted to get the boy out of the way in order to say something important to the father, so I sent him out to buy me some cigarettes. I made it clear as I could to the father that such a first reconciliation was far from being the end of the conflict. He could expect that his son would prove even more troublesome in the near future. Since there was no time then for a longer interview, I advised him to come back to me as soon as his son misbehaved again in order to consult me before he undertook any disciplinary measures. At the boy's suggestion, we arranged that he and the father should go straight from me to his employer so that he could get back to work that afternoon. The boy seemed relieved and pleased. Father and son went away arm in arm as though a lasting harmony had been established.

Early the next morning I found the father in despair, waiting for me at the door of the clinic. He poured out a flood of complaints. "It's no use. We can't do a thing with that boy. He must go to the reform school. You saw how broken-up he was yesterday, and now it's the same old story again. Kindness doesn't work with him."

I asked calmly, "But what's the matter?" You will understand that I was not especially disturbed. I had told him the day before that something more was bound to happen. I was surprised, however, that it had happened so quickly. The father continued. "We went away entirely reconciled. On the way I gave him a good talking-to, to the effect that he must keep on being good now since I had forgiven him. He listened and said nothing, so that I had to keep myself in hand not to get angry again.

I didn't give his employer any explanation because he thinks that the boy was sick. Instead of beginning work in the afternoon as he should have, he went bumming around until late that night."

You will remember that I had sent the boy out for cigarettes in order to call the father's attention to the fact that backsliding was to be expected. Now it had occurred. Although the father should have been prepared for this by my talk, he had lost control of himself, had reproached his son severely, and had jeopardized what we had achieved on the preceding day. It is understandable that the father's participation made the boy seem to play the role of the "ungrateful prodigal." Such critical situations are usually misunderstood by parents and often by educators. Since the real situation is seldom properly recognized, we find ourselves on the wrong track and endanger the success of all our pedagogical efforts.

What occurs in these dissocial young people has a great deal to do with unconscious guilt feelings. It is comprehensible that a boy who has been accustomed to severe punishment for his misdemeanors should feel distrustful when the punishing person, the father, suddenly shows a right-about-face attitude. This change is not trusted and is therefore put to further tests; confidence is established only when the boy is convinced that the punishment is really abandoned. The dissocial youth is not satisfied when he gets kind and gentle treatment from his superiors; he aggravates them through increasingly annoying behaviour. Instead of understanding this, the parents may take this behaviour as proof that he cannot be influenced through kindness and consideration. They begin again with severity, and soon the old situation is restored, and no improvement can be expected. However, if the father shows real understanding and does not let himself make the mistake of falling back into the old attitude, then a critical situation arises for the youth. The antagonistic conduct, motivated by defiance of the father, has no longer any meaning. When the dissocial behavior begins as an expression of distrust, it is as though the child said to the parents, "Treat me the way you used to."

It is only when the provocative behaviour fails to achieve its aim that this pattern which supports the delinquency breaks down. Then gradually the manifestations of delinquency recede. The period of time necessary for this is indefinite; it varies according to how deeply the motivation is anchored in the unconscious. We are dealing here with a process which I have often observed but for which no adequate theory has been worked out. Such a theory can be evolved only when a sufficient number of such cases has been analyzed.

Let us go back to our case. I now saw that the father because of his emotional situation could not be counted on as a therapeutic helper and that I must work without him. I learned that the boy was at present at work and asked the father to send him to meet me that evening. I often have young people who work come to meet me on my way home in the evening. He met me punctually and was cordial though not communicative. He belonged to that group of people who talk little, but who are pleased to have someone with them. I asked him how he was and how he had got along with his work the past two days. He lied to me with a glib assurance about everything he had done the day before whereas I knew that he had not been in the workshop. We mentioned his father and he remarked that I really did not know his father. When I asked what he meant, he said, "You think he's a lot better than he really is." "Is he so bad then?" "No, but he is not good to me. He nagged me all the way home yesterday. He said I had to be good now that he'd forgiven me."

We have here an indication why the boy had reverted to his former behaviour so quickly. The father, who tried to talk him into something, seemed to him not to be the understanding person he had appeared in our interview. He had forced the boy back again into a bad position. As we talked, we walked slowly along the street. It began to rain and I thought I had better take a trolley. He was unwilling to leave me and came along. Among other things, we talked about music, whereupon he lost some of his reticence and told me that his family was musical; his father played the violin, his brother the piano, and he himself the flute. When we reached his transfer point where I urged him to leave, he remained, saying he would go the whole way home with me. Just before we got out, he asked me when and where we could meet again. I gave him an appointment for three days later, whereupon he said, "That's too far off. Can't it be sooner?" I said, "Yes, if you want to meet me tomorrow evening at seven on Blank Street." He went with me to my door and said, "Please give my regards to your wife." My wife had never been mentioned; he did not even know that I was married, but took it for granted. I stood by the door watching him as he walked away. After about fifty steps, he turned and raised his hat and I did likewise. This was repeated several times, until he reached the corner. The next evening he was there right on the dot. He proposed that we walk rather than ride so that we need not part so soon. Walking this distance took about an hour. Again he did not talk much but he invited me to come to his house some evening to hear some music. It was not certain that his father would play, but his brother had already promised to accompany him on the piano. I said that I was a very severe musical critic and that he and his brother must really get up a good programme before they could expect me to come. You will understand that I wanted to turn his own impulse to account pedagogically and I therefore utilized this interest, which would keep him occupied at home over a long period of time.

Since I was very busy during this period I could give him only a half hour three times a week and this had to be on my way home in the evening. If I were going to be able to achieve anything remedial with him under such unfavourable circumstances, he must develop some strong emotional feeling for me. It was not wise to question him directly. The only way I could appraise his feelings was to put them to the test, and so I told him to come to meet me two hours earlier than I knew I could be there. When I got there, he was gone. I learned that he had waited more than an hour and a half. He was not irritated when he left, but had left a request that I should let him know when and where we might meet again. We met the next day. I decided to praise him for his long wait as soon as a good opportunity presented itself. I did not have long to wait. He was friendly, did not reproach me, but on the contrary said he understood that I had a great deal to do and could not always keep appointments. Again we walked. He talked about his employer and told me jubilantly of some new work which had been entrusted to him. Through it all, I could see clearly a new feeling of his own importance. He talked also of the disagreeable things in the shop. Another worker was jealous of him and was cross and grouchy if he whistled a tune, something he had of late especially enjoyed. Then he began to talk about home. He became particularly expansive over the musical programme. He was very pleased with his brother, who was co-operating with him very well. This showed me the direction in which I could reward him. I thought it well to settle on a date, but since I wanted things to become a little more stable at home I put it off until Sunday, two weeks following. He was very happy to know that I would come on a certain day and was not impatient that he had to wait so long. We walked along in silence; he was lost in his thoughts and I was busy watching him. After a while I asked him what he was thinking about. He was embarrassed and did not want to tell me. When I pressed him, he said that it was really too stupid, he was not thinking about anything in particular, perhaps I'd only laugh at him if he told me but things were always like that with him. At first something would seem very important to him; he could not express it to his own satisfaction, he could only intimate it. If the other person did not show any interest, he would suddenly feel he had made too much fuss about something unimportant and would be embarrassed and unable to open his mouth. I made him understand that I did not expect anything remarkable from him and if it cost him too much effort he should remain silent. We went a little further and then he began timidly, "If my father were only like you, I would never have done all those things." I took that as an opening for talking about his relationship to his father. What he said was in substance only what we already know. The next three interviews were concerned mostly with various members of the family and in many points they clarified his relationship to his father.

One Saturday, after a week's separation, he turned up beaming. His pay had been raised a third. This was even more surprising since he had already received a slight increase in pay two weeks before. This, in addition to the fact that he had been entrusted with more important work, shows us that he had developed a new attitude toward his work.

Now to the Sunday visit! The family were all at home. The boy was greatly excited and I tried to put him at ease by asking them to begin. They played better than one would have expected. The boy was on fire with enthusiasm. I let him see plainly that I was pleased, but did not overdo my appreciation. The situation was natural; the whole family was happy, as I could read in their faces, and they were more than cordial to me. During a short pause, we sat around the table discussing various things, the mother's household affairs, the father's work, and the like, but nothing was said about his son's former or present behaviour. I stayed for nearly three hours.

The father, pleased with the outcome, came with me part of the way home. He was just as enthusiastic now as he had been despairing several weeks before. And just as then I had to curb his despair because all was not lost, so now I had to curb his enthusiasm because all was not yet won. Unpleasant surprises were not yet excluded. He said, "It seems like a dream to me that I could have been so discouraged that I wanted to put that boy in an institution. I didn't know what else to do. It's just like old times now. He works regularly and his employer told me he was completely satisfied with him. He comes home in the evening promptly, gets out his flute, and the two boys play together for hours. We're really a united family again. I can't tell you how happy I am that everything is all right once more."

The next evening I met the boy again. I did not have much time for him as I had an appointment. He went on the street car with me, talked over details of my visit, and closed with, "I went to bed right afterwards and I had to think it all over again, it was so nice." We continued meeting a few weeks longer, and though he walked all the way home with me, he did not come into my house because I wished to avoid that. Our meetings were interrupted by my vacation. During such a period, I do not give up the relationship already established but I keep in touch with the boy through letters. He was an enthusiastic letter writer. He wrote at least once a week, and if I replied immediately, twice. In one of these letters he reported that his mother and sister had gone to visit relatives. The mother had wanted to hire a woman to help with the housework while she was gone but he had thought this unnecessary and had offered to keep house himself. He told me about the bachelor housekeeping and how his father and brother must take orders from him. It they did not behave, he made a scene, and his father gave in more quickly than his brother, with whom he often had to be severe. Gradually the letters became cooler in tone although they arrived as frequently as before. When I came home, I let him know and he came to our next appointment with his old enthusiasm. He asked how I was and seemed pleased when I told him that we could meet in our usual way two days later. He did not come but wrote me a note excusing himself and asking if we could postpone the meeting until two days later. I agreed but he failed to turn up again and sent no excuse. I was not annoyed by his not coming. However, I cannot say that I was pleased with his release from me because it seemed to have occurred too quickly. I became a little anxious about him and feared that he had fallen back into his old ways. I was far from thinking that a permanent result had been accomplished. I wrote to him and received an immediate reply. He said that things were going well and that at present he was working overtime in the evening and therefore could not meet me. In a few weeks the rush would be over and he would be glad to see me again. By chance I met his father and he spoke with approbation of the excellent behaviour of the boy and said he hoped it would continue.

For several weeks I did not see him. At Christmas he came to see me, sent me a card at New Year's, and then I did not hear from him for many weeks. In the spring I met him by chance in the street car. He was in the best of spirits. For the next year and a half I had letters from him now and then, especially at holiday times. As far as his retraining went, the task was finished. He continued to do well for three years. We must recognize, however, that this boy had many other adjustments to make, among them a satisfactory heterosexual relationship.

Without an analysis of this boy, we can never be sure of the real reasons for the delinquency; we can only point to possible or apparent causal factors. The surprising features in this case, which are certainly not convincing without analysis, are the quickness and permanence of the therapy. It is clear that this therapeutic result was accomplished through the transference.

It seemed clear that we were dealing in this case with an act of revenge against the father. The boy felt inferior to the brother because as a student he had advantages which were denied an apprentice. Yet it is not entirely clear why at seventeen he reproached his father and made him responsible for the fact that he had become a shoemaker, when at fourteen he had put up such a stubborn resistance against his father's wish to keep him in school. We know from both the father and the son that the job of shoemaker's apprentice was not agreeable to the boy. At that time, the incentive to be a shoemaker's apprentice must have been stronger than the wish to continue in school. This incentive later disappeared. A sixteen-year-old boy is no longer in the same psychological situation as a fourteen-year-old. We must therefore try to reconstruct the psychological situation of the boy when he began his apprenticeship. One of his statements gives us a clue. As we stood at my door the first evening, he said, "Please give my regards to your wife." This is not just a chance remark nor one called forth by mere politeness as we had never spoken of my wife. Either he had noticed my wedding ring or he took it for granted that I was married. In any case, my marriage was a fact to this boy: else he would not have sent his greetings to my wife. This assumption is further understandable since he had put me in the place of his father. We recall how he said to me later, "If my father acted toward me the way you do, then I wouldn't have done these things." It is in this connexion that we can understand that the greetings to my wife were in reality for his mother. When such utterances come forth without any demonstrable external stimulus, they come out of the unconscious and must somehow involve a great deal of affect. Can we assume that there was such a strong tie to his mother? She had been dead for a long time and the stepmother had long been a member of the family circle. We might risk this possible conclusion because we can find some grounds for it. In the first place a feminine habitus, an anxious, shy behaviour, had already made us think of an infantile incestuous tie. The relationship to his stepmother was very good, as we learned first from his father, then from the boy, and finally from our own observation. His love for his own mother he seemed to have transferred completely to his stepmother. The infantile incestuous tie was still in operation, the wave of repression in adolescence was stronger than normal—that is to say, he had not succeeded in giving up his love object within the family in favour of one outside. We see the attitude to women in this boy is to turn away from them. In such cases the father remains the unconscious rival for the mother's love. The antagonism is repressed because one must love one's father. When, because of this repressed and unconscious antagonism and rivalry, the boy refused to go to school, he achieved satisfaction for his unconscious desire for revenge against his father. He knew that this would upset his father, particularly since he was a chief clerk and wished his son to have a similar position. The boy was not satisfied, however, with being unwilling to study; he went further and became a shoemaker like the stepmother's father. We know that the stepmother was tenderly attached to her own father. If the boy became a shoemaker, then he would force his stepmother to value him more than she did *his* own father, even as much as she did *her* father. We now realize that the father's efforts to keep him at his studies would have proved in vain even if he had not failed in school.

Two years later, when the dissocial behaviour began, he was in a different psychological state. We can imagine that the affective motive which had led him to be a shoemaker had been weakened by the unpleasant experience of being an apprentice. This must have been hard for a child of middle-class family who undoubtedly felt himself socially degraded, especially since he went to the workshop directly out of school. Furthermore he was always comparing himself with his student brother. The brother's vacation in a camp had made a deep impression on him. His sacrifice for his stepmother, that he became a shoemaker, was also in vain; she took his brother, not him, to visit her relatives. It would be comprehensible if hate had sprung up in him against his stepmother and had found an outlet in aggression toward her. But we see nothing of this. We must remember in this connexion that between the time of leaving school and becoming an apprentice, and the time of running away when he was sixteen, two years had elapsed. During this period he had lived through an interval of puberty and was in another developmental phase. Although the power of repression was still strong, the surge of libido had markedly strengthened his masculine aggression. He had no conscious hate feelings against his mother which would have been the case had the incestuous tie to her not abated. The loosening of this tie makes an approach to his father possible. He had actually tried to return to his father. He induced his father to give him money, and rationalized this by the fact that his brother had been given travelling money also. This gave him the same relationship to the father that the brother had. That he chose an objectionable way to bring himself closer to his father does not alter the fact. He did not recognize that he had taken an unfortunate path; he realized only that he had failed. We can imagine the conscious and unconscious struggle that raged in the boy: the disagreeable experiences as an apprentice, the father's disapproval of his being a shoemaker, the effort to hold his father as love object although his father had repulsed him and was at the same time a rival for the love of the stepmother; the futility of the sacrifice for his stepmother, and finally the feeling that the way back to his father was barricaded against him. It is not surprising that the boy, who saw his whole life plan disturbed, should think about killing himself. That he only carried his suicidal intentions out symbolically in the running away was due to his self-love, in psychoanalytical terms, his narcissism. This enabled him after much hesitation to find a way out of his torment.

SANCTIONS FOR SUPEREGO LACUNAE OF ADOLESCENTS

ADELAIDE M. JOHNSON

Weakness of conscience and other superego defects have long been considered basic factors contributing to antisocial behavior. These superego disturbances are variously attributed to learning from and identifying with deficiencies of parental superego functioning, physical and psychological traumatization during superego formation and consolidation, and constitutional factors. Prior to the publication of Johnson's article, from which the following is excerpted, it was common to attribute severe superego defects to "constitutional psychopathic inferiority." Although the "psychopath" was often described as one who lacked any capacity for inner control, serious observers considered such a blanket statement inaccurate inasmuch as superego defects, like ego defects, were rarely total (see Karpman, 1950, 1951, 1952, 1953, 1955; Lippman, 1954).

When Johnson introduced the term "superego lacunae" to describe Szurek's (1942) observations, clinicians, finding it a useful formulation for explaining certain types of delinquency as well as a wide variety of other acting-out behaviors, accorded the concept wide acceptance. It should be emphasized, however, that it relates more to the choice *of a particular piece of behavior than to the motivational forces underlying that behavior. Johnson and Szurek (1952) observed that the child's superego weakness, which was circumscribed, frequently corresponded to lacunae in the superego of the parents, who appeared to derive unconscious gratification from their child's misbehavior. This formulation has since been amply confirmed by clinical observations. Inasmuch as neither conscious nor unconscious duplicity in parent-child interaction is limited to delinquency (Litin, Giffin and Johnson, 1956), Johnson has applied this formulation to other types of symptomatology.*

The other readings in this section make clear that the concept of superego lacunae is only one of several factors contributing to acting out, the developmental aspects of which were the theme of the first monograph of the Journal of the American Academy of Child Psychiatry *(Rexford, 1966).*

Reprinted from *Searchlights on Delinquency,* ed. K. R. Eissler. New York: International Universities Press, 1949, pp. 225–234.

The problems discussed in this paper are not peculiar to adolescents, although most of the material will be drawn primarily from my experiences with that age group.

It is essential to define the character problems involved: those of adolescents in conflict with parents or some other external authority because of an acting out of forbidden, antisocial impulses. There is rarely a generalized weakness of the superego in the cases under consideration but rather a lack of superego in certain circumscribed areas of behavior, which may be termed superego lacunae. For instance, a child may be entirely dependable about regular school attendance or honesty at work, but engage in petty stealing or serious sexual acting out. Frequently, mild or severe neurotic conflicts accompany such superego lacunae.

I shall attempt to illustrate that the parents may find vicarious gratification of their own poorly-integrated forbidden impulses in the acting out of the child, through their conscious, or more often unconscious, permissiveness or inconsistency toward the child in these spheres of behavior. The child's superego lacunae correspond to similar defects of the parents' superego which in turn were derived from the conscious or unconscious permissiveness of their own parents. These conclusions are the result of the collaborative study and treatment of the significant parent as well as the adolescent patient as reported briefly by Szurek (1942).

The literature reveals a variety of descriptions and discussions of the etiology of such superego defects. Reich (1925) was the first to introduce the term "impulsive character" into psychoanalytic literature. Alexander (1930b) introduced the concept of the need for self-punishment as a motive for "acting out." Other authors stress the patient's receiving insufficient love and warmth so that a strong identification with the unloving parents is impossible. This lack of love is commonly considered the basic cause of superego defects.

Schmideberg (1938) believed that people who act out their conflicts have a greater constitutional inability to tolerate frustration than the more inhibited persons. Greenacre (1945) reported in some detail a number of cases of psychopathic personality but without concomitant study of the parents. She found that the fathers of such patients were usually ambitious and prominent, and the mothers usually frivolous and superficial, giving little attention to the home. She discussed the interrelationships of such parents with the child in respect to its superego development but did not speak of defects in the parents' superego.

Aichhorn (1925) and Healy and Bronner (1936) stated that some antisocial children have identified themselves with the gross ethical distortions of these parents. These observers saw the gross pathological correlations but apparently did not stress the implications in the subtler cases with which we are concerned in this paper. Healy and Bronner attributed the child's inability to develop a normal superego to the coldness and rejection of the parents, so that one child in a family may steal and another will not, depending upon the one being unloved and the other loved. Even granting that unloved children may not develop a "normal superego", it does not follow that coldness of parents alone can lead to the superego lacunae under discussion. Some very cold parents create such great guilt in children that a punitive, hostile superego is developed. On the other hand there are warm parents whose child may act out antisocially.

At the Institute for Juvenile Research our collaborative therapy of purely neurotic children and their parents revealed certain unmistakable but subtle parent-child interrelationships in which one provided the other with an unconscious impetus to the neurosis. The confusing literature on delinquency and the dissatisfaction with our results in treating delinquent children stimulated a research into the subtle family relationships for a clue such as we had found in the purely neurotic cases. It seemed logical to seek some hidden links between the superego of the parent and the child, even in cases where the parent himself did not act out.

Szurek (1942) stated the problem briefly and brilliantly in an understandable and simple way for both the gross *and* the subtler pathologies. Due to limitations of space he could not present the large amount of available evidence for his thesis. He saw the problem as a defect in personality organization—a defect in conscience:

> Clinical experience with children showing predominantly behavior which is a problem to others and *concurrent therapeutic effort with the parent* leaves the impression that the genesis of some of the human characteristics included in the definition of psychopathic personality is no greater mystery than other syndromes in psychopathology. Almost literally, in no instances in which adequate psychiatric therapeutic study of *both* parent and child has been possible has it been difficult to obtain sufficient evidence to reconstruct the chief dynamics of the situation. Regularly the more important parent—usually the mother, although the father is always in some way involved—has been seen *unconsciously* to encourage the amoral or antisocial behavior of the child. The neurotic needs of the parent whether of excessively dominating, dependent, or erotic character are vicariously gratified by the behavior of the child, or in relation to the child. Such—neurotic—needs of the parent exist either because of some current inability to satisfy them in the world of adults, or because of the stunting experiences in the parent's own childhood—or more commonly,

> because of a combination of both of these factors. Because their parental needs are unintegrated, unconscious, and unacceptable to the parent himself, the child in every instance is sooner or later frustrated and thus experiences no durable satisfactions. Because the indulgence or permissiveness of the parent in regard to marked overt hostility or to some mastery techniques, for example, is uncertain and inconsistent, control over the former, or acquisition of the latter, by the child is similarly uncertain and confused. If a discipline of the parent is administered with guilt, it permits the child to exploit and subtly to blackmail the parent until the particular issue between them is befogged and piled high with irrelevant bickerings and implied or expressed mutual recriminations (pp. 5–6).

The astonishing observation emerging repeatedly in our studies was the subtle manner in which one child in a family of several children might unconsciously be singled out as the scapegoat to act out the parent's poorly integrated and forbidden impulses. Analytic study of the significant parent showed unmistakably the peculiar meaning this child had for the parent and the tragic mode in which both the parent and the child were consciously, but much more often *unconsciously,* involved in the fatal march of events. As therapists, we could not avoid feeling sympathy for these consciously well-intentioned parents whose unconscious needs were unwittingly bringing down disaster on the family. This was strikingly illustrated in several families that had an adopted child as well as one or more children of their own. The acting out of the parent through the adopted child was always rationalized as inherited behavior.

Although not emphasized by Szurek, another fact that became obvious was that not only was the parent's forbidden impulse acted out vicariously by the unfortunate child, but this very acting out, in a way so foreign to the conscious wishes of the parent, often served as a channel for hostile, destructive impulses that the parent felt toward the child. In many cases, parents may reveal blatantly the child's acting out to schools, family friends, and neighbors in a way most destructive for the child's reputation. This becomes one of the greatest sources of rage in the child. The press recently reported a young adolescent girl hanging herself because her mother, missing $10.00, telephoned the school authorities to search the girl's purse.

Thus the parents' unconscious condoning of the acting out of asocial impulses by the child may serve the two-fold purpose of allowing the parent vicarious gratification of forbidden impulses as well as the expression of hostile destructive impulses felt toward the child.

Similarly the child consciously, but more often unwittingly, exposes the parents to all degrees of suffering through acting out. This acting out may often be an exaggerated picture of the unconscious impulses of the parent.

We must first understand the behavior of a well-integrated parent and the subtle conscious and unconscious ways in which this behavior directs the child's superego development, in order to be able to recognize the evidences of such destructive sanctions in less integrated parents. To be sure, the dissolution of the Oedipus conflict puts the real seal on the superego, but it is well to be aware of all the preoedipal and oedipal subtleties in the family which are part and parcel of this development. To the child in the early and middle latency period there may be alternative modes of reacting on an ego level, but when the superego is involved, the child normally is reared as if there could be *no* alternative reaction in regard to the suppression of the impulses to theft, murder, truancy, etc. The well-integrated, mature mother issuing an order to a child does not immediately check to see if it has been done, or suggest beforehand that if it is not done, there will be serious consequences.

Such constant checking or such a warning means to the child that there is an alternative to the mother's order and an alternate image of *him* in the mother's mind. Identification with the parent does not consist merely of identification with the manifest behavior of the parent. It necessarily includes a sharing by the child of the parent's conscious and unconscious concept of the child as one who is loved and honest or sometimes unloved or dishonest. It is essential to appreciate this fact if we are to understand the etiology of superego defect and plan a rational therapy. Angry orders or suspiciousness or commands colored by feelings of guilt convey to the child the doubtful alternative image of him in the parent's mind. The mature mother expects the thing to be done, and later, if she finds the child has side-stepped her wishes, she insists without guilt on her part that it be done. The mother must have this undoubting, firm, unconscious assurance that her child will soon make her intention his own in accordance with her own image of him. This, however, produces a rather rigid and inflexible attitude in the young child.

In adolescence the superego is normally still fairly rigid and the child is greatly disturbed when adults express doubts about it. Nothing angers adolescents more than to be warned about or accused of indiscretions of which overtly they were not guilty. Such lack of good faith in them threatens to break down their repressive defenses and lowers their self-esteem and feeling that they would do the right thing. It suggests an alternative mode of behavior which at that age frightens them.

With these simple basic concepts in mind, it becomes relatively easy to see what is happening in some rather simple cases of superego defect and to present the evidence for what Szurek stated in his article. It should be made clear that it is not within the scope of this paper to discuss the multiple determined types of character defenses which the child may evolve and use. Nor can the particular mode of therapy dealing with such character defenses be here included. These topics have been discussed in previous papers (Fenichel, 1941; Greenacre, 1945).

Let us return to our simple cases of superego defect. How is truancy initiated? It is not just that parents are cold and rejecting, as so many authors imply. How does the specific idea of leaving home originate? At six the little girl may say angrily: "You don't love me—nobody loves me—I hate you all." Quite often the child will receive such replies as: "Well, why don't you just pack your bag and go live some place else if you think we're so awful?" We know that some parents even follow this up by packing the little one's suitcase, which at first may terrify the child. The suggestion to leave home comes more frequently from inside the home than outside, for not many small children tell others at school that their parents are mean or get suggestions from other children to leave home.

If little children (especially up to the age of 11 or 12 let the thought that they are unloved come into consciousness at all, they then do not express that thought outside the family circle, from feelings of both guilt and pride.

When we carefully examine the cases of a first or a repeated running away, we often find that it was the parents who unconsciously made provocative suggestions from a variety of motives such as hostility, or a need of vicarious gratification, or both.

As, for example, six-year-old Stevie, who had been running away since he was four. His father seemed to know an inexplicable amount of detail concerning the boy's episodes of exploration. He reported that during these same two years he himself had been unable to continue his work as driver of a transcontinental truck, a job in which he revelled. Instead his present job confines him to the city. It was striking to observe this father with the little boy. He asked Stevie to tell of his most recent running away. When the child guiltily hesitated, his father started him on his way with an intriguing reminder. As the boy gave his account, his father was obviously fascinated—even occasionally prompting the child. Toward the end the father suddenly and angrily cut the child off saying, "That's enough, Stevie; now you see what I mean, Doctor?" Stevie could not help but see his father's great interest and pleasure when he told his tale each time he returned home, even though at the end of his account he received his whipping. The father was a kind, well-intentioned man who rightly feared for his little son's safety, but he was quite unconscious of the fact that the stimulus of his own thwarted need to travel was easily conveyed to the small, bright boy of whom the father said: "Stevie's really a good kid—he would follow me around the top of a wall 50 feet high."

No better example of how an adult can initiate such running away can be found than the story of how Aichhorn (1925) deliberately resorted to such provocation as a technique of treatment. In handling the transference he consciously used a simple provocative mechanism to get a boy to run away from the institution, since he could not make any positive contact with the adolescent. This very narcissistic boy, with no positive feeling for Aichhorn, constantly complained about the institution. Aichhorn made subtle suggestions about the attractiveness of the outside world, and an hour later the boy ran away. As Aichhorn had anticipated, some days later the boy returned, having found the outside world uninviting and then entered at once into a positive relationship with Aichhorn.

Let us now attempt to discover how stealing is initiated.

One of my patients, a woman who had been in analysis for nine months, came in very angry at her nine-year-old daughter. The reason for the anger was that the child had been found stealing some money from the teacher's desk the day before. The patient stated that she knew Margaret had taken nickels from her purse off and on since she was six or seven but had said nothing, feeling that "she would outgrow it". When I asked why she had said nothing, she said it was never serious, so she had felt the less said the better. It was stated earlier in this paper that the mature mother does not anticipate trouble nor check up constantly on her child. On the other hand, neither does she let something amiss go by when she observes it, but instead handles it promptly without anxiety or guilt. She can neither be the nagging, checking detective, nor the permissive, lax condoner. During this hour, my patient told me a dream she had had over the weekend. In the dream she went into Saks and stole a beautiful pair of slippers. In the discussion I commented that I was struck with the fact that in her dream she did not even project the theft onto someone else and wondered if possibly her mother had been permissive with little thefts. Then my patient told me, for the first time, of numerous thefts all through her childhood and adolescence, and that her mother had always protected her. For instance, during one year of her adolescence she had stolen at least two dozen lipsticks from stores. The prohibitions which had been so poorly integrated in her own life were unconsciously permitting and condoning her daughter's stealing. It was a revealing experience for my patient when three months later her mother came for a visit, to observe her mother's little deceptions and permissions with the two grandchildren, such deceptions as my patient had herself hitherto ignored. She did what she could to stop them and decided to limit long visits from her mother until the children were much older. In a very short time her daughter stopped all thefts as my patient, through her analysis, was able to make a definite stand without anxiety or vacillation. The child, formerly so unhappy and unpopular, later became an outstanding pupil in her school.

We see in this mother's behavior an attitude commonly found among parents of children who steal. The parent whose own superego is defective is the one who will say "he will outgrow it", and often the parent who is not involved in the acting out is the one who finally insists upon bringing the child to treatment. "He will outgrow it" is the permissive, protective attitude that keeps the problem active.

There are many such parents whose own poorly integrated prohibitions permit them to let slight offenses go by, only to react with sudden and guilty alarm at the first signs of criticism from outside the home by then angrily accusing the punishing their child. The child, confused and angry, in turn feels betrayed, and may in his own mind review his parents' similar deceptions. If he has the courage and is not too ashamed, he may point this out to the parent, and in this way the vicious circle of hostile, mutual blackmail, and corruption is started.

The fantasies, hopes, and fears which parents express in reaction to some behavior of their child is one of the commonest ways in which a child is influenced toward a healthy or a maladapted career. The horrified comments or anxiety over some behavior of the child are well-known to every one. How commonly we hear the parent of the little child, caught in some minor offense, angrily say, "You are beyond me—I can't handle you any more—if this doesn't stop, you will end in the reform school." Or the child who is just beginning to misbehave is likened to his uncle who came to a bad end. We become "good" or "bad" depending upon our parents' fantasies about us.

A professional worker recently told me that seventeen years ago she visited her friends who had a nine-month-old baby boy. The worker took the little boy on her lap and when he reached up and put his hands around her neck, the child's mother with a really frightening expression said, "I hope my son won't be a killer." The worker told me that by the age of fifteen years that boy had committed murder.

However I do not intend to use evidence here of the more tragic cases which have come to our attention, but will confine the discussion to fairly simple examples.

In *Psychoanalytic Therapy,* written by the Staff of the Institute for Psychoanalysis of Chicago, I reported the case of seventeen-year-old Ann who suffered from great anxiety and whose mother had written fraudulent excuses for the girl's absences from the school. The girl refused treatment, and I treated only the mother. It was possible to analyze not only much of the mother's destructive hostility to Ann, but also in the transference, to manage and thwart the mother's attempts to corrupt the analyst and pull her into the vicious circle. Two years later, Ann is in college and making an excellent adjustment.

Another case is that of a sixteen-year-old girl who came to treatment because of several years of severe depression and the occasional idea that she was being poisoned at the school cafeteria. As her depression subsided and her anger toward me came out, she went home one day and told her mother she was so angry at the therapist, she was going to kill her. The mother said, with horror, "Oh, Marion, don't bring any more tragedy on the family." Marion rushed back to me greatly frightened saying, "My mother actually believed I would murder–what is wrong with her?" At that point I succeeded in also getting the mother into treatment with another analyst. It was fortunate that I did so, for Marion's father had died psychotic, and the maternal grandmother had been promiscuous. Marion's mother was acting out ominous impulses through this girl and blaming them all on Marion's heredity from her father.

When one parent advises a child to keep something from the other parent, it is a frequent and destructive factor in creating deceptions and stealing. "Here, I'll give you $2.00, but don't tell your father." One could list an endless array of such sanctions. In treatment, these children will always try to get the therapist to lie to the parents. The parents' "more sensible superegos" unconsciously overlook the fact that to the rigid superego of a six- or nine-year-old, this does not look "sensible" but dishonest.

If we break a promise to a child without a sincere statement of the facts and a regretful apology, we undermine his ability to identify with us as adults of sound integrity.

There is an additional etiological factor in these cases which is puzzling. In work with adolescents from all social strata, I was impressed, as was Szurek, with the fact that sometimes the child's parents had a similar partial superego defect, that is, the mother was promiscuous or the father committed some thefts, etc. But there are other cases in which the parents had never actually done any of this acting out so far as we could find, and yet we could see them unconsciously initiating this with the child. These parents, let us say, had some neurotic conflicts about thefts, promiscuity, etc., like many of us, but why did such parents permit themselves to act these conflicts out through the child, while many neurotic parents do not? With this question in mind, whenever I had a parent in treatment, I explored the relation to her own parents very closely.

Where did the parent get the permission to act out through the child? Since the parent did not act out herself, she must have had a fairly strong conscience. Yet what caused this poorly integrated prohibition to appear in the next generation?

I frequently found that the present parent had gone along for years developing a good conscience, was secure about controlling her own impulses, and then something arose that led her parents to surprising suspicions and accusations. Since the parent under treatment already had a good conscience, he or she could not respond to this permissive accusation by acting out, yet was enraged at the injustice and defamation. The rage and the permission would then come out unconsciously by being displaced onto the daughter or son. The parent's acting out through the child may also occur when the parent with a well-developed conscience *later* observed dishonesty, erotic acting out, or some other disturbing behavior in *her* parents and felt much pain and confusion about their actions. Our parent in question already had a good conscience and too much guilt to do likewise herself, but the confusion, anger, and permission cannot be normally integrated into her personality and appears later through her own child.

EGO DISTURBANCES

Fritz Redl

Redl, while recognizing the complexity of the concept, ego (see Hartmann, Kris and Loewenstein, 1947), deplores the lack of clinical precision characteristic of so many descriptions of ego disturbances, particularly because the ambiguity affects the clinician in his efforts to offer ego support.

In the course of a varied career devoted to working with delinquents in the context of gangs, clubs, summer camps, and institutions, Redl and Wineman (1966) described more than twenty specific disturbances of ego functions. What they found in their special group went beyond what had been observed in the psychoanalytic treatment of primarily middle-class neurotics with relatively intact ego functioning. Redl focuses on a population suffering from a form of individual psychopathology unlike that of Aichhorn's (1925) neurotic delinquents or Johnson's (1949) patients with circumscribed superego lacunae.

In the following selection, Redl, in his usual lively style, illustrates the need for specificity in the concept of ego weakness and in the formulation of ego support. He cites the marked differences between the boy with deficient impulse control but adequate reality testing and the one with defective reality orientation who has no difficulty controlling impulses.
Here, he deals with frustration tolerance, the loss of ego control to group-psychological intoxication, apperception of the inherent structure of situations and things, and remaining "reasonable" under the impact of unexpected change. Elsewhere, he and Wineman (1957) describe other ego tasks observed to be deficient in their delinquent patients: coping with insecurity, anxiety, and fear; sublimation deafness; newness panic; controlling the floodgates of the past; disorganization in the face of guilt; learning from experience; to name a few.

Teasing out the precise aspect of ego function requiring specific differential therapeutic attention in lieu of global support for a vaguely defined "weak ego" transforms an impossible task into a difficult one.

Reprinted from *American Journal of Orthopsychiatry,* 21, 1951, pp. 273–279.

The concept of the "ego" and the functions it has to perform has grown in complexity over the years—so much so that nothing but a book in its own right could do justice to all that has been described, postulated, and said about it.

It is hopeless to try to find a short definition of the term "ego" with which a whole roomful of people would easily agree and that would, at the same time, be precise enough for theoretical speculation. Nor would it be feasible to try to follow the development that this concept has undergone since its earliest formulations by Sigmund Freud. For the sake of creating some kind of starting point for discussion, however, I shall at least try to suggest what I mean by "ego." By "ego," I refer to that part of our personalities that has primarily two duties to fulfill: to establish a relationship with the world in which we live; and to see to it that we behave reasonably in line with it without too serious inner conflict.

This rather crude "job analysis" of the ego obviously suggests that it has a variety of functions available by which to do these jobs. The first basic function seems to be of a cognitive nature. As the "research arm" of the personality, it seems to be the ego's task to perceive, assess, predict, and so forth what social and physical reality will do to us "if." However, it is not only the "outside world" that must be brought into the realm of ego awareness. If it is to do its other job, the ego's research department must also supply it with adequate data about the dictates of the conscience and about the nature and intensity of strivings, in short, of the "inner reality." At least it seems always tacitly assumed that impulses or superego particles that would not be accessible to the self-perceptive department of the ego would also be outside the reach of its power.

This "research arm" of the ego seems to be coordinated to some sort of "executive branch," which has the task of exerting force, in order to keep impulses and behavior in line. Just where it derives the energies to do this still perplexes us.

The importance of the ego, and with it the focal role of ego psychology, has increased tremendously since its early "part-time employment" as a guardian on the borderline between inside and outside reality, and the details of this development, as well as the most recent speculations about it, are a most fascinating story indeed.

This short paper, however, sets itself a limited task: to lure the practitioner into becoming much more impressed with the need to be very specific in the use of the term "ego disturbance" and to stimulate the clinician to seek a much wider repertoire of techniques whenever he is confronted with the task of "ego support."

Deficiencies of the Current Concept of Ego Disturbance

No matter how elaborate the speculations of the theoretician about ego functions may be, it seems to me that the concept of "ego disturbances," when used in connection with actual clinical material, shrivels up into a rather oversimplified little gadget, hardly able to do the job we expect of it. My main criticisms of the current use of the term in connection with case material are three.

First, the term "ego disturbance" frequently confuses qualitative and quantitative aspects and lumps them together as though they were the same, so much so that the terms "ego weakness" and "ego disturbance" are often used synonymously. It is obvious that this mixture must lead to a great deal of diagnostic and prognostic confusion. If Johnny, for instance, attacks me in a prepsychotic temper tantrum, his attack can be blamed on disturbance of his ego functions. For the clinician, however, it would be of paramount importance to know more specifically just where the disturbance lies. Johnny might, for instance, perceive me correctly as the person I am and the role I play in his life, but his ego may not have "strength" enough to hold his terrific impulse upsurgence or frustration onrush in check. The same behavior may result with a youngster whose ego is perfectly able to cope with an onrush of impulsivity but who is so "confused" about the difference between present and past that the mere role similarity between me, Johnny's camp director, and his foster father of earlier childhood years stirs up old images instead of a correct reality appraisal. In both cases, the behavioral results will be highly similar. Clinically, however, the two are very different.

Second, the most frequent breakdown of the concept of "ego disturbances" parallels our concept of "ego functions," of course. However, most of these "functions of the ego" have been derived from the psychoanalysis of the neuroses of children from the middle- or upper-classes. In order to be amenable even to the very basic requirements of analytic therapy, most egos have to be intact, and their functioning can be described in terms of the usual list of "ego-defense mechanisms," which become disturbances primarily if they get out of hand. The kind of children I refer to seem to have a variety of seriously disturbed functions that obviously belong to the realm of the "ego," but we would never arrive at them from the study of the ego of the neurotic, which is still more or less intact. I think there are many more "ego functions" than we have assumed in the past, which we simply take for granted and which may be separately disturbed. I shall try to describe a few of them shortly.

Third, in blaming symptomatology on "ego disturbances" we usually automatically assume that things go wrong only if an ego or part of it does not function or is too weak to assert its role. We seem to forget a wide variety of behavioral disturbances that seem to me to arise from overfunctioning of ego activities, at least in certain areas. For example, I would call it a job of the normal ego to be aware of large parts of the id. The unusual self-perception that we find in certain types of schizophrenic stages has puzzled us for a long time. For, although obviously part of a pathological state, it seems a hypertrophic development rather than a "disturbance." Similarly, we find that certain egos that are totally in the service of delinquent superegos have terrifically overdeveloped skills of appraisal of the world as far as delinquent enterprises are concerned. Some of my toughest customers, for instance, have skills in "casing the joint," acuities of observation of job-relevant facts, that are certainly overdevelopments rather than disturbances or undevelopments of ego functions. The fact that the subsequent behavior can be called "disturbed" has misled us into assuming that these children suffer from "ego disturbances," whereas partial "ego hypertrophy" would be a more correct term. Not all disturbances that happen to be connected with "poor adjustment to reality" are by that very fact also real "ego disturbances," and before the term "ego disturbance" assumes any practical sense, a much more specific description of symptomatology as well as causality is indicated.

Ego Disturbance—Just Where?

It would not do simply to mention obvious and understandable weaknesses of our present conceptualizations. The job to be done is really to work on a much more specific psychology of ego disturbances than we have yet attained. To arrive at it, we have to extend our studies much beyond the usual classical psychoanalytic interview or play situation, and we have to create settings in which we can see ego functions and their disturbances in operation, even when conscious or unconscious expression of them within regular treatment channels is practically not to be had.

We have tried to do just this in various projects. The observations presented in this paper were all made in the framework of the following three projects: the Detroit Group Project, an agency for group therapy with children on a small-club basis; the Detroit Group Project Summer

Camp; and Pioneer House, a residential treatment home for ego-disturbed children. I must forfeit the fascination of dwelling either on the treatment designs or on the intakes and other details of these projects and can, of course, not even try to list some of the findings. In a nutshell, I think we can describe about thirty very distinct forms of "disturbance" of ego functions, all of which may be independently observed in varying degrees. For illustration, I shall select only a few.

Inability to Cope with Frustration Aggression

We frequently, and rightly, consider the inability of a child to "hold his own" under the impact of impulse onrushes an "ego disturbance." The healthy ego is supposed to have considerable energy and to be able to use it at times of emergency.

What I want to imply here is that some of our children are able to maintain reasonable ego intactness in the face of certain rather heavy impulse doses but still lose all control in the face of typical "frustration aggression." For instance, Johnny may successfully cope with the temptation to yield to an urge for the possession of somebody else's toy; he may be able to hold his own under the impact of quite sizable doses of temptation in this realm. However, when confronted with the slightest "frustration," like simple interruption of a game for a meal, his ego reacts with total loss of control. This seems to suggest that the ability to cope with frustration-produced aggression may be a separate function of the ego and may be disturbed by itself, even though in other areas more complex ego functions are quite intact.

Loss of Ego Control Through Group-Psychological Intoxication

We usually assume that the amount of "ego control" that a child has achieved in a certain area remains reasonably constant for the time being. This is an illusion indeed. We have all the evidence to support a theory to the contrary. It is clearly visible that, under certain group-atmospheric conditions, some of our children suffer total losses of ego control even in areas in which their egos otherwise seem to be intact. For example, a youngster with a considerable desire to "behave reasonably in line with dining-table expectations," especially in the presence of certain staff members, may be thrown totally out of control the moment the "group mood" has reached a certain level of hilarity, especially if, for a variety of other reasons, the "contagion index" for the whole group has gone up for the time being. In short, Johnny, who ordinarily wouldn't think of taking a chance by breaking a rule of table behavior that has just been reinforced, suddenly goes haywire under the impact of that element of "group-psychological intoxication," which is so familiar to the practitioner and yet so hard to describe.

This item has an importance far beyond the situational implication in each case. In fact, we have arrived at a desire to define something like the "group-intoxicational breaking point" of every child's usual ego control and thus could arrive at the following rather puzzling fact: A child with a relatively low level of ego control sometimes has a rather high melting point at whatever level he has achieved; that is, although he has lower ego control than his neighbor, whatever ego control he has is group psychologically more indestructible than is the other fellow's. Another child with a very high level of ego control but a very low melting point under group-atmospheric conditions is more of a risk to the practitioner than is the first child. Instead of talking about ego strength and ego weakness even in specific areas, we should therefore introduce as a further variable the concept of "group-psychological melting point" of whatever ego-function levels are otherwise in action. In short, the highness or lowness of the group-psychological melting point of existing ego functions is in itself as important an item clinically as the functioning or disturbance itself.

Apperception of the Inherent Structure of Situations and Things

Most anybody, if overwhelmed by a sudden onrush of aggressive impulsivity, may suffer a temporary loss of control. In such a state of mind he is likely to use anything at hand as a weapon against his opponent. Such a situation seems so simple because whatever contribution the ego may have tried to make is flooded by the obvious impulse intensity with which he deals, so that it looks as if all that has happened is an overpowering of the ego through impulsivity onrush. It becomes easy, however, to see how much more complex the situation really is if we vary the intensity of the impulsive side of the picture so that the cognitive signal functions of the ego can more clearly emerge. The following illustration may clarify what I have in mind: In the early months at Pioneer House, the children, entering their toy room even in a mild state of restlessness or hilarity far removed from their usual more dangerous aggressive moods, would have reacted to practically any toy in the same way. A piece of wood, as well as a typewriter, would have suffered the same fate as a piece of clay: It would have been joyously thrown around, banged up, and finally trampled under. In a later development, with increased specification of ego function, the same medium degree of restless hilarity would not have led to the same scene. One of them would have perceived immediately the potential of the typewriter for typing a "dirty" insult to an opponent or an adult; another, the use of the piece of wood as a source of fun, first cutting a gun out of it, and then throwing the scraps at the people around. In short, in the second case, the youngsters would have been able to show more "civilized" reactions to the inherent structures of the toys they were confronted with, not because their impulsivity had been reduced, but because the ego function of perceiving the inherent structures of situations and things had improved. It can well be seen of what tremendous importance for the whole problem of sublimation and socialization this very special ability of the ego may become, and it can easily be seen how an attack upon this type of ego disturbance would require entirely different strategy and techniques from those for any one of the others.

Remaining "Reasonable" Under the Impact of Uexpected Change

Very often the concept of "ego control" is narrowly identified with the task of the ego to visualize the limitations that the "reality principle" sets and to enforce the limitations of reality against a recalcitrant id. This definition of task seems to me much too narrow. What if the ego is suddenly in the embarrassing position of having to set limitations when reality does not set any? Many an ego I know, which does a reasonably good job of "reality-limitation enforcement," would miserably flunk this other task. In the children I am thinking of, this other disturbance usually did not become visible until we had exposed them to the treatment process itself. Briefly, this is what we saw: Some of our children were reasonably able to take some reality limitations in some areas of their lives. The deficiencies of their egos suddenly became overt when limitations were taken away. In that case, their egos proved entirely unable to cope with the task presented to them. The result was that the offering of freedom, presents, or love would, in many of them, produce terrific amounts of anxiety. The old, well-known "fear of one's own impulses" would emerge, and reckless, aggressive demands would result.

Example 1. A child who manages well to keep his hostile impulses against other children subdued in the face of a sharp disciplinary regime may become entirely reckless the moment organization pressures are removed. It would not do to call this youngster simply "ego-disturbed." His ego is good enough to signal clearly and demand submission sharply in the face of direct reality limitations. What it lacks is the resourcefulness to substitute for the sudden disappearance of outside reality limitations a limitational system of its own.

Example 2. Some children have been deeply deprived in terms of love from adults and of possessions and toys. When given what they have long needed, they may go through periods of partial regression and exaggerated dependency, but on the whole that is all. Under the impact of the diet they need, their egos soon gain strength and are able to unfold in many ways.

Not so the "toughies" I am thinking of at the moment. They have been equally deprived in terms of adult love, possessions, and toys. Of course, because of their very disturbances, they also have developed strong defenses against open acceptance of what they originally needed. So we know it will take quite some time until we can get them to accept our offerings. But that is not the problem I want to concentrate on here. The trouble I want to talk about begins after we succeed in breaking down their defenses. At the very point at which they openly and greedily accept the fact that old reality frustrations have ceased and at which they begin to "take" to our affectionate and giving attitudes toward them, we suddenly see their egos in further fits of despair. They have learned how to deal with some reality limitations, though not too well. They seem entirely at a loss, however, in dealing with sudden disappearances of limitations. The demands of these children for love and total possession of adults, for gifts and permissiveness, assume such terrific and absolute proportions that nobody can or should try to fulfill them. In short, these children, when getting what they obviously need, may suddenly be found lacking in ego functions that are necessary for the new, therapeutically created situation. We could not have seen before that these ego functions are disturbed. The ability of the ego to set self-demand limitations when reality is unexpectedly granting seems to be as essential a function of the ego as is the old stand-by of signaling barriers from the outside.

I can hardly exaggerate the impact that the functioning or nonfunctioning of this phase of ego effectiveness must have on the clinician's strategy and especially on the problem of permissiveness versus interference, as well as total treatment design. If this item is not calculated accurately, the basically best treatment design may easily leave the child's ego in a panic that is more than it can handle.

SOME CURRENT THEORIES OF DELINQUENT SUBCULTURES

RICHARD A. CLOWARD AND LLOYD E. OHLIN

It is equally valid to consider the problem of antisocial behavior from the sociological as from the psychological point of view. The one perspective complements and even enriches the other (Finch, 1962). Just as sociologists can point to conditions contributing to antisocial behavior, so can psychologists help to explain why various people are affected in different ways by similar sociological influences.

Cloward and Ohlin, seeking reasons for the formation of delinquent subcultures, differentiate three principal orientations: (a) criminal, which is organized primarily for material gain, (b) conflict, which is founded on violence, and (c) retreatist, which emphasizes the consumption of drugs.

Cloward and Ohlin's view of the sources of the delinquent subcultures focuses on the adjustment problems that stem from the marked disparity between the goals to which lower-class youth is led to aspire and the opportunities for achievement that are actually available. They postulate that adolescents who organize into delinquent subcultures have internalized conventional goals but then find that legitimate avenues of access to these goals are blocked. In brief, Cloward and Ohlin hypothesize that when such youngsters are unable to revise their aspirations downward, they are confronted with intense frustration which stimulates the exploration of antisocial alternatives which, in turn, lead to the delinquent subculture.

In arriving at their opinion, Cloward and Ohlin critically explore other sociological theories of the sources of delinquent subcultures. Three such critical reviews are presented here as a sociological complement to the various psychological points of view already represented.

Reprinted with permission of the Macmillan Company from *Delinquency and Opportunity: A Theory of Delinquent Gangs* by Richard A. Cloward and Lloyd E. Ohlin. New York: Free Press of Glencoe, 1960, pp. 48–76, 108–110, © The Free Press, a corporation, 1960.

Masculine Identification and Delinquent Subcultures

Sex differences are not just biological; they also reflect differences in social definitions of masculinity and femininity. Part of "growing up" entails learning the social roles prescribed for the members of each sex. Sometimes young people seeking to make an appropriate sex identification encounter serious obstacles; tendencies toward aberrant behavior may result. This problem of adjustment arises from efforts to conform to cultural expectations under conditions in which conformity is hampered or precluded.

A number of observers have suggested that "ganging," especially among adolescent males in our society, and particularly "compulsive masculinity" may be understood as reactions to obstacles to masculine identification. Talcott Parsons (1954), for example, asserts that certain features of the American kinship system and the relatively sharp segregation of kinship and occupational roles create barriers to masculine identification. Our kinship system tends to be female-centered. In the middle class, adult males feel compelled to invest great energy in their occupational roles. This reduces the amount of their involvement in kinship activities. Since the occupational tasks of the father are almost invariably performed outside the home, he is not readily available as a masculine model for his sons. In some sectors of the lower class, particularly among Negro families, female-centered households result from the great occupational instability and familial transience of adult males. The problem is intensified among all social classes by the fact that occupations are becoming highly specialized, complex, and esoteric. Since occupational activity is an important component of the masculine role, boys have trouble forming a clear masculine self-image.

Under such conditions, boys presumably gravitate toward the mother as the central object of identification. When they reach adolescence, and encounter especially strong cultural expectations that they behave as males, they experience the most acute strain. Engulfed by a feminine world and uncertain of their own identification, they tend to "protest" against femininity. This protest may take the form of robust and aggressive behavior, and even of malicious, irresponsible, and destructive acts. Such acts evoke maternal disapproval and thus come to stand for independence and masculinity to rebellious adolescents. This is the process designated by such terms as "masculine protest" or "compulsive masculinity":

> Our kinship situation, it has been noted, throws children of both sexes over-

> whelmingly upon the mother as *the* emotionally significant adult. In such a situation, "identification" in the sense that the adult becomes a "role model" is the normal result. For a girl this is normal and natural, not only because she belongs to the same sex as the mother, but because the functions of housewife and mother are immediately before her eyes and are tangible and relatively easily understood by a child . . . Thus the girl has a more favorable opportunity for emotional maturing through positive identification with an adult model, a fact which seems to have much to do with the well-known earlier maturity of girls. The boy, on the other hand, has a tendency to form a direct feminine identification, since his mother is the model most readily available and significant to him. But he is not destined to become an adult woman. Moreover, he soon discovers that in certain vital respects women are considered inferior to men, that it would hence be shameful for him to grow up to be like a woman. Hence when boys emerge into what Freudians call the "latency period," their behavior tends to be marked by a kind of "compulsive masculinity." They refuse to have anything to do with girls. "Sissy" becomes the worst of insults. They get interested in athletics and physical prowess, in the things in which men have the most primitive and obvious advantage over women. Furthermore, they become allergic to all expression of tender emotion; they must be "tough." This universal pattern bears all the earmarks of a "reaction formation." It is so conspicuous, not because it is simply "masculine nature," but because it is a defense against a feminine identification [Parsons, 1954, pp. 304–305].

Inadequacies of the Theory

Exponents of the theory that problems of masculinity generate delinquency have concentrated on the dynamics of the adjustment problem rather than on its relation to delinquent conduct. As a result, their explanations fail to take explicit account of the five questions that we believe a theory of delinquent subcultures must answer.

Definition–In the first place, this theory provides no clear definitions of the types of deviant behavior that are supposedly explained by problems of masculine identification. Parsons, for example, is concerned principally with the relations between *aggressive* behavior and various features of Western family and social organization. He does not claim explicitly that the problem of masculinity explains delinquency; he simply observes that female-centered family systems result in "a strong tendency for boyish behavior to run in antisocial if not directly destructive directions, in striking contrast to that of pre-adolescent girls" (p. 306). Other theorists, principally Cohen (1955) and Miller (1958), explicitly claim that problems of masculine identification can be a source of delinquent behavior. However, neither Cohen nor Miller defines the precise forms of delinquency to which problems of masculine identification lead. Cohen relates these problems to the emergence of "malicious, non-utilitarian, negativistic, and hedonistic behavior" among middle-class boys whereas Miller relates them to tough, aggressive, and irresponsible acts among lower-class boys. Neither writer relates the problems simultaneously to *delinquent* and *collective* conduct. But it is not enough to suggest that problems of masculine identification produce deviant acts; it must also be shown that they generate collective patterns that are normally construed by officials as transgressions of legal prohibitions.

Distribution—The relative diffuseness of the behavior which the masculine-identity crisis is said to explain makes it difficult to use this crisis as a basis for describing the distribution of delinquency. An emphasis upon toughness, aggressiveness, and hedonism may or may not result in delinquent acts or norms. Toughness may be displayed in many ways that are not subject to legal sanctions; the same may be said of aggressiveness and hedonism. Thus a description of the distribution of values stressing toughness would not necessarily provide a description of the distribution of delinquent acts or norms. Proponents of the masculine-identity-crisis theory have not as yet been able to show a correspondence between the distribution of values emphasizing masculinity and the distribution of norms prescribing delinquent acts. Indeed, there is considerable doubt as to the distribution of the masculine-identity crisis itself, as we shall presently see.

The Problem of Adjustment—Difficulties arise in defining masculine identification as the problem of adjustment underlying the development of delinquent subcultures when we apply our three criteria of relevance—distribution, significance, and permanence. As we have noted, there is no firm agreement among theorists as to where in the social structure this problem occurs most frequently or in most acute form. Theorists even differ concerning the distribution of the female-centered family, which, it is claimed, gives rise to the masculinity crisis. Parsons apparently feels that it can be found at both middle- and lower-class levels. There is, he claims, "a strong tendency to instability of marriage and a 'mother-centered' type of family structure . . . both in Negro and white population elements [of the lower class]" (p. 185). He also notes the existence of a "suburban matriarchy": "In certain suburban areas, especially with an upper-middle-class population, the husband and father is out of the home a very large proportion of the time. He tends to leave by far the greater part of responsibility for children to his wife" (p. 13). Other theorists, however, regard the female-centered household as a more prominent feature of one class than of the other. Cohen, for example, says:

> It should be emphasized that Parsons advances this view as an explanation of delinquency *in general;* however, it seems to us that the circumstances to which he attributes delinquency are most marked in the middle class [1955, p. 162].

Miller, on the other hand, asserts:

> The genesis of the intense concern over "toughness" in lower-class culture is probably related to the fact that a significant proportion of lower-class males are reared in a predominantly female household and lack a consistently present male figure with whom to identify and from whom to learn essential components of a "male" role. Since women serve as a primary object of identification during the preadolescent years, the almost obsessive lower-class concern with "masculinity" probably resembles a type of compulsive reaction-formation [1958, p. 9].

The distribution of female-centered households is, of course, important to establish. If such households are equally prevalent in the middle and lower classes, then the theorist is confronted with the problem of explaining why delinquent subcultures arise in one stratum but not in the other.

Evidence is lacking as to the significance and the permanence of problems of masculinity. Plausible arguments may be advanced to support or reject the proposition that this problem intimately engages the major concerns of adolescents and strikes them as a permanent threat to the achievement of long-range personal goals.

The Evolution of Subcultural Solutions–The formation of a delinquent subculture, as we have pointed out, involves the emergence of delinquent norms. Disaffected persons partially withdraw sentiments supporting the legitimacy of official norms and draw together in a new group. There is little doubt that barriers to masculine identification may produce a tendency for adolescent males to assert their fundamental maleness by engaging in aggressive deviant conduct. But there is an important difference between deviant acts and delinquent acts. Furthermore, the masculine-crisis theory fails to explain why delinquent *norms* are a logical outcome of barriers to masculine identification.

Failure to specify the relation between problems of masculine identification and the emergence of delinquent norms leads to a further theoretical difficulty: it makes it impossible to identify the conditions that result in the differentiation of delinquent subcultures. Delinquent subcultures, as we have said, vary in significant respects. Nothing in the masculinity-crisis theory helps us to specify the intervening variables that determine the outcome of generalized pressures resulting from this problem of adjustment.

Persistence and Change–No effort has been made to show the relevance of problems of masculine identification to the persistence or change of different types of delinquent subculture. If the theory is valid, changes in delinquent patterns would be related to changes in problems of masculine identification. If delinquency rates are increasing, the theorist would have to show that boys are experiencing greater difficulty developing a sense of masculinity; if the rates are decreasing, he would have to show that problems of masculine identity are diminishing. Data in confirmation of these hypothesized relationships are not available.

In summary, we are inclined to think that the masculine-identity theory, although it explains "compulsive masculinity," is not an adequate explanation of the formation of delinquent norms. It may be that problems of masculine identification have a reinforcing effect on other motivations leading to the development of delinquent subcultures or play a part in motivating individuals to become actively involved in *established* delinquent subcultures. However, we do not feel that these problems are central to an explanation of the origins or differentiation of delinquent subcultures among lower-class male adolescents.

Adolescence and Delinquent Subcultures

The transition from adolescence to adulthood poses many problems of adjustment for boys in our society. Attempts to explain delinquency as a product of these difficulties have usually been based on three related propositions: (1) any major change in status constitutes a crisis in the life of the individual; (2) the severity of the crisis depends on the availability of socially institutionalized means to facilitate the change; (3) aberrant behavior may result from this crisis.

Passage from childhood to adulthood is generally regarded as one of the most prominent instances of status transition in human society. Although the achievement of adulthood is a stressful period in most societies, it is generally acknowledged to be especially difficult in Western societies because of the extreme complexity of the occupational structure. A young man usually cannot take over an adult occupation simply because he wants to do so or because his father wishes him to be his successor.

Our occupational system is technical and specialized; the successful pursuit of many occupational roles requires years of formal training and preparation. Furthermore, until young males acquire the values, knowledge, and skills that are prerequisite to adult occupational activities, they ordinarily must forego other adult roles. Since they usually cannot support a wife and children during this period, they are forced to postpone participation in the roles of husband and father despite their biological and emotional readiness to discharge these roles. Thus male adolescents are cut off from adult roles and relegated to a prolonged preparatory status in which they are no longer children but are not yet adults.

Although the adolescent is barred from immediate access to adult roles, every effort is made to ensure that he does not relinquish his aspirations for eventual adult status. Even though he is formally deprived of the major rewards of adult status–money, personal autonomy, sexual relations, and the like–he is at the same time imbued with the belief that these are rewards worth having. He is thus led to orient himself toward ends which are not immediately available to him by socially approved means. Despite his aspirations and his physical and emotional readiness, he is forced to remain in a state of social, economic, and legal dependency.

The frustrations that build up under these conditions exert constant pressure for deviant behavior. A common reaction is the boisterous ganging tendency of male adolescents, voicing their protests against the adult world in all manner of aberrant acts. Among his compeers, the adolescent can play semi-adult roles free from the disapproving and depriving attitudes of the adult world. Here he can "act the adult"–even if the resulting behavior is awkward and exaggerated, recognized as adult only by his contemporaries.

One of the most detailed expositions of this adjustment problem as a source of delinquent subcultures can be found in *The Gang: A Study in Adolescent Behavior,* (1958) by Bloch and Niederhoffer. They summarize their position as follows:

> The adolescent period in all cultures, visualized as a phase of striving for the attainment of adult status, produces experiences which are much the same for all youths, and certain common dynamisms for expressing reaction to such subjectively held experiences. The intensity of the adolescent experience and the vehemence of external expression depend on a variety of factors, including the general societal attitudes towards adolescence, the duration of the adolescent period itself, and the degree to which the society tends to facilitate entrance into adulthood by virtue of institutionalized patterns, ceremonials, rites, and rituals, and socially supported emotional and intellectual prepara-

> tion. When a society does not make adequate preparation, formal or otherwise, for the induction of its adolescents to the adult status, equivalent forms of behavior arise spontaneously among adolescents themselves, reinforced by their own group structure, which seemingly provides the same psychological content and function as the more formalized rituals found in other societies. This the gang structure appears to do in American society, apparently satisfying deep-seated needs experienced by adolescents in all cultures. Such, very briefly, is our hypothesis [1958, p. 17].

Inadequacies of the Theory

Definition—Like the masculine-identification theory, the theory that conflict in the transition to adulthood is the source of delinquent subcultures fails to identify clearly the pattern of deviant behavior to be explained. Bloch and Niederhoffer consistently equate "adolescent gangs" with "delinquent gangs." It is true that most delinquent gangs are composed of adolescents, but one can hardly say that all adolescent groups are composed of delinquents. Nevertheless, Bloch and Niederhoffer do not distinguish between adolescent groups whose behavior is within the limits of conventional tolerance and delinquent groups as such.

Distribution—Failure to delimit the object of inquiry inevitably confounds the task of describing its distribution in the social structure. This is clearly apparent in the somewhat ambiguous assertions by Bloch and Niederhoffer regarding the distribution of delinquency. At the outset, they argue that delinquency is rather widely diffused throughout the social structure and, furthermore, that it is extremely difficult to distinguish middle-class from lower-class delinquency.

> It became extremely difficult upon occasion to draw a clear line of distinction between . . . lower- and middle-class groups. If, for example, conflict or hostility to the out-group is one of the criteria of gang behavior, middle-class groups are certainly not exempt from such characterization . . . As far as the commission of delinquent acts is concerned, middle-class adolescents, singly or in groups, participate in a variety of delinquent episodes, including such illegal activities as auto theft, operating a motor vehicle without a license, disorderly conduct . . . In respect to the type of organization structure, there is little to distinguish, in one sense, between middle- and lower-class adolescent groups. Although middle-class groups of teen-agers are not as apt to have the formal, almost military structure characteristic of certain lower-class "war gangs" . . . they do have similar and well-defined informal patterns of leadership and control [p. 7–9].

Despite these apparent class similarities, Bloch and Niederhoffer appear to agree with the majority of observers that the problem of delinquency is more serious in the lower class. They base their belief on the observation that delinquent acts in the lower class tend to develop strong subcultural supports.

> . . . [I]n recognizing the group nature of delinquent acts, it is significant to note that the lower-class youth, exposed to powerful instigating forces of his own milieu and subcultural setting, does tend to develop a unique delinquent subculture of his own . . . Differences in the qualitative nature of delinquency, as well as the character of the psychological and sociological reinforcement of the delinquent act, would appear to follow as a result of . . . class and cultural differences. In this sense, therefore, *viz.,* that delinquent acts in a lower-class setting receive strong sanctioned support and approval, [the] view that the locus of much delinquency is in the lower-class gang may not be seriously disputed [p. 15].

The assertion that lower-class delinquency receives "strong sanctioned support and approval" identifies a difference that goes to the heart of the problem of defining and locating delinquent subcultures. Indeed, it is principally this difference that permits us to say, with Bloch and Niederhoffer, that the most serious delinquency problem exists in the lower class. Whether or not delinquent norms are part of the structure of the group is, it seems to us, a crucial criterion in distinguishing between delinquent and nondelinquent subcultures. If members of a group have not qualified or partially withdrawn their support of the legitimacy of conventional norms, then we would not call the group a delinquent subculture.

Having alluded to this crucial distinction, however, Bloch and Niederhoffer do not then incorporate it in their analysis of delinquent behavior. Rather than focus upon the forces which transform adolescent groups into specifically delinquent gangs, they attempt to account for the features that are common to all adolescent groups, delinquent and otherwise:

> From the foregoing discussion, it would appear that many of the . . . features which distinguish the [lower-class] gang from middle-class cliques are primarily a matter of degree. Actually, what we are concerned with here are the general characteristics of the adolescent group process itself. May we assume that there are certain common features of this grouping process which appear to function irrespective of class, ethnic, and cultural level? Examination of the evidence of group behavior, characteristic of adolescents not only on different class levels within the same culture but even within widely divergent cultures, would seem to suggest that adolescence produces certain remarkable similarities in the group behavior of the young person striving for adulthood [p. 10].

Our objection to statements of this kind is based, not on the assertion that "adolescence produces certain remarkable similarities," whatever the individual's society or position within a given society, but on the implication of this assertion, that delinquency, being a manifestation of adolescence, is also more or less the same wherever it arises. Indeed, Bloch and Niederhoffer also have difficulty with this point, for, as we noted, they seem to agree that lower-class delinquency is different from delinquency elsewhere in the social structure principally because it is rooted in subcultural norms. Their failure to define the object of inquiry thus leads to considerable confusion regarding its distribution.

The Problem of Adjustment—According to Bloch and Niederhoffer, adolescent cultures arise because the young encounter barriers in access to adult status. This status crisis is a significant one which produces a great deal of discontent and frustration. It appears to result in marked tendencies toward ganging and unruly behavior, particularly among males. The adolescent culture is one "of negation in which the positive values of the prevailing culture are distorted and inverted for uses best suited to a philosophy of youthful dissidence and protest" (p. 13). Probably few people would question this general explanation of turbulence during adolescence. It is, however, a rather long step from "youthful dissidence and protest" to systematic, recurrent thievery, organized street warfare, and habitual drug use. Treating "youthful dissidence" and these other phenomena as if they were similar is rather like lumping the social drinker and the chronic alcoholic under the same rubric. The theory of adolescent protest may help to explain the emergence of "youth culture," but it does not explain the conditions under which *delinquent* subcultures develop.

The experience of frustration in adolescent strivings toward adulthood seems to be so widespread in our society that it is hard to decide where it is most frequent and acute. In the absence of definitive data to show that this adjustment problem is concentrated among lower-class males in large cities, plausible arguments can be advanced for either a middle- or a lower-class concentration. For example, one might argue that the middle-class adolescent experiences more conflict because he generally has to delay much longer than the lower-class boy before assuming adult roles. His expected occupational roles as an adult generally require much longer periods of preparatory training. The lower-class boy is permitted to participate in adult roles and rewards much closer to the time when he is physically and emotionally ready to do so. On the other hand, it might be argued that the lower-class boy feels more frustrated because he has been trained to delay gratification as has the middle-class boy, who has been led to anticipate a prolonged period of training as essential and encouraged to accept intermediate substitutes for eventual adult rewards.

The problem of the transition to adulthood is obviously not a permanent one. Although the adolescent crisis is acute, adult status is bound to come in time. Given the temporary quality of this problem of adjustment, current theories of adolescent frustration as explanations of delinquent subculture do not seem convincing to us.

The Evolution of Subcultural Solutions—How does the theory of adolescent status crisis account for the origin of delinquent norms? The "adolescent protest," like the "masculine protest," may lead to delinquent acts—assaults, vandalism, and the like—in many adolescent groups, but these acts may or may not be supported by specifically delinquent norms. In our opinion, most adolescents who engage in such acts acknowledge the legitimacy of the conventional norms from which their behavior departs. Most adolescent groups in which delinquent acts occur, therefore, cannot properly be called delinquent subcultures. Thus the adolescent status-crisis theory does not provide an answer to the critical question of how delinquent norms originate.

Indeed, Bloch and Niederhoffer themselves do not seem wholly certain that the problem of adolescent status transition is the chief source of lower-class delinquent norms, for they introduce a further problem of adjustment experienced by lower-class youth—namely, discontent arising from a marked discrepancy between aspirations and opportunities for upward social mobility.

> The lower-class boy . . . absorbs dominant *middle-class values* which set goals for him, *but sees on every hand that he is unable to pursue these ends.* To many a lower-class boy, the socially approved objectives for desired manhood are so far-fetched, so unattainable, that they constitute a sort of chimera, a never-never land about which he can dream but actually not hope to achieve. The patterns of living of his father and other adult male figures in his environment appear to offer testimony as to the futility of achieving the goals which the popular cult of American success so stridently affirms in the classroom, the movies, TV, and other popular channels of mass enlightenment. What models are offered in the lives of parents and others in his environment, who are closely bound to a limited and constricted routine of seemingly unrewarded toil, appear uninspired and, for many youths, hardly worth the effort. Recognizing the limitations on his strivings, the values of the working-class youth may be an actual negation of the very things which the calculated prudence of the middle class hopes to foster among its own young [p. 109].

Where previously these authors stressed barriers to adult status, they now point to barriers to *middle-class* adult status. The problem of the lower-class adolescent, they say, is not simply one of becoming a lower-class adult. Rather, it is a problem of leaving his class of origin and becoming affiliated with a class higher in the social structure. Pressures toward deviance arise because legitimate routes to success-goals are limited or closed to lower-class youth. As a result, frustrated adolescents may seek higher status by alternative, though illegal, paths. In their analysis of a lower-class gang known as the Pirates, for example, Bloch and Niederhoffer note that the members engaged in "glorification of racketeers." Anticipating lack of access to middle-class status, these lower-class boys apparently withdrew sentiments supporting the legitimacy of conventional norms, for they developed "contempt for the doctrine that hard work leads to success and happiness. The gang stopped reading Horatio Alger long ago. The squalor of the lower-class worker's life compared to the glamour of the racketeer leaves no choice. The big man, the big shot, is the realistic ideal from which to shape life" (p. 170). Rejecting the goal of conventional lower-class adult status but cut off from middle-class adult status, potential delinquents orient themselves toward an illegitimate opportunity structure—the rackets.

It appears, then, that Bloch and Niederhoffer, while explicitly suggesting that delinquent subcultures arise from adolescent strivings toward immediate adult gratifications, have in fact advanced a theory based on the discrepancy between aspirations for culturally defined success-goals and the realistic possibilities of achieving those goals by legitimate means. It is the latter problem of adjustment that they use to account for the withdrawal of sentiments supporting official norms.

A test of the explicit Bloch-Niederhoffer hypothesis would require a comparison of the propensities toward delinquency exhibited by lower-class youth who wish to become lower-class adults and by middle-class youth who wish to become middle-class adults. If such a comparison showed that lower-class youth experience greater stress, it might then be said that the distribution of the adolescent crisis parallels the class distribution of delinquent subcultures. Unfortunately, Bloch and Niederhoffer do not provide the necessary data for such a comparison, nor do we find supporting data elsewhere in the literature on adolescence. But whatever we may eventually discover with respect to this comparison, it remains true that the Bloch and Niederhoffer account does not rest exclusively on the hypothesis that adolescent role strains are responsible for delinquency. Instead they imply that the dual problem of achieving adult status *and* middle-class status is the adjustment dilemma to which delinquent subcultures in the lower class are a response.

When we consider the adolescent-crisis theory as a basic for identifying the conditions accounting for the emergence of the three types of subculture among lower-class youth, statements found in the literature prove somewhat confusing. Bloch and Niederhoffer assert that most lower-class delinquency is rational, disciplined, and utilitarian:

> The present authors' investigations of literally hundreds of juvenile crimes, including burglaries and robberies, expose the overwhelming number committed by lower-class gangs. Inevitably, money or valuable property was taken. If the scene of the crime was ransacked, it was because the perpetrators turned the place over in their search for the hiding place of the money. It is true that often other articles in addition to the money were taken. But these, too, were apt to be useful to the gang in some way . . . Rarely was there evidence to corroborate the non-utilitarian motives which Cohen ascribes to lower-class crime. Perhaps with boys younger than twelve, this may be true, reflecting their immaturity and lack of social intelligence rather than class membership [p. 178].

They do not, of course, deny the existence of the conflict and retreatist forms of delinquent subculture; they simply assert the primacy of the criminal pattern. (They do, however, note historical changes in the rates of each pattern, suggesting that the conflict pattern is tending to become ascendent.)

This emphasis on utilitarian delinquency does not seem to be consistent with their theoretical analysis. It is not clear why the frustrations of adolescence should yield disciplined, utilitarian behavior. In fact, one might expect the reverse: that negativistic, aggressive, destructive–i.e., "conflict"–behavior would result from the stresses of adolescence. As a matter of fact, this is precisely what the cross-cultural comparisons presented by Bloch and Niederhoffer show, as witness the following examples:

> *Manus:* In the study of the Manus people, it has been demonstrated that rites are inadequate in preparing adolescents in that society for the abrupt transition from a happy childhood to the anxiety-ridden life they lead as adults. This should be fertile territory for the growth of gangs. Here again we find evidence of the formation of groups of dissident and roistering adolescent males . . . *"the terror of their own village girls, the scourge of neighboring villages."*
>
> *Comanche:* There were deviant individuals who by their depredations and reckless courage earned the sobriquet of "the contrary ones." Both Herbert

> Bloch and Abraham Kardiner point out that while such gangs or individuals represent a definite threat to the peace and harmony of the community, they are tolerated because this same reckless behavior is demanded of the "contrary ones" in war. In this, non-conforming "delinquent" activity, whether gang or individual, is channeled into constructive paths [pp. 134–135, emphasis added].

Their illustrations of delinquency from the American scene, by contrast, stress utilitarian behavior: "In gangs dedicated to burglaries, robberies and larcenies, there are careful preparations involving 'casing the job,' practicing rehearsals, coordination of efforts according to a master plan. Long hours are spent acquiring mechanical and electrical skills, checking the patrol habits of the policeman on the post. Surely this is not short-run hedonism!" (p. 180). With this last statement we must agree. But how, then, are we to reconcile these accounts of utilitarian behavior among many lower-class gangs with the unruly behavior of the Manus and Comanche adolescents, or with accounts of urban "fighting gangs"?

Persistence and Change—Bloch and Niederhoffer present a discussion of the "rising trend of modern delinquency." However, instead of using their theory of the adolescent crisis to account for this development, they invoke psychological explanations: "Considerable recent evidence suggests rather strongly that the rising trend of modern delinquency is characterized by pathological states of minds. The frequency of psychopathies and emotional disturbances among young offenders may be reaching significant proportions" (p. 148). Whatever the merits of this explanation, it seems unrelated to the general theory that delinquent subcultures—and changes in them—result from the status deprivations of adolescence.

Logically, proponents of the adolescent-crisis theory of delinquency must account for changes in delinquency rates on the basis of changes in the relationship of adolescent and adult roles. If delinquency rates are increasing, has there been a corresponding increase in the difficulties associated with the transition from adolescence to adulthood? Unfortunately, Bloch and Niederhoffer do not pursue this line of inquiry, nor have relevant data been reported elsewhere in the literature on adolescence.

Lower-Class Culture and Delinquent Subcultures

American criminologists have frequently attributed the emergence of delinquent and criminal subcultures to value conflicts. Briefly, this point of view asserts that societies often contain several value systems which vary in their relative dominance so that conformity with a subordinate value system evokes sanctions from the agents of the dominant value system. One variant of the traditional "value conflict" or "culture conflict" theory has recently been advanced by Walter B. Miller (1958). Unfortunately, Miller has not concerned himself with many of the theoretical issues raised by former proponents and critics of this tradition, so that many unresolved problems remain in his work.

Miller's thesis may be reduced to three main propositions: (1) The lower class is characterized by distinctive values. (2) These vary markedly from the middle-class values which undergird the legal code. (3) The result is that conformity with certain lower-class values may automatically result in violation of the law. As Miller puts it, "Engaging in certain cultural practices which comprise essential elements of the total life pattern of lower-class culture automatically violates certain legal norms. Examples of this may be seen in the use of profanity, in hanging around or loitering, and in the serial-mating pattern characteristic of many homes." In other words, the lower-class way of life as such is intrinsically law-violating; it runs counter to the definitions of conformity that prevail in other sectors of the society.[1] This view is clearly implied in Miller's statement: "Many school [personnel] tend to see the future lives of [lower-class youth] in terms of only two major alternatives–an essentially lower-class or an essentially middle-class way of life. A third alternative–and one which is far more feasible in a large proportion of cases–is to train and prepare the youngsters for a law-abiding lower-class way of life" (Kvaraceus and Miller, 1959). The task of the school in this perspective is to help youngsters to overcome the general propensities toward law-violating behavior which are a "normal" consequence of socialization in the lower class.

The "focal concerns," values, or preoccupations which characterize the lower class and which predispose its members to law-violating behavior are defined by Miller as follows:

> *Trouble:* Concern over 'trouble' is a dominant feature of lower-class culture . . . 'Trouble' in one of its aspects represents a situation or a kind of behavior which results in unwelcome or complicating involvement with official authorities or agencies of middle-class society . . . For men, 'trouble' frequently involves fighting or sexual adventures while drinking; for women, sexual involvement with disadvantageous consequences. Expressed desire to avoid behavior which violates moral or legal norms is often based less on an explicit commitment to 'official' moral or legal standards than on a desire to avoid 'getting into trouble,' e.g., the complicating consequences of the action.

[1] See Miller's remarks in Kvaraceus and Miller (1959 pp. 68–69).

> *Toughness:* The concept of 'toughness' in lower-class culture represents a compound combination of qualities or states. Among its most important components are physical prowess, evidenced both by demonstrated possession of strength and endurance and athletic skill; "masculinity," symbolized by a complex of acts and avoidance [bodily tattooing, absence of sentimentality; non-concern with 'art,' 'literature'; conceptualization of women as conquest objects, etc.]; and bravery in the face of physical threat. The model for the 'tough guy'–hard, fearless, undemonstrative, skilled in physical combat–is represented by the movie gangster of the thirties, the 'private eye,' and the movie cowboy.
>
> *Smartness:* 'Smartness' . . . involves the capacity to outsmart, outfox, outwit, dupe, 'take,' 'con' another or others, and the concomitant capacity to avoid being outwitted, 'taken,' or duped oneself. In its essence, smartness involves the capacity to achieve a value entity–material goods, personal status–through a maximum of mental agility and a minimum of physical effort.
>
> *Excitement:* For many lower-class individuals the rhythm of life fluctuates between periods of relatively routine or repetitive activity and sought situations of great emotional stimulation. Many of the most characteristic features of lower-class life are related to the search for excitement or 'thrill.' Involved here are the wide-spread use of gambling of all kinds . . . The quest for excitement finds . . . its most vivid expression in the . . . recurrent 'night on the town' . . . a patterned set of activities in which alcohol, music, and sexual adventuring are major components.
>
> *Fate:* Related to the quest for excitement is the concern with fate, fortune, or luck. Here also a distinction is made between two states–being 'lucky' or 'in luck,' and being unlucky or jinxed. Many lower-class persons feel that their lives are subject to a set of forces over which they have relatively little control. These are not equated directly with the supernatural forces of formally organized religion, but relate more to a concept of 'destiny' or man as a pawn of magical powers . . . This often implicit world view is associated with a conception of the ultimate futility of directed effort toward a goal . . .
>
> *Autonomy:* The extent and nature of control over the behavior of the individual–an important concern in most cultures–has a special significance and is distinctively patterned in lower-class culture . . . On the overt level there is a strong and frequently expressed resentment of the idea of external controls, restrictions on behavior, and unjust or coercive authority . . . Actual patterns of behavior, however, reveal a marked discrepancy between expressed sentiment and what is covertly valued. Many lower-class people appear to seek out highly restrictive social environments wherein stringent external controls are maintained over their behavior . . . Lower-class patients in mental hospitals will exercise considerable ingenuity to insure continued commitment while voicing the desire to get out; delinquent boys will frequently 'run' from a correctional institution to activate efforts to return them; to be caught and returned means that one is cared for [1958, p. 8–13].

Proponents of culture-conflict theories have differed in their views regarding the relation of such conflict to delinquency. For example, Wirth (1931) says that culture conflict is relevant to delinquency only when two conflicting value systems are simultaneously internalized; this produces feelings of anxiety and insecurity which may result in delinquent behavior. Miller, however, seems to view delinquency among lower-class youth as the outcome of an *external* clash of cultural codes. He asserts that delinquents have internalized only the distinctive code of the lower class but that the power structure of the society enforces the middle-class code. Their efforts to conform to their own values thus bring them into conflict with the agents of middle-class norms, with the result that lower-class youngsters are defined as delinquent. This point of view is strongly reminiscent of Sellin's classic discussion of "external cultural conflict" (1938):

> A few years ago, a Sicilian father in New Jersey killed the sixteen-year-old seducer of his daughter, expressing surprise at his arrest since he had merely defended his family honor in a traditional way. In this case a mental conflict in the sociological sense did not exist. The conflict was external and occurred between cultural codes or norms. We may assume that where such conflicts occur, violations or norms of one cultural group or area migrate to another and that such conflict will continue so long as the acculturation process has not been completed [p. 68].

Although it seems unlikely that there are many lower-class persons today so completely unacculturated to the "core" values of American society as this Sicilian father, Miller nevertheless adheres closely to the position implied by this incident with respect to certain lower-class values:

> A large body of systematically interrelated attitudes, practices, behaviors, and values characteristic of lower-class culture are designed to support and maintain the basic features of the lower-class way of life. In areas where these differ from features of middle-class culture, action oriented to the achievement and maintenance of the lower-class system may violate norms of the middle class and be perceived as deliberately non-conforming or malicious by an observer strongly cathected to middle-class norms. This does not mean, however, that violation of the middle-class norm is the dominant component of motivation; *it is a byproduct of action primarily oriented to the lower-class system* [1958, p. 19].

Yet the lower class is now composed principally of persons who are at least one generation removed from foreign-born ancestors. These people, in common with middle-class persons, have been exposed to the cultural impact of universal public education and the mass media of our society. Although middle- and lower-class value systems are not identical, they are nevertheless parts of the same society and thus have much in common. This is a point to which we will return later in this discussion, for it bears directly on the adeqquacy of the theory of culture conflict.

INADEQUACIES OF THE THEORY

Definition—The culture-conflict theory, like the adolescent-status and masculine-identity theories, is an attempt to explain *all* types of delinquent act, whether or not these acts are supported by subcultural norms. Thus there is a tendency to classify as delinquent any group in which delinquent acts occur. Miller defines delinquency as *"behavior by nonadults which violates specific legal norms or the norms of a particular societal institution with sufficient frequency and/or seriousness so as to provide a firm basis for legal action against the behaving individual or group"* (Kvaraceus and Miller, 1959 p. 54). He notes, further, that the members of all lower-class adolescent "street-corner" groups commit acts which fit this definition as part of their ordinary activities:

> The cutomary set of activities of the adolescent street-corner group includes activities which are in violation of laws and ordinances of the legal code. Most of these center around assault and theft of various types [the gang fight; auto theft; assault on an individual; petty pilfering and shoplifting; 'mugging'; pocketbook theft] [p. 17].

It would appear that for Miller the only basis for differentiating delinquent and nondelinquent groups is that members of the former engage in delinquent acts more frequently. Thus Miller says that "delinquent gangs" are simply a variant of street-corner groups: "What has been called the 'delinquent gang' . . . defined on the basis of frequency of participation in law-violating activity . . . should not be considered a legitimate unit of study per se, but rather as one particular variant of the adolescent street-corner group" (p. 14).

The problem with a definition that focuses exclusively upon delinquent acts is that it encompasses many street-corner groups whose core members generally disapprove of, or at best merely tolerate, the delinquencies of other members. In such groups, delinquent acts are not a requirement or a desideratum for membership. By Miller's definition, a social or athletic group which becomes involved in a delinquent episode is no less delinquent than are groups which are organized specifically for theft, street warfare, or other illegal activities. Failure to recognize the relationship between a delinquent act and the social and cultural structure of the group in which it occurs thus leads to serious problems of definition.

Distribution—Miller's concept of delinquency also can be criticized on the ground that an extraordinarily wide range of adolescents are caught in the net. Delinquent subcultures, as we have said, tend to be confined to adolescent males in lower-class urban areas, but this certainly cannot be said of delinquent acts. Delinquent acts, as such, occur throughout the social structure; although the rates differ, they are committed by females, middle-class adolescents, and residents in rural areas. It is unreasonable to assume that a single theory can account for such diverse behavior. If we focus on delinquent norms, by contrast, the theoretical task becomes much more manageable, for the emergence of delinquent norms tends to be restricted to certain social locations. Furthermore, an emphasis on supporting norms—that is, on the cultural structure of the delinquent group—makes it possible to draw meaningful distinctions among various types of gang, which cannot be done when the act alone is taken as the criterion of delinquency.

The Problem of Adjustment—How, then, are we to account for delinquent acts which are so widely dispersed throughout the social structure? Miller suggests that conformity with lower-class values in a middle-class world is such an adjustment problem. But what of middle-class adolescents who commit delinquent acts? Miller offers the rather unconvincing answer that middle-class adolescent groups are taking over many of the focal concerns of the lower class and thus are finding themselves at odds with the values of their own class. Miller feels that the preoccupation with the diffusion of middle-class values in our society has caused us to underestimate the upward diffusion of lower-class values, particularly with the development of mass media of communication (Kvaraceus and Miller, 1959). It is certainly a debatable question whether the mass media disseminate middle-class or lower-class values. In any case, middle-class groups embraced by Miller's definition of delinquent gang present a major problem for theories based on the culture-conflict theme.

Miller's theory can also be challenged on the ground that the conflict between lower-class and middle-class values is not so significant and persistent a problem in the life experience of delinquents as he supposes. Serious delinquencies, such as burglary, robbery, assault, gang killings, and drug addiction, violate lower-class as well as middle-class values. Miller's examples of deviance arising from culture conflict—"the use of profanity, . . . hanging around or loitering, . . . the serial-mating pattern characteristic of many homes"—tend to be relatively innocuous forms of conduct from the standpoint of both lower- and middle-class norms. Furthermore, the focal concerns of lower-class groups as outlined by Miller—trouble, toughness, smartness, excitement, fate, and autonomy—do not seem to differ from middle-class preoccupations so much that simple conformity to these values would "automatically" lead to serious law violations. Miller's analysis suggests a degree of cultural independence of the two classes that has probably not prevailed since the mass immigrations of the nineteenth and early twentieth centuries.

The Evolution of Subcultural Solutions—Perhaps the most serious defect of the culture-conflict theory of delinquent gangs lies in its failure to account for the origins of delinquent norms. Under what conditions do the focal concerns of lower-class youngsters become transformed into specifically delinquent prescriptions? Miller, like earlier theorists in the culture-conflict tradition, has concentrated on explaining delinquent as opposed to nondelinquent acts. This leaves the problem of identifying the conditions under which delinquent acts come to be buttressed by a stable set of delinquent norms. In order to explain how patterned delinquent subcultures emerge—how lower-class "focal concerns" become sufficiently "intensified," "maximized," or "distorted" to lead to subcultural delinquency —Miller turns to two additional problems of adjustment.

He first explores the consequences of socialization in the female-centered households and introduces a version of the problem of masculine identification. In order to assert their masculinity, he contends lower-class boys from female-entered households tend to exaggerate delinquent aspects of the lower-class value system.[2] Miller also points to discrepancies between the aspirations of lower-class youth and the realistic possibilities for achievement as a source of frustration and anxiety. It should be noted that this second problem runs counter to his frequent emphasis on the relative isolation of lower- and middle-class value systems. Success themes are at the core of the middle-class value system in America, and there is much in Miller's work to indicate that lower-class youth are exposed to these themes and take them quite seriously. In this connection, Miller suggests a typology of lower-class youth based on the gap between aspirations and possibilities of achievement:

1. *'Stable' lower class.* This group consists of youngsters who, for all practical purposes, do not aspire to higher status or who have no realistic possibility of achieving such aspirations.
2. *Aspiring but conflicted lower class.* This group represents those for whom family or other community influences have produced a desire to elevate their status, but who lack the necessary personal attributes or cultural

[2] See Kvaraceus and Miller (1959), Chapter 11, and Miller (1958), pp. 13–14.

'equipment' to make the grade, or for whom cultural pressures effectively inhibit aspirations.

3. *Successfully aspiring lower class.* This group, popularly assumed to be the most prevalent, includes those who have both the will and the capacity to elevate their status [Kvaraceus and Miller, 1959, p. 72].

The first two categories in this typology are marked by internal contradictions. With respect to the stable lower class (type 1), there is a considerable difference between those "who do not aspire to higher status" and those who do aspire but "have no realistic possibility of achieving such aspirations." Those who do not aspire avoid frustrations arising from position discontent; those who aspire but are cut off from appropriate avenues to higher status experience acute frustrations. To preserve this distinction it might be preferable to describe type 1 as follows: This group consists of youngsters who, for all practical purposes, do not aspire to higher status or who, because of expectations of failure, have revised their aspirations downward.

The definition of type 2 also blurs important distinctions. Miller says that persons in this category "desire to elevate their status" but that various "cultural pressures effectively inhibit aspirations." Thus it is not clear what he intends to convey about the aspiration levels of this category. It would appear from other elements in the definition that this type should properly consist of lower-class youth who aspire to but are cut off from success, either because they "lack the necessary personal attributes or 'cultural equipment' to make the grade" or because opportunity is objectively limited. To the extent that their aspirations persist under conditions limiting achievement, acute frustrations would be experienced. This group, then, should be clearly distinguished from type 1 and type 3. Type 3 includes those who aspire and who possess traits and abilities that are likely to bring them success.

According to Miller, discrepancies between aspirations and possibilities of achievement are a major source of pressures toward delinquent behavior: "The lower-class youngster who is 'stalled' in regard to his achievement aspiration is . . . likely to become delinquent" (Kvaraceus and Miller, 1959 p. 136). This statement and others that call attention to social and cultural dislocations within lower-class environments obviously conflict with Miller's hypothesis that delinquency is basically a consequence of conformity to lower-class values. It is perhaps sufficient at this point for us to note that the theory of culture conflict does not prove adequate by itself to account for the emergence of delinquent subcultures. It is necessary to introduce other types of adjustment problem to differentiate the responses of lower-class youngsters to their living conditions.

Nothing in Miller's account of lower-class life helps to explain the differentiation of delinquent subcultures. Even if his definition of lower-class values were accepted, it is not at all clear why this conflict would result alternatively in criminal, conflict, or retreatist adaptations.

Persistence and Change—The culture-conflict theory addresses the problem of the persistence of delinquent norms more directly than the problem of their origins. Delinquent norms are regarded as "given"; Miller, for example, is concerned primarily with how these norms are taken over by the child. His theory assumes the existence of delinquent norms whose dictates must be followed by new members as the price of admission to the group:

> The *demanded* response to certain situations recurrently engendered within lower-class culture may call for the commission of illegal acts. For many youngsters the bases of prestige are to be found in toughness, physical prowess, skill, fearlessness, bravery, ability to con people, gaining money by wits, shrewdness, adroitness, smart repartee, seeking and finding thrills, risk, danger, freedom from external constraint, and freedom from superordinate authority. These are the explicit values of the most important and essential reference group of many delinquent youngsters. These are the things he respects and strives to attain. The lower-class youngster who engages in a long and recurrent series of delinquent behaviors that are sanctioned by his peer group is acting so as to achieve prestige within his reference system [Kvaraceus and Miller, 1959, p. 59]. [3]

It is apparent, however, that a theory of the persistence of a cultural tradition is not a sufficient explanation of the origin of that tradition. To maintain that delinquent norms are an exaggeration of aspects of the

[3] Miller's statement that "the *demanded* response to certain situations recurrently engendered within lower-class culture may call for the commission of illegal acts" sounds very much as though he were referring to *delinquent norms* as such—that is, to norms that prescribe the commission of various delinquent acts. Here again we find an ambiguity in Miller's work, for the distinction between lower-class norms in general and delinquent norms is unclear. Furthermore, it should be noted that lower-class focal concerns, such as the emphasis upon masculinity, are not delinquent or criminal. Miller has not shown why efforts to be masculine result in delinquent or criminal behavior. There are many ways of exhibiting masculinity that do not entail legal violations. If ways are chosen that entail law violations, then these *choices* require explanation.

In this connection Miller's work has similarities to that of Shaw (1930, 1931) Shaw et al, (1940), Shaw and McKay, (1942), and Sutherland (1937, 1947, 1949), who were also very much in the culture-conflict tradition. They, too, took delinquent codes as *given* and focused on the transmission of these codes from one generation to another.

lower-class value system simply shifts the original question to the problem of accounting for the development of different value systems within the same society and of the relative dominance of one over the others. Miller alludes to a historical continuity between contemporary lower-class values in the United States and the traditional values of depressed groups in other parts of the world, asserting that "lower-class culture is a distinctive tradition many centuries old with an integrity of its own" (Miller, 1958). But at some juncture the theorist must identify the social conditions from which these values develop as a solution to the adjustment problems of everyday life. The historical-continuity theory of lower-class values as a source of delinquent norms can be attacked on many points. We should like to point out here that it ignores the extent to which lower-class and delinquent cultures today are predictable responses to conditions in our society rather than persisting patterns taken over from foreign cultures.

The culture-conflict hypothesis poses special problems when one considers the sources of change in the patterns of delinquent activity. Culture-conflict theorists typically account for a reduction in delinquency by referring to acculturation—a process in which serious value conflicts are gradually eliminated. It is somewhat harder, however, for culture-conflict theorists to explain an increase in the amount of delinquency and a change in its content. Logically these changes must be explained by the infusion of new value conflicts into the system or by some type of breakdown in the diffusion of existing values, although no account of such a breakdown has been offered. In conclusion, therefore, we are not disposed to accept the hypothesis that culture conflict is the most characteristic and significant adjustment problem underlying the development of delinquent subcultures.

The Evolution of Delinquent Subcultures

When a social system generates severe problems of adjustment for occupants of a particular social status, it is possible that a collective challenge to the legitimacy of the established rules of conduct will emerge. This is especially likely to occur where a democratic ideology exists, espousing equality of opportunity and universally high aspirations for success. Since discrepancies between aspiration and opportunity are likely to be experienced more intensely at some social positions than at others, persons in status locations where the discrepancy is most acute may develop a common perception and sense of indignation about their disadvantages as contrasted with the advantages of others. Interaction among those sharing the same problem may provide encouragement for the withdrawal of sentiments in support of the established system of norms. Once freed of allegiance to the existing set of rules, such persons may devise or adopt delinquent means of achieving success.

A collective delinquent solution to an adjustment problem is more likely to evolve by this process in a society in which the legitimacy of social rules can be questioned apart from their moral validity. For example, it would be relatively unlikely to develop in a tradition-bound, self-sufficient folk society where a complex network of closely integrated moral sentiments reinforce acceptance of the dominant norms. In such a society an intricate interweaving of sacred and secular motivations defines whatever is as right. In the secular, competitive, impersonal, mass society of the modern Western world, on the other hand, the necessity for highly specialized activities has enormously complicated the task of maintaining a cohesive and stable order. It has become more and more difficult to identify universally shared moral sentiments which will guarantee allegiance to the dominant norms of the society. The long, complex chains of relationships required to integrate the social and economic life of the society permit the development of special beliefs, values, and norms at different social locations and the dissolution of links in the established structure of beliefs, values, and norms. What seems expedient, rational, and efficient often becomes separable for the imputation of legitimacy. Under such conditions it is difficult for persons at different social positions to agree about the forms of conduct that are both expedient and morally right. Once this separation takes place, the supporting structure of the existing system of norms becomes highly vulnerable. When the individual defines his commitment to the dominant system of norms on the basis of expediency rather than moral validity, his sentiments may become attached to some competing set of norms more to his advantage. It is even possible that he may attribute legitimacy on the grounds of expediency to rules of conduct that he regards at the same time as morally inferior to some competing set of norms.

To understand the growth of delinquent subcultures, we must identify more explicitly the social conditions within which this alienation from established norms and acceptance of illegitimate models of behavior occurs. It seems evident that the members of a newly emerging delinquent subculture must pass through a complex process of change in attitudes toward themselves, other persons, and the established social order before such a major shift in allegiance can take place. First, they must be freed from commitment to and belief in the legitimacy of certain aspects of the existing organization of means. They must be led to question the validity of various conventional codes of conduct as an appropriate guide for their own actions before accepting a model of behavior involving forbidden acts. Secondly, they must join with others in seeking a solution to their adjustment problems rather than attempt to solve them alone. Thirdly, they must be provided with appropriate means for handling the problems of guilt and fear which new recruits to the subculture sometimes experience as a result of engaging in acts of deviance. Finally, they must face no obstacles to the possibility of joint problem-solving.

PART VI
PSYCHOPHYSIOLOGIC DISORDERS

Psychophysiologic disorders are, in general, physiological maladaptations to situations which have been the source of chronic emotional stress. They were studied in adults for many years before efforts were made to observe and understand them in children. The symbolic expression of repressed feelings through the disorder of body functions, originally called hysteria, is distinguished from psychophysiologic disorders in that: (1) organs are innervated by the autonomic or involuntary nervous system; (2) the symptoms are physiologic rather than psychologically symbolic in origin; (3) actual structural changes are often produced; and (4) pregenital rather than phallic fixations are primary in the personality make-up.

In 1943, Dunbar, who was of the opinion that a specific personality type was a predisposing factor and thus determined the "choice" of somatic illness, popularized the term "psychosomatic" with her personality profiles. She advanced the major premise that mental stimuli, just as bacteria and toxins, bring about body changes.

Alexander (1950) and his group subsequently challenged these conceptualizations and developed a model based on the concept of a specific conflict rather than personality type. Perhaps the best-known example is that of the individual who represses oral-receptive longings with reaction formations of great activity leading to increased gastric secretion and peptic ulcer. Alexander felt that unknown factors involving constitutional predisposition were also important (organ susceptibility seemed significant inasmuch as many people with this particular kind of conflict and personality did not develop peptic ulcer). As others have noted (Engel, 1963; Prugh, 1963), physiological and psychological phenomena cannot be discussed interchangeably—they are two levels of organization which, though interrelated, exhibit different laws of operations. Mirsky's (1958) work has further confirmed the operation of predisposing biological and psychological factors which act together and predictably, i.e., a person with a high blood pepsinogen level and a conflict picture of repressed oral longings, when subjected to stress, often exhibits the clinical picture of ulcer.

Observing the interaction of biological and psychological components of ulcerative colitis in children, McDermott and Finch (1967) noted that, in spite of significant improvement of personality functioning, the disease typically continued on an unremitting course. This led them to speculate that other factors, perhaps autoimmunological, once emotionally triggered, become dissociated from psychological influences and irreversible.

Thus far, there is little evidence that particular personality types are pathognomonic of specific psychosomatic disorders in children. The often cited "conflict" appears to be the nonspecific dependency problem. But again, the question is to what extent these problems are primary and to what degree they are secondary to the chronic debilitating disease. Much of the work has centered on the mother-child relationship. Sperling (1949) describes the "psychosomatic type" of object relationship in which the mother relates to the child positively only through his illness. Other authors (Fries, 1944; Garner et al., 1959; Gerard, 1953) have noted the combination of the dominating mother and overly dependent child who reacts with symptoms when his dependent needs are threatened. Certainly, we are offered a wide range of theories attempting to explain the mother-child interaction involved in psychophysiological disorders.

While the mechanism of the emotional factors is still not clear, and that of the biological factors even less so, interaction of the two is generally accepted as necessary to the genesis of the classical psychophysiologic disorders. Unfortunately, there are still painfully few systematic studies and too much dogmatism regarding all these disorders.

ANOREXIA NERVOSA

WILLIAM W. GULL

It was Sir William Gull, the 19th-century physician who, with Victorian charm, coined the diagnostic term, anorexia nervosa. He deliberately chose to emphasize that somatic factors were secondary to mental. In identifying the variability of the emotional picture among patients and recognizing its relationship to family and environment, Gull was a man ahead of his time. Yet, since his observations preceded Freud's description of unconscious mental functioning and psychic conflicts, he could not be more specific except to identify emotions as significant etiologic factors. In his formulation of the disease, he, in fact, omitted any reference to developmental histories.

Gull (1868) was especially interested in diseases in which "morbid brain force" pervaded the various members of a family "as if in different individuals different portions of the gray matter were the seed of the same kind of morbid action, the equivalent of mental disorder in one, occurring as colon disorder in another, and so on." His idea of morbid nerve force was a psychophysiologic concept which enabled later observers to add to his formulation their understanding of the psychodynamics of the disease.

While there has been much disagreement among authors regarding the underlying etiology of anorexia nervosa, Bruch (1961a, 1962b) has conjectured that, as in obesity, the patients cannot recognize when they are hungry or satiated and cannot differentiate the need for food from other sensations of discomfort. Lipton (1966) wonders whether hunger stimuli and sexual impulses may be mixed together at a preconscious level, thus accounting for the fact that the patients do not report hunger impulses.

It is generally agreed that the significance of the common acute onset of this disorder at puberty represents a fear of assuming the adult role, including the sexual role, and that there may be fears of oral impregnation, oral aggression, and cannibalistic impulses within this need to remain a child. While typically occurring in girls, with amenorrhea a cardinal feature, anorexia nervosa has also been described in boys (Falstein, Feinstein and Judas, 1956). The type and degree of underlying emotional disturbance has been variously described as obsessive-compulsive, schizophrenic, depressive, hys-

Reprinted from *Transactions, Clinical Society of London,* 7, 1874, pp. 22–27.

terical, and phobic. Branch and Bliss (1967) note that the different classes of anorectic patients become malnourished in their own distinctive ways–an adolescent anorectic patient may worry excessively about obesity and diets to increase self-respect and escape ridicule; the hysterical patient develops a somatic disturbance which interferes with the ingestion of food; the phobic patient fears obesity and refuses to eat; the obsessional ruminates about food and obesity and pursues a ritualistic diet; the depressed patient loses his appetite and stops eating, the schizophrenic develops delusions that his food is contaminated or poisoned. Aspects of family dynamics and involvement, as they affect anorexia, have also been studied, and are included in comprehensive reviews of the syndrome (Kaufman and Heiman, 1964).

In an address on medicine, delivered at Oxford in the autumn of 1868, I referred to a peculiar form of disease occurring mostly in young women, and characterized by extreme emaciation, and often referred to latent tubercle, and mesenteric disease. I remarked that at present our diagnosis of this affection is negative, so far as determining any positive cause from which it springs; that it is mostly one of inference from our clinical knowledge of the liability of the pulmonary or abdominal organs to particular lesions, and by proving the absence of these lesions in the cases in question. The subjects of this affection are mostly of the female sex, and chiefly between the ages of 16 and 23. I have occasionally seen it in males at the same age.

To illustrate the disease I may give the details of two cases, as fair examples of the whole.

Miss A., aet. 17, under the care of Mr. Kelson Wright, of the Chapham Road, was brought to me on January 17, 1866. Her emaciation was very great. It was stated that she had lost 33 lbs. in weight. She was then 5 st. 12 lbs. Height, 5 ft. 5 in. Amenorrhoea for nearly a year. No cough. Respirations throughout chest everywhere normal. Heart-sounds normal. Resps. 12; pulse, 56. No vomiting nor diarrhoea. Slight constipation. Complete anorexia for animal food, and almost complete anorexia for everything else. Abdomen shrunk and flat, collapsed. No abnormal pulsations of aorta. Tongue clean. Urine normal. Slight deposit of phosphates on boiling. The condition was one of simple starvation. There was but slight variation in her condition, though observed at intervals of three or four months. The impulse was noted on these several occasions as 56 and 60. Resps. 12 to 15. The urine was always normal, but varied in sp. gr., and was sometimes as low as 1005. The case was regarded as one of simple anorexia.

Various remedies were prescribed–the preparations of cinchona, the bichloride of mercury, syrup of the iodide of iron, syrup of the phosphate of iron, citrate of quinine and iron, & c.–but no perceptible effect followed their administration. The diet also was varied, but without any effect upon the appetite. Occasionally for a day or two the appetite was voracious, but this was very rare and exceptional. The patient complained of no pain, but was restless and active. This was in fact a striking expression of the nervous state, for it seemed hardly possible that a body so wasted could undergo the exercise which seemed agreeable. There was some peevishness of temper, and a feeling of jealousy. No account could be given of the existing cause.

Miss A. remained under my observation from January, 1866, to March, 1868, when she had much improved, and gained in weight from 82 to 128 lbs. The improvement from this time continued, and I saw no more of her medically. As she recovered she had a much younger look, corresponding indeed to her age, 21; whilst photographs taken when she was 17, give her the appearance of being near 30. Her health has continued good.

It will be observed that all the conditions in this case were negative, and may be explained by the anorexia which led to starvation, and a depression of all the vital functions; viz., amenorrhoea, slow pulse, slow breathing. In the stage of greatest emaciation one might have been pardoned for assuming that there was some organic lesion, but from the point of view indicated such an assumption would have been unnecessary.

This view is supported by the satisfactory course of the case to entire recovery, and by the continuance of good health.

Miss B., aet. 18, was brought to me October 8, 1868, as a case of latent tubercle. Her friends had been advised accordingly to take her for the coming winter to the South of Europe.

The extremely emaciated look, much greater indeed than occurs for the most part in tubercular cases where patients are still going about, impressed me at once with the probability that I should find no visceral disease. Pulse 50, Resp. 16. Physical examination of the chest and abdomen discovered nothing abnormal. All the viscera were apparently healthy. Notwithstanding the great emaciation and apparent weakness, there was a peculiar restlessness, difficult, I was informed, to control. The mother added, 'She is never tired.' Amenorrhoea since Christmas, 1866. The clinical details of this case were in fact almost identical with the preceding one, even to the number of the pulse and respirations.

I find the following memoranda frequently entered in my note-book:—'pulse 56, resp. 12; January, 1868, pulse 54, resp. 12; March, 1869, pulse 54, resp. 12; March, 1870, pulse 50, resp. 12.' But little change occurred in the case until 1872, when the respirations became 18 to 20, pulse 60.

After that date the recovery was progressive, and at length complete.

The medical treatment probably need not be considered as contributing much to the recovery. It consisted, as in the former case, of various so-called tonics, and a nourishing diet.

Although the two cases I have given have ended in recovery, my experience supplies one instance at least of a fatal termination to this malady. When the emaciation is at the extremest, oedema may supervene in the lower extremities—the patient may become sleepless—the pulse become quick, and death be approached by symptoms of feeble febrile reaction. In one such case the *post-mortem* revealed no more than thrombosis of the femoral veins, which appeared to be coincident with the oedema of the lower limbs. Death apparently followed from the starvation alone. This is the clinical point to be borne in mind, and is, I believe, the proper guide to treatment. I have observed that in the extreme emaciation, when the pulse and respiration are slow, the temperature is slightly below the normal stardard. This fact, together with the observations made by Chossat on the effect of starvation on animals, and their inability to digest food in the state of inanition, without the aid of external heat, has direct clinical bearings; it being often necessary to supply external heat as well as food to patients. The best means of applying heat is to place an india-rubber tube, having a diameter of 2 inches and a length of 3 or 4 feet, filled with hot water along the spine of the patient, as suggested by Dr. Newington, of Ticehurst.

Food should be administered at intervals varying inversely with the exhaustion and emaciation. The inclination of the patient must be in no way consulted. In the earlier and less severe stages, it is not unusual for the medical attendant to say, in reply to the anxious solicitude of the parents, 'Let her do as she likes. Don't force food.' Formerly, I thought such advice admissible and proper, but larger experience has shown plainly the danger of allowing the starvation-process to go on.

As regards prognosis, none of these cases, however exhausted, are really hopeless whilst life exists; and, for the most part, the prognosis may be considered favourable. The restless activity referred to is also to be controlled, but this is often difficult.

It is sometimes quite shocking to see the extreme exhaustion and emaciation of these patients brought for advice; yet, by warmth and steady supplies of food and stimulants, the strength may be gradually resuscitated, and recovery completed.

After these remarks were penned, Dr. Francis Webb directed my attention to the Paper of Dr. Lasègue (Professor of Clinical Medicine in the Faculty of Medicine of Paris, and Physician to La Pitié Hospital), which was published in the 'Archives Générales de Médecine,' April, 1873, and translated into the pages of the 'Med. Times,' September 6 and 27, 1873.

It is plain that Dr. Lasègue and I have the same malady in mind, though the forms of our illustrations are different. Dr. Lasègue does not refer to my address at Oxford, and it is most likely he knew nothing of it. There is, therefore, the more value in his Paper, as our observations have been made independently. We have both selected the same expression to characterize the malady.

In the address at Oxford I used the term *Apepsia hysterica,* but before seeing Dr. Lasègue's Paper, it had equally occurred to me that *Anorexia* would be more correct.

The want of appetite is, I believe, due to a morbid mental state. I have not observed in these cases any gastric disorder to which the want of appetite could be referred. I believe, therefore, that its origin is central and not peripheral. That mental states may destroy appetite is notorious, and it will be admitted that young women at the ages named are specially obnoxious to mental perversity. We might call the state hysterical without committing ourselves to the etymological value of the word, or maintaining that the subjects of it have the common symptoms of hysteria. I prefer, however, the more general term 'nervosa,' since the disease occurs in males as well as females, and is probably rather central than peripheral. The importance of discriminating such cases in practice is obvious; otherwise prognosis will be erroneous, and treatment misdirected.

In one of the cases I have named the patient had been sent abroad for one or two winters, under the idea that there was a tubercular tendency. I have remarked above that these wilful patients are often allowed to drift their own way into a state of extreme exhaustion, when it might have been prevented by placing them under different moral conditions.

The treatment required is obviously that which is fitted for persons of unsound mind. The patients should be fed at regular intervals, and surrounded by persons who would have moral control over them; relations and friends being generally the worst attendants.

THE ROLE OF BODILY ILLNESS IN THE MENTAL LIFE OF CHILDREN

Anna Freud

Felix Deutsch (1959b) articulated the broad view that every case of physical illness can be regarded as having psychological components. He saw these not only as causing or precipitating an illness, but as contributing to its continuation. He described how the patient's reaction to his illness could exacerbate symptoms and how environmental reactions to illness could affect the patient adversely.

Anna Freud's article, which follows, emphasizes how much more serious emotional reactions to physical illness are in children than in adults. This is both because the child is engaged in developmental tasks which will tend to become conceptually and emotionally attached to the illness experience, and because he is only gradually beginning to differentiate the psyche from the soma. Owing to this incomplete differentiation and the interposition of regression and secondary gain, it is at times difficult to tell when a child is becoming physically ill and when he has fully recovered from an illness. Jessner, in her studies of children undergoing routine elective tonsillectomy, observed that prehospital adjustment relates directly to the severity of disturbed reactions in children (Jessner, Blom, and Waldfogel, 1952). In a paper on latency-age children, Jessner (1959) noted that illness drew attention to the body, altering the body and self images, and at the same time curtailing motor expression and mastery of the outside world, both of which are necessary for the consolidation of ego functions in latency. The ensuing helplessness, regression, and defenses against anxiety can interfere with the basic developmental process. How children react to illness is, of course, largely determined by their previous level of anxiety, their emotional ties, and their degree of maturity, as well as by whether they have integrated former traumatic experiences.

Anna Freud's paper makes a significant contribution in pointing up that the child has two ways of reacting to his sick body's heightened demand for libidinal cathexis. One is to claim extra love and attention from the mother;

Reprinted from *The Psychoanalytic Study of the Child,* 7. New York: International Universities Press, 1952, pp. 69–81.

the other is to withdraw from the object world and concentrate on the body and its needs. She calls the second type of reaction a beneficial process. Jessner (1959) has gone on to suggest that children of the second type experience a grief reaction, and that this is an integrative process in which illness may not only spur *maturation, but also widen the horizon, heighten sensitivity, and bring forth a greater depth of feeling and increased capacity for empathy and sublimation. As Greenacre (1957) has observed, it does not seem accidental that so many great artists, scientists, and political leaders have experienced childhood illness that began with a number of profound and grave transformations. Finally, Solnit (1960) has suggested that hospitalization as well as illness may have maturational effects. In his opinion, the potential for psychological damage and* benefit *are high for preschoolers in the hospital. He notes that problems of separation, ambivalence, and self-control having to do with the mother-child relationship, which are most common under the age of five, can sometimes be resolved by carefully planned separation at the time of hospitalization.*

Others have discussed various aspects of the role of the hospital experience in the child's life, as well as the impact and meaning of illness to the child at different developmental levels (Bergmann and Freud, 1965; Bowlby, 1961a; Bowlby, Robertson, and Rosenbluth, 1952; Heinicke and Westheimer, 1965; Robertson, 1958, 1962; Spitz, 1945, 1946c).

When trying to evaluate the role of bodily illness in the mental life of children, we find ourselves hampered by the lack of integration in the material at our disposal. With the present-day division between professional teaching, nursing, child guidance work, child analysis and pediatrics, there is little or no opportunity for the trained worker in one of these fields to function, even in the role of observer, in one of the other services for children. Nursery workers, schoolteachers, and child analysts see nothing of the children under their care when they are ill; while pediatricians and sick-nurses lose contact with their young patients when they are healthy. It is only the mothers who have the opportunity to see their children in health, illness, convalescence, deviating from the norm bodily and mentally, and returning to it. On the other hand, during severe bodily illness the mother's own emotional upset and her inevitable concentration on bodily matters act as distorting factors and leave little room for objective observation of the child's psychological reactions.

In recent years a number of analytic authors have made attempts to deal with the effects of hospitalization on young children, a series of studies which culminated in a documentary film. But in the case of these studies, the interest of the investigators was directed toward the misery and anxiety which arise invariably when young children are removed from their parents, placed in unfamiliar surroundings, and handled and cared for by strangers; hospitalization merely serving as the prototype of a first, short-term separation from home. Instructive as these investigations are as a demonstration of separation anxiety and its consequences, they did not produce—nor were meant to do so—additional knowledge concerning reactions to illness and pain in infantile life.

Data are less scarce where the aftereffects of illness are concerned. When describing the neurotic disorders of their children, parents date back the onset of the trouble frequently to some bodily illness after which the child appeared to be "different." Mood swings, changes in the relationship to parents and siblings, loss of self-confidence, temper tantrums often appear for the first time during convalescence after a severe illness. Symptoms such as bed wetting, soiling, feeding and sleeping troubles, school phobias, which had existed and been overcome earlier in life, may reappear. Some children who had been considered brilliant in their intellectual performance before illness reappear afterward in school comparatively dull and apathetic; others surprise their parents and teachers by emerging from the same experience curiously ripened and matured. It is true that changes of this kind may happen after a period of hospitalization. But it is equally true that they happen as well where hospitalization does not take place, i.e., in children who have remained under the care of their mothers during illness and been nursed at home. When considering the effects of bodily illness on the life of the child, it is important to note that hospitalization is no more than one factor among several other potentially harmful and upsetting influences.

The Effects of Nursing, Medical and Surgical Procedures

Before we can arrive at a correct assessment of this potentially traumatic experience of illness, we have to work our way through the action of a large number of factors which, though they are mere by-products of the situation, are for the child's mind inextricably intermixed with it. The child is unable to distinguish between feelings of suffering caused by the disease inside the body and suffering imposed on him from outside for the sake of curing the disease. He has to submit uncomprehendingly, helplessly, and passively to both sets of experiences. In certain instances, factors of the latter kind, with their high emotional significance, may even be the decisive ones in causing a child's psychological breakdown during illness, or in determining the aftereffects.

Change of emotional climate during illness.—There are few parents who do not, imperceptibly or grossly, change their own attitude to the ill child. There are some parents, with ascetic leanings, who are afraid of over-indulging and thereby "spoiling" the child at such times, and consequently leave him severely alone, to "sleep out" his indisposition with the minimum of fussing. The majority of parents adopt an opposite attitude. The ill child may find himself more loved and fondled than at any other time of his life; for a child of a large family, an infectious disease, with consequent isolation from siblings, may be the one occasion when he is in sole possession of his mother's time and care. The mother, owing to her anxiety for the child's health may suspend all considerations of discipline and good behavior and indulge the child's wishes to the extreme. Or, on the contrary, in her preoccupation with the child's body, she may forget the most elementary principles of psychological handling which she had applied in times of health: Shocks, forcible feeding or evacuation of the bowels, sudden separations (for hospitalization), deceptions (before operations) count for nothing with her, so long as they ensure that her child recovers. The child, on the other hand, reacts to such unexpected handling as to traumatic experiences, he feels bewildered by the upsetting of formerly immovable emotional and moral standards or finds himself unable to renounce the incidental emotional gains after recovery.

The experience of being nursed.—The child's reaction to the experience of being nursed is understood best in terms of comparison with the better known and frequently described reactions of adults to the corresponding situation. [1] A normal adult who is nursed through a severe illness cannot help feeling at the same time that he is exposed to a series of indignities. He has to renounce ownership of his own body and permit it to be handled passively. He is dressed and undressed, fed, cleaned, washed, helped with urination and defecation, turned from one side to the other, his nakedness exposed to nurse and doctor, regardless of sex, of decencies, and conventional restrictions. He is, as it were, under orders, subjected to a hygienic routine which implies a major disregard for his personal attitudes and preferences. Characteristically enough, many adults sum up this

[1] Compare, in this connection, *The Middle of the Journey* by Lionel Trilling, with its striking description of an adult intellectual returning to responsibility for his own health after having been looked after and nursed during a severe illness.

experience as being "treated as a baby," or as a "complete return to the conditions of their childhood."

On the other hand it would be a mistake to conclude from such statements that the situation of being nursed, by virtue of its similarity to infantile experiences, is less upsetting to the child than to the adult. Observation, as well as theoretical considerations show that the opposite may well be the case. The gradual mastering of various bodily functions, such as independent eating, independent bowel and bladder evacuation, the ability to wash, dress, undress, etc., mark for the child highly significant stages in ego development as well as advances in detaching his own body from that of the mother and possessing it at least in part. A loss of these abilities, when occasioned by the nursing procedures (or by the weakened bodily condition itself), means an equivalent loss in ego control, a pull back toward the earlier and more passive levels of infantile development. Some children who have built up strong defenses against passive leanings oppose this enforced regression to the utmost, thereby becoming difficult, intractable patients; others lapse back without much opposition into the state of helpless infancy from which they had so recently emerged. Newly acquired and, for that reason, precariously anchored ego achievements are lost most frequently under these conditions. Many mothers report that after a period of illness their young infants have to be retrained so far as their toilet habits are concerned, weaned once more from spoon feeding, from clinging to the constant company of the mother, etc.

Restrictions of movement, diet, etc.—In contrast to the comparative ease with which ego skills and abilities are renounced under the impact of being "nursed," children defend their freedom of movement in the same situation to the utmost wherever they are not defeated by the type or intensity of the illness itself. It is well known that, at least under the conditions of home nursing, children with minor indispositions cannot be kept in bed consistently, or at least not lying down in bed. Young toddlers who have only recently learned to walk are known to stand up stubbornly in their beds for the whole course of even severe illnesses (for instance meales) until exhaustion forces them to adopt the lying position. Recently some enlightened pediatricians have accepted this state of affairs and treat their child patients, whenever possible, without enforcing bed rest.

The psychological significance of the children's negative attitude in this respect becomes apparent in those extreme instances when child patients have to be immobilized after surgery or in the course of orthopedic treatment. Several analytic authors have observed and discussed the consequences of such extreme restraint of movement of limbs and have pointed out the possible connection with the emergence of stereotyped, tic-like movements elsewhere in the body (D. Levy 1928, 1944), the difference of this mechanically enforced from psychologically enforced restraint (Mahler, Luke and Daltroff, 1945), and their bearing on the blocking of aggression discharge as well as on the discharge of stimulation in general with consequent overerotization of the whole body (Greenacre, 1944). Bergmann (1945), in an observational study carried out during three years' work in an orthopedic ward, gives a vivid description of the defense mechanisms which enable the immobilized children to bear the restraint and even to increase their docility when the restraining measures have to be increased. On the other hand she describes the rages and temper tantrums which appear when the restraint is partially, not wholly, lifted, or when chance deprivations outside the expected medical procedure are added to it unexpectedly. She emphasizes, further, a twofold relationship between the immobilized limbs and other parts of the body. According to her experience, on the one hand, the restraint of one limb may spread in the form of inhibitions to other, nonaffected parts; on the other hand, certain ego skills, speech, etc., may undergo an accelerated development to compensate for motor restriction of one limb. The same processes as they occur in children with pulmonary tuberculosis are presented in a highly interesting study by Dubo (1950).

These authors' observations are confirmed by much nonrecorded experience of parents and teachers. The heightening of aggression during and after motor restraint (in plaster casts, etc.) is especially well known to the general public. The most usual ways in which this dammed-up aggression appears are restlessness, heightened irritability, the use of bad language, etc. [2]

In comparison with this massive blocking of a whole system of discharge, the food restrictions imposed on children during illness are of monor importance. Normally, in acute illnesses, the physiological lessening of the child's appetite prepares the way for the acceptance of a reduced diet; it is only the children with strong oral fixations, for whom food and deprivation of food have heightened libidinal significance, who react to the situation with fantasies of being badly treated, unloved, rejected. In chronic illnesses (such as diabetes, kidney trouble, colitis, aller-

[2] The present author has analytic knowledge of a girl who was immobilized during her latency period for orthopedic reasons. She used to pay her friends out of her pocket money for every new swear word which they brought home from school. The use of "bad language" was the only outlet left for her otherwise paralyzed aggression.

gies) where dietary restrictions have to be maintained for long periods of time, children are known to feel "different," singled out, discriminated against, or, in defense against being passively deprived, to develop ascetic self-denying tendencies.

On the whole, considerably less harm is done by the necessity of withholding desired foods than by an anxious mother, urging or even forcing unwelcome food on an ill child. It is these latter situations which turn even minor, short illnesses into starting points for serious and prolonged eating difficulties, usually by reviving feeding battles which have raged between mother and child in the nursing period.

For some children the taking of medicines presents a major difficulty. Though the bad taste or smell of the drug is in the foreground so far as the child's conscious reasons are concerned, analytic investigation invariably discloses behind these rationalizations the existence of repressed ideas of being attacked by the mother through the symbol of the drug (Melanie Klein), of being poisoned, impregnated, by her. Laxatives which force the bowels to move, though the child intends otherwise, may form the connecting link between reality and these unconscious fantasies.

In this connection it is interesting to remember that the punitive character of these restrictive measures has always been known to parents and has been exploited by them. To send a child to bed, confine him to his room, deprive him of favorite dishes have been used as punishments over the ages. In certain societies even the forcible administration of laxatives is used for the same purpose.

Operations.—Ever since the discovery of the castration complex, analysts have had ample opportunity in their therapeutic work to study the impact of surgical operations on normal and abnormal development. By now it is common knowledge among analysts that any surgical interference with the child's body may serve as a focal point for the activation, reactivation, grouping, and rationalization of ideas of being attacked, overwhelmed and (or) castrated. The surgeon's action, from minor surgery to major operations, is interpreted by the child in terms of his level of instinct development, or in regressive terms. What the experience means in his life, therefore, does not depend on the type or seriousness of the operation which has actually been performed, but on the type and depth of the fantasies aroused by it. If, for example, the child's fantasies are concerned with his aggression against the mother, projected onto her person, the operation is experienced as a retaliatory attack made by the mother on the inside of the child's body (Melanie Klein); or the operation may be used to represent the child's sadistic conception of what takes place between the parents in intercourse, with the child in the role of the passive sexual partner; or the operation is experienced as mutilation, i.e., as punishment for exhibitionistic desires, for aggressive penis envy, above all for masturbatory practices and oedipal jealousies. If the operation is actually performed on the penis (circumcision, if not carried out shortly after birth), castration fears are aroused, whatever the level of libidinal development. In the phallic phase, on the other hand, whatever part of the body is operated on will take over by displacement the role of an injured genital part. [3] The actual experience of the operation lends a feeling of reality to the repressed fantasies, thereby multiplying the anxieties connected with them. Apart from the threatening situation in the outer world, this increase of anxiety presents an internal danger which the child's ego has to face. Where the defense mechanisms available at the time are strong enough to master these anxieties, all is well; where they have to be overstrained to integrate the experience, the child reacts to the operation with neurotic outbreaks; where the ego is unable to cope with the anxiety released, the operation becomes a trauma for the child.

In a symposium on the Emotional Reactions of Children to Tonsillectomy and Adenoidectomy (Jessner and Kaplan, 1949), a representative group of analysts, psychiatrists, pediatricians, and psychologists discussed the subject in the light of these ideas with a view to lessening the traumatic potentialities of the three main factors involved in the situation: reaction to anesthesia, to hospitalization, and to the operative procedure itself. Finding the optimal time for carrying out an operation; careful preparation before the event (Fries, 1946); avoidance of separation anxiety (Jackson, 1942,); psychiatric support, facilities for expression of feeling were brought forward as the most important precautionary measures (Levy, 1945; Pearson, 1942).

When studying the aftereffects of childhood operations in the analysis of adult patients, we find that it is not the castration fear, but the feminine castration wish in a male child which is most frequently responsible for serious postoperative breakdowns or permanent postoperative character changes. In these instances the surgical attack on the patient's body acts like a seduction to passivity to which the child either submits, with

[3] By deciding on the length of preparation time before an operation, two factors have to be taken into account. A preparation period which is too lengthy leaves too much room for the spreading-out of id fantasies; where the interval between knowledge and performance of operation is too short, the ego has insufficient time for preparing its defenses.

disastrous results for his masculinity, or against which he has to build up permanent pathologically strong defenses.

Pain and Anxiety

The mental interpretation of pain.—The manner in which the child invests bodily events with libidinal and aggressive cathexis and significance creates a phenomenon which has baffled many observers. Parents and others who deal with young children frequently comment on the remarkable individual differences in children's sensitiveness to bodily pain; what is agonizing to one child may be negligible to another. The analytic study of such behavior reveals as different, not the actual bodily experience of pain, but the degree to which the pain is charged with psychic meaning. Children are apt to ascribe to outside or internalized agencies whatever painful process occurs inside the body or whatever hurt happens to the body (accidental hurts, falls, knocks, cuts, abrasions, surgical interference as discussed above, etc.). Thus, so far as his own interpretation is concerned, the child in pain is a child maltreated, harmed, punished, persecuted, threatened by annihilation. The "tough" child "does not mind pain," not because he feels less or is more courageous in the real sense of the word, but because, in his case, latent unconscious fantasies are less dominant and therefore less apt to be connected with the pain. Where anxiety derived from fantasy plays a minor or no part, even severe pain is borne well and forgotten quickly. Pain augmented by anxiety, on the other hand, even if slight in itself, represents a major event in the child's life and is remembered a long time afterward, the memory being frequently accompanied by phobic defenses against its possible return.

According to the child's interpretation of the event, young children react to pain, not only with anxiety, but with other affects appropriate to the content of the unconscious fantasies, i.e., on the one hand with anger, rage and, revenge feelings, on the other hand with masochistic submission, guilt, or depression.

The correctness of these assumptions is borne out by the fact that after analytic therapy formerly oversensitive children become more impervious to the effect of pain.

Pain and anxiety in infants.—Where the direct observation of infants in the first year of life is concerned, the relative proportion of physiological and psychological elements in the experience of pain is an open question. At this stage, any tension, need, or frustration is probably felt as "pain," no real distinction being made yet between the diffuse experience of discomfort and the sharper and more circumscribed one of real pain arising from specific sources. In the first months of life, the threshold of resistance against stimulation is low, and painful sensations assume quickly the dignity of traumatic events. The actual response of the infant, whether it occurs instantaneously, or after a time lag of varying length, or remains invisible altogether, is no reliable guide to an assessment of the shock caused by the pain.

From what age onward the bodily event is supposed to carry psychic meaning for the infant will depend altogether on the analytic observer's theoretical assumptions concerning the date when unconscious fantasies begin to exist.

For the observer of children under the conditions of medical treatment it is interesting to note that older infants (two to three years) may react with almost identical distress to the experience of injections or inoculations and to the experience of sunlight treatment, although the former involves pain (plus anxiety) whereas the latter is merely anxiety-raising without any pain involved.

Passive devotion to the doctor.—It is the psychological meaning of pain which explains why doctors and other inflictors of pain are not merely feared but in many cases highly regarded and loved by the child. The infliction of pain calls forth passive masochistic responses which hold an important place in the child's love life. Frequently the devotion of the child to doctor or nurse becomes very marked on the days after the distress caused by a painful medical procedure has been experienced.

Reaction to pain as a diagnostic factor.—With young boys in the oedipal stage, their reaction to bodily pain provides a useful key to the differential diagnosis between genuine phallic masculinity and the misleading manifestations of reactive overstressed phallic behavior designed to ward off passive feminine castration ideas. The masculine boy is contemptuous of bodily pain which means little to him. The boy who has to defend himself against passive leanings cannot tolerate even slight amounts of pain without major distress.

The Effects of Illness

Changes in libido distribution.—The casual observer, while following with his attention the loud, manifest reactions to anxiety and pain, nursing procedures and restrictions, is in danger of disregarding another process which, silent and under the surface, is responsible for most important alterations during illness: i.e., the heightened demand of the ill body for libidinal cathexis. Some observant mothers know the mental signs heralding this state and are able to diagnose from them the onset of a disease even before any significant bodily symptoms have appeared.

There are two ways for the patient to react to this demand from the side of the body. Many children, who, when healthy, are in good contact with their surroundings, full of interest in their toys and occupations, and in the happenings of everyday life, begin their sicknesses by withdrawing from the environment, lying down on the floor or curling up in a corner, listless and bored. [4] At the height of the illness they lie in bed without moving, their faces turned to the wall, refusing toys, food, as well as any affectionate advances made to them. Though these reactions occur in certain children regularly, even with harmless sore throats, stomach upsets, raised temperatures, and the most common infectious children's diseases, the impression given by such a child in a state of withdrawal is that of a seriously ill person. Anxious mothers are terrified by this complete reversal in their child's behavior and feel him to be in grave danger. In reality the manifestation is not a physiological but a psychological one and not commensurate with the severity of the illness. It is a change in libido distribution during which cathexis is withdrawn from the object world and concentrated on the body and its needs. Despite its frightening suggestion of malignancy, this process is a beneficial one serving the purpose of recovery.

There are other children who, for some unknown reason rooted in their individual libido economy, use a different manner to achieve the same result. Unable to give their own ill body the additional narcissistic cathexis which it demands from them, they claim this surplus of love and attention from the mothers who nurse them through the illness, i.e., they become demanding, exacting, clinging far beyond their years. In doing so they make use of a natural process dating back to the first year of life, when the mother's libidinal cathexis of the infant's body is the main influence in protecting it from harm, destruction, and self-injury (Hoffer, 1950b). For the surface observer, children of this type are extremely "fussy" when ill, those of the former type are undemanding.

In both cases the gradual return to health is accompanied by a gradual regularization of these movements of libido, though not without difficulties and reversals during which the child appears "cranky." Occasionally the abnormal distribution of libido proves irreversible for a cer-

[4] This refers to cases where such listlessness cannot be accounted for on physiological grounds.

tain length of time and produces some of the puzzling personality changes after illness which have been pointed out above.

The child's body as the mother's property. Hypochondria.—Some mothers find it difficult to resign themselves to the fact that their children, even after the toddler stage, cannot really be trusted to take care of their own bodies and to observe the rules serving health and hygiene. Whenever a mother reports with pride that her child washes hands before eating without being told to do so, analytic exploration will reveal that the child in question is a severe obsessional, and his apparently sensible cleanliness a compulsive and magical defense against imaginary dangerous contact. Children who protect themselves against colds and drafts ward off fears of death; those who choose their foods carefully do so on the basis of fears of being poisoned; those who refrain from eating too much or too many nourishing foods are obsessed by anxieties concerning pregnancy. The average normal child will observe none of these precautionary measures; he will eat with dirty hands, stuff himself, brave wet and cold weather, eat green apples and other unripe fruits unless forced, urged, or prevented by his mother. In illness he will at best co-operate with her; at worst he will fight the care taken of him and proceed to use his own body as he pleases. So far as health, hygiene, and the nursing care are concerned, the mother's ownership of the child's body extends from earliest infancy, when the mother-child unity is an important factor in the libido economy of both, through all the phases of childhood into adolescence. At this last stage, before independence is finally reached, recklessness in matters of health provides one of the familiar battle grounds for bitter struggles between the adolescent and his mother.

It is interesting to observe that this state of affairs is reversed more or less completely where motherless, orphaned, and institutional children are concerned, even in those cases where competent professional nursing care is provided. Far from enjoying the freedom from anxious motherly supervision (as the observer might expect from the mothered child's revolt against her care) motherless children proceed to care for their own bodies in an unexpected manner. In an institution known to the author, it was difficult sometimes to prevail upon a child to shed his sweater or overcoat in hot weather; his answer was that he "might catch cold." Rubber boots and galoshes were asked for and conscientiously worn by others so as "not to get their feet wet." Some children watched the length of their sleep anxiously, others the adequacy of their food. The impression gained was that all the bogeys concerning the child's health, which had troubled their mothers' minds in the past, had been taken over by the young children themselves after separation or bereavement and activated their behavior. In identification with the temporarily or permanently lost mother, they substituted themselves for her by perpetuating the bodily care received from her.[5]

When watching the behavior of such children toward their bodies, we are struck with the similarity of their attitudes to that of the adult hypochondriac, to which perhaps it provides a clue. The child actually deprived of a mother's care adopts the mother's role in health matters, thus playing "mother and child" with his own body. The adult hypochondriac who withdraws cathexis from the object world and places it on his body is in a similar position. It is the overcharging of certain body areas with libido (loving care) which makes the ego of the individual hypersensitive to any changes which occur in them. With children, analytic study seems to make it clear that in the staging of the mother-child relationship, they themselves identify with the lost mother, while the body represents the child (more exactly: the infant in the mother's care). It would be worth investigating whether the hypochondriacal phase which precedes many psychotic disorders corresponds similarly to a regression to, and reestablishment of, this earliest stage of the mother-child relationship.

Summary

In carrying further the author's and other writers' studies of separation anxiety (hospitalization), this paper surveys the other factors which play a part in the child's reaction to bodily illness. The effects of the various nursing, medical, and surgical procedures which are open to modification are distinguished from those elements which are inherent in the process of illness itself, such as the effects of pain and the inevitable changes of libido distribution. Lastly, a comparison is drawn between the stage of deprived children who care for their bodies in identification with their lost mothers, and the adult hypochondriac who overcathects his body with libido after it has been withdrawn from the object world.

In summarizing these factors, which play an important role in every normal development, the author wishes once more to stress how serious a measure hospitalization is, separating the child from the rightful owner of his body at the very moment when this body is threatened by dangers from inside as well as from the environment.

[5] A most instructive example of this behavior is the instance of a motherless boy of six years who in a long drawn out nightly attack of vomiting and diarrhea was heard to say to himself: "I, my darling." When asked what he meant, he answered: "That I love myself. It is good to love oneself, isn't it?"

DISTURBED COMMUNICATION IN EATING DISORDERS

HILDE BRUCH

Twenty-five years ago the emphasis was on finding an endocrinological basis for obesity. Hilde Bruch started her investigations at that time and, since 1939, has published a series of papers on her studies of over 200 children. This report emphasizes the often neglected facets of awareness of, and communication through, body "messages."

Disturbances in eating are perhaps more directly associated with mental state than any other psychosomatic disorders. There are cultural counterparts to Bruch's patients who equate their large size with strength and power. In many sections of the world, particularly those where malnutrition predominates, obesity is considered a sign of royalty, of wealth and power in men, of beauty in women. In the United States, as opposed to much of the rest of the world, high socioeconomic status is associated with an absence of obesity.

Food can serve to give symbolic expression to emotional conflicts characteristic of the various stages of development. Levy (1943) and Anna Freud (1947) have described how food is used as substitute satisfaction for parental affection and closeness in early childhood, as a focus for conflict over growing up. Stunkard (1967) noted that obesity often occurs in adolescence—a critical time for imprinting concepts of the body as loathesome and grotesque, the symbol of all failures and disappointments. Many agree with Bruch that obesity serves as a defense, providing the child with a sense of strength and safety against feelings of distorted and stunted body image. Of course, overeating may play a role in a variety of conflicts.

In another paper, Bruch (1958b), approaches the issue of constitutional predisposition to obesity. She delineates three groups of obese children: (1) those who have inherited obesity as a normal state and to whom it is no psychological handicap; (2) those who react to a traumatic emotional experience, such as death or separation, by overeating; and (3) those for whom it is a "way of life" in which the family as well as the child are involved. Re-

Reprinted from *American Journal of Orthopsychiatry,* 38, 1963, pp. 99–102.

cently the cycle has turned to reconsideration of physiological in addition to intrapsychic and interpersonal factors; that is, there is some evidence from work with animals that marked obesity is often predicated on a derangement in the dynamics of fat metabolism.

In 1941, in my paper, "Obesity in Childhood and Personality Development," I described the interaction between environmental and intrapsychic factors that had resulted not only in an abnormal bodily shape but also in peculiar behavior and personality traits. Contrary to the then popular opinion that fat people are cheerful and easygoing, the obese children I had studied appeared to be fundamentally unhappy and maladjusted. They were timid, retiring and clumsy, and helpless in the face of teasing and humiliation by their age group.

These observations were not entirely new. Levy (1936) and Mittelman (1938), among others, had described immaturity, overdependence, and lack of aggressiveness as outstanding features. Endocrine theories so dominated the clinical approach to obesity, however, that this behavior was simply attributed to the endocrine dysfunction.

Our studies at Babies Hospital had indicated that theories about the endocrine origin of obesity were in error. On the other hand, we recognized as an important etiological factor the intense emotional involvement with the fat child on the part of the parents, usually more marked in the mother. Parents showed anxious concern with the physical well-being of the child, who was stuffed with food and protected against any physical exertion, which was looked upon as dangerous. These observations stimulated an inquiry into the developmental life experiences of these children, in particular the interpersonal relationships within the family. The findings were published in 1940 (Bruch).

The 1941 paper was my first attempt to define the forces within the child that led to this abnormal development. The marked retardation of social and emotional development in these children stood in striking contrast to their expansive growth and accelerated physical and, in many cases, intellectual development. The very existence of obesity in a child was taken as a concrete illustration of the fact that the conflicts that Allen (1937) had called the "dilemma of growth" had not been resolved. I concluded: "Obesity in a child may thus be understood as a disturbance in the maturation of the total personality and as a somatic compensation for thwarted creative drives, whereby the total size of the body becomes an expressive organ of the conflict" (p. 474). I was aware at that time that this expressed the problem only very generally.

Since then I have tried to understand more specifically what goes on within individuals who become obese and whose behavior shows many features comparable to what is observed in pre-schizophrenic development. The age of my patients increased; I had the opportunity of studying adolescents and adults, and also, more and more often, those suffering from anorexia nervosa and severe weight fluctuations.

Follow-up observations on the early unselected group showed that obesity in childhood was not a uniform condition (1955). In approximately two-thirds of the cases—regardless of whether they had lost weight, remained obese or had grown even fatter—severe psychiatric difficulties were observed, but the difficulties varied considerably. The developmental form of obesity, beginning in childhood or early adolescence, tends toward schizophrenic development, with frank psychosis a not infrequent occurrence (1957, 1958a). A close association with schizophrenia is also observed in anorexia nervosa and other severe eating disorders. I shall concern myself here chiefly with this group of patients.

Severe Eating Disorders

The psychoanalytic approach widened and deepened the field of inquiry. At first, it was exciting to uncover the hidden motives and symbolic meaning of the traditional clinical symptoms—overeating, inactivity and passive dependency—and to recognize that behind the placid obese facade were hidden the turmoils of rage and hostility, but also megalomanic daydreams of success and aggressive self-assertion (1952). The patients, too, seemed to benefit from having their difficulties approached dynamically, instead of having them pointed out as punishment for being fat and greedy. But then the disappointment came. They did not put the insight they acquired so eagerly to constructive use but resorted to their old pattern of overeating. This happened not only with my patients but also with those analyzed by others. Meyer, for example, concluded a brilliant discussion of the psychodynamics of anorexia nervosa and bulemia by stating "with regard to treatment, I must confess pessimism" (1957, 1959).

As I inquired whether something was missing in the traditional psychoanalytic approach, a new question arose, namely, how does a body function develop so that it lends itself to later use, or actually misuse, as a pseudosolution for conflicts and problems in the social and interpersonal field. Gradually I noticed that underlying the manifold psychodynamic pattern and the symbolic meaning of food and eating there was a conceptual disturbance. This misconception is the patient's conviction of being the misshapen product of somebody else's action. Obese patients suffer from a genuine lack of identity, of not even "owning" their own bodies, and they lack awareness of their bodily sensations and interpersonal effectiveness. The specific aspect of this delusional self-conception in patients with severe eating disorders is their inability to recognize hunger and satiety.

Traditionally the clinician assumes that a human being has an inborn knowledge of how his body feels. In psychoanalysis we refer to these supposedly inherent body sensations as "drives" or "instincts," and explain disorders as "fixation" at certain levels. Once one begins to inquire systematically, it is amazing how many fat or anorectic patients will answer, with an immediate sense of recognition, that this lack of bodily sensation is exactly what they have suffered from all their lives, and that they never knew when to stop eating, except by being told or by gradually learning from observing others what the polite or socially approved behavior was. Conversely, during an eating binge they were compulsively driven to eat against their desire not to become fat, and they experienced neither hunger nor pleasure nor satisfaction from eating.

Stunkard had described a similar phenomenon as "the denial of hunger" (1959). He felt that such patients denied their hunger sensations in the face of social disapproval. In my opinion, we are dealing with an incorrect learning experience that goes back to the earliest phases of development.

My deduction from clinical observation is in agreement with findings in experimental work. Hebb (1949) writes that the sensation of hunger in rats and other animals is not inborn but needs to be learned. This point has found amazingly little recognition in clinical research. On the contrary, different psychoanalytic schools of thought have developed from neglect of this very fact. Controversies between the libidinal and interpersonal theories are mere constructions, since biological development without close and continuous interaction with another person is impossible. Thus, it is an unrealistic abstraction to speak of "drives" apart from the intrinsic interpersonal component, or of "interpersonal relations" apart from the biological bodies involved. Yet, recent work on the significance of disturbed family interaction for schizophrenia has focused exclusively on the resulting disturbances in the sociointerpersonal field, without taking note of the equally significant distortions in the biological field.

Disturbances in body concept with a falsified awareness of bodily needs (propioceptor impulses) seem to me to link severe developmental eating disorders and schizophrenia, whether or not the psychosis becomes clinically manifest. To visualize how the disturbed cognitive perception of bodily needs is related to the conflicting and misleading communication within the family group, a simplified model of human development was necessary. Current theories, particularly in psychoanalysis, suffer from the use of terms denoting adult emotions in describing a child's development, and the mistaking of words and concepts invented to cope with complex situations for the cause of the condition they describe (Freud, 1914a). Clinical preoccupation has been with the content of the disturbed experience, and not with the functional process underlying it.

On the basis of my clinical observations, I concluded that two basic forms of behavior must be differentiated, regardless of the specific content of the behavior or whether it belongs to the biological or interpersonal field, namely, behavior *in response* to stimuli from the outside, and behavior that is *initiated* or *originates* inside the individual. I learned later that similar subdivisions are used in experimental psychology, where they are called *elicited* and *emitted* behavior. This means that healthy integrated development requires from the environment both adequate stimulation and appropriate response to the signs and signals that originate in the child.

The histories of obese patients rarely give evidence of gross neglect or absence of love and affection; on the contrary, more often than not, the conventional term "overprotectiveness" describes the situation. The trouble is that the ministrations of the mother, or her substitute, are derived from what *she* feels the child needs and are directed at forcing the child to do what she wills. Under such circumstances, not only are signals indicating nutritional needs inappropriately and inconsistently appeased, but many other signals initiated by the child are disregarded altogether or evoke an inappropriate response. An appropriate, re-enforcing response, however, is needed if a child is to develop a sense of trust in his own activities and impulses, along with the spontaneity and initiative essential for his self-reliance and effectiveness in social situations.

If the mother's response is so one-sided that she alone initiates behavior and remains impervious to all signs and signals initiated by the child, the child will become an individual who lives entirely by responding to stimuli from others—be it with passive compliance or rigid negativism—and who lacks the faculty of experiencing as effective the sensations, thoughts, feelings, and actions that originate within himself. In other words, we are confronted with the essential matrix of schizophrenic development. The specific factor in eating disturbances is the prominent involvement of the nutritional function.

Summary

The overt clinical picture of patients with disturbed eating habits varied widely, from severe psychosis to seemingly adequate functioning except for the abnormal weight. Nevertheless, none of them could correctly differentiate sensations indicating nutritional need from other bodily states and emotional feelings (Bruch 1961b, 1962a). Their experience, in varying degrees, was that they functioned under the influence, and in the service of, some one else. Delineating this conceptual confusion, which in turn was the result of disturbed communication early in life, is of utmost importance for treatment. Correction of this misconception is a prerequisite for effective psychotherapy with lasting result.

THE ASTHMATIC CHILD AND THE PSYCHOSOMATIC PROBLEM OF ASTHMA: TOWARD A GENERAL THEORY

PETER H. KNAPP

In the sense that allergy and emotion have so long been recognized as its etiological factors, the claim that asthma has both biological and psychological components is perhaps sounder than for other diseases. Nevertheless, the precise nature of the etiology of asthma still remains obscure. If allergens play a role in the predisposition to asthma, there is by no means a one-to-one relationship between allergic phenomena and asthmatic attacks. Then too, we know that emotions can modify susceptibility and sensitivity to allergens.

Knapp's paper, taken from a book devoted to the subject of asthma, presents a comprehensive review of the literature. In addition, with his customary clarity, Knapp, utilizing the interplay of ego psychology and physiological concepts, offers a model of asthma as a psychosomatic disorder of children. He doubts that there is a specific personality type characteristic of the asthmatic, and prefers to speak of the degree to which the total personality is involved in the psychosomatic disturbance. But one need only review the literature further to find speculations and statements about the "personality type." French and Alexander (1941) opened up this Pandora's box with their famous study of 27 cases treated at the Chicago Institute for Psychoanalysis. Their thesis was that when the primitive cry is normally modified into speech, it retains the original function of maintaining the bond between the child and its mother. In asthma, they said, when there is danger of losing the mother (either by physical separation or by giving in to dangerous, unacceptable temptations), the cry or its derivative is suppressed, thereby triggering the attack. Others (Gerard, 1948; Sperling, 1963b) have subsequently suggested that the mother's anxiety over the crying infant results in a displacement toward asthma, as well as an ego which is handicapped in its development. While Knapp questions theories of the "rejecting mothers" of asthma-prone children, Sperling (1968) notes that the critical arrest of development at the phase of separation and self-assertion, the anal phase, coin-

Reprinted from *The Asthmatic Child: Psychosomatic Approach to Problems of Treatment*, ed. H. I. Schneer. New York: Hoeber Division of Harper & Row, 1963, pp. 234–255.

cides with the most common time of onset of asthma, the age of two to four. Jessner, Lamont, Long, Rollins, Whipple, and Prentice (1955) note that these children have fantasies of mother meeting all their needs, even of breathing; but this total surrender is frightening to them inasmuch as it symbolizes helplessness, frustration, and death, as well as satisfaction and safety. Asthma may be "outgrown" (Lamont, 1963) at puberty because of an emotional revision of the parent-child relationship. Theories have ranged from those involving learning and conditioning (Lipton, Steinschneider and Richmond, 1966) to those in which asthma is considered a part of total family problems (Mohr, Salesnick and Augenbraun, 1963).

William Golding, in his brilliant, savage novel, *Lord of the Flies,* describes the disintegration of a fictional group of children marooned in a future war. Their most civilized member epitomizes the intellectual, whose rational influence succumbs during a growing reversion to barbarism. This figure is fat, awkward, wears spectacles, and is called Piggy. In addition, he has asthma. The disorder appears to symbolize something about his personal civilized state of being, the restraints upon inner primitiveness within him, and his residual outer weakness.

My own experience has been primarily with adult asthmatics, more than 80 in number, seen for varying periods of time, from one or two consultative interviews to hundreds of psychoanalytic sessions with 4 individuals. I have studied occasional child patients and have had some contact with the children of my adult patients but, for the most part, have relied on reports and reconstructions of childhood events. This essentially adult-oriented work supplements the direct investigations of children reported here and elsewhere. In contrast to children, adults can tell more about themselves and are better subjects for physical experimentation. It is easier to observe the child's environment, however, and often easier, too, to follow his course in time and relate this to environmental change.

Asthma as a psychosomatic problem has been studied as long and as intensively as any other disorder. Investigations of asthma reflect many of the strengths and weaknesses of the psychosomatic field. They consist of a melange of observations, frequently from widely different viewpoints, evolving slowly from the anecdotal to the systematic stage, but seldom, to date, experimental in the true sense, and they are strewn with the wrecks of premature explanatory theories. Often, as remarked elsewhere (1957b), these follow an implicit model of the germ theory and try to find, in one or another facet of the syndrome, a *bacillus asthmaticus psychosomaticus.*

Before attempting any more comprehensive explanatory view, it is neccessary to have some idea of the facts to be explained. Some of these will be grouped under the following topics: (1) the role of allergic predisposition, (2) the role of life experience, (3) the nature of the habitual personality in asthma, (4) emotional factors in the acute attack, and (5) the transition from acute to chronic asthma.

Allergic Predisposition

Agreement is virtually unanimous among those who have worked with asthmatics, and particularly emphatic from those who have seen manifestations of illness appear within weeks or months of birth, that allergic predisposition, or diathesis, is a necessary condition for the subsequent development of asthma (Creak and Stephan, 1958; Deutsch, 1951; French and Alexander, 1941; Gerard, 1946; Hurst, 1943; Jessner et al., 1955; Razran, 1961; Stein and Ottenberg, 1958). One must, however, beware of using catchall terms. The exact scope of the concept awaits definition. An extremely thorough study by Schwartz, in Denmark, brings forward conclusive evidence for an inherited factor in asthma and a genetic relationship between asthma, vasomotor rhinitis, Resnier's prurigo, and possibly urticaria and Quincke's edema in females (Schwartz, 1952), The same author concluded, however, that eczema, migraine, psoriasis, gastrointestinal allergy, ichthyosis, and epilepsy were genetically unrelated to asthma. It may be that we shall ultimately have to think of diatheses in the plural, rather than in the global singular. In any case, as deGara (1959) points out, further controlled research is needed.

The precise mechanisms involved in hypersensitivity are equally unclear. Recent years have seen a resurgence of interest in immunologic processes. Evidence suggests that they may be both more complex and more pervasive than has hitherto been suspected. Classic sensitivity reactions to external allergens, with elaboration of a histaminelike substance, do not appear to play a simple uncomplicated role in most clinical "allergic" phenomena (Samter, 1961). Certainly they do not in asthma, where antihistamine medication is of little use. On the other hand, more subtle types of reaction, particularly of the auto-immune kind, have been implicated in a wide number of disorders, including rheumatic fever, scleroderma, disseminated lupus erythematosus, ulcerative colitis, thyroiditis, and acquired hemolytic anemia, among others (cf. Kirsner, 1960 and DeGara,

1959). Much remains to be elucidated about the steps evolved in any such processes, and, indeed, in the whole transformation from potential to actual allergic disease. One crude estimate places the number of "atopic individuals" in the United States at about 35 million, "but only 6 to 8 million of these actually have 'atopic disease' " (Samter, 1961). This selectivity may be, in part, due to variations in allergic endowment, which may distribute itself in a spectrum rather than in an all-or-none fashion (Lippard, 1939). In the absence of a reliable quantitative measure, it is hard to be sure. A biochemical tool, of the sort the pepsinogen assay has proved to be in the study of gastrointestinal disorders, is badly needed (Pilot and Spiro, 1961).

A final question is that of the relationship between the parasympathetic nervous system and hypersensitivity. Opinions vary widely among different workers, from those who lay most of "clinical allergic" symptomatology at the door of parasympathetic activity to those who feel that the parasympathetic system plays a negligible role. Of great interest is recent evidence that parasympatheticomimetic agents may enhance and localize allergic types of reaction (Kirsner, 1960; Samter, 1961).

The Role of Life Experience

An additional obvious hypothesis is that the future of an allergic "soil" will depend, in part, upon the presence or absence of appropriate cultivation. Reinforcing factors during life are probably crucial. Such reinforcement may, of course, be purely within the allergic sphere itself, traumatic early exposure to large amounts of allergen, and persistent, even if subtle, re-exposure. The evidence is impressive, however, that social and psychologic stimuli can influence the course, especially of respiratory disorders, whether in a planned way, as was the case of the early and still classic experiments of Sir James MacKenzie with the paper rose (1886), or in the innumerable experiments of nature, reported clinically, in which exacerbations followed change, not in the allergic, but in the emotional field. The same seems true of at least some remissions. Many workers (Abramson, 1954; Bukantz, 1961; Clarkson, 1937; Hallovitz, 1954; Jessner, et al., 1955; Purcell et al., 1961; Rogerson et al., 1935; Strauss, 1935) have remarked on the improvement of children when removed from their homes. In one instance it was even possible to show that heavy exposure of a group of children in the hospital to house dust, which had been incriminated in their asthma, failed to cause them to relapse (Bloom et al., 1958).

As in the case of the allergic predisposition, it seems less valuable to debate the existence of psychologic influences in asthma than to ask how they reinforce the asthmatic response, and to what extent. A simple model for attacking the question is that of classic conditioning. Considerable evidence has come out of Russia to indicate that a number of visceral responses may be influenced by the process of conditioned-reflex formation (Bykov, 1957; Razran, 1961). Early work indicated that it was possible to induce asthma in guinea pigs by this technique (Noelpp-Eschenhagen and Noelpp, 1954; Ottenberg and Stein, 1958), although the identity of the "conditioned" attacks with those induced by sensitization has become more doubtful as methods for studying pulmonary functions have become more precise (Schiavi et al., 1961). Similar caution must be observed in assessing the few attempts at using the same techniques to influence the bronchospastic response in humans (Dekker et al., 1957). In our laboratory, Sloanaker and Luminet have been attempting to pair ordinarily neutral sensory stimuli with induced bronchospastic and bronchodilating agents introduced into a closed breathing circuit without the knowledge of the human subject. Preliminary results have been suggestive, and the method offers a potentially valuable tool for precise investigation of psychophysiologic mechanisms.

Learning is a complex matter, and asthma is a complicated response. It is subject to many influences at various levels with respect to the organism: the classic Pavlovian model may prove to be too simple to be applied to the complex asthmatic response. Even so, this would not invalidate the clinical evidence of reinforcement by life experience. Such "learning" was implicit in Deutsch's early suggestion (1939) that respiratory infection in a child, coinciding with a critical conflict, might sensitize the pulmonary apparatus. It would seem necessary to broaden this hypothesis, as Deutsch himself did subsequently when he outlined the conditions necessary for establishing a "psychosomatic unit" (1955). From retrospective adult material it has been suggested that the subjects might have had their olfactory-nasal-respiratory apparatus "sensitized," or pathologically "conditioned," in a number of ways, varying from person to person. Among these were included identification of the subject with another asthmatic person (Knapp, 1957b).

In one case reported by Oberndorf (1935), the history suggested possible identification with a neighbor. Usually, it is a relative, often the mother, so that the task of disentangling heredity from identification becomes difficult. One five-year-old child who was referred to me for study had a history of mild asthma and eczematous dermatitis—both symptoms surprisingly similar to those from which his mother had suffered in her childhood. He had an additional symptom, to which I shall refer later, namely fecal incontinence. The main interest in him arose from the fact that he was an adopted child. One could not help wondering whether the relationship to his adoptive mother had not had a striking influence on his symptomatic course. Although that may have been so, he did not contravene what was stated in the earlier section of this chapter. Upon checking the adoption-agency records, we found that he had had, in his first four months of life, a definite, though mild, infantile eczema.

On the clinical evidence, in many cases, it is apparent that identification plays an important, if not exclusive, role. An earlier report discussed an asthmatic mother (Knapp and Nemetz 1960) whose son lived alone with her, frequently in the same bedroom, watching her gasp through the night with asthma. When he later developed mild asthma, the mother looked at him and almost lost her sense of identity, so convinced was she that she saw herself in the dyspneic child. Another mother, who had spent much of her childhood fighting off the memories of repeated respiratory and ear infections during several traumatic years of her early childhood, finally succumbed to asthma and severe depressive conflict after her second son was born. He was given, for a first name, her maiden name. She felt that he "took after her," and she often brought him to her therapeutic sessions. It was he who, at about six, developed mild but definite asthmatic symptoms. In both of these cases and in two others seen briefly, modification of the mothers' attitudes to the children's asthma seemed partially responsible for the relatively mild course of symptoms in the children. Such is not always true, as in some of the cases reported by Coolidge (1956) and in one earlier case of ours (1957b), whose mother and grandmother had both died asthmatic deaths. Since the time of the earlier report, this patient, who, at the height of her asthmatic attacks used to cry, "Mama, take me with you," entered a hospital in another city, concealed her severe steroid dependence, did not ask for steroid medication, and died in a sudden drastic status asthmaticus.

Not only maternal identification but maternal attitudes, in many areas, have attracted much attention in the study of childhood asthma. Attempts at global characterization of mothers as "rejecting" (Gellhorn, 1942; Miller and Baruch, 1948; Strauss, 1935) or "engulfing" (Abramson, 1954) seem to have outrun the evidence as to exactly how mothers of asthmatics may differ from other mothers in whom such attitudes are not unknown. A number of studies have concentrated on the detailed ways in which mothers appeared to influence the process of the illness. M. Sperling

(1949) and Mohr et al. (1961) give examples of mothers almost unable to accept their children or to relate to them except through the avenue of somatization and illness. Benjamin (1960) and his co-workers report on identical twins in whom there was striking variation of both maternal attitudes and the severity of asthmatic symptoms. Their asthma apparently developed out of an allergic background; the differences between them suggest modulating effects of early environmental experience upon the course of the disease. Lipton and Lieberman (1963), in their report of identical twins provide striking confirmation of this point. Bell (1958) also describes the differences between parental attitudes and influences in a sick asthmatic patient, whose whole life had come to center around her illness, and a longitudinally studied asthma-prone boy who developed vastly greater ability to master asthmatic episodes and certain bodily developmental processes.

The Habitual Personality

In asthmatic children, whatever the basis of their established illness, it was early thought that the intelligence level was unusually high (Clarkson, 1937; Rogerson et al., 1935). Subsequent controlled studies, however, have failed to confirm this finding (Bukantz, 1961; Chobot et al., 1939; Harris and Shure, 1956). Nor is there, in our experience (1957a) and in that of others (French and Alexander, 1941), any single and simple personality type among asthmatics of the sort claimed in some earlier studies (Brown and Goitein, 1943).

Nevertheless, within the gamut of widely divergent personalities found in asthmatic subjects, certain characteristic fantasies and concerns are reported with great frequency. These relate to water and drowning, claustral confinement, birth and rebirth, odors, weeping, and the voice (Deutsch, 1953; French and Alexander, 1941; Knapp and Nemetz, 1957b; McDermott and Cobb, 1939; Stein and Ottenberg, 1958). The most plausible assumption at present is that the prominence of such preoccupations depends upon the extent to which the total character of a patient is involved in his disease process. One must be cautious. Deutsch (1947), in a brilliant essay, demonstrates the outpouring of water and birth symbolism in *Water Babies* by Charles Kingsley, who, as far as is known, suffered from hay fever which was only moderately incapacitating. The extent to which an individual can express fantasies in cognitive terms as against bodily symptoms undoubtedly follows its own laws, which are not simple. Such "asthmatic" concerns and fantasies are common in children, as Jessner et al. report (1955). Further empirical research may help us understand to what extent they are secondary to the actual physiologic experiences accompanying allergic disease, and to what extent they are primary in the sense of reflecting underlying impulses that are playing a part in the disorder.

Certain types of conflictual impulses do appear to be unusually common in asthmatic subjects. Anal conflict—over defecation per se, dirt, smearing, contaminating uncleanliness, and other derivatives—has been noted in many reports, including our own (Bacon, 1956; Deutsch, 1951, 1953; Dunbar, 1938; Knapp, 1960, 1957b). Some authors, particularly Abramson (1963), have commented on the frequency with which asthma develops at the age when toilet conflicts are apt to be at their height, and have remarked on the physiologic analogies between the retentive-expulsive struggle in asthma and that seen in bowel evacuation (Bell, 1958; Deutsch, 1951). Occasional instances have been encountered in which asthmatic and lower-bowel disease seem closely intertwined. One sufferer wrote: "My bowels, which you know were always wretched . . . have been getting worse, since I am always troubled with a dysentery, in addition to unusual weakness" (Sullivan, 1927, p. 48). Some months earlier he had written:

> The disease was consumption and about seven weeks ago after much pain and suffering she died. She was such a kind, loving mother to me, and my best friend. Ah. Who was happier than I when I could still utter the sweet name, mother, and it was heard? And to whom now can I speak it? Only to the silent image resembling her evoked by the power of the imagination. I have passed very few pleasant hours since my arrival here, having during the whole time been suffering from asthma, which may, I fear, develop into consumption; to this is added melancholy—almost as great an evil as my malady itself [1927, p. 60].

The writer was Beethoven, in a period filled with personal sorrow and with illness, including the onset of his enigmatic hearing loss.

Berkovitz (unpublished) reports interesting and extensive psychoanalytic observations on one individual suffering from both regional ileitis and asthma. One of my patients, in her adolescence, suffered the outbreak of a virulent ulcerative colitis—one of the disorders, as mentioned previously, in which auto-immune responses are now suspected. Her childhood history was one of entanglement with a mother, herself nearly psychotic, who appeared to have been responsible for enormous anal fixation. Since the age of three the patient had suffered from hay fever, followed by asthma. These manifestations appeared in her history as almost incidental disabilities, mild, and, one might suspect, unreinforced. After a colectomy, however, followed by a struggle in psychotherapy with gross, severe, sexual conflict, her respiratory symptoms became somewhat more prominent.

The striking nature of anal preoccupation in asthmatics has, perhaps, obscured the presence in many of them of marked oral concerns, conflicts over eating, being fed, longings for certain desired foods, and terrors of bad, poisonous ones (Jessner et al., 1955; Knapp, 1960, 1957b). Furthermore, in seven cases I observed there was a striking history of persistent childhood enuresis. Bostock (1958) attempts to link asthma and enuresis as related phenomena, although neither his nor my evidence really indicates that it is numerically more frequent among asthmatics. It is interesting that Fink and Schneer (1963) found it in more than a third of their patients, who came from a lower social and economic group. The fact that I happened to uncover a history of enuresis in three out of four psychoanalytic patients after treatment had started may lead me to weigh the importance of this symptom unduly. The fourth analytic patient did not report it, but it may be relevant to note that his older son, aged 11, had been in prolonged psychotherapy because of marked encopresis, and his younger son, aged nine, does, in fact, have enuresis. Such clinical hints suggest that along with asthma, in many individuals, there may be generalized difficulties in the regulation of certain instinctual bodily processes.

One of my patients was a rigid, isolated, markedly asthmatic male, whose illness had developed in the wake of severe respiratory infection at the age of four. Throughout his childhood and in many periods of adult life, he had been tended through long asthmatic nights by his mother, who was also asthmatic. At the age of 14, he began visiting a doctor for injections. He reported, retrospectively, a sudden resolve to get well, which he implemented by a program of exercise, including walking more than 10 miles to and from his medical appointments. He became asthma-free and remained so for 12 years. During this time he had an episode of renal colic, presumably on the basis of a kidney stone. His over-all health was sufficiently good for him to be taken into the Army during World War II. While stationed in the far North at an isolated outpost, he developed what seems to have been a near homosexual panic, marked by insomnia, great fears of violence, intensified drinking, and marked discomfort in the sleeping quarters with his fellow soldiers. His nights became wild. At times he crawled around in a semidelirium, thinking that he was an animal. In this setting, he had a recurrence of his asthma. Respiratory symptoms alternated with those of abdominal and low back distress. The evidence from psychotherapeutic interviews suggested that, during the former periods, he was strongly identified with his mother; in the latter, with his chronically ill, dying father. This patient also, after two years of treatment, confessed that throughout his life, until and including the present, he had been persistently enuretic.

His history points up the fascinating and enigmatic fluctuations encountered during the course of asthma. Rackeman's figures (cf. Creak and Stephan, 1958) suggest that more than 50 per cent of asthmatic children recover symptomatically, "growing out" of it in one way or another. The effort of Lamont (1963) and his colleagues to predict which patients will and which will not do so promises to throw real light on the importance of psychologic factors in the ultimate outcome.

It must be noted that while some patients are growing out of asthma, others are growing in. Still others oscillate between periods of health and illness, as did the patient just described and a number of others in the group. It has been possible to identify parallel oscillations in certain personality features. The most common pattern, which I have seen in both males and females, is the occurrence, during periods of relative health, of prominent masculine features in the patient's identification, along with powerful, aggressive impulses, which I have interpreted as representing both anal and phallic strivings. This configuration, which often appears highly unstable, may break down and be replaced by a more passive feminine one. In one carefully studied case this included open transvestitism (1960). Emergence of this "passive core" seems to coincide with heightened vulnerability to the outbreak of asthma. I have tentatively designated such a condition as "readiness to regress" (1960).

Emotional Factors in the Acute Attack of Asthma

The dramatic events of an acute asthmatic paroxysm are terrifying. They have obvious reverberations, after the fact, on the emotions of the frightened, helpless victim. They may be precipitated by purely biologic stimuli—allergy, infection, or cold or irritating air. At times—as in the celebrated self-report by Professor Trousseau, the dust in whose stable was enhanced by rage at his stableman—it appears that symbolic stimuli, generating emotions, may collaborate with or overshadow biologic ones. An equally obvious fact is that not all "emotion," in a purely nonspecific sense, acts to aggravate established asthma. Certain types of arousal, indeed, appear at times to act to overcome the asthmatic state. Emotions interact with asthma in a highly selective way.

There are other aspects to this interaction. Terror is struck not only in the patient but in those around him. In both children and adults, as Sperling also remarks (1953), there is a quasi-voluntary, controlling quality in the behavior of the asthmatic. Elsewhere, Nemetz and I mentioned one of our patients who claimed to have the ability to "think herself into asthma" (1960), and I am interested in Abramson's (1963) report that this phenomenon is common in children. Awareness and conflicts become centered in the process of illness. Thus it has not only dynamic precipitants, varying from instance to instance, but it serves adaptive purposes, and it becomes an avenue by which large amounts of excitation are expressed. Furthermore, there may be considerable disorganization of behavior, suggesting, even in young children, a breakdown of established patterns of behavior; that is, in some spheres at least, regression.

Regression is a complex term, applicable to a variety of reemerging patterns of response which mingle past with present. It is tempting to think also that certain physiologic regulatory mechanisms break down. Michaels (1944) and Margolin (1953) advance this notion in their attempts to understand a variety of psychosomatic processes. The best analysis of such a reversion is that of Schur (1953, 1955). He speaks of "resomatization," apropos of states in which anxiety ceases to become a flexible, cognitive stimulus and becomes a massive state of excitation, like those encountered in early childhood. The disordered, exaggerated, maladaptive, and uncontrolled asthmatic respiratory response may represent, in part at least, some similar re-emergence of physiologic mechanisms normally held in control.

In any event, more is necessary for asthma than mere psychologic distress and mere breakdown of overt behavior. Some sort of violent arousal takes place, often betraying itself by violent emotions. Anger and anxiety are the two most common affects (Gerard, 1946; Hurst, 1943; Knapp and Nemetz, 1960). At times they are embedded in a diffuse excitement. In my limited experience, this type of reaction, which may be subtle and masked in the adult, is common and often flagrant in the acute attack of asthma in a child (Jessner et al., 1955). The excitement, periodically growing to a crescendo, in the fatal case reported by Schneer (1963), gives a further suggestion of this sort of powerful emotional arousal.

I was asked to see a five-and-a-half-year-old girl after she had been admitted to the hospital in acute, drastic asthma which had necessitated placing her in an oxygen tent. Both parents gave a history of mild hay fever. The patient had developed asthma a year before, when both parents had had to go away suddenly because of the serious illness and eventual death of the mother's sister to whom the patient had been attached.

The little girl referred to her attacks as "being dead." Their onset was marked by great excitement. The mother expressed surprise that the doctors were able to treat the girl at all in her absence, so hyperactive and restless was she. In particular, she used to shriek. Concerning shrieking, when the child was 12 to 18 months of age, the mother reported, she and the patient had gone through what she called "the battle of screaming." Screaming occurred when the little girl could not communicate, or when she wanted her own way. The mother felt that she should "try to teach her in every way that screaming wasn't the way to get things," and then added that she couldn't stand hearing the child scream: "I just can't tolerate it . . . It goes through me like a knife." She used to carry the patient upstairs when she screamed and bring her down only after it was over, sometimes repeating this tactic half a dozen times in an afternoon.

Gerard (1953) reports that among a group of mothers of children with psychosomatic illnesses, those of asthmatics appeared to have suppressed the crying of their infants. Some of my cases confirmed such a history; others did not, even though apparently detailed information about the earliest years was obtained. The data clearly bear out the hypothesis of French and Alexander (1941) that asthma occurs in the presence of a suppressed impulse to cry for the mother.

Actually this is a double hypothesis, stressing the importance of crying, that is, sensitization of the vocal apparatus, and the intended object of the cry, the fear of maternal estrangement. Questions arise on both counts. Assuming, at least in some cases, vocal sensitization, precisely how does that lead to asthma? And how does one explain the extensive clinical evidence that asthma may remit when the child leaves his mother? It may recur, not in a situation of threatened estrangement, but in one of threatened or actual reunion, as Jessner, among others, reports (1955). At the least, such observations suggest intense ambivalence toward the mother, a state of affairs partly covered by French and Alexander when they speak of "the cry of fear or rage" (1941). Jessner and her group, however, also comment upon urges in their patients toward fusion with the mother—urges which seem threatening even though pleasurable. A further body of evidence points to the presence, in asthmatic symptomatology, of impulses to take in, the fantasy of incorporating another person (See Deutsch, 1953, 1959a; Fenichel and Rapaport, 1953; Sperling 1949, 1953).

Thus, two alternative hypotheses about the acute attack of asthma have been suggested. The first postulates a process similar to conversion, in which unconscious, conflict-laden impulses to cry out translate themselves somehow into asthma. The second also proposes a process similar to conversion, but one in which unconscious, conflict-laden impulses to take in, through the respiratory apparatus, similarly express themselves.

Several logical possibilities exist: (1) that neither hypothesis is valid; (2) that one refers to primary phenomena, the other only to secondary ones; (3) that both are valid in certain instances, though essentially unrelated; and (4) that both are valid and in some way related. Empiric research, particularly with respect to environmental attitudes toward crying, may be able to decide the matter. Later, I shall return to some adult psychoanalytic observations and other considerations which favor the last possibility—(4) above—that crying and incorporative conflict are both important in asthma and related to each other.

The Transition from Acute to Chronic Asthma

For asthma to be translated from the acute to the chronic state, some noxious process must persist. This may, of course, be an offending biologic agent. Can symbolic stimuli and emotional conflict serve the same end? We must avoid falling into a dualistic, psychosomatic trap. Asthma, once started for whatever reason, has a decided mechanical inertia. In part, this arises from a vicious circle which occurs when one attempts to expel air for whatever reason; the raised intrathoracic pressure tends to collapse the larger airways and, by negative feedback, to make expiration correspondingly more difficult. Furthermore, respiration is not a mere matter of lung function. As mentioned elsewhere (1960), the feeling of dyspnea stirs up central mechanisms which tend further to aggravate the respiratory effort; in the "panicky state" so often reported by asthmatics, the breathing becomes progressively less efficient. Finally, it is possible that long-term metabolic and glandular defects play a part. The sympathetic and adrenocortical systems may well be important in "defense" against the psychophysiologic dysfunction of asthma. Not only may an individual wish to perpetuate asthmatic symptoms that are serving some adaptive purpose for him, but his state of depression and discouragement conceivably may hinder full mobilization of these long-term defensive processes.

An increasing number of patients with severe asthma—not always of exactly the same degree—slip readily into dependence upon treatment by steroid preparations, whatever relationship such treatment may have to naturally occurring bodily defenses. The group of workers in Denver (Bukantz, 1961; Purcell et al., 1961) suggest that steroid-dependent children may represent a type of asthmatic actually biologically different from others, prone to develop illness at an earlier age and of a more irreversible sort. Evidence on this point does not yet seem decisive. Ratings by parents show the degree of "neurosis" to be less in steroid-dependent children. Other contributors to the present volume have stressed the need to check this impression by detailed clinical observations, particularly ones which will permit inferences about unconscious processes. It may be that such children represent only ones with an earlier established and more thoroughly "learned" response, into which more conflict is channelized. Social and psychologic contributions to their disease may not be less; they may merely have led to earlier and more massive somatic expression.

Toward a General Theory of Asthma

The Parasympathetic Nervous System, Riddance Processes, and Crying

Among the many adaptive functions of the organism, those that concern direct contact with the environment and concrete interchange with it—touching, tasting, ingesting, eliminating—are supported by the parasympathetic nervous system. Its functions in this respect contrast with those of the sympathetic nervous system, which assists functions of mobility and mastery, the flight or fight reactions of Cannon (1932). Considerable attention has been paid to ingestive, or oral, behavior. Evidence has been accumulated that, just as the sympathetic nervous system is "backed up" by metabolic and endocrine systems in its functions, so also is the parasympathetic in the sphere of food assimilation, where digestive hormones, for example, play an important role. Such considerations led to the concept of the "vago-insulin" system, as Gellhorn called it (1942).

Less attention has been paid to mechanisms by which the organism eliminates substances such as natural or exogenous toxins. These may be called riddance processes. As a broad tendency, elimination was mentioned as one of the three "vectors" in Alexander's original conceptualizations (1950) but the idea of widespread, interlocking mechanisms serving riddance purposes, comparable to the ones serving ingestive needs, has not been so clearly stated, although it is obvious that they must be vital to life. Rado (1956) is one of the few authors who has called attention to these processes. They are varied in their manifestations but closely interwoven in the sense of having overlapping functions. Some of these concern the gastrointestinal tract, some the skin, some respiration, some possibly generalized inflammatory responses to noxious invaders. Some such processes are voluntary, such as scratching or spitting; some are quasi-voluntary, such as vomiting or defecation; some, I suggest, are purely involuntary. The suggestion is further made that allergic processes belong in this general adaptive category and are related functionally, not merely fortuitously, to parasympathetic nervous responses.

Such a set of interrelated processes appears to be activated in asthma. This view, essentially an adaptive one, was offered by Wolff, who spoke of the "blocking out, and washing away" responses in the respiratory apparatus.

> Conspicuous among the defensive protective reactions are those involving the nose and airways. It has been observed that in reaction to assault, certain individuals occlude their air passages and limit the ventilatory exchange by vasodilation, turgescence, hypersecretion, and smooth and skeletal muscle contractions [1950].

This point of view tells only part of the story. What is missing is the relationship of such processes to intaking and retentive tendencies—fantasies which are found in all humans and are prominent among asthmatics. Human fears concern not only external attack, or invasion, which mobilizes reactions toward flight or battle (warding-off responses); other fears seem inwardly focused, in the sense of distress over what is inside, which the organism has been impelled to take in but which must then be eliminated.

Another aspect of the processes of environmental interchange, subserved by the parasympathetic nervous system, here comes to the fore; that is, the reciprocal relationship between intake and riddance, the balance between appetite and disgust. Excessive ingestion, in fantasy as well as in fact, can stimulate the urge toward riddance. This truism can be documented in everyday as well as in clinical experience. Such urges may be closely related in time to the onset of an attack of asthma. This may be preceded by the sense of having eaten or drunk too much, or by fantasies of taking substances into the body, or merely by the sense of "letting go," becoming capable of being filled with longed-for substances or being open to penetration, whether these wishes are cast in strictly oral terms or have an added sexual coloration (1960, Knapp and Nemetz 1957b, 1960). At times the relationship to riddance becomes striking, as we have remarked (1957b) and Abramson (1963) emphasizes, the ordinary compartmentalization of parasympathetic nervous responses is breached, and an attack of asthma ends in vomiting.

If the notion of a powerful impulse to suck something into the lungs and its counterpart, the urge to expel, seems farfetched, one need only look at the population of socially acceptable addicts who spend much of their time and energy doing just this. I refer to heavy smokers, a group we are currently studying, in whom these tendencies are outstanding.

But what of crying, which, as we have seen, in its specifically vocal form has intrigued those who have studied asthma? Can this function be related in any way to what has been said about parasympathetic function and riddance processes? At the risk of piling speculation upon speculation, I shall say that it can. The physiology of weeping is obscure, but what is known about it suggests that it is a function served peripherally by the parasympathetic nervous system. A profound "parasympathetic storm" has, as one consequence, weeping. Conversely, in children it is not uncommon to see a temper tantrum, with its storm of tears, also end in vomiting. Lacrimation is accompanied by engorgement in the upper respiratory passages; since we lack suitable methods for observation of functions deep in the lungs, particularly in association with emotional observations, the case is not ironclad with respect to the linkages in asthma. Adaptively, tears serve the function of protecting a most vital organ, the eye, by ridding it of irritants or other invaders. There are, in short, many functional interrelationships between weeping, parasympathetic function, and riddance processes.

True, there is more to crying than tears. Lacrimation and vocalization tend to differentiate during development, although one may not be justified in making an absolute differentiation between them. They probably start in a violent common matrix. The scream of the infant seems to involve, physiologically, massive arousal of both branches of the autonomic system, in so far as they have matured. Viewed as an expressive phenomenon, it appears as a primitive core out of which different emotional expressions later separate. Vocal crying, specifically, differentiates into both the distress call and the battle cry. Though these active communicative processes rid the individual of distressing stimuli, they have only a tangential relation to "riddance" as the term has been used here. But it is just these active, violent aspects of crying which are most frequently absent in the asthmatic; instead, the depression, the sadness, the fullness in the chest, and the sense of being on the edge—though seldom over the edge—of tears are apparent. In such a state the hypothetic parasympathetic riddance functions of weeping would seem to be maximal. At the same time, there is the holding back of tears. Not only does the individual restrain the scream of rage which might destroy the person whom he needs, but he fails to rid himself of his longings and of the sensations that accompany them. In so doing, he may also struggle to retain whatever he wanted to take into his chest.

The longing to take something in, as fantasy, is inevitably closely allied to the urge to cry, as affect expression, and vice versa (1960b). Our clinical evidence suggests that both fantasy and affect, in many cases, represent aspects of a common struggle over urges toward intake and retention, in competition with powerful riddance impulses, being expressed in the previously sensitized pulmonary apparatus.

SUMMARY: A SCHEMATIC THEORY

The outlines of a general psychosomatic theory of asthma have been implied in what has been said thus far. Any such theory cannot emphasize only one of the hereditary, developmental, psychodynamic, or adaptive facets mentioned. The schema outlined in Figure 1, a modification of an earlier one (1960), groups many of the concepts which have been mentioned and endeavors to provide a skeleton for understanding some of the varied phenomena of asthma.

The schema assumes a number of necessary conditions, which, if met sequentially, lead to the development of asthmatic illness.

Allergic Predisposition. The first of these is allergic predisposition. Research in this field should ascertain exactly what immunologic mechanisms are involved, how they are distributed, how activated, and how related to autonomic nervous processes.

Reinforcement. Reinforcement by the environment is a second condition. This implies the channelization of the allergic response in a variety of ways toward the pulmonary apparatus. It also implies influence by the key figures in the early environment–usually the mother–on somatization as a mode of response to neurotic conflict. There may be other defects in learning, such as failure to acquire smooth control of involuntary processes, particularly of excretion, which interact with the potentiality of the asthmatic to break down in the respiratory sphere. Crucial research, particularly of a prospective sort, is necessary to determine the extent and manner of this type of environmental reinforcement.

Sensitized Pathway. The term "sensitized pathway" is applied to a third condition–the resultant of the two earlier ones. By sensitized is meant

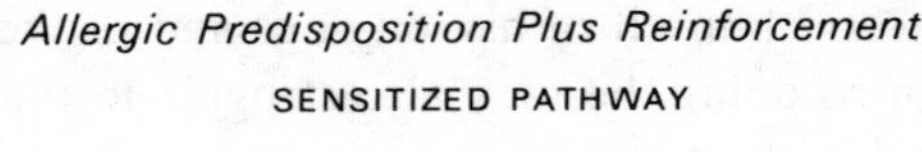

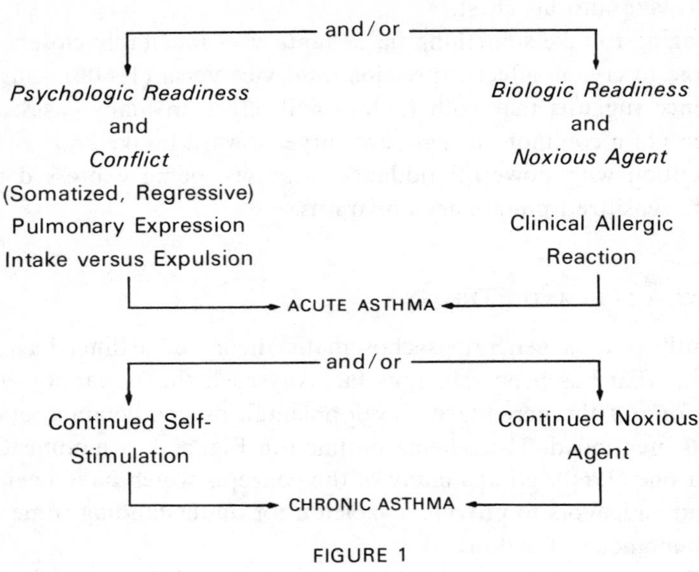

FIGURE 1
Asthma: A Schema

rendered vulnerable by whatever means. The term is deliberately chosen to include both psychic and somatic sensitizing experiences. By pathway is meant the pulmonary apparatus, a peripheral-organ system with central connections, an avenue for entry of biologic stimuli into the organism and for the expression of emotional conflict and impulses arising essentially from central sources. Such a sensitized pathway appears to be accompanied by no simple, single "personality of asthma." However, various characteristic problems and preoccupations are encountered in asthmatics. Their prominence seems to depend upon the degree to which the total personality is involved with the psychosomatic disturbance. How far these may reflect reactions to the asthmatic experience and how far they may result from conflictual impulses that play a part in the asthmatic process are, again, matters for future research.

Acute asthma. Acute asthma is seen as involving the breakdown of adaptive and defensive patterns used by the organism against the maladaptive asthmatic response. Such a breakdown may occur in the symbolic or the physiologic sphere, or in both. If in the symbolic sphere, particular stimuli for a given individual mobilize powerful emotional conflicts. These become focused in pulmonary expression, which serves to defend against other dangers and to make an adaptive demand upon the environment. Through the pulmonary apparatus is expressed a primitive psychophysiologic urge to take something into the body, activating powerful psychophysiologic urges toward riddance. Crying is a complex process which involves the parasympathetic nervous system and which also serves riddance functions. Conflict over crying is often, although not always, involved in this struggle to take in, retain, and expel.

Such a view does not suggest that, in the sense of their total personality or their use of voluntary mechanisms, asthmatics, child or adult, are "hysterical." It is, however, similar to the view proposed by Schur in certain dermatoses (1955) and by Deutsch in a number of other psychosomatic states (1953). In so far as symbolic stimuli and the emotions they arouse provoke asthma, it suggests that the complex can be regarded as a conversion process, using a predisposed organ system.

Transition from Acute to Chronic Asthma. The change from acute to chronic asthma is seen as being dependent upon multiple reverberating self-stimulating mechanisms (which may also operate at several of various levels), mechanical or emotional aggravation of the maladaptive process, persistent noxious stimulation in the biologic or symbolic spheres, and faulty revival of bodily or psychologic defenses.

AN EXPERIMENTAL APPROACH TO THE PSYCHOPATHOLOGY OF CHILDHOOD: ENCOPRESIS

E. JAMES ANTHONY

These two excerpts from a research project illustrate the psychopathological considerations in encopresis, a term coined in 1926 to designate cases of fecal soiling in children over two years old who manifest no organic illness. While there are few reports and little is known of the prevalence of the disorder, it is considered only about one tenth as frequent as enuresis. It is a symptom appearing to have a multitude of underlying causes, and each authority seems to have focused on a limited group of these. Prugh (1963) noted that both clinging to the infantile pleasure of self-stimulation of the anorectal mucosa and rebellion by withholding (both characteristic of the toddler) may persist as unconscious conflicts in older children, leading to soiling based on conversion mechanisms of the external musculature. Richmond (1954) has described encopretic children as unusually obedient and conforming, often neat in all spheres except the gastrointestinal. Except for their soiling, they tend to control overt manifestations of aggression and hostility and to impress adults favorably with their behavior.

The earlier notion that latency-age encopresis "must" mean psychosis no longer prevails. However, the prognosis is considered more favorable in the three- and four-year-old child than later on when the symptom becomes a part of the character structure. These two degrees of severity might parallel, respectively, the discontinuous and the retentive groups to which Anthony refers. Shirley (1938) has suggested that the child not only uses encopresis as a means of obtaining continued parental attention, but that he has learned to use retention and expulsion of feces as a means of avenging himself against or communicating with the parents. Anthony's systematic investigation of this and other syndromes (1958, 1959) shows the accessibility of childhood disorders to well-designed research into these hypotheses.

Reprinted from *British Journal of Medical Psychology,* 30, 1957, pp. 156–162, 172–174.

Definition of a "New" Symptom

The symptom known as encopresis has a comparatively short history. It was first described thirty years ago by Weissenberg (1926), although cases of psychogenic soiling had been recognized before that (Fowler, 1882). As is usual with symptoms, once carefully defined, it was more frequently diagnosed. But this factor alone would not account for the larger numbers seen more recently in all clinics. It is possibie that this increase is a false one and related to increased referrals from pediatricians. The instrumentalists of the back-passage had been accustomed to wash out the colon religiously, the rationale of which it was difficult to understand. It was like Mrs. Partington attempting to sweep out the Atlantic Ocean with her broom, which makes one inclined to think that it is a policy of despair that now sends us these children in greater numbers. It is, of course, equally possible that the increase is genuine and originates from some radical cultural shift in child-rearing methods. As previously stated, recent work would suggest that such a shift has in fact occurred. My own numbers do not represent in any way a normal intake. When I first broadcast my research intentions, the clinic trickle was rapidly converted into an appreciable stream as referring agencies rushed to rid themselves of their most unpopular customers. Clinicians on the whole, perhaps out of disgust, prefer neither to treat them nor to write about them. The literature as compared with enuresis is surprisingly scanty, and what there is seems superficial, as if the children had been observed from a respectable distance.

For the purposes of this research, I have demanded incontrovertible evidence of the regular passage of a formed motion of normal or near-normal consistency (defined in the American literature, I am sorry to say for those who like them, as having the consistency of ripe bananas) into the clothes, bedclothes, or any receptacle not intended for the purpose. Defecation, however successfully, into cupboards, fireplaces, the inside of pianos (one case) would, therefore, be included in this investigation as encopresis.

Clinical Consideration and Classifications

Although at first regarded as a monosymptomatic condition, encopresis is now recognized as a syndrome, in which the soiling acts as a nucleus around which there clusters a constellation of ancillary and related symptoms. As the child grows older, there is a tendency for these to disappear, and for the nucleus to remain tightly encapsulated for a while before its final disappearance during puberty.

Altogether about 100 cases have passed through the research clinic, of which seventy-six were set aside for the full investigation. In this experimental group, there were only thirteen girls, giving a sex ratio of about 6:1, which is in excess of the usual clinic ratio. The ages ranged from four to 15. Three criteria were made use of in classifying the cases:

(1) The continuity or discontinuity of the encopretic symptom with the training period.

(2) The association or dissociation of the encopresis with enuresis.

(3) The presence or absence of fecal retention either as a persistent or intermittent phenomenon.

The frequencies are given in Table 1.

TABLE 1

CLINICAL TYPES OF ENCOPRESIS, n = 76

	No. of cases
(1) Continuous associated	25
(2) Continuous dissociated	5
(3) Retentive	16
(4) Discontinuous associated	11
(5) Discontinuous dissociated	19
Total no. continuous cases	30
Total no. discontinuous cases	30

The frequencies do not in any way represent the natural distribution of the symptom in the population, but are research artifacts. The discontinuous types were easy to collect, but it took much longer to find thirty continuous cases to match with the others. Unmatched cases were excluded.

Clinical Descriptions

The clinical pictures that follow are mildly exaggerated in order to accentuate the points of difference between two conditions sharing the same presenting symptom and generally regarded as similar. I will consider prototypes of "continuous", "discontinuous" and "retentive" groups of children.

The "continuous" child is a dirty child coming from a dirty family, burdened with every conceivable sort of social problem. The child's messiness forms an integral part of the general messiness and is, to some extent, camouflaged by it. Symptom tolerance in these families is surprisingly high and the parents are usually driven to the clinic, reluctantly and resentfully, by social agencies. Mother's general attitude is one of "I couldn't care less". She can give very little useful data on training history and is frequently unable to recall which of the children in her large family soil and wet. The child's early history is often so full of gastrointestinal disease that it is not surprising that data on continence is difficult to elicit. The family morale is maintained by recourse to such vague somatic concepts as "weakness" of bladder and bowel, but it is abundantly clear that the weakness lies in the maternal control. The fact that this type of case is commonly found among the lowest of the social classes would suggest the operation, in part at least, of some cultural factors, although these are liable to be inundated beneath the welter of florid psychopathology. Defecation cues are weak or absent and mother's awareness of them singularly inept. Any passing distraction seems capable of smothering it, and distractions are numerous in the life of this overactive, aggressive, dysinhibited child, who soils and smears and breaks and takes with little concern for the rights and feelings of others, and with often a complete absence of guilt, shame or disgust. As he grows older, he may tone down a lot, but the aggressive-regressive mixture is always there to distinguish him from the less rigid types of the "discontinuous" child. According to Whiting & Child (1953), he may be said to have a positive anal fixation. These children remain, as far as one knows, impulsive and infantile, but no one at present is at all certain what course their future psychiatric history takes. One thing is fairly sure: they undoubtedly help to breed further generations of encopretics and enuretics. The dirty mothers of these children do nothing with the dirt except live comfortably with it and teach their children to live comfortably with it. Most of them have come from "wet and dirty" families and they seem to have stepped from one problem situation into another.

The "discontinuous" child is the compulsive child of a compulsive family. He is overcontrolled and inhibited in his emotional life and scrupulous with regard to his habits. The toilet "leakage" is his dark secret and towards it he manifests a mixture of shame and anxiety. He is always very much on the defensive about his symptom and is therefore difficult to contact therapeutically. His reticence gradually resolves with treatment, and the words, especially dirty ones, then come pouring out. The defecation cues are loud and clear but disregarded, so that causal explanations tend to centre on such epithets as "lazy," "casual," etc. As he grows older, his rigidity becomes more marked, and he may ultimately develop the rituals and compulsions of a full-blown obsessional state. A small number of older obsessional cases gives a history of soiling in childhood, although retention is the more common admission. These "discontinuous" cases usually have normal stools, but a few are subject to episodic retention and may have had periods of constipation in early childhood.

The mothers tend to be rigid and authoritarian in their outlook, and to establish sadomasochistic relationships with their children and their husbands. They are prone to dichotomize their concepts, and the world for them is sharply divided into categories of good and bad, clean and dirty; the good being clean and the bad dirty. Their families contain two types of children, clean ones and dirty ones, and the dirty ones are made the scapegoat for all mother's ambivalent feelings towards dirt. It requires little psychological exploration to ascertain that, through their children, they vicariously gratify some of their own strongly forbidden dirty impulses. For example, one of these meticulously clean mothers could hardly keep her punishing hands off her encopretic child when he soiled. During his remissions, however, the skin over her face would break out into an unpleasant and itchy form of rash at which she would scratch away savagely. It was "terrible" for a woman like her to have a dirty skin or dirty child, and she was equally ashamed of both. Another woman, a typical "encopretic mother," said to me: "If you knew how clean I was at home, doctor, you would say I was the last person in the world to have a dirty child." It needed only a short clinical acquaintance with her to realize that, on the contrary, she was probably destined to have other encopretic children in the future. Occasionally the husband may provide himself as an alternative scapegoat and, appropriately for the role, he is often a lavatory attendant, a coalman or a dustman, who may smell as much as the child. (The sense of smell is acute in these women.) "One brings it from outside and the other brings it from inside and I've got to shovel it up after both of them." If the enjoyment is not obvious, the reluctance to abandon this way of life is very much so. One encopretic mother hated the dirt of her husband—a lavatory attendant with piles. (Piles appear to be an occupational hazard with these men; they constantly indulge in lurid details about their appendages, boasting of their size in the manner of fishermen.) Nevertheless, she eschewed any thought of leaving him and of ending her dirt-shovelling, cat-and-dog, sadomasochistic existence with him. This type of mother is highly reminiscent of Bunyan's famous character in *The Pilgrims' Progress,* the muckraker, "the person with a muck-rake in his hand who would look no way but downwards"; "and they offered him a celestial crown for his muck-rake, but the man did neither look up, nor regard, but raked to himself the straws, the small sticks and dust of the floor".

The "retentive" child really belongs to a subgrouping of both the main clinical categories, since either of them may, at times, include elements of retentiveness. He undergoes a severe toilet training, and responds to it not with soiling or a precarious continence, but with stubborn constipation which later gives way to encopresis ("Obstipatio paradoxa"). For a while he may show a pseudobowel control largely through being constipated most of the time. Mother may later give a history of a clean period, but, on closer inquiry, this reveals itself correctly as a retentive one. The struggle between mother and child is an intense affair. It was described by one of the protagonists in the following way: "We fight every day. He turns red and sweats, and crosses his legs together. I try and force his buttocks apart but although he's only four, his leg muscles seem stronger than my arms. But I won't give in. He's got to see who's master. Once I let him beat me, he'll always get his own way."

The two obstinacies are evenly matched until mother brings up reinforcements in the shape of enemata, suppositories, purgatives and "roughage." The child's internal opposition runs parallel with its external counterpart, making an intolerable situation for the compulsive woman, who is ready to do battle on every issue and will yield no ground. It becomes the principal matter in her life. Engaged in it, she is almost immune from real disasters and tragedies which may involve her. The provocation is admittedly severe. This is the type of child who will wait for his mother to change his nappies and then immediately soil them. He will sit like Patience for hours on his pot, and then deposit his feces on the floor besides it. He will react against the time, the place and the position. He will arch his back, cross his legs, clench his fists and redden with the effort of retention. His four abdominal quadrants are loaded with hard feces. Periodically he passes a voluminous stool, the size of which becomes a dramatic highlight in the history of the case. One mother reiterated in every session the claim that her child had once filled "three potfuls" in one sitting. Xrays reveal a distended colon as far as the anal sphincter, but no evidence of Hirschsprung's disease; hence the term "psychogenic megacolon" (Richmond et al., 1954).

Three phases in the development of the condition are clinically discernible. An intense voluntary resistance emerges out of the prodromal syndrome in the toddler, which may last up to two or three years. This is followed by an apparent surrender and a period of good bowel behaviour with perhaps occasional constipation. But the "battle of the bowel", seemingly won in the nursery, is destined to be lost on the playing fields at school. The discipline and control of the classroom, the alien toilet and the affects released in play combine to bring about a recrudescence or retention with overflow. No longer, however, is the retention associated with an active and voluntary resistance. The latter has now been internalized and opposition to the act is involuntary and effortless. As one of the children put it: "Every time I go near the toilet, something down below seems to tighten up, and I can't make it let go however much I try. And I do try for Mummy's sake because I know how worried she gets about it, and I want to please her." The past history in this case was of a fierce mother-child battle at the age of four of which the patient, at the age of eight, had no conscious recollection.

Tables 2-4 summarize the clinical characteristics of the two main categories and their relation to the type of training given.

TABLE 2
DIFFERENTIATING FACTORS, "CONTINUOUS" TYPE

(1) Usually associated with enuresis
(2) Low-pressure toilet training
(3) Low levels of aspiration and achievement for mother
(4) Social and emotional regression marked
(5) Obsessional traits usually absent
(6) Antisocial behaviour
(7) "Leakage symptoms" generally prominent
(8) "Reaction formations" usually absent
(9) Reaction to encopresis shameless
(10) Child usually rejected and neglected
(11) Infantilizing tendency on mother's part
(12) Educational backwardness characteristic
(13) Parents frequently psychopathic
(14) Emotionally dysinhibited
(15) *Weak aversion reaction*

TABLE 3

DIFFERENTIATING FACTORS, "DISCONTINUOUS" TYPE

(1) Usually dissociated from enuresis
(2) High-pressure toilet training
(3) High levels of aspiration and achievement for mother
(4) Social and emotional regression much less marked
(5) Obsessional traits usually present
(6) Antisocial behaviour absent
(7) "Leakage symptoms" seldom present
(8) "Reaction formations" usually a striking feature
(9) Reaction to encopresis—shame, guilt and anxiety
(10) Child usually overprotected
(11) Maternal tendency to hurry child through infancy
(12) Child usually doing well at school
(13) Parents generally obsessional
(14) Emotionally inhibited
(15) *Strong aversion reaction*

TABLE 4

TYPE OF ENCOPRESIS IN RELATION TO TOILET TRAINING*

Type of encopresis	Coercive training (%)	Cooperative training (%)	Neglectful training (%)
Continuous (n = 30)	26.7	6.6	66.7
Retentive (n = 16)	75	25	0
Discontinuous (n = 30)	63.3	13.3	23.4
Total n = 70			

* The differences for each clinical type are significant at the 1% level.

I will now turn from disturbances of function to disturbances of attitude towards the toilet function and its products.

Disturbed Attitudes to Function

Small children, as Freud (1910) first showed, are particularly prone to construct theories about the way in which the intimate bodily functions work. In this inquiry I found that they also theorize on the way the body, chiefly the hidden parts of it, fail to work. If cautiously approached, every child with encopresis will reveal his own idiosyncratic explanations for the dysfunction of his bowel. It is an inadequate and anxious picture to which the mother contributes her share when she attempts to force the child into conformity, with horrifying descriptions of impending intestinal catastrophes that he was building up inside him. Her own fantasies play their part in this, for, together with her frequent gastrointestinal ailments, they furnish a conception of the hidden, inner world which is threatened or threatening. The more disturbed the child, the more frightening will this concept be. In the diagram that follows (Figure 1), a five-year-old boy tried to explain to me what happened when he became constipated. He was a very disturbed child at the height of a bowel battle with his obsessional mother. His father suffered from chronic pulmonary tuberculosis and had been two years in a sanatorium. He was closely identified with his damaged father, who had treated his symptom much more sympathetically, and had given him a "lecture" on his constipation before he had left him, at the age of three, to deal with his punitive mother alone. His description was clearly an elaboration of this remembered "lecture." In normal defecation, the fecal lumps queue up quietly at the point of exit. With retention, there is a damming up of the lungs and the head, giving rise to shortage of breath, horrid white phlegm, occasionally blood, headaches and catarrh in the nose. If left too long, the lumps hardened to form a "cannon-ball". "One day," he remarked cheerfully, "it will come out with such a pop that it will knock Mummy right over and kill her." The "battle of the bowel" is not waged without ammunition on the child's side!

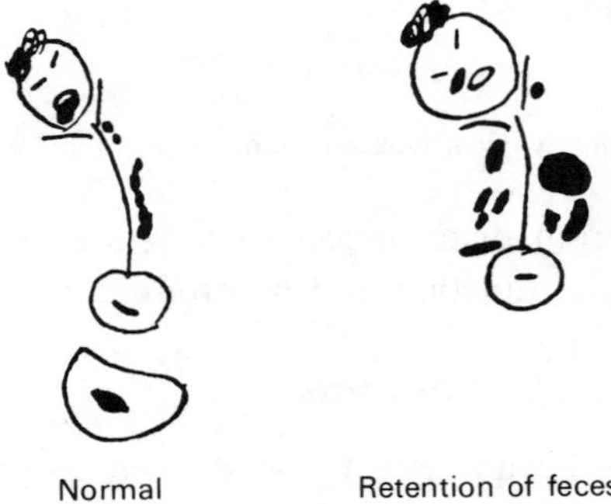

FIGURE 3

Five-Year-Old Encopretic Child's Concept of Alimentary Events

Disturbed Attitudes to Feces

Children often tend to interpret the outside world in animistic terms (Piaget, 1929). In the present investigation, I found a similar tendency with regard to intestinal events and products. In Table 5, the stages in intestinal animism are related to Piaget's stages in general animism and show an interesting correspondence.

TABLE 5

Stages	Ages	Piaget's Animistic Scale	Comparable Stages in Intestinal Animism
1	Under 5	Everything is alive	Everything inside the body is alive
2	Under 7	Everything that moves is alive	Feces inside body are alive. Feces outside body are not alive
3	Under 9	Everything that moves by itself is alive	Feces that control themselves are alive Feces controlled by the child are not alive
4	Over 10 or 11	Clear biological concept of life	Clear biological concept of feces

These animistic attitudes are not difficult to elicit if one uses Piaget's method of free interrogation and follows the child passively into his magical systems of belief.

Not only, however, does the child bring his feces to life in this striking way (Anthony, 1956), but he also endows them with special feelings, which may be roughly divided into positive, negative and neutral. Examples of each of these are given below.

Positive Attitudes

L.S. 6.4. "I sometimes think my biggies fall asleep in my tummy; it's so nice and warm there. Sometimes I'd like to cuddle them. They're rubber aren't they?"

P.L. 5.8. "When I do a really big job, mummy always says to me: 'Good girl!' She should really say: 'Good job!' because it's jobby that does it not me." ("But you let him out from inside, don't you?") "No. When he grows up and becomes a big jobby, he just knocks on the door. Sometimes I say it's not time yet. Please wait till school's over. Sometimes he's nice and waits, but sometimes he just says 'Oh bother school', and just comes out. And then everyone's cross with me when they should really be cross with Mr. Jobby." (Adds rather affectionately) "He does get me into lots of trouble, but he's not so bad really. He just doesn't think!"

Negative Attitudes

M.B. 6.1. "My mum says it ends up in the sea. I think the fish might gobble it up. Then it will be a ghost and haunt me." ("Where will it stay?") "It might stay in the toilet and wait for me."

A.L. 5.6. "When I drop it down in the toilet, I'm sometimes afraid it will jump back and bite me on the bottom." ("Why would it do that?") "Because it's cross from being sent away, I suppose." ("Couldn't you pull the chain and send it right away?") "That would make him much crosser. I hate pulling the chain. It only gets stuck in the pipes and can't breathe."

N.D. 5.1. "It smells horrid. I hate it. My mummy hates it too. I could squash it. I hate it. It hurts coming out."

Neutral Attitudes

S.T. 5.10. "You know the noise my tummy makes. Well, it's all my plops squeaking. They squeak if they're hungry." ("Are they alive?") "O yes. They're alive because they're inside me. But they die as soon as they come out. That's why they like to stay inside." ("Are they ever naughty inside?") "No. They are not naughty." ("Are they good, then?") "No. They are not good. They are never naughty or good. They don't do anything. They just stay inside." ("But are they alive inside?") "O yes. They're alive inside, but they die when they come out." ("What keeps them alive inside?") "Because it's all alive there." ("Why is that?") "Because it is."

Relation of Animistic Phantasies to Type of Toilet Training

When these attitudes were correlated with the type of toilet training received by the child, a significant relationship was found between the quality of the animistic phantasies and the amount of pressure experienced (Table 6).

TABLE 6
ANIMISTIC FEELINGS TOWARD FECES IN RELATION TO THE TYPE OF TOILET TRAINING

Response to Piagetian "Interrogation"	Coercive training (%)	Cooperative training (%)	Neglectful training (%)
Expression of erotic, affectionate, solicitous feelings towards feces (n = 18)	11.1	33.4	55.5
Neutral feelings towards feces (n = 15)	26.6	26.6	46.8
Fearful or hateful feelings towards feces (n = 15)	73.3	6.7	20.0

Total n = 48, children under 10.

Discussion and Conclusions

According to Freud (1913a), the predisposition to anal fixation was determined to a large extent by the nature of the toilet training experienced by the child, and he emphasized that both a coercive and early, or a neglectful and late training could equally lead to this development. He felt unsure that this was sufficiently explanatory and therefore postulated a further "constitutional" factor–the so-called "anal stamp." Fenichel (1945b) clarified the position further by classifying the fixation factors into those resulting from excessive gratification, frustration, or an alteration of either of these, and those in which "concurrence" of instinctual and security gratifications occurred.

Let us admit at once that no absolute evidence can be offered for the causal relationship between toilet training and bowel dysfunction and, even less so, between toilet training and the formation of a particular character trait, but as Prugh and others have pointed out (1954) most available evidence does indicate "a suggestive correlation".

One has to bear in mind the following exceptions to the causal theory as simply stated:

(1) Not all children who experience an abnormal (in the sense of coercive or neglectful) type of toilet training develop bowel dysfunction or abnormal character traits.

(2) Not all children who have bowel dysfunction or abnormal traits experience an abnormal toilet training.

(3) Primitive children who have had a toilet training judged to be abnormal by the standards that are in use do not appear especially prone to develop bowel dysfunctions or abnormal character traits.

There could be two possible explanations for the insufficiency of the training hypothesis, the first being that possibly more than one cause is implicated and that the major one obscures the clear appreciation of the minor one; the second, that "since child-rearing methods generally harmonize with other cultural influences . . . it is not possible to say that adult personality is related specifically to childhood experiences" (Argyle, 1957, p. 45), so that other common factors may be involved.

From the findings of this research, it has emerged that toilet training is the most important and the most influential of the variables involved. The additional factors seem largely to belong to the group of "immeasurable" variables associated with the "potting couple" and which may help to modify the training pressure. From this point of view, it seems important that Huschka's criteria (1942) should be interpreted within the context of the total mother-child situation, and not in any simple chronological sense. The same spurious norms may be used in one instance by a pathologically motivated and anally preoccupied mother, and in another by a culturally motivated mother, anxious to keep in step with her neighbours but otherwise warm and understanding. Because of this, the same means may not bring about the same ends, and, consequently, the one-to-one relationship between means and ends is lost.

In this paper I have been mainly concerned with bowel training and its sequelae. That the same arguments may apply equally to bladder training has been shown in a paper by Bostock & Shackleton (1951) on the relationship between toilet training and enuresis. They found definite significant associations between urinary incontinence and coercive training, between coercive training and unwantedness, and between unwantedness and urinary incontinence. As a result of these findings, they elaborated a concept of enuresis as the "end-product of a total situation . . . [with] its roots in the total personality of the child, and this includes the whole attitude of the parent to the child from the moment that breast feeding and toilet training commences" (p. 111). They single out two types of mothers responsible for the enuretic outcome—the unwanting mother who compensates for her lack of love by multiplying and intensifying her ministrations, and the other, a compulsively clean and perfectionist mother, who tions, and the other, a compulsively clean and perfectionist mother, who is "spurred to achieve early a high degree of toilet cleanliness" and who adheres to the letter rather than to the spirit of any instruction given.

Nevertheless, she is a wanting mother. I would include both these as subdivisions of the high-pressure group. The prognosis is probably better with the wanting than with the unwanting mother, but no figures are available to support such a belief. The authors attempt to interpret their results in the light of learning theory. According to them the subsequent development of enuresis "depends largely upon the degree of later frustration to which the toddler will be subjected, *but the mother has created the necessary predisposition*" (my italics) by means of her frustrating training techniques. The later frustrations lead to a habit disintegration and the regression to such "sterotypies" as enuresis and encopresis. Why is the act of urination picked out before defecation? Having reduced these complex and "over-determined" issues to their simple formulation, the authors answer, somewhat weakly, that this is probably due to "availability". "The act of defecation is less susceptible to control by the higher centres than that of micturition" (sic). Their thinking follows closely on that of Maier. Their symptomatic stereotypes are also "peculiarly strong and persistent," less subject to the influence of rewards and punishments, and stubborn to eradicate. Treatment consists in the removal of frustrating factors and in conditioning. They make no attempt to differentiate between continuous and discontinuous types of enuresis, which explains why they only saw the high-pressure type of mother.

The final discussion concerns the child's contribution to the formation of his symptoms. However abnormal the mother or her training behaviour, we have to remember that it is the child and not the mother who soils. There are factors in the child that respond to the mother's handling. There are Freud's "constitutional" factors. The child may be unduly responsive to disturbed family relationships, to incidental traumata during and after the training period, to sensitization by gastrointestinal illnesses. He may, with mother's help, mismanage his own anal phase, or react to various components in an extreme way. The developmental task is full of problems to which even a normal child may succumb temporarily. He is preoccupied with his fantasies apart from what mother is doing to him or for him. He "appears to over-value his feces in a magical narcissistic fashion, and at times marked anxiety over their loss 'down the toilet' or in other ways may be manifest. His fantasies of omnipotence regarding this object, the stool, and its fantasied use in attacks upon others *may lead to an animistic misunderstanding,* related to fears or retaliation involving fantasied physical damage to his own anal region or the interior of his body" (my italics) (Prugh et al., 1954). This description of the normal child passing through his anal phase is so reminiscent of the older encopretic child as he appears in this research, that it almost appears as if nothing has been added to the state of encopresis that was not already present during the anal phase of his development. As we have seen, the mother's management helps to intensify these feelings towards his feces in a positive or negative direction.

Diagnosis, Treatment and Prognosis

The perceptual battery can separate two disparate groups within a monosymptomatic clinical state. Clearly no one will want to use it simply for this purpose. Once the clinician is aware of these differences, and finds them important clinically, he will dispense with such ponderous aids. So often in child psychiatry one works on dark hunches, and if occasionally one can go along with the laboratory, so much the better. It is of some value to the clinician to know that his clinical judgments have experimental support; it subscribes to his scientific well-being. On the other hand, the diagnostic label of "pregenital conversion" may seem unhelpful to him, although like Warson et al. (1954) he may be interested in relating encopresis to the psychosomatic disorder and the hysterical symptom and finding elements of both in it. I would agree, after a clinical experience of about a hundred cases, with Prugh et al. (1954) that these children do not appear to be using their bowels symbolically for defensive purposes, but that the symptom ensued from a "less well-differentiated handling of tensions which could no longer be successfully dealt with in more mature fashion."

The treatment implications are of greater importance. The "continuous" child does not need psychotherapy, but habit training under happier conditions. He requires a warm, interested but relaxed, person operating under a more consistent regime than was ever available at home. He can be reasonably stabilized in a period of three to five months, although relapes are not infrequent with return to the old environment.

In the course of retraining, he needs to develop a normal degree of disgust, and he can obtain this, nondidactically, by identification with the normal adult who trains him. Failures in retraining occur when cases are severely complicated by unwantedness and backwardness. Nocturnal types of encopresis may be particularly recalcitrant.

The "discontinuous" child is a different proposition altogether. He is generally a deeply disturbed child who needs prolonged psychotherapy and some measure of protection from his mother. Once a sadomasochistic union has been fully established, the situation may become very intractable to treatment. A disappearance of the exaggerated disgust reaction is the first hopeful therapeutic sign, but it is at this stage, when he may swing over to "dirty" behaviour, that the mother requires expert handling if she is not to withdraw the child from therapy.

Many therapeutically heartbreaking situations in the past may be avoided by careful selection of cases for treatment. It would be illuminating to find out how many therapist-hours have been wasted doing psychotherapy with the "continuous" group, or carrying out physical and training procedures with the "discontinuous" group, for want of careful understanding of the treatment requirements.

The intensity of the disgust reaction may be of some prognostic value. Where it is weak, the encopretic child seems very liable to develop a passive and inadequate personality, which, if allowed to progress, can prove as difficult to influence therapeutically as the rigid character of the strong reactor. On the whole, I would agree with Whiting & Child (1953) in considering the "continuous," positively fixated type as being more amenable to unlearning the bad habits and in reforming good ones. In a healthy environment these cases often resolve spontaneously, especially if normalizing group influences are at work. The "discontinuous," negatively fixated types are difficult treatment problems, who may defy all attempts at psychotherapy and end, eventually, as severe compulsive neurotics with contamination phobias and washing rituals, ultimately needing a leucotomy knife to eradicate their intense disgust reactions.

It would therefore seem that the transformation of the disgust reaction in the child, from weak or strong to the normal for the environment, is one of the most important therapeutic undertakings in the treatment of these children and one with far-reaching consequences.

PART VII

CHILDHOOD PSYCHOSIS

Forty years ago, psychotic children were generally classified as mental defectives and relegated to custodial institutions. Today they are the subjects of extensive and intensive study and given highly specialized care. Despite this attention, our understanding of childhood psychosis remains limited and fraught with problems. Because differential etiological factors have not been established, classification presents difficulties; controversy over nomenclature continues. There is less disagreement with respect to its major clinical signs and symptoms. As for etiology, although the emphasis *of various workers on the nature-or-nurture controversy persists, it is generally agreed that hereditary factors may be predisposing in many cases and that postnatal elements may cause them to emerge, that is, that these two kinds of determinants do not exist in isolation from each other (Benjamin, 1961). Thus, psychosis may resemble the psychophysiological disorders (see Part V) in that, probably, there is a common biological factor which must be acted upon by certain environmental influences to become fully operative.*

Included in this section are classical descriptions of autistic and symbiotic psychosis, a borderline case, and a clinical study which views psychosis in terms of its organicity.

CHILDHOOD SCHIZOPHRENIA

LAURETTA BENDER

Bender, one of the pioneers in the study of childhood psychosis, emphasizes the primacy of the biological process. She suggests that the symptomatic expressions of the common underlying disorders are inevitable consequences of the disturbance in homeostatic balance. Her conceptualization—that the final clinical picture of the disorder may take several symptomatic forms according to whether the defenses used are pseudodefective, pseudoneurotic, or pseudopsychopathic—has been developed elsewhere (Bender, 1959). This special viewpoint, although controversial, has left a major imprint on the field and has stimulated further research into the relationship between biological and psychological factors.

Bender believes that environmental traumata are precipitating, but not causal factors, because the disorder is based on dysmaturation of the nervous system and not on learned experience. At the opposite pole are the environmentalists who think that parental influences are primary if not causal factors (see, for example, the "atypical child" described by Rank, 1949, and Pavenstedt, 1955). Bender states that parental "psychopathology" is a result *of the child's difficulties. This is in sharp contrast to the concepts of those who view the child's behavior as reactive to parental attitudes, or to those who see the picture as the result of a mutually reinforcing interactional withdrawal of parent and child. Bettelheim (1967), while generally taking a position opposite to that of Bender, agrees with her that autism is a defense against anxiety. Yet, he feels that this anxiety is not a secondary reaction to an organic, inborn impairment, but that it has its source in the child's evaluation of the conditions of his life as being utterly destructive. Ekstein and Friedman (1968), looking beyond Bender's work, believe that schizophrenia is not an abstract entity, but a unique phenomenon in each individual, always more and other than the sum of its biological, physiological, and psychological processes.*

Reprinted from *American Journal of Orthopsychiatry,* 17, 1947, pp. 40–56.

More than one hundred preadolescent children, who have presented the clinical picture of childhood schizophrenia, have been observed on the Children's Ward of the Psychiatric Division of Bellevue Hospital in the past ten years. Our own definition of childhood schizophrenia (Bender, 1942) has been a clinical entity, occurring in childhood before the age of eleven years, which

> reveals pathology in behavior at every level and in every area of integration or patterning within the functioning of the central nervous system, be it vegatative, motor, perceptual, intellectual, emotional, or social. Furthermore, this behavior pathology disturbs the pattern of every functioning field in a characteristic way. The pathology cannot therefore be thought of as focal in the architecture of the central nervous system, but rather as striking at the substratum of integrative functioning or biologically patterned behavior.

At present the only concept we can have of this pathology is in terms of field forces in which temporal rather than spatial factors are emphasized. Within the concept of field forces, one can accept some idea of a focal disorder, since no one integrated function is even completely lost or inhibited, and since there are different degrees of severity of disturbance in the life history of any child and between two different children. This also differs with the period of onset.

The diagnostic criteria for the 100 schizophrenic children which make up this study have been rigid. In each child it has been possible to demonstrate characteristic disturbances in every patterned functioning field of behavior. Every schizophrenic child reacts to the psychosis in a way determined by his own total personality including the infantile experiences and the level of maturation of the personality. This reaction is usually a neurotic one determined by the anxiety stirred up by the disturbing phenomena in the vaso-vegetative, motility, perceptual, and psychological fields. Interferences in normal developmental patterns and regressive phenomena with resulting primitive reactions are related to both the essential psychosis and the reaction of the anxiety-ridden personality.

There are, of course, children in whom the differential diagnosis is very difficult. Those with some form of diffuse encephalopathy or diffuse developmental deviations in which the normally strong urges for normal development push the child into frustration and reactive anxiety may present many schizophrenic features in the motility disturbances, intellectual interferences, and psychological reactions. Some children with a deep anxiety due to disturbances in interpersonal relationships may react with profound biological disturbance and regressive behavior akin to the schizophrenic. The common feature is the anxiety and the fact that the developing child is a biological social entity with only a certain number of ways of reacting to life traumas and always reacts holistically whether the trauma arise internally or externally or at whatever point in the developmental curve. Schizophrenia adds nothing to childhood experiences or behavior which an otherwise normal child might not also be capable of under some other condition.

Schizophrenia in childhood may otherwise be defined as a form of encephalopathy appearing at different points in the developmental curve, interfering with the normal developmental pattern of the biological unit and the social personality in a characteristic way and, because of frustration, causing anxiety to which the individual must react according to his own capacities.

In every schizophrenic child, we can see disturbances in the vaso-vegetative functioning. They may be either excessively labile or unresponsive in their vasomotor behavior; they may flush, perspire, or be colorless with blue cold extremities; they react to minor and major illnesses in an unpredictable way. A simple cold may make them appear to be in a state of shock for a short time, and they may completely recover in an hour or two. They may react with no temperature fluctuation to a severe infection or show an excessive response to a slight illness. Hoskins (1946) has emphasized the difficulties that lie in the integration or control or cooperation in the different fields of vasomotor, vegetative, or endocrine functions in the adult. The rapidly growing organism of the child seems to accentuate these problems although little specific work has been done on children. Leonard Gold (1943) showed that there was a disturbance in equilibrium of the autonomic nervous system in that the sympathetic was more sluggish than the para-sympathetic. In nine of our patients the autonomic nervous system maintained its own homeostasis and was sluggish in its recuperative powers once it was thrown out of equilibrium by mecholyl chloride as compared with 19 nonschizophrenic problem children.

The physiological rhythms of daily living lose their normal rhythmic pattern. This is seen in the sleeping, eating, and elimination habits. Mothers complain of it as a part of the early disorder in behavior, and we observe it in trying to adapt the children to the ward routine suitable for the normal child. Growth discrepancies are marked. The children are too big or too little, too fat or too thin. The growth problems become interrelated with the psychological problems because of both the essential schizophrenic process and the reactive anxiety. Stuart, in whom schizophrenia began in the first two years, when anxiety is at its height in relationship to oral activities, was, at eight and a half years, as tall as a 12 year old boy and was obese. Most of his activities and preoccupations centered on oral problems with biting, spitting, excessive verbalization with obscenities, and overeating. He distressed his mother by identifying her as "horse face."

Menstruation has occurred in several girls at age seven and 10 years without other gross endocrine anomalies, but with the onset of schizophrenia. Delay in the onset of menses in girls with schizophrenia at puberty is well known. Precocious or delayed puberty in boys also occurs. Unevenness in the somatic growth and nonspecific endocrine dyscrasias would seem to explain the dysplastic features of many adult schizophrenics. It remains to be determined whether in such cases the clinical picture of schizophrenia was apparent in the stage of childhood at which the deviation in physical development asserted itself. Such cases have been referred to as a constitutional type of schizophrenia (Bowman, 1933), and it has been shown that they have a schizoid type of prepsychotic personality in childhood which may well have been a childhood schizophrenia.

Electroencephalograms show a disproportionate number of dysrhythmic records with periodic bursts of slow-high voltage waves, but as yet, one cannot interpret the EEG as a projection of a specific cortical pattern disorder in schizophrenia.

Characteristic disturbances in patterned motor behavior or motility can be demonstrated in every schizophrenic child. Mothers will tell us in retrospect of unevenness in the motor development of the child. They complain of motor awkwardness and poor control of limbs. The child seemed insecure and unhappy in gaining new motor patterns and expressed anxiety to a distressing degree in forming new motor habits independent of the mother, such as walking alone, climbing stairs, stepping over or off of small objects, or using swings, tricycles, or even being left alone in a carriage or high chair. The motor independence may have been established and lost again with the onset of the schizophrenic illness. This is probably one of the most significant early causes for the reactive anxiety and guilt on the part of the mother who cannot understand why she cannot make her child independent in his motor habits when he seems otherwise quite normal in his physical development.

Early or primitive reflex patterned activities may outlive the stage to which they belong and be retained throughout childhood as a mode of play or of expressing anxiety, etc. A good example of this is the choreo-athetotic activities of the hands of the infant which is normal in the first few months, and is used as a play pattern in the latter half of the first year as the child discovers its hands and relates them to the visual motor patterns and eating-grasping patterns. In children who develop schizophrenia in the first two years of life, this motor pattern is retained and seems compulsively determined, along with other motor reflex patterns. Later in childhood, it may assume the pattern of mannerisms. Some children will relate them to oral habits, biting and sucking the fingers until they are sore and abscessed. Others relate them to jumping activities either in play or anger, as in temper tantrums. Seven-year-old Richard, schizophrenic since his second year, says, "It is my nervousness and it makes me happy. If I didn't do it, I wouldn't be nervous but maybe I wouldn't be happy." It occurred most characteristically in him after an elaborately patterned and symbolic play situation. Whatever the pattern, it is always a pattern and not an isolated neurological sign of known brain pathology such as choreoathetosis.

There are postural reflex responses (Schilder, 1931; Bender and Schilder, 1941; Hoff and Schilder, 1927) which are nearly specific for childhood schizophrenia. Postural reflexes are tested by having the child stand with his arms outstretched in front of him and his eyes closed while the head is turned on the neck by the examiner. The primitive response to this test is to turn the body so as to bring it in line again with the head. So long as the examiner continues to turn the head, the child will continue to turn on the longitudinal axis. This is a normal response for the young child from the time he is old enough to stand alone and cooperate with the test procedure without losing his balance (otherwise he will resist the test) until the age of six years in the average normal child. After this, the normal child will accept the turning of the head without rotating the body and, after an initial displacement of the arms, will correct the displacement. This is a highly sensitive test procedure for many types of motor disabilities in children (Teicher, 1941). The schizophrenic child responds with a graceful fluid whirling which he quickly accepts as a new pattern of activity, if he has not already discovered it himself, and will carry it on spontaneously. Sometimes the examiner need only put his finger on the top of the head which suggests a pivot. This should not be misunderstood as an acquired trained pattern in a child anxious to please the adult. Normal children do not usually respond in this way. The schizophrenic child finds that the test stimulus conforms with his own impulse tendencies. Rotating and whirling motor play in all planes make up a large part of their activity. It finds expression in their dreams and all other forms of fantasies, and is the nucleus of many of their psychological problems such as fear of or preoccupation with losing their limbs, inability to determine the periphery of their own body or the boundaries of their personality or "ego boundaries," their relationship to the reality of the outer world, to determine their own center of gravity, to relate themselves to time and space, or even be sure of their own identity.

There are two other related phenomena. The schizophrenic child shows a physical or bodily dependence which can be seen by simple physical contact. He seeks instantly to use the body or the motility of the adult and will either lean so completely on the other person as to fall to the ground if that support is withdrawn or will readily sink completely and passively into the lap and arms of the accepting adult as though to melt his very body into that of the other and thereby identify himself with the other's more secure center of gravity. With the same impulse, he clings to and holds on to the adult at every opportunity. The second phenomenon is a cohesiveness of the body surface such that there seems to be no limiting membrane between the two proximating skin surfaces. One can obtain complete motor compliance from the child by contact through the palmar surfaces and induce *cerea flexibilitas* or push the child about at will. Sometimes negativism or ambivalence may lead to an initial resistance to such phenomena but it is quickly overcome. The examining adult must lend himself sympathetically to the relationship since he must always be an active and passive participant in every patient-physician relationship. The child's motor compliance (Schilder, 1939) suggests a strong need or impulse to be completely dependent upon the body of another person as though seeking a dependable center of gravity which can be used to control his own disorganizing impulses and undetermined ego boundaries.

The schizophrenic child of three to five or six years may become largely preoccupied with motor play which is composed of many interrevolving systems of reflex activity. Effort to get the child to conform to the pattern of life about him by acquired habit patterns may give the impression of awkwardness and dissociated behavior, but when left to his own devices, he carries on endless rhythmic and graceful dancing behavior with changing tempos.

There are also some unconnected impulsive activities, best described as darting, which are sudden and usually at a tangent from the other rhythmic activities. It is as though there were two impulses for activity, one that keeps the child at a constant rhythmic play about a changing center or multiple centers which he is trying to fixate, and the other in which he tries to escape from the organized center of gravity and its determined reflex pattern. In articulate children, this desire to escape may be expressed in psychological as well as motor terms. They strive either to escape from the dependence on the mother (due to the disease process with its motor insecurity and frustrated oral cravings) or to escape from whatever environment they are in and feel is confining them, or again, to escape from their own identity and the frustrating disorder of the psychosis. Ten-year-old Francine wrote a letter to her doctor: "For the doctor, I am sure I will escape though and go to the real world. It is better there. He isn't a guardian angel and neither is this a guardian angel hospital meant for all who come here. I, Francine, that is what they call me, was very unhappy there. It was a terrible world. I thought it was a real one but it seems it isn't. I may some day go to the real one."

An uncertain control of the facial musculature leads to grimacing, carefully patterned, and belonging in some way to the total psychological problem. Various oral mannerisms, often with associated oral or vocal noises, are common. If there is some inequality in the physical make-up in the child (common to all organic patterns and all individuals), it tends to be exaggerated in the schizophrenic child while the normal child compensates for inequalities. Thus, inequalities of the head or face may be reflected into the musculature as a mannerism so marked as to confuse the diagnosis. Other so-called "soft neurological signs" which do not make a syndrome are not uncommon in schizophrenia and can be explained in the same way. The voice is wooden-like in quality, mechanically modulated, and seems not to belong to the child. It has something of a ventriloquistic character as though it too could not be sure of the ego boundary or center or identity of the child which is producing it.

The child's inability to locate the periphery of his body seems related to his inability to take care of his body secretions, body extensions, and his clothes. He has no concern about nasal secretions, saliva, tears, urine and feces, and they drip from him without his awareness. Hair is neglected, but that the problem is something more than simple neglect is evidenced by the observation that many schizophrenic children cut their hair with the schoolroom scissors.

It is clear that it is impossible to discuss problems of motor activity, concern or awareness of body functional problems, body image problems, and other perceptual problems separately. The perceptual problems of schizophrenic children are easily seen, as one need only observe their visual motor patterning with the use of pencil and paper. Most schizophrenic children are highly productive with the various projective techniques although they tend to lose this as they deteriorate, and some, in whom schizophrenia has started early and progressed rapidly, may never show any productivity.

In the study of the genesis of visually perceived form (1938), it was determined that a vortical movement is the basis for the organization of the visual field and is the beginning of all form. The young child starts with a large whole arm circular scribble; action is the initial impulse for form. It is never unpatterned and the pattern always includes action or motor elements and visual or form elements and spatial and temporal elements. At three or four, the child begins to control the vortical movement into discrete circles, also related to each other concentrically and directionally on a horizontal plane. At four, a modified circle is a square; at five, a triangle; at six, a diamond. A point is the center of a circle. The vertical plane is obtained at four or five by rotating the horizontal plane circle-wise (Fabian, 1945).

With the use of gestalt figures which give sufficient play to these problems, and which may be copied, these genetic features can be determined. One can also determine the disorders in visual motor pattern in pathological states. The schizophrenic child copying these figures shows many of the same problems which are shown in his motility. There is a tendency to use old primitive responses interlocked with the more mature capacities which are expected from the maturational level of the child. There is therefore an excessive use of the vortical movement even with good diamond forms. A series of figures on a horizontal plane may be pulled around into a vortical figure. The boundaries of circles are uncertain and may be gone over several times. The centers of circles are uncertain; there are no points but many little circles, and for the same reason angular and crossed forms are fragmented. Action cannot be readily controlled and figures are elaborated, enlarged, repeated. The total product makes a pattern itself with a great deal of fluidity to it based upon vortical movement. The perceptual patterns lose their boundaries and therefore their relationship to the background. One may speak here, too, of a motor compliance and cohesiveness between the boundaries of two objects. There is also an effort to explore and fixate depth or third and fourth dimensions. In this well-patterned fluid matrix, are areas in which the pattern is broken; a part of a figure is separated from the whole mass. It is as though in a circular stream of rippling water a pebble was thrown, causing a new wave movement. One's best understanding is to think in terms of a disturbance in the time factor being of biological origin and related to this disease process alone. Other forms of behavior such as regressive, projective and introjective, elaborative, inhibitive, distractive and concretistic, are efforts on the part of the personality to orient itself to this pathology and, if possible, control it.

The spontaneous art of schizophrenic children is a field so fertile that its study would bring us not only a very advanced understanding of the disease entity, but also of many normal human problems. The characteristic pathology of schizophrenia with the impulse to action, the reactive anxiety with the desire to understand and correct the pathology, and the accelerated creativeness of the six to twelve-year-old child all combine so that often the schizophrenic child shows remarkable art ability which may express itself in various fields—graphic art, dancing, music, and verbalization.

The schizophrenic child usually employs three topics for his spontaneous graphic art, the human figure, natural scenes, and abstractions. The latter two subjects are extremely intriguing, but cannot be discussed here.

When the child draws the human form, it is essentially a projection of his body image and its problems; it is a self-portrait. It is not surprising that the schizophrenic child with his body image problems, motility, and perceptual disturbances, uncertainty as to his identity, and his drive for action, finds ready expression for his problems in drawing the human form. The techniques that are used have a wide range even in one child. The most primitive use of vortical movement with graduated variations may be the sole form used to draw a human figure, but it expresses just that whirling motility, impulse to action, fluid ego boundary and uncertain center of gravity which represents the schizophrenic child and his problems. He is by no means limited to this technique device. Without training and by sheer self experimentation, these children develop the most amazing capacity to express human form in action, always related to some total situation which is immediately evident from the picture itself. Not all develop the gifts, of course; some express the problems crudely, unesthetically, but nevertheless express it. In others, the gift is dramatic and bears no relationship to the child's endowment but seems to be a hypertrophied capacity arising from the disease. It is fleeting and deteriorates with the progress of the illness or diminishes if the child improves, and as he passes into puberty. The problems which are expressed in the drawings of the human form are his identity and relationship to people about him, the accelerated impulse to motion, action, whirling, dancing, and aggression, the functions of different parts of the body, the boundaries and peripheries and extensions of the body; i.e.—multiplicity of heads and limbs, facial expression of anxiety and terror—feeling of external influence, changing states of consciousness, interpersonal relationships, and social problems.

It is a never-ending source of amazement to see a child who is perhaps underdeveloped, infantile in motor play, physically dependent, unconcerned with his body excreta and clothing, unsure of his own identity, inarticulate to the point of mutism, unable to make any school or social adjustment, but who will cover paper with the most expressive human forms in all kinds of motor patterns and in the most intricate interhuman and social relationships, and experimenting–Picasso-like–in techniques and art forms.

The study of the genesis of the thought and language disturbance of the schizophrenic child will help clarify many of the problems of schizophrenic thought and language in general. When schizophrenia occurs in the first few years or before language is well established, there is usually more or less retardation, inhibition or blocking, often with complete mutism which may appear as an initial symptom but may later be partially overcome with a return of speech that is distorted; or speech may gradually "deteriorate" or "regress" by use of simpler language forms, dropping out of connection words, loss of more recently acquired language forms, and fragmentary speech. Language may be used as a repetitive expression of anxiety with questions concerning identity and orientation, but never waiting or attending to an answer or ceasing to use it as a means of communication or interpersonal relationship; it is used as a chanting accompaniment of motor play. There are occasional explosive expletives, aggressive or obscene in nature. Language may be only experimentally imitative, echoing, repetitive or perseverative, compulsive and obsessional. Isolated words may be played or experimented with, and new word forms created, at first varying only slightly from recognizable words and having some significant sign value in the child's emotional problems. Using the third person pronoun for himself and confusing or evading all other pronouns may represent an echolalic repetition of language as he hears it, or may represent concretistic use of language forms, regression to infantile levels, or expressing his difficulties with identity of himself and orientation to the world. When language returns after a period of mutism, it may show all types of deviation as though the child were experimenting with all forms of aphasia and language pathology (Despert, 1940; Curran and Schilder, 1935; Kanner, 1943; Despert, 1942).

On the other hand, the child who has already mastered language may show an increased activity in the field of language and in thinking processes. In some there is an early precocious language development. In psychometric tests, his language development may be beyond the level anticipated for his endowment. In this field, too, the drive for action expresses itself. There is no better way of describing the thought processes than to say that they are vortical, gyrating, circling about a nuclear point of gravity which cannot be fixated. There seems to be experimentation with many alternate thought forms and ideas, and only some fragments can be projected since the recording apparatus of speech is slower than the field of language action. Thus what we hear sounds fragmented, dissociated, bizarre; occasional tangent, darting expletives may break through.

Symbol formation is a part of normal thought and language development. Just as there are form disturbances in all other fields of language, so there are in symbol formation in the schizophrenic child. The function of symbol formation (Schilder, 1938a) normally is to use the biologically determined perceptual motor patterns as a sign reference for emotional, psychological, and personality problems. Thus the motile circle in visual motor patterns is used to express body image problems projected and integrated by the maturating child into the human form. At times, unacceptable human traits or partial traits, such as oral aggression in response to aggressive parents, are symbolized as animal forms (Bender and Rapoport, 1944). For the young child whose problems are those relating to his relationship with his mother, the family and the outer world, the circle becomes a boat upon a motile flowing ocean, the boat is the mother, the sun is the father and the child himself is inside the boat (Bender and Wolfson, 1943). This can and is elaborated indefinitely to meet the needs of the individual child. For seven-year-old Richard, schizophrenic since his second year, the circle is a "rat-cheese-hole" dealing with his problems of introjection, anality, an aggressive father image and his anxiety concerning aggression. If the circle becomes a square, it is still a "rat-cheese-hole" but it is now derived from electric wall plugs and the rat will be electrocuted by the wires if he goes into the hole. One sees in such symbolization tendencies for condensation or the superimposing of many levels of thinking and of many psychological problems, mixing of abstract and concrete thinking, and of regressive and accelerated drives. At the same time, the child becomes fixated on his symbolic forms and cannot leave them because they never solve his problems. For the normal child, his symbol formation is quickly digested by ceasing to be concrete and becoming abstract, contributing to his growth once they are experienced. Symbols become either amnestic or appear as dreams and recognized fables, fairy stories and fantasies. In the schizophrenic child, such symbol formations are the best examples of the patterned form that the schizophrenic thought disorder tends to take to express, by condensation, all the problems which concern the child.

The psychological problems of childhood schizophrenia are different from those of the adolescent or adult. They are appropriate for the period of childhood and also for critical developmental periods within childhood which may be the period of onset of the illness. The significant problems are identity, body image and body function problems, object relationship and interpersonal relationship both in the family and the larger social world, orientation in time and space, meaning of language and, finally, the problem of anxiety. The disturbance in identification processes; that is, difficulties in identifying one's self and thereby relating to the rest of the world, is the essential psychological problem. The resulting anxiety is a reactive problem, and the symptom formation is related to both.

The youngest schizophrenic children, those in the first two or three years of life, show disturbances in the vegetative rhythms and habit patterns, in motility, and in object relationship. Mothers are most distressed by this inability of the child to relate to herself, to siblings, play material, food or clothes. Language has no objective use for sign value, communication, or interpersonal relations. Kanner (1943) speaks of "autistic disturbances in affective contact." The child may be fixated on one kind of object relationship such as round objects which can be spun like a top. Robert who was seen by me at age four and again at five and a half, could only relate himself to buttons, silver dollars, and "pepper-pot tops." For the child between three and five, whose language is not inhibited, we may get a revealing expression of the psychological problems which may again be fixated on one or another problem at a time, as Richard's rat-cheese-holes, or they may show a spread over almost every problem of childhood. Five-and-a-half-year-old Judy says, "I say, hello, doctor, have you any new toys? Let me open your radiator with this screw driver. I say let me open it. I say, so what! Can I copy your animals? I am in a doctor's office. You and I are twins, aren't we? I am coloring this camel brown. I said I am coloring it brown. I said I am coloring it brown. Have you a little scissors? Have you a big scissors? I say, have you a big scissors? Well here's what I will use, what do you think. It is called a knife. How does my voice sound? What? What? Judy what? Is that your name? I'm cutting out this camel. Is it pretty enough to hang on the wall? Can you cut as pretty as this? My sister says, camel talk, Isn't that funny? Camel talk. My voice sounds like up in the library. Doesn't it? In the hospital my voice sounds like up in the library. Can you say li-bra-ri-an? The library is where you get books."

An eleven-year-old girl (Bender, 1937) had been placed in a shelter with her brother and sisters because of a crisis in the family. When the mother called for the children, the child refused to go with her, saying, "I have two sisters and one brother . . . Their mother came for them but my mother didn't come for me. My mother didn't take me home because she didn't come for me. Another lady came for them. It was their mother. She didn't have the same look. She was darker. She didn't have my mother's hat or clothes. My mother told me she didn't come. My mother is a colored woman with nice brown hair and brown eyes. She is not so dark. The one that came wasn't so nice and I knew it wasn't my mother. The other children thought so. I am different from the other children. I'm dumber. They catch it before I do. I am harder to catch on anything. They don't want me to play with them. They like me a lot. They like me more and more. There ain't no others. I like them lots and lots and lots. I am an oddicle person because I belong catching one before they do. I don't think my sister is my sister. She went home with her mother. She plays my sister." Later, she said, "I want to go home with my mother, I made a mistake. Her eyes seemed bigger, she looked taller, her feet were bigger, she had a long head and she was blacker. She didn't speak with the same voice as my mother. People on the street seemed to be talking about my mother, I imagined it wasn't nice, maybe something like I was being mean to my mother. The girls would lay on the bed and make up things about my mother. They weren't my sisters. They were the ones that went home with the woman who says she was our mother."

The sexual problems of early childhood may be accentuated in schizophrenia with excessive and open masturbation and preoccupation with the functions of elimination. There may be distressing preoccupations with masturbatory impulses and internalized objects in the pelvic region. One young boy, whenever alone, would cry out "Every minute, every minute, I can't get it out, a big one, too, Jesus Christ, every minute, it's getting bigger." He would not explain, but compress his thighs and writhe in his chair and point to his buttocks, and only say "There is something in my arms, there is clay—they feel stiff." There is never the complaint that someone outside is responsible for these experiences. Verbal hallucinations akin to the adult's are so uncommon as to be of no diagnostic value. When present, they seem to have the same mechanism as in nonschizophrenic children, are neurotically determined, and clearly represent a voice of conscience usually related to the introjected body and to unsatisfactory ego-ideals. They readily disappear with treatment (Bender and Lipkowitz, 1940). In childhood we look for introjection instead of projection (Rapoport, 1944). The introjected object is often the good and/or bad mother, the devil or guardian angel, the whole of hell or the world at war, "a little man with a big old long hat? and Francine's

(Rapoport, 1944) "brain bodies" which her bad mother put in her to make her have a baby.

These are the internalized objects which Melanie Klein (1932) has found important in the normal development of the early infantile period. In childhood schizophrenia, they can be demonstrated and usually persist until nearly puberty. They have considerable influence on the child; in adults they are treated as hallucinations or persecutory objects.

It is a general principle that all of the normal mechanisms of early childhood will be used as points of fixation in childhood schizophrenia. They will be exaggerated by repetition, by finding expression in various forms, by condensing with other mechanisms and carried into later periods of development.

In the same way, the problem of aggression is very important to children especially in the parent-child relationship and sibling relationships. A nine-year-old says, "I want a hammer to kill my bed. I'm mad at it, it won't come to me at night and I have to go find it when I want it. I'm mad at my mother too, she takes food to bed and eats it in bed. If my grandmother found out, she'd kill her. I got a gun to shoot somebody's head off and a razor to cut my finger off. My thumb hurts. I hope I get an operation on my throat, it hurts. I want a very terrible operation on my throat to get something out. It might be poison. I ate something I thought it was candy. Is that a lady or a man doll? What a funny face. It must be a skeleton. They kill people, jump on your back and bite you all to pieces. Know why I want to get hurt? Because my family won't leave me alone. My sisters tell lies about me. They beat me. I want to get hurt real bad. I dreamed a fox was after me. I fell on top of a stump and hurt me. A fox came behind me. I jumped off the roof. But the fox couldn't jump. I landed right on my head and got hurt. I liked that. When you get hurt and wake up, it is beautiful. I dreamed you tried to tiptoe down the stairs and tripped and fell down and half killed yourself. My mother doesn't love me. She shouldn't have had me. I should have stayed in her guts. I am in my own gizzard. I think I will go back to heaven where I came from."

Anxiety is the nucleus of the schizophrenic problem in the earlier stages. It is the reactive mechanism of the threatened personality, threatened by the disrupting effects of the schizophrenic process in all the functioning fields of the personality, the ego, or the biological unit. The way the individual deals with this anxiety determines much of the symptom formation. The presence of a severe anxiety in a child, unaccounted for by a reality situation, is in itself suggestive of schizophrenia. The suffering on the part of the child and those about him is proportionate to this anxiety and the resulting symptom formation.

Our therapeutic approach at present is directed essentially at the anxiety and secondary symptom formation. In the child, we also attempt to help in the integration of the pattern of behavior and the promotion of such identification processes as are possible. So long as the anxiety is evident, the child shows considerable affect. The excessive impulse to action drives the child as much toward social contacts as away from it. The great anxiety also leads him to cling physically and psychologically. Failure to get satisfaction from such contact may gradually lead to withdrawal but not until there has been a long period of illness. The gyrating thought process of such children, and the tendency to experiment in the hope that they can seek a solution to their problems, leads to what may well be called an ambivalence in personality relationships. Their great charm results in a strong reciprocal relationship. The most dearly beloved of the problem children on the ward in the past ten years have usually been schizophrenic children.

In discussing the disturbances in the interpersonal relationships of the schizophrenic child, we cannot omit comments on the reactions of the mothers, and also of others in the child's world. The mother of the schizophrenic child, especially the child in whom the process has developed insidiously over a long period, shows a specific mechanistic patterning due to her efforts to help the child in his distorted identification processes, to understand what is happening and to identify herself with the child. The mother bears an intolerable burden of anxiety and guilt, and is more bewildered than the child himself. She will try every mechanism for denying, evading, displacing, or absolving the child's psychosis. The motor and physical dependence of the child, his intriguing charm, his distressing anxiety, all bind the child to the mother while she cannot identify with his problems or follow his disturbed thought process and development.

The relationship between siblings, when one is schizophrenic, is particularly difficult because the essential problem in sibling relationship is identification. But the negative and positive features in such a relationship are exaggerated and disturbed. In the same way, other children are both attracted to the schizophrenic child and his exaggeration of childhood problems and frightened by his anxiety and inability to solve his problems. Two schizophrenic children have a strong tendency to identify with each other even though the identification has its difficulties. An eight-year-old girl says, "Do you like Melvin? I hate him. Everybody tries to make him be my boy friend."

In the family situation the problem is further complicated by strong hereditary tendencies. In many of the schizophrenic children in this study, there were other schizophrenic individuals in the family which, of course, amplified the problems of identification and anxiety in the family circle even among those who were not psychotic. (To be reported in more detail in a subsequent report.)

By contrast with adults, one can often make an unusually good contact with schizophrenic children. There is generally a searching, penetrating, even aggressive clinging dependence. They are attractive, intriguing, and appear gifted. They attempt to solve their problems by an excessive identification or interpenetrating relationship. Six-year-old Martin for a while would eat only what I fed him. He was given an Indian suit in the hospital and would not permit it to be removed for sleeping or bathing except by me. If permitted he would sit all day in the corner of my office with his thumb in his mouth, and if put out of the room, would be content if only the toe of his shoe could be pushed over the door sill. At such periods the sight of his mother threw him into a screaming panic. Now, at 16, he is still glad to see me (the process is quiescent now) and talks vaguely of his problems.

In the classification of childhood schizophrenia, the most important factor is the age of onset of the illness. The second factor is the progression or severity of the illness, whether it is rapid and profound or slow and slight, accelerating or regressive, and if the progression is steady or subject to remissions or arrests.

As to the age of onset, there are three critical periods. 1) The first two years of life not uncommonly includes the onset of a mental illness in children which subsequently proves to be schizophrenia. The development is reported by the mother to have been uneven and there may be no point at which the child appeared normal and then regressed. If the progress is rapid and profound, it is difficult to differentiate from organic deficiencies (Bender and Yarnell, 1941b). However, there are no gross somatic deficiencies such as microcephaly; the motility disorder is typical of the schizophrenic child and does not make any other neurological syndrome; the disorder in object relationship is conspicuous and there is evidence of excessive anxiety; there may be no language development at all, but if there is, it may be lost again or misused as a play pattern. Some children, in whom the onset is clearly set in the first two years by the mother, may continue to develop to good intellectual levels, be physically precocious and demonstrate profound motility and psychological disorders, and show anxiety continuously.

2) From three to four and a half years is the most common period of onset. This group is more readily recognized because of the normal development up to this period. The regression may be insidious and very slow, or abrupt and very rapid, so that in six months the child may lose all he has gained in three years, especially the socially oriented behavior patterns, leaving him well developed physically with good gait and exaggerated graceful motility, but having lost many of his acquired habit patterns, language, object relationship, with increased anxiety and physical dependence on the mother. Subsequently, the anxiety may also be lost. It is then we speak of deterioration. Having regressed as far as possible, the child may then slowly begin to regain some patterned behavior but now distorted by the schizophrenic patterning. A variety of unevenness in the patterned disorder may occur. The child may show increased activity with anxiety, emotional instability, irritability, excitement, unprovoked aggression (usually oral) and temper tantrums with fears, phobias, disturbed sleep, accelerated language development, and considerable preoccupation with all of the psychological problems of identity, body functions, physical and social orientation. There will be an aggressive dependence on the mother and all adults. There may be a general acceleration of the developmental tendencies in all fields including physical growth, a general regression, or any mixture of the two. Regressive mental illnesses or infantile dementia commonly starting at this age have been recognized for some time as Heller's disease (Bender, 1941b; Kanner, 1932).

It is difficult if not impossible to differentiate this group of cases from what appears to be the more rapidly and evenly regressive schizophrenia or from some of the regressive organic dementias. The family history and ultimate course of the disorder may help in diagnosis. In general, those children with onset of schizophrenia before age five, who show severe interference or regression in fundamental habit patterns, language, object relationship, and motility, and show a loss of anxiety, are the most severe cases. In our experience they do not indicate a tendency to remissions nor do they respond much to shock treatment. On the other hand, children in whom the onset may be just as early but who show the accelerated type of response with a great deal of anxiety, may pass through very severe disturbances, respond to shock therapy and psychotherapy, have good remissions and return to their homes and schools. They may withstand the pubertal period and be relatively well, though on clinical examination still show residual signs of schizophrenia in motility, thought disturbances, some defect in object relationship, and in the handling of their emotional life. They remain dependent on their family. It appears that the prognosis for schizophrenia for even this infantile type is as good as it is in adults, which means that a third to a half will make a fair to good social recovery or remission but remain vulnerable. However, this prognosis is possible only if the criteria for diagnosis are clearly delineated and those children who have the milder forms of schizophrenia and those subject to remissions are also diagnosed. The prognosis is improved by early recognition and active treatment.

Children of school age are often brought to the psychiatrist's attention with the history of onset apparently at six to eight years. In most of these, however, it is probable that the onset was three to four years and only recognized when the child was brought to school and into community activities.

3) The third common childhood period of onset is the prepubertal period, age 10 to 11½. In these children the clinical picture is quite different. While in the infantile period, we have difficulties in differentiating between schizophrenia and organic brain disorders, at the prepubertal period the differentiation must be made with the neuroses, especially anxiety states and obsessional-compulsive states. With the obsessional-compulsive thinking added to the psychological problems of the schizophrenic child with his disturbance in identification and orientation, he evolves persecutory systems in which he suspects that either he or his parents are changed and that other children are against him because he cannot identify with them. His efforts to control his motility lead to mannerisms which may appear compulsive. Inability to keep track of the periphery of his body leads to a breakdown in personal habits and care. In some cases the behavior is like delinquency; the child truants, wanders away from home and enters strange dwellings in an effort to orient himself.

His problems in identification are now not only to orient himself in his family, but his family in the social group. His concern about body function includes a concern about his mental processes and his own psychological problems, states of consciousness, life and death, social aggression. He may be suicidal and threaten the welfare of siblings or children his own age level. These problems are often graphically expressed in behavior, in language directly or symbolically, and in art media. There is a good deal of concern with language. Many children read a great deal, most of them show accelerated development in language fields in contrast to performance functioning. The budding sexual problems lead to diffuse exaggerated identifications, most clearly seen in girls who identify with their brothers. In the past few years they have fantasied themselves in war experiences and the love life of their adolescent brothers. This problem leads to a disrupting ambivalence in all their relationships.

Similarly, there is a tendency to identify with negative characters, such as our enemies during the war. One boy cooperated dramatically with shock treatment because he said we were turning him into a good Jap. The problems are the same as those of early childhood, but are dealt with by a ten-year-old experience and abilities. By this time introjected superegos tend to become projected. Hallucinations are not clear and are not concerned with sexual matters, but there is a tendency to be vaguely aware of the various perceptions being projected just beyond the body periphery. The anxiety tends to focus at this point with considerable concern as to whether they themselves or something outside themselves is identified with this distressing feeling that something is going on which they cannot control.

In conclusion, may I say that the problems of the schizophrenic child are the problems of all growing children, but the patterning is modified by mixed tendencies to expansions and contractions, accelerations and regressions which follow configurational tendencies specific for schizophrenia.

EARLY INFANTILE AUTISM

LEO KANNER AND LEONARD I. LESSER

One of the historic landmarks in child psychiatry occurred in 1943, when Kanner first described early infantile autism as a discrete form of childhood psychosis. He subsequently differentiated it from mental retardation and from psychosis and listed its cardinal signs and symptoms. Kanner's description of the syndrome is still accepted as a model, although his ideas of the origin and treatability have been subject to question. His characterization of the parents of autistic children as themselves "successful autistics"–cold, compulsive, intellectual people, having in common upper social class standing–raised questions about the interactional etiology of the disorder.

Early notions that autism was simply a reaction to parental rejection, aloofness, or distance, gave way to more complicated theories of environmental pathology. Bettelheim (1967) cautions against blaming the pathology of severe childhood psychosis on parents alone. He suggests that, in addition, some specific attitude or event has created in each child the conviction that he is threatened with total destruction. As Escalona (1963) says: "The controversy as to whether infantile autism is 'due to' inadequate mothering or 'due to' inborn deficit loses its significance. . . . It is caused by the absence of those vital experiences in early childhood which we regard as the necessary condition for ego synthesis" (p. 243).

It is true today that autism, perhaps the most serious pathology found in children, remains as much of a research challenge as it did when Kanner first described it. But whereas Kanner insisted on separating autism from retardation, we have learned that the two indeed do often coexist.

The syndrome, while relatively rare, has had a particular fascination for students of childhood psychopathology, perhaps because those afflicted often have special abilities, along with severe pathology. Among the more recent reviews and reconceptualizations of the disorder is Rimland's (1964) book, Infantile Autism.

Reprinted from *Pediatric Clinics of North America,* 5 (3), 1958, pp. 711–730.

In 1938 a number of children were observed whose unusual characteristics seemed worthy of special consideration and whose clinical picture appeared to comprise a psychotic illness heretofore undescribed. During the ensuing five years, 11 such children were studied in detail, and the observations were reported in 1943 under the title *Autistic Disturbances of Affective Contact* (Kanner, 1943). In this and subsequent publications, the syndrome was noted to be recognizable as early as the first or second year of life. Two outstanding characteristics, extreme aloneness and a desire for the preservation of sameness, were delineated and established as essential diagnostic criteria. The designation, "early infantile autism", was suggested by the unmistakable evidence of typical symptoms in the first two years of life and the self-centered and, at least in the beginning, often impenetrable aloneness.

The first reports met with some skepticism, but, subsequently, numerous confirmatory reports were published. In addition to our own cases, autistic children were studied in this country by Despert (1938, 1951, 1957), Mahler (1952, Mahler et al. 1949), Weil (1953), Murphy (unpublished), Rank (1949, 1955), and others; in Canada by Cappon (1953); in England by Creak (1951, 1952); in France by Stern and Schachter (1952, 1953); and in The Netherlands by van Krevelen (1952a, 1952b) and Grewel (1954). A number of workers have discussed the theoretical implications for language and perceptual function of the phenomena shown by the autistic child. It therefore seems justified to state that the specificity of early infantile autism is now rather commonly accepted, with some differences, however, in diagnostic allocation.

Case Histories

Two case histories are introduced to show the typical symptomatology and to indicate the wide range of later development.

Case 1. Margaret J. was brought by her parents on March 8, 1943, at the age of five years 10 months. She was referred with the complaint that "she is a behavior problem in the sense that in a small public school she has made herself so objectionable that the school refuses to take her back."

The mother recalled that Margaret showed *"peculiar traits" when she was less than one year old.* "For instance, when we would sit on a certain chair upon which she did not like us to sit or which she felt should be occupied by another member of the family, she would scream. She always insisted on entering the garden through a certain door. She would notice when the dishes on a tray were not in the accustomed order." She seemed friendly and smiled, but never looked at a person. She never addressed her parents as "Mommy" or "Papa." She rolled a great deal in her crib and banged her head against the bars.

Margaret was a planned and wanted child. The pregnancy was uneventful. She was delivered at term by low forceps and was healthy at birth. There was no indication of birth trauma. She was placed at the breast and given a supplementary feeding for six weeks. She always loved to eat and presented no feeding problem, but drank little milk. She was easily toilet-trained. Past illnesses included a mild, uncomplicated case of measles and a "cold with high fever way after she was one year old." There was no history of injuries, operations or convulsions.

Her general development was said to be slow. She stood at 10 months and walked at 22 months, after a phase of crawling. At 18 months an x-ray examination of the long bones ruled out rickets.

She talked before she walked. She could repeat short sentences, but had no interest in making conversation. "She did not use the right pronouns. She said 'You,' meaning 'I,' and still occasionally does. For a long time we were distressed because she did not use a definite Yes or No in an answer. When asked if she wanted milk, she replied, 'Margaret wants her milk.' " Formation of plurals and tenses presented no difficulties.

At three and a half "she cried a lot and was given to tantrums. She would get up and touch things in the same order–every morning." She was entered in nursery school because it was felt that she was spoiled and needed more discipline. At the beginning she showed no interest in the other children, but stayed at the edge of the group or by herself, happily swinging or playing alone. After some time she improved sufficiently in her relationships to be tried in a public kindergarten. Her adjustment there was poor. Though she cooperated in music and rhythm, she could not become interested in reading. When a story was read at school, she paid no attention, giggled hysterically and disturbed the group. It soon became apparent that she would not "make the grade." Her career at this school was terminated abruptly when she urinated and defecated in a waste paper basket. "She was quite hysterical about it and thought it was a good joke."

In reference to more recent behavior, the mother said, "She has the most amazing memory I have ever seen. She notices many details; for instance, she knows how many tiles there are in the bathroom. She has to hear a nursery rhyme only once, then recognizes the tune. She can tell Victrola records from the type of sealing . . . She counts very well, knows her colors, and can identify pictures, especially of airplanes. She draws well, usually with her left hand. She cuts with her right hand. She starts to read from right to left and sometimes looks at pictures turned upside down.

"Recently her behavior has changed somewhat. She used to touch the floor all the time, but got over that. Now she pops her eyes and giggles. She is terrified by an elevator. During the train trip to the clinic she was interested in everything; noticed people, and talked. She shows a particular interest in body discharges. She asked a taxi driver who cleared his throat, 'Did you have phlegm in your throat?' She is very observant and interested if somebody goes to the bathroom."

Margaret is the younger of two children. The mother, a college graduate librarian, is a high-strung, intelligent person who worries a great deal and is devoted to her children and family. She describes her husband, a successful advertising copywriter, as "not too warm a person who is considered by many people as conceited, but who is devoted to his family." Both parents are sociable people and have many friends. The family is financially comfortable. There is one brother, William, who was characterized at that time as "a perfectly normal boy who is in good rapport with people and makes friends very easily."

Physical examination at our clinic revealed a well developed, attractive child, with abundant, coarse brunette hair. There were no physical or neurological abnormalities noted. X-ray examination of the skull was read as normal.

Margaret entered the consultation room without looking at any person and asked, "Who is that?", meaning the examiner. She shook hands, but did not look at the person with whom she shook hands. She was deeply absorbed in her play with blocks, with which she built a certain pattern. She showed good manual dexterity, using both hands alternately. She named each of the blocks and was anxious to place them in particular positions to each other, following a certain purposefulness and certain rules, which she made up for herself. As long as she was left alone, she was completely happy and satisfied, talking to herself, plainly, but for the outsider, incoherently. From time to time she looked in self-abandonment into the air, asking, "What made the ceiling crack itself?" When anyone interfered with her realm, by moving or taking a block, she became angry, shouted, "Don't!", then jumped up, becoming aggressive, hitting and kicking, and showing her typical reaction of frustration mixed with anger. She put her fingers in her mouth and twisted her hair with the other hand, standing motionless and staring into space. As soon as one restored the changed or missing object, she snapped out of the reaction. This pattern of behavior could be provoked by any interference with her occupation.

In the second interview Margaret, upon returning, amazed everyone by demanding the same blocks. She recalled exactly the names which she had given them the day before and proceeded to arrange them in precisely the same pattern. She asked for the same puzzles and assembled them exactly as on the previous day. When given crayons and paper, she drew airplanes, while mumbling, "Airplanes flying over Europe and the Philippines."

The next day, when seen in her hospital room, she was lying on her bed, sucking her fingers, and rolling in ecstasy from side to side. She used personal pronouns correctly and showed a good vocabulary. She moved gracefully and quickly. A complete Binet test could not be given because of insufficient responsiveness, but the general impression was that she was of at least normal intelligence.

Placement in a special school was recommended, and this recommendation was accepted by the parents.

During an interview in February, 1944, it was learned that Margaret had returned to public school and had indeed made a surprising adjustment. She passed thereafter from the second through the sixth grades; then she entered a private school in upper New York State. There she was noted to be insecure, tense and anxious.

On a Wechsler Bellevue Scale, given in 1944, she attained a full scale intelligence quotient of 110.

She was seen again with her mother in December, 1953, at the age of 16 years seven months.

She had made amazing progress and developed a great deal of insight into her own personality. She spoke of herself as "a plugger" and indicated that she put considerable pressure on herself in order to do well. She said, "Up to last year the fundamentals of learning have been easy because of my good memory, but this year it's the interpretation, and this is difficult for me." She had ambitions to go to college and added, "I may be hitching my wagon to a star." About her relationships with other children she said, "The girls in school are very nice and very friendly, and I have a good time with them. There are some points in which I am not close to them. I feel I'm not as mature as I should be; I don't have the interest in boys that most girls my age have."

In the fall of 1953 Margaret entered a well known women's college and graduated in 1957. She selected subjects in which rote memory rather than spontaneous production was essential. She took part in routine activities, though she made few, if any real friendships. She is a serious, rather literal-minded young woman who augurs to do reasonably well in an occupation in which no demand is made on give-and-take relationship with other people.

Case 2. Elaine C. was brought by her parents on April 12, 1939, at seven years two months, because of "unusual development." "She doesn't adjust. She stops at all abstractions. She doesn't understand other children's games, doesn't retain interest in stories read to her, wanders off and walks by herself, is especially fond of animals of all kinds, occasionally mimics them by walking on all fours and making strange noises."

Elaine was born on February 3, 1932, at term. She appeared healthy, took feedings well, stood at seven months and walked at less than a year. She could say four words at the end of her first year, but made no progress in linguistic development for the following four years. Deafness was suspected, but was ruled out. Because of febrile illness at 13 months, her increasing difficulties were interpreted as possible postencephalitic behavior disorder. Others blamed the mother, who was accused of inadequate handling of the child. Feeblemindedness was another diagnosis. For 18 months she was given anterior pituitary and thyroid preparations. "Some doctors," struck by Elaine's intelligent physiognomy, "thought she was a normal child and said that she would outgrow this."

At two years she was sent to a nursery school, where "she independently went her way, not doing what the others did. She, for instance, drank the water and ate the plant when they were being taught to handle flowers." She developed an early interest in pictures of animals. Though generally restless, she could concentrate for hours on looking at such pictures, "especially engravings."

When she began to speak by about five years, she started out with complete though simple sentences that were "mechanical phrases" not related to the situation of the moment or related to it in a peculiar metaphorical way. She had an excellent vocabulary and knew especially the names and "classifications" of animals. She did not use pronouns correctly, but used plurals and tenses well. She "could not use negatives, but recognized their meaning when others used them."

There were many peculiarities in her relation to situations:

"She can count by rote. She can set the table for numbers of people if the names are given her or enumerated in any way, but she cannot set the table for three. If sent for a specific object in a certain place, she cannot bring it if it is somewhere else but still visible."

She was "frightened" by noises and anything moving toward her. She was so afraid of the vacuum cleaner that she would not even go near the closet where it was kept, and when it was used, ran out into the garage, covering her ears with her hands.

Elaine was the older of two children. Her father, aged 36, studied law and the liberal arts in three universities (including the Sorbonne), was an advertising copywriter, "one of those chronically thin persons, nervous energy readily expended." The mother, aged 32, a "self-controlled, placid, logical person," had done editorial work for a magazine before marriage.

Elaine had been examined by a Boston psychologist at nearly seven years of age. The report stated, among other things:

"Her attitude toward the examiner remained vague and detached. Even when annoyed by restraint, she might vigorously push aside a table or restraining hand with a scream, but she made no personal appeal for help or sympathy. At favorable moments she was competent in handling her crayons or assembling pieces to form pictures of animals. She could name a wide variety of pictures, including elephants, alligators and dinosaurs. She used language in simple sentence structure, but rarely answered a direct question. As she plays, she repeats over and over phrases which are seemingly irrelevant to the immediate situation."

When examined in April, 1939, she shook hands with the physician upon request, without looking at him, then ran to the window and looked out. She automatically heeded the invitation to sit down. Her reaction to questions–after several repetitions–was a parroting of the whole question or, if it was too lengthy, of the end portion. She had no real contact with the persons in the office. Her expression was blank, though not unintelligent, and there were no communicative gestures. At one time, without changing her physiognomy, she said suddenly, "Fishes don't cry." After a time she got up and left the room.

She was placed at the Child Study Home of Maryland, where she was observed for three weeks. While there, she soon learned the names of all the children, knew the color of their eyes, the bed in which each slept, and many other details about them, but never entered into any relationship with them. When taken to the playgrounds, she was extremely upset and ran back to her room. She was very restless, but, when allowed to look at pictures, play alone with blocks, draw, or string beads, she could entertain herself contentedly for hours. Any noise, any interruption disturbed her. Once, when on the toilet seat, she heard a knocking in the pipes; for several days thereafter, even when put on a chamber pot in her own room, she did not move her bowels, anxiously listening for the noise. She frequently ejaculated stereotyped phrases, such as, "Dinosaurs don't cry"; "Crayfish, sharks, fish and rocks"; "Butterflies live in children's stomachs, and in their panties, too"; "Fish have sharp teeth and bite little children"; "There is war in the sky"; "Gargoyles bite children and drink oil"; "I will crush old angle worm, he bites children"; "Needle head. Pink wee-wee. Has a yellow leg. Cutting the dead deer. Poison deer. Poor Elaine. No tadpoles in the house. Men broke deer's leg."

A few excerpts from the observations follow.

"Her language always has the same quality. Her speech is never accompanied by facial expression or gestures. She does not look into one's face. Her voice is peculiarly unmodulated, somewhat hoarse; she utters words in an abrupt manner. Her utterances are impersonal. She never uses the personal pronouns of the first and second persons correctly. She does not seem able to conceive the real meaning of these words. Her grammar is inflexible. She uses sentences just as she has heard them, without adapting them grammatically to the situation of the moment. When she says, "Want me to draw a spider," she means, "I want you to draw a spider." She affirms by repeating a question literally, and she negates by not complying. Her speech is rarely communicative. She has no relation to children, has never talked to them, been friendly with them or played with them. She moves among them like a strange being, as one moves between the pieces of furniture of a room. She insists on the repetition of the same routine always. Interruption of the routine is one of the most frequent occasions for her outbursts. Her own activities are simple and repetitious. She is able to spend hours in some form of daydreaming and seems to be very happy with it. She is inclined to rhythmical movements which always are masturbatory. She masturbates more in periods of excitement than during calm happiness. Her movements are quick and skillful."

Elaine was placed in a private school in Pennsylvania. In a progress letter the father reported "rather amazing changes": "She is a tall husky girl with clear eyes that have long since lost any trace of that animal wildness they periodically showed in the time you knew her. She speaks well on almost any subject, though with something of an odd intonation. Her conversation is still rambling talk, frequently with an amusing point, and it is only occasional, deliberate, and announced. She reads very well, but she reads fast, jumbling words, not pronouncing words, not pronouncing clearly, and not making proper emphases. Her range of information is really quite wide, and her memory almost infallible. It is obvious that Elaine is not normal. Failure in anything leads to a feeling of defeat, of despair, and to a momentary fit of depression."

The father's optimism proved to be premature. The next communication concerning Elaine came from a psychiatric evaluation center in New York state where she was admitted September 7, 1950. Her behavior there was described as follows:

"From the time of admission the patient was a serious behavior problem. She was overactive, distractible, spontaneously assaultive on many occasions and talked in an irrational manner with a flat degree of affect. She ran through the wards without clothing, threw furniture about and banged her head on the wall, had episodes of laughing and screaming during the night and imitated various animal sounds. She made frequent reference to animals and to being killed or butchered. In conversation with her she showed a good choice of vocabulary but could not maintain a conversation along a given topic. EEG made on her did not show any definite abnormality. Her disturbed and unpredictable behavior continued, and she failed to profit by the program of the institution. Considerable time was spent with her in the occupational therapy department in trying to make an individual appeal, but her conduct continued in the same degree.

"In view of her behavior making her a source of danger to herself and others, and since her instability and irrational behavior was of sufficient degree to constitute a mental illness, the matter was referred to the Department of Mental Hygiene who concurred and instructed that she be certified to a state hospital for care and treatment."

The Clinical Picture

Among the 150 children observed at the Children's Psychiatric Service of the Johns Hopkins Hospital, the case studies offer individual differences in specific features, family constellations, and step-by-step development over the course of years. Even a superficial review, however, reveals the emergence of a number of essential characteristics which together constitute a unique clinical syndrome. These may be grouped into two primary or cardinal features: *extreme self-isolation* and an *anxiously obsessive desire for the preservation of sameness.* A number of secondary features may be considered derivatives of these.

The common denominator, as pointed out in the original paper, is "the children's inability to relate themselves in the ordinary way to people and situations from the beginning of life." The children are described by their parents as "having always been self-sufficient," "like in a shell," "happiest when left alone," "acting as if people weren't there," "perfectly oblivious to everything about him," "giving the impression of silent wisdom," "failing to develop the usual amount of social awareness," "acting almost as if hypnotized." This does not represent a departure or withdrawal from previous relationships, but rather, from the start, an *extreme autistic aloneness* which, whenever possible, disregards, ignores, shuts out anything that comes to the child from the outside. Direct physical contact or such motion or noise as threatens to disrupt the aloneness is either treated as if it were not there or painfully resented as a distressing interference.

The parents of autistic children can almost invariably recall the child's *failure to assume an anticipatory posture* when picked up from the crib or to show the usual body molding when carried in the parent's arms. The parents have the sensation of lifting and carrying a sack of flour rather than a child.

Food, as the first intrusion brought to the child from the outside, is often resisted or refused. The history of *early feeding difficulties* is commonly obtained. Occasionally tube feeding is reported to have been tried. This problem usually disappears after a few months, often abruptly.

Language is a function of human relatedness which ordinarily serves for communication. Autistic children seem to feel no need for communication. Approximately one third of these children remain "mute," but even in these the rare utterance of a whole sentence in an emergency situation attests to the child's ability to store up and use language.

In the "speaking" children, language is not used initially to convey meaning to others. Phonation, articulation and naming of objects present no difficulty. Many parents proudly tell about the facility with which the child repeats an inordinate number of miscellaneous items such as nursery rhymes, prayers, lists of animals, roster of presidents, the alphabet forward and backward, and even French lullabies. Aside from repetitions of sentences, these children are usually late in putting words together as tools for receiving and imparting meaningful messages. When sentences are finally formed, they are for a long time mostly parrot-like repetitions of previously heard word combinations. They are sometimes echoed immediately, but just as often "stored" by the child and uttered at a later date—a phenomenon termed *delayed echolalia.*

The apparent irrelevance of utterances of these children is more understandable when one regards them as metaphorical expressions. They differ from the usual metaphors of poetry and etymology in being idiomatic for the autistic child, not primarily intended as a means of inviting other people to understand and share in the child's symbols.

Donald T. at seven years of age was asked the Binet question: "If I were to buy four cents' worth of candy and give the storekeeper 10 cents, how much money would I get back?" He obviously knew the answer. His reply, however, was not "six cents," but, "I'll draw a hexagon." Two years previously, at five years of age, Donald had been scribbling with crayons; all the while he kept saying with conviction, "Annette and Cecile make purple." It was learned that Donald at home had five bottles of paint. He named each one after one of the Dionne quintuplets. Blue became "Annette," the red became "Cecile." After that Annette became the word for blue and Cecile for red. Purple, not being one of the five colors, remained purple.

This concept amplifies the long-felt assumption that similar mechanisms prevail in the "irrelevant," "incoherent", and "metaphorical" language of adult schizophrenics.

Grammatical structuring often appears in bizarre ways. Affirmation is indicated by the literal repetition of the question. "Yes" is a concept that requires many years for these children to acquire. It is not initially understood as a general symbol of assent. Donald learned to say "Yes" when his father told him that he would put him on his shoulders if he said "Yes." This word came to mean only the desire to be put on his father's shoulders. It took many months before he could detach the word "Yes" from the specific situation, and it took much longer before he was able to use it as a general term of affirmation.

The same type of literalness exists also with regard to prepositions. Alfred, when asked, "What is this picture about?", replied, "People are moving about." John F. corrected his father's statement about pictures on the wall; the pictures were "*near* the wall." Donald T., when requested to put something *down,* promptly put it on the floor.

There is no difficulty with plurals or tenses. The absence of spontaneous sentence formation and the echolalia-type reproduction have given rise to a peculiar grammatical phenomenon. Personal pronouns are repeated just as heard, with no change to suit the altered situation. A child once told by his mother, "Now I will give you your milk," expresses the desire for milk in exactly the same words. Consequently he comes to speak of himself as "You" and the person addressed as "I." Not only the words but also the intonation is retained. The pronominal fixation remains until about the sixth year of life, when the child gradually learns to speak of himself in the first person and of the person addressed in the second person. In the transition period he may revert to the earlier form or at times refer to himself in the third person.

Autistic children do not face or address those who attempt to communicate with them, even though they may echo what is said. It often takes numerous reiterations of a question to elicit even an echoed response. A considerable proportion of the children are initially thought of as deaf or hard of hearing.

The child's *obsessive desire for the maintenance of sameness* is continually illustrated by the monotonously repetitious nature of his noises, motions, and verbal utterances. There is great limitation in the variety of his spontaneous behavior. His entire life activity becomes a series of rituals. Furthermore, he forces the other people in his world to be even more obsessive than he is. While he may make an occasional concession, he does not grant this privilege to others. Parents report how difficult it has been to "teach" the children to walk or talk. Long after they have abandoned their efforts, the child surprises them by suddenly performing these tasks with skill, then incorporating them into his routine.

The environment must be kept whole or unaltered. Anything broken, dolls "improperly" dressed, and cracks in the wall bring forth comment and unhappiness. People must also be "whole." A visible scar or wart evokes instant comment. There is no sympathy or solicitude for the person as such. The attitude is rather one of annoyance—again, not with the person, but with the fact itself.

Once blocks, beads, or sticks have been assembled in a certain way, they are often regrouped later in exactly the same way, even though there was no definite design. The children's memories are phenomenal in this respect. After a lapse of several days, a multitude of blocks could be rearranged, most astonishingly, by Donald T. and Margaret J. in precisely the same pattern, with the same color of each block turned up, with each picture or letter on the upper surface of each block facing in the same direction as before. The absence of a block or presence of a supernumerary block was noticed immediately, and there was an imperative demand for restoration of the missing piece. If someone removed a block, the child struggled to get it back, hitting the hand which held it and going into a crescendo of panic tantrum until he regained it and then, promptly and with sudden calm after the storm, returned to the design and replaced the block.

At home the furniture arrangement, the location of bed and chairs, the dishes, the books on the bookshelf must remain in their precise positions. Parts of the human body are considered to have specific arrangements. A person's foot belongs on the floor and is not to be placed on a chair. Legs are not to be crossed.

Anthony F. was given the Séguin Formboard test which he completed in 25 seconds, but he became disgusted with the star-shaped form and stated, "Star, you are bad. You should be in the sky!"

The retention of sequences is as important to the children as the maintenance of appearances and space relations.

Malcolm H., when taken for a walk, "insists on covering the same ground that has been covered on previous walks." Donald T., at the age of nine-and-a-half years, had been "going to school" since the age of six, when the principal had agreed to let him attend. On one afternoon the session was dispensed with. No one in the family knew about this. Donald went to school as usual. Though no other child was in the classroom, he sat down in his seat, took out his books, did some writing, and left when the bell rang.

From the foregoing, it can be seen that an autistic child may *relate skillfully to objects.* He is interested in them, can play with them happily for hours, can be fond of them, can have power and control over them or get angry with them. Certain children may spin everything that can possibly be spun, meanwhile jumping up and down in ecstasy while the objects whirl about. Other children sense and exercise this same power over their own bodies by rolling, whirling, rocking, and other rhythmic movements. These actions and the accompanying ecstatic fervor strongly suggest the presence of masturbatory orgastic gratification.

The children's *relationship to people* is altogether different. Upon entering a playroom or office, such a child goes immediately after blocks or toys without paying the least attention to anyone present. The child is aware of the people there, but considers them not differently from the way he considers the desk, bookshelf, or filing cabinet. If addressed, he does not bother to look up. Conversation elicits no interest. If the adults do not intrude into his domain, he will at times, while moving between them, gently touch a hand or a knee just as he will pat the desk or couch. Should an adult forcibly intrude himself by taking a block away or stepping on an object that the child needs, he becomes angry *at the hand or foot,* which is dealt with per se and not as part of a person. Once he retrieves the object, his mood changes abruptly to one of placidity. If pricked with a pin, he may show anger and fear toward the *pin,* but not toward the person who pricks him.

The relationship to members of the household or to other children is essentially the same. The mother or father may leave the child without protest on his part. When they return, he does not seem to have been aware of their absence.

After many outbursts of frustration, he reluctantly learns to compromise and comply in matters of daily routine. When there is company, he moves among the people "like a stranger." When with other children, he does not play with them. He plays alone while they are around, maintaining no bodily, physiognomic, or verbal contact with them. He does not take part in competitive games. He is just there, and if sometimes he happens to stroll as far as the periphery of a group, he soon removes himself and remains alone. At the same time he quickly becomes familiar with the names of all the children of the group and may know the color of each child's hair and other details about each of them.

Even though most of these children are initially considered feeble-minded, they are all unquestionably *endowed with good cognitive potentialities,* which are masked by the basic disorder. Their facial expressions suggest good intelligence, serious-mindedness, and an anxious tenseness. When alone with objects, there is often a placid smile sometimes accompanied by happy though monotonous humming and singing. The astounding vocabulary of the speaking children, the unusual memory for events, the excellent rote memory for poems and names, and the precise recollection of complex patterns and sequences bespeak good intelligence in the sense in which this word is commonly used. Binet or similar testing can rarely be carried out because of limited accessibility, but the children perform surprisingly well on the Séguin Formboard.

Physical Examination

Careful physical and neurological examinations have thus far failed to reveal any consistent findings that would differentiate a group of autistic children from a similar-sized group picked at random. Neither can generalizations be made on the basis of prenatal or paranatal difficulties. Of the first 100 cases seen in our clinic, difficult labor was reported in 11, precipitous labor in two, prolonged labor in seven, and placenta previa in two. Four were delivered by cesarean section, and one sustained a fracture of an arm at birth. Difficulties in breathing were stated to be present in three of those and in three others who were delivered without mishap. As for congenital anomalies, one had a clubfoot, and one had strabismus. One boy began having grand mal seizures at five years of age. Twelve were reported to have been premature; of these, eight weighed less than six pounds at birth.

Electroencephalographic studies have been carried out only sporadically. In one series of 28 cases so studied, 21 were stated to be normal, three definitely abnormal, and four equivocal.

It should be kept in mind that examinations for integrity of the central nervous system are still in their clinical infancy, and a negative result with current methods cannot be regarded as a conclusive demonstration of the lack of central nervous system pathology.

Nosology

The nosological position of the autistic illness remains a matter of some uncertainty. There is no clinical resemblance to any of the known organic neurological conditions. Autistic children do not appear physically ill at any specific period. Even those patients who have withdrawn to the point of functional idiocy or imbecility show, especially in their behavior with puzzles and formboards, residues of planned mental activity which should deter one from thinking in terms of a degenerative organic process.

The possibility of prenatal organic damage has been investigated, but thorough physical and laboratory examinations have thus far yielded no consistent clue of any kind.

The concept that early infantile autism is basically an aphasic phenomenon has been ruled out by the not too uncommon observation that the "mute" children sometimes surprise their parents by uttering whole, well formed sentences in emergency situations.

Van Krevelen (1952a) has suggested that the condition represents an "oligophrenia with concomitant emotional defects." The observation that a few of the patients who originally tested at an idiot or imbecile level achieved intelligence quotients well above 100 in their early teens would cast considerable doubt on this view.

The relation between early infantile autism and schizophrenia is difficult to determine. The extreme emotional isolation from other people, which is the foremost characteristic of early infantile autism, bears so close a resemblance to schizophrenic withdrawal that the thought of a relationship can hardly be dismissed. The demand that a period of relatively normal adjustment must precede withdrawal as a criterion for the diagnosis of schizophrenia has been revised. Studies of onset, content and course of schizophrenia in children, such as those of Ssucharewa (1932) and Grebelskaya-Albatz (1934, 1935) in Russia and Despert (1938, 1951, 1957) in this country, differentiate between cases with acute and insidious onset. Mahler (1952, Mahler et al. 1949), on the basis of phenomenology and the nature of the mother-child relationship, worked out the helpful division between autistic and symbiotic infantile psychoses.

Early infantile autism may then be looked upon as the earliest possible manifestation of childhood schizophrenia in the broadest sense of this term. Stern and Schachter (1953) have suggested that, for the present, the condition be considered a specific phenomenon. This might seem practical in the sense that inclusion in a broader diagnostic group would tend to shove out of focus current studies regarding its developmental and symptomatic peculiarities. At all events, it seems advisable to keep in mind the specificity of the syndrome, regardless of any preferred nosological allocation.

Etiological Considerations

The first 100 autistic children seen in our clinic were selected for a consideration and statistical evaluation of the significant etiological factors. Of this group, 80 were boys and 20 were girls. The vast majority were of Anglo-Saxon or Jewish descent. As previously noted, exploration of somatic factors by means of complete physical and laboratory examinations has thus far furnished no clues that might point to specific acquired or constitutional organic anomalies.

Considering the 200 parents of these children from a genetic standpoint, it was observed that only one in the entire group had a major mental illness, a postpartum psychosis in a mother, following the birth of her autistic child's older sibling. One mother and one father were alcoholics, and one was epileptic. One father, a prominent lawyer, had twice interrupted his college studies because of anxiety neurosis. Another father, a well-known scientist, had had convulsions in infancy and later showed marked digital tremors. Of the 400 grandparents, three committed suicide, two had unidentified "nervous breakdowns," one had Friedreich's ataxia, and one had an obsessive-compulsive neurosis. Of the 373 uncles and aunts accounted for, six had psychotic episodes, two were reported to be feeble-minded, and one epileptic.

Among the children's own 131 siblings, 117 were considered normal. Of the others, seven had physical illnesses which were presumably unrelated. In addition to these, one was designated as a psychopathic personality, and two were severe stutterers. It is significant that three of our patients have siblings who, though not seen in our clinic, could be diagnosed as autistic children. One has, in addition, a brother who shows definite schizoid tendencies in his behavior.

These figures indicate that, from a genetic point of view, a meaningful positive correlation between early infantile autism and the occurrence of psychiatric or neurological disease in the patient's ancestry is unlikely.

The children in this series almost invariably come from intelligent and sophisticated stock. Among the 100 fathers studied, 96 were high school graduates, and, of these, 74 were college graduates. Their occupations included 31 businessmen, 12 engineers, 11 physicians, 10 lawyers, eight tradesmen, five chemists, five military officers, four writers, three doctors of philosophy in science and two in humanities, two teachers, two rabbis, one publisher, one forester, and one photographer.

Of the 100 mothers, 92 were high school graduates, and, of these, 49 were college graduates. Many continued to work after marriage. Their occupations included teacher, librarian, artist, social worker, writer, psychologist, physician, lawyer, chemist and others.

In considering the personalities of these parents, one may think of them as "successfully autistic" persons. This suggests the possibility that they may represent mild or latent manifestations, while their children show the manifest forms of the disorder. One of the fathers in this group, a physician engaged in research, described mildly schizoid trends in his grandparents, more severe ones in his parents and himself, and a full-blown picture of autism in his child. These parents, as a rule, are cold, humorless perfectionists who prefer reading, writing, playing music or "thinking" to seeking out the presence of other people. They are polite, dignified, impressed by seriousness, and disdainful of "small talk." They describe themselves and their marital partners as undemonstrative. Matrimonial life is a rather cool and formal affair. The parents treat each other with faultless respect, talk things over earnestly and calmly, and give to outsiders the impression of mutual loyalty.

The parents' behavior toward the children accentuates the emotional frigidity and mechanization of care. Lack of genuine maternal warmth is often conspicuous in the first visit to the clinic. Many of the fathers hardly know their autistic children. They are outwardly friendly, admonish, teach, observe objectively, but rarely step down from the pedestal of adulthood to indulge in childish play. Obsessive devotion to duty, rules, and job serve most of the parents as a substitute for the enjoyment of life. At the same time, their preoccupation with scientific and literary abstractions is accentuated by the large proportion of the parents and grandparents who have appeared in *Who's Who* and have attained considerable distinction in scientific, artistic, and literary fields.

Autistic children could rarely be thought of as rejected children. Childbearing was accepted as a part of matrimony, but the parents did not seem to know what to do with the children once they arrived. They lacked the warmth which their babies needed. The children did not seem to fit into their established scheme of living. The mothers felt duty-bound to carry out to the letter the rules and regulations given by their physicians. They were anxious to do a good job, and this meant mechanized service of the kind rendered by an overconscientious gasoline service station attendant.

Approximately 10 per cent of these parents do not fit the stereotype. In addition, those who do have reared other normal or, in any event, nonpsychotic children. Moreover, similarly frigid parents are often seen whose children are not autistic.

A control study of parents of nonautistic children revealed considerably lower levels of educational and professional attainment. Neither did they show the detachment, obsessiveness, or coldness usually present in the parents of autistic children.

The dynamic aspects of the interplay between the patients and parents have been studied by a number of authors, and on the basis of these studies three viewpoints have emerged. One regards the parental behavior as a reaction to the child's peculiarities, and of no etiological significance per se. At the other extreme, the parents, particularly the mother, could be considered the basic source of pathogenicity. The assumption is that a healthier maternal attitude would have precluded the disorder. A third group of investigators feels that the patient, endowed with an innate disability to relate himself to people, is further influenced adversely by the personality deviations of the parents and their resulting manner of handling him; this in no way discounts the possibility of a reciprocal relationship which, in turn, causes the parent to shrink from the child or to overprotect him in a more or less stilted fashion.

Course and Prognosis

It has now been possible to follow the destinies of autistic patients for a number of years, to compile data, and to reflect on the course and prognosis of the disorder.

In 1951 Darr and Worden published a case report of a patient 28 years after she had been evaluated (at the age of four) at the Henry Phipps Psychiatric Clinic by Drs. Meyer and Richards. Though no formal diagnosis was made, the child's behavior and the parents' personalities corresponded in every detail to the typical findings in early infantile autism. Dr. Meyer suggested "a natural, direct and affectionate handling without any pushing or undue demands." The mother carried this out by hiring a succession of different people to take care of the child. The child took piano and voice lessons, learned to speak Spanish fluently, and was able to take care of her personal needs. But at the same time, she lacked any intuitive social sense, had temper tantrums when thwarted, seemed most comfortable when she lived by precise routine, and showed marked hypochondriac tendencies which caused her to go into seclusion when contact with people became too upsetting. On a home visit for the Christmas holidays there was an acutely psychotic exacerbation of her symptoms. Deep coma insulin and electroshock resulted in a brief period of remission. A second series, instituted because of a recurrence of her outbursts and occasional assaultive episodes, brought no improvement. After nine months of group and intensive individual psychotherapy, it was reported that she had established no particular relationship with either patients or personnel in the private sanitarium where she was being treated. There was an apparent lack of relatedness to other persons, real or imaginary, in the content of her psychosis. The authors state specifically that "none of her productions has indicated delusional content."

This report represents the first opportunity to follow an autistic child into adulthood, and describes in detail "one example" of how such a person has adjusted over a period of years.

Mahler (1952), on the basis of her extensive experience with autistic children, wrote the following impressions regarding the course and prognosis of the "autistic infantile psychosis":

> Establishment of contact and substitution therapy over a long . . . time may sometimes give spurts of impressive and gratifying results. But they are usually followed by an insuperable plateau of arrested progress, which usually taxes the patience and frustrates the renewed hopes of the parents. Impatient reactions and pressures are then exercised and progress forced. But if the autistic type is forced too rapidly into social contact,—he is often thrown into a catatonic state and then into a fulminant psychotic process . . . If such catastrophic reactions cannot be avoided, it seems that such autistic infants are better off if allowed to remain in their autistic shell, even though in 'a daze of restricted orientation' they may drift into a very limited degree of reality adjustment only. Diagnosis of their 'original condition', of course, then usually escapes recognition; they are thrown into the category of the feeble-minded [p. 303].

In 1955 Kanner and Eisenberg published the results of a long-term follow-up study of 42 autistic children selected from those originally evaluated. They concluded:

> Every point of Mahler's statement was borne out by our follow-up studies: the spurts of gratifying results, the insuperable plateau, and the more or less permanent capsulation, occurring in different patients under different circumstances. Our findings suggest strongly that there are, from the beginning, differences in the intensity of autistic aloneness and fragmentation. We have as yet been unable to match them even approximately with somatic, genetic, or dynamic factors which might possibly be held responsible. But they do exist, and it would be a mistake to assume, as has sometimes been done, that autistic children are expected to be exactly alike. In this respect, a clear distinction between primary and secondary features proves of great value. Presence of the primary signs of aloneness, and insistence on sameness is a sure diagnostic guide and holds the group together, regardless of the number and nature of the secondary manifestations [p. 232].

The children ranged in age from eight to 24 years, with an average age of 14 years. The interval between the first visit and the follow-up visit averaged eight and a half years. Of this group, none was reliably known to have had hallucinations or delusions. The main pathologic state was found in the area of inability "to relate in the ordinary way to other human beings." Even the relatively "successful" children exhibited a lack of social perceptiveness, perhaps best characterized as a lack of *savoir-faire.* This was illustrated by the following incident involving one of the patients: Attending a football rally of his junior college, and called upon to speak, he shocked the assembly by stating that he thought the team was likely to lose—a prediction that was correct, but unthinkable in the setting. The ensuing round of booing dismayed this young man, who was totally unable to comprehend why the truth should be unwelcome.

This amazing lack of awareness of the feelings of others, who seem not to be conceived of as persons like the self, runs like a red thread through our case histories. We might cite a four-year-old boy whose mother came to us with the account that on a crowded beach he would walk straight toward his goal irrespective of whether this involved walking over newspapers, hands, feet, or torsos, much to the discomfiture of the owners. The mother was careful to point out that he did not intentionally deviate from his course in order to walk on others, but neither did he make the slightest attempt to avoid them. It was as if he did not distinguish people from things, or at least did not concern himself with the distinction.

From a prognostic standpoint it is clinically useful to regard speech as an index of the ability to relate, or, conversely, of the degree of autistic isolation. It was observed that those patients who spoke by the age of five eventually demonstrated a far greater degree of social adjustment than those who failed to speak. Of the 42 children followed up, there were 23 speaking and 19 nonspeaking children.

In the speaking group, the children had begun to talk at the usual time or slightly thereafter. Articulation was normal and phonation either normal or of a sing-song "Donald Duck" quality. Their rote memories were excellent, and the grammatical peculiarities described were in evidence.

Among the "mute" children, the differences in speech development as observed in first and in subsequent visits were impressive. "Some of the patients had completely renounced the use of speech; they were either mute throughout, or began to avail themselves sparingly of the linguistic tool only after five years of age, or—having said a few words—abandoned articulate language altogether" (p. 232).

Eighteen of the 19 children who did not talk by the fifth year were "still firmly enveloped in their autistic shell" and would, as Mahler pointed out, "impress a casual observer as essentially feeble-minded . . . It is necessary to emphasize that, in this group, the present condition has come about regardless of the manner in which the patients had been handled. In fact, two of them had received intensive psychotherapy in good treatment centers; in both instances, slight apparent progress had given rise to guarded temporary optimism" (p. 234). Only one of the 19 originally mute children has emerged sufficiently to attend public school. Of the other 18, seven were placed in institutions for mental defectives, seven were kept in their respective homes in a state close to biological helplessness, two were placed on farms, and two in psychiatric state hospitals.

The 23 speaking children fared somewhat better. Ten were reported to be doing poorly. Of these, five were placed in state hospitals, three in schools for retarded children, one on a farm, and one remained at home. However, "most of them, even at the low ebb to which they have receded, still show remnants which distinguish them from the demented or pseudo-demented level of the mute autistic children" (p. 235). The remaining 13 had reached a plateau which allowed them to function at home and in their respective communities.

Of this group, one has completed high school, served two years in the military service, married and fathered a child, and is at present devoting himself to a career in musical composition. Another, who showed a special aptitude for mathematics and an intelligence quotient of 150, was able to attain a degree from The Johns Hopkins University in three years and is now pursuing postgraduate studies. Margaret J., whose case history has been abstracted, has graduated from college. The other 10 are attending elementary or high schools. All in this group are isolated, strange persons, who continue to relate well to objects such as books and blackboards, have few, if any, real friends, and still maintain a somewhat tenuous contact with reality. Because of increased accessibility, they all have shown substantial increases in formal intelligence quotient ratings. However, considering the clinical picture as a whole, one would not be particularly optimistic about their future.

In a more recent publication, Eisenberg (1957a) confirmed these observations with an enlarged group of 63 children. The outcome was classified into three categories: "good" (patient functioning well academically and socially); "fair" (patient able to attend school at about grade level, but distinctly deviant in personality); and "poor" (maladaptive functioning characterized by apparent feeble-mindedness and/or grossly disturbed psychotic behavior).

> Of the total group of 63, three were classified as having a good, 14 a fair, and 46 a poor outcome. Thus about 27% were functioning at a fair to good social level . . . Of the former (speaking) group, 16 (50%) achieved a fair adjustment whereas only one (3%) of the latter (non-speaking) group did so . . . So different is the prognosis in the two clinical groups that the thought presents itself that we may be dealing with two syndromes rather than one [p. 79].

Despert (1951) has suggested a correlation between failure to assume an anticipatory posture prior to being picked up in infancy and the degree of isolation in the child. Since this finding precedes the development of speech, it should prove useful as a still earlier prognostic sign.

Diagnosis

There is no single pathognomonic sign in early infantile autism, but, taken in aggregate, the historical and behavioral features present so striking a picture that one should encounter little difficulty in making the diagnosis. The characteristic findings of extreme aloneness and preoccupation with preservation of sameness, becoming manifest within the first two years of life, are invariably present. Other symptoms vary from case to case.

Deafness can be ruled out by proper otologic and audiometric examinations. Heller's and other degenerative diseases become evident with the passage of time. Aphasic disorders become separated clinically from infantile autism when children with the latter disorder use well formed phrases or sentences in emergency situations. Moderate or severe mental retardation poses more of a problem in differential diagnosis, particularly when the children exhibit behavioral oddities which bear superficial resemblance to some of the "secondary" symptoms often observed in autistic patients.

The various forms of childhood schizophrenia share with early infantile autism the loss of affective contact and autistic thinking. However, in other forms of childhood schizophrenia there is usually a later onset and a period of normal development preceding it. Communicational and affective perception are not usually as deeply disturbed as in the autistic children. In the broader schizophrenic group there may also be a wider variety of symptoms, such as symbiotic features, possibly because development proceeded further before the onset of the illness.

ON CHILD PSYCHOSIS AND SCHIZOPHRENIA: AUTISTIC AND SYMBIOTIC INFANTILE PSYCHOSES

MARGARET S. MAHLER

Various people (Benedek, 1949; Greenacre, 1959) have used the term "symbiosis" in a psychological sense, but Mahler's name has become inextricably associated with the concept. The paper reprinted here, and her subsequent ones, have gone far in refining our understanding of the dynamics of psychosis in children. Symbiotic psychosis, together with autistic psychosis (Kanner, 1943, 1944, 1949b), constitute the two "developmental psychoses" which occur in the first five years of life. They have in common a primary disturbance in object relations and in ego boundaries. Questions may be raised as to whether autistic and symbiotic psychosis are really different manifestations of the same illness, occurring at either end of the period of most concentrated relation to a primary object, the mother, or whether they are indeed qualitatively separate and distinct from each other. In any event, they both have their onset around the time of this normal but crucial phase of development.

The Group for the Advancement of Psychiatry (1966) has proposed that child psychosis be divided into two groups—autistic and interactional. Mahler's concept of symbiotic psychosis would appear to be the prototype of the latter group. She notes that both groups have in common a state brought about by a sense of disintegration set off by psychotic alienation from the human libidinal object (1958).

In the course of her writings on child psychosis, Mahler has considered both extrinsic parental pathology as the principal etiological determinant and intrinsic factors within the child which prevent the successful development and resolution of the symbiotic mother-child relationship (1965, 1968).

It seems that psychosis is the sad prerogative of the human species. It is not confined to adults alone. Animals are born with well-developed in-

Reprinted from *The Psychoanalytic Study of the Child,* 7. New York: International Universities Press, 1952, pp. 286–305.

stincts which guarantee their independent individual survival soon after birth. In the human young, however, these animal instincts (in terms of sense of track) have atrophied and became unreliable and, as Freud stated, the ego had to take over the role of adaptation to reality which the id neglects. The somatic corollary of ego development is the central nervous system which is in a very immature state at birth. The neonate appears to be an almost purely biological organism with instinctual responses to stimuli, not on a cortical, but essentially on a reflex and thalamic level. There exist only somatic defense mechanisms which consist of overflow and discharge reactions whereby cortical inhibition is undeveloped. Thus we may say that at birth there exists only a rudimentary ego, incapable of retaining stimuli in any degree of tension, or else, that prevalence of the undifferentiated phase of personality development persists for a comparatively long period of extrauterine existence (Hartmann et al., 1946). Yet the psychobiological rapport between the nursing mother and the baby complements the infant's undifferentiated ego. This normal empathy on the part of the mother is the human substitute for the instinct on which the animal can rely for survival. In the quasi-closed system or unit, the mother executes vitally important ministrations without which the human young would be unable to survive. The intrauterine, parasite-host relationship within the mother organism (Deutsch, 1945) must be replaced in the postnatal period by the infant's being enveloped, as it were, in the extrauterine matrix of the mother's nursing care, a kind of *social symbiosis.*

The young infant is readily thrown into affectomotor storm-rage reactions which, if not relieved by the mother's ministrations, may result in a state of organismic distress. This organismic distress is phenomenologically quite similar to the panic reactions of later life. As a second stage of his homeostatic insufficiency, the young infant may exhaust his life energy and may lapse into a kind of semistupor reminiscent of his fetal existence (Ribble, 1941). The newborn and young infant must be gradually brought out of this tendency toward vegetative splanchnic regression, out of the tendency to lapse into this exhausted semistuporous state, into an increased sensory awareness of, and contact with his environment (Greenacre, 1946; Spitz, 1946). In terms of energy or libidinal cathexis, this means that a progressive displacement of energy quantities from the inside of the body (particularly from the abdominal organs toward the periphery of the body) has to occur so that the perceptual conscious system, as Freud calls the surface of the body, the peripheral rind of the ego containing the sense organs, may receive cathexis. The turning from predominantly proprioceptive awareness to increased sensory awareness of the outer world occurs through the medium of affective rapport with the mother. The baby's libido position thus proceeds from the stage of fetal narcissism to primary body narcissism, a stage in which representation of the mother's body plays a large part. Thus, to repeat, the infant's rudimentary and very vulnerable homeostatic equipment after birth must be enveloped by the now extrauterine matrix of a mother's or a mother substitute's nursing care.

The Body Ego in Infantile Psychosis

The core of ego development, the first orientation toward external reality, is the differentiation of the body image, which is the psychic representation of the bodily self (Schilder, 1938b). Through the rhythmically recurring experience of painful accumulation of tension in the inside of his own body, followed by regularly repeated experiences of gratification which the infant cannot provide for himself hallucinatorily beyond a certain point, the infant eventually becomes dimly aware of the fact that satisfaction is dependent on a source outside of his bodily self. Thus the infant recognizes an orbit beyond the boundaries of the self, that of external reality, represented by the mother. Bodily contact with the mother, that is, fondling and cuddling, is an integral prerequisite for the demarcation of the body ego from the nonself within the stage of somatopsychic symbiosis of the mother-infant dual unity. Under normal circumstances, infants do not only treat parts of the mother's body as if they were their own, but, as Anna Freud and Dorothy Burlingham (1944) pointed out: "We assume, on the basis of much evidence, that the child's feeling of oneness with the mother's body has a parallel in the mother's feeling that the baby's body belongs to her" (p. 7). In terms of libidinal and aggressive cathexis, this implies that the baby's instinctual drives vicariously aim at the mother's body, particularly her eyes, mouth, hand, face, and breast, as if they were his own. He experiments with the feel of the mother's body, comparing it with the feel of his own. However, this learning about one's own body contour as separate from the mother's represents a relatively high degree of ego differentiation, an ability to neutralize and direct aggression, and a relatively advanced sensory perceptive awareness of the environment. Even this vague sensory discrimination represents a degree of development of the sense of reality—a state which is by no means reached or maintained by all cases of infantile psychosis.

In Early Infantile Psychosis Grave Distortion of the Mother-Child Relationship Seems the Essential Cause for "Ego Alienation from Reality"

Freud (1924b) considered the ego's alienation from reality the pivotal disturbance in adults' or adolescents' psychoses. Ferenczi (1913) has described how the infant's sense of reality proceeds—through the stages of magic hallucinatory omnipotence toward gestural and word magic—until, very gradually, he is able to accept and to master realistically his expanding external orbit. It seems obvious to those who have the opportunity to treat deeply disturbed children that the infantile ego's alienation from, or arrest of recognition of, reality is an occurrence inherent in the brittle and weak organization of the infantile personality (proclivity to ego fragmentation). To understand the dynamics in infantile psychosis, observation and study of the most important transitory step in the adaptation to reality is necessary; namely, that step in the development of the sense of reality in which the mother is gradually left outside the omnipotent orbit of the self. This step is preliminary to, and perhaps alternates with, the process of endowing the mother with object-libidinal cathexis. The toddler gradually delimits his own individual entity from the primal mother-infant symbiotic unit. He separates his own self (and his mental representation) from that of the mother. This stage in ego development is a very vulnerable one, particularly in children in whose early life the somatopsychic symbiosis has been pathological. (Compare Spitz, 1951.)

The Importance of Constitutional (Intrinsic) Factors in the Genesis of Infantile Psychosis

In regard to the question of heredity versus early frustrational and traumatic etiology of infantile psychosis, we may say that it is very difficult to ascertain whether the grave disturbance in a case of early infantile psychosis has been caused by the mother's pathology and lack of empathy, or by the infant's great innate ego deviation, be it an inherent lack of contact with his living environment, or an inordinate need for symbiotic parasitic fusion with the adult. It is a fact that time and again we see schizophrenic children whose mothers appear not to lack warmth, genuine love, or acceptance of the individual child, nor do they appear to be exceptionally possessive, infantilizing, and restrictive. Human nature provides a mutuality between the infant and his mother by which part of the environment seems to damage a constitutionally sound baby only if the baby is very young; on the other hand (as the famous Dennis experiment has shown and as everyday life experience demonstrates) the constitutionally sound baby, beyond the fourth, fifth, and sixth month, automatically coerces the adult's empathy (Greenacre, 1944). The infant's contact-seeking gestures appeal to woman's most basic biological longing. Hence, emotional gratification as well as food are readily given unless maternal psychopathology has rendered the adult partner unable to respond. In other words, it seems that such basic damage to the ego which results in infantile psychosis occurs in children who have a hereditary or constitutional "Anlage" for it, or in whom an intrinsic factor is prevalent. There *are* infants with an inherently defective tension-regulating apparatus which probably cannot be adequately complemented by either the most quantitatively or qualitatively efficient mothering. It seems that there *are* infants with an inherent ego deficiency which from the very beginning—that is to say, from the stage of the undifferentiated phase—predisposes them to remain or become alienated from reality; there are others whose precarious reality-adherence depends on delusional symbiotic fusion with the mother image.

Autistic Infantile Psychosis

From the points of view of object relationship and development of the sense of reality, we may describe two clinically and dynamically distinct groups of early child psychosis: in one group of early child psychosis the mother, as representative of the outside world, seems never to have been perceived emotionally by the infant, and the first representation of outer reality, the mother as a person, as a separate entity, seems not to be cathected. The mother remains a part object seemingly devoid of specific cathexis and not distinguished from inanimate objects. This type of infantile psychosis was first described by Kanner (1943, 1944, 1949b) and given the name of "Early Infantile Autism." In autistic infantile psychosis there are no signs of affective awareness of other human beings. Behavior which would point to affective perception of ministrations coming from the mother—from the outside world—is absent. In the anamnesis of these children, one finds descriptions of the earliest behavior which betray that there was no anticipatory posture at nursing, no reaching-out gestures, and no specific smiling response. One finds the following data: "I never could reach my baby."—"He never smiled at me."—"The minute she could walk, she ran away from me."—"It hurt me so when I saw other babies glad to be in their mother's arms; my boy always tried to creep away from my lap as soon as he could."—"He never greeted me when I entered, he never cried, he never even noticed when I left the room."—"She never was a cuddly baby, she never liked caresses, she did not want anybody to embrace or to kiss her."—"She never made any personal appeal for help at any time."—This last remark, of a very observant mother of one of these autistic children, described the disturbance as seen in terms of social behavior.

Let me give you the example of my little patient Lotta, aged three years and four months, who suffered from an *inherent* autistic disturbance. She provoked multiple traumatizations from a mother who herself lived in a hateful dependency on her own mother. There were severe feeding deprivations; a lip injury from spoon feeding occurred at a very early age. There was a strict and unloving regime of precocious toilet training. A vulvovaginitis followed the first signs of Lotta's beginning to "touch herself." Thus, traumatic overstimulation crowded out normal zonal libidinization in all areas of psychosexual development. Yet these traumatizations, I believe, could not have occurred if there had not been great intrinsic ego pathology. Daily struggles over constipation, with digital removal of the feces, was just one indication of the kind of atmosphere which prevailed. At the age of three and a half Lotta had no language, no gestural communication, no hand, mouth and eye integration (Hoffer, 1949). She neither fed nor handled herself and she showed a terrified startle reaction at any chance touch *of* or *by* another person. By the usual intelligence rating she would have ranked among the lower imbeciles. However, Lotta's habits were compulsively neat, her motor and manipulative skills were age-adequate, her knowledge of, her memory for, her static inanimate environment were phenomenal.

During therapy, by using every conceivable device, she was slowly brought to sensory perception of the outer world by gradually accepting contact with the analyst's body. Yet no normal identification occurred but instead there was extensive mirroring and parrot-like word formation. Word formation was autistic, and speech was not used for intercommunication but only for commands and signals—and it was used toward objects as freely as toward the analyst.

She seemed to catch up rapidly with isolated fragments of her arrested ego development. She went through repetitious, aggressive exploration of her inanimate environment—banging the doors, switching the lights on and off, and fingering everything as blind people do.

There were bizarre discrepancies of body-ego integration as the disconnected fragments of her personality forged ahead at fantastically uneven rates. Let me give you an illustration:

At the stage of treatment when Lotta went through repetitious testing of her environment, she would indeed tax the patience of her mother. A little flashlight was provided for her by the analyst in order to drain away some of the disturbing behavior from the overstrained home situation. She became quite attached to the little flashlight. At the same time, Lotta started to put everything she liked into her mouth. Thus she mouthed the little flashlight like a teething baby. When driving from the office at that time, her mother, as usual, used the automatic lighter to light her cigarette. Lotta, unnoticed, got hold of the glowing lighter and put it to her mouth, causing severe scorching of her lips. [1] She showed practically no reaction. Her pain sensitivity seemed grossly below normal. This, among other signs, is, I believe, and indication of the lack or deficiency of peripheral cathexis in autistic child patients. In contrast, proprioceptive stimuli, visceral pain was keenly felt and reacted to (Mahler, 1950).

To repeat: it seemed, in Lotta's case at least, unavoidable that autonomous ego functions emerged, were put together and existed simultaneously, like a patchwork of loosely connected parts held together in a static way, without the specific matrix of "affective correlation" in the course of treatment.

This bizarre picture of scattered ego functions and the clinically clearly discernible lack of peripheral cathexis make us realize that, in autistic infantile psychosis, the vicissitudes of libido and aggression cannot be traced merely in terms of the hierarchy of zonal stages. Instead, we can in some cases trace during treatment the course of libido and aggression from the splanchnic-visceral position through progressive cathexis in cranial direction, outward onto the periphery of the body, the skin, and the sense organs, i.e., the perceptual conscious system (Mahler, 1950). The instinctual forces, both libido and aggression, exist in an unneutralized form, due to the absence of the synthetic function of the ego. There is an inherent lack of contact with the human environment.

Whenever Lotta was in great distress, her whole little body shook with tearless sobs, yet she neither sought nor accepted help from anyone, but threw herself flat on the floor and pressed against the solid support of it. Likewise she would cling to the familiar high chair, but not to father or mother. This autistic psychotic child was characterized (as were all those whom I observed) by a peculiar inability to discriminate between living

[1] Compare Hartmann, Kris, and Loewenstein (1946)

and inanimate objects, even in a perceptual sense (compare Stirnimann, 1947).

Symbiotic Infantile Psychosis

There is, however, another group of infantile psychosis in which the early mother-infant symbiotic relationship is marked but does not progress to the stage of object-libidinal cathexis of the mother. The mental representation of the mother remains, or is regressively *fused with*—that is to say, is *not* separated from the self. It participates in the delusion of omnipotence of the child patient.

Children of the symbiotic group rarely show conspicuously disturbed behavior in the first year of life except, perhaps, disturbances of sleep. They may be described by their mothers as crybabies or oversensitive infants. Their disturbance becomes apparent either gradually or fulminantly, at such crossroads of personality development at which maturational function of the ego would usually effect separation from the mother and would enable the child to master an ever-increasing segment of reality, independently of her. As soon as ego differentiation and psychosexual development confront the child and thus challenge him with a measure of separation from and independence of the mother, the illusion of the symbiotic omnipotence is threatened, and severe panic reactions occur. These reactions usually manifest themselves in the third or fourth year, or else at the height of the oedipal conflict. In other words, it would seem that a break with reality is touched off by the maturational growth of motor co-ordination which harbors the inherent challenge of motor independence, or else the complicated and differential emotional demands of the oedipal situation throw the symbiotic psychotic child into the described affective panic. In symbiotic child psychosis, unneutralized libidinal and aggressive forces have remained narcissistically vested in fused systems of mother-father-child unit, reminiscent of the primary unit (mother-infant). Landmarks of fragmentation of the ego are traumatizations through sickness, separation (for instance placement in a nursery school), birth of a sibling, and also all kinds of changes of a minor nature which upset the precarious psychobiological balance of such children. Thereby the cumulative effect of previous traumata very often plays a role. The world is hostile and threatening because it has to be met as a separate being. Separation anxiety overwhelms the brittle ego of the "symbiotic psychotic child." His anxiety reactions are so intense and so diffuse that they are reminiscent of the organismic distress of early infancy. Clinically, such children show all the signs of abysmal affective panic. These severe panic reactions are followed by restitutive productions which serve to maintain or restore the narcissistic fusion, the delusion of oneness with the mother and/or father. Restitution in symbiotic psychosis is attempted by somatic delusions and hallucinations of reunion with the narcissistically loved and hated omnipotent mother image, or sometimes by hallucinated fusion with a condensation of father-mother images. In the symbiotic infantile psychosis, reality testing remains fixated at, or regresses to, the omnipotent delusional stage of the symbiotic mother-infant relationship. The boundaries of the self and the nonself are blurred. Even the mental representation of the body-self is unclearly demarcated. These are the cases, I believe, of whom Bender (1947) was thinking when she described their body contour melting in one's own. The autistic child's body, in contrast, is uniquely unyielding and feels like a lifeless object in one's arms (Rank and Macnaughton, 1950).

A peculiar hypercathexis of one part of the body is often encountered in symbiotic psychotic children. It seems to occur in those cases of symbiotic infantile psychosis, in which parental psychopathology—the extrinsic factor in the genesis of the symbiotic psychosis—is rather prominent. In these, but by no means in all symbiotic cases, the adult partner very often seems to be able to accept the child only as long as it belongs as a quasi-vegetative being, as an appendage to her or his body.

STEVE'S mother, for instance, had a good deal of insomnia during pregnancy, due to her fears lest the baby be a boy, because her own brother had turned out so badly. Steve did not sleep enough to suit his mother. Whenever his eyes were open, she would hold him tightly in her arms for hours and would walk up and down with him until her arms were aching and numb and she could not feel her arms any more.

Is it a mere coincidence that Steve's most conspicuous symptom was going about compulsively asking everyone and also himself: "Are these my hands?" "Are those your hands?" "Can these hands kill?" "I am many people."? In his weird histrionics he compulsively enacted many characters all day long.

At four-and-a-half years, the child's extreme dependency—which his mother had previously enjoyed—so harassed her that she placed him in a boarding school, though he was still wholly dependent on her. At that time, overt and continual masturbation seems to have been the last straw to break the camel's back, as far as the mother was concerned.

In the case of one of my schizophrenic patients, the mother was pictured by the child in analysis as a "multi-pronged monster," a "giant medusa or spider," who would "wind her fat legs around my body and squash me," with all the manifestations of horror that only a schizophrenic patient can display. At the beginning of the treatment, the mother lived in another country and thus had no contact with me. Later, when she came for an interview with me, she sought my reassurance against her excessive guilt feeling, because Babette's condition might be due to the "terrible thing I did with her when she was a small baby." She went on to relate then that, since her husband frustrated her and treated her very badly, she would compensate her sensual needs—as she put it—by taking the chubby, smooth little baby between her legs, and masturbating, rubbing the little body up and down her genitals.

A psychotic child's father, whose own legs were crippled (and whose death wishes toward the son were quite overt) related to the psychiatrist that he would sneak to the crib of the infant boy night after night and examine his legs in the fear of finding something wrong with the baby son's legs. This schizophrenic child's main somatic delusions centered upon his legs.

It seems to me that these strange coincidences—this precise dovetailing of the somatic memory—traces in these pathological delusional body sensations of the symbiotic child, and the way in which the aggressive erotic appersonation was effected by the parent partner—cannot be without causal connection. The peculiar hypercathexis of one part of the body which we encountered in many symbiotic children often corresponds to the type of overstimulation which occurred during symbiotic relationships. This finding is noteworthy and deserves further careful investigation (Greenacre, 1944).

Concerning the Question of "Child Schizophrenia"

I now wish to take up a point implied by the title of this paper. I believe that all clinical evidence disproves the contention of certain psychiatrists and psychoanalysts that schizophrenia does not occur before puberty because the schizophrenic picture is based on the psychotic elaboration of the homosexual conflict. First of all, I believe that the main cause of proclivity for alienation of the ego from reality and fragmentation is the above-described grave disturbance—a specific conflict of the mother-child relationship, be it autistic or symbiotic. Second, I believe—and have much clinical evidence to show—that bisexual conflict can be, and often is prominent in the symptomatology, the production, and even the immediate genetic cause of the psychotic breakdown of the ego in childhood.[2] To establish the latter point, I would like to give two very condensed case reports.

GEORGE was just under seven when admitted to our Children's Service with fulminant symptoms of delusions and hallucinations. He had developed fairly normally to the age of three, when a sister was born. He began to have night terrors. At about the same time he began to have what his mother aptly described as "talking tantrums." He would pace the room, talking angrily to himself about something which seemed entirely irrelevant to his environment. He would mumble: "I'm a pussy cat. I'm a pussy cat. Elaine is big. I'm a pussy cat." Shortly after the baby came, he wanted to wear her clothes and often wanted to wear his mother's. He insisted that he wanted to be a girl, preferred female animals and asked his mother perseverative questions as to why he should not be a girl. At about the same time he began to be afraid of the holes in a fence which he passed, or wherever he encountered any. His father frequently used this fear as a threat, often telling him he would put him in a hole. He tried to get reassurance from his father by asking frequently: "Do you love me?"

George became a very good but asocial student. He often spoke of his sister and, again and again, of his pet kitten in school. "I have a cat at home. It's a girl cat. I like my cat. I'm a girl cat." His fear of, and wish for, castration could be traced back to his mother's pregnancy. First he developed a strange interest in barrels. He stopped and touched barrels and looked at them with extreme interest. After his preoccupation with barrels he became fascinated by pipes of all sorts which again he would have to stop and touch, commenting on their size, shape, or other characteristics. He would play with his father's pipes for long periods. After a few months he developed a similar preoccupation with electrical appliances. He would endlessly pretend to be plugging in a cord into a socket. Later he developed an intense interest in fires, and this was prevalent at the time of his hospitalization. He needed the fire to burn and to kill his sister in his hallucinations–yet in the next breath would profess to love her dearly.

In the hospital his hallucinatory and delusional restitution attempts per-

[2] Dr. Greenacre in a personal communication, originally designated as discussion remarks to this paper, said the following: ". . . in children suffering from severe and early traumata there is a condition of increased plasticity of the body responsiveness which may under certain conditions produce a severe bisexual identification. There are then bodily hallucinations of bisexual nature which persist and play an important part in the child's fantasy during the early latency period . . ."

tained to incorporative and destructive tendencies toward his sister and mother. In his clearer periods he would state: "I'm afraid of killing my mother. I have ideas of wanting to kill her. Yes, I think of killing her, and these thoughts upset me so. That gives me bad feelings in my head. It makes me so upset when I am home. Doctor, you are supposed to take that out."

On the ward he seemed to be hallucinating almost constantly. While sitting next to the nurse whom he loved and hated most, he unzipped his overalls and began pulling at the nurse's skirt as though gathering up something. He then put his hands in his overalls as if pouring in what he had gathered. This went on for a short time, then he zipped up his overalls and sat there smiling. "I've got a Hollinger [name of the nurse] in there . . . that's what I've got in there."

George was hilariously elated for the rest of the day and sat off in a corner, communicating with the introjected beloved (Klein, 1932).

It is obvious that this youngster in his childish way was making the same type of restitutive efforts to solve, albeit psychotically, his bisexual conflict as do adult schizophrenics.

This example of the bisexual conflict before puberty is far from rare. From a repertoire of such cases we select another one.

CLIFFORD, age seven, was a patient of the Children's Service, when he was six and a half, with a mixed type of childhood schizophrenia. For the first fourteen months of his life his development seemed normal, though he was never a cuddly baby and, in retrospect, seemed to have shown the characteristics of a case of early infantile autism during his second, third, and fourth years. At three and a half he became intensely jealous of his eight-month-old sister. His speech did not develop. He used stereotype phrasing which he would perseverate in a sing-song voice, and spoke of himself exclusively in the third person. He became obsessed with mechanical and electrical equipment. At five, restitutive symbiotic mechanisms became increasingly marked. Whereas up to then he had defended his secluded, autistic world, now he insisted on sharing his parents' bed and sought close contact with both of them. His bisexual conflict manifested itself in a similar way as that described in the case of George. Clifford began to bite the nurses suddenly and impulsively, for example, when he passed them in the hall. He said he "loved" the nurses, called them each carefully by name and sought their company for a type of ritualized converation consisting mostly of identifying them by name and telling his name, then naming other personnel on the ward. As his biting was discouraged, he began to dress in two handkerchiefs arranged as a skirt, a nurse's cap, and insisted, "Don't call me Clifford, call me Miss Clifford. I'm a nurse." He became anxious if this was not done, and for a period of time insisted on being called "Miss Clifford" or "Nurse Clifford."

This phase of behavior was introduced in the therapeutic sessions by a denial. "I don't want to be a girl. Girls wear dresses, boys wear pants. I don't want to be like my sister. Girls and boys are different." The above was repeated at home, but was quickly followed, as in the hospital, by the period of insistence upon wearing his younger sister's clothes and being called "Miss Clifford" also by his family.

The Function of Autism as Contrasted with that of the Mechanism of Symbiotic-Parasitic Fusion in Child Psychosis

Whereas in the symbiotic infantile psychosis panic reactions are most prominent, all observers emphasize in contrast the seemingly self-sufficient contentedness of the autistic child if only he be left alone. Any approach, any change in the environment, in the social setting, is resented as an irritating intrusion. The autistic position is defended by catatonic-like temper tantrums (Geleerd, 1945). Aggressive and destructive acts seem not to be aimed at the interfering person as a whole. The autistic child shoves away the "hand" that is in his way as he would a wooden block.

What is the nature, what is the function of this pseudo self-sufficiency of early infantile autism? It would seem that autism is the basic defense attitude of these infants, for whom the beacon of emotional orientation in the outer world—the mother was primary love object—is nonexistent. Early infantile autism develops, I believe, because the infantile personality, devoid of emotional ties to the person of the mother, is unable to cope with external stimuli and inner excitations which threaten from both sides his very existence as an entity. Autism is therefore the mechanism by which such patients try to shut out, to hallucinate away (negative hallucination) the potential sources of sensory perception, particularly those which demand affective response. If we observe such psychotic children clinically, the most striking feature is their spectacular struggle against any demand for human (social) contact which might interfere with their hallucinatory delusional need to command a static, greatly constricted segment of their inanimate environment in which they behave like omnipotent magicians (Mahler et al., 1949). It would seem that their capacity to master their inner feelings (proprioceptive excitation), their own thought processes, their own motility, their highly selective and restricted sensory awareness all but overtax their undifferentiated ego. They cannot cope with stimulation from the external world. They cannot mediate between two sets of stimuli. In short, it seems as though these patients experience outer reality as an intolerable source of irritation, without specific or further qualification.

The mechanisms which are characteristic in the *symbiotic* infantile psychosis, on the other hand, are the introjective-projective mechanisms and their psychotic elaboration, the symptomatology of which we have described in a previous paper as Group II of "schizophrenia-like" clinical pictures in children (Mahler et al., 1949b). These mechanisms aim at a restoration of the symbiotic parasitic delusion of oneness with the mother and thus are the diametric opposites of the function of autism. As far as our research could ascertain up to date, the lack of separation of the representation of the self from the representation of nonself is clinically not discernible in the first two years of life (Jacobson, 1953). Hence, clinical evidence for symbiotic conflict of the order and unequivocality which points to autistic disturbance in the first two years of life cannot be expected. But it seems that the symbiotic psychosis candidates are characterized by an abnormally low tolerance for frustration and, later, by a more or less evident lack of emotional separation or differentiation from the mother. Clinical symptoms manifest themselves between the ages of two and a half to five, with a peak of onset in the fourth year of life. These infants' reality ties depended mainly upon the early delusional fusion with the mother (unlike those of the autistic who had no reality ties to begin with). Reactions set in, as we described above, at those points of the physiological and psychological maturation process at which separateness from the mother must be perceived and faced. Figuratively speaking, it seems that from the third year onward the growing discrepancy between the rate of maturation of partial ego functions versus lag of developmental individuation causes the brittle ego of these children to break into fragments (Mahler, 1947, 1949). Agitated, catatonic-like temper tantrums and panic-stricken behavior dominate the picture; these are followed by bizarrely distorted reality testing and hallucinatory attempts at restitution. The aim is restoration and perpetuation of the delusional omnipotence phase of the mother-infant fusion of earliest times—a period at which the mother was an ever-ready extension of the self, at the service and command of "His Majesty, the Baby." In their stereotyped speech productions, one can discern the predominance of hallucinatory soliloquies with the introjected object, and their actions dramatize the same introjective reunion. These are the cases which demonstrate with obtrusive explicitness the mechanisms described by Melanie Klein (1932). The manifestations of love and aggression in these children's impulse-ridden behavior seem utterly confused. They crave body contact and seem to want to crawl into you—yet they often shriek at such body contacts or overt demonstrations of affection on the part of the adult, even though they themselves may have asked or insisted on being kissed, cuddled and "loved." On the other hand, their biting, kicking, and squeezing the adult is the expression of their craving to incorporate, unite with, possess, devour, and retain the "beloved." In other words, the restitutive mechanisms with which they wish to recapture the eluding reality are conspicuously aberrant and different from anything we observe in chronically aggressive, nonpsychotic children, or panic-stricken phobic cases—the two categories which might conceivably pose a differential diagnostic problem (Mahler, 1947).

We cannot better illustrate this desperate attempt to perpetuate the symbiotic fusion when it conflicts with the struggle for separation and individuation, accompanied by the bisexual conflict than in the words and behavior of a patient.

ALMA came to our attention on the ward at the age of fourteen. Onset of her psychosis could be traced back to the age of four and a half. At that time she had a high temperature and was hospitalized for ten days because of measles complicated by pneumonia. Her inclination to "somatization" and to bodily symbolization occurred in what seemed to be infantile pregnancy fantasies. These were indicated by the fact that during the entire period of hospitalization of ten days she had no bowel movement. After her return home her abdomen protruded enormously, as verified by several observers. From then on Alma seemed quite different: weak, sick, whimpering, and crying. During her first three days at home, she defecated constantly and her abdomen returned to normal size. Following this expulsion of feces, but not during it, she began to stutter. She became fussy about food, consistently refused all solids (warding off of oral sadistic fantasies?), and vomited frequently. She began school at the age of six but seemed to make no friends. At seven, according to her story, an older man made sexual advances to her. It is difficult to determine whether there had actually been an advance of a sexual nature or whether she had interpreted the episode in this way.

At ten, following a bad dream, Alma became very disturbed. Her "nervousness" followed upon seeing the movie "Snow White and the Seven Dwarfs." After this movie, the patient had a dream from which she woke screaming and ran to her mother. It took a long time and much coaxing to persuade Alma to explain what was bothering her: *She heard a voice saying: "Strangle your mother, strangle your mother."* She therefore was afraid to sleep in her own room and insisted on sleeping with her father, thereby displacing her mother to another room. She was taken to a psychiatrist at this point.

Alma began to feel that her friends did not like her because something was wrong with *her face. She felt* it was too skinny; later she felt that it *looked much older* than her age (approximately the age of her mother). She has become overly solicitous about her mother's health, and also overargumentative. On the ward she was constantly looking into the mirror and said that the whole ward (or world?) was a mirror image of herself. She said: "All things are two substances, soul and sex; some people and some things are primarily 'sex' (mainly women), some people combine the sex and soul feelings together (mainly men). The same feeling I have toward my mother, pertains to sex feeling." In a letter she said: ". . . *Maybe then* [at ten] *I for the first time separated from my mother and I was afraid of reality and therefore didn't give it a chance.* [3] And I cut myself off and forgot soul feelings. Like maybe *when I saw 'Snow White and the Seven Dwarfs,' somehow I was the witch and fed the girl the apple*—and I saw the prince and I saw soul and sex feelings which (feelings) in reality concern men.—*Maybe somehow I wanted to get my mother out of myself by strangulation and at the same time strangling or punishing myself* [for and by] *killing Snow White.*—All I know is, after I said, "Strangle your mother," subconsciously *I equated my mother to the witch and sort of broke away from my mother.* I felt weird inside; strange; empty: an afraid weirdness. [Then] I was no more afraid of myself anymore for a few seconds. But *for a whole year I constantly threw up and always felt like dizzy.* [4] Maybe subconsciously I was strangling myself (as the witch) or was it mother—or was it Snow White—or was it the mice that Ma killed [5]—but I imagine it was me—I thought I would sleepwalk and kill her. [6] After a few seconds I didn't feel empty but different."

One could hardly ask for a more explicit description of the steps which introduced the gradual loss of reality, the psychotic break with reality,

[3] We know from the anamnesis that in fact the first real separation and prepsychotic reaction to facing reality apart from mother occurred when Alma was four-and-a-half-years old.

[4] We again know from the anamnesis that this vomiting off and on and refusing solids (in warding off obviously oral sadistic incorporative fantasies by ejection) began at four and a half.

[5] Alma was horror-stricken when her mother actually exterminated mice in their kitchen.

[6] This was the rational reason Alma gave for sleeping with her father; to be protected from her dangerous impulse.

and the subsequent restitution mechanisms in this symbiotic psychosis. There is confusion between the self and the mother and a lack of direction between libidinal and aggressive tendencies. Both the mother and the self are confused and *fused* as the goal of unneutralized instinctual forces.

The introjected persecuting mother makes Alma fear that she looks much older than she is; she has sex feelings toward the mother, has the impulse to strangle the mother—in herself and in the outside—and then she says either that she is her mother's mirror image or again that the world is her own mirror image. "It is as if I have to live with my reflection (like when I look in the mirror) [the mother in herself] and I have to face my reflection when I see people because they are my walking or live reflections." The fusion of all three representations—self, mother and world—is expressed in her own words: "What if I am the living reflection of my mother and when I look in the mirror it is a double exposure. And I see my reflection in others and it makes me miserable . . . I go around in circles. There is no escape. I live in a world that has a plane surface, flat like my reflection in the mirror and the people I see in this world are the living reflection of myself and this sex-person that I see in the mirror isn't me. I refuse to accept that person."

The crux of the pathogenic struggle to give up the symbiotic-parasitic fusion with the parental image is clearly expressed, and the Kleinian mechanisms are strikingly illustrated by the patient when she says: "After I said, 'Strangle your mother,' subconsciously I equated my mother to the witch and sort of broke away from my mother." "But for a whole year I *constantly threw up* and always felt like dizzy. Maybe subconsciously I was strangling myself [or the mother in herself] and felt guilty for strangling myself—or was it mother—or was it Snow White [whom the witch tried to kill]—or was it the mice that Ma killed—but I imagine it was me. After a few seconds I didn't feel empty, but I felt different."

This is but a brief excerpt of the wealth of material this young girl produced. Though these productions stem from a time when she was an adolescent, we cite them here because she was actually describing the genesis of her psychosis in retrospect (as verified by her mother, sister and father) and because, with her queer talent for introspection, she has described all the aspects and functions of the symbiotic-parasitic hallucinatory mechanisms of restitution.[7]

[7] They are identical with those in symbiotic cases like George's, Betty's, etc., whom we studied or analyzed respectively from the age of five to eleven (Mahler, 1947).

Differential Diagnostic Considerations

I believe that the two types of infantile psychosis—the *autistic* versus the *symbiotic*—can, in many cases, be clearly differentiated in the beginning. Later the pictures tend to overlap. Differential diagnosis in retrospect may be attempted by reconstruction and appraisal of the earliest mother-infant relationship. The specific factor in differential diagnosis is the mother's role as reflected in the baby's nursing behavior during the process of individuation, during the period when the infant's body ego and representation of the self should emerge from the primal somato-psychic symbiotic stage and the fused representation (Jacobson, 1953). As described above, the autistic baby behaves quite differently during the nursing period from either the normal infant or the symbiotic baby. We stated that the primarily symbiotic child often cannot be detected before awareness of separateness from the mother image throws these infants into a state of panicky separation anxiety. When we meet cases of child psychosis at a later stage, it seems that pure cases of autistic child psychosis, as well as pure cases of symbiotic-parasitic psychosis, are rather rare, whereas mixed cases are frequent; by this time, symbiotic mechanisms have been superimposed on basic autistic structures and vice versa.

AN INVESTIGATION OF CHILDHOOD SCHIZOPHRENIA: A RETROSPECTIVE VIEW

WILLIAM GOLDFARB

In defining two relatively distinct groups of childhood psychosis, organic and nonorganic, Goldfarb has pursued and refined the concepts of central nervous system substrates for childhood psychosis. His massive longitudinal studies constitute perhaps the most systematic experimental approach to date, and their results support the premise of the heterogeneity of the psychoses—that they are actually different complexes, each with its own symptomatology and, probably, etiology. Goldfarb's findings suggest that the physiological predisposition to ego disturbances varies, unfolding into a distinct entity only through complementary interplay with family pathology. Kallman (1956) has studied this genetic predisposition further, emphasizing both the inheritance of a vulnerability and a lowered general capacity to compensate adequately for this vulnerability. Hartmann (1953) and Bergman and Escalona (1949) have also considered the nature of the physiological defect in psychological terms.

Goldfarb breaks through the nature-nurture controversy of etiology by relating the one to the other. The complementary interplay within a family of the two kinds of predisposing factors indicates that further clinical research in depth is sorely needed.

It is my intention to summarize the investigations in childhood schizophrenia carried on over the past ten years at the Ittleson Center for Child Research. These investigations have not constituted a very rigidly organized and totally preplanned program of research. However, primary research objectives were carefully enunciated, and each of the studies did emerge naturally out of previous ones. In this sense, they did add up to

Reprinted from *Archives of General Psychiatry,* 11, 1964, pp. 620–634.

an interrelated chain of explorations. The investigations were ordered by an evolving set of concepts and derivative hypothetical propositions. Ordinarily, when in the midst of an investigative task, the investigator is likely to dissociate the scientific undertaking from its philosophical implications. I particularly welcome the opportunity to describe the major findings of the Ittleson studies, therefore, since a distillation of the data and trends as they emerged sequentially might illuminate the scientific logic and perspective of the total endeavor. What questions did we ask? How did we set about answering them?

Paradoxically, even as we have become more conscious of the complexity of the phenomena that needed to be encompassed in a coherent study of any child designated as schizophrenic, the child himself has become more comprehensible to us. This improvement in understanding has stemmed in large measure from seeing schizophrenic children in actual process of living. The schizophrenic child became less mysterious when studied with an eye on his special adaptive strategies for dealing with his physical and social world. It is also true that, so viewed, he became more human and stimulated more familiar feelings of empathy and engagement in the observer. In the vistas afforded the observer when he examines the schizophrenic child in pertinent life process, this very disordered child is certainly not totally unlike the normal child in social and emotional response. The schizophrenic child merely seems to be equipped with a narrower repertoire of responses than is the normal child.

In our investigations into childhood schizophrenia, we have, therefore, deliberately developed our hunches within the context of psychiatric treatment based on the conscious, meaningful use of social processes. We have preferred to regard the aberrations of schizophrenic children as highly unique strategies on their part—always in adaptive response to intrapsychic and interactional processes—and oftentimes most feasibly studied on a case basis. Our therapeutic intention thus had an implicit significance far beyond its specific expression in our healing effort. It affected our speculations about childhood schizophrenia, the questions we asked, and the appeal of specific explanations for the disorders manifested by the schizophrenic child.

Clinical treatment of the children and their families encouraged alertness to the heterogeneity of schizophrenic children and their individual differences in genetic background, congenital disposition, psychosocial experience, capacity, defensive characteristic, and response to treatment. It is important to grasp that the phrase, childhood schizophrenia, tells you little about each schizophrenic child's ego strengths and limitations, his unique ontogenetic development, and the kind of therapeutic program he requires. The most profitable conceptual model engendered by a detailed view of all the factors, many of which are particularly open to view in therapy, would seem to be one in which each schizophrenic child's adaptive aberrations are seen as highly individualized accommodations to the very special requirements of his psychosocial environment. (I shall try to illustrate this point in a discussion of the process of "explanation" in reference to childhood schizophrenia.)

As will be seen, our investigations proceeded naturally from description of the schizophrenic child's behavior to efforts to explain it; i.e., to outline causes for the behavior. The children were diagnosed as schizophrenic if they showed a commonly accepted set of symptoms, such as impaired relationships, disturbances in personal identity, resistance to change, marked anxiety, perceptual difficulties, communicative defects, bizarre motility, unusual preoccupations, and sometimes, severe intellectual retardation. Yet detailed observation demonstrated great diversity among the children diagnosed as schizophrenic and, of even greater interest, wide fluctuations in all the symptoms within the same child. On further observation, these inconstancies and variations in behavioral phenomena could be linked to specific temporal and spatial circumstances. The most common behavior, for example, which was ascribed to the schizophrenic child was human withdrawal. Now, social withdrawal in these children was never absolute in the sense of being unvarying and free from external control. In fact, in our clinical experience, total and unalterable social withdrawal was never seen. [1] The fluctuations in social response can only be understood in terms of historical or developmental factors. Increasingly it became our scientific conviction that the observer needs to know why the schizophrenic child alters his social responses, and the historical course followed by the child as he becomes more or less withdrawn from moment to moment. Even more urgently, the adaptive value of the social withdrawal to the schizophrenic child at any given time needed to be understood. What special problems in adaptation had been posed for the schizophrenic child? What capacities did he have for meeting these adaptive tasks, and how did he finally adjust his capacities to the task? Why, that is, under what circumstances, did he resort to withdrawal?

[1] This has been confirmed in a systematic study of peer interaction among schizophrenics (Goldfarb and Radin, 1964) and even more dramatically demonstrated in current studies of relational and communicative behavior of schizophrenic children and their mothers (Levy et al., 1962; Meyers et al., 1963).

We may similarly ask "why" about most of the schizophrenic child's symptoms. This is another way of asking what causes the complex of phenomena we label childhood schizophrenia. To illustrate the intricacies in delineating cause in childhood schizophrenia, I ask you to join me in some clinical reflections of our therapeutic and child caring staffs. Let us view the sudden and changing adjustment of a 9-year-old schizophrenic girl whom we shall call Jane. She had been admitted two years previously with a plethora of symptoms, among which we shall stress, for the present, extreme withdrawal, sudden outbursts of aggression to other children, flat and inappropriate affective expression, multiple fears, extremely loose associations, and marked disorientation. She clung to her mother and violently resisted separations. In the first two years of treatment she improved perceptibly. She became less withdrawn, less suspicious, more confident in learning and self-care. Until the moment of the incident to be described, however, she persisted stubbornly in her efforts to possess the female counselors exclusively for herself.

With this very brief background, I now refer you to a specific sequence of events. In the first place, the staff reported in a progress conference that in the most recent period Jane had withdrawn increasingly from both the adults and children about her. However, she had attached herself to "Mary," a 12-year-old girl who was the oldest member of the group. They spent all their time together playing what the other children called "the sick mother games." One of these games involved a continuous and compulsive re-enactment of a fantasy of a mother caring for a little baby. In this play, the children assumed a shifting set of identities in which each in turn became the mother or the child and elaborately enacted an encompassing symbiotic relationship. Staff members became concerned over the total isolation of the pair from other children and the adults in the center. Jane and Mary were utilizing each other for illusory fulfillment and for gratification of the urge for total omnipotent absorption of a maternal object, with consequent loss of contact with reality. However, it is important to note that what brought the incident into special focus was the emotional intensity of the staff reaction which combined puzzlement, anxiety, and even some guilt.

In the staff discussion, some were inclined to intrude actively by separating the children physically and to discourage their playing together. Others were more properly disposed to view the mutual symbiosis as a defensive manifestation and to discourage unnecessary and aggressively manipulative intrusion by anxious or guilty adults. The appropriate question for us was why these children had to seek each other out for objects of gratification. It has been our experience that a child cannot compete with an adult in this regard provided the adult makes himself available as a parental object. When the child-caring adults explored their own behavior it became quite clear that they had indeed become inaccessible to the two children. For dynamic reasons of their own, they had reacted with anger and disgust to Jane's excessive demands for attention and body closeness. They had suppressed overt expression of these feelings; but they had withdrawn from Jane to an extent they had not recognized. Suffice it to say that Jane's behavior could not be understood without reference to the immediate social climate available to her. As a matter of fact, a shift in the adult feelings and their behavior with Jane resulted in a rapid dissolution of the Jane-Mary dyad.

Beyond our interest in the immediate social circumstances, we questioned why Jane was disposed toward defensive strategies which involved fantasies of psychic fusion with other objects. This led naturally to a detailed study of Jane's relationships to her own parents. We learned that Jane had lived in a completely unstructured atmosphere, one in which incredibly little direction, guidance, and clarity of communication had been offered. The mother was one of our most perplexed parents and was incapable of ordering a structured environment. She had never been able to oppose Jane's demands for her constant attendance and even physical contact throughout the 24 hours of the day. All other relationships were excluded. (Jane slept with the parents till the age of 3. When Jane was given her own bedroom at that age, she resisted violently and her parents finally yielded to her demands.) It was concluded that the extremely unstructured family environment, which at no point encouraged experiences of separation, accounted for Jane's ravenous demands, her fantasies of omnipotent possession of her mother, her disorientation, her confused body awareness, her fluctuant fusing of self and maternal object, her helplessness when physically alone, and her violent resistance to separations.

To explain the "perplexed" family environment, Jane's parents were explored psychodynamically. Jane's mother was a bright college graduate who presented a picture of helplessness with Jane. She was unable to counter any of Jane's demands and seemed unable to gratify Jane in a posed, appropriate way. What emerged in treatment of the mother was an unyielding craving for nurturance for herself, and thus an identification with Jane's tyrannizing demands. She also harbored enormous, unconscious rage, since Jane's demands were experienced as traumatic rather than maternally gratifying. She could not accept consciously her fury to Jane, however, and her resultant behavior was total assertive paralysis.

What about the father? He showed himself to be an ineffective, unusually inactive individual, both in relation to his wife and to his children. For psychodynamic reasons of his own, he made no move to intrude on Jane's total possession of her mother. (Throughout Jane's life, he acceded to the sleeping arrangement in which he was discharged from his bed and Jane slept with her mother.)

This account of Jane, a schizophrenic girl, is necessarily abbreviated; but does serve to illustrate a number of principles basic to the investigation of cause in childhood schizophrenia. The symptoms of childhood schizophrenia are biological events in the sense of being behavioral processes with adaptive significance. Thus the restitutive value to Jane of her absorption of Mary has been noted. It also represented an accommodation to immediate psychosocial circumstances, specifically the resentful withdrawal of the counselors. Beyond this, the immediate events at the Center were facilitated by a predisposing set of circumstances. Her addictive craving for physical union with her mother, like an altered metabolism, dominated her thoughts and wishes. Further, her stubborn demands for a highly undifferentiated relationship with her mother had been rather firmly fixed by an unusual set of familial circumstances during her early years. Obviously, explanations of purposeful behavior in a child, disordered or not, must refer to the value of the behavior to the child and, beyond this, to the functional impact of the behavior on the psychosocial community which elicits the behavior.

It is also justifiable to talk of levels of cause in which time is the referent. Thus, there are always both immediate and more distant causes. In Jane's case, the emotional withdrawal of the adults at the Center is an immediate cause. Jane's experience in early life within her family is a distant cause. More distantly, perhaps, would be the influence of genetic factors. I am sure you would agree, however, that any attempt to explain the purposeful behavior of a schizophrenic child such as Jane by reference solely to a single factor, remote in time, will not throw satisfactory light on adaptive phenomena which are linked to very specific points in time and space.

Up to now, I have stressed that it is more pertinent to study the schizophrenic child in life process than it is to study the professional abstraction termed "childhood schizophrenia." I have implied that the childhood schizophrenic is not characterized by a specific disease entity but rather that he is a child with ego manifestations and, particularly, deficits to which we assign the characterizing label. Each schizophrenic child's manifestations express his efforts to survive within the demands, expectations, and boundaries of inner and outer predisposition and structure. This point of view represents a kind of field theory in which the individual child's intrapsychic organization and his outward behavior always reflect accommodations to his environment, especially his family. Of course, the schizophrenic child also plays his own unique role in the family. The approach can best be implemented through the longitudinal study of individual children.

However, the individual case studies provided hunches for systematic investigation. If we now proceed to more experimental and observational investigation, which of necessity analyzes more arbitrary segments of behavior than the case study, it is obvious that the investigator may focus selectively on different aspects of the schizophrenic child and his world. In regard to etiologies, one might look at either immediate or distant factors. Again one might concentrate on the child in terms of his own adaptive capacities or on his family as a psychosocial unit. We have preferred to focus on the reciprocating influence of the child and his environment. We were not in a position to observe a growing child in process of becoming "schizophrenic." Generally speaking, therefore, our program of investigation utilized postulational methods. In other words, a general conceptual model for schizophrenia was first formulated on the basis of the data and material of clinical and therapeutic observation. From this model, a set of postulates were deduced and utilized as propositions to explore experimentally. To bridge the gap between our speculative theories and our continuing clinical observations, we formulated assumptions that were operational and definitions that were empirical. Hopefully this will become clear as I refer briefly to the substantive findings of our investigations.

Our studies of schizophrenic children moved forward through a series of overlapping stages. To assist you as I present the more expanded summary of the investigations, I should like first to outline very briefly the argument and the four approximately sequential steps followed by the projects:

Stage 1. Because of the universally acknowledged problems of classification and the obvious behavioral heterogeneity of schizophrenic children, our first objective was a precise *descriptive differentiation of schizophrenic children* from normal children in behavioral functions that a child requires in order to orient himself to reality and to seek gratification of elementary needs. We anticipated additionally that this study would offer leads for a system of subdividing the children, would suggest etiologic possibilities, and would enable us to initiate a longitudinal study of the children.

Stage 2. The study of purposeful behavior alerted us to the important *processes of self-awareness* which accompany every action of the child. We, therefore, began to explore self-awareness in children as an accompaniment of goal directed behavior.

Stage 3. This led directly to a study of *processes for monitoring and controlling purposeful action and the awareness of self in action.*

Stage 4. In studying the impairments in their adaptive response, in self-awareness, and in control processes, it seemed most probable that factors within the child and in his psychosocial environment were contributing causes. We began to study *cause in childhood schizophrenia in terms of a multiplicity of factors* and concentrated particularly on neurological factors in the child and on psychosocial factors in the family. In recent years we have invested more of our attention in the detailed study of the relational behavior of schizophrenic children in interaction with their surrounding environment, beginning with an analysis of communicational interactions of schizophrenic children and their mothers.

1. *Descriptive Differentiation of Schizophrenic Children in Terms of Adaptive Functions.*—The first phase of investigations, therefore, contrasted a group of schizophrenic children with a group of normal children in behavioral functions for contacting, testing, and manipulating reality (Goldfarb, 1961). It was proposed that the diagnosis of childhood schizophrenia refers to observed deficits in adaptation at all levels, that is, perceptual, integrative, and executive. Interest thus centered on self-regulative functions such as sensation, perception, categorical behavior, motor response, and language. The schizophrenic children are not distinguished from normals in visual and auditory acuity. Similarly there is evidence of elementary pain sensibility (Goldfarb, 1958a). However, the schizophrenic children are very impaired in the organization of sensory stimuli into forms and patterns. This is demonstrated through tests which measure the ability to perceive wholes when fragmented stimuli are presented (Street Figures) and the ability to separate figures from ground (Gottschaldt test). The perceptual impairment is also shown in tests of ability to differentiate body cues (Esthesiometer, Finger Location test)—cues which are prerequisite for the achievement of an integrated body image. Similarly, the schizophrenic children as a group are deficient in conceptual functions. Defects in these higher processes are demonstrated in tests of categorical response (e.g., Weigl test); orientation to time, place, and person; and body representation (Human Figure Drawing). The schizophrenic child's impairments in ego are reflected in a lowering of his

functional intelligence as manifested in his performance in tests of intelligence. (Wechsler Intelligence Scale for Children.) Finally, the schizophrenic child is inferior in psychomotor response (Lincoln-Oseretsky test). In summary a very extensive battery of observations has confirmed a massive impairment in abilities to assign patterned form to stimulus input, to organize the incoming information into working categories, and to execute adaptive acts on the basis of these schemata.

From the beginning, we have had an interest in understanding how the schizophrenic child deals with the task of bridging distance between himself and others, and we have studied his modes of communication. We have been particularly interested in the various aspects of voice and speech which are necessary for emotional and connotative communication. They enable the child to articulate multiple levels of meaning in a way that is comprehensible to others. Schizophrenic children are always aberrant in this capacity for metacommunicative expression (Goldfarb, 1961, Goldfarb, et al. 1956). It is of significance, however, that the speech deficiencies differ from one schizophrenic child to another and that what is often termed "schizophrenic" speech really refers to speech that is a variant from normal expectancy. It is also true that the absence of such standard cues for multilevel expression has the effect of further alienating the listener from the schizophrenic child. What is then referred to as "flat" speech in the schizophrenic child may be any one of a number of idiosyncratic speech forms.

2. *Self-Awareness Process.*—All these studies unequivocally show that schizophrenic children suffer defects in orientative and manipulative functions that are normally the foundation of self-regulative behavior. These impairments are in turn linked to extreme defects in self awareness. Impairments in self-awareness are most dramatically represented in the schizophrenic child's difficulties in achieving a unified body image, clearly articulated and constant in respect to time. Aside from the experimental findings which confirm major gaps in ability to perceive, discriminate, localize, and give meaning to body percepts, the children present us with a continuous flood of naturalistic evidence that they do not possess integrated and stable body awareness. The body is experienced as broken, fragmented, disintegrating, and lacking intact body boundaries. Confusion may refer to sex or body size or the rhythmic predictability of body processes. Schemata for categorizing body sensations are absent and these sensations remain very vague and diffused, so that comfort-discomfort, pain-pleasure, tension-complacency, beginnings and endings are not articulated.

The disturbances in goal directed behavior, on the one hand, and in awareness of self, on the other, are manifestly linked. This association reminds us more positively that in the normal child self-regulative functions are accompanied by a set of inner feelings and images. We have termed these internal feelings and images self-awareness. The child moves his lips and eventually learns "I am moving my lips." The inner embodiment of self thus derives from the child's recognition of himself as the performer of purposeful action. He not only hears a sound but also communicates to himself "I know I hear a sound." Or on seeing, he communicates to himself "I know that I see." He gradually becomes aware of his own responsibility and capacity for intended response and eventually conceptualizes the boundaries between himself and the outer world.

Rather early too, he recognizes the permanence, the wholeness, and predictability of the self and the nonself. He experiences a feeling state of inner and outer familiarity. Schizophrenic children repeatedly remind us of the significance of such experimental familiarity, for in its absence, massive reactions of panic and anger are to be observed. (Because these reactions are in response to a very elemental experience of unfamiliarity, I have called these states "Primordial anxiety."

3. *Control Processes.*—The findings I have just reported stimulated speculation about processes for monitoring or controlling adaptive action and its accompanying inner state, self-awareness.

All purposeful conduct is guided by reports fed back to the organism in the course of action. The feedback for control purposes may be conscious or it may be unconscious. The monitoring stimuli may be completely internal; e.g., the kinesthetic information released by the movement of a leg which guides coordinated walking. Or the monitoring information may be initiated by the outer environment in response to the organism's activity. This kind of response by the outer environment acts to reinforce behavior in the natural repertoire of children in a differential way through the use of rewards and punishments. So defined, goal directed conduct in the child involves inbuilt machinery for informational feedback (perception), processing (conceptualizing), and differential response to reward and punishment. In addition it is a social process since the child adapts to the external environment in accord with the reinforcement contingencies provided by a human environment which responds to the child's behavior by pertinent and discriminable word and action.

In view of the schizophrenic child's deficiencies in self-regulative conduct, we found ourselves intensely interested in the control processes available to him. Aberrations have been noted in four areas of control of purposive behavior; namely

A. Receptor behavior
B. Conceptual behavior
C. Hedonic behavior
D. External psychosocial reinforcement

A. Receptor Aberrations: Clinical observations showed that schizophrenic children avoided the use of the distance receptors (vision, hearing) as a basis for orienting themselves, and they made relatively more use of proximal receptors (Goldfarb, 1956). It was proposed that this failure to utilize vision and hearing reduced the capacity of the children to anticipate and to conceptualize. In an experiment (Pollack and Goldfarb, unpublished) for the measurement of optikinetic nystagmus, using a rotating drum, we have been able to demonstrate the gating out of visual stimuli. In this experiment, normal children typically showed optikinetic nystagmus, such as one ordinarily shows on watching a moving object. However, schizophrenic children did not show an equal degree of optikinetic response, so that we have inferred an avoidance of visual engagement. Their diminished use of the eyes for guiding purposeful action has been further supported by experiments testing oculomotor response and another experiment which tested the improvement of discriminative response to tactile stimuli with eyes open over the response with eyes closed (Goldfarb, 1961). A similar exclusion of hearing in the control and monitoring of speech by the schizophrenic has been demonstrated in the delayed feedback experiment (Goldfarb, 1961, 1958b). In this experiment, the artificial delay in return of air conducted sound of the child's speech to the speaker alters the speech of the normal child; but does not alter that of the schizophrenic child.

Longitudinal studies of schizophrenic children have confirmed that reduced responsiveness to vision and hearing are a defensive adjustment to earlier hypersensitivity. This agrees with an auditory startle experiment comparing the responses of normal and schizophrenic children to a sudden loud sound (100 db sound at 3,000 cycles per second). In the startle experiment, the most marked extremes of hypersensitivity and hyposensitivity are found exclusively in the schizophrenic group (Goldfarb, 1961). There seems little doubt that schizophrenic children manifest alterations in the availability of hearing and seeing as instruments for monitoring executive action.

B. Conceptual Aberrations: Not only do the restrictions in perceptual response limit the possibilities for anticipatory behavior, but there is also evidence of defect in many schizophrenic children in capacity for abstraction and categorization of incoming stimuli (Goldfarb, 1961). It has seemed to us that this defect in integrative processing often reflects a primary cognitive defect. However, in the case of other schizophrenic children, motivational determinants often appear to be limiting their will to conceptualize entirely or to be restricting compliant acceptance of cultural generalizations.

C. Hedonic Aberrations: The schizophrenic children are extremely deficient in responses of pleasure and pain (Goldfarb, 1958a). The narrowing of pleasurable and painful response refers to inner feelings of awareness, to communication of these feelings, and thus to the availability of these feelings for purposes of organizing and integrating action. This means the dynamic force behind integrated behavior is lacking. Even more significantly, this deficiency limits the schizophrenic child's accessibility to the learning essential for growth of ego; inasmuch as the environment can barely provide appropriate contingencies for reinforcing behavioral differentiation. It is extremely difficult to ascertain his inner thoughts and feelings and even more, how to punish and how to reward him.

D. Aberrations in Psychosocial Reinforcements: The study of receptor aberrations illuminates the schizophrenic child's insufficient use of stimulus information released by his own actions for purposes of monitoring these actions. Similarly, he defensively dampens the impact of information from the external material and social environment. However, it has also seemed to us that the families of many schizophrenic children do not offer responses to the children's behavior that are clearly articulated, discernible, pertinent, and reinforcing. We have particularly been impressed clinically and in controlled, direct observation, by a parental response characterized by parental passivity, lack of spontaneity, absence of empathy with reduced awareness of the child's needs for gratification, and unusual absence of control and discipline. This is a "grey" environment which does not enhance the development of complex functions and discriminations. We have labelled this type of parental paralysis "parental perplexity" (Goldfarb et al., 1958c; Meyers and Goldfarb, 1961).

The environmental possibilities for facilitating refined discriminative response and awareness are diminished when the social environment's (parents') own range of responsiveness is narrowed. We have speculated that the child requires the referential feedback from his external environment through his extroceptors, as much as the information released within himself by his own actions, in order to sustain and coordinate his purposeful action. To test this hunch, we turned to the important area of communication. In one study of speech, we were able to demonstrate that the speech of mothers of schizophrenic children is abnormal compared to the speech of mothers of normal children (Goldfarb, unpublished). This confirms the proposition that the maternal speech model available to the schizophrenic child is a poor one for him to imitate if he is to attain culturally demanded speech forms. However, I have also proposed that the speech of some of the parents of schizophrenic children is so narrow in range or so lacking in differentiated form and patterning as to provide insufficient vocal anchoring to the child in his own attempts to attain complex speech forms. It was not feasible to test this hypothesis experimentally by using an actual mother of a schizophrenic as a source of response contingencies. However, a speech expert in our research team with a finely attuned ear was able to train herself to duplicate the speech of one of our mothers. This mother had such incredibly restricted range of phonative, tonal, and melodic expression that affective and connotative significance was totally lacking in her speech. A rotation experiment was designed in which the normal child conversed with the adult who alternately employed her normal speech pattern and the monotone speech imitating that of the mother of the schizophrenic child (Goldfarb, unpublished). Typically, when the adult responded in "flat" monotone speech, the speech of the normal preschool child deteriorated perceptibly. He lost the normal vocal forms he was able to demonstrate when the adult used normal speech. Older normal children showed similar shifts but were less vulnerable or dependent on adult speech. In accord with the delayed feedback results and conclusions, schizophrenic children showed no shifts in speech under the varying conditions of adult response.

As we investigated the highly fluctuant processes of self-awareness in schizophrenic children as these processes grow out of adaptive conduct, it became increasingly clear that self-awareness in itself was a behavioral and adaptive process dependent for its integrity on monitoring processes similar to those described more generally for all behavior. The knowledge "I know I am doing" in the course of "doing" implies a continuous return of perceptual information, and a categorization of the information by conceptual generalization. Although this has been known and reported more or less explicitly by others (Erikson, 1950; Meade, 1934; Sullivan, 1953), it came to us as an exquisite personal discovery that awareness of self (comparable to personal identity) is not an established, unalterable "thing" each person possesses under all circumstances. Rather, it refers to a social process highly dependent at every moment in time on outer cues as well as internal information. In the event that the guiding effects of a constant input of stimuli was altered or lacking, the child became utterly confused and then apprehensive to an incredible degree. Examples of this sequence of events were noted in situations in which the eyes or ears were covered, or the physical setting was altered or became unstructured, or the same person presented himself to the child in different settings.

I have already suggested that the delayed feedback experiment confirms the proposition that schizophrenic children do not employ auditory feedback for the monitoring of speech. When the auditory sidetone is delayed, the speech of schizophrenic children does not change, whereas the speech of the normal child is undermined. This by no means implies that hearing is totally excluded by the schizophrenic child. It seems rather to be screened out in relation to the specific act of speech. That there is hearing is verified by other changes in functions of orientation and recognition. Self-awareness in the schizophrenic children is interfered with while that in normals is not. The schizophrenic children cannot recognize the voice, become very confused, and then extremely frightened.

The inner experience of awareness of the self as a unitary continuing whole requires a constant anchoring to a world of inner and outer perceptions. When the usual perceptual environment is altered, frightening feelings of disorientation and unfamiliarity may be expected. It is also true that the entire range of internal imagery and feeling, as well as the verbal articulation of these inner events represented in phrases such as "I like," or "I dislike," or "I hate," or "I feel miserable," are related to processes of self-awareness. They, too, are internal discriminative and categorical responses which are socially determined. They are elaborated and refined under the reinforcing influence of a responsive environment which uses an elaborate system of communicative cues.

It thus seemed to us that a variety of factors could influence the proficiency with which the child adapts and is conscious he is adapting. Similarly, a variety of factors, inside and outside the schizophrenic child, could contribute to his deficiencies in self-directive action and awareness. These were seen to include intrinsic limitations in perceptual and integrative capacities as a result of cerebral dysfunction and extrinsic limitations in the environment's responses for purposes of reinforcement of the child's behavior. I should like now to go on to a discussion of studies pertaining to this model of etiology, which developed at this phase of our investigations.

4. *Organismic and Environmental Factors: The Hypothesis of Multiple Causation.*—In initiating our investigations, we were conscious of the necessity for achieving a suitable degree of homogeneity in diagnosis and classification. We already had on hand the descriptive systems of a number of important workers, and it seemed to us we had a suitable set of criteria for diagnostic classification. In preparation for this report, I have reviewed our early diagnostic notes. These early diagnostic criteria, which still pertain in our clinical selection, may again be summarized briefly as follows: conspicuous defects in human relationships (withdrawal or inappropriate response), unusual preoccupations, defects in self-awareness, bizarre mannerisms, deviant motility, disturbances in communication (mutism, echoic vocalizations, symbolic defects, deviations in melody and intonation), marked resistance to change, cognitive and perceptual impairments, panic states.

Yet it is perfectly clear that each of these criteria is broadly defined and each is subject to varying interpretation. Nor do all workers agree that all of the criteria apply in all cases. In actual fact, the criteria mentioned constitute a very gross filter indeed, and the children whom it succeeds in extracting turn out to be extremely heterogeneous, whether viewed globally or in terms of single, carefully defined functions. On the one hand, one sees a child totally lacking in speech, restless, whirling spontaneously, disinterested in any person or object, undiscriminating of all persons and to all appearances lacking in fantasy or cognitive capacity. On the other hand, another child is very verbal, extremely bright, but obsessively perseverating, overly distrustful and suspicious. He is dominated by projective fears of his own destruction by the other people in his environment and protects himself by a complicated system of magic rituals. In these two brief illustrations, the children are truly distinguished in their capacities, social responsiveness, range of pleasure, the substantive content of their anxieties, sensory responsiveness, defensive behavior. Their two families differ as psychosocial units; and, as it developed, one child improved dramatically in treatment, and the other child remained clinically unchanged. One does not have to proceed beyond clinical experience, therefore, to be certain that schizophrenic children differ among themselves in symptoms, developmental course, and in ultimate status.

Of course, such descriptive heterogeneity does not in itself imply etiologic heterogeneity. Yet schizophrenic children do fluctuate dramatically in behavior, and it has frequently been possible to link these behavioral fluctuations with psychosocial factors impinging on the child. It has also been possible to explain the specific behavior as an adaptive accommodation of the schizophrenic child, with his own predispositions and capacities, to specific environmental tasks.

Such an approach, of course, is disposed to relate the descriptive heterogeneity of a group of schizophrenic children to etiologic heterogeneity. We have preferred the hypothesis that there are multiple and, preferably, combined causes for the many behavioral impairments of diagnosed schizophrenic children. Two general categories of cause were proposed, namely intrinsic organismic causes within the child himself and extrinsic psychosocial or environmental factors. Organismic factors, asserting themselves at birth, include the factors of heredity and reproductive complication. Psychosocial factors are particularly represented in the influences of the child's family. Each schizophrenic child may be viewed as a reflection of varying combinations of both these factors. The combinations were considered along a continuum. At one end of the continuum intrinsic inadequacies in the child would be primary; and at the other end psychosocial factors would be dominant. This is a heuristic model, of course, but one which conformed with our clinical experience. Thus, clinically, we would place at one pole of the continuum the severely incapacitated child whose family is well functioning as a climate for rearing children and in whom we find increased evidence of cerebral dysfunction. At the other pole would be the child in whom we find no evidence of neurological or other somatic disturbance but whose family is extremely disordered.

In our earliest observations, we were impressed by what seemed like gross anatomic and structural deviation in many of the schizophrenic children. This clinical observation was confirmed by a comparative study of anatomic stigmata in schizophrenic and normal children (Botstein and Goldfarb, unpublished). The schizophrenic children showed a significantly higher incidence of physical stigmata and were also more typically characterized by multiple stigmata. We interpreted these findings to reflect a factor of somatic inadequacy in some of the children.

Following this, to explore the possibility of neurological impairment in the schizophrenic children, a series of classical neurological tests were standardized for purposes of experimental use (Goldfarb, 1961; Pollack and Goldfarb, 1957; Pollack and Krieger, 1958). In a comparison of neurological test responses of diagnosed schizophrenic and normal children, the schizophrenic children were inferior in motor coordination, perceptual discrimination, body imagery, muscle tone, balance, posture, and righting behavior. We were conscious of the possibility that functional factors might have produced some of the disordered responses. For example, it was conceivable that extremes of impulsivity or inhibition could affect motor coordination. Similarly, excessive emotional compliance and passivity might have facilitated the absence of good body tone. Or the deficiencies in self-awareness might be responsible for the directional confusion and disordered body image. Nevertheless, such defects are found more typically among children with brain damage rather than among normals; and primary cerebral dysfunction was inferred to be a contributing factor in the adaptive deficiences of some of the children.

At the same time, independent neurological appraisal was made by a child neurologist who had no access to any other case material. When the neurologist was required to give a summed estimate in which subtle manifestations were given weight, a very high percentage of the children were considered to give positive evidence of neurological disability in either examination or history (Goldfarb, 1961).

In a subsequent study (Taft and Goldfarb, 1964), a more controlled comparison of the reproductive histories of schizophrenic children, their siblings, and normal controls confirmed the greatest incidence of prenatal and perinatal complications in the schizophrenic group. This study used three sources of information, that is, hospitals, physicians, and mothers. The most telling evidence of reproductive complication in the histories of diagnosed childhood schizophrenics came from hospital records which were made at birth and could not, of course, have anticipated which of the children would become known as schizophrenic.

Using the neurological diagnosis for subdividing the children into those with ("organic") and those without ("nonorganic") neurological impairment, two groups of children with extremely different ego capacities emerge. The "nonorganic" children surpass the "organic" children in many functions. In comparing the schizophrenic subdivisions and normals, the capacity gradient from highest to lowest is: normals superior to "nonorganic" schizophrenics who are in turn superior to "organic" schizophrenics. Although other factors are probably operating, this capacity gradient reflects the behavioral restrictions imposed on the "organic" child by his cerebral dysfunction. He is most impaired in perception, discrimination of body cues, orientation to his own body, postural and righting responses, conceptualization, and psychomotor ability.

Of special interest are a number of behavioral variations that are found overwhelmingly in the "organic" subcluster of schizophrenic children.

What particularly brings these observations to our attention is the fact that, while they have been referred to in the past as characteristics of childhood schizophrenia, they are in fact more uniquely linked to cerebral dysfunction. Two deviations of this kind are offered as illustrative. One is the occurrence of the whirling phenomenon, stressed in Bender's writings (1947), in which the child tends to whirl his entire body when his head is turned passively. The other is the phenomenon of extreme receptor hypersensitivity, manifested either in reactions of excruciating discomfort (hypersensitivity) or a total defensive exclusion (hyposensitivity) when an intense sensory stimulus is presented. In the auditory startle experiment, previously mentioned, the very extreme reactions are found almost exclusively in the "organic" schizophrenic group (Goldfarb, 1961).

In view of the descriptive imprecision of the diagnosis of childhood schizophrenia, the experiments were evaluated to determine what functional impairments might be considered characteristic of childhood psychosis (Goldfarb, 1961). Using the criterion of observational and experimental data which did not differentiate "organic" and "nonorganic" schizophrenic children but did distinguish both groups from the normal, the findings point to three major behavioral deviations of diagnostic significance in our data: (1) abnormal receptor behavior, in which the central finding is auditory and visual inattention (exclusion of the distance receptors), (2) deficient self-awareness, and (3) deficient communication. These findings do not preclude the likelihood of other characteristic phenomena in childhood psychosis, since our data were limited by the very methods employed. A delineation of levels of socialization, for example, is now being attempted on the basis of clinical observation. However the three adaptive impairments noted above may be considered among the primary impairments of schizophrenic children, provided primary characteristics are defined as those common to all schizophrenic children and totally absent in normal children.

The specification of the two clusters of schizophrenic children by the criterion of neurological impairment has been of inestimable value in the study of the families of schizophrenic children. If one accepted the view that a variety of causes could produce similar adaptive impairments in children, then it seemed reasonable to assume that psychosocial influences of the family in regard to the deviations of schizophrenic children might differ from child to child. Further, such influences might be determining factors in the case of some of the children and less so in the case of others. To treat the whole group of schizophrenic children as one, therefore, would tend to becloud the actual impact of family environment. Therefore, assays of family interaction were made separately for "organic" and "nonorganic" subclusters.

In one series of investigations, a method of participant observation of the families was developed (Behrens and Goldfarb, 1958; Behrens and Sherman, 1959; Goldfarb, 1961). In this method a trained family observer visits the family for three hours, including a meal time. All family members, including the child, are present. The observer focuses on interactions between the parents in their roles as marital partners and parents, between the children and parents on the family as a whole. The families are then rated on a large number of scales appraising interactions. The summed rating (Family Adequacy Score) is presumed to represent a quantified estimate of the families' capacity to supply sufficient and appropriate contingencies for the reinforcement of the innumerable facets of normal ego development in the child. With these scales it has been possible to test the postulate that psychosocial factors are more characteristic determinants in the case of the "nonorganic" children than in the case of the "organic" children (Goldfarb, 1961, 1962). This hunch has indeed been confirmed. The Family Adequacy Scales demonstrate the superior psychosocial adequacy of families of normal children over those of the schizophrenic group as a whole. What is even more pertinent is the differentiation of "organic" and "nonorganic" children. The families of the children with cerebral dysfunction, the "organic" group, are not significantly different from those of the normal children. However, the families of the "nonorganic" children are typically inferior to those of normal children in their interactional conduct. This finding would in itself buttress the Ittleson Center diagnostic differentiation of schizophrenic subclusters on the basis of neurological assay.

Our etiologic differentiation of schizophrenic children received further support in an investigation of the psychiatric status of the parents and siblings (Meyers and Goldfarb, 1962). Twice as many mothers of the "non-organic" children as mothers of the "organic" schizophrenic children are schizophrenic; and the mean adjustment rating of the siblings of the "nonorganic" children is lower than that of the siblings as the "organic" schizophrenic children. (Fathers are not distinguished.) In this study we were able to demonstrate the force of psychosocial impact of the schizophrenic parent since families in which one or both parents are schizophrenic showed lower family adequacy ratings than those families of schizophrenic children in which neither parent was schizophrenic.

Most recently, we have been engaged in a systematic effort to test the transactional nature of the symptoms of the schizophrenic child by analyzing how the schizophrenic child and his mother affect each other by their behavioral and communicational interactions (Levy et al., 1962; Meyers et al., 1963). A standardized 20 minute visit is fully recorded by movies and tape. This procedure, which was derived from Levy's early study of the behavioral relations of nursing babies and their mothers (Levy, 1958), uses observations of small specimens of behavior to the highest extent and exhaustively exploits their possibilities as independent sources of information.

This method of relational analysis would seem to us to contain dramatic possibilities for discovery, for it views directly the moment of mutual impingement between mother and child. It lends itself to an analysis of the kind and quality of reinforcement contingencies provided the child by his mother and, on the other hand, the stimulus value of the child's responses to his mother.

Our first program restricted itself to the analysis of communicational clarity. An extensive system for classifying and coding communicational clarity has been developed, and we are now classifying errors in communication in the mother-schizophrenic child interaction. An example, out of the large number of errors that we have coded, is discordance between the mother's expression and the child's level of comprehension. Consider the following: A mother visits her 10-year-old boy at the Ittleson Center. He greets her with a French word *"Combien."* (We learn after the visit that this apparently meaningless word was an error on his part. He had actually had a French lesson that day and had meant to say *"Comment allez vous?"* in an effort to win his mother's praise.) His mother does not, on the one hand, express her puzzlement about *"Combien"* and does not insist on an explanation that clarifies for her so that he may sound less incoherent. On the other hand, she misses entirely his natural desire for praise. She says "Are you speaking French already?" and then "You couldn't have learned it all in a couple of days. There must still be some left to do." This remark distresses him, since he thinks she is saying he has not studied his lessons, whereas she is actually using an adult variety of sarcastic humor to imply you cannot learn language after two lessons, which were all he had. He says "I did really my studies." Eight minutes later, he persists "Mommy, how come you said I couldn't learn it all yet?"

This type of communicational analysis should eventually throw a great deal of light on the task each communicant in the mother-schizophrenic child dyad presents to the other. On the other hand, we are impressed that more and more of the errors we are finding, such as the error in reciprocal comprehension noted above, do occur–in much milder form, of course—in ordinary mother-child relationships. Our study thus has a great bearing on communication among normal mother-child dyads.

If I may recapitulate, I have identified two clusters of children among schizophrenic children and have attempted to document their investigative value. Each of these classes of disorder, to be sure, is nonspecific and in themselves inclusive of many varieties of children. Now I should like to emphasize that the symptoms of all the children in both subclusters can only be understood in terms of intrapsychic and interpersonal dynamics, that is, in terms of their adaptive and survival value for each child. Each schizophrenic child needs to be explored longitudinally in terms of physiological and ego predisposition and in terms of the interplay between the child and his family. This essential kind of interactional analysis is as applicable to clinical research of the "organic" children as of the "nonorganic" children. As an example, we have been able to find clear illustrations of the value of a transactional approach in recent clinical investigations of the longitudinal development of children who show sensory hypersensitivity. It is clear in each case that the hypersensitivity represents a specific challenge for the parents; and on the other hand, the parents' responses to the hypersensitivity represent an adaptive task to the children. In the case of the schizophrenic children, the net impact of the environmental response has been aversive so that the hypersensitive receptor modality is avoided.

I have now concluded the essential logic of our explorations. I want to mention one further study which is of primary importance, since it will ultimately improve our understanding of schizophrenic children. Along with other observers, we have been concerned about the ultimate destiny of children diagnosed as schizophrenic. In clarifying this matter, an answer would also be found to the question of relationship between childhood schizophrenia of very early onset and adult schizophrenia. In view of the absence of precise diagnosis in the first place and the highly selective character of each sampling, significant follow-up would entail clear, detailed, reliable description of the specific group of children included in follow-up. At the Ittleson Center we are in the midst of a longitudinal investigation of a group of schizophrenic children which should ultimately total about 100 children. Systematic behavioral observations are repeated at regular intervals. The focus is on the observation and recording of patterns of longitudinal change of individual children. Though extremely difficult, the summation of individuals in process of change has a unique validity and is particularly feasible in a comprehensive treatment setting.

In addition to establishing what the ultimate clinical status of diagnosed schizophrenic children will be, the data will permit us to elaborate in great detail their growth in many behavioral dimensions.

In concluding, even as I have been recalling the longitudinal trajectory of our research effort, I am conscious that I have presented few entirely novel hunches. However, it has been my conviction that our speculations became part of a scientific methodology only insofar as we have been able to implement them empirically in the form of appropriate experimental and observational operations. In so doing, we have been able to move continuously from one stage of research knowledge to another. Finally, we have, in fact, enjoyed that unique satisfaction that comes to the investigator when it would seem he has found harmonious accord between data and hypothesis.

THE SPACE CHILD

RUDOLF EKSTEIN AND DOROTHY G. WRIGHT

The psychological phenomenon of schizophrenia seems best understood if viewed through the window of therapeutic interaction–the bridge between the world of primary and secondary process. The treatment situation with the borderline child provides a particularly favorable setting for the study of disturbed ego functioning.

It seems fitting to close the section on psychosis with this clinical vignette, which illustrates the inner workings of psychosis through the long-term treatment of 11-year-old Tom. Such studies are rare, perhaps because of the controversial nature of the disease entity. Ekstein's term, "schizophrenoid," is one of many used to designate borderline disturbances; some others are: schizophreniclike, prepsychotic, schizoid, atypical (Geleerd, 1946, 1958; Rosenfeld and Sprince, 1963, 1965; Weil, 1953).

Ekstein assigns special significance to the ego's distancing mechanisms of space and time (projection and introjection), that is, lengthening or shortening the distance between it and the object. While this case illustrates the concept that the borderline patient is one in whom there are marked, sudden, and frequent fluctuations in ego states without gross precipitating phenomena, the question may be raised as to whether children who remain *severely neurotic or mildly psychotic should also be included under this diagnositc category. Ekstein (1966) points up the primitive, unintegrated defenses of these youngsters. He notes that, within a span of several sessions, the ego organization of the borderline child fluctuates in its use of autistic, symbiotic, and neurotic relationship modes, thereby reflecting the coexistence of different ego organizations. He adds, "The timing and content of the space fantasies, which appear so frequently in the treatment of these children, have led us to assign to them a special psychological meaning as distance defenses, whose collective function it is to achieve maximal distance from the unconscious conflict and the conscious ego. Space fantasy is the safety valve which permits the maintaining of the neurotic relationship while at the same time representing a necessary return to more regressed modes of relationship."*

Reprinted with permission from *Bulletin of the Menninger Clinic,* 16, 1952, pp. 211–224, copyright 1952 by the Menninger Foundation.

From the Pullman car little Tommy watched his parents on the train platform. He attempted nervously to get their attention and finally began to pound on the window. He got more and more frightened, and amidst pounding and sobbing he yelled to his travelling companion: "They won't even look at me." Only as the train started to move did the parents look up and wave goodby, while Tommy pressed his tear-stained face against the glass. Tommy could not have characterized better his psychological situation upon returning to the residential treatment center from a short vacation with his parents. He described thus the psychological distance he felt between himself and his parents.

At that time he had been in our center almost two years receiving intensive analytic psychotherapy three hours weekly. His parents, prominent citizens of a North American city, had brought him to us when he was nine after unsuccessful attempts at treatment elsewhere. He had suffered from severe asthmatic attacks since the age of twenty-one months. He could neither play nor get along with other children, and expressed fears about an impending disaster. The parents complained about his rebellious attitude and their inability to manage him.

The parents were described by the social worker as conscientious, intellectual, without spontaneity, shy, cool, compulsive, and at the same time eager to help their only child. They could hardly be described as "rejecting" parents despite their inability to give, to contact him. Whether their difficulty was a consequence of his illness rather than a cause of it cannot be answered unequivocally.

Their initial concern was the child's asthma. They had taken him to specialists and after a fruitless placement in Arizona brought him to us for a psychiatric evaluation, consultation, and possible placement.

The examining psychiatrist summarized his findings as follows:

> Although of superior intelligence and capable of achieving a high educational level, play activities reveal marked disorganization and very intense destructive phantasying. Intellectual activity is over-stressed and isolated from ordinary events. Affect is flattened and somewhat inappropriate. Capacity for interpersonal relationships is almost absent. Diagnostic impression: Childhood Schizophrenia.

This pessimistic diagnosis was shared by other psychiatrists. The psychologist spoke of "A rather severe neurotic illness in which intellectualizing, obsessive-compulsive and hysterical defenses are used in order to try to control unusually strong aggressive urges and sexual conflicts." Of his fantasying she said that "It has at times a psychotic-like quality."

We wish to consider certain selected aspects of psychotherapy with this "schizophrenoid" child, a label we suggest for him in order to underline the severity of the illness, and to by-pass at present the diagnostic problem.[1]

Beginning Treatment

At first the boy spent weeks in bed with severe asthmatic attacks and presented more of a medical than a psychiatric problem. For most of the first two years he was so disturbed and frightened that he required 24-hour care. He needed a constant special companion because of his intense anxiety, his open threats and attempts at suicide, his constant provoking behavior, and his phobias—alone, he dared not cross the street which separates two of the buildings of our center. While this scared little boy needed a personal policeman to protect him from the wrath of the world and from his own anxieties, he would not permit the companion to enter his room at times.

Most of his communications to children, companions, teachers, and other professional personnel at the center consisted of fantasies which were frightful and in many ways seemed a complete contradiction to his actual behavior. In these fantasies he was a Five-Star General, commanded countless space ships, was out to destroy the world, sailed to faraway regions of space, destroyed stars, and invaded different solar systems. At the same time he was an unusually endowed little boy who had practically learned by heart the Book of Knowledge, knew more about school subjects than most of the other children, and put brilliant questions to the personnel.

So inaccessible did he seem at first that the psychotherapist avoided his fantasy world and remained on the level of his reality problems, his everyday fears and his needs in the living situation. After some months of such treatment the decision was reached to accept his fantasies and try to enter his psychological world. This seemed a dangerous shift in technique

[1] Abraham suggested in 1908 in his paper "The Psychosexual differences between Hysteria and Dementia Praecox," that an abnormal psychosexual constitution in the direction of auto-erotism was the cause for dementia praecox. He added that future research might help to elucidate the intellectual disturbances seen in the clinical picture of dementia praecox. It is as if he foresaw the development of modern ego psychology as represented, for example, by Erikson's *Childhood and Society*, published in 1950. *Our diagnostic interest in Tommy concerns the shifting ego states as they emerge during and because of treatment.* We think then of childhood schizophrenia as an ego illness despite the preference of some authors to use this diagnosis only for adults whose illness might develop out of such childhood disturbances as seen in Tommy's illness.

since his fantasy world seemed so overwhelming that to accept it might mean breaking down the remnants of his contact with us and wiping out the limits of reality.

However, as we changed our attitude toward him, we discovered underneath the manifest content of the fantasies the story of his life, and of his family situation. All the problems of love, of secret longing, of sensual gratification, were hidden behind a world of aggression between and among monsters. He talked for many hours about an old man who did not need and did not want to be married: in other words a man who had no sexual life whatsoever. This man, however, was so tremendously wise and clever that he could rule the solar system, the stars, and could ward off any invasion from Mars or any other planet.

Space Defense

The boy talked about faraway battles, faraway victories, faraway defeat, and rarely did he return to earth. At that time he was as far away from the psychotherapist as he was from his own unconscious conflicts. The problem of distance that he proposed to us at that time suggested one specific aspect of the strategy for our psychotherapy with this particular child. The authors decided not to concern themselves primarily with the problem of the content of his fantasies, even though they seemed clearly to suggest presentations of the primal scene or violent danger that is implied in thoughts about sexuality, but rather with the problem of defense.

While in real life he presented himself as a timid, scared little boy who needed protection from everyone, he was in his fantasy world an aggressive, deadly, faraway monster. Between these two there seemed to be no connection unless one could go by space ship from here to Mars.

The psychotherapist expressed sorrow for the old man who tried to win all his battles. True enough he might win his battles, but how lonesome he must be, how sad for him that he never had a mother or father, as Tommy had stated, and that he never had any friends on earth and did not want to think of marriage. How sad to think that he had only one gratification, that of believing that he could destroy everybody. The psychotherapist's main concern was with the distance between the psychological world of this faraway monster and that of the little fellow who was yearning to be loved and accepted by his parents, by the children and the teachers in the school.

When we speak of distance, we refer to it in the physical, emotional, metaphoric sense, since his way of describing the man far away, his using the metaphor of hundreds and thousands of light years, seemed to be nothing but an allusion to a psychological problem which he could not present in any other way. The mode of his defense, the way his ego attempted to master internal problems rather than the content of the conflict was attacked by psychotherapeutic work.

The therapist occasionally heard from Tommy that the old man wondered if, after one of his victories when it would be quite clear that no one could defeat him, he might come down and visit earth. By implying that the old General could win all battles only if he gave up forbidden sexual striving, Tommy revealed how difficult it was for him to bring the old man, the sexless, aggressive beast down to earth.

Tommy suggested to the psychotherapist one day that Tommy was not there any longer. He had gone far away to Arizona to do research to improve the atomic bomb, in order to protect America and to destroy its enemies. The boy who was left behind was simply a friend of Tommy's named Oscar Pumphandle. While he had a different name now, he stated that he still had some connection with the "real" Tommy. As a matter of fact he was going to visit Tommy once in a while, but never would he, Oscar Pumphandle, tell any of Tommy's secrets to the psychotherapist. He could not do it because if he did, he would lose Tommy's friendship.

The forbidden instinctual impulses, at first thousands of light years away, had returned to earth. The split was now not between the humble, frightened, asthmatic-ridden boy on earth and the old destructive General in space, but rather between two boys, both on earth and about a thousand miles apart. There was still tremendous distance between the forbidden and the overt, but the distance was reduced now.

Again the psychotherapist commented primarily on the distance and did not refer to the content of research, as symbolically presented through the secret explosion of the atomic bomb in the Arizona desert. The therapist suggested that Tommy in Arizona was perhaps scared of psychotherapy and wouldn't he, Oscar Pumphandle, suggest to Tommy that psychotherapy was not so dangerous and Tommy might return. Oscar Pumphandle said that Tommy was not scared since he was a great researcher into atomic explosions. As a matter of fact, according to Oscar Pumphandle Tommy was not sick at all. Actually no one was sick, and if any one was, it was Oscar Pumphandle. What was his illness? His illness was that he made too many jokes. The only help Oscar Pumphandle wanted from the therapist was to help him not to make too many jokes.

It was the first indication on the child's part that he was aware of his defensive system. He defended himself by distance. The undesirable, the unconscious, forbidden and repressed were sent far away. The other line of defense consisted of denial, in suggesting that what seemed to the therapist a psychological reality was nothing but a joke. Even the choice of the name, a funny name, a good joke on the psychotherapist, contained both a repressed and re-repressing force. The funny name of the joker gave away what the secret research was about.

The psychotherapist, recognizing the defensive problem in the transference, slowly conveyed to him that it was not Tommy who was afraid of the therapist but rather Oscar Pumphandle who was afraid of Tommy. They were not really such good friends. Each time they got together they had tremendous struggles, and Oscar could not call Tommy back because he was afraid of what would happen. This changed the situation indeed. Tommy came back, and with his coming we had a new problem. The shy little boy suddenly seemed to permit the other part of him, the forbidden one, to come back and the result for a while was utter chaos. The psychotherapist felt like the sorcerer's apprentice who loosed the uncontrollable devil. Tommy was at first as helplessly exposed to his own inner impulses as the therapist was to his aggressive provoking behavior. Only as the therapist turned into the sorcerer again could the flood of impulses be limited. The child attempted to masturbate openly during psychotherapeutic hours, began to steal and to destroy equipment, blew up car tires, expressed hate for staff members, organized gangs with other children, and turned from a timid youngster into a vicious little monster.

We now had an administrative and educational problem as well as a psychotherapeutic one. If he could not have the support of his defense through distance, he needed the support of the therapist and the limits that would be enforced in the educational setting. The therapist told the child that she would not permit him to be destructive. She had to let him know and feel that the personnel at Southard School was strong enough to protect him from his own destructiveness and to help him grow up. At the same time, however, she accepted him without condemnation.

After a number of weeks of these episodes, Tommy began to talk more and more about himself, and one day suddenly started to talk about his parents. Until then he seemed convinced that he had no parents or rather, that he had parents much as fish have parents. One of his fantasies was that his parents had been dinosaurs who battled each other. He had survived by hiding in a little hole while the army of dinosaurs swept across the country and destroyed everything in their way. His fantasy seemed to be that, by chance and because of his smallness and timidity, he had managed to survive and live without parents.

We see then that the lonesome old man was in a way the lonesome, helpless child in reverse and at the same time someone who was not abandoned but rather had chosen lonesomeness, someone who was not weak but terribly powerful and strong so he could win any battle as long as he would give up childhood sexuality and childhood helplessness and dependency.

The fantasies and the distance problem of time and space shifted and reflected the transference situation. We do not suggest that certain changes occurred in definite stages and that he started on a new problem, or a new type of fantasy as soon as one was worked through. There were no sharp delineations, but certain regressive moves in the types of fantasies, while always continuing, became less frequent. One could differentiate definitely certain changes in his use of a complicated syndrome of mechanisms of distance which could be taken as indicators of psychotherapeutic progress. [2]

For example, the boy would sometimes return to types of fantasies such as the one concerning dinosaurs, but a new element in the fantasy would indicate that "distance" now had new meaning in the transference situation. Fantasies now contained a new element: He told the therapist that things were worse again. The newspaper headlines warned that soon there might be a destructive atomic war and our civilization might come to an end and he needed to do something in order to get away. He spoke of a farm in the mountains, far away from present civilization and, "incidentally", a dinosaur farm where he could be occupied with his buddies raising dinosaurs. This is a reversal, indeed, of the idea that the dinosaurs had reared him. He wanted to go there because he felt that his interest in fossils, his great knowledge about geology and about archaeology would be rewarding, and that he would be safe. He felt his therapist ought to change in the transference situation. Since she liked him and he liked her, she should not be destroyed by our contemporary civilization. As long as she kept the rules of this safer world which he had invented, she could stay there with him and would not be punished. We note again a reversal

[2] Anna Freud in her paper "Observations on Child Development" (1951) states: "In the analytic literature on the subject of libido development, it is stressed repeatedly that the oral, anal, and phallic phases merge into each other at the points of transition, and that they should only be thought of as distinct from each other in the sense that in each phase one of the component urges is highly cathected with libido and therefore prominent, whereas the others, earlier as well as later trends, though they may exist, have a low cathexis and therefore play a minor part. Such warnings are useful to the analyst to whom the libidinal phases often appear as closed-off entities when seen in retrospect" (p. 22).

This observation could be paraphrased for the shifting defensive fantasies, and for the amount of cathexis which is given to one particular type of fantasy, while the others coexist, but with less intensity.

of the situation. He took her along, and the two travelled together in his fantasies to the far reaches, and while true enough, this again was an escape from reality, an escape from the contemporary world, a reaction to extreme anxiety, it revealed at the same time a different attitude toward the therapist, a change of the transference situation.

Change in Transference Situation

In the beginning of treatment he used the therapist as a kind of *tabula rasa,* writing his fantasies on her, without seeming to notice her. He had spent many weeks alone in his room, too scared to be outside yet unable to tolerate the presence of recreational workers in his room. If one were to speak of transference at that time, one would have to state that he was as distant from his therapist as he was from his parents, whose pending visit at that time frightened him immensely, and as was the old General in space from our earth.

The only way the therapist could enter his psychological world at first was to be willing to tolerate and to watch it. But now she was accepted as an equal partner and was permitted to assume roles in his fantasy world. We saw now on a different level how the patient was tortured not only by powerful instinctual strivings but also by an equally strong and cruel superego. He described an inner situation which was ruled by the Talion Principle.

It was not the content particularly that changed, only the form that content took. A decisive step forward was the different use of defense syndromes in describing, revealing and disguising the inner situation.

He had moved from the days when he had represented his sexual conflict only in symbolic form to a situation where he was able to talk openly with his psychotherapist about sex, about the creation of new life. One day, during one of these discussions on problems of sex he asked the psychotherapist what would happen if either his testicles or his penis would be surgically removed. The therapist reassured him and told him that no one would remove the genitals of little boys. Very much to her amazement the boy came back during the next hour in an obvious state of panic. He had not described an external danger but rather an internal one. He had also described his reaction to the psychotherapist whom he experienced as a tempting and seductive mother figure. He told her: "You cannot help me. Psychotherapy will never help me. I need a mental hospital forever and ever. I need a closed ward, and I need more than that; I need a neurosurgeon to open my brain all around and look for the swollen emotions and cut them out and perhaps that would make me all right." Only as she was able to ponder the question aloud as to what he thought he had done that would need such cruel punishment did the panic subside and the child regain control of the situation.

The freedom she gave him to discuss sexual material heightened sexual tension, was experienced as sexual temptation, and he was not only fighting his erections during the hour but felt terribly sinful about it. What he needed was not reassurance—though it was intended by the therapist to reduce an external danger—but recognition and a chance to admit his "bad" thoughts and feelings. He needed help so he could cope with the inner danger. Since he felt she was responsible for this, he could not accept her as helper at that point but thought of the neurosurgeon, the punitive father figure.

Decisive, it seemed, in the treatment of this child was the problem of the analysis of his defenses, the specific problem of the defensive distance which was re-introduced by the child over and over and characterized a specific ego problem. The internal struggle continued, but on different levels of distance. [3]

The shifting psychotherapeutic situation permitted us to observe the emergence of different self concepts of the child. During the first phase he created a picture of the unacceptable part in himself through the fantasies about the old General. On earth we met a helpless child, the counterpart of the destructive hero in space.

This self concept slowly and at times also violently grew into another one, where the unacceptable part was a child explorer and inventor in a desert a thousand miles away and the acceptable one, participating in the therapeutic session, was a joking youngster. Again, as the therapeutic situation developed, a different concept evolved where both the acceptable and unacceptable aspect of the personality blended together and produced a delinquent youngster who challenged his environment.

Only as the educators and the psychotherapist were able to set limits, could the boy master the chaos, and in the period to follow he could ex-

[3] Distance problems are observed in all psychotherapeutic situations or patient groups. Some of the space fantasies of this child occur indeed in other children, and are actually nurtured through science fiction, science fiction movies, and other similar literary productions. This child differed from others, or his therapeutic experience differed from other ones, inasmuch as a specific process could be observed in which distance, while oscillating, became smaller. Spatial and temporal distance were specific aspects of the defensive system of the ego. The same held true for the content of his fantasies which were always traceable to actual experience, like the manifest dream content can be traced to day residues. Even Tommy's dinosaurs had their place in actual experience: huge plaster cast monuments in the zoo of his home town.

press for the first time thoughts about the childhood home, about his parents, and his feelings of rejection.

As he faced his thoughts about the parents, he also moved on in the transference situation. He spoke more openly about the therapist, and once, when feeling that she could not help him when experiencing her as seductive, he expressed utter lack of confidence in psychotherapy.

In this later period, in spite of his open and direct expressions of hostility, suspicion, and fear, and requests for direct gratifications, he was able to bring more immediate experiences into the therapeutic situation. Change in the transference situation expressed itself in the fact that the psychotherapist now more than ever was an experienced part of the child's psychological world. [4]

It is interesting that in his attempt to describe to the psychotherapist what she meant to him, he reintroduced the problem of distance: his need to divide her into her bad and her good aspects.

For example, during one session, his teeth set, his stare directed at the therapist's breasts, he suddenly accused her of being a witch, thought that she ought to be burned. Then he changed and said that she was not really a witch but had witches inside of her. He had done research on witches and told her that she was an undesirable person since she had witches inside her which made her brain say things to him that he did not like to hear. She also made him do things which he did not want to do. He began to draw a picture of a witch. The picture he drew was of a phallic witch, having male genitals but also breasts, riding on a broom, and possessing a large witch's hat. He connected the witch's brain which he placed in her stomach with her male genitals and her breasts. The brain of the witch which was controlled by breasts and genitals was connected with the brain of the therapist, and thus controlled the therapist. He suggested that most people had two or three witches but his therapist had at least six witches. Witches had to be burned.

Therapeutic interviews of this period revealed that some direct content interpretations were experienced by the patient as seductive and overpermissive; and, what seemed more interesting than his condemnation of the therapist, his struggle against her, and his flight from her, is the method that he was employing now in order to express the condemna-

[4] When we speak about transference situations we are using the concept "transference" in a double sense. Certain expressions of the child refer to early preoedipal phases of his life and are reflected in a "transference neurosis." Other expressions toward the psychotherapist are a transfer, not from the repressed past to the present, but rather from present relationships with parents or educators in the environment to the therapist.

tion of her. He had to maintain his love for her and projected on to her superior forces as responsible for her seductiveness which operated in the same way and dominated her in the same way as instinctual forces dominated his own life and were experienced by him.

His beginning awareness and understanding of the psychotherapist was blended with powerful projective elements, and his picture of her, while suggesting a mother introject, was also a projective description of himself.

Signs of Improvement

When a few weeks later the child's parents were to visit him he prepared himself for the event. During the first visit he had refused to see them and was panic stricken. During the second visit he met them as a joking little boy who could control his anxiety only when being funny and entertaining them with little jokes.

For this third visit the child elaborated a new fantasy. He spoke about the Martian agent who had come to earth, and was to return to Mars in his space ship. In the beginning of therapy he had used this fantasy, but then the space ship was destroyed and he could not return to Mars. It was as if the space ship expressed the distance from the parents and his own home; and its being destroyed meant that he had given up all hope that he could ever go back to them. Now he suggested that he had a space ship, that it was buried and maybe he might be able to go back to Mars. He insisted that he would return in the near future. He wanted to leave the earth because the earth was too warlike and he described Mars as peaceful.

When the psychotherapist reminded him of the early stories of the General conducting catastrophic wars in space, he said that they were just "science fiction stuff" and he insisted that the Martian people were quite peaceful. We learned that the Martian, whose anatomy he drew for us, was not sexless as the old General in space had been. Among other things, the boy stated that the Martian urinated through the rectum because the genital sexual regions had to be pure. The new Martian man in many ways was a picture, a new self-concept of the patient. The child described copulation on Mars in such a way as to deny the joy of sex life. When the therapist asked him once why he was against enjoyment in the case of Martian men, the child lost patience with her and said to her: "You are supposed to be a therapist and interested in the mind and mental things, and here you are asking questions about sexual matters." He said that he was a space explorer and not a biologist. This new concept of himself not only put the psychotherapist in her place but also indicated in which way he felt he could be accepted by his parents, in which way he was lovable and could accept himself and he indicated also his problem, the exploration of space, of distance, of defense.

An example, quoted from the psychotherapeutic record, concerns the child's play with a wild horse through which he indicated to us how he attempted to cope with his fluctuating defense system. Tommy built feverishly and frantically a wall of blocks around a wild horse. While this wall was being built by men, the horse rushed around and trampled everything that was in his way. Luckily enough for the time being the horse trampled only other animals to death and men were spared. The game lasted a number of days and consisted in constantly building up walls and tearing them down again. At one point the psychotherapist referred to the horse as a representation of the wild and untamable in Tommy, but he rejected the interpretation as if to say that he did not want to tell her about the wild horse but rather about his attempt to tame the horse. Constantly he built up and tore down the walls which held the animal and thus he described his inner situation, the shifting ego strength he used successfully and unsuccessfully, at some point later, in order to contain the wild horse.

We cannot better illustrate the progress that Tommy made during these two years than by quoting another example recorded just before the third visit of his parents.

He asked if the therapist thought that his parents would think he was different. The therapist assured him that they hardly could think otherwise from the way that he acted now. On the other hand, she added, it was possible that he might feel he had to withdraw and act as he had in the past. She did not know for sure what he might do but indicated that she would accept him both ways. Tommy didn't think that he would withdraw. He was less anxious and quite cheerful. He had been depressed and frightened before their last visit. Tommy asked what he had said last time. The therapist recalled how unhappy he had been and how scared he was.

Tommy said: "Well, let's dramatize that interview. I will be Mrs. W. and you will be Tommy."

Tommy: "Well, Tommy, you don't look very happy today. Is there something wrong?"

Therapist: "Yes, Mrs. W., I'm so worried about my parents' visit."

Tommy: "What in particular are you worried about, Tommy?"

Therapist: "Well, I'm afraid they won't like me as the kind of boy I am."

Tommy: "Well, why don't you think they will like you as you are?"

Therapist: "Well, the way I figure it I tried so hard to be the kind of child my parents wanted me to be and I failed and that's why I am sick."

Tommy: "Yes, there is probably something to that. How do you feel about it now?"

Therapist: "Well, I feel I have changed some and I don't know if they will like me as I am now."

Tommy: "But you told me worrying about whether or not they would like you is what made you sick before. Why don't you forget about what kind of boy your parents want and just act like you feel like acting?"

Therapist: "You think if I do that my parents will be upset?"

Tommy: "Well, they will understand better when they see the social worker and she can explain to them that it is important for a boy to be himself."

Therapist (pretending that she was crying): "But, Mrs. W., I hardly know my parents."

Tommy: "Of course you don't. It will take a long time for you to know them and they to know you."

Then Tommy stopped for a minute and asked the therapist if he cried last time with very big tears. He then went on to predict how he would act this time with his parents. Actually, his asthma symptoms had almost completely cleared up by then. He needed no special companions and made good progress in school. He had more satisfactory contacts with children and staff. His fantasy life did not have the intensive quality it had in the beginning. He was much improved.

After this interview he went on a vacation with his parents and the incident described in the beginning of this presentation occurred as he was returning to treatment. It was as if the myth of birth without parents, of a lonesome life far away in space, of constant hostility, conquest, and fear had given way to a more realistic myth about his childhood. At the end of the treatment phase which we have described in this paper he reacted to his parents in very much the same way perhaps that adult patients "reconstruct" their frustrating childhood and the picture of their parents while in the initial stages of analysis. His situation was complicated, of course, by the fact that many of the elements of the picture he had about his parents and about childhood, and about himself were aspects of a grim reality which we could not deny.

We are aware that child psychotherapists occasionally overidentify themselves with the child's fate and experience parents as rejecting and hostile and, therefore, are more prone to accept the "myth" which the child offers.

Comment on Treatment Technique

The reconstruction of the early childhood situation, however, does not seem to be decisive, but rather *the way in which reconstruction takes place.* This presentation may help clarify the fact that the main attempt of the therapist is not aimed at the reconstruction of the trauma or of the series of traumata but rather that such a reconstruction allows the psychotherapeutic process to take place. During the psychotherapeutic process we discover the main modes of defense which the suffering child has been using consciously and unconsciously in order to master, successfully in part and unsuccessfully in others, the problems of growth and development.

Tommy offered an unusual example of a situation in which the way he had used to master his situation indicated new therapeutic possibilities. We have attempted to describe more fully these aspects of the therapeutic process which refer to his unusual pattern of *defense through distance.* His treatment, which is still in progress, stimulates many more questions which we have scarcely touched on.

We assumed responsibility for his treatment when he was in the middle of what is called the latency period, although he never quite succeeded in reaching it. It is not the authors' intention to speculate about the nature of the unsuccessful attempts at instinct mastery. The present communication concerns primarily technical problems as they arose out of the specific use he made of his fantasy life, and the specific use of distance in his fantasies. The primary concern of the therapist with the mode of space defense seems to be responsible for the progress Tommy made, from the lonesome, destructive space child to the little boy who could stand the pain of separation without escaping again into a distant world of disaster.

PART VIII

MENTAL RETARDATION

The most generally accepted definition of mental retardation is that of the American Association of Mental Deficiency, which defines it as an entity referring to subaverage intellectual functioning, having its origin during the developmental period, and associated with impairment of adaptive behavior.

An I.Q. score in itself, as Reissman's (1962) article in this section emphasizes, is not the ultimate diagnostic criterion of mental retardation. It is estimated that—using an I.Q. of 70 or below as the criterion—three per cent of the population of the United States are retarded. Perhaps it is significant that 75 to 85 per cent of this group are estimated as being mildly retarded. The old classification of degrees of retardation as idiot, imbecile, and moron, has given way to that of severe, moderate, and mild retardation. From the modern standpoint, retardation is viewed as relating to difficulties in a dynamic process of evolving intelligence at distinct stages of development. Numerous theories have been proposed to relate intellectual development and mental retardation. Piaget's (1962) stages of sensorimotor, preoperational, and concrete operations in developmental sequence, for example, can be seen as points of fixation leading to severe, moderate, or mild retardation in which the individual has never intellectually reached the stage of abstract operations.

Many myths still persist concerning retardation, its causes, and effects. And while the controversy between concepts of nature or nurture has given way, as with psychosis, to theories of multiple causation, the need remains for detailed study of the interaction of genetic, constitutional, and environmental factors.

FIRST DEVELOPMENTS OF THE YOUNG SAVAGE OF AVEYRON

JEAN M. ITARD

The following excerpt is taken from a report submitted to the French Minister of Health in 1801 by a young medical officer of the French National Institute for the Deaf and Dumb. It is of major importance in the history of emotional and mental disorders in children. In describing his work of–as we would say today–fostering ego development in a primitive child, Itard suggested a close association between mental retardation and mental illness. Rejecting the popular belief of the time in devils and spirits, he treated young Victor for more than five years on the assumption that the boy's "idiocy" was caused by lack of social stimulation. Itard's surprisingly modern diagnostic assessment and therapeutic goals, even certain elements in his approach, set the stage for the education and training of the retarded for some time thereafter. They were introduced in the United States in 1848, by Itard's pupil Séguin.

Many authors have puzzled over the nature of Victor's pathology and Itard's disappointment in his minimal improvement. While Gesell (1940b) argued that the failure of speech development was evidence that Victor was indeed mentally defective, others (Silberstein and Irwin, 1962) felt that the diagnosis was more complicated than "simple mental deficiency," and related it to studies of deprivation (see Spitz, 1945). The case raises, once again, questions about the interrelationship of intellectual and emotional functioning.

A child of eleven or twelve, who some years before had been seen completely naked in the Caune Woods seeking acorns and roots to eat, was met in the same place toward the end of September 1799 by three sportsmen who seized him as he was climbing into a tree to escape from their pursuit. Conducted to a neighboring hamlet and confided to the care of a widow, he broke loose at the end of a week and gained the mountains, where he wandered during the most rigorous winter weather, draped rather than covered with a tattered shirt. At night he retired to solitary places but during the day he approached the neighboring villages, where of his own accord he entered an inhabited house situated in the Canton of St. Sernin.

There he was retaken, watched and cared for during two or three days and transferred to the hospital of Saint-Afrique, then to Rodez, where he was kept for several months. During his sojourn in these different places he remained equally wild and shy, impatient and restless, continually seeking to escape. He furnished material for most interesting observations, which were collected by credible witnesses whose accounts I shall not fail to report in this essay where they can be displayed to the best advantage. [1] A minister of state with scientific interests believed that this event would throw some light upon the science of the mind. Orders were given that the child should be brought to Paris. He arrived there towards the end of September 1800 under the charge of a poor respectable old man who, obliged to part from the child shortly after, promised to come and take him again and act as a father to him should the Society ever abandon him.

The most brilliant and irrational expectations preceded the arrival of the Savage of Aveyron at Paris. A number of inquisitive people looked forward with delight to witnessing the boy's astonishment at the sights of the capital. On the other hand many people otherwise commendable for their insight, forgetting that human organs are by so much less flexible, and imitation made by so much more difficult, in proportion as man is removed from society and from his infancy, believed that the education of this child would only be a question of some months, and that he would soon be able to give the most interesting information about his past life. In place of all this what do we see? A disgustingly dirty child affected with spasmodic movements and often convulsions who swayed back and forth ceaselessly like certain animals in the menagerie, who bit and scratched those who opposed him, who showed no sort of affection for those who attended him; and who was in short, indifferent to everything and attentive to nothing.

[1] If the expression *Savage* has been understood until now to mean a man but slightly civilized, it will be agreed that this term has never been more truly merited. I will then keep to this name by which he has always been designated until I have given an account of the motives which determined me to give him another.

It can easily be understood that a creature of this kind could excite only a momentary curiosity. People ran in crowds, they saw him without observing him, they passed judgment on him without knowing him, and spoke no more about him. In the midst of this general indifference the administrators of the National Institute of the Deaf and Dumb and its celebrated director never forgot that society, in taking over this unfortunate youth, had contracted towards him binding obligations that must be fulfilled. Sharing then the hopes which I founded upon a course of medical treatment, they decided that this child should be confided to my care.

But before the details and results of this decision are presented I must begin with an account of our starting point and recall and describe this first period, in order that the progress we have made may be better appreciated. By thus contrasting the past with the present, we can determine what ought to be expected from the future. Obliged then to return to facts already known, I will state these briefly; and that I may not be suspected of having exaggerated for the purpose of contrast, I will venture here to give a careful analysis of the description given of the boy, in a meeting to which I had the honor of being admitted, by a doctor whose genius for observation is as famous as his profound knowledge of mental diseases.

Proceeding first with an account of the sensory functions of the young savage, citizen Pinel showed that his senses were reduced to such a state of inertia that the unfortunate creature was, according to his report, quite inferior to some of our domestic animals. His eyes were unsteady, expressionless, wandering vaguely from one object to another without resting on anybody; they were so little experienced in other ways and so little trained by the sense of touch, that they never distinguished an object in relief from one in a picture. His organ of hearing was equally insensible to the loudest noises and to the most touching music. His voice was reduced to a state of complete muteness and only a uniform guttural sound escaped him. His sense of smell was so uncultivated that he was equally indifferent to the odor of perfumes and to the fetid exhalation of the dirt with which his bed was filled. Finally, the organ of touch was restricted to the mechanical function of the grasping of objects. Proceeding then to the state of the intellectual functions of this child, the author of the report presented him to us as being quite incapable of attention (except for the objects of his needs) and consequently of all those operations of the mind which attention involves. He was destitute of memory, of judgment, of aptitude for imitation, and was so limited in his ideas, even those relative to his immediate needs, that he had never yet succeeded in opening a door or climbing upon a chair to get the food that had been raised out of reach of his hand. In short, he was destitute of all means of communication and attached neither expression nor intention to his gestures or to the movements of his body. He passed rapidly and without any apparent motive from apathetic melancholy to the most immoderate peals of laughter. He was insensible to every kind of moral influence. His perception was nothing but a computation prompted by gluttony, his pleasure an agreeable sensation of the organ of taste and his intelligence the ability to produce a few incoherent ideas relative to his wants. In a word, his whole life was a completely animal existence.

Later, reporting several cases collected at Bicêtre of children incurably affected with idiocy, citizen Pinel established very strict parallels between the condition of these unfortunate creatures and that of the child now under consideration, and convincingly established a complete and perfect identity between these young idiots and the Savage of Aveyron. This identity led to the inevitable conclusion that, attacked by a malady hitherto regarded as incurable, he was not capable of any kind of sociability or instruction. This was the conclusion which citizen Pinel drew but which, nevertheless, he accompanied by that philosophic doubt which pervades all his writings, and which accompanies the predictions of the man who estimates the science of prognosis at its true worth, seeing in it nothing but a more or less uncertain calculation of probabilities and conjectures.

I never shared this unfavorable opinion and in spite of the truth of the picture and the justice of the parallels I dared to conceive certain hopes. I founded them for my part upon the double consideration of the cause and the curability of this apparent idiocy. I cannot go further without dwelling a moment upon these two considerations. Moreover, they bear upon the present and depend upon a series of facts which I must relate, and to which I shall see myself obliged more than once to add my own reflections.

If it were proposed to solve the following problem of metaphysics: *to determine what would be the degree of intelligence and the nature of the ideas of an adolescent, who, deprived from his childhood of all education, had lived entirely separated from individuals of his own species,* unless I am greatly mistaken the solution of the problem would be found as follows. There should first be assigned to that individual nothing but an intelligence relative to the small number of his needs and one which was deprived, by abstraction, of all the simple and complex ideas we receive by education, which combine in our mind in so many ways solely by means of our knowledge of signs, or reading. Well, the mental picture of this adolescent would be that of the Wild Boy of Aveyron and the solution of the problem would consist in exhibiting the extent and the cause of his intellectual state.

But in order to justify still further my opinion of the existence of this cause, it is necessary to prove that it has operated for a number of years, and to reply to the objection that can be made and that has already been made to me, that the so-called savage was merely a poor imbecile whom his parents in disgust had recently abandoned at the entrance to some woods. Those who lend themselves to such a supposition had not observed the child shortly after his arrival in Paris. They would have seen that all his habits bore the mark of a wandering and solitary life. He had an insurmountable aversion to society and to its customs, to our clothing, our furniture, to living in houses and to the preparation of our food. There was a profound indifference to the objects of our pleasures and of our fictitious needs; there was still in his present state, in spite of his new needs and dawning affections, so intense a passion for the freedom of the fields that during a short sojourn at Montmorency he would certainly have escaped into the forest had not the most rigid precautions been taken, and twice he did escape from the house of the Deaf and Dumb in spite of the supervision of his governess. His locomotion was extraordinary, literally heavy after he wore shoes, but always remarkable because of his difficulty in adjusting himself to our sober and measured gait, and because of his constant tendency to trot and to gallop. He had an obstinate habit of smelling at anything that was given to him, even the things which we consider void of smell; his mastication was equally astonishing, executed as it was solely by the sudden action of the incisors, which because of its similarity to that of certain rodents was a sufficient indication that our savage, like these animals, most commonly lived on vegetable products. I said most commonly, for it appeared by the following incident that in certain circumstances he had devoured small dead animals. A dead canary was given him and in an instant the bird was stripped of its feathers big and little, opened with his nail, sniffed at and thrown away.

Other indications of an entirely isolated, precarious and wandering life are the nature and the number of scars with which the child's body is covered. To say nothing of the scar which is visible on his throat and which I shall mention elsewhere as having another origin and meriting particular attention, there could be counted four upon his face, six along his left arm, three at some distance from the right shoulder, four at the margin of the pubis, one upon the left buttock, three on one leg and two on the other which makes twenty-three altogether. Of these some appeared to be due to bites of animals and the others to scratches which were more or less large and deep, forming numerous and ineffaceable evidences of the long and total abandonment of this unfortunate creature. When considered from a more general and philosophic point of view, these scars bear witness equally against the feebleness and insufficiency of man when left entirely to himself, and in favor of the resources of nature which, following apparently contradictory laws, work openly to repair and conserve that which she tends secretly to impair and to destroy.

Let us add to all these facts derived from observation those not less authentic to which the inhabitants of the country near the woods in which he was found have testified. We shall find that in the first days following his entrance into society, his only nourishment was acorns, potatoes and raw chestnuts, that he made no sort of sound, that in spite of the most active supervision he succeeded several times in escaping, that he showed a great repugnance to sleeping in a bed, etc. We shall find above all that he had been seen more than five years before entirely naked and fleeing at the approach of men, which presupposes that he was already, at the time of his first appearance, habituated to this manner of life, which could only be the result of at least two years' sojourn in uninhabited places. Thus this child had lived in an absolute solitude from his seventh almost to his twelfth year, which is the age he may have been when he was taken in the Caune woods. It is then probable, and almost proved, that he had been abandoned at the age of four or five years, and that if, at this time, he already owed some ideas and some words to the beginning of an education, this would all have been effaced from his memory in consequence of his isolation.

This is what appeared to me to be the cause of his present state. It can be seen why I augured favorably from it for the success of my treatment. Indeed, considering the short time he was among people, the Wild Boy of Aveyron was much less an adolescent imbecile than a child of ten or twelve months, and a child who would have the disadvantage of anti-social habits, a stubborn inattention, organs lacking in flexibility and a sensibility accidentally dulled. From this last point of view his situation became a purely medical case, and one the treatment of which belonged to mental science, that sublime art created in England by Willis and Crichton, and newly spread in France by the success and writings of Professor Pinel.

Guided much less by the spirit of their doctrine than by their precepts, which could not be adapted to this unforeseen case, I classified under five principal aims the mental and moral education of the Wild Boy of Aveyron.

1st Aim. To interest him in social life by rendering it more pleasant to him than the one he was then leading, and above all more like the life which he had just left.

2nd Aim. To awaken his nervous sensibility by the most energetic stimulation, and occasionally by intense emotion.

3rd Aim. To extend the range of his ideas by giving him new needs and by increasing his social contacts.

4th Aim. To lead him to the use of speech by inducing the exercise of imitation through the imperious law of necessity.

5th Aim. To make him exercise the simplest mental operations upon the objects of his physical needs over a period of time afterwards inducing the application of these mental processes to the objects of instruction.

MENTAL RETARDATION IN HISTORICAL PERSPECTIVE

HOWARD W. POTTER

Within his own discipline of child psychiatry, Potter is considered an early crusader against the neglect of the study and treatment of retardation as a clinical entity. He is of the opinion that the simple and severe forms of mental retardation are unrelated. Sarason (1958) in his review of research efforts to differentiate mental retardation from mental deficiency, points up that the latter has a neurological underpinning. Tredgold (1908) suggested that all *mental retardation had an organic basis, although it was not always readily demonstrable. Reports of the Group for the Advancement of Psychiatry (1959, 1963) discuss the qualitative difference between mild and severe retardation. They conclude that organicity and severe retardation occur together in the same proportion throughout various levels of the population, but that mild and "nonorganic" forms, also closely associated, are concentrated in the lower socioeconomic classes, where disadvantaged children are found.*

Beyond the question of whether the retarded are more vulnerable to emotional disorder than the nonretarded, Potter approaches intelligence as an ego function and causes us to wonder whether the retarded, generally, tend to use certain defenses over others, and whether they are prone to particular kinds of emotional disorders. Sorely needed are studies among the retarded on the role of anxiety in the dynamics of "adaptation," differences in managing the series of developmental tasks of childhood, and differences in coping mechanisms.

Garfield (1963) notes that the term mental retardation is frequently used as if it denoted some restricted or uniform type of behavior. The literature abounds in generalization pertaining to the behavior of the retarded as a group, and in stereotyped descriptions of their personalties. Rather than indulge in such simplistic generalizations, we need to raise such questions as: How important is limited intelligence in the eventual development of emotional disturbance? Does subnormal cognitive ability limit the individual's ability to cope with the normal frustrations and necessary adjustments of

Excerpted from "The Needs of Mentally Retarded Children for Child Psychiatry Services." *Journal of the American Academy of Child Psychiatry,* 3, 1964, pp. 353–363.

everyday life? To what extent is awareness of intellectual inferiority responsible for anxiety formation and feelings of insecurity? Are individuals with limited intellectual ability more prone to certain types of behavioral disturbances or to using basic adjustive defenses than nonretarded individuals? Or is the behavior a result of early parent-child relationships, parental rejection, hostility, and the like? Some reviews of the psychopathology of mental retardation do exist (Garfield, 1963; Beier, 1964). But unfortunately, as Sarason and Gladwin (1958) and Feldman (1946) have emphasized, the mental defective has rarely been studied with regard to the importance of early experiences and parental influences for subsequent behavior, nor have his experiences, feelings, and attitudes been explored as thoroughly as those of the nonretarded.

The portion of the article dealing specifically with child psychiatry services and with training programs in child psychiatry have been omitted. In the following excerpt, Potter reviews the social, psychological, and medical attitudes toward mental retardation, thereby putting the subject in perspective. In addition, he gives a critical survey of the literature and makes a plea for sharpening the distinction between the mildly and severely retarded.

For the sake of clarity, a few comments on terminology are in order. Feeble-mindedness, Mental Deficiency, and Mental Retardation are generic terms, inclusive of all persons whose cognitive functions are impaired and whose subnormal intelligence is congenital or was acquired during infancy or childhood. These generic terms may or may not have clinical implications but are rather useful for administrative purposes. Feeble-mindedness is the oldest and first used of these generic terms; it began to appear in the literature during the latter half of the nineteenth century, coincident with the establishment of tax-supported institutions for "idiots and other feeble-minded persons." Feeble-mindedness was not defined in terms of mental test scores until 1916, when Terman (1916) declared "all who test below 70 I.Q. should be considered feeble-minded." Mental Deficiency began to replace feeble-mindedness as a generic term in the 1920s, and mental retardation began to replace mental deficiency during the early years of the 1950s. Mental deficiency carried with it the I.Q. 70 cutoff point that had been established for feeble-mindedness in 1916, while the cutoff point for mental retardation varies a point or two below I.Q. 70, depending upon which intelligence test is used (American Association on Mental Deficiency, 1961).

As early as 1672 a description of "degrees of stupidity," bearing a close resemblance to mild, moderate, severe, and profound mental retardation of today, appeared in a textbook on mental disorders, *De Anima Brutorum,* by Sir Thomas Willis, one of the most astute physicians of seventeenth-century London. A quotation from this book, Chapter XIII, "De Stupiditate sive Morosis," follows:

> Stupidity hath many degrees; for some are accounted unfit or incapable as to all things, and others as to some things only. Some being wholly fools in the learning of letters, or the liberal sciences, are yet able enough for mechanical arts. Others of either of these incapable, yet easily comprehend agriculture, or husbandry and country business. Others unfit almost for all affairs, are only able to learn what belongs to eating or the common means of living. Others merely dolts or driveling fools, scarce understand anything at all, or do anything knowingly.

Idiocy (from the Greek *Idioteia,* meaning uncouthness) and *Imbecility* (from the Latin *Imbecilitas,* meaning weakness of mind and body) have appeared in medical writings since antiquity, were used interchangeably, and stood for some kind of gross pathology in body structure and gross distortions of behavior.

However, neither Sir Thomas's recognition and brilliant description of degrees of intellectual subnormality nor the discovery of cretinism in the Swiss Alps by Paracelsus fifty years before (1616) aroused any active interest in idiocy among either the medical profession or the laity until the turn of the nineteenth century, when Itard undertook his epoch-making endeavor to cure Victor of his idiocy. Itard, an adherent of Locke's concept of the mind as a *tabula rasa,* directed his efforts toward "educating the mind" through the vigorous pursuit of a systematic program of sensory input and habit training. His report, *De l'education d'un homme sauvage,* was published in 1801.

In 1837 Seguin, a former student of both Itard and Esquirol, founded in Paris the first school for the education of idiots. His book, *The Moral Treatment, Hygiene, and Education of Idiots and Other Backward Children,* published in 1846, is a landmark in the literature on mental deficiency.

Shortly before the mid-point of the nineteenth century, under the leadership of Seguin, and his American counterpart, Samuel Gridley Howe, both of whom had had a rich and successful experience in the re-education of deaf mutes, widespread interest was focused on ways and means through sensory input and habit training to bring about some significant functional improvement of idiots and imbeciles. (And that this can be achieved is being rediscovered now, 100 years later.)

Causology attracted but little attention until the Parisian School of Neurology and Psychiatry turned its attention to searching clinical and pathological investigations of idiocy. The brilliant descriptions of the clinical and pathological characteristics of a number of neurological diseases associated with idiocy, published during the last two decades of the nineteenth century, are classics in the literature of neurology. Bourneville's (1893) reports received worldwide recognition and established beyond doubt that many cases of idiocy were basically some form of brain pathology or anomalous development. Bourneville's case material did not include that which we call today mild mental retardation, for the simple reason that mild mental retardation (morosis) had not been generally recognized.

By the last decade of the nineteenth century and the earlier years of the twentieth century, less seriously handicapped retardates were coming to be recognized and filtering into the institutions in increasing numbers. Their limitations in the "learning of letters" was self-evident and most came to the "idiot asylums" as social misfits, neglected children, or both. In terms of I.Q. levels, they were probably high-grade imbeciles or low-grade morons.

It was not until the second decade of the twentieth century that mild mental retardation came to be recognized in any significant numbers. Goddard of the Training School, Vineland, New Jersey, had introduced the Binet-Simon scale for testing intelligence to America in 1908. Immediately, the test was applied to increasing numbers of school children and, based on the test results, Goddard introduced the Moron (the mildly retarded) to America in 1910. (Moron, from the Greek *Moron,* meaning foolish.)

By 1916, Terman, professor of education at Stanford University, had modified the Binet-Simon test, and the Stanford Revision of the Binet-Simon Intelligence Scale became the standard test for many years.

In the introduction to *The Measurement of Intelligence,* Terman (1916) stated: "Only very recently . . . have scientific workers begun to appreciate fully the importance of intelligence tests as a guide to educational procedure." It has now long since been recognized that nomenthetic tests of intelligence are indeed indispensable guides for the educator.

But in this same book, Terman goes far afield from the pragmatic application of his test to the operational aspects of educational programs. After explaining how an Intelligence Quotient is calculated, he goes on to say: "All who test below 70 I.Q. by the Stanford Revision of the Binet-Simon Scale should be considered feeble-minded" (p. 79). Thus by an edict and a stroke of the pen, the category feeble-mindedness (mental deficiency, mental retardation) was defined in terms of the I.Q. and gained wide acceptance with little or no debate. Terman's magical cutoff point–I.Q. 70–has been written into the laws of many states or is incorporated into regulations of Bureaus and Commissions in defining mental retardation and regulating the placement of children in institutions and "special" classes in the public schools.

A second quote from the same book: "Of the feeble-minded, those between 50 and 70 I.Q. include most of the morons [mild mental retardation] . . ., those between 20 or 25 and 50 are ordinarily to be classed as imbeciles [moderate and severe mental retardation], and those below 20 or 25, as idiots [profound mental retardation]" (p. 79). Thus by a second pronouncement, Terman placed mildly retarded children and the most profoundly retarded ones, and all the retardates in between these two extremes, in one and the same category.

Five years before Terman published his book, Davenport reported on his genealogical studies of mental defectives. When Davenport made this study, the Binet-Simon test had been employed for some two years or more, and Goddard had introduced the moron; it was this group of institutionalized subjects whose ancestral records Davenport explored. Davenport's study was a highly biased one; sociopathy, alcoholism, criminality, prostitution, ineffective or irregular employment, and other social transgressions among the subject's ancestors were interpreted as *prima-facie* evidence of mental deficiency. In his monograph *Heredity in Relation to Eugenics* (1911), Davenport came to the conclusion that "low mentality is due to the absence of some factor that determines normal development . . . Two mentally defective parents will produce only mentally defective offspring" (p. 66). It is likely that both Davenport (1911) and Goddard (1912, 1914) closely followed and subscribed to Morel's (1857) theory of degeneration, which has long since been disproven.

By the end of the second decade of the twentieth century, most clinicians viewed all feeble-mindedness as representing some known or unknown pathological deviation from "normality." It came to be generally accepted that morosis (mild mental retardation) was undoubtedly an attenuated form of idiocy; the superb clinical blunder of the ages! It was hypothecated that most morons were feeble-minded because of bad heredity expressed in some degree of cerebral agenesis, and that the rest were feeble-minded because of some encephalopathy due to infection, trauma, or toxic agents. The ghost of these 1920 concepts about morosis still hovers over mild mental retardation in some quarters today!

Since the moron was a relatively new recruit to the ranks of feeble-mindedness in 1920, and in alarming numbers, too, institutionalized morons became the focus for dozens of "researchers," and the subject matter of hundreds of publications and reports over the next two decades or more. The moron supply was a dependable one too, for ever since the Davenport report it had become public policy to get the moron into an institution whenever possible and to keep him there lest he propagate more of his own kind if released to the community. Social investigators swarmed over the countryside eagerly recording both fact and "old wives' tales" about the families of institutionalized morons. Brains of morons were scrutinized for gross and histological anomalies. Hundreds of morons became subjects of neuroendocrine explorations, and tons of endocrine substances were fed to the point of satiation. The moron's body fluids came in for biochemical tests and assays extant at that time. All this, and more too, ended up as "negative"; the moron proved out to be just like his "normal" control in his brain structure, his body chemistry, and his metabolism. More recently the cellular geneticists and the experts in intermediary metabolism have taken a look at mild mental retardation and have had nothing exciting to report. But with all of this, there survives in too many places a lurking suspicion that all is not well with the mild retardate's physiology, metabolism, brain structure, or chromosomes.

Of course it has long since been proven, and additional scientific proof is being discovered in recent years, that encephalopathy, cerebral agenesis, and deviant metabolism are responsible for the pronounced and more serious forms of mental retardation. There is, indeed, no valid reason to argue the point.

There are relatively few articles and reports in psychiatric literature that bear on mental retardation, but some of them merit attention. A hint at psychogenic causology is found in Thomas Willis's textbook, *De Anima Brutorum* (1672). "Stupidity or Morosis, or Foolishness . . . signifies a defect of the intellect and judgment . . . this eclipse of the superior soul proceeds from the imagination and the memory being hurt and the failing of these depends upon the faults of the animal spirits and the brain itself."

A thoughtful reading of Itard's report (1801) convinces one that he recognized the significance of motivation, needs, and transference, in his therapeutic work with Victor. Much of his effort, too, was directed toward fostering ego development and the strengthening of ego controls through the use of identification. Itard's monography might well be called the first published report on relationship psychotherapy. To demonstrate that even a severely mentally retarded subject such as Victor was responsive to psychotherapeutic efforts was a momentous achievement.

In 1860, Griesinger published the second edition of his textbook, *Mental Pathology and Therapeutics.* In his chapter, "Idiocy in General," he introduces the concept of psychogenic causology in mental subnormality:

> Cases where the mental development remains stationary from want of any external mental impulse–from extreme neglect and inattention–association with other dements, unfavorable outward relations, etc., finally certain cases where the mental development does not progress, because in weakly children there exists such an excessive degree of emotional irritability, of timidity and fear, that a state of passionate excitement is awakened by every attempt at mental influence, even by any lively sensorial impression, so that development of the normal process of perception is rendered impossible. Although few of the latter cases originally belong to the idiotic states, still they have the same practically important result–arrest of mental development" [pp. 348–349].

The earlier annals (1876–1900) of the American Association on Mental Deficiency are rich in their references to training and education procedures based upon the dynamics of modern psychotherapy.

In 1922, both Potter and Wallace published articles on the significance of personality structure in the social adaptation of mildly impaired young adult retardates.

Potter (1927a) reported on a study of the erotic behavior of idiots and suggested that most were fixed at an infantile level of psychosexuality characterized by diffuse forms of autoerotism.

In the same year, Potter (1927b) stated in another paper, "in certain instances there may be such an overwhelming narcissism in the infant as to prevent the outflow and onflow of that portion of the libido which perhaps furnishes at least a part of the urge needed for the development of intelligence, and, as a result, the intelligence becomes fixed at an incomplete level of development" (p. 698).

In 1933, L. P. Clark, in his monograph on *The Nature and Treatment of Amentia,* states:

> If we say that mental deficiency consists of some failure in the process of acquiring, absorbing and using knowledge for an adaptive mastery of reality, what are the specific defects behind this failure? Brain lesions or defects, a pathological variation in the germ cell, arrested neuron development, etc., have been indicated as the basis for mental arrest. None of these can indicate, however, just how the fundamental cause leads to the difficulties which the ament is seen to have, nor do they contain possibilities for understanding the individual in such a way as to help him in his problem of getting along in the world . . . There is found in all mental defectives a weak ego structure in

> association with an impounding of libido within the personality and an inbinding of primary narcissism, thus limiting the psychic energy available for object relationships which in turn dilutes the motivation for learning or acquisition [pp. 36–37].

In 1933, Potter identified childhood schizophrenia and noted that schizophrenic children are commonly found in institutions for mental defectives where they are usually regarded as "excitable imbeciles" or "idiot-savants."

In more recent years, and especially since World War II, perhaps stimulated by the unique maternal deprivation studies of Spitz (1946, 1959), a wealth of material directly or indirectly bearing on mental retardation and of particular interest to the child psychiatrist has been appearing in the literature. Many studies are reported by pediatricians, psychiatrists, educators, and psychologists showing that the infant's development and functioning may be affected physically, intellectually, emotionally, and socially by maternal or sociocultural deprivation (Kirk, 1958; Bowlby, 1951; Bakwin, 1942, 1949; Ribble, 1943; Brodbeck and Irwin, 1946; Rheingold, 1933; Levy, 1947; Goldfarb, 1945a, 1945b; Simonsen, 1947; Sarason and Gladwin, 1958; Skeels and Dye, 1938c-39; Theis, 1924; Bornstein, 1930; Clarke, 1958; Despert and Pierce, 1946; Kanner, 1952; Mundy, 1957).

In a recent study of 159 mentally retarded children, ages three to six, three quarters of whom "had evidence of organic brain disease," Webster (1963) reports that all had some clinical evidence of retarded emotional development.

Some psychoanalytic studies have been reported by Woodward, et al. (1958), Menninger and Chidester (1936), Green (1961), and a few others (Stacy and DeMartino, 1957) showing substantial improvement even in tested intelligence.

Perhaps a hundred or so reports (Stacy and DeMartino, 1957) have been published on the technique and effect of group therapy with mental retardates.

Follow-up studies (Camp and Waite, 1932; McKay, 1942; Davies, 1930, 1959; Kennedy, 1948; Saenger, 1957; Fernald, 1919; Storrs, 1929; Wolfson, 1956; Windle, 1962) have shown that not only do most of the mildly retarded make excellent social adjustments in adult life, but that also in some, tested intelligence has risen to well within normal ranges.

Odd though it may seem, there is a dearth of communications in the literature on the problem of anxiety in mental retardates, and the role that anxiety plays in the psychodynamics of the adaptational problems so common in those handicapped by subnormal intellectual endowment.

In reviewing the literature, it again is obvious that child psychiatry has been especially remiss in meeting its responsibilities to the intellectually handicapped child. With remarkably myopic vision, the intrapsychic aspects of adaptative problems of these children have been ignored. Little or no thought has been given to psychogenic causology in mental retardation. Child psychiatrists and psychoanalysts preoccupied with ego development have ignored an area of human pathology or deviation which might well be a rewarding area of investigation.

The author maintains that mild mental retardation is unrelated to the more disabling forms of intellectual deficits except that it has been assigned an ordinal position on the one and same I.Q. ladder. Many biological structures and functions, including intelligence, are susceptible to mensuration by some relatively precise measuring or quantifying instrument. The "normal ranges" of pulse rate, blood pressure, blood sugar level, coagulation time, brain weight, body weight, stature, and a host of other functions and structures are a matter of record. The "normal range" is a serviceable guide for clinicians, but the extent to which a deviation is an indicator of "abnormality" is a matter of clinical judgment.

Sixty years of experience of competent psychologists have gone into the construction of mental tests and in measuring intelligence. For classification purposes, the intelligence quotient has long since been adopted as the unit for measured intelligence. Whatever the defects and inadequacies of the test may be, and the experts are well aware of these, experience has demonstrated the intelligence quotient to be a useful guide and certainly one that most clinicians would not willingly discard.

Mild mental retardation is a classification based exclusively on the intelligence quotient computed from the responses to the various items in a standardized nomenthetic type of intelligence test. In the *Manual on Terminology and Classification in Mental Retardation,* Second Edition, published by the American Association on Mental Deficiency in 1961, mild mental retardation is defined as greater than minus two standard deviation units of measured intelligence but not more than three; this range of minus deviation units represents an intelligence quotient, based on the use of the Stanford-Binet test, Forms L and M, ranging from 52 to 67 inclusive. Mild mental retardation, in terms of its defined I.Q. range, is essentially synonomous with "moderate retardation" as defined in the *Diagnostic and Statistical Manual,* published in 1952 by the American Psychiatric Association, and closely approximates the moron as defined by Terman (1916).

As a general proposition, mildly retarded children closely resemble, rather than differ from, "normal" children and significantly differ from, rather than resemble, more seriously handicapped and limited mental retardates. Unlike the latter, mildly retarded children seldom have any evidence of retarded development in infancy and the preschool years; encephalopathy and inborn errors of metabolism are but rarely encountered; and all of them are potentially capable of independent living, self-support, and socially effective behavior in their adult years. It seems to be the consensus of most sophisticated clinicians that "mild retardation" represents a normal physiological variation in the minus direction on the distribution curve of tested intelligence for any population group. In fact, the only difference between mildly retarded children and children who are not retarded is that the former are, relatively speaking, slow learners in structured educational situations (the classroom) and their capacity for abstract thinking, limited.

At a conservative estimate, 75 of every 100 children classified as mentally retarded are within the category of "mild retardation." In other words, three quarters of all retarded children closely resemble "normal" children. Ordinarily one would expect to find somewhere in the neighborhood of 250 mildly retarded children in each 10,000 school children in the United States. Only some two or three per cent of mildly retarded children are admitted to residential centers for retardates.

According to the statistical data on *Patients in Public Institutions for the Mentally Retarded* (1960), published by the United States Public Health Service, however, an estimate based on a scrutiny of a number of statistical tabulations places the number of the mildly retarded who have not reached their fifteenth birth at only 4½ per cent (7,000) of the total institutional census. There are 108 such institutions in the United States, and about 90 per cent of these carry a patient census not in excess of 2,000. Thus one might reasonably expect to find, at the most, 90 mildly retarded children in the great majority of these residential centers. It is highly probable that all institutionalized mildly retarded children are anxiety ridden in one way or another, since either their disturbed behavior, or broken, disorganized homes, or both, precipitated their admission.

The proportion of mildly retarded children who are never institutionalized but are emotionally disturbed or socially maladjusted is probably not less than 10 per cent. But this is merely an educated guess. The prevalence of adaptational difficulties and emotionally disturbed personality is probably greater among mildly retarded children than in "normal" children for the following reasons:

a. A large share of the mildly retarded come from the culturally and socially deprived strata of society where emotional deprivation is a common experience, where motivation for intellectual achievement is at a low ebb, and where opportunity for identification with intellectual proficiency is rather meager.

b. Those from middle- and upper-class homes, where scholastic achievement has great prestige in our culture, are commonly subject to parental repudiation and rejection or frantic coercion.

c. Their limited intellectual capacities often go unrecognized, and as a result demands are made upon them both at home and in school which they are unable to fulfill.

d. Mildly retarded children are particularly apt to erect an anxiety-burdened self-image of exaggerated inadequacy and ineptitude. Many develop a sense of futility and build up a significant element of repressed hostility and guilt.

THE HIDDEN I.Q.

FRANK REISSMAN

Reissman falls into the growing tradition of those psychologists, who have expressed concern over the unfairness of using standardized tests in evaluating the intelligence of lower-class children. In his opinion, a diagnosis of mental retardation, solely on the grounds of I.Q., is unwarranted in that it is based on but one laboratory test performance with a particular examiner at a particular time. He challenges the validity of I.Q. tests in terms of two variables: motivation of the examinee, and the culture-bound nature of the tests. Reissman here considers the effects of the "blunting" of the lower-class child's intellectual life. He draws attention to the influence of social-class differences in child-rearing practices on attitudes toward performance, curiosity, and approaches to problem-solving. Reissman uses Hebb's (1949) theory of stimulus deprivation as a model, questioning its validity. Pasamanick (1959), in his perinatal studies, discusses the problem of socioculturally determined disorders from the standpoint of physical deprivation—poor nutrition and medical care.

Reissman, in aggreement with Benton (1956) who describes certain forms of "temporary" mental retardation, challenges the notion of irreversibility of poor performance. There have been other cross-cultural studies which relate to Reissman's speculations. Sarason (1959) found that Italian youngsters with poor performance had always been given tasks without explanation, setting a style or model for their limited approach to problem solving. Sarason mentions that other cultures value physical ability more highly than mental, that depending on these and other variables, the distribution of mentally retarded individuals differs considerably from one setting to the other.

Investigators are currently trying to devise culture-free and culture-fair tests. What we urgently need is research to find out what the organism needs at what particular point in its development so that we may adapt our social programs and educational institutions to the needs of all children.

Reprinted from *The Culturally Deprived Child.* New York: Harper & Row, 1962, pp. 49–62.

A few years ago a birthday party for a member of the staff at a well-known psychological clinic played a novel role in the test performance of a Negro child. Prior to the party, this boy, whom we shall call James, had been described on the psychological record as "sullen, surly, slow, unresponsive, apathetic, unimaginative, lacking in inner life." This description was based on his behavior in the clinic interviews and on his performance on a number of psychological measures including an intelligence test and a personality test. His was not an unusual record; many culturally deprived children are similarly portrayed.

On the day of the birthday party, James was seated in an adjoining room waiting to go into the clinician's office. It was just after the lunch hour, and James had the first afternoon appointment. The conclusion of the lunch break on this particular day was used by the staff to present a surprise birthday cake to one of the clinicians who happened to be a Negro. The beautifully decorated cake was brought in and handed to the recipient by James' clinician who was white, as were all the other members of the staff. The Negro woman was deeply moved by the cake—and the entire surprise. In a moment of great feeling, she warmly embraced the giver of the cake. James inadvertently perceived all this from his vantage point in the outer office. That afternoon he showed amazing alacrity in taking the tests and responding in the interview. He was no longer sullen and dull. On the contrary, he seemed alive, enthusiastic, and he answered questions readily. His psychologist was astonished at the change and in the course of the next few weeks retested James on the tests on which he had done so poorly. He now showed marked improvement, and she quickly revised not only the test appraisal of him on the clinical record card, but her general personality description of him as well.

The high point of their new, positive relationship came some months later when he confided to her that she had gotten off on the wrong foot with him on the first day in the first three minutes of contact. She was taken aback and said, "What do you mean? I was very friendly, I told you my name and asked you yours." He responded, "Yeh, and I said James Watson and right away you called me Jimmy and you bin callin' me Jimmy ever since. My names is James, 'cept to my very good friends maybe. Even my mother calls me James." Then he went on to tell her how he had changed his opinion of her on the day of the birthday party because of the close relationship he had seen between her and the Negro psychologist.

This little story illustrates a number of things: First, it shows that *the test is a social situation.* The testing situation, whether it be a psychological test or any other kind of test, for that matter, reflects a relationship between people, a relationship that is often remarkably subtle. And when anything hampers this relationship, the result is likely to show in the test score itself. This can occur on an individual test as well as a group test, an I.Q. test as well as a personality test, a subject matter examination as well as a psychological measure.

It also shows how the behavior evidenced in the clinical situation tends to be seen by the psychologist as indicative of the basic personality of the child. This is frequently done with little awareness of how much this behavior is a product of the particular relationship of the psychologist to the child, and of the testing situation as such. Children from different cultural backgrounds respond very differently to clinical situations and to the idea of being tested or evaluated.

The anecdote also points up the fact that a well-meaning, clinically trained, unprejudiced psychologist can have poor rapport with a deprived child, not because of deficient psychological technique, but because of limited knowledge about certain cultural attitudes. In this case, the attitude in question is the feeling held by many Negro people that the informality intended by shortened nicknames signifies a lack of respect when it takes place across cultural lines. This does not suggest that the child himself was aware of this reasoning, but that, rather, he was simply reflecting his parents' wish that he be called by his full name.

The importance of having Negro psychologists on the staff of a clinic is shown in a pertinent way by the anecdote. The Negro child need not himself have a Negro clinician, but her presence in the clinic was indirectly influential.

Finally, the story neatly illustrates the fact that scores on tests are not fixed and can be reversed dramatically when the relationship to the tester is improved. There is apparently a hidden I.Q. and a hidden personality that is often not revealed by the test and the clinical interview. In our story, James' I.Q. score rose considerably in the retesting, and his personality began to appear in a totally new light.

The I.Q. Controversy

Currently there is considerable questioning of some of the basic assumptions of the I.Q. test. Consistent with the incident we have just reported, the old notion that the I.Q. is relatively stable or constant is under heavy fire. There is increasing recognition that I.Q. scores of underprivileged children do not reflect their ability, because the test items include words that are not in the experience repertoire of these children.

But there are many other assumptions involved that have not been as fully questioned, and perhaps it would be a good idea to briefly trace the history of the I.Q. controversy.

At first the issue revolved around whether the lower I.Q. of deprived children was a result of heredity or environment. Research indicated that environmental factors were apparently decisive in producing the higher middle-class I.Q. Then Davis questioned the applicability of the I.Q. tests to deprived groups (1948). He wondered if the tests might not be impregnated with middle-class problems and language, and thus not be fair to underprivileged youngsters.

What Davis did was to take various intelligence test problems on which the deprived did poorly, and reword them in terms equally familiar to all children. For example:

Instead of "Cub is to bear as gosling is to 1 ( ) fox, 2 ( ) grouse, 3 ( ) goose, 4 ( ) rabbit, 5 ( ) duck," he substituted, "Puppy goes with dog like kitten goes with 1 ( ) fox, 2 ( ) goose, 3 ( ) cat, 4 ( ) rabbit, 5 ( ) duck."

The required understanding of the relationship of the concepts is not altered by the revised form. If the child does not know the word "gosling," he can never demonstrate his grasp of the relationship required in this question. In other words, until the change was made, this item was functioning as a vocabulary test for the disadvantaged child (Eells et al., 1951).[1] The reformulation changed not only the vocabulary involved, but also the structure of the sentence to read "puppy *goes with* dog like kitten *goes with* ______." "Goes with" is substituted for "is to." This made the problem more understandable to the underprivileged children.

Surprisingly enough, however, even though Davis' changes produced a test that was more attuned to them, disadvantaged youngsters did not improve markedly. Something else apparently was deterring them. It remained for Haggard to clear up the mystery (1954).

The Big Three: Practice, Motivation, Rapport

Haggard reasoned that although deprived children may have taken

[1] Robert Havighurst, one of Davis' colleagues, points out that items requiring knowledge of the following words may touch the experience of the middle-class child but not that of the deprived child: fireplace, chandelier, wall-paper, salad fork, dining room. Words which might be more familiar to deprived children, such as pump, coal stove, kerosene lamp, rain barrel, rarely appear on intelligence tests.

many I.Q. tests, they really did not know how to take these tests properly: they lacked meaningful, directed practice. They also lacked motivation, and their relationship to the examiner was typically distant and beset by fears.

Haggard decided to control each of these factors. He gave both deprived and non-deprived children three one-hour training periods in taking I.Q. tests. These practice periods included careful explanation of what was involved in each of the different types of problems found on the I.Q. tests. The explanations were given in words that were familiar to both groups. Haggard also offered special rewards for doing well, and he trained his examiners to be responsive to the deprived children as well as to the middle-class youngsters, thus greatly enhancing the rapport. [2]

Under these conditions the I.Q.'s of the disadvantaged children improved sharply. *This occurred with only three hours of practice* (Haggard, 1954). And it occurred even on the old I.Q. tests with the middle-class-biased items. Apparently more important than the content of the test items was the attitude of the children toward the test situation and the examiner.

Haggard also showed that when test items were read aloud to the deprived children while they followed in their test booklets, these children did much better (Haggard, 1954). Deprived children are notoriously poor readers. Consequently, their typically inadequate intelligence test performance is partly a result of that difficulty rather than of limited intelligence.

It might be asked at this point, why all the fuss–if deprived children cannot read well, what difference does it make if we say they are less intelligent, or that they are deficient in reading? The answer is that it makes a huge difference because of the contrasting implications of deficiencies in intelligence and deficiencies in reading ability. Reading skill, it is gener-

[2] In the area of motivation, it is clear that middle-class children are more motivated to do well on examinations of the I.Q. sort because of the general emphasis on success and competition in middle-class life. Even where an examination is not directly related to a reward or a threat, the middle-class child strives to perform well. Part of the difference in I.Q. scores of middle-class and deprived children is due to differences in strength of motivation to perform well on an examination rather than to differences in intelligence.

This point is indirectly verified in a study by Douvan (1956). At first, an examination was given to both deprived and middle-class youngsters without any indication of its importance, or of an offering of a meaningful reward for satisfactory work. The result was typical: the middle-class group showed far greater motivation than the deprived group. Later, the test was rerun, but this time a reward was offered for successful work on the test. The result: the motivation of the deprived group increased much more than that of the middle-class group. Thus, when the test situation promised rewards that were direct, immediate, practical, and meaningful, deprived children responded at a higher level than where such rewards were absent. But less so with middle-class youth, who are more often motivated to perform at close to their maximum level even while rewards are absent.

ally accepted, can be improved fairly easily, certainly in the child, and to some degree even in the adult, where motivation is present. On the other hand, the old assumption was that intelligence, while it is affected by experience and knowledge, is much less easily changed or improved. Perhaps not much can be done in schools to help deprived children if they suffer from low intelligence; but the outlook is much more positive if the problem is poor reading. [3]

I.Q. Assumptions Discriminate Against the Deprived

Walter Murray, one of Davis' coworkers, is currently continuing the analysis of basic assumptions underlying the I.Q. He questions the following assumptions which function either directly or indirectly to penalize the deprived child:

1. The I.Q. is measured by the use of brief exercises that have to be executed fairly quickly; while "many of the problems that individuals are expected to solve in real life require much time and concentration," this type of task is excluded from the I.Q. test.

The brief exercises and the general accent on speed in particular work against the deprived child. His style is slow and cautious. It takes him a long time to become involved in problems, and his potential will not easily be evidenced in short, speed-oriented tasks. He will, in all likelihood, show his ability only after he is absorbed in a problem. Many non-deprived children have a similar work orientation, of course, and rural children find the speed emphasis equally distasteful.

Davis (1948) notes that speed is affected by cultural attitudes concerning the importance or unimportance of speed, and by personality factors, such as "competitiveness, conscientiousness, compulsiveness, exhibitionism, and anxiety." *These personality characteristics are less frequently associated with the deprived child's personality pattern.*

[3] It might be objected, of course, that in Haggard's investigation the underprivileged youngsters improved more than did the middle-class because the latter had the higher I.Q. scores and thus could not improve upon them. There are two answers to this objection, one of which is somewhat technical: Haggard points out that through the use of a special statistical method (the Johnson-Neyman technique), the effect of the higher I.Q. of the middle-class children was held constant or removed. (Haggard, personal communication).

Secondly, and less technical, the argument overlooks a fundamental assumption underlying most intelligence tests, namely, that the I.Q. is relatively stable, and that it certainly *cannot be raised easily.* Haggard's study shows, on the contrary, that in a period of five days, which included only three one-hour practice sessions, the I.Q. of large numbers of deprived youngsters could be significantly increased. What seems to be involved here is that if the individual or group is not functioning with high motivation, or if efficient test-taking techniques have not been developed, or if rapport with the examiner is not good, the resulting *performance* can rather readily be improved.

2. The I.Q. score is based on the accuracy of the final answer to the I.Q. question, not the method of thinking involved in arriving at this answer. Murray (1960) states, "In most tests the final score or judgment of the student's intelligence, is based on the number of correct responses. Little or no attention is given to the method by which the student attacked the problem or the kinds of considerations he made use of in attempting to solve it"[4] (cited in Riessman [1962, p. 55]).

The deprived child does not possess, as one psychologist put it recently, "good avoidance conditioning for wrong answers." He does not have a good sense for what is likely to be a poor answer, because he has limited test-taking skills. The teacher and the psychologist are typically oriented toward getting the right answer and are less interested in the thinking processes involved, particularly when the thinking does not lead to the correct result.

3. Intelligence is assumed to develop and increase with age; items which do not show an improvement with age are excluded from the I.Q. tests.

The assumption that intelligence increases with age has an indirect effect on the measurement of the I.Q. of the deprived child. Characteristically his measured I.Q. has been found to *fall* with age. This is, apparently, because he has not been exposed to the experiences and vocabulary presumed to be normal in the culture, and on which all the I.Q. tests are based. Now, if it were possible to have I.Q. exercises that were not dependent on these experiences, and that measured skills that did not improve with the age of the child, the underprivileged child might fare better.

4. It is assumed that intelligence is best demonstrated in a school environment. I.Q. tests have tended to become tests of scholastic aptitude. Intelligence may be relatively unimportant in business, industry, agriculture, etc., but this does not on the surface appear to be a very sound assumption.

With regard to the highly academic character of the I.Q. test, Tyler (1951) notes that

> . . . so far as problem-solving exercises are concerned, the typical intelligence tests lean heavily on academic, school-type problems, whereas lower-class

[4] Haggard (1953) reports the following: In one study, children were asked to give the reasons for their answers to intelligence test items. In the case of one analogy item, 35 of the 60 children tested marked the "correct" response, but not one of these children gave the "correct" reason for marking it. The reasons given were on the basis of rhyming, synonym, etc., but not on the basis of making the analogy—the process which the test constructor assumed was being measured.

> children frequently have had more experience than have middle-class children in dealing with the kinds of practical problems encountered on the street and in the playground. That is to say, it seems clear . . . that youngsters who do not show up well on intelligence tests do possess abilities that indicate some skill in solving practical problems and that suggest potentialities for further education if the schools had broad enough goals to utilize talents of these kinds [p. 43].

Early Environment and the Changeability of the I.Q.

Few people still maintain the old assumption that the I.Q. is necessarily stable or constant throughout life. There is too much evidence showing that it can be changed under varying conditions. But an allied view has been advanced that is related to the "constancy" assumption.

This argument holds that the underprivileged child has been immersed in an early "impoverished" environment in which there is insufficient stimulation, thus producing a *basic retardation,* so that, in effect, his I.Q. remains relatively low throughout life. [5]

One version of this argument maintains that the early environment of the deprived child produces behavior similar to that sometimes found in institutional children and in children brought up in isolation from society. At its extreme, this view sees the behavior of deprived children as being similar to that found in the stimulus deprivation experiments, where volunteers are put in special respiratory tanks for twenty-four hours. (Following these experiments, the subjects are unable to concentrate, their I.Q. performance and problem-solving ability temporarily deteriorates, and they are in a general fog.) The stimulus deprivation thesis presumes that the underprivileged child has suffered some similar lack of stimulation over a long period of time, particularly in his early life, and that this accounts for his low I.Q. There are three levels at which this argument may be challenged:

1. In the first place, the stimulus-depriving tank analogy seems extremely far-fetched because, whatever one may say about the environment of these children, it certainly is not lacking in stimulation per se. Witness the crowded homes and streets, the noise, parties, TV sets, the sports, games, fights, etc.

[5] Hebb (1949, Chapter II), a leading psychologist, makes the assumption that the early childhood period is of decisive importance in determining later intelligence. He believes that Negro and poor white children have had insufficient stimulation in their early development, and that this accounts for their lower *functioning* intelligence at a later age. He accepts the intelligence test performance as an accurate indicator of operating intelligence, although he believes it to be a completely inaccurate index of *capacity*–inherent intelligence.

2. Moreover, the family life includes a good deal of sibling interaction, physical punishment, definite toilet training, masturbation inhibition, breast feeding, and various responsibility demands. Regardless of the particular evaluation one may wish to place on these practices, they do appear to provide stimulation. This environment seems quite distinct from that of children reared in isolation from society.

3. Haggard's findings further call into question the inference concerning "basic retardation," because if the I.Q. can be so markedly improved by only three hours of special training, surely the childhood experiences cannot have been so limiting or irreversible. It might also be added that much of the behavior of deprived children in non-academic spheres gives evidence of considerable spontaneity, a trait not ordinarily associated with a history of deficient stimulation.

Creativity and the I.Q.

Eric Fromm (1947) says of intelligence tests that "they measure not so much the capacity for reason and understanding, as the capacity for quick mental adaptation to a given stituation; 'mental adjustment tests' would be the adequate name for them" (p. 75).

The items used on the tests do not require any intrinsic interest or curiosity on the part of the subject. On the contrary, if he becomes too interested in any one item he will probably take too much time on it and possibly give an unconventional response that might be marked as being wrong. The motivation called for on the test is not interest in the specific questions as such, but rather an overall competitive motivation to do well. But the intelligence of certain kinds of people may not really be tapped unless they are deeply involved in the specific problem on which they are working. This is more likely to be the case with disadvantaged individuals.

Psychologists have come to disagree with the notion that a high I.Q. is the mark of "giftedness" or creativity. Dr. Westcott (1960) at Vassar College has developed a specific test for measuring creativity that has been validated in terms of actual creative accomplishments of the students—accomplishments such as writing a piece of music, poetry, and the like. He finds little relationship between creativity and I.Q. scores.

The I.Q. of deprived individuals is generally relatively low, but their creativity is often shown in non-academic ways: A prominent labor union economist, Solomon Barkin, Research Director of the Textile Workers' Union of America, has said that he has seen a number of wage incentive schemes that seemed to him foolproof, with no way of adapting them so that they would benefit the workers. But he has never seen a plan that in practice could not be adapted or "jimmied" in their favor. He reports that a number of times he had objected to management proposals for incentive plans as unfavorable to the workers, only to be told by the men involved, "Don't worry, we'll figure out how to jimmy it." He, himself, could not see any possibility for manipulation of the scheme, yet in every case, within a year, the men in the shop had been able to figure out ways of "beating the system" that he, an expert, could not envision. We are not discussing the ethics of the actions, but the creativity manifested.

We have frequently observed children in deprived neighborhoods playing basketball by tieing a fruit basket, with the bottom removed, to a fire escape. This requires a fair amount of creative ingenuity.

Action Implications

As a result of the re-evaluation of the standard I.Q. tests and their particular limitations for underprivileged children, a number of recommendations have come forth:

1. One suggestion is to employ performance tests wherever possible, since these appear to be less affected by the vocabulary limitations of the deprived child. Unfortunately, while these tests have a number of advantages, their use does not overcome the problems of rapport, motivation, and test-taking skill encountered with underprivileged youngsters.

2. Davis (1948) and Eells (1951) have developed a "culture fair" games test which in many ways seems more appropriate for underprivileged groups. While some deprived individuals fare better on this test, others do not. The problems of rapport, motivation, and practice appear here again, although the motivation problem is partially reduced by making the test a game.

3. Murray (1960) and others have suggested that the deficiencies of the standard I.Q. tests be corrected. He feels that the tests are potentially valuable tools, and rejects the argument advanced by some that they should be discarded because of their weaknesses. Not only can the tests be improved, but different dimensions of intelligence can be tapped. Items employed need not be brief; tasks showing no change with age can be utilized; time limits may be removed or lengthened; less academic, bookish problems can be employed; the thinking involved in solving the problems can be evaluated along with the accuracy of the final answer; items that discriminate between deprived and middle-class groups can be removed from the tests, just as items discriminating between the sexes are removed

in test construction; emotionally loaded items can be selected, and the responses to them compared with the more value-free items. These are just a few of the possible changes that might be introduced to strengthen the tests.

4. Haggard's study, in which the measured I.Q. of deprived children was raised considerably with only three hours of special training, highlights the need for giving these children directed practice, and developing new test-taking habits. Deprived children are less test-conscious and are not accustomed to being evaluated. They have poor auditory habits, do not concentrate sufficiently on the examiner's instructions, do not pick up the examinations readily, and, in general, are lethargic, apathetic, and ill at ease in the test situation. Sometimes they hurry through the test, just to get it over with and to remove themselves from the situation. Some deprived children are more serious about the test, but they are usually over-cautious, anxious and slow.

Simple, undirected practice in test-taking will not overcome these difficulties. In the course of their school careers, deprived youngsters receive much practice, but it is unmotivated, meaningless practice. Experience is a good teacher only when one knows what to learn from it; by itself, practice can merely reinforce bad habits.

5. Haggard's research also demonstrates the great need for rapport. Haggard trained his examiners so that they would know how to work with deprived youngsters. This kind of training is decisive for clinicians and teachers. The clinician has to know how to elicit questions from the deprived child, and how to provide answers in terms that are clearly understood, are repeated often, with numerous examples. He must realize that simply giving the child the test instructions, and having him nod that they are understood, is by no means any guarantee. Deprived children, unless they are at ease with the examiner, are much more likely to be passive in the test situation.

Rapport is also dependent upon the examiner having confidence that the child *can* do well. In a sense, the clinician has to convey to the deprived child that he understands why the child has not done well in the past, but that now the conditions are different, and the child will therefore be able to show his real ability. This should not be false, or artificial; in fact, the examiner should believe this and let the child perceive his optimistic, but not demanding or pressing, expectation.

6. The teacher might choose to ignore the standard I.Q. results because of the limitations of the test, and instead attempt to discover the "hidden I.Q." of the deprived child. This can best be done by noting the child's

contributions in discussing a topic which interests him a good deal, such as popular music or the world series. Role-playing (acting out situations) and physical tasks in general are useful for estimating his potential intelligence.

A good deal of the behavior of underprivileged individuals outside the school context indicates considerable intelligence in terms of dealing with problems and interests close to their own lives. Their intelligence is more fully shown in games such as dominoes, in sports, in humor, and in gossip. They are often surprisingly perceptive in sensing various subtle forms of discrimination, and the children demonstrate much misdirected ingenuity in avoiding truant officers and the law. In general, it might be said that they are rather "human smart," and their "hidden I.Q.'s" are best seen in their human relations.

EFFECTS OF ADOPTION ON CHILDREN FROM INSTITUTIONS

HAROLD M. SKEELS

Skeels' dramatic findings have shaken the pessimistic attitudes toward retardation that prevailed in the earlier part of the century. These represented the simplistic approach that genetic transmission, i.e., the inheritance of a unitary factor, was common to the entire retarded population. Goddard (1912) considered the squalor and poverty of the Kallikak home sufficient evidence to support the theory of the genetic transmission of mental deficiency. He could, of course, just as easily have used the same evidence toward the theory that retardation is caused by lack of environmental stimulation. Other myths about retardation, interestingly enough initiated by leaders and pioneers in the field, include Fernald's statement that feeblemindedness is the mother of crime, pauperism, and degeneracy.

Our hope today is that primary prevention–school enrichment programs, better parental care, family planning, and genetic counselling–will reduce the number of retarded in the future, and that secondary prevention–early recognition of emerging retardation–will forestall permanent handicaps.

We are discovering that too many institutions do not use preventive measures or rehabilitate. On the contrary, they do not even allow for the normal growth and development which might occur in an appropriate family setting. In many cases, they perpetuate retardation iatrogenically. Skeels' program of alternate placement is by no means ideal and is associated with the enormous problems of the social realities, i.e., our inability to find enough ideal foster placements. Yet it has demonstrated stunning effects. Provence and Lipton (1962) have proposed that we identify the most deleterious aspects of institutional care and devote our efforts to altering them.

The National Institute of Mental Health is presently carrying on three follow-up studies of adults who were reared away from their own parents. The purpose is to determine the adult status of children previously stud-

Reprinted with permission from *Children,* 12(1), 1965, pp. 33–34. U.S. Department of Health, Education, and Welfare, Welfare Administration, Children's Bureau.

ied by the Iowa Child Welfare Research Station, State University of Iowa, in cooperation with the Children's Division, Iowa Board of Control of State Institutions, which initiated modes of intervention in infancy or early childhood. These include follow-up studies of:

I. A longitudinal study of 100 adopted children (Skodak and Skeels, 1949). The follow-up of this study is being carried on by the original investigators.

II. A study of the effects of differential stimulation on mentally retarded children (Skeels and Dye, 1938c–1939). The follow-up of this study is also being carried on by the original investigator.

III. A study of the mental development in adoptive homes of children whose biological mothers were mentally retarded (Skeels and Harms, 1948). The follow-up of this study is being carried on by Lowell W. Schenke, psychologist, Iowa Board of Control of State Institutions, with one of the original investigators (the writer) serving as consultant.

In all three of these studies, the children selected for study were considered to be biologically sound and without demonstrable abnormality as determined through diagnostic evaluation by competent pediatricians. With the inclusion of the present followup studies, they cover a life span of 30 years, the present ages of the subjects being within a range of 25 to 35 years.

Adopted Children

In regard to the follow-up of Study I, all adoptive parents and adopted children have been located after a lapse of 16 years since the last contacts of the earlier study. Interviews with adoptive parents and their adult adopted children are nearing completion. Analysis of the data will start in the near future.

Preliminary indications are that these adoptive children as adults are achieving at levels consistently higher than would have been predicted from the intellectual, educational, or socio-economic level of the biological parents, and equal to the expectancy for children living in the homes of natural parents capable of providing environmental impacts similar to those which have been provided by the adoptive parents.

Mentally Retarded Children

In regard to follow-up of Study II, all subjects have been located after a lapse of 21 years, all interviews completed, with the data presently being processed.

Preliminary findings of this follow-up study are particularly startling. In the original study, 13 children in an experimental group, all mentally retarded at the beginning of the study, were at an early age transferred from one institution to another which provided a much higher degree of one-to-one emotional relationship between mother-surrogates and the children. Later, 11 of these children were placed in adoptive homes.

A contrast group of 12 children, initially at a higher level of intelligence than those in the experimental group, remained in a relatively nonstimulating institutional environment over a prolonged period of time. In the initial study, the children in the experimental group showed a decided increase in rate of mental growth, whereas the children in the contrast group showed progressive mental retardation.

In the adult follow-up study, the two groups continued to be remarkably divergent. All 13 children in the experimental group are self-supporting, and none is a ward of any institution, public or private. Eleven of the 13 children are married, and nine of these have children.

Of the 12 children in the contrast group, one died in adolescence following continued residence in a State institution for the mentally retarded; four are still wards of institutions–one of these is in a mental hospital and three are in institutions for the mentally retarded. Among those no longer wards of institutions, only two have married, and one of these is divorced. Two of the four females in the contrast group were sterilized in late adolescence to preclude the possibility of procreation if later placed out to work.

In education, disparity between the two groups is great. In the experimental group, the median grade completed is the 12th; in the contrast group, the third. Four subjects in the experimental group have had one year or more of college work, one of the boys having received a B.A. degree. Occupationally, the experimental group ranges from professional and semiprofessional positions to semiskilled labor or domestic work. In the contrast group, 50 per cent of the subjects are unemployed, and those that are employed are, with the exception of one person, unskilled laborers.

One girl in the experimental group who initially had an I.Q. of 35 has subsequently graduated from high school and taken one semester of work at a college. She is married and has two boys. These boys have been given intelligence tests and have achieved I.Q. scores of 128 and 107.

If this girl had had the continuing experience characteristic of those in the contrast group, she would have remained all these years on a custodial ward in an institution for the mentally retarded or have been sterilized in late adolescence or early adulthood and subsequently placed out on a nonskilled labor type of domestic employment.

In fact, "but for the grace of God," any one of the cases in the experimental group might have experienced the impact of deprivation of those in the contrast group, and vice versa.

Cost to the State

We are also studying the cost to the State of each subject in the experimental group and the contrast group of Study II—based on information as to per capita cost for institutional care per month or year for each of the years from 1932 to 1963. Preliminary indications are shocking.

In the experimental group, the median total cost is less than $1,000 whereas in the contrast group it is 10 times that, with a range from $7,000 to $24,000. One case in the contrast group can be cited of a person who has been a ward of the State institution for over 30 years. The total cost to the State in this instance has been $24,113.

In the 1930's, the monthly per capita cost at State children's institutions and at mental hospitals ranged around $17 per month. This has progressively increased over the years until the present figure is considerably more than $200 per month. We can speculatively extrapolate on the cost to the State of the subjects in Study II had our comparisons started in 1963 instead of 1932. Assuming that costs were constant from 1963 to 1993, the case in the example cited would have cost the State $100,000.

Mentally Retarded Parents

As already mentioned, Study III involved children whose biological mothers were considered to be mentally retarded. The children had been separated from their natural mothers in early infancy, either by voluntary release or by court commitment, and had been placed in adoptive homes before they were two years old. The study included a total of 87 cases. I.Q. scores were obtained on each of the mothers, none of whom achieved higher than 75. The range extended down to an I.Q. of 32.

After a time interval of 21 years, efforts are under way to locate the adoptive parents and children of this study, and indications are that all or most of them will be found. Several interviews have already been completed.

In the follow-up, in addition to securing information on the adult status of the children, intelligence tests are being administered to the second generation—the grandchildren of the mentally retarded, biological grandmothers.

Preliminary findings in this follow-up study suggest that the first generation (the children of the original study) compares favorably in occupational status as adults with the Iowa population of comparable ages according to 1960 census figures. The second-generation children are scoring average and above on intelligence tests.

Some Implications

Since the preliminary findings of these three follow-up studies are substantiated by reports of many supporting studies published in the past 20 years, it would seem that we have adequate knowledge for designing programs of intervention to counteract the devastating effects of poverty, sociocultural deprivation, maternal deprivation, or a combination of these ills. This means making expenditures for the tremendous costs of a curative nature. It does not, of course, preclude further research and exploratory studies to determine the optimum modes of intervention and the most appropriate ages for initiating such procedures.

PARENTS' FEELINGS ABOUT RETARDED CHILDREN

LEO KANNER

Kanner's indictment of the medical profession highlights some important problems clinicians must face as more and more children are being kept at home and educated in the community. Now that automatic placement at the time of diagnosis has gone by the boards, the question of whether or not to institutionalize the retarded child is perhaps the hardest part of parent counseling.

Solnit (and Stark, 1961; Omwake and Solnit, 1961) and others (Dembo et al., 1956; Wright, 1960) have also considered dynamic factors behind the problems of working with parents of handicapped children. They believe that the period just following the diagnosis is a critical one, one in which we frequently see underlying currents of "mourning" for the perfect child the parents had expected, and their grief over his loss. Solnit states that they must be helped through the phase before they can actively participate in whatever decision needs to be made.

Family assessment must be individualized. It is of vital importance that the mental health professional differentiate between those cases in which retardation is (1) "accidental"–an organic form occurring in a normal family; (2) those in which it is organic, but has evoked a pathological reaction with secondary emotional problems superimposed on child and parent; and (3) those cases in which family pathologies have indeed been inextricably involved in the etiological development of the retardation itself. Kanner, in this and his other work on mental retardation (1949a), directs us to the second kind of retardation–the development of secondary emotional disorders in cases of primary simple retardation.

There was a time when, confronted with the task of dealing with retarded children, the educator's, psychologist's, or physician's main effort consisted of an examination of the child and advice to the family. No

Reprinted from *American Journal of Mental Deficiency,* 56, 1953–1954, pp. 375–383.

matter how expertly and conscientiously this was done, it somehow did not take in the whole magnitude of the problem. Parents were told of the child's low I.Q. in mournful numbers and were urged to think in terms of ungraded classes or residential school placement. The I.Q. figures may have been correct, and the suggestions may have been adequate, and yet, very often, a major, highly important and, in fact, indispensable part of the job was somehow neglected.

It is recognized more and more that professional, and at the same time humane, attention should be given to the attitudes and feelings of people who are understandably puzzled by the lag in their child's development and progress. Whenever parents are given an opportunity to express themselves, they invariably air their emotional involvements in the form of questions, utterances of guilt, open and sometimes impatient rebellion against destiny, stories of frantic search for causes, pathetic accounts of matrimonial dissensions about the child's condition, regret about the course that has been taken so far, anxious appraisals of the child's future, and tearful pleas for reassurance. It takes a considerable amount of cold, hard-boiled, pseudoprofessorial detachment to turn a deaf ear on the anxieties, self-incriminations, and concerns about past, present, and future contained in such remarks. We have learned to take them into serious consideration and to treat them as the genuine, deep-seated, intrinsic perplexities that they are. We have learned to distinguish between abrupt, brutal frankness and a sympathetic statement of fact, between a dictatorial, take-it-or-leave-it kind of recommendation and the sort of presentation which would appeal to parents as the most constructive and helpful procedure, best suited under the existing circumstances.

I know that it is difficult to speak in generalities about a subject which entails individual sentiments. I know from experience that every couple who comes with a retarded child carries along a set of specific curiosities which must be understood and satisfied. For this reason, it may perhaps serve the purpose of this address if I were to introduce a few definite instances and, in so doing, to discuss the principal implications as they come along in the life of the retarded child and in the minds of his family.

Johnny Jones was brought to our clinic at the age of eight years. He was referred to us by his pediatrician with the request for a psychometric evaluation. Johnny was in his third year in school, had been demoted once, and after that had been given courtesy promotions, even though he did not master the required curriculum of his grade. The psychologist's examination showed that Johnny had a test age of six years and an I.Q. of 75. It was obvious that, with his endowment, he could not possibly be expected to do better than low first grade work. It would have seemed easy to say to the parents that Johnny should be in an ungraded class because of his low intelligence. It would have been very easy to give them the numerical result of the test and, if they balked, to offer them an authoritative explanation of the Binet-Simon or any other scale that had been employed. However, there was one big fly in the ointment. Mr. and Mrs. Jones were both college graduate people and moved in highly intellectual and sophisticated circles. Mr. Jones was a competent representative of a pharmaceutical firm and his wife had been a librarian prior to her marriage. They could see logically that their son had not been able to accomplish the scholastic functions expected of a child his age. But for years they had struggled against the very thought that something might be amiss with their Johnny's academic possibilities. As a result, they had kept looking for interpretations of his failures other than the one interpretation which they dreaded because they could not accept it emotionally. They had found fault with the "school system." There couldn't be anything wrong with the child; the problem must lie somewhere in the *method of instruction:* Johnny's teachers were either too young and inexperienced or too old and unfamiliar with modern educations. They were alternately critical of what they chose to call either old-fashioned drilling or new-fangled frills. When, in the course of time, they had been convinced that the other children in Johnny's group got along all right under the same educational regime, they tried to seek the culprit in *Johnny's body.* After considerable search, they found one doctor who persuaded them that Johnny would do better if his tonsils and adenoids were taken out. They cherished this bit of wisdom because it fitted into their emotional pattern. They could say to themselves that, after all, their Johnny was all right and would learn better after the repair of a physical imperfection. This did not work. In order to satisfy their need for prestige, they began to pounce on *Johnny himself.* They decided that the child must be lazy. They scolded him, deprived him of privileges and sat with him for hours trying to hammer his homework into him. They pointed out to him how well his numerous cousins did without all the help such as he received from them. The child, smarting from the constant rebuff and rebuke, sat there, unable to grasp the parental instructions and, not knowing why he could not conform, came to think of himself as a wretched, miserable, ungrateful creature who let his parents down. He gave up completely. He lost all confidence in himself and, in order to find some compensation for his anguish, he took to daydreaming. Eventually, the parents thought that Johnny's salvation stared them in the face when they came upon an article in *The Reader's Digest* which told them that a certain drug, named glutamic acid, could brighten up children and make them learn better. They obtained the drug and got him to swallow tablet after tablet. For a time, they called off the dogs of daily tutoring and pushing, with the idea that glutamic acid would do the trick. Johnny, relieved of the pressures, perked up for a while and seemed brighter. He felt that being offered the tablets, however ill-tasting they were, was better than being hovered over impatiently at the desk. The parents came to feel that the money they paid to the druggist was about the best investment they had ever made. But in the long run they realized that, as far as learning was concerned, there was no noticeable departure from the status quo. They felt disillusioned and finally decided to take the child to the clinic.

Betty Brown was a placid, likable little girl whose physical characteristics and marked developmental retardation had led the child's pediatrician to make the correct diagnosis of mongolism. He was able to help the parents to understand and accept Betty's limitations. The Browns were warm-hearted people and genuinely fond of their three children, of whom Betty was the youngest. Michael and Anne were healthy and bright and held out every promise of good academic achievement. They sensed their sister's handicaps, were helped by their parents to make the necessary allowances and, being secure in the warmth of a comfortable emotional climate, adjusted nicely to Betty's need for her mother's special attention. Anne, in fact, welcomed and invited opportunities to be mother's little helper in her ministrations to Betty.

This constellation of attitudes might have made for an ideal mode of family living. But a "bull in the china shop" charged into this peaceful home in the shape of Betty's paternal grandmother who lived a few doors away from the Browns. The elder Mrs. Brown stubbornly refused to acknowledge the doctor's diagnosis. She had always been a bit critical of her daughter-in-law but had found it difficult to hold on to a specific hatrack on which to hang her expressions of disapproval. Betty's failure to develop properly came to her as a godsend. She made up her mind that there was nothing wrong with Betty herself and that the whole trouble stemmed from the child's mother's inadequate methods of training. She offered no concrete suggestions. She did not substantiate her recriminations. But every morning, with clock-like regularity, she appeared at the home, looked at the child with a mien of profound commiseration, and uttered the same reproachful phrase: "When are you going to start making something of the child?"

Mrs. Brown took this as long as she could. She discarded as utterly futile her initial attempts to convey to her tormentor the reality of Betty's condition. She decided to remain silent. But eventually she could stand it no longer. It is not easy to be confronted daily with insult added to painful injury. She turned for help to her husband, imploring him to do something about his mother's stereotyped antics. All that he had to offer was the advice that she "pay no attention." After a few months, she brought Betty to our clinic. In reality, she brought herself and her misery rather than the child. She was obviously depressed and was seeking help for herself, which by that time she needed desperately.

Alan Smith was his parents' only child. He was severely retarded in his development. The Smiths, feeling that Alan would need all of their attention, had decided to deprive themselves of further offspring. There was also the dread of a possible repetition of the tragedy. But most pathetic of all was the boy's mother's constant self-searching for some shortcomings of her own which might be responsible for her son's intellectual defect. When she brought him to the clinic, she asked: "Doctor, did I have something to do with it? Did I do something wrong?" She eagerly gulped down the acquittal but went on: "Well–maybe before he was born–did I do something then?" When told that her child's retardation was not determined by anything that she had done, she was still puzzled. She wondered: "If it isn't what I have *done,* maybe it's what I *am* that brought it about." Again she seemed grateful for authoritative absolution. But still she went on. If she had not contributed to the fact of Alan's retardation, then she was surely guilty of not recognizing it in time, of pushing him beyond his capacity, of losing patience with him, of doing things for him which he might have learned to do for himself. Furthermore, she had been ashamed of his backwardness and tried to hide it from her friends and neighbors, and then she was ashamed of having felt shame. Of course, she could not gain peace through mere verbal reassurance, however thirstily she lapped it up. She needed many opportunities to talk herself out, more chances for his confessional type of expiation, and help in the suggested efforts to return to her previous social and communal life from which she had removed herself in sacrificial isolation because of her feelings of shame and guilt and remorse.

Larry White was brought to our clinic at the age of seven-and-a-half years. His parents were distressed by his poor progress in school and by the suggestion that he be placed in an ungraded class. Larry was their only child who had come to them after eight years of married life. His birth, preceded by a miscarriage and much gynecological maneuvering, was greeted with jubilation. His mother, previously an efficient office manager, took Larry over as the biggest assignment of her career. Her feeding methods made and kept him nice and chubby. Speech development was somewhat delayed but this, she reasoned, is true of many children who later become regular chatterboxes. His faulty articulation was handled by sending him to a "teacher of expression and dramatics." He did well in nursery school and kindergarten. He was a happy, sociable, and well-mannered child.

Then the parents experienced their great shock. Larry could not do his first grade work, failed of promotion and finally was recommended for a special class. At first, the mother blamed his eyesight but three successive examinations convinced her that his vision was not at fault. The mother tried to do his homework with him, and each attempt made her more impatient. She then employed a tutor for him. When his scholastic performance showed no improvement, the parents began to transfer the blame to Larry himself. The father found comfort in the formula that Larry was "mentally lazy." The mother began to nag and punish him and deprive him of privileges. Larry became rebellious under the many-sided pressures, was increasingly restless, at times even destructive, and developed behavior ostensibly intended to get even with his critics and oppressors.

His I.Q. was 77.

The mother reported that her nephews and nieces all had superior intelligence and remarked significantly: "I can't understand. Why does this happen to me?" The father, more genuinely fond of the child, said: "I think he is perfect apart from school," and added that his wife was disturbed because Larry obviously was not a genius. Thereupon she said categorically: "I want him to go to college. We can afford it."

It is clear that one could not use a sledge hammer in dealing with Larry's parents. Merely telling them that their son was not ready for first grade work did not solve the essential problem. They had known this for some time. But they needed help in learning to accept the child as he was without a sense of personal shame and failure. Larry's mother felt shamed and socially disgraced by having a child whom her society considers inferior. She felt guilty because the unpleasant thought must have kept obtruding itself that, after all her gynecological difficulties, she should perhaps have remained childless. She felt frustrated because her one great asset, her efficiency, had suffered defeat.

Examples such as these can be produced almost indefinitely. But even the small number of cited instances suffices to bring out a few highly important considerations. It is, of course, necessary for the expert to make the best possible use of the available test methods in order to obtain a scientifically valid assessment of a child's developmental potentialities. The application of these tests requires skill, experience, patience, and a setting in which the tested child would be at his ease and cooperate to his best ability. Many pitfalls must be avoided, such as testing a child during his regular naptime, failure to take into account an existing impairment of hearing or vision, psychometric examination immediately preceding or following a convulsion, or difficulty in allaying a child's acute anxiety which may manifest itself in speechless timidity or noisy defiance.

When a test has been completed satisfactorily and the child's intellectual endowment has been ascertained with reasonable accuracy, it is the expert's duty to report and explain his findings to the child's parents. It should hardly seem necessary to point out that such a report, if it involves the disclosure of a child's retardation, should be made tactfully, lucidly, and truthfully. But I have known parents who, without any concern for their emotional readiness, were thrown into a panic by the words feebleminded, imbecile, or moron hurled at them as if from an ambush. I have also known good-natured doctors who did not have the heart to confront the parents with the true state of affairs and mumbled something to the effect that Johnny or Janie may "outgrow" the developmental lag or "catch up" with other children of his or her age.

I once had a long-distance telephone call from a physician in a small town, who asked me to see a six-year-old boy who was markedly retarded. For several years, he had "played along" with Billy's parents, who were his personal friends. He minimized, if not ridiculed, their apprehensions. When Billy did not begin to talk long past the expected time, he reminded the parents of a cousin of his who had not talked until the age of four years but then made up for lost time and eventually graduated from high school and college. He advised: "If Billy won't talk, just don't give him the things he wants unless he asks for them verbally." When this method did not work and the parents wondered whether they should have Billy tested, he said some unkind words about "all that psychology stuff." But when Billy was to be enrolled in the first grade, the school authorities refused to accept him. The heartbroken parents were enraged at the physician who, they felt, had either been inexcusably ignorant or had knowingly betrayed their trust in him. When I saw them, they asked again and again, "*Why* didn't he tell us?"

Adequate examination and the issuance of correct information are indeed indispensable. But they by no means constitute the whole of the expert's responsibility. The cited examples show that the mere procedure of Binetizing and Simonizing a child, the mere determination of an intelligence quotient, the mere pronouncement of the test result, do not in themselves take care of the significant matter of family sentiments. It is true that each situation is unique and that different parents come with different problems. Yet it is possible to pick out from the large welter of cases several recurrent puzzlements which are voiced almost invariably. Allow me to enumerate some of the questions which are asked regularly with a great deal of feeling and to which the inquirers hope to get straightforward answers, without evasion and without hedging:

What is the cause of our child's retardation?

Have we personally contributed to his condition?

Why did this have to happen to us?

What about heredity?

Is it safe to have another child?

Is there any danger that our normal children's offspring might be similarly affected?

How is his (or her) presence in the home likely to affect our normal children?

How shall we explain him (or her) to our normal children?

How shall we explain him (or her) to our friends and neighbors?

Is there anything that we can do to brighten him (or her) up?

Is there an operation which might help?

Is there any drug which might help?

What about glutamic acid?

Will our child ever talk?

What will our child be like when he (or she) grows up?

Can we expect graduation from high school? From grammar school?

Would you advise a private tutor?

Should we keep our child at home or place him (or her) in a residential school?

What specific school do you recommend?

If a residential school, how long will our child have to remain there?

Will our child become alienated from us if placed in a residential school?

Will our child ever be mature enough to marry?

Do you think that our child should be sterilized and, if so, at what age?

These are some of the questions asked commonly by the parents of retarded children. The questions vary, of course, depending on the degree of the child's retardation, on the presence or absence of other children in the family, on the parents' financial resources, on their ideas about social prestige, on their degree of acceptance or rejection of the child.

It is not possible to answer every one of these questions unequivocally.

Science has not advanced sufficiently—and probably never will—to make omniscient persons of the consulted physician or psychologist. Aside from the fact that causes of retardation are not always the same in all instances and that there may be multiple contributing factors in the same instance, the search for an ultimate cause often runs against the barrier of our incomplete knowledge. I have never encountered a parent who respected me less because, in answer to the question about the cause of his or her child's retardation, I made no secret of my inability to supply a definite answer. Intelligent parents usually realize fully that would-be erudite terms, such as innate, congenital, or constitutional, though literally correct, often beg rather than answer their question. What most of them hope to hear is, indeed, not so much a piece of etiological wisdom in words of Greek or Latin origin as an authoritative and sympathetic endorsement of themselves, of their human and parental competence, of their right not to blame themselves for what has happened.

Parents whose first child happens to be seriously retarded, are almost invariably plagued by the question whether or not they should have another child. There is a conflict between the strong desire to enjoy the pleasure of having a healthy child and the simultaneous fear that things may go wrong again. The parents always wait for an opportunity to present this question to the person whom they consult about their handicapped offspring. They are disappointed if this opportunity is not forthcoming. It is not an easy thing to help in the solution of this conflict. For one thing, the question is not merely a desire for information. Behind it is sometimes a scheme, of which the parents themselves are not necessarily aware, to throw the whole burden of responsibility on the adviser. If the second child should also be afflicted, the parents are clear of any blame. They can point an accusing finger at the adviser who had told them what they wanted to hear. It has been my policy to remind parents that every childbirth entails a risk, that no one could possibly have predicted that their first child would be born handicapped. Though experience teaches that lightning does not usually strike twice in the same place, the risk, however small, must rest with the parents. But if they do decide in favor of having another child, they should do so only if they are capable of freeing themselves of any anticipation of disaster. Such constant dread before and after the arrival of the new baby would create an attitude not conducive to a wholesome relationship with even the healthiest and sturdiest child.

There is no time to go into a discussion of all the questions which have been enumerated above. But the introductory examples show how profoundly the feelings of parents are involved in their types of curiosity, in the handling of their retarded children, and in their need for understanding and guidance. Like all human beings, the parents of retarded children react to their feelings. Their own life experiences, which have helped to shape their personalities, have contributed to the manner in which they adjust to pleasant and unpleasant realities in general, and to the presence of a handicapped child in particular.

In essence, one may distinguish three principal types of reaction:

1. Mature acknowledgement of actuality makes it possible to assign to the child a place in the family in keeping with his specific peculiarities. The child is accepted as he is. The mother neither makes herself a slave to him, nor does she take her inevitable frustrations out on him. She goes on functioning in her accustomed way. She continues her associations with her friends and acquaintances. The father shares her fondness for the child. Both parents manage to appraise the needs of their normal children as well and to distribute their parental contributions accordingly.

2. Disguises of reality create artificialities of living and planning which tend to disarrange the family relationships. The fact of the handicap is seen clearly but is ascribed to some circumstances, the correction of which would restore the child to normalcy. Some culprit is assumed in the child's character or body or in the educational inadequacy of the trainers. The child's poor scholastic progress in the regular grades is interpreted as a manifestation of laziness or stubbornness which must be exorcised with painfully punitive methods; the full burden is placed on the child himself. His low marks, his failure of promotion, the school's recommendation that he be placed in an ungraded class, are taken as a result of the blameworthy effrontery of a willfully unaccommodating child. Parental pressures to speed up his lagging speech development, to correct his indistinct articulation, and to improve his homework heap misery on the child, who finds it impossible to gain parental approval.

Instead of, or in addition to, the child himself, his body comes in for frantic attempts at correction. Tongues are clipped, prepuces are amputated, tonsils are evicted, with the notion that somehow such measures will undo the reality of his handicap. Thyroid extract, recommended by some physicians with hazy etiologic notions, and chiropractic adjustments of an allegedly misplaced vertebra are still much too frequently employed as a means of disguising reality.

3. Complete inability to face reality in any form leads to its uncompromising denial. The formula goes something like this: "There is absolutely nothing the matter with the child. Those who are anxious about his development are merely pessimistic spreaders of gloom. Some children

walk or talk sooner than others, and some take their time." This is often the reaction especially of fathers who have no knowledge of children and do not wish to be bothered about them. They are away at work most of the day, have a glimpse of the child when he is asleep, hear the child's laughter on the rare occasion when they pick him up, and conclude with a shrug of the shoulder: "I can't see anything unusual."

A busy surgeon, the father of three children, could not see anything unusual about his youngest child, a severely withdrawn, autistic boy whom his mother brought to our clinic against her husband's wishes. The surgeon finally came, after several invitations. He had no idea of the child's developmental data; he left all this to his wife, he declared complacently. I tried to get an emotional rise at least by making him angry. I asked whether he would recognize any one of his three children if he met him unexpectedly in the street. He thought for a while, scratched his head, and then said calmly: "Well, I don't really know if I would." He felt that his wife's concern about the child was all nonsense, but if she wanted to bring him to the clinic, that was all right, too; after all, this was her own business.

Any slightest acquaintance with the elementary principles of psychology is enough to indicate that all these different types of attitudes and resulting practices are deeply anchored in the emotional backgrounds of the individual parents and other relatives. Smothering overprotection, cold rejection, nagging coercion, or open neglect defended as proper tactics necessary to cope with the child's handicap, are, in the main, fundamental, dynamically evolved reactions which seize on the handicap as a readily accessible, superficial explanation.

All of this leads to the inescapable conclusion that the study and treatment of exceptional children would be sorely incomplete if the emotional factors of family relationships were left out of the consideration. In every instance, the place of the exceptional child in the family structure calls for a thorough overhauling, often with the urgent need for interviews with the parents. Frequently enough, the parents themselves beg for such an overhauling; they do so by asking seemingly specific or insignificant questions, and are most appreciative if such hints are understood and they are given an opportunity to talk themselves out before an experienced and sympathetic listener.

PART IX
BRAIN DYSFUNCTION

This section does not focus on the relatively uncommon gross, organic neurological disorders in children, but rather on "organicity" as a concept bridging a variety of diagnostic classifications in childhood psychopathology.

In the 1930's, the term "brain-injured" was used to differentiate children with severe organic forms of mental deficiency. Later, it began to be used with regard to children of normal intelligence who demonstrated behavior and learning problems. The concept was broadened considerably, into one of the most fiercely controversial diagnostic categories in childhood psychopathology. Kahn (1934) coined the term "organic drivenness," suggesting brain-stem disorder as the basis of hyperactivity in children. Eponyms such as the "Strauss syndrome" (Strauss and Lehtinen, 1950), the concept of central nervous system immaturity and maturational lags (Bender et al., 1963), and aphasia (Strauss, 1954) have also been used.

Pasamanick's (1961) article approaches the general epidemiological issues, the question of broader public health problems underlying the wide variety of syndromes. Eisenberg (1957) examines the most controversial segment of Pasamanick's "continuum of reproductive causality," the "Gray area" in which certain behavioral manifestations are thought by some to be pathognomic of brain damage. Gottschalk (1953) offers clinical reports on epileptic children with demonstrable psychological and neurological symptoms. He re-examines epilepsy as an idiopathic disturbance.

PSYCHIATRIC IMPLICATIONS OF BRAIN DAMAGE IN CHILDREN

LEON EISENBERG

The early view that brain damage has a one-to-one relationship with aberrations in behavior—that "All brain lesions, wherever localized, are followed by a similar kind of disordered behavior" (Strauss and Lehtinen, 1950)—no longer prevails. Here again, modern investigators are taking into consideration the role of the environment (Benjamin, 1961). Birch (1964) prefers to think in terms of many varieties of brain-damaged children, rather than of a "minimally brain-damaged child." Laufer et al. (1957) have defined the hyperkinetic syndrome as representing not acute or chronic brain syndrome as we had known it before, but a controversial overlapping area.

Eisenberg challenges those who have attempted to draw conclusions from symptoms manifested by large groups of children. He notes that the expression of any given kind of brain damage is determined by the interaction of the environment and the organic factor in the individual. Kennedy and Ramirez (1964) find this thesis substantiated in their study of monkeys. Pathological examination of the brains of monkeys who had been subjected to the same objective condition or risk, i.e., asphyxia early in life, revealed differing amounts of damage and, in some cases, no discernible damage. When the animals were permitted to develop, their behavior was as varied as the anatomical findings; some were normal and some showed massive disturbance in learning and motor functioning.

Eisenberg surveys the soft symptoms and signs associated with brain damage in the hope that once we recognize the complexity of the causes of the syndrome, our diagnoses will be more accurate and our treatment more appropriate.

The disturbances in behavior associated with brain damage provide a particularly striking instance of a psychobiological disorder. At first

Reprinted from *Psychiatric Quarterly,* 31, 1957, pp. 72–92.

glance, it might seem as if the problem would be solely neurological. Yet clinical experience soon dispels naive expectations of a one to one correlation between tissue loss and behavior pathology. Children with the lesser tissue destruction may exhibit the more disorganization in behavior. This seeming paradox does not justify the conclusion that brain substance has little to do with psychological function, but suggests a need to re-examine our notions of the relationship between structure and functions.

Basic to an understanding of the clinical facts, is the concept that the patient is a psychobiological entity, subject both to biological and to social influences and manifesting a psychological continuity of his own. The outcome of brain injury, then, will be determined by factors operating in all these spheres. To begin with, one observes the quantitative and qualitative alterations in brain function produced by damage to its structure. On a second level, the behavior observed is influenced by the reorganization of the previous personality of the patient in the face of his functional deficit. On still a third level, the social environment has a profound influence on the patient's performance—and, under certain conditions, the decisive influence. It is the interaction between these three classes of factors that determines the outcome in each particular case. It need, therefore, not be a surprise that study of intracranial pathology *alone* does not suffice to account for the vicissitudes of clinical behavior.

From this viewpoint, the interest of the psychiatrist in the phenomena associated with brain injury is not merely a question of the "psychogenic" factors that play upon the child or his "adjustment" to his illness. It is rather that brain injury constitutes a compelling demonstration of the complexity of psychophysiological interrelationships—and it is this aspect of the problem that will be the primary concern of the following discussion.

The Clinical Problem

Obviously, there is no single pattern of behavior that is produced by brain injury, for the area or areas damaged, the extent of the damage, and perhaps also the type of damage, are important determinants of the features of each case. Nevertheless, it is possible to describe, in general, certain signs and symptoms which are frequently found. It must be admitted at the outset that these signs and symptoms per se are *not* pathognomonic for organic impairment of the central nervous system. Similar difficulties may be observed in nonbrain-damaged children. But the much greater frequency of their occurrence in cases of brain injury, their greater severity, their presence in combination, and their appearance following injury justify us in regarding them as related to brain damage. It will not be possible to consider the features of given syndromes which follow the havoc wrought by specific etiologic agents. The uniqueness of such syndromes suggests a predilection on the part of specific agents for preferential destruction of particular central nervous tissue. This may partially explain such clinical observations as the much greater severity and poorer prognosis of the behavior disorders seen following the epidemic encephalitis of the 1920's (Bond and Smith, 1935) as compared, for instance, with post-traumatic syndromes (Blan, 1936). However, the present concern is with the common features of brain-damaged children (H. Bakwin and R. M. Bakwin, 1953; Kanner, 1948).

In the motor sphere, one of the most outstanding characteristics is *hyperkinesis.* Hyperkinetic children are constantly on the move, unable to sit still, fingering, touching, mouthing objects. They are frequently destructive, at times by design, at others inadvertently, because of impulsive and poorly controlled movements. Their overactivity thrusts them at all times into the center of the group so that they are typically described as attention-seeking. This aspect of their behavior has been vividly described, by Kahn and Cohen (1934) in the term "organic drivenness." These authors ascribe the constant activity to a "surplus of inner impulsions." Whatever its etiology, the hyperkinesis becomes a primary source of conflict with the social environment, which inevitably finds this behavior difficult to tolerate.

A parallel disorder may be seen in the sensory sphere. Brain-injured children tend to display *a very short attention span* and *marked distractibility.* They seem at the mercy of every extraneous sound or sight. Their interest flits from object to object in the environment, resting for only a very brief period on each. This makes for great difficulty in school where the task of learning becomes extraordinarily difficult because of inability to exclude irrelevant sensory impressions. This factor must, of course, be borne in mind in evaluating the results of intelligence testing. Tasks requiring sustained application are often failed even when, not only each of the individual operations, but also the sequence of the ensemble, would be within the child's grasp, except for his inability to stay with the problem until its completion. This inference can be substantiated when either good rapport with the examiner or the judicious use of drugs lowers the pitch of nervous activity.

A third feature that is often present is *marked lability of mood.* Frustration threshold is reduced. When this threshold is exceeded, outbursts of angry behavior result. Mercurial changes of mood from tears to laughter are sometimes seen. Unprovoked frenzies of rage, in which for no apparent reason the child strikes out blindly at all about him, often inflicting harm on others, can be noted. When these attacks terminate, the child may be bewildered by what he has done and genuinely apologetic for it–only to undergo another uncontrollable crisis not long afterward. The lack of adequate provocation and the disproportionate destructiveness suggest the escape of the lower, more primitive rage mechanisms from cortical control.

Antisocial behavior, in the form of lying, stealing, truancy, cruelty, and sexual offenses, may be a prominent feature. Often, though not always, the behavior seems inexplicable in terms of the customary determinants of similar behavior in non-brain-damaged children. That is, the behavior lacks understandable motivation and may be discordant with the child's previous social adjustment. Furthermore, the individual episodes may turn on and off abruptly and may appear to be beyond the control of the remorseful child. The lack of adequate motivation, the abruptness, and the lack of integration with the child's total personality suggest an automaticity in the antisocial behavior. It seems to resemble in some respects the complex, highly organized and sustained episodes of dissociated behavior that may be observed in cases of psychomotor (temporal lobe) epilepsy (Livingston, 1954; Jasper et al., 1938; Gibbs et al., 1948).

There may be a greater or lesser degree of *intellectual deficit,* depending, in part, upon the extent and location of the damage. The intellectual loss, when present, has a tendency to be patchy in distribution, in that some abilities are more gravely impaired than others (Shaffer and Lazarus, 1952). Thus, the pattern of the test performance may be more indicative of brain damage than the aggregate score, which fails to distinguish between primary development failure and secondary deterioration, unless a pre-injury control value is available. Tasks requiring abstract thought are particularly apt to be difficult for these children, whereas concrete problems may be successfully completed. In sorting tests, such children reveal uncommon responses and tend to group objects by unusual, accidental and insignificant details. They may exhibit perseveration in responses and often display meticulous and pedantic behavior as if they are desperately trying to keep a chaotic inner world in order by limiting outer stimuli (Strauss 1942, 1944). The distinction between figure and ground appears to be blurred, and tests which require the child to recognize figural outlines on a background of extraneous lines and shapes are useful in bringing this disability to the fore.

Finally, brain-injured children frequently display manifest *anxiety,* (Bender, 1951). Slightly unfamiliar situations, tasks that tax their abilities, or disapproving attitudes toward them precipitate sweating, tremor, tachycardia, and hyperpnea. Anxiety, which may key the normal child to a higher pitch of adaptive alterness, appears to have a destructive effect upon the functioning of the brain-damaged. The anxiety may mount to the proportions of panic—the so-called catastrophic reaction—if it is not possible to remove the child from the tension-producing situation or to offer him meaningful emotional support in the midst of it. This constitutes an important problem in management. Learning obviously requires new and necessarily tension-producing experiences; at the same time, if the anxiety generated exceeds the low level of tolerance, learning is not only blocked, but function may be reduced to a lower level than before.

These, then, are some of the signs and symptoms that may be found in the presence of brain injury: hyperkinesis; distractibility; emotional lability; antisocial behavior; intellectual deterioration, particularly in abstract functions; and overwhelming anxiety. To what extent can one account for these clinical manifestations in terms of present conceptions of neurophysiological, psychological and social function?

Neurophysiologic Considerations

In evaluating the functional consequences of damage to central nervous system structure, it must first of all be stressed that the brain is a highly complex and delicately-integrated structure, the proper working of each of its parts dependent upon the proper working of most, if not all, of the others. This is by no means an unparalleled situation in biology, though it is the most exquisite example of it, for so much simpler a unit as the chromosome exhibits similar characteristics. Not only will the loss, or modification by mutation, of a given gene alter the expression of the remaining genes, but the mere shift in position of genes on the chromosome (that is, a redistribution of the *same* genic material) may result in alteration of the genotype. At the cortical level, this can be seen, for example, in the fact that isolation of a given area of the cortex, which is otherwise left intact, results in the appearance of "suppression bursts" in the electrocorticogram (Henry and Scoville, 1952) "which may be a factor in the mechanism underlying focal cortical seizures," (Echlin, et al., 1952). This conception of the *interdependence of functional areas and their subordination to total integration* must be borne in mind if the error is to be avoided of regarding the injured brain as merely the same brain minus the functions specific to the area destroyed. This error rests upon the faulty analogy of the brain to a telephone switching center, for, in such a model, the loss of circuits affects only the functions they subserve and does not change the others, except insofar as the alternative routes are eliminated.

As Coghill (1929) so beautifully demonstrated, the development of function in the embryo proceeds, not in the pattern of building individual reflex arcs one upon the other until total function is achieved, but rather in a diametrically opposite fashion. From the first, the organism responds as a whole, wherever a stimulus is applied. Growth is associated with the progressive differentiation of more and more delicately selective and appropriate responses to specific stimuli, both by facilitation of appropriate channels and inhibition of maladaptive ones. Tissue loss, then, is followed by the reorganization of remaining structures on a more primitive level, still attempting to serve the same general biological purposes, but in a less effective manner. This is the conception of "dedifferentiation" in Goldstein's terminology (1939) or of "dissolution of function" in Hughling Jackson's (1932).

The integrative neurological basis of behavior is apparent from other considerations (Lashley, 1952). A square is seen as a square, whether it is large or small, light or dark, in the center or at the periphery of the visual field. Thus, there is an equivalence of excitation patterns, irrespective, of the anatomic field to which they are projected, a feature incompatible with the trunk-line theory of nervous function. Similarly, in the motor sphere, behavior is organized, not in terms of isolated pathways to particular muscles, but rather in terms of function. Damage to individual motor units will be followed by a more or less successful attempt to achieve the same goal by employing the available alternate muscle groups. *The neural organization of behavior is thus in terms of over-all organismic needs.* This both allows us to understand the persistence of adequate function in the presence of tissue destruction in subordinate areas and prepares us to find that damage to the higher integrative mechanism has catastrophic effects for the individual.

A second important—and inadequately appreciated—principle of neural organization is the *vital role played by inhibition.* The simplest reflect pattern, the stretch reflex, which involves only two neurons in the arc between stimulus and response, has built into it simultaneous inhibition of antagonistic muscles (Lloyd, 1941, 1946). Evocation of the flexion reflex will cause prompt and total cessation of activity in extensor muscles, just as effectively as if the motor nerve had been severed (Fulton, 1949). Inhibition is prominent at successively higher levels of the central nervous system through the brain stem (Magoun, 1947) to the "suppressor areas" of the cortex (Dusser de Barenne 1941a, 1941b; Hines, 1937) and to the "centrencephalic" area of Penfield and Jasper (Penfield, 1946, 1952; Hunter and Jasper, 1949), the excitation of which causes prompt suspension of all ongoing purposive behavior.

Attentiveness to a task, the prerequisite for efficient learning, is associated, first of all, with the sensitization of the specific receptor area by background subthreshold excitation (Lashley, 1952; Jasper, 1952). At the same time, however, there is a decrease in the input to other, nonrelevant cortical areas. For example, in straining to hear a distant sound, we become more aware of auditory, and less aware of other, sensations. The decreased awareness may be "passive (withdrawal of interest) or "active" (inhibition). The latter state of affairs may be observed when we "put out of mind" an unwelcome thought or sensation. Just such tasks are exceedingly difficult for a brain-injured child, who appears to have little ability to focus on stimulus A by excluding stimulus B. It is probable that this deficiency is in part responsible for the blurring of figure-ground discrimination, because the child attends as closely to irrelevant as he does to relevant stimuli.

In the motor sphere, the overactivity displayed by the brain-injured child can be understood as a consequence of his inability to inhibit, or even delay, upsurging inner impulses. Such children have great difficulty in postponing present gratification for future gain, and it is this that provides one of the most vexing problems in management. When one considers that it is during the delay between a need and its satisfaction that the most complex human functions appear, one can understand the handicap that this disability constitutes for the brain-injured.

Learning, itself, is as dependent upon inhibition as it is upon facilitation. This can be illustrated by the dog who is conditioned to salivate at the sound of a bell. If a bell of a particular frequency is reinforced by the provision of food and a second bell not reinforced, the dog, after a number of trials no longer responds to the second bell. What has happened is that the previous general response has become specific for a given frequency by inhibiting responses to other frequencies (Pavlov, 1928b). Recent experiments with human subjects have given a clear demonstration of cortical inhibition during such conditional discrimination (Morrell and Ross, 1953).

The task of distinguishing between auditory cues is a limited example of the more general conceptual problem of distinguishing similarity from identity. Brain-injured children, given objects to sort, often classify them—as has been noted—on the basis of the possession of common but irrelevant details. On the other hand, they are unable to recognize general regularities because of their preoccupation with these same details (Strauss and Werner, 1942). These conceptual difficulties once again involve failure of the inhibitory mechanism to function properly. Indeed, it has been demonstrated that "patients with cerebral lesions show striking inability to learn conditioned responses, which normal subjects learn regularly and promptly" (Reese et al., 1953, p. 790).

A third and final general consideration is the so-called "mass action" effect of tissue loss. If, for a moment, the problem of localization is ignored, there is some indication that the volume of tissue loss, almost without regard to its distribution, is an important determinant of the resulting functional impairment. This mass effect does not appear until after considerable destruction has occurred (Lashley, 1929). The basis for this phenomenon would appear to lie in the following considerations: With the exception of the strictly private sensory pathways from receptors to primary receiving areas in the cortex, most nervous pathways are routes employed in common by impulses originating from many different points. Each path, however, can be employed by only one pattern of impulses at any given time. Under normal operating conditions, the number of available paths is large enough so that the chance of getting a "busy signal" is small enough to permit efficient function. But if a significant number of these common routes are destroyed—or are usurped by pathological trains of impulses—messages originating elsewhere cannot be transmitted to their destinations. (The problem then becomes one that is familiar to communication engineering and can be analyzed statistically.) (Wiener, 1948). We would expect, therefore, that the brain-damaged individual would be unable to handle complex tasks or handle multiple single tasks simultaneously, whereas the same problems, broken down and presented singly, could be carried through. It would further follow that the elimination of extraneous stimuli would also facilitate the successful completion of tasks.

These, then, are some of the general effects of brain lesions upon integration, inhibitory mechanisms and transmission efficiency. Attention will now be turned to the more specific effects of lesions that impinge on the neural mechanisms underlying (a) alertness or wakefulness, (b) emotional responses and (c) higher intellectual functions.

Fundamental contributions from Magoun's laboratories (Magoun, 1952; Starzl et al., 1951; Lindsley et al., 1950; Moruzzi and Magoun,

1949), report isolating an "activating system" in the brain stem reticular formation which is necessary for the *maintenance of the waking state.* Stimulation of this center rouses the sleeping animal and causes a simultaneous desynchronization of the EEG from sleep to waking patterns. The arousal reaction produced by strong sensory stimuli depends on collateral projections to this area, for it can be produced after the classical sensory pathways have been sectioned at the tegmental level, but it disappears after destruction of the activating system. The somnolent and akinetic states observed in human subjects with brain stem lesions can now be understood in terms of damage to this "wakefulness center" (Cairns et al., 1941; Cairns, 1952; Myer and Hunter, 1952). A second ascending influence on the cortex has been described, the "diffuse thalamocortical projection system," whose function is to enhance or inhibit the elaboration of impulses, once they have reached their primary destination in the cortex (Jasper, 1949).

However, it is evident from mere introspection that wakefulness and alertness are not simply matters determined by subcortical elements, for the normal subject can voluntarily retard or induce sleep in himself and can choose to increase or decrease his attentiveness to peripheral stimuli. The neurophysiological substrate for this voluntary mechanism has recently been clarified by the work of French et al. (1955), who have demonstrated projections from ("suppressor") areas of the cerebral cortex extending precisely to the brain stem activating system. Cortical stimulation has now been shown to be capable of interrupting the sleep electroencephalogram and of causing arousal by way of cortico-reticulo-cortical pathways (Segundo et al., 1955).

Consciousness, from the neurophysiological standpoint, *is now seen to depend upon a reciprocal relation between cortex and brain stem* that (1) maintains the cortex on the *qui vive* for incoming stimuli and (2) differentially alters it for particular stimuli. Brain stem lesions are apparently implicated in the disturbances in vigilance, alertness, and "set" displayed by brain-damaged patients. The wide variability among patients may result from the fact that the inhibitory and facilitatory mechanisms are so closely interwoven anatomically in this system that small shifts in the site of lesions can produce markedly different effects. An additional experimental finding of clinical significance is the great sensitivity of the brain stem mechanism to drugs (French et al., 1955). It opens the possibility of selectively altering the dysfunction of this mechanism without impairing cortical functions.

The *affective disturbances* associated with neurologic lesions are currently the focus of much interest (Langworthy, 1955). It has long been known that stimulation of the hypothalamus in animals produces the somatic and visceral components of rage reactions (Bard, 1928). It early became clear that this "sham rage" differs from the physiological state in that it is unmotivated, transient, and cannot be conditioned; it is clearly a reflection of the role of the hypothalamus as a co-ordinating center for the *expression* of rage, but does not justify the conclusion that it is the source of the emotion or the seat of the experience felt. (Masserman, 1946). More recently, attention has centered upon the "visceral" or limbic brain, a higher co-ordinating center for emotional experience, though still not its final integrator (MacLean 1952, 1955). Lesions at specific sites within the closed circuit of the visceral brain have been reported variously to produce, depending on the site, hyperactivity, tameness, and changes in sexual behavior in experimental animals (Fulton, 1951; Kluver and Bucy, 1939; Pribram and Fulton, 1954). Stimulation within this anatomical complex can produce the behavioral concomitants of emotional reactions, but these are again unconnected with the conditions that normally incite them (Hess 1954; Hess and Akert, 1955; Smith, 1945; Ingram, 1952).

Physiological emotional states clearly reflect the role of the neocortex, as the analyzer by which the subtle implications of external events take on meaning to the individual. Emotional experience cannot but be profoundly altered when lower centers are divorced from cortical control (Landis 1950, 1952). The changes in emotional state frequently observed in brain-damaged children imply dysfunction in cortical-subcortical relations. The apparently unmotivated emotional outbursts which have been described in those children suggest the presence of a discharging pathological focus in the "visceral" brain. The patient cannot be held responsible for such behavior when it occurs; but it by no means follows that we are helpless to alter the reaction pattern. Reenforcement by means of repetition of the measures that are normally effective for producing inhibition of socially unacceptable behavior may serve to bring the autonomously discharging focus under at least partial cortical control.

When one turns to the problem of the intellectual deficits associated with brain damage, the key question that emerges is that of localization of function. Evolutionary considerations lead to the expectation that higher functions will be most significantly depressed following destruction of the frontal lobes, but clinical verification of this prediction has not been forthcoming (Hebb, 1945). There is, however, good evidence to support the view that the entire cerebral cortex plays the dominant role in intellectual activity. Battersby and his collaborators, studying patients with cerebral neoplasms, have demonstrated a significant loss in "abstract attitude" and figure-ground discriminations in patients with hemispheric lesions, as compared with patients with simple increase in cerebrospinal fluid pressure or cord tumors (Battersby et al., 1953). They could not distinguish in their tests, patients with frontal, from those with temporal or occipital tumors. Teuber (1951, 1952, 1955) suggests that there is a continuum from specificity to "mass effects" in cerebral lesions. Citing his own work on patients with cerebral gunshot wounds, he describes, in occipital lesions, "specific deficits" (scotomata): "diffuse deficits," still confined to their particular system (depression in critical flicker fusion frequency); and "nonspecific deficits" (difficulties in figure-ground discriminations). The first two types of deficits are to be found only in patients with occipital lesions, but the last type appears whenever marked cortical damage is present. This modified notion of localization is in keeping with Harlow's studies (1952), on monkeys with experimental cortical lesions. He concludes that "although no specific intellectual function is localized in any single cortical area, the different cortical areas play markedly unequal roles in the mediation of our diverse intellectual processes".

The intellectual difficulties of the brain-injured child, then, can be related to the loss or malfunction of cortical tissue. In part the deficits may be specific; but the deterioration in "general functions" cannot be ascribed to particular cortical areas. This conclusion brings us back to the considerations which initiated this discussion of the relationship between structure and function. The *central nervous system* is not to be regarded as a network of telephone circuits but rather as a *complex of transient electrical fields whose reciprocal interrelation is the essence of normal function.* This comparison is the more applicable the higher the function that is studied; and it leads to the anticipation that any distortion in the feltwork of the cortex will alter the social adaptability of the organism. But it is also true that distortions in the social setting, to which the child endeavors to adapt, will, in their turn, produce pathological changes in his behavior and its physiological substrate.

The production of experimental behavior disorders in animals with structurally intact nervous systems illustrates the dramatic effect of input pattern on brain function (Kempf, 1953; Finger, 1944). The multiplicity of methods for inducing experimental "neuroses" share the general feature that the animal is faced with tasks that it cannot solve. It may be required to make discriminations beyond its sensory capacities, or the cues given to it may be made so inconsistent that choice becomes meaningless. The result is an animal whose behavior becomes bizarrely maladaptive and whose visceral physiology is disordered. *Extrinsic influences have produced nervous dysfunction no less total than that which can be caused by intrinsic lesions.* But if this holds true for lower animals, it applies with manifold greater force to man whose *human* characteristics are *social* products. The brain-injured child, handicapped by his organic disorders, is by his handicap that much more subject to deleterious psychosocial influences, since his adaptive flexibility is restricted.

Psychosocial Factors

Thus, *knowledge of the relation between nervous structure and function,* however useful it may be, *cannot suffice for an understanding of the problems of the brain-damaged child.* Tissue destruction imposes limits which function cannot transcend, but the degree to which the patient realizes his remaining potential will depend upon the ways in which he is influenced by his environment, including the adequacy of the treatment available to him. It cannot be too strongly stressed that evaluation of the patient's behavior is impossible without psychiatric study of the setting in which it occurs and the meaning of that setting to the patient.

Precisely because of his handicap, the brain-damaged child is in need of emotional support, above and beyond the requirements normal for his age. Unlike the brain-injured adult, who may compensate in part by drawing upon previously developed skills and who may seek an environment that puts minimal stress on his inadequacies, the child has no such choice (Brown, 1952). He inevitably regresses to a lower functional level; yet he may be expected to face a school situation that makes no allowance for, and is unable to comprehend, his difficulties. His behavior, impulsive, demanding, often antisocial, is particularly apt to provoke rejection. Its very lability and unpredictability make it the more difficult to accept, for the fact that he does so well one day and is so difficult on another leads to the feeling that "he could do better if he would." His failure to do so is regarded as a sign of basic intransigence. An impatient attitude and unjustified blame by the teacher increase the child's anxiety and result both in more disturbed behavior and in less ability to learn. Unless therapeutic intervention occurs, this self-perpetuating cycle is likely to end only with expulsion from school or persistent truancy.

The important role of social factors in governing the manifest behavior of the brain-damaged child is nowhere more clearly evident than at home. The same youngster who is a holy terror in an unsympathetic, rigid, and rejecting home may be transmuted into a friendly and reasonably competent child in a warm, supportive foster home or residential school. In other cases, the feelings induced in parents by their child's affliction may lead to smothering overprotectiveness. The child learns little or no self-sufficiency because things are done for him before he has a chance to try them on his own. His parents are unable to exert effective and consistent discipline. This, coupled with the organically-induced difficulty in establishing internal controls, keeps the patient perpetually infantilized and prone to tantrums, behavior that may be mistakenly regarded as intrinsic to his disease.

Parental attitudes will help determine the child's own attitude toward his illness. The extent and severity of the problem he faces require that a high level of motivation be sustained if treatment is to achieve its full goals. Yet one sees children, whose organic handicaps are not too great, but who are crushed and defeated by parental perfectionism and who feel that nothing can help them. With such children, the primary task of therapy is to win them over into a relationship of trust and beginning hopefulness, for it is only then that they are willing to try. The child who is strong enough to rebel may release his resentment against unreasonable expectations in antisocial channels; his surface bravado is accompanied by a cynical and fatalistic outlook toward the future. Other children may wallow in self-pity, encouraged by an attitude at home that continually curses the fate that selected them as its victims. In all these situations, *environmental pathology becomes the crucial determinant of the disturbances in behavior.*

Diagnosis

From these considerations it should be evident that a knowledge of the neuro- and psychodynamics of brain damage in children carries important consequences for treatment. It becomes, therefore, all the more important that the clinician be sensitive to the diagnosis. It is an unfortunate, and perhaps somewhat unavoidable, consequence of the rapid expansion of interest in psychogenic behavior disorders that there is a growing tendency to ascribe all difficult behavior to purely psychological factors, often even in the presence of unequivocal evidence of brain injury. Children with cerebral palsy, postencephalitic and postmeningitic states, lead encephalopathy, and even brain tumors have been appearing at the Harriet Lane Home Clinic (Baltimore) in increasing numbers with the label "emotional block" pinned to them by previous examiners. Differential diagnosis is no mere academic issue; the successful resolution of the problem—and in some cases the preservation of the patient's life—depends on diagnostic accuracy.

Correct diagnosis is suggested, in the first instance, by a history of behavior that, on careful clinical psychiatric examinations, exhibits the characteristics associated with brain damage. In a high percentage of such cases, the taking of a detailed medical history will reveal the presence of etiologic factors. Neurological examination is likely to uncover confirmatory signs precisely in proportion to its detail and refinement. It cannot consist merely of a cursory survey of reflexes but must assess complex motor and sensory activity (Schilder, 1937). Marked "scatter" on standard intelligence tests suggests an organic pattern though, as Strauss and Lehtinen (1950) point out, "with few exceptions there does not exist at this moment a pattern or type of response characteristic and specific for the brain-injured child on standardized test of intelligence, academic achievement, or visuomotor performance" (p. 104). This test must be supplemented by special psychological tests of abstractive and synthetic abilities (Strauss and Werner, 1942; Bender, 1940). In addition, Rorschach responses may reveal signs of organicity (Fisher, 1955). The EEG, though usually nonspecific for etiology, may give definite evidence of intracranial pathology (Cohn, 1949). In special cases, pneumo-encephalography or arteriography may be indicated.

There is obviously a spectrum of cases that extends from those of unquestionable organic etiology to those in which final evaluation must rest upon clinical judgment. But, in all cases, the initial survey must include a thoroughgoing evaluation of psychodynamic factors in the family unit, for these are not only of importance in assessing the cause of behavior but may actually be the decisive factors in determining outcome. The aim is not only to interrupt pathological trends that may interfere with therapeutic efforts, but also to capitalize upon healthy features of family life that may facilitate therapeutic efforts.

Summary

The brain is an instrument of enormous subtlety and complexity that mediates the relationship between the child and his world. Damage to its structure has profound implications for all levels of psychobiological function. Treatment of the disorders associated with brain injury, therefore, requires attention to biological, psychological, and social factors and is a challenge to the psychiatrist as a medical specialist. It serves to emphasize his need to comprehend the roots of behavior in the broadest sense if he is to discharge his function adequately. The reward he can hope to achieve is the restoration of a child to his full human rights.

EFFECTS OF INTENSIVE PSYCHOTHERAPY ON EPILEPTIC CHILDREN

LOUIS GOTTSCHALK

Many famous people—Buddha, Socrates, Caesar, Alexander the Great, Mohammed, Napoleon, Doestoevski—were epileptic. Nevertheless, throughout history, epilepsy has been considered a stigma, a sign of devils, of visitation from the gods. While the stigma still remains with respect to jobs, legislation, and so forth, the public attitude toward the disorder has gradually become more enlightened.

Freud (1928) assumed that epilepsy is characterized by preformed organic channels of discharge which are used when normal outlets for emotional tension are inhibited or blocked. Thus, it is possible that this, one of the "classical" forms of neurological disorder, may indeed serve to clarify the relationship of mind and body. In all the literature, however, there has, until recently, been virtually no mention of epileptic children.

Gottschalk provides perhaps the most detailed clinical reports, to date, of how psychological factors influence the form and frequency of epilepsy, formerly thought to be a discrete neurological disorder. In another report (1956), he hypothesizes that "A grand mal seizure is a kind of mass reflex which is the end product of a potential series of noxious stresses (trauma, electric shock, drugs, metabolic disturbances, emotional problems) to the organism, but it is not specific to any one kind of stress" (pp. 378-379). His work challenges earlier theories concerning the relationship of personality to epilepsy. Clark (1926) made sweeping generalizations about a "defective primary endowment" consisting of egocentricity, supersensitiveness, marked emotional poverty, and rigidity, as characteristic of the epileptic patient. Rorschach (1942) himself described an epileptic protocol to contribute to the idea that there was such a thing as an epileptic personality. Lennox and Gibbs (1941), however, disagreed and noted that there was no greater frequency of personality problems among noninstitutionalized epileptic patients than in the general population.

Conversely, there have been theories that epileptic seizures are in themselves expressions of conflict. Some clinicians hold that convulsive phenomena can

Reprinted from *AMA Archives of Neurology and Psychiatry,* 70, 1953, pp. 361–384.

be specific regressive reactions to life situations in people with a particular personality makeup. However, it is generally believed that there is no universal symbolic expression for punishment, orgasm, death, rebirth, or any single conflict expressed by the convulsive disorder itself. Other controversies continue with respect to epileptic "equivalents." Most clinicians agree with Gottschalk that the dynamics of the patient with epilepsy must be evaluated individually, and that there is no "typical" epileptic patient, but that, as in his second clinical case illustration, individual conflicts and cerebral disorders combine to produce certain seizure patterns. Thus, there has been a movement, as in other psychosomatic research, from early questions of "typical personality pattern" to careful psychophysiological experiments on the interrelationships and mechanisms of interactions. Recent work extends from efforts to identify emotional states which are linked to seizure patterns on the electroencephalogram (Kemph et al., 1963) to identification of family patterns and reactions (Zegans et al., 1964).

The psychiatric study of genuine epilepsy has produced information which strongly suggests that psychologic factors play a role in the elaboration or exacerbation of epileptic phenomena. The literature on psychopathology of epilepsy has been thoroughly reviewed elsewhere (Mittelman, 1947; Schick, 1949). Various studies, mostly clinical, have led to the development and elaboration of hypotheses concerning the psychobiological functions of both the aura (Hendrick, 1940; Lennox & Cobb, 1933) and the seizure manifestations (Barker, 1948; Bartemeier, 1943; Clark, 1915, 1917, 1931; Cobb, 1940, 1944; Greenson, 1944; Heilbrunn, 1950; Jelliffe & White, 1935; Jelliffe, 1935; Kardiner, 1932; Menninger, 1926; Schilder, 1928).

If psychopathological hypotheses of the origin of the epileptic syndrome have some basis in fact, there should be a possibility through psychologic means of modifying the frequency and/or form of the seizures in certain epileptic patients. The neurophysiological correlates of epileptogenic phenomena, such as the electroencephalogram, may possibly also be modifiable through psychologic means. Barker and Barker (1949) and others, Higgens et al., 1950, for instance, have collected evidence that exploratory psychologic investigations may modify the cerebral bioelectric activity of known epileptic patients. They have interviewed epileptic subjects during electroencephalographic recordings and have reported that appropriate emotional stresses can lead to transitory electroencephalographic seizure discharges. Such observations have not been substantially confirmed.

Purpose of the Investigation

The present study was developed to test several relevant hypotheses.

1. Psychologic factors, as well as other factors, contribute to the form and frequency of the clinical manifestations of chronic idiopathic convulsive conditions in children.

2. Psychotherapy can modify the form and frequency of the convulsive manifestations of idiopathic epilepsy in children.

3. The form and frequency of the child's convulsive manifestations vary, not only with the status of the child's intrapersonal neurotic conflicts, but also with the status of the neurotic conflicts in key members of the family (or others).

Sources of Case Material and General Comments on Procedures

Epileptic children, instead of adults, were chosen as subjects, in the expectation that the children might have more potential for change in psychologic, behavioral, and physiological activity than have adults.

The three children participating in this study were referred for psychiatric evaluation to the Child Psychiatry Clinic, Michael Reese Hospital. The children were chosen primarily for two reasons: The diagnosis of "idiopathic epilepsy" had been established by careful neurological examinations, and the parents of the children were agreeable to cooperating in a psychotherapeutic program of indefinite duration. It is important to add that the psychiatric problems of these children did not appear, on superficial inspection, any more pronounced than those of other children with convulsive manifestations referred to the Clinic. Furthermore, they were the only three epileptic children whom I treated during the period of this study.

The type of therapy these children received may be categorized generally as "psychoanalytic psychotherapy." K. (Case 1) was seen most frequently, on the average of three to four times a week; N. (Case 2) and R. (Case 3) were seen once a week. Each child was seen for a total of more than 100 therapeutic sessions.

K. and N., boys five and 10 years of age respectively, were seen in a playroom setting by the therapist, the patients using the play materials only when they chose to do so. R., an adolescent boy, age 17, was seen in an interviewing room for adults. He usually sat in a chair. Occasionally he lay on a couch, if he so desired.

One or both parents of each child were interviewed before psychotherapy of the children was started by the psychiatrist, and they were seen at subsequent intervals by the psychiatrist when indicated. The mothers of K., N., and R. and the father of N. were studied and treated collaboratively by psychiatric social workers.

Evaluation of the efficacy of a therapeutic agent under any circumstances, is acknowledged to be a complicated and exacting procedure requiring careful assessment of the criteria of improvement. Evaluation of psychotherapeutic effects, because of various subjective considerations involved, is still in the process of being established on a reasonably objective, if not a quantitative, footing. The present study was an attempt to improve on previous evaluations of psychotherapeutic efforts in persons with epilepsy by including, besides a report on the clinical changes during and after treatment, the results of electroencephalographic studies and objective psychologic tests in the children who received intensive psychotherapy. In tabulation of the clinical changes, particular attention was paid to modifications in the frequency and form of epileptic seizures and other habitual behavior of the patient in reaction to stressful situations.

The advisability of suitable control studies was considered. One control arrangement might have been to study three or more comparable epileptic subjects not receiving formal psychotherapy but treated only according to a standard medical regimen. It was considered impossible, however, to match perfectly children receiving psychotherapy with other children in respect to variables that might be relevant and etiologically significant, e.g., sex, age at onset of epilepsy, type of seizures, type of electroencephalographic tracings, genetic background, sibship, child-parent relationships, and life experiences. It was felt that the only way of ascertaining that psychotherapy received by the epileptic children and/or their parents was of relevance in effecting clinical changes observed in the children was to use the three children as their own controls. Any evidence in a child of an increase in the seizure threshold could be considered a valid criterion of symptomatic improvement. Indicators of increase in the seizure threshold would be: decrease in seizure frequency, decrease in the amount of anticonvulsant medication required, decrease in the ability of psychologic or other stress to precipitate seizures, and improvement in the electroencephalogram. The method of intraindividual controls was not regarded as a solution to the need for scientific rigorousness in assessing the effect of psychotherapy on a small group of subjects. Rather, it was thought to be a compromise until larger groups of subjects could be appropriately studied.

Electroencephalographic studies were done either at the Epilepsy Clinic, Illinois Neuropsychiatric Institute, or the Electroencephalography Laboratory, Michael Reese Hospital. Psychologic tests were administered at the Psychology Laboratory, Institute for Psychosomatic and Psychiatric Research and Training, Michael Reese Hospital.

The following case summaries will give for each patient the pertinent identifying data, frequency and duration of psychotherapeutic sessions, descriptive classifications of the seizures and personality disorder, known and presumptive pathogenic etiological factors in the epileptic syndrome, and reviews of the clinical manifestations, electroencephalographic patterns, and psychologic text findings before, during and after the period of psychotherapy.

Summary of Cases

Case 1

K., a boy born June 17, 1945, was started in psychotherapy in April, 1950, at the age of four years 10 months. He was seen four times a week for 60 hours and thereafter three times a week, for a total of 140 sessions. The therapy was terminated in June, 1951, because at the time he was considered to be in no further need of treatment.

The diagnostic categories which best describe his condition are (1) idiopathic epilepsy, with atypical and possible petit mal seizures, and (2) inhibited, infantile character disorder.

Clinical Manifestations Before Psychotherapy. His typical ictal manifestations included (1) daily, generally nocturnal, sudden, explosive episodes of twitching and jerking of the hands, arms and facial musculature, with or without loss of consciousness, and (2) frequent daily transient trance-like states, with brief periods of disturbance of consciousness. All these convulsive manifestations had their onset and development gradually between March and May, 1948, when K. was approaching the age of three.

He had certain other patterns of behavior not demonstrated to be of ictal nature. These included nocturnal, and occasional diurnal, enuresis; night terrors; temper tantrums; inarticulate, and frequently unintelligible, speech with occasional stuttering; avoidance of, or hostile activity toward, other children; negativism; feeding difficulty (recalcitrance to eating as much food as his mother wished), and general retardation in learning.

Possible Pathogenic Factors in the Epileptic Syndrome. There was no familial history of epilepsy or relevant history of trauma or infection of the central nervous system. All neurological examinations had revealed nothing significant. An electroencephalographic report at the age of four years two months noted a spike seizure focus in the left temporal area. The birth and infantile development were normal, as determined from the hospital and well-baby clinic records. The mother personally reported, however, that he had been a particularly feeble nursling, showing little inclination to suckle on either the breast or the bottle as long or as vigorously as she thought he should. He walked at nine months, vocalized before that, but did not begin to verbalize intelligibly until nearly three years of age.

The onset of changes in K's personality occurred abruptly in March, 1948, when he was approaching three years of age. Previously a very docile, passive child, he began to be rebellious, negativistic, and demanding of indulgence. Coincident with these behavioral changes, ictal manifestations appeared. This abrupt change in his characteristic behavior occurred while the mother was trying to effect a sudden change in her manner of handling him—from anxious overprotection to forceful insistence on his developing independence and self-reliance in isolated areas. For instance, she had begun making him walk to the store on his own, instead of always carrying him.

In May, 1948, he had a short bout of chickenpox, followed by aggravation of his irritable and negativistic behavior and ictal manifestations. Further aggravation of his personality and ictal disorder occurred after a tonsillectomy and adenoidectomy in October, 1948, surgical operations which the parents had secured on advice from a physician that they would remedy the child's "nervousness."

Collaborative psychiatric studies of the mother by a social worker indicated that, although a capable and maternal woman, the mother had been obsessed from K.'s birth with the irrational fear that he was a weakling and that he was destined to die in infancy. In consequence of this fear, she infantilized him considerably. He was still occasionally having a bedtime bottle at the time of his beginning psychologic treatment. On the other hand, though the mother was overprotective for fear that he might be injured, she was also fearful he might hurt, or even kill, someone if allowed freedom to express himself. She therefore restricted his more vigorous neuromuscular activities, e.g., crawling, climbing, and running in and out of the house, and personally supervised all his outside play activities and interactions with other children. In contrast to these special attitudes and feelings she had about K., she volunteered freely that she had had no such problems in nursing and rearing the patient's only sibling, a sister three years older than he. The mother revealed that sometimes she reacted toward K. as though he were one of her younger male siblings, whom she had had to accept the responsibility of rearing after the untimely death of her own mother, when she was 12. She also reacted to K. at times as though she were dealing with her father, who had been harsh, impetuous, and demanding. One memory that for her was particularly associated with feelings of humiliation and of rebellion toward males was that her father habitually had her wash his feet when he returned from work. A situation which mobilized and reinforced latent doubts she had about how safe a mother she was for a boy was the fact that her first pregnancy had terminated in the miscarriage of a male fetus.

The patient's father was a laborer in a steel factory. Though considered a reliable provider and conscientious family man, he took only passing interest in his son. He spent all his free time with cronies at work or in the company of his own father, for whom he had a strong dependent attachment.

Effect of Anticonvulsant Medication Before the Start of Psychotherapy. K. was taken to the Epilepsy Clinic, Illinois Neuropsychiatric Institute, in August, 1949, and the anticonvulsant medication was started—diphenylydantoin (Dilantin) sodium 0.03 gm. four times a day, and phenobarbital, 0.03 gm. three times a day. His seizure manifestations persisted but in definitely milder form. His behavior disorder continued essentially unchanged or worsened.

Changes in Clinical Manifestations During and After Psychotherapy. The first interview with K., in April, 1950, revealed that he was short for his age but of about average physique. His face appeared pale, and he bore an air of grim preoccupation, lacking completely any animation. His initial investigatory activity of the playroom and its contents was cautious and circumscribed. Verbalization was either absent or restricted to brief remarks. He indicated either by gestures or by expectant waiting his apparent interest in some toys, e.g., blocks or an automobile. He would not use any such toys at first unless the therapist used them with him or nonverbally indicated it was acceptable for him to do so by himself.

It became clear in the early playroom sessions that many bodily movements, such as speaking, eating, or excreting, were associated with ideas of hurting or being hurt, and that the performance of such activities was interfered with because of the fear of retaliation and loss of security. As he began to learn in the treatment situation, essentially nonverbally, that he was not in danger and that the activities and ideas generated by him were not dangerous, he began to talk more and to express himself in play more freely.

Then, in his play, and increasingly in his vocalization and verbalization, he demonstrated a wish to be big, strong, and powerful. This trend was associated with his expressing fearful ideas that he might be too powerful—that he might hurt those on whom he depended for support and indulgence. He became interested in a toy drum and by gestures and looks indicated he wanted to pound on it, but he would not venture to do so at first. When he was satisfied that the therapist had a permissive attitude toward this striving, he chose to strike the drum gently with matchsticks rather than with the much heavier regular drumsticks, which were available. Even then, K. quailed at the little noise he personally originated. A moment later he smiled, then chuckled anxiously at the discovery that no dire consequences resulted. His boldness grew, and he spent periods building with blocks a small tower alongside a much taller tower. Invariably, when the tall tower got knocked down, accidentally or not, he knocked over the small tower purposely. With this type of play, the content of his growing verbal communications dealt with the relative sizes of objects, big and little, and their relative utility and advantages. Eventually, when even bolder, the scope of his playroom activities included periodic experimentation with a dart-shooting toy pistol. He then showed another pattern of activity: he would exhibit various kinds of trick shooting and gun play, punctuated with shouts of glee, and would then suddenly manifest signs of tension, peer around anxiously, and abruptly terminate and avoid this sort of play for a while. On one such occasion, when he had been merrily holding the gun behind him and shooting the dart forward between his legs and the state of tension and avoidance had suddenly ensued, he was asked why he was afraid of something when he seemed to find it fun to learn how to use parts of his body. He shook his head fearfully and stated frankly he did not know. Soon after this episode, while playfully lying prone on a table in the room and talking about a water-pistol fight he had had with a playmate, he began to move his hips in a coital manner while holding his hands together in a peculiar fashion in front of him to indicate they were not involved in this performance. When no remarks were made about this activity, he suddenly asked to go to the toilet to urinate. On returning to the playroom, he hastily reported spontaneously that he only touched his penis when he had to urinate. Later, his conflicting association of genitourinary activities with ideas of injuring someone or being injured came to the fore.

In the working through of the conflict of expressing various activities and self-imposed, autonomous inhibitions against talking about or carrying out such activities, some compromise solutions appeared. About this time, for a brief period, he made a furious effort to avoid coming to further psychotherapeutic sessions. This occurred because of a terrible fear that he might lose the security of parents or their surrogates if he continued to express inhibited wishes so freely. His wish to withdraw from treatment and his feeling of insecurity were altered by the therapist's indicating to him that his mother and father approved of his telling the therapist about his worries and by reminding him that his mother was seeing someone at the Clinic for her worries, too.

A two- to three-month period occurred during which he manifested transient muscular jerks and facial grimaces in the playroom (possibly partial duplications of the seizures he had had at home). These manifestations gave way to a period of hand washing, which was actually the most prolonged deviant motor expression observed. It cannot be proved that these motor acts—muscular twitches, grimaces, and handwashing activity—constituted either alternate modes of discharging pent-up and conflictual tensions or epileptiform activity. It can be stated with certainty, however, that one mode of such habitual motor activity was superseded by another and that one or the other invariably preceded the verbalization of some new idea, fantasy, or feeling or followed the performing of some new, increasingly skilled, and organized pattern or behavior. For example, muscular twitches and facial grimaces appeared immediately after he formlessly smeared with paint or cut with scissors for the first time. These movements suddenly reappeared later, immediately after he painted or cut out his first formed and structured productions.

His speaking habits also underwent modifications during the period of observation. After verbal communication became a regular accompaniment of other playroom activities, he would have sudden periods (sometimes lasting for several sessions) of relative muteness, always after some psychologic stress at home or in the playroom. His relative silence usually heralded the introduction of new psychologic material, and this was often communicated first in nonverbal activities and play. When he was not mute, interferences in the smooth, coordinated flow of verbalization, such as stuttering, were observed during periods when the expression of a strong emotion, usually anger, was for some reason or other blocked. When the therapist dealt with the unexpressed emotion openly, for example, by indicating acceptance of its expression or by exposing its irrational origin, the stuttering was regularly alleviated or eliminated completely.

K.'s testing out of his fantasies of great power and awful danger to others who frustrated him became a more and more integrated process. Instead of reacting to the termination of a therapeutic session or the realization that the therapist saw other children by making, for example, a clay ball and chewing it up and spitting it out, he accepted these realities without such primitive signs of distress. Frustrating situations of a more mature sort he then verbalized in terms of wanting to take the place of his father, who slept next to his mother, or, again, in his own words, "Why can't I marry my mother and have her for myself?" He acted out these situations in the playroom in the form of rivalry with me. For instance, he climbed up on the playroom table and laughed and said that now he was much taller than the therapist and that the therapist had to do what he wanted. Later, showing increased ability to delay immediate satisfaction of wishes, he remarked during his play that in time he would really grow as tall as, or taller, than, the therapist. Subsequent modifications of these fantasies of growing up included his often-expressed desire to have a horse to ride as big as "Hopalong Cassidy's." Eventually, and over a period of time, he began asking for information about processes such as childbirth and procreation, and these questions were subsequently elaborated, discussed, and worked through.

During the course of treatment there was seen a gradual, but certain, alteration in the frequency and form of his ictal manifestations and behavioral disorders, the changes coinciding in time with particular aspects of his treatment. At first, nocturnal epileptiform seizures were occurring almost nightly during the first 15 minutes of going to sleep; they consisted of incoordinate muscle jerkings, often preceded by a yell. The duration of these phenomena decreased to a few minutes and, finally, to momentary, mild to insignificant twitches of an arm, a leg, a finger, or a toe while he was falling asleep. At this point, after one-and-a-half to two months of psychotherapy, night terrors became infrequent and nocturnal enuresis stopped. K. then showed a tendency to want to hug and kiss his mother. Soon after this period, however, he had transient recurrences of nocturnal fits and increases in diurnal temper tantrums, which appeared whenever his mother frustrated him in some receptive demand. On one occasion his mother weaned him completely from the bottle, and on another occasion she took toys away from him and returned them to children from whom K. had forcefully acquired them; on occasions of this sort, K. kicked, screamed, and bit at his mother. These reactions quieted after a time, aided undoubtedly by the mother's less anxious management of the boy. Then a new series of temper tantrums, this time without nocturnal jerkings, occurred coincidentally with his dealing with sibling rivalry situations in the playroom setting. During this series of temper outbursts he threw rocks at a boy and scratched his sister. On still another occasion, after asking his mother to let him sit on her lap, he scratched, bit, and spit at her soon after sitting there, without apparent provocation so far as the mother knew. This series of temper outbursts culminated in a single recurrence of a prolonged nocturnal grand mal seizure–the last during the period of psychotherapy. The latter shower of temper tantrums and the prolonged nocturnal grand mal seizure occurred at a time when the mother was presenting material to her social service therapist about her fears that she would hurt or injure the patient as she had feared she might hurt her younger male siblings. The mother was discussing also at this time a recurring, frightening dream of hers about a strange, vicious man who enucleated a little boy's eyes. This dream was presented by the mother to the social worker when the mother was discussing her strong feeling of urgent need to protect helpless children against potential physical harm.

An indication of K.'s increase in frustration tolerance and seizure threshold is afforded by an example of a situation occurring during the latter part of psychotherapy. K. had told his mother spontaneously that he did not want to grow up to be a big boy, and therefore he argued he should be allowed to sleep with her in the place of his father. He kept asking her whether she did not have a penis, too. When the mother frankly answered his questions about her genital apparatus and refused to have him sleep with her instead of the father, he became briefly furious and called her a "dirty rat." But with this predominantly verbal temper flash, his reactions of anger subsided. No seizure occurred. Shortly thereafter he evidenced no further protestations about the matter and expressed affectionate feelings toward her. Previously, the frustration associated with such an attempt at problem solving might have been followed by an epileptic seizure.

Summary: After 140 analytic treatment sessions, over a period of 14 months, the clinical changes which occurred may be enumerated as follows:

1. Psychologic treatment began April, 1950. No further seizures occurred after September, 1950; and with the gradual withdrawal of all anticonvulsant medication during February and March, 1951, there was no recurrence of epileptic seizures. The seizure-free period at the time of this report has been longer than two years.

2. Enuresis and night terrors stopped. Play and social relations with other children improved. Normal investigative activity and success in the development of manual and intellectual skills occurred. School adjust-

ment in kindergarten and first grade was moderately above average, intellectually and socially. Feeding difficulties no longer persisted.

3. There was no further stuttering, and speech was much more articulate and intelligible. Some fluctuating, mild speech disturbance persisted, consisting essentially of a tendency to mispronounce certain consonants. The latter was improving gradually.[1]

Psychodynamic Formulation of K.'s Personality Disorder. K. had an infantile, receptive, demanding orientation toward people, developed as a protection against the idea that he might be injured expressing independence and vigorous assertiveness or injure a source of security, such as the mother. This orientation was, furthermore, a means of insuring himself a continual supply of parental, particularly maternal, support, protection, and tenderness. There resulted an inhibition of the usual learning activities, effective aggression, speech development, and sphincter control. The advantage of such an orientation was the obtaining of some support, protection, and indulgence from the mother. The disadvantage was that the expected indulgences and infantilization could not be forthcoming from the mother forever.

K.'s interpersonal relations with his parents were found to contribute significantly to his intrapersonal conflict and his overt behavior patterns. The mother's hostile, depreciatory fantasies toward K. and her defensive restriction and overprotection of him were, indeed, a realistic basis for his fears that any of his feelings or actions might be harmful. The father's preference for the role of a son, rather than the role of a father, afforded K. limited avail from his parent.

The treatment procedure provided evidence that K. was especially vulnerable to frustrations in receiving continued infantile support and indulgence from the mother and to the restrictions by the mother in his experimental and investigatory activities. Such frustrations eventuated in explosive attacks of impotent rage, directed outwardly and toward himself, and/or convulsive seizures. These formulations appeared to be correlated with the incidence of the epileptic spells, the behavior maladjustments, and some of the retarded developmental characteristics of this boy.

Psychologic Tests

Stanford-Binet Scale Form L: The results are tabulated.

[1] In the opinion of Dr. Joseph Wepman, a speech diagnostician and therapist, who examined the patient after the termination of psychotherapy, the speech diagnosis was "dysalia due to faulty auditory discrimination and lack of development." It was his prognosis that "the speech will become fairly adequate within two years with no teaching or formal training."

	Feb. 15, 1950 (Before Psychotherapy)	Aug. 15, 1951 (After Psychotherapy)
Chronological Age	4 yr.-8 mo.	6 yr.-2 mo.
Mental Age	4 yr.-8 mo.	6 yr.-4 mo.
Intelligence Quotient	100	103
Basal	Year 4	Year 6
Highest Successes	Year 6	Year 7

ELECTROENCEPHALOGRAPHIC REPORT

1. Before Psychotherapy (August, 1949; age 4 years 2 months): "The record reveals 6- to 7-cps activity in all leads, with constant spike seizure activity in the left temporal region, spreading to the left parietal area. The sleep record also shows the spiking in this area. The impression is that of a spike seizure focus in the left temporal area, spreading to the left parietal area." (F. A. Gibbs)

2. Before Psychotherapy (April, 1950; age, 4 years 10 months): "The record shows 8- to 9-cps activity in all leads, with frequent spike seizure discharges in the left parietal area, spreading to the left temporofrontal area during secobarbital-induced sleep. The impression is that of a spike seizure focus in the left parietal area." (F. A. Gibbs)

3. After Psychotherapy (April, 1951; age, 5 years 10 months): "The record shows 8- to 10-cps activity in all leads. There is no focus of abnormality and no seizure discharges. Sleep activity is normal. The impression is that of a normal electroencephalogram, both during waking and during sleep. The record shows great improvement over the two previous records." (F. A. Gibbs)

Rorschach Test (Dr. Samuel J. Beck). Only one Rorschach test was made on this boy, two months after psychotherapy was terminated. It indicated that the child reacts to his unacceptable impulses with anxiety and a rigid pattern of defense. He is vulnerable to emotionally toned, exciting stimuli. He reacts to such stimuli with withdrawal—at one extreme to the level of complete blocking (one of his full rejections of a card). He also reacts to these stimuli with unstable, but not explosive, behavior, however, in the form of some concretistic, immature thinking, immature language, and self-evaluative attitude. That the personality structure is at the level of neurosis is attested by a 'color-shock pattern.'

"Anxiety is mobilized in relation to the 'father' figure, to which he responds, 'looks like a giant, looks bad,' and also to the 'mother' figure, although not so severely. A confusion of the concept of man and woman occurs twice.

"His problem of mastering uncontrolled impulses is complicated by his relative lack of creative resources and his overly rigid pattern of inhibitions."

Case 2.

N., a 10-and-a-half-year-old boy with epilepsy, born Sept. 18, 1938, was treated psychotherapeutically from March, 1949, to June, 1951. He was seen regularly once a week for a total of a little more than 100 therapeutic sessions. The treatment was terminated, not because psychotherapy was considered completed but because the therapist had to leave the city for military service.

The diagnostic categories which roughly describe N.'s pathological condition include (1) idiopathic epilepsy with frequent daily "psychic or atypical" seizures, occasional psychomotor fits, and very rare grand mal seizures, and (2) a hysterical character disorder.

Clinical Manifestations Before Psychotherapy. His ictal manifestations included psychic, atypical fits, precipitated usually only by looking through an ordinary window screen, or occasionally by looking at checkered or striped patterns on clothes, tablecloths, etc. (These seizures will henceforth be designated as "screen spells.") These fits consisted of spells of staring through the screen and were accompanied by uncoordinated, generally symmetrical shaking of the upper extremities. According to the parents, the arm movements looked to them like a bird's flapping its wings. Sometimes the arm movements, with accompanying head and neck motions, suggested to the parents protective or warding off actions against some threat to the child's head and neck. These seizures lasted from one to 45 minutes. N. would generally remain standing, would only rarely fall or bite his tongue, could not be communicated with during the spell, and could not recall what he had been doing during the spell. These episodes had had their onset in November, 1943, when he was five years of age, soon after the father had to leave home to enter active duty in the Army.

Psychomotor seizures, of recent origin, appeared at the age of 10 years. Typical in their pattern, lasting from 15 to 30 minutes, these were paroxysmal episodes of complicated and rather highly organized motor activity, with a prominent destructive component, e.g., tearing clothes to shreds or breaking furniture. He had no notion what led to these seizures and could not be communicated with during them. After the seizures he could not recall what he had done during them.

Grand mal seizures were rare. The first one had occurred at the age of nine years, and one such seizure had occurred each year thereafter, accompanied by tonic and clonic phases and biting of the tongue on two occasions. The grand mal seizures all evolved during "screen spells."

Possible Pathogenic Factors in the Epileptic Syndrome. There was no familial history of epilepsy or migraine and no relevant history of trauma or infection. His birth and development during infancy were free from known symptomatic disease. All neurological examinations revealed a normal state, except for bilateral constriction of the peripheral visual fields ("tubular vision"), first appearing at the age of 10 years four months and lasting two months. Thorough neurological and opthamologic studies revealed a disturbance of the form fields, and not of the color fields, in this visual symptom, but no detectable structural or anatomical basis for it. The visual field defect cleared up soon after the advent of psychotherapy and did not recur. The first electroencephalographic recording, done when he was six years old, showed 3-cps spike and wave discharges.

N. was described by his parents as a boy who, except for his seizures, was customarily conforming to their standards, though clinging and demanding of indulgence. He was adjudged by psychiatrists who had seen him previously on consultation as "very immature and rather effeminate" and as a "boy with whom it was difficult to establish close rapport." He was an only child.

Psychiatric studies of the mother revealed that she was a compulsive, perfectionistic person, whose relationships with others were characterized by very little investment on her part, except for what support and approval others might give her. She was inclined to be overindulgent and unduly intimate in N.'s rearing. She kept in constant attendance during his baths and frequently undressed in front of him or slept with him up to the time he began psychologic treatment. On the other hand, she showed poor tolerance to the least signs of hostility he manifested toward her. She encouraged him to learn to cook and do housework. She had a tendency to tell him in what respects she considered the father inadequate.

The father was a passive, self-depreciative person who had difficulties in dealing with men in competitive situations or in adequately asserting himself when someone's demands were actually excessive, e.g., an employer's. As the oldest son in the family, the father had had to take over the financial support of his siblings at the age of 15 because of the economic failures of the paternal grandfather, a temperamental, chronic alcoholic. In psychotherapeutic sessions with a male social worker, it developed that the father had the idea the patient wanted to replace him, just as the father had replaced the paternal grandfather. The father defended himself against rivalry with his son by constantly giving him gifts, exposing him—if not pushing him—to the mother's confusing intimacy, aloofness, and compulsive demands for cleanliness and orderliness. Though the father wanted to do so, he had difficulty in experiencing a warm interest in and real companionship with his son.

Events Occurring at the Onset of Patient's Seizures. The onset of N.'s first seizures ("Screen Spells") occurred at the age of five years, in 1943, shortly after the father departed for active duty in the army. Interviews with the mother revealed that at this time she turned to the patient for security and that she also directed some of her anger aroused by her husband's leaving at the patient. Her inconsistent seductiveness and compulsive restraint were most pronounced toward him at this time.

No life situations of significance are known to have occurred during the time of onset of N.'s grand mal seizures, at the age of nine years, and his psychomotor seizures, at the age of 10 years.

Effect of Anticonvulsant Medication on Clinical Manifestations Before Start of Psychotherapy. From the time of onset of his first seizures, i.e., the "screen spells," many of the standard anticonvulsant regimens, including use of a ketogenic diet and administration of bromides, phenobarbital, diphenylhydantoin, or trimethadione (Tridione), or combinations of these, had been tried. Such medication had effected no essential change in the frequency or form of his seizures. However, at the time psychotherapy was started, in March, 1949, he had not taken any medication regularly for about one year, being given only a capsule of phenobarbital (30 mg.), usually after a fit.

Because of the distressing effect on his parents of the destructive aspects of his psychomotor seizures at the time psychotherapy was started, another trial of diphenylhydantoin medication was made—diphenylhydantoin, in a dose of 0.09 gm. twice a day. With the disappearance of the psychomotor spells after the first five or six months of psychologic treatment, the administration of diphenylhydantoin was discontinued. No anticonvulsant drug of any sort was administered during the remainder of the course of psychotherapy.

Changes in Clinical Manifestations During and After Psychotherapy. At the initial interview, N. was observed to be large for his age, plump, pink-skinned, with regular facial features. He wore glasses. Throughout the session he kept a knit cap on his head. He was restless and moved about the playroom continually, sometimes apparently for purposes of exploration and orientation, but oftener without discernible reason. He glanced out of the playroom window through the window screen furtively, without any immediate or discernible reaction. He then began playing actively with a dart gun and holster, while explaining he had seen several doctors previously at the Clinic. It seemed, he explained, that he had "hypnotic powers," could hypnotize himself by looking through a screen, "a habit, very silly." He went on to say that he wanted to get rid of the habit because Dr. H., his pediatrician, told his mother he should. As soon as any questions were asked, he regularly responded with the remark, "I don't know," but often later would spontaneously elaborate with a more detailed and pertinent answer. He volunteered tensely that he liked to come and see doctors, psychiatrists, because he liked "to be amused." When his next responses were awaited without his implicit plea to be entertained being satisfied, he remarked petulantly, "I love to play and amuse myself." He did so for a while with different play materials. Returning to the gun and holster and strapping it onto himself, he tried pulling out the gun rapidly and pulling the trigger, observing that he had to practice because he "might be slow on the draw, the gun could get caught in the holster . . . happens sometimes to cowboys." At the close of the session he said he had to shoot the dart gun four or five more times. He did so and then observed, in a tone of threatening reminder, "I like to be amused so much; do I have to go?"

Summary: During the first three months of treatment, the "screen spells," which had occurred one to several times a day, became decreasingly frequent and disappeared for about six months. In the meantime the psychomotor seizures became more frequent, the number ranging from two to eight a month. No grand mal seizures occurred during this period. Then, as the patient began to be able to communicate the various components of his psychomotor seizures, i.e., the thing he was doing and what feeling he had about it at the moment just preceding his psychomotor spell, and what he did, thought, and felt during and after the seizure, his psychomotor seizures disappeared fairly rapidly. No further frank psychomotor episodes occurred after the fifth month of psychotherapy. In view of this, the diphenylhydantoin sodium, which had been administered with the beginning of psychotherapy, was then discontinued. In these circumstances, no recurrence of the psychomotor fits was noted. Situations which previously had been followed by psychomotor spells were then followed by typical temper tantrums, which the patient could describe and discuss fully. He could also give a more detailed report of his emotional reactions during the temper tantrums. The incidence of these temper tantrums gradually decreased during therapy and became progressively milder and briefer. During the last 18 months of treatment they occurred only rarely.

On the other hand, as psychomotor seizures waned and disappeared, the "screen spells," which had practically stopped at home, began to recur about the fifth to the sixth month of treatment, tending for a while to be confined to the therapeutic sessions in the playroom. Much less frequent than previously, but definitely paroxysmal in nature, these spells began to change in character during the therapeutic sessions. The patient could terminate one of these seizure states if the therapist requested him to do so. He began to be able to communicate freely his thoughts, fantasies, and feelings during the seizure. Although sometimes he would deny knowing what neuromuscular activities he had just performed, when the therapist described to him what he had done, he began to integrate this information into his discussion and evaluation of the matter. Oftener, he spontaneously volunteered observations about one or another aspect of his motor activity during the spells. In these circumstances, he demonstrated the ability to control the time when a "screen spell" would start; i.e., he could prevent or let the paroxysmal motor activity occur while looking through the screen, he could generally stop such activity at will, and frequently he interrupted it to talk with the therapist and then resumed the motor activity characteristic of this convulsive state.

Furthermore, the form and pattern of these seizures changed. Instead of the stereotyped extensor movements of his arms and the flexor movements of his head and neck, this paroxysmal motor activity became more complex and highly organized, and he was able to verbalize, simultaneously with this activity, appropriate ideation and feeling. When, for instance, the "screen spell" consisted mainly of coital movements with flexor movements of his head and neck, he observed that he was moving "like a hula dancer," and much of his interseizure and other intraseizure verbalizations were related to inhibited heterosexual aims. During the period when he was talking about masturbatory problems, there occurred seizures during which he manipulated his genitals through his trouser pockets or clutched and grabbed at his buttocks with one hand and with the other hand fingered his genitals. Another time, when he was obviously enraged and anxious, he had a "screen spell" during which he stood before the window screen, his arms akimbo, hitting his thighs and knees forward on the wall, ducking, and often banging his forehead on the edge of the raised window. Suddenly he interrupted this activity and reported anxiously that he felt as though the wall had moved outward, that he had knocked it out by the strength of his movements. [2]

3. Various modifications in the characteristic behavior of the patient occurred. He began to communicate his ideas and feelings more intelligibly. He confided being terrified at times by his own "crazy thoughts," predominantly destructive urges. Instead of exhibiting a habitually submissive behavior and seeking to be entertained, he became increasingly assertive and spontaneously made bids for more independence and self-determination. He got a part-time job after school as a delivery boy. He tested his parents in various ways. He went through a brief period of mimicking and caricaturing his father and his mother in their usual ways of interacting with him. He began asking many questions of the therapist, generally with evidence of much anxiety. He eventually asked the therapist for sexual information and revealed his own anal theories of conception and birth. Frequently, in the playroom, when the therapist could help him formulate a question or the reason for very strong unacceptable impulses, a "screen spell" was averted or aborted.

At the time of discontinuation of psychotherapy, he had achieved a more congenial companionship with his father, and his adjustment at school with his friends was better. The situation with his mother was improved, but he was experiencing distressful, ambivalent feelings about her. "Screen spells" now occurred infrequently at home, and they occurred rarely in the playroom. As previously mentioned, no psychomotor spells had recurred for two years.

It is perhaps interesting that each of the two grand mal seizures that occurred during this period of 28 months of psychotherapy appeared at a time when N. made decisive efforts toward independence and self-reliance. The first grand mal spell occurred after 18 months of treatment, specifically after an interruption of therapy during summer vacation. Continuation of treatment had been made contingent on his own decision to come (at his insistence), and without either parent accompanying him, as one had pre-

[2] With repeated observations on, and communications with, N. during, before, and after his "screen spells," I became aware of the inadequacies of the current terminologies referable to explosive neuromuscular, ideational, emotional, and vegetative discharges in subjects with demonstrable interseizure electroencephalographic abnormalities. To what extent "hysterical" seizures and "temper tantrums," and even less striking behavioral activities, shade into, may be superimposed on, or may be indistinguishable from "true, or genuine, epileptic" phenomena is difficult to evaluate. (Attention has already been called to the similarity of these various kinds of sudden, transient activities [Bartemeier, 1943].) The present report does not propose to deal extensively with the semantic confusion and difficulties in differential diagnosis in this borderland region of investigation of neurology and psychiatry or neurophysiology and psychology, but the matter is brought up at this time to indicate a problem in nomenclature, designation, and connotation which will need further clarification.

viously done regularly. The therapist telephoned him, and N. stated that he had decided to continue treatment and come to the therapeutic sessions without either parent. The next day—the day before his appointment—he had a major seizure at home. The day after final termination of psychotherapy, also, although he was superficially gleeful about the ending of treatment, because he regarded the termination as a sign of maturation and development, he had another grand mal seizure. N. understood that the therapist was leaving for military service, as N.'s father once had done, but he did not consider this of any consequence. One year after the termination of psychotherapy, in July, 1952, at the age of 13 years 10 months; with his parents' permission he went away from home to a summer resort to work as a bus boy and waiter. There he soon had a series of three or four grand mal seizures, each one occurring after he felt compelled to stare through window screens. Initially, he had a typical "screen spell," during the course of which a frank grand mal fit occurred.

The psychotherapeutic investigation of this patient provided some information as to the origin of the looking behavior as a trigger for the "screen spells." Seeking to look at his parents having sexual relations had been a temptation presented to him between the ages of three and 10, when he had occupied a bedroom adjacent to his parents' room, his bed being so situated that he could see his parents' bed in the next room. The adjoining doorway lacked a door when he was three to six years of age, but a clear view was irregularly obscured by a decorative, checkered screen! He had no conscious memory of witnessing parental intercourse, but he had a strong forbidding urge to do so. In his looking through window screens he had confusing fantasies of being beaten by God or some powerful person and fantasies of assuming either the male or the female role in the sexual act. His concept of the sexual act was that it was a sadomasochistic performance. He anxiously confessed that he had a powerful urge to see women tortured. He wondered why gangsters did not have sexual relations with women they killed. He attributed magical and omnipotent powers to the acts of looking and being looked at, reacted as though he could control or hurt others by looking, and feared equally potent retaliation through being looked at by others. The following further observations relevant to the psychologic activating factors of N.'s spells can be made.

Screen Spells. A characteristic chain of events was observed to culminate in screen spell in the playroom.

1. N. would be either engaging the therapist in some play or talking

with the therapist. In this interaction an incident would occur which N. would presumably experience as a "deprivation,"[3] the depriving agent being either someone that N. was telling the therapist about or the therapist himself, e.g., the therapist or someone else did not fulfill some explicit or implicit demand of N.'s.

2. The pattern of N.'s immediate activities would abruptly change, whatever he was doing and/or saying. He would turn and walk toward the window, on reaching it would glance slightly upward through the screen, and would often reiterate that at times he was unaccountably and irresistibly drawn to the screen.

3. Generally, staring less than one-half minute through the screen did not lead to a typical screen spell. During this half-minute, verbal interchange with N. was open. When questioned, he never saw any relation between his feeling of compulsion to go to the screen and the context of the immediately preceding interactions with the therapist. He never volunteered that he experienced any feeling of anger, fear, or frustration. In fact, he usually denied any such feeling when he was asked. But an accurate and acceptable interpretation of the preceding situation and N.'s presumably covert aims and feelings could at this point prevent the development of a screen spell.

4. If N. looked through the screen for longer than about one-half minute, a screen spell of varying duration invariably occurred.

Grand Mal Seizures. Grand mal seizures were never observed in the playroom. In all instances in which they occurred, however, it was observed by his parents, or other observers, that grand mal fits developed sometime during prolonged screen spells. Psychiatric investigation added the information that the infrequent grand mal seizures tended to occur during a period when N. had been making efforts, often premature, toward independence from parental control and support.

Psychomotor Seizures. No psychomotor seizures were observed during sessions in the playroom. Retrospective verbal comments by N. about the situations and his personal feelings and aims just preceding the onset of such seizures gave evidence that a sequence of events obtained somewhat similar to those with the screen spells. That is, N. experienced some "deprivation," which was shortly followed by a psychomotor seizure. The deprivation, as reported by N., was typically of trivial variety. For example, on one occasion he reported that he had been listening to a cowboy

[3] The term "deprivation" is used in a broad sense to include any state or situation in which one could reasonably infer that N. experienced a lack of indulgence, failure to reach a goal, or frustrating experience.

radio thriller and the program was interrupted by the announcer making a commercial; N. felt furious, briefly, at the interruption, and a psychomotor seizure ensued. N. could not report what he did during the seizure. Only his parents could give a description of the behavioral details. Nor could N. recall any of his thoughts or feelings during the seizure episode. On another occasion, he reported he had been bouncing a tennis ball against a backboard. He missed several shots, felt furious, and started to break his tennis racket. A psychomotor seizure, with the usual wantonly destructive components, followed.

A perhaps essential differentiating characteristic of the intervening variables in the psychologic trigger associated with the psychomotor seizures as distinguished from the screen spell was the fact that N. could report feeling angry (out of proportion, of course, to the situation) just before the onset of the psychomotor spell, whereas he was aware of no emotion or frustration just before the onset of a screen spell—only a compulsion to go to and look out of a window screen.

Electroencephalographic Report.

1. Before Psychotherapy (January, 1945; age, 6 years 4 months): "The record shows 10-cps activity, with short runs of 4- to 6-cps activity, and an occasional petit mal seizure discharge, slightly more pronounced in the right hemisphere, but no reliable focus of abnormal activity. During spontaneous sleep, petit mal discharges appear more numerous. There is large build-up with hyperventilation. The impression is that of an electroencephalogram which is fairly normal in frequency, with petit mal seizure discharges." (F. A. Gibbs)

2. Before Psychotherapy (July, 1945; age, 6 years 10 months): "The record is similar to one taken in January, 1945, with occasional petit mal seizures discharges. Placing of the screen in front of the patient produces no changes clinically or in the electroencephalogram and no more seizures discharges than before. The impression is that of petit mal discharges." (F. A. Gibbs)

3. Before Psychotherapy (December, 1948; age, 10 years 3 months): "The record shows 9- to 10-cps waves in the occipital region and bursts of 3- to 4-cps waves in all leads, most pronounced in the occiput. No focus of abnormality is found. There is a moderate build-up with hyperventilation. The impression is that of an abnormal curve consistent with a diagnosis of epileptic disorder of unspecified type." (H. M. Serota)

4. During Psychotherapy (September, 1949; age, 11 years): "The record shows bilateral 9- to 10- cps occipital rhythm, reflected in the anterior leads. High-amplitude, 6-cps waves appear in frequent sequences, diffusely.

Slower waves, of 3- to 4-cps frequency and often spike-like in form, arise principally from the occipitoparietal region bilaterally. There is moderate build-up with hyperventilation. The impression is that of paroxysmal discharges, highly consistent with a convulsant disorder." (H. M. Serota)

5. After Psychotherapy (October 16, 1951; age, 13 years 1 month): "A sleep record was not obtained. There is 9- to 10-cps activity, with considerable irregular slow activity and occasional sharp wave-and-spike activity of low to medium voltage. In longitudinal leads, spikes and sharp waves are primarily seen in the right parietal area. Slow activity tends to appear in the right parietal area and in the temporal area bilaterally. There are occasional diffuse complex paroxysmal bursts. With hyperventilation there are improvement of alpha rhythm and reduction of slow activity. The impression is that of focal slow activity in the right parietotemporal region, with paroxysmal spikes and sharp waves of low voltage in the right parietal area. The character of the minor paroxysmal abnormalities suggests a deep or subcortical, rather than a superficial, lesion, probably right-sided, as does the continuous slow activity. It is suggested that the lesion is either deep to the right temporoparietal cortex or in a subcortical system having the same projection." (J. P. Toman)

Psychological Tests. Stanford-Binet Scale, Form L: The results were tabulated.

	June 27, 1945 (Before Psychotherapy)	Sept. 19, 1951 (After Psychotherapy)
Chronological age	6-9	13-0
Mental age	7-0	14-0
Intelligence quotient	104	108

Rorschach Tests (Dr. Samuel J. Beck). Two Rorschach tests are evaluated.

Rorschach Test 1 was done when the boy was 10 years three months of age (before psychotherapy). The findings reveal that the patient rigidly inhibits the expression of feelings. There is a relative absence of association to human forms. He shows an inability to verbalize personal matters. In summary, there is a striking inadequacy of personality development, marked furthermore, by perceptual departures, attention lapses, and rigid thinking processes. When emotional stresses occur, such symptomatic behavior is to be expected.

Rorschach Test 2 was done when the patient was 12 years 11 months of age (after psychotherapy). The findings show that psychologic conflict and free anxiety are definitely more prominent, although rigid defenses and a tendency to withdraw from human relationships persists. But in the second test the expression of feelings and impulses is out in the open. In contrast to the results in the first test, there is considerably more willingness to master primitive urges, in spite of consequent painful tensions and anxiety. Psychotherapy should be continued.

Case 3.

R., an adolescent boy, born July 24, 1930, was 17 years 10 months of age when psychotherapy was started, on May 18, 1948. He was seen regularly once a week for two years and thereafter about once every two weeks for a total of a little more than 100 therapeutic sessions.[4] His psychotherapeutic treatment was interrupted May 2, 1951, because the therapist had to leave the city permanently.

Diagnostic categories which roughly describe or classify his personality disorder include (1) idiopathic epilepsy, grand mal type, and (2) schizoid character disorder.

Clinical Manifestations Before Psychotherapy. Ictal manifestations before the period of psychotherapy consisted of grand mal seizures, which began at the age of 17 months and occurred once or twice a month.

Other notable behavior and personality manifestations were presented: 1. Calling telephone operators impulsively and making obscene and hostile remarks to them. This behavior began in August, 1947, occurred about 30 times, and lasted four months until R. was apprehended by the police and referred to the juvenile court. Incidentally, he was referred to the psychiatric clinic for treatment because of these episodes. 2. Occasional uncontrollable and inappropriate giggling for brief periods. These spells were observed at home and during therapeutic sessions for the first six months. 3. Insistence on his being subsidized so as to get training as a musician. R. was evaluated by his music teachers at school as having limited aptitude and very little skill as a musician at that time. (His instrument of choice then was the trumpet.) Furthermore, he was in the process of failing his senior year in high school.

[4] It was the impression of the therapist that when any more frequent treatment interviews were attempted with R., there was mobilized either such anxiety, or regression to such a dependent orientation, that either treatment progress was acutely interfered with or the frequency of convulsions was acutely increased.

Possible Pathogenic Factors in the Epileptic Syndrome. There was no familial history of epilepsy or migraine or history of birth trauma. At the age of six months he had had a severe attack of pneumonia, requiring a month's hospitalization. At the age of 17 months he had his first grand mal seizure, and these attacks continued to occur on the average of about 12 a year until the ages of eight to 13, when their frequency ranged from 25 to 40 a year. A decrease in the annual seizure frequency to 20 to 30 a year followed the administration of regular anticonvulsant medication, started at the age of 13.

At the age of four years, a developmental visual defect was first noted, i.e., ambylopia and esophoria of the left eye; this has persisted unimproved. In addition to these findings, ophthalmologic examinations revealed "an old chorioretinitis" in the left eye.

At the age of six years he fell off his bicycle and hurt his left hip. Medical examination revealed aseptic necrosis of the head of the left femur (Legg-Perthes disease; osteochondrosis of the capital epiphysis of the femur). He became completely dependent on his mother for day-to-day care. When he was seven years old, his mother became pregnant, and she felt she was unable to care for him efficiently during the latter part of her pregnancy. It was at this time that he was hospitalized for treatment of his hip disease for seven months; this resulted in a structural recovery of the joint lesion and the full use of his extremity. In the hospital, he had feeding difficulties, often refusing to eat. At the age of eight years, on returning from the hospital, he first learned that he had a baby sister, two months of age. Although at first he expressed interest in his new sibling, he shortly became upset, when he found he was receiving considerably less of his mother's usual attention. The frequency of his seizures was immediately greater and continued so during the ensuing years. An electroencephalogram obtained at the age of 16½ years was considered consistent with the diagnosis of an epileptic disorder.

The parents' attitude towards R. was that he was incurably tainted. The mother was too ashamed ever to tell relatives that R. had epilepsy. She kept him from meeting them. She did not allow him to participate in any physical recreation whatever during his years of schooling. She would not let him seek any kind of gainful employment for fear he would have a seizure. Collaborative psychiatric treatment of the mother by a psychiatric social worker revealed that she showed intense and pervasive hostility, feelings of inferiority, unusually strong desires to improve or maintain social status, and fears of impoverishment. (The father actually did have to struggle to make a living as a newspaper vendor.) She constantly refused to permit the patient independence and emphasized his physical limitations. Yet she criticized his failure to achieve independence. Furthermore, she incited trouble between the patient and his sister, provoking them to fight with one another for her attention.

Events Occurring at Onset of Patient's Seizures. The available data indicate only that R.'s seizures began at the age of 17 months, nine months after a severe bout of pneumonia, requiring hospitalization. An increase in the frequency of seizures at the age of 8 years, from an average of 12 to one of 25 or 40 a year, was temporally related to a long period of hospitalization for Legg-Perthes disease and the birth of a sibling.

Effect of Anticonvulsant Medication on Clinical Manifestations Before and at the Beginning of Psychotherapy. At the age of 13 years, R. began receiving anticonvulsant medication in the form of diphenylhydantoin sodium and phenobarbital, in variable dosage, with some reduction in the seizure frequency, i.e., from 35 or 40 to 20 or 30 seizures a year. For about one year before psychotherapy was started, he was receiving diphenylhydantoin sodium, 1½ grains (0.9 gm) four times a day, and phenobarbital, 1½ grains three times a day.

In 1946 he had a total of 22 major seizures; in 1947, a total of 23 grand mal attacks.

Within one month after psychotherapy was started in May, 1948, the anticonvulsant medication was changed to use of diphenylhydantoin sodium, 1½ grains five times a day, and no phenobarbital was administered. The total number of seizures during 1948 was 27. These seizures, in contrast to those in preceding years, began, during the latter part of 1948, to occur as a series of several a day, with increasing length of the seizure-free intervals, instead of as isolated seizures at more frequent intervals.

Changes in Clinical Manifestations During and After Psychotherapy. At the initial interview R. presented an unkempt and strangely ape-like appearance. At first he was very slow moving and sat stiffly in his chair, with a fixed facial expression. Gradually he tended to flex his extremities and body to assume a position with his head resting on his arms, which were folded on the table. From this position he would glance up at the examiner from time to time without moving the rest of his body. At first his verbal spontaneity was very low, and intervals of two to three minutes would follow his laconic replies to questions. He gradually showed more spontaneity and talked at greater length, but relative retardation in the frequency and latency of his verbalizations continued. There were few variations in facial expression or bodily posture until emotion-provoking subjects came under discussion. Then he would straighten up, cross his legs, and look away. His cheeks would redden slightly. He would drum with his fingers on the table or on his arms and hum in a distracted fashion, and yet respond relevantly to the conversation. He talked about his seizures. He described his aura, stating that he experienced a sudden feeling of hunger, slight nausea, and "shivering," with cold sensations up and down his spine and the back of his legs. The attitude expressed toward his seizures was one of rebellious resignation. He did not know why he had made the telephone calls to telephone operators. He felt ashamed and guilty at having said abusive things to "people who did not deserve them." He passed off further discussion of this matter with the remark that these episodes were "like my grand mal seizures–I don't know what causes them." He then mentioned his annoyance and chronic rivalry with his only sibling, a sister eight years younger than he. He stated that his parents, especially his mother, formed an alliance with his sister against him.

During the first year of psychotherapy, R.'s activities in the treatment sessions consisted primarily of testing out how reliable a person the therapist was. By devious, rather than direct, means he began extracting proof from the therapist that he was acceptable and likable. He spent many sessions gazing dreamily at the therapist and occasionally asking questions about situations at school and at home. His declarative statements were generally limited to difficulties in getting along with his sister and the unreliability of his mother. Because he was so disorganized and insecure, he was permitted to proceed in this way. His questions became more frequent, stereotyped, and irrelevant, and he became more animated and demanding. He would ask for the chemical formula of medical drugs or the definition of words.

A dramatic elimination of R.'s seizures occurred for a period of six months, as long as the therapist was permissive and continued giving verbal responses when R. signaled with a question that he wanted the therapist to say something, anything. Eventually, with a refusal on the part of the therapist to answer the more irrelevant questions and his insistence on determining their underlying motivation, the patient had frequent seizures, several occurring a day. The seizures closely followed commonplace, extratreatment incidents which had special, often symbolic, significance for R.; e.g., his mother changed the dairy from which she bought chocolate milk for the family, his sister forgot to buy the ice cream she was supposed to get for supper, or he read in a musicians' periodical that certain union members were in default of their dues and therefore subject to suspension from the musician's union.

Then R. began to be aware of his inordinate need for support and acceptance. He told episodes of his childhood that revealed a strong sense of parental, particularly maternal, rejection. He reported feelings of confusion about his worthiness. On the other hand, he related isolated instances from his earlier childhood (before his sister's birth), when he felt soothingly protected and indulged by his mother. In association with these memories, he reported recurring daydreams of himself as a great and highly celebrated person.

From the beginning of psychiatric treatment, R. had expressed wonder that people made such a stir about the difference in the sexes. He now declared there was no essential difference between male and female. Certainly, he insisted, they both had a penis. He thought he had seen his sister's penis. Such open naïveté about anatomical differences in the sexes in a 17-year-old boy might have been considered suspect. But the evidence was convincing that, so far as the patient's reportable knowledge of such matters was concerned, he knew of only one sex, anatomically speaking, and could not believe that there should be any other structural possibility. His first dream during treatment indicated that he was curious to know but that his acquisition of information was blocked.

"I was going up some dark stairs. At the top there was a dark corridor. On either side was a door. I knew one was a men's toilet. The other was for women. The door to the women's room was a little open, and I started toward it and woke up with a start. But this is a dream. I've had it many times. I always wake up at that point."

The origin of this specific inhibition of acquiring information could then be supplied by the patient in certain memories of childhood. Until he was five years of age his mother had regularly taken baths with him because, as he understood it, she wanted to be near enough to him to protect him if he had a seizure at such a time. When he began to ask questions about anatomical differences and childbirth, she abruptly stopped taking baths with him and watched over him from the outside of the tub. She warned him never again to come into her room when she was dressing or when she was bathing. She emphatically denied that there was any difference in the roles of the sexes in childbearing and did not supply information pertaining to any mutual contribution of the sexes in procreation. R.'s view of childbirth was, for instance, that some people can have babies and some cannot, regardless of sex. The sharp interruption in his day-to-day experience of receiving his mother's care, occasioned by his long hospitalization and the arrival of a baby sister when he was seven or eight years old, reinforced an early, chronic childhood premonition he had had (the basis of which was not learned and cannot now be established without speculation) of some sense of catastrophic deprivation. Therefore, various life experiences, such as the withholding of information he requested, the denial of a tension-relieving verbal reply when he made a verbal request, his mother's changing of his brand of chocolate milk, the refusal of someone to do all his homework for him, and the refusal of the therapist to let him study his clinic chart, were presumably experienced by him as serious deprivations and evidence of the unreliability of a parent or a parent surrogate. Situations of this sort, or with some common denominator, were repeatedly found to trigger his gastric aura and his grand mal seizures. Biochemical or other factors apparently determined whether one or several such life experiences were adequate to precipitate a seizure. After the therapist had achieved some degree of success in illustrating and promoting partial understanding of his inordinate demands for acceptance and support and his feelings of deprivation, a notable decrease in the seizure frequency occurred.

That the period of psychotherapy played a key role in bringing about symptomatic improvement is evidenced by the fact that with psychotherapy this boy, whose seizures had never previously been controlled adequately by anticonvulsant medication, had about one half the usual number of fits in 1949 and 1950 and had no seizures whatever in 1951 or 1952 on approximately his usual dose of anticonvulsant medication. Incipient strivings to emancipate himself from his deep insecurities and from the home where his conflicting drives and maladaptations were nurtured are perhaps indicated by his last dreams in treatment, when he was dealing with the problem of achieving some financial and emotional independence of his parents:

"I had something like a chicken, although much smaller than a chicken. More like a homing pigeon. I let it go out of the house to fly around where it wanted to, and to test out whether it could find its way back.

"I had some gas balloons, tied a note to them with my name and address, and let them go out of the window. I was just curious to find out whether the notes would be returned to me, so I could find out how far the balloons had gone."

His associations centered around his wish to become independent of his family and of his anxieties about certain realistic aspects of an epileptic person's getting and keeping regular employment.

During the period of treatment, the patient graduated from high school and attended one year of junior college. He continued his study of music—on his own—and actually did satisfy the qualifications and become a member of the Chicago musicians' union. Later, because of difficulties in securing employment as a musician, he studied to be a masseur, by this time getting some, perhaps misguided, encouragement and financial support from his parents. Blocked in obtaining employment as a masseur, he finally accepted employment as a clerk and was holding his first position of gainful employment when psychotherapy was stopped.

At this time, still a strange-looking person, and still in conflict psychologically, he was no longer so unkempt, retarded, or frankly withdrawn and dissociated. He could communicate his wants, feelings, and fantasies and could appraise his life circumstances more realistically.

The psychologic factors associated with R.'s seizures may be summarized. R. was fixated at a dependent stage of development. His demands for food, affection, and support had hostile components. The mobilizations of receptive and dependent impulses occasioned both guilt and fear of loss of love. Examples of R.'s often disorganized and devious attempts to solve his conflicts are described. Parental attitudes of rejection and fear about R. and the meaning of his seizures contributed to his insecurity. Everyday events that R. experienced as evidence of the unreliability of a parent or parent surrogate were found to trigger his gastric aura (a sudden feeling of hunger and slight nausea), which, in turn, was often followed by a grand mal seizure.

Electroencephalographic Report

1. Before Physiotherapy: (a) December, 1946 (age, 16 years 5 months). "The record shows bilateral 10½-cps occipital rhythm, with a suggestion of 3- to 4-cps occipital rhythm. There is no build-up with hyperventilation. The impression is that of a possible abnormal curve, with numerous artifacts. The patient cooperated with difficulty" (H. M. Serota). (b) January, 1947 (age, 16 years 6 months). "The record shows an 11- to 12-cps occipital rhythm, with occasional bursts of 4- to 5-cps bilateral frontal activity. There is a large build-up with hyperventilation. The impression is that of an abnormal curve consistent with the diagnosis of a convulsive disorder" (H. M. Serota). (c) April, 1947 (age, 16 years 9 months). "The record shows a 10-cps occipital rhythm, with definite 3- to 5-cps fronto-parietal rhythm in paroxysmal bursts and slow random potentials. There is a slight build-up on hyperventilation. The impression is that of a definitely abnormal curve consistent with the diagnosis of a convulsive disorder." (H. M. Serota)

2. During Psychotherapy (July, 1949; age, 19 years): "The record shows

a 12-cps occipital rhythm, with diffuse occasional 4- to 5-cps activity. There is a moderate build-up with hyperventilation. The impression is that of an abnormal curve consistent with diagnosis of an epileptic disorder. However, the record shows definite improvement over the curves for January and April, 1947, with a tendency toward diminution of slow and paroxysmal activity." (H. M. Serota)

3. After Psychotherapy (May, 1951; age, 20 years 10 months): "The waking record shows 9- to 10-cps occasional slow and sharp activity in the frontal and temporal leads, especially in the left anterior temporal area. The sleeping record shows low-voltage fast and irregular slow activity. With hyperventilation there is paroxysmal sharp and slow activity. The impression is that, except for the hyperventilation sensitivity, this record shows some improvement over previous electroencephalograms." (J. P. Toman)

Psychological Tests. Weschsler-Bellevue Intelligence Scale: The results are tabulated.

	Nov. 25, 1946 (Before Psychotherapy)	Aug. 13, 1951 (After Psychotherapy)
Intelligence quotient	93	96
Verbal	117	120
Performance	67	70
Chronological age	16-4	21

The remarkable aspect of the results of these two tests is their extreme similarity. The only significant difference is the marked improvement in arithmetic. The shifts in the performance series, for better or for worse, are not very great, although an improvement in picture arrangement (social comprehension and grasp of cause-and-effect relationships) may be important for this boy.

Rorschach Tests (Dr. Samuel J. Beck). Two Rorschach tests are evaluated.

"The first Rorschach test was done when the boy was 17 years four months of age (before psychotherapy). The data of the test reveal a withdrawal of emotional contact and expression from the outer world, erratic perception and attention, and regressive thinking. In addition, there are a rigid character structure and inhibition of pleasurable responses.

"Anxiety is mobilized most acutely to the 'mother' figure but is also apparent toward the 'father' figure, toward which an ambivalent attitude is suggested.

"His vulnerability to the color stimuli suggests a reactive or neurotic personality structure.

"The second Rorschach test was done when the patient was 21 years one month of age (after psychotherapy). It indicates that strong urges and feelings have been freed from repression and that the patient can now enjoy relations with other persons. On the other hand, there persists many signs of disturbances in personality functioning, e. g., serious inaccuracies, deviations in thinking, unique or irrelevant elaborations, and flight of attention. His response to the test has progressed from an immature to a 'neurotic' reaction pattern, in which there is now evidence that when he experiences strong emotions he has conflicts about expressing them.

"Although there is considerable improvement in this patient's personality, the whole picture is not that of a well-integrated person."

Comment

Modifications in Seizure Frequency Induced by Psychotherapy

A review of the changes in seizure frequency and the requirements of anticonvulsant medication during and after the period of psychotherapy provides evidence that the seizure threshold of each patient was increased. It cannot be proved in this study that the passage of time alone or in combination with an anticonvulsant medication was not of some consequence in effecting this change. The evidence that the psychotherapeutic activities contributed to the clinical changes is provided by the fact that variations in the psychotherapeutic management of each child were associated with reversible changes in the frequency of his convulsive manifestations. Moreover, there were notable differences in the dosage of anticonvulsant medication the children received before psychotherapy and the types of convulsive behavior they manifested. Nevertheless, they all showed a decrease in seizure frequency with psychotherapy.

It is unfortunate that critical intergroup control experiments could not be run in such a study as this, so as to demonstrate decisively and exactly the effect on seizure rate of passage of time alone, and of psychotherapy alone, on large groups of perfectly matched pairs of patients. But the infeasibility of such an attempt is obvious. As a result, in this investigation some compromise in scientific rigorousness, such as the use of a patient as his own control, seemed necessary.

Some comment on the interseizure electroencephalographic studies is necessary. Such records supply neurophysiological evidence of the paroxysmal or epileptic nature of each child's convulsions. They do not help to clarify with certainty which behavioral manifestations were accompanied by disordered cerebral electrical potentials and which were not. But they do substantiate the idea that each of these three patients had a deviant or pathological pattern of electroencephalographic activity.

When N. (Case 2) was at an age when he was having only "screen spells," the electroencephalographic reports indicate that the form of cerebral electrical discharges recorded from his scalp were typical of "petit mal" discharges. But most readers would hardly recognize the patient's "screen spells" as typical petit mal seizures. These "screen spells" had features indistinguishable from such syndromes as hysterical convulsions of fugue states. To these conditions is imputed primarily, if not solely, a psychogenic basis. It is my opinion, based on both the interseizure electroencephalograms and repeated observations of the "screen spells," that the occurrence of these "screen spells" was determined both by biological factors–structural and/or functional–and by experiental, or psychologic factors. Not one, but an interplay of all these factors, was necessary for the ictal phenomena to occur.

The improvement in the electroencephalograms of K. (Case 1) with psychotherapy is interesting. This child happened to be the one receiving the most intensive psychotherapy in terms of sessions (three to four a week). He showed the most dramatic change in personality of the three patients treated. Furthermore, he was the youngest child. It would be tempting to conclude that the beneficial effect of psychotherapy was reflected, at a neurophysiological level, in his electroencephalogram. To draw such a conclusion would be unjustifiable, however, for a "fairly large percentage of patients" with a spike discharge focus in the midtemporal area have, within five years, a presumably spontaneous disappearance of this focus (Gibbs–Personal Communication). The significance of the improvement in the electroencephalograms in Case 3 must also await evaluation. Further studies must be made to establish whether or not psychologic procedures can modify paroxysmal electroencephalographic patterns.

Modifications in the Form of the Seizures During Psychotherapy

The idea that the form of epileptic seizures in a patient may change in relation to other events is not new. The administration of one type of anticonvulsant drug has been observed to inhibit the occurrence of one kind of seizure and increase the frequency of a different form of paroxysmal manifestations (Gibbs, F. A., 1947 Toman et al., 1947; Toman, 1951;). Psychotherapy has been reported to modify the form of the convulsive episodes in a patient with petit mal seizures. In this report, the chronological sequence of changes in the form of paroxysmal manifestations during psychotherapy were petit mal seizures, grand mal seizures, psychomotor "acting out", narcolepsy, and various conversion manifestations or anxiety attacks (Barker, 1948).

The present study gives additional evidence that children subject to convulsive tendencies may show, in relation to intervening events such as psychotherapy, alternative forms of repetitive, explosive behavior, and sensory activity. In Case 1, the disappearance of nocturnal grand mal seizures and petit-mal-like spells was followed by temper tantrums, then facial tics, and finally, sudden hand-washing episodes. At the time psychologic treatment was terminated, all such behavior had been absent about four months. No frank seizures have recurred in more than two years.

In Case 2 (N.) interesting variations in the form of seizures occurred. Psychomotor fits replaced "screen spells," and finally grand mal spells tended to replace all other types of seizures. The previously stereotyped form of the boy's bizarre "screen spells" changed, so that new and varied motor and sensory phenomena occurred and alternated with one another.

In Case 3 (R.) the impulsive making of abusive telephone calls and uncontrollable giggling disappeared, and grand mal spells persisted; finally, all frank seizure activity disappeared.

It has not been ascertained what characteristic motor or sensory activity is a direct expression of abnormal electrical cerebral discharges, what activity is merely associated with an abnormally discharging brain, and what activity is not related to an established paroxysmal cerebral dysrhythmia. No crucial evidence is available to distinguish in any one epileptic patient when a characteristic type of behavior is ictal and when it is nonictal. A recent attempt has been made to differentiate "psychogenic" and "epileptic" seizures in patients with generalized convulsions by a hypnotic-recall technique and electroencephalograms (Peterson et al., 1950; Summer et al., 1952). The assumption is made that if a patient can recall details of his seizure during hypnosis the seizure is "psychogenic"; if he cannot do so, it is "epileptogenic." Such an assumption is unwarranted. The hypnotic-recall technique demonstrates only which seizure phenomena are possible of recall under hypnosis. It does not give information as to which convulsions are epileptic—which are accompanied by paroxysmal or otherwise deviant cerebral electrical discharges. There are many epileptic manifestations, also, in which recall of the convulsive behavior may not be seriously affècted, e.g., in many minor seizures, in certain initial seizure phenomena of major seizures (Penfield and Kristiansen, 1951), and in Jacksonian and focal convulsions.

Psychologic Conflicts as Precipitants of Seizures

That external or internal psychologic stress may precipitate an epileptic seizure is generally accepted, but the phenomenon is not well understood or accounted for.

Textbook classifications of the epileptic syndromes have recognized that type of genuine seizure which is triggered by a psychologic or sensory event. These seizures have been labeled "reflex epilepsy" and "affective epilepsy." (Wilson, 1940). Various stressful psychologic stimuli are routinely used to elicit experimental seizures in animals whose brains have been traumatized, one standard method being vigorous prodding of the animal with a stick (Kopeloff et al., 1947).

Clinical and therapeutic studies of epileptic persons have been reported as showing a relation of psychologic stress to onset of epileptic seizures in some patients (Fremont-Smith, 1934; Gowers, 1901; Mettelman 1947; Pond, 1952). Mittelman (1947) has recently reviewed the theoretical views and clinical evidence relevant to such matters. Ingenious attempts to correlate the arousal of emotional conflict with paroxysmal or abnormal electroencephalographic activity have given suggestive, but not conclusive, evidence that psychologic conflict or stress can, in some persons, initiate epileptic behavior (Barker and Barker, 1950).

The data collected in the present study are indeed compatible with the view that epileptic seizures and/or behavioral disorders occurring in a patient with epilepsy may be precipitated by an event or events of psychologic nature.

An attempt will be made to synthesize the common denominators of psychologic events that eventuated in seizures, or seizure-like activity, in these three children. The personal situation, generally the first in a sequence of personal events, that repeatedly led to paroxysmal behavior in these patients may be described as the blocking of any drive or strong emotion from gratification or expression by either an internal, autonomous inhibiting factor or an external agent and/or situation. The aim of the drive, whether to get support or protection, to escape a situation, to fight, or to attack, apparently made no difference as to its adequacy in activating the chain of events leading to a seizure. The important feature was the blocking of such an aim, or the blocking of the conventional manner of communication of a feeling associated with such an aim.

Other psychiatrically oriented reports on the psychogenesis of epilepsy have tended to single out one impulse, or drive, as the one which was blocked or conflictual, e.g., a need to express anger (Freud, 1928; Bartemeier, 1932), desire for sexual activity (Greenson, 1944), or desire for dependence (Heilbrunn, 1950). In the present investigation, the operation of a single specific conflictual drive as the constant psychologic precipitant in epileptic seizures could not be substantiated.

An objection to the concept that any blocked drive or emotion can elicit an epileptic episode in a person so predisposed might be that this concept in no way distinguished the psychologic conflict leading to an epileptic episode from that reportedly leading to other states of somatic dysfunction, e.g., asthma, hypertension, peptic ulcer, or colitis. Further study of this matter is necessary before final conclusions can be drawn. It is possible, after all, that epileptic children do not vary significantly in the range of psychologic conflicts that can trigger their episodes of somatic dysfunction from children with other recurring episodic bodily dysfunctions.

How do these epileptic children differ from children without symptomatic disease? Is not such a psychologic conflict common in all people? It is acknowledged that such a conflict is probably universal. Two points distinguished these epileptic children from other children in general:

1. Neurophysiologically, their seizure threshold was lower than that of other children. Psychologically, they had a predisposition to paroxysmal, explosive neuromuscular, and sensory activity.

2. Their impulses and emotions were more primitive, less mature, than those of other children of comparable age. Consequently, perhaps psychologic conflicts were more overwhelming.

In the present study evidence for the latter point accrued from two sources. One was the clinical judgment of the therapist; the other was the standardized evaluation via psychologic tests. The analysis, by Dr. Samuel Beck, of the Rorschach protocols showed clearly in each child a decided immaturity, in which drives or emotions were poorly integrated with the total personality. These tests revealed, furthermore, a chronic blocking of gratification or expression of motivational needs. In summary, the Rorschach test findings tended to corroborate the clinical finding that the epileptic children studied had special vulnerabilities to the mobilizing of unacceptable drives.

Effect of Psychotherapy on Epileptic Manifestations

That reports of psychotherapeutic attempts in the management of epilepsy in children have been few has been noted (Lennox, 1941; Kanner, 1948). Lennox (1941) stated: "I have encountered no convincing reports in the medical literature of successful treatment of epilepsy by psychotherapy." In fact, he cautions, "Formal analysis should not be attempted in a child" (p. 125).

Previous surveys have indicated that roughly 20 per cent of persons whose seizures begin in the first decade of life have remissions during other types of treatment, lasting two years or longer (Turner, 1907; Lennox, 1932; Wilkins, 1937). In the present study, the seizures of two of the children have not yet recurred, during a period of more than two years. The probability of observing two or more than two-year remissions in three patients is approximately 1:10.

The experience with these epileptic children offers some evidence that psychoanalytic psychotherapy was decisively beneficial in the treatment of their epilepsy. The results do not give evidence that psychotherapy is superior to other forms of treatment, such as anticonvulsant medication. I feel, nevertheless, that it is justifiable to generalize from the findings that psychotherapy judiciously combined with anticonvulsant medication may effect greater reduction in the seizure manifestations of certain patients than the use of anticonvulsant medication alone. Further studies are necessary to determine which epileptic persons may benefit from psychotherapy, and to what extent they can benefit.

In any event, the success of psychologic treatment of these three children is offered as evidence that psychologic, as well as other factors, may play a decisive role in the development of epileptic phenomena.

Summary

1. The seizure frequencies of three epileptic children decreased notably during and after a course of psychotherapy. The seizures of two of the children have not recurred for two years.

2. The form of the ictal manifestations of the children, as well as the seizure frequency, was modified during psychotherapy.

3. The above findings constitute evidence that psychologic factors, as well as other factors, can contribute to the form and frequency of seizures and associated clinical manifestations. Evidence is given which supports the hypothesis that interpersonal events, as well as intrapersonal conflicts, can activate epileptic behavior.

EPIDEMIOLOGIC STUDIES ON THE COMPLICATION OF PREGNANCY AND THE BIRTH PROCESS

BENJAMIN PASAMANICK AND HILDA KNOBLOCH

This article, based on a number of studies and a wealth of data accumulated by Pasamanick and his co-workers, extends the concept of organicity and attempts to provide bridges between organic, genetic, and cultural approaches to childhood psychopathology. The authors suggest that psychopathology in children is organic and that minor brain damage is sufficient to disrupt the child's behavioral development. They stress that most abnormalities of pregnancy, as well as most emotional disorders of children, occur predominantly in the lower socioeconomic level of our society. They incline to the view that, whereas much brain damage has its origins in the prenatal period, life experience and the sociocultural milieu play an equally important role. Their conclusions, that what we see in the children of the poor is a result of a double handicap: organic lesion and cultural deprivation, parallel Eisenberg's (1964).

In the conduct of such studies, one must remain alert to the distinction between correlation and causation, and exercise caution about basing a diagnosis of organicity on behavioral symptoms and signs. Not all brain-damaged children exhibit the commonly ascribed behavior characteristics, but many children without brain damage do, inasmuch as children manifest anxiety through motoric hyperactivity.

We have found in our clinical experience that the most difficult diagnostic issue involves the question of "normal organicity." It is the area in which clinicians often hotly disagree and become polarized in their clinical approaches. While it is crucial that large-scale epidemiologic and longitudinal studies such as Pasamanick's continue, it is vital to balance these with individual in-depth studies of children with disorders ascribed to minimal brain damage. Only in this way shall we be able to relate a child's biological, social, and psychological experiences to each other and avoid emphasizing one aspect of his clinical picture and its development at the expense of another.

The hypothesized association of abnormalities of pregnancy and the birth process with neuropsychiatric disorders of childhood would appear to present a valuable opportunity for epidemiologic investigation. Essentially we are offering for consideration a chronological review of our own still incomplete chain of studies and a summary of our major findings to date. We believe they warrant serious attention as evidence for the existence of potent precursors of neuropsychiatric disorder.

The hypothesis basic to the series of studies to be described stems from a number of propositions: (1) Since prematurity and complications of pregnancy are associated with fetal and neonatal death, usually on the basis of injury to the brain, there must remain a fraction so injured who do not die. (2) Depending upon the degree and location of the damage, the survivors may develop a series of disorders. These extend from cerebral palsy, epilepsy, and mental deficiency through all types of behavioral and learning disabilities which are a result of lesser degrees of damage sufficient to disorganize behavioral development and lower thresholds to stress (Knobloch and Pasamanick, 1956a). (3) Further, these abnormalities of pregnancy are associated with certain life experiences, usually socioeconomically determined, and consequently (4) they themselves and their resulting neuropsychiatric disorders are found in greater aggregation in the lower strata of our society.

It should be explicitly noted at this point that retrospective epidemiologic research and clinical investigation of the individual patient rely upon data gathered, and possibly interpreted, in a manner that may introduce biases. In clinical work, unselected information secured from the patient or the parent of a patient cannot be compared to that secured from even a well-matched, healthy control. Such information, particularly on early childhood and before, is therefore not a very good source from which to draw diagnoses (Pasamanick, 1953).

Even cause and effect are frequently confounded in our psychodynamic formulations. In a study to be described later, we found a high positive correlation between the irritability and tension displayed by a mother during her interview with a nurse and the degree of neurological damage found in her infant by a physician. Since we know clinically that most of the neurological signs discernible during infancy disappear with maturation, it is possible to conceive that had this infant been presented as a behavior-disordered child ten or fifteen years later, its difficulties could have been attributed to the mother's behavior. The clinician must keep his head above the multiplicity of variables operating through time upon his patients and not be drowned, grasping at a single straw of causation (Pasamanick and Knobloch, 1960).

In naturalistic epidemiologic investigation, an attempt is made to isolate the independent variable through partialing it out in the experimental sample. This is done by selecting a control sample similar in all aspects except for the variable under scrutiny and then determining how both samples differ in the dependent variables. Contrasted with this is the experimental study in which both samples are drawn from the same population and the independent variable is intentionally altered. While the latter type of study is much more likely to offer definitive conclusions, the naturalistic study is frequently the only method available for research on human populations, particularly in the chronic disorders. It is possible, however, to demonstrate that the results of such a study, interwoven with additional factors, present so weighty an argument for a given chain of causality that no other conclusion seems valid under the circumstances (Pasamanick, 1950).

The New Haven Study

We first became interested in the influence of prenatal factors during the course of a longitudinal study of Negro child development in New Haven (Pasamanick, 1946). In a group of Negro infants born during one of the middle war years, we found adaptive behavioral development proceeding at rates normal for white infants according to the Gesell developmental techniques. Not only was this finding contrary to previous published studies, but also no explanation of the disparity could be found in environmental associations such as the education or geographic origin of the parents, number of siblings, quality of housing, or skin color. However, when the growth curves were examined we noted (also contrary to previous findings) that from birth the subjects were progressing according to the best available white rates in both weight and height.

On the basis of this we hypothesized that the mothers of these infants had received an adequate prenatal diet because of war time rationing, and because of employment opportunities that bettered their economic status. This hypothesis was supported by further examinations of the children, continued into their eighth year of life (Knobloch and Pasamanick, 1953). At seven years of age, the subjects had a mean intellectual functioning equal to that of the mean white scores as measured on the Stanford-Binet and Arthur performance tests (Nash et al., unpublished data).

In two areas of behavioral development, language and gross motor behavior, we did find significant differences from the white norms. The lowered language scores found at two years were shown to be due to impaired verbal responsiveness, possibly a result of inhibition caused by a white examiner, while verbal comprehension remained unimpaired (Pasamanick and Knobloch, 1955). During the course of another study to be described later we found that the seeming acceleration in gross motor behavior that had also been described by other investigators was not present (Knobloch and Pasamanick, 1959b). (Motor behavior of white and Negro infants at the midcentury is comparable and is significantly accelerated over the norms established a decade or two ago. This may be due to changes in child-rearing methods, but no definitive explanation is available at this time.)

Retrospective Studies

Following this investigation, we began a series of retrospective studies (Lilienfeld et al., 1955) of the relationship between prenatal experience and certain neuropsychiatric disorders (cerebral palsy, epilepsy, mental deficiency, behavior disorders, reading disabilities, tics, and speech disorders). More than 8,000 children were involved in these studies. For each study, a large population of children diagnosed as having the particular clinical entity under scrutiny was selected from the case files of hospital outpatient clinics, institutions, and public schools. The clinical data from the case histories was abstracted and coded for internal comparison studies. We then searched the birth certificate register to single out for further examination those children who had been born in Baltimore, where these studies were conducted, and for whom birth records were available.

A series of controls to whom the cases could be compared was also selected. In all but one of the studies, the control was the next surviving infant in the birth certificate register of the same race, sex, and socioeconomic status as the case, who was born in the same hospital to a mother of the same age. In the behavior disorder study the control was the next child alphabetically of the same sex in the same school class as the case. This controlled for teacher bias in reporting and automatically controlled for race, since the study was done prior to integration.

Information about the parents and their socioeconomic status was derived from the children's birth certificates. For those children born in hospitals, information was gathered from hospital records on such items as number of previous pregnancies; abortions; stillbirths; premature and neonatal deaths; complications of pregnancy, labor, and delivery; operative delivery procedures; birth weight; and neonatal course.

In retrospective studies of this type, direct comparisons of current behavior between cases and controls are not made, but information that has been recorded in the past is examined. By this method, associations between prior conditions and current clinical entities can be demonstrated by showing significant differences between cases and controls in the incidence of various prior abnormalities under consideration. If those cases selected as controls from the birth certificate files had any of the clinical neuropsychiatric entities under investigation, any difference in the histories between the cases and the controls would be more significant in the face of the possibility that the control patient group was contaminated by clinical cases. The point has been raised repeatedly that studies of this nature are inherently flawed by the poor quality and almost universal under-reporting of complications or abnormalities. This fact presents a bias against the hypothesis being tested. While relationships might be obscured or missed, the finding of significant differences is evidence for true associations.

Thus far, five of the clinical entities studied in these children have been found to be significantly associated both with complications of pregnancy and prematurity. These are cerebral palsy (Lilienfeld and Pasamanick, 1955), epilepsy (Lilienfeld and Pasamanick, 1954), mental deficiency (Pasamanick and Lilienfeld, 1955a), behavior disorders (Pasamanick et al., 1956c), and reading disabilities (Kawi and Pasamanick, 1958). A sixth condition, tics (Pasamanick and Kawi, 1956c) was found to be significantly associated with complications of pregnancy, but not with prematurity. The seventh entity, childhood speech disorder (Pasamanick et al., 1956b), when not associated with cerebral palsy or mental deficiency, showed no significant relation to abnormalities of pregancy or prematurity, although slight differences in the predicted direction were found for pregnancy abnormality.

No difference was found between the cases and controls in the incidence of prolonged and difficult labor and of operative procedures during delivery, such as mid or high forceps, Caesarean section, breech extraction, or internal version and extraction—the types of situation that have previously been hypothesized as responsible for birth trauma. Rather, the associations occurred with the prolonged and probably anoxia-producing complications of pregnancy such as the toxemias and maternal bleeding.

Two other general observations can be made. First, the incidence of abnormalities of pregnancy was much higher in the nonwhites than in the whites. Second, the differences between cases and controls tended to be greater in the more severe clinical conditions, e.g., cerebral palsy and epilepsy, and to decrease as the handicap became milder.

It should also be noted that in all the conditions studied, except speech disorders, there was a much higher prevalence of the clinical entities in males, perhaps a further lead as to the etiologic role of brain injury as a precursor of these disorders.

As in most epidemiologic studies there were a number of byproducts that permitted us to examine other possible etiologic factors and to seek for the internal consistency necessary to help support the major tests of the hypothesis.

In the investigation of epilepsy we found that although differences between cases and controls were in the expected direction among Negroes, they were not statistically significant. This is probably at least partially attributable to the fact that the rate of pregnancy abnormality among Negro mothers and their offspring, both cases and controls, was so high that the number of cases available did not constitute a sample large enough to yield significant results.

In addition to direct evidence from morbidity statistics that postnatal insult following such conditions as lead intoxication, head injury, and infection is probably more common among Negroes than among whites, there is also indirect evidence for this in the findings of this study (Pasamanick and Knobloch, 1955). The younger a patient at the onset of convulsive seizures, the more likely is the condition to be due to brain damage sustained early in the development of the individual. In the white patients, there was a positive association between prenatal and paranatal complications and the onset of seizures in the first year of life. In the Negro epileptics, however, this relationship between age and onset of seizures and abnormalities of pregnancy was not observed.

Since we had data available on the occurrence of epilepsy in the families of our cases, we thought it might be fruitful to see what light our results cast on the genetic hypothesis. It is reasonable to assume that if prenatal and paranatal factors play a significant role in the causation of some forms of epilepsy, and genetic factors in others, our cases in which the pregnancy factors were absent should have had more epileptic parents than those cases in which these factors were present. This was not found to be true, and makes it necessary to re-examine the genetic hypothesis in epilepsy. May not the familial aggregation of epilepsy be a reflection of the occurrence of familial aggregation of the prenatal and paranatal factors under discussion in this report? Prematurity, stillbirth, and neonatal death have been so described, and the socioeconomic factors with which these and other abnormalities are associated are usually a lifelong experience.

In the study of mental deficiency, although there was significantly more prematurity among the retarded Negro children, there was no significant difference between cases and controls as far as complications of pregnancy were concerned. However, when we examined the relationship between the degree of mental deficiency and these pregnancy abnormalities, a most revealing association was discovered (Lilienfeld and Pasamanick, 1956). Almost every one of the Negro children in the group with I.Q.'s under 50 had been exposed to one or more abnormalities of pregnancy. For those above I.Q. 50, no such difference existed between cases and controls. This is in contrast to the white cases, where differences existed at all levels of deficiency. The most likely explanation for these results is that the Negro group with I.Q.'s from 50 to 80 must have been diluted by the inclusion of cases who had no real brain disease but who merely reflected the widespread sociocultural retardation known to exist among Negro children (Pasamanick and Knobloch, 1958). We also found that very young mothers and older women had a significantly higher risk of producing mentally defective children. Increasing birth order also increased the risk of mental deficiency.

Among the behavior disorders investigated, the highest association with the complications under consideration was found for both racial groups in those children called hyperactive, confused, and disorganized (Rogers et al., 1955). These accounted for 40 per cent of the school referrals in Baltimore. When this diagnostic category was removed, there were no longer any significant differences between white cases and controls. In the Negroes, however, differences were still present for the remainder of the cases. It may be that in nonwhites cerebral injury is so pervasive that it infiltrates all types of behavior disorder.

A number of socioeconomic and familial variables were examined in this study. Items previously incriminated by other writers, such as family composition, parental age and education, employment, and housing, were not found to be different among the cases and controls (Pasamanick, 1956a).

The reading disorder investigation was confined to white children, since any sample of Negro children would have been heavily contaminated by cases whose disorders were a result of sociocultural retardation (Kawi, 1958). As a test of internal consistency we looked at association with degree of reading disability. The greater the disability, the more abnormalities of pregnancy were found in the background.

In the study of speech disorders, from which no significant association was found with complications of pregnancy, we did encounter a finding that helped confirm previous impressions. Contrary to our expectation, there was no greater incidence of speech disorders among males which was in marked contrast to the other neuropsychiatric disorders studied. We also found a significantly higher proportion of multiple pregnancies among the speech disorder cases, as well as an increased risk of disorder in the higher birth orders, both associations explainable on psychologic grounds.

It has been known for some time that the neuropsychiatric disorders under discussion are more common among the lower socioeconomic strata of our population, including Negroes and other disadvantaged minority groups (Pasamanick and Knobloch, 1957). We suspected that this discrepancy extended to the complications associated with these disorders. Of particular interest to us were prematurity and abnormalities of the prenatal and paranatal periods.

An examination of the distribution of prematurity in Baltimore in relation to socioeconomic status, as defined by census tract, demonstrated a significant negative correlation with socioeconomic status in the white groups (Rider et al., 1955). The incidence was 5 per cent in the highest economic tenth compared to 7.6 per cent in the lowest. In the nonwhites, it was 11.4 per cent. In examining the distribution of complications of pregnancy and birth in the white population, only the lower and upper economic fifth were compared. The findings were striking (Pasamanick et al., 1956b). The incidence of complications in the white upper economic fifth was 5 per cent and in the white lower fifth 14.6 per cent. In the nonwhites, it was 50.6 per cent.

These higher rates of prematurity and complications of pregnancy among Negroes over even the lowest white socioeconomic group are so marked that some workers in this field maintain that they must be attributable to some innate racial characteristic. Since average Negro socioeconomic status is generally lower than that in the lowest white groups, it seems more parsimonious to eliminate the postulated racial factors, and to hypothesize that prematurity and pregnancy complication rates increase exponentially below certain socioeconomic thresholds.

Prospective Studies

Thus far, except for the longitudinal study of Negro child development, we have been discussing a series of retrospective investigations of associations. These are subject to the possibility that the factors studied as dependent variables might have helped produce the factors studied as independent variables through some means other than the one hypothesized. A somewhat better test of the hypothesis is possible through the prospective investigation in which the dependent variable of the retrospective studies becomes the independent variable and the independent, in turn, becomes the dependent examined repeatedly through time (Pasamanick, 1952).

Some eight years ago we entered upon such a study in which the independent variable was prematurity. In this study a socioeconomically stratified sample of five hundred prematurely born children delivered in one year in Baltimore and their full-term matched controls were followed from birth. A detailed description of the study design and analysis has already been published (Knobloch and Pasamanick, 1956), but some of the findings of the Gesell Developmental Examination given at 40 weeks of age are germane to our present discussion.

When adjustments were made for differences between the whites and nonwhites in the distribution of birth weights, no significant differences were found between the races in the incidence of neurologic and intellectual defect (Knobloch et al., 1956). However, as was predicted by our hypothesis, the incidence of abnormality increased as the birth weight decreased. The frequency of serious neurologic abnormality was significantly higher in the prematures than in the controls, and there was a high negative correlation of intellectual potential with degree of prematurity. Forty-four per cent of the infants with birth weights under 1500 gm. had an abnormal condition of sufficient magnitude to cause serious concern about the prognosis for future development. The comparable incidence for the rest of the premature group was 8.6 per cent, and for the full-term infants, 2.6 per cent.

In addition, significantly more of the prematures exhibited the syndrome of "minimal damage." This syndrome describes a group of children who in infancy show distinct and definite deviations in neurologic patterning, but in whom clinical experience indicates that complete compensation for the neurologic abnormalities will occur with maturation. According to the hypothesis these children, found among both prematures (16.3 per cent) and controls (10 per cent), are the ones who should exhibit at a later date the integrational defects seen in behavior and learning disorders.

We have recently had occasion to do an item analysis of the 46 individual neurologic patterns investigated in our study of prematures; it has given us a clinical picture of what may be a fairly specific entity and it is now being tested by further studies (Knobloch and Pasamanick, 1959c). Unfortunately, most of these neurologic items are difficult or impossible to secure on a retrospective historical basis in clinical practice. They include such items as substitutive patterns, excessive extension in, and abruptness of, release, difficulty in retaining, maldirected reaching, increased tendon reflexes, hypertonicity, and so on. However, some of the behavior patterns that can be secured by anamnesis (such as sucking and feeding difficulties, and excessive startle,), and which are as discriminating as the neurologic items, deviate in the same direction.

Some of our findings in studies on perception in known brain-injured school-age children may provide an explanation of the sources of difficulty in minimally brain-injured individuals, as well as a basis for some objective diagnostic measures. While studying different measures of visual perception (including light thresholds [Mark, 1958], critical flicker fusion [Mark et al., 1958], asynchronism [Mark, 1958], and apparent movement thresholds [Nash et al., unpublished data]) we found, in addition to threshold differences, significant intraindividual response variability. These studies were strengthened by threshold measurements in other sense modalities, including the proprioceptive. The findings are probably related to the so-called "scatter of function" referred to in intelligence testing. It is possible to hypothesize, therefore, that organic dysfunction readily manifests itself in a lack of consistency of one sort or another, and indeed, it is easy to conceptualize how increased variability in the relatively simpler primary functions, such as light perception, may actually give rise to dysfunction in processes such as conditioning and memory, as well as in more complex behavior patterns.

We turn now to the question of intellectual potential, as examined in our study of prematures in Baltimore. The general developmental quotient for our controls at 40 weeks of age was 105.4 for the whites and 104.5 for the nonwhites. It is noteworthy that the distribution of the general developmental quotients was not affected by differences in the education of the parents, economic status, or race. But when the first 300 of the approximately one thousand children involved in the study were reexamined at approximately three years of age, distinct racial differences were observed. The mean developmental quotient for the white controls rose significantly to 110.9; it fell to 97.4 for the nonwhites. This indicated the need for a special analysis of the data to see whether this change could be explained.

One method of evaluating this change with age between the two racial groups was to compare the distribution of intellectual potential in the infant population with the distribution shown by intelligence tests given to school-age children (Knobloch and Pasamanick, 1959a). A representative distribution of general developmental quotients for the infant population of Baltimore was evolved by adjusting for differences in birth weight, race, and economic status in the infant sample. Approximately 90 per cent of the infant population had developmental quotients between 90 and 120. When this distribution was compared with that found on the Stanford-Binet testing in the literature, there was evidence of a widening band in the older age group.

Two points about this widening are important. First, relatively little increase occurred at the upper range of the intelligence quotient scale, in contrast to a marked increase in the percentage of school-age children who had I.Q.'s less than 85. This increase occurred largely in the I.Q. group between 50 and 70, frequently considered retarded on a genetic basis, but increases also occurred in the group with I.Q.'s between 70 and 85, those ordinarily felt to be part of the normal human variation, but to occupy their position in the curve on the basis of inferior hereditary endowment. Second, in the infant group there was a sharp, abrupt rise at a level of 80 or 85, while in the older group this curve was relatively smooth and the increase started at a lower level, in the 50 to 55 I.Q. range.

Another method of evaluating the increase in number of children with I.Q.'s below 80 was by analysis of the individual infants in the Baltimore group who had developmental quotients below 80. Almost all these infants were organically impaired either neurologically or physically. They also had a history of a significantly higher proportion of the chronic complications of pregnancy and a markedly higher percentage of birth weights less than 1500 gm., compared to the remainder of the infants. In contrast, as already stated, there is a tendency to label older children with low intelligence quotients "familial morons," because of the absence of any objective neurologic findings and because other family members also appear to be intellectually dull (probably a reflection of their inferior socioeconomic status). These findings help to confirm those of our retrospective study of mental defectives. They also add to our impression that intelligence tests used in later life are greatly influenced by life experiences that tend to limit opportunities for acquiring the kinds of information the tests seek to evaluate. They even raise the question as to whether or not the distribution of intelligence really follows the broad bell-shaped curve that has been found for a few biological characteristics such as height and weight. (Indeed, examination shows that many biological functions, as measured by vital metabolic indexes, are far from being normally distributed. Such measurements, for example, as blood pH, sugar, iodine, and a number of electrolytes are certainly not normally distributed. In a large population, the range may be broad, but almost all the individuals fall into a narrow middle range even more constricted than the distribution found in our infants (Knobloch and Pasamanick, 1961).

While the evidence is obviously far from complete, it tends to support the view that the range of normal human intellectual potential is much narrower than has been thought. Except for a few hereditary clinical deficiencies and for exogenous injury to neural integration, behavioral variation does not seem to be the result of genetically determined structural origin. We believe that it is now possible to entertain a new *tabula rasa* theory which hypothecates that at conception individuals are much alike in intellectual endowment except for the few rare hereditary neurologic defects. It appears to be life experience and the sociocultural milieu influencing biological and physiological function that in the absence of organic brain damage make human beings significantly different behaviorally from each other (Knobloch and Pasamanick, 1960).

It might be pertinent at this point to raise the question of the value of the infant testing in predicting future development, since previous investigators have indicated that low correlations of about 0.2 or less are obtained between various psychological examinations at nine months of age and again at about three years. Re-examinations of approximately a third of the group studied as premature at three years of age and of the New Haven Negro children and other groups followed by us indicate that when the Gesell developmental examination is used as a neurologic tool by physicians trained in its administration, the correlation between developmental quotients derived from testing at nine months and those derived from testing at preschool age (up to seven years) is fairly high, approximating 0.5. In those infants diagnosed at nine months as clinically abnormal it is 0.75, indicating that the examination is effective in picking out infants in need of supervision (Knobloch, 1958).

A parenthetical note apropos of maternal deprivation and the effects of hospitalization might be inserted at this point. In the study referred to in the introduction of this report, we found that, in addition to a linear positive relationship of maternal tension to degree of brain damage, there was a similar direct relationship of brain injury to illness (Knobloch et al., 1959). This was accompanied by a significantly higher rate of hospitalization that could be related directly to the amount of cerebral injury. It should be apparent by now that the psychologic effects of early hospitalization may not be simply a result of maternal deprivation, but may contain, within the complex mother-child system, the additional variable of brain injury in a significant number of the cases. The interactions between behavioral dysfunction in the infant as a symptom of minimal cerebral injury and maternal tension, illness, hospitalization, and psychologic injury, eventually followed by further dysfunction and tension, should be considered as possible causes of behavioral difficulties later in childhood. Further, since a large number of children exhibit no significant difficulties after hospitalization, we must consider the possibility that it may be largely those children having some brain injury, with a consequent lowering of thresholds to stress, who are affected by hospitalization during infancy. On examining the intelligence test data and clinical descriptions of Goldfarb's institutionalized group (1955), it becomes apparent that one or more of his group were grossly defective, and that an additional number probably were brain-injured and had therefore remained in the institution instead of being placed in foster homes. Probably the factor of brain injury rather than maternal deprivation per se created the statistically significant differences in psychologic functioning in the institutionalized group. Our own studies of institutionalized infants, while indicating significant and increasing retardation in behavioral development during the stay in an institution, are equivocal as to evidence of any permanent damage (Pasamanick, 1946).

Conclusions

We submit that the epidemiologic evidence derived from the studies described above is sufficiently strong to indicate that there exists a continuum of reproductive insult, at least partially socioeconomically determined, resulting in a continuum of reproductive casualty, extending from death through varying degrees of neuropsychiatric disability. We also submit that this evidence—which supports the findings of other studies—is strong enough to warrant the institution of preventive programs in the prenatal period and preferably even before conception (Pasamanick, 1959).

These programs should be geared to the elimination and modification of such results of poverty and deprivation as malnutrition, infection, and other forms of stress, prenatally in the mother and postnatally in the child. In addition, it seems apparent to us that psychosocial deprivation and faulty stimulation in childhood require fully as much attention, if not more, in preventive programs. Hopefully, such programs would be established on a controlled experimental basis so that the hypotheses offered could be tested definitively.

REFERENCES

Aberle, D. F. and Naegele, K. D. (1952), Middle class fathers' occupational role and attitudes toward children. *Amer. J. Orthopsychiat.,* 22:366-378.

Abraham, K. (1907), The experiencing of sexual traumas as a form of sexual activity. In: *Selected Papers.* New York: Basic Books, 1953, pp. 47-63.

________ (1916), The first pregenital stage of the libido. In: *Selected Papers.* New York: Basic Books, 1953, pp. 248-279.

________ (1924a), A short study of the development of the libido, viewed in the light of mental disorders. In: *Selected Papers.* New York: Basic Books, 1953, pp. 418-501.

________ (1924b), The influence of oral erotism on character formation. In: *Selected Papers.* New York: Basic Books, pp. 393-417.

________ (1955), *Clinical Papers and Essays in Psychoanalysis.* New York: Basic Books.

Abramson, H. A. (1954), Evaluation of maternal rejection theory in allergy. *Ann. Allergy,* 12:129-140.

________ (1963), Some aspects of the psychodynamics of intractable asthma in children. In: *The Asthmatic Child,* ed. H. I. Scheer. New York: Harper & Row.

Abse, D. W. (1950), *The Diagnosis of Hysteria.* London: Bristol Wright.

Abt, I. A. (1915), Hysteria in children. *Med. Clin. Chicago,* 1:477-487.

Ackerman, N. W. (1953), Psychiatric disorder in children—diagnosis and etiology in our time. In: *Current Problems in Psychiatric Diagnosis,* ed. P. M. Hoch and J. Zubin. New York: Grune & Stratton, pp. 205-230.

Adelson, J. (1964), The mystique of adolescence. *This Volume,* pp. 214-220.

Adler, A. (1953), Co-editor's introduction: Problems regarding our knowledge of hysteria in childhood. *Nerv. Child,* 10:211-213.

Aichhorn, A. (1925), *Wayward Youth.* New York: Viking Press, 1935. See also, *This Volume,* pp. 507-521.

Ainsworth, M. D. and Bowlby, J. (1954), Research strategy in the study of mother-child separation. *Courrier de la Centre International de L'Enfance,* 4:105-129.

Alexander, F. (1930a), *The Psychoanalysis of the Total Personality.* New York: Nervous and Mental Disease Monograph No. 52.

________ (1930b), The neurotic character. *Intenat. J. Psycho-Anal.,* 11:292-311.

________ (1950), *Psychosomatic Medicine: Its Principles and Application.* New York: Norton.

Allen, F. H. (1937), The dilemma of growth. *Arch. Neurol. Psychiat.,* 37:859-867.

Allport, F. H. (1934), The J-curve hypothesis of conforming behavior. *J. Soc. Psychol.,* 5: 141-183.

Allport, G. W. (1937), *Personality: a Psychological Interpretation.* New York: Henry Holt.

Alpert, A. (1959), Reversibility of pathological fixations associated with maternal deprivation in infancy. *The Psychoanalytic Study of the Child,* 14:169-185. New York: International Universities Press.

American Association on Mental Deficiency (1961), *A Manual on Terminology and Classification in Mental Retardation,* 2nd ed. Willimantic, Conn.

American Psychiatric Association (1952), *Diagnostic and Statistical Manual: Mental Disorders.* Washington.

Anderson, J. E. (1936), *The Young Child in the Home: A Survey of Three Thousand American Families.* New York: Appleton-Century.

Angel, A. (1934), Aus der analyse einer bettnaesserin. *Ztschr. f. Psychoanal. Paed.,* 8:216-228.

Anthony, E. J. (1956), The significance of Jean Piaget for child psychiatry. *Brit. J. Med. Psychol.,* 29:20-34.

________ (1957), The system makers: Piaget and Freud. *Brit. J. Med. Psychol.,* 30:255-269.

________ (1957), An experimental approach to the psychopathology of childhood: encopresis. *This Volume,* pp. 610-625.

________ (1967), Psychoneurotic disorders. In: *Comprehensive Textbook of Psychiatry,* ed. A. M. Freedman and H. I. Kaplan. Baltimore: Williams & Wilkins, pp. 1387-1406.

Anthony, J. (1958), An experimental approach to the psychopathology of childhood: autism. *Brit. J. Med. Psychol.,* 31:211-225.

——— (1959), An experimental approach to the psychopathology of childhood: sleep disturbances. *Brit. J. Med. Psychol.,* 32:19-37.

Arey, L. B. (1944), *Developmental Anatomy.* Philadelphia: Saunders.

Argyle, M. (1957), *The Scientific Study of Social Behaviour.* London: Methuen.

Aries, P. (1965), *Centuries of Childhood.* New York: Vintage.

Arlow, J. A. and Brenner, C. (1964), *Psychoanalytic Concepts and the Structural Theory.* New York: International Universities Press.

Aubry, J. (1955), *La Carence des Soins Maternels.* Paris: Presses Universitaires de France.

Azam, E. (1876), Le dédoublement de la personnalité. Suite de l'histoire de félida. *Rev. Scientifique,* 11:265-269.

Babinski, J. (1908), My conception of hysteria and hypnotism (pithiatism). *Alienist & Neurologist,* 29:1-29.

Bachmann, F. (1927), Uber kongenitale wortblindheit (angeborene leseschwache). *Abhandl. a. d. Neurol.,* 40:1-72.

Bacon, C. L. (1956), The role of aggression in the asthmatic attack. *Psychoanal. Quart.,* 25:309-324.

Bakwin, H. (1928), Enuresis in children. *Arch. Ped.,* 45:664-672.

——— (1942), Loneliness in infants. *Amer. J. Dis. Child.,* 63:30-40.

——— (1949), Emotional deprivation in children. *J. Ped.,* 35:512-521.

——— and Bakwin, R. M. (1953), *Clinical Management of Behavior Disorder in Children.* Philadelphia: Saunders, pp. 433-444.

Balint, M. (1937), Fruehe entwicklungsstadien des ichs. Primaere objektliebe. *Imago,* 23:270-288.

Bard, P. (1928), A diencephalic mechanism for the expression of rage with special reference to the sympathetic nervous system. *Amer. J. Physiol.,* 84:490-513.

Barker, W. (1948), Studies on epilepsy: the petit mal attack as a response within the central nervous system to distress in organism-environment integration. *Psychosom. Med.,* 10:73-94.

——— and Barker, S. (1950), Experimental production of human convulsive brain potentials by stress-induced effects upon neutral integrative function: dynamics of the convulsive reaction to stress. *A. Res. Nerv. Ment. Dis., Proc.,* 29:90-113.

Barron, D. H. (1950), Genetic neurology and the behavior problem. In: *Genetic Neurology,* ed. P. Weiss. Chicago: University of Chicago Press.

Barry, H., Jr. (1949), Significance of maternal bereavement before age of eight in psychiatric patients. *Arch. Neurol. Psychiat.,* 62:630-637.

——— and Lindemann, E. (1960), Critical ages for maternal bereavement in psychoneuroses. *Psychosom. Med.,* 22:166-181.

Bartemeier, L. H. (1932), Some observations on convulsive disorders in children. *Amer. J. Orthopsychiat.,* 2:260-267.

——— (1943), Concerning the psychogenesis of convulsive disorders. *Psychoanal. Quart.,* 12:330-337.

Battersby, W. S., Krieger, H. P., Pollack, M. and Bender, M. B. (1953), Figure-ground discriminations and the 'abstract attitude' in patients with cerebral neoplasms. *Arch. Neurol. Psychiat.,* 70:703-712.

Baudouin, C. (1929), Ein fall von bettnaessen. *Ztschr. f. Psychoanal. Paed.,* 3:323-324.

Beach, F. A. and Jaynes, J. (1954), Effects of early experience upon the behavior of animals. *Psychol. Bull.,* 51:239-263.

Behrens, M. and Goldfarb, W. (1958), Study of patterns of interaction of families of schizophrenic children in residential treatment. *Amer. J. Orthopsychiat.,* 28:3000-312.

——— and Sherman, A. (1959), Observations of family interaction in the home. *Amer. J. Orthopsychiat.,* 29:243-248.

Beier, D. (1964), Behavioral disturbances in the mentally retarded. In: *Mental Retardation,* eds. H. Stevens and R. Heber. Chicago: University of Chicago Press, pp. 453-487.

Beitel, R. J. (1939), Case report: hysterical amblyopia combined with monocular divergent squint. *Amer. J. Optometry,* 16:366-369.

Bell, A. (1958), Some thoughts on postpartum respiratory experiences and their relationship to pregenital mastering, particularly in asthmatics. *Int. J. Psycho-Anal.,* 39:159-166.

________ (1961), Some observations on the role of the scrotal sac and the testicles. *J. Amer. Psychoanal. Assn.,* 9:261-286.

Bell, J. E. (1945), Emotional factors in the treatment of reading difficulties. *J. Consult. Psychol.,* 9:125-131.

Bender, L. (1937), Behavior problems in children of psychotic parents. *Genetic Psychology Monograph* No. 18.

________ (1938), A visual motor gestalt test and its clinical use. *Amer. Orthopsychiat. Assn. Monogr. Series,* No. 3.

________ (1940), The Goodenough test (drawing a man) in chronic encephalitis in children. *J. Nerv. Ment. Dis.,* 91:277-286.

________ (1942), Childhood schizophrenia. *Nerv. Child,* 1:138-140.

________ (1947), Childhood schizophrenia. *This Volume,* pp. 628–646.

________ (1951), The psychological treatment of the brain-damaged child. *Quart. J. Child Behav.,* 3:123-132.

________ (1959), The concept of pseudo-psychopathic schizophrenia in adolescents. *Amer. J. Orthopsychiat.,* 29:491-509.

________ Cobrinik, L., de Hirsch, K. and Jansky, J. (1963), Symposium: the concept of plasticity and its relationship to learning disorders. *Amer. J. Orthopsychiat.,* 33:305-308.

________ and Lipkowitz, H. H. (1940), Hallucinations in children. *Amer. J. Orthopsychiat.,* 10:471-490.

________ and Rapoport, J. (1944), Animal drawings of children. *Amer. J. Orthopsychiat.,* 14:512-527.

________ and Schilder, P. (1941), Mannerisms as organic motility syndrome (paracortical disturbances). *Confinia Neurologica,* 3:321-330.

________ ________ (1951), Graphic art as a special ability in children with a reading disability. *J. Clin. Exper. Psychopath.,* 12:147-156.

________ and Kaiser, S. (1936), Studies in aggressiveness. *Genetic Psychology Monograph* No. 18.

________ and Wolfson, W. (1943), The nautical theme in the art and fantasy of children. *Amer. J. Orthopsychiat.,* 13:462-467.

________ and Yarnell, H. (1941), An observation nursery: a study of 250 children in the psychiatric division of Bellevue Hospital. *Amer. J. Psychiat.,* 97:1158-1174.

Bender, M. B. (1952), *Disorders in Perception, With Particular Reference to the Phenomena of Extinction and Displacement.* Springfield, Ill.: Charles C. Thomas.

Benedek, T. (1938), Adaptation to reality in early infancy. *Psychoanal. Quart.,* 7:200-215.

________ (1949), The psychosomatic implications of the primary unit: mother-child. *Amer. J. Orthopsychiat.,* 19:642-654.

________ (1956), Toward the biology of the depressive constellation. *J. Amer. Psychoanal. Assn.,* 4:389-427.

________ (1959a), Sexual functions in women and their disturbance. In: *American Handbook of Psychiatry,* ed. S. Avieto, Vol. I. New York: Basic Books.

________ (1959b), Parenthood as a developmental phase: a contribution to the libido theory. *J. Amer. Psychoanal. Assn.,* 7:389-417.

Benedict, R. (1934), *Patterns of Culture.* Boston: Houghton Mifflin.

________ (1946), *The Chrysanthemum and the Sword: Patterns of Japanese Culture.* Boston: Houghton, Mifflin.

________ (1949), Continuities and discontinuities in cultural conditioning. *This Volume,* pp. 203–213.

Benjamin, E. (1930), Die trotzperiode als psychopathologisches phanomen. *Grundlagen und Entwicklungsgeschichte der kindlichen Neurose.* Leipzig: Georg Thieme, Chapter III.

________ (1942), Period of resistance in early childhood: Its significance for the development of the problem child. *Amer. J. Dis. Child.,* 63:1019-1079.

Benjamin, J. D. (1944), A method for distinguishing and evaluating formal thinking disorders in schizophrenia. In: *Language and Thought in Schizophrenia,* ed. J. S. Kasanin. Berkeley and Los Angeles: University of California Press, pp. 65-88.

________ (1950), Methodological considerations in the validation and elaboration of psychoanalytical personality theory. *Amer. J. Orthopsychiat.,* 20:139-156.

——— (1952), Directions and problems in psychiatric research. *Psychosom. Med.,* 14:1-9.

——— (1958a), Some considerations in biological research in schizophrenia. *Psychosom. Med.,* 20:427-445.

——— (1958b), Some developmental observations relating to the theory of anxiety. Paper read at the Panel on Early Psychic Functioning at the December, 1958, meeting of the American Psychoanalytic Association. To be published.

——— (1961), The innate and the experiential in child development. *This Volume,* pp. 2-19.

——— and Tennes, K. (1958), A case of pathological head nodding. Paper read at the December, 1958, meeting of the American Psychoanalytic Association. To be published.

——— (1959), Prediction and psychopathological theory. In: *Dynamics of Psychotherapy in Childhood,* ed. J. Jessner and E. Pavenstedt. New York: Grune & Stratton, pp. 6-77.

——— (1960), Report on panel on research meeting of American Psychoanalytic Association, December, 1960.

——— (1965), Developmental biology and psychoanalysis. In: *Psychoanalysis and Current Biological Thought,* ed. N. S. Greenfield and W. C. Lewis. Madison, Wisc.: University of Wisconsin Press, pp. 57-80.

Bennett, C. C. (1938), An inquiry into the genesis of poor reading. *Teach. Coll. Contr. Educ.* No. 755.

Benon, R. (1953), Neuro-psychiatrie infantile chez l'enfant: la crise d'hysterie (child neuro-psychiatry: hysteria). *Bull. Med., Paris,* 67:361.

Benton, A. (1956), The concept of pseudo-feeblemindedness. *Arch. Neurol. Psychiat.,* 75:379-388.

Bergman, P. and Escalona, S. K. (1949), Unusual sensitivites in very young children. *The Psychoanalytic Study of the Child,* ¾:333-352. New York: International Universities Press.

Bergmann, T. (1945), Observation of children's reactions to motor restraint. *Nerv. Child,* 4:318-328.

——— and Freud, A. (1965), *Children in the Hospital.* New York: International Universities Press.

Berkovitz, I. (unpublished), Psychoanalytic findings in a man with regional ileitis and asthma.

Berman, I. R. and Bird, C. (1933), Sex differences in speed of reading. *J. Applied Psychol.,* 7:221-226.

Bernfeld, S. (1929), *The Psychology of the Infant,* translated by R. Hurwitz. New York: Bretano.

——— (1944), Freud's earliest theories and the school of Helmholtz. *Psychoanal. Quart.,* 13:341-362.

Bernheim, H. (1897), *Suggestive Therapeutics.* New York: Putnam.

Bernstein, L. (1957), The effects of variations in handling upon learning and retention. *J. Comp. Physiol. Psychol.,* 50:162-167.

Bettelheim, B. (1962), *Symbolic Wounds: Puberty Rights and the Envious Male.* New York: Collier Books.

——— (1967), *The Empty Fortress.* New York: The Free Press. Beverly, B. I. (1933), Incontinence in children. *J. Pediat.,* 2:718-725.

Biermann, G. (1955), Erbrechen und nabelkoliken als konversionshysterisches syndrom in reifungsalter junger mädchen and seine projektion im Rorschach-formdeutverfahren. *Psyche (Stuttgart),* 9:453-480, 537-559. (Vomiting and umbilical colics as a syndrome of conversion hysteria in girls at the age of maturation and its manifestation in the Rorschach test.) *Exc. Med.,* Sec. 8, Vol. 9, No. 2634, June 1956.

Binet, A. (1892), *Les Alterations de la Personnalité.* Paris: F. Alcan.

Binois, R. and Salsac, C. (1951), Paralysie hystérique de l'accommodation chez un enfant de 8 ans. *Maroc Medical* (Casablanca), 30:590.

Birch, H. (1964), The problem of brain damage in children. In: *Brain Damage in Children: The Biological and Social Aspects,* ed. H. Birch. Baltimore: Williams & Wilkins Co., pp. 3-12.

——— Thomas, A., and Chess, S. (1964), Behavioral development in brain-damaged children: three case studies. *Arch. Gen. Psychiat.,*

Blan, A. (1936), Mental changes following head trauma in children *Arch. Neurol. Psychiat.,* 35:723-769.

Blanchard, P. (1928), Reading disabilities in relation to maladjustment. *Ment. Hyg.*, 12:772-788.

________ (1929), Attitudes and educational disabilities. *Mental Hyg.*, 13:550-563.

________ (1935), Psychogenic factors in some cases of reading disability. *Amer. J. Orthopsychiat.*, 5:361-374.

________ (1936a), Reading disabilities in relation to difficulties of personality and emotional development. *Ment. Hyg.*, 20:384-413.

________ (1936b), Emotional factors in a disability for reading and writing words. In: *Readings in Mental Hygiene,* ed. E. Groves and P. Blanchard. New York: Holt, pp. 283-301.

________ (1946), Psychoanalytic contributions to the problems of reading disabilities. *This Volume,* pp. 487–504.

Blau, A. (1946), The master hand; a study of the origin and meaning of right and left sidedness and its relation to personality and language. *J. Amer. Orthopsychiat. Assn.*, 16:455-480.

Blauvelt, H. (1955), Dynamics of the mother-newborn relationship in goats. In: *Group Processes, 1st Conference.* New York: Josiah Macy, Jr., Foundation.

Bleyer, A. (1928), A clinical study of enuresis. *Amer. J. Dis. Child.*, 36:989-997.

Bloch, H. and Niederhoffer, A. (1958), *The Gang: A Study in Adolescent Behavior.* New York: Philosophical Library, p. 17.

Bloom, G. C., Long, R. T., Lamont, J. H., et al. (1958), A psychosomatic study of allergic and emotional factors in children with asthma. *Amer. J. Psychiat.*, 114:890-899.

Blos, P. (1941), *The Adolescent Personality.* New York: Appleton-Century-Crofts.

________ (1954), Prolonged adolescence: the formulation of a syndrome and its therapeutic implications. *Amer. J. Orthopsychiat.*, 24:733-742.

________ (1958), Preadolescent drive organization. *J. Amer. Psychoanal. Assn.*, 6:47-56.

________ (1962), *On Adolescence: A Psychoanalytic Interpretation.* New York: Free Press of Glencoe. See also *This Volume.* pp. 221–233.

Blum G. S. and Miller, D. R. (1952), Exploring the psychoanalytic theory of the "oral character." *J. Personal.*, 20:287-304.

Blume, D. (in preparation), A study of the eye of the dog.

Bond, E. D. and Smith, L. H. (1935), Post-encephalitic behavior disorders: a ten year review of the Franklin School. *Amer. J. Psychiat.*, 92:17-31.

Bornstein, B. (1930), Zur psychogenese der pseudodebilität. *Int. Z. Psychoanal.*, 16:378-399.

________ (1934), Enuresis und kleptomanie als passagères symptom. *Zeitschr. f. Psychoanal. Paed.*, 8:229-237.

________ (1935), Phobia in a two-and-a-half-year-old child. *Psychoanal. Quart.*, 4:93-119.

________ (1949), The analysis of a phobic child. *The Psychoanalytic Study of the Child,* 3/4:181-226. New York: International Universities Press.

Bostock, J. and Shackleton, M. (1951), Enuresis and toilet training. *Med. J. Aust.*, 2:110-113.

________ (1958), Exterior gestation, primitive sleep, enuresis, and asthma: a study in aeteology (I and II). *Med. J. Aust.*, 2:149-156.

Botstein, A. and Goldfarb, W. (unpublished), Physical stigmata in schizophrenic children.

Bourneville, D. (1893), Recherches sur l'idiotic. In: *Recherches Clinques et Therapeutiques Sur L'hysterie et L'idiotie.* Paris: Bureaux due Progres Medical.

Bourru, H. and Burot, P. (1888), *Variations de la Personnalité.* Paris: Bailliere.

Bowlby, J. (1946), *Forty-Four Juvenile Thieves.* London: Bailliere, Tindall & Cox.

________ (1951), *Maternal Care and Mental Health.* Geneva: World Health Organization Monograph #2.

________ (1953), Some pathological processes set in train by early mother-child separation. *J. Ment. Sci.*, 99:265-272.

________ (1958), The nature of the child's tie to his mother. *Int. J. Psycho-Anal.*, 39:350-373.

________ (1960a), Grief and mourning in infancy and early childhood. *The Psychoanalytic Study of the Child,* 15:9-52. New York: International Universities Press.

________ (1960b), Separation anxiety. *Int. J. Psycho-Anal.*, 41:89-113.

________ (1961a), Childhood mourning and its implications for psychiatry. *This Volume,* pp. 263-289.

——— (1961b), Processes of mourning, *Int. J. Psycho-Anal.*, 42:317-340.

——— (1969), *Attachment and Loss,* Vol. I, Attachment. New York: Basic Books.

——— Robertson, J. and Rosenbluth, D. (1952), A two-year-old goes to the hospital. *The Psychoanalytic Study of the Child,* 7:82-94. New York: International Universities Press.

Bowman, K. M. and Kasanin, J. (1933), Constitutional schizophrenia. *Amer. J. Psychiat.,* 90:645-658.

Brain, W. R. (1945), Speech and handedness. *Lancet,* 2:837-842.

Branch, C. H. and Bliss, E. (1967), Anorexia nervosa. In: *Comprehensive Textbook of Psychiatry,* ed. A. Freedman and H. Kaplan. Baltimore: Williams & Wilkins, pp. 1062-1063.

Brenton, M. (1966), *The American Male.* New York: Coward-McCann.

Breuer, J. and Freud, S. (1895), Studies in hysteria. *Standard Edition,* 2:3-335. London: Hogarth Press, 1955.

Bridger, W. H. and Reiser, M. F. (1959), Psychophysiologic studies of the neonate. *Psychosom. Med.,* 21:265-276.

Broadbent, W. H. (1872), On the cerebral mechanism of speech and thought. *Med. Chir. Trans.,* 55:145-194.

Broadwin, I. T. (1932), A contribution to the study of truancy. *Amer. J. Orthopsychiat.,* 2:253-259.

Brodbeck, A. and Irwin, O. (1954), An exploratory study on the acquisition of dependency behavior in puppies. *Bull. Ecol. Soc. Amer.,* 35:73.

——— ——— (1946), The speech behavior of infants without families. *Child Developm.,* 17:145-146.

Brody, S. (1956), *Patterns of Mothering.* New York: International Universities Press.

——— (1964), *Passivity.* New York: International Universities Press.

Bronfenbrenner, U. (1958), Socialization and social class through time and space. In: *Readings in Social Psychology,* ed. E. E. Maccoby, T. M. Newcomb and E. I. Hartley. New York: Holt.

Bronner, A. (1921), *The Psychology of Special Abilities and Disabilities.* Boston: Little, Brown, p. 77.

Brown, E. A. and Goitein, P. L. (1943), Some aspects of mind in asthma and allergy: comparative personality study of two groups of clinical cases. *J. Nerv. Ment. Dis.,* 98:638-647.

Brown, F. (1961), Depression and childhood bereavement. *J. Ment. Sci.,* 107:754-777.

Brown, J. R. (1952), Management of patients with brain damage. *Neurology,* 2:273-283.

Brownfield, E. D. (1956), An investigation of the activity and sensory responses of healthy newborn infants. Ph.D. thesis, Cornell University.

Bruch, H. (1940), Obesity in childhood, V: the family frame of obese children. *Psychosom. Med.,* 2:141-206.

——— (1941), Obesity in childhood and personality development. *Amer. J. Orthopsychiat.,* 11:467-474.

——— (1952), Psychological aspects of reducing. *Psychosom. Med.,* 14:337-346.

——— (1955), Fat children grown up. *Amer. J. Dis. Child.,* 90:501.

——— (1957), *The Importance of Overweight.* New York: Norton.

——— (1958a), Developmental obesity and schizophrenia. *Psychiat.,* 21:65-70.

——— (1958b), Obesity. *Psychiatric Clinic of North America,* 5:613-627.

——— (1961a), Conceptual confusion in eating disorders. *J. Nerv. Ment. Dis.,* 133:46-54.

——— (1961b), Transformation of oral impulses in eating disorders: A conceptual approach. *Psychiat. Quart.,* 35:458-481.

——— (1962a), Falsification of bodily needs and body concept in schizophrenia. *Arch. Gen. Psychiat.,* 6:18-24.

——— (1962b), Perceptual and conceptual disturbances in anorexia in the male child. *Amer. J. Orthopsychiat.,* 26:751-770.

——— (1963), Disturbed communication in eating disorders. *This Volume,* pp. 585-590.

Brückner, G. H. (1933), Untersuchungen zur tierpsychologie, insbesondere zur auflösung der familie. *Ztschr. f. Psychol.,* 128:1-110. (also *Schielderupp-Ebbe: Ztschr. f. Psychol.,* no. 88, 1922 and no. 92, 1923).

Brunswick, R. M. (1940), The preoedipal phase of the libido development. *Psychoanal. Quart.,* 9:293-319.

Buhler, C. (1935), *From Birth to Maturity.* London: Routledge & Kegan Paul.

Bühler, Ch. (1927), *Das Seelenleben der Jugendliehen,* ed. 4. Jena.

________ (1928), Kindheit und Jugend. *Psychological Monograph,* 3:304.

Bühler, K. (1942), *Die Geistige Entwicklung Des Kindes,* 4th ed. Jena, pp. 106, 116.

Bukantz, S. C. (1961), An integrated psychosomatic approach to a study and treatment of intractable bronchial asthma in children. Presented at New England Society Allergy, Boston.

Burlingham, D. T. (1935), Child analysis and the mother. *Psychoanal. Quart.,* 4:69-92.

________ and Freud, A. (1942), *Young Children in Wartime.* London: Allen & Unwin. (American ed.: Freud, A. and Burlingham, D.: *War and Children.* New York: International Universities Press, 1942.)

________ (1944), *Infants Without Families.* London: Allen & Unwin. (American ed.: Freud, A. and Burlingham, D.: *Infants Without Families.* New York: International Universities Press, 1944.)

Burt, C. (1921), *Mental and Scholastic Tests.* London: King & Sons.

Busemann, A. (1928), Über das so genannte trotzalter des kindes. *Ztschr. f. pädagog. Psychol.,* 29:42-49.

________ (1929), Uber die ursachen des "ersten trotzalters" und der erregungsphasen überhaupt. *Ztschr. f. pädagog. Psychol.,* 30:276-281.

Buxbaum, E. (1947), Activity and aggression. *Amer. J. Orthopsychiat.,* 17:161-166.

________ (1964), The parents' role in the etiology of learning disabilities. *The Psychoanalytic Study of the Child,* 9:421-447. New York: International Universities Press.

Buytendijk, F. J. J. (1947), Das erste lächeln des kindes. *Psyche,* 2:57-70.

Bykov, K. M. (1957), *The Cerebral Cortex and the Internal Organs.* New York: Chemical Publishing.

Cairns, H. (1952), Disturbances of consciousness with lesions of the brain stem and diencephalon. *Brain,* 75:109-146.

________ and Oldfield, R. C., Pennybacker, J. B. and Whitteridge, D. (1941), Akinetic mutism with an epidermoid cyst of the third ventricle. *Brain,* 64:273-290.

Caldwell, B. M. (1967), What is the optimal learning environment for the young child? *Amer. J. Orthopsychiat.,* 37:8-21.

Camp, B. and Waite, T. (1932), Report of four cases of mental deficiency on parole. *Amer. Assn. Study Feebleminded,* 37:381-394.

Campbell, M. F. (1934), A clinical study of persistent enuresis. *N. Y. State J. Med.,* 34:190-194.

Camuset, L. (1882), Un cas de dédoublement de la personnalité. Période amnésique d'une année chez un jeune homme hystérique. *Ann. Med. Psychologiques,* 6th Ser., 7:75-86.

Cannon, W. B. (1932), *The Wisdom of the Body.* New York: Norton.

Cappon, D. (1953), Clinical manifestations of autism and schizophrenia in childhood. *Canad. M.A.J.,* 69:44-49.

Carmichael, L. (1954), The onset and early development of behavior. In: *Manual of Child Psychology,* by L. Carmichael. New York: Wiley.

Carter, J. W., Jr. (1937), A case of reactional dissociation (hysterical paralysis). *Amer. J. Orthopsychiat.,* 7:219-224.

Casler, L. (1961), *Maternal Deprivation: A Critical Review of the* Literature. [*Society for Research in Child Development,* Monogr. 26.2].

Caulfield, E. (1943), Pediatric aspects of the Salem witchcraft tragedy: a lesson in mental health. *Amer. J. Dis. Child.,* 65:788-802.

Cazden, C. B. (1966), Subcultural differences in child language: an inter-disciplinary review. *Merrill-Palmer Quart.,* 12:185-219.

Chance, B. (1913), Developmental alexia: two cases of congenital word blindness. *N. Y. Med. J.,* 97:697-699.

Chapin, H. D. (1915a), Are institutions for infants necessary? *J. Amer. Med. Assn.,* 64:1-3.

________ (1915b), A plea for accurate statistics in infants' institutions. *Arch. Peds.,* 32:724-726.

Charcot, J. M. and de la Tourette, G. (1892), Hypnotism in the hysterical. In: *A Dictionary of Psychological Medicine,* ed. H. D. Tuke. Philadelphia: Blakiston, 1:606-610.

Charles, M. S. and Fuller, J. L. (1956), Developmental study of the electroencephalogram of the dog. *Electroencephalog. & Clin. Neurophysiol.,* 8:645.
Chesher, E. C. (1937), Aphasia; Technique of clinical examinations. *Bull. Neurol. Inst. New York,* 6:134.
Chess, S. (1964), Mal de Mere. *Amer. J. Orthopsychiat.,* 34:613-614.
——— (1968), Temperament and learning ability of school children. *Amer. J. Public Health,* 58: 2231-2239.
——— Hertzig, M., Birch, H. G., and Thomas, A. (1962), Methodology of a study of adaptive functions of the preschool child. *J. Amer. Acad. Child Psychiat.,* 1:236-245.
——— Thomas, A., and Birch, H. G. (1966), Distortions in developmental reporting made by parents of behaviorally disturbed children. *J. Amer. Acad. Child Psychiat.,* 5:226-234.
——— ——— (1967), Behavior problems revisited: findings of an anterospective study. *This Volume,* pp. 56-65.
——— and Hertzig, M. (1960), Implications of longitudinal study of child development for child psychiatry. *Amer. J. Psychiat.,* 117:434-441.
——— Rutter, M., and Birch, H. G. (1963), Interaction of temperament and environment in the production of behavioral disturbances in children. *Amer. J. Psychiat.,* 120:142-148.
Chobot, R., Spadaveccguam, R. and DeSanctis, R. M. (1939), Intelligence rating and emotional pattern of allergic children. *A.M.A. Amer. J. Dis. Child.,* 57:830.
Christoffel, V. H. (1934), Zur biologie der enuresis. *Zeitschr. f. Kinderpsych.,* 1:104.
Claiborne, J. H. (1906), Types of congenital symbol amblyopia. *J.A.M.A.,* 47:1813.
Claparède, E. (1917a), Bradylexie bei einem sonst normalen kinde. *Neurol. Centrabl.,* 36:572.
——— (1917b), La Psychologie de l'intelligence. *Scientia,* 11:353-367.
——— (1933), La genèse de l'hypothese. *Arch. Psychol.,* 24:1-155.
Clark, L. P. (1915), A study of certain aspects of epilepsy compared with the emotional life and impulsive movements of the infant. *Interstate Med. J.,* 22:969.
——— (1917), *Clinical Studies in Epilepsy.* Utica, N. Y.: State Hospitals Press.
——— (1926), A further contribution to the psychology of the essential epileptic. *J. Nerv. Ment. Dis.,* 63:575-585.
——— (1931), The psychobiologic concept of epilepsy. *J. Res. Nerv. Ment. Dis., Proc.,* 7:65.
——— (1933), *The Nature and Treatment of Amentia.* Baltimore: Wood.
——— (1947), *Anatomical Pattern as the Essential Basis of Sensory Discrimination.* Springfield, Ill.: Charles C Thomas.
Clarke, A. (1958), *Genetic and Environmental Studies of Intelligence.* Glencoe, Ill.: Free Press.
Cloward, R. A. & Ohlin, L. E. (1960), Some current theories of delinquent subcultures. *This Volume,* pp. 540-564.
Cobb, S. (1940), Psychiatric approach to the treatment of epilepsy. *Amer. J. Psychiat.,* 96:1009-1022.
——— (1944), *Borderlands of Psychiatry, Harvard Monographs in Medicine and Public Health,* No. 4. Cambridge, Mass.: Harvard University Press.
——— and Butler, A. (1949), Clinic on psychosomatic problems: psychogenic deafness in a disturbed boy. *Amer. J. Med.,* 7:221-227.
Coghill, G. E. (1929), *Anatomy and the Problem of Behavior.* London: Cambridge University Press, p. 113.
Cohen, A. K. (1955), *Delinquent Boys: The Culture of the Gang.* Glencoe, Ill.: Free Press, p. 162.
Cohen, M. B. (1966), Personal identity and sexual identity. *Psychiatry,* 29:1-14.
Cohn, R. (1949), *Clinical Electroencephalography.* New York: McGraw-Hill, p. 639.
——— (1951), On certain aspects of the sensory organization of the human brain. II. A study of rostral dominance in children. *Neurology,* 1:119-122.
Coleman, J. S. (1966), *Equality of Educational Opportunity.* Wash., D. C.: U.S. Government Printing Office.
Coleman, R. W., Kris, E. and Provence, S. (1952), The study of variations of early parental

attitudes. *The Psychoanalytic Study of the Child,* 8:20-47. New York: International Universities Press.

Colm, H. N. (1959), Phobias in children. *Psychoanal. & Psychoanal. Rev.,* 40:65-84.

Committee on Child Psychiatry (1966), *Psychopathological Disorders in Childhood: Theoretical Considerations and a Proposed Classification,* Report #62. New York: Group for the Advancement of Psychiatry.

Compayré, G. (1893), *L'Evolution Intellectuelle et Morale de L'Enfant.* Paris: Hachette.

Conel, J. L. R. (1939), The brain structure of the newborn infant and consideration of the senile brain. In: Association for Research in Nervous and Mental Disease. Research Publications, Vol. 19: *The Inter-relationship of Mind and Body.* Baltimore: Williams & Wilkins, pp. 247-255.

Coolidge, J. C. (1956), Asthma in mother and child as a special type of intercommunication. *Amer. J. Orthopsychiat.,* 26:165-178.

________ Hahn, P. B. and Peck, A. L. (1957), School phobia: neurotic crisis, a way of life? *Amer. J. Orthopsychiat.,* 27:296-306.

________ Tessman, E., Waldfogel, S. and Willer, M. L. (1962), Patterns of aggression in school phobia. *The Psychoanalytic Study of the Child,* 17:319-333. New York: International Universities Press.

Cramer, J. P. (1959), Common neuroses of childhood. In: *American Handbook of Psychiatry,* ed. S. Arieti. New York: Basic Books, 1:797-815.

Creak, M. (1938), Hysteria in childhood. *Brit. J. Child Dis.,* 35:85-95.

________ (1951), Psychoses in childhood. *J. Ment. Sci.,* 97:545-554.

________ (1952), Psychoses in childhood. *Proc. Roy. Soc. Med.,* 45:797-800.

________ and Stephan, J. (1958), The psychological aspects of asthma in children. Pediatric Clinics of North America, *Behavior Disorders.* Philadelphia: Saunders.

Critchley, M. (1953), *The Parietal Lobes.* Baltimore: Williams & Wilkins, 1966.

Curran, F. J. and Schilder, P. (1935), Paraphasic signs in diffuse lesions of the brain. *J. Nerv. Ment. Dis.,* 82:613-636.

Darr, G. C. and Worden, F. G. (1951), Case report 28 years after an autistic disorder. *Amer. J. Orthopsychiat.,* 21:559-570.

Davenport, C. (1911), *Heredity in Relation to Eugenics.* New York: Holt.

David, M. and Appell, G. (1958), Personal communication.

Davies, S. (1930), *Social Control of the Mentally Deficient.* New York: Crowell.

________ (1959), *The Mentally Retarded in Society.* New York: Columbia University Press.

Davis, A. (1948), *Social-Class Influences Upon Learning.* Cambridge: Harvard University Press.

Davis, C. M. (1928), Self-selection of diet by newly-weaned infants. *Amer. J. Dis. Child.,* 36:651-679.

________ (1935a), Choice of formulas made by three infants throughout the nursing period. *Amer. J. Dis. Child.,* 50:385-394.

________ (1935b), Self-selection of food by children. *Amer. J. Nursing,* 35:403-410.

Dawes, L. G. (1953), The psychoanalysis of a case of "grand hysteria in Charcot" in a girl of fifteen. *Nerv. Child.,* 10:272-305.

De Ajuriaguerra, J. (1951), A propos des troubles de l'apprentissage de la lecture; critiques méthodologiques. *Enfance,* 4:389-399.

Dearborn, W. F. (1931), Ocular and manual dominance in dyslexia. *Psychol. Bull.,* 28:704.

DeGara, P. F. (1959), The hereditary predisposition in man to develop hypersensitivity: a critical review. In: *Mechanisms of Hypersensitivity,* ed. J. H. Shaffer, et al. Boston: Little, Brown.

de Hirsch, K., Jansky, J. J. and Langford, W. S. (1966), *Predicting Reading Failure.* New York: Harper & Row.

Dekker, F., Pelser, H. E. and Groen, J. (1957), Conditioning as a cause of asthmatic attacks. *J. Psychosom. Res.,* 2:58-66.

Dembo, T., Leviton, G. L. and Wright, B. A. (1956), Adjustment to misfortune: a problem of social psychological rehabilitation. *Artificial Limbs,* 3:4-62.

Denenberg, V. H. (1964), Critical periods, stimulus input, and emotional reactivity. *Psychol. Rev.,* 71:335-351.

De Sandoval, D. M. (1953), Servicio medico-social; caso de desfloramiento en una niña con histeria de conversion. (Medico-social service; case of defloration in a female with conversion hysteria.) *Bol. Med. Hosp. Infant. Mex.,* 10:226-231.

Despert, J. L. (1938), Schizophrenia in children. *Psychiat. Quart.,* 12:366-371.

________ (1940), Comparative study in thinking in schizophrenic children and children of pre-school age. *Amer. J. Psychiat.,* 97:189-213.

________ (1942), Prophylactic aspects of schizophrenia in childhood. *Nerv. Child,* 1:199-231.

________ (1951), Some considerations relating to the genesis of autistic behavior in children. *Amer. J. Orthopsychiat.,* 21:335-350.

________ and Pierce, H. (1946), The relation of emotional adjustment to intellectual function. *J. Genet. Psychol.,* 34:5-56.

________ and Sherwin, A. C. (1957), Further examination of diagnostic criteria in schizophrenic illness and psychoses of infancy and early childhood. Read at American Psychiatric Association, May, 1957, unpublished.

Deutsch, F. (1939), The choice of organ in organ neurosis. *Int. J. Psycho-Anal.,* 20:252-262.

________ (1947), Artistic expression and neurotic illness. Paper read at Smith College, July 27, 1947.

________ (1951), Thus speaks the body: some psychosomatic aspects of the respiratory disorder: asthma. *Acta Med. Orient.,* 10:67-86.

________ (1953), Basic psychoanalytic principles in psychosomatic disorders. *Acta Psychotherapeutica,* 1:102-111.

________ (1959a), *On the Mysterious Leap from the Mind to the Body.* New York: International Universities Press.

________ (1959b), Symbolization as a formative stage of the conversion process. In: *On the Mysterious Leap from the Mind to the Body,* ed. F. Deutsch. New York: International Universities Press, pp. 75-97.

________ and Murphy, W. F. (1955), *The Clinical Interview.* New York: International Universities Press, p. 320.

Deutsch, H. (1932), *Psychoanalysis of the Neurosis.* London: Hogarth Press.

________ (1937), Absence of grief. *Psychoanal. Quart.,* 6:12-22.

________ (1945), *The Psychology of Women,* Vol. II. New York: Grune & Stratton.

Deutsch, M. (1965), The role of social class in language development and cognition. *Amer. J. Orthopsychiat.,* 35:78-88.

Dewey, J. and Bentley, A. F. (1949), *Knowing and the Known.* Boston: Beacon Press.

Dollard, J. and Miller, N. (1950), *Personality and Psychotherapy.* New York: McGraw-Hill.

Douvan, E. (1956), Social status and success striving, *J. Abnormal Social Psychol.,* 54:219-223.

________ and Adelson, J. (1958), The psychodynamics of social mobility in adolescent boys. *J. Abnormal & Social Psychol.,* 56:31-44.

________ ________ (1966), *The Adolescent Experience.* New York: Wiley.

Drews, E. M. (1954), The significance of the reversal error in reading. Unpublished dissertation, University of Michigan.

Dubo, S. (1950), Children with pulmonary tuberculosis. *Amer. J. Orthopsychiat.,* 20:520-528.

Dufay (1876), La notion de la personnalité. *Rev. Scientifique,* 11:69-71.

Dunbar, H. F. (1938), Psychoanalytic notes relating to syndromes of asthma and hay fever. *Psychoanal. Quart.,* 7:25-68.

________ (1943), *Psychosomatic Diagnosis.* New York: Hoeber, pp. 481-541. Durfee, H. and Wolf, K. (1933), Anstaltspflege and entwicklung im ersten lebensjahr. *Zeit. f. Kinderforschung,* 42:273-320.

Dusser de Barenne, J. G., Garol, H. W. and McCulloch, W. S. (1941a), Functional organization of sensory and adjacent cortex of the monkey. *J. Neurophysiol.,* 4:324-330.

________ and McCulloch, W. S. (1941b), Suppression of motor responses obtained from area 4 by stimulation of area 4-S. *J. Neurophysiol.,* 4:313-323.

Duvall, E. M. (1946), Conceptions of parenthood. *Amer. J. Sociol.,* 52:193-203.

Eames, T. H. (1935), A frequency study of physical handicaps in reading disability and unselected groups. *J. Educ. Res.,* 29:1-5.

Earle, A. M. and Earle, B. V. (1961), Early maternal deprivation and later psychiatric illness. *Amer. J. Orthopsychiat.,* 31:181-186.

Echlin, F. A., Arnet, V. and Zoll, J. (1952), Paroxysmal high voltage discharges from isolated or partially isolated human and animal cerebral cortex. *EEG Clin. Neurophysiol.,* 4:147-164.

Ederer, S. and Von Lederer, E. (1933), Zur pathogenese der enuresis. *Jahrb. f. Kinderhlk.,* 138:21-30.

Editorial (1953), Dedication. *Psychosom. Med.,* 15:372.

Eells, K., et al. (1951), *Intelligence and Cultural Differences.* Chicago: University of Chicago Press, p. 18.

Eisenberg, L. (1957a), The course of childhood schizophrenia. *A.M.A. Arch. Neurol. Psychiat.,* 78:69-83.

________ (1957b), Psychiatric implications of brain damage in children. *This Volume,* pp. 774-787.

________ (1958), School phobia: a study in the communication of anxiety. *Amer. J. Psychiat.,* 114:712-718.

________ (1964), Behavioral manifestations of cerebral damage in childhood. In: *Brain Damage in Children: The Biological and Social Aspects,* ed. H. Birch. Baltimore: Williams & Wilkins, pp. 61-73.

Eissler, K. R. (1949a), Some problems of delinquency. In: *Searchlights on Delinquency.* New York: International Universities Press, pp. 3-25.

________ ed. (1949b), *Searchlights on Delinquency.* New York: International Universities Press.

Ekstein, R. (1966), *Children of Time and Space.* New York: Appleton.

________ Bryant, K. and Friedman, S. W. (1958), Childhood schizophrenia and allied conditions. In: *Schizophrenia: A Review of Syndrome,* ed. L. Bellak. New York: Logos Press, pp. 555-693.

________ and Friedman, S. (1968), Cause of the illness or cause of the cure? *Int. J. Psychiat.,* 5:224-229.

________ and Wright, D. G. (1952), The space child. *This Volume,* pp. 710-723.

Elkin, H. (unpublished), Manuscript on the Arapaho.

Elkonin, D. B. (1957), The physiology of higher nervous activity and child psychology. In: *Psychology in the Soviet Union,* Ed. B. Simon. London: Routledge & Kegan Paul.

Ellingson, R. J. (1958), Electroencephalograms of normal, full-term newborns immediately after birth with observations on arousal and visual evoked responses. *EEG & Clin. Neurophysiol.,* 10:31-50.

Ellis, A. (1949), Results of a mental hygiene approach to reading disability problems. *J. Consult. Psychol.,* 13:56-61.

________ (1950), An introduction to the principals of scientific psychoanalysis. *Genet. Psychol. Monogr.,* 41:147-212.

Engel, F. (1963), *Psychophysiological Development and Health and Disease.* Philadelphia: Saunders.

Engel, G. L. (1954), Selection of clinical material in psychosomatic medicine. The need for a new physiology. *Psychosom. Med.,* 16:368-373.

________ Reichsman, F., and Segal, H. L. (1956), A study of an infant with a gastric fistula. *Psychosom. Med.,* 18:374-398.

________ (1961), Is grief a disease? A challenge for medical research. *Psychosom. Med.,* 23:18-22.

English, O. S. and Pearson, G. H. J. (1945), *Emotional Problems of Living.* New York: Norton.

________ ________ (1937), *Common Neuroses of Children and Adults.* New York: Norton.

________ ________ (1963a), Irrational fears and phobias. *This Volume,* pp. 375-381.

________ ________ (1963b), Difficulties in learning. *This Volume,* pp. 445-456.

Erikson, E. H. (1940), Studies in the interpretation of play. *Gen. Psychol. Monogr.,* 22:557-671.

________ (1950), *Childhood and Society.* New York: Norton. See also *This Volume,* pp. 109-132.

________ (1951), Sex differences in the play configurations of preadolescents. *Amer. J. Orthopsychiat.,* 21:667-692.

——— (1953), Growth and crises of the "healthy personality". In: *Personality in Nature, Society and Culture,* 2nd edition, ed. C. Kluckhohn and H. Murray. New York: Knopf, pp. 185-225.

——— (1954), The dream specimen of psychoanalysis. *J. Amer. Psychoanal. Assn.,* 2:5-55.

——— (1956), The problem of ego identity. *J. Amer. Psychoanal. Assn.,* 4:56-121.

——— (1958), *Young Man Luther.* New York: Norton.

——— (1959), Identity and the Life Cycle. [*Psychological Issues,* Monogr. 1.] New York: International Universities Press, pp. 1-171.

——— ed. (1963), *Youth, Change and Challenge.* New York: Basic Books.

Escalona (1949), Discussion In: Jessner & Kaplan (1949)

——— (1952a), Problems in psychoanalytic research. *Int. J. Psycho-Anal.,* 33:1-11.

——— (1952b), Earliest phases of personality development: a research report. *Child Res. Monogr.* 17:1-72.

——— (1963), Patterns of infantile experience and the developmental process. *The Psychoanalytic Study of the Child,* 18:197-244. New York: International Universities Press.

——— and Heider, G. M. (1959), *Prediction and Outcome: A Study in Child Development.* New York: Basic Books.

Esersky, J. M., Plotitscher, A. I. and Furmanow, A. M. (1931), Probleme der klinik und der genese der enuresis nocturna bei kindern. *Ztschr. f. Kinderforsch.,* 38:233-255.

Eustis, R. S. (1947), The primary etiology of the specific language disabilities. *J. Peds.,* 31:448-455.

Eysenck, H. J., ed. (1960a), *Behaviour Therapy and the Neuroses: Readings in Modern Methods of Treatment Derived from Learning Theory.* London: Pergamon Press.

——— (1960b), Personality and behaviour therapy. *Proc. Roy. Soc. Med.,* 53:504-508.

Fabian, A. A. (1945), Vertical rotation in visual-motor performance – its relationship to reading reversals. *J. Ed. Psychol.,* 36:129-154.

Fairbairn, W. R. D. (1952), *Psycho-Analytic Studies of the Personality.* London: Tavistock.

——— Feinstein, S. C., and Judas, I. (1956), Anorexia nervosa in male child. *Amer. J. Orthopsychiat.,* 26:751-772.

Farnham, M. F. (1953), Cases of hysteria in childhood. *Nerv. Child,* 10:232-237.

Federn, P. (1940), The determination of hysteria versus obsessional neurosis. *Psychoanal. Rev.,* 27:265-270.

Feldman, F. (1946), Psychoneurosis in the mentally retarded. *Amer. J. Ment. Def.,* 51:247-254.

Fenichel, O. (1941), *Problems of Psychoanalytic Technique.* New York: Psychoanalytic Quarterly, Chapter V, p. 71, Comments on the analysis of the transference; Chapter VI, pp. 80-81, Working through and some special technical problems.

——— (1945a), Neurotic acting out. *Collected Papers,* 2:296-304. New York: Norton, 1954.

——— (1945b), *Psychoanalytic Theory of the Neurosis.* New York: Norton.

——— and Rapaport, A. (1953), Respiratory introjection. In: *Collected Papers of Otto Fenichel.* New York: Norton, p. 221.

Ferenczi, S. (1913), States in the development of the sense of reality. In: *Contributions to Psychoanalysis.* Boston: Richard C. Badger, 1916.

——— (1926a), *Hysteric Materialization. Further Contributions to the Theory and Technique of Psychoanalysis.* London: Hogarth Press.

——— (1926b), The problem of acceptance of unpleasant ideas–advances in knowledge of the sense of reality. *Hysteric Materialization. Further Contributions to Theory and Technique of Psychoanalysis.* London: Hogarth Press.

Fernald, G. M. and Keller, H. (1921), The effect of kinaesthetic factors in the development of word recognition in the case of non-readers. *J. Educ. Res.,* 4:355-377.

Fernald, W. (1919), Aftercare study of the patients discharged from Waverly for a period of 25 years. *Ungraded,* 5:25-31.

Finch, S. M. (1962), The psychiatrist and juvenile delinquency. *J. Amer. Acad. Child Psychiat.,* 1:619-635.

Finger, F. W. (1944), Experimental behavior disorders in the rat. In: *Personality and the Behavior Disorders,* ed. J. McV. Hunt, 1:413-430. New York: Ronald.

Fink, G. and Schneer, H. I. (1963), Psychiatric evaluation of adolescent asthmatics. In: *The Asthmatic Child,* ed. H. I. Schneer. New York: Harper & Row.

Fisher, J., Gonda, T. A. and Little, K. B. (1955), The Rorschach and central nervous system pathology: a cross-validation study. *Amer. J. Psychiat.,* 111:487-492.

Flavell, J. H. (1963), *The Developmental Psychology of Jean Piaget.* Princeton, N. J.: Van Nostrand.

Fodor, N. (1946), Hysterical color blindness—caused by infantile sexual guilt. *J. Clin. Psychopathol.,* 8:279-289.

Foss, B. M., ed. (1961-1965), *Determinants of Infant Behavior,* Vols. 1-3. New York: Wiley.

Fowler, G. B. (1882), Incontinence of faeces in children. *Amer. J. Obstet.,* 15:984-988.

Fraga-Arroyo, R. and Herrera, J. G. (1947), Presentacion de 5 casos de histeria en niños con manifestaciones mortoras. *Rev. Cubana de Pediatria,* 19:479-486.

Fraiberg, S. (1950), On the sleep disturbances of early childhood. *This Volume,* pp. 310–339.

________ (1952), A critical neurosis in a two and a half year old girl. *The Psychoanalytic Study of the Child,* 7:173-213. New York: International Universities Press.

________ (1959), *The Magic Years.* New York: Scribners.

________ (1968), Parallel and divergent patterns in blind and sighted infants. *The Psychoanalytic Study of the Child,* 23:264-300. New York: International Universities Press.

François, P. (1953), Baisse d'acuité visuelle et petits pitiates (Low visual field in hysteria in children). *Bull. des Sociétés D'Ophthalmologie de France.* No. 4, pp. 434-435.

Fredericson, E. (1952), Perceptual homeostasis and distress vocalization in puppies. *J. Personal.,* 20:472-477.

Fremont-Smith, F. (1934), The influence of emotion in precipitating convulsions: preliminary report. *Amer. J. Psychiat.,* 13:717-723.

French, J. D., Hernandez-Peon, R. and Livingston, R. B. (1955), Projections from cortex to cephalic brain stem (reticular formation) in monkey. *J. Neurophysiol.,* 18:74-95.

French, T. (1936), A clinical study in the course of a psychoanalytic treatment. *Psychoanal. Quart.,* 5:148-194.

________ and Alexander, F. (1941), Psychogenic factors in bronchial asthma. *Psychosom. Med. Monogrs.,* Vol. 4. Washington, D. C.: National Research Council.

Freud, A. (1926), An hysterical symptom in a child of two years and three months. *Int. J. Psycho-Anal.,* 7:227-229.

________ (1935), Psychoanalysis and the training of the young child. *Psychoanal. Quart.,* 4:15-24.

________ (1936), *The Ego and the Mechanisms of Defense.* New York: International Universities Press, rev. ed., 1966.

________ (1945), Indications for child analysis. *The Psychoanalytic Study of the Child,* 1:127-150. New York: International Universities Press.

________ (1946), The psychoanalytic study of infantile feeding disturbances. *This Volume,* pp. 296-309.

________ (1949), Aggression in relation to emotional development. *The Psychoanalytic Study of the Child,* 3/4:37-42. New York: International Universities Press.

________ (1951), Observations on child development. *The Psychoanalytic Study of the Child,* 6:18-30. New York: International Universities Press.

________ (1952), The role of bodily illness in the mental life of children. *This Volume,* pp. 572-584.

________ (1955), Safeguarding the emotional health of our children In: *Casework Papers, 1954,* ed. Family Service Association of America, National Conference of Social Welfare. New York: Columbia University Press.

________ (1958), Child observations and prediction of development: a memorial lecture in honor of Ernst Kris. *The Psychoanalytic Study of the Child,* 13:92-116. New York: International Universities Press.

________ (1960a), Discussion of Dr. Bowlby's Paper (1960). *The Psychoanalytic Study of the Child,* 15:53-62. New York: International Universities Press.

________ (1960b), Introduction to Kata Levy's Paper. *The Psychoanalytic Study of the Child,* 15:378. New York: International Universities Press.

——— (1962), Assessment of childhood disturbances. *The Psychoanalytic Study of the Child,* 17:149-158. New York: International Universities Press.

——— (1965), *Normality and Pathology in Childhood.* New York: International Universities Press. See also *This Volume,* pp. 133-156.

——— and Burlingham, D. (1943), *War and Children.* New York: International Universities Press.

——— (1944), *Infants without Families.* New York: International Universities Press.

Freud, S. (1894), On the grounds for detaching a particular syndrome from neurasthenia under the description "anxiety neurosis". *Standard Edition,* 3:85-117. London: Hogarth Press, 1962.

——— (1895), A reply to criticisms of my paper on anxiety neurosis. *Standard Edition,* 3:120-139. London: Hogarth Press, 1962.

——— (1896a), Further remarks on the neuropsychoses of defence. *Standard Edition,* 3:157-185. London: Hogarth Press, 1962.

——— (1896b), Heredity and the aetiology of the neuroses. *Standard Edition,* 3:141-156. London: Hogarth Press, 1962.

——— (1896c), The aetiology of hysteria. *Standard Edition,* 3:187-221. London: Hogarth Press, 1962.

——— (1897), *The Origins of Psychoanalysis, Letters to Wilhelm Fliess, Drafts and Notes.* Letter No. 69. New York: Basic Books, 1954, pp. 215-218.

——— (1898), Sexuality in the aetiology of the neuroses. *Standard Edition,* 3:260-297. London: Hogarth Press, 1962.

——— (1900), The interpretation of dreams. *Standard Edition,* 4 & 5. London: Hogarth Press, 1953.

——— (1901), Psychopathology of everyday life, *Standard Edition,* 6. London: Hogarth Press, 1960.

——— (1905a), My views on the part played by sexuality in the aetiology of the neuroses. *Standard Edition,* 7:269-279. London: Hogarth Press, 1953.

——— (1905b), Three essays on the theory of sexuality. *Standard Edition,* 7:123-243. London: Hogarth Press, 1953.

——— (1905c), *Jokes and their Relation to the unconscious. Standard Edition,* 8:3-238. London: Hogarth Press, 1960.

——— (1908), Hysterical phantasies and their relation to bisexuality. *Standard Edition,* 9:155-166. London: Hogarth Press, 1959.

——— (1909a), Analysis of a phobia in a five-year-old boy. *Standard Edition,* 10:1-149. London: Hogarth Press, 1955.

——— (1909b), Minutes of the Vienna Psychoanalytic Society, November 17, 1909. *The Life and Works of Sigmund Freud,* ed. E. Jones. New York: Basic Books, 1955.

——— (1910), *Three essays on the theory of sexuality. Standard Edition,* 7:125-243. London: Hogarth Press, 1953.

——— (1911), Formulations on the two principles of mental functioning. *Standard Edition,* 12:213-226. London: Hogarth Press, 1958.

——— (1913a), The predisposition to obsessional neurosis: a contribution to the problem of choice of neurosis. *Standard Edition,* 12:311-326. London: Hogarth Press, 1958.

——— (1913b), Totem and taboo. *Standard Edition,* 13:1-161. London: Hogarth Press, 1955.

——— (1914a), On narcissism: an introduction. *Standard Edition,* 14:69-102. London: Hogarth Press, 1957.

——— (1914b), On the history of the psychoanalytic movement. *Standard Edition,* 14:1-66. London: Hogarth Press, 1957.

——— (1915a), Instincts and their vicissitudes. *Standard Edition,* 14:111-140. London: Hogarth Press, 1957.

——— (1915b), Repression. *Standard Edition,* 14:141-158. London: Hogarth Press, 1957.

——— (1916), Some character types met within psychoanalytic work. *Standard Edition,* 14:309-333. London: Hogarth Press, 1957.

——— (1916-1917), Introductory lectures on psycho-analysis. *Standard Edition,* 15 & 16. London: Hogarth Press, 1963.

________ (1917), Mourning and melancholia. *Standard Edition,* 14:239-258. London: Hogarth Press, 1957.

________ (1918 [1914]), From the history of an infantile neurosis. *Standard Edition,* 17:1-122. London: Hogarth Press, 1955.

________ (1920a), The neuro-psychoses of defense. *Standard Edition,* 3:43-61. London: Hogarth Press, 1962.

________ (1920b), Beyond the pleasure principle. *Standard Edition,* 18:1-64. London: Hogarth Press, 1955.

________ (1922), The etiological significance of sexual life. *This Volume,* pp. 79-82.

________ (1923), *The Ego and the Id. Standard Edition,* 19:3-66. London: Hogarth Press, 1961.

________ (1924a), Footnote to: Further remarks on the defence neuropsychoses. *Standard Edition,* 3:157-185. London: Hogarth Press, 1962.

________ (1924b), The loss of reality in neurosis and psychosis. *Standard Edition,* 19:181-187. London: Hogarth Press, 1961.

________ (1925a), *An Autobiographical Study.* London: Hogarth Press, 1935.

________ (1925b), Creative writers and day-dreaming. *Standard Edition,* 9:141-153. London: Hogarth Press, 1959.

________ (1926), Inhibitions, symptoms and anxiety. *Standard Edition,* 20:77-174. London: Hogarth Press, 1959.

________ (1927), Fetishism. *Standard Edition,* 21:149-157. London: Hogarth Press, 1961.

________ (1928), Dostoevsky and parricide. *Standard Edition,* 21:177-194. London: Hogarth Press, 1961.

________ (1930), Civilization and its discontents. *Standard Edition,* 21:59-145. London: Hogarth Press, 1961.

________ (1933), New introductory lectures on psychoanalysis. *Standard Edition,* 22:3-182. London: Hogarth Press, 1964.

________ (1937), Analysis terminable and interminable. *Standard Edition,* 23:211-253. London: Hogarth Press, 1964.

________ (1938), Splitting of the ego in the process of defense. *Standard Edition,* 23:271-278. London: Hogarth Press, 1964.

________ (1940), An outline of psycho-analysis. *Standard Edition,* 23:141-207. London: Hogarth Press, 1964.

________ (1953), *A General Selection from the Works of Freud,* ed. J. Rickman. London: Hogarth Press.

Friedenberg, E. (1959), *The Vanishing Adolescent.* Boston: Beacon Press.

Friedlander, K. (1957), *The Psychoanalytic Approach to Juvenile Delinquency.* New York: International Universities Press.

Fries, M. E. (1944), Psychosomatic relationships between mother and infant. *Psychosom. Med.,* 6:159-162.

________ (1946), The child's ego development and the training of adults in his environment. *The Psychoanalytic Study of the Child,* 2:85-112. New York: International Universities Press.

________ and Woolf, P. J. (1953), Some hypotheses on the role of the congenital activity type in personality development. *The Psychoanalytic Study of the Child,* 8:48-62. New York: International Universities Press.

Fromm, E. (1947), *Man For Himself.* New York: Rinehart, p. 75.

Fuller, J. L., Easler, C. A. and Banks, E. M. (1950), Formation of conditioned avoidance responses in young puppies. *Amer. J. Physiol.,* 160:462-466.

Fulton, J. F. (1949), *Physiology of the Nervous System,* 3rd ed. New York: Oxford University Press, pp. 93-104.

________ (1951), *Frontal Lobotomy and Affective Behavior.* New York: Norton, p. 160.

Gallagher, J. R. (1960), General principles of clinical care of adolescent patients. *Pediatric Clinics of North America,* Vol. 7, No. 1. Philadelphia: Saunders.

Gann, E. (1945), *Reading Difficulty and Personality Organization.* New York: King's Crown Press.

Gantt, W. H. (1944), *Experimental Basis for Neurotic Behavior.* New York: Hoeber.

Garfield, S. L. (1963), Abnormal behavior in mental deficiency. In: *Handbook of Mental Deficiency,* ed. N. R. Ellis. New York: McGraw-Hill, pp. 574-601.

Garner, A. and Wenar, C. (1959), *The Mother-Child Interaction in Psychosomatic Disorders.* Urbana, Ill.: University of Illinois Press.

Garsche, G. (1953), Grundzüge des normalen elektroencephalogramms im kindesalter. *Klin. Wochenschrift,* 31:118-123.

Gates, A. I. (1922), *The Psychology of Reading and Spelling, with Special Reference to Disabilities.* New York: Teachers College, Columbia University.

——— (1927), *The Improvement of Reading.* New York: Macmillan.

——— (1936), *The Improvement of Reading,* Rev. Ed. New York: Macmillan.

——— (1941), The role of personality maladjustment in reading disability. *J. Genet. Psychol.,* 59:77-83.

Geleerd, E. R. (1945), Some observations on temper tantrums in children. *Amer. J. Orthopsychiat.,* 15:238-246.

——— (1946), A contribution to the problem of psychosis in children. *The Psychoanalytic Study of the Child,* 2:271-291. New York: International Universities Press.

——— (1958), Borderline states in childhood and adolescence. *The Psychoanalytic Study of the Child,* 13:279-295. New York: International Universities Press.

Gellhorn, E. (1942), *Autonomic Regulations: The Significance for Physiology, Psychology and Neuropsychiatry.* New York: Interscience.

Gerard, M. W. (1937), Child analysis as a technique in the investigation of mental mechanisms. *Amer. J. Psychiat.,* 94:653-663.

Gerard, M. W. (1939), Enuresis: a study in etiology. *This Volume,* pp. 418-430.

——— (1946), Bronchial asthma in children. *Nerv. Child,* 5:327-331.

——— (1948), Bronchial asthma in children. In: *Studies in Psychosomatic Medicine: An Approach to the Case and Treatment of Vegetative Disturbances,* ed. F. G. Alexander and T. M. French. New York: Ronald Press, pp. 243-248.

——— (1953), Genesis of psychosomatic symptoms in infancy. In: *The Psychosomatic Concept in Psychoanalysis,* ed. F. Deutsch. New York: International Universities Press, pp. 82-95.

Gerard, R. (1955), Biological roots of psychiatry. *Science,* 122:225-230.

Gero, G. (1933), Review of Dembo, T. (1931). Der aerger als dynamisches problem. *Psychol. Forschung,* 15:1-144.

——— (1936), The construction of depression. *Int. J. Psycho-Anal.,* 17:423-461.

Gerstmann, J. (1940), Syndrome of finger agnosia, disorientation for right and left, agraphia and acalculia; local diagnostic value. *A.M.A. Arch. Neurol. Psychiat.,* 44:398-408.

Gesell, A. (1940a), *The First Five Years of Life.* New York: Harper & Row. See also *This Volume,* pp. 66-78.

——— (1940b), *Wolf Child and Human Child.* New York: Harper & Row.

——— and Amatruda, C. S. (1941), *Developmental Diagnosis.* New York: Hoeber.

——— and ——— (1947), *Developmental Diagnosis: Normal and Abnormal Child Development, Clinical Methods, and Pediatric Applications,* 2nd ed. New York: Hoeber.

——— and Gesell, B. C. (1912), *The Normal Child and Primary Education.* Boston: Ginn.

——— and Ilg., G. (1937), *Feeding Behavior of Infants.* Philadelphia: Lippincott.

——— and ——— (1943), *Infant and Child in the Culture of Today.* New York: Harper & Row.

——— and ——— (1946), *The Child from Five to Ten.* New York: Harper & Bros.

——— and Ames, L. B. (1956), *Youth: The Years from Ten to Sixteen.* New York: Harper & Bros.

——— and Thompson, H. (1934), *Infant Behavior.* New York: McGraw-Hill.

Gibbs, E. L., Gibbs, F. A. and Fuster, B. (1948), Psychomotor epilepsy. *Arch. Neurol. Psychiat.,* 60:331-339.

Gibbs, F. A. (1947), New drugs of value in the treatment of epilepsy. *Ann. Int. Med.,* 27:548-554.

Giffin, M. E., Johnson, A. M. and Litin, E. M. (1954), Specific factors determining antisocial acting out. *Amer. J. Orthopsychiat.,* 24:668-684.

Gill, M. M., ed. (1967), *The Collected Papers of David Rapaport.* New York: Basic Books.
Gillette, W. R. (1882), Hysteria in early childhood. *N.Y. Med. J.,* 36:261-263.
Glasser, W. (1969), *Schools Without Failure.* New York: Harper & Row.
Glidewell, J. C., Domke, H. R., and Kantor, M. D. (1963), Screening in schools for behavior disorders: use of mother's report of symptoms. *J. Educ. Res.,* 56:508-515.
Glover, E. (1930), Introduction to the study of psychoanalytic theory. *Int. J. Psycho-Anal.,* 11:470-484.
Glueck, S. and Glueck, E. (1950), *Unravelling Juvenile Delinquency.* Boston: Harvard University Press.
________ (1956), *Physique and Delinquency.* New York: Harper and Row.
Goddard, H. (1912), *The Kallikak Family.* New York: The Macmillan Co.
________ (1914), *Feeblemindedness: Its Causes and Consequences.* New York: Macmillan
Gold, L. (1943), Autonomic balance in patients treated with insulin shock as measured by mecholyl chloride. *Arch. Neurol. Psychiat.,* 50:311-317.
Goldfarb, W. (1943), Effects of early institutional care on adolescent personality. *J. Exper. Educ.,* 12:106-129.
________ (1944a), Infant rearing as a factor in foster home placement. *Amer. J. Orthopsychiat.,* 14:162-167.
________ (1944b), Effects of early institutional care on adolescent personality: Rorschach data. *Amer. J. Orthopsychiat.,* 14:441-447.
________ (1945a), Effects of psychological deprivation in infancy and subsequent stimulation. *Amer. J. Psychiat.,* 102:18-33.
________ (1945b), Psychological deprivation in infancy and subsequent development. *Amer. J. Orthopsychiat.,* 15:247-255.
________ (1955), Emotional and intellectual consequences of psychological deprivation in infancy: a revaluation. In: *Psychopathology of Childhood,* ed. P. H. Hoch and J. Zubin. New York: Grune & Stratton.
________ (1956), Receptor preferences in schizophrenic children. *A.M.A. Arch. Neurol. Psychiat.,* 76:643-652.
________ (1958), Pain reactions in group of institutionalized schizophrenic children. *Amer. J. Orthopsychiat.,* 28:77-85.
________ (1961), *Childhood Schizophrenia.* Cambridge, Mass.: Commonwealth Fund, a division of Harvard University Press.
________ (1962), Families of schizophrenic children. In: *Mental Retardation.* Baltimore: Williams & Wilkins, pp. 256-269.
________ (1964), An investigation of childhood schizophrenia: a retrospective view. *This Volume,* pp. 688-709.
________ (unpublished), Study of speech of mothers of schizophrenic children.
________ (unpublished), External guides for speech in normal and schizophrenic children.
________ and Braunstein, P. (1958), Reactions to delayed auditory feedback in schizophrenic children. In: *Psychopathology of Communication,* ed. P. H. Hoch and J. Zubin. New York: Grune & Stratton, pp. 49-63.
________ Braunstein, P. and Lorge, I. (1956), Study of speech patterns in group of schizophrenic children. *Amer. J. Orthopsychiat.,* 26:544-555.
________ and Klopfer, B. (1944), Rorschach characteristics of institutional children. *Rorschach Research Exchange,* 8:92-100.
________ and Radin, S. S. (1964), Group behaviour of schizophrenic children. *Int. J. Soc. Psychiat.,* 10:199-208.
________ Sibulkin, L., Behrens, M., and Jahoda, H. (1958), Parental perplexity and childhood confusion. In: *New Frontiers in Child Guidance,* ed. A. H. Esman. New York: International Universities Press, pp. 157-170.
Golding, W. (1955), *Lord of the Flies.* New York: Coward-McCann.
Goldman, F. (1948), Breastfeeding and character formation. *J. Personal.* 17:83-103.
________ (1950), Breastfeeding and character formation, II: The etiology of the oral character in psychoanalytic theory. *J. Personal.* 19:189-196.
Goldstein, K. (1939), *The Organism.* New York: American Book Company, pp. 131-156.
________ (1957), Das lacheln des kindes und das problem des verstehen des anderen ich.

In: *Recontre/Encounter/Begegnung.* Utrecht/Antwerp: Spectrum, pp. 181-197.

Goodenough, F. L. (1931), *Anger in Young Children.* [*Institute of Child Welfare,* Monogr. 9.] Minneapolis: University of Minnesota Press.

Goodglass, H. and Quadfasel, F. A. (1964), Language ·laterality in left-handed aphasics. *Brain,* 77:521-548.

Gottschalk, L. (1953), Effects of intensive psychotherapy on epileptic children. *This Volume,* pp. 788-824.

——— (1956), The relationship of psychologic state and epileptic activity. *The Psychoanalytic Study of the Child,* 11:352-380. New York: International Universities Press.

Gouin Décaire, T. (1965), *Intelligence and Affectivity in Early Childhood.* New York: International Universities Press.

Gowers, W. R. (1901), *Epilepsy and Other Chronic Convulsive Diseases: Causes, Symptoms, Treatment,* ed. 2. London: J. & A Churchill.

Graham, F. K., Matarazzo, R. G. and Caldwell, B. M. (1956), Behavioral differences between normal and traumatized newborns, II. Standardization, reliability and validity. *Psychol. Monogr.,* 70:17-33.

Gary, C. T. (1922), *Deficiencies in Reading Ability: Their Diagnosis and Remedies.* Boston: Little, Brown.

Grebelskaja-Albatz, E. (1934), Zur klinik der schizophrenic des fruhen kindesalters. I. *Schweiz. Arch. f. Neurol. u. Psychiat.,* 34:244-253.

——— (1935), Zur klinik der schizophrenic des fruhen kindesalters. II. *Schweiz. Arch. f. Neurol. u. Psychiat.,* 35:30-40.

Green, R. and Money, J. (1961), Effeminacy in pre-pubertal boys. *Pediatrics,* 27:286-291.

Green, S. (1961), Ego structure of the adolescent retardate. *Int. Record of Med.,* 174:205-211.

Greenacre, P. (1941), The predisposition to anxiety. *Psychoanal. Quart.,* 10:66-94 and 610-638.

——— (1944), Infant reactions to restraint: Problems in the fate of infantile aggression. *Amer. J. Orthopsychiat.,* 14:204-218. (Also in: *Trauma, Growth and Personality.* New York: Norton, 1952, pp. 83-105.)

——— (1945), Conscience in the psychopath. *Amer. J. Orthopsychiat.,* 15:495-509.

——— (1946), The biological economy of birth. *The Psychoanalytic Study of the Child,* 1:31-51. New York: International Universities Press.

——— (1952b), *Trauma, Growth and Personality.* New York: Norton.

——— (1956), Experiences of awe in childhood. *The Psychoanalytic Study of the Child,* 11:9-30. New York: International Universities Press.

——— (1957), The childhood of the artist. *The Psychoanalytic Study of the Child,* 12:47-72. New York: International Universities Press.

——— (1959), On focal symbiosis. In: *Dynamic Psychopathology in Childhood,* ed. L. Jessner and E. Pavenstedt. New York: Grune & Stratton, pp. 243-256.

Greenblatt, M., Emory, P. E., and Glueck, B. C., Jr. (1967), *Poverty and Mental Health.* Psychiatric Research Report #21. Washington, D. C.: American Psychiatric Association.

Greenson, R. R. (1944), On genuine epilepsy. *Psychoanal. Quart.,* 13:139-159.

Gregory, I. (1958), Studies of parental deprivation in psychiatric patients. *Amer. J. Psychiat.,* 115:432-442.

Grenlich, W. W., et al. (1942), Somatic and endocrine studies of pubertal and adolescent boys. *Society for Research in Child Development,* Vol. 7, No. 3. Washington, D. C.: National Research Council.

Grewel, F. (1954), *Infantile Autism.* Amsterdam. J. Muusses te Purmurend.

Griesinger, W. (1860), *Mental Pathology and Therapeutics,* 2nd ed. London: New Sydenham Society.

Grinker, R. R. (1953), Some current trends and hypotheses of psychosomatic research. In: *The Psychosomatic Concept in Psychoanalysis,* ed. F. Deutsch. New York: International Universities Press, pp. 37-62.

Grotjahn, M. (1949), The primal crime and the unconscious. In: *Searchlights on Delinquency,* ed. K. R. Eissler. New York: International Universities Press, pp. 306-314.

Group for the Advancement of Psychiatry (1959), *Basic Considerations in Mental Retardation: A Preliminary Report.* New York: G.A.P. Report #56.

________ (1963), *Mental Retardation: A Family Crisis—The Therapeutic Role of the Physician.* New York: G.A.P. Report #56.

________ (1966), *Psychopathological Disorders in Childhood: Theoretical Considerations and a Proposed Classification.* New York: G.A.P. Report #62, Vol. 6.

Gull, W. (1868), The address on medicine. *Lancet,* 2:171-176.

________ (1874), Anorexia nervosa. *This Volume,* pp. 567-571.

Guttman, S. (1965), Some aspects of scientific theory construction and psychoanalysis. *Int. J. Psycho-Anal.,* 46:129-136.

Haggard, E. A. (1953), Techniques for the development of unbiased tests. *Proceedings: 1952 Conference on Testing Problems.* Princeton: Educational Testing Service, pp. 93-117.

________ (1954), Social status and intelligence. *Genet. Psychol. Monogr.,* 49:141-186.

Hallgren, B. (1950), Specific dyslexia ("congenital word blindness"). A clinical and genetic study. *Acta Psychiat. et Neurol.,* Supplementum 65, Copenhagen.

Hallowitz, D. (1954), Residential treatment of chronic asthmatic children. *Amer. J. Orthopsychiat.,* 24:576-587.

Hamill, R. C. (1929), Enuresis. *J.A.M.A.,* 93:254-257.

Harlow, H. F. (1952), *Functional Organization of the Brain in Relation to Mentation and Behavior in the Biology of Mental Health and Disease.* New York: Hoeber, pp. 244-256.

________ (1958), The nature of love. *Amer. Psychologist,* 13:673-685.

________ and Zimmerman, R. R. (1959), Affectional response in the infant monkey. *Science,* 130:421-432.

________ (1962), The heterosexual affectional system in monkeys. *Amer. Psychologist,* 17:1-9.

________ and Harlow, M. K. (1962), Social deprivation in monkeys. *Scientific Amer.,* 207:136-146.

Harmon, P. J., Personal communication.

Harms, E. E. (1945), Childhood schizophrenia and childhood hysteria. *Psychiat. Quart.,* 19:243-257.

________ (1963), *Problems of Sleep and Dreams in Children.* New York: Pergamon Press.

Harrington, M. (1962), *The Other America.* New York: Macmillan.

Harris, I. (1961), *Emotional Blocks to Learning.* New York: Free Press of Glencoe.

Harris, M. C. and Shure, N. (1956), A study of behavior patterns in asthmatic children. *J. Allergy,* 27:312-323.

Harrison, S. I. (1970a), Is psychoanalysis "our science": reflections on the scientific status of psychoanalysis. *J. Amer. Psychoanal. Assn.,* 18:125-149.

________ (1970b), Reared in the wrong sex. *J. Amer. Acad. Child Psychiat.,* 9:44-102.

________ et al. (1965), Social class and mental illness in children: choice of treatment. *Arch. Gen. Psychiat.,* 13:411-417.

Hartmann, H. (1933), Ein experimenteller beitrag zur psychologie der zwangsneurose (Über das behalten erledigter und unerledigter handlungen). *Jahr. f. Psychiatrie u. Neurol.,* 50:243-254.

________ (1939), *Ego Psychology and the Problem of Adaptation.* New York: International Universities Press, 1958.

________ (1947), On rational and irrational action. *Psychoanalysis and the Social Sciences,* ed. G. Róheim, 1:359-392. New York: International Universities Press.

________ (1950), Comments on the psychoanalytic theory of the ego. *The Psychoanalytic Study of the Child,* 5:74-96. New York: International Universities Press.

________ (1953), Contributions to the metapsychology of schizophrenia. *The Psychoanalytic Study of the Child,* 8:177-198. New York: International Universities Press.

________ (1958), Comments on the scientific aspects of psychoanalysis. *The Psychoanalytic Study of the Child,* 13:127-146. New York: International Universities Press.

________ (1964), *Essays on Ego Psychology.* New York: International Universities Press.

________ (1947), On rational and irrational action. *Psychoanalysis and the Social Sciences,* ed. G. Róheim, 1:359-392. New York: International Universities Press.

________ and Kris, E. (1945), The genetic approach in psychoanalysis. *The Psychoanalytic Study of the Child,* 1:11-30. New York: International Universities Press.

________ and Loewenstein, R. M. (1946), Comments on the formation of psychic structure. *This Volume,* pp. 83-108.

——— (1964), *Papers on Psychoanalytic Psychology* [*Psychological Issues,* Monogr. # 14.]. New York: International Universities Press.

Head, H. (1926), *Aphasia and Kindred Disorders of Speech.* Cambridge: Cambridge University Press.

Healy, W. and Bronner, A. F. (1936), *New Light on Delinquency and Its Treatment.* New Haven: Yale University Press.

Hebb, D. O. (1945), Man's frontal lobes: critical review of methods in analysis of cerebral function. *Arch. Neurol. Psychiat.,* 54:10-24.

——— (1949), *The Organization of Behavior.* New York: Wiley.

——— (1955), The mammal and his environment. *Amer. J. Psychiat.,* 111:824-831.

Heilbrunn, G. (1950), Psychodynamic aspects of epilepsy. *Psychoanal. Quart.,* 19:145-157.

Heinicke, C. M. (1956), Some effects of separating two-year-old children from their parents: a comparative study. *Human Relations,* 9:105-176.

——— and Westheimer, I. (1965), *Brief Separations.* New York: International Universities Press.

Hendrick, I. (1940), Psychoanalytic observations on the aura of 2 cases with convulsions. *Psychosom. Med.,* 2:43-52.

——— (1942), Instinct and the ego during infancy. *Psychoanal. Quart.,* 11:33-58.

——— (1949), Discussion. In: Jessner & Kaplan (1949).

Henry, C. E. and Scoville, W. B. (1952), Suppression burst activity from isolated cerebral cortex in man. *EEG Clin. Neurophysiol.,* 4:1-22.

Henry, J. (1947), Environment and symptom formation. *Amer. J. Orthopsychiat.,* 17:628-632.

Hermann, K. and Voldby, H. (1946), The morphology of handwriting in congenital word-blindness. *Acta Psychiat. et Neurol.,* 21:349-363.

Hersher, L., Moore, U. and Richmond, J. B. (1958), The effect of postpartum separation of mother and kid on maternal care in the domestic goat. *Science,* 128:1342-1343.

Hess, E. H. (1962), Imprinting and the critical period concept. In: *Roots of Behavior,* ed. E. L. Bliss. New York: Harper & Bros., pp. 254-263.

Hess, W. R. (1954), *Diencephalon: Autonomic and Extrapyramidal Functions.* New York: Grune & Stratton, p. 79.

——— and Akert, K. (1955), Experimental data on role of hypothalamus in mechanism of emotional behavior. *Arch. Neurol. Psychiat.,* 73:127-129.

Hetzer, H. and Wolf, K. (1928), Babytests. Eine testserie für das erste lebensjahr. *Zeitschr. für Psychologie,* 107:62-104.

——— (1929), Entwicklungsbedingte erziehungsschwierigkeiten. *Ztschr. Pädagog. Psychol.,* 30:77-85.

Higgins, J., Lederer, H. and Rosenbaum, M. (1950), Life situations, emotions and idiopathic epilepsy. *A. Res. Nerv. Ment. Dis.,* 29:137-147.

Hildreth, G. (1945), A school survey of eye-hand dominance. *J. Appl. Psychol.,* 29:83-88.

Hilgard, J. R. and Newman, M. F. (1959), Anniversaries in mental illness. *Psychiatry,* 22:113-121.

——— and Fisk, F. (1960), Strength of adult ego following childhood bereavement. *Amer. J. Orthopsychiat.,* 30:788-798.

Hincks, E. (1926), *Disability in Reading and Its Relation to Personality.* Cambridge, Mass.: Harvard University Press.

Hines, M. (1937), The "motor" cortex. *Bull. Johns Hop. Hosp.,* 40: 313-336.

Hirschberg, J. C. (1957), Parental anxiety accompanying sleep disturbances in young children. *Bull. Menn. Clin.,* 21:129-139.

Hoff, H. and Schilder, P. (1927), Die lagerreflexes des menschen. Vienna.

Hoffer, W. (1949), Mouth, hand and ego integration. *The Psychoanalytic Study of the Child,* 3/4:49-56. New York: International Universities Press.

——— (1950a), Development of the body ego. *The Psychoanalytic Study of the Child,* 5:18-23. New York: International Universities Press.

——— (1950b), Oral aggressiveness and ego development. *Int. J. Psycho-Anal.,* 31:160-168. (also in *The Yearbook of Psychoanalysis,* 7:123-131. New York: International Universities Press, 1951.)

——— (1952), The mutual influences in the development of ego and id: earliest stages. *The Psychoanalytic Study of the Child,* 7:31-41. New York: International Universities Press.

Hollingshead, A. B. and Redlich, F. C. (1958), *Social Class and Mental Illness.* New York: Wiley.

Hollingworth, L. (1923), *Special Talents and Defects.* New York: Macmillan.

Holt, J. (1964), *How Children Fail.* New York: Dell.

Holt, R. R., ed. (1967), *Motives and Thought: Psychoanalytic Essays in Honor of David Rapaport.* [*Psychological Issues,* Monogr. 18/19.] New York: International Universities Press.

Homburger, A. (1926), *Psychopathologie des Kindesalters.* Berlin: Springer.

Hooker, D. (1939), Fetal behavior. In: *The Inter-relationship of Mind and Body,* Association for Research in Nervous and Mental Disease. Research Publications, Vol. 19. Baltimore: Williams & Wilkins Co., pp. 237-243.

________ (1950), Spinal cord regeneration. In: *Genetic Neurology,* ed. P. Weiss. Chicago: University of Chicago Press.

Hoskins, R. G. (1946), *The Biology of Schizophrenia.* New York: Norton.

Hunter, J. and Jasper, H. H. (1949), Effects of thalamic stimulation in unaesthetized animals. *EEG Clin. Neurophysiol.,* 1:305-324.

Hurst, A. (1943), Asthma in childhood. *Brit. Med. J.,* 1:403-406.

Huschka, M. (1942), The child's response to coercive bowel training. *Psychosom. Med.,* 4:301-308.

Huxley, J. (1961), *Humanist Frame.* London: Allen & Unwin. New York: Harper & Bros., 1962.

Hyman, H. H. (1953), The value systems of different classes: a social psychological contribution to the analysis of stratification. In: *Class, Status and Power: A Reader in Social Stratification,* ed. R.V Bendix and S. M. Lipset. Glencoe, Ill.: Free Press of Glencoe, Inc., pp. 426-442.

Illingworth, R. S. and Holt, K. S. (1955), Children in hospital: some observations on their reactions with special reference to daily visiting. *Lancet,* 2:1257-1262.

Ingham, H. V. (1949), A statistical study of family relationships in psychoneurosis. *Amer. J. Psychiat.,* 106:91-92.

Ingram, W. R. (1952), Brain stem mechanisms in behavior. *EEG Clin. Neurophysiol.,* 4:397-406.

Inkeles, A. (1960), Industrial man: the relation of status to experience, perception, and value. *Amer. J. Sociol.,* 66:20-21 and Table 9.

Irvine, R. (1941), An ocular policy for public schools. *Amer. J. Ophth.,* 24:779-787.

Itard, J. (1801), *The Wild Boy of Aveyron.* New York: Century, 1932. See *This Volume,* pp. 726-732.

Jackson, J. H. (1932), *Selected Writings,* ed. J. Taylor. 2:3-118. London: Hodder & Stoughton. 12:56-67.

________ (1945), Prophylactic considerations for the neonatal period. *Amer. J. Orthopsychiat.,* 15:89-102.

Jackson, J. H. (1932), *Selected Writings,* ed. J. Taylor. 2:3-118. London: Hodder & Stoughton.

________ (1944), A survey of psychological, social, and environmental differences between advanced and retarded readers. *J. Genet. Psychol.,* 65:113-131.

Jacobson, E. (1943), Depression: the Oedipus conflict in the development of depressive mechanisms. *Psychoanal. Quart.,* 12:541-560.

________ (1946), The effect of disappointment on ego and superego formation in normal and depressive development. *Psychoanalyt. Rev.,* 33:129-147.

________ (1950), Development of the wish for a child in boys. *The Psychoanalytic Study of the Child,* 5:139-152. New York: International Universities Press.

________ (1953), Contribution to the metapsychology of cyclothymic depression. In: *Affective Disorders: Psychoanalytic Contribution to Their Study,* ed. P. Greenacre. New York: International Universities Press., pp. 49-83.

________ (1957), On normal and pathological moods. *The Psychoanalytic Study of the Child,* 12:73-113. New York: International Universities Press.

James, M. (1960), Premature ego development: some observations upon disturbances in the first three years of life. *Int. J. Psycho-Anal.,* 41:288-294.

James, W. T. and Cannon, D. J. (1952), Conditioned avoiding responses in puppies. *Amer. J. Physiol.,* 168:251-253.

Janet, P. (1876), La notion de personnalité. *Rev. Sci.* 11.

———— (1907), *The Major Symptoms of Hysteria,* 2nd ed. New York: Macmillan, 1929.

———— (1937), Psychological strength and weakness in mental diseases. *Factors Determining Human Behavior.* Cambridge. Harvard University Press, pp. 64-106.

Jasper, H. H., Solomon, P. and Bradley, C. (1938), Electroencephalographic analyses of behavior problem children. *Amer. J. Psychiat.,* 95:641-658.

———— (1949), Diffuse projection systems: the integrative action of the thalamic reticular system. *EEG Clin. Neurophysiol.,* 1:405-420.

———— (1952), Electrical activity and mechanisms of cerebral integration. In: *The Biology of Mental Health and Disease.* New York: Hoeber, pp. 226-243.

Jelliffe, S. E. (1935), Dynamic concepts and the epileptic attack. *Amer. J. Psychiat.,* 92:565-574.

———— and White, W. A. (1935), *Diseases of the Nervous System: Textbook of Neurology and Psychiatry,* 6th ed. Philadelphia: Lea & Febiger.

Jensen, R. A. and Wert, A. D. (1945), Conversion hysteria in children. *J. Lancet,* 65:172-175.

Jersild, A. T. and Holmes, F. B. (1935a), *Children's Fears.* [Child Development, Monogr. 20]. New York: Bureau of Publications, Teachers College, Columbia University.

———— and ———— (1935b), Methods of overcoming children's fears. *J. Psychol.,* 1:75-104.

———— Markey, F. V. and Jersild, C. L. (1933), *Children's Fears, Dreams, Wishes, Daydreams, Likes, Pleasant and Unpleasant Memories.* [Child Development, Monogr. 12]. New York: Columbia University Press.

Jessner, L. (1959), Some observations on children hospitalized during latency. In: *Dynamic Psychopathology in Childhood,* ed. L. Jessner and E. Pavenstedt. New York: Grune & Stratton, pp. 257-268.

———— & Kaplan (1949), Reaction of children to tonsillectomy and adenoidectomy—preliminary report. In: *Problems of Infancy and Childhood,* ed. M.J.E. Senn. New York: Josiah Macy Jr. Foundation.

———— Blom, G. and Waldfogel, S. (1952), Emotional implications of tonsillectomy and adenoidectomy on children. *The Psychoanalytic Study of the Child,* 7:126-169. New York: International Universities Press.

———— Lamont, J., Long, R., Rollins, N., Whipple, B. and Prentice, N. (1955), Emotional import of nearness and separation for the asthmatic child and his mother. *The Psychoanalytic Study of the Child,* 10:353-375. New York: International Universities Press.

Johnson, A. M. (1949), Sanctions for superego lacunae of adolescents. *This Volume,* pp. 522-531.

———— Falstein, E. I., Szurek, S. A., and Svendsen, M. (1941), School phobia. *This Volume,* pp. 410-417.

———— and Szurek (1952), The genesis of antisocial acting out in children and adults. *Psychoanal. Quart.,* 21:313-343.

Johnston, P. W. (1942), The relation of certain anomalies of vision and laternal dominance to reading disability. *Monographs Soc. Res. in Child Devel.,* Vol. 7, No. 2. Washington, D. C.: National Research Council.

Jones, E. (1923), The child's unconscious. In: *Papers on Psychoanalysis,* Chapter 36. London: Wood.

———— (1924), Editorial preface to *Collected Papers.* In: *Collected* Papers, 1:4. London: Hogarth Press, 1946.

———— (1935), Early female sexuality. In: *Papers on Psychoanalysis,* 5th ed. London: Bailliere, Tindall & Cox, 1948, pp. 485-495.

———— (1953), *The Life and Work of Sigmund Freud,* 1:265-267. New York: Basic Books.

Jones, H. E. (1940), Personal reactions of the yearbook committee. *39th Yearbook, National Society for the Study of Education,* 1:454-456.

Jones, H. G. (1960), Learning and abnormal behavior. In: *Handbook of Abnormal Psychology,* ed. H. J. Eysenck. London: Pitman, pp. 488-528.

Jones, M. C. (1924a), The elimination of children's fears. *J. Exper. Psychol.,* 7:382-390.

———— (1924b), A laboratory study of fear: the case of Peter. *Pedagog. Seminar,* 31:308-316.

Jones, M. M. W. (1944), Relationship between reading deficiencies and left-handedness. *School & Soc.,* 60:238-239.

Josselyn, I. (1954), The ego in adolescence. *Amer. J. Orthopsychiat.,* 24:223-237.

Kagan, J. and Moss, H. A. (1959), Parental correlates of child's I.Q. and height. *Child Development,* 52:365-398.

Kagan, J. (1964), Acquisition and significance of sex typing and sex role identity. In: *Review of Child Development Research,* ed. M. L. Hoffman and L. W. Hoffman. New York: Russell Sage Foundation, 1:137-167.

________ and Moss, H. A. (1962), *Birth to Maturity: A Study in Psychological Development.* New York: Wiley.

Kahn, E. and Cohen, L. (1934), Organic drivenness: a brain stem syndrome and an experience. *New England J. Med.,* 210:748-756.

Kaila, E. (1932), Die reaktionen des säuglings auf das menschliche gesicht. *Ann. Univ. Aboensis,* 17:1-114.

Kallman, F. and Roth, B. (1956), Genetic aspects of preadolescent schizophrenia. *Amer. J. Psychiat.,* 112:599-606.

Kanner, L. (1932), *Child Psychiatry.* Springfield, Ill.: Charles C Thomas.

________ (1941), *In Defense of Mothers.* New York: Dodd Mead.

________ (1943), Autistic disturbances of affective contact. *Nerv. Child,* 2:217-250.

________ (1944), Early infantile autism. *J. Pediat.,* 25:211-217.

________ (1948), *Child Psychiatry* (2nd ed.), Springfield, Ill.: Charles C Thomas.

________ (1949a), *A Miniature Textbook of Feeblemindedness.* New York: Child Care Publications.

________ (1949b), Problems of nosology and psychodynamics of early infantile autism. *Amer. J. Orthopsychiat.,* 19:416-426.

________ (1952), Emotional interference with intellectual functioning. *Amer. J. Ment. Def.,* 56:701-707.

________ (1953), Parents' feelings about retarded children. *This Volume,* pp. 761-771.

________ (1960), Arnold Gesell's place in the history of developmental psychology and psychiatry. In: *Child Development and Child Psychiatry,* ed. C. Shagass and B. Pasamanick. Psychiatric Research Reports #13, pp. 1-9. Washington, D. C.: American Psychiatric Association.

________ and Eisenberg, L. (1955), Notes on the follow-up studies of autistic children. In: *Psychopathology of Childhood,* ed. P. H. Hoch and I. Zubin. New York: Grune & Stratton, pp. 227-239.

________ and Lesser, L. I. (1958), Early infantile autism. *This Volume,* pp. 647-669.

Kardiner, A. (1932), The bio-analysis of the epileptic reaction. *Psychoanal. Quart.,* 1:375-483.

Karlin, I. W. (1935), Incidence of spina bifida occulta in children with and without enuresis. *Amer. J. Dis. Child.,* 49:125-194.

Karpman, B. (1950), The psychopathic delinquent child, Round table, 1949. *Amer. J. Orthopsychiat.,* 20:223-265.

________ (1951), Psychopathic behavior in infants and children: a critical survey of the existing concepts, Round table, 1950. *Amer. J. Orthopsychiat.,* 21:223-272.

________ (1952), A differential study of psychopathic behavior in infants and children, Round table, 1951. *Amer. J. Orthopsychiat.,* 22:223-267.

________ (1953), Psychodynamics of child delinquency, Round table, 1952. *Amer. J. Orthopsychiat.,* 26:1-69.

________ (1955), Psychodynamics of child delinquency: further contributions, round table, 1953. *Amer. J. Orthopsychiat.,* 25:238-282.

Katan, A. (1937), The role of "displacement" in agoraphobia. *Int. J. Psycho-Anal.,* 32:41-50, 1951.

________ (1946), Experiences with enuretics. *The Psychoanalytic Study of the Child,* 2:241-255. New York: International Universities Press.

Kaufman, M. and Heiman, M., ed. (1964), *Evolution of Psychosomatic Concepts Anorexia Nervosa: A Paradigm.* New York: International Universities Press.

Kawi, A. A. and Pasamanick, B. (1958), Association of factors of pregnancy with reading disorders in childhood. *J.A.M.A.,* 166:1420-1423.

Kellogg, W. N. and Kellogg, L. A. (1933), *The Ape and the Child.* New York: McGraw-Hill, p. 182.

Kempf, E., ed. (1953), Comparative conditioned neuroses. *Ann. N. Y. Acad. Sci.,* 56:141-380.

Kemph, J. P., Zegans, L. S., Kooi, K. A. and Waggoner, R. W. (1963), The emotionally disturbed child with a convulsive disorder. *Psychosom. Med.,* 25:441-449.

Kennard, M. A. (1948), Myelinization of the central nervous system in relation to function. In: *Problems of Early Infancy.* New York: Josiah Macy, Jr. Foundation, pp. 78-81.

Kennedy, C. (1957), Physiologic characteristics of human cerebral maturation. In: *Etiologic Factors in Mental Retardation,* Ross Pediatric Research Conference No. 23. Columbus, Ohio: Ross Laboratories, pp. 17-23.

——— and Ramirez, L. (1964), Brain damage as a cause of behavior disturbance in children. In: *Brain Damage in Children: The* Biological and Social Aspects, ed. H. Birch. Baltimore: Williams & Wilkins, pp. 13-23.

Kennedy, R. (1948), *The Social Adjustment of Morons in a Connecticut City.* Hartford, Conn.: Mansfield Southbury Training Schools, Social Service Dept.

Kerr, J. (1897), School hygiene, in its mental, moral and physical aspects. *J. Roy. Stat. Soc.,* 60:613-680.

Kessler, J. W. (1966), *Psychopathology of Childhood.* Englewood Cliffs, N. J.: Prentice-Hall.

Kirk, S. (1958), *Early Education of the Mentally Retarded.* Urbana, Ill.: University of Illinois Press.

Kirsner, J. B. (1960), Experimental hypersensitivity reactions in the colon and the problem of ulcerative colitis. *Amer. J. Dig. Dis.,* 5:868-879.

Klapp, O. E. (1962), *Heroes, Villains, and Fools: The Changing American Character.* Englewood Cliffs, N. J.: Prentice-Hall.

Klein, E. (1945), Reluctance to go to school. *The Psychoanalytic Study of the Child,* 1:263-279. New York: International Universities Press.

Klein, M. (1931), A contribution to the theory of intellectual inhibition. *Int. J. Psycho-Anal.,* 12:206-218.

——— (1932), *The Psychoanalysis of Children.* London: Hogarth Press.

——— (1935), A contribution to the psychogenesis of manic-depressive states. In: *Contributions to Psychoanalysis.* London: Hogarth Press, 1948.

——— (1940), Mourning and its relation to manic-depressive states. In: *Contributions to Psychoanalysis.* London: Hogarth Press, 1948.

Kleitman, N. (1963), *Sleep and Wakefulness.* Chicago: University of Chicago Press.

Klemm, E. (1951), Neurotische halsmuskelkontraktur eines 9 jährigen mädchens ein beitrag zur hysteria in kindesalter (Hysteria in children: neurotic contracture of neck musculature in girl 9 years old). *Arch. für Kinderheilkunde* (Enke), 141:134-141.

Kluckhohn, C. (1951), Values and value orientations. In: *Toward a General Theory of Action,* ed. T. Parsons and E. A. Shils. Cambridge, Mass.: Harvard University Press, p. 395.

Klüver, H. (1955), Porphyrins in relation to the development of the nervous system. In: *Biochemistry of the Developing Nervous System: Proceedings of the First International Neurochemical Symposium, Held at Magdalen College, Oxford, July 13-17, 1954,* ed. H. Waelsch. New York: Academic Press, pp. 137-144.

——— and Bucy, P.C. (1939), Preliminary analysis of functions of the temporal lobes in monkeys. *Arch. Neurol. Psychiat.,* 42:979-1000.

Knapp, P. H. (1960), Acute bronchial asthma. II. Psychoanalytic observations on fantasy, emotional arousal, and partial discharge. *Psychosom. Med.,* 22:88-105.

——— (1963), The asthmatic child and the psychosomatic problem of asthma: toward a general theory. *This Volume,* pp. 591-609.

——— and Nemetz, S. J. (1957a), Personality variations in bronchial asthma. *Psychosom. Med.,* 19:443-465.

——— (1957b), Sources of tension in bronchial asthma. *Psychosom. Med.,* 19:466-485.

——— (1960), Acute bronchial asthma. I. Concomitant depression and excitement, and varied antecedent patterns in 406 attacks. *Psychosom. Med.,* 22:42-56.

Knobloch, H. (1958), Pneumonencephalograms and clinical behavior. *Pediatrics,* 22:13-19.

——— and Pasamanick, B. (1953), Further observations of the behavioral development of Negro infants. *J. Genet. Psychol.,* 83:137-157.

——— (1956), *A Developmental Questionnaire for Infants 40 Weeks of Age: An Evaluation.* Monogr. 61, Society for Research in Child Development. Yellow Springs: Antioch Press.

________ (1959b), Distribution of intellectual potential in an infant population. In: *Epidemiology of Mental Disorder,* ed. B. Pasamanick. Washington, D. C.: American Association for the Advancement of Science, pp. 249-272.

________ (1959b), The relationship of race and socioeconomic status to the development of motor behavior patterns in infancy. In: *Social Aspects of Psychiatry, ed.* B. Pasamanick. [Psychiatric Research Report No. 10.] Washington, D. C.: American Psychiatric Association, pp. 123-132.

________ (1959c), The syndrome of minimal cerebral damage in infancy. *J.A.M.A.,* 170:1384-1387.

________ (1960), Environmental factors affecting human development, before and after birth. *Pediatrics,* 26:210-218.

________ (1961), Some thoughts on the inheritance of intelligence. *Amer. J. Orthopsychiat.,* 31:454-473.

________ Harper, P. A., and Rider, R. V. (1959), The effect of prematurity on health and growth. *Amer. J. Pub. Health,* 49:1164-1173.

________ Rider, R., Harper P. and Pasamanick, B. (1956), The neuropsychiatric sequelae of prematurity: A longitudinal study. *J.A.M.A.,* 161:581-585.

Kohn, M. L. (1959a), Social class and parental values. *Amer. J. Sociol.,* 64:337-351.

________ (1959b), Social class and the exercise of parental authority. *Amer. Sociol. Rev.,* 24:352-366.

________ (1963), Social class and parent-child relationships: an interpretation. *This Volume,* pp. 189-202.

________ and Carroll, E. E. (1960), Social class and the allocation of parental responsibilities. *Sociometry,* 23:372-392.

Kopeloff, N., Kopeloff, L. M., and Pacella, B. L. (1947), The experimental production of epilepsy in animals. In: *Epilepsy: Psychiatric Aspects of Convulsive Disorders,* ed. P. H. Hoch and R. P. Knight. New York: Grune & Stratton, p. 163.

Korner, A. F. (1964), Some hypotheses regarding the significance of individual differences at birth for later development. *The Psychoanalytic Study of the Child,* 19:58-72. New York: International Universities Press.

Kozol, J. (1967), *Death at an Early Age: The Destruction of the Hearts and Minds of Negro Children in Boston Public Schools.* Houghton Press.

Kraepelin, E., (1904), *Psychiatrie.* Leipzig: Barth.

Kretschmer, E. (1926), *Hysteria.* New York: Nervous Mental Disease Monograph Series, No. 44.

Kris, E. (1947a), Methodology of clinical research, Round Table Discussion. *Amer. J. Orthopsychiat.,* 17:210-214.

________ (1947b), The nature of psychoanalytic propositions and their validations. In: *Freedom and Experience,* ed. S. Hook and M. R. Kobnitz. Ithica: Cornell University Press, pp. 239-259.

________ (1950b), The significance of Freud's earliest discoveries. *Int. J. Psycho-Anal.,* 31:108-116.

________ (1952), *Psychoanalytic Explorations in Art.* New York: International Universities Press.

________ (1954), Introduction (pp. 29-30) and footnotes (pp. 216-217). In: *The Origins of Psychoanalysis. Letters to Wilhelm Fliess, Drafts and Notes.* New York: Basic Books.

Kris, M. (1957), The use of prediction in a longitudinal study. *The Psychoanalytic Study of the Child,* 12:175-189. New York: International Universities Press.

Kubie, L. S. (1960), Psychoanalysis and Scientific Method. *J. Nerv. and Mental Dis.,* 131:495-512.

Kussmaul, A. (1877), Disturbance of speech. In: *Cyclopaedia of the Practice of Medicine,* ed. H. von Ziemssen, 14:770-778. New York: Williamwood.

Kvaraceus, W. C. and Miller, W. B. (1959), *Delinquent Behavior: Culture and the Individual.* Washington, D. C.: National Education Association, pp. 68-69.

LaBarre, W. (1956), They shall take up serpents. The Southern snake cult. A study in culture and psychopathology. Department of Anthropology, Duke University, Durham, N. C.

Lacey, J. I. and Wilder, (1956), The evaluation of autonomic responses: toward a general solution. *Ann. N. Y. Acad. Sc.,* 67:123-164.

Lamont, J. H. (1963), Which children outgrow asthma and which do not. In: *The Asthmatic Child: Psychosomatic Approach to Problems and Treatment,* ed. H. I. Schneer. New York: Hoeber Medical Division of Harper & Row, pp. 16-26.

Lampl-de Groot, J. (1947), The preoedipal phase in the development of the male child. *The Psychoanalytic Study of the Child,* 2:75:83. New York: International Universities Press.

Landes, R. (1938), *The Ojibwa Woman.* New York: Columbia University Press, pp. 1-50.

Landis, C., Zubin, J. and Mettler, F. A. (1950), The functions of the human frontal lobe. *J. Psychol.,* 30:123-138.

——— (1952), The frontal lobes and anguish: a new formulation of an old problem. *J.N.M.D.,* 115:203-214.

Langworthy, O. R. (1933), Development of behavior patterns and myelinization of the nervous system in the human fetus and infant. Publications 139-143. Carnegie Institution of Washington.

——— (1955), Newer concepts of the central control of emotions. A review. *Amer. J. Psychiat.,* 111:481-486.

Lapouse, R. and Monk, M. A. (1958), An epidemiologic study of behavior characteristics in children. *Amer. J. Public Hlth.,* 48:1134-1144.

Lashley, K. S. (1929), *Brain Mechanisms and Intelligence: A Quantitative Study of Injuries to the Brain.* Chicago: University of Chicago Press, p. 186.

——— (1938), Experimental analysis of instinctive behavior. *Psychol. Rev.,* 45:445-472.

——— (1952), Patterns of organization in the central nervous system. *Res. Publ. A.R.N.M.D.,* 30:529-547.

Laubenthal, F. (1941), Zur erbhygienischen bewertung der kongenitalen wort blindheit. *Der Erbarzt,* 9:156.

Laufer, M., Denhoff, E. and Salomons, G. (1957), Hyperkinetic impulse disorder in children's behavior problems. *Psychosom. Med.,* 19:38-49.

Launay, C. (1952a), Étude d'ensemble des inaptitudes à la lecture. *Semaine hôp. Paris,* 28:1463-1474.

——— (1952b), Étude d'une classe d'enfants de 6 à 7 ans inaptes à la lecture. *Semaine hôp. Paris,* 28:1459-1463.

Lazarus, A. A. (1960), The elimination of children's phobias by deconditioning. In: *Behaviour Therapy and the Neuroses,* ed. H. J. Eysenck. Oxford: Pergamon Press, pp. 114-122.

——— and Rachman, S. (1957), The use of systematic desensitization in psychotherapy. *S. African Med. J.,* 31:934-937.

Lennox, W. G. (1932), Epilepsy. In: *Nelson New Loose-Leaf Medicine,* 6:261. New York: Nelson.

——— (1941), *Science and Seizures: New Light on Epilepsy and Migraine.* New York: Harper & Bros.

——— and Cobb, S. (1933), Epilepsy. XIII. Aura in epilepsy; a statistical review of 1,359 cases. *Arch. Neurol. Psychiat.,* 30:374-387.

Levy, D. M. (1925), Resistant behavior of children. *Amer. J. Psychiat.,* 4:503-507.

——— (1928), Finger sucking and accessory movements in early infancy. *Amer. J. Psychiat.,* 7:881-918.

——— (1934), Experiments on the sucking reflex and social behavior of dogs. *Amer. J. Orthopsychiat.,* 4:203-224.

——— (1936), Aggressive-sumbissive behavior and the Fröhlich syndrome. *Arch. Neurol. & Psychiat.,* 36:991-1020.

——— (1937a), Attitude therapy. *Amer. J. Orthopsychiat.,* 7:103-113.

——— (1937b), Primary affect hunger. *Amer. J. Psychiat.,* 94:644-652.

——— (1938), Release therapy in young children. *Psychiat.,* 1:381-389.

——— (1939), Trends in therapy: release therapy. *Amer. J. Orthopsychiat.,* 9:713-736.

——— (1940), Psychotherapy and children. *Amer. J. Orthopsychiat.,* 10:905-910.

——— (1943), Maternal overprotection. *This Volume,* pp. 290-295.

——— (1944), On the problem of movement restraint, tics, stereotyped movements hyperactivity. *Amer. J. Orthopsychiat.,* 14:644-671.

——— (1945), Psychic trauma of operations in children. *Amer. J. Dis. Child.,* 69:7-25.

——— (1950), On evaluating the "specific event" as a source of anxiety. In: *Anxiety,* ed. P. H. Hoch and J. Zubin. New York: Grune & Stratton, pp. 140-149.

________ (1951a), Critical evaluation of the present state of child psychiatry. *Amer. J. Psychiat.,* 108:481-494.

________ (1951b), Observations of attitudes and behavior in child health center; sample studies of maternal feelings, dependency, resistant behavior, and innoculation fears. *Amer. J. Pub. Health,* 41:182-190.

________ (1953), The early development of independent and oppositional behavior. In: *Midcentury Psychiatry,* ed. R. Grinker. Springfield, Ill.: Charles C Thomas, pp. 113-122.

________ (1955), Oppositional syndromes, and oppositional behavior. *This Volume,* pp. 340-359.

________ (1958), *Behavioral Analysis.* Springfield, Ill.: Charles C Thomas.

________ Meyers, D. and Goldfarb, W. (1962), Relational behavior of schizophrenic children and their mothers: a methodological study. Read before the Orthopsychiatry Association, March, 1962.

________ and Tulchin, S. H. (1923), I. The resistance of infants and children during mental tests. *J. Exper. Psychol.,* 6:304-322. II. 8:209-224, 1925.

Levy, K. (1934), Vom bettnässen des kindes. *Zeitschr. f. Psychoanal. Paed.,* 8:178-195.

________ (1960), Simultaneous analysis of a mother and her adolescent daughter: the mother's contribution to the loosening of the infantile object tie. With an introduction by Anna Freud. *The Psychoanalytic Study of the Child,* 15:378-391. New York: International Universities Press.

Levy, R. (1947), effects of institutional vs. boarding home care on a group of infants. *J. Personal.,* 15:233-241.

Lewin, K. (1935), *A Dynamic Theory of Personality.* New York: McGraw-Hill.

________ (1936), *Principles of Topological Psychology.* New York: McGraw-Hill.

________ (1948), *Resolving Social Conflicts.* New York: Harper and Bros.

Lewis, H. (1954), *Deprived Children.* Oxford University Press.

Liddell, H. S. (1944), Conditioned reflex method and experimental neurosis. In: *Personality and the Behavior Disorders,* ed. J. McV. Hunt, 1:389-412. New York: Ronald Press.

Lilienfeld, A. M. and Pasamanick, B. (1954), Association of maternal and fetal factors with the development of epilepsy. I. Abnormalities in the prenatal and paranatal periods. *J.A.M.A.,* 155:719-724.

________ (1955), The association of prenatal and paranatal factors with the development of cerebral palsy and epilepsy. *Amer. J. Obst. & Gynec.,* 70:93-101.

________ (1956), The association of maternal and fetal factors with the development of mental deficiency. II. Relationship to maternal age, birth order, previous reproductive loss and degree of mental deficiency. *Amer. J. Ment. Defic.,* 60:557-569.

________ and Rogers, M. (1955), Relationship between pregnancy experience and the development of certain neuropsychiatric disorders in childhood. *Amer. J. Pub. Health,* 45:637-643.

Linch, A. (1956), The influence of certain cultural factors in a segment of the patient population of the University of North Carolina Memorial Hospital Psychiatric Center. Presented at the Annual Meeting of the American Orthopsychiatric Association, New York.

Lindemann, E. (1944), Symptomatology and management of acute grief. *Amer. J. Psychiat.,* 101:141-148.

Lindsley, D. B., Schreiner, L. H., Knowles, W. B. and Magoun, H. W. (1950), Behavioral and EEG changes following chronic brain stem lesions in the cat. *EEG Clin. Neurophysiol.,* 2:483-498.

Linton, R. (unpublished), Class notes on the Marquesans.

Lippard, V. W. (1939), Immunologic response to ingestion of foods by normal and by eczematous infants. *A.M.A. Amer. J. Dis. Child.,* 57:524-540.

Lippman, H. (1932), The treatment of enuresis. Address delivered at the Minnesota State Conference of Social Work, September 24, 1932.

________ (1954), Antisocial acting out, Symposium. *Amer. J. Orthopsychiat.,* 24:667-696.

Lipset, S. M. (1959), Democracy and working-class authoritarianism. *Amer. Sociol. Rev.,* 24:482-501.

Lipton, E. L., Richmond, J. B., and Lustman, S. L. (1955), Autonomic function in the neonate and psychosomatic disease (abstract). *A.M.A. Amer. J. Dis. Child.,* 90:491.

________ Weinberger, H. and Hersher, L. (1958), An approach to the evaluation of neonate autonomic responses. Paper presented at the Annual Meeting of the American Psychosomatic Society, Cincinnati, March 31, 1958.

——— and Steinschneider, A. (1964), Studies on the psychophysiology of infancy. *Merrill-Palmer Quart.* 10:103-117.

——— and Richmond, J. (1966), Psychophysiologic disorders in children. In: *Review of Child Development Research,* ed. L. Hoffman and M. Hoffman, 2:169-220. New York: Russell Sage Foundation.

Litin, E. M., Giffin, M. E., and Johnson, A. M. (1956), Parental influences in unusual sexual behavior in children. *Psychoanal. Quart.,* 25:37-55.

Littman, R. A., Moore, R. C. A. and Pierce-Jones, J. (1957), Social class differences in child rearing: a third community for comparison with Chicago and Newton. *Amer. Sociol. Rev.,* 22:694-704, esp. p. 703.

Livingston, S. (1954), *The Diagnosis and Treatment of Convulsive Disorders in Children.* Springfield, Ill.: Charles C Thomas, pp. 111-113.

Lloyd, D. P. C. (1941), A direct central inhibitory action of dromically conducted impulses. *J. Neurophysiol.,* 4:184-190.

——— (1946), Integrative pattern of excitation and inhibition in two-neuron reflex arcs. *J. Neurophysiol.,* 9:439-444.

Loewenstein, R. (1938), L'origine du masochisme et la theorie des pulsions. *Rev. Franc. de Psa.,* 10:293-321.

——— (1940), On vital and somatic drives. *Int. J. Psycho-Anal.,* 21:377-400.

——— (1957), Some thoughts on interpretation in the theory and practice of psychoanalysis. *The Psychoanalytic Study of the Child,* 12:127-150. New York: International Universities Press.

——— et al., eds. (1966), *Psychoanalysis—A General Psychology: Essays in Honor of Heinz Hertmann.* New York: International Universities Press.

Lorenz, K. (1935), Der kumpan in der umwelt des vogels. *J. fuer Ornithol.,* 83:137-213.

——— (1950), The comparative method in studying innate behaviour patterns. In: *Physiological Mechanisms in Animal Behaviour,* ed. J. F. Danielli and R. Brown, Society of Experimental Biology Symposium. Cambridge: Cambridge University Press, Series #4, pp. 221-268.

——— (1952), *King Solomon's Ring.* London: Methuen.

——— (1958), Personal communication.

——— (1965), *Evolution and Modification of Behavior.* Chicago: University of Chicago Press.

——— (1966), *On Aggression.* New York: Harcourt, Brace & World.

Lovibond, S. H. (1964), *Conditioning and Enuresis.* New York: Macmillan.

Lowrey, L. G. (1940), Personality distortion and early institutional care. *Amer. J. Orthopsychiat.,* 10:576-585.

——— (1950), In: Symposium, 1950, training in the field of orthopsychiatry: findings of the membership study in relation to training and membership. *Amer. J. Orthopsychiat.,* 20:667-693.

Luce, G. G. and Segal, J. (1966), *Sleep.* New York: Coward-McCann.

Lucretius (Titus Lucretius Carus) (1951), *De Rerum Natura.* Translated as *The Nature of the Universe,* by R. E. Latham. Harmonsworth: Penguin Books, pp. 105-106.

Luisa Palacios, T. S., De Sandoval, D. M. and Herrera, C. (1953), Servicio medico social; un caso de histeria de conversion (Medico-social service; case of conversion hysteria). *Bol. Med. Hosp. Infant. Mex.,* 10:479-486.

Lustman, S. L. (1963), Some issues in psychoanalytic research. *The Psychoanalytic Study of the Child,* 18:51-74. New York: International Universities Press.

Macciotta, G. (1931), Spasmophilic forms of enuresis in children. *Pediatria,* 38:1145. (Quoted from *Child. Devel. Abs.,* 5:46.)

Maccoby, E. (1966), *Development of Sex Differences.* Stanford: Stanford University Press.

MacFarlane, J. W., Allen, L., and Honzik, M. P. (1962), *A Developmental Study of the Behavior Problems of Normal Children between Twenty-one Months and Fourteen Years.* [University of California Publications in Child Development, Volume II.] Berkeley: University of California Press.

McGuinness, A. C. (1935), The treatment of enuresis in childhood. *Med. Clin. North Amer.,* 19:287-294.

MacKenzie, J. N. (1886), The projection of the so-called "rose cold" by means of an artificial rose. *Amer. J. Med. Sci.,* 91:45-57.

MacLean, P. D. (1952), Some psychiatric implications of physiological studies on frontotemporal portions of limbic system (visceral brain). *EEG Clin. Neurophysiol.,* 4:407-418.

________ (1955), The limbic system ("visceral brain") and emotional behavior. *Arch. Neurol. Psychiat.,* 73:130-134.

Maenchen, A. (1955), Sleep disturbances and ego developments. Unpublished manuscript presented to the American Psychoanalytic Association, December, 1955. Abstracted by M. R. Friend (1956), Panel reports, On sleep disturbances in children. *J. Amer. Psychoanal. Assn.,* 4:514-525.

Magoun, H. W. (1952), An ascending reticular activating system in the brain stem. *Arch. Neurol. Psychiat.,* 67:145-154.

________ and Rhines, R. (1947), *Spasticity: The Stretch Reflex and the Extra-pyramidal Systems.* Springfield, Ill.: Charles C Thomas, p. 59.

Mahler, M. (1945), Ego psychology applied to behavior problems. In: *Modern Trends in Child Psychiatry,* ed. N. D. C. Lewis and B. L. Pacella. New York: International Universities Press, pp. 43-56

________ (1947), Various clinical pictures of schizophrenic children. Paper read at the Schilder Society, New York (unpublished).

________ (1949), Remarks on psychoanalysis with psychotic children. *Quart. J. Child Behavior,* 1:18-21.

________ (1950), Discussion remarks to papers by Anna Freud and Ernst Kris. Symposium on Problems of Child Development, Stockbridge, Mass. (unpublished).

________ (1952), On child psychosis and schizophrenia: Autistic and Symbiotic Infantile Psychoses. *The Psychoanalytic Study of the Child,* 7:286-305. New York: International Universities Press. See also *this Volume,* pp. 670-687.

________ (1958), Autism and symbiosis: two extreme disturbances of identity, *Int. J. Psycho-Anal.,* 39:77-83.

________ (1963), Thoughts about development and individuation. *The Psychoanalytic Study of the Child,* 18:307-324. New York: International Universities Press.

________ (1965), On early infantile psychosis: the symbiotic and autistic syndromes. *J. Amer. Acad. Child Psychiat.,* 4:554-568.

________ (1968), *On Human Symbiosis and the Vicissitudes of Individuation.* New York: International Universities Press.

________ and Gosliner, B. J. (1955), On symbiotic child psychosis: genetic, dynamic and restitutive aspects. *The Psychoanalytic Study of the Child,* 10:195-212. New York: International Universities Press.

________ Luke, J. A., and Daltroff, W. (1945), Clinical and follow-up study of the tic syndrome in children. *Amer. J. Orthopsychiat.,* 15:631-647.

________ Ross, J. R., Jr., and Fries, de Z. (1949), Clinical studies in benign and malignant cases of childhood psychosis (schizophrenialike). *Amer. J. Orthopsychiat.,* 19:295-305.

Margolin, S. G. (1953), Genetic and dynamic psychophysiological determinants of pathophysiological processes. In: *The Psychosomatic Concept in Psychoanalysis,* ed. F. Deutsch. New York: International Universities Press, pp. 3-36.

Mark, H. J., Meyer, P. and Pasamanick, B. (1958), Variability of critical flicker fusion thresholds in brain injured children. *A.M.A. Arch. Neurol. Psychiat.,* 80:682-688.

________ (1958), Asynchronism and apparent movement thresholds in brain-injured children. *J. Consult. Psychol.,* 22:173-177.

________ and Pasamanick, B. (1958), Variability of light perception thresholds in brain injured children. *J. Abnorm. & Soc. Psychol.,* 57:25-28.

Marmor, J. (1953), Orality in the hysterical personality. *J. Amer. Psychoanal. Assn.,* 1:656-671.

________ ed. (1968), *Modern Psychoanalysis: New Directions and Perspectives.* New York: Basic Books.

Masserman, J. H. (1946), *Principles of Dynamic Psychiatry.* Philadelphia: Saunders, pp. 101-103.

Masterson, J. F. (1967), *The Psychiatric Dilemma of Adolescence.* Boston: Little, Brown.

McDermott, J. F. and Finch, S. M. (1967), Ulcerative colitis in children: reassessment of a dilemma. *J. Amer. Acad. Child Psychiat.,* 6:512-525.

——— et al. (1965), Social class and mental illness in children: observation of blue collar families. *Amer. J. Orthopsychiat.,* 35:500-508.

McDermott, N. T. and Cobb, S. (1939), A psychiatric survey of 50 cases of bronchial asthma. *Psychosom. Med.,* 1:203-244.

McGraw, M. B. (1946), Maturation of behavior. In: *Manual of Child Psychology,* ed. L. Carmichael. New York: Wiley, pp. 332-369.

McKay, B. (1942), A study of IQ changes in a group of girls paroled from a state school for mental defectives. *Amer. J. Ment. Def.,* 46:496-500.

Mead, M. (1939), *From the South Seas: Studies of Adolescence and Sex in Primitive Societies.* New York: Morrow.

——— (1949), *Male and Female.* New York: Morrow.

——— (1954a), Cultural discontinuities and personality transformation. *J. Social Issues,* Supplement Series #8, pp. 3-16.

——— (1954b), Research on primitive children. In: *Manual of Child Psychology,* 2nd ed., ed. L. Carmichael. New York: Wiley, pp. 735-780.

——— and Wolfenstein, M., eds. (1955), *Childhood in Contemporary Cultures.* Chicago: University of Chicago Press.

Meade, G. H. (1934), *Mind, Self and Society.* Chicago: University of Chicago Press.

Meek, L. (1925), *A Study of Learning and Retention in Young Children.* New York: Teachers College, Columbia University.

Meili, R. (1957), *Anfange der Charakterentwicklung.* Bern & Stuttgart: Huber.

——— (1959), A longitudinal study of personality development. In: *Dynamic Psychopathology in Childhood,* ed. L. Jessner and E. Pavenstedt. New York: Grune & Stratton, pp. 106-123.

Menninger, K. A. (1926), Psychoanalytic study of a case of organic epilepsy. *Psychoanal. Rev.,* 13:187-199.

——— and Chidester, L. (1936), The application of psychoanalytic methods of the study of mental retardation. *Amer. J. Orthopsychiat.,* 6:616-625.

Meyer, A. (1903), An attempt at analysis of the neurotic constitution. *Amer. J. Psychol.,* 14:354-367. (Reprinted in *The Commonsense Psychiatry of Dr. Adolf Meyer: Fifty-Two Selected Papers,* ed. A. Lief. New York: McGraw-Hill, 1948, pp. 103-116.)

Meyer, B. C. and Weinroth, L. A. (1957), Observations on psychological aspects of anorexia nervosa: report of a case. *Psychosom. Med.,* 19:389-398.

——— (1959), Discussion of: Psychological and physiological aspects of marked obesity in a young adult female. *J. Hillside Hosp.,* 8:206-209.

Meyers, D. and Goldfarb, W. (1961), Studies of perplexity in mothers of schizophrenic children. *Amer. J. Orthopsychiat.,* 3:551-564.

——— (1962), Psychiatric appraisal of parents and siblings of schizophrenic children. *Amer. J. Psychiat.,* 118:902-915.

——— Levy, D. M., and Goldfarb, W. (1963), Analysis of communication between mothers and their schizophrenic children: problem of clarity of communication. Read before the American Orthopsychiatric Association Institute of Research in Childhood Schizophrenia, March, 1963.

Michaels, J. J. (1944), A psychiatric adventure in comparative pathophysiology of the infant and adult. *J. Nerv. Ment. Dis.,* 100:49-63.

——— (1955), *Disorders of Character: Persistent Enuresis, Juvenile Delinquency and Psychopathic Personality.* Springfield, Ill.: Charles C Thomas.

Middlemore, M. P. (1941), *The Nursing Couple.* London: Hamish Hamilton Medical Books.

Miller, D. (1969), *The Age Between.* London: Cornmarket-Hutchinson.

Miller, D. R. and Swanson, G. E. (1958), *The Changing American Parent.* New York: Wiley.

Miller, H. and Baruch, D. (1948), Psychosomatic studies of children with allergic manifestations. I. Maternal rejection: a study of 63 cases. *Psychosom. Med.,* 10:275-278.

Miller, S. M. and Riessman, F. (1961), The working class subculture: a new view. *Social Problems,* 9:86-97.

Miller, W. B. (1958), Lower class culture as a generating milieu of gang delinquency. *J. Social Issues,* 14:5-19.

Minuchin, S. et al. (1968), *Families of the Slums: An Exploration of Their Structure and Treatment.* New York: Basic Books.

________ (1953), Psychoanalysis and the biological sciences. In: *20 Years of Psychoanalysis,* ed. F. Alexander and H. Ross. New York: Norton, pp. 155-176.

Mittelmann, B. (1938), Juvenile adiposgenital dystrophy: neurologic and psychopathologic aspects. *Endocrinology,* 23:637-655.

________ (1947), Psychopathology of epilepsy. In: *Epilepsy: Psychiatric Aspects of Convulsive Disorders,* ed. P. H. Hoch and R. P. Knight. New York: Grune & Stratton, pp. 136-148.

Mohr, G. J. (1928), Emotional factors in nutrition work with children. *Ment. Hyg.,* 12:366-367.

________ Richmond, J. B., Garner, A. M., and Eddy, E. J. (1955), A program for the study of children with psychosomatic disorders. In: *Emotional Problems of Early Childhood,* ed. G. Caplan. New York: Basic Books, pp. 251-268.

________ Selesnick, S. and Augenbraun, B. (1963), Family dynamics in early childhood asthma: some mental health considerations. In: *The Asthmatic Child: Psychosomatic Approach to Problems and Treatment,* ed. H. I. Schneer. New York: Hoeber Medical Division of Harper & Row, pp. 103-117.

________ Tausend, H., Selesnick, S. and Augenbraun, B. (1961), Studies of eczema and asthma in the preschool child. Presented at American Psychiatric Association Meeting, Chicago, May, 1961.

________ and Waterhouse, E. H. (1929), Enuresis in children. *Amer. J. Dis. Child.,* 37:1135-1145.

Moltz, H. (1960), Imprinting: empirical basis and theoretical significance. *Psychol. Bull.,* 57:291-314.

Money, J., Hampson, J. G. and Hampson, J. L. (1955), An examination of some basic sexual concepts: the evidence of human hermaphroditism. *Bull. Johns Hop. Hosp.,* 98:43-57.

________ ed. (1965), *Sex Research: New Developments.* New York: Holt, Rinehart & Winston.

________ (1966), *The Disabled Reader: Education of the Dyslexic Child.* Baltimore: Johns Hopkins Press.

Monroe, M. (1928), *Methods for Diagnosis and Treatment of Cases of Reading Disability.* Clark University Press.

________ (1932), *Children Who Cannot Read.* Chicago: University of Chicago Press.

Montague, M. F. A. (1950), Constitutional and prenatal factors in infant and child health. In: *Symposium on the Healthy Personality,* ed. M. J. E. Senn. New York: Josiah Macy, Jr. Foundation, pp. 148-210.

Morel, B. (1857), *Traite des Degenerescences Physiques, Intellectuelles et Morales de L'Espece Humaine.* Paris: Bailliere.

Morgan, W. P. (1896), A case of congenital word blindness. *Brit. Med. J.,* 2:1378-1379.

Morrell, F. and Ross, M. H. (1953), Central inhibition in cortical conditioned reflexes. *Arch. Neurol. Psychiat.,* 70:611-616.

Moruzzi, G. and Magoun, H. W. (1949), Brain stem reticular formation and activation of the EEG. *EEG Clin. Neurophysiol.,* 1:445-473.

Mowrer, O. H. (1953), *Psychotherapy: Theory and Research.* New York: Ronald Press.

________ and Mowrer, W. (1938), Enuresis: a method for its study and treatment. *Amer. J. Orthopsychiat.,* 8:436-459.

Mundy, L. (1957), Environmental influence on intellectual function as measured by intelligence tests. *Brit. J. Med. Psychol.,* 30:194-201.

Murie, A. (1944), *The Wolves of Mt. McKinley.* Washington, D. C.: Government Printing Office.

Murphy, L. B. and Collaborators (1962), *The Widening World of Childhood: Paths Toward Mastery.* New York: Basic Books.

Murphy, R. C. and Preston, C. E. (unpublished), Three autistic brothers. Presented at American Orthopsychiatric Association.

Murray, C. D. (1930), Psychogenic factors in the etiology of ulcerative colitis and bloody diarrhea. *Amer. J. Med. Sci.,* 180:239-248.
Murray, W. (1960), Some major assumptions underlying the development of intelligence tests. Unpublished.
Muus, R. E. (1962), *Theories of Adolescence.* New York: Random House.
Myer, J. S. and Hunter, J. (1952), Behavior deficits following diencephalic lesions. *Neurology,* 2:112-129.
Nagera, H. (1966a), *Early Childhood Disturbances, the Infantile Neurosis and the Adulthood Disturbances.* [*The Psychoanalytic Study of the child,* Monogr. 2.] New York: International Universities Press.
———— (1966b), Sleep and its disturbances approached developmentally. *The Psychoanalytic Study of the Child,* 21:393-447. New York: International Universities Press.
———— (1969), Children's reaction to the death of important objects: a developmental approach. *The Psychoanalytic Study of the Child,* 25:360-400. New York: International Universities Press.
Nash, E., Nash, H., Knobloch, H. and Pasamanick, B. Unpublished data.
Nelson J. B. (1956), Anlage of productiveness in boys: womb envy. *This Volume,* pp. 360-372.
Nielson, J. M. (1941), *A Textbook of Clinical Neurology.* New York: Hoeber, p. 235.
Noelpp-Eschenhagen, I. and Noelpp, B. (1954), New contributions to experimental asthma. *Progress in Allergy,* 4:361-456. Basel: Karger.
Norton, A. (1952), Incidence of neurosis related to maternal age and birth order. *Brit. J. Soc. Med.,* 6:253-258.
Nunberg, H. (1930), The synthetic function of the ego. *Psycho-anal.,* 12:123-140, 1931.
———— (1932), *Allgemeine Neurosenlebre auf Psychoanalytischer Grundlage.* Hans Huber, Chapter III.
Oberndorf, C. P. (1935), The psychogenic factors in asthma. *N. Y. J. Med.,* 35:41-48.
Offer, D. (1967), Normal adolescents. *Arch. Gen. Psychiat.,* 17:285-290.
O'Gorman, G. (1970), *The Nature of Childhood Autism.* New York: Appleton-Century-Crofts.
Olden, C. (1952), Notes on child rearing in America. *The Psychoanalytic Study of the Child,* 7:387-392. New York: International Universities Press.
Olson, W. C. (1949), *Child Development.* Boston: Heath.
Oltman, J. E., McGarry, J., and Friedman, S. (1952), Parental deprivation and the "broken home" in dementia praecox and other mental disorders. *Amer. J. Psychiat.,* 108:685-694.
Omwake, E. and Solnit, A. (1961), "It isn't fair:" the treatment of a blind child. *The Psychoanalytic Study of the Child,* 16:352-404. New York: International Universities Press.
Orton, S. T. (1925), Word-blindness in school children. *Arch. Neurol. Psychiat.,* 14:585-615.
———— (1928a), An impediment to learning to read. *School & Soc.,* 28:286-290.
———— (1928b), Specific reading disability–strephosymbolia. *J.A.M.A.,* 90:1095-1098.
———— (1937), *Reading, Writing and Speech Problems in Children.* New York: Norton.
Ottenberg, P., Stein, M., Lewis, J., and Hamilton, C. (1958), Learned asthma in the guinea pig. *Psychosom. Med.,* 20:395-400.
Paine, R. S. (1965), The contribution of developmental neurology to child psychiatry. *J. Amer. Acad. Child Psychiat.,* 4:353-386.
Parkes, C. M. (1959), Morbid grief reactions: a review of the literature. D.P.M. Dissertation, University of London. (Version for publication in preparation.)
Parsons, T. (1954), *Essays in Sociological Theory,* rev. ed. Glencoe, Ill.: Free Press of Glencoe, pp. 304-305.
———— and Bales, R. F. (1955), *Family, Socialization and Interaction Process.* Glencoe, Ill.: Free Press of Glencoe, esp. p. 45.
Pasamanick, B. (1946), A comparative study of the behavioral development of Negro infants. *J. Genet. Psychol.,* 69:3-44.
———— (1950), The epidemiologic investigations of some prenatal factors in the production of neuropsychiatric disorders. In: *Field Studies in the Mental Disorders,* ed. J. Zubin. New York: Grune & Stratton, pp. 173-212.
———— (1952), Patterns of research in mental hygiene. *Psychoanal. Quart.,* 26:577-589.

________ (1953), The scope and limitations of psychiatry. In: *Basic Problems in Psychiatry,* ed. J. Wortis. New York: Grune & Stratton, pp. 26-51.

________ (1956), The epidemiology of behavior disorders of childhood. In: *Neurology and Psychiatry in Childhood.* Research Publications of the Association for Nervous and Mental Disease. Baltimore; Williams & Wilkins, 34:397-403.

________ (1959), Research on the influence of sociocultural variables upon organic factors in mental retardation. *Amer. J. Ment. Def.,* 64:316-320.

________ Constantinou, F. K. and Lilienfeld, A. M. (1956), Pregnancy experience and the development of childhood speech disorders: an epidemiologic study of the association with maternal and fetal factors. *A.M.A. Amer. J. Dis. Child.,* 91:113-118.

________ and Kawi, A. (1956), A study of the association of prenatal and paranatal factors with the development of tics in children: a preliminary investigation. *J. Pediat.,* 48:596-601.

________ and Knobloch, H. (1955), Language development in Negro children and some implications for the testing of intelligence. *J. Abnorm. & Soc. Psychol.,* 50:401-402.

________ (1957), Some early organic precursors of racial behavioral differences. *J. Nat. Med. Assn.,* 49:372-375.

________ (1958), The contribution of some organic factors to school retardation in Negro children. *J. Negro Educ.,* 27:4-9.

________ and Knobloch, H. (1960), Brain injury and reproductive casualty. *Amer. J. Orthopsychiat.,* 30:298-305.

________ (1961), Epidemiologic studies on the complication of pregnancy and the birth process. *This Volume,* pp. 825-837.

________ Knobloch, H., and Lilienfeld, A. M. (1956), Socioeconomic status and some precursors of neuropsychiatric disorders. *Amer. J. Orthopsychiat.,* 26:594-601.

________ and Lilienfeld, A. M. (1955), Association of maternal and fetal factors with the development of mental deficiency. I. Abnormalities in the prenatal and paranatal periods. *J.A.M.A.,* 159:155-160.

________ Rogers, M. E., and Lilienfeld, A. M. (1956c), Pregnancy experience and the development of childhood behavior disorder. *Amer. J. Psychiat.,* 112:613-617.

Odier, C., *Anxiety and Magical Thinking.* New York: International Universities Press, 1956.

Pavenstedt, E. (1955), History of a child with an atypical development, and some vicissitudes of his treatment. In: *The Emotional Problems of Early Childhood,* ed. G. Caplan. New York: Basic Books, pp. 379-405.

________, chrmn. (1962), Symposium on research in infancy and early childhood. *J. Amer. Acad. Child Psychiat.,* 1:# 1, whole issue.

________ (1965), A comparison of the child-rearing environment of upper-lower and very low-lower class families. *Amer. J. Orthopsychiat.,* 35:89-98.

Pavlov, I. P. (1928a), *Lectures on Conditioned Reflexes.* New York: Liveright.

________ (1928b), *Lectures on Conditioned Reflexes.* Translated by W. H. Gantt. New York: International Publishers, pp. 205-212.

Pearson, G. H. J. and English, O. S. (1937), *Common Neuroses of Children and Adults.* New York: Norton, p. 162.

________ (1941), Effect of operative procedures on the emotional life of the child. *Amer. J. Dis. Child.,* 62:716-729.

________ (1952), A survey of learning difficulties in children. *The Psychoanalytic Study of the Child,* 7:322-386. New York: International Universities Press.

________ (1954), *Psychoanalysis and the Education of the Child.* New York: Norton.

Peiper, A. (1956), *Die Eigenart der Kindlichen Hirntätigkeit,* 2nd ed. Leipzig: Thieme.

________ (1963), *Cerebral Function in Infancy and Childhood,* 3rd ed. New York: Consultants Bureau.

Penfield, W. (1952), Epileptic automatism and the centrencephalic integrating system. *Res. Publ. A.R.N.M.D.,* 30:513-528.

________ and Jasper, H. (1946), Highest level seizures. *Res. Publ. A.R.N.M.D.,* 26:252-271.

________ and Kristiansen, K. (1951), *Epileptic Seizure Patterns: A Study of the Localizing Value of Initial Phenomena in Focal Cortical Seizures.* Springfield, Ill.: Charles C Thomas, p. 10.

Peterson, D. B., Sumner, J. W., Jr., and Jones, G. A. (1950), Role of hypnosis in differentiation of epileptic from convulsive-like seizures. *Amer. J. Psychiat.,* 107:428-433.

Petö, E. (1937), Säugling und mutter. *Zeit. f. Psa. Pad.,* 11:244-252.

Piaget, J. (1928), *Judgment and Reasoning in the Child.* New York: Harcourt, Brace.

——— (1929), *The Child's Conception of the World.* New York: Harcourt, Brace. London: Routledge & Kegan Paul, 1951.

——— (1930), *The Child's Concept of Physical Causality.* London: Kegan Paul.

——— (1932a), *The Language and Thought of the Child.* London: Routledge.

——— (1932b), *The Moral Judgment of the Child.* London: Kegan Paul.

——— (1952), *The Origins of Intelligence in Children.* New York: International Universities Press.

——— (1954), *The Construction of Reality in the Child.* New York: Basic Books.

——— (1962a), The stages of the intellectual development of the child. *This Volume,* pp. 157-166.

——— (1962b), The relation of affectivity to intelligence in the mental development of the child. *This Volume,* pp. 167-175.

Pilot, M. L. and Spiro, H. M. (1961), Comments on the use of blood pepsin (pepsinogen) as a research technique. *Psychosom. Med.,* 23:420-425.

Pollack, M. and Goldfarb, W. (1957), The face-hand test in schizophrenic children. *A.M.A. Arch. Neurol. Psychiat.,* 77:635-642.

——— and Krieger, H. P. (1958), Oculomotor and postural patterns in schizophrenic children. *A.M.A. Arch. Neurol. Psychiat.,* 79:720-726.

Pollack, R. and Goldfarb W. (unpublished), Study of optikinetic nystagmus in schizophrenic children.

Pollock, G. H. (1961), Mourning and adaptation. *Int. J. Psycho-Anal.,* 42:341-361.

Pond, D. A. (1952), Psychiatric aspects of epilepsy in children. *J. Ment. Sci.,* 98:404-410.

Potter, H. (1922), Personality in the mental defective with a method for its evaluation. *Ment. Hyg.,* 6:487-497.

——— (1927a), An introductory study of the erotic behavior of idiots. *J. Nerv. Ment. Dis.,* 65:497-507.

——— (1927b), Mental deficiency and the psychiatrist. *Amer. J. Psychiat.,* 83:691-698.

——— (1933), Schizophrenia in children. *Amer. J. Psychiat.,* 12:1253-1269.

Potter, H. W. (1964), Mental retardation in historical perspective. *This Volume,* pp. 733-743.

Powers, D. A. (1955), A functional loss of memory in a preadolescent boy. *North Carolina Med. J.,* 16:99-101.

Pratt, K. C. (1954), The neonate. In: *Manual of Child Psychology,* 2nd ed., ed. L. Carmichael. New York: Wiley, pp. 215-291.

Preston, M. I. (1939), The reaction of parents to reading failures. *Child Dev.,* 10:173-179.

——— (1940), The school looks at the non-reader. *Elem. School J.,* 40:450-458.

Pribram, K. H. and Fulton, J. F. (1954), An experimental critique of the effects of anterior cingulate ablation in monkey brain. *Brain,* 77:34-44.

Proctor, J. T. (1958), Hysteria in childhood. *This Volume,* pp. 431-442.

Provence, S. and Lipton, R. (1962), *Infants in Institutions.* New York: International Universities Press.

Prugh, D. G., (1963), Toward an understanding of psychosomatic concepts in relation to illness in children. In: *Modern Perspectives in Child Development,* ed. A. Solnit and S. Province. New York: International Universities Press, pp. 246-367.

——— Staub, E. M., Sands, H. H., Kirschbaum, R. M., and Lenihan, E. A. (1953), A study of the emotional reaction of children in families to hospitalization and illness. *Amer. J. Orthopsychiat.,* 23:70-106.

Prugh, G. P., et al. (1954), On the significance of the anal phase in pediatrics and child psychiatry. Workshop. In: *Case Studies in Childhood Emotional Disabilities,* ed. G. E. Gardiner. American Orthopsychiatric Association.

Purcell, K., Bernstein, L., and Bukantz, S. (1961), A preliminary comparison of rapidly remitting and persistently steroid-dependent asthmatic children. *Psychosom. Med.,* 23:305-310.

Purtell, J. J., Robins, E., and Cohen, M. E. (1951), Observations on clinical aspects of hysteria: a quantitative study of 50 hysteric patients and 156 control subjects. *J.A.M.A.,* 146:902-909.

Rabinovitch, R. D. (1954), An evaluation of present trends in psycho-therapy with children. *J. Psychiat. Soc. Work,* 24:11-9.

________ Drew, A. L., DeJong, R. N., Ingram, W., and Withey, L. (1956), A research approach to reading retardation. *This Volume,* pp. 457-486.

Rachman, S. and Costello, C. G. (1961), The etiology and treatment of children's phobias: a review. *This Volume,* pp. 394-409.

Rado, S. (1956), *Psychoanalysis of Behavior.* New York: Grune & Stratton.

Rangell, L. (1965), The scope of Heinz Hartmann. *Int. J. Psycho-Anal.,* 46:5-30.

Rank, B. (1949), Adaptation of the psychoanalytic technique for the treatment of young children with atypical development. *Amer. J. Orthopsychiat.,* 19:130-139.

________ (1955), Intensive study and treatment of preschool children who show marked personality deviations, or "atypical development," and their parents. In: *Emotional Problems of Early Childhood,* ed. G. Caplan. New York: Basic Books, p. 491-501.

________ and Macnaughton, D. (1950), A clinical contribution to early ego development. *The Psychoanalytic Study of the Child,* 5:53-65. New York: International Universities Press.

Rao, L. (1955), cited by Craigie, E. H.: Vascular patterns of the developing nervous system. In: *Biochemistry of the Developing Nervous System.* New York: Academic Press, pp. 28-51.

Rapaport, D. (1944), *Manual of Diagnostic Psychological Testing.* New York: Macy Foundation.

________ (1950), On the psycho-analytic theory of thinking. *Int. J. Psycho-Anal.,* 31:161-170.

________ (1951a), *Organization and Pathology of Thought.* New York: Columbia University Press.

________ (1951b), The autonomy of the ego. *Bull. Menn. Clin.,* 15:113-123.

________ (1958), The theory of ego-autonomy: A generalization. *Bull. Menn. Clin.,* 22:13-35.

________ (1959a), The structure of psychoanalytic theory (a systematizing attempt). In: *Psychology: A Study of a Science,* ed. S. Koch, Vol. 3. New York: McGraw-Hill.

________ (1959b), A historical survey of psychoanalytic ego psychology. In: *Identity and the Life Cycle,* ed. E. H. Erikson. [*Psychological Issues,* Monogr. 1, pp. 5-17.] New York: International Universities Press.

________ (1960), *The Structure of Psychoanalytic Theory: A Systematizing Attempt.* [*Psychological Issues,* Monogr. 6.] New York: International Universities Press.

Rapoport, J. (1944), Phantasy objects in children. *Psychoanal. Rev.,* 31:316-321.

Razran, G. (1961), The observable unconscious and the inferable conscious in current Soviet psychophysiology: interoceptive conditioning, semantic conditioning and the orienting reflex. *Psychol. Rev.,* 68:81-147.

Redl, F. (1951), Ego disturbances. *This Volume,* pp. 532-539.

________ and Wineman, D. (1951), *Children Who Hate.* New York: Free Press of Glencoe.

________ (1952), *Controls From Within.* New York: Free Press of Glencoe.

________ (1957), *The Aggressive Child.* New York: Free Press of Glencoe.

________ (1966), *When We Deal With Children.* New York: Free Press of Glencoe.

Reese, W. G., Doss, R. and Gantt, W. H. (1953), Autonomic responses in differential diagnosis of organic and psychogenic psychosis. *Arch. Neurol. Psychiat.,* 70:778-793.

Reich, W. (1925), *Der triebhafte Charakter.* Internationaler Psychoanalytischer Verlag, Wien.

Reissman, F. (1962), The hidden I.Q. *The Culturally Deprived Child.* New York: Harper & Row. *This Volume,* pp. 744-755.

________ Pearl, A. and Cohen, J., eds. (1964), *Mental Health of the Poor.* Glencoe, Ill.: Free Press of Glencoe.

Rexford, E., ed. (1966), *A Developmental Approach to Problems of Acting Out: A Symposium.* [*J. Amer. Acad. Child Psychiat.,* Monogr. 1.] New York: International Universities Press.

Rheingold, H. (1933), Mental and social development of infants in relation to the number of other infants in the boarding home. *Amer. J. Orthopsychiat.,* 13:41-45.

Ribble, M. A. (1941), Disorganizing factors in infant personality. *Amer. J. Psychiat.,* 98:459-463.

________ (1943), *The Rights of Infants.* New York: Columbia University Press.

________ (1944), Infantile experience in relation to personality development. In: *Personality and the Behavior Disorders,* ed. J. McV. Hunt. New York: Ronald Press, pp. 621-651.

Ricciuti, H. N. and Benjamin, J. D. (1957), Sorting behavior and conceptual thinking in pre-school children. *Abstr. Amer. Psychol.,* 12:365.

Richfield, J. (1954), On the scientific status of psychoanalysis. *Scit. Month.,* 79:306-309.

Richmond, J. B., Eddy, E. and Garrards, S. (1954), The syndrome of fecal soiling and mega-colon. *Amer. J. Orthopsychiat.,* 24:391-401.

———— Grossman, H. J., and Lustman, S. L. (1953), A hearing test for newborn infants. *Pediatrics,* 11:634-638.

———— and Lipton, E. L. (1959), Some aspects of neurophysiology of the newborn and their implications for child development. *This Volume,* pp. 39-55.

Richter, D. (1955), The metabolism of the developing brain. In: *Biochemistry of the Developing Nervous System,* ed. H. Waelsch. New York: Academic Press, pp. 225-250.

Rider, R. V., Taback, M. and Knobloch, H. (1955), Associations between premature birth and socioeconomic status. *Amer. J. Pub. Health,* 45:1022-1028.

Riese, H. (1962), *Heal the Hurt Child.* Chicago: University of Chicago Press.

Riese, W. (1954), Auto-observation of aphasia, reported by an eminent nineteenth century medical scientist. *Bull. Hist. Med.,* 28:237-242.

Riesen, A. H. (1947), The development of visual perception in man and chimpanzee. *Science,* 106:107-108.

Rimland, B. (1964), *Infantile Autism.* New York: Appleton-Century-Crofts.

Ripin, R. (1930), A study of the infant's feeding reactions during the first six months of life. *Arch. Psychol.,* 116:44.

Robbins, E. and O'Neal, P. (1953), Clinical features of hysteria in children with a note on prognosis. A two to seventeen year follow-up study of 41 patients. *Nerv. Child,* 10:246-271.

Robbins, L. C. (1963), The accuracy of parental recall of aspects of child development and of child-rearing practices. *J. Abnormal & Soc. Psychol.,* 66:261-270.

Robertson, James (1953a), Film: A two-year-old goes to hospital. London: Tavistock Child Development Research Unit. New York: New York University Film Library.

———— (1953b), Some responses of young children to loss of maternal care. *Nursing Times,* 49:382-386.

———— (1958), *Young Children in Hospital.* London: Tavistock Publications. New York: Basic Books, 1959.

———— (1962), *Hospitals and Children.* London: Bollancz, Ltd.

———— and Bowlby, J. (1952), Responses of young children to separation from their mothers. II. Observations of the sequences of response of children aged 18 to 24 months during the course of separation. *Courrier du Centre International de l'Enfance,* 2:131-142.

Robertson, Joyce (1956), A mother's observations on the tonsillectomy of her four-year-old daughter. With comments by Anna Freud. *The Psychoanalytic Study of the Child,* 11:410-433. New York: International Universities Press.

Robinson, H. M. (1946), *Why Pupils Fail in Reading.* Chicago: University of Chicago Press.

Rogers, M. E., Lilienfeld, A. M., and Pasamanick, B. (1955), *Prenatal and Paranatal Factors in the Development of Childhood Behavior Disorders.* Copenhagen: Munksgaard.

Rogerson, C. H., Hardcastle, D. H. and Duguid, K. (1935), A psychological approach to the problem of asthma and the asthma-eczema-prurigo syndrome. *Guy's Hosp. Rep.,* 85:289-308.

Róheim, G. (1932), Psychoanalysis of primitive cultural types. *Int. J. Psycho-Anal.,* 13:1-224, in particular, Chapt III, on the Aranda, The Children of the Desert.

Rollman-Branch, H. S. (1960), On the question of primary object need. *J. Amer. Psychoanal. Assn.,* 8:686-702.

Rønne, H. (1936), Congential word-blindness in school-children. *Tr. Ophth. Soc. U. Kingdom,* 56:311-333.

Root, N. (1957), A neurosis in adolescence. *The Psychoanalytic Study of the Child,* 12:320-334. New York: International Universities Press.

Rorschach, H. (1942), *Psychodiagnostics.* Bern, Switzerland: Huber.

Rosen, H. and Lidz, T. (1949), Emotional factors in the precipitation of recurrent diabetic acidosis. *Psychosom. Med.,* 11:211-215.

Rosenfeld, S. K. and Sprince, M. P. (1963), An attempt to formulate the meaning of the concept "borderline". *The Psychoanalytic Study of the Child,* 18:603-635. New York: International Universities Press.

________ (1965), Some thoughts on the technical handling of borderline children. *The Psychoanalytic Study of the Child,* 20:495-517. New York: International Universities Press.

Rosenthal, R. (1966), *Experimental effects in Behavioral Research.* New York: Appleton-Century-Crofts.

Ross, S., Fisher, A., and King, D. (in preparation), The effect of early enforced weaning on sucking behavior of puppies.

Roudinesco, J., David, M., and Nicolas, J. (1952), Responses of young children to separation from their mothers. *Courrier de la Centre International de l'Enfance,* 2:66-78.

Ruegamer, W. R., Bernstein, L. and Benjamin, J. D. (1954), Growth, food utilization, and thyroid activity in the albino rat as a function of extra handling. *Science,* 120:184-185.

Rutherford, W. J. (1909), The aetiology of congenital word-blindness; with an example. *Brit. J. Child Dis.,* 6:484-488.

Rutter, M. (1969), Concepts of autism: a review of research. *J. Child Psychol. & Psychiat.,* 9:1-25.

________ Birch, H. G., Thomas, A., and Chess, S. (1964), Temperamental characteristics in infancy and the later development of behavioral disorders. *Brit. J. Psychiat.,* 110:651-661.

Sadger (1910), Über Urethralerotik. *Jahrb. Psychoanal. Psychopathol. Forsch.,* 2:409-450.

________ (1918), Über Pollutionen und Pollutionstraüme. *Fortschr. Med.,* 36:14-15.

Saenger, G. (1957), *The Adjustment of Severely Retarded Adults in the Community.* Albany, N. Y.: State Interdepartmental Health Resources Board.

Samter, M. (1961), The state of allergy—1961: a reappraisal. *Therapeutic Notes,* 68:283-286.

Sandler, J. (1962), Research in psychoanalysis. *Int. J. Psycho-Anal.,* 43:287-291.

Sarason, S. (1959), *Psychological Problems in Mental Deficiency.* New York: Harper & Row, 3rd ed.

________ Davidson, K. S., Lighthall, F. F., Waite, R. R., and Ruebush, B. K. (1960), *Anxiety in Elementary School Children.* New York: Wiley.

________ and Gladwin, T. (1958), Psychological and cultural problems in mental subnormality: a review of research. *Genet. Psychol. Monogr.,* 57:1-284.

Schachter, M. (1933), Die pathogenese der enuresis. *Jahrb. f. Kinderhlk.,* 140:234-235.

Schaefer, E. S. (1959), A circumplex model for maternal behavior. *J. Abnormal & Soc. Psychol.,* 59:226-234.

Schaffer, H. R. (1958), Objective observations of personality development in early infancy. *Brit. J. Med. Psychol.,* 31:174-183.

________ and Callender, W. M. (1959), Psychologic effects of hospitalization in infancy. *Pediatrics,* 24:528-539.

Scheibel, M. E. and Scheibel, A. B. (1964), Some neural substrates of postnatal development. In: *Review of Child Development Research,* 1:481-519. ed. H. L. Hoffman and L. W. Hoffman. New York: Russell Sage Foundation.

Schiavi, R. C., Stein, M. and Sethi, B. B. (1961), Respiratory variables in response to a pain-fear stimulus and in experimental asthma. *Psychosom. Med.,* 23:485-492.

Schick, A. (1949), A contribution to the psychopathology of genuine epilepsy. *Psychoanal. Rev.,* 36:217-239.

Schilder, P. (1928), *Introduction to a Psychoanalytic Psychiatry.* [*Nervous and Mental Disease Monogr.* 50.] New York: Nervous and Mental Disease Publishing Company.

________ (1931), *The Relation Between the Personality and Motility of Schizophrenia in Brain and Personality.* [Part II. *Nervous and Mental Disease Monogr.* 53.] New York: Nervous and Mental Disease Publishing Company.

________ (1935), *The Image and Appearance of the Human Body.* London: Paul, French, Trubner.

________ (1937), The psychological implications of motor development in children. *Proc. Child Res. Clin. Woods Schools,* 4:38-59.

________ (1938a), The child and the symbol. *Scientia,* 64:21-26.

________ (1938b), *The Image and Appearance of the Human Body.* New York: International Universities Press, 1951.

________ (1939), Psychology of schizophrenia. *Psychoanal. Rev.,* 26:380-398.

________ (1944), Congenital alexia and its relation to optic perception. *J. Genet. Psychol.,* 65:67-88.

Schlossmann, A. (1920), Zur frage der säuglingssterblichkeit. *Anstalten Münchner Med. Wochenschrift,* 67:1318-1320.

Schmideberg, M. (1934), Intellektuelle hemmung und esstorung. *Zeit. J. Psa. Päd.,* 8:109-116.

——— (1938), The mode of operation of psychoanalytic therapy. *Int. J. Psycho-Anal.,* 19:310-320.

Schneer, H. I. (1963), The death of an asthmatic child. In: *The Asthmatic Child,* ed. H. I. Schneer. New York: Harper & Row.

Schnurmann, A. (1949), Observations of a phobia. *The Psychoanalytic Study of the Child,* 3/4:253-270. New York: International Universities Press.

Schuler, E. A. and Parenton, V. J. (1943), A recent epidemic of hysteria in a Louisiana high school. *J. Soc. Psychol.,* 17:221-235.

Schur, M. (1953), The ego in anxiety. In: *Drives, Affects, Behavior,* ed. R. Loewenstein. New York: International Universities Press, pp. 67-103.

——— (1955), Comments on the metapsychology of somatization. *The Psychoanalytic Study of the Child,* 10:119-164. New York: International Universities Press.

——— (1960), Discussion of Dr. Bowlby's Paper (1960), *The Psychoanalytic Study of the Child,* 15:63-84. New York: International Universities Press.

——— (1966), *The Id and the Regulatory Principles of Mental Functioning.* New York: International Universities Press.

Schwartz, M. (1952), Heredity in bronchial asthma: a clinical and genetic study of 191 asthma probands and 50 probands with Baker's asthma. *Acta. Allergol.,* Suppl. 2, pp. 288.

Scott, J. P. (1951), The relationships between developmental change and social organization among mammals. *Anat. Rec.,* 111:489-490.

——— (1953), The process of socialization in higher animals. In: *Interrelations Between the Social Environment and Psychiatric Disorders.* New York: Milbank Memorial Fund, pp. 82-102.

——— (1957), The genetic and environmental differentiation of behavior. In: *The Concept of Development,* ed. D. B. Harris. Minneapolis: University of Minnesota Press, pp. 59-77.

——— (1958a), *Animal Behavior.* Chicago: University of Chicago Press.

——— (1958b), *Aggression.* Chicago: University of Chicago Press.

——— (1958c), Critical periods in the development of social behavior in puppies. *This Volume,* pp. 20-38.

——— (1962), Critical periods in behavioral development. *Science,* 138:949-958.

——— Fredericson, E. and Fuller, J. L. (1951), Experimental exploration of the critical period hypothesis. *J. Person.,* 1:162-183.

——— and Fuller, J. L. (1950), *Manual of Dog Testing Techniques.* Bar Harbor, Me.: Jackson Laboratory.

——— and Marston, M. V. (1950), Critical periods affecting the development of normal and maladjustive social behavior of puppies. *J. Genet. Psychol.,* 77:25-60.

Sears, R. R., Maccoby, E. E., and Levin, H. (1957), *Patterns of Child Rearing.* Evanston, Ill.: Row, Peterson, pp. 44-447.

Seguin, E. (1846), *The Moral Treatment, Hygiene and Education of Idiots and Other Backward Children.* New York: Columbia Universities Press.

Segundo, J. P., Naguet, R. and Buser, P. (1955), Effects of cortical stimulation on electrocortical activity in monkeys. *J. Neuro-physiol.,* 18:236-245.

Seitz, P. F. D. (1954), The effects of infantile experience upon adult behavior in animal subjects: effects of litter size during infancy upon adult behavior in the rat. *Amer. J. Psychiat.,* 110:916-927.

Sellin, T. (1938), *Culture Conflict and Crime.* New York: Social Science Research Council, p. 68.

Sexton, P. (1961), *Education and Income.* New York: Viking Press.

Shaffer, G. W. and Lazarus, R. S. (1952), *Fundamental Concepts in Clinical Psychology.* New York: McGraw-Hill, pp. 136-161.

Shaw, C. R. (1930), *The Jack-Roller.* Chicago: University of Chicago Press.

——— (1931), *The Natural History of a Delinquent Career.* Chicago: University of Chicago Press.

________ and McKay, H. D. (1942), *Juvenile Delinquency and Urban Areas.* Chicago: University of Chicago Press.

________ et al. (1940), *Delinquency Areas.* Chicago: University of Chicago Press.

Shaw, M. (1961), Definition and identification of academic underachievers. In: *Guidance for the Underachievers with Superior Ability.* Washington, D. C.: Office of Educational Bulletins.

Sheffield, H. B. (1898), A contribution to the study of hysteria in childhood as it occurs in the U.S.A. *New York Med. J.,* 68:412-416, 433-436.

Sheldon, W. H. (1949), *Varieties of Delinquent Youth.* New York: Harper & Row.

Shen, S. C. (1957), Enzyme synthesis in the central nervous system during embryogenesis. In: *Etiologic Factors in Mental Retardation,* Ross Pediatric Research Conference No. 23. Columbus, Ohio: Ross Laboratories, pp. 24-27.

Shirley, H. F. (1938), Encopresis in Children. *J. Pediat.,* 12:367-380.

Shuttleworth, F. K. (1938), The adolescent period: a graphic and pictorial atlas. Monograph, *Society for Research in Child Development,* Vol. 3, No. 3. Washington, D. C.: National Research Council.

Sicard, J. A. (1925), Enuresis. *Ann. de Med.,* 17:470-477.

Sigel, I. E., Chrmn. (1968), Papers from the 1967 Merrill-Palmer conference on research and teaching of infant development. *Merrill-Palmer Quart.,* 14:#1, whole issue.

Silber, E., et al. (1961), Adaptive behavior in competent adolescents. *Arch. Gen. Psychiat.,* 5:354-365.

Silberstein, R. M. and Irwin, H. (1962), Jean-Marc-Gaspart Itard and the savage of Aveyron: an unsolved diagnostic problem in child psychiatry. *J. Amer. Acad. Child Psychiat.,* 1:314-322.

Simonsen, K. M. (1947), *Examination of Children from Children's Homes and Day Nurseries by the Bühler-Hetzer Developmental Test.* University of Copenhagen, Faculty of Medicine.

Simpson, B. R. (1939), The wandering I.Q. *J. Psychol.,* 7:351-367.

Skeels, H. M. (1938), Mental development of children in foster homes. *J. Consult. Psychol.,* 2:33-43.

________ (1940), Some Iowa studies of the mental growth of children in relation to differentials of the environment: a summary. *39th Yearbook, National Society for the Study of Education,* 2:281-308.

________ (1965), Effects of adoption on children from institutions. *This Volume,* pp. 756-760.

________ and Dye, H. B. (1938-1939), A study of the effects of differential stimulation on mentally retarded children. (Proceedings and addresses of the American Association on Mental Deficiency.) *J. Psychoasthenics,* 44:114-136.

________ and Harms, I. (1948), Children with inferior social histories; their mental development in adoptive homes. *J. Genet. Psychol.,* 73:283-294.

________ Updegraff, R., Wellman, B. L., and Williams, H. M. (1938), A study of environmental stimulation; an orphanage preschool project. *University of Iowa Studies in Child Welfare,* Vol. 15, No. 4.

Skodak, M. (1939), Children in foster homes. *University of Iowa Studies in Child Welfare,* Vol. 16, No. 1.

________ and Skeels, H. M. (1949), A final follow-up study of one hundred adopted children. *J. Genet. Psychol.,* 75:85-125.

Skydsgaard, H. B. (1942), *Den Konstitutionelle Dyslexi "Ordblindhed".* Kobenhavn: Busck.

Sluckin, W. (1965), *Imprinting and Early Learning.* Chicago: Aldine.

Smith, L. C. (1950), A study of laterality characteristics of retarded readers and reading achievers. *J. Exper. Educ.,* 18:321-329.

Smith, W. K. (1945), The functional significance of the rostral cingular cortex as revealed by its responses to electrical excitation. *J. Neurophysiol.,* 8:241-255.

Solms, H. (1948), Beitrag zur lehre von der sog. kongenitalen wortblindheit. *Monatschr. f. Psychiat. u. Neurol.,* 115:1-54.

Solnit, A. (1960), Hospitalization: an aid to physical and psychological health in children. *Amer. J. Dis. Child.,* 99:155-163.

________ and Stark, M. (1961), Mourning and the birth of a defective child. *The Psychoanalytic Study of the Child,* 16:523-537. New York: International Universities Press.

Sontag, L. S., Baker, C. T., and Nelson, V. P. (1955), Personality as a determinant of performance. *Amer. J. Orthopsychiat.,* 25:555-562.
Spencer, B. and Gillen, F. J. (1927), *The Arunta.* New York: Macmillan, 2 vols.
Sperling, M. (1949), The role of the mother in psychosomatic disorders in children. Psychosom. Med., 11:377-385.
________ (1953), Food allergies and conversion hysteria. *Psychoanal. Quart.,* 22:525-538.
________ (1963), A psychoanalytic study of bronchial asthma in children. In: *The Asthmatic Child: Psychosomatic Approach to Problems and Treatment,* ed. H. I. Schneer. New York: Hoeber Medical Division of Harper & Row, pp. 138-165.
________ (1968), Asthma in children: an evaluation of concepts and therapies. *J. Amer. Acad. Child Psychiat.,* 7:44-58.
Spiegel, L. (1951), A review of contribution to a psychoanalytic theory of adolescence: individual aspects. *The Psychoanalytic Study of the Child,* 6:375-393. New York: International Universities Press.
Spitz, R. A. (1945), Hospitalism. *This Volume,* pp. 237-262.
________ (1946a), Anaclitic depression. *The Psychoanalytic Study of the Child,* 2:313-342. New York: International Universities Press.
________ (1946b), Hospitalism—a follow-up report. *This Volume,* pp. 258-262.
________ (1950), Anxiety in infancy, a study of its manifestations in the first year of life. *Int. J. Psycho-Anal.,* 31:138-143.
________ (1951), The psychogenic diseases in infancy. *The Psychoanalytic Study of the Child,* 6:255-275. New York: International Universities Press.
________ (1957), *No and Yes. On the Genesis of Human Communication.* New York: International Universities Press.
________ (1959), *A Genetic Field Theory of Ego Formation.* New York: International Universities Press.
________ (1960), Discussion of Dr. Bowlby's Paper (1960). *The Psychoanalytic Study of the Child,* 15:85-94. New York: International Universities Press.
________ (1965), *The First Year of Life.* New York: International Universities Press.
________ and Wolf, K. M. (1946), The smiling response: a contribution to the ontogenesis of social relations. *Genet. Psychol. Monogr.,* 34:57-125.
Spock, B. (1963), *Baby and Child Care.* New York: Pocket Books.
Ssucharewa, G. (1932), Ueber den verlauf der schizophrenien in kindesalter. *Ztschr. ges. Neurol. u. Psychiat.,* 142:309-321.
Stacy, C. L. and DeMartino, M. F. (1957), *Counselling and Psychotherapy with the Mentally Retarded.* Glencoe, Ill.: Free Press.
Starr, P. H. (1953), Some observations on the diagnostic aspects of childhood hysteria. *Nerv. Child,* 10:214-231.
Starzl, T. E., Taylor, C. W. and Magoun, H. W. (1951), Collateral afferent excitation of reticular formation of brain stem. *J. Neurophysiol.,* 14:479-496.
Stein, M. and Ottenberg, P. (1958), Role of odors in asthma. *Psychosom. Med.,* 20:60-65.
Stendler, C. (1950), Sixty years of child training practices. *J. Pediat.,* 36:122-134.
Stengel, E. (1939), Studies on the psychopathology of wandering. *Brit. J. Med. Psychol.,* 18:250-254.
________ (1941), On the aetiology of the fugue states. *J. Ment. Sci.,* 87:572-599.
________ (1943), Further studies on pathological wandering. *J. Ment. Sci.,* 89:224-241.
Stephenson, S. (1907), Six cases of congenital word-blindness affecting three generations of one family. *Opthalmoscope,* 5:482-484.
Sterba, E. (1941), An important factor in eating disturbances of childhood. *Psychoanal. Quart.,* 10:365-372.
Sterba, R. (1942), *Introduction to the Psychoanalytic Theory of the Libido.* #68. New York: Nervous and Mental Disease Monographs.
Stern, E. (1952), A propos d'un cas d'autisme chez un jeune enfant. *Arch. franc. Pediat.,* 9:157-164.
________ and Schachter, M. (1953), Zum problem des frühkindlichen autismus. *Prax. Kinderpsychol. u. Kinderpsychiat.,* 2:113-119.

Stern, W. (1930), *Psychology of Early Childhood up to the Sixth Year of Age.* Translated by Anna Barwell, 2nd ed. New York: Henry Holt.

Stevenson, H. W. (1967), Developmental psychology. In: *Annual Review of Psychology,* 18:88-93. Palo Alto: Annual Reviews Inc.

Stewart, R. S. (1950), Personality maladjustment and reading achievement. *Amer. J. Orthopsychiat.,* 20:410-417.

Stirnimann, F. (1947), Das kind und seine früheste umwelt. *Psychologische Praxis,* Vol. 6. Basel: S. Karger Verlag.

Stoddard, G. D. (1940), Intellectual development of the child: an answer to the critics of the Iowa studies. *School and Society,* 51:529-536.

Stoller, R. J. (1968), *Sex and Gender.* New York: Science House.

Stolz, H. R. and Stolz, L. M. (1951), *Somatic Development of Adolescent Boys.* New York: Macmillan.

Stolz, L. M. (1958), Youth: the Gesell institution and its latest study. *Contemp. Psychol.,* 3:10-13.

Stone, C. P. and Baker, R. G. (1939), The attitudes and interests of premenarchial and postmenarchial girls. *J. Genet. Psychol.,* 54:27-71.

Storrs, H. (1929), A report on an investigation made of cases discharged from Letchworth Village. *Amer. Assn. Study of Feebleminded,* 34:220-232.

Strachey, J. (1930), Some unconscious factors in reading. *Int. J. Psycho-Anal.,* 11:322-331.

Strauss, A. A. and Werner, H. (1942), Disorders of conceptual thinking in the brain-injured child. *J. Nerv. Ment. Dis.,* 96:153-172.

________ (1944), Ways of thinking in brain-crippled deficient children. *Amer. J. Psychiat.,* 100:639-647.

________ and Lehtinen, L. (1950), *Psychopathology and Education of the Brain Injured Child.* New York: Grune & Stratton.

________ (1952), The education of the brain-injured child. *Amer. J. Ment. Def.,* 56:712-718.

________ (1954), Aphasia in children. *Amer. J. Phys. Med.,* 33:93-99.

Strauss, E. B. (1935), A problem in methodology. *Guy's Hosp. Rep.,* 85:309-316.

Stuart, H. (1946), Normal growth and development during adolescence. *New England J. Med.,* May, 1946.

Stunkard, A. (1959), Obesity and the denial of hunger. *Psychosom. Med.,* 21:281-289.

________ (1967), Obesity. In: *Comprehensive Textbook of Psychiatry,* ed. A. Freedman and H. I. Kaplan. Baltimore: Williams & Wilkins, pp. 1059-1062.

Sturniman, A. (1933), *Das Erste Erleben des Kindes.* Fauenfeldt: Huber.

Sullivan, H. S. (1953), *Interpersonal Theory of Psychiatry.* New York: Norton.

Sullivan, J. W. N. (1927), *Beethoven: A Study of Greatness.* New York: Mentor Books.

Sumner, J. W., Jr. Cameron, R. R., and Peterson, D. B. (1952), Hypnosis in differentiation of epileptic from convulsive-like seizures. *Neurology,* 2:395-402.

Sutherland, E. H., ed. (1937), *The Professional Thief.* Chicago: University of Chicago Press.

________ (1947), *Principles of Criminology.* Philadelphia: J. P. Lippincott.

________ (1949), *White Collar Crime.* New York: Dryden Press.

Sylvester, E. (1945), Analysis of psychogenic anorexia in a four-year-old. *The Psychoanalytic Study of the Child,* 1:167-187. New York: International Universities Press.

________ and Kunst, M. S. (1943), Psychodynamic aspects of the reading problem. *Amer. J. Orthopsychiat.,* 13:69-76.

Szurek, S. (1942), Genesis of psychopathic personality traits. *Psychiat.,* 5:1-6.

Taft, L. T. and Goldfarb, W. (1964), Prenatal and perinatal factors in childhood schizophrenia. *Develop. Med. Child Neurol.,* 6:32-43.

Tapia, F., Jekel, J., and Domke, H. R. (1960), Enuresis: an emotional symptom? *J. Nerv. Ment. Dis.,* 130:61-66.

Teicher, J. D. (1941), Preliminary survey of motility in children. *J. Nerv. Ment. Dis.,* 94:277-304.

Terman, L. (1916), *The Measurement of Intelligence.* New York: Houghton, Mifflin.

Teuber, H. L. (1952), Some observations on the organization of higher functions after penetrating brain injury in man. In: *The Biology of Mental Health and Disease.* New York: Hoeber, pp. 259-262.

——— (1955), Patterns of cerebral localization. Paper presented at Psychology Colloquium, Johns Hopkins University, March 4, 1955.

——— Battersby, W. S. and Bender, M. B. (1951), The performance of complex visual tasks after cerebral lesions. *J. Nerv. Ment. Dis.,* 114:413-429.

Theis, S. (1924), *How Foster Children Turn Out.* New York: State Charities Aid Assn., Publication No. 165.

Thomas, A., Chess, S., and Birch, H. G. (1968), *Temperament and Behavior Disorders in Children.* New York: New York University Press.

——— Hertzig, M., and Korn, S. (1963), *Behavioral Individuality in Early Childhood.* New York: New York University Press.

Thompson, L. J. (1966), *Reading Disability: Developmental Dyslexia.* Springfield, Ill.: Charles C. Thomas.

Thorndike, E. L. (1911), *Animal Intelligence: Experimental Studies.* New York: Macmillan.

——— (1914), *Educational Psychology,* Vol. III. New York: Columbia University Press.

Thorpe, W. H. (1956), *Learning and Instinct in Animals.* London: Methuen.

Tilton, J. R. (1966), *Annotated Bibliography on Childhood Schizophrenia, 1954-1964.* New York: Grune & Stratton.

Tinbergen, N. (1951), *The Study of Instinct.* Oxford: Clarendon Press.

Tolman, E. C. (1932), *Purposive Behavior.* New York: Century.

Toman, J. E. P., (1951), Neuropharmacologic considerations in psychic seizures. Neurology, 1:444-460.

——— Loewe, S. and Goodman, L. S. (1947), Physiology and therapy of convulsive disorders: the effect of anticonvulsant drugs on electro-shock seizures in man. *Arch. Neurol. Psychiat.,* 58:312-324.

Tredgold, A. F. (1908), *A Textbook of Mental deficiency.* Baltimore: Williams & Wilkins, 8th ed., 1952.

Tulchin, S. (1935), Emotional factors in reading disabilities in school children. *J. Educ. Psychol.,* 26:443-454.

Turner, W. A. (1907), *Epilepsy: A Study of the Idiopathic Disease.* London: Macmillan.

Tyler, R. W. (1951), Can intelligence tests be used to predict educability. In: *Intelligence and Cultural Differences,* ed. K. Eells, et al. Chicago: University of Chicago Press, p. 43.

Updegraff, R. (1932), The determination of a reliable intelligence quotient for the young child. *J. Genet. Psychol.,* 41:152-166.

U.S. Public Health Service (1960), *Patients in Public Institutions for Mental Defectives.* Washington, D. C.: U. S. Government Printing Office.

Van Buren, A. (1960), Exhausted mother gets lots of advice. *Ann Arbor News,* February 22, 1960.

Van Der Leeuw, P. J. (1958), The preoedipal phase in the male. *The Psychoanalytic Study of the Child,* 13:352-374. New York: International Universities Press.

Van Gennep, A. (1960), *The Rites of Passage.* Chicago: University of Chicago Press.

van Krevelen, D. A. (1952a), Een geval van "early infantile autism". *Nederl. tijdschr. v. Geneesk.,* 96:202-206.

——— (1952b), Early infantile autism. *Ztschr. Kinderpsychiat.,* 19:91-97.

——— (1953a), Zur psychopathologie der fuges–im besonderen bei fugendlichen (Psychopathology of the fugue with special reference to adolescence.) *Wiener Z. für Nervenheilkunde und deren Grenzgebiete,* 7:354-362.

——— (1953b), De psychopathologie van de fugue. (The psychopathology of the fugue.) *Ned. Tijdschr. Genessk.,* 97:2524-2530. Abstract: *Exc. Med.,* Sec. 8, Vol. 7, No. 4152., 1954.

——— (1955), Hysterie bij kinderen voorheen en thans (Hysteria in children, past and present.) *Ned. Tijdschr. Geneesk.,* 99:1890-1894.

Variot, G. and Lecomte (1906), Un cas de typhlolexie congénitale. *Gaz. d. Hôp.,* 79:1479-1481.

Waelder, R. (1930), The principle of multiple function: observations on over-determination. *Psychoanal. Quart.,* 5:45-62, 1936.

——— (1943), Lectures on various theoretical departures from psychoanalytic theory. Presented before the Philadelphia Psychoanalytic Society. As quoted by English and Pearson (1945).

________ (1962), Psychoanalysis, scientific method and philosophy. *J. Amer. Psychoanal. Assn.,* 10:617-637.

Wahl, C. W. (1954), Some antecedent factors in the family histories of 392 schizophrenics. *Amer. J. Psychiat.,* 110:668-676.

________ (1956), Some antecedent factors in the family histories of 568 male schizophrenics in the Navy. *Amer. J. Psychiat.,* 113:201-210.

Waldfogel, S., Coolidge, J. C., and Hahn, P. B. (1957), The development, meaning and management of school phobia. *Amer. J. Orthopsychiat.,* 27:754-780.

________ Tessman, E. and Hahn, P. B. (1959), Learning problems, III: A program for early intervention in school phobia. *Amer. J. Orthopsychiat.,* 29:324-333.

Walker, C. F. (1947), Hysteria in childhood. *Amer. J. Orthopsychiat.,* 17:468-476.

Wallace, G. (1922), A report of a study of 100 feebleminded girls with a mental rating of eleven years. *Amer. Assn. Study of Feebleminded,* 27:177-185.

Wallerstein, R. S. (1964), The role of prediction in theory building in psychoanalysis. *J. Amer. Psychoanal. Assn.,* 12:675-691.

Walton, H. J. (1958), Suicidal behavior in depressive illness; a study of etiological factors in suicide. *J. Ment. Sci.,* 104:884-891.

Warren, A. B. and Jones, V. (1943), Effect of acrophobia upon reading ability as measured by reading comprehension and eye-movements in reading. *J. Genet. Psychol.,* 63:3-14.

Warson, S. R., et al. (1954), The dynamics of encopresis. *Amer. J. Orthopsychiat.,* 24:402-415.

Watson, J. B. (1919), *Psychology from the Standpoint of a Behaviorist.* Philadelphia: Lippincott.

________ (1928), *Psychological Care of Infant and Child.* London: Allen & Unwin.

________ and Morgan, J. J. B. (1917), Emotional reactions and psychological experimentation. *Amer. J. Psychol.,* 28:163-174.

________ and Raynor, R. (1920), Conditioned emotional reactions. *This Volume,* pp. 382-393.

Webster, T. (1963), Problems of emotional development in young retarded children. *Amer. J. Psychiat.,* 120:37-43.

Wechsler, D. (1944), *Measurement of Adult Intelligence,* 3rd ed. Baltimore: Williams & Wilkins.

________ (1949), *Wechsler Intelligence Scale for Children: Manual Psychological Corporation.* New York.

Weil, A. P. (1953), Clinical data and dynamic considerations in certain cases of childhood schizophrenia. *Amer. J. Orthopsychiat.,* 23:518-529.

Weiss, P., ed. (1950), *Genetic Neurology.* Chicago: University of Chicago Press.

Weissenberg, S. (1926), Ueber enkopresis. *Z. Kinderheilkunde,* 40:674-677.

Weiner, I. B. (1970), *Psychological Disturbance in Adolescence.* New York: Wiley-Interscience.

Wenar, C. (1963), The reliability of developmental histories: summary and evaluation of evidence. *Psychosom Med.,* 25-505-509.

Werner, H. (1957), The concept of development from a comparative and organismic point of view. In: *The Concept of Development,* ed. D. B. Harris. Minneapolis: University of Minnesota Press, pp. 125-148.

Werry, J. S. and Wollersheim, J. P. (1967), Behavior therapy with children: a broad overview. *J. Amer. Acad. Child Psychiat.,* 6:346-370.

Westcott, M. R. (1960), A method for the study of creativity as a special case of problem solving. Paper presented at the Eastern Psychological Association, New York City, April 16, 1960.

Westman, J. C., Arthur, B., and Scheidler, E. P. (1965), Reading retardation: an overview. *Amer. J. Dis. Child.,* 109:359-369.

White, M. S. (1957), Social class, child-rearing practices, and child behavior. *Amer. Sociol. Rev.,* 22:704-712.

Whitehorn, J. C. (1947), The concepts of "meaning" and "cause" in psychodynamics. *Amer. J. Psychiat.,* 104:289-292.

Whiting, J. W. and Child, I. L. (1953), *Child Training and Personality.* New Haven: Yale University Press.

Wiener, N. S. (1948), *Cybernetics.* New York: Wiley.

Wilkins, L. (1937), Epilepsy in childhood: II. The incidence of remissions. *J. Peds.,* 10:329-340.

Williams, F. E. (1936), *Papuans of the Trans-Fly.* Oxford: Clarendon Press.

Williams, R. M., Jr. (1951), *American Society: A Sociological Interpretation.* New York: Knopf.

Willis, T. (1672), *De Anima Brutorum,* translated by S. Pordage. London: Dring, Harper & Leigh, 1683.

Wilson, S. A. K. (1940), *Neurology.* Baltimore: William Wood, Vol. 2.

Windle, C. (1962), Prognosis of mental subnormals. *Amer. J. Ment. Def.,* Monogr. Suppl., Vol. 66.

Wing. J. K. (1966), *Childhood Autism: Clinical, Educational, and Social Aspects.* New York: Pergamon Press.

Winkler, H. (1929), *Der Trotz, sein Wesen und seine Behandlung.* Munich: Reinhardt.

Winnicott, D. W. (1930), Enuresis. *Proc. Roy. Soc. Med.,* 23:255-256.

———— (1931), *Clinical Notes on Disorders of Childhood.* London: Heinemann.

———— (1953), Transitional objects and transitional phenomena: a study of the first not-me possession. *Int. J. Psycho-Anal.,* 34:89-97.

———— (1955), Metapsychological and clinical aspects of regression within the psycho-analytical set-up. *Int. J. Psycho-Anal.,* 36:16-26.

Wirth, L. (1931), Culture conflict and misconduct. *Social Forces,* 9:484-492.

Witmer, H., ed. (1946), *Psychiatric Interviews with Children.* Commonwealth.

Witmer, L. (1907), A case of chronic bad spelling: amnesia visualis verbalis, due to arrest of postnatal development. *Psychol. Clin.,* 1:53-64.

Witty, P. and Kopel, D. (1939), *Reading and the Educative Process.* Boston: Ginn.

Wolf, K. M. (1953), Observation of individual tendencies in the second year of life. In: *Problems of Infancy and Childhood.* New York: Josiah Macy, Jr. Foundation, pp. 121-140.

Wolfenstein, M. (1953), Trends in infant care. *This Volume,* pp. 176-188.

Wolff, E. and Lachman, G. S. (1938), Hysterical blindness in children (a report of two cases). *Amer. J. Dis. Child.,* 55:743-749.

Wolff, G. (1916), Uber "kongenitale wortblindheit." *Cor.-Bl. f. Schweiz. Arzte,* 46:237-238.

Wolff, H. (1950), Quoted in S. Cobb, *Emotions and Clinical Medicine.* New York: Norton, p. 137.

Wolff, P. H. (1959), Observations on newborn infants. *Psychosom. Med.,* 21:110-118.

———— (1960), *The Developmental Psychologies of Jean Piaget and Psychoanalysis.* [*Psychological Issues,* Monogr. 5.] New York: International Universities Press.

———— (1966), *The Causes, Controls and Organization of Behavior in the Neonate.* [*Psychological Issues,* Monogr. 17.] New York: International Universities Press.

Wolpe, J. (1958), *Psychotherapy by Reciprocal Inhibition.* Palo Alto: Stanford University Press.

———— and Rachman, S. (1960), Psychoanalytic "evidence": a critique based on Freud's case of Little Hans. *J. Nerv. Ment. Dis.,* 131:135-148.

Wolpe, Z. S. (1953), Psychogenic visual disturbance in a four year old child. *Nerv. Child,* 10:314-325.

Wolfson, I. (1956), Follow-up studies of 92 male and 131 female patients who were discharged from the Newark State School in 1946. *Amer. J. Ment. Def.,* 61:224-238.

Woodward, K., et al. (1958), Psychiatric study of mentally retarded children of preschool age. *Amer. J. Orthopsychiat.,* 28:376-393.

Woodworth, R. S. (1941), Heredity and environment. *Bulletin 47, Social Science Research Council.*

World Health Organization (1962), *Deprivation of Maternal Care: A Reassessment of its Effects.* [*Public Health Paper,* #14.] Geneva: World Health Organization.

Wright, B. A. (1960), Value changes in acceptance of disability. In: *Physical Disability: A Psychological Approach.* New York: Evanston, pp. 98-137.

Wulff, M. (1928), A phobia in a child of eighteen months. *Int. J. of Psycho-Anal.* 9:354-359.

———— (1951), The problem of neurotic manifestations in children of preoedipal age. *The*

Psychoanalytic Study of the Child, 6:169-179. New York: International Universities Press.

Yarrow, L. J. (1961), Maternal deprivation: toward an empirical and conceptual re-evaluation. *Psychol. Bull.,* 58:459-490.

Yasuma, E. R. (1951), Hysterical amblyopia in children and young adults. *Arch. Ophthal.,* 45:70-76.

Yntema, C. L. and Hammond, W. S. (1955), Experiments on the origin and development of the sacral autonomic nerves in the chick embryo. *J. Exper. Zool.,* 129:375-414.

Zegans, L. S., Kooi, K. A., Waggoner, R. W. and Kemph, J. P. (1964), Effects of psychiatric interview upon paroxysmal cerebral activity, and autonomic measures in a disturbed child with petit mal epilepsy. *Psychosom. Med.,* 26:151-161.

Zeigarnik, B. (1927), Untersuchungen zur handlungs–und affektpsychologie: das behalten erledigter und unerledigter handlungen. *Psychol. Forschung,* 9:1-85.

Zilboorg, G. (1937), Consideration on suicide with particular reference to that of the young. *Amer. J. Orthopsychiat.,* 7:15-31.

SUBJECT INDEX

Achievement testing, in reading retardation, 467–469
Acting out, in adolescence, and attitudes of parents, 522–531
Action, as ego function, 87
Activity, and masculinity, 369
Adaptive behavior
  at five years old, 74–75
  at four years old, 68–69
Adolescence
  causes of delinquency in, 507–521
  conflicts settled in, 230–231
  delinquent subcultures in, 540–564
  ego disturbances in, 532–539
  Identifications in, 106
  individuation in, 231–232
  institutionalized patterning in, 228–229
  mystique of, 214–220
  physical changes in, 225–228
  pregenital impulses in, 141
  psychoanalytic view of, 221–233
  and puberty, 221–233
  role confusion in, 120–122
  superego lacunae in, 522–531
Adoption
  during latency period, 141
  effects of, 756–760
Affect
  and autonomic concomitants of emotion, 50
  disorders with brain dysfunction, 782–783
  intelligence related to, 167–175
  and neurologic mechanisms in emotional states, 783
Aggression
  in childhood, 97–98
  and eating habits, 306–307
  frustration-induced, coping with, 536
  and negativism, 352–353, 358
  and reading disabilities, 494, 496
  in schizophrenia, 641
Agoraphobia, 396
Allergies, and asthma, 593–594
Ambivalence
  origin of, 95
  preoedipal, 141
Anal phase
  conflicts in, and sleep disorders, 319–322, 330–335
  and wish for babies, in boys, 365
Anal pleasures, and eating habits, 307–308, 319
Anger
  as grief reaction, 270–271
  as primal emotion, 393
  see also Hostility
Animal phobias, 396
  as conditioned responses, 383–393, 402
Animal studies
  maternal care of newborn in, 54
  with puppies, 20–38
  responses to loss in, 270–271
  separation of mother and young in, 349–350
Animistic fantasies, in encopresis, 620–621
Anniversary reactions, 270, 287
Anorexia nervosa, 567–571
  oppositional syndromes in, 355–356
Antisocial disorders, 505–564
  and brain dysfunction, 777
  and causes of delinquency, 507–521
  and delinquent subcultures, 540–564

Antisocial disorders (continued)
and ego disturbances, 532–539
and superego lacunae of adolescents, 522–531
Anxiety
in brain dysfunction, 778
in childhood, 99–100
in mental retardates, 740
and negativism, 358–359
and pain, 580–581
and phobias, 396, 397–398, 411, 412
in schizophrenia, 641–642
Art work, in schizophrenia, 635–637
Asthma, 591–609
allergic predisposition to, 593–594
as conditioned response, 595
and crying, 606–607
emotional factors in acute attack, 600–603
general theory of, 604–607
identification in, 596–597
parasympathetic nervous system in, 604–605
and personality, 597–600
riddance processes in, 605–606
role of life experience in, 594–597
schematic theory of, 607–609
transition from acute to chronic state, 603–604
Autism, infantile, 647–669, 674–677
case histories of, 648–655, 675–676
clinical picture of, 655–660
compared to symbiotic psychosis, 682–687
course and prognosis of, 664–668
diagnosis of, 668–669
etiology of, 662–664
and intelligence, 660
language in, 656–658
nosology of, 661–662
object relations in, 659
and obsession for sameness, 658–659
physical examination in, 660–661
and relationship to people, 659–660
Autonomic nervous system
neonatal, 47–50
in schizophrenia, 630
Autonomy
in adolescence, 217–219
and negativism, 357
vs. shame and doubt, 113–115
Aveyron, young savage of, 726–732
Babies, wish for, in boys, 365
Behavior problems in children
anterospective study of, 56–65
and maternal complications in pregnancy, 831
Behaviorism
and asthma development, 595
and conditioned emotional reactions, 382–393
cultural conditioning, 203–213
and enuresis, 418
and learning disorders, 451
Bladder training. *See* Toilet training
Body image, in infantile psychosis, 672, 696–697
Body independence, development lines in, 141–147
Bowel training. *See* Toilet training
Brain development
in newborn, 41–45
in puppies, 27–28
Brain dysfunction, 773–837
as clinical problem, 775–778
diagnosis of, 786–787
neurophysiologic considerations in, 778–785
and pregnancy complications, 825–837
psychiatric implications of, 774–787
psychosocial factors in, 785–786
and psychotherapy in epilepsy, 788–824
Breast feeding, attitudes toward, 181–184

Castration fear, 103–104, 396
after surgery, 578–580
Catatonia, negativism in, 341, 353
Central nervous system
development in puppies, 27–29
neonatal, 41–45; defects in, 53–54
see also Brain dysfunction
Cognition, development of, 14–16
Communication, disturbed, and eating disorders, 585–590
Companionship, development of 147–148
Compulsion neurosis, infantile model for, 114
Compulsive wandering, 277
Conditioning. *See* Behaviorism
Conflict, psychic, 85–86

and epileptic seizures, 822–823
and learning disorders, 453–455
and psychosomatic disorders, 565
and reading disabilities, 494
Consciousness, neurologic mechanisms in, 782
Constitution concept, 56, 57
and psychoanalysis, 2
Constitutional factors, in infantile psychoses, 673–674
Creativity
and intelligence, 752–753
and productivity, 360–372
in schizophrenia, 635–637
Critical periods, in development of puppies, 20–38
Crying, and asthma, 606–607
Cultural conditioning, continuities and discontinuities in, 203–213
Culture conflict theories, of delinquent subcultures, 553–562

Danger, defense against, 100
Darkness, prolonged, effects of, 45
Daydreaming, 150
and learning disorders, 454–455
Defense mechanisms, 100
after loss, 274, 277
Delinquency
causes of, 507–521
and ego disturbances, 532–539
incidence of childhood loss in, 280–288
Delinquent subcultures, 540–564
and adolescence, 545–553
evolution of, 562–564
and lower-class culture, 549–552, 553–562
and masculine identification, 541–545, 559
Dependency
and negativism, 344
and school phobias, 414–417
Depression
anaclitic, 140, 237
and early parental loss, 286
Deprivational experiences in infancy, 93, 95–97, 140, 836–837
and intelligence testing, 744–755
and mental retardation, 740
and mourning, 263–289
see also Institutions
Despair
vs. ego integrity, 126–127
as response to loss, 267, 268
Detachment, as response to loss, 267, 268, 273
Development in childhood, 1–233
affectivity related to, 167–175
and behavior problems, 56–65
and concept of developmental lines, 133–156
and critical periods in puppies, 20–38
and cultural conditioning, 203–213
disorders of, 235–372
and eight ages of man, 109–132
at five years old, 73–78
at four years old, 67–73
innate and experiential interactions in, 2–19
intellectual development stages in, 157–166
and neurophysiology of newborn, 39–55
and psychic structure formation, 83–108
sexual development in, 79–82
social class affecting, 189–202
and trends in infant care, 176–188
Differentiation, concept of, 90–91
Dogs, critical periods in development of, 20–38
Dominance, and submission, 207–209
Dominated overprotected children, 293
Doubt and shame, vs. autonomy, 113–115
Dream functions, in sleep disturbances, 317–318
Drives, instinctual, 9
and eating habits, 299–302

Ear development, in puppies, 26
Eating
and aggressive instinct, 306–307
and anal pleasures, 307–308, 319
and anorexia nervosa, 567–571
and attitudes toward breast feeding, 181–184
and attitudes toward weaning, 181–184
in autistic children, 656
behavior in puppies, 30–34
development from suckling to rational eating, 142–144

Eating (continued)
disturbed communication in disorders of, 585–590
and effects of weaning, 303
and fantasies of phallic phase, 308–309
infantile disturbances in, 296–309
as instinctive process, 299–302
and oral pleasures, 305–306
problems in overprotected children, 294
and reactions to food restrictions, 577–578
resistance to, in newborn, 342–343
rigidity in schedules of, 300–302
and stages of object love, 302–304
Echolalia, delayed, 656
Ego
concept of, 86
disturbances of, 532–539
formation of, 95–102
functions of, 87
and id impulses in childhood, 136
integrity of, vs. despair, 126–127
precocious development of, 113, 140
splitting of, after loss, 274, 278
in undifferentiated phase, 91
Egocentricity, in infancy, 135
development to companionship, 147–148
Electroencephalography
in epilepsy, 800, 809–810, 817–818
in schizophrenia, 631
Emotional factors
in asthma acute attack, 600–603
in reading disabilities, 460, 488–504; cases illustrating, 498–503
Emotional reactions, conditioned, 382–393
removal of, 391–392
Encopresis, 432–433, 610–625
animistic phantasies in, 620–621
in "continuous" child, 613, 616
in "discontinuous" child, 613–615, 617
and disturbed attitudes to feces, 619
and disturbed attitudes to function, 617–618
negative attitudes in, 620
neutral attitudes in, 620
positive attitudes in, 619–620
in "retentive" child, 615–616
treatment of, 624–625
Enuresis, 418–430, 622–623
Environment
and changes in intelligence, 751–752
and development, 2–19
interaction with temperament, 59–65
and neural function, 44–45
self related to, 92–95
Enzymes in nervous system, in newborn, 43
Epigenetic chart, of psychosocial stages, 127–132
Epilepsy
electroencephalograms in, 800, 809–810, 817–818
grand mal seizures in, 808–809
and maternal complications of pregnancy, 830
psychologic tests in, 799, 810, 818
psychotherapy in, 788–824
screen spells in, 807–808
Equilibration, and intelligence, 158
Experiential and innate, interactions between, 2–19
External events, translated into internal experience, 133–135, 137
Eyes
and learning disorders, 449–450, 458–459
and reading disorders, 490
development in puppies, 25, 26
and development of visual learning, 45
hysterical disorders of, 433
visual motor pattern in schizophrenia, 634–635, 698

Facial musculature, in schizophrenia, 634
Families. *See* Parents
Fantasies, in phallic phase, and eating habits, 308–309
Fathers. *See* Parents
Fear
castration, 103–104, 396; after surgery, 578–580
in childhood, 99
irrational, 375–381
nocturnal, and enuresis, 425–426
as primal emotion, 393
and thumb-sucking, 392
See also Phobias

Feeding, *see* Eating
Feminine attributes in males, 360–372
Femininity, and passivity, 369
Five-year-old children, characteristics of, 73–78
Fixation, after loss, 274
Foundling home children, compared to nursery children in penal institution, 245–258
Four-year-old children, characteristics of, 66–73
Friendships, development of, 147–148
Frustration and aggression, coping with, 536

Games, role of, 151
Generativity, vs. stagnation, 125–126
Genetic and experiential factors, in development, 2–19
Genitality, 123–124
Gerstmann syndrome, 475, 476–477
Gratifications, in childhood, 92, 94–95, 98, 101–102
Group actions, and loss of ego control, 536–537
Guilt, vs. initiative, 116–118

Health matters, childhood concepts of, 147
Hearing test, for newborn, 46
Heart rate
  neonatal, stimuli affecting, 48–49, 51
  in puppies, 28
Heller's disease, 644
Heredity
  and developmental patterns in puppies, 34
  and experiential factors in development, 2–19
Hobbies, role of, 151–152
Hospitalism, 237–262; *see also* Institutions
Hostility
  and learning disorders, 446
  and reading disabilities, 493–494, 496
Hunger, denial of, 588
Hyperkinetic children, 776
Hypochondria, 583–584
Hysteria, 431–442
  and choice of neurosis, 438–440
  epidemics of, 432
  incidence of, 434–435
  in males, 439
  oral and oedipal material in, 440–442
  and schizophrenia, 442

Id
  concept of, 86
  and ego responses in childhood, 136
  functions of, 87
  in undifferentiated phase, 91
Idealization of parents, 104–105
Identification
  in asthma patients, 596–597
  concept of, 101, 104–106
  masculine, and delinquent subcultures, 541–545, 559
  in schizophrenia, 639–640
Identity vs. role confusion, 120–122
Idiocy, 735
Immobilization, prolonged, reactions to, 576–577
Impulses, in schizophrenia, 633–634
Individuality, in behavior problems, 56–65
Individuation
  in adolescence, 231–232
  breakdowns in, 140
Indulged overprotected children, 293
Industry, vs. inferiority, 118–120
Infant care, trends in, 176–188, 191–193
Inferiority, vs. industry, 118–120
Inhibitory therapy, in phobias, 403–404
Initiative, vs. guilt, 116–118
Innate and experiential, interactions between, 2–19
Instinctual drives, 9
  and eating habits, 299–302
Institutions
  adoption from, effects of, 756–760
  foundling home children compared to nursery children in penal institution, 245–258
  effects of hospitalization, 836–837
  hospitalism, 237–262
  intelligence in institutionalized children, 837
  reactions to hospitalization, 573–580
  studies of hospitalized infants, 167, 172
Integration, concept of, 90–91
Integrity, vs. despair, 126–127
Intellectual development
  affectivity related to, 167–175

Intellectual development (continued)
  concrete operations in, 163–164
  formal operations in, 164–166
  and object relations, 170–172
  in pre-operation stage, 161–163
  in sensori-motor stage, 159–161, 169–170
  stages of, 157–166
Intelligence
  and autism, 660
  and brain dysfunction, 777, 783–784
  changeability of, 751–752, 834–836
  and creativity, 752–753
  definitions of, 158–159
  and epilepsy, 800, 810
  in institutionalized children, 837
  and learning disorders, 445–448
  after maternal complications of pregnancy, 831
  testing of, in reading retardation, 462–467, 488
  validity of tests for, 744–755
  See also Mental retardation
Internal experience, compared to external events, 133–135, 137
Interpersonal relationships, *see* Social behavior
Intimacy, vs. isolation, 122–125
Introjection, 111
Isolation, vs. intimacy, 122–125

Language
  of autistic children, 656–658
  at five years old, 75–77
  at four years old, 69–71
  of parents of psychotic children, 700
  in schizophrenia, 637–638
  speech disorders after maternal complications of pregnancy, 831–832
  vocalization in puppies, 29–30
Latency period, 105–106, 120
  adoptions in, 141
Learning
  neurologic mechanisms in, 780
  psychoanalytic hypotheses of, 98
Learning disorders, 443–504
  focusing attention in, 454–455
  and hostility, 446
  and intelligence, 445–448
  intrapsychic conflicts in, 453–455
  and object relations, 451
  and painful conditioning experiences, 451
  and permissive upbringing, 455–456
  and physical impairment, 449–450
  and reading readiness, 448–449
  and relationship with parents, 452, 490
  and relationship with teacher, 451–452, 490
  and school phobias, 411
  tutoring in, 452–453
  See also Reading disabilities
Learning theory. *See* Behaviorism
Libido
  development of, 80–81
  physical illness affecting, 581–582
Life cycle, epigenetic chart of, 127–132
Light, neonatal responses to, 46
Loss
  in childhood, incidence in psychiatric patients, 280–288
  responses to, 270–275
Love, adolescent, 121
Lying, childhood concepts of, 174

Males, feminine attributes in, 360–372
Masculinity
  and activity, 369
  and delinquent subcultures, 541–545, 559
Masturbation
  attitudes toward, 177–179, 187
  enuresis as substitute for, 426–427
Maturational crisis, in infants, 9–11
Megacolon, psychogenic, 615
Mental retardation, 725–771
  and hidden I.Q., 744–755
  historical perspective of, 733–743
  incidence of, 742
  and maternal complications of pregnancy, 830–831
  and maternal deprivation, 740
  mild, 736, 741–742
  and parents' feelings about children, 761–771
  terminology of, 734–735
  in young savage of Aveyron, 726–732
Middle-class parents, child-rearing by, 189–202
Moral feelings, and affectivity, 173–174
Morons, 736
Mothers, *see* Parents

Motor behavior
  at five years old, 73-74
  at four years old, 67-68
  in hyperkinesis, 776
  in schizophrenia, 631-634
  see also Sensorimotor behavior
Mourning, in childhood, 263-289
Myelinization, in newborn, 42-43

Negativism, 340-359
  inner, 353
Nervous system
  parasympathetic, in asthma, 604-605
  in schizophrenia, 630-635
  see also Autonomic *and* Central nervous system
Neurological appraisal, in reading retardation, 472-477, 489
Neuromuscular responses, neonatal, association with autonomic responses, 49-50
Neurophysiology
  and brain dysfunction, 778-785
  in newborn, 39-55
Neurotic disorders, 373-442
  feeding disturbances, 302-309
  reading disabilities, 460, 488-504
Newborn
  autonomic function in, 47-50
  central nervous system of, 41-45
  maturational crisis in, 9-11
  neurophysiology of, 39-55
  responses to stimulation, 48-53
  sensorimotor behavior in, 13-14, 45
  sleep patterns in, 11-12
  smiling response, in 12-13
Normal development, 1-233
  See also Development in childhood
Nursery school, adaptation to, 154-156

Obesity in childhood, 585-590
Object cathexis, 98
Object constancy, as phase in development, 140-141
Object loss, responses to, 270-275
Object relations
  in autistic children, 659
  in childhood, 94
  and eating habits, 302-304
  and learning disorders, 451
  stages of, 170-172
Occupational differences, in middle-class and working-class parents, 196-197
Occupational identity, in adolescence, 121
Odors
  neonatal responses to, 46
  reactions to, in puppies, 26
Oedipus complex, 81-82, 103
  and phobic disorders, 395-396
Operations, and intelligence, 158-159
Oppositional syndromes and behavior, 340-359
Oral pleasures, feeding related to, 305-306
Oral sadism, and eating habits, 306
Organic drivenness, concept of, 776
Organic feeding disturbances, infantile, 298-299
Organic syndromes, *see* Brain dysfunction
Organicity, concept of, 825
Orphanages, effects of, *see* Institutions
Overprotection, maternal, 290-295

Pain, childhood reactions to, 580-581
Parasympathetic nervous system, in asthma, 604-605
Parents
  of adolescents with superego defects, 522-531
  areas of difference between child and adult, 135-137
  of asthmatic children, 591-592
  of autistic children, 663-664
  and behavior problems in children, 61, 64, 65
  of brain-damaged children, 786
  child's body as mother's property, 583-584
  dependency on mother, in school phobias, 414-417
  of encopretic children, 613, 614, 615
  of enuretic children, 427-428, 622-623
  of epileptic children, 799, 802, 812
  and feeding disturbances in children, 304, 589
  feelings about retarded children, 761-771
  idealization of, 104-105
  and learning disorders in child, 452, 490

Parents (continued)
maternal care of newborn, in animals, 54
maternal deprivation in infancy, *see* Deprivational experiences in infancy
maternal overprotection, 290–295
mother-child interactions, 94, 96, 111, 135, 139, 172, 224, 252, 303–304
and psychosomatic disorders in children, 566
of psychotic children, 628, 692–693, 706–707; speech of, 700
reactions of boys to feminine functions of mothers, 361–372
roles as child and father, 204–213
social class and parent-child relationships, 189–202
and symbiotic psychoses in infants, 673
tension reduction by mothers, 9–10
Passivity, and femininity, 369
Penal institution, nursery children in, compared to children in foundling home, 245–258
Perception, as ego function, 87
Permissive upbringing, and learning disorders, 455–456
Perseveration, in infancy, 345
Personality
and asthma development, 591, 597–600
formation of, 175
interaction of temperament with environment, 59–65
and psychosomatic disorders, 565
Phallic phase of development, 102–103
fantasies of, and eating habits, 308–309
Phobias, 375–381
anxiety in, 396, 397–398, 411, 412
behavior theory of, 401–403
behavior therapy of, 403–405
as conditioned response, 383–393, 402
etiology and treatment of, 394–409
psychoanalytic theory of, 395–401; reinterpretation of, 405–408
and reading disabilities, 497–498
school, 405–406, 410–417
Physical illness
childhood reactions to, 572–584
and negativism, 348
Play activities, and ability to work, 148–150
Pleasure, and eating, 300–301
Posture
in autistic children, 656
and reflexes in schizophrenia, 632
Pregnancy complications
and behavior disorders, 831
and brain damage, 825–837
and epilepsy, 830
and mental retardation, 830–831
and speech disorders, 831–832
Premature births, incidence of, 832
Preoedipal period
development in, 141
in males, 365
Productivity, and creativity, 360–372
Projection, mechanisms in, 111
Protest, as response to loss, 267, 268, 270
Psychiatric evaluation, in reading retardation, 469–472
Psychic conflict, 85–86; *see also* Conflict, psychic
Psychic energy, 93
Psychic structure, formation of, 83–108
Psychoanalytic theory
and reading disabilities, 487–504
views on adolescence, 221–233
Psychometric evaluation, in reading retardation, 462–467
Psychophysiologic disorders, 47–48, 565–625
anorexia nervosa, 567–571
asthma, 591–609
disturbed communication and eating disorders, 585–590
encopresis, 610–625
and mother-child relationships, 566
and personality types, 565
and reactions to physical illness, 572–584
Psychoses in childhood, 627–723
adaptive functions in, 695–696
age of onset, 643–646
aggression in, 641
and anxiety, 641–642
art work in, 635–637
autism, infantile, 647–669, 674–677; *see also* Autism
body ego in, 672, 696–697

case reports of, 680–682
control processes in, 697–702
constitutional factors in, 673–674
diagnosis of, 629–630
differential diagnosis of, 687
environmental and organismic factors in, 702–709
etiology of, 702–709
genetic research in, 17–18
and hysteria, 442
identification in, 639–640
impulses in, 633–634
infantile, 670–687
interpersonal relationships in, 642–643
language and thought in, 637–638
mother-child relationship in, 673
motor behavior in, 631–634
nervous system in, 630–635
parents of children with, 692–693, 706–707
postural reflexes in, 632
psychological problems in, 638–642
retrospective view of, 688–709
self-awareness in, 672, 696–697, 700
sexual problems in, 640–641
space child, 710–723
symbiotic psychoses, 670–687
transference in, 717–720
visual motor pattern in, 634–635, 698
Psychosocial stages, epigenetic chart of, 127–132
Psychosomatic disorders, *see* Psychophysiologic disorders
Psychotherapy, in epilepsy, 788–824
Puberty and adolescence, 221–233; *see also* Adolescence
Puppies, critical periods in development of, 20–38

Rage, *see* Anger
Reading disabilities
achievement testing in, 467–469
and aggression, 494, 496
contents of books affecting, 497–498
diagnostic criteria for, 459
emotional factors in, 460, 488–504; cases illustrating, 498–503
and eye defects, 490
and hostility, 493–494, 496
after maternal complications in pregnancy, 831
neurological appraisal in, 472–477, 489
from neurological deficits, 461
and phobias, 497–498
primary, 461; remedial reading therapy in, 478–483
psychiatric evaluation in, 469–472
psychoanalytic contributions to, 487–504
psychometric evaluation in, 462–467, 488
and relationship with parents or teachers, 451–452, 490, 494
remedial reading therapy in, 477–485
research approach to, 457–486
secondary, 461; remedial reading therapy in, 483–485
single determining factors in, 459–460
and strephosymbolia, 450, 458
terminology in, 458–459
Reading habits, in overprotected children, 294
Reading readiness, 448–449
Regression, and enuresis, 430
Religion, trust as factor in, 112–113, 115
Repetitious movements, in infancy, 345
Repression
concept of, 100
after loss, 274
Resistance, and negativism, 341–359
Responsibilities in childhood, conditioning for, 205–207
Retardation, mental, 725–771; *see also* Mental retardation
Riddance processes, in asthma, 605–606
Role confusion, vs. identity, 120–122

Sadism, oral, and eating habits, 306
Sameness, obsession for, in autistic children, 658–659
Savage of Aveyron, 726–732
Scapegoating, 525
Schizophrenia, *see* Psychoses in childhood
School
adaptation to nursery school, 154–156
and learning disorders, 443–504
oppositional school syndromes, 355
School phobia, 405–406, 410–417

School phobia (continued)
and dependency on mother, 414-417
and learning disorders, 411
Self, and environment, 92-95
Self-awareness, in schizophrenia, 672, 696-697, 700
Sense organs, development in puppies, 26-27
Sensory deprivation, effects of, 45
Sensorimotor behavior
in brain dysfunction, 776
in infants, 13-14, 45-47; and intelligence, 159-161, 169-170
see also Motor behavior
Separation anxiety, 140
Separation from mother, *see* Deprivational experiences in infancy
Sexuality
and adolescent development, 223-231
and childhood development, 79-82
and feminine attributes in males, 360-372
immature, in infants, 135
in overprotected children, 294
and phobic disorders, 397
in primitive societies, 209-210, 212
and roles in children and adults, 209-210
in schizophrenia, 640-641
in young adults, 122-125
Shame and doubt, vs. autonomy, 113-115
Sibling relationships, in schizophrenia, 642-643
Smiling, social, in infants, 12-13
Sleep patterns, disturbances
in early childhood, 310-339
and anal period conflicts, 319-322
dream function in, 317-318
onset of, and traumatic situation, 312-319
profound disorder in 18-month-old girl, 322-338
neonatal, 11-12
in overprotected children, 294
Social behavior
in autistic children, 659-660
at five years, 77-78
at four years, 71-73
in puppies, 29-30; food associated with, 32-33
in schizophrenia, 642-643
see also Antisocial behavior
Social class, and parent-child relationships, 189-202
Sociological theories, of delinquent subcultures, 540-564
Soiling, fear of, and sleep disorders, 319-322, 330-335
Sound, neonatal responses to, 46
Space child, 710-723
Speech, *see* Language
Stagnation, vs. generativity, 125-126
Stealing, in adolescence, 528-529
Strephosymbolia, 450, 458
Subcultures, delinquent, 540-564
Sublimation
in preadolescence, 141
and reading disabilities, 494, 496
Submission, and dominance, 207-209
Sucking frustration, in puppies, 33-34
Suicidal patients, 286
Superego
concept of, 86
defects in adolescence, 522-531
formation of, 102-106
functions of, 87
Surgery, childhood reactions to, 578-580
Symbiotic psychoses, infantile, 670-687
compared to autism, 682-687
Symbols
formation in schizophrenia, 638
function in childhood, 161

Tantrums, and negativism, 352
Teachers, and learning and reading disorders in children, 451-452, 490, 494
Temperament, interaction with environment, 59-65
Tension
accumulation of, and hysteria, 439
reduction of, by mothers, 9-10
Thought
in autism, 660
and development of cognition, 14-16
as ego function, 86
in schizophrenia, 637-638
Thumb-sucking
attitudes toward, 177-181, 187
as compensatory device, 392
Time, childhood concepts of, 136

Toilet training
  attitudes toward, 178, 179, 184–187
  conflicts in, 98–99
  and development of bladder and bowel control, 144–146
  and encopresis, 622–623
  and enuresis, 418–430
  in institutionalized children, 259
  and sleep disturbances, 320–322, 330–335
Tonsillectomy, childhood reactions to, 579
Tooth eruption, in puppies, 24–25
Toys, and play activities, 148–150
Transference, in schizophrenic children, 717–720
Truancy, causes of, 527–528
Trust, basic, vs. mistrust, 109–113

Undifferentiated phase, in development, 91–92

Vision, *see* Eyes

Wandering, compulsive, 277
Weaning
  changes in attitudes toward, 181–184
  effects of, 303
Whining, in puppies, 29–30
Womb envy, 360–372
Work ability, play activities related to, 148–150
Working-class parents, child-rearing by, 189–202

NAME INDEX

Aberle, D. F., 196
Abraham, K., 4, 6, 276, 296, 297, 306, 396, 397, 712
Abramson, H. A., 594, 596, 598, 605
Abse, D. W., 438, 442
Abt, I. A., 441
Ackerman, N. W., 133
Adelson, J. B., 214–220, 221
Adler, A., 433, 434
Aichhorn, A., 507–521, 523, 528, 532
Ainsworth, M. D., 266
Akert, K., 783
Alexander, F., 88, 508, 523, 565, 591, 593, 597, 602, 604
Allen, F. H., 586
Allport, F., 90, 354
Alpert, A., 140
Amatruda, C. S., 66, 477
Ambrose, A., 289
American Association of Mental Deficiency, 725, 734, 739, 741
Anderson, J. E., 193
Anderson, S., 232–233
Angel, A., 421
Anthony, E. J., 157, 373, 610–625
Appell, G., 10
Arey, L. B., 42
Argyle, M., 622
Aries, P., 176
Arlow, J. A., 79
Arthur, B., 444
Aubry, J., 267
Augenbraun, B., 592
Azam, E., 86

Babinski, J., 434
Bachmann, F., 459
Bacon, C. L., 598
Baker, C. T., 487
Baker, R. G., 222
Bakwin, H., 239, 240, 420, 740, 776
Bakwin, R. M., 776
Bales, R. F., 200
Balint, M., 94
Barcroft, 46
Bard, P., 783
Barker, S., 789, 822
Barker, W., 789, 821, 822
Barkin, S., 752
Barron, D. H., 45, 46
Barry, H., Jr., 281, 282, 284, 285, 286
Bartemeier, L. H., 806, 822
Baruch, D., 596
Battersby, W. S., 783–784
Baudouin, C., 421
Beach, F. A., 18
Beck, S. J., 800, 810, 818, 823
Behrens, M., 706
Beier, D., 734
Beitel, R. J., 433
Bell, A., 362, 597, 598
Bell, J. E., 503
Bender, L., 56, 96, 239, 240, 374, 459, 476, 628–646, 678, 705, 773, 778, 787
Bender, M. B., 473, 476
Benedek, T., 41, 93, 94, 96, 110, 228, 290, 670
Benedict, R., 203–213
Benjamin, E., 351
Benjamin, J. D., 2–19, 56, 361, 394, 627, 774
Bennett, C. C., 476
Benon, R., 433
Bentley, A. F., 3
Benton, A., 744

Bergman, P., 14, 56, 688
Bergmann, T., 573, 577
Berkovitz, I., 598
Berman, I. R., 488
Bernfeld, S., 297
Bernheim, H., 431
Bernstein, L., 18
Bettelheim, B., 360, 628, 647
Beverly, 420
Bibring, G., 301
Biermann, G., 433, 434
Binet, A., 86
Binois, R., 433
Birch, H. G., 56–65, 774
Bird, C., 488
Blan, A., 776
Blanchard, P., 458, 460, 487–504
Blau, A., 460
Blauvelt, H., 54
Bleyer, A., 419
Bliss, E., 568
Bloch, H., 546–553
Blom, G., 572
Bloom, G. C., 594
Blos, P., 203, 214, 221–233
Blum, G. S., 296
Blume, D., 26
Bodel, P., 174
Bond, E. D., 776
Bornstein, B., 311, 319, 397, 398–399, 400, 406, 407, 421, 740
Bostock, J., 599, 622
Botstein, A., 703
Bourneville, D., 736
Bourru, H., 86
Bowlby, J., 20, 140, 237, 263–289, 382, 573, 740
Bowman, K. M., 631
Brain, W. R., 476
Branch, C. H., 568
Brenner, C., 79
Brenton, M., 360
Breuer, J., 4, 431, 434
Bridger, W. H., 2, 51
Broadbent, W. H., 459
Broadwin, I. T., 411
Brodbeck, A., 32, 740
Brody, S., 296, 360
Bronfenbrenner, U., 191–193, 199, 200, 201
Bronner, A., 490, 491, 505, 523
Brown, E. A., 597
Brown, F., 282, 283, 285, 286
Brown, J. R., 785
Brownfield, E. D., 49, 50
Bruch, H., 291, 567, 585–590
Brückner, G. H., 349–350
Brunswick, R. M., 94, 360, 364, 365
Bucy, P. C., 783
Buhler, C., 149, 252, 351
Buhler, K., 158
Bukantz, S. C., 594, 597, 603
Burlingham, D. T., 96, 237, 267, 273, 672
Burot, P., 86
Burt, C., 491
Busemann, A., 351
Butler, A., 434
Buxbaum, E., 97, 290
Bykov, K. M., 595

Cairns, H., 782
Caldwell, B. M., 237
Callender, W. M., 267
Camp, B., 740
Campbell, M. F., 420
Camuset, L., 86
Cannon, D. J., 27
Cannon, W. B., 604
Cappon, D., 648
Carmichael, L., 45, 46, 54
Carroll, E. E., 191
Carter, J. W., Jr., 434
Casler, L., 238
Caulfield, E., 432, 438
Cazden, C. B., 189
Chapin, H. D., 238
Charcot, J. M., 431
Charles, M. S., 28
Chesher, E. C., 474
Chess, S., 56–65
Chidester, L., 740
Child, I. L., 613, 625
Chobot, R., 597
Christoffel, V. H., 420, 421
Claiborne, J. H., 458
Claparède, E., 158, 169, 458
Clark, L. P., 44, 739, 788
Clarke, A., 740
Clarkson, 594, 597
Clausen, J. A., 191
Cloward, R. A., 540–564
Cobb, S., 434, 597, 789
Coghill, G. E., 46, 779

Cohen, A. K., 542–543, 544
Cohen, L., 776
Cohen, M. B., 371
Cohn, R., 476, 787
Coleman, J. S., 443
Coleman, R. W., 56, 290
Colm, H. N., 375
Compayre, G., 252
Conel, J. L. R., 42, 43
Coolidge, J. C., 405, 410, 596
Costello, C. G., 374, 382, 394–409, 418
Cramer, J. P., 373
Creak, M., 432, 434, 593, 600, 648
Critchley, M., 476, 477
Curran, F. J., 637

Daltroff, W., 577
Darr, G. C., 664
Davenport, C., 737
David, M., 10
Davies, S., 740
Davis, A., 747, 753
Davis, C. M., 296, 302
Dawes, L. G., 432
De Ajuriaguerra, J., 459
Dearborn, W. F., 476
DeGara, P. F., 593
De Hirsch, K., 458
DeJong, R. N., 457–486
DeMartino, M. F., 740
De Sandoval, D. M., 433
Dekker, F., 595
Dembo, T., 761
Denenberg, V. H., 20
Despert, J. L., 637, 648, 661, 668, 740
Deutsch, F., 572, 593, 595, 597, 598, 602
Deutsch, H., 189, 272, 274, 277, 421, 671
Devereux, G., 208
Dewey, J., 3
Dollard, J., 394
Douvan, E. 217, 748
Drew, A. L., 457–486
Drews, E. M., 460
Dubo, S., 577
Dufay, 86
Dunbar, H. F., 565, 598
Durfee, H., 239, 240
Dusser de Barenne, J. G., 780
Duvall, E. M., 194–195
Dye, H. B., 740, 757

Eames, T. H., 476
Earle, A. M., 286
Earle, B. V., 286
Echlin, F. A., 778
Ederer, S., 419
Eells, K., 753
Eisenberg, L., 395, 405, 410, 665, 668, 773, 774–787, 825
Eissler, K. R., 505, 507
Ekstein, R., 628, 710–723
Elkin, H., 211
Elkonin, D. B., 53, 54
Ellingson, R. J., 52
Ellis, A., 394, 398, 460, 476
Engel, F., 565
Engel, G. L., 50, 53, 269
English, O. S., 375–381, 394, 434, 437, 440, 445–456, 457, 487, 493
Erikson, E. H., 8, 17, 79, 98, 109–132, 176, 230, 368, 700, 712
Escalona, S. K., 9, 14, 56, 394, 647, 688
Esersky, J. M., 420
Eustis, R. S., 473
Eysenck, H. J., 382, 394, 397, 401, 402, 403, 405

Fabian, A. A., 635
Fairbairn, W. R. D., 277
Falstein, E. I., 410–417, 567
Farnham, M. F., 442
Federn, P., 439, 440, 441, 442
Feinstein, 567
Feldman, F., 734
Fenichel, O., 79, 230, 297, 434, 438, 527, 602, 621
Ferenczi, S., 95, 438, 673
Fernald, W., 740, 756
Finch, S. M., 506, 540, 566
Finger, F. W., 784
Fink, G., 599
Fisher, A., 33
Fisher, J., 787
Flavell, J. H., 133
Fodor, N., 433
Foss, B. M., 39
Fowler, G. B., 611
Fraga-Arroyo, R., 437
Fraiberg, S., 310–339
Francois, P., 433
Fredericson, E., 21, 29, 30
Fremont-Smith, F., 822
French, J. D., 95, 782

French, T., 591, 593, 597, 602
Freud, A., 8, 79, 83, 100, 106, 133–156, 224, 231, 235, 237, 263, 273, 277, 290, 291, 296–309, 373, 439, 440, 441, 493, 494, 495, 572–584, 585, 672, 716
Freud, S., 4–7, 8–9, 10, 18–19, 79–82, 84–107, 123, 128, 223, 224, 267, 269, 270, 273, 275, 278, 297, 313, 315, 317–318, 375, 380, 381, 395–397, 420, 431, 434, 438, 496, 502, 508, 589, 617, 623, 671, 673, 788, 822
Friedenberg, E., 214, 220
Friedlander, K., 507
Friedman, S., 628
Fried, M. E., 2, 50, 56, 566, 579
Fromm, E., 752
Fuller, J. L., 21, 24, 27, 28
Fulton, J. F., 779, 783

Gallagher, J. R., 226, 227
Gann, E., 460
Gantt, W. H., 403
Garfield, S. L., 733, 734
Garner, A., 566
Garsche, G., 11
Gates, A. I., 460, 489, 490, 491, 492, 496, 503
Geleerd, E. R., 682, 710
Gellhorn, E., 596, 604
Gerard, M. W., 374, 418–430, 566, 591, 593, 601, 602
Gerard, R., 42
Gerö, G., 97, 276
Gerstmann, J., 475, 477
Gesell, A., 46, 66–78, 133, 193, 252, 256, 296, 298, 299, 300, 303, 311, 340, 477, 726
Gesell, B. C., 66
Gibbs, E. L., 777
Gibbs, F. A., 800, 809, 820
Giffin, M. E., 410, 522
Gill, M. M., 79
Gillen, F. J., 212
Gillette, W. R., 440, 441
Gladwin, T., 734, 740
Glasser, W., 444
Glidewell, J. C., 59
Glover, E., 88
Glueck, E., 283, 285, 287, 506
Glueck, S., 283, 285, 287, 506
Goddard, H., 736, 756
Goitein, P. L., 597
Gold, L., 630
Goldfarb, W., 237, 239, 266, 688–709, 740, 837
Golding, W., 592
Goldman, F., 296
Goldstein, K., 779
Goodenough, F. L., 340
Goodglass, H., 474
Gottschalk, L., 773, 788–824
Gouin-Décarie, T., 157, 170, 171
Gowers, W. R., 822
Graham, F. K., 46, 50, 53
Gray, C. T., 491
Grebelskaya-Albatz, E., 661
Green, R., 360, 740
Greenacre, P., 10, 97, 361, 442, 523, 527, 573, 577, 670, 671, 674, 679, 680
Greenblatt, M., 189
Greenson, R. R., 789, 822
Gregory, I., 280, 281, 286
Grenlich, W. W., 227
Grewel, F., 648
Griesinger, W., 739
Grotjahn, M., 363
Group for the Advancement of Psychiatry, 133, 236, 670, 733
Gull, W., 567–571
Guttman, S., 394

Häberlin, 351
Haggard, E. A., 747–748, 749, 750, 752, 754
Hallgren, B., 459, 477
Hallowitz, D., 594
Hamill, R. C., 420
Hammond, W. S., 43
Harlow, H. F., 20, 237, 263, 266, 784
Harman, P. J., 26, 27
Harms, E. E., 310, 442
Harms, I., 757
Harrington, M., 189
Harris, I., 444, 487
Harris, M. C., 597
Harrison, S. I., 83, 189, 361, 394
Hartmann, H., 8, 15, 17, 79, 83–108, 146, 156, 230, 298, 394, 532, 671, 688
Havighurst, R., 747
Head, H., 474

Healy, W., 505, 523
Hebb, D. O., 42, 45, 588, 744, 751, 783
Heilbrunn, G., 789, 823
Heiman, M., 568
Heinicke, C., 267, 573
Hendrik, I., 91, 94, 119, 789
Henry, C. E., 778
Henry, J., 438
Hermann, K., 475
Herrera, J. G., 437
Hess, E. H., 20
Hess, W. R., 783
Hetzer, H., 240, 351
Higgins, J., 789
Hildreth, G., 476
Hilgard, J., 274, 287
Hincks, E., 491
Hinde, R., 289
Hines, M., 780
Hirschberg, J. C., 311
Hoff, H., 632
Hoffer, W., 139, 146, 582
Hollingworth, L., 491
Holmes, F. B., 408
Holt, J., 444
Holt, K. S., 267
Holt, R. R., 79
Homburger, A., 419
Hooker, D., 43, 45
Hoskins, R. G., 630
Howe, S. G., 735
Hunter, J., 782
Hurst, A., 593, 601
Huschka, M., 622
Huxley, J., 131
Hyman, H. H., 197

Ilg, G., 66, 252, 296, 298, 299, 300, 303, 340
Illingworth, R. S., 267
Ingham, H. V., 281
Ingram, W., 457–486, 783
Inkeles, A., 195
Irvine, R., 460
Irwin, H., 726
Irwin, O., 740
Itard, J. M., 726–732, 735, 738

Jackson, H., 779
Jackson, J. H., 297, 458, 503, 579
Jacobson, E., 269, 276, 365, 683, 687
James, M., 140
James, W. T., 27
Janet, P., 86, 89, 169, 431, 434, 435
Jansky, J. J., 458
Jasper, H. H., 777, 780, 782
Jelliffe, S. E., 789
Jensen, R. A., 432, 435
Jersild, A. T., 376, 377, 408
Jessner, L., 572, 573, 579, 592, 593, 594, 597–598, 599, 602
Johnson, A. M., 291, 405, 410–417, 522–531, 532
Johnston, P. W., 460, 476
Jones, E., 4, 367, 491
Jones, H. E., 240
Jones, H. G., 397, 401, 402, 403, 404
Jones, M. C., 382, 394, 408, 460
Jones, V., 498
Josselyn, I., 228
Judas, 567

Kagan, J., 58, 360, 487
Kahn, E., 773, 776
Kaila, E., 12
Kaiser, S., 96
Kallman, F., 688
Kanner, L., 66, 290, 432, 439, 637, 639, 644, 647–669, 670, 674, 740, 761–771, 776, 823
Kaplan, 579
Kardiner, A., 553, 789
Karlin, I. W., 419
Karpman, B., 522
Kasatkin, 54
Katan, A., 134, 418
Kaufman, M., 568
Kawi, A. A., 829
Kellogg, L. A., 348
Kelloff, W. N., 348
Kempf, E., 784
Kemph, J. P., 789
Kennard, M. A., 44
Kennedy, C., 42, 43, 44, 53, 774
Kennedy, R., 740
Kerr, J., 459
Kessler, J. W., 235
King, D., 33
King, J. A., 32
Kirk, S., 740
Kirsner, J. B., 593, 594
Klapp, O. E., 215
Klein, E., 396, 397, 406

Klein, M., 39, 139, 276, 278–279, 297, 306, 441, 496, 578, 641, 681, 684
Kleitman, N., 310
Klemm, E., 433
Klopfer, B., 239
Kluckhohn, C., 190
Kluver, H., 43, 783
Knapp, P. H., 591–609
Knobloch, H., 825–837
Kohn, M. L., 189–202
Kopel, D., 460
Kopeloff, N., 822
Kozol, J., 444
Kraepelin, E., 373
Kretschmer, E., 434
Krieger, H. P., 703
Kris, E., 4, 8, 17, 56, 83–108, 290, 394, 532
Kris, M., 58
Kristiansen, K., 821
Kubie, L., 394
Kunst, M. S., 493
Kussmaul, A., 458, 459
Kvaraceus, W. C., 554, 557, 558, 559, 560, 561

La Barre, W., 437
Lacey, J. I., 48
Lachman, G. S., 433
Lamont, J., 592, 600
Lampl-de Groot, J., 365
Landes, R., 207
Landis, C., 783
Langford, W. S., 458
Langworthy, O. R., 42, 783
Lapouse, R., 59
Lashley, K. S., 92, 779, 780, 781
Laubenthal, F., 460
Laufer, M., 774
Launay, C., 459
Lazarus, A. A., 404–405
Lazarus, R. S., 777
Lecomte, G., 458
Lehtinen, L., 773, 774, 787
Lennox, W. G., 788, 789, 823, 824
Lesser, L. I., 647–669
Levy, D. M., 33, 264, 290–295, 340–359, 462, 577, 579, 585, 586
Levy, K., 420
Levy, R., 740
Lewin, K., 169
Lewis, H., 284
Liddell, H. S., 403
Lieberman, 597
Lilienfeld, A. M., 828, 829, 831
Linch, A., 437
Lindemann, E., 269, 282, 284
Lindsley, D. B., 781
Linton, R., 210
Lipkowitz, H. H., 640
Lippard, V. W., 594
Lippman, H., 420, 522
Lipset, S. M., 198
Lipton, E. L., 2, 39–55, 56, 567, 592, 597
Lipton, R., 237, 756
Litin, E. M., 410, 522
Littman, R. A., 192
Livingston, S., 777
Lloyd, D. P. C., 779
Loewenstein, R. M., 8, 83–108, 532
Long, R., 592
Lorenz, K., 13, 20, 21, 263, 340
Lovibond, S. H., 418
Lowrey, L. G., 239, 240, 462
Luce, G. G., 310
Lucretius, 19
Luisa Palacios, T. S., 433
Luke, J. A., 577
Lustman, S. L., 48, 51, 394

Macciotta, G., 420
Maccoby, E., 192, 360
MacFarlane, J. W., 58, 235
MacKenzie, J., 594
MacLean, P. D., 783
Maenchen, A., 311
Magoun, H. W., 780, 781
Mahler, M., 95, 139, 140, 291, 341, 577, 648, 661, 665, 670–687
Margolin, S. G., 601
Mark, H. J., 834
Marmor, J., 79, 439, 440, 441, 442
Marston, M. V., 20
Masserman, J. H., 88, 783
Masterson, J. F., 214
McDermott, J. F., 189, 566
McDermott, N. T., 597
McGraw, M. B., 46
McGuinness, A. C., 420
McKay, B., 740
McKay, H. D., 561
Mead, M., 203, 214, 360
Meade, G. H., 700

Meek, L., 491
Meili, R., 14
Menninger, K. A., 740, 789
Meyer, A., 263, 264, 288
Meyer, B. C., 587
Meyers, D., 690, 699, 706
Michaels, J. J., 418, 601
Middlemore, M. P., 297
Miller, D. R., 176, 189, 198, 214
Miller, H., 596
Miller, N., 394
Miller, S. M., 198
Miller, W. B., 542–543, 544, 554–562
Minuchin, S., 189
Mirsky, 17, 565
Mittelman, B., 586, 789, 822
Mohr, G. J., 47, 297, 420, 592, 597
Moltz, H., 20
Money, J., 360, 361, 458
Monk, M. A., 59
Monroe, M., 443, 459, 460, 476, 488, 490, 491
Montague, M. F. A., 2
Moore, R. C. A., 192
Morel, B., 737
Morgan, J. J. B., 383
Morgan, W. P., 458, 459
Morrell, F., 780
Moruzzi, G., 781
Moss, H. A., 58, 487
Mowrer, O. H., 394, 418
Mowrer, W., 418
Mundy, L., 740
Murie, A., 23
Murphy, L. B., 58, 360, 369
Murphy, R. C., 648
Murray, W., 749, 750, 753
Muus, R. E., 214
Myer, J. S., 782

Naegele, K. D., 196
Nagera, H., 133, 235, 263, 310, 373
Nash, E., 827, 834
Nelson, J. B., 360–372
Nelson, V. P., 487
Nemetz, S. J., 596, 597, 601, 605
Niederhoffer, A., 546–553
Nielson, J. M., 489
Noelpp, B., 595
Noelpp-Eschenhagen, I., 595
Norton, A., 284
Nunberg, H., 8, 488

Oberndorf, C. P., 595
Odier, C., 167
Ohlin, L. E., 540–564
Olden, C., 176
Olson, W. C., 459
Oltman, J. E., 284
Omwake, E., 761
O'Neal, P., 432, 434, 437, 439
Orton, S. T., 450, 458, 476, 489, 492
Ottenberg, P., 593, 595, 597

Paine, R. S., 39
Paracelsus, 735
Parenton, V. J., 432
Parkes, C. M., 275
Parsons, T., 200, 541–542, 543
Pasamanick, B., 744, 773, 825–837
Pavenstedt, E., 39, 189, 628
Pavlov, I. P., 382, 780
Pearson, G. H. J., 375–381, 394, 434, 437, 445–456, 457, 460, 487, 493, 579
Peiper, A., 11, 39
Penfield, W., 780, 821
Peterson, D. B., 821
Peto, E., 297
Piaget, J., 14, 16, 105, 133, 157–175, 619, 725
Pierce, H., 740
Pierce-Jones, J., 192
Pilot, M. L., 594
Pollack, M., 698, 703
Pollock, G. H., 271
Pond, D. A., 822
Potter, H. W., 733–743
Powers, D. A., 432
Pratt, K. C., 46
Prentice, N., 592
Preston, M. I., 490
Pribram, K. H., 783
Proctor, J. T., 431–442
Provence, S., 56, 237, 290, 756
Prugh, D. G., 267, 286, 565, 610, 621, 623, 624
Purcell, K., 594, 603
Purtell, J. J., 433, 437, 439

Quadfasel, F. A., 474

Rabinovitch, R. D., 457–486
Rachman, S., 374, 382, 394–409, 418

Rackeman, 600
Radin, S. S., 690
Rado, S., 604
Ramirez, L., 774
Rangell, L., 83
Rank, B., 628, 648
Rao, L., 44
Rapaport, A., 602
Rapaport, D., 8, 15, 17, 83, 394
Rapaport, J., 462, 638, 640, 641
Raynor, R., 374, 382–393, 394, 397, 402, 403, 418
Razran, G., 593, 595
Redl, F., 507, 532–539
Reese, W. G., 781
Reich, W., 381, 523
Reichsmann, F., 50
Reiser, M. F., 2, 51
Reissmann, F., 189, 198, 443, 725, 744–755
Rexford, E., 522
Rheingold, H., 740
Ribble, M. A., 32, 671, 740
Ricciuti, H. N., 15
Richfield, J., 394
Richmond, J. B., 39–55, 56, 592, 610, 615
Richter, D., 43
Rider, R. V., 832
Riese, H., 189
Riese, W., 458
Riesen, A. H., 45
Rimland, B., 647
Ripin, R., 240
Robbins, E., 58, 432, 434, 437, 439
Robertson, J., 136, 267, 289, 573
Robinson, H. M., 444
Rogers, M. E., 831
Rogerson, C. H., 594, 597
Róheim, G., 212
Rollins, N., 592
Rollman-Branch, H. S., 266, 286
Ronne, H., 459
Root, N., 273
Rorschach, H., 788
Rosenbluth, D., 573
Rosenfeld, S. K., 710
Rosenthal, R., 487
Ross, M. H., 780
Ross, S., 33
Roudinesco, J., 267
Ruegamer, W. R., 18
Rutherford, W. J., 458
Rutter, M., 57, 60

Sadger, 421
Saenger, G., 740
Salsac, C., 433
Samter, M., 593, 594
Sandler, J., 83
Sarason, S., 396, 397, 734, 740, 744
Schachter, M., 420, 648, 662
Schaefer, E. S., 200
Schaffer, H. R., 266, 267
Scheibel, A. B., 39
Scheibel, M. E., 39
Scheidler, E. P., 444
Schenke, L. W., 757
Schiavi, R. C., 595
Schick, A., 789
Schilder, P., 94, 96, 459, 476, 489, 632, 633, 637, 638, 672, 787, 789
Schlossman, A., 238
Schmideberg, M., 297, 523
Schneer, H. I., 599, 601
Schnurmann, A., 399, 407
Schuler, E. A., 432
Schur, M., 9, 79, 263, 442, 601
Schwartz, M., 593
Scott, J. P., 18, 20–38, 54
Scoville, W. B., 778
Segal, H. L., 50
Segal, J., 310
Seguin, E., 735
Segundo, J. P., 782
Seitz, P. F. D., 54
Selesnick, S., 592
Sellin, T., 556
Serota, H. M., 809, 810, 817, 818
Sexton, P., 443
Shackleton, M., 622
Shaffer, G. W., 777
Shaw, C. R., 561
Shaw, M., 443
Sheffield, H. B., 432
Sheldon, W. H., 506
Shen, S. C., 43
Sherman, A., 706
Shirley, H. F., 610
Shure, N., 597
Shuttleworth, F. K., 226
Sicard, J. A., 419
Siegel, I. E., 39
Silber, E., 214

Silberstein, R. M., 726
Simonsen, K. M., 740
Simpson, B. R., 240
Skeels, H. M., 237, 240, 740, 756–760
Skodak, M., 240, 757
Skydsgaard, H. B., 459
Sluckin, W., 20
Smith, L. H., 476, 776
Smith, W. K., 783
Solms, H. 459
Solnit, A., 573, 761
Sontag, L. S., 487
Spencer, B., 212
Sperling, M., 566, 591, 596, 601, 602
Sperry, 487
Spiegel, L., 218
Spiro, H. M., 594
Spitz, R. A., 8, 12, 13, 20, 32, 37, 40, 45, 93, 140, 167, 172, 237–262, 263, 277, 382, 440, 441, 573, 671, 673, 726, 740
Spock, B., 193, 296
Sprince, M. P., 710
Ssucharewa, G., 661
Stacy, C. L., 740
Stark, M., 761
Starr, P. H., 432, 434
Starzl, T. E., 781
Staver, 487
Stein, M., 593, 595, 597
Steinschneider, A., 2, 39, 592
Stendler, C., 176
Stengel, E., 277
Stephan, J., 593, 600
Stephenson, S., 458
Sterba, E., 297, 308, 319
Sterba, R., 79
Stern, E., 648, 662
Stern, W., 252
Stevenson, H. W., 39
Stewart, R. S., 460
Stirnimann, F., 677
Stoddard, G. D., 240
Stoller, R. J., 361
Stolz, L. M., 66, 225, 226
Stone, C. P., 222
Storrs, H., 740
Strachey, J., 297, 492, 496
Strauss, A. A., 472, 773, 774, 777, 781, 787
Strauss, E. B., 594
Stuart, H., 226, 227
Stunkard, A., 585, 588
Sturniman, A., 420
Sullivan, H. S., 700
Sully, J., 346
Sumner, J. W., 821
Svendsen, M., 410–417
Swanson, G. E., 176, 189, 198
Sylvester, E., 297, 493
Szeminska, N., 162
Szurek, S. A., 410–417, 522, 523, 524–525

Taft, L. T., 704
Tapia, F., 418
Teicher, J. D., 632
Tennes, K., 3, 14
Terman, L., 447, 734, 736–737, 741
Teuber, H. L., 784
Theis, S., 740
Thomas, A., 56–65
Thompson, H., 66, 256
Thompson, L. J., 458
Thorndike, E. L., 382
Thorpe, W. H., 30
Tinbergen, N., 20
Tolman, E. C., 252
Toman, J. P., 810, 818, 820
Tredgold, A. F., 733
Trilling, L., 575
Tulchin, S. H., 346, 492
Turner, W. A., 824

Ulrich, 487
Underhill, R., 206
Updegraff, R., 240

Van Buren, A., 418
Van der Leeuw, P. J., 365
Van Gennep, A., 203
Van Krevelen, D. A., 433, 648, 661
Variot, G., 458
Voldby, H., 475

Waelder, R., 8, 394, 438
Wahl, C. W., 284
Waite, T., 740
Waldfogel, S., 405, 410, 572
Walker, C. F., 437
Wallace, G., 739
Wallerstein, R. S., 394
Walton, H. J., 286
Warren, A. B., 498

Warson, S. R., 432, 624
Watson, J. B., 374, 382–393, 394, 397, 402, 403, 418
Webster, T., 740
Wechsler, D., 462
Weil, A. P., 648, 710
Weiner, I. B., 214
Weiss, P., 44
Weissenberg, S., 611
Wenar, C., 58
Wepman, J., 799
Werner, H., 14, 781, 787
Werry, J. S., 395
Wert, A. D., 432, 435
Westcott, M. R., 752
Westheimer, I., 573
Westman, J. C., 444
White, M. S., 192
White, W. A., 789
Whitehorn, J. C., 457, 461
Whiting, J. W., 613, 625
Wiener, N. S., 781
Wilder, 48
Wiley, J., 217
Wilkins, L., 824
Williams, F. E., 212
Williams, R. M., 190, 191
Willis, T., 735, 738
Wilson, S. A. K., 822
Windle, C., 46, 740
Wineman, D., 532
Winkler, H., 345
Winnicott, D. W., 138, 140, 148, 421, 432, 440
Wirth, L., 556
Withey, L., 457–486
Witmer, H., 498
Witmer, L., 458
Witty, P., 460
Wolf, K. M., 12, 13, 14, 51, 53, 237, 239, 240, 241
Wolfenstein, M., 176–188, 203, 296
Wolff, E., 433
Wolff, G., 458
Wolff, H., 605
Wolff, P. H., 11, 14, 39, 157
Wolfson, I., 740
Wolfson, W., 638
Wollersheim, J. P., 395
Wolpe, J., 382, 397, 398, 401, 402, 403, 408
Wolpe, Z. S., 433
Woodward, K., 740
Woodworth, R. S., 240, 241
Woolf, P. J., 2
Worden, F. G., 664
World Health Organization, 238
Wright, B. A., 761
Wright, D. G., 710–723
Wulff, M., 319, 433, 441

Yarnell, H., 239, 240, 643
Yarrow, L. J., 238
Yasuma, E. R., 433
Yntema, C. L., 43

Zegans, L. S., 789
Zeigarnik, B., 97
Zilboorg, G., 286, 363